Language Arts Standards

The **Tennessee Curriculum Standards** ensure that all students throughout the state of Tennessee are provided opportunities to learn communication and critical thinking skills. The English I course integrates reading, writing, speaking and listening, and viewing and representing.

To help you understand what is required in English I, refer to the chart below. Each Standard and Learning Expectation, which makes up the Curriculum Standards, appears in a yellow box and is followed by an explanation. To the right you will find an example from *Elements of Literature*.

WRITING

1.0 The student will develop the structural and creative skills necessary to produce written language that can be read and interpreted by various audiences.

1.01 Write to acquire knowledge, clarify thinking, synthesize information, improve study skills, gain confidence, and promote life-long communication.

You should write to learn to solidify your thoughts and help you communicate.

EXAMPLE: Writing to Communicate

In the Writing Workshop on pages 834–841, you will clarify your thinking about a real-world situation that needs to be changed. Then, you will write an essay that helps you clarify your position and communicates your thinking to readers.

1.02 Write frequently for a variety of purposes including narration, description, persuasion, exposition, and personal, creative expression.

Whether you want to persuade, to inform, to entertain, or to express, you are required to write different kinds of compositions.

EXAMPLE: Writing for a Variety of Purposes

The eleven Writing Workshops in this book guide you through the process of writing a persuasive essay, a research paper, a short story, and more. Also, in every Response and Analysis section that follows the reading selections, you will find at least one writing assignment.

1.03 Identify and write for a variety of audiences.

You are required to write a variety of papers for a variety of audiences.

EXAMPLE: Identifying Purpose and Audience

The Writing Workshops ask you to specify your purpose and audience (see "Your Readers Await You" on page 383).

1.04 **Recognize that language has several levels of usage determined by audience, purpose and occasion.**

You should learn to use language that is suitable for your audience, purpose, and occasion.

EXAMPLE: Using Language Appropriately for Context, Purpose, and Audience

Many of the Writing Workshops deal with aspects of context, purpose, and audience in the prewriting and revision stages of the writing process. See, for example, "Consider Purpose, Audience, and Tone" (pages 456 and 834–835) and "Evaluate and Revise Your Draft" (page 831).

1.05 **Approach writing tasks systematically and use elements of the writing process as appropriate.**

You should learn how to break down the writing process into manageable steps: prewriting, drafting, revising, editing, proofreading, and publishing. Peer review, as part of the revision stage, allows you to exchange drafts with a partner and evaluate and comment upon each other's texts.

EXAMPLE: Writing a Short Story

The Writing Workshop on pages 154–161 walks you through planning, writing, revising, and publishing a short story. The rubric in this and in other workshops provides guidelines for evaluating and revising the content and organization of your writing. You can apply these specific and helpful guidelines to your own work or to a peer's work.

1.06 **Practice a variety of prewriting activities to generate, focus and organize ideas.**

You are required to employ prewriting—the stage of the writing process in which you brainstorm for ideas, gather information, and organize your notes to help you write your first draft.

EXAMPLE: Prewriting

Every Writing Workshop helps you generate, gather, and organize ideas for writing. For example, "Writing an Autobiographical Narrative" on pages 78–85 asks you to start by thinking about important places or events from your past.

1.07 **Use a variety of appropriate organizational strategies to develop writing on various topics.**

You should organize your ideas by jotting them down in outlines, diagrams, and webs.

EXAMPLE: Keeping Order

For a list of organizational patterns, see "Text Structures" on pages 1157–1158 of the Handbook of Reading and Informational Terms.

1.08 **Develop organized pieces of writing containing focused, well-developed ideas.**

This standard asks that you create written works that follow a logical order and that contain clear and elaborated ideas.

EXAMPLE: Organizing Writing

Each Writing Workshop includes instruction on how to develop ideas and how to organize a particular paper. See pages 320–322 for information on how to identify similarities and differences and how to use the block method or the point-by-point method to organize a comparison-contrast paper.

1.09 **Demonstrate effective writing style by the use of vivid words, a variety of sentence structures, and appropriate transitions.**

You should enhance your writing by choosing just the right word, using different kinds of sentences, and using certain words to help your reader follow your ideas.

EXAMPLE: Improving Your Style

See "Writing Effective Sentences" on pages 1181–1184 for help combining related sentences, varying sentence structure, and improving sentence style.

1.10 **Evaluate and revise writing to focus on purpose, organization, development, transitions, unity, and audience awareness.**

This standard asks you to check that you have thoroughly treated and logically organized your content.

EXAMPLE: Editing for Effect

Each Writing Workshop includes a rubric for evaluating and revising writing. See page 561 for an example of a rubric that addresses organization, unity, and audience awareness.

1.11 **Recognize and demonstrate knowledge of standard English: usage, mechanics and standard spelling, and sentence structure.**

When you write, you will be evaluated not only on what you say but also on how you say it. To demonstrate mastery of this benchmark, you will need to correct any errors in spelling, punctuation, sentence structure, and grammar.

EXAMPLE: Using Standard American English

The Language Handbook on pages 1159–1205 serves as a ready reference for questions about spelling, capitalization, punctuation, grammar, and sentence structure. Be sure to consult the handbook for help in editing your drafts. In addition, twelve Grammar Link features (for example, page 76) provide you with the opportunity to practice and master various language conventions.

1.12 **Identify and begin to use a variety of resources to revise and edit writing.**

You should learn how to use different books and materials to improve your writing.

EXAMPLE: Using Resources

The entry "Dictionary" (pages 1149–1150) in the Handbook of Reading and Informational Terms explains how to use print or electronic dictionaries to determine the precise meanings of words.

1.13 **Research information from various sources to prepare presentations or reports which use summarizing, paraphrasing, direct quotations, citation of sources, and bibliographic sources.**

Whatever question you are investigating, you are asked to learn to choose and use the best and most appropriate resources.

EXAMPLE: Determining and Using Research Sources

On pages 55–59 you will find information on how to choose reliable print and electronic resources. See pages 711–712 for information about summarizing, quoting, and paraphrasing and pages 715–717 for information about citing sources and direct quotations.

1.14 **Continue to respond actively and imaginatively to literature.**

After you read a literary work, you are asked to write an interpretation or critique of it.

EXAMPLE: Responding to Literature

Throughout the text, you will write brief responses to literature (for example, a free-verse poem on page 554, a sequel on page 357, a comparison on page 536, and an analysis of style on page 621).

1.15 **Demonstrate an understanding of and respect for multicultural and ethnic diversity in language.**

You are required to show that you understand how writers who come from various cultures express themselves.

EXAMPLE: Discussing Ethnic Diversity

Read Pat Mora's "Legal Alien/Extranjera legal" (page 549), a poem about cultural identity in the United States. Then, see the Response and Analysis to understand how one writer uses language to express herself.

READING

2.0 The student will develop the reading skills necessary for word recognition, comprehension, interpretation, analysis, evaluation, and appreciation of the written text.

2.01 Develop an understanding of and respect for multicultural, gender, and ethnic diversity in language use, patterns, and dialects.

As you read, you are asked to explore words and expressions as they are used in different contexts and by people of different communities.

EXAMPLE: Appreciating Diversity

Read "To Da-duh, in Memoriam" (pages 607–622) to explore the use of regional dialect.

2.02 Discern reading strategies appropriate to text.

This standard requires you to employ reading strategies as you read literary and informative texts.

EXAMPLE: Reading Skills

On page A30 of the Table of Contents, you'll find these two categories: Reading Skills for Literary Texts and Reading Skills for Informational Texts. Beneath each is an extensive list of the skills in this textbook that will help you increase your reading fluency and comprehension.

2.03 Extend reading vocabulary.

You should expand your vocabulary by finding words, such as synonyms, homographs, and homophones, that are related in various ways to other words.

EXAMPLE: Building Vocabulary

Several exercises in every chapter help you develop your reading vocabulary. You will also find several practice activities that show you how to map unfamiliar words. See "Semantic Map: Charting Words" on page 454.

2.04 Use comprehension strategies to enhance understanding, to make predictions, and to respond to literature.

You are asked to master the use of comprehension strategies, such as making predictions, to help you grasp what you read.

EXAMPLE: Making Predictions

See pages 16, 261, 348, and 1100 for instruction on making predictions.

2.05 Improve comprehension by interpreting, analyzing, synthesizing, and evaluating written text.

You should critically analyze a piece of writing and judge its merits. You should also pull together, or synthesize, the ideas from several works.

EXAMPLE: Synthesizing Written Text

The four nonfiction selections linked to the short story "The Sniper" offer practice and instruction on comparing, contrasting, and connecting sources to understand an issue more clearly (pages 281–293).

2.06 Use oral reading in individual and group presentations.

You should demonstrate the application of the strategies necessary to present an effective reading.

EXAMPLE: Presenting an Oral Interpretation

"Presenting a Poem" (pages 564–565) gives step-by-step instruction for delivering an oral interpretation of a poem.

2.07 Read independently for a variety of purposes.

You should choose books to expand your literary base, to acquire general or specific knowledge, or to find out how to do specific tasks.

EXAMPLE: Reading Independently

At the end of each collection, you will find recommendations for fiction and nonfiction books in the Read On section (for example, on pages 153 and 319).

2.08 Use cognitive strategies to evaluate text critically.

You are asked to master the use of comprehension strategies, such as making predictions, to help you grasp what you read.

EXAMPLE: Synthesizing from Multiple Texts

In Collection 9, you will read and analyze an American crisis—the assassination of President John F. Kennedy—from different perspectives: a short story, eyewitness accounts, a speech to Congress, a biography, and an encyclopedia article.

2.09 Develop skills in making inferences and recognizing unstated assumptions.

You are asked to show that you can read between the lines to come to conclusions.

EXAMPLE: Making Inferences

See pages 108, 686, and 1152 for information on making inferences.

2.10 Discern the purposes, main ideas, biases, points of view, and persuasive devices found in various texts.

You should demonstrate that you can determine an author's purpose and perspective and also that you understand how an author constructs writing in an attempt to achieve that purpose.

EXAMPLE: Understanding Emotional and Logical Appeals

Turn to "Evaluating an Author's Argument: Intent and Tone" on page 818, where you will find examples of how authors can use logical and emotional appeals, connotations, and loaded language to influence their readers.

2.11 Interpret ideas, recognize logical relationships, and make judgments based on sufficient evidence.

You are required to evaluate a text and to determine whether the author uses enough information or the right kind of information to support an argument or idea.

EXAMPLE: Understanding Historical Texts

Turn to "Primary and Secondary Sources: Through Whose Eyes?" on page 674. Then, read the explanation of primary and secondary sources and the steps you can take to analyze and evaluate them for accuracy, authenticity, and bias.

2.12 Select resource material in order to apply it effectively.

You are required to use sources that are reliable, accurate, and current when researching.

EXAMPLE: Determining and Evaluating Research Sources

Instruction on pages 674–675 will help you select and evaluate resources you might use when researching a topic.

2.13 Read, interpret, and respond in a variety of ways to various genres.

You are asked to read and respond to many different types of literary and informational texts.

EXAMPLE: Responding to a Variety of Texts

See the Response and Analysis sections that appear after each major selection for a variety of ways to respond to the essays, short stories, poems, drama, fables, letters, interviews, biographies, and articles in the book. See pages 434, 703, and 813–814 for examples.

2.14 Identify and interpret literary elements and figurative language.

You are asked to analyze the literary elements and figurative language of a work in order to gain a deeper understanding of it.

EXAMPLE: Analyzing Literary Devices

A feature called Literary Focus introduces a literary device with most of the selections. Questions after each selection then ask you to analyze and evaluate the author's use of the literary device. See "Foreshadowing: Hints About What's Ahead" (page 16) before the story "The Most Dangerous Game" and questions following the story (page 36).

2.15 Interact with text to form a personal interpretation.

As you read and listen to selections, you should answer questions that will help you connect the content of the text to your life.

EXAMPLE: Connecting Texts to Your Life

The Make the Connection/Quickwrite feature that accompanies many selections introduces you to an idea that connects the content of the selection to your own world. After many selections, a writing assignment on the Response and Analysis pages has you return to this idea and write about it as part of your response to the text.

VIEWING AND REPRESENTING

3.0 The student will use, read, and view media/technology and analyze content and concepts accurately.

3.01 Access and demonstrate multiple technological reference sources.

You are required to demonstrate that you can access and use technology to help you find and employ information.

EXAMPLE: Technological Reference Sources

The Writing Workshop "Writing a Research Paper" lists technological reference sources and how to evaluate them (see pages 708–711).

3.02 Develop media applications for a variety of audiences and purposes.

You should learn how to develop a variety of different presentations to suit your goal and your listeners.

EXAMPLE: Using Media to Publish Your Work

The Publishing sections of the Writing Workshops often provide suggestions for using the media to publish your work (see page 327 for suggestions on using e-mail).

3.03 Use media to view, to read, to write, to communicate, and to create.

Learn how to use media for a variety of purposes.

EXAMPLE: Reading and Creating with Media

See pages 55–59 for practice on how to read and use a Web site. See pages the Publishing sections in the Writing Workshops for ideas on how to use media to publish your works (for example, page 85).

3.04 Analyze the impact of media on daily life.

You are required to learn how the media use techniques that influence our daily thinking.

EXAMPLE: Comparing and Contrasting Media Coverage

In the "Comparing Media Coverage" lesson on pages 320–327, you are asked to compare the news coverage of a single event reported by two news media. You will use specific points of comparison appropriate for the types of communication being evaluated.

3.05 Research, organize, interpret, and present information from print and non-print media.

You should learn to use a variety of sources (from books to the Internet) to research a topic.

EXAMPLE: Using Sources

For the Writing Workshop "Writing a Research Paper" on pages 706–725, you will read, organize, interpret, and present information from print and non-print media.

3.06 Utilize multimedia to create, to display, and to explain information.

You are required to use, design, and develop a media project to share information.

EXAMPLE: Creating a Multimedia Presentation

For help in completing a multimedia project, see the media tutorials on the *Elements of Literature* Internet site.

3.07 Explore the advantages and limitations of the computer as a communication tool.

You should learn how to communicate using the computer effectively.

EXAMPLE: Using a Computer

The Computer Tips in the Writing Workshops will help you explore the advantages of using a computer in your writing (see pages 161, 389, 712, 714, and 725).

3.08 Recognize the differences between using print and non-print media as a means of communication.

You are asked to differentiate between print and computers, television, radio, and other forms of media so that you understand the effectiveness of each medium.

EXAMPLE: Comparing Media

The Writing Workshop "Comparing Media Coverage" guides you through evaluating the differences between print and non-print media (pages 320–327).

3.09 Explain creative strategies used in the production of print and non-print media.

You should be able to explain how writers and media artists create their work so that you can use these techniques yourself.

EXAMPLE: Recognizing Film Techniques

The sections on "Identifying Narrative Techniques in Film" and "Identifying Film Techniques" on page 1041 describe creative strategies used by filmmakers.

SPEAKING AND LISTENING

4.0 The student will express ideas clearly and effectively in a variety of oral contexts and apply active listening skills in the analysis and evaluation of spoken ideas.

4.01 Demonstrate skills in analysis, interpretation, and evaluation of literary works through spoken language.

You are required to discuss and present your responses.

EXAMPLE: Presenting an Analysis

The Listening and Speaking Workshop on pages 564–565 guides you through the preparation for presenting an oral interpretation of a poem.

4.02 Demonstrate confidence and poise in various speaking situations.

You are asked to demonstrate a variety of speaking skills to help you gain confidence and to communicate effectively.

EXAMPLE: Public Speaking

For tips on speaking, see "Deliver Your Narrative" (page 87), "Practice Your Presentation" (page 465), and "Guidelines to Improve Delivery" (page 565).

4.03 Follow and give oral directions.

This standard asks you to listen to and follow instructions as well as give clear directions to an audience.

EXAMPLE: Following Instructions

One way to practice following and giving instructions is to participate in a partner or group activity. See pages 137, 220, and 390–393 for examples.

4.04 Utilize appropriate verbal and non-verbal feedback in a variety of situations.

You are asked to show mastery in giving appropriate verbal and nonverbal feedback to others.

EXAMPLE: Verbal and Nonverbal Techniques

You can use the instruction in "Analyzing and Evaluating Speeches" (pages 1048–1051) to evaluate a historically significant speech. You can adapt the criteria in this workshop to provide feedback for a peer's speech.

4.05 Demonstrate effective listening skills through note-taking.

You will need to organize a speaker's main points by outlining the content of the speech or lecture.

EXAMPLE: Organizing Information

See "Outlining" (pages 1154–1155) in the Handbook of Reading and Informational Terms. There you will find instruction on creating an outline that shows the relationships between key ideas.

4.06 Demonstrate critical listening skills essential for comprehension and evaluation.

To really listen, you should ask yourself questions, note gestures, and make eye contact.

EXAMPLE: Listening Actively

You will listen actively as you conduct an interview. See pages 124, 709, and 843.

4.07 Present oral summaries and/or analysis of material read or viewed.

You are required to summarize and state what you have discovered about a print or nonprint text.

EXAMPLE: Summarizing

Summarizing is defined on page 711. Steps for summarizing are given on pages 1102–1103.

4.08 Engage in problem solving through group discussions.

You are asked to work with others to find solutions to problems.

EXAMPLE: Solving Problems as a Group

Several features pose a question and ask students to discuss answers as a group. See page 42 for an example.

4.09 Present and support ideas/opinions in group discussions.

You are required to ask good questions, respond to others with relevant information, and encourage others to talk in group discussions.

EXAMPLE: Participating in a Classroom Discussion

All of the Thinking Critically and Extending and Evaluating questions on the Response and Analysis pages give you practice in class discussion. (See, for example, the questions about "The Scarlet Ibis" on page 428.)

4.10 Develop an understanding of and respect for diversity in language use, patterns, and dialects across cultures, ethnic groups, geographic regions, and social roles.

As you read, you should explore words as they are used in different contexts and by people of different communities.

EXAMPLE: Appreciating Differences in Language

See the "Glossary of Usage" (pages 1201–1205) for formal and informal word usages. See "To Da-duh, in Memoriam" on pages 609–619 for an example of a story with dialect.

4.11 Demonstrate appropriate language structure, tone and voice control in oral communication.

You are asked to demonstrate that you understand how word choice, tone, and verbal techniques affect communication.

EXAMPLE: Understanding Verbal Communication

The chart on page 1050 discusses three verbal delivery techniques (emphasis, pauses, enunciation).

Taking the English I End-of-Course Assessment and the Writing Assessment, Grade 11

You have probably already taken national or statewide standardized tests. These tests become more important as you approach graduation, especially if you plan to go to college.

This year, for example, you will take the **English I End-of-Course Assessment.** This test will measure your ability to respond to questions about reading selections and student essays. You need good reading and writing skills to succeed in all your school subjects, so this is an important test.

Another statewide test you will take is the **Writing Assessment.** However, you will not take the Writing Assessment this year; it will be given in grade eleven. This test will measure your ability to respond to a writing prompt. Even though you have a few more years before you take the writing test, practicing for this test now will help you become familiar with the testing process and will help you succeed in writing tasks that you complete this year. By practicing now, you will be prepared later to take the writing test in grade eleven.

Use the tips and practice items in this section to help you understand the types of questions you will encounter on the English I End-of-Course Assessment and on the Writing Assessment, Grade 11.

English I End-of-Course Assessment

For the English I End-of-Course Assessment, you will answer 60 multiple-choice questions about fiction and nonfiction reading selections, including student drafts and essays. The test will take approximately 90 minutes to complete.

TYPES OF MULTIPLE-CHOICE QUESTIONS

The multiple-choice questions on the English I End-of-Course Assessment will measure your reading and writing skills. You will be given criterion-referenced items, which will assess how well you perform according to specific standards—in this case, the Tennessee English/Language Arts Curriculum Standards for English I.

Some of the types of questions you will see on the English I End-of-Course Assessment include:

Grammar Conventions. These questions ask you to show your awareness of grammar rules. You might be asked to

- correct sentence fragments by using sentence combining techniques
- correct run-on sentences
- recognize correct subject/verb agreement
- select correct pronoun/antecedent agreement
- identify shifts in verb tense or point of view
- identify misplaced modifiers
- point out correct uses of punctuation

Content. Content questions ask you to examine the ideas within a piece of writing or a picture. You might be asked to

- identify different types of conflict
- select a sentence that does not support the main idea of a paragraph
- recognize the difference between a strong supporting idea and a weak one
- distinguish between fact and opinion
- identify an audience for a selection
- identify a writer's biases or beliefs

Word Choice. These questions ask you about the use of words in sentences. You might be asked to

- choose the most vivid words
- use the proper form of comparative and superlative adjectives
- distinguish between *your* and *you're*, *it's* and *its*, or *they're*, *their*, and *there*
- use words such as *effect* and *affect*, *stationary* and *stationery*, and *accept* and *except* appropriately
- choose the correct pronoun case

Organization. Organization questions ask you about the writing process and how you organize your ideas. You might be asked to

- identify the stages of the writing process: prewriting, drafting, revising, proofreading, and publishing
- think of an appropriate title for an essay
- choose the best method to combine sentences
- determine the best order of sentences within a passage
- revise a sentence to show correct parallelism
- use appropriate transitions

Meaning. Meaning questions ask you to analyze a selection. You might be asked to

- determine the main idea or theme of a selection
- identify causes and effects
- draw conclusions
- recognize literary elements, such as character, simile, tone, alliteration
- make generalizations
- identify the point of view of a selection
- explain symbols within a selection
- complete analogies
- use context clues to determine the meaning of a word
- make inferences

Technique. These questions ask you to recognize a writer's or presenter's style. You might be asked to

- identify how the author reveals a character to the reader
- identify the writer's or speaker's point of view
- point out literary techniques
- evaluate supporting details
- select the best presentation skill for a speech

TIPS FOR TAKING MULTIPLE-CHOICE TESTS

Multiple-choice questions are the most common type of question found on standardized tests. Teachers and other education professionals suggest these tips for success:

STEP 1   **Watch your time.** Since you have about 90 minutes to complete 60 questions, you should allow yourself one minute to answer each question. That way, you will have 30 minutes to read passages and to return to those questions you found difficult. You may even have time to review your answers.

STEP 2   **Read everything carefully.** Stay focused and alert as you read, and don't skip anything. Pay special attention to the **directions** that tell you what to do; the literary and informational **reading passages;** and **each question in full,** including all answer choices.

STEP 3   **There are no trick questions.** Don't waste time wondering what a question "really" means. *Do* look closely for words that limit the correct choice in some way:

- *Not* and *except* require you to choose an answer that is false or opposite in some way.

- *Always* and *never* signal that a choice applies in all or no situations.

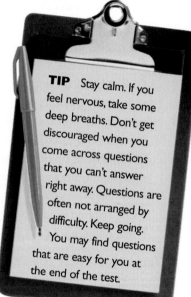

TIP   Stay calm. If you feel nervous, take some deep breaths. Don't get discouraged when you come across questions that you can't answer right away. Questions are often not arranged by difficulty. Keep going. You may find questions that are easy for you at the end of the test.

STEP 4   **Trust yourself.** Read the question carefully and try to predict the right answer. Then, read all of the answer choices. If you're not sure of the right answer, eliminate answers that are obviously wrong. Make your best guess about the choices that remain. If you really can't decide, mark the question to review later, and go on to the next item.

STEP 5   **Mark answers carefully.** Double-check to make sure you've selected the letter that goes with the answer you've chosen. Be careful also to match each question number on the test with the same number on your answer form.

STEP 6   **Review your work.** If you have time, go back to answer any questions that you skipped. Erase any stray marks you have made on your answer form.

PRACTICE ENGLISH I EOC ASSESSMENT

The English I End-of-Course Assessment consists of several reading selections and drafts of students' papers. After each selection, you will find a set of multiple-choice questions that relate to that selection.

This practice test includes three reading selections and three passages from a student's essay. Each is followed by questions like those you might find on the English I End-of-Course Assessment.

Directions: Read Selection I, an excerpt from Oliver Stone's "Where I Find My Heroes." Then, answer questions I through 6.

Oliver Stone became a movie director after serving in the Vietnam War. His films have explored historical subjects, such as the Vietnam War and President Kennedy's assassination.

It's not true that there are no heroes anymore—but it is true that my own concept of heroism has changed radically over time. When I was young and I read the Random House biographies, my heroes were always people like George Washington and General Custer and Abraham Lincoln and Teddy Roosevelt. Men generally, and
5   doers. Women—with the exception of Clara Barton, Florence Nightingale, and Joan of Arc—got short shrift. Most history was oriented toward male heroes.

But as I've gotten older, and since I've been to war, I've been forced to reexamine the nature of life and of heroism. What is true? What are the myths?

The simple acts of heroism are often overlooked—that's very clear to me not only
10   in war but in peace. I'm not debunking all of history: Crossing the Delaware *was* a magnificent action. But I am saying that I think the meaning of heroism has a lot to do with evolving into a higher human being. I came into contact with it when I worked with Ron Kovic, the paraplegic Vietnam vet, on *Born on the Fourth of July*. I was impressed by his life change, from a patriotic and strong-willed athlete to
15   someone who had to deal with the total surrender of his body, who grew into a non-violent and peaceful advocate of change in the Martin Luther King, Jr., and Gandhi tradition. So heroism *is* tied to an evolution of consciousness. . . .

Since the war, I've had children, and I'm wrestling now with the everyday problems of trying to share my knowledge with them without overwhelming them. It's
20   difficult to be a father, to be a mother, and I think that to be a kind and loving parent is an act of heroism. So there you go—heroes are everyday, common people. Most of what they do goes unheralded, unappreciated. And that, ironically, *is* heroism: not to be recognized.

continued

continued

Who is heroic? Scientists who spend years of their lives trying to find cures
25   for diseases. The teenager who says no to crack. The inner-city kid who works
at McDonald's instead of selling drugs. The kid who stands alone instead of
joining a gang, which would give him an instant identity. The celebrity who
remains modest and treats others with respect, or who uses his position to help
society. The student who defers the immediate pleasure of making money and
30   finishes college or high school. People who take risks despite fears. People in
wheelchairs who don't give up. . . .

"Where I Find My Heroes" by Oliver Stone from *McCall's Magazine*, November 1992. Copyright © 1992 by **Oliver Stone**. Reprinted by permission of the author.

MEANING

1 What does Oliver Stone admire about Ron Kovic?

A his fearlessness

B his intelligence

C his patriotism and strength of will

D his ability to change and grow

EXPLANATION: Stone doesn't mention fearlessness or intelligence, so you can eliminate A and B. Stone does say that Kovic was patriotic and strong-willed (C); however, what impresses Stone is Kovic's ability to *change* from a patriotic and strong-willed athlete to a different kind of person. **The correct answer is D.**

MEANING

2 What does the phrase "given short shrift" have to do with how Oliver Stone thinks women were treated by history?

F Florence Nightingale is an example of how women were usually treated in historical texts.

G The role of women in history was often ignored or overlooked.

H Women were just as likely to be treated as heroes as men were.

J History was often oriented toward female heroes.

EXPLANATION: Florence Nightingale is listed as an exception to being given "short shrift," so you can eliminate F. Stone says that history was oriented toward *male* heroes, so H and J can be eliminated. **The correct answer is G.**

MEANING

3 The experience of having children has helped Stone realize that

A history tends to focus on male heroes

B celebrities like him need to behave modestly

C heroism can involve taking risks

D being a good parent is one type of heroism

EXPLANATION: Although Stone does believe the statements made in A, B, and C, there is no evidence in the text that being a parent has caused Stone to reach these conclusions. Judging from what Stone says about the challenging experience of parenting, it follows that this experience has caused him to realize that good parents are heroes. **D is the correct answer.**

MEANING

4 With which of these statements would Stone most likely agree?

F Heroes are always regular, ordinary people.

G You cannot be a hero without changing yourself completely.

H Heroism must be measured by the effect a person has on others.

J Heroism can be displayed in an almost infinite number of ways.

EXPLANATION: This question requires you to make an educated guess based on the clues in the selection. Since Stone says that a celebrity can be a hero, he probably wouldn't agree with F. Since Stone cites solitary acts of heroism, such as staying away from a gang, H is a poor choice. G is possible, but the many different types of heroes listed by Stone suggest that **J is the answer.**

TECHNIQUE

5 What is the intent of the italicized paragraph at the beginning of this article?

A to warn against believing the opinions of the writer

B to give people background information about the writer

C to encourage people to watch the films Oliver Stone has made

D to persuade people to think about who the writer is before accepting his opinions

EXPLANATION: Measure each description of purpose against the content of the paragraph. The paragraph doesn't try to warn or persuade you, so you can eliminate A and D. Does the paragraph say that Stone's films should be seen (C)? No. But it does contain information about who Oliver Stone is, suggesting that giving people background about Stone is the paragraph's intent. **The correct answer is B.**

CONTENT

6 All of these sentences express Stone's vision of heroism except:

F Heroes can put off immediate gratification.

G Heroes must receive recognition for important work.

H Heroes show the ability to change.

J Heroes do important work without appreciation.

EXPLANATION: Skim through the text looking for the presence of each idea. You will find that the ideas listed in F, H, and J are present in the selection. However, Stone never expresses the view that heroes must receive recognition. **G is the correct answer.**

Directions: Read Selection 2, which is a traditional West African poem. Then, answer questions 7 and 8.

Old Song

Do not seek too much fame,
but do not seek obscurity.
Be proud.
But do not remind the world of your deeds.
Excel when you must,
but do not excel the world.
Many heroes are not yet born,
many have already died.
To be alive to hear this song is a victory.

MEANING

7 **According to this poem, a hero is someone who**
  A is not afraid of death
  B tries to do his best, but does not boast about success
  C values pride above all else
  D accomplishes great deeds, but strives to avoid any notice

EXPLANATION: Look at each description of a hero in the answer choices, and compare each one against the information presented in the poem. Line 4 places limitations on pride, so C can be eliminated. Lines 8 and 9 imply that merely staying alive is a heroic act, so A can be eliminated. Since line 2 warns against purposely seeking obscurity, D is incorrect. **B is the correct answer.**

MEANING

8 **One theme of this poem is "What Makes a Hero." Another possible theme for this poem would be:**
  F Strike a balance.
  G Strive to overcome great odds.
  H Express your individuality.
  J Seek to earn fame.

EXPLANATION: To find which of these themes is a possible match, check whether each one is consistent with the poem's message. Since the poem does not touch upon overcoming odds or expressing your individuality, G and H are incorrect. The poem's message about fame is different than the one expressed in J. **F is the correct answer.**

ORGANIZATION

9 **Read this paragraph from a student's essay.**

> (1) My mother is a hero because she has the courage to face a difficult challenge and to commit to success. (2) My mother married at a very young age, and by the time she was twenty-two she had two kids. (3) Extra time and money were scarce, but my mother never gave up on her dream to earn a biology degree. (4) As soon as my sister Caitlin and I started elementary school, my mother enrolled at the local university.

What is the topic sentence of this paragraph?
A 1
B 2
C 3
D 4

EXPLANATION: The first sentence (A) explains why the student's mother is a hero. The rest of the sentences in the paragraph (B, C, and D) support the first sentence by showing how the student's mother is a hero. **A is the correct answer.**

CONTENT

10 **Read this paragraph from a student's paper.**

> (1) My mother had bravely taken on a challenge. (2) She knew, though, that courage alone would not be enough. (3) Success would also require a long-term commitment to hard work. (4) Many young people today will do anything to get out of hard work.

Which sentence does not need to be in this paragraph?
F 1
G 2
H 3
J 4

EXPLANATION: The first three sentences (F, G, and H) discuss the mother's challenge and her commitment to hard work. J does not need to be in the paragraph; it discusses the student's view of how young people react to hard work. **J is the correct answer.**

WORD CHOICE

11 **Read this sentence from a student's essay.**

> After years of this <u>tiring</u> routine, my mother finally earned her degree.

Select a more vivid adjective to replace the underlined one.
A monotonous
B exhausting
C painful
D constant

EXPLANATION: B, *exhausting,* is a vivid adjective meaning *tiring.* **B is the correct answer.**

Directions: Read Selection 3, which is an excerpt from a novel. Then, answer questions 12–16.

from Great Expectations

1. When I had exhausted the garden, and a greenhouse with nothing in it but a fallen-down grape-vine and some bottles, I found myself in the dismal corner upon which I had looked out of window. Never questioning for a moment that the house was now empty, I looked in at another window, and found myself, to my great surprise, exchanging a broad stare with a pale young gentleman with red eyelids and light hair.

2. This pale young gentleman quickly disappeared, and reappeared beside me. . . .

3. "Come and fight," said the pale young gentleman.

4. What could I do but follow him? I have often asked myself the question since: but, what else could I do? His manner was so final, and I was so astonished, that I followed where he led, as if I had been under a spell.

5. "Stop a minute, though," he said, wheeling round before we had gone many paces. "I ought to give you a reason for fighting, too. There it is!" In a most irritating manner he instantly slapped his hands against one another, daintily flung one of his legs up behind him, pulled my hair, slapped his hands again, dipped his head, and butted it into my stomach.

6. The bull-like proceeding last mentioned, besides that it was unquestionably to be regarded in the light of a liberty, was particularly disagreeable just after bread and meat. I therefore hit out at him, and was going to hit out again, when he said, "Aha! Would you?" and began dancing backwards and forwards in a manner quite unparalleled within my limited experience. . . .

7. My heart failed me when I saw him squaring at me with every demonstration of mechanical nicety, and eyeing my anatomy as if he were minutely choosing his bone. I never have been so surprised in my life, as I was when I let out the first blow, and saw him lying on his back, looking up at me with a bloody nose and his face exceedingly fore-shortened.

8. But, he was on his feet directly, and after sponging himself with a great show of dexterity began squaring again. The second greatest surprise I have ever had in my life was seeing him on his back again, looking up at me out of a black eye.

9   His spirit inspired me with great respect. He seemed to have no strength, and he never once hit me hard, and he was always knocked down; but, he would be up again in a moment, sponging himself or drinking out of the water-bottle, with the greatest satisfaction in seconding himself according to form, and then came at me with an air and a show that made me believe he really was going to do for me at last. He got heavily bruised, for I am sorry to record that the more I hit him, the harder I hit him; but, he came up again and again and again, until at last he got a bad fall with the back of his head against the wall. Even after that crisis in our affairs, he got up and turned round and round confusedly a few times, not knowing where I was; but finally went on his knees to his sponge and threw it up, at the same time panting out, "That means you have won."

10   He seemed so brave and innocent, that although I had not proposed the contest I felt but a gloomy satisfaction in my victory. . . . I said, "Can I help you?" and he said "No thankee," and I said "Good afternoon," and *he* said "Same to you."

by Charles Dickens

MEANING

12 The theme of this incident is <u>best</u> stated as

  F everything has a logical explanation

  G sometimes events happen for reasons that are unclear

  H fighting is a way to settle arguments

  J it is difficult to get to know a stranger

EXPLANATION: F doesn't fit the passage; there's no logical explanation for the fight. H mentions fighting, but the boys do not argue, and the fighting settles nothing. J is too broad; it doesn't address the fight. **G is the best choice.**

WORD CHOICE

13 "My heart failed me when I saw him . . . eyeing my anatomy as if he were <u>minutely</u> choosing his bone." (paragraph 7)
Which of the following could replace <u>minutely</u> in this sentence?

  A quickly

  B doubtfully

  C precisely

  D playfully

EXPLANATION: Test each meaning in context. **The correct answer, C, fits best.**

ORGANIZATION

14 Which would be the best title for the excerpt from *Great Expectations?*

F "A Strange Encounter"

G "A Hard-Earned Victory"

H "A Fight for My Life"

J "A Terrifying Experience"

EXPLANATION: G, H, and J can be eliminated as possible titles. The narrator says the fight was easily won, so it was not a hard-earned victory (G), a fight for his life (H), or a terrifying experience (J). F describes the passage from the narrator's perspective; it was a strange encounter. **Therefore, F is the correct answer.**

GRAMMAR

15 Choose the sentence that uses correct pronoun/antecedent agreement.

A Readers love to hear stories about their youth.

B The boy or the narrator offered their apologies.

C Everyone wanted to tell their side of the story.

D Both of the boys probably hurt his fist in the fight.

EXPLANATION: B is incorrect because the sentence should contain a singular pronoun (*his*) when two antecedents are separated by *or*. C is incorrect because it should use a singular pronoun (*his*) with *everyone*. D is incorrect because it should use a plural pronoun (*their*) with *both*. **A is correct;** the plural pronoun *their* agrees with the antecedent *readers*.

GRAMMAR

16 Read the following.

In the window of the empty house.

The narrator saw a young boy staring out at him.

What is the best way to write the underlined section to correct the sentence fragment?

F house; the narrator

G house, so the narrator

H house, the narrator

J house; and the narrator

EXPLANATION: F would produce a sentence that is punctuated incorrectly. G and J would have incorrect punctuation as well as illogical conjunctions, making the sentence difficult to understand. H is the best way to correct the sentence fragment. It correctly includes a comma after the introductory prepositional phrase. **H is the correct answer.**

Writing Assessment

As stated previously, you will not take the Writing Assessment this year. Instead, you will take it in grade eleven, so you have two years to prepare. For the Writing Assessment, you will be asked to write an essay in response to a writing prompt within twenty-five minutes. For the Writing Assessment given in grade eleven, you will write a **persuasive essay.** A persuasive essay uses evidence and reasons to convince a reader to support a point of view. A well-written persuasive essay has a clear, central focus and support.

The Writing Assessment measures your writing skills. Scorers will look at what you write and how you write. Therefore, your essay will be scored based on its **content** and on your use of **writing conventions.** You will receive a score from 6 (outstanding) to 1 (deficient). The following rubric tells you which content and convention elements scorers will look for in your paper.

CONTENT AND CONVENTIONS RUBRIC

A 6 PAPER IS OUTSTANDING. A 6 paper

- is well organized
- is developed in a logical way
- explains the main idea clearly
- uses many different sentence structures
- shows that you know how to use language well to get across an idea
- has few errors in mechanics, usage, and sentence structure

A 5 PAPER IS STRONG. A 5 paper

- is generally well organized
- is generally developed in a logical way
- explains the main idea
- uses a few different sentence structures
- shows that you know how to use language to get across an idea
- has just a few errors in mechanics, usage, and sentence structure

A 4 PAPER IS COMPETENT. A 4 paper

- is satisfactorily organized

- is satisfactorily developed

- explains the main idea somewhat

- shows that you know how to use language satisfactorily to get across an idea to your readers

- has some errors in mechanics, usage, or sentence structure

A 3 PAPER IS LIMITED. A 3 paper reveals one or more of the following weaknesses:

- is not well organized

- is not well developed

- does not explain the main idea well

- has limited or inappropriate word choice

- has many errors in mechanics, usage, or sentence structure

A 2 PAPER IS FLAWED. A 2 paper reveals one or more of the following weaknesses:

- is poorly organized

- is not developed

- has few if any details to support the main idea

- has serious errors in mechanics, usage, sentence structure, or word choice that make the paper difficult to read

A 1 PAPER IS DEFICIENT. A 1 paper has serious writing errors or is not clear.

A 0 PAPER IS UNSCORABLE. A 0 paper could not be scored because it is blank, unreadable, off topic, or written mostly in another language.

STEPS TO COMPLETING A WRITING PROMPT

Here are the key steps for writing a response to a persuasive writing prompt. Use these steps when you take the Writing Assessment and when you complete persuasive writing assignments for this class and others.

STEP 1   **Analyze the prompt.** Look for key verbs (such as *persuade, convince,* or *support*) that define the task. Notice whether the prompt asks you to do more than one thing. Also, identify your audience because you want to make sure that you address their needs.

STEP 2   **Plan what you will say.** Spend some time thinking before you write. On scratch paper, brainstorm ideas. Use a graphic organizer or outline to map main points and support. Number your points in the order you think you will use them.

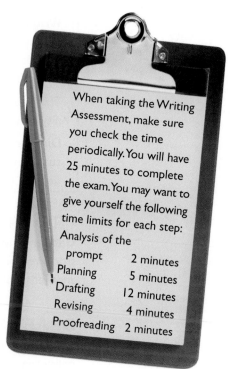

STEP 3   **Draft your essay.** Try to present your ideas clearly and in an easy-to-follow order. Each paragraph of your essay should clearly relate to your main idea. Use relevant details to support and elaborate ideas. Create a strong introduction and conclusion. If necessary, include a call to action, telling your audience what they should do after reading your essay. Don't forget to vary the kinds of sentences (short, long, simple, compound, complex) you use.

STEP 4   **Revise and edit your draft.** Look for places where you can add transitions or combine sentences to make ideas flow smoothly. Eliminate repetition and wordiness. Strengthen your paper with added support and improved order.

STEP 5   **Proofread your essay.** Find and correct errors in grammar, usage, and mechanics. Make all corrections neatly. You want to make sure your essay is readable.

A SAMPLE WRITING PROMPT

Prompts for the Writing Assessment are made up of two parts: the writing situation and the directions for writing. The writing situation introduces you to the subject about which you will write. The directions for writing give you an aspect or aspects of the topic to consider. Read the following sample writing prompt.

> *Writing Situation:* Many people believe that community service can provide students with valuable learning experiences. Your school board members are considering a new policy that will require high school students to perform twenty hours of community service each year in order to graduate.
>
> Think about how you would feel if you were required to perform a community service.
>
> *Directions for Writing:* Write a letter to the school board members persuading them to adopt or reject the policy. Defend your position with detailed reasons.

PREWRITING: ORGANIZING YOUR IDEAS

Gather your ideas. Decide whether you are for or against the policy. Then, brainstorm reasons to support your position. You might want to use a word web or another graphic organizer to organize your ideas.

DRAFTING: GETTING IT DOWN ON PAPER

Time to write. Now it is time to draft your essay. First, introduce your topic—a policy requiring community service for high school students—and your position in an **opinion statement.** Use your notes to provide support for your position. End your essay by restating your position and asking readers to accept it.

REVISING AND PROOFREADING: POLISHING YOUR DRAFT

The final step. Before you write your final essay, read it a couple of times. Make sure that your points are clear and expressed with style. Also, proofread it to catch mistakes in grammar, usage, mechanics, and spelling. Remember that scorers of the Writing Assessment will be looking for

- good sentence formation
- clearly organized paragraphs
- correct capitalization, punctuation, and spelling

A SAMPLE ESSAY
Here is one writer's response to the prompt presented on page TN30.

Dear School Board Members: — **Business letter greeting**

    I strongly endorse the proposed policy requiring high school students to complete twenty hours of community service each year. — **Opinion statement**
I think that twenty hours of community service work definitely should be made a graduation requirement. Across the state, twenty-six — **Supporting fact**
school districts have instituted similar policies successfully, and the movement is growing nationwide. The people students work with——children or hospital patients, for example—will greatly benefit from the time students spend with them, but for several reasons I think the biggest beneficiaries will be the students themselves.

    First, community service work opens students to new experi- — **Reason 1**
ences and people they might not meet otherwise. As a volunteer at Parkway Hospital on Saturday mornings, I play with young children — **Personal experience**
on the pediatric floor. It is eye-opening to observe these children and their parents coping with life-threatening diseases. My experiences in pediatrics have taught me a lot about the power of hope and laughter and love.

    Another benefit of community service is that students may — **Reason 2**
discover interests and talents that may lead to career choices. After volunteering in a veterinarian's office, my friend Iris decided to become — **Examples**
a veterinarian. My brother enjoyed tutoring in an after-school program so much that he decided to become a teacher.

    Most important, community service teaches students an essen- — **Reason 3**
tial value: the importance of helping others. With any luck, the high school community service requirement will be the beginning of a life

Example

time habit. *For example, my mother did volunteer work when she was younger, and she still does volunteer work today. In fact, she even involves our dog Misty in her volunteer work by taking Misty to visit residents of nursing homes once a month.* Unfortunately, we students need to combat the stereotype of teenagers as selfish. Volunteering does help others, but in turn it makes us feel good about ourselves.

Personal experience

Helping the children at Parkway Hospital not only makes them happy, but it also makes me happy.

Conclusion and call to action

For all of these reasons, I urge you to make community service a requirement at Howard High School. It is far better, I believe, for students to spend twenty hours a year helping people than to spend that time watching TV or wandering the malls. Twenty hours a year is not a lot of time to devote to our community, but the effects can be huge and lasting. I believe that doing community service can change us for the better.

Business letter closing

Sincerely yours,

Kate LeMay

EVALUATING: REVIEWING YOUR WORK

When you have finished your paper, how can you tell whether it will earn a high score? Evaluate your writing by comparing it with the characteristics of an excellent paper below.

- The paper is interesting, clear, and focused.
- The ideas are thoroughly explained and supported with appropriate details and examples.
- The organization of ideas is strong and moves the reader smoothly and naturally through the paper.
- Language use is mature and effective.
- Knowledge of language and its rules adds to the effectiveness of the paper.

HOLT
ELEMENTS OF
LITERATURE®

Third Course

HOLT, RINEHART AND WINSTON

A Harcourt Education Company

Orlando • **Austin** • New York • San Diego • Toronto • London

Program Authors

Dr. Kylene Beers is the senior program author for *Elements of Literature*. A former middle school teacher who is now a senior reading researcher in the School Development program at Yale University, Dr. Beers has turned her commitment to helping struggling readers into the major focus of her research, writing, speaking, and teaching. She is the author of *When Kids Can't Read: What Teachers Can Do* and *Aliteracy: The Glitch in Becoming a Nation of Readers* and from 1999 to 2006 was the editor of the National Council of Teachers of English (NCTE) literacy journal *Voices from the Middle*. Additionally, Dr. Beers is the co-editor of *Into Focus: Understanding and Creating Middle School Readers*. Having authored chapters in numerous books and articles in *English Journal, Journal of Adolescent and Adult Literacy, School Library Journal, Middle Matters,* and *Voices from the Middle*, she is a recognized authority on struggling readers, who speaks both nationally and internationally. Dr. Beers has served as the chair of the National Adolescent Literacy Coalition (2005–2007) and has served as a member of the review boards for *English Journal, The ALAN Review,* the Special Interest Group on Adolescent Literature of the International Reading Association, and the Assembly on Literature for Adolescents of the NCTE. She is the 2001 recipient of the Richard W. Halle Award given by NCTE for outstanding contributions to middle school literacy.

Dr. Lee Odell helped establish the pedagogical framework for writing, listening, and speaking for *Elements of Literature*. Dr. Odell is Professor of Composition Theory and Research and, since 1996, Director of the Writing Program at Rensselaer Polytechnic Institute. He began his career teaching English in middle and high schools. More recently he has worked with teachers in grades K–12 to establish a program that involves students from all disciplines in writing across the curriculum and for communities outside their classrooms. Dr. Odell's most recent book (with Charles R. Cooper) is *Evaluating Writing: The Role of Teachers' Knowledge About Text, Learning, and Culture.* He is past chair of the Conference on College Composition and Communication and of NCTE's Assembly for Research.

Writers

Robert Anderson is a playwright, novelist, screenwriter, and teacher. His plays include *Tea and Sympathy; Silent Night, Lonely Night; You Know I Can't Hear You When the Water's Running;* and *I Never Sang for My Father.* His screenplays include *The Nun's Story* and *The Sand Pebbles.* Mr. Anderson has taught at the Writers' Workshop at the University of Iowa, the American Theater Wing Professional Training Program, and the Salzburg Seminar in American Studies. He is a past president of the Dramatists Guild of America, a past vice president of the Authors League of America, and a member of the Theater Hall of Fame.

John Malcolm Brinnin, author of six volumes of poetry that have received many prizes and awards, was a member of the American Academy and Institute of Arts and Letters. He was a critic of poetry, a biographer of poets, and for a number of years the director of New York's famous Poetry Center. His teaching career included terms at Vassar College, the University of Connecticut, and Boston University, where he succeeded Robert Lowell as Professor of Creative Writing and Contemporary Letters. Mr. Brinnin wrote *Dylan Thomas in America: An Intimate Journal* and *Sextet: T. S. Eliot & Truman Capote & Others.*

Kathleen Daniel has edited and directed middle school and secondary literature and language programs for over forty years, specializing in literature anthologies. She currently works as a writer, editor, and educational consultant.

Flo Ota De Lange and **Sheri Henderson**
Flo Ota De Lange is a former teacher with a thirty-year second career in psychotherapy, during which she studied learning processes in children and adults. Those careers led to her third career, as a writer.

Sheri Henderson brings to the program twenty years of experience as a California middle-school research practitioner and full-time reading and language arts teacher at La Paz International School in Saddleback Valley Unified School District. She regularly speaks at statewide and national conferences.

Since 1991, DeLangeHenderson LLC has published over fifty titles designed to integrate the teaching of literature with standards requirements and state and national tests.

Madeline Travers Hovland, who taught language arts for several years, is a writer of educational materials. She studied English at Bates College and received a master's degree in education from Harvard University.

John Leggett is a novelist, biographer, and former teacher. He went to the Writers' Workshop at the University of Iowa in the spring of 1969.

In 1970, he assumed temporary charge of the program, and for the next seventeen years he was its director. Mr. Leggett's novels include *Wilder Stone, The Gloucester Branch, Who Took the Gold Away?, Gulliver House,* and *Making Believe.* He is also the author of the highly acclaimed biography *Ross and Tom: Two American Tragedies* and of a biography of William Saroyan, *A Daring Young Man.* Mr. Leggett lives in Napa Valley, California.

David Adams Leeming was for many years a Professor of English and Comparative Literature at the University of Connecticut. He is the author of several books on mythology, including *Mythology: The Voyage of the Hero; The World of Myth;* and *Encyclopedia of Creation Myths.* For several years, Dr. Leeming taught English at Robert College in Istanbul, Turkey. He also served as secretary and assistant to the writer James Baldwin in New York and Istanbul. He has published the biographies *James Baldwin* and *Amazing Grace: A Life of Beauford Delaney.*

Mara Rockliff is a writer and editor with a degree in American civilization from Brown University. She has written dramatizations of classic stories, collected in a book called *Stories for Performance.* She has also published feature stories in national newspapers and is currently writing a novel for young adults.

Diane Tasca, a graduate of Temple University, earned a doctorate in English from the University of Illinois. Over the past thirty years, Dr. Tasca has taught various college courses in composition, literature, and performance and has developed, written, and edited instructional materials for high school and college language arts textbooks. A member of the San Francisco Bay Area theater community, she has performed in numerous plays and assisted playwrights with the development of new dramatic works. She currently teaches drama at Foothill College in Los Altos Hills, California.

Senior Program Consultant

Carol Jago teaches English at Santa Monica High School, in Santa Monica, and directs the California Reading and Literature Project at UCLA. Her classroom experience began with middle school and has included journalism, remedial reading and writing, and honors and advanced placement. She has written a weekly education column for the *Los Angeles Times* and edits the quarterly journal of the California Association of Teachers of English, *California English*. She is the author of several books, including a series on contemporary writers in the classroom: *Alice Walker in the Classroom, Nikki Giovanni in the Classroom,* and *Sandra Cisneros in the Classroom.* She is also the author of *With Rigor for All: Teaching the Classics to Contemporary Students, Beyond Standards: Excellence in the High School English Classroom, Cohesive Writing: Why Concept Is Not Enough, Classics in the Classroom: Designing Accessible Literature Lessons,* and *Papers, Papers, Papers: An English Teacher's Survival Guide.*

ADVISORS

Cynthia A. Arceneaux
Administrative Coordinator
Office of Deputy Superintendent,
    Instructional Services
Los Angeles Unified School District
Los Angeles, California

Dr. Julie M. T. Chan
Director of Literacy Instruction
Newport-Mesa Unified School
    District
Costa Mesa, California

Al Desmarais
English Department Chair and
    Curriculum Specialist in
    Language Arts
El Toro High School
Saddleback Valley Unified School
    District
Lake Forest, California

José M. Ibarra-Tiznado
ELL Program Coordinator
Bassett Unified School District
La Puente, California

Dr. Ronald Klemp
Instructor
California State University,
    Northridge
Northridge, California

Fern M. Sheldon
K–12 Curriculum and Instruction
    Specialist
Rowland Unified School District
Rowland Heights, California

Jim Shields
Instructor
El Toro High School
Saddleback Valley Unified School
    District
Lake Forest, California

CRITICAL REVIEWERS

Paulette Dewey
Toledo Public School
Toledo, Ohio

Terry Filippo
Pendleton High School/
    Clemson University
Pendleton, South Carolina

R. E. Fisher
Westlake High School
Atlanta, Georgia

Robert V. Gardner
Chaparral High School
Temecula, California

Janice Gauthier
Everett High School
Everett, Massachusetts

Sandra J. Gilligan
Passaic High School
Passaic, New Jersey

Kimberly Hoelterhoff
Temple City High School
Temple City, California

Victor Jaccarino
Herricks High School
New Hyde Park, New York

Barbara Kimbrough
Kane Area High School
Kane, Pennsylvania

Dr. Louisa Kramer-Vida
Oyster Bay-East Norwich SD
Oyster Bay, New York

Mary Ann Liberati
East Greenwich High School
East Greenwich, Rhode Island

Cynthia Marr
Arlington High School
Riverside, California

Faith Nitschke
Hoover High School
Fresno, California

Toni Lee Olson
Nogales High School
La Puente, California

Norm Rush
Chaffey High School
Ontario, California

Brenda Scheidler
Evansville-Vanderburgh School Corp.
Evansville, Indiana

Mary Ellen Snodgrass
Hickory High School
Hickory, North Carolina

David Trimble
Norwin High School
N. Huntingdon, Pennsylvania

Donna Walthour
Greensburg Salem High School
Greensburg, Pennsylvania

John Williamson
Ft. Thomas Schools
Ft. Thomas, Kentucky

FIELD-TEST PARTICIPANTS

Sandra J. Gilligan
Passaic High School
Passaic, New Jersey

Lee Lowery
Highlands High School
Fort Thomas, Kentucky

Pamela Rockich
Barberton High School
Barberton, Ohio

Ellen Schunks
North County High School
Bonne Terre, Missouri

Casey Williams
Highlands High School
Fort Thomas, Kentucky

CONTENTS IN BRIEF

COLLECTION 1

Into the Unknown

LITERARY FOCUS
Analyzing Plot and Setting

INFORMATIONAL READING FOCUS
Developing Research Questions Based on Reading

On Your Own

LITERARY FOCUS	INFORMATIONAL READING FOCUS
Analyzing Character	Using Primary and Secondary Sources

COLLECTION 3

Truth and Consequences

LITERARY FOCUS
Analyzing Narrator and Voice

INFORMATIONAL READING FOCUS
Synthesizing Sources: Main Ideas and Supporting Evidence

Friends and Enemies

LITERARY FOCUS
Comparing Themes

INFORMATIONAL READING FOCUS
Synthesizing Sources:
Drawing Conclusions

Hard Choices

LITERARY FOCUS
Analyzing Irony and Ambiguity

INFORMATIONAL READING FOCUS
Evaluating an Argument

COLLECTION 6

Ties That Bind

LITERARY FOCUS
Analyzing Symbolism and Allegory

INFORMATIONAL READING FOCUS
Synthesizing Sources: Works by One Author

ALL SELECTIONS AND FEATURES SUPPORT YOUR TENNESSEE STANDARDS

COLLECTION 7

Imagine

LITERARY FOCUS
Analyzing Poetry

THE SOUNDS OF POETRY

COLLECTION 8

Crossing Borders

LITERARY FOCUS
Literary Criticism: Evaluating Style

INFORMATIONAL READING FOCUS
Evaluating Arguments: Pro and Con

Turning Points

LITERARY FOCUS
Literary Criticism: Using Biographical and Historical Approaches

INFORMATIONAL READING FOCUS
Using Primary and Secondary Sources

Heroes and Monsters

LITERARY FOCUS
Analyzing Epic and Myth

INFORMATIONAL READING FOCUS
Evaluating an Argument: Intent and Tone

COLLECTION 12

Creating Computer Games

INFORMATIONAL READING FOCUS
Consumer and Workplace Documents

by Flo Ota De Lange *and* Sheri Henderson

Contents **A17**

Resource Center

ALL SELECTIONS AND FEATURES SUPPORT YOUR TENNESSEE STANDARDS

SELECTIONS BY ALTERNATIVE THEMES

Selections are listed here in alternative theme groupings.

JOURNEYS

LOYALTY AND BETRAYAL

NATURE

PASSAGES

ROOTS

WAR AND PEACE

SELECTIONS BY GENRE

FICTION

FABLE

FOLK TALE

MYTH

NOVEL EXCERPT

SHORT STORY

DRAMA

COMEDY

TRAGEDY

POETRY

EPIC

SONG

NONFICTION AND INFORMATIONAL TEXT

AUTOBIOGRAPHY

BIOGRAPHY

ENCYCLOPEDIA ARTICLE

HISTORY BOOK

INTERVIEW

SKILLS, WORKSHOPS, AND FEATURES

SKILLS

ELEMENTS OF LITERATURE ESSAYS

LITERARY SKILLS

READING SKILLS FOR LITERARY TEXTS

READING MATTERS

READING SKILLS FOR INFORMATIONAL TEXTS

VOCABULARY SKILLS

WORKSHOPS

WRITING WORKSHOPS

LISTENING AND SPEAKING WORKSHOPS

FEATURES

A CLOSER LOOK

SKILLS, WORKSHOPS, AND FEATURES

GRAMMAR LINK

INTRODUCING THE COLLECTION THEME

LANGUAGE HANDBOOK

SKILLS REVIEW

TEST SMARTS

WRITER'S HANDBOOK

Elements of Literature on the Internet

TO THE STUDENT

At the *Elements of Literature* Internet site, you can read texts by professional writers and learn the inside stories behind your favorite authors. You can also build your word power and analyze messages in the media. As you move through *Elements of Literature*, you will find the best online resources at **go.hrw.com.**

Here's how to log on:

1. Start your Web browser, and enter **go.hrw.com** in the Address or Location field.

2. Note the keyword in your textbook.

INTERNET

More About Plot

Keyword: LE7 9-1

3. Enter the keyword and click "go."

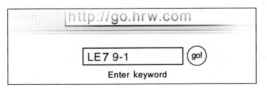

FEATURES OF THE SITE

More About the Writer
Author biographies provide the inside stories behind the lives and works of great writers.

More About the Literary Element
Graphic organizers present visual representations of literary concepts.

Interactive Reading Model
Interactive Reading Workshops guide you through high-interest informational articles and allow you to share your opinions through pop-up questions and polls.

More Writer's Models
Interactive Writer's Models present annotations and reading tips to help you with your own writing. Printable Professional Models and Student Models provide you with quality writing by real writers and students from across the country.

Vocabulary Practice
Interactive vocabulary-building activities help you build your word power.

Projects and Activities
Projects and activities help you extend your study of literature through writing, research, art, and public speaking.

Speeches
Video clips from historical speeches provide you with the tools you need to analyze elements of great speechmaking.

Media Tutorials
Media tutorials help you dissect messages in the media and learn to create your own multimedia presentations.

Collection 1

Into the Unknown

Literary Focus:

Analyzing Plot and Setting

Informational Reading Focus:

Developing Research Questions

Based on Reading

Time Transfixed (1939) by René Magritte.
Oil on canvas (146.3 cm × 97.5 cm).

The Art Institute of Chicago.

Elements of Literature

Plot *by* John Leggett
TIME AND SEQUENCE

Hooking Your Curiosity

When we talk about stories, plot is the element to start with, for plot is story itself. **Plot** is a series of related events, like links in a chain. Each event hooks our curiosity and pulls us forward to the next event.

Conflict: The Fuel of Narrative

In most stories, we care about what happens next because we're hooked by a **conflict,** or struggle. In an **external conflict** the struggle takes place between two characters, between a character and a group, or between a character and something nonhuman—a typhoon or a computer virus, for example. An **internal conflict** takes place within a character's mind or heart: A desire to win someone's friendship might conflict with a fear of rejection.

Conflict is the fuel of narrative. The greater the conflict, the more we care about the outcome.

The Bare Bones of a Plot

Stories, like houses and human beings, need a structure, or framework, to hold them together. Plots are usually built on four major parts, which we might think of as their bare bones.

1 The first part of a plot is called the **basic situation,** or **exposition.** This is the opening of the story, when the characters and their conflict are introduced.

Young William didn't mind his hard work as the king's stableboy because he loved horses. The king, however, was miserable because his kingdom had been invaded by a large fire-breathing dragon who smelled to high heaven.

2 The second part of a plot is the **complication.** Now the main character takes some action to resolve the conflict but meets with more problems or complications: danger, hostility, fear, or even a new threatening situation.

William set out to kill the dragon in order to help the king. While he was riding into the woods, several robbers tried to hijack his horse. Poor William felt himself losing courage.

3 The third part of a story is the **climax.** This is the key scene in the story—that tense or exciting or terrifying moment when our emotional involvement is greatest. Now we learn what the outcome of the conflict is going to be.

When he had just about decided to give up the chase and return home, William found himself staring down the dragon's throat. Closing his eyes, he hurled his sword into the dragon's windpipe. The monster gagged and began to die.

4 The final part of the story is the **resolution.** Sometimes this is called the **denouement** (dā′noo·män′). The resolution occurs at the end of the story. Now all the struggles are over, and we know what is going to happen to the characters.

SKILLS FOCUS

Literary Skills
Understand plot structure and development of time and sequence.

INTERNET
More About Plot
Keyword: LE7 9-1

When he returned to the palace with the dragon's head, William became a hero, although he had to spend the next two weeks soaking himself to get rid of the smell of a very dead dragon.

It's All in the Timing

Events in real life can go on and on, but stories cannot. That's why the plot of a story is framed by time. A story may cover fifty happy years in a marriage or five nerve-racking moments in a submarine, but every work of fiction is defined by a time span, a period of time that suits the writer's purpose.

Most stories are told in **chronological order,** the order in which events unfold in real time. The writer starts at the beginning and tells about each event in the order in which it happens. Yet writers frequently use other techniques to manipulate time and control our emotions, especially our feelings of suspense. For example, they might slow down time to emphasize a moment of danger, or they might speed up time to skip over events that don't move the story along.

Playing with Time

You have also read stories in which writers interrupt the flow of events to present an episode from the past. Such a scene is called a **flashback.** For example, a story might begin with a description of a woman hiding in an abandoned house. The writer might then use a flashback to show why the woman is hiding. A flashback could also be used to strengthen our understanding of the character by revealing a powerful memory.

Writers can play with time in another way as well. Instead of going back to the past, they can jump ahead days or years into the future by using a literary device called a **flash-forward.**

Finally, writers can bring the future into the present by using **foreshadowing,** hints or clues that suggest what is to come in the story. Foreshadowing can make a story more exciting by increasing suspense. For instance, a man is barely aware of wolves howling in the distance, but the reader wonders about them. Days later the man is pursued by those wolves. The reader realizes the howling foreshadowed the man's now-desperate situation.

So, whether writers make us look back or think ahead, they hook us into a story by playing with time.

Practice

Choose a children's story or a fairy tale that is familiar to you. First, draw a **plot diagram** like the one shown here, and add labels describing the key parts of the story's plot. Then, use your imagination to write a **flashback** that could occur in one part of the story.

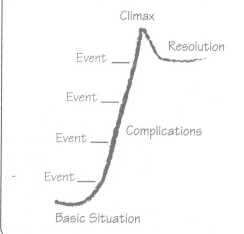

Introducing the Collection Theme

Into the Unknown

Make the Connection

Quickwrite

When you hear the phrase "into the unknown," what do you think about? Make a two-column chart. In the first column, list the different types of unknowns you've faced in your life—or will face in the future, such as attending college or getting your first job. In the second column, jot down words and phrases describing each unknown and your feelings about it. Save your chart.

Exploring the Theme: Into the Unknown

Like many TV shows, movies, and computer games, this collection revolves around characters and people who enter into the unknown. In "The Most Dangerous Game," a castaway on a mysterious island confronts unknown dangers. In the short story "Dog Star" and the article "Far-out Housekeeping on the ISS," scientists brave life in the vast unknown of outer space. The narrator in "A Christmas Memory" enters the unknown world of adolescence—away from home and alone.

   In "Initiation," the story you are about to read, a teenager faces an initiation rite for a high school sorority—and the unknowns of being an insider or an outsider. An initiation rite is a type of test someone must pass to join a special group. Some initiation rites are tough, mean, or even violent, whereas others are just silly and embarrassing. In many high schools and colleges today, certain types of initiation rites are banned.

Literary Focus

Plot

Remember what you know about plot—that **conflict** leads to **complications,** a **climax,** and then a **resolution.** Remember, too, that there are **internal conflicts,** struggles within the heart and mind of a character, and **external conflicts,** struggles between a character and outside forces. As you read "Initiation," look for the point when the main character faces her most powerful conflict—one that leads her into the unknown.

Adolescence (1947) by Milton Avery (1893–1965). Daniel J. Terra Collection, 1992.3. Oil and graphite on canvas. 30 x 40 in. © 2007 Milton Avery Trust/Artists Rights Society (ARS), New York.

SKILLS FOCUS

Literary Skills
Understand internal and external conflicts.

Initiation

Sylvia Plath

The basement room was dark and warm, like the inside of a sealed jar, Millicent thought, her eyes getting used to the strange dimness. The silence was soft with cobwebs, and from the small, rectangular window set high in the stone wall there sifted a faint bluish light that must have been coming from the full October moon. She could see now that what she was sitting on was a woodpile next to the furnace.

Millicent brushed back a strand of hair. It was stiff and sticky from the egg that they had broken on her head as she knelt blindfolded at the sorority altar a short while before. There had been a silence, a slight crunching sound, and then she had felt the cold, slimy egg-white flattening and spreading on her head and sliding down her neck. She had heard someone smothering a laugh. It was all part of the ceremony.

Then the girls had led her here, blindfolded still, through the corridors of Betsy Johnson's house and shut her in the cellar. It would be an hour before they came to get her, but then Rat Court would be all over and she would say what she had to say and go home.

For tonight was the grand finale, the trial by fire. There really was no doubt now that she would get in. She could not think of anyone who had ever been invited into the high school sorority and failed to get through initiation time. But even so, her case would be quite different. She would see to that. She could not exactly say what had decided her revolt, but it definitely had something to do with Tracy and something to do with the heather birds. ❶

What girl at Lansing High would not want to be in her place now? Millicent thought, amused. What girl would not want to be one of the elect,[1] no matter if it did mean five days of initiation before and after school, ending in the climax of Rat Court on Friday night when they made the new girls members? Even Tracy had been wistful when she heard that Millicent had been one of the five girls to receive an invitation.

"It won't be any different with us, Tracy," Millicent had told her. "We'll still go around together like we always have, and next year you'll surely get in."

"I know, but even so," Tracy had said quietly, "you'll change, whether you think you will or not. Nothing ever stays the same."

---

1. **elect** (e·lekt´) *n.*: specially chosen group; here, those elected to be part of the sorority.

PLOT

❶ What is the situation at the beginning of the story? What **conflicts** are hinted at?

New Green (2004) by
Alex Katz (b. 1927). Oil
on canvas. 60 x 144 in.
Art © Alex Katz/Licensed by
VAGA/New York, NY.

And nothing does, Millicent had thought. How horrible it would be if
one never changed . . . if she were condemned to be the plain, shy
Millicent of a few years back for the rest of her life. Fortunately there was
always the changing, the growing, the going on.

It would come to Tracy, too. She would tell Tracy the silly things the
girls had said, and Tracy would change also, entering eventually into the
magic circle. She would grow to know the special ritual as Millicent had
started to last week.

"First of all," Betsy Johnson, the vivacious[2] blonde secretary of the
sorority, had told the five new candidates over sandwiches in the school
cafeteria last Monday, "first of all, each of you has a big sister. She's the
one who bosses you around, and you just do what she tells you." ❷

"Remember the part about talking back and smiling," Louise Fullerton
had put in, laughing. She was another celebrity in high school, pretty and
dark and Vice-President of the Student Council. "You can't say anything
unless your big sister asks you something or tells you to talk to someone.
And you can't smile, no matter how you're dying to." The girls had
laughed a little nervously, and then the bell had rung for the beginning
of afternoon classes.

---

2. **vivacious** (vi•vā′shəs) adj.: lively; spirited.

PLOT

❷ This paragraph
begins a lengthy
flashback, a scene
that interrupts the
present action to
show what happened
in the past. When did
this conversation with
Betsy take place?

It would be rather fun for a change, Millicent mused, getting her books out of her locker in the hall, rather exciting to be part of a closely knit group, the exclusive set at Lansing High. Of course, it wasn't a school organization. In fact, the principal, Mr. Cranton, wanted to do away with initiation week altogether, because he thought it was undemocratic and disturbed the routine of school work. But there wasn't really anything he could do about it. Sure, the girls had to come to school for five days without any lipstick on and without curling their hair, and of course everybody noticed them, but what could the teachers do?

Millicent sat down at her desk in the big study hall. Tomorrow she would come to school, proudly, laughingly, without lipstick, with her brown hair straight and shoulder length, and then everybody would know, even the boys would know, that she was one of the elect. Teachers would smile helplessly, thinking perhaps: So now they've picked Millicent Arnold. I never would have guessed it.

A year or two ago, not many people would have guessed it. Millicent had waited a long time for acceptance, longer than most. It was as if she had been sitting for years in a pavilion outside a dance floor, looking in through the windows at the golden interior, with the lights clear and the air like honey, wistfully watching the gay couples waltzing to the never-ending music, laughing in pairs and groups together, no one alone. ❸

THEME

❸ What have you learned so far about the way Millicent used to see herself and the way she sees herself now?

But now at last, amid a week of fanfare and merriment, she would answer her invitation to enter the ballroom through the main entrance marked "Initiation." She would gather up her velvet skirts, her silken train, or whatever the disinherited princesses wore in the story books, and come into her rightful kingdom . . . The bell rang to end study hall.

"Millicent, wait up!" It was Louise Fullerton behind her, Louise who had always before been very nice, very polite, friendlier than the rest, even long ago, before the invitation had come.

"Listen," Louise walked down the hall with her to Latin, their next class, "are you busy right after school today? Because I'd like to talk to you about tomorrow."

"Sure. I've got lots of time."

"Well, meet me in the hall after home room then, and we'll go down to the drugstore or something."

Walking beside Louise on the way to the drugstore, Millicent felt a surge of pride. For all anyone could see, she and Louise were the best of friends.

"You know, I was so glad when they voted you in," Louise said.

Millicent smiled. "I was really thrilled to get the invitation," she said frankly, "but kind of sorry that Tracy didn't get in, too."

Tracy, she thought. If there is such a thing as a best friend, Tracy has been just that this last year.

"Yes, Tracy," Louise was saying, "she's a nice girl, and they put her up on the slate, but . . . well, she had three blackballs against her."

"Blackballs? What are they?"

"Well, we're not supposed to tell anybody outside the club, but seeing as you'll be in at the end of the week I don't suppose it hurts." They were at the drugstore now.

"You see," Louise began explaining in a low voice after they were seated in the privacy of the booth, "once a year the sorority puts up all the likely girls that are suggested for membership . . . "

Millicent sipped her cold, sweet drink slowly, saving the ice cream to spoon up last. She listened carefully to Louise, who was going on, ". . . and then there's a big meeting, and all the girls' names are read off and each girl is discussed."

"Oh?" Millicent asked mechanically, her voice sounding strange.

"Oh, I know what you're thinking," Louise laughed. "But it's really not as bad as all that. They keep it down to a minimum of catting.[3] They just talk over each girl and why or why not they think she'd be good for the club. And then they vote. Three blackballs eliminate a girl."

"Do you mind if I ask you what happened to Tracy?" Millicent said.

Louise laughed a little uneasily. "Well, you know how girls are. They notice little things. I mean, some of them thought Tracy was just a bit *too* different. Maybe you could suggest a few things to her."

---

3. **catting** (kat′iŋ) *v.* used as *n.*: making mean, nasty comments.

"Like what?"

"Oh, like maybe not wearing knee socks to school, or carrying that old bookbag. I know it doesn't sound like much, but well, it's things like that which set someone apart. I mean, you know that no girl at Lansing would be seen dead wearing knee socks, no matter how cold it gets, and it's kiddish and kind of green to carry a bookbag." ❹

"I guess so," Millicent said.

"About tomorrow," Louise went on. "You've drawn Beverly Mitchell for a big sister. I wanted to warn you that she's the toughest, but if you get through all right it'll be all the more credit for you."

"Thanks, Lou," Millicent said gratefully, thinking, this is beginning to sound serious. Worse than a loyalty test, this grilling over the coals. What's it supposed to prove anyway? That I can take orders without flinching? Or does it just make them feel good to see us run around at their beck and call?

"All you have to do really," Louise said, spooning up the last of her sundae, "is be very meek and obedient when you're with Bev and do just what she tells you. Don't laugh or talk back or try to be funny, or she'll just make it harder for you, and believe me, she's a great one for doing that. Be at her house at seven-thirty."

And she was. She rang the bell and sat down on the steps to wait for Bev. After a few minutes the front door opened and Bev was standing there, her face serious.

"Get up, gopher," Bev ordered.

There was something about her tone that annoyed Millicent. It was almost malicious.[4] And there was an unpleasant anonymity[5] about the label "gopher," even if that was what they always called the girls being initiated. It was degrading, like being given a number. It was a denial of individuality. ❺

Rebellion flooded through her.

"I said get up. Are you deaf?"

Millicent got up, standing there.

"Into the house, gopher. There's a bed to be made and a room to be cleaned at the top of the stairs."

Millicent went up the stairs mutely.[6] She found Bev's room and started making the bed. Smiling to herself, she was thinking: How absurdly funny, me taking orders from this girl like a servant.

Bev was suddenly there in the doorway. "Wipe that smile off your face," she commanded.

---

4. **malicious** (mə·lish′əs) *adj.:* intentionally harmful; cruel.
5. **anonymity** (an′ə·nim′ə·tē) *n.:* namelessness; lack of individuality.
6. **mutely** (myo͞ot′lē) *adv.:* without speaking; silently.

PLOT

❹ Why was Tracy blackballed? What **complication** does Tracy's blackballing create for Millicent?

THEME

❺ What details point to Millicent's growing uncertainty about the initiation?

There seemed something about this relationship that was not all fun. In Bev's eyes, Millicent was sure of it, there was a hard, bright spark of exultation.[7]

On the way to school, Millicent had to walk behind Bev at a distance of ten paces, carrying her books. They came up to the drugstore, where there already was a crowd of boys and girls from Lansing High waiting for the show.

The other girls being initiated were there, so Millicent felt relieved. It would not be so bad now, being part of the group.

"What'll we have them do?" Betsy Johnson asked Bev. That morning Betsy had made her "gopher" carry an old colored parasol through the square and sing "I'm Always Chasing Rainbows."

"I know," Herb Dalton, the good-looking basketball captain, said.

A remarkable change came over Bev. She was all at once very soft and coquettish.[8]

"You can't tell them what to do," Bev said sweetly. "Men have nothing to say about this little deal."

"All right, all right," Herb laughed, stepping back and pretending to fend off a blow.

"It's getting late." Louise had come up. "Almost eight-thirty. We'd better get them marching on to school."

The "gophers" had to do a Charleston step[9] all the way to school, and each one had her own song to sing, trying to drown out the other four. During school, of course, you couldn't fool around, but even then, there was a rule that you mustn't talk to boys outside of class or at lunch time . . . or any time at all after school. So the sorority girls would get the most popular boys to go up to the "gophers" and ask them out, or try to start them talking, and sometimes a "gopher" was taken by surprise and began to say something before she could catch herself. And then the boy reported her and she got a black mark.

Herb Dalton approached Millicent as she was getting an ice cream at the lunch counter that noon. She saw him coming before he spoke to her, and looked down quickly, thinking: He is too princely, too dark and smiling. And I am much too vulnerable. Why must he be the one I have to be careful of?

I won't say anything, she thought, I'll just smile very sweetly.

She smiled up at Herb very sweetly and mutely. His return grin was rather miraculous. It was surely more than was called for in the line of duty.

"I know you can't talk to me," he said, very low. "But you're doing fine, the girls say. I even like your hair straight and all."

---

7. **exultation** (egz′əl·tā′shən) *n.*: rejoicing; triumph.
8. **coquettish** (ko·ket′ish) *adj.*: flirtatious. (A coquette is a woman who flirts with men.)
9. **Charleston** (chärls′tən) **step:** The Charleston is a lively dance from the 1920s.

Bev was coming toward them, then, her red mouth set in a bright, calculating[10] smile. She ignored Millicent and sailed up to Herb.

"Why waste your time with gophers?" she caroled gaily. "Their tongues are tied, but completely."

Herb managed a parting shot. "But that one keeps *such* an attractive silence." ➏

Millicent smiled as she ate her sundae at the counter with Tracy. Generally, the girls who were outsiders now, as Millicent had been, scoffed at the initiation antics as childish and absurd to hide their secret envy. But Tracy was understanding, as ever.

"Tonight's the worst, I guess, Tracy," Millicent told her. "I hear that the girls are taking us on a bus over to Lewiston and going to have us performing in the square."

"Just keep a poker face outside," Tracy advised. "But keep laughing like mad inside."

Millicent and Bev took a bus ahead of the rest of the girls; they had to stand up on the way to Lewiston Square. Bev seemed very cross about something. Finally she said, "You were talking with Herb Dalton at lunch today."

"No," said Millicent honestly.

"Well, I *saw* you smile at him. That's practically as bad as talking. Remember not to do it again."

Millicent kept silent.

"It's fifteen minutes before the bus gets into town," Bev was saying then. "I want you to go up and down the bus asking people what they eat for breakfast. Remember, you can't tell them you're being initiated."

Millicent looked down the aisle of the crowded bus and felt suddenly quite sick. She thought: How will I ever do it, going up to all those stony-faced people who are staring coldly out of the window . . .

"You heard me, gopher."

"Excuse me, madam," Millicent said politely to the lady in the first seat of the bus, "but I'm taking a survey. Could you please tell me what you eat for breakfast?"

"Why . . . er . . . just orange juice, toast and coffee," she said.

"Thank you very much." Millicent went on to the next person, a young businessman. He ate eggs sunny side up, toast and coffee.

By the time Millicent got to the back of the bus, most of the people were smiling at her. They obviously know, she thought, that I'm being initiated into something.

---

10. **calculating** (kal′kyoo•lāt′iŋ) *adj.*: plotting; scheming.

Introducing the Collection Theme

PLOT

➏ How does Herb add a new level of **conflict** to Millicent and Bev's relationship?

Christy (2004) by Alex Katz (b. 1927). Oil on canvas. 96 × 33.5 in.

Art ©Alex Katz/Licensed by VAGA/New York, NY.

Finally, there was only one man left in the corner of the back seat. He was small and jolly, with a ruddy, wrinkled face that spread into a beaming smile as Millicent approached. In his brown suit with the forest-green tie he looked something like a gnome or a cheerful leprechaun.[11]

"Excuse me, sir," Millicent smiled, "but I'm taking a survey. What do you eat for breakfast?"

"Heather birds' eyebrows on toast," the little man rattled off.

"*What?*" Millicent exclaimed.

"Heather birds' eyebrows," the little man explained. "Heather birds live on the mythological moors[12] and fly about all day long, singing wild and sweet in the sun. They're bright purple and have *very* tasty eyebrows."

Millicent broke out into spontaneous[13] laughter. Why, this was wonderful, the way she felt a sudden comradeship with a stranger.

"Are you mythological, too?"

"Not exactly," he replied, "but I certainly hope to be some day. Being mythological does wonders for one's ego."

The bus was swinging into the station now; Millicent hated to leave the little man. She wanted to ask him more about the birds.

And from that time on, initiations didn't bother Millicent at all. She went gaily about Lewiston Square from store to store asking for broken crackers and mangoes, and she just laughed inside when people stared and then brightened, answering her crazy questions as if she were quite serious and really a person of consequence. So many people were shut up tight inside themselves like boxes, yet they would open up, unfolding quite wonderfully, if only you were interested in them. And really, you didn't have to belong to a club to feel related to other human beings. ❼

One afternoon Millicent had started talking with Liane Morris, another of the girls being initiated, about what it would be like when they were finally in the sorority.

"Oh, I know pretty much what it'll be like," Liane had said. "My sister belonged before she graduated from high school two years ago."

"Well, just what *do* they do as a club?" Millicent wanted to know.

"Why, they have a meeting once a week . . . each girl takes turns entertaining at her house . . ."

"You mean it's just a sort of exclusive social group . . ."

"I guess so . . . though that's a funny way of putting it. But it sure gives a girl prestige[14] value. My sister started going steady with the captain of the football team after she got in. Not bad, I say."

THEME

❼ How does Millicent's encounter with the little man change her feelings about the initiation?

---

11. **gnome** (nōm) **or a cheerful leprechaun** (lep′rə•kôn)*n.:* In folklore a gnome is a small, misshapen creature, and a leprechaun is a mischievous elf.
12. **moors** (mŏŏrz) *n.:* open, rolling areas of land, usually covered with heather, a plant with small, pinkish purple flowers.
13. **spontaneous** (spän•tā′nē•əs) *adj.:* arising naturally; unplanned.
14. **prestige** (pres•tēᴣh′)*n.* used as *adj.:* relating to status or the power to impress because of wealth or success.

No, it wasn't bad, Millicent had thought, lying in bed on the morning of Rat Court and listening to the sparrows chirping in the gutters. She thought of Herb. Would he ever have been so friendly if she were without the sorority label? Would he ask her out (if he ever did) just for herself, no strings attached?

Then there was another thing that bothered her. Leaving Tracy on the outskirts. Because that is the way it would be; Millicent had seen it happen before.

Outside, the sparrows were still chirping, and as she lay in bed Millicent visualized them, pale gray-brown birds in a flock, one like the other, all exactly alike.

And then, for some reason, Millicent thought of the heather birds. Swooping carefree over the moors, they would go singing and crying out across the great spaces of air, dipping and darting, strong and proud in their freedom and their sometime loneliness. It was then that she made her decision.

Seated now on the woodpile in Betsy Johnson's cellar, Millicent knew that she had come triumphant through the trial of fire, the searing[15] period of the ego which could end in two kinds of victory for her. The easiest of which would be her coronation[16] as a princess, labeling her conclusively as one of the select flock. ❽

The other victory would be much harder, but she knew it was what she wanted. It was not that she was being noble or anything. It was just that she had learned there were other ways of getting into the great hall, blazing with lights, of people and of life.

It would be hard to explain to the girls tonight, of course, but she could tell Louise later just how it was. How she had proved something to herself by going through everything, even Rat Court, and then deciding not to join the sorority after all. And how she could still be friends with everybody. Sisters with everybody. Tracy, too. ❾

The door behind her opened and a ray of light sliced across the soft gloom of the basement room.

"Hey, Millicent, come on out now. This is it." There were some of the girls outside.

"I'm coming," she said, getting up and moving out of the soft darkness into the glare of light, thinking: This is it, all right. The worst part, the hardest part, the part of initiation that I figured out myself.

But just then, from somewhere far off, Millicent was sure of it, there came a melodic fluting, quite wild and sweet, and she knew that it must be

---

15. **searing** (sir′iŋ) *v.* used as *adj.:* burning; scorching.
16. **coronation** (kôr′ə•nā′shən) *n.:* crowning.

PLOT

❽ The **flashback** ends at the start of this paragraph. What day is it now?

THEME

❾ What decision has Millicent made about joining the sorority, now that she has faced the unknown? Why?

the song of the heather birds as they went wheeling and gliding against wide blue horizons through vast spaces of air, their wings flashing quick and purple in the bright sun.

Within Millicent another melody soared, strong and exuberant,[17] a triumphant answer to the music of the darting heather birds that sang so clear and lilting over the far lands. And she knew that her own private initiation had just begun. **10**

---

17. **exuberant** (eg·zo͞o′bər·ənt) *adj.:* joyful.

THEME

10 What do you think the narrator means by saying that Millicent's "own private initiation had just begun"?

Meet the Writer
Sylvia Plath

A Stormy Life

Sylvia Plath (1932–1963) was a golden girl—beautiful, intelligent, and popular. Beneath that shining exterior, however, Plath struggled with episodes of depression. When "Initiation" was accepted for publication by *Seventeen* magazine, the nineteen-year-old Plath wrote, "This news makes me feel that I am maybe not destined to deteriorate, after all."

Despite the depression that sometimes plagued her, Plath graduated with the highest honors from Smith College and went to Cambridge University in England on a Fulbright grant. There, she fell in love with and married the brooding, handsome English poet Ted Hughes. Their stormy relationship produced two children and a great deal of poetry, but eventually their marriage fell apart, and Hughes moved out.

Overcome by loneliness and despair, Plath took her own life in the winter of 1963, at the age of thirty. Shortly before her death, *The Bell Jar,* an ambitious and haunting novel that Plath based on her earlier experiences of collapse and recovery, was published. In her last weeks she worked feverishly on a series of intensely personal poems that were later compiled by Hughes and published in *Ariel* (1965). This powerful collection of poetry cemented Plath's status as a celebrated and influential poet.

After You Read

Response and Analysis

Reading Check

1. What are the tests the girls being initiated into the sorority must pass?

Thinking Critically

2. Millicent compares joining the sorority to entering a "magic circle" or "her rightful kingdom." What do these phrases tell you about her view of the sorority? What does she hope to gain by becoming a member?

3. What is Millicent's **internal conflict**? What **external conflicts** does she face? Which of these conflicts do you think is the most significant? Explain.

4. At the end of the story, Millicent is inspired by the thought of heather birds "wheeling and gliding against wide blue horizons." How do the heather birds differ from the sparrows, which the narrator mentions twice? Why does Millicent decide to identify with the heather birds and not the sparrows?

5. In your Quickwrite chart you made notes about the various unknowns in your life. The unknown takes several forms in this story, too. Think about how the collection theme "Into the Unknown" relates to this story by answering the following questions:

   • In what ways does Millicent venture into the unknown by participating in the initiation rite? What does she discover about herself as a result?

   • What kinds of unknowns does Millicent face at the end of the story, when she prepares to confront the waiting group of sorority members? Using clues in the story, predict how Millicent will feel after she confronts the group.

Extending and Evaluating

6. This story takes place in the 1950s. How could the **plot** be updated to take place today? What do you see as the main differences between high school students and initiation rites in the 1950s and teenagers and their rites today?

> ## Exploring the Theme
> ### Into the Unknown
>
> In the rest of this collection, you'll read about characters and people who confront the unknown. As you read, think about the types of unknowns these individuals face and the different ways they respond to the strange or the unfamiliar.

SKILLS FOCUS

Literary Focus
Analyze internal and external conflicts.

Before You Read

The Most Dangerous Game

Make the Connection
Quickwrite ✏️

Some of the most exciting narratives pit villain against hero in a life-or-death struggle. The tension in such stories often depends as much on the character of the bad guy or gal as on that of the hero. Write a few sentences describing a villain from a novel, story, or movie. Why does the character fascinate you?

Literary Focus
Foreshadowing: Hints About What's Ahead

People call them cliffhangers or nail-biters. They are stories of suspense that keep you glued to your chair. One way that writers create suspense is through **foreshadowing,** the use of clues that hint at later events in the story. Foreshadowing makes you curious, even anxious, to know what will happen next—it keeps you turning the pages. Once you've finished reading, you can piece together the clues and enjoy the story all the more. In this suspenseful tale the ominous foreshadowing will hook you early on.

Reading Skills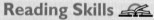
Making Predictions: Matching Wits with the Writer

When you read a suspense-filled story, you make predictions about what is going to happen, often without even realizing it. A **prediction** is a type of inference, a guess based on evidence. Some of the things readers base predictions on include

- clues the writer plants

- their own experience of life
- their understanding of how stories work

Before you start this famous adventure story, read its **title** again. What do you predict the title might mean? Be sure to compare your predictions with those of your classmates. (How many different interpretations did you have for the word *game*?) Then, as you read, stop at the open-book signs (📖) at the end of some paragraphs, and continue to make predictions.

Vocabulary Development

receding (ri·sēd′iŋ) *v.* used as *adj.*: becoming more distant.

disarming (dis·ärm′iŋ) *adj.*: removing or lessening suspicions or fears.

prolonged (prō·lôŋd′) *v.* used as *adj.*: extended.

imprudent (im·prōōd′′nt) *adj.*: unwise.

surmounted (sər·mount′id) *v.*: overcame.

unruffled (un·ruf′əld) *adj.*: calm; not disturbed.

invariably (in·ver′ē·ə·blē) *adv.*: always; without changing.

diverting (də·vurt′iŋ) *adj.*: entertaining.

impulse (im′puls′) *n.*: sudden desire to do something.

protruding (prō·trōōd′iŋ) *v.* used as *adj.*: sticking out.

SKILLS FOCUS

Literary Skills
Understand foreshadowing.

Reading Skills
Make predictions.

INTERNET

Vocabulary Practice

Keyword: LE7 9-1

THE MOST DANGEROUS GAME

"Sailors have a curious dread of the place."

Richard Connell

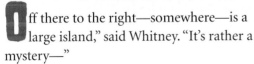ff there to the right—somewhere—is a large island," said Whitney. "It's rather a mystery—"

"What island is it?" Rainsford asked.

"The old charts call it Ship-Trap Island," Whitney replied. "A suggestive name, isn't it? Sailors have a curious dread of the place. I don't know why. Some superstition—"

"Can't see it," remarked Rainsford, trying to peer through the dank tropical night that was palpable as it pressed its thick warm blackness in upon the yacht.

"You've good eyes," said Whitney, with a laugh, "and I've seen you pick off a moose moving in the brown fall bush at four hundred yards, but even you can't see four miles or so through a moonless Caribbean night."

"Nor four yards," admitted Rainsford. "Ugh! It's like moist black velvet."

"It will be light in Rio," promised Whitney. "We should make it in a few days. I hope the jaguar guns have come from Purdey's.[1] We should have some good hunting up the Amazon. Great sport, hunting."

"The best sport in the world," agreed Rainsford.

"For the hunter," amended Whitney. "Not for the jaguar."

"Don't talk rot, Whitney," said Rainsford. "You're a big-game hunter, not a philosopher. Who cares how a jaguar feels?"

"Perhaps the jaguar does," observed Whitney.

"Bah! They've no understanding."

"Even so, I rather think they understand one thing—fear. The fear of pain and the fear of death."

"Nonsense," laughed Rainsford. "This hot weather is making you soft, Whitney. Be a realist. The world is made up of two classes—the hunters and the huntees. Luckily, you and I are the hunters. Do you think we've passed that island yet?"

"I can't tell in the dark. I hope so."

"Why?" asked Rainsford.

"The place has a reputation—a bad one."

"Cannibals?" suggested Rainsford.

"Hardly. Even cannibals wouldn't live in such a Godforsaken place. But it's gotten into sailor lore, somehow. Didn't you notice that the crew's nerves seemed a bit jumpy today?"

"They were a bit strange, now you mention it. Even Captain Nielsen—"

"Yes, even that tough-minded old Swede, who'd go up to the devil himself and ask him for a light. Those fishy blue eyes held a look I never saw there before. All I could get out of him was: 'This place has an evil name among seafaring men, sir.' Then he said to me, very gravely:

'Don't you feel anything?'—as if the air about us was actually poisonous. Now, you mustn't laugh when I tell you this—I did feel something like a sudden chill.

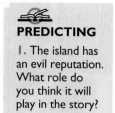

PREDICTING

1. The island has an evil reputation. What role do you think it will play in the story?

"There was no breeze. The sea was as flat as a plate-glass window. We were drawing near the island then. What I felt was a—a mental chill, a sort of sudden dread."

"Pure imagination," said Rainsford. "One superstitious sailor can taint the whole ship's company with his fear."

"Maybe. But sometimes I think sailors have an extra sense that tells them when they are in danger. Sometimes I think evil is a tangible thing—with wavelengths, just as sound and light have. An evil place can, so to speak, broadcast vibrations of evil. Anyhow, I'm glad we're getting out of this zone. Well, I think I'll turn in now, Rainsford."

"I'm not sleepy," said Rainsford. "I'm going to smoke another pipe on the afterdeck."

"Good night, then, Rainsford. See you at breakfast."

"Right. Good night, Whitney."

There was no sound in the night as Rainsford sat there but the muffled throb of the engine that drove the yacht swiftly through the darkness, and the swish and ripple of the wash of the propeller.

Rainsford, reclining in a steamer chair, indolently[2] puffed on his favorite brier.[3] The sensuous drowsiness of the night was on him. "It's so dark," he thought, "that I could sleep without closing my eyes; the night would be my eyelids—"

An abrupt sound startled him. Off to the

---

1. **Purdey's** (pʉr′dēz): British manufacturer of hunting equipment.

2. **indolently** (in′də·lənt·lē) *adv.:* lazily.
3. **brier** (brī′ər) *n.:* tobacco pipe made from the root of a brier bush or tree.

right he heard it, and his ears, expert in such matters, could not be mistaken. Again he heard the sound, and again. Somewhere, off in the blackness, someone had fired a gun three times.

Rainsford sprang up and moved quickly to the rail, mystified. He strained his eyes in the direction from which the reports had come, but it was like trying to see through a blanket. He leapt upon the rail and balanced himself there, to get greater elevation; his pipe, striking a rope, was knocked from his mouth. He lunged for it; a short, hoarse cry came from his lips as he realized he had reached too far and had lost his balance. The cry was pinched off short as the blood-warm waters of the Caribbean Sea closed over his head.

He struggled up to the surface and tried to cry out, but the wash from the speeding yacht slapped him in the face and the salt water in his open mouth made him gag and strangle. Desperately he struck out with strong strokes after the receding lights of the yacht, but he stopped before he had swum fifty feet. A certain coolheadedness had come to him; it was not the first time he had been in a tight place. There was a chance that his cries could be heard by someone aboard the yacht, but that chance was slender and grew more slender as the yacht raced on. He wrestled himself out of his clothes and shouted with all his power. The lights of the yacht became faint and ever-vanishing fireflies; then they were blotted out entirely by the night.

Rainsford remembered the shots. They had come from the right, and doggedly he swam in that direction, swimming with slow, deliberate strokes, conserving his strength. For a seemingly endless time he fought the sea. He began to count his strokes; he could do possibly a hundred more and then—

Rainsford heard a sound. It came out of the darkness, a high screaming sound, the sound of an animal in an extremity of anguish and terror.

He did not recognize the animal that made the sound; he did not try to; with fresh vitality he swam toward the sound. He heard it again; then it was cut short by another noise, crisp, staccato.

"Pistol shot," muttered Rainsford, swimming on.

Ten minutes of determined effort brought another sound to his ears—the most welcome he had ever heard—the muttering and growling of the sea breaking on a rocky shore. He was almost on the rocks before he saw them; on a night less calm he would have been shattered against them. With his remaining strength he dragged himself from the swirling waters. Jagged crags appeared to jut into the opaqueness.[4]

He forced himself upward, hand over hand. Gasping, his hands raw, he reached a flat place at the top. Dense jungle came down to the very edge of the cliffs. What perils that tangle of trees and underbrush might hold for him did not concern Rainsford just then. All he knew was that he was safe from his enemy, the sea, and that utter weariness was on him. He flung himself down at the jungle edge and tumbled headlong into the deepest sleep of his life.

---

4. **opaqueness** (ō·pāk′nis) *n.*: here, darkness. Something opaque does not let light pass through.

Vocabulary
receding (ri′sēd′iŋ) *v.* used as *adj.*: becoming more distant.

For a seemingly endless time he fought the sea.

When he opened his eyes he knew from the position of the sun that it was late in the afternoon. Sleep had given him new vigor; a sharp hunger was picking at him. He looked about him, almost cheerfully.

"Where there are pistol shots, there are men. Where there are men, there is food," he thought. But what kind of men, he wondered, in so forbidding a place? An unbroken front of snarled and ragged jungle fringed the shore.

He saw no sign of a trail through the closely knit web of weeds and trees; it was easier to go along the shore, and Rainsford floundered along by the water. Not far from where he had landed, he stopped.

Some wounded thing, by the evidence a large animal, had thrashed about in the underbrush; the jungle weeds were crushed down and the moss was lacerated; one patch of weeds was stained crimson. A small, glittering object not far away caught Rainsford's eye and he picked it up. It was an empty cartridge.

"A twenty-two," he remarked. "That's odd. It must have been a fairly large animal too. The hunter had his nerve with him to tackle it with a light gun. It's clear that the brute put up a fight. I suppose the first three shots I heard was when the hunter flushed his quarry[5] and wounded it. The last shot was when he trailed it here and finished it."

He examined the ground closely and found what he had hoped to find—the print of hunting boots. They pointed along the cliff in the direction he had been going. Eagerly he hurried along, now slipping on a rotten log or a loose stone, but making headway; night was beginning to settle down on the island.

Bleak darkness was blacking out the sea and jungle when Rainsford sighted the lights. He came upon them as he turned a crook in the coastline, and his first thought was that he had come upon a village, for there were many lights. But as he forged along, he saw to his great astonishment that all the lights were in one enormous building—a lofty structure with pointed towers plunging upward into the gloom. His eyes made out the shadowy outlines of a palatial château;[6] it was set on a high bluff, and on three sides of it cliffs dived down to where the sea licked greedy lips in the shadows.

"Mirage," thought Rainsford. But it was no mirage, he found, when he opened the tall spiked iron gate. The stone steps were real enough; the massive door with a leering gargoyle for a knocker was real enough; yet about it all hung an air of unreality.

He lifted the knocker, and it creaked up stiffly, as if it had never before been used. He let it fall, and it startled him with its booming loudness. He thought he heard steps within; the door remained closed. Again Rainsford lifted the heavy knocker and let it fall. The door opened then, opened as suddenly as if it were on a spring, and Rainsford stood blinking in the river of glaring gold light that poured out. The first thing Rainsford's eyes discerned was the largest man Rainsford had ever seen—a gigantic creature, solidly made and black-bearded to the waist. In his hand the man held a long-barreled revolver, and he was pointing it straight at Rainsford's heart.

Out of the snarl of beard two small eyes regarded Rainsford.

"It's clear that the brute put up a fight."

---

5. **flushed his quarry:** drove the animal he was hunting out of its hiding place.

6. **château** (sha·tō′) *n.:* large country house.

"Don't be alarmed," said Rainsford, with a smile which he hoped was disarming. "I'm no robber. I fell off a yacht. My name is Sanger Rainsford of New York City."

The menacing look in the eyes did not change. The revolver pointed as rigidly as if the giant were a statue. He gave no sign that he understood Rainsford's words or that he had even heard them. He was dressed in uniform, a black uniform trimmed with gray astrakhan.[7]

"I'm Sanger Rainsford of New York," Rainsford began again. "I fell off a yacht. I am hungry."

The man's only answer was to raise with his thumb the hammer of his revolver. Then Rainsford saw the man's free hand go to his forehead in a military salute, and he saw him click his heels together and stand at attention. Another man was coming down the broad marble steps, an erect, slender man in evening clothes. He advanced to Rainsford and held out his hand.

In a cultivated voice marked by a slight accent that gave it added precision and deliberateness, he said: "It is a very great pleasure and honor to welcome Mr. Sanger Rainsford, the celebrated hunter, to my home."

Automatically Rainsford shook the man's hand.

"I've read your book about hunting snow leopards in Tibet, you see," explained the man. "I am General Zaroff."

Rainsford's first impression was that the man was singularly handsome; his second was that there was an original, almost bizarre quality about the general's face. He was a tall man past middle age, for his hair was a vivid white; but his thick eyebrows and pointed military moustache were as black as the night from which Rainsford had come. His eyes, too, were black and very bright. He had high cheekbones, a sharp-cut nose, a spare, dark face, the face of a man used to giving orders, the face of an aristocrat. Turning

to the giant in uniform, the general made a sign. The giant put away his pistol, saluted, withdrew.

"Ivan is an incredibly strong fellow," remarked the general, "but he has the misfortune to be deaf and dumb. A simple fellow, but, I'm afraid, like all his race, a bit of a savage."

"Is he Russian?"

"He is a Cossack,"[8] said the general, and his smile showed red lips and pointed teeth. "So am I.

"Come," he said, "we shouldn't be chatting here. We can talk later. Now you want clothes, food, rest. You shall have them. This is a most restful spot."

Ivan had reappeared, and the general spoke to him with lips that moved but gave forth no sound.

"Follow Ivan, if you please, Mr. Rainsford," said the general. "I was about to have my dinner when you came. I'll wait for you. You'll find that my clothes will fit you, I think."

It was to a huge, beam-ceilinged bedroom with a canopied bed big enough for six men that Rainsford followed the silent giant. Ivan laid out an evening suit, and Rainsford, as he put it on, noticed that it came from a London tailor who ordinarily cut and sewed for none below the rank of duke.

The dining room to which Ivan conducted him was in many ways remarkable. There was a medieval magnificence about it; it suggested a baronial hall of feudal times, with its oaken panels, its high ceiling, its vast refectory table where two-score men could sit down to eat. About the hall were the mounted heads of many

PREDICTING

2. What do Zaroff's remarks about Cossacks suggest about how he will behave later in the story?

---

7. **astrakhan** (as′trə·kən) *n.:* curly fur of very young lambs.

8. **Cossack** (käs′ak′): member of a group from Ukraine, many of whom served as horsemen to the Russian czars and were famous for their fierceness in battle.

Vocabulary

disarming (dis·ärm′iŋ) *adj.:* removing or lessening suspicions or fears.

animals—lions, tigers, elephants, moose, bears; larger or more perfect specimens Rainsford had never seen. At the great table the general was sitting, alone.

"You'll have a cocktail, Mr. Rainsford," he suggested. The cocktail was surpassingly good; and, Rainsford noted, the table appointments were of the finest—the linen, the crystal, the silver, the china.

They were eating borscht, the rich red soup with sour cream so dear to Russian palates. Half apologetically General Zaroff said: "We do our best to preserve the amenities[9] of civilization here. Please forgive any lapses. We are well off the beaten track, you know. Do you think the champagne has suffered from its long ocean trip?"

"Not in the least," declared Rainsford. He was finding the general a most thoughtful and affable host, a true cosmopolite.[10] But there was one small trait of the general's that made Rainsford uncomfortable. Whenever he looked up from his plate he found the general studying him, appraising him narrowly.

"Perhaps," said General Zaroff, "you were surprised that I recognized your name. You see, I read all books on hunting published in English, French, and Russian. I have but one passion in my life, Mr. Rainsford, and it is the hunt."

"You have some wonderful heads here," said Rainsford as he ate a particularly well-cooked filet mignon. "That Cape buffalo is the largest I ever saw."

"Oh, that fellow. Yes, he was a monster."

"Did he charge you?"

"Hurled me against a tree," said the general. "Fractured my skull. But I got the brute."

"I've always thought," said Rainsford, "that the Cape buffalo is the most dangerous of all big game."

For a moment the general did not reply; he was smiling his curious red-lipped smile. Then he said slowly: "No. You are wrong, sir. The Cape buffalo is not the most dangerous big game." He sipped his wine. "Here in my preserve on this island," he said in the same slow tone, "I hunt more dangerous game."

Rainsford expressed his surprise. "Is there big game on this island?"

The general nodded. "The biggest."

"Really?"

"Oh, it isn't here naturally, of course. I have to stock the island."

"What have you imported, general?" Rainsford asked. "Tigers?"

The general smiled. "No," he said. "Hunting tigers ceased to interest me some years ago. I exhausted their possibilities, you see. No thrill left in tigers, no real danger. I live for danger, Mr. Rainsford."

The general took from his pocket a gold cigarette case and offered his guest a long black cigarette with a silver tip; it was perfumed and gave off a smell like incense.

"We will have some capital hunting, you and I," said the general. "I shall be most glad to have your society."

"But what game—" began Rainsford.

"I'll tell you," said the general. "You will be amused, I know. I think I may say, in all modesty, that I have done a rare thing. I have invented a new sensation. May I pour you another glass of port, Mr. Rainsford?"

"Thank you, general."

The general filled both glasses and said: "God makes some men poets. Some He makes kings, some beggars. Me He made a hunter. My hand was made for the trigger, my father said. He was a very rich man, with a quarter of a million acres in the Crimea,[11] and he was an

> **PREDICTING**
>
> 3. What do you **predict** the most dangerous game will be?

---

9. **amenities** (ə·men′ə·tēz) *n.*: comforts and conveniences.

10. **cosmopolite** (käz·mäp′ə·līt′) *n.*: knowledgeable citizen of the world.

11. **Crimea** (krī·mē′ə): peninsula in Ukraine jutting into the Black Sea.

Casanova (1997) by Julio Larraz. Oil on canvas (60″ × 69″).
Courtesy of the Nohra Haime Gallery, New York.

ardent sportsman. When I was only five years old, he gave me a little gun, specially made in Moscow for me, to shoot sparrows with. When I shot some of his prize turkeys with it, he did not punish me; he complimented me on my marksmanship. I killed my first bear in the Caucasus[12] when I was ten. My whole life has been one <u>prolonged</u> hunt. I went into the army—it was expected of noblemen's sons—and for a time commanded a division of Cossack cavalry, but my real interest was always the hunt. I have hunted every kind of game in every land. It would be impossible for me to tell you how many animals I have killed."

---

12. **Caucasus** (kô′kə·səs): mountainous region between southeastern Europe and western Asia.

Vocabulary
prolonged (prō·lôŋd′) *v.* used as *adj.*: extended.

The general puffed at his cigarette.

"After the debacle[13] in Russia I left the country, for it was imprudent for an officer of the czar to stay there. Many noble Russians lost everything. I, luckily, had invested heavily in American securities, so I shall never have to open a tearoom in Monte Carlo[14] or drive a taxi in Paris. Naturally, I continued to hunt—grizzlies in your Rockies, crocodiles in the Ganges,[15] rhinoceroses in East Africa. It was in Africa that the Cape buffalo hit me and laid me up for six months. As soon as I recovered I started for the Amazon to hunt jaguars, for I had heard they were unusually cunning. They weren't." The Cossack sighed. "They were no match at all for a hunter with his wits about him and a high-powered rifle. I was bitterly disappointed. I was lying in my tent with a splitting headache one night when a terrible thought pushed its way into my mind. Hunting was beginning to bore me! And hunting, remember, had been my life. I have heard that in America businessmen often go to pieces when they give up the business that has been their life."

"Yes, that's so," said Rainsford.

The general smiled. "I had no wish to go to pieces," he said. "I must do something. Now, mine is an analytical mind, Mr. Rainsford. Doubtless that is why I enjoy the problems of the chase."

"No doubt, General Zaroff."

"So," continued the general, "I asked myself why the hunt no longer fascinated me. You are much younger than I am, Mr. Rainsford, and have not hunted as much, but you perhaps can guess the answer."

"What was it?"

"Simply this: Hunting had ceased to be what you call a sporting proposition. It had become too easy. I always got my quarry. Always. There is no greater bore than perfection."

The general lit a fresh cigarette.

"No animal had a chance with me anymore. That is no boast; it is a mathematical certainty. The animal had nothing but his legs and his instinct. Instinct is no match for reason. When I thought of this, it was a tragic moment for me, I can tell you."

Rainsford leaned across the table, absorbed in what his host was saying.

"It came to me as an inspiration what I must do," the general went on.

"And that was?"

The general smiled the quiet smile of one who has faced an obstacle and surmounted it with success. "I had to invent a new animal to hunt," he said.

"A new animal? You're joking."

"Not at all," said the general. "I never joke about hunting. I needed a new animal. I found one. So I bought this island, built this house, and here I do my hunting. The island is perfect for my purposes—there are jungles with a maze of trails in them, hills, swamps—"

"But the animal, General Zaroff?"

"Oh," said the general, "it supplies me with the most exciting hunting in the world. No other hunting compares with it for an instant. Every day I hunt, and I never grow bored now, for I have a quarry with which I can match my wits."

Rainsford's bewilderment showed in his face.

"I wanted the ideal animal to hunt," explained the general. "So I said: 'What are the attributes of an ideal quarry?' And the answer was, of course: 'It must have courage, cunning, and, above all, it must be able to reason.'"

---

13. **debacle** (di·bä′kəl) *n.*: overwhelming defeat. Zaroff is referring to the Russian Revolution of 1917, in which the czar and his government were overthrown.
14. **Monte Carlo** (mänt′ə kär′lō): gambling resort in Monaco, a country on the Mediterranean Sea.
15. **Ganges** (gan′jēz): river in northern India and Bangladesh.

Vocabulary

imprudent (im·prōōd′′nt) *adj.*: unwise.
surmounted (sər·mount′id) *v.*: overcame.

Tropical Storm with Tiger—Surprise by Henri Rousseau (Le Douanier) (1844–1910).
National Gallery, London/SuperStock.

"But no animal can reason," objected Rainsford.

"My dear fellow," said the general, "there is one that can."

"But you can't mean—" gasped Rainsford.

"And why not?"

"I can't believe you are serious, General Zaroff. This is a grisly joke."

"Why should I not be serious? I am speaking of hunting."

"Hunting? Good God, General Zaroff, what you speak of is murder."

The general laughed with entire good nature. He regarded Rainsford quizzically. "I refuse to believe that so modern and civilized a young man as you seem to be harbors romantic ideas about the value of human life. Surely your experiences in the war—"

"Did not make me condone[16] coldblooded murder," finished Rainsford stiffly.

Laughter shook the general. "How extraordinarily droll you are!" he said. "One does not

---

16. **condone** (kən·dōn′) *v*.: overlook an offense; excuse.

expect nowadays to find a young man of the educated class, even in America, with such a naive, and, if I may say so, mid-Victorian point of view. It's like finding a snuffbox in a limousine. Ah, well, doubtless you had Puritan ancestors. So many Americans appear to have had. I'll wager you'll forget your notions when you go hunting with me. You've a genuine new thrill in store for you, Mr. Rainsford."

"Thank you, I'm a hunter, not a murderer."

"Dear me," said the general, quite <u>unruffled</u>, "again that unpleasant word. But I think I can show you that your scruples[17] are quite ill-founded."

"Yes?"

"Life is for the strong, to be lived by the strong, and if need be, taken by the strong. The weak of the world were put here to give the strong pleasure. I am strong. Why should I not use my gift? If I wish to hunt, why should I not? I hunt the scum of the earth—sailors from tramp ships—lascars,[18] blacks, Chinese, whites, mongrels—a thoroughbred horse or hound is worth more than a score of them."

"But they are men," said Rainsford hotly.

"Precisely," said the general. "That is why I use them. It gives me pleasure. They can reason, after a fashion. So they are dangerous."

"But where do you get them?"

The general's left eyelid fluttered down in a wink. "This island is called Ship-Trap," he answered. "Sometimes an angry god of the high seas sends them to me. Sometimes, when Providence is not so kind, I help Providence a bit. Come to the window with me."

PREDICTING

4. Think about the information presented at the beginning of the story. How might Zaroff find men to hunt?

---

17. **scruples** (skrōō′pəlz) *n.:* feelings of doubt or guilt about a suggested action.
18. **lascars** (las′kərz) *n.:* East Indian sailors employed on European ships.

(Opposite) *The Snake Charmer* by Henri Rousseau (1844–1910).
Oil on canvas (160 cm × 189.5 cm).
Musée d'Orsay, Paris.

Rainsford went to the window and looked out toward the sea.

"Watch! Out there!" exclaimed the general, pointing into the night. Rainsford's eyes saw only blackness, and then, as the general pressed a button, far out to sea Rainsford saw the flash of lights.

The general chuckled. "They indicate a channel," he said, "where there's none; giant rocks with razor edges crouch like a sea monster with wide-open jaws. They can crush a ship as easily as I crush this nut." He dropped a walnut on the hardwood floor and brought his heel grinding down on it. "Oh, yes," he said, casually, as if in answer to a question, "I have electricity. We try to be civilized here."

"Civilized? And you shoot down men?"

A trace of anger was in the general's black eyes, but it was there for but a second, and he said, in his most pleasant manner: "Dear me, what a righteous young man you are! I assure you I do not do the thing you suggest. That would be barbarous. I treat these visitors with every consideration. They get plenty of good food and exercise. They get into splendid physical condition. You shall see for yourself tomorrow."

"What do you mean?"

"We'll visit my training school," smiled the general. "It's in the cellar. I have about a dozen pupils down there now. They're from the Spanish bark *San Lucar* that had the bad luck to go on the rocks out there. A very inferior lot, I regret to say. Poor specimens and more accustomed to the deck than to the jungle."

He raised his hand, and Ivan, who served as waiter, brought thick Turkish coffee. Rainsford,

---

Vocabulary
unruffled (un·ruf′əld) *adj.:* calm; not disturbed.

with an effort, held his tongue in check.

"It's a game, you see," pursued the general blandly. "I suggest to one of them that we go hunting. I give him a supply of food and an excellent hunting knife. I give him three hours' start. I am to follow, armed only with a pistol of the smallest caliber and range. If my quarry eludes me for three whole days, he wins the game. If I find him"—the general smiled—"he loses."

"Suppose he refuses to be hunted?"

"Oh," said the general, "I give him his option, of course. He need not play that game if he doesn't wish to. If he does not wish to hunt, I turn him over to Ivan. Ivan once had the honor of serving as official knouter[19] to the Great White Czar, and he has his own ideas of sport. Invariably, Mr. Rainsford, invariably they choose the hunt."

"And if they win?"

The smile on the general's face widened. "To date I have not lost," he said.

Then he added, hastily: "I don't wish you to think me a braggart, Mr. Rainsford. Many of them afford only the most elementary sort of problem. Occasionally I strike a tartar.[20] One almost did win. I eventually had to use the dogs."

"The dogs?"

"This way, please. I'll show you."

The general steered Rainsford to a window. The lights from the windows sent a flickering illumination that made grotesque patterns on the courtyard below, and Rainsford could see moving about there a dozen or so huge black shapes; as they turned toward him, their eyes glittered greenly.

"A rather good lot, I think," observed the general. "They are let out at seven every night. If anyone should try to get into my house—or out of it—something extremely regrettable would occur to him." He hummed a snatch of song from the Folies-Bergère.[21]

"And now," said the general, "I want to show you my new collection of heads. Will you come with me to the library?"

"I hope," said Rainsford, "that you will excuse me tonight, General Zaroff. I'm really not feeling at all well."

"Ah, indeed?" the general inquired solicitously.[22] "Well, I suppose that's only natural, after your long swim. You need a good, restful night's sleep. Tomorrow you'll feel like a new man, I'll wager. Then we'll hunt, eh? I've one rather promising prospect—"

Rainsford was hurrying from the room.

"Sorry you can't go with me tonight," called the general. "I expect rather fair sport—a big, strong black. He looks resourceful— Well, good night, Mr. Rainsford; I hope you have a good night's rest."

The bed was good and the pajamas of the softest silk, and he was tired in every fiber of his being, but nevertheless Rainsford could not quiet his brain with the opiate[23] of sleep. He lay, eyes wide open. Once he thought he heard

> "If I find him"
> —the general
> smiled—
> "he loses."

---

19. **knouter** (nout'ər) *n.:* person who beats criminals with a knout, a kind of leather whip.
20. **strike a tartar:** get more than one bargained for. A tartar is a violent, unmanageable person.
21. **Folies-Bergère** (fô′lē ber·zher′): famous nightclub in Paris.
22. **solicitously** (sə·lis′ə·təs·lē) *adv.:* in a concerned manner.
23. **opiate** (ō′pē·it) *n.:* anything that tends to soothe or calm someone. An opiate may also be a medicine containing opium or a related drug used to relieve pain.

Vocabulary
invariably (in·ver′ē·ə·blē) *adv.:* always; without changing.

stealthy steps in the corridor outside his room. He sought to throw open the door; it would not open. He went to the window and looked out. His room was high up in one of the towers. The lights of the château were out now, and it was dark and silent, but there was a fragment of sallow moon, and by its wan light he could see, dimly, the courtyard; there, weaving in and out in the pattern of shadow, were black, noiseless forms; the hounds heard him at the window and looked up, expectantly, with their green eyes. Rainsford went back to the bed and lay down. By many methods he tried to put himself to sleep. He had achieved a doze when, just as morning began to come, he heard, far off in the jungle, the faint report of a pistol.

General Zaroff did not appear until luncheon. He was dressed faultlessly in the tweeds of a country squire. He was solicitous about the state of Rainsford's health.

"As for me," sighed the general, "I do not feel so well. I am worried, Mr. Rainsford. Last night I detected traces of my old complaint."

To Rainsford's questioning glance the general said: "Ennui. Boredom."

Then, taking a second helping of crêpes suzette,[24] the general explained: "The hunting was not good last night. The fellow lost his head. He made a straight trail that offered no problems at all. That's the trouble with these sailors; they have dull brains to begin with, and they do not know how to get about in the woods. They do excessively stupid and obvious things. It's most annoying. Will you have another glass of Chablis, Mr. Rainsford?"

"General," said Rainsford firmly, "I wish to leave this island at once."

The general raised his thickets of eyebrows; he seemed hurt. "But, my dear fellow," the general protested, "you've only just come. You've had no hunting—"

"I wish to go today," said Rainsford. He saw the dead black eyes of the general on him, studying him. General Zaroff's face suddenly brightened.

He filled Rainsford's glass with venerable Chablis from a dusty bottle.

"Tonight," said the general, "we will hunt—you and I."

Rainsford shook his head. "No, general," he said. "I will not hunt."

The general shrugged his shoulders and delicately ate a hothouse grape. "As you wish, my friend," he said. "The choice rests entirely with you. But may I not venture to suggest that you will find my idea of sport more <u>diverting</u> than Ivan's?"

He nodded toward the corner where the giant stood, scowling, his thick arms crossed on his hogshead of chest.

"You don't mean—" cried Rainsford.

"My dear fellow," said the general, "have I not told you I always mean what I say about hunting? This is really an inspiration. I drink to a foeman worthy of my steel—at last."

The general raised his glass, but Rainsford sat staring at him.

"You'll find this game worth playing," the general said enthusiastically. "Your brain against mine. Your woodcraft against mine. Your strength and stamina against mine. Outdoor chess! And the stake is not without value, eh?"

"And if I win—" began Rainsford huskily.

"I'll cheerfully acknowledge myself defeated if I do not find you by midnight of the third day," said General Zaroff. "My sloop will place you on the mainland near a town."

The general read what Rainsford was thinking. "Oh, you can trust me," said the Cossack.

PREDICTING
5. Who will be the general's next victim?

---

24. **crêpes suzette** (krăp soo·zet′) *n.*: thin pancakes folded in a hot orange-flavored sauce and served in flaming brandy.

Vocabulary
diverting (də·vurt′iŋ) *adj.*: entertaining.

"I will give you my word as a gentleman and a sportsman. Of course you, in turn, must agree to say nothing of your visit here."

"I'll agree to nothing of the kind," said Rainsford.

"Oh," said the general, "in that case— But why discuss that now? Three days hence we can discuss it over a bottle of Veuve Clicquot,[25] unless—"

The general sipped his wine.

Then a businesslike air animated him. "Ivan," he said to Rainsford, "will supply you with hunting clothes, food, a knife. I suggest you wear moccasins; they leave a poorer trail. I suggest too that you avoid the big swamp in the southeast corner of the island. We call it Death Swamp. There's quicksand there. One foolish fellow tried it. The deplorable[26] part of it was that Lazarus followed him. You can imagine my feelings, Mr. Rainsford. I loved Lazarus; he was the finest hound in my pack. Well, I must beg you to excuse me now. I always take a siesta after lunch. You'll hardly have time for a nap, I fear. You'll want to start, no doubt. I shall not follow till dusk. Hunting at night is so much more exciting than by day, don't you think? Au revoir,[27] Mr. Rainsford, au revoir."

General Zaroff, with a deep, courtly bow, strolled from the room.

From another door came Ivan. Under one arm he carried khaki hunting clothes, a haversack of food, a leather sheath containing a long-bladed hunting knife; his right hand rested on a cocked revolver thrust in the crimson sash about his waist. . . .

Rainsford had fought his way through the bush for two hours. "I must keep my nerve. I must keep my nerve," he said through tight teeth.

He had not been entirely clearheaded when the château gates snapped shut behind him. His whole idea at first was to put distance between himself and General Zaroff, and, to this end, he had plunged along, spurred on by the sharp rowels[28] of something very like panic. Now he had got a grip on himself, had stopped, and was taking stock of himself and the situation.

He saw that straight flight was futile; inevitably it would bring him face to face with the sea. He was in a picture with a frame of water, and his operations, clearly, must take place within that frame.

"I'll give him a trail to follow," muttered Rainsford, and he struck off from the rude paths he had been following into the trackless wilderness. He executed a series of intricate loops; he doubled on his trail again and again, recalling all the lore of the fox hunt and all the dodges of the fox. Night found him leg-weary, with hands and face lashed by the branches, on a thickly wooded ridge. He knew it would be insane to blunder on through the dark, even if he had the strength. His need for rest was imperative and he thought: "I have played the fox; now I must play the cat of the fable." A big tree with a thick trunk and outspread branches was nearby, and taking care to leave not the slightest mark, he climbed up into the crotch and stretching out on one of the broad limbs, after a fashion, rested. Rest brought him new confidence and almost a feeling of security. Even so zealous a hunter as General Zaroff could not trace him there, he told himself; only the devil himself could follow that complicated trail through the jungle after dark. But, perhaps, the general was a devil—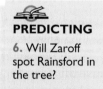

PREDICTING

6. Will Zaroff spot Rainsford in the tree?

An apprehensive night crawled slowly by like a wounded snake, and sleep did not visit

---

25. **Veuve Clicquot** (vöv klē·kô′): brand of fine champagne.
26. **deplorable** (dē·plôr′ə·bəl) *adj.:* regrettable; very bad.
27. **au revoir** (ō′rə·vwär′): French for "goodbye."

---

28. **rowels** (rou′əlz) *n.:* small wheels with spurs that horseback riders wear on their heels.

Rainsford, although the silence of a dead world was on the jungle. Toward morning, when a dingy gray was varnishing the sky, the cry of some startled bird focused Rainsford's attention in that direction. Something was coming through the bush, coming slowly, carefully, coming by the same winding way Rainsford had come. He flattened himself down on the limb, and through a screen of leaves almost as thick as tapestry, he watched. The thing that was approaching was a man.

It was General Zaroff. He made his way along with his eyes fixed in utmost concentration on the ground before him. He paused, almost beneath the tree, dropped to his knees and studied the ground. Rainsford's impulse was to hurl himself down like a panther, but he saw the general's right hand held something metallic—a small automatic pistol.

The hunter shook his head several times, as if he were puzzled. Then he straightened up and took from his case one of his black cigarettes; its pungent incenselike smoke floated up to Rainsford's nostrils.

Rainsford held his breath. The general's eyes had left the ground and were traveling inch by inch up the tree. Rainsford froze there, every muscle tensed for a spring. But the sharp eyes of the hunter stopped before they reached the limb where Rainsford lay; a smile spread over his brown face. Very deliberately he blew a smoke ring into the air; then he turned his back on the tree and walked carelessly away, back along the trail he had come. The swish of the underbrush against his hunting boots grew fainter and fainter.

Then pent-up air burst hotly from Rainsford's lungs. His first thought made him feel sick and numb. The general could follow a trail through the woods at night; he could follow an extremely difficult trail; he must have uncanny powers; only by the merest chance had the Cossack failed to see his quarry.

Rainsford's second thought was even more terrible. It sent a shudder of cold horror through his whole being. Why had the general smiled? Why had he turned back?

Rainsford did not want to believe what his reason told him was true, but the truth was as evident as the sun that had by now pushed through the morning mists. The general was playing with him! The general was saving him for another day's sport! The Cossack was the cat; he was the mouse. Then it was that Rainsford knew the full meaning of terror.

"I will not lose my nerve. I will not."

He slid down from the tree and struck off again into the woods. His face was set and he forced the machinery of his mind to function. Three hundred yards from his hiding place he stopped where a huge dead tree leaned precariously[29] on a smaller living one. Throwing off his sack of food, Rainsford took his knife from its sheath and began to work with all his energy.

The job was finished at last, and he threw himself down behind a fallen log a hundred feet away. He did not have to wait long. The cat was coming again to play with the mouse.

---

29. **precariously** (pri·ker′ē·əs·lē) *adv.:* unsteadily; in an unstable manner.

Vocabulary
impulse (im′puls′) *n.:* sudden desire to do something.

Following the trail with the sureness of a bloodhound came General Zaroff. Nothing escaped those searching black eyes, no crushed blade of grass, no bent twig, no mark, no matter how faint, in the moss. So intent was the Cossack on his stalking that he was upon the thing Rainsford had made before he saw it. His foot touched the <u>protruding</u> bough that was the trigger. Even as he touched it, the general sensed his danger and leapt back with the agility of an ape. But he was not quite quick enough; the dead tree, delicately adjusted to rest on the cut living one, crashed down and struck the general a glancing blow on the shoulder as it fell; but for his alertness, he must have been smashed beneath it. He staggered, but he did not fall; nor did he drop his revolver. He stood there, rubbing his injured shoulder, and Rainsford, with fear again gripping his heart, heard the general's mocking laugh ring through the jungle.

"Rainsford," called the general, "if you are within the sound of my voice, as I suppose you are, let me congratulate you. Not many men know how to make a Malay man-catcher. Luckily for me, I too have hunted in Malacca.[30] You are proving interesting, Mr. Rainsford. I am going now to have my wound dressed; it's only a slight one. But I shall be back. I shall be back."

When the general, nursing his bruised shoulder, had gone, Rainsford took up his flight again. It was flight now, a desperate, hopeless flight, that carried him on for some hours. Dusk came, then darkness, and still he pressed on. The ground grew softer under his moccasins; the vegetation grew ranker, denser; insects bit him savagely. Then, as he stepped forward, his foot sank into the ooze. He tried to wrench it back, but the muck sucked viciously at his foot as if it were a giant leech. With a violent effort, he tore loose. He knew where he was now. Death Swamp and its quicksand.

His hands were tight closed as if his nerve were something tangible that someone in the darkness was trying to tear from his grip. The softness of the earth had given him an idea. He stepped back from the quicksand a dozen feet or so, and, like some huge prehistoric beaver, he began to dig.

Rainsford had dug himself in in France,[31] when a second's delay meant death. That had been a placid pastime compared to his digging now. The pit grew deeper; when it was above his shoulders, he climbed out and from some hard saplings cut stakes and sharpened them to a fine point. These stakes he planted in the bottom of the pit with the points sticking up. With flying fingers he wove a rough carpet of weeds and branches and with it he covered the mouth of the pit. Then, wet with sweat and aching with tiredness, he crouched behind the stump of a lightning-charred tree.

He knew his pursuer was coming; he heard the padding sound of feet on the soft earth, and the night breeze brought him the perfume of the general's cigarette. It seemed to Rainsford that the general was coming with unusual swiftness; he was not feeling his way along, foot by foot. Rainsford, crouching there, could not see the general, nor could he see the pit. He lived a year in a minute. Then he felt an impulse to cry aloud with joy, for he heard the sharp crackle of the breaking branches as the cover of the pit gave way; he heard the sharp scream of pain as the pointed stakes found their mark. He leapt up from his place of concealment. Then he cowered back. Three feet from the pit a man was standing, with an electric torch in his hand.

"You've done well, Rainsford," the voice of the general called. "Your Burmese tiger pit has

---

30. **Malacca** (mə·lak′ə): state in what is now the nation of Malaysia in southeastern Asia.

31. **dug himself in in France:** dug a hole for shelter from gunfire during World War I (1914–1918).

Vocabulary
protruding (prō·trood′iŋ) v. used as adj.: sticking out.

claimed one of my best dogs. Again you score. I think, Mr. Rainsford, I'll see what you can do against my whole pack. I'm going home for a rest now. Thank you for a most amusing evening."

At daybreak Rainsford, lying near the swamp, was awakened by the sound that made him know that he had new things to learn about fear. It was a distant sound, faint and wavering, but he knew it. It was the baying of a pack of hounds.

Rainsford knew he could do one of two things. He could stay where he was and wait. That was suicide. He could flee. That was postponing the inevitable. For a moment he stood there, thinking. An idea that held a wild chance came to him, and, tightening his belt, he headed away from the swamp.

The baying of the hounds drew nearer, then still nearer, nearer, ever nearer. On a ridge Rainsford climbed a tree. Down a watercourse, not a quarter of a mile away, he could see the bush moving. Straining his eyes, he saw the lean figure of General Zaroff; just ahead of him Rainsford made out another figure whose wide shoulders surged through the tall jungle weeds. It was the giant Ivan, and he seemed pulled forward by some unseen force. Rainsford knew that Ivan must be holding the pack in leash.

They would be on him any minute now. His mind worked frantically. He thought of a native trick he had learned in Uganda. He slid down the tree. He caught hold of a springy young sapling and to it he fastened his hunting knife, with the blade pointing down the trail; with a bit of wild grapevine he tied back the sapling. Then he ran for his life. The hounds raised their voices as they hit the fresh scent. Rainsford knew now how an animal at bay feels.

He had to stop to get his breath. The baying of the hounds stopped abruptly, and Rainsford's heart stopped too. They must have reached the knife.

He shinnied excitedly up a tree and looked back. His pursuers had stopped. But the hope that was in Rainsford's brain when he climbed died, for he saw in the shallow valley that General Zaroff was still on his feet. But Ivan was not. The knife, driven by the recoil of the springing tree, had not wholly failed.

"Nerve, nerve, nerve!" he panted, as he dashed along. A blue gap showed between the trees dead ahead. Ever nearer drew the hounds. Rainsford forced himself on toward that gap. He reached it. It was the shore of the sea. Across a cove he could see the gloomy gray stone of the château. Twenty feet below him the sea rumbled and hissed. Rainsford hesitated. He heard the hounds. Then he leapt far out into the sea. . . .

PREDICTING

7. Trapped between his deadly pursuer and the sea, Rainsford jumps. Is the game over? Who has won?

When the general and his pack reached the place by the sea, the Cossack stopped. For some minutes he stood regarding the blue-green expanse of water. He shrugged his shoulders. Then he sat down, took a drink of brandy from a silver flask, lit a perfumed cigarette, and hummed a bit from *Madama Butterfly.*[32]

General Zaroff had an exceedingly good dinner in his great paneled dining hall that evening. With it he had a bottle of Pol Roger and half a bottle of Chambertin. Two slight annoyances kept him from perfect enjoyment. One was the thought that it would be difficult to replace Ivan; the other was that his quarry had escaped him; of course the American hadn't played the game—so thought the general as he tasted his after-dinner liqueur. In his library he read, to soothe himself, from the works of Marcus Aurelius.[33] At ten he went up to his bedroom. He was deliciously tired, he said to himself as he locked himself in. There was a little moonlight, so before turning on his light, he went to the window and looked down at the courtyard. He could see the great hounds, and he called: "Better luck another time," to them. Then he switched on the light.

A man, who had been hiding in the curtains of the bed, was standing there.

"Rainsford!" screamed the general. "How in God's name did you get here?"

"Swam," said Rainsford. "I found it quicker than walking through the jungle."

The general sucked in his breath and smiled. "I congratulate you," he said. "You have won the game."

Rainsford did not smile. "I am still a beast at bay," he said, in a low, hoarse voice. "Get ready, General Zaroff."

The general made one of his deepest bows. "I see," he said. "Splendid! One of us is to furnish a repast[34] for the hounds. The other will sleep in this very excellent bed. On guard, Rainsford. . . ."

He had never slept in a better bed, Rainsford decided. ■

---

32. *Madama Butterfly:* famous Italian opera by Giacomo Puccini (1858–1924).

33. **Marcus Aurelius** (mär′kəs ô·rē′lē·əs): emperor of Rome from A.D. 161 to 180, who wrote about the philosophy of Stoicism, which held that people should make themselves indifferent to both pain and pleasure.

34. **repast** (ri·past′) *n.:* meal.

Meet the Writer

Richard Connell

Famous for One Story

By the time he dreamed up Rainsford's epic battle of wills with General Zaroff, Richard Connell (1893–1949) was already a seasoned writer, accustomed to seeing his work in print. He began writing early: As a ten-year-old cub reporter, he covered local baseball games for the newspaper his father edited in Poughkeepsie, New York. During his student days at Harvard, Connell wrote for both the college newspaper and *The Harvard Lampoon,* the school's famous humor magazine. He went on to write hundreds of short stories, as well as novels and screenplays. Despite Connell's tremendous output, only one story—"The Most Dangerous Game" (1924)—is still widely read. The story has not only fascinated readers for decades but has also intrigued filmmakers. This suspenseful tale has inspired four movies in the past seventy years.

What accounts for the story's enduring popularity? Nothing in it is especially believable—not the characters, not the plot, not even the violence. We are never really afraid that Rainsford will be chewed up by one of those hounds. Perhaps the answer is that "The Most Dangerous Game" is an adventure story, with all the appeal of a Hollywood scare-o-rama, complete with an elegant villain, his huge brute of a manservant, a castle, a dark jungle, bloodthirsty animals, and hideous mantraps. It is a fine example of a macho escape story. When we read it, we escape reality for a short time. We spend an hour or two away from real life and its problems.

Despite its literary flaws, people rarely forget this story.

What do you think of it?

After You Read   Response and Analysis

Reading Check

1. Fill out a story map like the one below to review the **plot** of this famous chase story:

Characters:
Conflict: What do the characters want, and what problems do they face?
Main events: 1. 2. 3. [etc.]
Climax:
Resolution:

SKILLS FOCUS

Literary Skills
Analyze plot structure and foreshadowing.

Reading Skills
Make predictions.

Writing Skills
Write a story sequel.

INTERNET

Projects and Activities

Keyword: LE7 9-1

Thinking Critically

2. Did you **predict** the meaning of the story's **title**? What is the most dangerous game?

3. To hook our curiosity, writers drop clues that **foreshadow** what is going to happen later in a story.
   - What clues at the start of the story foreshadow danger for Rainsford?
   - How does Rainsford and Whitney's discussion about hunting at the start of the story foreshadow later developments?
   - What details in the physical description of Zaroff foreshadow the truth about his nature?

4. In your opinion, what happens to Zaroff? Do you think Rainsford changes his mind about hunting by the end of the story? Explain.

5. List the unknowns Rainsford encounters in the story, and think about how he reacts to each one. What enables him to triumph in the face of the unknown?

6. **Compare and contrast** the **characters** of Rainsford and Zaroff. Fill out a Venn diagram like the one below, listing the characteristics of each man in his circle. In the shaded area, list the characteristics the two men share.

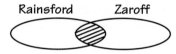

7. Think back to the villain you described in your Quickwrite. How does Zaroff compare with that evil character?

Extending and Evaluating

8. Look back at Zaroff's arguments for hunting men (pages 24–26). What is your opinion of his comments?

9. Think about Zaroff's civilized tastes and his favorite game. Do Zaroffs—people whose refined manners mask their true nature—exist in real life? Explain.

WRITING

The Sequel

In the morning, Rainsford awakes in Zaroff's bed. What happens next? Write a sequel to Rainsford's adventure. Does he stay on Ship-Trap Island and turn it into a theme park? Does he go home with a new taste for danger? You might let Rainsford tell his own story, using "I."

After You Read | Vocabulary Development

Prefixes: Important Beginnings

What's the difference between *net* and *Internet*? Just a **prefix**—a few letters added to the beginning of a word that can greatly change a word's meaning. Knowing what a prefix means can help you define a new word. The chart below contains a number of common prefixes, some of which you'll find in the Word Bank words:

Prefix	Meaning	Example
bi–	two	bicycle
di–, dis–	no; not; away; apart	dishonest; dismiss
im–, in–	no; not; in	improper; include
inter–	between; among	international
mis–	badly; not; wrongly	misunder-standing
pre–	before	prearrange
pro–	forward; before	promote; proclaim
re–	back; again	return; redo
sur–	over; above	surface
un–	not; reverse of	untrue

PRACTICE

Use the prefix chart at the left as you answer these questions:

1. What's the difference between *preceding* and *receding*? (Hint: The Latin word *cedere* originally meant "to go.")

2. How might a disarming smile affect you?

3. What's the difference between a long discussion and a prolonged discussion?

4. Give an example of an imprudent choice and a prudent one.

5. Use the meanings of the prefixes *sur*– and *dis*– to explain the difference between *surmounted* and *dismounted*.

6. What happens when a person remains unruffled in a tense situation? What happens if a person becomes ruffled?

7. If team A invariably loses to team B, what are team A's chances of remaining undefeated in a given season?

8. Ann, knowing that the Latin word *vertere* means "to turn," tells Joyce, "If you find that kids' movie diverting, you are reverting to childish behavior." Explain what Ann means.

9. Why might problems result from something you did on an impulse? If problems did result, would you want to redo or undo your actions?

10. Why would a protruding branch block the view from your window?

SKILLS FOCUS

Vocabulary Skills
Use prefixes to understand word meanings.

Can Animals Think?

Developing Research Questions Based on Reading

Doing research is largely a question-and-answer process. You begin by looking at a subject and assessing what you already know about it. Then, you ask questions on topics you want to know more about and do research to answer those questions.

Asking good questions is the key to doing research that will lead to an interesting, informative report. When you generate research questions, your main goals should be to stay focused on a limited topic and to ask productive questions.

Helpful Hints

Here are some guidelines to help you develop research questions based on informational materials:

- Try using a **KWL** chart to begin your research. In the **K** column, list what you already know about the topic. In the **W** column, list the questions you have—what you want to learn. (When you've finished your research, complete the **L** column by telling what you've learned.)

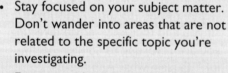

K	W	L

- Stay focused on your subject matter. Don't wander into areas that are not related to the specific topic you're investigating.
- Focus on subsections of an informational article, which may be indicated by subheads. In this way you will narrow the scope of your subject so that you can explore it in more depth.

- Ask the **5W-How? questions** rather than yes-or-no questions: Who was involved? What happened? When and where did it happen? Why and how did it happen? Such questions will help you get more information about your subject.
- Ask questions that can be answered within the scope of your research. Don't ask about issues so far-reaching that you cannot present a complete answer.

Remember: When you research, you aim to build your understanding of a subject from general, superficial knowledge to more specific, in-depth knowledge. Your research will be only as good as the questions you ask.

Vocabulary Development

balmy (bäm′ē) *adj.:* mild; pleasant.

intangible (in·tan′jə·bəl) *adj.:* cannot be touched or held.

awry (ə·rī′) *adv.:* in the wrong manner.

devious (dē′vē·əs) *adj.:* sneaky; deceptive.

beguile (bē·gīl′) *v.:* charm; deceive.

Connecting to the Literature

In "The Most Dangerous Game," General Zaroff has outwitted every animal he has hunted. So just how smart are animals? In the following article, Eugene Linden presents anecdotes—both amusing and heartwarming—that will make you think. Read on for glimpses into the often surprising thought processes of animals.

SKILLS FOCUS

Reading Skills
Generate research questions.

INTERNET
Interactive Reading Model
Keyword: LE7 9-1

Can Animals Think?

from *Time*, September 6, 1999

Eugene Linden

THE FIRST TIME Fu Manchu broke out, zookeepers chalked it up to human error. On a balmy day, the orangutans at the Omaha Zoo had been playing in their big outdoor enclosure. Not long thereafter, shocked keepers looked up and saw Fu and his family hanging out in some trees near the elephant barn. Later investigation revealed that the door that connects the furnace room to the orangutan enclosure was open. Head keeper Jerry Stones chewed out his staff, and the incident was forgotten. But the next time the weather was nice, Fu Manchu escaped again. Fuming, Stones recalls, "I was getting ready to fire someone."

Orangutans at a zoo in Tampa, Florida.

The next nice day, alerted by keepers desperate to keep their jobs, Stones finally managed to catch Fu Manchu in the act. First, the young ape climbed down some air-vent louvers into a dry moat. Then, taking hold of the bottom of the furnace door, he used brute force to pull it back just far enough to slide a wire into the gap, slip a latch, and pop the door open. The next day, Stones noticed something shiny sticking out of Fu's mouth. It was the wire lock pick, bent to fit between his lip and gum and stowed there between escapes.

Fu Manchu's jailbreaks made headlines in 1968, but his clever tricks didn't make a big impression on the scientists who specialize in looking for signs of higher mental processes in animals. At the time, much of the action in animal intelligence was focused on efforts to teach apes to use human languages. No researcher cared much about ape escape artists.

And neither did I. In 1970, I began following studies of animal intelligence, particularly the early reports of chimpanzees who learned how to use human words. The big breakthrough in these experiments came when two psychologists,[1] R. Allen and Beatrix Gardner, realized their chimps were

---

1. **psychologists** (sī·kälʹə·jists) *n.:* specialists who study the mind and emotions.

Vocabulary
balmy (bämʹē) *adj.:* mild; pleasant.

having trouble forming wordlike sounds and decided to teach a young female named Washoe sign language instead. Washoe eventually learned more than 130 words from the language of the deaf called American Sign Language.

Washoe's success spurred more language studies and created such ape celebrities as Koko the gorilla and Chantek the orangutan. The work also set off a fierce debate in scientific circles about the nature of animal intelligence—one that continues to this day. Indeed, it has been easier to defeat communism than to get scientists to agree on what Washoe meant three decades ago when she saw a swan on a pond and made the signs for "water bird." Was she inventing a phrase to describe waterfowl, or merely generating signs vaguely associated with the scene in front of her?

I began to wonder whether there might be better windows on animal minds than experiments designed to teach them human signs and symbols. When I heard about Fu Manchu, I realized what to me now seems obvious: If animals can think, they will probably do their best thinking when it serves their purposes, not when some scientist asks them to.

Lending a Helping Tail

Why would an animal want to cooperate with a human? The behaviorist[2] would say that animals cooperate when, through reinforcement, they learn it is in their interest to cooperate. This is true as far as it goes, but I don't think it goes far enough. Certainly with humans, the intangible reinforcement that comes with respect, dignity, and accomplishment can be far more motivating than material rewards.

---

2. **behaviorist** (bē·hāv′yər·ist) *n.:* specialist who studies behavior.

Gail Laule, a consultant on animal behavior with Active Environments Inc., uses rewards to encourage an animal to do something, but also recognizes that animals are more than windup toys that blindly respond to tempting treats. "It's much easier to work with a dolphin if you assume that it is intelligent. . . . That was certainly the case with Orky," says Laule, referring to her work with one of the giant dolphins called orcas or killer whales. "Of all the animals I've worked with, Orky was the most intelligent. . . . He would assess a situation and then do something based on the judgments he made."

Like the time he helped save a member of the family. Orky's mate Corky gave birth in the late 1970s, but the baby did not thrive at first, and the keepers took the little killer whale out of the tank by stretcher for emergency care and feeding. Things began to go awry when they returned the orca to the tank. The boom operator halted the stretcher when it was still a few feet above the water. Suddenly the baby began throwing up, through both its mouth and its blowhole. The keepers feared it would aspirate[3] some vomit, which could bring on a fatal case of pneumonia, but they could not reach the baby dangling above.

Orky had been watching the procedure, and, apparently sizing up the problem, he swam under the stretcher and allowed one of the men to stand on his head. This was remarkable since Orky had never been trained to carry people on his head like Sea World's Shamu. Then, using the amazing power of

---

3. **aspirate** (as′pə·rāt′) *v.:* breathe in.

Vocabulary
intangible (in·tan′jə·bəl) *adj.:* cannot be touched or held.
awry (ə·rī′) *adv.:* in the wrong manner.

Orky, a killer whale like the ones above, once helped save his baby.

his tail flukes to keep steady, Orky provided a platform that allowed the keeper to reach up and release the bridle so that the 420-pound baby could slide into the water within reach of help.

The Keeper Always Falls for That One

A sad fact of life is that it is easier to spot evidence of intelligence in <u>devious</u> behavior than in acts of cooperation or love.

While psychologists have studied various forms of animal deception, zookeepers are its targets every day. Helen Shewman, of the Woodland Park Zoo in Seattle, Washington, recalls that one day she dropped an orange through a feeding porthole for Meladi, one of the female orangutans. Instead of moving away, Meladi looked Helen in the eye and held out her hand. Thinking that the orange must have rolled off somewhere inaccessible, Helen gave her another one. When Meladi

shuffled off, Helen noticed that she had hidden the original orange in her other hand.

Tawan, the colony's dominant male, watched this whole charade, and the next day he too looked Helen in the eye and pretended that he had not yet received an orange. "Are you sure you don't have one?" Helen asked. He continued to hold her gaze and held out his hand. Relenting, she gave him another, then noticed that he had been hiding his orange under his foot.

Countless creatures draw on their abilities not only to secure food and compete with their peers, but also to deal with, deceive, and <u>beguile</u> the humans they encounter. Every so often, they do something extraordinary, and we gain insight into our own abilities and what it's like to be an orangutan or an orca.

Vocabulary
devious (dē′vē·əs) *adj.:* sneaky; deceptive.
beguile (bē·gīl′) *v.:* charm; deceive.

Reading Check

1. How did Fu Manchu get out of his enclosure?

2. What did Orky do that was so remarkable?

3. How did Meladi and Tawan deceive their zookeeper?

Test Practice

1. What is the **main idea** of "Can Animals Think"?

   A Studying animal behavior is interesting.

   B Animals are most likely to show intelligence not to please us but to serve their own needs.

   C Apes have had a difficult time mastering the sounds of human speech.

   D Human beings cannot or will not recognize animal intelligence.

2. If you wanted to do further research on the topic of animal intelligence, which question would help limit your investigation?

   F Do we value intelligence more than it deserves to be valued?

   G Will humans ever be able to communicate extensively with animals?

   H What are other instances in which orcas have made judgments?

   J What does *intelligence* mean?

3. Why is *How did the Gardners teach Washoe sign language?* a more useful first research question than *Did Washoe like learning sign language?*

   A It is a broad question about Washoe.

   B It will lead you to detailed information rather than a yes-or-no answer.

   C It covers a lengthy period of time.

   D It includes the psychologists who worked with Washoe.

4. Which research question would yield the *most* useful information about the intelligence of apes?

   F Who was smarter, Chantek or Koko?

   G What intelligent actions have observers seen orangutans perform in the wild?

   H How many times did Fu Manchu try to escape his enclosure?

   J What did Helen Shewman do the next time an orangutan tried to trick her into giving him an extra orange?

SKILLS FOCUS

Reading Skills
Generate research questions.

Constructed Response

Make a list of five questions that most intrigue you about animal intelligence. Once you have your list, share your questions with a few classmates. Which questions seem most likely to yield good research results?

Synonyms and Connotations

Is your town small, little, tiny, teeny, puny, or dinky? Do you live in a large, vast, gigantic, or sprawling city? How do you decide which is the best word to use when you are faced with what can seem like a dizzying number of choices?

The English language is filled with **synonyms**—words that mean the same thing or almost the same thing. When you choose a word or when you examine why a writer uses a particular word, you should think about its precise meaning as well as its context. You should also think about the word's **connotations,** or emotional overtones. *Dinky,* above, has negative connotations because it suggests something small, shabby, and insignificant. You would not like your beloved small town to be called dinky by a big-city visitor.

Look, for example, at what Gail Laule says about Orky in "Can Animals Think?":

> "He would <u>assess</u> a situation and then do something based on the <u>judgments</u> he made."

If you were using your own words to express that idea to a friend, you might have said that Orky would "think about" the situation. Why might *assess* be a better word to use to describe Orky's behavior? *Think* is a general word; it can be used in many different contexts. For example, *think* can mean "reflect." You might think about how a piece of advice applies to your life. *Assess,* however, is more precise. It implies the process of evaluation or calculation. *Assess* conveys the idea that Orky thinks logically. The word suits the scientific context of the sentence because the statement is an observation made by a specialist in animal behavior.

PRACTICE

Use a dictionary and a thesaurus to create a synonym chart, like the one below, for each word in the Word Bank. Write a sentence for each synonym. If there are slight (or not so slight) differences in meaning among the synonyms, or differences in connotation, try to make your sentences show that.

Word Bank

- balmy
- intangible
- awry
- devious
- beguile

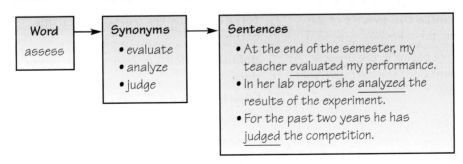

Word	Synonyms	Sentences
assess	• evaluate • analyze • judge	• At the end of the semester, my teacher <u>evaluated</u> my performance. • In her lab report she <u>analyzed</u> the results of the experiment. • For the past two years he has <u>judged</u> the competition.

SKILLS FOCUS

Vocabulary Skills
Understand connotations of synonyms.

Dog Star

Make the Connection
Quickwrite 🖉

Have you ever had a special relationship with an animal? Why do people love their pets so much? Jot down qualities that can make an animal a best friend.

Literary Focus
Flashback: Time Past, Time Present

It's impossible to turn back time. In your imagination, though, you can easily jump from the present to the past. When this jumping back happens in a story or movie, it's called a **flashback,** a scene that interrupts the present action of the plot to show what took place before.

One reason writers use flashbacks is to explain what led up to the present moment in a story. Flashbacks can also show the emotional impact of memories or past events. They can help writers create suspense, surprise, or mystery as well. As you read "Dog Star," think about Arthur C. Clarke's reasons for choosing to tell his story with a flashback.

SKILLS FOCUS

Literary Skills
Understand flashback.

Reading Skills
Understand chronological order.

INTERNET

More About
Arthur C. Clarke

Keyword: LE7 9-1

Reading Skills 📖
Chronological Order

Most stories follow **chronological order**—relating a series of events in time order, from start to finish. In "Dog Star," however, the writer interrupts the present time with a long flashback. To help you **organize the events** of this story, consider the following questions:

• The narrative begins in the present. At what moment does the narrative shift to the past?

• At what point does the narrator return to the present?

• How much time has passed between the final events in the flashback and the present moment in the story?

Background

Astronomers study space through powerful telescopes in observatories. The narrator of this story (published in 1962) is an astronomer. His dog, Laika, is named after the first animal sent into space—in 1957 aboard *Sputnik II,* a Russian satellite. The Dog Star, also known as Sirius, is the brightest star in the sky, located in the constellation Canis Major.

Vocabulary Development

desolating (des'ə·lāt'iŋ) *v.* used as *adj.*: producing a feeling of loneliness and sadness.

astronomers (ə·strän'ə·mərz) *n.*: scientists who study the stars and planets.

stellar (stel'ər) *adj.*: of or like a star.

luminous (lōō'mə·nəs) *adj.*: shining; glowing.

misanthropic (mis'ən·thräp'ik) *adj.*: disliking other human beings.

terrestrial (tə·res'trē·əl) *adj.*: earthly; of this world.

default (dē·fôlt') *n.*: failure to do something.

labyrinthine (lab'ə·rin'thin) *adj.*: like a maze; complicated.

DOG STAR

ARTHUR C. CLARKE

Oddly enough, I was not frightened— at first.

When I heard Laika's frantic barking, my first reaction was one of annoyance. I turned over in my bunk and murmured sleepily, "Shut up." That dreamy interlude lasted only a fraction of a second; then consciousness[1] returned—and, with it, fear. Fear of loneliness, and fear of madness.

---

1. consciousness (kän′shəs·nis) *n.:* state of being awake or aware.

For a moment, I dared not open my eyes; I was afraid of what I might see. Reason told me that no dog had ever set foot upon this world, that Laika was separated from me by a quarter of a million miles of space—and, far more irrevocably, five years of time.

"You've been dreaming," I told myself angrily. "Stop being a fool—open your eyes! You won't see anything except the glow of the wall paint."

That was right, of course. The tiny cabin was empty, the door tightly closed. I was alone with my memories, overwhelmed by the transcendental[2] sadness that often comes when some bright dream fades into drab reality. The sense of loss was so desolating that I longed to return to sleep. It was well that I failed to do so, for at that moment, sleep would have been death. But I did not know this for another five seconds, and during that eternity I was back on Earth, seeking what comfort I could from the past.

No one ever discovered Laika's origin, though the Observatory staff made a few inquiries and I inserted several advertisements in the Pasadena newspapers. I found her a lost and lonely ball of fluff, huddled by the roadside one summer evening when I was driving up to Palomar. Though I have never liked dogs, or indeed any animals, it was impossible to leave this helpless little creature to the mercy of the passing cars. With some qualms, wishing that I had a pair of gloves, I picked her up and dumped her in the baggage compartment. I was not going to hazard the upholstery of my new '92 Vik, and felt that she could do little damage there. In this, I was not altogether correct.

When I had parked the car at the Monastery—the astronomers' residential quarters, where I'd be living for the next week—I inspected my find without much enthusiasm. At that stage, I had intended to hand the puppy over to the janitor; but then it whimpered and opened its eyes. There was such an expression of helpless trust in them that—well, I changed my mind.

Sometimes I regretted that decision, though never for long. I had no idea how much trouble a growing dog could cause, deliberately and otherwise. My cleaning and repair bills soared; I could never be sure of finding an unravaged pair of socks or an unchewed copy of the *Astrophysical Journal*. But eventually Laika was both house-trained and Observatory-trained: She must have been the only dog ever to be allowed inside the two-hundred-inch dome. She would lie there quietly in the shadows for hours, while I was up in the cage making adjustments, quite content if she could hear my voice from time to time. The other astronomers became equally fond of her (it was old Dr. Anderson who suggested her name), but from the beginning she was my dog, and would obey no one else. Not that she would always obey me.

---

2. **transcendental** (tran´sen·dent´'l) *adj.:* extraordinary; supreme.

Vocabulary

desolating (des´ə·lāt´iŋ) *v.* used as *adj.:* producing a feeling of loneliness and sadness.

astronomers (ə·strän´ə·mərz) *n.:* scientists who study the stars and planets.

She was a beautiful animal, about ninety-five percent Alsatian.[3] It was that missing five percent, I imagine, that led to her being abandoned. (I still feel a surge of anger when I think of it, but since I shall never know the facts, I may be jumping to false conclusions.) Apart from two dark patches over the eyes, most of her body was a smoky gray, and her coat was soft as silk. When her ears were pricked up, she looked incredibly intelligent and alert; sometimes I would be discussing spectral types or stellar evolution with my colleagues, and it would be hard to believe that she was not following the conversation.

Even now, I cannot understand why she became so attached to me, for I have made very few friends among human beings. Yet when I returned to the Observatory after an absence, she would go almost frantic with delight, bouncing around on her hind legs and putting her paws on my shoulders—which she could reach quite easily—all the while uttering small squeaks of joy which seemed highly inappropriate from so large a dog. I hated to leave her for more than a few days at a time, and though I could not take her with me on overseas trips, she accompanied me on most of my shorter journeys. She was with me when I drove north to attend that ill-fated seminar at Berkeley.

We were staying with university acquaintances; they had been polite about it, but obviously did not look forward to having a monster in the house. However, I assured them that Laika never gave the slightest trouble, and rather reluctantly they let her sleep in the living room. "You needn't worry about burglars tonight," I said. "We don't have any in Berkeley," they answered, rather coldly.

In the middle of the night, it seemed that they were wrong. I was awakened by a hysterical, high-pitched barking from Laika which I had heard only once before—when she had first

seen a cow, and did not know what on earth to make of it. Cursing, I threw off the sheets and stumbled out into the darkness of the unfamiliar house. My main thought was to silence Laika before she roused my hosts—assuming that this was not already far too late. If there had been an intruder, he would certainly have taken flight by now. Indeed, I rather hoped that he had.

For a moment I stood beside the switch at the top of the stairs, wondering whether to throw it. Then I growled, "Shut up, Laika!" and flooded the place with light.

She was scratching frantically at the door, pausing from time to time to give that hysterical yelp. "If you want out," I said angrily, "there's no need for all that fuss." I went down, shot the bolt, and she took off into the night like a rocket.

It was very calm and still, with a waning Moon struggling to pierce the San Francisco fog. I stood in the luminous haze, looking out across the water to the lights of the city, waiting for Laika to come back so that I could chastise her suitably. I was still waiting when, for the second time in the twentieth century, the San Andreas fault woke from its sleep.[4]

Oddly enough, I was not frightened—at first. I can remember that two thoughts passed through my mind, in the moment before I realized the danger. Surely, I told myself, the geophysicists[5] could have given us *some* warning. And then I found myself thinking, with great surprise, "I'd no idea that earthquakes make so much noise!"

---

4. **second time . . . its sleep:** The San Andreas fault is a vast system of cracks running for about six hundred miles along California's coast. The fault's northern end was the center of a disastrous earthquake in San Francisco in 1906. The earthquake in "Dog Star" is fictional.
5. **geophysicists** (jē′ō·fiz′ə·sists) *n.:* scientists who study such aspects of the earth as the weather, earthquakes, and volcanoes.

Vocabulary

stellar (stel′ər) *adj.:* of or like a star.
luminous (loo′mə·nəs) *adj.:* shining; glowing.

---

3. **Alsatian** (al·sā′shən): British name for German shepherd, a large dog resembling a wolf.

It was about then that I knew that this was no ordinary quake; what happened afterward, I would prefer to forget. The Red Cross[6] did not take me away until quite late the next morning, because I refused to leave Laika. As I looked at the shattered house containing the bodies of my friends, I knew that I owed my life to her; but the helicopter pilots could not be expected to understand that, and I cannot blame them for thinking that I was crazy, like so many of the others they had found wandering among the fires and the debris.

After that, I do not suppose we were ever apart for more than a few hours. I have been told—and I can well believe it—that I became less and less interested in human company, without being actively unsocial or <u>misanthropic</u>. Between them, the stars and Laika filled all my needs. We used to go for long walks together over the mountains; it was the happiest time I have ever known. There was only one flaw; I knew, though Laika could not, how soon it must end.

We had been planning the move for more than a decade. As far back as the nineteen-sixties it was realized that Earth was no place for an astronomical observatory. Even the small pilot instruments on the Moon had far outperformed all the telescopes peering through the murk and haze of the <u>terrestrial</u> atmosphere. The story of Mount Wilson, Palomar, Greenwich, and the other great names was coming to an end; they would still be used for training purposes, but the research frontier must move out into space.

I had to move with it; indeed, I had already been offered the post of Deputy Director, Farside Observatory. In a few months, I could hope to solve problems I had been working on for years. Beyond the atmosphere, I would be like a blind man who had suddenly been given sight.

It was utterly impossible, of course, to take Laika with me. The only animals on the Moon were those needed for experimental purposes; it might be another generation before pets were allowed, and even then it would cost a fortune to carry them there—and to keep them alive. Providing Laika with her usual two pounds of meat a day would, I calculated, take several times my quite comfortable salary.

The choice was simple and straightforward. I could stay on Earth and abandon my career. Or I could go to the Moon—and abandon Laika.

After all, she was only a dog. In a dozen years, she would be dead, while I should be reaching the peak of my profession. No sane man would have hesitated over the matter; yet I did hesitate, and if by now you do not understand why, no further words of mine can help.

In the end, I let matters go by <u>default</u>. Up to the very week I was due to leave, I had still made no plans for Laika. When Dr. Anderson volunteered to look after her, I accepted numbly, with scarcely a word of thanks. The old physicist[7] and his wife had always been fond of her, and I am afraid that they considered me indifferent and heartless—when the truth was just the opposite. We went for one more walk together over the hills; then I delivered her silently to the Andersons, and did not see her again.

Takeoff was delayed almost twenty-four hours, until a major flare storm had cleared the Earth's orbit; even so, the Van Allen belts were still so active that we had to make our exit through the North Polar Gap.[8] It was a

---

6. **Red Cross:** international society that aids people during wars or disasters.

7. **physicist** (fiz'ə·sist) *n.*: scientist who studies forms of matter and energy.
8. **Van Allen belts . . . North Polar Gap:** The Van Allen belts, discovered by the American physicist James Van Allen, are two bands of radiation surrounding the earth. The North Polar Gap refers to an area above the North Pole where the radiation is weaker.

Vocabulary

misanthropic (mis'ən·thräp'ik) *adj.*: disliking other human beings.

terrestrial (tə·res'trē·əl) *adj.*: earthly; of this world.

default (dē·fôlt') *n.*: failure to do something.

miserable flight; apart from the usual trouble with weightlessness, we were all groggy with antiradiation drugs. The ship was already over Farside before I took much interest in the proceedings, so I missed the sight of Earth dropping below the horizon. Nor was I really sorry; I wanted no reminders, and intended to think only of the future. Yet I could not shake off that feeling of guilt; I had deserted someone who loved and trusted me, and was no better than those who had abandoned Laika when she was a puppy, beside the dusty road to Palomar.

The news that she was dead reached me a month later. There was no reason that anyone knew; the Andersons had done their best, and were very upset. She had just lost interest in living, it seemed. For a while, I think I did the same; but work is a wonderful anodyne,[9] and my program was just getting underway. Though I never forgot Laika, in a little while the memory ceased to hurt.

Then why had it come back to haunt me, five years later, on the far side of the Moon? I was searching my mind for the reason when the metal building around me quivered as if under the impact of a heavy blow. I reacted without thinking, and was already closing the helmet of my emergency suit when the foundations slipped and the wall tore open with a short-lived scream of escaping air. Because I had automatically pressed the General Alarm button, we lost only two men, despite the fact that the tremor—the worst ever recorded on Farside—cracked all three of the Observatory's pressure domes.

I had deserted someone who loved and trusted me . . .

It is hardly necessary for me to say I do not believe in the supernatural;[10] everything that happened has a perfectly rational explanation, obvious to any man with the slightest knowledge of psychology. In the second San Francisco earthquake, Laika was not the only dog to sense approaching disaster; many such cases were reported. And on Farside, my own memories must have given me that heightened awareness, when my never-sleeping subconscious[11] detected the first faint vibrations from within the Moon.

The human mind has strange and labyrinthine ways of going about its business; it knew the signal that would most swiftly rouse me to the knowledge of danger. There is nothing more to it than that; though in a sense one could say that Laika woke me on both occasions, there is no mystery about it, no miraculous warning across the gulf that neither man nor dog can ever bridge.

Of that I am sure, if I am sure of anything. Yet sometimes I wake now, in the silence of the Moon, and wish that the dream could have lasted a few seconds longer—so that I could have looked just once more into those luminous brown eyes, brimming with an unselfish, undemanding love I have found nowhere else on this or on any other world. ■

---

9. **anodyne** (an′ō·dīn′) *n.*: something that relieves pain.

10. **supernatural** (soo′pər·nach′ər·əl) *n.*: forces or events that are not explained by the known laws of nature.

11. **subconscious** (sub·kän′shəs) *n.*: mental activity that occurs without our awareness.

Vocabulary
labyrinthine (lab′ə·rin′thin) *adj.*: like a maze; complicated.

Meet the Writer

Arthur C. Clarke

The First Citizen of the Future

If the future is another country, Arthur C. Clarke (1917–   ) is its first citizen. Here are some of his credentials: He predicted many of the scientific developments of the second half of the twentieth century—such as satellites orbiting Earth and the moon landing—and he warned the world about the Y2K computer bug. Clarke has even predicted a few events that haven't happened yet. He expected humans to land on Mars in the 1990s; he has since revised the date to 2021. Soon after that, he says, dinosaurs will be re-created from computer-generated DNA, and mini-raptors will replace watchdogs.

Clarke was born in Minehead, England. At age thirteen, he built a telescope out of an old lens and a cardboard tube. Since his early start as an amateur astronomer, Clarke has written dozens of books of science fiction and science fact. In 1968, he was nominated for an Academy Award for writing the film version of his novel *2001: A Space Odyssey.*

Clarke says that he wants to be known not as a prophet but, rather, as an extrapolator —that is, someone who predicts the future based on what is happening in the present. In old age, when many others dwell nostalgically on the past, he continues to look hopefully into the future.

“ If an elderly but distinguished scientist says that something is possible, he is almost certainly right, but if he says that it is impossible, he is very probably wrong. **”**

Arthur C. Clarke looks forward to celebrating his one hundredth birthday in December 2017 in a hotel orbiting the earth.

For Independent Reading

Arthur C. Clarke has written and edited more than ninety books, with about 100 million copies in print. In his exciting novel *Childhood's End,* the Overlords eliminate threats to humans—such as disease and poverty—but then they become a threat to humankind as well by controlling the minds of children. In Clarke's famous *2001: A Space Odyssey,* you'll take a journey with the crew of a spacecraft run by an all-too-human computer named HAL.

The World Is Not a Pleasant Place to Be

Nikki Giovanni

the world is not a pleasant place
to be without
someone to hold and be held by

5 a river would stop
its flow if only
a stream were there
to receive it

an ocean would never laugh
if clouds weren't there
10 to kiss her tears

the world is not
a pleasant place to be without
someone

Reading Check

1. At what moment in the story does the **flashback** begin? (What present event triggers the flashback?) At what moment in the story are we back in present time?

2. Create a time line showing the events of the story in **chronological order.** Start with the earliest events in the story at the left end of your time line, and finish at the right end with the final event.

Thinking Critically

3. **Flashbacks** can serve several different purposes. For example, they can reveal a character's past or explain the cause of an event. What purposes does the flashback in this story serve?

4. Just before the flashback begins, there is a **foreshadowing** of what is about to happen in the present. Find the sentence in the fourth paragraph that foreshadows what is about to occur. Explain the clue.

5. List the details the **narrator** tells you about himself. Then, consider his actions. How would you **characterize** the narrator?

6. How would you describe Laika's **character**? Are there points in the story where she seems more like a person than like a dog? Explain.

7. The narrator has a terrible **internal conflict** to resolve in choosing between Laika and his career. Does the author suggest that the narrator made a mistake by choosing an unknown future in space over life with Laika? Support your answer with details from the story.

8. At the end of the story, how does the narrator explain what happened in the lunar observatory? Do you think he really believes his own explanation, or does the reason he woke up remain unknown? Support your answer.

9. What different meanings can you propose for the story's **title**?

10. Does this story have something to say about love's power to conquer even time? Explain what you think is the story's major revelation, or **theme.**

11. What do you think the narrator's response would be to the message of "The World Is Not a Pleasant Place to Be" (see the **Connection** on page 52)? Would you count a pet as "someone" who can make the world a pleasant place? Check your Quick-write notes.

Extending and Evaluating

12. Would the story have been as effective if the writer had told it in strict chronological order instead of using a **flashback**? Explain your response.

WRITING

Blasts from the Past

Often something that we see, hear, or smell—a kite in the sky, a song on the radio, an apple pie baking in the oven—will trigger a memory, and suddenly we find ourselves flashing back to the past. Write a short **autobiographical narrative** about a past event in your own life. Has something in particular ever sparked your memory of the event?

▶ Use "Writing an Autobiographical Narrative," pages 78–85, for help with this assignment.

SKILLS FOCUS

Literary Skills
Analyze plot structure, flashback, and foreshadowing.

Reading Skills
Understand chronological order.

Writing Skills
Write an autobiographical narrative.

Vocabulary Development

Word Derivations: Back to the Source

The English language is made up of many words that originated in other languages, such as Latin, Greek, and French. You can use a **dictionary** to trace the **derivation,** or origin, of any word. (The derivation is also called the **etymology.**) The derivation usually appears in brackets after the entry word. The oldest form of the word appears last. (Be sure to check the meanings of the abbreviations used in your dictionary. *Gr* usually stands for "Greek," and *L* usually stands for "Latin.")

Look at the sample derivation below for *desolate.* (We are using *desolate* because most dictionaries do not have a separate listing for *desolating.*) The symbol "<" means "derived from or came from."

> **desolate** [ME *desolat* < L *desolare* < *de–*, intens.
> + *solare*, to make lonely < *solus*, alone]

You can read the above derivation as follows: *Desolate* comes from the Middle English *desolat,* which comes from the Latin *desolare,* which comes from a combination of the prefix *de–* (an intensive, or word part that emphasizes a meaning) and *solare,* which means "to make lonely." *Solare,* in turn, comes from the Latin *solus,* which means "alone."

Word Bank

desolating
astronomers
stellar
luminous
misanthropic
terrestrial
default

PRACTICE 1

Use a dictionary to research the **derivation,** or origin, of each Word Bank word (except *desolating* and *labyrinthine*). Write the oldest form of the word and the language from which the word originally derives.

Words and Myths: Telling Tales

When we talk about a herculean task, we're referring to the mythological muscleman Hercules. Many words in English have their origins in Greek, Roman, and Norse myths. We often associate other words, such as *labyrinth,* with these famous stories. A famous labyrinth (or maze) was built by Daedalus to house the Minotaur, a monster with the body of a man and the head of a bull. The Greek hero Theseus escaped from the labyrinth and killed the Minotaur. (For more about words from myths, see pages 816 and 832.)

Word Bank

labyrinthine

SKILLS FOCUS

PRACTICE 2

Vocabulary Skills
Understand word derivations. Identify words from myths.

Labyrinth and *labyrinthine,* an adjective meaning "like a maze" or "complicated," can be used both literally and figuratively (*the labyrinth of his mind,* for example). List as many things as you can that could be called labyrinthine—either literally or figuratively.

Far-out Housekeeping on the ISS

Researching Questions

Once you've generated research questions (see the guidelines on page 38), you're ready to look for the answers. Remember to consult as many reliable sources as possible.

Using Print Resources

Here are some useful resources you can find in a library or on the Internet:

- **Reference books**—such as encyclopedias, atlases, almanacs, and biographical references—contain specialized information. They are usually organized in a logical way, such as in alphabetical or chronological order. Examples include
  American Men and Women of Science
  National Geographic Atlas of the World
  The World Almanac and Book of Facts
- Other **nonfiction sources,** such as biographies, autobiographies, and history books, can help you get the full story. Use the library catalog to find these books.
- **Periodicals**—newspapers and magazines—can be excellent sources of information, especially for up-to-date facts. Libraries have either the *Readers' Guide to Periodical Literature,* a print index, or electronic indexes to help you locate articles on a particular subject.

Surfing the Web

The **Internet** provides up-to-the-minute information on a vast range of topics. Here are some useful research tips:

- Use a **search engine** to get a list of Web sites related to your topic. Often you can click on a site name on the list and go directly to the site. If your search produces too many results, narrow it by choosing a more specific search term. You may need to try a different search engine to locate useful Web sites.
- Go directly to a **Web site** if you know the URL (uniform resource locator), the site's Internet address.

Checking Out a Web Site

On a Web page, look for **links** that lead directly to other sources on your topic. **Internal links** connect to other pages in the same site. **External links** lead to different Web sites. Usually you can reach a link by clicking on it. Look for these types of links:

- Some links are highlighted words or phrases within the text of an article. They may be underlined, in a color, or in italics.
- Other highlighted links may be listed in a side column or at the end of an article.
- **Audio** or **video links** connect to material you can listen to or watch.
- **Icons** are images, such as symbols or pictures, that function as links.

SKILLS FOCUS

Reading Skills
Use research sources, including print resources and the Internet.

Connecting to the Literature

When Arthur C. Clarke published "Dog Star" in 1962, he was imagining that people could live in space. Today people actually do live in space, on the International Space Station (ISS). This Internet article talks about real-life housekeeping in space.

go.
hrw
.com

INTERNET

Interactive
Reading Model

Keyword: LE7 9-1

Back **Forward** **Stop** **Reload** **Search**

Location: http://science.nasa.gov/headlines/y2000/ast29nov_1.htm

Science @NASA

Inform Inspire Involve
science.nasa.gov

NASA Science News home

◁ Listen to this story

Click on the **audio link** to listen to the article.

Far-out Housekeeping on the ISS

Title of article.

Life in space is a daring adventure, but somebody still has to cook dinner and take out the trash. Science@NASA interviews two astronauts about the thrill and routine of daily life in orbit.

November 29, 2000—It's open for business! And even though the construction crews aren't done yet, the International Space Station's first occupants have moved in and set up housekeeping. If all goes as

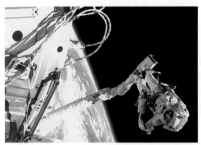

planned, the arrival of Expedition 1 in orbit earlier this month signaled the beginning of a new era. From now on, there will always be humans in space.

Living in space is a daunting adventure with plenty of derring-do and glamour. Hollywood spacefarers rarely have to take out the trash or clean the kitchen. But, what about real-life astronauts? Are there chores to do on the ISS? In a recent interview with Science@NASA, Dr. Edward Lu and Coast Guard Lieutenant Commander Daniel Burbank—two astronauts who helped build the space station—discussed the excitement and the day-to-day routine of life in orbit.

"Space really is the most hostile environment humans have ever tried to live in," said Burbank. "You depend on the Station and the people on the ground for everything you need to survive. It is complicated and everything has to work!" It's a risky adventure with very little margin for error, but, said the astronauts, the thrill of being there is something that neither would give up.

HOT FOODS AND FRESH FRUIT

So what is it like being there for months or years at a time? For example, what does the ISS crew eat, and how is it cooked?

Click on links **within the article** to learn more about a subject.

All food is delivered by the American space shuttle or Russian Progress vehicle. The crew helps select the foods they want from a wide-ranging menu.

(Right) The biggest challenge at mealtime for astronauts: catching your food! In this image Astronaut Loren Shriver (STS-46) demonstrates how objects act in free-fall while enjoying a snack of candy-coated peanuts. Residents of the ISS have more nutritious choices, too, including fresh fruits shuttled from Earth.

According to Vicki Kloeris, subsystem manager for shuttle and space station food at the Johnson Space Center, food aboard Space Station will come in several forms. "Most of the food will be processed and packaged in pouches or cans. Some will be dehydrated and the astronauts add hot water and eat. Some will be in pouches and cans and you simply heat and eat. A small amount will be fresh food delivered by the shuttle and Progress." The fresh food will include fruits and veggies, but nothing that requires

Back

Forward

Stop

Reload

Search

Location: http://science.nasa.gov/headlines/y2000/ast29nov_1.htm

refrigeration. ISS will contain more than one oven when it is fully operational. In the early stages, food is being cooked using either a small food warmer built by the Russians or a U.S.-built portable food warmer, about the size of a suitcase.

ISS, PHONE HOME

Information gained from the experiences of the Russian MIR space station crews indicates that isolation is one of the biggest problems a long-duration crew will face. To prevent this on ISS, the crew members will be encouraged to phone home. And while working on ISS will not exactly be like spending a couple of weeks away from home on business in the Big Apple or the Windy City, sailors traveling around the British Empire in the 17th and 18th centuries were more isolated than the ISS crew will be.

"Each crew member will have a video telephone call from home each week," said Burbank. "And the crew will be receiving and sending daily e-mail messages to and from family and friends. No one should feel isolated from home and family."

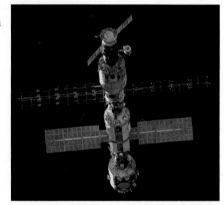

(Right) Members of the STS-106 crew, including Lu and Burbank, snapped this picture of the ISS from the space shuttle Atlantis in September 2000. [more information]

WHO TAKES OUT THE TRASH?

A recent Science@NASA story about water recycling on the ISS covered the great lengths that ISS designers are taking to minimize how much water and other consumables must be launched from Earth. Water-recycling efficiencies of greater than 95% are the goal.

But other wastes cannot be recycled so efficiently, particularly solid waste from food containers, experiments, empty fuel containers, and other ISS activities. So: Who takes out the trash?

Again, Progress and Shuttle come to the rescue. Every arrival of Shuttle brings fresh supplies. And when it leaves, it becomes the world's most expensive trash hauler! Bags and containers of sealed trash will be brought back to Earth.

More exciting, perhaps, is how the Russian Progress disposes of trash. Again, when it arrives, it brings fresh supplies (but no crews, since it is just a supply vehicle). And when the fresh supplies are unloaded, the trash bags are piled in and Progress is sealed. After it disconnects from ISS, it is placed into a lower orbit and makes a controlled reentry during which it and the trash are incinerated over the ocean.

R&R IN SPACE

Crews will be busy during their tours of duty on ISS. But all work and no play. . . . So what constitutes relaxation and recreation for the men and women living aboard ISS?

"Crew members will be allowed to take a certain amount of personal gear up with them," said Lu. "So things like checkers or chess sets, CDs and tape players, and the like are allowed. You can listen to your favorite music if you like. DVD movies will also be available for viewing."

So it's not exactly like home! And you can't take an evening walk outside to watch the sunset. But the "sailors" on ISS will have it better than those intrepid explorers that left Europe in the 15th century looking for new lands, or the Polynesian sailors that charted and settled the vast Pacific Ocean, or the Asian explorers and settlers who walked the land bridge from Siberia into Alaska and opened two new continents for their people.

They do, however, share two important traits. First, they are the vanguard of their respective civilizations, doing what they believe will improve the well-being of their people.

And second, they all had to forge ahead and ignore the shrill voices behind them warning that "beyond this point, there be dragons!"

Web Links

Click on one of the underlined **links** in this box to go to a related Web page.

Water on the Space Station—The first Science@NASA article in this series about the practical challenges of extended living in space. This article looks at how water will be conserved and recycled on the space station—including the crew's own urine!

Breathing Easy on the Space Station—The second Science@NASA article in this series about the practical challenges of extended living in space. The systems and methods used to ensure safe, breathable air for the crew are examined in this article.

Microscopic Stowaways on the Space Station—The third Science@NASA article in this series about the practical challenges of extended living in space.

International Space Station—NASA's Web page for the International Space Station.

Advanced Life Support Web Page—from the Johnson Space Flight Center.

Environmental Control and Life Support Systems—describes the life-support systems being developed at Marshall Space Flight Center.

Join our growing list of subscribers—sign up for our express news delivery and you will receive a mail message every time we post a new story!!!

 More Headlines

Click on the **icon** to reach a related Web page.

For lesson plans and educational activities related to breaking science news, please visit Thursday's Classroom.

Author: Ron Koczor
Production Editor: Dr. Tony Phillips
Curator: Bryan Walls
Media Relations: Steve Roy
Responsible NASA official: Ron Koczor

Reading Check

1. Describe how food is brought to the International Space Station and how trash is removed.

2. According to the article, what traits do space travelers share with explorers who lived in earlier centuries?

Test Practice

1. If you wanted to learn more about living in space on a long-term basis, which search term would be the *most* useful?
   - **A** History of space exploration
   - **B** Space stations
   - **C** Astronauts
   - **D** Spacesuits

2. Which source would provide the *most* up-to-date information about extended living in space?
   - **F** An interview with astronauts who lived on the Mir space station
   - **G** A science textbook
   - **H** A history book about important space missions
   - **J** A Web page about new technology used on the ISS

3. If you wanted to find out more about how crews spend their free time in space, which source would be the *most* helpful?
   - **A** A newspaper article about plans for future space missions
   - **B** An autobiography describing an astronaut's experiences in space

   - **C** An encyclopedia entry about the history of the U.S. space program
   - **D** A Web page about the purpose of the U.S. space shuttle

4. If you wanted to learn about oxygen supplies for the ISS crew, which **link** on this Web page would be *least* likely to provide information?
   - **F** Breathing Easy on the Space Station
   - **G** Advanced Life Support Web Page
   - **H** Environmental Control and Life Support Systems
   - **J** Water on the Space Station

5. If you wanted to find out more about the handling of wastes on the ISS, which link would be the *most* useful?
   - **A** The Nasa News icon "More Headlines"
   - **B** The internal link "All food"
   - **C** The internal link "water recycling on the ISS"
   - **D** The audio link "Listen to this story"

Constructed Response

Generate a list of questions based on "Far-out Housekeeping on the ISS." (You might have questions about the experiences of the crews in the time since the article was written.) Then, choose one question, and research it in a library and on the **Internet.** Did you find information easily? What sources did you use? What additional resources could you have used to answer the question?

SKILLS FOCUS

Reading Skills
Generate research questions, and research the answers.

Elements of Literature

Setting *by* John Leggett
PUTTING US THERE

A storyteller, like a travel agent, can help gather us up from wherever we are and put us down in another setting on earth or, for that matter, on another planet or on the moon (as Arthur C. Clarke does in "Dog Star"). That other setting may be a spot we've always wanted to visit, such as a beach in Hawaii, or a place where we don't want to be, such as the deck of a sinking ship.

Setting tells us where and when a story takes place. Setting can include the locale of a story, the weather, the time of day, and the time period (past, present, or future). Setting can even include people's customs—how they live, dress, eat, and behave. One purpose of setting is to provide background—a place where the characters can live and act. Think, for example, of Ship-Trap Island in "The Most Dangerous Game," which provides a background filled with peril for Rainsford's contest with Zaroff. A good setting helps to make a story vivid and memorable.

Setting and Character

Places where people live can reveal a great deal about their characters. In "The Most Dangerous Game," for example, Connell tells us that General Zaroff lives in a "palatial château." The dining room has "a medieval magnificence about it," with its "oaken panels," "high ceiling," and table set with the "finest" silver and china. The interior of Zaroff's castle gives the impression that the general is a civilized and cultured gentleman of refined taste. Other details of the setting hint at another, very different side of Zaroff, however. The towers of the castle plunge "upward into the gloom," and the cliffs below the castle dive "down to where the sea licked greedy lips in the shadows." A "tall spiked iron gate" guards the entrance to the castle. Although Zaroff is a man of culture and elegance on the outside, these eerie details hint at the evil lurking inside him. The setting helps us understand one of Connell's points in the story: Evil is sometimes masked by polished manners, hidden from view by deceptive appearances. As Connell does, writers can use setting to help reveal meaning in their stories.

Setting, Mood, and Tone

Setting can also provide **mood,** or **atmosphere**—it can affect the way we feel. Some settings make us fearful or uneasy (midnight, a lonely house, the scraping of a branch against the window). Other settings make us feel happy (morning, a garden, the song of a bird). The emotional effect created by a story's atmosphere draws us into the plot and makes us care about the characters.

Writers can also use setting to help express a **tone,** or attitude toward a subject or character. Imagine, for example, that a writer places a character in a home decorated with fake antiques and huge, poorly painted portraits of family members. We can tell from the setting that the writer is mocking the character's pretentious manners. By contributing to the tone, setting helps shape our reactions to a story.

SKILLS FOCUS

Literary Skills
Understand setting and how it affects character, mood, and tone.

INTERNET

More About Setting

Keyword: LE7 9-1

How Is Setting Created?

One of the wonders of language is that it can summon up a place for us immediately. It can take us to Ship-Trap Island in "The Most Dangerous Game" and into Zaroff's château. Language can reach us through our five senses and put us right in the middle of the action, along with the characters themselves.

To create a believable setting or one that can make us feel pleasure, mystery, or fear, the writer must select the right details or images. **Images** are words or phrases that call forth a response from our senses—sight, smell, touch, hearing, and taste.

Suppose a writer wants us to imagine a setting as ordinary as the drugstore where Tamara is telling J. D. she never wants to see him again. We would get tired of reading a long list of all the objects on the drugstore shelves. Similarly, we would get tired of reading a list of all the trees, rocks, and puddles in the mountain pass where Casey is waiting to ambush the noon stagecoach. However, our own imagination will supply many details if the writer prompts us with the right images. In the drugstore scene the right image might be a row of bottles, each bearing the label "Poison." In the mountain pass the right image might be a circling vulture or the muddy water that seeps into the outlaw's cracked boots.

When a writer supplies a few right images, we will provide the rest of the scenery. We might draw from our own experience, or we might go beyond our memory into our imagination. There we will find all kinds of images—desert islands, palaces, and planets where we have never been.

This exercise of our imagination is what makes reading fiction a more personal and mind-enhancing experience than, for all its lazy pleasures, watching the ready-made images of movies and television.

Practice

Think of a story that you've read in which the setting captured your imagination. Fill in a chart like the one here to describe the setting and show its role in the story:

SETTING
Title of story:
Where story takes place:
When story takes place:
Details of setting that reveal **character**:
Details of setting that reveal **mood** or **tone**:

HE DIDN'T KNOW HOW TO APPRECIATE NATURE.

Before You Read

A Christmas Memory

Make the Connection
Quickwrite ✏️

"A Christmas Memory" is a story about two unlikely friends. The story reveals something about the nature of friendship and the enduring power of love—even when, to the rest of the world, the friendship seems odd, and the love is not noticed at all.

What do friends give each other? Think about your oldest friendship—why do some friendships last while others don't? Jot down your ideas on friendship, and save your notes.

Literary Focus
Setting Makes It Real

Literary Skills
Understand setting and how it affects mood.

Reading Skills
Identify sensory details.

INTERNET

Vocabulary Practice
•
More About Truman Capote
•
Keyword: LE7 9-1

Setting can include the time when a story takes place, the weather, and the customs of the people—how they live, what they eat, how they dress, what they believe. Setting can help reveal character, affect the plot, contribute to a story's **mood** (or emotional effect), and enhance its meaning. In some stories the setting is so crucial that the story could not take place anywhere else.

Truman Capote opens "A Christmas Memory" by asking us to imagine a setting: "a morning in late November . . . more than twenty years ago" (he was referring to the early 1930s), a kitchen in a "spreading old house in a country town," and in the fireplace the season's first roaring fire. Capote's vivid description of the setting brings the characters to life and makes us feel as if we are there with them just as "fruitcake weather" begins.

Reading Skills 📖
Reading for Details

One of the first rules of good writing is "Show, don't tell." Through the use of **sensory details** (images that appeal to our senses of sight, taste, smell, hearing, and touch), writers reveal character and help their readers visualize actions and setting. As you read "A Christmas Memory," look for telling details in Capote's description of the setting—sensory details and comparisons that convey a feeling, or **mood,** and reveal a great deal about the characters. The questions at the open-book signs will help you.

Vocabulary Development

inaugurating (in·ô′gyə·rāt′iŋ) v.: formally beginning.

exhilarates (eg·zil′ə·rāts′) v.: gladdens; excites.

dilapidated (də·lap′ə·dāt′id) adj.: shabby; falling apart.

paraphernalia (par′ə·fər·nāl′yə) n.: equipment; gear.

sacrilegious (sak′rə·lij′əs) adj.: disrespectful toward religion.

carnage (kär′nij) n.: widespread killing; slaughter.

prosaic (prō·zā′ik) adj.: ordinary.

disposition (dis′pə·zish′ən) n.: usual frame of mind; temperament.

suffuse (sə·fyo͞oz′) v.: spread over or through.

noncommittal (nän′kə·mit′′l) adj.: not admitting or committing to any particular purpose or point of view.

A CHRISTMAS MEMORY

We are each other's best friend.

TRUMAN CAPOTE

Christmas Morning (1930) by Charles E. Burchfield. Watercolor on paper (30″ × 22⅛″).

*I*magine a morning in late November. A coming of winter morning more than twenty years ago. Consider the kitchen of a spreading old house in a country town. A great black stove is its main feature; but there is also a big round table and a fireplace with two rocking chairs placed in front of it. Just today the fireplace commenced its seasonal roar.

A woman with shorn white hair is standing at the kitchen window. She is wearing tennis shoes and a shapeless gray sweater over a summery calico dress. She is small and sprightly, like a bantam hen; but, due to a long youthful illness, her shoulders are pitifully hunched. Her face is remarkable—not unlike Lincoln's, craggy like that, and tinted by sun and wind; but it is delicate too, finely boned, and her eyes are sherry-colored and timid. "Oh my," she exclaims, her breath smoking the windowpane, "it's fruit-cake weather!"

The person to whom she is speaking is myself. I am seven; she is sixty-something. We are cousins, very distant ones, and we have lived together—well, as long as I can remember. Other people inhabit the house, relatives; and though they have power over us, and frequently make us cry, we are not, on the whole, too much aware of them. We are each other's best friend. She calls me Buddy, in memory of a boy who was formerly her best friend. The other Buddy died in the 1880s, when she was still a child. She is still a child.

"I knew it before I got out of bed," she says, turning away from the window with a purpose-ful excitement in her eyes. "The courthouse bell sounded so cold and clear. And there were no birds singing; they've gone to warmer country, yes indeed. Oh, Buddy, stop stuffing biscuit and fetch our buggy. Help me find my hat. We've thirty cakes to bake."

It's always the same: A morning arrives in November, and my friend, as though officially <u>inaugurating</u> the Christmas time of year that <u>exhilarates</u> her imagination and fuels the blaze of her heart, announces: "It's fruitcake weather! Fetch our buggy. Help me find my hat."

The hat is found, a straw cartwheel corsaged with velvet roses out-of-doors has faded; it once belonged to a more fashionable relative. To-gether, we guide our buggy, a <u>dilapidated</u> baby carriage, out to the garden and into a grove of pecan trees. The buggy is mine; that is, it was bought for me when I was born. It is made of wicker, rather unraveled, and the wheels wobble like a drunkard's legs. But it is a faithful object; springtimes, we take it to the woods and fill it with flowers, herbs, wild fern for our porch pots; in the summer, we pile it with picnic <u>paraphernalia</u> and sugar-cane fishing poles and roll it down to the edge of the creek; it has its winter uses, too: as a truck for hauling firewood from the yard to the kitchen, as a warm bed for Queenie, our tough little orange and white rat terrier who has survived distemper and two rattlesnake bites. Queenie is trotting beside it now.

Three hours later we are back in the kitchen hulling a heaping buggyload of windfall pecans.[1] Our backs hurt from gathering them: How hard they were to find (the main crop having been shaken off the trees and sold by the orchard's owners, who are not us) among the concealing leaves, the frosted, deceiving grass. Caarackle! A cheery crunch, scraps of miniature thunder sound as the shells collapse and the golden mound of sweet, oily, ivory meat mounts in the milk-glass bowl. Queenie begs to taste, and now

---

1. **windfall pecans:** pecans blown down from the trees by wind.

Vocabulary

inaugurating (in·ô′gyə·rāt′iŋ) *v.*: formally beginning.

exhilarates (eg·zil′ə·rāts′) *v.*: gladdens; excites.

dilapidated (də·lap′ə·dāt′id) *adj.*: shabby; falling apart.

paraphernalia (par′ə·fər·nāl′yə) *n.*: equipment; gear.

and again my friend sneaks her a mite, though insisting we deprive ourselves. "We mustn't, Buddy. If we start, we won't stop. And there's scarcely enough as there is. For thirty cakes." The kitchen is growing dark. Dusk turns the window into a mirror: Our reflections mingle with the rising moon as we work by the fireside in the firelight. At last, when the moon is quite high, we toss the final hull into the fire and, with joined sighs, watch it catch flame. The buggy is empty; the bowl is brimful.

READING FOR DETAILS

1. Which **senses** does the author appeal to in the description of the kitchen in this paragraph? What **mood** is created?

We eat our supper (cold biscuits, bacon, blackberry jam) and discuss tomorrow. Tomorrow the kind of work I like best begins: buying. Cherries and citron, ginger and vanilla and canned Hawaiian pineapple, rinds and raisins and walnuts and whiskey and oh, so much flour, butter, so many eggs, spices, flavorings: Why, we'll need a pony to pull the buggy home.

But before these purchases can be made, there is the question of money. Neither of us has any. Except for skinflint sums persons in the house occasionally provide (a dime is considered very big money); or what we earn ourselves from various activities: holding rummage sales, selling buckets of handpicked blackberries, jars of homemade jam and apple jelly and peach preserves, rounding up flowers for funerals and weddings. Once we won seventy-ninth prize, five dollars, in a national football contest. Not that we know a fool thing about football. It's just that we enter any contest we hear about: At the moment our hopes are centered on the fifty-thousand-dollar Grand Prize being offered to name a new brand of coffee (we suggested "A.M."; and, after some hesitation, for my friend thought it perhaps sacrilegious, the slogan "A.M.! Amen!"). To tell the truth, our only *really* profitable enterprise was the Fun and Freak

Museum we conducted in a backyard woodshed two summers ago. The Fun was a stereopticon[2] with slide views of Washington and New York lent us by a relative who had been to those places (she was furious when she discovered why we'd borrowed it); the Freak was a three-legged biddy chicken[3] hatched by one of our own hens. Everybody hereabouts wanted to see that biddy: We charged grown-ups a nickel, kids two cents. And took in a good twenty dollars before the museum shut down due to the decease of the main attraction.

But one way and another we do each year accumulate Christmas savings, a Fruitcake Fund. These moneys we keep hidden in an ancient bead purse under a loose board under the floor under a chamber pot[4] under my friend's bed. The purse is seldom removed from this safe location except to make a deposit, or, as happens every Saturday, a withdrawal; for on Saturdays I am allowed ten cents to go to the picture show. My friend has never been to a picture show, nor does she intend to: "I'd rather hear you tell the story, Buddy. That way I can imagine it more. Besides, a person my age shouldn't squander their eyes. When the Lord comes, let me see Him clear." In addition to never having seen a movie, she has never: eaten in a restaurant, traveled more than five miles

2. **stereopticon** (ster′ē·ǎp′ti·kən) *n.:* old-fashioned kind of slide projector.
3. **biddy chicken:** hen; female chicken.
4. **chamber pot** *n.:* Before indoor plumbing and toilets, people used pots, usually kept in their bedrooms, or chambers.

Vocabulary

sacrilegious (sak′rə·lij′əs) *adj.:* disrespectful toward religion.

from home, received or sent a telegram, read anything except funny papers and the Bible, worn cosmetics, cursed, wished someone harm, told a lie on purpose, let a hungry dog go hungry. Here are a few things she has done, does do: killed with a hoe the biggest rattlesnake ever seen in this county (sixteen rattles), dip snuff[5] (secretly), tame hummingbirds (just try it) till they balance on her finger, tell ghost stories (we both believe in ghosts) so tingling they chill you in July, talk to herself, take walks in the rain, grow the prettiest japonicas[6] in town, know the recipe for every sort of old-time Indian cure, including a magical wart-remover.

READING FOR DETAILS
2. What does the description of the hiding place for the Fruitcake Fund tell you about Buddy and his friend?

Now, with supper finished, we retire to the room in a faraway part of the house where my friend sleeps in a scrap-quilt-covered iron bed painted rose pink, her favorite color. Silently, wallowing in the pleasures of conspiracy, we take the bead purse from its secret place and spill its contents on the scrap quilt. Dollar bills, tightly rolled and green as May buds. Somber fifty-cent pieces, heavy enough to weight a dead man's eyes. Lovely dimes, the liveliest coin, the one that really jingles. Nickels and quarters, worn smooth as creek pebbles. But mostly a hateful heap of bitter-odored pennies. Last summer others in the house contracted to pay us a penny for every twenty-five flies we killed. Oh, the carnage of August: the flies that flew to heaven! Yet it was not work in which we took pride. And, as we sit counting pennies, it is as though we were back tabulating dead flies. Neither of us has a head for figures; we count slowly, lose track, start again. According to her calculations, we have $12.73. According to mine, exactly $13. "I do hope you're wrong, Buddy. We can't mess around with

thirteen. The cakes will fall. Or put somebody in the cemetery. Why, I wouldn't dream of getting out of bed on the thirteenth." This is true: She always spends thirteenths in bed. So, to be on the safe side, we subtract a penny and toss it out the window.

Of the ingredients that go into our fruitcakes, whiskey is the most expensive, as well as the hardest to obtain: State laws forbid its sale. But everybody knows you can buy a bottle from Mr. Haha Jones. And the next day, having completed our more prosaic shopping, we set out for Mr. Haha's business address, a "sinful" (to quote public opinion) fish-fry and dancing cafe down by the river. We've been there before, and on the same errand; but in previous years our dealings have been with Haha's wife, an iodine-dark Indian woman with brassy peroxided hair and a dead-tired disposition. Actually, we've never laid eyes on her husband, though we've heard that he's an Indian too. A giant with razor scars across his cheeks. They call him Haha because he's so gloomy, a man who never laughs. As we approach his cafe (a large log cabin festooned[7] inside and out with chains of garish-gay naked light bulbs and standing by the river's muddy edge under the shade of river trees where moss drifts through the branches like gray mist) our steps slow down. Even Queenie stops prancing and sticks close by. People have been murdered in Haha's cafe. Cut to pieces. Hit on the head. There's a case coming up in court next month. Naturally these goings-on happen at night when the colored lights cast crazy patterns and the Victrola[8] wails. In the daytime Haha's is shabby

---

5. **snuff** *n.*: powdered tobacco inhaled by sniffing.
6. **japonicas** (jə·pän′i·kəz) *n.*: flowering shrubs.

7. **festooned** (fes·tōōnd′) *v.* used as *adj*: decorated.
8. **Victrola** (vik·trō′lə): old term for a record player.

Vocabulary

carnage (kär′nij) *n.*: widespread killing; slaughter.

prosaic (prō·zā′ik) *adj.*: ordinary.

disposition (dis′pə·zish′ən) *n.*: usual frame of mind; temperament.

Bouquet and Stove (1929) by Yasuo Kuniyoshi.

His eyes tilt more. Would you believe it? Haha is smiling! Laughing, too. "Which one of you is a drinkin' man?"

"It's for making fruitcakes, Mr. Haha. Cooking."

This sobers him. He frowns. "That's no way to waste good whiskey." Nevertheless, he retreats into the shadowed cafe and seconds later appears carrying a bottle of daisy-yellow unlabeled liquor. He demonstrates its sparkle in the sunlight and says: "Two dollars."

We pay him with nickels and dimes and pennies. Suddenly, jangling the coins in his hand like a fistful of dice, his face softens. "Tell you what," he proposes, pouring the money back into our bead purse, "just send me one of them fruitcakes instead."

"Well," my friend remarks on our way home, "there's a lovely man. We'll put an extra cup of raisins in *his* cake."

The black stove, stoked with coal and firewood, glows like a lighted pumpkin. Eggbeaters whirl, spoons spin round in bowls of butter and sugar, vanilla sweetens the air, ginger spices it; melting, nose-tingling odors saturate the kitchen, <u>suffuse</u> the house, drift out to the world on puffs of chimney smoke. In four days our work is done. Thirty-one cakes, dampened with whiskey, bask on window sills and shelves.

Who are they for?

and deserted. I knock at the door, Queenie barks, my friend calls: "Mrs. Haha, ma'am? Anyone to home?"

Footsteps. The door opens. Our hearts overturn. It's Mr. Haha Jones himself! And he *is* a giant; he *does* have scars; he *doesn't* smile. No, he glowers at us through Satan-tilted eyes and demands to know: "What you want with Haha?"

For a moment we are too paralyzed to tell. Presently my friend half finds her voice, a whispery voice at best: "If you please, Mr. Haha, we'd like a quart of your finest whiskey."

Vocabulary

suffuse (sə·fyōz′) *v.*: spread over or through.

Friends. Not necessarily neighbor friends: Indeed, the larger share are intended for persons we've met maybe once, perhaps not at all. People who've struck our fancy. Like President Roosevelt. Like the Reverend and Mrs. J. C. Lucey, Baptist missionaries to Borneo who lectured here last winter. Or the little knife grinder who comes through town twice a year. Or Abner Packer, the driver of the six o'clock bus from Mobile, who exchanges waves with us every day as he passes in a dust-cloud whoosh. Or the young Wistons, a California couple whose car one afternoon broke down outside the house and who spent a pleasant hour chatting with us on the porch (young Mr. Wiston snapped our picture, the only one we've ever had taken). Is it because my friend is shy with everyone *except* strangers that these strangers, and merest acquaintances, seem to us our truest friends? I think yes. Also, the scrapbooks we keep of thank-you's on White House stationery, time-to-time communications from California and Borneo, the knife grinder's penny postcards, make us feel connected to eventful worlds beyond the kitchen with its views of a sky that stops.

Now a nude December fig branch grates against the window. The kitchen is empty, the cakes are gone; yesterday we carted the last of them to the post office, where the cost of stamps turned our purse inside out. We're broke. That rather depresses me, but my friend insists on celebrating—with two inches of whiskey left in Haha's bottle. Queenie has a spoonful in a bowl of coffee (she likes her coffee chicory-flavored and strong). The rest we divide between a pair of jelly glasses. We're both quite awed at the prospect of drinking straight whiskey; the taste of it brings screwed-up expressions and sour shudders. But by and by we begin to sing, the two of us singing different songs simultaneously. I don't know the words to mine, just: *Come on along, come on along, to the dark-town strutters' ball.* But I can dance: That's what I mean to be, a tap-dancer in the movies. My dancing shadow

rollicks on the walls; our voices rock the chinaware; we giggle as if unseen hands were tickling us. Queenie rolls on her back, her paws plow the air, something like a grin stretches her black lips. Inside myself, I feel warm and sparky as those crumbling logs, carefree as the wind in the chimney. My friend waltzes round the stove, the hem of her poor calico skirt pinched between her fingers as though it were a party dress: *Show me the way to go home*, she sings, her tennis shoes squeaking on the floor. *Show me the way to go home.*

Enter: two relatives. Very angry. Potent with eyes that scold, tongues that scald. Listen to what they have to say, the words tumbling together into a wrathful tune: "A child of seven! whiskey on his breath! are you out of your mind? feeding a child of seven! must be loony! road to ruination! remember Cousin Kate? Uncle Charlie? Uncle Charlie's brother-in-law? shame! scandal! humiliation! kneel, pray, beg the Lord!"

Queenie sneaks under the stove. My friend gazes at her shoes, her chin quivers, she lifts her skirt and blows her nose and runs to her room. Long after the town has gone to sleep and the house is silent except for the chimings of clocks and the sputter of fading fires, she is weeping into a pillow already as wet as a widow's handkerchief.

READING FOR DETAILS

3. What details in this paragraph help convey the feelings of Buddy's friend?

"Don't cry," I say, sitting at the bottom of her bed and shivering despite my flannel nightgown that smells of last winter's cough syrup, "don't cry," I beg, teasing her toes, tickling her feet, "you're too old for that."

"It's because," she hiccups, "I *am* too old. Old and funny."

"Not funny. Fun. More fun than anybody. Listen. If you don't stop crying you'll be so tired tomorrow we can't go cut a tree."

She straightens up. Queenie jumps on the bed (where Queenie is not allowed) to lick her cheeks.

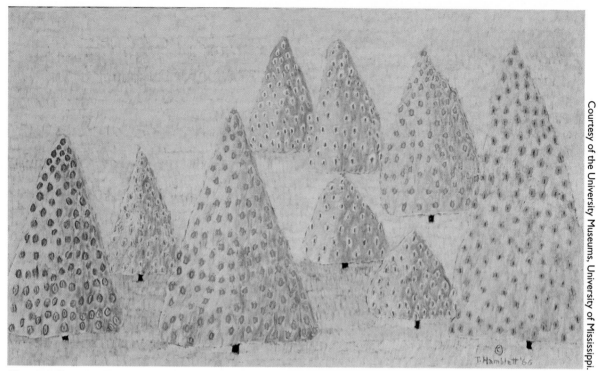

Christmas Trees by Theora Hamblett. Drawing.

"I know where we'll find real pretty trees, Buddy. And holly, too. With berries big as your eyes. It's way off in the woods. Farther than we've ever been. Papa used to bring us Christmas trees from there: carry them on his shoulder. That's fifty years ago. Well, now: I can't wait for morning."

Morning. Frozen rime[9] lusters the grass; the sun, round as an orange and orange as hot-weather moons, balances on the horizon, burnishes[10] the silvered winter woods. A wild turkey calls. A renegade hog grunts in the undergrowth. Soon, by the edge of knee-deep, rapid-running water, we have to abandon the buggy. Queenie wades the stream first, paddles across, barking complaints at the swiftness of the current, the pneumonia-making coldness of it. We follow, holding our shoes and equipment (a hatchet, a burlap sack) above our heads. A mile more: of chastising thorns, burs and briers that catch at our clothes; of rusty pine needles brilliant with gaudy fungus and molted feathers. Here, there, a flash, a flutter, an ecstasy of shrillings remind us that not all the birds have flown south. Always, the path unwinds through lemony sun pools and pitch vine tunnels. Another creek to cross: A disturbed armada[11] of speckled trout froths the water round us, and frogs the size of plates practice belly flops; beaver workmen are building a dam. On the farther shore, Queenie shakes herself and trembles. My friend shivers, too: not with cold but enthusiasm. One of her hat's ragged roses sheds a petal as she lifts her head and inhales the pine-heavy air. "We're almost there; can you smell it, Buddy?" she says, as though we were approaching an ocean.

And, indeed, it is a kind of ocean. Scented acres of holiday trees, prickly-leafed holly. Red berries shiny as Chinese bells: Black crows swoop upon them screaming. Having stuffed our burlap

---

9. **frozen rime:** frost.
10. **burnishes** (bᴜr′nish·iz) *v.:* polishes.

---

11. **armada** (är·mä′də) *n.:* group, as of warships.

sacks with enough greenery and crimson to garland a dozen windows, we set about choosing a tree. "It should be," muses my friend, "twice as tall as a boy. So a boy can't steal the star." The one we pick is twice as tall as me. A brave, handsome brute that survives thirty hatchet strokes before it keels with a creaking, rending cry. Lugging it like a kill, we commence the long trek out. Every few yards we abandon the struggle, sit down, and pant. But we have the strength of triumphant huntsmen; that and the tree's virile, icy perfume revive us, goad us on. Many compliments accompany our sunset return along the red clay road to town; but my friend is sly and <u>noncommittal</u> when passersby praise the treasure perched in our buggy: What a fine tree and where did it come from? "Yonderways," she murmurs vaguely. Once a car stops and the rich mill owner's lazy wife leans out and whines: "Giveya twobits cash for that ol tree." Ordinarily my friend is afraid of saying no; but on this occasion she promptly shakes her head: "We wouldn't take a dollar." The mill owner's wife persists. "A dollar, my foot! Fifty cents. That's my last offer. Goodness, woman, you can get another one." In answer, my friend gently reflects: "I doubt it. There's never two of anything."

Home: Queenie slumps by the fire and sleeps till tomorrow, snoring loud as a human.

A trunk in the attic contains: a shoe box of ermine tails[12] (off the opera cape of a curious lady who once rented a room in the house), coils

Morning Haze (1909) by Leonard Ochtman.

National Museum of American Art, Washington, D.C.

of frazzled tinsel gone gold with age, one silver star, a brief rope of dilapidated, undoubtedly dangerous candylike light bulbs. Excellent decorations, as far as they go, which isn't far enough: My friend wants our tree to blaze "like a Baptist window," droop with weighty snows of ornament. But we can't afford the made-in-Japan splendors at the five-and-dime. So we do what we've always done: sit for days at the kitchen table with scissors and crayons and stacks of colored paper. I make sketches and my friend cuts them out: lots of cats, fish too (because they're easy to draw), some apples, some watermelons, a few winged angels devised from saved-up sheets of Hershey-bar tinfoil. We use safety pins to attach these creations to the tree; as a final touch, we sprinkle the branches with shredded cotton (picked in August for this purpose). My friend, surveying the effect, clasps her hands together. "Now honest, Buddy. Doesn't it look good enough to eat?" Queenie tries to eat an angel.

Vocabulary

noncommittal (nän′kə·mit′′l) *adj.*: not admitting or committing to any particular purpose or point of view.

---

12. **ermine** (ur′min) **tails:** black-tipped white tails of certain kinds of weasels, used to trim clothes.

After weaving and ribboning holly wreaths for all the front windows, our next project is the fashioning of family gifts. Tie-dye scarves for the ladies, for the men a home-brewed lemon and licorice and aspirin syrup to be taken "at the first Symptoms of a Cold and after Hunting." But when it comes time for making each other's gift, my friend and I separate to work secretly. I would like to buy her a pearl-handled knife, a radio, a whole pound of chocolate-covered cherries (we tasted some once, and she always swears: "I could live on them, Buddy, Lord yes I could— and that's not taking His name in vain"). Instead, I am building her a kite. She would like to give me a bicycle (she's said so on several million occasions: "If only I could, Buddy. It's bad enough in life to do without something *you* want; but confound it, what gets my goat is not being able to give somebody something you want *them* to have. Only one of these days, I will, Buddy. Locate you a bike. Don't ask how. Steal it, maybe"). Instead, I'm fairly certain that she is building me a kite—the same as last year, and the year before: The year before that we exchanged slingshots. All of which is fine by me. For we are champion kite-fliers who study the wind like sailors; my friend, more accomplished than I, can get a kite aloft when there isn't enough breeze to carry clouds.

Christmas Eve afternoon we scrape together a nickel and go to the butcher's to buy Queenie's traditional gift, a good gnawable beef bone. The bone, wrapped in funny paper, is placed high in the tree near the silver star. Queenie knows it's there. She squats at the foot of the tree, staring up in a trance of greed: When bedtime arrives she refuses to budge. Her excitement is equaled by my own. I kick the covers and turn my pillow as though it were a scorching summer's night. Somewhere a rooster crows: falsely, for the sun is still on the other side of the world.

"Buddy, are you awake?" It is my friend, calling from her room, which is next to mine; and an instant later she is sitting on my bed holding a candle. "Well, I can't sleep a hoot," she declares. "My mind's jumping like a jack rabbit. Buddy, do you think Mrs. Roosevelt will serve our cake at dinner?" We huddle in the bed, and she squeezes my hand I-love-you. "Seems like your hand used to be so much smaller. I guess I hate to see you grow up. When you're grown up, will we still be friends?" I say always. "But I feel so bad, Buddy. I wanted so bad to give you a bike. I tried to sell my cameo Papa gave me. Buddy—" she hesitates, as though embarrassed. "I made you another kite." Then I confess that I made her one, too; and we laugh. The candle burns too short to hold. Out it goes, exposing the starlight, the stars spinning at the window like a visible caroling that slowly, slowly daybreak silences. Possibly we doze; but the beginnings of dawn splash us like cold water: We're up, wide-eyed and wandering while we wait for others to waken. Quite deliberately my friend drops a kettle on the kitchen floor. I tap-dance in front of closed doors. One by one the household emerges, looking as though they'd like to kill us both; but it's Christmas, so they can't. First, a gorgeous breakfast: just everything you can imagine—from flapjacks and fried squirrel to hominy grits and honey-in-the-comb. Which puts everyone in a good humor except my friend and me. Frankly, we're so impatient to get at the presents we can't eat a mouthful.

READING FOR DETAILS

5. This paragraph includes interesting **figures of speech**, or comparisons, describing the stars and the dawn. What are the comparisons, and why are they effective?

Well, I'm disappointed. Who wouldn't be? With socks, a Sunday school shirt, some handkerchiefs, a hand-me-down sweater, and a year's subscription to a religious magazine for children, *The Little Shepherd*. It makes me boil. It really does.

My friend has a better haul. A sack of satsumas,[13] that's her best present. She is proudest, however, of a white wool shawl knitted by her married sister. But she *says* her favorite gift is the kite I built her. And it *is* very beautiful; though not as beautiful as the one she made me, which is blue and scattered with gold and green Good Conduct stars; moreover, my name is painted on it, "Buddy."

"Buddy, the wind is blowing."

The wind is blowing, and nothing will do till we've run to a pasture below the house where Queenie has scooted to bury her bone (and where, a winter hence, Queenie will be buried, too). There, plunging through the healthy, waist-high grass, we unreel our kites, feel them twitching at the string like sky fish as they swim into the wind. Satisfied, sun-warmed, we sprawl in the grass and peel satsumas and watch our kites cavort. Soon I forget the socks and hand-me-down sweater. I'm as happy as if we'd already won the fifty-thousand-dollar Grand Prize in that coffee-naming contest.

"My, how foolish I am!" my friend cries, suddenly alert, like a woman remembering too late she has biscuits in the oven. "You know what I've always thought?" she asks in a tone of discovery, and smiling not at me but a point beyond. "I've always thought a body would have to be sick and dying before they saw the Lord. And I imagined that when He came it would be like looking at the Baptist window: pretty as colored glass with the sun pouring through, such a shine you don't know it's getting dark. And it's been a comfort: to think of that shine taking away all the spooky feeling. But I'll wager it never happens. I'll wager at the very end a body realizes the Lord has already shown Himself. That things as they are"—her hand circles in a gesture that gathers clouds and kites and grass and Queenie pawing earth over her bone—"just what they've always seen,

was seeing Him. As for me, I could leave the world with today in my eyes."

This is our last Christmas together.

Life separates us. Those who Know Best decide that I belong in a military school. And so follows a miserable succession of bugle-blowing prisons, grim reveille-ridden[14] summer camps. I have a new home too. But it doesn't count. Home is where my friend is, and there I never go.

And there she remains, puttering around the kitchen. Alone with Queenie. Then alone. ("Buddy dear," she writes in her wild hard-to-read script, "yesterday Jim Macy's horse kicked Queenie bad. Be thankful she didn't feel much. I wrapped her in a Fine Linen sheet and rode her in the buggy down to Simpson's pasture where she can be with all her Bones. . . .") For a few Novembers she continues to bake her fruitcakes single-handed; not as many, but some: And, of course, she always sends me "the best of the batch." Also, in every letter she encloses a dime wadded in toilet paper: "See a picture show and write me the story." But gradually in her letters she tends to confuse me with her other friend, the Buddy who died in the 1880s; more and more, thirteenths are not the only days she stays in bed: A morning arrives in November, a leafless birdless coming of winter morning, when she cannot rouse herself to exclaim: "Oh my, it's fruitcake weather!"

And when that happens, I know it. A message saying so merely confirms a piece of news some secret vein had already received, severing from me an irreplaceable part of myself, letting it loose like a kite on a broken string. That is why, walking across a school campus on this particular December morning, I keep searching the sky. As if I expected to see, rather like hearts, a lost pair of kites hurrying toward heaven. ■

---

13. **satsumas** (sat′sə·mäz′) *n.*: oranges.

14. **reveille-ridden** (rev′ə·lē rid′'n): ruled by the drum or bugle signal used to rouse sleeping people in a military or summer camp. The writer uses this phrase to suggest a tightly disciplined camp.

Meet the Writer

Truman Capote

"A Turtle on Its Back"

Truman Capote (1924–1984) said he was "sort of dragged up" by assorted elderly relatives who lived in "dirt-road Alabama." He was born in New Orleans, but his father deserted the family, and the boy was moved from place to place while his mother lived in New York. For several years, Capote attended military schools, which he hated. When he was seventeen, he abandoned formal schooling for good and moved to New York City to learn to write. He came to national prominence when he was just twenty-four years old, with the publication of his first novel, *Other Voices, Other Rooms* (1948).

Capote's most famous novel is probably *Breakfast at Tiffany's* (1958). It was made into a movie starring Audrey Hepburn as Holly Golightly, the story's unpredictable and "lost" heroine, who goes to New York from the South to make her fortune. His most talked-about book is not fiction at all, but an account of a mass murder that took place in Kansas. Called *In Cold Blood* (1965), the book took Capote six years to research and write and involved him in much controversy. Capote called the book a nonfiction novel—a narrative that reads like a novel but with events that are all true.

In an interview in *The New York Times Magazine*, Capote once said that his frustrations during his early years made him feel "like a turtle on its back."

> **❝**I always felt that nobody was going to understand me, going to understand what I felt about things. I guess that's why I started writing. At least on paper I could put down what I thought.**❞**

My Father Is a Simple Man
Luis Omar Salinas

I walk to town with my father
to buy a newspaper. He walks slower
than I do so I must slow up.
The street is filled with children.
5   We argue about the price
of pomegranates, I convince
him it is the fruit of scholars.
He has taken me on this journey
and it's been lifelong.
10   He's sure I'll be healthy
so long as I eat more oranges,
and tells me the orange
has seeds and so is perpetual;°
and we too will come back
15   like the orange trees.
I ask him what he thinks
about death and he says
he will gladly face it when
it comes but won't jump
20   out in front of a car.
I'd gladly give my life
for this man with a sixth
grade education, whose kindness
and patience are true . . .
25   The truth of it is, he's the scholar,
and when the bitter-hard reality
comes at me like a punishing
evil stranger, I can always
remember that here was a man
30   who was a worker and provider,
who learned the simple facts

The Jazz Musician by William Low.
Courtesy of the Artist.

in life and lived by them,
who held no pretense.°
And when he leaves without
35   benefit of fanfare° or applause
I shall have learned what little
there is about greatness.

---

13. **perpetual** (pər·pech′o͞o·əl) *adj.*: continuing
    forever.
33. **who held no pretense:** who didn't show off.
35. **fanfare** (fan′fer′) *n.*: noisy display to draw
    attention (literally, a flourish of trumpets).

After You Read   Response and Analysis

Reading Check

1. What do you know about Buddy? What is his relationship to the old woman he calls "my friend"?

2. Why do Buddy and his friend make fruitcakes each year?

3. What obstacles must they overcome to make their gifts?

4. What does Buddy's friend discover after flying her kite on their last Christmas Day together?

Thinking Critically

5. How would you describe the **character** of Buddy's friend? Consider
   - what she says
   - the way her face is described
   - the things she does and has never done
   - Buddy's description of her as "still a child"

6. Look carefully at the sensory details in Capote's description of the kitchen at different points in the story. What **mood**—or feeling—do these details of **setting** convey in each scene? 📖

7. Which details in the description of Mr. Haha Jones's cafe make it seem like a threatening place? Does the **setting** accurately reflect Haha Jones's character? Explain your answer. 📖

8. As friends, what do Buddy and his cousin give to each other, and what do they get in return? In your opinion, why does this friendship have a lasting effect on Buddy, as he leaves home for the unknown world of adolescence? Support your answer with evidence from the story, and check your Quickwrite notes. ✏️

9. Explain the reference to kites in the last paragraph. What do kites represent for Buddy? What does this reference tell you about Buddy's feelings concerning the death of his friend?

10. In what ways is Buddy's friend similar to the speaker's father in "My Father Is a Simple Man" (see the **Connection** on page 74)? Do you think Buddy learns about "greatness" from his friend? Explain.

Extending and Evaluating

11. Do you think that Buddy's friend is a realistic character, or do you think that people like her don't exist in real life? Explain your response.

WRITING

There's No Place Like Home

People's homes reveal a great deal about their characters. We learn, for example, that Buddy's friend "sleeps in a scrap-quilt-covered iron bed painted rose pink," which may suggest her simplicity, her desire for beauty, or her own rosy, childlike personality. Write a **description** of the home of someone you know. Use **sensory details** to make the setting vivid and to create a mood. Be sure to convey the person's character through your description of his or her home. If you want to, you can create your own fictional character and setting.

▶ Use "Describing a Place," pages 456–463, for help with this assignment.

SKILLS FOCUS

Literary Skills
Analyze setting and how it affects mood.

Reading Skills
Identify sensory details.

Writing Skills
Write a description of a place.

After You Read Vocabulary Development

Vocabulary Resource File

PRACTICE

Begin a vocabulary resource file you can refer to when you're writing and at a loss for words. Put each Word Bank word on a separate index card (or create a file on your computer). As in the example below, include the definition and sample sentences using the word. When you learn new words, add them to your file.

inaugurating *(verb)*
Definition: *formally beginning*
Examples
The principal will be <u>inaugurating</u> a new school policy tomorrow.
The theater will be <u>inaugurating</u> its first season with a performance of *Romeo and Juliet*.

Grammar Link

Verb Tenses: What Time Is It?

The tense of a verb indicates the time of the action or the state of being expressed by the verb. Different tenses serve different purposes. "A Christmas Memory" is told in the present tense, although Capote uses the past and future tenses at times.

Tense	Example	Purpose
Present	"On the farther shore, Queenie <u>shakes</u> herself and <u>trembles</u>."	• expresses an action that is occurring now • shows a customary action • expresses a general truth
Past	"'I <u>made</u> you another kite.'"	• expresses an action that occurred in the past but is not occurring now
Future	"'Buddy, do you think Mrs. Roosevelt <u>will serve</u> our cake at dinner?'"	• expresses an action that will occur

SKILLS FOCUS

Vocabulary Skills
Use words in context.

Grammar Skills
Identify and use verb tenses.

PRACTICE

1. Choose two paragraphs without dialogue in the story. Rewrite them in the past tense. How does the change in tense change the feeling of the story? Why do you think Capote chose to write in the present tense?

2. Take a sample of your writing, and underline the verbs. Label each verb tense. Are your tenses consistent?

▶ **For more help, see Tense, 3d and 3e, in the Language Handbook.**

FICTION

Just a Little Guy

In J.R.R. Tolkien's fantasy **The Hobbit,** Bilbo Baggins is just a little guy—a hobbit— who is minding his own business. Then one day the wizard Gandalf and a gang of thirteen dwarfs arrive at his door and carry him off. So begins Bilbo's great adventure, an adventure with some big challenges for a little guy: bee pastures, giant spiders, icy waterfalls, and the dreaded dragon Smaug.

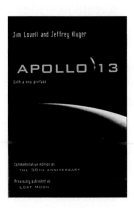

NONFICTION

A Space Odyssey

It was a routine journey—the fifth time U.S. astronauts had set out for the moon. But on April 13, 1970, Jim Lovell, Fred Haise, and Jack Swigert felt a strange explosion in their spacecraft. The lights dimmed, and the air got thinner. The three astronauts abandoned ship—for a tiny lunar module with room and supplies for only two. **Apollo 13,** co-written by Jim Lovell and Jeffrey Kluger, tells the story of the epic journey.

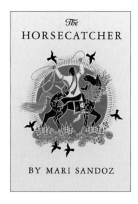

FICTION

A Cheyenne Adventure

Has anyone ever had dreams for your future that you don't necessarily share? This is the situation that Young Elk, a Cheyenne youth, faces. His family wants him to become a warrior, but Young Elk wants to follow in the footsteps of Old Horsecatcher, a great man among the Cheyenne people, who tames wild horses with a gentle hand. In Mari Sandoz's **The Horsecatcher,** you'll meet a young man who will do anything—including tread on enemy territory, wrangle with untamed horses, and risk both life and honor—to stay true to his own spirit.

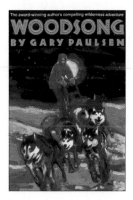

NONFICTION

Man's Best Friend

Can you imagine enduring a temperature of -50°F—or lower—on a dog-sled race that covers more than a thousand miles? Gary Paulsen brings an adventure like this to life in his book **Woodsong.** In this account of his experiences during the Iditarod, a dog-sled race through Alaska, Paulsen whisks us along on his long and lonely journey. His only companions are a team of dogs, and they turn out to be the best friends he has ever had.

Writing an Autobiographical Narrative

Writing Assignment
Write an autobiographical narrative that reveals an experience's significance for you.

It is human nature to want to share what happens in our lives. Many magazines and books—like this one—contain stories written by people who want to share their meaningful life experiences. You can share an experience that is important to you with others by writing an **autobiographical narrative**.

Prewriting

Search Your Memory for Experiences

Magic Moments Your autobiographical narrative will be based on a specific, meaningful experience from your life. To come up with some experiences that you might write about, jog your memory by visiting a specific place that was important to you when you were younger, thinking about the first time you did something—rode a bike, for example—or listing special occasions you remember well.

Choose an Experience

Do the Write Thing Ask yourself the following questions to evaluate each experience that you thought of.

- Is this experience important to me? Why?

- What specific details can I give about this experience?

- Is the experience too private or embarrassing to share?

   When you finish, look over what you wrote about each experience. Choose the experience that brought out the most detailed and positive responses from you.

Define Your Purpose and Audience

Your Side of the Story In an autobiographical narrative your **purpose** is to relate the **sequence of events** that make up a personal experience and to express to your audience the **significance** of those events. Your **audience** consists of the people you think might read your autobiographical narrative. Ask yourself the questions below and on the next page to get a feel for your audience.

1. **Who is my intended audience?** Your audience might include classmates, teachers, friends, parents, or even total strangers.

SKILLS FOCUS

Writing Skills
Write an autobiographical narrative.

2. What will the audience need to know to understand the experience?
Plan to provide background information to help your readers understand your narrative, if necessary.

Gather Details

Let Your Memory Be Your Guide To search your memory for the details that will bring your narrative to life, answer the questions and use the tips in the chart below. List all of the vivid details you can recall about events, people, places, thoughts, and feelings. The second column contains details from one writer's answers to the questions.

ADDING DETAILS	
Questions/Tips	**Examples**
Events What sequence of events make up the experience? Were there important events that led up to or followed the experience? **TIP:** Match the **pace** of your narrative to the pace of the actual events—a quick pace for rapid events, a slow pace for more drawn-out events.	Sequence of events: walking in park, practicing building fires with Dad Later events: camp contest, camping in mountains
Places Where did the events happen? **TIP:** Use **concrete sensory details** to create effective images of the sights, sounds, and smells of the places you are describing.	city park on cool summer morning; wilderness; thickly leaved trees; pines and aspens; smell of trees
People Who was involved in the events? What did those people look like? What did they do and say? **TIP:** Use sensory details to describe **actions** and **gestures**. Use **dialogue**, actual words people say, to show each person's personality.	me—ages five, eleven, fourteen; Dad—young man dressed for work, wearing glasses; what Dad said as he taught me
Thoughts and Feelings What did I think and feel as the events unfolded? **TIP:** Use **interior monologue**, "thinking out loud," to share your thoughts with readers.	happiness during times with Dad; pleasure at collecting wood; luck for having such a dad; special bond

Organize Details

Ducks in a Row Now, take a look at the events that you listed. When you write your narrative, discuss the events in **chronological order,** or time order. Events that came before your experience will appear first in your narrative because they will help your audience understand what led up to your experience. You will discuss events that came after your experience later in your narrative to show how that experience related to other parts of your life.

Guide readers through the events by including in your narrative transitional words and phrases that suggest changes in time (*at first, to begin, then*) and place (*around, nearby, across from*). Also, keep in mind that the tone of your writing should be informal, as if you were talking to friends.

Consider the Significance of Your Experience

And So It Ends You chose a particular experience to write about because it was important to you in some way. You will want to share this significance with your readers, too. To consider the meaning of your autobiographical narrative, ask yourself these questions.

- Did the experience change me? If so, how?

- What did I learn from the experience?

- Has my **perspective,** my thoughts and feelings about the event, shifted over time? If so, how?

DO THIS

Thinking about your answers to the questions above, write a sentence telling what the experience meant to you. The writer narrating her experience with her father as he taught her to build a campfire developed the following statement about the meaning of her experience.

> A simple lesson in building campfires defined the relationship my dad and I have shared.

You don't have to include the sentence you wrote about the meaning of your experience in your final draft, but it will remind you of the controlling impression you want to create as you write. The **controlling impression** is the main idea or feeling you want to communicate about your experience. Every detail in the narrative should contribute to that impression. In the Writer's Model on the next page, the writer doesn't state her controlling impression directly. Instead, she expresses the controlling impression indirectly throughout the narrative through her choice of details.

SKILLS FOCUS

Writing Skills
Establish a controlling impression.

PRACTICE & APPLY 1 Follow the guidelines in this section to choose an experience, analyze your audience, and gather and organize details for your autobiographical narrative.

Writing

Writing an Autobiographical Narrative

A Writer's Framework

Introduction

- Begin with an engaging opening.
- Supply background information so readers understand the context of the narrative.
- Hint at the significance of the experience.

Body

- Discuss the sequence of events that make up your experience.
- Discuss the important events that led up to or followed your experience.
- Include plenty of details about people, places, and events.

Conclusion

- Look back at the experience from the present time.
- Reflect on what you learned or how you changed as a result of this experience.
- Reveal the significance of the experience.

A Writer's Model

A Campfire Girl

Do people make campfires anymore? I suppose they do, but building campfires is prohibited in many places now. Even if rangers do not ban campfires, environmentally aware people agree that no one should be allowed to pick the ground bare of wood and scar the land with fire rings. Still, I am a campfire girl at heart. Even though I dutifully use camp stoves in the mountains and in the campgrounds, I still love a small blaze to warm my hands, to dry soggy socks, and to stare into when the night sky, far from the glow of city lights, is deep black.

My love for campfires all started because of a leisurely stroll in a park in New York City. When I was a tidy little skirt-wearing five-year-old, my family lived in New York for a summer. My father and I would go out early, when it was still cool, to walk the dog. Dad would be dressed for work, his shoes treading the asphalt path as I happily did a quickstep along beside him.

One morning as my father threw sticks for the dog, I started picking up sticks of my own. Always ready to play and teach, my dad crouched down and said, "Here, let me show you the right way to build a campfire. Once you learn how, you can build a fire in the middle of a tornado." He took my sticks and helped me gather others, graduated in size from tiny twigs to hefty branches. Gently propping the twigs

(continued)

INTRODUCTION
Engaging opening
Background information
Hint at meaning

BODY
First event of experience

People and place details
Feelings

Second event of experience

Dialogue

Specific action with sensory details

(continued)

Specific movement

Dialogue

Thought

Later important event

Specific movement

Sensory details
Interior monologue

Later important event

Feelings

Sensory details

Sensory detail
CONCLUSION
A look back from the present

Significance of the experience

together, he started with a teepee shape. I watched his careful hands gently place slightly larger sticks on top of the others. "Don't pack the sticks too tightly together," he warned, "or the air can't flow and feed the fire." (This was the theory at least; we did not light our fires there in the middle of the city.) While I worked on the tepee and other structures—the log cabin, the **A**—the sounds of the city faded away.

Several years later at summer camp, we had a contest: Who could make a campfire the fastest using just one match? I have no doubt that my lessons in the park in New York City laid the foundation for my championship fire building at camp. I used the **A** structure. I blew gently on my kindling, giving the flame just enough air to turn the kindling into bright embers and make flames lick at the larger sticks. As other girls struggled to start a fire, I thought, "You're one lucky girl to have the dad you have. Some of my friends might have neat dads, but not like mine."

On later camping trips with my father, when I was no longer a tidy little girl, but a rugged teenager in jeans and work boots, I took special pleasure in collecting wood, placing each size in a separate pile. Then I would place the kindling and get it burning, making a small cook fire. Dad and I never built great, big bonfires in rings with three- to four-foot diameters. We made campfires just big enough for the heavy skillet we packed into the wilderness. (It cooked so much better than the aluminum pans that came in camp mess kits.) We ate many meals over our fires—usually potatoes and onions and just-caught trout. I can almost hear the sizzle of the fresh fish frying now.

That day in the city park, my dad could not have known of the backpacking trips he and I would share now—nine years later. Still, I see those little piles of sticks as my introduction to life outdoors. The thickly leaved trees of the park have given way to fragrant pines and aspen overhead, but the kinship I experienced with my dad remains the same. I was his campfire girl, sharing in his love of the outdoors and a well-built campfire. We were building something to warm us then and now.

go.
hrw
.com

INTERNET

More Writer's Models

Keyword: LE7 9-1

PRACTICE & APPLY 2 Write your autobiographical narrative, organizing details about people, places, and events chronologically. Refer to the framework on page 81 and the Writer's Model above as guides.

Revising

Evaluate and Revise Your Draft

Do Look Back To improve the draft of your autobiographical narrative, you must read it and read it again. Looking at your paper twice will help you strengthen the logic and coherence of its content and organization as well as its style. As you look over your draft, keep your **audience** and **purpose** in mind. Also, consider the **formality** of your words. Since you are telling your own true story, remember that the overall tone of your paper will be informal and personal.

First Reading: Content and Organization On your first reading, concentrate on evaluating and revising your autobiographical narrative's content and organization. Use the guidelines in the chart below as a **think sheet**.

> **PEER REVIEW**
>
> Exchange your paper with a peer before you revise, and ask him or her to evaluate how effectively your narrative communicates the significance of your experience.

Rubric: Writing an Autobiographical Narrative

Evaluation Questions	▶ Tips	▶ Revision Techniques
❶ Does the introduction include an engaging opening, background information, and a hint at the significance of the experience?	▶ **Bracket** the engaging opening and background information. **Underline** the hint about the significance.	▶ **Add** an engaging opening and background information. **Add** a sentence or two that suggests the significance of the event.
❷ Does the narrative include details about events, people, and places?	▶ **Circle** details. If you have fewer than three circles in each paragraph, revise.	▶ **Add** details about events, people, and places to the paragraph. **Elaborate** on existing details with sensory language or dialogue.
❸ Does the narrative include details about the narrator's thoughts and feelings?	▶ **Highlight** sentences that contain the narrator's thoughts or feelings. If there isn't at least one such detail in the narrative, revise.	▶ **Elaborate** on details by answering the questions, "What did I think?" or "How did I feel?" Consider using interior monologue.
❹ Is the order of the events clear?	▶ **Number** the events in chronological order.	▶ **Rearrange** events in chronological order, if necessary, and **add** transitional words and phrases to show the order.
❺ Does the conclusion discuss the significance of the experience?	▶ **Underline** sentences in the conclusion that reveal the meaning of the experience.	▶ **Add** sentences that indirectly or directly explain the importance of the experience.

Second Reading: **Style** The second time you read through your draft, focus on evaluating and revising your style—the way you express yourself. Using the style guidelines in the chart below, check to see that you have used **precise language** in your narrative. For example, suppose you wrote the words *wide street.* Try to think of a more precise noun and a more descriptive adjective to better show the scene you are trying to bring to life—*tree-lined boulevard,* for example.

Style Guidelines

Evaluation Question	▶ Tip	▶ Revision Technique
● Does the narrative include precise language?	▶ Pick four sentences in each paragraph. In each, **circle** the nouns and adjectives. Are the nouns and adjectives vivid and precise?	▶ **Replace** at least two imprecise nouns and adjectives per paragraph with more precise language. (Use a dictionary or thesaurus if necessary.)

ANALYZING THE REVISION PROCESS
Study these revisions, and answer the questions that follow.

replace

                                   leisurely stroll
My love for campfires all started because of a ~~walk~~ in a park

add

                        a tidy little skirt-wearing five-year-old
in New York City. When I was ~~five~~, my family lived in New

York for a summer. My father and I would go out early, when

it was still cool, to walk the dog. Dad would be dressed for

elaborate

                                    happily
work, his shoes treading the asphalt path as I did a quickstep

along beside him.

Responding to the Revision Process
1. In the first sentence, why is "leisurely stroll" an improvement over "walk"?

2. How do the additions in the second and fourth sentences affect the reader's image of the narrator?

SKILLS FOCUS

Writing Skills
Use precise language.

PRACTICE & APPLY 3 Evaluate and revise the content, organization, and style of your essay, using the guidelines on these pages. Consider peer comments, too.

Publishing

Proofread and Publish Your Autobiographical Narrative

To Err Is Human Proofread your paper before you prepare a clean copy for publishing. Read your paper aloud slowly, focusing on each word you have written to make sure each sentence is complete. You might even ask for assistance in proofreading from a peer. Find and eliminate errors in grammar, mechanics, and usage. Such errors can prevent readers from enjoying or even understanding your ideas.

Get the Word Out You've just completed the story of a personal experience that is meaningful to you. Your work is something to be proud of and to share with other people. Try some of the following suggestions for reaching readers besides your teacher and classmates.

- Mail or e-mail your paper to interested relatives or friends. If your narrative is about an event in their lives or about someone your readers know, they might be especially interested in reading it. You might even consider giving your paper as a gift to someone else who was involved in the experience you describe.

- Look for magazines that publish this kind of personal essay. Well-written, authentic stories from students' lives are often welcomed in magazines for young people.

- If your narrative is about school life, consider submitting your narrative to your school's literary magazine or your school newspaper.

Reflect on Your Autobiographical Narrative

Count the Ways Use the following questions to look back at your autobiographical narrative and assess what you've learned in the process of writing it.

- How did writing this paper help you to understand this experience better or in a new way?

- Are you satisfied with how you expressed the meaning of your experience? Why or why not? What would you do differently if you wrote another autobiographical narrative?

PRACTICE & APPLY 4 Proofread your narrative to eliminate mistakes. Make a clean copy of your paper and publish it, using one of the suggestions above. Finally, answer the reflection questions.

TIP Proofreading will help ensure that your autobiographical narrative follows the **conventions** of standard American English. For example, look for and fix misplaced modifiers that describe people, places, and events in your narrative. For more on **misplaced modifers,** see Placement of Modifiers, 5g, in the Language Handbook.

SKILLS FOCUS

Writing Skills
Proofread, especially for misplaced modifiers.

Presenting an Oral Narrative

You have probably already told many true stories aloud, such as what happened when the family car broke down on vacation or how your team won the baseball championship. When you tell a story aloud, you are giving an **oral narrative.**

Adapt Your Autobiographical Narrative

Try a New Twist Because your audience will be listening to your narrative instead of reading it, you'll need to change it as you prepare for your presentation. Keep in mind the **occasion**—a speech for your class—and follow these suggestions to adapt your narrative.

- **Word Choice** Use **vocabulary** that sounds natural. Avoid words that might be unfamiliar to listeners, who won't be able to stop and look them up in a dictionary.

- **Setting** Locate events in **specific places.** For instance, say "in the cafeteria line" or "by my locker" rather than "at school."

- **Details** Readers have time to linger over language to form mental images of what a writer describes. Listeners don't. Look carefully at the **sensory details** you used in your written narrative to describe the sights, sounds, and smells of the events and people's actions. Read sensory passages aloud, and ask yourself whether your language is vivid enough to create images in listeners' minds.

One writer decided that a more vivid description of starting a fire would interest her listeners. For her oral presentation, she changed "enough air to turn the kindling into bright embers and make flames lick at the larger sticks" to "enough air to turn the little pieces of wood into bright orange coals and make yellow and blue flames lick at the bigger sticks."

- **Organization** Use **chronological order** in your oral narrative, just as you did in your written one. You can even use the same transitional words and phrases you included in your paper to help listeners follow the events of your experience.

- **Conclusion** If you didn't directly state the **significance** of your experience in the conclusion of your written narrative, do so in the conclusion to your oral narrative. Strongly suggesting or indirectly stating the significance is acceptable in a written narrative that readers can re-read, but not in an oral narrative that they have to understand immediately.

SKILLS FOCUS

Listening and Speaking Skills
Present an oral narrative.

Deliver Your Narrative

Show and Tell When you wrote your autobiographical narrative, you expressed the significance of your experience through words alone. Since you'll deliver your narrative orally, you can also use **verbal and nonverbal techniques**—ways of using your voice as well as your face and body—to show how the experience made you feel and what it meant to you.

Use Verbal Techniques How you use your voice can give the audience as much information as what you say. The following chart explains some of the basic verbal techniques you can use.

VERBAL TECHNIQUES

Technique	Uses	Examples
Pitch	• change pitch for different characters • use pitch to show feelings	• a high pitch might represent a young child • a low pitch might show feelings of fright
Volume	• change volume for different characters • use volume to create mood	• a loud voice might represent a pushy character • a quiet voice might create a suspenseful mood
Rate, or Pace	• use rate to show emotions or create a mood • use a pace that reflects the speed at which various events occurred	• speaking slowly can create drama and suspense • speaking quickly (but distinctly) can communicate excitement or a quick series of events

Use Nonverbal Techniques You will also use facial expressions and gestures to add meaning to your oral narrative. A gesture such as forming an **A** with the hands can illustrate a method of placing sticks for a fire. Use your eyes to show emotion, and keep your listeners involved by making frequent eye contact with them.

Be sure to tailor your gestures and tone to your audience. For instance, exaggerated facial expressions and a "cutesy" voice might be appropriate for small children, but not for your classmates.

Take Note Sound natural and relaxed by delivering your narrative **extemporaneously,** using **concise notes**—notes that say a lot in a few words. Make note cards with short phrases or single words that remind you of details, and arrange the note cards in the order in which you will present them.

SKILLS FOCUS

 Adapt your written autobiographical narrative into an oral narrative. Practice your narrative, and then present it to your class.

Listening and Speaking Skills
Use effective verbal and nonverbal techniques.

So You Want to Be an Astronaut?
Richard Knight

Richard Knight explains the problems that would-be space tourists will face.

All but the most hardened skeptics[1] now admit that, sooner or later, space tourism will become a reality. But the question is: when exactly?

The answer is: probably not for quite a while yet.

MirCorp, the company which has leased the Mir space station, is offering one place on its mission to the station in September—it announced the spare seat earlier this year. But the return fare will cost up to £20 million[2]—and costs are not the only problems facing future space cadets.

The Body

According to Royal Air Force space expert Derek Clark, our bodies are not built for spaceflight and any would-be tourist will have to accept certain health risks and discomforts.

Just getting to space is a physically demanding experience. Passengers will be pinned to the backs of their seats by a 3G force (increasing each tourist's apparent weight threefold) for 4 minutes 40 seconds from launch to orbit while being buffeted as they crash through the atmosphere.

However, since extreme forces beyond 3G (which might be experienced in an emergency) can either starve the brain of oxygen or cause it to hemorrhage,[3] each tourist will probably have to be fitted with a tailor-made G-suit.

In space, where there is almost no gravity, blood equalizes around the body, rather than being pulled into our legs. The effect is to give the brain more blood than usual. Our bodies cope with this by reducing blood mass through increased urination, reduced liquid intake, and nosebleeds. Passengers will take a day to get over this unpleasant process. Back on Earth, they will find their reduced blood mass is again drawn downwards, causing them to faint.

SKILLS FOCUS

Pages 88–91 cover
Reading Skills
Generate research questions.

---

1. **skeptics** (skep′tiks) *n.*: people who doubt something.
2. **£20 million**: sum approximately equal to $30 million.
3. **hemorrhage** (hem′ər·ij′) *v.*: bleed heavily.

Before facing that challenge, however, 50 percent of space tourists will have spent most of their time feeling ill because of space sickness (an extreme form of travel sickness). This would contribute to weight loss: Each passenger will lose about 5 pounds on their first day in space and will continue to lose weight daily.

This is also because, with no gravity to fight against, muscles will deteriorate[4] fast, most seriously around the heart. In fact, tourists who stay in space long enough will find their hearts have become irreversibly weakened—which is the fate of some Mir astronauts. Each passenger would have to exercise for 6 hours a day to halt muscle deterioration.

Painful kidney stones are more likely to develop in space, and there is a need to protect would-be astronauts against infection. So tourists will either be isolated for a month prior to flight or given regular medicals during the lead-up. Having second thoughts, by any chance?

The Mind

Tourists will need to be quizzed by psychologists[5] in order to check whether they have the right mental stuff. This is because passengers may feel a profound sense of isolation as they look at Earth from space. Gazing out, they will be able to use the tips of their thumbs to blot the Earth from view, making everything they have ever known disappear.

As the sun rises and sets 16 times a day in space, sleep patterns will also be disrupted, possibly unhinging passengers. Some will suffer claustrophobia[6] from being confined to a narrow capsule in which one cannot walk, open a window or—of course—get out!

Another problem is that former astronauts are statistically more likely to suffer serious accidents when they return to Earth. This might be because, having flown to space and taken such a huge risk, they feel invincible[7] and take greater chances than normal. *Still* feel like going?

---

4. **deteriorate** (dē·tir′ē·ə·rāt′) *v.:* become weak or damaged.
5. **psychologists** (sī·käl′ə·jists) *n.:* specialists who study the mind and emotions.
6. **claustrophobia** (klôs′trə·fō′bē·ə) *n.:* abnormal fear of being in an enclosed place.
7. **invincible** (in·vin′sə·bəl) *adj.:* all-powerful; unbeatable.

Enough Demand?

Do sufficient numbers of people really want to travel to destination space? It is likely to be enormously expensive: Will enough people be able to find the money? Once the market is proved, the money required to fuel passenger space planes should be more forthcoming than it is at present. For now, however, we can only guess when the first scheduled flight beyond the atmosphere will take off . . . phew![8]

—**from** *The Times* **(London), April 22, 2000**

---

8. **For now . . . phew!** After the publication of this article, Dennis A. Tito, an American, became the first space tourist, blasting off into space on April 28, 2001. Paying $20 million for the trip, he joined a Russian crew on an eight-day journey to the International Space Station.

---

1. Which of the following questions is answered in the article?

   A What causes heart damage during prolonged space travel?

   B Why might space travelers develop kidney stones?

   C What can space travelers do to avoid becoming depressed?

   D What will the interior of a passenger space plane look like?

2. Which of the following research questions about space tourism is the *most* narrow and focused?

   F What kinds of people want to be astronauts?

   G In the future, will space tourism become as routine as international airplane flights are now?

   H How does a G-suit prevent a person from being injured during liftoff?

   J How effective are the U.S. government's current plans for the space program budget?

3. Assume your initial research question is *How do people feel once they return to earth after traveling in space?* Which follow-up question will *best* help you narrow your research?

A Do people visit doctors frequently after space flights?

B Are people satisfied with their lives once they are back on earth?

C Do people ever regret traveling in space?

D What specific physical effects do people experience after a space flight, and how long do the effects last?

4. If you wanted to do further research on the effects of space travel on the mind, which question would give you the *most* relevant information?

F Will space tourists returning to earth be tested by psychologists?

G Is there a cure for claustrophobia?

H How do disrupted sleep patterns affect the human mind?

J Which former astronauts have had serious accidents?

5. Which research question about the effects of space travel on the body follows *most* directly from the information in the article?

A When will doctors and nurses be trained to work in space?

B Does gravity have harmful effects on our bodies when we are on earth?

C What are the symptoms of space sickness, and how long does it last?

D What kinds of circulation problems do people face on earth?

6. If you wanted to use a search engine to learn how tourists will be transported to space, which would be the *most* helpful search term?

F Mir space station

G space planes

H space missions

J Royal Air Force

Constructed Response

7. Generate two original research questions from "So You Want to Be an Astronaut?" and explain why you believe one might be a more promising line of inquiry and further research than the other.

Collection 1: Skills Review

Vocabulary Skills

Multiple-Meaning Words

DIRECTIONS: Choose the answer in which the underlined word is used in the same way it is used in the sentence from "The Most Dangerous Game."

1. "'I suppose the first three shots I heard was when the hunter flushed his quarry and wounded it.'"
   A Shawna's face flushed with shame.
   B We flushed the pipes with cleanser.
   C The sudden noise flushed the sparrow out of his tree.
   D Flushed and feverish, Dan cried.

2. "But as he forged along, he saw to his great astonishment that all the lights were in one enormous building. . . ."
   F The horseshoes were forged in the blacksmith's shop.
   G The detective said that the signature on the check had been forged.
   H After lengthy negotiations the two companies forged a merger.
   J The runner in last place suddenly forged ahead and grabbed the lead.

3. "'Here in my preserve on this island,' he said in the same slow tone, 'I hunt more dangerous game.'"
   A The wild-animal preserve has become a popular tourist attraction.
   B The ice cream was topped with a fruit preserve.
   C Salt can preserve certain meats.
   D The president swears to "preserve, protect, and defend the Constitution."

4. "The door opened then, opened as suddenly as if it were on a spring. . . ."
   F We hiked to the spring and camped out in the woods.
   G My dogs spring to the door when they hear my key in the lock.
   H The child opened the box, and a clown on a spring popped up.
   J New houses spring up each day as more people move to the town.

5. "'A twenty-two,' he remarked. 'That's odd. It must have been a fairly large animal too. The hunter had his nerve with him to tackle it with a light gun.'"
   A Eli is a tackle on the football team.
   B I tackled cleaning the garage, since someone had to do it.
   C The fisherman packed up his tackle box as the boat docked.
   D In the game, Claudia managed to tackle her opponent from behind.

6. "There was no sound in the night as Rainsford sat there but the muffled throb of the engine. . . ."
   F Sometimes we sing so much that our voices sound hoarse.
   G The child was so tired that he fell sound asleep in the car.
   H Karen gave me sound advice.
   J The silence was broken by the sound of shattering glass.

SKILLS FOCUS

Vocabulary Skills
Understand multiple-meaning words.

Collection 1: Skills Review
Writing Skills

DIRECTIONS: The following paragraph is from a draft of a student's autobiographical narrative. Read the questions below it, and choose the best answer to each question.

(1) Of all the events of my childhood, the one I remember best is my first ride on the school bus. (2) It took our bus forty-five minutes to get from my house to the school. (3) As I stepped up the gritty black steps and looked for an empty seat, I saw countless strange faces glaring back at me. (4) I sat near the back of the bus next to a shy-looking kid with glasses that sat crookedly on his nose. (5) As the bus got rolling, I soon found myself in the midst of a raging paper war. (6) "When will this ever stop?" I wondered to myself as a thick, wet paper wad struck the back of my neck. (7) "Get under here!" the boy next to me shouted, signaling me to duck under the backpack he had put over his head for protection. (8) As we crouched, we laughed together at the chaos around us. (9) When we arrived, I promised to meet him after school so we could ride home together.

1. To improve the coherence of this paragraph, which sentence might the writer delete?
   - **A** 2
   - **B** 4
   - **C** 7
   - **D** 8

2. If the writer wanted to add sensory details to the paragraph, which of the following would be appropriate?
   - **F** The bus had room for sixty-four.
   - **G** I hated waiting for the bus even more than I hated riding in it.
   - **H** I waded through crumpled litter and gray, chewed gum to get to my seat.
   - **J** My friend's mom worked at the school, so she didn't ride the bus.

3. Why did the student put *"When will this ever stop?"* in quotation marks?
   - **A** It sets the pace of the story.
   - **B** It is the title of the story.

   - **C** It is an important event.
   - **D** It is interior monologue.

4. Which of the following sentences might the writer add to explain the significance of this experience?
   - **F** I never met a single person I liked on that school bus.
   - **G** In the midst of flying trash, I had somehow found a friend.
   - **H** The bus system is in need of a strict disciplinary program.
   - **J** The school bus is an efficient mode of transportation.

5. Imagine that you have been asked to present this experience as an oral narrative. Which of the following gestures would be appropriate to make when saying, "Get under here!"?
   - **A** clapping your hands
   - **B** giving the thumbs-up sign
   - **C** waving your hands toward you
   - **D** pointing at the audience

SKILLS FOCUS

Writing Skills
Write an autobiographical narrative.

On Your Own

Literary Focus:

Analyzing Character

Informational Reading Focus:

Using Primary and
Secondary Sources

INTERNET

Collection
Resources

Keyword: LE7 9-2

April (1990–1991) by Chuck Close.
Oil on canvas (100" × 84").

The Eli and Edythe L. Broad Collection. © Chuck Close.
Photograph © Bill Jacobson Studio.

Elements of Literature

Character *by* John Leggett
REVEALING HUMAN NATURE

Creating characters—telling what human beings are like—is the whole point of writing stories. A story is interesting to us as readers largely because of what it tells us about people and how we behave.

A magazine editor once told me that all you need to tell a story is a character, an adjective, and a series of choices that the character must make. Of course, people are much more complex than a single adjective can suggest, and that is the joy, and the difficulty, of storytelling. How does a writer build a character out of words—someone who will seem to become flesh and blood and rise off the page?

Interpreting Characters' Words

The most obvious method of characterization is the characters' **speech.** Think of how you can recognize your friends from what they say and how they say it. Think of how Joe can be counted on to talk about what things cost, whereas Sally talks about their beauty. Think of how Alice reveals her nature by using long, fancy words and Sam reveals his by using short, slangy ones. Here are four ways writers use speech to reveal character:

1 When characters tell their own stories through **first-person narration,** they speak directly to the reader. They present facts—describing events in the story and perhaps even their backgrounds—but they also tell us what they think and feel. As they talk, they reveal their personal traits.

2 Reading the characters' **dialogue** in a story is like listening in on a conversation. We can learn about the characters not only by what they say about themselves, but by how they respond to each other.

3 In a **dramatic monologue,** a type of poem, a speaker addresses one or more silent listeners, often discussing a specific problem or situation. As the words come tumbling out, however, the speaker tells us a great deal about his or her life and values. We also learn about the speaker's relationship with the listener(s).

4 In a play this kind of self-revealing speech is a **soliloquy.** It is delivered by a character alone onstage, addressing himself or herself. Shakespeare's plays, such as *Romeo and Juliet* (see page 901), contain a number of soliloquies in which characters reveal their deepest thoughts to the audience in this way.

Other Clues to Character

1 Writers also use **appearance** to create character. We can tell so much about Scrooge, for example, from the way Charles Dickens describes his features:

The cold within him froze his old features, nipped his pointed nose, shriveled his cheek, stiffened his gait; made his eyes red, his thin lips blue. . . .

Clearly Dickens wants us to think of Scrooge as a character whose cold heart is reflected in his whole appearance.

SKILLS FOCUS

Literary Skills
Understand characterization.

INTERNET

More About Character

Keyword: LE7 9-2

The kinds of clothes a character wears can give us hints too. As readers we will respond one way to a character wearing a pinstriped suit and another way to a character wearing faded jeans.

2 In fiction a writer can even take us into the characters' minds to reveal their **private thoughts.** We might learn, for example, how one character secretly feels when he sees the bully picking on the smallest kid in the schoolyard or how another character feels as she watches her grandmother's coffin being lowered into the ground.

3 We can learn about characters by watching **how other characters in the story feel about them.** We might learn, for instance, that a salesman is a good guy in the eyes of his customers and a generous tipper in the eyes of the local waiter, but he is cranky and selfish in the eyes of his family.

4 One of the most important ways that we learn about characters is from their **actions,** from what we see them doing. For instance, when we first meet Scrooge on Christmas Eve, he is working on his accounts—an action that instantly reveals his obsession with money.

Direct and Indirect Characterization

Some writers also use **direct characterization** to tell us about the people who inhabit their fictional worlds. This means that a writer tells us directly what a character is like or what a person's motives are. In a famous listing of adjectives, Dickens tells us directly what kind of person Scrooge is:

Oh, but he was a tightfisted hand at the grindstone, Scrooge! a squeezing, wrenching, grasping, scraping, clutching, covetous old sinner!

Most modern writers do not rely on direct statements about their characters. They usually use the other methods listed here, which are called **indirect characterization.** This means that a writer *shows* us a character but allows us to interpret for ourselves the kind of person we are meeting. In fiction as in life itself, it is much more satisfying to discover for ourselves what people are truly like.

Practice

Who is the most unforgettable character you've ever met in a story? Write a few sentences about why you find the character so memorable. Before you begin writing, jot down your ideas on a chart like the one here:

Most memorable character	
Most outstanding character trait	
Character's appearance	
Important statements	
Important thoughts	
Important actions	
Reactions of other characters	

Introducing the Collection Theme

On Your Own

Make the Connection

Quickwrite

Think about the pressure you or students in your school may feel to be "the same"—to act, think, or dress the same way others do. Do you think the pressure to be the same comes from outside forces or from personal desires? Do you think being the same makes most people happy, or would they really prefer to act on their own? Jot down your thoughts.

Exploring the Theme: On Your Own

Whether you were taking responsibility or taking a stand, making a mistake or making sense of things, you've probably found yourself "on your own" at some point in your life, just like the characters and people described in this collection. Characters on their own in "Thank You, M'am" and "Marigolds" get into trouble. Teenagers, like David Levitt in "Feeding Frenzy," strike out on their own to help their communities. The narrator in "Helen on Eighty-sixth Street" must come to terms, by herself, with her parents' divorce.

"Harrison Bergeron," the story you are about to read, is about a teenager who rebels against a dehumanizing system. He pays a heavy price for deciding to be himself and acting on his own.

Literary Focus

Characters in Action

Writers reveal character in a variety of ways—through a character's appearance, words, and, most dramatically, actions. This story is named for the main character, Harrison Bergeron. To understand him, you need to learn about his family and the very strange society he has the misfortune to live in. You really get to know him, though, by watching what he does on his own. As you read, be alert to all the details you are given about Harrison's character.

Pause (1996) by Edward Paschke (1939–2004). Oil on canvas. 28 x 35 in. ©Ed Paschke, 1996.

SKILLS FOCUS

Literary Skills
Understand how character traits are revealed through appearance, words, and actions.

Harrison Bergeron

Kurt Vonnegut

The year was 2081, and everybody was finally equal. They weren't only equal before God and the law. They were equal every which way. Nobody was smarter than anybody else. Nobody was better looking than anybody else. Nobody was stronger or quicker than anybody else. All this equality was due to the 211th, 212th, and 213th Amendments to the Constitution, and to the unceasing vigilance of agents of the United States Handicapper General. ❶

Some things about living still weren't quite right, though. April, for instance, still drove people crazy by not being springtime. And it was in that clammy month that the H-G men took George and Hazel Bergeron's fourteen-year-old son, Harrison, away.

It was tragic, all right, but George and Hazel couldn't think about it very hard. Hazel had a perfectly average intelligence, which meant she couldn't think about anything except in short bursts. And George, while his intelligence was way above normal, had a little mental handicap radio in his ear. He was required by law to wear it at all times. It was tuned to a government transmitter. Every twenty seconds or so, the transmitter would send out some sharp noise to keep people like George from taking unfair advantage of their brains. ❷

George and Hazel were watching television. There were tears on Hazel's cheeks, but she'd forgotten for the moment what they were about.

On the television screen were ballerinas.

A buzzer sounded in George's head. His thoughts fled in panic, like bandits from a burglar alarm.

"That was a real pretty dance, that dance they just did," said Hazel.

"Huh?" said George.

"That dance—it was nice," said Hazel.

"Yup," said George. He tried to think a little about the ballerinas. They weren't really very good—no better than anybody else would have been, anyway. They were burdened with sash weights and bags of birdshot, and their faces were masked, so that no one, seeing a free and graceful gesture or a pretty face, would feel like something the cat drug in. George was toying with the vague notion that maybe dancers shouldn't be handicapped.

THEME

❶ What does the first paragraph tell you about individuals in this society?

THEME

❷ According to the information in this paragraph, how does the government control people? What is the government trying to prevent?

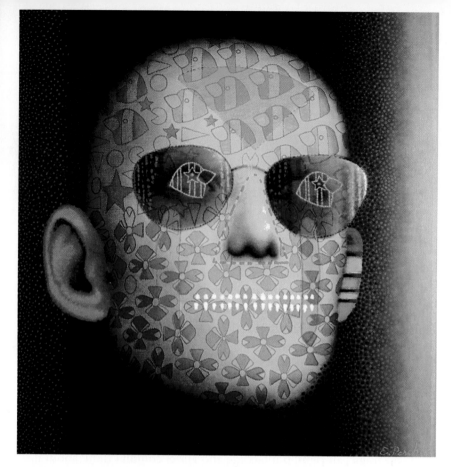

Bird Eye (1996) by
Edward Paschke
(1939–2004). Oil on
linen. 36 x 40 in.
©Ed Paschke, 1996.

But he didn't get very far with it before another noise in his ear radio
scattered his thoughts.

George winced. So did two out of the eight ballerinas.

Hazel saw him wince. Having no mental handicap herself, she had to
ask George what the latest sound had been.

"Sounded like somebody hitting a milk bottle with a ball-peen
hammer,"[1] said George.

"I'd think it would be real interesting, hearing all the different sounds,"
said Hazel, a little envious. "All the things they think up."

"Um," said George.

"Only, if I was Handicapper General, you know what I would do?" said
Hazel. Hazel, as a matter of fact, bore a strong resemblance to the
Handicapper General, a woman named Diana Moon Glampers. "If I was
Diana Moon Glampers," said Hazel, "I'd have chimes on Sunday—just
chimes. Kind of in honor of religion."

"I could think, if it was just chimes," said George.

"Well—maybe make 'em real loud," said Hazel. "I think I'd make a
good Handicapper General."

"Good as anybody else," said George.

---

1. ball-peen hammer *n.:* hammer with a ball-shaped head.

"Who knows better'n I do what normal is?" said Hazel.

"Right," said George. He began to think glimmeringly about his abnormal son who was now in jail, about Harrison, but a twenty-one-gun salute in his head stopped that. ❸

"Boy!" said Hazel, "that was a doozy, wasn't it?"

It was such a doozy that George was white and trembling, and tears stood on the rims of his red eyes. Two of the eight ballerinas had collapsed to the studio floor and were holding their temples.

"All of a sudden you look so tired," said Hazel. "Why don't you stretch out on the sofa, so's you can rest your handicap bag on the pillows, honeybunch." She was referring to the forty-seven pounds of birdshot in a canvas bag which was padlocked around George's neck. "Go on and rest the bag for a little while," she said. "I don't care if you're not equal to me for a while."

George weighed the bag with his hands. "I don't mind it," he said. "I don't notice it anymore. It's just a part of me."

"You been so tired lately—kind of wore out," said Hazel. "If there was just some way we could make a little hole in the bottom of the bag, and just take out a few of them lead balls. Just a few."

"Two years in prison and two thousand dollars fine for every ball I took out," said George. "I don't call that a bargain."

"If you could just take a few out when you came home from work," said Hazel. "I mean—you don't compete with anybody around here. You just set around."

"If I tried to get away with it," said George, "then other people'd get away with it—and pretty soon we'd be right back to the Dark Ages again, with everybody competing against everybody else. You wouldn't like that, would you?"

"I'd hate it," said Hazel.

"There you are," said George. "The minute people start cheating on laws, what do you think happens to society?"

If Hazel hadn't been able to come up with an answer to this question, George couldn't have supplied one. A siren was going off in his head. ❹

"Reckon it'd fall all apart," said Hazel.

"What would?" said George blankly.

"Society," said Hazel uncertainly. "Wasn't that what you just said?"

"Who knows?" said George.

The television program was suddenly interrupted for a news bulletin. It wasn't clear at first as to what the bulletin was about, since the announcer, like all announcers, had a serious speech impediment. For about half a minute, and in a state of high excitement, the announcer tried to say, "Ladies and gentlemen——"

He finally gave up, handed the bulletin to a ballerina to read.

Introducing the Collection Theme

THEME

❸ In this society, what makes a person normal or abnormal?

THEME

❹ Why do you think a siren goes off in George's head at this moment?

Cyborg and Binary
Digits (2000) by
Darren Winter.

"That's all right——" Hazel said of the announcer, "he tried. That's the big thing. He tried to do the best he could with what God gave him. He should get a nice raise for trying so hard."

"Ladies and gentlemen——" said the ballerina, reading the bulletin. She must have been extraordinarily beautiful, because the mask she wore was hideous. And it was easy to see that she was the strongest and most graceful of all the dancers, for her handicap bags were as big as those worn by two-hundred-pound men.

And she had to apologize at once for her voice, which was a very unfair voice for a woman to use. Her voice was a warm, luminous, timeless melody. "Excuse me——" she said, and she began again, making her voice absolutely uncompetitive.

"Harrison Bergeron, age fourteen," she said in a grackle squawk,[2] "has just escaped from jail, where he was held on suspicion of plotting

2. **grackle squawk:** loud, harsh cry, like that of a grackle (blackbird).

to overthrow the government. He is a genius and an athlete, is under-handicapped, and should be regarded as extremely dangerous."

A police photograph of Harrison Bergeron was flashed on the screen—upside down, then sideways, upside down again, then right side up. The picture showed the full length of Harrison against a background calibrated[3] in feet and inches. He was exactly seven feet tall.

The rest of Harrison's appearance was Halloween and hardware. Nobody had ever borne heavier handicaps. He had outgrown hindrances[4] faster than the H-G men could think them up. Instead of a little ear radio for a mental handicap, he wore a tremendous pair of earphones, and spectacles with thick wavy lenses. The spectacles were intended not only to make him half blind, but to give him whanging headaches besides.

Scrap metal was hung all over him. Ordinarily, there was a certain symmetry,[5] a military neatness to the handicaps issued to strong people, but Harrison looked like a walking junkyard. In the race of life, Harrison carried three hundred pounds.

And to offset his good looks, the H-G men required that he wear at all times a red rubber ball for a nose, keep his eyebrows shaved off, and cover his even white teeth with black caps at snaggletooth random. ❺

"If you see this boy," said the ballerina, "do not—I repeat, do not—try to reason with him."

There was the shriek of a door being torn from its hinges.

Screams and barking cries of consternation[6] came from the television set. The photograph of Harrison Bergeron on the screen jumped again and again, as though dancing to the tune of an earthquake.

George Bergeron correctly identified the earthquake, and well he might have—for many was the time his own home had danced to the same crashing tune. "My God—" said George, "that must be Harrison!"

The realization was blasted from his mind instantly by the sound of an automobile collision in his head.

---

3. **calibrated** (kal′ə•brāt′id) *v.* used as *adj.*: marked with measurements.
4. **hindrances** (hin′drən•siz) *n.*: obstacles; things that restrain or prevent an activity.
5. **symmetry** (sim′ə•trē) *n.*: balanced arrangement.
6. **consternation** (kän′stər•nā′shən) *n.*: fear; bewilderment.

CHARACTER

❺ What does the description of Harrison's appearance in the preceding four paragraphs tell you about him?

6 What do you think Harrison means when he says, "Now watch me become what I *can* become"? What does this statement tell you about his **character**?

When George could open his eyes again, the photograph of Harrison was gone. A living, breathing Harrison filled the screen.

Clanking, clownish, and huge, Harrison stood in the center of the studio. The knob of the uprooted studio door was still in his hand. Ballerinas, technicians, musicians, and announcers cowered[7] on their knees before him, expecting to die.

"I am the Emperor!" cried Harrison. "Do you hear? I am the Emperor! Everybody must do what I say at once!" He stamped his foot and the studio shook.

"Even as I stand here—" he bellowed, "crippled, hobbled, sickened—I am a greater ruler than any man who ever lived! Now watch me become what I *can* become!" **6**

Harrison tore the straps of his handicap harness like wet tissue paper, tore straps guaranteed to support five thousand pounds.

Harrison's scrap-iron handicaps crashed to the floor.

Harrison thrust his thumbs under the bar of the padlock that secured his head harness. The bar snapped like celery. Harrison smashed his headphones and spectacles against the wall.

He flung away his rubber-ball nose, revealed a man that would have awed Thor, the god of thunder.

"I shall now select my Empress!" he said, looking down on the cowering people. "Let the first woman who dares rise to her feet claim her mate and her throne!"

A moment passed, and then a ballerina arose, swaying like a willow.

Harrison plucked the mental handicap from her ear, snapped off her physical handicaps with marvelous delicacy. Last of all, he removed her mask.

She was blindingly beautiful.

"Now—" said Harrison, taking her hand, "shall we show the people the meaning of the word *dance*? Music!" he commanded.

The musicians scrambled back into their chairs, and Harrison stripped them of their handicaps, too. "Play your best," he told them, "and I'll make you barons and dukes and earls."

The music began. It was normal at first—cheap, silly, false. But Harrison snatched two musicians from their chairs, waved them like batons as he sang the music as he wanted it played. He slammed them back into their chairs.

The music began again and was much improved.

Harrison and his Empress merely listened to the music for a while—listened gravely, as though synchronizing[8] their heartbeats with it.

They shifted their weights to their toes.

---

7. cowered (kou'ərd) *v.*: drew back or crouched in fear and helplessness.
8. synchronizing (siŋ'krə•nīz'iŋ) *v.*: causing to occur at the same rate or time.

Harrison placed his big hands on the girl's tiny waist, letting her sense the weightlessness that would soon be hers.

And then, in an explosion of joy and grace, into the air they sprang!

Not only were the laws of the land abandoned, but the law of gravity and the laws of motion as well.

They reeled, whirled, swiveled, flounced, capered, gamboled, and spun.

They leaped like deer on the moon.

The studio ceiling was thirty feet high, but each leap brought the dancers nearer to it.

It became their obvious intention to kiss the ceiling.

They kissed it.

And then, neutralizing gravity with love and pure will, they remained suspended in air inches below the ceiling, and they kissed each other for a long, long time. ❼

It was then that Diana Moon Glampers, the Handicapper General, came into the studio with a double-barreled ten-gauge shotgun. She fired twice, and the Emperor and the Empress were dead before they hit the floor.

Diana Moon Glampers loaded the gun again. She aimed it at the musicians and told them they had ten seconds to get their handicaps back on.

It was then that the Bergerons' television tube burned out.

Hazel turned to comment about the blackout to George. But George had gone out into the kitchen for a can of beer.

George came back in with the beer, paused while a handicap signal shook him up. And then he sat down again. "You been crying?" he said to Hazel.

La Nuit (1983) by Edward Paschke (1939–2004). Musée National d'Art Moderne, Centre Georges Pompidou, Paris. Oil on paper. 1.01 meters x 1.52 meters. ©Ed Paschke, 1983.

CHARACTER

❼ What actions does Harrison take to defy the authorities? What is your opinion of his actions?

THEME

❽ What does the ending reveal about what happens to people in this society who act on their own?

"Yup," she said.

"What about?" he said.

"I forget," she said. "Something real sad on television."

"What was it?" he said.

"It's all kind of mixed up in my mind," said Hazel.

"Forget sad things," said George.

"I always do," said Hazel.

"That's my girl," said George. He winced. There was the sound of a riveting-gun in his head.

"Gee—I could tell that one was a doozy," said Hazel.

"You can say that again," said George.

"Gee—" said Hazel, "I could tell that one was a doozy." ❽

Meet the Writer
Kurt Vonnegut

A Good Citizen

Kurt Vonnegut (1922–   ) has long been concerned about the ways in which people treat one another in a high-tech world. His novels are mostly social satires that raise tough questions about morality, freedom, and what we should value. "I consider writing an act of good citizenship," he has said.

During World War II, Vonnegut was held prisoner in the underground meat locker of a slaughterhouse in Dresden, Germany. He used that experience in his most famous novel, *Slaughterhouse-Five, or the Children's Crusade* (1969), which carries a strong message against all war.

For Independent Reading

Looking for more stories by Kurt Vonnegut? Pick up a copy of *Welcome to the Monkey House*, a collection of Vonnegut's stories and essays that includes "EPICAC," about a computer that falls in love, and "Report on the Barnhouse Effect," about a man with astonishing powers.

After You Read

Response and Analysis

Reading Check

1. Why was Harrison put in jail, and what happens to him at the end of the story?

Thinking Critically

2. Review your responses to the questions that appear in the side margins of the story. What details about Harrison's appearance and actions make him seem like a superhuman **character,** the kind you might find in comics or movies? Do you think Harrison, like many other superhuman characters, wants to save people from evil, or do you think his motives are not so pure?

3. In your Quickwrite notes, you jotted down your thoughts about the pressures people feel to conform. In this story, how has the government tried to eliminate competition and make everyone the same? What details in the story make us **infer,** or guess, that all does not work very smoothly in this society in which everyone is "equal every which way"?

4. Think about how the collection theme "On Your Own" relates to this story. What attitudes about equality is Vonnegut mocking in the story? (Consider, for example, the character of Hazel and the comments she makes.) In your opinion, what statement is he making about individuality?

Extending and Evaluating

5. What is the difference between believing that all people are equal under the law and believing that all people are the same?

6. Technology is now more a part of people's lives than ever before. Do you think this story has something to say to us today about the role of technology in our lives? Explain your answer.

Diderot (1989) by Nam June Paik (1932–2006). Mix-No Metals (video sculpture—twelve antique television cabinets, twelve color television monitors, two laser disk players and books). 120.1 x 72 in. Photo ©Christie's Images Limited 1998.

Exploring the Theme
On Your Own

In the rest of this collection, you'll read about the experiences of characters and people who are on their own in some way. As you read each selection, think about how being on their own affects these individuals.

SKILLS FOCUS

Literary Skills
Analyze how character traits are revealed through appearance, words, and actions.

Before You Read

Thank You, M'am

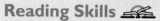

Make the Connection

Quickwrite ✏️

There's a saying "When the going gets tough, the tough get going." In very difficult circumstances some people do indeed get going. They have a spirit that moves them ahead—pushing them to do heroic deeds. What makes these people so tough, so strong in spirit? Why do they turn out to be good? Why do others go so wrong? Jot down your thoughts about these hard questions.

Literary Focus

Dialogue: What Do They Say?

You get to know people best by talking with them and listening as they speak to others. In the same way, characters in a story reveal themselves to one another—and to the reader—through **dialogue,** or conversation. As a reader you eavesdrop on those conversations and form your own opinions about the characters.

In "Thank You, M'am" you eavesdrop on a brief encounter between two strangers. By the story's end they have learned some important things about each other. Notice what these two people say to each other—and what they don't say. Then, decide what you think of them.

Literary Skills
Understand how character traits are revealed through dialogue.

Reading Skills
Make inferences.

Reading Skills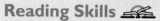

Making Inferences: Educated Guesses

Most good writers don't tell you directly what their characters are like. Instead, authors often allow you to make your own inferences about characters from what they say and do. When you **make an inference,** you use your observations and prior experience to guess about something you don't know for sure. However, an inference isn't just a random guess. It's an educated guess—because it's based on evidence in the text. After you read this story, skim through it again, and jot down clues that you think reveal something important about the characters. Look at what they *say* (or what they don't say) and how they *act*.

> "Well, you didn't have to snatch *my* pocketbook to get some suede shoes."

go.
hrw
.com

INTERNET

More About Langston Hughes

Keyword: LE7 9-2

Thank You, M'am

Langston Hughes

Mom Alice (1944) by William Johnson. Oil on paperboard (25″ × 30¼″).

She was a large woman with a large purse that had everything in it but a hammer and nails. It had a long strap, and she carried it slung across her shoulder. It was about eleven o'clock at night, dark, and she was walking alone, when a boy ran up behind her and tried to snatch her purse. The strap broke with the sudden single tug the boy gave it from behind. But the boy's weight and the weight of the purse combined caused him to lose his balance. Instead of taking off full blast as he had hoped, the boy fell on his back on the sidewalk and his legs flew up. The large woman simply turned around and kicked him right square in his blue-jeaned sitter. Then she reached down, picked the boy up by his shirt front, and shook him until his teeth rattled.

After that the woman said, "Pick up my pocketbook, boy, and give it here."

She still held him tightly. But she bent down enough to permit him to stoop and pick up her purse. Then she said, "Now ain't you ashamed of yourself?"

Firmly gripped by his shirt front, the boy said, "Yes'm."

The woman said, "What did you want to do it for?"

The boy said, "I didn't aim to."

She said, "You a lie!"

By that time two or three people passed, stopped, turned to look, and some stood watching.

"If I turn you loose, will you run?" asked the woman.

"Yes'm," said the boy.

"Then I won't turn you loose," said the woman. She did not release him.

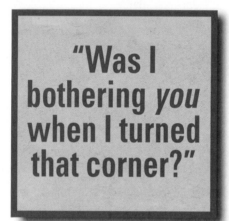

"Was I bothering *you* when I turned that corner?"

"Lady, I'm sorry," whispered the boy.

"Um-hum! Your face is dirty. I got a great mind to wash your face for you. Ain't you got nobody home to tell you to wash your face?"

"No'm," said the boy.

"Then it will get washed this evening," said the large woman starting up the street, dragging the frightened boy behind her.

He looked as if he were fourteen or fifteen, frail and willow-wild, in tennis shoes and blue jeans.

The woman said, "You ought to be my son. I would teach you right from wrong. Least I can do right now is to wash your face. Are you hungry?"

"No'm," said the being-dragged boy. "I just want you to turn me loose."

"Was I bothering *you* when I turned that corner?" asked the woman.

"No'm."

"But you put yourself in contact with *me*," said the woman. "If you think that that contact is not going to last awhile, you got another thought coming. When I get through with you, sir, you are going to remember Mrs. Luella Bates Washington Jones."

Sweat popped out on the boy's face and he began to struggle. Mrs. Jones stopped, jerked him around in front of her, put a half nelson about his neck, and continued to drag him up the street. When she got to her door, she dragged the boy inside, down a hall, and into a large kitchenette-furnished room at the rear of the house. She switched on the light and left the door open. The boy could hear other roomers laughing and talking in the large house. Some of their doors were open, too, so he knew he and the woman were not alone. The woman still had him by the neck in the middle of her room.

She said, "What is your name?"

Digestive System (1989) by James Romberger. Pastel on paper (57″ × 60″).

"Roger," answered the boy.

"Then, Roger, you go to that sink and wash your face," said the woman, whereupon she turned him loose—at last. Roger looked at the door—looked at the woman—looked at the door—*and went to the sink.*

"Let the water run until it gets warm," she said. "Here's a clean towel."

"You gonna take me to jail?" asked the boy, bending over the sink.

"Not with that face, I would not take you nowhere," said the woman. "Here I am trying to get home to cook me a bite to eat, and you snatch my pocketbook! Maybe you ain't been to your supper either, late as it be. Have you?"

"There's nobody home at my house," said the boy.

"Then we'll eat," said the woman. "I believe you're hungry—or been hungry—to try to snatch my pocketbook."

"I want a pair of blue suede shoes," said the boy.

"Well, you didn't have to snatch *my* pocketbook to get some suede shoes," said Mrs. Luella Bates Washington Jones. "You could've asked me."

"M'am?"

The water dripping from his face, the boy looked at her. There was a long pause. A very long pause. After he had dried his face and not knowing what else to do, dried it again, the boy turned around, wondering what next. The door was open. He could make a dash for it down the hall. He could run, run, run, *run*!

The woman was sitting on the daybed. After a while she said, "I were young once and I wanted things I could not get."

There was another long pause. The boy's mouth opened. Then he frowned, not knowing he frowned.

The woman said, "Um-hum! You thought I was going to say *but*, didn't you? You thought I was going to say, *but I didn't snatch people's pocketbooks*. Well, I wasn't going to say that." Pause. Silence. "I have done things, too, which I would not tell you, son—neither tell God, if He didn't already know. Everybody's got something in common. So you set down while I fix us something to eat. You might run that comb through your hair so you will look presentable."

In another corner of the room behind a screen was a gas plate and an icebox. Mrs. Jones got up and went behind the screen. The woman did not watch the boy to see if he was going to run now, nor did she watch her purse, which she left behind her on the daybed. But the boy took care to sit on the far side of the room, away from the purse, where he thought she could easily see him out of the corner of her eye if she wanted to. He did not trust the woman *not* to trust him.

And he did not want to be mistrusted now.

"Do you need somebody to go the store," asked the boy, "maybe to get some milk or something?"

"Don't believe I do," said the woman, "unless you just want sweet milk yourself. I was going to make cocoa out of this canned milk I got here."

"That will be fine," said the boy.

She heated some lima beans and ham she had in the icebox, made the cocoa, and set the table. The woman did not ask the boy anything about where he lived, or his folks, or anything else that would embarrass him. Instead, as they ate, she told him about her job in a hotel beauty shop that stayed open late, what the work was like, and how all kinds of women came in and out, blondes, redheads, and Spanish. Then she cut him a half of her ten-cent cake.

"Eat some more, son," she said.

When they were finished eating, she got up and said, "Now here, take this ten dollars and buy yourself some blue suede shoes. And next time, do not make the mistake of latching onto *my* pocketbook *nor nobody else's*—because shoes got by devilish ways will burn your feet. I got to get my rest now. But from here on in, son, I hope you will behave yourself."

She led him down the hall to the front door and opened it. "Good night! Behave yourself, boy!" she said, looking out into the street as he went down the steps.

The boy wanted to say something other than "Thank you, m'am" to Mrs. Luella Bates Washington Jones, but although his lips moved, he couldn't even say that as he turned at the foot of the barren stoop and looked up at the large woman in the door. Then she shut the door. ■

He could make a dash for it down the hall. He could run, run, run, *run*!

Meet the Writer

Langston Hughes

A Lonely Child

Langston Hughes (1902–1967) was a lonely child who moved often and felt distant from his parents, who eventually divorced. Hughes was born in Joplin, Missouri, and graduated from high school in Ohio. His father wanted to discourage his son's "impractical" dream of being a writer, so he sent him to Columbia University in New York City to study engineering.

The young writer was not happy, and he left college to join the crew of a ship that sailed to Europe and Africa. Eventually Hughes graduated from Lincoln University in Pennsylvania, but to support his writing, he worked at a variety of jobs: The man who was later known as one of the great original voices in American literature was also a cook, sailor, beachcomber, launderer, doorman, and busboy.

Although Hughes traveled to many parts of the world, he is chiefly associated with Harlem, in New York City, where he participated in the great flowering of African American art and writing known as the Harlem Renaissance. His most creative work was done at his typewriter near a third-floor rear-apartment window over-looking a Harlem backyard. You can easily imagine this setting as his inspiration for "Thank You, M'am."

Although he wrote stories, Hughes is probably best known as a poet. In an early collection of his poems, he wrote:

> **"**I have felt that much of our poetry has been aimed at the heads of the highbrows, rather than at the hearts of the people.**"**

Hughes chose to let ordinary people speak for themselves. As in "Mother to Son" (see the **Connection** on page 114), his poems are often written in dialect, and many include slang—his speakers say what is on their minds, and they say it in the language they use every day.

For Independent Reading

If you would like to know more about Langston Hughes's interesting life, look for Arnold Rampersad's very readable biography, *The Life of Langston Hughes*.

*In Hughes's poem "Mother to Son," a mother is talking to her son. The poem is an example of a **dramatic monologue,** a poem in which a speaker addresses one or more silent listeners. During the course of a dramatic monologue, the speaker reveals important thoughts and feelings.*

Mother to Son

Langston Hughes

Well, son, I'll tell you:
Life for me ain't been no crystal stair.
It's had tacks in it,
And splinters,
5   And boards torn up,
And places with no carpet on the floor—
Bare.
But all the time
I'se been a-climbin' on,
10 And reachin' landin's,
And turnin' corners,
And sometimes goin' in the dark
Where there ain't been no light.
So boy, don't you turn back.
15 Don't you set down on the steps
'Cause you finds it's kinder hard.
Don't you fall now—
For I'se still goin', honey,
I'se still climbin',
20 And life for me ain't been no crystal stair.

Proletarian (1934) by Gordon Samstag.
Oil on canvas (48⁵⁄₁₆″ × 42″).
The Toledo Museum of Art, Toledo, Ohio.
Museum Purchase Fund (1935.34).

Reading Check

1. Write down the **main events** of this story as if you were reporting them for a newspaper. Answer these questions:

- *What* happened?
- *Whom* did it happen to?
- *When* and *where* did it happen?
- *Why* did it happen?

Then, compare your list of events with your classmates' lists.

Thinking Critically

2. What does the **dialogue** between Roger and Mrs. Jones, as well as their actions, reveal about their **character traits**? Make a chart like the one here, showing what you **infer** from each character's words, silences, and actions.

	Mrs. Jones	Roger
Words		
Silences		
Actions		
What they reveal		

3. At the end of the story, what do you think the boy wants to say, other than "Thank you, m'am"? In your opinion, why can't he even say "thank you"?

4. How does the **setting** of Mrs. Jones's home—her furnished room, the gas plate, the ten-cent cake, the noisy tenement—contribute to your sense of the kind of person she is? What details can your imagination add to her surroundings?

5. Compare the character traits revealed by Mrs. Jones in the **dialogue** in the story with the traits revealed by the mother in "Mother to Son," Langston Hughes's **dramatic monologue** (see the **Connection** on page 114). Both women talk about difficulties in their own lives. What important message is each character trying to convey to her listener?

6. Look at your Quickwrite notes about what makes some people turn out to be good while others go wrong. What do you think made Mrs. Jones so good?

Extending and Evaluating

7. Based on your own experience, do you believe that these events could happen as Hughes describes them? Why or why not?

Literary Criticism

8. Review the biography of Langston Hughes on page 113. Do you think the way Mrs. Jones and the mother in "Mother to Son" approach life might reflect Hughes's own attitude toward life? Explain your answer.

WRITING

A Letter from Roger

Left on his own, Roger gets in trouble at the beginning of the story. What do you think Roger will be like when he is on his own ten years after his encounter with Mrs. Jones? What might he write in a letter to her? Compose a **letter** from Roger. Write as "I." Be sure to state the purpose of his communication after all these years.

SKILLS FOCUS

Literary Skills
Analyze how character traits are revealed through dialogue.

Reading Skills
Make inferences.

Writing Skills
Write a letter.

Vocabulary Development

Synonyms: Accept No Substitutes?

Although a **synonym** is a word that has the same or almost the same meaning as another word, synonyms are not always interchangeable. Often synonyms will have subtle but distinct shades of difference in meaning.

PRACTICE

Here are three words from the first paragraph of the story: *large, carried,* and *fell.* Find the sentences in which the words are used. Then, make a chart like the one below for each word. Could the synonyms work just as well in each sentence?

barren	
Definition	*empty; devoid of life*
Synonyms	*bare, sterile*
Substitutions	*He turned at the [bare/sterile] stoop.*
Response to substitutions	*Bare could work because it can refer to a lack of objects. Sterile doesn't work because it suggests cleanliness, not emptiness. Barren is best; it reminds me of something empty and lifeless.*

Grammar Link

Modifiers: Precise Meanings

Modifiers make your writing more specific. Notice how adjectives help you visualize those blue suede shoes that Roger wants. **Adjectives** (and adjective phrases) answer the question *what kind? which one? how many?* or *how much?* **Adverbs** (and adverb phrases) answer the question *where? when? how often? in what way?* or *to what extent?* The modifiers in these sentences from Hughes's story are single words, compound words, and phrases:

1. "The large woman simply turned around and kicked him right square in his blue-jeaned sitter."

2. "He looked as if he were fourteen or fifteen, frail and willow-wild, in tennis shoes and blue jeans."

PRACTICE

For each numbered sentence at the left, tell whether the underlined modifiers are acting as adjectives or adverbs. Then, rewrite each sentence three times, replacing the underlined modifiers with words and phrases of your own. Each time, give Mrs. Jones or the boy a totally different appearance. (For example, you might put Roger in hiking boots and a plaid shirt.)

When you write a description of a character, use precise adverbs and adjectives. Don't overdo it with modifiers, though. Sometimes a simple word is best.

▶ **For more help, see Using Modifiers, 5a–g, in the Language Handbook.**

SKILLS FOCUS

Vocabulary Skills
Understand shades of meaning of synonyms.

Grammar Skills
Use precise modifiers.

Teaching Chess, and Life ◆ Community Service & You ◆ Feeding Frenzy

Using Primary and Secondary Sources: Whose View?

Research sources generally fall into two basic categories: primary sources and secondary sources.

- A **primary source** is a firsthand account. In primary sources, writers present their experiences, opinions, and ideas. Primary sources include auto-biographies, letters, interviews, oral his-tories, eyewitness news reports, essays, editorials, and speeches.

- A **secondary source** is a secondhand account, often based on more than one viewpoint. In secondary sources, writers summarize, interpret, or analyze events in which they did not participate. Ex-amples of secondary sources include en-cyclopedias and other reference works, textbooks, biographies, many magazine articles, and most newspaper articles.

Using the Sources

Follow these steps to get the most out of your sources:

- **Analyze.** First, decide whether the work is a primary or a secondary source. Then, look for the **main idea** of the work. Ask yourself, "How does the author support the main idea? Who is the author's audience? What is the author's purpose?"

- **Evaluate.** Look for clues indicating whether the author is presenting ob-jective **facts** or subjective **opinions.** Is the factual information accurate? With primary sources especially, check the accuracy of the information by reading other sources. Evaluate the author's opinions as well. Do you agree with the author's message?

- **Elaborate.** When you elaborate, you add information, usually in the form of details. You might present your own ideas on the topic, or you might do further research. Check to see if a secondary source has a **bibliography** or list of **works cited.** These contain other useful sources of information.

Vocabulary Development

mentorship (men′tər·ship) *n.*: advice or lessons from a mentor, or wise teacher.

intimidating (in·tim′ə·dāt′iŋ) *v.* used as *adj.*: frightening.

endeavors (en·dev′ərz) *n.*: serious attempts, efforts, or undertakings.

legislation (lej′is·lā′shən) *n.*: law or body of laws.

bureaucratic (byoor′ə·krat′ik) *adj.*: re-lating to rigid government routine.

undaunted (un·dôn′tid) *adj.*: not discouraged by a difficulty or setback.

Connecting to the Literature

Mrs. Jones in "Thank You, M'am" helps a boy who might otherwise end up on the wrong path. In the follow-ing primary and secondary sources, you'll meet people who also help others, and you'll learn about com-munity service in the process.

SKILLS FOCUS

Reading Skills Understand the uses of primary and secondary sources.

INTERNET
Interactive Reading Model
Keyword: LE7 9-2

TEACHING CHESS, AND LIFE

from an essay adapted by *The New York Times*, September 3, 2000

Carlos Capellan

If you were to walk down West 160th Street in Washington Heights, you would see drug dealers whistling to people in cars and handing off small packages to passersby. As you walk further down the block, you would see residents who are too scared to sit and talk to their neighbors on the front steps. These families stay inside most of the time. You would see parents pick up their children from P.S. 4 and hurry off the block before trouble can start. This is my block and this is my neighborhood.

Many kids my age in Washington Heights wind up in gangs, as drug dealers, in jail, or dead. I decided long ago that I would not end up in one of those situations because of the consequences I saw others suffer. I have stuck by this decision with help from several important people. One of the most influential people in my life is my former chess coach and current boss, Jeremy Chiappetta, who has taught me a lot about chess and more about life.

Carlos Capellan, an assistant chess coach, shares a laugh with students during chess practice at Intermediate School 90.

As an eighth-grader at a gang-infested junior high school, I joined the chess team as a way to stay out of trouble. I already knew the coach, Mr. Chiappetta, because he was my social studies teacher.

As a ninth- and tenth-grader, I volunteered to help Chia with his chess team at Intermediate School 90 on West 168th Street. During these years, I matured. I learned how to present myself in a positive way: taking off my hat inside buildings, judging when it was appropriate to make jokes (I had to learn this lesson a few times), and knowing how to speak in certain situations.

At one tournament I learned an important lesson from Chia. It was the last round of the U.S. Amateur Team East. I was playing for a top prize and was nervous. In the middle of the game I found a winning combination and I began to slam the pieces out of happiness. Then a big hand stopped the game clock and pulled me away. It was Chia. I could tell that he was angry, but I did not realize what I had done wrong. We talked about the meaning of sportsmanship. I apologized for my rudeness to my opponent and forfeited the game. I didn't win a prize.

With Chia's <u>mentorship</u>, I learned from my mistake. As a coach at I.S. 90, I've had to teach the same lesson to others. It makes me feel good about myself because I like helping the younger kids learn the game Chia taught me to love. ❶

Chia left I.S. 90 the year I became an eleventh-grader. He recommended me as an assistant chess coach, for which I am paid. This is my second year at I.S. 90 as an assistant coach. My responsibilities include teaching chess strategies and tactics three days a week. I also chaperone the team at tournaments almost every weekend.

All of this would not have been possible if not for Mr. Chiappetta. He turned me to chess and kept me involved. He gave me the opportunity to earn money doing something I love. Chess has kept me off the streets. It has challenged me and taught me to think in new ways. Because of chess, I was recently honored by the *Daily News* as one of the "21 New Yorkers to Watch in the 21st Century." Chess has made me a mentor to younger students, giving me the chance to become their Chia. ❷

> **❶ ELABORATE**
>
> Have you ever helped or taught a younger person? Were your feelings about the experience similar to Carlos's? Explain.

> **❷ EVALUATE**
>
> How would you evaluate the impact Chia had on Carlos's life?

Vocabulary
mentorship (men′tər·ship) *n.*: advice or lessons from a mentor, or wise teacher.

SECONDARY SOURCE MAGAZINE ARTICLE

Community Service & You

from *Career World,* September 1998

T. J. Saftner

Imagine you read the following help-wanted ad in your local newspaper:

Change the World Around You! Individual required to help out at nonprofit organization. No experience necessary. Interesting work with excellent benefit package. Short workweek and flexible hours.

Would you apply? What if the ad also said, "Must be willing to work without pay"? Before you say "No way!" consider this:

Last weekend, millions of Americans worked at soup kitchens, shelters, playgrounds, museums, prisons, and schools—and they didn't earn a cent. But they didn't go home empty-handed either. What these people received for their contribution wasn't money—according to a survey by Independent Sector—but a chance to learn new skills, prove their reliability, demonstrate their creativity, and build their self-esteem.

Record numbers of young people are getting involved in community service to gain a sense of belonging in their community, to foster personal development, and to help do all that needs to be done in today's world—

Pilots and volunteers unload food and supplies for the city of Watsonville, California, after the Loma Prieta earthquake.

women's shelter. She spends one evening a month at the shelter, serving dinner and talking to the women.

Not only can you make a contribution to your community and make a difference in someone's life, you can learn new skills, network° for future job contacts, and gain some valuable experience—all of which can help you in your future endeavors. Stephanie says her experience has helped to broaden her understanding of different kinds of people as well as social issues.

from tutoring young readers, to building houses, to working at a blood drive.

Making a Difference

Volunteering can sound a little <u>intimidating</u> when you're a teenager. But look what's going on *already* in youth volunteerism:

Youth Service America is an alliance of organizations committed to community and national service whose goal is to "encourage the vitality, creativity, and goodwill of young people."

In 1995, Youth Service America joined basketball star Chris Webber and 1,000 young people in a massive river-cleanup project. In 1996, Youth Service America worked with four local nonprofit organizations to help construct playgrounds in Atlanta, Denver, Minneapolis, and Philadelphia.

Though these and many other events have attracted media attention, millions of young people volunteer without being recognized in the media for their efforts. Why do they do it?

Stephanie Star, a senior at Highland Park High School in the Chicago area, says, "It just feels good. You get a lot out of helping other people." Stephanie volunteers at a battered

Making a Move

Volunteering can be a long-term commitment or an afternoon event. There are many areas available for community service: churches, soup kitchens, shelters, schools, the environment, politics, and lots more. You might be phoning, organizing, cooking, working with the young or the old. Whatever you do, it will most certainly affect someone's life. Who knows . . . it might even be your own. ●

● **ANALYZE**
Who is the author's **audience**? What is the author's **purpose** in writing this article?

° **network** *v.*: meet people or share information, often to advance a career.

Vocabulary
intimidating (in·tim′ə·dāt′iŋ) *v.* used as *adj.*: frightening.
endeavors (en·dev′ərz) *n.*: serious attempts, efforts, or undertakings.

Feeding Frenzy

from *People*, June 2, 1997

Peter Ames Carlin *and* Don Sider

When 15-year-old David Levitt makes his weekly appearance at the Haven of Rest food bank in Pinellas Park, Florida, he is greeted as a good Samaritan.[1]

No one knows better than Levitt how to get food to the hungry. Since 1994 the surplus food-sharing program he designed as an 11-year-old for the Pinellas County public schools has sent more than a quarter-million pounds of cafeteria leftovers to the county's shelters and food banks. Singled out for praise last year by President Clinton, Levitt, a freshman at Seminole High, is currently backing state legislation to protect donors of surplus food from liability lawsuits.[2] "It's a no-brainer," says State Representative Dennis Jones, who is shepherding Levitt's bill toward certain passage when the state legislature meets next spring. "You wonder why it's taken so long for someone to do it."

The same question crossed Levitt's mind in 1993, when he first read about Kentucky Harvest, a nonprofit organization that funnels leftover food from restaurants and other businesses to charities. He was only a sixth-grader, but Levitt understood that a nation that regularly sends 30 million people to bed hungry shouldn't toss nearly 20 percent of its edible food into the garbage.

Buttonholing[3] Osceola Middle School principal Fred Ulrich outside class one day, he asked if he could start a Harvest program using cafeteria leftovers. "I figured he didn't know me," says Levitt, "so he couldn't be mean."

> ● **ANALYZE**
>
> List three **facts** in the previous two paragraphs. Then, find two **opinions.**

Ulrich wasn't mean. He was merely realistic, pointing out that district health regulations prohibited using previously served food. ("Red tape,[4] red tape," Levitt sighs.) But, encouraged by his mother, Sandy, Levitt attended a Pinellas County school-board meeting and made his case for a local Harvest program. He not only won the board's approval but a spontaneous ovation to boot.

The board's approval, alas, merely gained him entrance to the bureaucratic maze. Next he had to contend with state health-department rules governing the handling of secondhand food. For a time it seemed that packaging requirements would doom the program—the state demanded specific containers, and the schools had no money to

---

3. **buttonholing** *v.* used as *adj.*: speaking intently with another person, often in an attempt to persuade him or her to do something.
4. **red tape** *n.*: complicated official forms and regulations.

Vocabulary

legislation (lej′is·lā′shən) *n.*: law or body of laws.

bureaucratic (byoor′ə·krat′ik) *adj.*: relating to rigid government routine.

---

1. **good Samaritan** *n.*: person who unselfishly helps others. The term comes from a Bible parable (Luke 10:30–37).
2. **liability lawsuits:** legal actions brought against a person or group to make up for loss or damage that has occurred.

pay for them. <u>Undaunted</u>, Levitt wrote to a major corporation, which promptly shipped eight cases of plastic bags to his doorstep, and on November 8, 1994, Levitt helped make the school's first delivery: cartons of milk and bags of salad for Haven of Rest. *"That,"* he says, "was satisfaction."

The younger child (sister Jamie is 18) of Sandy Levitt, a bookkeeper, and her husband, Rich, vice president of a medical-supply company, Levitt grew up in Seminole, a suburb of St. Petersburg, earning A's and B's in school and playing volleyball and a handful of musical instruments. "David's a typical teenager," notes his mother. Eventually he would like to attend the U.S. Air Force Academy and learn to fly. "That's today," he says. "Call me tomorrow—I might change."

What doesn't change is his ability to make things happen. And while he's fortunate to have a mother who helps push his projects along (Sandy is "the silent driving force," according to her husband), Levitt's energy has won him plenty of fans. "David has drawn attention to hunger and the availability of food in the community," says Mary Dowdell, director of Tampa Bay Harvest. Adds Stan

Curtis, the Kentucky stockbroker who started the first Harvest program: "Any parent in America would be glad to have him as a son."

Including the First Dad,[5] who invited Levitt to the White House last spring as part of a Points of Light ceremony.[6] Taking his medal from Hillary Rodham Clinton, Levitt wasn't shy about pushing his agenda. "What," he asked the First Lady, "do you do with the White House leftovers?"

---

5. **First Dad:** the president, if he has children; in this case, President Clinton.
6. **Points of Light ceremony:** awards ceremony sponsored by the Points of Light Foundation to honor people who have performed outstanding community service. The foundation, begun in 1990, took its name from a phrase used by former president George Herbert Walker Bush to describe private acts of goodwill: "a thousand points of light."

Vocabulary
undaunted (un·dôn′tid) *adj.*: not discouraged by a difficulty or setback.

David Levitt gathers bread for his Harvest program.

Reading Check

1. In "Teaching Chess, and Life," what lesson did Carlos Capellan learn after he slammed his chess pieces down during a tournament?

2. Give examples of how young people can benefit from doing volunteer work, according to "Community Service & You."

3. What motivated David Levitt to develop his food-sharing program, as described in "Feeding Frenzy"?

Test Practice

1. Which of the following statements is the *most* accurate **evaluation** of "Teaching Chess, and Life"?

   A The author uses both fact and opinion to make his point.

   B The author includes only opinions in his article.

   C The author includes facts that can't be checked for accuracy.

   D Because he does not support his point, the author fails to show why Chia has been so influential.

2. If the author of "Community Service & You" wrote a work that was a **primary source** instead of a **secondary source**, the writer would —

   F write only about his or her experience as a volunteer

   G write only about Stephanie Star's experience as a volunteer

   H interview volunteers who constructed playgrounds

   J provide a detailed report about the Independent Sector survey

3. Which sentence *best* expresses the **main idea** of "Feeding Frenzy"?

   A Good deeds should be given public recognition.

   B Many government regulations serve no purpose.

   C A good cause is worth pursuing, even in the face of difficulties.

   D Millions of people in America go to bed hungry.

4. Of the three articles, which gives the *best* picture of the difficulties faced by those who wish to do community service?

   F "Teaching Chess, and Life," because it tells about at-risk young people.

   G "Community Service & You," because it includes the statement "Volunteering can sound a little intimidating when you're a teenager."

   H "Feeding Frenzy," because it describes the obstacles to starting a food-sharing program.

   J "Teaching Chess, and Life," because the author needed Chia's help.

SKILLS FOCUS

Reading Skills
Use primary and secondary sources.

Constructed Response

Elaborate on the benefits of community service, as discussed in these articles, by doing your own original research. Interview someone, recommended by your teacher or a family member, who does volunteer work. Ask the volunteer to explain the benefits of his or her work. Then, use the primary-source information from the interview to extend the ideas presented in the articles. Write one or two paragraphs about the value of community service, and present a report to the class.

After You Read   Vocabulary Development

Mapping an Unfamiliar Word

PRACTICE 1

Making a word map like the one here, which organizes some ideas about *legislation,* will help you get to know a new word better. Fill out this map for *legislation,* and then make word maps of your own for the other words in the Word Bank. You will have to make up your own questions for each word.

Word Bank

intimidating
endeavors
legislation
bureaucratic
undaunted

Meaning
•

legislation

What kinds of things are controlled by legislation?
•
•

Sample sentence
•

What legislation directly affects me?
•
•

Word Origins: What's in a Word?

In "Teaching Chess, and Life," Carlos Capellan views Mr. Chiappetta as his mentor. The word *mentor,* which means "wise teacher," comes to us courtesy of Greek mythology. In Homer's great epic the *Odyssey* (see page 750), the goddess Athena assumes the form of Mentor and gives advice to Odysseus, Homer's hero, and to Odysseus's young son, Telemachus. Today a mentor is a teacher, a coach, or anyone else who acts as an advisor to other people.

Word Bank

mentorship

PRACTICE 2

Like *mentor,* the following words and phrases from the selections have interesting histories. Investigate the history of each one, and write a sentence or two about its origin and present meaning. To start, you may consult each selection's footnotes, but you will need to do your own research using a dictionary or other reference sources.

tournament	chaperone	good Samaritan
buttonholing	red tape	

SKILLS FOCUS

Vocabulary Skills
Create word maps.
Understand word origins.

Helen on Eighty-sixth Street

Make the Connection

Quickwrite ✏️

We all have hopes and dreams. Some come true, some don't. What happens when our wishes don't come true, when we have to accept a loss or when we are disappointed in love or friendship? Jot down some of your hopes and dreams. Have any of them come true yet? What do these hopes and dreams tell you about yourself?

Literary Focus

Determining Character Traits: Got to Be Me

When characters tell their own stories, they also tell you a lot about their **character traits**—their personalities, values, likes, and dislikes. In "Helen on Eighty-sixth Street," the narrator, Vita, announces right off the bat, "I hate Helen. That's all I can say." While this statement reveals that Vita and Helen are not friends, Vita's forceful way of talking also tells you that she is outspoken and that she has strong feelings. As you read Vita's narration, determine more of her character traits, both from what she says and from the way she says it.

Reading Skills

Understanding Allusions

Allusions are references to features of a culture—for example, to literature and history—that writers expect their readers to recognize. The writer of this story frequently alludes to Greek mythology.

You may have already read some myths; in this textbook you'll find stories from the Greek epic the *Odyssey* (page 750). For more help with allusions, you can consult these resources in this text:

- A Closer Look, page 129
- the story's footnotes, pages 128–133

Don't get bogged down identifying allusions. Sometimes you can just guess what a name or event refers to by looking at the context clues.

Vocabulary Development

embodies (em·bäd′ēz) v.: conveys the impression of; represents.

odyssey (äd′i·sē) n.: extended journey marked by wandering, adventure, and changes of fortune.

litany (lit″n·ē) n.: repetitive prayer or recitation.

incantation (in′kan·tā′shən) n.: chant of words or phrases that is meant to produce a magical result.

stifled (stī′fəld) v. used as *adj.*: smothered.

scourge (skʉrj) n.: cause of serious trouble or great suffering.

polytheism (päl′i·thē·iz′əm) n.: belief in more than one god.

ramparts (ram′pärts′) n.: broad embankments surrounding a castle, fort, or city for defense against attack.

supplication (sup′lə·kā′shən) n.: humble plea or request.

enunciate (ē·nun′sē·āt′) v.: pronounce; articulate.

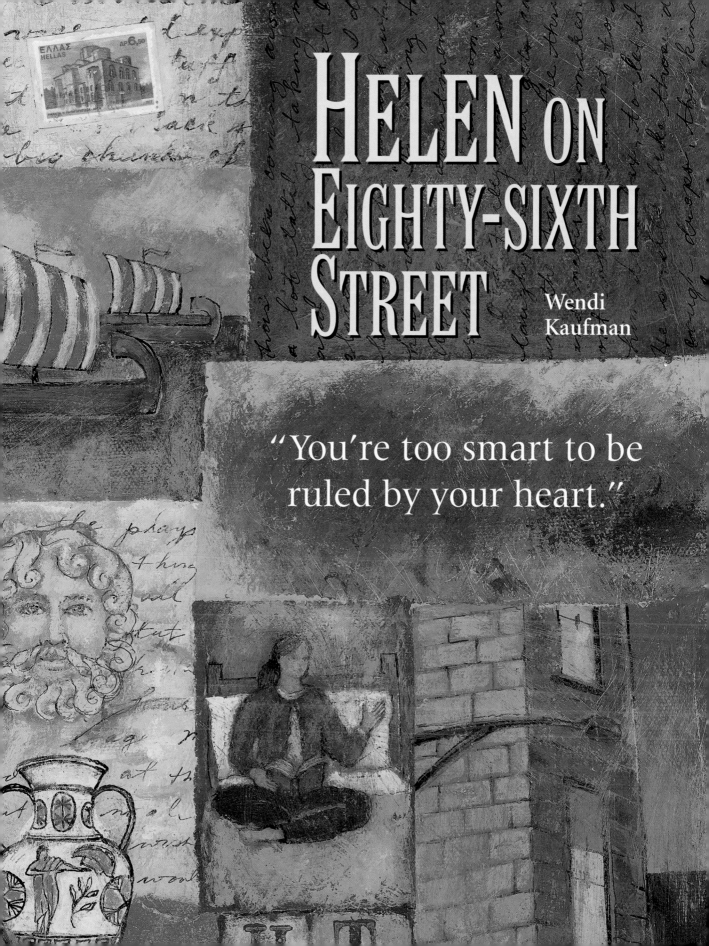

HELEN ON EIGHTY-SIXTH STREET

Wendi Kaufman

"You're too smart to be ruled by your heart."

I hate Helen. That's all I can say. I hate her. Helen McGuire is playing Helen, so Mr. Dodd says, because, out of the entire sixth grade, she most embodies Helen of Troy. Great. Helen McGuire had no idea who Helen of Troy even was! When she found out, well, you should have seen her—flirting with all the boys, really acting the part. And me? Well, I know who Helen was. I am unhappy.

My mother doesn't understand. Not that I expected she would. When I told her the news, all she said was "Ah, the face that launched a thousand ships." She didn't even look up from her book. Later, at dinner, she apologized for quoting Marlowe. Marlowe is our cat.[1]

At bedtime I told my mother, "You should have seen the way Helen acted at school. It was disgusting, flirting with the boys."

Mom tucked the sheets up close around my chin, so that only my head was showing, my body covered mummy style. "Vita," she said, "it sounds like she's perfect for the part."

So, I can't play Helen. But, to make it worse, Mr. Dodd said I have to be in the horse. I can't believe it. The horse! I wanted to be one of the Trojan women—Andromache, Cassandra, or even Hecuba. I know all their names. I told Mr. Dodd this, and then I showed him I could act. I got really sad and cried out about the thought of the body of my husband, Hector, being dragged around the walls of my city. I wailed and beat my fist against my chest. "A regular Sarah Heartburn"[2] was all he said.

"Well, at least you get to be on the winning team," my mother said when I told her about the horse. This didn't make me feel any better.

"It's better than being Helen. It's better than being blamed for the war," she told me.

Mom was helping me make a shield for my costume. She said every soldier had a shield that was big enough to carry his body off the field. I told her I wasn't going to be a body on the field, that I was going to survive, return home.

"Bring the shield, just in case," she said. "It never hurts to have a little help."

Mom and I live on West Eighty-sixth Street. We have lived in the same building, in the same apartment, my entire life. My father has been gone for almost three years. The truth is that he got struck with the wanderlust—emphasis on "lust," my mother says—and we haven't heard from him since.

"Your father's on his own odyssey," my mother said. And now it's just me and Mom and Marlowe and the Keatses, John and John,[3] our parakeets, or "pair of Keats," as Mom says. When I was younger, when Dad first left and I still believed he was coming back, it made me happy that we still lived in the same building. I was happy because he would always know where to find us. Now that I am older, I know the city is not that big. It is easy to be found and easy to stay lost.

And I also know not to ask about him. Sometimes Mom hears things through old friends—that he has traveled across the ocean, that he is living on an island in a commune

---

1. **Marlowe:** The cat is named after Christopher Marlowe (1564–1593), an English dramatist. "The face that launched a thousand ships" is from one of Marlowe's plays and alludes to the Greek army's pursuit of Helen of Troy.
2. **Sarah Heartburn:** humorous reference to Sarah Bernhardt (1844–1923), a French actress known for her emotional style.

3. **Keatses, John and John:** The parakeets are named after the English Romantic poet John Keats (1795–1821).

Vocabulary

embodies (em·bäd′ēz) v.: conveys the impression of; represents.

odyssey (äd′i·sē) n.: extended journey marked by wandering, adventure, and changes of fortune.

with some people she called "the lotus-eaters,"[4] that he misses us.

Once I heard Mr. Farfel, the man who's hanging around Mom now, ask why she stayed in this apartment after my father left. "The rent's stabilized,"[5] she told him, "even if the relationship wasn't."

At school, Helen McGuire was acting weird because I'm going to be in the horse with Tommy Aldridge. She wanted to know what it's like: "Is it really cramped in there? Do you have to sit real close together?"

I told her it's dark, and we must hold each other around the waist and walk to make the horse move forward. Her eyes grew wide at this description. "Lucky you," she said.

Lucky me? She gets to stand in the center of the stage alone, her white sheet barely reaching the middle of her thighs, and say lines like "This destruction is all my fault" and "Paris, I do love you." She gets to cry. Why would she think I'm lucky? The other day at rehearsal, she was standing onstage waiting for her cue, and I heard Mrs. Reardon, the stage manager, whisper, "That Helen is as beautiful as a statue."

At home Old Farfel is visiting again. He has a chair in Mom's department.[6] The way she describes it, a chair is a very good thing. Mom translates old books written in Greek and Latin. She is working on the longest graduate degree in the history of Columbia University. "I'll be dead before I finish," she always says.

---

4. **lotus-eaters** *n.:* in the *Odyssey,* people who eat the fruit of the lotus tree, a sort of drug, which causes them to forget forever their homes and families. The Greek soldier Odysseus enters the land of the Lotus Eaters on his journey home from the Trojan War. (See page 758.)

5. **rent's stabilized:** In New York City, rent stabilization is a form of government-controlled rent regulation. Rent-stabilized apartments are less expensive than other types and are therefore much sought after.

6. **chair in Mom's department:** A chair is an important teaching position at a university.

A CLOSER LOOK

The Beautiful Helen

According to Greek mythology, the god Zeus fell in love with Leda, a mortal woman, and visited her in the form of a swan. Their daughter Helen grew up to be the most beautiful woman on earth. Helen married Menelaus, king of Sparta, but Paris, a handsome young prince, fell in love with her and ran away with her to Troy, his kingdom in Asia Minor. Helen's husband, Menelaus, banded together with other Greek kings and warriors under the leadership of his brother, Agamemnon. They sailed to Troy in a thousand ships to fetch Helen home.

For ten long years the Greeks camped outside the walls of Troy, but they were unable to break down the thick walls of the city. Finally the Greeks tricked the Trojans. They built a huge wooden horse with a hollow belly and hid some soldiers in it. They left the horse on the beach at Troy and pretended to sail away. The Trojans thought that the Greeks had at last retreated and had left the horse as a gift. They wheeled the huge horse into their city. That night the Greeks crept out of the horse, opened the city gate to their comrades, and slaughtered the Trojans. The old king, Priam, was killed. The Trojan women, including Queen Hecuba and her daughter Cassandra, were dragged into slavery. The queen of Troy had already seen her beloved son Hector killed by Achilles, his bleeding body dragged three times in the dust around the walls of the city.

In "Helen on Eighty-sixth Street," a class reenacts the tale of the beautiful Helen of Troy.

Old Farfel has been coming around a lot lately, taking Mom and me to dinner at Italian places downtown. I don't like to be around when he's over.

"I'm going to Agamemnon's apartment to rehearse," I told Mom.

Old Farfel made a small laugh, one that gets caught in the back of the throat and never really makes it out whole. I want to tell him to relax, to let it out. He smells like those dark cough drops, the kind that make your eyes tear and your head feel like it's expanding. I don't know how she can stand him.

"Well, the play's the *thing*," Old Farfel said. "We're all just players strutting and fretting our hour on the stage."[7] Mom smiled at this, and it made me wish Old Farfel would strut his hours at his apartment and not at our place. I hate the way he's beginning to come around all the time.

When I get back from rehearsal, Mom is spinning Argus.[8] It's what she does when she gets into one of her moods. Argus, our dog, died last summer when I was away at camp. My mother can't stand to part with anything, so she keeps Argus, at least his ashes, in a blue-and-white vase that sits on our mantel.

Once I looked into the vase. I'd expected to see gray stuff, like the ash at the end of a cigarette. Instead, there was black sand and big chunks of pink like shells, just like at the beach.

My mother had the vase down from the mantel and was twirling it in her hands. I watched

---

7. **Well, the play's . . . on the stage:** references to lines in Shakespeare's plays *Hamlet* and *Macbeth*.

8. **Argus:** Odysseus's old dog. When Odysseus returns home after twenty years, Argus is the only one who recognizes him. (See page 794.)

the white figures on it turn, following each other, running in a race that never ends.

"Life is a cycle," my mother said. The spinning made me dizzy. I didn't want to talk about life. I wanted to talk about Helen.

"Helen, again with Helen. Always Helen," my mother said. "You want to know about Helen?"

I nod my head.

"Well, her father was a swan and her mother was too young to have children. You don't want to be Helen. Be lucky you're a warrior. You're too smart to be ruled by your heart."

"And what about beauty? Wasn't she the most beautiful woman in the world?" I asked.

Mom looked at the Greek vase. "Beauty is truth, truth beauty—that is all ye need to know."[9]

She is not always helpful.

"Manhattan is a rocky island," Mom said at dinner. "There is no proper beach, no shore." My mother grew up in the South, near the ocean, and there are times when she still misses the beach. Jones, Brighton, or even Coney Island beaches don't come close for her. I know when she starts talking about the water that she's getting restless. I hope this means that Old Farfel won't be hanging around too long.

Every night I write a letter to my father. I don't send them—I don't know where to send them—but, still, I write them. I keep the letters at the back of my closet in old shoe boxes. I am on my third box. It's getting so full that I have to keep the lid tied down with rubber bands.

I want to write "Mom is talking about the water again. I think this means she is thinking of you. We are both thinking of you, though we don't mention your name. Are you thinking of us? Do you ever sit on the shore at night and wonder what we're doing, what we're thinking? Do you miss us as much as we miss you?"

---

9. **Beauty is truth . . . know:** The last two lines of Keats's poem "Ode on a Grecian Urn" are "'Beauty is truth, truth beauty'—that is all / Ye know on earth, and all ye need to know."

But instead I write, "I am in a play about the Trojan War. I get to wear a short white tunic, and I ambush people from inside a big fake horse. Even though we win the war, it will be many, many years before I return home. Until I see my family again. In this way, we are the same. I will have many adventures. I will meet giants and witches and see strange lands. Is that what you are doing? I wish you could come to the play."

Old Farfel is going to a convention in Atlanta. He wants Mom to go with him. From my bed, I can hear them talking about it in the living room. It would be good for her, he says. I know that Mom doesn't like to travel. She can't even go to school and back without worrying about the apartment—if she turned the gas off, if she fed the cat, if she left me enough money. She tells him that she'll think about it.

"You have to move on, Victoria," he tells her. "Let yourself go to new places."

"I'm still exploring the old places," she says.

He lets the conversation drop.

Mom said once that she traveled inside herself when Dad left. I didn't really understand, but it was one of the few times I saw her upset. She was sitting in her chair, at her desk, looking tired. "Mom, are you in there?" I waved my hand by her face.

"I'm not," she said. "I'm on new ground. It's a very different place."

"Are you thinking about Dad?"

"I was thinking how we all travel differently, Vita. Some of us don't even have to leave the house."

"Dad left the house."

"Sometimes it's easier to look outside than in," she said.

That night I dreamed about a swan. A swan that flies in circles over the ocean. This is not the dark water that snakes along the West Side Highway and slaps against the banks of New Jersey but the real ocean. Open water. Salty, like tears.

At play practice, I watch the other girls dress up as goddesses and Trojan women. They wear gold scarves wound tight around their necks and foreheads. They all wear flowers in their hair and flat pink ballet slippers. I wear a white sheet taken from my bed. It is tied around the middle with plain white rope. I also wear white sneakers. I don't get to wear a gold scarf or flowers. Mr. Dodd wrote this play himself and is very picky about details. Tommy Aldridge, my partner in the horse, was sent home because his sheet had Ninja Turtles on it. "They did not have Ninja Turtles in ancient Greece," Mr. Dodd said.

Mr. Dodd helps Helen McGuire with her role. "You must understand," he tells her, "Helen is the star of the show. Men have traveled great distances just to fight for her. At the end, when you come onstage and look at all the damage you've caused, we must believe you're really upset by the thought that this is all your fault."

Helen nods and looks at him blankly.

"Well, at least try to think of something really sad."

Old Farfel is taking Mom out to dinner again. It's the third time this week. Mom says it is a very important dinner, and I am not invited. Not that I would want to go, but I wasn't even asked. Mom brought in takeout, some soup and a cheese sandwich, from the coffee shop on the corner.

I eat my soup, alone in the kitchen, from a blue-and-white paper cup. I remember once at a coffee shop Mom held the same type of cup out in front of me.

"See this building, Vita?" she said. She pointed to some columns that were drawn on the front of her cup. It wasn't really a building—more like a cartoon drawing. "It's the Parthenon,"[10] she said. "It's where the Greeks made sacrifices to Athena."

"How did they make sacrifices?" I asked.

"They burned offerings on an altar. They believed this would bring them what they wanted. Good things. Luck."

I finish my soup and look at the tiny building on the cup. In between the columns are the words "Our Pleasure to Serve You." I run my fingers across the flat lines of the Parthenon and trace the roof. I can almost imagine a tiny altar and the ceremonies that were performed there.

It is then that I get an idea. I find a pair of scissors on Mom's desk and cut through the thick white lip of the cup toward the lines of the little temple. I cut around the words "Our Pleasure to Serve You." Then I take the temple and the words and glue them to the back of my notebook. The blue-and-white lines show clearly against the cardboard backing. I get Argus's big metal water bowl from the kitchen and find some matches from a restaurant Old Farfel took us to for dinner.

In my room I put on my white sheet costume and get all my letters to Dad out from the back of the closet. I know that I must say something, to make this more like a ceremony. I think of any Greek words I know: *spanakopita, moussaka, gyro.* They're only food words, but it doesn't matter. I decide to say them anyway. I say them

10. **Parthenon:** temple of Athena, the Greek goddess of wisdom and warfare, who sided with the Greeks during the war. The Parthenon was built in the fifth century B.C.

over and over out loud until they blur into a litany, my own incantation: "*Spanakopitamoussakaandgyro, Spanakopitamoussakaandgyro, Spanakopitamoussakaandgyro.*"

As I say this, I burn handfuls of letters in the bowl. I think about what I want: to be Helen, to have my father come back. Everything I have ever heard says that wishes are granted in threes, so I throw in the hope of Old Farfel's leaving.

I watch as the words burn. Three years of letters go up in smoke and flame. I see blue-lined paper turn to black ashes; I see pages and pages, months and years, burn, crumble, and then disappear. The front of my white sheet has turned black from soot, and my eyes water and burn.

When I am done, I take the full bowl of ashes and hide it in the vase on the mantel, joining it with Argus. My black hands smudge the white figures on the vase until their tunics become as sooty as my own. I change my clothes and open all the windows, but still Mom asks, when she comes home, about the burning smell. I told her I was cooking.

She looked surprised. Neither of us cooks much. "No more burnt offerings when I'm not home," she said. She looked upset and distracted, and Old Farfel didn't give that stifled laugh of his.

It's all my fault. Helen McGuire got chicken pox. Bad. She has been out of school for almost two weeks. I know my burning ceremony did this. "The show must go on," Mr. Dodd said when Achilles threw up the Tater Tots or when Priam's beard got caught in Athena's hair, but this is different. This is Helen. And it's my fault.

I know all her lines. Know them backward and forward. I have stood in our living room, towel tied around my body, and acted out the entire play, saying every line for my mother. When Mr. Dodd made the announcement about Helen at dress rehearsal, I stood up, white bedsheet slipping from my shoulders, and said in a loud, clear voice, "The gods must have envied me my beauty, for now my name is a curse. I have become hated Helen, the scourge of Troy."

Mr. Dodd shook his head and looked very sad. "We'll see, Vita. She might still get better," he said.

Helen McGuire recovered, but she didn't want to do the part because of all the pockmarks that were left. Besides, she wanted to be inside the horse with Tommy Aldridge. Mr. Dodd insisted that she still be Helen until her parents wrote that they didn't want her to be pressured, they didn't want to *do any further damage*, whatever that means. After that, the part was mine.

Tonight is the opening, and I am so excited. Mom is coming without Old Farfel. "He wasn't what I wanted," she said. I don't think she'll be seeing him anymore.

"What is beautiful?" I ask Mom before the play begins.

"Why are you so worried all the time about beauty? Don't you know how beautiful you are to me?"

"Would Daddy think I was beautiful?"

"Oh, Vita, he *always* thought you were beautiful."

"Would he think I was like Helen?"

She looked me up and down, from the gold lanyard[11] snaked through my thick hair to my too tight pink ballet slippers.

"He would think you're more beautiful than Helen. I'm almost sorry he won't be here to see it."

"*Almost* sorry?"

---

11. **lanyard** (lan′yərd) *n.*: here, a decorative cord.

Vocabulary

litany (lit″n·ē) *n.*: repetitive prayer or recitation.

incantation (in′kan·tā′shən) *n.*: chant of words or phrases that is meant to produce a magical result.

stifled (stī′fəld) *v.* used as *adj.*: smothered.

scourge (skʉrj) *n.*: cause of serious trouble or great suffering.

"Almost. At moments like this—you look so good those ancient gods are going to come alive again with envy."

"What do you mean, come alive again? What are you saying about the gods?"

"Vita, Greek polytheism is an extinct belief," she said, and laughed. And then she stopped and looked at me strangely. "When people stopped believing in the gods, they no longer had power. They don't exist anymore. You must have known that."

Didn't I get the part of Helen? Didn't Old Farfel leave? I made all these things happen with my offering. I know I did. I don't believe these gods disappeared. At least not Athena.

"I don't believe you."

She looked at me, confused.

"You can't know for sure about the gods. And who knows? Maybe Daddy will even be here to see it."

"Sure," she said. "And maybe this time the Trojans will win the war."

I stand offstage with Mr. Dodd and wait for my final cue. The dry-ice machine has been turned on full blast and an incredible amount of fake smoke is making its way toward the painted back-drop of Troy. Hector's papier-mâché head has accidentally slipped from Achilles' hand and is now making a hollow sound as it rolls across the stage.

I peek around the thick red curtain, trying to see into the audience. The auditorium is packed, filled with parents and camcorders. I spot my mom sitting in the front row, alone. I try to scan the back wall, looking for a sign of him, a familiar shadow. Nothing.

Soon I will walk out on the ramparts, put my hand to my forehead, and give my last speech. "Are you sure you're ready?" Mr. Dodd asks. I think he's more nervous than I am. "Remember," he tells me, "this is Helen's big moment. Think loss." I nod, thinking nothing.

"Break a leg," he says, giving me a little push toward the stage. "And try not to trip over the head."

The lights are much brighter than I had expected, making me squint. I walk through the smoky fog toward center stage.

"It is I, the hated Helen, scourge of Troy."

With the light on me, the audience is in shadow, like a big pit, dark and endless. I bow before the altar, feeling my tunic rise. "Hear my supplication," I say, pulling down a bit on the back of my tunic.

"Do not envy me such beauty—it has wrought only pain and despair."

I can hear Mr. Dodd, offstage, loudly whispering each line along with me.

"For this destruction, I know I will be blamed."

I begin to recite Helen's wrongs—beauty, pride, the abdication of Sparta—careful to enunciate clearly. "Troy, I have come to ask you to forgive me."

I'm supposed to hit my fist against my chest, draw a hand across my forehead, and cry loudly. Mr. Dodd has shown me this gesture, practiced it with me in rehearsal a dozen times—the last line, my big finish. The audience is very quiet. In the stillness there is a hole, an empty pocket, an absence. Instead of kneeling, I stand up, straighten my tunic, look toward the audience, and speak the line softly: "And to say goodbye."

There is a prickly feeling up the back of my neck. And then applause. The noise surrounds me, filling me. I look into the darkened house and, for a second, I can hear the beating of a swan's wings, and, then, nothing at all. ■

Vocabulary

polytheism (päl′i·thē·iz′əm) n.: belief in more than one god.

ramparts (ram′pärts′) n.: broad embankments surrounding a castle, fort, or city for defense against attack.

supplication (sup′lə·kā′shən) n.: humble plea or request.

enunciate (ē·nun′sē·āt′) v.: pronounce; articulate.

Meet the Writer

Wendi Kaufman

"Is Vita Based on Me?"

Wendi Kaufman (1964–   ) lives in Virginia, but her written "voice" was shaped by her childhood experiences—growing up in a small town in upstate New York. Kaufman is a graduate of George Mason University's master-of-fine-arts program. She is currently a correspondent for National Public Radio. Here is what she says about "Helen on Eighty-sixth Street":

❝ I was reading the *Odyssey* and thought the stage production of a mythic tale would make a good backdrop for a short story. The *Odyssey* was originally an oral tale, an epic poem recited for hundreds of years before it was finally written down. I wanted to somehow incorporate that incantatory tone, to have my story sound like it was being spoken out loud—that's where the voice of Vita, the narrator, comes from.

Vita is twelve years old. I remember that as a hard age, a time on the cusp, when you're stuck in that middle ground between child and teen, and it's difficult to know where you belong, to find your own place. Vita wants to be Helen of Troy because she wants everything that Helen represents: beauty, popularity, adoration. I think these are things that many of us have desired at one time or another. The truth about Vita is that she *is* beautiful. She is warm, funny, knows her own mind, and is capable of great love—what could be more beautiful than that? She just doesn't know it yet.

I grew up in a sleepy town in the Hudson River Valley, about an hour from New York City, the kind of place Washington Irving wrote about. I always felt it was a boring town, a place where nothing ever happened. What I didn't realize was that the most important things were happening around me every day, the drama of daily life. As an adult, I have lived all over the country and have had many different experiences, but it is those childhood years, those early memories and discoveries, that I return to and write about most often.

Is Vita based on me? Not really. But as a young girl, I did love reading mythology. Myths are great stories for young writers. The plot twists, the drama—it's all there. Myths run the gamut of human emotion and experience. Love, loss, deceit, regret, betrayal, there's something in there for everybody. I would recommend them to any young writer—and to a few old ones.

For me, writing is an experience of the imagination, that chance to take a kernel of an idea or experience and explore it by becoming anyone or saying anything. That's what I love about writing. As for advice for young writers? Simple: Read, read, read. And, of course, keep writing. There are things that come out on the page, when pen hits paper, that you weren't expecting, that you didn't plan for. Those are the moments we all strive for.

Writing is about possibilities, about the freedom of the blank page. I can remember reading *Little Women* in the fourth grade and crying my eyes out. That was the first time I realized the power of literature. Never underestimate that power. **❞**

Reading Check

1. What is Vita's family situation?
2. What are her three wishes?
3. How does each wish turn out?

Thinking Critically

4. As Vita tells us her story, we learn a great deal about her. We find out, for example, how she feels about herself and what she wants. Find passages in which Vita reveals what she is like. Based on those passages, what would you say are her three or four most important **character traits**?

5. Explain how Vita feels about her father's leaving her on her own with her mother. Does she really believe her father will return? As she deals on her own with her parents' divorce, what do her thoughts and statements reveal about her **character**?

6. Describe Vita's triumphs and losses. Which do you think are more important to her—the triumphs or the losses? Explain why.

7. Think about Vita and what she has learned by the story's end. How would you state the **theme** of this story—what truth does Vita's experience reveal to you?

8. Make a list of all the story's **allusions**—references to Greek mythology, to literature, even to New York City. With a partner, discuss how you figured out the meaning of each allusion. What resources in the text helped you? Are any of these allusions still puzzling you? (For example, what are those swan's wings at the story's end?)

SKILLS FOCUS

Literary Skills
Analyze character traits from what characters say about themselves.

Reading Skills
Understand allusions.

Writing Skills
Write a description. Write a short story.

Vocabulary Skills
Understand word meanings.

Grammar Skills
Understand and use coordinating conjunctions.

Extending and Evaluating

9. Vita's mother tells her, "You don't want to be Helen. Be lucky you're a warrior. You're too smart to be ruled by your heart." What do you think of this advice?

10. This story can be boiled down to the following facts: A girl wants to star in the sixth-grade play. She misses her father, who has left the family, and she hopes that he will attend the play. Do you think the author's decision to add the myth of Helen of Troy to the story was a good idea? (Does the myth contribute to your understanding of Vita, or does it instead make the story too complicated?) Explain your answer.

WRITING

Impossible Dream?

Vita's dream of playing Helen in the school production comes true. Write about an ambition, hope, or dream of your own. Describe the dream, and explain how you tried to make it a reality. Did you succeed? Is it still too early to tell? Has your old dream been replaced by a more achievable one? (Be sure to check your Quickwrite notes.)

Trading Places

Write your own brief **story** about a character who wants to be like someone in a myth, novel, or movie you know. In your story, make it clear who your **character** wants to be and why. Create an interesting **conflict,** and end your story by having your character make an important discovery.

▶ Use "Writing a Short Story," pages 154–161, for help with this assignment.

Word Knowledge: Questions About Words

PRACTICE

How much do you know about the meanings of the Word Bank words? Make up two questions about each word, and organize your answers in a chart like the one below. After you have completed charts for all the words, invite a partner to answer your questions.

stifled	
Questions	**Answers**
When is a cough sometimes stifled?	• during a play • during a speech
What other things are some-times stifled?	• sobs • screams • protests

Word Bank

embodies
odyssey
litany
incantation
stifled
scourge
polytheism
ramparts
supplication
enunciate

Grammar Link

Coordinating Conjunctions: Getting It Together

Coordinating conjunctions join words, phrases, or clauses of equal importance. Suppose the following phrases are Kaufman's notes:

> Told Helen McGuire it's dark. Hold each other around waist. Walk to make horse move forward.

Here is how she puts these notes together in one sentence using coordinating conjunctions:

> "I told her it's dark, and we must hold each other around the waist and walk to make the horse move forward."

Here are two other sentences from the story that use coordinating conjunctions. Break these sentences into shorter ones to see how many details the writer combines:

1. "I will meet giants and witches and see strange lands."
2. "I change my clothes and open all the windows, but still Mom asks, when she gets home, about the burning smell."

PRACTICE

Using each coordinating conjunction listed below, summarize the main events in "Helen on Eighty-sixth Street." Be sure to compare your summaries with those of your classmates.

and	or	yet
so	for	
nor	but	

▶ **For more help, see The Compound Subject and The Compound Verb, 8e–f, and Run-on Sentences, 9b, in the Language Handbook.**

Elements of Literature

Character Interactions *by* John Leggett
GIVE-AND-TAKE

A story with a suspenseful, fast-moving plot allows us to escape, at least briefly, from the tedium of our daily lives. For fiction to be more than just escape reading, though, it needs vivid, complex characters whose problems and triumphs draw forth our emotions and reveal some truth about humankind.

Characters in Conflict

Often a story revolves around one main character. Usually we care about this character, who may remind us of a person we know or even of ourselves.

What sets the main character's story in motion is **conflict.** The main character wants something, and the obstacles and choices he or she faces form the plot. We call the main character the **protagonist.** The character or force the protagonist struggles against and must overcome is the **antagonist.**

When the conflict is with an outside force—another person, society, a creature from the deep—it's an **external conflict.** When the protagonist faces a conflict within himself or herself—fear or self-doubt, for example—the character must overcome an **internal conflict.** Frequently an external conflict results in an internal struggle.

While the focus of our attention in a story is the conflict between the protagonist and the antagonist, writers often include **subordinate characters** who add depth and complication to the plot.

Imagine a situation in which Dorothy, our protagonist, is locked in a room by her antagonist, Uncle Godfrey. In an hour, Dorothy is due to sing in a contest to win a music scholarship. Her uncle is trying to prevent her from pursuing her music career because he wants her to work on the family's alligator farm. Dorothy's external conflict with her uncle creates an internal conflict for her as well. Her career goals conflict with her gratitude to her uncle for raising her and with her desire to obey him.

Enter a subordinate character: Dorothy's best friend, Madeleine, who pressures Dorothy to abandon her singing career and to become her partner in a get-rich-quick scheme. The way Dorothy resolves her conflicts with her uncle and with Madeleine will not only affect the plot but also reveal Dorothy's values and personality traits.

Motivation: The Driving Force

Motivation is what drives a character's actions. It explains behavior and reveals personality. What would motivate Dorothy to give up her singing career and become Madeleine's partner? Would it be loyalty to her best friend, or if she is ambitious, could it be greed?

Writers rarely make direct statements about a character's motivation. Instead, they plant clues and rely on readers to make inferences from those clues. If a writer doesn't provide motivation, a character's actions may seem unbelievable or the story may seem boring.

Rounding Out Character

A **flat character** has only one or two character traits. If Uncle Godfrey's only motivation for locking up Dorothy is to get free labor on the farm, then we would view him as a flat character. Selfish and cruel, he is no more complicated than a character in a cartoon or fairy tale (think of the wicked stepmother in *Cinderella*).

Watch how our view of Uncle Godfrey changes if we learn that he is dying of a rare disease. Fearing that he won't be able to maintain the farm and that Dorothy's inheritance will become worthless, he wants her to look after the alligators. Proud and independent, however, he hides his diagnosis because he doesn't want Dorothy's pity. Suddenly we see him as a **round character,** a figure who has several sides to his personality. Uncle Godfrey has become complex, as have our reactions to him and to the story.

Characters and Change

In most stories, as the characters struggle to resolve their conflicts, they learn something about themselves or other people or even the world. As a result, they take action or change their behavior or their attitudes. Such characters are called **dynamic** because they grow or change.

Static characters don't progress or change. At the end of the story, they are the same as they were in the beginning. Subordinate characters are often static because a story doesn't revolve around them. Instead, their role is to further the plot or to help us understand the main character.

A static character, Madeleine exits the story in pursuit of wealth, never changing her perspective or values. Dorothy, however, learns not to judge people too quickly. Discovering that Uncle Godfrey is ill, she realizes that sometimes people hide their emotions and fears. The changes that a dynamic character undergoes contribute to the **meaning** of the story.

The next time you read a story, think about the characters' choices—and those of the writer as well. If you had been in the shoes of either the protagonist or his or her creator, would you have made a different choice?

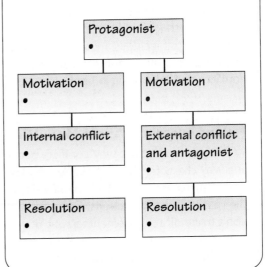

Practice

Think of a story you've read in which the protagonist faces powerful conflicts. Use a chart like the one here to map out the conflicts and their resolutions, as well as the protagonist's motivations:

- Protagonist
  - •
- Motivation
  - •
- Internal conflict
  - •
- Resolution
  - •
- Motivation
  - •
- External conflict and antagonist
  - •
- Resolution
  - •

Before You Read

Marigolds

Make the Connection

Quickwrite ✏️

This story is about the passage from childhood to adulthood, a journey that is often marked by conflict. In fact, negotiating this passage can demand as much courage as a struggle with an outside enemy. Before you read this story, write down your response to the following question: What fears and conflicts do most young people deal with as they move into adult life? Keep your notes for use later on.

Literary Focus

Conflict: Battles Within and Without

Conflict, or struggle, is the heart of a story. When characters struggle against something outside themselves, their conflicts are **external.** Characters with **internal conflicts** struggle to resolve contradictory desires or to battle personal problems, such as fear or anger. The most intense conflicts occur when characters face both kinds of battles.

"Marigolds" includes a violent external confrontation, but important internal conflicts also take place in Lizabeth.

Reading Skills

Making Inferences About Motivation

When you think about why conflicts occur and why characters behave as they do, you are trying to determine their **motivation,** the reasons for their actions. Often writers don't make direct statements about their characters. Instead, they expect you to make **inferences,** or educated guesses, based on clues in the text, such as a character's actions and words. As you read "Marigolds," think about the characters' motivations. The questions at the open-book signs will help you.

Background

In the 1930s, a terrible economic depression swept the world. The booming stock market had collapsed in 1929, causing businesses to shut down all over America and factories to close their doors. Banks failed. People lost their life savings. Life was hard for almost every American during those years. As the narrator of this story says, however, the Great Depression was nothing new to her family: For the black families of rural Maryland, all times were hard times.

Vocabulary Development

arid (ar′id) adj.: lacking enough water for many types of plants to grow; dry.

futile (fyoot′'l) adj.: useless; vain.

impoverished (im·päv′ər·ishd) v. used as adj.: poor; poverty-stricken.

poignantly (poin′yənt·lē) adv.: with a sharp sadness or pain; movingly.

clarity (klar′ə·tē) n.: clearness.

placidly (plas′id·lē) adv.: calmly; quietly.

inciting (in·sīt′iŋ) v. used as n.: stirring up.

malicious (mə·lish′əs) adj.: showing a desire to harm another; spiteful.

contrition (kən·trish′ən) n.: deep feelings of guilt and repentance.

MARIGOLDS

Eugenia W. Collier

Miss Lottie didn't like intruders, especially children.

The Magic Garden (1978) by Romare Bearden. Watercolor and collage (10⅛″ × 7″).

When I think of the hometown of my youth, all that I seem to remember is dust—the brown, crumbly dust of late summer—arid, sterile dust that gets into the eyes and makes them water, gets into the throat and between the toes of bare brown feet. I don't know why I should remember only the dust. Surely there must have been lush green lawns and paved streets under leafy shade trees somewhere in town; but memory is an abstract painting—it does not present things as they are, but rather as they *feel*. And so, when I think of that time and that place, I remember only the dry September of the dirt roads and grassless yards of the shantytown where I lived. And one other thing I remember, another incongruency[1] of memory—a brilliant splash of sunny yellow against the dust—Miss Lottie's marigolds.

Whenever the memory of those marigolds flashes across my mind, a strange nostalgia comes with it and remains long after the picture has faded. I feel again the chaotic emotions of adolescence, illusive as smoke, yet as real as the potted geranium before me now. Joy and rage and wild animal gladness and shame become tangled together in the multicolored skein[2] of fourteen-going-on-fifteen as I recall that devastating moment when I was suddenly more woman than child, years ago in Miss Lottie's yard. I think of those marigolds at the strangest times; I remember them vividly now as I desperately pass away the time. . . .

I suppose that futile waiting was the sorrowful background music of our impoverished little community when I was young. The Depression that gripped the nation was no new thing to us, for the black workers of rural Maryland had always been depressed. I don't know what it was that we were waiting for; certainly not for the prosperity that was "just around the corner," for those were white folks' words, which we never believed. Nor did we wait for hard work and thrift to pay off in shining success, as the American Dream promised, for we knew better than that, too. Perhaps we waited for a miracle, amorphous[3] in concept but necessary if one were to have the grit to rise before dawn each day and labor in the white man's vineyard until after dark, or to wander about in the September dust offering one's sweat in return for some meager share of bread. But God was chary[4] with miracles in those days, and so we waited—and waited.

We children, of course, were only vaguely aware of the extent of our poverty. Having no radios, few newspapers, and no magazines, we were somewhat unaware of the world outside our community. Nowadays we would be called culturally deprived and people would write books and hold conferences about us. In those days everybody we knew was just as hungry and ill clad as we were. Poverty was the cage in which we all were trapped, and our hatred of it was still the vague, undirected restlessness of the zoo-bred flamingo who knows that nature created him to fly free.

Perhaps we waited for a miracle . . .

---

3. **amorphous** (ə·môr′fəs) *adj.*: vague; shapeless.
4. **chary** (cher′ē) *adj.*: not generous.

Vocabulary

arid (ar′id) *adj.*: lacking enough water for many types of plants to grow; dry.

futile (fyoot′'l) *adj.*: useless; vain.

impoverished (im·päv′ər·ishd) *v.* used as *adj.*: poor; poverty-stricken.

---

1. **incongruency** (in′kän′groo·ən·sē) *n.*: inconsistency; lack of agreement or harmony.
2. **multicolored skein** (skān): The writer is comparing her many feelings to a long, coiled piece (skein) of many- (multi) colored yarn.

As I think of those days I feel most poignantly the tag end of summer, the bright, dry times when we began to have a sense of shortening days and the imminence of the cold.

By the time I was fourteen, my brother Joey and I were the only children left at our house, the older ones having left home for early marriage or the lure of the city, and the two babies having been sent to relatives who might care for them better than we. Joey was three years younger than I, and a boy, and therefore vastly inferior. Each morning our mother and father trudged wearily down the dirt road and around the bend, she to her domestic job, he to his daily unsuccessful quest for work. After our few chores around the tumbledown shanty, Joey and I were free to run wild in the sun with other children similarly situated.

For the most part, those days are ill-defined in my memory, running together and combining like a fresh watercolor painting left out in the rain. I remember squatting in the road drawing a picture in the dust, a picture which Joey gleefully erased with one sweep of his dirty foot. I remember fishing for minnows in a muddy creek and watching sadly as they eluded my cupped hands, while Joey laughed uproariously. And I remember, that year, a strange restlessness of body and of spirit, a feeling that something old and familiar was ending, and something unknown and therefore terrifying was beginning.

One day returns to me with special clarity for some reason, perhaps because it was the beginning of the experience that in some inexplicable[5] way marked the end of innocence. I was loafing under the great oak tree in our yard, deep in some reverie which I have now forgotten, except that it involved some secret, secret thoughts of one of the Harris boys across the yard. Joey and a bunch of kids were bored now with the old tire suspended from an oak limb, which had kept them entertained for a while.

"Hey, Lizabeth," Joey yelled. He never talked when he could yell. "Hey, Lizabeth, let's go somewhere."

I came reluctantly from my private world. "Where you want to go? What you want to do?"

The truth was that we were becoming tired of the formlessness of our summer days. The idleness whose prospect had seemed so beautiful during the busy days of spring now had degenerated to an almost desperate effort to fill up the empty midday hours.

"Let's go see can we find some locusts on the hill," someone suggested.

Joey was scornful. "Ain't no more locusts there. Y'all got 'em all while they was still green."

The argument that followed was brief and not really worth the effort. Hunting locust trees wasn't fun anymore by now.

"Tell you what," said Joey finally, his eyes sparkling. "Let's us go over to Miss Lottie's."

The idea caught on at once, for annoying Miss Lottie was always fun. I was still child enough to scamper along with the group over rickety fences and through bushes that tore our already raggedy clothes, back to where Miss Lottie lived. I think now that we must have made a tragicomic spectacle, five or six kids of different ages, each of us clad in only one garment—the girls in faded dresses that were too long or too short, the boys in patchy pants, their sweaty brown chests gleaming in the hot sun. A little cloud of dust followed our thin legs and bare feet as we tramped over the barren land.

> **MOTIVATION AND CONFLICT**
>
> 1. What do you think **motivates** the children to go to Miss Lottie's house to annoy her?

Vocabulary

poignantly (poin′yənt·lē) *adv.*: with a sharp sadness or pain; movingly.

clarity (klar′ə·tē) *n.*: clearness.

---

5. **inexplicable** (in·eks′pli·kə·bəl) *adj.*: not explainable or understandable.

When Miss Lottie's house came into view we stopped, ostensibly[6] to plan our strategy, but actually to reinforce our courage. Miss Lottie's house was the most ramshackle of all our ramshackle homes. The sun and rain had long since faded its rickety frame siding from white to a sullen gray. The boards themselves seemed to remain upright not from being nailed together but rather from leaning together, like a house that a child might have constructed from cards. A brisk wind might have blown it down, and the fact that it was still standing implied a kind of enchantment that was stronger than the elements. There it stood and as far as I know is standing yet—a gray, rotting thing with no porch, no shutters, no steps, set on a cramped lot with no grass, not even any weeds—a monument to decay.

In front of the house in a squeaky rocking chair sat Miss Lottie's son, John Burke, completing the impression of decay. John Burke was what was known as queer-headed. Black and ageless, he sat rocking day in and day out in a mindless stupor, lulled by the monotonous squeak-squawk of the chair. A battered hat atop his shaggy head shaded him from the sun. Usually John Burke was totally unaware of everything outside his quiet dream world. But if you disturbed him, if you intruded upon his fantasies, he would become enraged, strike out at you, and curse at you in some strange enchanted language which only he could understand. We children made a game of thinking of ways to disturb John Burke and then to elude his violent retribution.

But our real fun and our real fear lay in Miss Lottie herself. Miss Lottie seemed to be at least a hundred years old. Her big frame still held traces of the tall, powerful woman she must have been in youth, although it was now bent and drawn. Her smooth skin was a dark reddish brown, and her face had Indian-like features and the stern

stoicism[7] that one associates with Indian faces. Miss Lottie didn't like intruders either, especially children. She never left her yard, and nobody ever visited her. We never knew how she managed those necessities which depend on human interaction—how she ate, for example, or even whether she ate. When we were tiny children, we thought Miss Lottie was a witch and we made up tales that we half believed ourselves about her exploits. We were far too sophisticated now, of course, to believe the witch nonsense. But old fears have a way of clinging like cobwebs, and so when we sighted the tumbledown shack, we had to stop to reinforce our nerves.

"Look, there she is," I whispered, forgetting that Miss Lottie could not possibly have heard me from that distance. "She's fooling with them crazy flowers."

"Yeh, look at 'er."

Miss Lottie's marigolds were perhaps the strangest part of the picture. Certainly they did not fit in with the crumbling decay of the rest of her yard. Beyond the dusty brown yard, in front of the sorry gray house, rose suddenly and shockingly a dazzling strip of bright blossoms, clumped together in enormous mounds, warm and passionate and sun-golden. The old black witch-woman worked on them all summer, every summer, down on her creaky knees, weeding and cultivating and arranging, while the house crumbled and John Burke rocked. For some perverse reason, we children hated those marigolds. They interfered with the perfect ugliness of the place; they were too beautiful; they said too much that we could not understand; they did not make sense. There was something in the vigor with which the old woman destroyed the weeds that intimidated us. It should have been a comical sight—the old woman with the man's hat on her cropped white head, leaning over the bright mounds, her big

---

6. **ostensibly** (ä·sten′sə·blē) *adv.:* seemingly; apparently.

7. **stoicism** (stō′i·siz′əm) *n.:* calm indifference to pleasure or pain.

Southern Limited (1976) by Romare Bearden. Collage.

backside in the air—but it wasn't comical, it was something we could not name. We had to annoy her by whizzing a pebble into her flowers or by yelling a dirty word, then dancing away from her rage, reveling in our youth and mocking her age. Actually, I think it was the flowers we wanted to destroy, but nobody had the nerve to try it, not even Joey, who was usually fool enough to try anything.

MOTIVATION

2. What reasons can you give to explain why Miss Lottie works so hard in her garden?

"Y'all git some stones," commanded Joey now and was met with instant giggling obedience as everyone except me began to gather pebbles from the dusty ground. "Come on, Lizabeth."

I just stood there peering through the bushes, torn between wanting to join the fun and feeling that it was all a bit silly.

"You scared, Lizabeth?"

I cursed and spat on the ground—my favorite gesture of phony bravado. "Y'all children get the stones, I'll show you how to use 'em."

I said before that we children were not consciously aware of how thick were the bars of our cage. I wonder now, though, whether we were not more aware of it than I thought. Perhaps we had some dim notion of what we were, and how little chance we had of being anything else. Otherwise, why would we have been so preoccupied with destruction? Anyway, the pebbles were collected quickly, and everybody looked at me to begin the fun.

"Come on, y'all."

We crept to the edge of the bushes that bordered the narrow road in front of Miss Lottie's place. She was working <u>placidly</u>, kneeling over the flowers, her dark hand plunged into the golden mound. Suddenly *zing*—an expertly aimed stone cut the head off one of the blossoms.

"Who out there?" Miss Lottie's backside came down and her head came up as her sharp eyes searched the bushes. "You better git!"

We had crouched down out of sight in the bushes, where we stifled the giggles that insisted on coming. Miss Lottie gazed warily across the road for a moment, then cautiously returned to her weeding. *Zing*—Joey sent a pebble into the blooms, and another marigold was beheaded.

Miss Lottie was enraged now. She began struggling to her feet, leaning on a rickety cane and shouting. "Y'all git! Go on home!" Then the rest of the kids let loose with their pebbles, storming the flowers and laughing wildly and senselessly at Miss Lottie's impotent rage. She shook her stick at us and started shakily toward the road crying, "Git 'long! John Burke! John Burke, come help!"

Then I lost my head entirely, mad with the power of <u>inciting</u> such rage, and ran out of the bushes in the storm of pebbles, straight toward Miss Lottie, chanting madly, "Old witch, fell in a ditch, picked up a penny and thought she was rich!" The children screamed with delight, dropped their pebbles, and joined the crazy dance, swarming around Miss Lottie like bees and chanting, "Old lady witch!" while she screamed curses at us. The madness lasted only a moment, for John Burke, startled at last, lurched out of his chair, and we dashed for the bushes just as Miss Lottie's cane went whizzing at my head.

I did not join the merriment when the kids gathered again under the oak in our bare yard.

Suddenly I was ashamed, and I did not like being ashamed. The child in me sulked and said it was all in fun, but the woman in me flinched at the thought of the <u>malicious</u> attack that I had led. The mood lasted all afternoon. When we ate the beans and rice that was supper that night, I did not notice my father's silence, for he was always silent these days, nor did I notice my mother's absence, for she always worked until well into evening. Joey and I had a particularly bitter argument after supper; his exuberance got on my nerves. Finally I stretched out upon the pallet[8] in the room we shared and fell into a fitful doze.

When I awoke, somewhere in the middle of the night, my mother had returned, and I vaguely listened to the conversation that was audible through the thin walls that separated our rooms. At first I heard no words, only voices. My mother's voice was like a cool, dark room in summer— peaceful, soothing, quiet. I loved to listen to it; it made things seem all right somehow. But my father's voice cut through hers, shattering the peace.

"Twenty-two years, Maybelle, twenty-two years," he was saying, "and I got nothing for you, nothing, nothing."

"It's all right, honey, you'll get something. Everybody out of work now, you know that."

"It ain't right. Ain't no man ought to eat his woman's food year in and year out, and see his children running wild. Ain't nothing right about that."

Where did I fit into this crazy picture?

---

8. **pallet** (pal′it) *n.:* small bed or pad laid directly on the floor.

Vocabulary

placidly (plas′id·lē) *adv.:* calmly; quietly.

inciting (in·sīt′iŋ) *v.* used as *n.:* stirring up.

malicious (mə·lish′əs) *adj.:* showing a desire to harm another; spiteful.

"Honey, you took good care of us when you had it. Ain't nobody got nothing nowadays."

"I ain't talking about nobody else, I'm talking about *me*. God knows I try." My mother said something I could not hear, and my father cried out louder, "What must a man do, tell me that?"

"Look, we ain't starving. I git paid every week, and Mrs. Ellis is real nice about giving me things. She gonna let me have Mr. Ellis's old coat for you this winter—"

"Damn Mr. Ellis's coat! And damn his money! You think I want white folks' leavings? Damn, Maybelle"—and suddenly he sobbed, loudly and painfully, and cried helplessly and hopelessly in the dark night. I had never heard a man cry before. I did not know men ever cried. I covered my ears with my hands but could not cut off the sound of my father's harsh, painful, despairing sobs. My father was a strong man who could whisk a child upon his shoulders and go singing through the house. My father whittled toys for us, and laughed so loud that the great oak seemed to laugh with him, and taught us how to fish and hunt rabbits. How could it be that my father was crying? But the sobs went on, unstifled, finally quieting until I could hear my mother's voice, deep and rich, humming softly as she used to hum to a frightened child.

MOTIVATION

3. Why does Lizabeth's father break down and cry?

The world had lost its boundary lines. My mother, who was small and soft, was now the strength of the family; my father, who was the rock on which the family had been built, was sobbing like the tiniest child. Everything was suddenly out of tune, like a broken accordion. Where did I fit into this crazy picture? I do not now remember my thoughts, only a feeling of great bewilderment and fear.

Long after the sobbing and humming had stopped, I lay on the pallet, still as stone with my hands over my ears, wishing that I too could cry and be comforted. The night was silent now except for the sound of the crickets and of Joey's soft breathing. But the room was too crowded with fear to allow me to sleep, and finally, feeling the terrible aloneness of 4 A.M., I decided to awaken Joey.

"Ouch! What's the matter with you? What you want?" he demanded disagreeably when I had pinched and slapped him awake.

"Come on, wake up."

"What for? Go 'way."

I was lost for a reasonable reply. I could not say, "I'm scared and I don't want to be alone," so I merely said, "I'm going out. If you want to come, come on."

The promise of adventure awoke him. "Going out now? Where to, Lizabeth? What you going to do?"

I was pulling my dress over my head. Until now I had not thought of going out. "Just come on," I replied tersely.

I was out the window and halfway down the road before Joey caught up with me.

"Wait, Lizabeth, where you going?"

I was running as if the Furies[9] were after me, as perhaps they were—running silently and furiously until I came to where I had half known I was headed: to Miss Lottie's yard.

The half-dawn light was more eerie than complete darkness, and in it the old house was like the ruin that my world had become—foul and crumbling, a grotesque caricature. It looked haunted, but I was not afraid, because I was haunted too.

"Lizabeth, you lost your mind?" panted Joey.

I had indeed lost my mind, for all the smoldering emotions of that summer swelled in me and burst—the great need for my mother who was never there, the hopelessness of our poverty

---

9. Furies (fyoor′ēz): in Greek and Roman mythology, spirits who pursue people who have committed crimes, sometimes driving them mad.

and degradation, the bewilderment of being neither child nor woman and yet both at once, the fear unleashed by my father's tears. And these feelings combined in one great impulse toward destruction.

"Lizabeth!"

I leaped furiously into the mounds of marigolds and pulled madly, trampling and pulling and destroying the perfect yellow blooms. The fresh smell of early morning and of dew-soaked marigolds spurred me on as I went tearing and mangling and sobbing while Joey tugged my dress or my waist crying, "Lizabeth, stop, please stop!"

MOTIVATION AND CONFLICT

4. Why does Lizabeth destroy the marigolds? Why do you think she cries as she does so?

And then I was sitting in the ruined little garden among the uprooted and ruined flowers, crying and crying, and it was too late to undo what I had done. Joey was sitting beside me, silent and frightened, not knowing what to say. Then, "Lizabeth, look."

I opened my swollen eyes and saw in front of me a pair of large, calloused feet; my gaze lifted to the swollen legs, the age-distorted body clad in a tight cotton nightdress, and then the shadowed Indian face surrounded by stubby white hair. And there was no rage in the face now, now that the garden was destroyed and there was nothing any longer to be protected.

"M-miss Lottie!" I scrambled to my feet and just stood there and stared at her, and that was the moment when childhood faded and womanhood began. That violent, crazy act was the last act of childhood. For as I gazed at the immobile face with the sad, weary eyes, I gazed upon a kind of reality which is hidden to childhood. The witch was no longer a witch but only a broken old woman who had dared to create beauty in the midst of ugliness and sterility. She had been born in squalor and lived in it all her life. Now at the end of that life she had nothing except a falling-down hut, a wrecked body, and John Burke, the mindless son of her passion. Whatever verve there was left in her, whatever was of love and beauty and joy that had not been squeezed out by life, had been there in the marigolds she had so tenderly cared for.

Of course I could not express the things that I knew about Miss Lottie as I stood there awkward and ashamed. The years have put words to the things I knew in that moment, and as I look back upon it, I know that that moment marked the end of innocence. Innocence involves an unseeing acceptance of things at face value, an ignorance of the area below the surface. In that humiliating moment I looked beyond myself and into the depths of another person. This was the beginning of compassion, and one cannot have both compassion and innocence.

The years have taken me worlds away from that time and that place, from the dust and squalor of our lives, and from the bright thing that I destroyed in a blind, childish striking out at God knows what. Miss Lottie died long ago and many years have passed since I last saw her hut, completely barren at last, for despite my wild <u>contrition</u> she never planted marigolds again. Yet, there are times when the image of those passionate yellow mounds returns with a painful poignancy. For one does not have to be ignorant and poor to find that his life is as barren as the dusty yards of our town. And I too have planted marigolds. ■

MOTIVATION

5. What motivates Lizabeth to tell this story? Why does she still think of Miss Lottie's marigolds?

Vocabulary

contrition (kən·trish′ən) *n.*: deep feelings of guilt and repentance.

Meet the Writer

Eugenia W. Collier

"I Must Have Done My Job Well"

"Marigolds" is a story that emerged from a difficult time in the life of its author, Eugenia W. Collier (1928–   ). Collier, who has taught English at Howard University, Baltimore Community College, and Morgan State University, tells how she came to write "Marigolds" and what the story means to her:

" When I talk with people about 'Marigolds,' someone usually asks me whether the story is autobiographical. I am always pleased with the question, because it means that I must have done my job well—convinced the reader that the incidents in the story are actually happening. However, I always end up admitting that Lizabeth and I are two very different people. I was born and bred in the city of Baltimore, and my family never had the economic problems of Lizabeth's. In some ways we are different in temperament: I was never as daring as Lizabeth, never a leader among my peers. However, I hope that through her I have captured an experience which most young people have—the painful passage from childhood to adulthood, a passage which can be understood only in retrospect. Also, I was tapping into another deeply human experience: hoping desperately for something (planting marigolds) and then having that hope destroyed.

I wrote 'Marigolds' at a time of profound unhappiness. One night I had a tremendous urge to write. I wrote nonstop until the story was finished—about twenty-four hours. Later I sent 'Marigolds' (along with a fee I could hardly afford) to a well-advertised literary agency, which returned the story (not the fee) with a note saying that it had no plot, no conflict, and no hope of publication. Discouraged, I put 'Marigolds' away. Five years later, doing research for a project on black writing of the 1960s, I read stories in *Negro Digest* which were similar in subject matter to 'Marigolds.' I submitted my story, and *Negro Digest* published it. It won the Gwendolyn Brooks Prize for Fiction, it was selected for inclusion in an anthology of black fiction, and since then it has been included in a number of collections. Of all the fiction I have written, 'Marigolds' remains my favorite. "

Forgive My Guilt

Robert P. Tristram Coffin

Not always sure what things called sins may be,
I am sure of one sin I have done.
It was years ago, and I was a boy,
I lay in the frostflowers with a gun,
5   The air ran blue as the flowers, I held my breath,
Two birds on golden legs slim as dream things
Ran like quicksilver on the golden sand,
My gun went off, they ran with broken wings
Into the sea, I ran to fetch them in,
10   But they swam with their heads high out to sea,
They cried like two sorrowful high flutes,
With jagged ivory bones where wings should be.

For days I heard them when I walked that headland
Crying out to their kind in the blue,
15   The other plovers were going over south
On silver wings leaving these broken two.
The cries went out one day; but I still hear them
Over all the sounds of sorrow in war or peace
I ever have heard, time cannot drown them,
20   Those slender flutes of sorrow never cease.
Two airy things forever denied the air!
I never knew how their lives at last were spilt,
But I have hoped for years all that is wild,
Airy, and beautiful will forgive my guilt.

Reading Check

1. What is the story's **setting**—that is, when and where does the story take place?

2. Who is Miss Lottie? Describe the children's daytime confrontation with her.

3. What does Lizabeth discover about her parents when she overhears their conversation?

4. What does Lizabeth do to Miss Lottie's flowers just before dawn?

Thinking Critically

5. Left on her own, Lizabeth faces **internal conflicts.** What personal monsters are troubling her?

6. Lizabeth felt ashamed after she led the first attack against Miss Lottie. Why doesn't her sense of shame prevent her from destroying the garden at the end of the story? How is her **motivation** for this destructive act different from her motivation for taunting Miss Lottie earlier?

7. The narrator doesn't tell us much about the effect on Miss Lottie of the **external conflict** over the marigolds. Using the details the narrator *does* provide, explain how you think Miss Lottie was affected.

8. Lizabeth says that destroying the marigolds was her last act of childhood. After that incident, why does she think of herself as standing on her own as an adult?

9. What does Lizabeth mean at the end of the story when she says that she too has planted marigolds? What do you think the marigolds have come to mean in the story? To

answer, consider the feelings that the characters have had about the marigolds throughout the story:

- Miss Lottie loves and cares for them.
- The children do not understand why they are there.
- Lizabeth wants to destroy them.

10. Lizabeth's parents are **subordinate characters,** but their late-night conversation has a big impact on her. "The world had lost its boundary lines," she says in reaction to their conversation. What does she mean? What situations might make a child feel that boundaries have been lost?

Extending and Evaluating

11. Compare Lizabeth's feelings at the end of the story with those of the speaker of "Forgive My Guilt" (see the *Connection* on page 150). What did both children discover? In both cases, did you find it credible that a single act could cause a child to make such an important discovery? Explain your answer.

WRITING

Turning Points

Write an **autobiographical narrative** about a turning point in your life, an incident—whether minor or major, happy or sad—that made you grow up a little. What fears or conflicts did you face? What was the outcome of the incident? Include a reflection telling how the event brought you a little closer to being an adult. (Be sure to check your Quickwrite notes.)

▶ Use "**Writing an Autobiographical Narrative,**" **pages 78–85, for help with this assignment.**

SKILLS FOCUS

Literary Skills
Analyze internal and external conflicts.

Reading Skills
Make inferences about character motivation.

Writing Skills
Write an autobiographical narrative.

After You Read — Vocabulary Development

Analogies: Same or Different?

You can gain a better understanding of many words by completing an **analogy.** In an analogy the relationship between the words in the first pair is the same as the relationship in the second pair. In some common types of analogies, the words in the pairs are **synonyms** (words with the same meaning) or **antonyms** (words with opposite meanings). For more help with analogies, see pages 279 and 672.

PRACTICE 1

Use a word from the Word Bank to complete each analogy below. The first one has been done for you.

Word Bank
arid
futile
impoverished
poignantly
clarity
placidly
inciting
malicious
contrition

1. HARSHLY : ROUGHLY :: _placidly_ : peacefully
2. BRAVERY : COURAGE :: _____ : regret
3. FLEXIBILITY : STIFFNESS :: _____ : vagueness
4. SOCIABLE : SHY :: _____ : wealthy
5. TARDY : PUNCTUAL :: _____ : wet
6. CHEERFUL : GLOOMY :: _____ : kind
7. FREQUENT : RARE :: _____ : useful
8. SWIFTLY : QUICKLY :: _____ : movingly
9. SINCERITY : FALSENESS :: _____ : suppressing

Figures of Speech: Making It Vivid

Collier's story is remarkable for its vivid figures of speech, which make the setting and the characters' feelings come alive. In a **figure of speech,** one thing is compared to another, very different thing. There are several kinds of figures of speech. A **simile** states the comparison using a word such as *like, as,* or *than:*

> "But old fears have a way of clinging like cobwebs. . . ."
> [Fears are compared to cobwebs.]

A **metaphor** compares two unlike things without using the word *like* or *as:*

> "Memory is an abstract painting. . . ."
> [Memory is directly compared to a painting.]

SKILLS FOCUS

Vocabulary Skills
Understand word analogies. Understand figures of speech (simile and metaphor).

PRACTICE 2

For each numbered item on the right, create at least one imaginative figure of speech. Remember that a figure of speech compares two *unlike* items.

1. The marigolds were _____.
2. The garden looked like _____.
3. The days were as empty as _____.

FICTION

A Sapling Stands Tall

In Betty Smith's novel, a tree grows in Brooklyn—and so does young Francie Nolan. Living in a poor neighborhood with her parents and brother, Francie finds joys and an assortment of troubles as she comes of age. Her experiences are sometimes painful, but they become the building blocks of wisdom. *A Tree Grows in Brooklyn* takes place between 1902 and 1919, but don't be surprised if Francie and the Nolan family remind you of people you know.

FICTION

A Beauty That Broke Hearts

Imagine having the kind of beauty that causes the death of fifty thousand men and the collapse of a great civilization. That is what happens to twelve-year-old Helen when she is kidnapped from her home and brought to the city of Troy. Clemence McLaren's novel *Inside the Walls of Troy* breathes new life into the ancient story of Helen, turning a mythical figure into a believable, flesh-and-blood young woman.

FICTION

Be Yourself

When you read the stories, poems, and plays in *American Dragons,* you'll hear the voices of twenty-five Asian American teenagers expressing their feelings. They are trying to figure out how to fit in and how to be themselves at the same time. In describing their struggles, they express a range of feelings—from rage to sorrow, from worry to wonder.

NONFICTION

The Boy Who Dreamed

Richard Wright's early years were plagued by hunger—for food, for knowledge, and for respect. He wrote stories filled with imagination and longing, and his intelligence left those around him feeling puzzled and threatened. After all, a black boy living in rural Mississippi in the 1920s couldn't go far in life—or could he? Wright's autobiography *Black Boy* is the stunning account of a young man who rose above oppression to live out his dreams.

Writing a Short Story

Writing Assignment
Write a short story in which you use your imagination to express yourself and entertain others.

Have you ever been envious of a classmate, like Vita is of Helen in "Helen on Eighty-sixth Street"? You may have read many short stories and said to yourself, "That could be me." In fact, your life is probably filled with incidents that you could turn into stories. Now is your chance. In this workshop you'll write a **short story** of your own.

Prewriting

Find a Story Idea

On Fancy's Wings   Short stories are works of **fiction.** The characters and events depicted in a short story might be based on real people and actual events, or they might be entirely the product of the writer's imagination. Brainstorm a list of ideas, and choose one as the starting point of your short story. You could write a story based on

- a great adventure you've always dreamed of having
- a historical event that fascinates or inspires you
- a personal experience from which you learned a lesson about life
- an incident from the life of a friend or relative

Plan Your Story

How to Begin   There are five basic ingredients for any story: **plot, characters, point of view, setting,** and **theme.** You will need to use all of these ingredients, or elements, in your short story, but you can *start* by considering any one of them.

Plot   What will happen in your story? The **plot** of a short story centers around a **conflict,** a struggle between opposing forces. Here are some of the different kinds of conflicts found in short stories.

TYPES OF CONFLICTS AND EXAMPLES	
External Conflict: character vs. character	Raul and Thomas compete for the final spot on the basketball team.
character vs. environment	Cassandra fights the storm as she tries to bring her small sailboat safely home.

(continued)

| character vs. situation | Shannon battles tradition to be allowed to play on a boys' baseball team. |
| **Internal Conflict:** character vs. himself or herself (a struggle between conflicting ideas and feelings within a character) | Jason is torn between his desire to help his friend pass an exam and his sense of right and wrong. |

The conflict builds through a sequence of events, called the **rising action,** to a **climax,** the emotional high point of the story. After the climax, events unwind in the **resolution,** which shows the outcome of the conflict and brings the story to an end.

As you develop your plot, use the techniques listed below.

- Use plenty of **narrative details** about the actions, movements, gestures, and feelings of the characters to bring your story to life.

- Arrange your plot events in **chronological order,** the order in which the events actually occur.

- Use **flashbacks** to provide the background information necessary for readers to understand the story.

- **Pace** the action of your plot to reflect the mood you're trying to create. For example, a slow and leisurely pace might depict the events of a lazy summer afternoon. A fast and furious pace might depict the chaotic events of a chase scene.

Characters Who are the people in your story? Because short stories are just that—short—they usually concentrate on one **main character.** As you think of your main character, jot down answers to the following questions to bring that character to life.

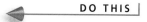 **DO THIS**

- What does your main character look like?

- What are his or her mannerisms?

- How does he or she act, think, feel, talk? (When characters in a story speak, they engage in **dialogue.** To be realistic, dialogue should sound the way real people talk.)

Supporting characters are developed in proportion to their importance in the story. In other words, if a supporting character appears briefly in your story, don't spend time developing that character. Give more detail about a supporting character who plays a key role in your story. To develop supporting characters, answer the same questions you answered to create your main character. You may not end up needing all the details, but you'll have them if you do.

Point of view Who will **narrate,** or tell, your story? Choose one of the following points of view, and use it consistently throughout your story.

 SKILLS FOCUS

Writing Skills
Write a short story. Develop plot, characters, point of view, setting, and theme.

- A **first-person narrator** is either the main character, who tells his or her own story, or a supporting character, who tells the main character's story. The narrator uses the first-person pronoun *I* to tell the story. If you choose to use the first-person point of view, you limit yourself to telling only what the narrator could logically know and what he or she feels, thinks, or experiences.

- A **third-person-omniscient narrator** is not a character in the story, but an outside observer who sees and knows all. This narrator can tell the thoughts, feelings, and actions of any character in the story. He or she can narrate events occurring at the same time in different places. The omniscient narrator can also use **shifting perspectives,** revealing several characters' thoughts, feelings, and attitudes toward the same character or event. Use third-person pronouns—*he, she, they*—if you choose this point of view.

Read the examples below to see the difference your choice of point of view can make in your story.

> **First Person:** I walked to Mrs. Hawkins's house and knocked firmly on the door. When she opened it, I could tell she was surprised to see me. I quickly handed her the sandwich bag I had stored the card in.
>
> **Third Person Omniscient:** As Li walked to Mrs. Hawkins's house, she felt nervous. She knocked firmly on the door. Mrs. Hawkins was surprised to see Li standing on her doorstep. Quickly, Li handed her the sandwich bag that contained the card.

Setting Where and when does your story take place? **Setting** can play a major role in a short story, or it can be relatively unimportant. Use **sensory details**—words describing the sights, sounds, and smells of the setting—to help readers form specific mental pictures.

Setting often plays a role in establishing **mood**—the feeling or atmosphere of the story. For example, the setting of an isolated, old house surrounded by thick forests on a stormy night would contribute to a story's eerie, threatening mood.

Theme What is the **theme** of your story? What idea about life does it illustrate? Most often, stories suggest a theme through the details of characters, plot, setting, and point of view. The themes of most literature, including short stories, have to do with the emotions and experiences that make us human, such as fear, courage, loss, greed, love, and forgiveness.

SKILLS FOCUS

Writing Skills
Use sensory details.

PRACTICE & APPLY 1 Use the instructions in this section to develop the plot, characters, setting, and theme of a short story. Add sensory details to enhance your story.

Writing

Writing a Short Story

A Writer's Framework

Beginning	Middle	End
• Begin with an intriguing event or an engaging introduction to the main character.	• Develop the events of the rising action.	• Make the resolution of the conflict believable.
• Establish the story's setting and the point of view.	• Use narrative and sensory details to develop characters and describe the setting.	• See that the resolution suggests the theme of the story.
• Introduce the conflict that gives rise to the story's plot.	• Bring the conflict to a head in an effective climax.	

A Writer's Model

The Long Lost Baseball Card

Li Hua, a thirteen-year-old baseball fanatic and rabid card collector, lay on her back in her bed. She was about to open the beat-up old book on baseball she'd paid a dollar for that morning at a garage sale. As she opened the dusty book, an object dropped out of it and hit her squarely on the end of her nose, making her sneeze and momentarily blinding her. She grabbed the object and held it away from her face. Her heart jumped in excitement when she saw that it was a Dizzy Dean baseball card. Dean was the great pitcher of the St. Louis Cardinals who won two games during the 1934 World Series. Fifteen minutes later, Li found the card on the Internet. It was worth well over a hundred dollars! What a find! Then she thought of Mrs. Hawkins, the kind woman who had sold her the book for a measly dollar, a book worth well over a hundred dollars, if you counted the card. Mrs. Hawkins's husband had died and she lived alone. She probably could use a hundred dollars.

Li remembered Mrs. Hawkins listening with a warm smile on her face while she rattled on about baseball and what a great find the book was. "I bought the book. The baseball card was in the book," Li said to herself. Mrs. Hawkins obviously doesn't know about the card. What harm would it do for me to keep it?"

Li picked up the phone to call Grandpa Lang and tell him about her discovery. Then, abruptly, she put it down. What would Grandpa Lang

(continued)

BEGINNING
Introduction to main character/Setting

Third-person point of view

Narrative and sensory details

Conflict suggested

MIDDLE

Interior monologue

Rising action

(continued)

say? Would he be excited about the card, or would he be ashamed of her for keeping it? She couldn't stand for Grandpa Lang to be ashamed of her. The mere thought of disappointing him was terrible. At the same time, the card was like a strong magnet drawing her to it. That night she lay awake late into the night, wondering what to do.

Internal conflict

As she tossed and turned, a scene from the past kept playing itself in her head. She and Grandpa Lang were standing in line to pay for the groceries they had bought. When it came time for Grandpa Lang to pay, he handed the cashier a ten-dollar bill. Grandpa didn't look at the change the cashier gave him. Instead, he stuffed it into his pocket, picked up the grocery bag, grabbed Li by the hand, and left the store. When they arrived at Grandpa Lang's house, Grandpa put the grocery bag on the table, emptied his pocket, and counted the change. "That young man gave me too much change," Grandpa Lang said. "He gave me change for a twenty instead of a ten. We must go back to the store, Li, and return the extra money."

Flashback

Narrative and sensory details

Early the next morning, Li walked like a girl with a mission to Mrs. Hawkins's house and knocked firmly on the door. When the small woman answered the door, Li handed her the sandwich bag she'd stored the card in. "Here," she said, "is a card I found in the book you sold me yesterday. It's very valuable, so I knew you would want it back."

Setting

Climax

"That's so sweet of you, dear," Mrs. Hawkins said with a smile. "You know, my late husband was a great baseball fan. He even played on a minor-league team when we were young. He must have put that old card in that book to mark his place. I just know he would want someone who loves baseball as much as he did to have it. That card belongs to you, dear, but thank you for being such an honest young lady. I know your family must be very proud of you."

Dialogue

Li couldn't believe her ears. Her eyes welled up with tears as she poured out her thanks to Mrs. Hawkins and promised her that the card would become a prized part of her collection. Her heart felt so full she thought it might burst as she walked homeward, toward the waiting phone. Now she could call Grandpa Lang. She knew he would be as proud of her as she was of herself.

END

Resolution

Sensory details

Theme

go.hrw.com

INTERNET

More Writer's Models

Keyword: LE7 9-2

PRACTICE & APPLY 2 Refer to the framework on page 157 and the Writer's Model above as you write the first draft of your short story. Return to the Prewriting section of this workshop as necessary to remind yourself of short story elements.

Revising

Revise Your Short Story

Author's Way Professional writers, authors who make their living by writing, are rarely satisfied with the first draft of anything they write. They spend hours rewriting, tweaking, and polishing their works, and even then they are not always satisfied. You should read and evaluate your story at least twice, once for content and organization and again for style. Use the charts below and on the next page as **think sheets** when you revise your story.

PEER REVIEW

Ask a classmate for feedback on your story's content, organization, and style. Have your classmate check for a consistent point of view.

▶ **First Reading: Content and Organization** The guidelines in the chart below can help you evaluate and revise the content and organization of your story.

Rubric: Writing a Short Story

Evaluation Questions	▶ Tips	▶ Revision Techniques
❶ Does the introduction introduce the story's main character? Does it establish the setting and the narrator's point of view?	▶ **Underline** the words that introduce the main character. **Circle** the words that establish the setting. **Put a star** next to the pronoun that reveals the narrator's point of view.	▶ **Add** details to introduce the main character and to establish the setting. **Add** pronouns that clearly show the point of view of the story's narrator.
❷ Does the introduction clearly introduce the story's conflict?	▶ **Highlight** the sentence or sentences that introduce the conflict.	▶ **Add** sentences that make the conflict clear.
❸ Is the plot fully developed and organized in chronological order? Does the climax bring the conflict to a head?	▶ **Number** the events in the rising action. **Bracket** the climax.	▶ **Add** events to make the rising action clearer. **Rearrange** events that are out of order. **Add** details to make the climax more effective.
❹ Is the main character adequately developed?	▶ **Put a check mark** beside any dialogue and the narrative and sensory details that develop the main character.	▶ **Add** dialogue and narrative and sensory details where necessary to develop the main character.
❺ Is the resolution believable? Is the story's theme clear by the end of the story?	▶ **Highlight** the resolution. **Underline** the sentence or sentences that suggest the theme.	▶ **Replace** unrealistic events or details with more believable ones. **Add** a sentence or two to make the theme clearer.

▷ **Second Reading: Style** Now, read and evaluate the style of your short story. Having good ideas for a plot, characters, and theme matters little if you don't engage the attention of your readers with a lively style. One way to ensure a lively, entertaining style is to use **vivid action verbs** that depict the action in your story with color and precision. Look at the examples below.

Dull Verbs	Vivid Verbs
walk	stroll
say	whisper
laugh	snicker

Style Guidelines

Evaluation Question	▸ Tip	▸ Revision Technique
● Does the writer use vivid action verbs to depict action precisely?	▸ **Put a star** by all of the verbs in a passage.	▸ **Replace** dull verbs with precise action verbs.

ANALYZING THE REVISION PROCESS

Study these revisions, and answer the questions that follow.

replace

> *welled up with tears*   *poured out her thanks to*
> Her eyes ~~watered~~ as she ~~thanked~~ Mrs. Hawkins and promised
>
> her that the card would become a prized part of her collection.
>
> Her heart felt so full she thought it might burst as she walked
>
> homeward, toward the waiting phone. *Now she could call*
> *Grandpa Lang. She knew he would be as proud of her as*
> *she was of herself.*

add

Responding to the Revision Process

1. What did the writer accomplish by making the two revisions to the first sentence?

2. Why did the writer add two sentences at the end of the story? Do you think this revision was necessary? Why or why not?

SKILLS FOCUS

Writing Skills
Revise for content and style.

PRACTICE & APPLY ③ Using the guidelines on these two pages, revise the content, organization, and style of your short story. Consider peer comments as you revise.

Publishing

Proofread and Publish Your Short Story

Tidy Tales After you've revised your short story, be sure to proofread it. Who will enjoy reading your short story if it is full of errors? You want your audience to focus on your story, not on mistakes you may have made. Check for and correct any errors in grammar, usage, and mechanics.

Welcome to the World of Publishing Your purpose for writing your short story was to express yourself and to entertain readers. Now that you've expressed your creative side to your classmates or teacher, it's time to publish your work so that others can read it. Here are some ways to present your story to a wider audience.

- Submit your story to a publication that accepts work from young writers. Your teacher or school librarian may have a list of such publications to get you started.

- Collect your class's short stories into a book. Arrange them in sections by theme: science fiction, adventure, drama, westerns, and mystery, for example. Then, put the book in the school library for others to read.

- Put your short story on the Internet by posting it to your own Web site, your school's Web site, or a site that accepts submissions from young writers.

- Rewrite your short story as a children's book. Simplify the plot and dialogue and add illustrations so that a younger audience will understand your story.

Reflect on Your Short Story

20/20 Hindsight Look back on what you've done, and reflect on what you've learned in the process of writing a short story. Use these questions to focus your thoughts.

- How did writing this short story help you understand the process that other authors go through when writing for publication?

- What short story elements do you think were the strongest in your story? Why?

 PRACTICE & APPLY 4 First, proofread your story, paying particular attention to your punctuation of dialogue. Then, publish your story for a wider audience. Finally, reflect on your short story by answering the questions above.

TIP Proofreading will help ensure that your essay follows the **conventions** of standard American English. For example, check to see that you have correctly punctuated dialogue in your story. For more on **using quotation marks,** see Quotation Marks, 13c–j, in the Language Handbook.

COMPUTER TIP

If you have access to a computer and advanced publishing software, use those tools to design and format your class's short stories so that they look more professional. For more on **page design,** see *Designing Your Writing* in the Writer's Handbook.

SKILLS FOCUS

Writing Skills
Proofread, especially for the correct use of quotation marks with dialogue.

Analyzing Character

DIRECTIONS: Read the following short story. Then, read and respond to the questions that follow.

During the Spanish Civil War (1936–1939), the Loyalists, who supported the government of Spain, fought against the Nationalists (Fascists), who were led by General Francisco Franco. "Old Man at the Bridge" is set during this conflict and shows the war's impact on the Spanish people.

Old Man at the Bridge

Ernest Hemingway

An old man with steel rimmed spectacles and very dusty clothes sat by the side of the road. There was a pontoon bridge across the river and carts, trucks, and men, women and children were crossing it. The mule-drawn carts staggered up the steep bank from the bridge with soldiers helping push against the spokes of the wheels. The trucks ground up and away heading out of it all and the peasants plodded along in the ankle deep dust. But the old man sat there without moving. He was too tired to go any farther.

It was my business to cross the bridge, explore the bridgehead beyond and find out to what point the enemy had advanced. I did this and returned over the bridge. There were not so many carts now and very few people on foot, but the old man was still there.

"Where do you come from?" I asked him.

"From San Carlos," he said, and smiled.

That was his native town and so it gave him pleasure to mention it and he smiled.

"I was taking care of animals," he explained.

"Oh," I said, not quite understanding.

"Yes," he said, "I stayed, you see, taking care of animals. I was the last one to leave the town of San Carlos."

He did not look like a shepherd nor a herdsman and I looked at his black dusty clothes and his gray dusty face and his steel rimmed spectacles and said, "What animals were they?"

"Various animals," he said, and shook his head. "I had to leave them."

I was watching the bridge and the African looking country of the Ebro Delta[1] and wondering how long now it would be before we would see the

---

1. **Ebro Delta:** the land at the mouth of the Ebro, the longest river entirely in Spain.

SKILLS FOCUS

Pages 162–165 cover **Literary Skills** Analyze character traits, internal and external conflicts, and motivation.

enemy, and listening all the while for the first noises that would signal that ever mysterious event called contact, and the old man still sat there.

"What animals were they?" I asked.

"There were three animals altogether," he explained. "There were two goats and a cat and then there were four pairs of pigeons."

"And you had to leave them?" I asked.

"Yes. Because of the artillery.[2] The captain told me to go because of the artillery."

"And you have no family?" I asked, watching the far end of the bridge where a few last carts were hurrying down the slope of the bank.

"No," he said, "only the animals I stated. The cat, of course, will be all right. A cat can look out for itself, but I cannot think what will become of the others."

"What politics have you?" I asked.

"I am without politics," he said. "I am seventy-six years old. I have come twelve kilometers now and I think now I can go no further."

"This is not a good place to stop," I said. "If you can make it, there are trucks up the road where it forks for Tortosa."

"I will wait a while," he said, "and then I will go. Where do the trucks go?"

"Towards Barcelona," I told him.

"I know no one in that direction," he said, "but thank you very much. Thank you again very much."

He looked at me very blankly and tiredly, then said, having to share his worry with some one, "The cat will be all right, I am sure. There is no need to be unquiet about the cat. But the others. Now what do you think about the others?"

"Why they'll probably come through it all right."

"You think so?"

"Why not," I said, watching the far bank where now there were no carts.

"But what will they do under the artillery when I was told to leave because of the artillery?"

"Did you leave the dove cage unlocked?" I asked.

"Yes."

---

2. **artillery** (är·til′ər·ē) *n.*: mounted guns, such as cannons.

"Then they'll fly."

"Yes, certainly they'll fly. But the others. It's better not to think about the others," he said.

"If you are rested I would go," I urged. "Get up and try to walk now."

"Thank you," he said and got to his feet, swayed from side to side and then sat down backwards in the dust.

"I was taking care of animals," he said dully, but no longer to me. "I was only taking care of animals."

There was nothing to do about him. It was Easter Sunday and the Fascists were advancing toward the Ebro. It was a gray overcast day with a low ceiling so their planes were not up. That and the fact that cats know how to look after themselves was all the good luck that old man would ever have.

---

1. Why did the old man at the bridge leave his home in San Carlos?
   A   He was taken prisoner by the enemy.
   B   He was fleeing an artillery attack.
   C   He needed medical attention.
   D   He wanted to get help for his animals.

2. The story's most serious **external conflict** is between —
   F   the old man and the narrator
   G   the two main characters and the war
   H   the old man and the soldiers at the bridge
   J   the narrator and the captain

3. The old man faces an **internal conflict** between —
   A   rescuing the cat and saving the goats and pigeons
   B   his loyalty to the government and his belief in the enemy's cause
   C   his desire to take care of his animals and the need to leave his home
   D   crossing the bridge to seek shelter and fleeing to Barcelona

4. The old man can *best* be **characterized** as —
   F   angry and determined
   G   tired and worried
   H   hopeful and encouraging
   J   unconcerned and unfriendly

5. What is the narrator's **motivation** for urging the old man to move on?

  A Concern for the old man's safety

  B The need to carry out his orders

  C Anger at the old man

  D A desire to reunite the old man with his family in Barcelona

6. Several times the narrator says that he was "watching" the bridge or the far bank of the river. What **character trait** does the narrator reveal through this description?

  F Curiosity

  G Bravery

  H Carelessness

  J Alertness

7. What does the old man reveal about himself when he says in his **dialogue** with the narrator, "I am without politics"?

  A He does not care about his native town.

  B He has not taken sides during the war.

  C He is rebelling against the leaders of his country.

  D He is trying to hide his beliefs from the narrator.

8. Which of the following words *best* describes the behavior of the narrator toward the old man?

  F Protective

  G Hostile

  H Indifferent

  J Loving

9. From what the narrator says in the last paragraph about the old man's luck, we can infer that the **narrator** feels —

  A sympathetic and optimistic

  B relieved and carefree

  C powerless and pessimistic

  D superstitious and frightened

10. At the end of the story, we can infer that the **narrator** —

  F leaves the old man to his fate

  G stays to guard the old man

  H deserts the army

  J searches for someone to travel with the old man

Constructed Response

11. At different points in the story, both the old man and the narrator "give up." Identify details and words from the story that show each character's feeling of defeat.

Collection 2: Skills Review

Vocabulary Skills

Context Clues

DIRECTIONS: Use the context clues in the following passages to identify the meaning of the underlined vocabulary words.

1. In "Helen on Eighty-sixth Street," Vita makes up an incantation in order to win the role of Helen and to bring her father back. Although the magical words she says are actually the names of Greek foods, Vita's prayer is heartfelt.
   In this passage, *incantation* means a —
   - **A** curse against an enemy
   - **B** speech praising a dead person
   - **C** blessing giving thanks
   - **D** chant to make something happen

2. In "Helen on Eighty-sixth Street," the audience can understand Vita's lines because she can speak precisely and clearly enunciate her words.
   In this passage, *enunciate* means —
   - **F** shout
   - **G** pronounce
   - **H** quote accurately
   - **J** mumble

3. In "Helen on Eighty-sixth Street," Vita sets forth on a kind of odyssey. However, instead of traveling throughout the world, she goes on a voyage of discovery into her own heart.
   In this passage, *odyssey* means —
   - **A** ordeal
   - **B** journey
   - **C** change
   - **D** education

4. In "Marigolds," Lizabeth tells about her impoverished hometown. People work hard but earn very little money, and many others have lost their jobs.
   In this passage, *impoverished* means —
   - **F** terrified
   - **G** guilty
   - **H** poor
   - **J** unlucky

5. "Feeding Frenzy" describes the obstacles David Levitt faced when he decided to start a food-sharing program. Undaunted, he did not give up and ultimately succeeded.
   In this passage, *undaunted* means —
   - **A** not discouraged
   - **B** proud
   - **C** judgmental
   - **D** furious

6. "Community Service & You" explains that you can learn new skills from volunteering that will help you in your future endeavors, such as finishing school or pursuing a career.
   In this passage, *endeavors* means —
   - **F** years
   - **G** obstacles
   - **H** undertakings
   - **J** knowledge

SKILLS FOCUS

Vocabulary Skills
Identify word meanings using context clues.

Collection 2: Skills Review

Writing Skills

DIRECTIONS: The following paragraph is from a draft of a student's short story. Read the questions below it, and choose the best answer to each question.

(1) After riding twenty-two hours on a train, Amanda was glad to hear the conductor's booming voice call out "Union Station, Chicago." (2) "Spending a month in Canada was great, but I can't wait to see my family!" she thought. (3) She had just enough time on her phone card to call her dad at his office to let him know she was in and needed a ride. (4) She dragged the suitcase to a pay phone and made the call. (5) "Honey, I'm swamped with work, so take the commuter train and I'll pick you up at the depot," Dad said.

1. What words did the writer use to establish the setting?
   A "Amanda was glad to hear . . . 'Union Station, Chicago.'"
   B "had just enough time on her phone card"
   C "I can't wait to see my family!"
   D "a month in Canada was great"

2. Which of the following sentences would add sensory details?
   F Amanda's family lived about thirty miles outside of Chicago.
   G Amanda had brought a souvenir for her grandmother.
   H The steamy Chicago summer heat hit her like a slap in the face.
   J Her dad ran his own business.

3. Why did the writer put sentence 5 in quotation marks?
   A The sentence is dialogue.
   B It is the title of the story.
   C It is the conflict of the story.
   D The sentence creates suspense.

4. Which of the following sentences, if added, would tell the conflict of the story?
   F A child clutched his parent's hand as he exited the train.
   G When Amanda hung up, she realized that she had only Canadian money.
   H Amanda thought about the photos she would show her family.
   J Inside the station, it was noisy, crowded, and hot.

5. Which of the following sentences could be added to effectively describe the appearance of the main character?
   A The chubby conductor smiled broadly at the departing passengers.
   B Her dad was a small, wiry man who worked too hard.
   C Amanda said goodbye to the woman she had sat next to on the train.
   D The tall, brown-eyed girl getting off the train was tired and hungry.

SKILLS FOCUS

Writing Skills
Write a short story.

Truth and Consequences

Literary Focus:
Analyzing Narrator and Voice

Informational Reading Focus:
Synthesizing Sources: Main Ideas and Supporting Evidence

INTERNET

Collection Resources

Keyword: LE7 9-3

In the Summer House (1958)
by George Tooker (b. 1920).
Egg tempera on gessoed panel.
20 x 24 in. Artwork © George Tooker.

Elements of Literature

Narrator and Voice *by* John Leggett

WHO'S TALKING?

When you read a story, you hear some-one—the narrator—telling the story. The narrator controls everything we know about the characters and events. There are three main types of narrators, or **points of view: omniscient** (äm·nish′ənt), **first person,** and **third person limited.**

Omniscient Point of View: The All-Knowing Storyteller

When the **omniscient point of view** is used, the narrator is not a character in the story and almost never refers to him-self or herself directly. *Omniscient* means "all-knowing," and the omniscient narra-tor is able to tell us everything about every character (including how each one thinks and feels). Let's look at a story told from the omniscient point of view:

One day a young woman looked out her apartment window and saw a man playing a saxophone. "Cool," she thought as she swayed to his tune. A big brown dog joined the man and howled along with the music.

Then a man in pajamas yelled from an-other window, complaining that the noise woke him up and he was going to call the police. This man, who worked the night shift and had to sleep all day, liked cats better than dogs anyway. The young saxo-phonist left.

The First-Person Point of View: "I" as the Storyteller

Unlike the all-knowing omniscient narra-tor, the **first-person narrator** is a char-acter in the story who talks to us, using *I,*

the first-person pronoun. (Literary critics sometimes use the term **persona** to refer to a first-person narrator.)

We get a very personal view of what is happening from a first-person narrator, but we know *only* what he or she thinks and experiences and is able—or chooses —to tell us. Always question whether a first-person narrator is **credible,** or can be trusted. An **unreliable narrator** is biased and does not (or cannot) tell the truth. Let's look at our story told by the man in pajamas, for example. Would you consider his opinion of the music reliable?

Oh, man! Just as I was finally dozing off, he starts playing that stupid saxophone. I've already been fired from one job be-cause I fell asleep on the night shift. Now it's going to happen again. I don't know which sounds worse, that tone-deaf saxo-phonist or that yowling dog. I'm going to call the police.

Third Person Limited: Focus on One Character

In the **third-person-limited point of view,** the storyteller zooms in on just one character but talks about the character in the third person, using *he* or *she.* With this point of view, we share one charac-ter's reactions to everything that happens in the story, but what we know about the other characters is limited. Suppose we hear our story from this point of view, focusing on the saxophone player:

He found a good spot in front of Park View Apartments and started playing soulfully on his sax. He wanted an audience and

SKILLS FOCUS

Literary Skills
Understand narrators, or points of view (omniscient, first person, and third person limited), tone, and voice.

INTERNET

More About Narrator and Voice

Keyword: LE7 9-3

needed money. After one song, he spotted a cute girl at a window, applauding madly. A dog howled with the music, but the sax player let him stay, hoping the dog might attract some donations. Then he heard a man yelling about calling the police—clearly not a music lover.

Tone: Watch That Attitude!

A story's tone can be described in a single word: joyous, somber, humorous, serious, angry, tender, ironic. **Tone** is the attitude a speaker or writer takes toward a subject, character, or audience.

If you change a story's point of view, you may change the tone as well. For example, how might the tone of the saxophonist's story be different if the young woman were telling the story instead of the man in pajamas?

Voice: One-of-a-Kind Style

Tone is one aspect of the **voice** that characterizes a piece of writing. Voice refers to the writer's use of language and overall style, and it's created by the writer's tone and choice of words (**diction**). Often you can identify the author of a piece of writing from the voice. Sometimes writers purposely switch voices, or their voice may change over time, but usually a writer's voice remains the same from work to work.

In fiction, narrators can also be said to have a voice, which is created by their manner of speaking, word choice, and tone. The narrator's voice can affect our view of characters and plot events and

shape the tone of the story as a whole. Imagine, if you will, the big brown dog telling our story.

Practice

Write a paragraph telling the saxophone story from the point of view of the young woman or the big brown dog. Use either the first-person or the third-person-limited point of view, and try to create a distinct voice. Remember to show what the character is thinking and feeling.

I remember well my sensation as we first entered the house. I knew instantly that something was very wrong. I realized that my father's chair had been sat in, as well as my mother's and my own. The porridge we had left on the table to cool had been partially eaten. None of this, however, prepared me for what we were about to discover upstairs. . . .

Truth and Consequences

Make the Connection

Quickwrite ✏️

Think about a mystery story you've read or seen on TV or in the movies. Summarize the story in a few sentences. What truth is revealed? What are the consequences? Then, explain whether you would recommend this mystery to a friend. In your opinion, what makes a mystery story good?

Exploring the Theme: Truth and Consequences

Every day we encounter real stories in the news or fictional stories, like the ones in this collection, that contain surprising—or even shocking—truths and consequences. In "The Interlopers" two bitter enemies face the consequences of a freakish act of nature. In "The Necklace" a high price is paid for hiding the truth. Two characters play a horrifying game of truth and consequences in "The Cask of Amontillado." You'll also read about the search for the true cause of Edgar Allan Poe's death.

"Full Circle," the story you're about to read, is a detective story—the kind of story often called a whodunit. In such stories an investigator tries to solve a mystery by uncovering the truth, and the consequences of the search usually come as shockers.

Literary Focus

Narrator and Voice

This story is told by Kinsey Millhone, the **first-person narrator** and hero of the popular mystery series written by Sue Grafton. As you read, you'll follow along with private detective Millhone and know only what she knows as she searches for the truth. You'll notice that Millhone is a bit tough and uses colorful slang when she speaks, just like many other fictional detectives. Pay attention to clues about her character—to her actions and words—as you read. Listen to her **voice**—her manner of speaking, word choice, and tone.

SKILLS FOCUS

Literary Skills
Understand the first-person narrator and voice.

Compression Ricard (1962). César Baldaccini (1921–1998). Musée National d'Art Moderne, Centre Georges Pompidou, Paris. Compressed automobile parts. 153 x 73 x 65 cm.

©2007 Artists Rights Society (ARS), New York/ADAGP, Paris.

Full Circle

Sue Grafton

The accident seemed to happen in slow motion . . . one of those stop-action sequences that seem to go on forever though in truth no more than a few seconds have elapsed. It was Friday afternoon, rush hour, Santa Teresa traffic moving at a lively pace, my little VW holding its own despite the fact that it's fifteen years out of date. I was feeling good. I'd just wrapped up a case and I had a check in my handbag for four thousand bucks, not bad considering that I'm a female private eye,[1] self-employed, and subject to the feast-or-famine vagaries[2] of any other free-lance work. ❶

I glanced to my left as a young woman, driving a white compact, appeared in my side view mirror. A bright red Porsche was bearing down on her in the fast lane. I adjusted my speed, making room for her, sensing that she meant to cut in front of me. A navy-blue pickup truck was coming up on my right, each of us jockeying for position as the late afternoon sun washed down out of a cloudless California spring sky. I had glanced in my rearview mirror, checking traffic behind me, when I heard a loud popping noise. I snapped my attention back to the road in front of me. The white compact veered abruptly back into the fast lane, clipped the rear of the red Porsche, then hit the center divider and careened directly into my path. I slammed on my brakes, adrenaline shooting through me as I fought to control the VW's fishtailing rear end. ❷

Suddenly a dark green Mercedes appeared from out of nowhere and caught the girl's car broadside, flipping the vehicle with all the expertise of a movie stunt. Brakes squealed all around me like a chorus of squawking birds and I could hear the successive thumps of colliding cars piling up behind me in a drumroll of destruction. It was over in an instant, a cloud of dust roiling up from the shoulder where the girl's car had finally come to rest, right side

---

1. **private eye** *n.:* slang for "private detective."
2. **vagaries** (vā′gə•rēz) *n.:* unexpected, unusual, or unpredictable events.

NARRATOR AND VOICE

❶ What does the **narrator** tell you about herself in this paragraph? What do you notice about her **voice**—her way of speaking and choice of words?

THEME

❷ What do you **predict** the cause of the loud popping noise will turn out to be?

Fire and Destruction
(1985) by Jüri Palm
(b. 1937). Art
Museum of Estonia,
Tallinn, Estonia.
Oil on canvas.
140.5 x 115 cm.

up, half-buried in the shrubbery. She had sheared off one of the support posts for the exit sign that now leaned crazily across her car roof. The ensuing silence was profound.

I pulled over and was out of my car like a shot, the fellow from the navy-blue pickup truck right behind me. There must have been five of us running toward the wreckage, spurred by the possibility of exploding gasoline, which mercifully did not ignite. The white car was accordion-folded, the door on the driver's side jammed shut. Steam billowed out from under the hood with an alarming hiss. The impact had rammed the girl head first into the wind-shield, which had cracked in a star-burst effect. She was unconscious, her face bathed in blood. I willed myself to move toward her though my instinct was to turn away in horror.

The guy from the pickup truck nearly wrenched the car door off its hinges in one of those emergency-generated bursts of strength that can't be duplicated under ordinary circumstances. As he reached for her, I caught his arm.

"Don't move her," I said. "Let the paramedics³ handle this."

He gave me a startled look but drew back as he was told. I shed my wind-breaker and we used it to form a compress, stanching the flow of blood from

---

3. **paramedics** (par′ə•med′iks) *n.:* people who provide emergency medical care.

the worst of her cuts. The guy was in his twenties, with dark curly hair and dark eyes filled with anxiety.

Over my shoulder, someone was asking me if I knew first aid, and I realized that others had been hurt in the accident as well. The driver from the green Mercedes was already using the roadside emergency phone, presumably calling police and ambulance. I looked back at the guy from the pickup truck, who was pressing the girl's neck, looking for a pulse.

"Is she alive?" I asked.

"Looks like it."

I jerked my head at the people on the berm[4] behind me. "Let me see what I can do down there until the ambulance comes," I said. "Holler if you need me." ❸

He nodded in reply.

I left him with the girl and moved along the shoulder toward a writhing man whose leg was visibly broken. A woman was sobbing hysterically somewhere close by and her cries added an eerie counterpoint to the moans of those in pain. The fellow from the red Porsche simply stood there numb, immobilized by shock.

Meanwhile, traffic had slowed to a crawl and commuters were rubbernecking as if freeway accidents were some sort of spectator sport and this was the main event. Sirens approached. The next hour was a blur of police and emergency vehicles. I spotted my friend John Birkett, a photographer from the local paper, who'd reached the scene moments behind the paramedics. I remember marveling at the speed with which news of the pileup had spread. I watched as the girl was loaded into the ambulance. While flashbulbs went off, several of us gave our accounts of the accident to the highway patrol officer, conferring with one another compulsively as if repetition might relieve us of tension and distress. I didn't get home until nearly seven and my hands were still shaking. The jumble of images made sleep a torment of sudden awakenings, my foot jerking in a dream sequence as I slammed on my brakes again and again.

When I read in the morning paper that the girl had died, I felt sick with regret. The article was brief. Caroline Spurrier was twenty-two, a senior psychology major at the University of California, Santa Teresa. She was a native of Denver, Colorado, just two months short of graduation at the time of her death. The photograph showed shoulder-length blond hair, bright eyes, and an impish grin. According to the paper, six other people had suffered injuries, none fatal. The weight of the young woman's death settled in my chest like a cold I couldn't shake.

---

4. **berm** (burm) *n.*: edge or shoulder of a road.

Introducing the Collection Theme

NARRATOR

❸ As the reader, you view the man from the pickup truck through the **first-person narrator's** eyes. What impression do you have of him?

My office in town was being repainted, so I worked at home that next week, catching up on reports. On Thursday, when the knock came, I'd just broken for lunch. I opened the door. At first glance, I thought the dead girl was miraculously alive, restored to health, and standing on my doorstep with all the solemnity of a ghost. The illusion was dispelled. A close look showed a blond woman in her midforties, her face etched with weariness.

"I'm Michelle Spurrier," she said. "I understand you were a witness to my daughter's accident."

I stepped back. "Please come in. I'm sorry for your loss, Mrs. Spurrier. That was terrible."

She moved past me like a sleepwalker as I closed the door.

"Please sit down. Can I get you anything?"

She shook her head, looking around with bewilderment as if she couldn't quite remember what had brought her here. She set her purse aside and sank down on my couch, placing her cupped hands across her nose and mouth like an oxygen mask.

I sat down beside her, watching as she breathed deeply, struggling to speak. "Take your time," I said.

When the words came, her voice was so low I had to lean closely to hear her. "The police examined Caroline's car at the impound lot[5] and found a bullet hole in the window on the passenger side. My daughter was shot." She burst into tears. ❹

I sat beside her while she poured out a grief tinged with rage and frustration. I brought her a glass of water and a fistful of tissues, small comfort, but all I could think to do. "What are the police telling you?" I asked when she'd composed herself.

She blew her nose and then took another deep breath. "The case has been transferred from traffic detail to homicide.[6] The officer I talked to this morning says it looks like a random freeway shooting, but I don't believe it."

"God knows they've had enough of those down in Los Angeles," I remarked.

"Well, I can't accept that. For one thing, what was she doing speeding down the highway at that hour of the day? She was supposed to be at work, but they tell me she left abruptly without a word to anyone."

"Where was she employed?"

"A restaurant out in Colgate. She'd been waiting tables there for a year. The shift manager told me a man had been harassing[7] her. He thinks she might have left to try to get away from him."

"Did he know who the guy was?"

She shook her head. "He wasn't sure. Some fellow she'd been dating.

---

5. **impound lot** *n.*: place where cars seized by the police are kept.
6. **homicide** (häm′ə•sīd′) *n.*: murder or manslaughter (killing someone without evil intentions).
7. **harassing** (hə•ras′iŋ) *v.*: making repeated threats or demands.

Apparently, he kept stopping by the restaurant, calling her at all hours, making a terrible pest of himself. Lieutenant Dolan tells me you're a private detective, which is why I'm here. I want you to find out who's responsible for this." ❺

"Mrs. Spurrier, the police here are very competent. I'm sure they're doing everything possible."

"Skip the public relations message," she said with bitterness. "I have to fly back to Denver. Caroline's stepfather is very ill and I need to get home, but I can't go unless I know someone here is looking into this. Please."

I thought about it briefly, but it didn't take much to persuade me. As a witness to the accident, I felt more than a professional interest in the case. "I'll need the names of her friends," I said.

I made a note of Mrs. Spurrier's address and phone number, along with the name of Caroline's roommate and the restaurant where she'd worked. I drew up a standard contract, waiving the advance. I'd bill her later for whatever time I put in. Ordinarily I bypass police business in an attempt to stay out of Lieutenant Dolan's way. As the officer in charge of homicide, he's not crazy about private eyes. Though he's fairly tolerant of me, I couldn't imagine what she'd had to threaten to warrant[8] the referral.

As soon as she left, I grabbed a jacket and my handbag and drove over to the police station, where I paid six dollars for a copy of the police report. Lieutenant Dolan wasn't in, but I spent a few minutes chatting with Emerald, the clerk in Identification and Records. She's a heavy black woman in her fifties, usually wary of my questions but a sucker for gossip.

"I hear Jasper's wife caught him with Rowena Hairston," I said, throwing out some bait. Jasper Sax is one of Emerald's interdepartmental foes.

"Why tell me?" she said. She was pretending disinterest, but I could tell the rumor cheered her. Jasper, from the crime lab, is forever lifting files from Emerald's desk, which only gets her in trouble when Lieutenant Dolan comes around.

"I was hoping you'd fill me in on the Spurrier accident. I know you've memorized all the paperwork."

She grumbled something about flattery that implied she felt flattered, so I pressed for specifics. "Anybody see where the shot was fired from?" I asked.

"No ma'am."

I thought about the fellow in the red Porsche. He'd been in the lane to my left, just a few yards ahead of me when the accident occurred. The man in the pickup might be a help as well. "What about the other witnesses? There must have been half a dozen of us at the scene. Who's been interviewed?"

Emerald gave me an indignant look. "What's the matter with you? You know I'm not allowed to give out information like that!"

---

8. **warrant** (wôr′ənt) v.: authorize; justify.

NARRATOR

❺ Since the story is told by a **first-person narrator,** you know only what the narrator knows. What questions do you have at this point in the story?

Freeway 280 (1977) by
Wayne Thiebaud
(b. 1920). Oil on
canvas. 20 x 24 in.
Private Collection. Art
©Wayne Thiebaud/Licensed
by VAGA, New York, NY.

"Worth a try," I said equably. "What about the girl's professors from the
university? Has Dolan talked to them?"

"Check it out yourself if you're so interested," she snapped.

"Come on, Emerald. Dolan knows I'm doing this. He was the one who
told Mrs. Spurrier about me in the first place. I'll make it easy for you.
Just one name."

She squinted at me suspiciously. "Which one's that?"

I took a flier,[9] describing the guy in the pickup, figuring she could
identify him from the list by age. Grudgingly, she checked the list and her
expression changed.

"Uh-oh," she said. "I might know you'd zero in on this one. Fellow in
the pickup gave a phony name and address. Benny Seco was the name,
but he must have made that up. Telephone was a fake, too. Looks like he
took off and nobody's seen him since. Might have been a warrant[10] out
against him he was trying to duck." **6**

"How about the guy in the Porsche?"

I heard a voice behind me. "Well, well, well. Kinsey Millhone. Hard at
work, I see."

---

9. **took a flier:** informal for "took a chance."
10. **warrant** (wôr′ənt) *n.:* in law, an order authorizing the police to make an arrest or
conduct a search.

THEME

6 How does Kinsey
Millhone succeed in
getting information
from Emerald?

Emerald faded into the background with all the practice of a spy. I turned to find Lieutenant Dolan standing in the hallway in his habitual pose: hands shoved down in his pants pockets, rocking on his heels. He'd recently celebrated a birthday, his baggy face reflecting every one of his sixty years.

I folded the police report and tucked it in my bag. "Mrs. Spurrier got in touch with me and asked me to follow up on this business of her daughter's death. I feel bad about the girl."

His manner shifted. "I do, too," he said.

"What's the story on the missing witness?"

Dolan shrugged. "He must have had some reason to give out a phony name. Did you talk to him at the scene?"

"Just briefly, but I'd know him if I saw him again. Do you think he could be of help?"

Dolan ran a hand across his balding pate. "I'd sure like to hear what the fellow has to say. Nobody else was aware that the girl was shot. I gather he was close enough to have done it himself."

"There's gotta be a way to track him down, don't you think?"

"Maybe," he said. "No one remembers much about the man except the truck he drove. Toyota, dark blue, maybe four or five years old from what they say."

"Would you object if I checked back with the other witnesses? I might get more out of them since I was there."

He studied me for a moment, then reached over to the file and removed the list of witnesses, which he handed to me without a word.

"Don't you need this?" I said, surprised.

"I have a copy."

"Thanks. This is great. I'll let you know what I find out." ❼

Dolan pointed a finger. "Keep in touch with the department. I don't want you going off half-cocked."[11]

I drove out to the campus area to the restaurant where Caroline Spurrier had worked. The place had changed hands recently, the decor downgraded from real plants to fake as the nationality of the food changed from Mexican to Thai. The shift manager, David Cole, was just a kid himself, barely twenty-two, tall, skinny, with a nose that belonged on a much larger face.

I introduced myself and told him I was looking into Caroline's death.

"Oh, yeah, that was awful. I talked to her mom."

"She says you mentioned some guy who'd been bugging her. What else can you tell me?"

---

11. **going off half-cocked:** acting thoughtlessly or too quickly.

THEME

❼ Why do you think Dolan helps Millhone in her search for the truth by giving her the witness list?

"That's about all I know. I mean, I never saw the guy myself. She was working nights for the last couple months and just switched back to days to see if she could get away from him."

"She ever mention his name?"

"Terry something, I think. She said he used to follow her around in this green van he drove. She really thought the dude was bent."

"Bent?"

"You know . . . twisted." He twiddled an index finger beside his head to indicate his craziness.

"Why'd she go out with him?"

"She said he seemed like a real nice guy at first, but then he got real possessive, all jealous and like that. In the end, I guess he was totally nuts. He must have showed up on Friday, which is why she took off."

I quizzed him, but couldn't glean much more from his account. I thanked him and drove over to the block of university housing where Caroline had lived. The apartment was typical of student digs; faintly shabby, furnished with mismatched items that had probably been languishing in someone's garage. Her roommate was a young woman named Judy Layton, who chatted despondently as she emptied kitchen cabinets and packed assorted cardboard boxes. I kept the questions light at first, asking her about herself as she wrapped some dinner plates in newspaper, shoving each in a box. She was twenty-two, a senior English major with family living in town.

"How long did you know Caroline?"

"About a year," she said. "I had another roommate, but Alice graduated last year. Caroline and I connected up through one of those roommate referral services."

"How come you're moving out?"

She shrugged. "Going back to my folks'. It's too late in the school year to find someone else and I can't afford this place on my own. My brother's on his way over to help me move."

According to her, Caroline was a "party-hearty" who somehow managed to keep her grades up and still have a good time.

"Did she have a boyfriend?"

"She dated lots of guys."

"But no one in particular?"

She shook her head, intent on her work.

I tried again. "She told her mom about some guy harassing her at work. Apparently she'd dated him and they'd just broken up. Do you have any idea who she might have been talking about?"

"Not really. I didn't keep track of the guys in her life."

"She must have mentioned this guy if he was causing such a fuss."

"Look. She and I were not close. We were roommates and that was it. She went her way and I went mine. If some guy was bugging her, she didn't say a word to me."

"She wasn't in any trouble that you knew about?"

"No."

Her manner seemed sullen and it was getting on my nerves. I stared at her. "Judy, I could use a little help. People get murdered for a reason. It might seem stupid or insignificant to the rest of us, but there was *something* going on. What gives?"

"You don't know it was murder. The policeman I talked to said it might have been some bozo in a passing car."

"Her mother disagrees."

"Well, I can't help you. I already told you everything I know." ❽

I nailed her with a look and let a silence fall, hoping her discomfort would generate further comment. No such luck. If she knew more, she was determined to keep it to herself. I left a business card, asking her to phone me if she remembered anything.

I spent the next two days talking to Caroline Spurrier's professors and friends. From the portrait that emerged, she seemed like a likable kid, funny, good-natured, popular, and sweet. She'd complained of the harassment to a couple of classmates without giving any indication who the fellow was. I went back to the list of witnesses at the scene of the accident, talking to each in turn. I was still tantalized by the guy in the pickup. What reason could he have to falsify his identity?

I'd clipped out the news account of Caroline Spurrier's death, pinning her picture on the bulletin board above my desk. She looked down at me with a smile that seemed more enigmatic with the passing days. I couldn't bear the idea of having to tell her mother my investigation was at an impasse,[12] but I knew I owed her a report.

I was sitting at my typewriter when an idea came to me, quite literally, in a flash. I was staring at the newspaper picture of the wreckage when I spotted the photo credit. I suddenly remembered John Birkett at the scene, his flash going off as he shot pictures of the wreck. If he'd inadvertently snapped one of the guy in the pickup, at least I'd have something to show the cops. Maybe we could get a lead on the fellow that way. I gave Birkett a call. Twenty minutes later, I was in his cubbyhole at the Santa Teresa *Dispatch,* our heads bent together while we scanned the contact sheets.[13] ❾

"No good," John said. "This one's not bad, but the focus is off. . . . I never really got a clear shot of him."

"What about the truck?"

---

12. **impasse** (im′pas′) *n.:* standstill; point at which no progress can be made.
13. **contact sheets** *n.:* sheets of paper containing rows of small prints of photographs.

NARRATOR

❽ The **narrator's** knowledge, along with the reader's, is restricted to what Judy Layton chooses to reveal. Do you think Judy is telling the truth when she says she's told the narrator everything she knows? Why or why not?

THEME

❾ What do you learn from this paragraph about the way Millhone tracks down leads in an investigation?

John pulled out another contact sheet that showed various views of the wrecked compact, the pickup visible on the berm behind. "Well, you can see it in the background, if that's any help."

"Can we get an enlargement?"

"You looking for anything in particular?"

"The license plate," I said.

The California plate bore a seven-place combination of numbers and letters that we finally discerned in the grainy haze of the two blowups. I should have called Lieutenant Dolan and had him run the license number, but I confess to an egotistical[14] streak that sometimes overrides common sense. I didn't want to give the lead back to him just yet. I called a pal of mine at the Department of Motor Vehicles and asked him to check it out instead. ❿

The license plate was registered to a 1984 Toyota pickup, navy blue, the owner listed as Ron Cagle with an address on McClatchy Way.

The house was stucco, dark gray, with the trim done in white. My heart was pounding as I rang the bell. The fellow's face was printed so indelibly in my memory that when the door was finally opened, I just stood there and stared. Wrong man. This guy was probably six foot seven, over two hundred pounds, with a strong chin, ruddy complexion, blue eyes, auburn hair, red moustache. "Yes?"

"I'm looking for Ron Cagle."

"I'm Ron Cagle."

"You are?" My voice broke in astonishment like a kid reaching puberty. "You're the owner of a navy-blue Toyota pickup?" I read off the number of the license plate.

He looked at me quizzically. "Yes. Is something wrong?"

"Well, I don't know. Has someone else been driving it?"

"Not for the last six months."

"Are you sure?"

He half laughed. "See for yourself. It's sitting on the parking pad just behind the house."

He pulled the door shut behind him, leading the way as the two of us moved off the porch and down the driveway to the rear. There sat the navy-blue Toyota pickup, without wheels, up on blocks. The hood was open and there was empty space where the engine should have been. "What's going on?" he asked.

"That's what I'm about to ask you. This truck was at the scene of a recent accident where a girl was killed."

---

14. **egotistical** (ē′go•tist′i•cäl) *adj.:* self-centered; conceited.

"Not this one," he said. "This has been right here."

Without another word, I pulled out the photographs. "Isn't that your license plate?"

He studied the photos with a frown. "Well, yes, but the truck isn't mine. It couldn't be." He glanced back at his pickup, spotting the discrepancy.[15] "There's the problem . . ." He pointed to the license. The plate on the truck was an altogether different set of numbers.

It took me about thirty seconds before the light finally dawned. "Somebody must have lifted your plates and substituted these."

"What would be the point?"

I shrugged. "Maybe someone stole a navy-blue Toyota truck and wanted plates that would clear a license check if he was stopped by the cops. Can I use your telephone?"

I called Lieutenant Dolan and told him what I'd found. He ran a check on the plates for the pickup sitting in the drive that turned out to match the numbers on a vehicle reported stolen two weeks before. An APB[16] was issued for the truck with Cagle's plates. Dolan's guess was

---

15. **discrepancy** (di•skrep′ən•sē) *n.:* inconsistency; difference.
16. **APB:** abbreviation for "all-points bulletin," an announcement sent out to alert police.

Dick's Union General (1971)
by Ralph Goings (b. 1928).
Oil on linen. 40 x 56 in.
Courtesy Louis K. Meisel Gallery.

that the guy had left the state, or abandoned the pickup shortly after the accident. It was also possible that even if we found the guy, he might not have any real connection with the shooting death. Somehow I doubted it.

A week passed with no results. The silence was discouraging. I was right back where I started from with no appreciable progress. If a case is going to break, it usually happens fast, and the chances of cracking this one were diminishing with every passing day. Caroline Spurrier's photograph was still pinned to the bulletin board above my desk, her smile nearly mocking as the days went by. In situations like this, all I know to do is go back to the beginning and start again.

Doggedly I went through the list of witnesses, calling everybody on the list. Most tried to be helpful, but there was really nothing new to add. I drove back to the campus to look for Caroline's roommate. Judy Layton had to know something more than she'd told me at first. Maybe I could find a way to worm some information out of her.

The apartment was locked, and a quick peek in the front window showed that all the furniture was gone. I picked up her forwarding address from the manager on the premises and headed over to her parents' house in Colgate, the little suburb to the north.

The house was pleasant, a story and a half of stucco and frame, an attached three-car garage visible at the right. I rang the bell and waited, idly scanning the neighborhood from my vantage point on the porch. It was a nice street, wide and treelined, with a grassy divider down the center planted with pink and white flowering shrubs. I rang the bell again. Apparently no one was home.

I went down the porch steps and paused in the driveway, intending to return to my car, which was parked at the curb. I hesitated where I stood. There are times in this business when a hunch is a hunch . . . when a little voice in your gut tells you something's amiss.[17] I turned with curiosity toward the three-car garage at the rear. I cupped my hands, shading my eyes so I could peer through the side window. In the shadowy interior, I saw a pickup, stripped of paint. ⓫

I tried the garage's side entrance. The door was unlocked and I pushed my way in. The space smelled of dust, motor oil, and primer. The pickup's license plates were gone. This had to be the same truck, though I couldn't think why it hadn't been dumped. Maybe it was too perilous[18] to attempt at this point. Heart thumping, I did a quick search of the cab's interior. Under the front seat, on the driver's side, I saw a handgun, a .45. I left it where it was, eased the cab door shut,

THEME

⓫ In your own words, explain what leads Millhone to search the garage.

---

17. **amiss** (ə•mis') *adj.:* wrong.
18. **perilous** (per'ə•ləs) *adj.:* dangerous.

and backed away from the truck. Clearly, someone in the Layton household had been at the murder scene.

I left the garage at a quick clip, trotting toward the street. I had to find a telephone and call the cops. I had just started my car, shoving it into gear, when I saw a dark green VW van pass on the far side of the divider and circle back in my direction, headed toward the Laytons' drive. The fellow driving was the man I'd seen at the accident. Judy's brother? The similarities were obvious, now that I thought of it. No wonder she'd been unwilling to tell me what was going on! He slowed for the turn, and that's when he spotted me.

If I'd had any doubts about his guilt, they vanished the minute he and I locked eyes. His surprise was replaced by panic, and he gunned his engine, taking off. I peeled after him, flooring it. At the corner he skidded sideways and recovered, speeding out of sight. I went after him, zigzagging crazily through a residential area that was laid out like a maze. I could almost chart his course ahead of me by the whine of his transmission. He was heading toward the freeway.

At the overpass, I caught a glimpse of him in the southbound lane. He wasn't hard to track, the boxy shape of the van clearly visible as we tore toward town. The traffic began to slow, massing in one of those inexplicable logjams on the road. I couldn't tell if the problem was a fender-bender in the northbound lane, or a bottleneck in ours, but it gave me the advantage I needed. I was catching him.

As I eased up on his left, I saw him lean on the accelerator, cutting to his right. He hit the shoulder of the road, his tires spewing out gravel as he widened the gap between us. He was bypassing stalled cars, hugging the shrubbery as he flew down the berm. I was right behind him, keeping as close to him as I dared. My car wasn't very swift, but then neither was his van. I jammed my accelerator to the floor and pinned myself to his tail. He was watching me steadily in his rearview mirror, our eyes meeting in a deadlock of determination and grit.

I spotted the maintenance crew just seconds before he did; guys in bright orange vests working with a crane that was parked squarely in his path. There was no way for him to slow in time and no place else to go. His van plowed into the rear of the crane with a crash that made my blood freeze as I slammed on my brakes. I was luckier than he. My VW came to a stop just a kiss away from death.

Like a nightmare, we repeated all the horror of the first wreck. Police and paramedics, the wailing of the ambulance. When I finally stopped shaking, I realized where I was. The road crew was replacing the big green highway sign sheared in half when Caroline Spurrier's car had smashed into it. Terry Layton died at the very spot where he killed her. **⑫**

Caroline's smile has shifted back to impishness in the photograph above my desk. I keep it there as a reminder, but of what I couldn't say. The brevity of life, perhaps, the finality of death . . . the irony of events that sometimes connect the two. We live in a world in which justice is skewed.[19]

---

19. **skewed** (sky o͞od) *v.:* twisted; distorted.

THEME

⑫ Do you think Terry Layton's death is a fitting consequence of his actions? Explain.

Meet the Writer
Sue Grafton

M Is for Mystery

The fictional detective Kinsey Millhone began her life in the 1982 novel *"A" Is for Alibi,* a book Sue Grafton (1940–) wrote after spending a number of miserable years working in Hollywood as a screenwriter. Since writing that first book, Grafton has been working her way through the alphabet— producing *"B" Is for Burglar, "C" Is for Corpse,* and so on—by publishing a Kinsey Millhone mystery almost every year or two for more than two decades. Some readers admire Kinsey Millhone so much that they've named their daughters after her. "Originally they were naming their dogs and cats Kinsey, so I think I'm moving up the food chain," remarks Grafton.

Grafton, who was born in Louisville, Kentucky, and was an English major at the University of Louisville, now divides her time between Santa Barbara, California, a town much like Santa Teresa in her fiction, and her hometown of Louisville. While Kinsey Millhone should not be mistaken for the author, Grafton admits the character is "a stripped-down version" of herself. "It is fun," Grafton says, to "get to live her life and mine."

After You Read

Response and Analysis

Reading Check

1. List the evidence in the story that proves Terry Layton murdered Caroline Spurrier.

Thinking Critically

2. The **first-person narrator** plays a key role in the story, because she is also the main character. Think about what Kinsey Millhone's actions, statements, and **voice** (her way of speaking) reveal about her. Then, using examples from the story, describe Millhone.

3. Why does Kinsey Millhone ultimately solve the case and discover the truth? Does she succeed because of her attitude, investigative skills, luck, or a combination of these or other factors? Explain your answer.

4. Explain why you think the author titled this story "Full Circle." Then, describe how the collection theme "Truth and Consequences" relates to the **title.** What does the title tell you about facing consequences in the story?

Extending and Evaluating

5. Because the story is told from the **first-person point of view,** we see events through Kinsey Millhone's eyes. How would the story be different if another character, such as Lieutenant Dolan or Judy Layton, were the narrator? Do you think the author made the right choice by deciding to have Millhone tell the story? Explain.

6. Review your Quickwrite notes in which you explained what makes a mystery story good. Then, evaluate "Full Circle." In your opinion, which parts of the story are the most successful? Are any details in the story not believable? Are you left with any unanswered questions about the characters, the murder, or the search for the murderer? (For example, why does Terry Layton stop at the crime scene?) Explain your response.

Exploring the Theme
Truth and Consequences

In the rest of this collection, you'll read about characters and people who face the truth in some way. As you read, think about why these individuals (or even the reader) have a hard time determining the truth. When the truth is hidden or revealed, what are the consequences?

SKILLS FOCUS

Literary Focus
Analyze the first-person narrator and voice.

Before You Read

The Interlopers

Make the Connection
Quickwrite 🖉

Most arguments can be settled when people agree to talk or compromise, but some disagreements become so bitter that they last for many years. Indeed, some regions of the world have been locked in conflict for generations. Write down a few examples of feuds that have torn families or even countries apart. What keeps such bitter hatred alive?

Literary Focus
Omniscient Narrator: Knowing It All

An **omniscient narrator** is someone who knows everything about everyone in the story. Since an omniscient narrator is not one of the characters, he or she can move easily from the mind of one character to the mind of the next. The narrator can also jump from place to place or zoom in and out. However, the fact that the narrator knows everything doesn't mean that you will learn all the information at once. Sometimes an omniscient narrator will save an important bit of information for the *very last moment* of the story.

Surprise Endings

A **surprise ending** resolves a story's conflict in a totally unexpected—yet logical—way. In Saki's story the surprise at the end may make you rethink the story.

Reading Skills 📖
Monitoring Your Reading

Good readers use the following strategies to get through a difficult sentence or passage. As you read Saki's story, have a notebook or some self-sticking notes handy so that you can follow these guidelines:

- When you don't understand a word, look for **context clues.**
- Break down long sentences into simpler ones.
- Look for the subject and verb in complicated sentences.
- Stop at the end of a passage you think is important, and **summarize** it.
- **Re-read** difficult passages.

Vocabulary Development

precipitous (prē·sip′ə·təs) *adj.*: very steep.

acquiesced (ak′wē·est′) *v.* (used with *in*): accepted; complied with.

marauders (mə·rôd′ərz) *n.*: people who roam in search of loot, or goods to steal.

exasperation (eg·zas′pər·ā′shən) *n.*: great annoyance.

pious (pī′əs) *adj.*: showing religious devotion.

retorted (ri·tôr′tid) *v.*: replied sharply.

condolences (kən·dō′ləns·iz) *n.*: expressions of sympathy.

languor (laŋ′gər) *n.*: weakness; weariness.

reconciliation (rek′ən·sil′ē·ā′shən) *n.*: friendly end to a quarrel.

succor (suk′ər) *n.*: help given to someone in distress; relief.

Moon Shadows (1992) by Lois Dodd. Oil on canvas (36″ × 50″).

THE INTERLOPERS

Saki

Ulrich von Gradwitz patrolled the dark forest in quest of a human enemy.

In a forest of mixed growth somewhere on the eastern spurs of the Carpathians,[1] a man stood one winter night watching and listening, as though he waited for some beast of the woods to come within the range of his vision and, later, of his rifle. But the game for whose presence he kept so keen an outlook was none that figured in the sportsman's calendar as lawful and proper for the chase; Ulrich von Gradwitz patrolled the dark forest in quest of a human enemy.

The forest lands of Gradwitz were of wide extent and well stocked with game; the narrow strip of <u>precipitous</u> woodland that lay on its outskirt was not remarkable for the game it

---

1. **Carpathians** (kär·pā′thē·ənz): mountain range that starts in Slovakia and extends through Poland, Ukraine, and Romania.

Vocabulary
precipitous (prē·sip′ə·təs) *adj.*: very steep.

harbored or the shooting it afforded, but it was the most jealously guarded of all its owner's territorial possessions. A famous lawsuit, in the days of his grandfather, had wrested it from the illegal possession of a neighboring family of petty landowners; the dispossessed party had never acquiesced in the judgment of the courts, and a long series of poaching affrays[2] and similar scandals had embittered the relationships between the families for three generations. The neighbor feud had grown into a personal one since Ulrich had come to be head of his family; if there was a man in the world whom he detested and wished ill to, it was Georg Znaeym, the inheritor of the quarrel and the tireless game snatcher and raider of the disputed border forest. The feud might, perhaps, have died down or been compromised if the personal ill will of the two men had not stood in the way; as boys they had thirsted for one another's blood, as men each prayed that misfortune might fall on the other, and this wind-scourged winter night Ulrich had banded together his foresters to watch the dark forest, not in quest of four-footed quarry, but to keep a lookout for the prowling thieves whom he suspected of being afoot from across the land boundary. The roebuck,[3] which usually kept in the sheltered hollows during a storm wind, were running like driven things tonight, and there was movement and unrest among the creatures that were wont to sleep through the dark hours. Assuredly there was a disturbing element in the forest, and Ulrich could guess the quarter from whence it came.

He strayed away by himself from the watchers whom he had placed in ambush on the crest of the hill and wandered far down the steep slopes amid the wild tangle of undergrowth, peering through the tree trunks and listening through the whistling and skirling[4] of the wind and the restless beating of the branches for sight or sound of the marauders. If only on this wild night, in this dark, lone spot, he might come across Georg Znaeym, man to man, with none to witness—that was the wish that was uppermost in his thoughts. And as he stepped round the trunk of a huge beech he came face to face with the man he sought.

The two enemies stood glaring at one another for a long silent moment. Each had a rifle in his hand, each had hate in his heart and murder uppermost in his mind. The chance had come to give full play to the passions of a lifetime. But a man who has been brought up under the code of a restraining civilization cannot easily nerve himself to shoot down his neighbor in cold blood and without a word spoken, except for an offense against his hearth and honor. And before the moment of hesitation had given way to action, a deed of Nature's own violence overwhelmed them both. A fierce shriek of the storm had been answered by a splitting crash over their heads, and ere they could leap aside, a mass of falling beech tree had thundered down on them. Ulrich von Gradwitz found himself stretched on the ground, one arm numb beneath him and the other held almost as helplessly in a tight tangle of forked branches, while both legs were pinned beneath the fallen mass. His heavy shooting boots had saved his feet from being crushed to pieces, but if his fractures were not as serious as they might have been, at least it was evident that he could not move from his present position till someone came to release him. The descending twigs had slashed the skin of his face, and he had to wink away some drops of blood from his eyelashes before he could take in a general view of

---

4. **skirling** (skurl'in) *v.* used as *n.*: shrill, piercing sound.

Vocabulary

acquiesced (ak'wē·est') *v.* (used with *in*): accepted; complied with.

marauders (mə·rôd'ərz) *n.*: people who roam in search of loot, or goods to steal.

---

2. **poaching affrays** (ə·frāz'): noisy quarrels or brawls about poaching, which means "fishing or hunting illegally on private property."

3. **roebuck** (rō'buk') *n.*: male (or males) of the roe deer, small deer that live in Europe and Asia.

the disaster. At his side, so near that under ordinary circumstances he could almost have touched him, lay Georg Znaeym, alive and struggling, but obviously as helplessly pinioned[5] down as himself. All round them lay a thick-strewn wreckage of splintered branches and broken twigs.

Relief at being alive and <u>exasperation</u> at his captive plight brought a strange medley of <u>pious</u> thank offerings and sharp curses to Ulrich's lips. Georg, who was nearly blinded with the blood which trickled across his eyes, stopped his struggling for a moment to listen, and then gave a short, snarling laugh.

"So you're not killed, as you ought to be, but you're caught, anyway," he cried, "caught fast. Ho, what a jest, Ulrich von Gradwitz snared in his stolen forest. There's real justice for you!"

And he laughed again, mockingly and savagely.

"I'm caught in my own forest land," <u>retorted</u> Ulrich. "When my men come to release us, you will wish, perhaps, that you were in a better plight than caught poaching on a neighbor's land, shame on you."

Georg was silent for a moment; then he answered quietly:

"Are you sure that your men will find much to release? I have men, too, in the forest tonight, close behind me, and *they* will be here first and do the releasing. When they drag me out from under these branches, it won't need much clumsiness on their part to roll this mass of trunk right over on the top of you. Your men will find you dead under a fallen beech tree. For form's sake I shall send my <u>condolences</u> to your family."

"It is a useful hint," said Ulrich fiercely. "My men had orders to follow in ten minutes' time, seven of which must have gone by already, and when they get me out—I will remember the hint. Only as you will have met your death poaching on my lands, I don't think I can decently send any message of condolence to your family."

"Good," snarled Georg, "good. We fight this quarrel out to the death, you and I and our foresters, with no cursed interlopers to come between us. Death and damnation to you, Ulrich von Gradwitz."

"The same to you, Georg Znaeym, forest thief, game snatcher."

Both men spoke with the bitterness of possible defeat before them, for each knew that it might be long before his men would seek him out or find him; it was a bare matter of chance which party would arrive first on the scene.

Both had now given up the useless struggle to free themselves from the mass of wood that held them down; Ulrich limited his endeavors to an effort to bring his one partially free arm near enough to his outer coat pocket to draw out his wine flask. Even when he had accomplished that operation, it was long before he could manage the unscrewing of the stopper or get any of the liquid down his throat. But what a heaven-sent draft[6] it seemed! It was an open winter,[7] and little snow had fallen as yet, hence the captives suffered less from the cold than might have been the case at that season of the year; nevertheless, the wine was warming and reviving to the wounded man, and he looked across with something like a throb of pity to where his enemy lay, just keeping the groans of pain and weariness from crossing his lips.

"Could you reach this flask if I threw it over to you?" asked Ulrich suddenly. "There is good wine in it, and one may as well be as comfortable as one can. Let us drink, even if tonight one of us dies."

---

6. **draft** *n.*: drink.
7. **open winter**: mild winter.

Vocabulary

exasperation (eg·zas′pər·ā′shən) *n.*: great annoyance.

pious (pī′əs) *adj.*: showing religious devotion.

retorted (ri·tôr′tid) *v.*: replied sharply.

condolences (kən·dō′ləns·iz) *n.*: expressions of sympathy.

---

5. **pinioned** (pin′yənd) *v.* used as *adj.*: pinned, as if chained or tied up.

"No, I can scarcely see anything; there is so much blood caked round my eyes," said Georg; "and in any case I don't drink wine with an enemy."

Ulrich was silent for a few minutes and lay listening to the weary screeching of the wind. An idea was slowly forming and growing in his brain, an idea that gained strength every time that he looked across at the man who was fighting so grimly against pain and exhaustion. In the pain and <u>languor</u> that Ulrich himself was feeling, the old fierce hatred seemed to be dying down.

"Neighbor," he said presently, "do as you please if your men come first. It was a fair compact. But as for me, I've changed my mind. If my men are the first to come, you shall be the first to be helped, as though you were my guest. We have quarreled like devils all our lives over this stupid strip of forest, where the trees can't even stand upright in a breath of wind. Lying here tonight, thinking, I've come to think we've been rather fools; there are better things in life than getting the better of a boundary dispute. Neighbor, if you will help me to bury the old quarrel, I—I will ask you to be my friend."

Georg Znaeym was silent for so long that Ulrich thought perhaps he had fainted with the pain of his injuries. Then he spoke slowly and in jerks.

"How the whole region would stare and gabble if we rode into the market square together. No one living can remember seeing a Znaeym and a von Gradwitz talking to one another in friendship. And what peace there would be among the forester folk if we ended our feud tonight. And if we choose to make peace among our people, there is none other to interfere, no interlopers from outside. . . . You would come and keep the Sylvester night[8] beneath my roof,

and I would come and feast on some high day at your castle. . . . I would never fire a shot on your land, save when you invited me as a guest; and you should come and shoot with me down in the marshes where the wildfowl are. In all the countryside there are none that could hinder if we willed to make peace. I never thought to have wanted to do other than hate you all my life, but I think I have changed my mind about things too, this last half-hour. And you offered me your wine flask. . . . Ulrich von Gradwitz, I will be your friend."

For a space both men were silent, turning over in their minds the wonderful changes that this dramatic <u>reconciliation</u> would bring about. In the cold, gloomy forest, with the wind tearing in fitful gusts through the naked branches and whistling round the tree trunks, they lay and waited for the help that would now bring release and <u>succor</u> to both parties. And each prayed a private prayer that his men might be the first to arrive, so that he might be the first to show honorable attention to the enemy that had become a friend.

Presently, as the wind dropped for a moment, Ulrich broke the silence.

"Let's shout for help," he said; "in this lull our voices may carry a little way."

"They won't carry far through the trees and undergrowth," said Georg, "but we can try. Together, then."

The two raised their voices in a prolonged hunting call.

"Together again," said Ulrich a few minutes later, after listening in vain for an answering halloo.

"I heard something that time, I think," said Ulrich.

Vocabulary

languor (laŋ′gər) *n.*: weakness; weariness.

reconciliation (rek′ən·sil′ē·ā′shən) *n.*: friendly end to a quarrel.

succor (suk′ər) *n.*: help given to someone in distress; relief.

---

8. **Sylvester night:** feast day honoring Saint Sylvester (Pope Sylvester I, d. 335), observed on December 31.

Chish Yah XV (1992) by Rick Bartow. Pastel and graphite on paper (20″ × 40″).

"I heard nothing but the pestilential[9] wind," said Georg hoarsely.

There was silence again for some minutes, and then Ulrich gave a joyful cry.

"I can see figures coming through the wood. They are following in the way I came down the hillside."

Both men raised their voices in as loud a shout as they could muster.

"They hear us! They've stopped. Now they see us. They're running down the hill toward us," cried Ulrich.

"How many of them are there?" asked Georg.

"I can't see distinctly," said Ulrich; "nine or ten."

"Then they are yours," said Georg; "I had only seven out with me."

"They are making all the speed they can, brave lads," said Ulrich gladly.

"Are they your men?" asked Georg. "Are they your men?" he repeated impatiently, as Ulrich did not answer.

"No," said Ulrich with a laugh, the idiotic chattering laugh of a man unstrung with hideous fear.

"Who are they?" asked Georg quickly, straining his eyes to see what the other would gladly not have seen.

"*Wolves.*" ■

---

9. **pestilential** (pes′tə·len′shəl) *adj.:* Strictly speaking, *pestilential* means "deadly; causing disease; harmful." Here, Georg uses the word to mean "cursed."

Meet the Writer

Saki

An Exotic Imagination

Hector Hugh Munro (1870–1916) wrote stories with snappy endings that were either wickedly funny or terrifying. Munro was born in Burma, where his father was an officer in the military police. When his mother died suddenly, he went to live with his grandmother and two stern aunts in a house in England whose windows were never opened. The aunts considered Hector sickly; he played with few children and was not sent to school until he was ten.

When he began writing stories, Munro took a foreign pen name, Saki, after the character who served wine to the gods in the then-popular poem the *Rubáiyát of Omar Khayyám*. (Omar Khayyám was a Persian poet.)

For Independent Reading

If you enjoyed "The Interlopers," try Saki's story "The Open Window," about a young girl with an unusual imagination.

The Granger Collection, New York.

CONNECTION / FABLE

The Trapper Trapped

Vai (African) traditional, retold by **Roger D. Abrahams**

Goat and Fox were quarreling, and Goat told Fox that he intended to get him into trouble so bad he would never be able to get out. Fox said, "All right; you do that, and I will return the favor to you."

Goat went for a walk and saw Leopard. Being frightened, Goat asked, "Auntie, what are you doing here?" "My little one is sick," said Leopard. Then Goat, thinking quickly, said, "Fox has medicine that will make your little one well." Leopard said to call Fox, so Goat went to Fox and said, "They are calling you."

"Who is calling me?" replied Fox. "I don't know," said Goat; "I think it is your friend. Go this way and you will run into him." Fox went down the path and at length came upon Leopard. Fox was frightened, and inquired: "Did you call me?" "Yes, my son. Goat came just a while ago and told me you had medicine that would make my little one well." "Yes," said Fox, "I have medicine that will cure your little one, but I must have a little goat horn to put it in. If you get me a goat horn, I will let you have the medicine." "Which way did Goat go?" asked Leopard. "I left him up there," replied Fox. "You wait here with my little one, and I will bring you the horn," said Leopard, and away she ran. Soon after, Leopard killed Goat and returned with his horns to Fox.

Beware, lest you fall into the trap you set for someone else.

Response and Analysis

Reading Check

1. Make a story map for "The Inter-lopers" by filling in a chart like the one here:

Title: "The Interlopers"
Characters:
Setting:
Conflicts:
Main events:
Climax and resolution:

2. Review the notes you made while you read the story. Did you find Saki's writing style difficult to understand? What reading strategies did you use to resolve your difficulties?

Thinking Critically

3. **Irony** is what we feel when something turns out to be different from what we expect or think appropriate. What is surprising and ironic about the ending of the story? What truth is revealed, and what do you predict the consequences will be?

4. Find places in the text where the word *interlopers* is used. What is an interloper? Who are the interlopers in the story? (Are there several kinds of interlopers in the story?)

5. Find instances when the **omniscient narrator** tells what Georg and Ulrich are thinking. What similarities between the **characters** are revealed by the narrator? How would your reaction to events in the **plot** be different if you didn't know what both characters were thinking?

6. **Tone**—the writer's attitude toward a subject or character—is affected by the choice of narrator. What tone does Saki create through the use of an **omniscient narrator**? How do you think the tone would be different if the story were told from the point of view of Ulrich or Georg?

7. Most fables have a **moral,** a message about how we should live our lives. What is the moral of "The Trapper Trapped" (see the **Connection** on page 194)? How does that moral compare with the message of "The Interlopers"?

Extending and Evaluating

8. Refer to your Quickwrite notes. Do you think Saki's story has a serious message about the kinds of feuds you described in your notes, or do you think the story is told just for entertainment? Give reasons for your answer.

WRITING

One More Twist

Saki's story has several surprising twists, the most stunning one being the **surprise ending.** Choose a point in the last two pages of the story, and create your own plot twist by changing the action and writing a **new ending.** You might decide not to have Ulrich and Georg reconcile; you might come up with a new twist beyond the final one. In your version, imitate Saki's omniscient narrator by showing what each character is thinking.

SKILLS FOCUS

Literary Skills
Analyze the omniscient narrator (or point of view).

Reading Skills
Monitor your reading.

Writing Skills
Write a surprise ending.

go.
hrw
.com

INTERNET

Projects and Activities

Keyword: LE7 9-3

Context Clues: Solving Word Mysteries

When you come across an unfamiliar word, **context clues**—the words and phrases around the word—can give you a good sense of that word's meaning. Here are a few ways in which context clues can point toward the meaning of an unfamiliar word—in this case, *interlopers:*

- Context clues may **define** the word.

  The people who interfered in the family's private concerns were accused of being <u>interlopers</u>.

- Context clues may **restate** the word.

  The <u>interlopers</u>, *intruders* on horseback, waved their swords as they rode into town.

- Context clues may provide **examples** of the word.

  Protecting the privacy of the millionaire, the guards viewed all strangers who approached the mansion as <u>interlopers</u>, *including curious tourists, journalists, and photographers.*

- Context clues may **compare** the word to something similar.

  Like mice, the <u>interlopers</u> slipped into the building unnoticed.

- Context clues may **contrast** a word with something dissimilar.

  Far from being welcome guests, the men at the party were seen as <u>interlopers</u>.

Look at the following passage from "The Interlopers," and note how the italicized context clues point toward the meaning of the Word Bank word *languor:*

> "An idea was slowly forming and growing in his brain, an idea that gained strength every time that he looked across at the man who was fighting so grimly against pain and *exhaustion.* In the pain and <u>languor</u> that Ulrich himself was feeling, the old fierce hatred seemed to be dying down."

Ulrich's "languor" is compared to Georg's "exhaustion," hinting that *languor* and *exhaustion* have similar meanings.

Word Bank

precipitous
acquiesced
marauders
exasperation
pious
retorted
condolences
languor
reconciliation
succor

SKILLS FOCUS

Vocabulary Skills
Understand and use context clues.

PRACTICE

Review the definition of each Word Bank word. Then, write an original sentence that provides **context clues** to the word's meaning. Use each of the following types of context clues at least once: definition, restatement, example, comparison, and contrast. You might want to exchange papers with a partner to evaluate each other's context clues.

The Necklace

Make the Connection

Quickwrite ✏️

All of us, at one time or another, have felt that the grass is greener on the other side of the fence—in other words, that someone else's life is better than our own. We believe that having what someone else has will make us happy—until we experience the unexpected negative results of envy. In a few lines, jot down your feelings about envy. Have you ever seen or felt its negative effects?

Literary Focus

Third-Person-Limited Point of View: Zooming In on One Character

Guy de Maupassant specialized in showing what makes human beings tick. It's not surprising, then, that he tells this famous story from the **third-person-limited point of view,** zooming in on the thoughts of a single character, Mathilde Loisel. We learn in the first seven paragraphs about Mathilde's past, her dreams, what makes her unhappy, what she envies in other people, and what she thinks will make her happy. We follow Mathilde so closely through a crisis in her life that the story's ending hits us almost as powerfully as it strikes the unsuspecting Mathilde.

Reading Skills 📖

Summarizing: A Plot Formula

Many short stories and movies have a plot that can be summed up with this formula: *Somebody wants . . . , but . . . , so . . .* The plot begins with *somebody* (the main character) who *wants* something desperately, *but* something or someone stands in the way (the conflict), *so* the character takes steps to overcome the obstacles. Remember that this formula may repeat itself several times in a story until the resolution of the plot. After you finish "The Necklace," decide how the story fits this pattern.

Background

"The Necklace" takes place in Paris in the late 1880s. At that time and in that place, social classes were all-important; people were born into a certain class, and that was usually where they remained for the rest of their lives.

Vocabulary Development

incessantly (in·ses′ənt·lē) *adv.:* constantly; continually.

disconsolate (dis·kän′sə·lit) *adj.:* causing sadness or depression; also, very unhappy.

vexation (vek·sā′shən) *n.:* disturbance; distress.

pauper (pô′pər) *n.:* very poor person.

adulation (a′jōō·lā′shən) *n.:* intense or excessive admiration or praise.

aghast (ə·gast′) *adj.:* terrified; horrified.

privations (prī·vā′shənz) *n.:* hardships; lack of the things needed for a happy, healthy life.

exorbitant (eg·zôr′bi·tənt) *adj.:* much too high in price or amount.

SKILLS FOCUS

Literary Skills
Understand the third-person-limited point of view.

Reading Skills
Summarize plot.

go.
hrw
.com

INTERNET

Vocabulary Practice
•
More About Guy de Maupassant
•

Keyword: LE7 9-3

THE NECKLACE

GUY DE MAUPASSANT

Interrupted Reading (c. 1870) by Jean-Baptiste-Camille Corot.
Oil on canvas mounted on board (92.2 cm × 65.1 cm).

She so much longed to please, be envied, be fascinating . . .

She was one of those pretty and charming girls, born, as if by an accident of fate, into a family of clerks. With no dowry,[1] no prospects, no way of any kind of being met, understood, loved, and married by a man both prosperous and famous, she was finally married to a minor clerk in the Ministry of Education.

She dressed plainly because she could not afford fine clothes, but she was as unhappy as a woman who has come down in the world; for women have no family rank or social class. With them, beauty, grace, and charm take the place of birth and breeding. Their natural poise, their instinctive good taste, and their mental cleverness are the sole guiding principles which make daughters of the common people the equals of ladies in high society.

She grieved incessantly, feeling that she had been born for all the little niceties and luxuries of living. She grieved over the shabbiness of her apartment, the dinginess of the walls, the worn-out appearance of the chairs, the ugliness of the draperies. All these things, which another woman of her class would not even have noticed, gnawed at her and made her furious. The sight of the little Breton girl[2] who did her humble housework roused in her disconsolate regrets and wild daydreams. She would dream of silent chambers, draped with Oriental tapestries[3] and lighted by tall bronze floor lamps, and of two handsome butlers in knee breeches, who, drowsy from the heavy warmth cast by the central stove, dozed in large overstuffed armchairs.

She would dream of great reception halls hung with old silks, of fine furniture filled with priceless curios,[4] and of small, stylish, scented sitting rooms just right for the four o'clock chat with intimate friends, with distinguished and sought-after men whose attention every woman envies and longs to attract.

When dining at the round table, covered for the third day with the same cloth, opposite her husband, who would raise the cover of the soup tureen, declaring delightedly, "Ah! a good stew! There's nothing I like better . . . ," she would dream of fashionable dinner parties, of gleaming silverware, of tapestries making the walls alive with characters out of history and strange birds in a fairyland forest; she would dream of delicious dishes served on wonderful china, of gallant compliments whispered and listened to with a sphinxlike[5] smile as one eats the rosy flesh of a trout or nibbles at the wings of a grouse.

She had no evening clothes, no jewels, nothing. But those were the things she wanted; she felt that was the kind of life for her. She so much longed to please, be envied, be fascinating and sought after.

She had a well-to-do friend, a classmate of convent-school days whom she would no longer go to see, simply because she would feel so

> She had no
> evening clothes,
> no jewels,
> nothing.

---

1. **dowry** (dou'rē) *n.:* property that a woman brings to her husband at marriage.
2. **Breton** (bret'n) **girl:** girl from Brittany, a region in northwestern France.
3. **tapestries** (tap'əs·trēz) *n.:* heavy woven cloths with decorative designs and pictures, used as wall hangings or furniture coverings.

---

4. **curios** (kyoor'ē·ōz') *n.:* unusual items.
5. **sphinxlike** *adj.:* mysterious. The sphinx was a creature in Greek mythology who asked riddles.

Vocabulary

incessantly (in·ses'ənt·lē) *adv.:* constantly; continually.

disconsolate (dis·kän'sə·lit) *adj.:* causing sadness or depression; also, very unhappy.

distressed on returning home. And she would weep for days on end from vexation, regret, despair, and anguish.

Then one evening, her husband came home proudly holding out a large envelope.

"Look," he said, "I've got something for you."

She excitedly tore open the envelope and pulled out a printed card bearing these words:

"The Minister of Education and Mme. Georges Ramponneau[6] beg M. and Mme. Loisel to do them the honor of attending an evening reception at the Ministerial Mansion on Friday, January 18."

Instead of being delighted, as her husband had hoped, she scornfully tossed the invitation on the table, murmuring, "What good is that to me?"

"But, my dear, I thought you'd be thrilled to death. You never get a chance to go out, and this is a real affair, a wonderful one! I had an awful time getting a card. Everybody wants one; it's much sought after, and not many clerks have a chance at one. You'll see all the most important people there."

She gave him an irritated glance and burst out impatiently, "What do you think I have to go in?"

He hadn't given that a thought. He stammered, "Why, the dress you wear when we go to the theater. That looks quite nice, I think."

He stopped talking, dazed and distracted to see his wife burst out weeping. Two large tears slowly rolled from the corners of her eyes to the corners of her mouth; he gasped, "Why, what's the matter? What's the trouble?"

By sheer willpower she overcame her outburst and answered in a calm voice while wiping the tears from her wet cheeks, "Oh, nothing. Only I don't have an evening dress and therefore I can't go to that affair. Give the card to some friend at the office whose wife can dress better than I can."

He was stunned. He resumed, "Let's see, Mathilde. How much would a suitable outfit cost—one you could wear for other affairs too—something very simple?"

She thought it over for several seconds, going over her allowance and thinking also of the amount she could ask for without bringing an immediate refusal and an exclamation of dismay from the thrifty clerk.

Finally, she answered hesitatingly, "I'm not sure exactly, but I think with four hundred francs I could manage it."

He turned a bit pale, for he had set aside just that amount to buy a rifle so that the following summer, he could join some friends who were getting up a group to shoot larks on the plain near Nanterre.[7]

However, he said, "All right. I'll give you four hundred francs. But try to get a nice dress."

As the day of the party approached, Mme. Loisel seemed sad, moody, ill at ease. Her outfit was ready, however. Her husband said to her one evening, "What's the matter? You've been all out of sorts for three days."

And she answered, "It's embarrassing not to have a jewel or a gem—nothing to wear on my dress. I'll look like a pauper. I'd almost rather not go to the party."

He answered, "Why not wear some flowers? They're very fashionable this season. For ten francs you can get two or three gorgeous roses."

She wasn't at all convinced. "No. . . . There's nothing more humiliating than to look poor among a lot of rich women."

But her husband exclaimed, "My, but you're silly! Go see your friend Mme. Forestier,[8] and ask her to lend you some jewelry. You and she know each other well enough for you to do that."

6. **Mme. Georges Ramponneau** (mà·dàm′ zhôrzh ràm′pə·nō) . . . **M.** (mə·syʉr′) . . . **Mme. Loisel** (mà·dàm′ lwä·zel′): M. and *Mme.* are abbreviations for "Monsieur" and "Madame" and are the French equivalents of *Mr.* and *Mrs.*

7. **Nanterre** (nä*n*·ter′): town near Paris.
8. **Forestier** (fô·rəs·tyā′).

Vocabulary

vexation (vek·sā′shən) *n.*: disturbance; distress.
pauper (pô′pər) *n.*: very poor person.

The New Necklace (1910) by William McGregor Paxton. Oil on canvas (91.76 cm × 73.02 cm).

She gave a cry of joy. "Why, that's so! I hadn't thought of it."

The next day she paid her friend a visit and told her of her predicament.

Mme. Forestier went toward a large closet with mirrored doors, took out a large jewel box, brought it over, opened it, and said to Mme. Loisel, "Pick something out, my dear."

At first her eyes noted some bracelets, then a pearl necklace, then a Venetian cross, gold and gems, of marvelous workmanship. She tried on these adornments in front of the mirror, but hesitated, unable to decide which to part with and put back. She kept on asking, "Haven't you something else?"

"Oh, yes, keep on looking. I don't know just what you'd like."

All at once she found, in a black satin box, a superb diamond necklace; and her pulse beat faster with longing. Her hands trembled as she took it up. Clasping it around her throat, outside her high-necked dress, she stood in ecstasy looking at her reflection.

Then she asked, hesitatingly, pleading, "Could I borrow that, just that and nothing else?"

"Why, of course."

She threw her arms around her friend, kissed her warmly, and fled with her treasure.

The day of the party arrived. Mme. Loisel was a sensation. She was the prettiest one there, fashionable, gracious, smiling, and wild with joy. All the men turned to look at her, asked who she was, begged to be introduced. All the Cabinet officials wanted to waltz with her. The minister took notice of her.

She danced madly, wildly, drunk with pleasure, giving no thought to anything in the triumph of her beauty, the pride of her success, in a kind of happy cloud composed of all the adulation, of all the admiring glances, of all the

---

Vocabulary

adulation (a'jōō·lā'shən) *n.*: intense or excessive admiration or praise.

A CLOSER LOOK
Separate Spheres

During the late nineteenth century the doctrine of "separate spheres" shaped French society. According to this idea, men were aggressive and intellectual, qualified to work in the public sphere of universities, business, and politics. Women were seen as weak and emotional, suited for the private sphere. They raised children and made sure that their homes were clean and beautiful. The law reinforced these boundaries: Husbands controlled their wives' property, and women could not vote or enter professions like the law or civil service. For middle- and upper-class women, supported by their husbands or fathers and aided by servants, this lifestyle was restrictive but not impossible. For poor women the situation was different. Millions of them became factory workers, laundresses, cooks, bread carriers, or seamstresses. These women led extremely difficult lives. At work, conditions could be hazardous, even fatal. Seamstresses endured daily shifts of thirteen hours or more; weavers were exposed to toxic substances; silk workers were surrounded by clouds of steam and frequently caught pneumonia. In the end, women received little in return for working strenuously and endangering their health. Many earned only about four hundred francs in an entire year, the cost of Mathilde Loisel's party dress.

Hush! (The Concert) (c.1875) by James Tissot. Oil on canvas (73.6 cm × 112.2 cm).
Manchester City Art Galleries, Manchester, England.

awakened longings, of a sense of complete victory that is so sweet to a woman's heart.

She left around four o'clock in the morning. Her husband, since midnight, had been dozing in a small, empty sitting room with three other gentlemen whose wives were having too good a time.

He threw over her shoulders the wraps he had brought for going home, modest garments of everyday life whose shabbiness clashed with the stylishness of her evening clothes. She felt this and longed to escape unseen by the other women, who were draped in expensive furs.

Loisel held her back.

"Hold on! You'll catch cold outside. I'll call a cab."

But she wouldn't listen to him and went rapidly down the stairs. When they were on the street, they didn't find a carriage; and they set out to hunt for one, hailing drivers whom they saw going by at a distance.

They walked toward the Seine,[9] disconsolate and shivering. Finally, on the docks, they found one of those carriages that one sees in Paris only after nightfall, as if they were ashamed to show their drabness during daylight hours.

It dropped them at their door in the Rue des Martyrs,[10] and they climbed wearily up to their apartment. For her, it was all over. For him,

---

9. **Seine** (sen): river that runs through Paris.
10. **Rue des Martyrs** (rü′ dā mär·tēr′): street in Paris. The name means "Street of the Martyrs." People who suffer for their beliefs or people who suffer for a long time are called martyrs.

The Boulevard Montmartre at Night (1897) by Camille Pissarro. Oil on canvas (53.3 cm × 64.8 cm).
© The National Gallery, London.

there was the thought that he would have to be at the Ministry at ten o'clock.

Before the mirror, she let the wraps fall from her shoulders to see herself once again in all her glory. Suddenly she gave a cry. The necklace was gone.

Her husband, already half undressed, said, "What's the trouble?"

She turned toward him despairingly, "I . . . I . . . I don't have Mme. Forestier's necklace."

"What! You can't mean it! It's impossible!"

They hunted everywhere, through the folds of the dress, through the folds of the coat, in the pockets. They found nothing.

He asked, "Are you sure you had it when leaving the dance?"

"Yes, I felt it when I was in the hall of the Ministry."

"But if you had lost it on the street, we'd have heard it drop. It must be in the cab."

"Yes, quite likely. Did you get its number?"

"No. Didn't you notice it either?"

"No."

They looked at each other aghast. Finally Loisel got dressed again.

"I'll retrace our steps on foot," he said, "to see if I can find it."

And he went out. She remained in her evening clothes, without the strength to go to bed, slumped in a chair in the unheated room, her mind a blank.

Her husband came in around seven o'clock. He had had no luck.

He went to the police station, to the newspapers to post a reward, to the cab companies, everywhere the slightest hope drove him.

That evening Loisel returned, pale, his face lined; still he had learned nothing.

"We'll have to write your friend," he said, "to tell her you have broken the catch and are having it repaired. That will give us a little time to turn around."

She wrote to his dictation.

At the end of a week, they had given up all hope.

And Loisel, looking five years older, declared, "We must take steps to replace that piece of jewelry."

The next day they took the case to the jeweler whose name they found inside. He consulted his records. "I didn't sell that necklace, madame," he said. "I only supplied the case."

Then they went from one jeweler to another hunting for a similar necklace, going over their recollections, both sick with despair and anxiety.

They found, in a shop in Palais Royal,[11] a string of diamonds which seemed exactly like the one they were seeking. It was priced at forty thousand francs. They could get it for thirty-six.

They asked the jeweler to hold it for them for three days. And they reached an agreement that he would take it back for thirty-four thousand if the lost one was found before the end of February.

Loisel had eighteen thousand francs he had inherited from his father. He would borrow the rest.

He went about raising the money, asking a thousand francs from one, four hundred from another, a hundred here, sixty there. He signed notes, made ruinous deals, did business with loan sharks, ran the whole gamut of moneylenders. He compromised the rest of his life, risked his signature without knowing if he'd be able to honor it, and then, terrified by the outlook of the future, by the blackness of despair about to close around him, by the prospect of all the privations of the body and tortures of the spirit, he went to claim the new necklace with the thirty-six thousand francs, which he placed on the counter of the shopkeeper.

When Mme. Loisel took the necklace back, Mme. Forestier said to her frostily, "You should have brought it back sooner; I might have needed it."

She didn't open the case, an action her friend was afraid of. If she had noticed the substitution, what would she have thought? What would she have said? Would she have thought her a thief?

Mme. Loisel experienced the horrible life the needy live. She played her part, however, with sudden heroism. That frightful debt had to be paid. She would pay it. She dismissed her maid; they rented a garret under the eaves.[12]

She learned to do the heavy housework, to perform the hateful duties of cooking. She washed dishes, wearing down her shell-pink nails scouring the grease from pots and pans; she

---

12. **garret under the eaves:** attic under the overhanging lower edges of a roof.

Vocabulary

aghast (ə·gast′) *adj.:* terrified; horrified.

privations (prī·vā′shənz) *n.:* hardships; lack of the things needed for a happy, healthy life.

---

11. **Palais Royal** (pà·lā′ rwä·yàl′): fashionable shopping district in Paris.

scrubbed dirty linen, shirts, and cleaning rags, which she hung on a line to dry; she took the garbage down to the street each morning and brought up water, stopping on each landing to get her breath. And, clad like a peasant woman, basket on arm, guarding sou[13] by sou her scanty allowance, she bargained with the fruit dealers, the grocer, the butcher, and was insulted by them.

Each month notes had to be paid, and others renewed to give more time.

Her husband labored evenings to balance a tradesman's accounts, and at night, often, he copied documents at five sous a page.

And this went on for ten years.

Finally, all was paid back, everything including the <u>exorbitant</u> rates of the loan sharks and accumulated compound interest.

Mme. Loisel appeared an old woman now. She became heavy, rough, harsh, like one of the poor. Her hair untended, her skirts askew, her hands red, her voice shrill, she even slopped water on her floors and scrubbed them herself. But, sometimes, while her husband was at work, she would sit near the window and think of that long-ago evening when, at the dance, she had been so beautiful and admired.

What would have happened if she had not lost that necklace? Who knows? Who can say? How strange and unpredictable life is! How little there is between happiness and misery!

Then, one Sunday, when she had gone for a walk on the Champs Élysées[14] to relax a bit from the week's labors, she suddenly noticed a woman strolling with a child. It was Mme. Forestier, still young looking, still beautiful, still charming.

Mme. Loisel felt a rush of emotion. Should she speak to her? Of course. And now that everything was paid off, she would tell her the whole story. Why not?

She went toward her. "Hello, Jeanne."

The other, not recognizing her, showed astonishment at being spoken to so familiarly by this common person. She stammered, "But . . . madame . . . I don't recognize . . . You must be mistaken."

"No, I'm Mathilde Loisel."

Her friend gave a cry, "Oh, my poor Mathilde, how you've changed!"

"Oh, my poor Mathilde, how you've changed!"

"Yes, I've had a hard time since last seeing you. And plenty of misfortunes—and all on account of you!"

"Of me . . . How do you mean?"

"Do you remember that diamond necklace you loaned me to wear to the dance at the Ministry?"

"Yes, but what about it?"

"Well, I lost it."

"You lost it! But you returned it."

"I brought you another just like it. And we've been paying for it for ten years now. You can imagine that wasn't easy for us who had nothing. Well, it's over now, and I am glad of it."

Mme. Forestier stopped short. "You mean to say you bought a diamond necklace to replace mine?"

"Yes. You never noticed, then? They were quite alike."

And she smiled with proud and simple joy.

Mme. Forestier, quite overcome, clasped her by the hands. "Oh, my poor Mathilde. But mine was fake. Why, at most it was worth only five hundred francs!" ■

---

13. **sou** (so͞o) *n.:* old French coin of little value.
14. **Champs Élysées** (shän zā · lē · zā′): famous avenue in Paris.

Vocabulary
exorbitant (eg · zôr′bi · tənt) *adj.:* much too high in price or amount.

Meet the Writer

Guy de Maupassant

Seeing Things Anew

Guy de Maupassant (gē də mō·pä·sän') (1850–1893), one of the world's greatest short story writers, was born in Normandy, the French province that is the setting for much of his fiction. After his parents separated, Maupassant was raised by his mother, who was a close friend of the great novelist Gustave Flaubert.

Flaubert set out to instruct the young Maupassant in the art of fiction. He explained that good writing depends upon seeing things anew, rather than recording what people before us have thought. Flaubert also gave his student this advice:

66 Whatever you want to say, there is only one word to express it, only one verb to give it movement, only one adjective to qualify it. 99

For years, Maupassant sent Flaubert his writing exercises every week, and then they met to discuss his work over lunch. With the success of his story "Ball of Fat," Maupassant, now age thirty, quit his job as a clerk with the naval ministry and began to put great energy into writing. He quickly achieved enormous popularity. For eleven years he wrote at a hectic pace and produced nearly three hundred stories and six novels. Advising writers, Maupassant said, "Get black on white."

His story "The Horla" has been called one of the most terrifying stories of madness ever written. It foretold Maupassant's own tragic fate of illness, insanity, and early death. He died in a Paris asylum when he was only forty-two years old.

For Independent Reading

Among Maupassant's many stories you might want to read "The Piece of String," in which a simple piece of string helps seal a man's fate. In "Two Friends" a carefree fishing trip proves fateful.

Reading Check

1. **Summarize** the plot using the *Somebody wants . . . , but . . . , so . . .* formula. Compare your summaries in class.

Thinking Critically

2. When Mme. Forestier reveals that the necklace was a fake, the reader feels the force of **irony**—the sense that something has turned out to be the opposite of what we expected. Explain what makes the story's closing sentences ironic.

3. Both Mathilde and Mme. Forestier hide the truth until the very end of the story. Explain why you think they hide the truth. What are the consequences of their actions? In what ways has Mathilde changed?

4. The **third-person-limited narrator** lets us see the world through the eyes of Mathilde Loisel. Does the narrator paint a mostly sympathetic or a mostly unsympathetic picture of Mathilde? Explain.

5. Think about this story's **point of view.** Explain how the story and our understanding of Mathilde would change if the story were told by her husband or by Mathilde herself.

6. The choice of narrator affects a story's **tone**—the writer's attitude toward a subject or character. What tone is created through Maupassant's use of a **third-person-limited narrator**? Consider whether the story is critical of Mathilde only or whether the writer is criticizing the values of a whole society.

7. How would you **characterize** Mathilde's husband? Consider what you know about him:
   - his loyalty to Mathilde
   - the way he indulges her
   - his years of sacrifice and hard work
   - his plans to buy something for himself

Extending and Evaluating

8. Look back at your Quickwrite notes about envy. Do you think Maupassant has painted a believable picture of the effects of envy? (Is the plot believable? Are the characters' motives convincing?) Why or why not?

WRITING

What's the Difference?

Do you think Mme. Forestier should return the difference in value between the original necklace and the one she received as a replacement? Take one side of this question, and write a statement for or against a payment to the Loisels. Be ready to defend your position in class.

Then and Now

Plan a twenty-first-century version of "The Necklace." The plot should focus on someone who borrows what he or she thinks is a valuable item and then briefly enters a different social world. Decide which point of view you will use to tell the story. Then, write a brief description of the major characters, the setting, and the plot. Try to come up with your own ironic ending.

SKILLS FOCUS

Literary Skills
Analyze the third-person-limited point of view.

Reading Skills
Summarize plot.

Writing Skills
Write a position statement.
Write a description.

INTERNET

Projects and Activities

Keyword: LE7 9-3

Vocabulary Development

Ranking Synonyms

PRACTICE

You can reinforce your ownership of a word by comparing the word with other words that have similar meanings. One way to compare words is to rank them from high to low intensity. For an example, see the chart below.

Work with a partner to make an "intensity scale" for each Word Bank word. We've done the first word for you. Add at least two words that are synonyms but show an increase or decrease in intensity. Be sure to compare and defend your intensity scales in class.

Word Bank

incessantly
disconsolate
vexation
pauper
adulation
aghast
privations
exorbitant

High Intensity	Medium Intensity	Low Intensity
incessantly	constantly	always

Grammar Link

Pronoun Problems

Some pronouns in English sound exactly like other words: *its* and *it's*; *their* and *they're*; *whose* and *who's*; *your* and *you're*. Words that sound alike are not a problem when you are speaking, but they can be troublesome when you are writing. To avoid making mistakes, you must be aware of the difference between a possessive pronoun and a pronoun contraction:

- A **possessive pronoun** (such as *its*, *their*, *whose*, *your*) shows ownership or relationship.

- A **pronoun contraction** (such as *it's*, *they're*, *who's*, and *you're*) is a shortened form of a pronoun and a verb (*it is*, *they are*, *who is*, and *you are*). A pronoun contraction *always* contains an **apostrophe.**

PRACTICE

Choose the correct pronoun from each underlined pair in parentheses.

1. "But her husband exclaimed, 'My, but (your/you're) silly!'"

2. "'(Its/It's) embarrassing not to have a jewel or a gem—nothing to wear on my dress.'"

3. "'Why not wear some flowers? (Their/They're) very fashionable this season.'"

4. "The next day they took the case to the jeweler (whose/who's) name they found inside."

Check the pronouns in your writing. Have you used a possessive where a contraction should have been used? Have you spelled a possessive pronoun with an apostrophe?

▶ **For more help, see Contractions, 14g, in the Language Handbook.**

SKILLS FOCUS

Vocabulary Skills
Identify degrees of intensity among synonyms.

Grammar Skills
Use possessive pronouns and pronoun contractions correctly.

Before You Read

The Cask of Amontillado

Make the Connection
Quickwrite

Poe was a master at writing stories of revenge. What experiences could lead someone to seek revenge? How could an obsession with vengeance lead to tragedy? Jot down your responses, and include examples from stories or movies.

Literary Focus
Unreliable Narrator

Writers sometimes assume a **persona,** which is a mask or a voice for a first-person narrator. When you read a story told by a **first-person narrator,** you need to ask yourself if you can trust the narrator. Sometimes a writer will purposely use an unreliable narrator to tell a story.

An **unreliable narrator** may not always know the whole truth or may purposely choose to deceive us. A narrator's actions, statements, and **voice**—his or her style of speaking, **diction** (word choice), and **tone** (attitude)—will provide you with clues about his or her reliability.

Reading Skills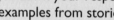
Drawing Conclusions

When you read, you act like a detective. You gather evidence and draw **conclusions,** or make judgments, based on that evidence. To decide if the narrator of Poe's story is unreliable, look closely at all the narrator *says* and *does*. Then, examine what his enemy, Fortunato, *says*. What details could support a charge of unreliability—even insanity? The questions at the open-book signs will help you.

Background

Centuries ago Christians in Italy buried their dead in catacombs—long, winding underground tunnels. Later wealthy families built private catacombs beneath their homes. Dark and cool, these chambers were suitable not only for burial but also for the storage of fine wines, such as amontillado (ə·män'tə·lä'dō). Poe's story is set during carnival, which is celebrated before the start of Lent, the season during which Christians give up various pleasures. During carnival, many people wear costumes and dance in the streets.

Vocabulary Development

precluded (prē·klōōd'id) v.: made impossible in advance; prevented.

impunity (im·pyōō'ni·tē) n.: freedom from punishment or harm.

retribution (re'trə·byōō'shən) n.: punishment.

immolation (im'ə·lā'shən) n.: destruction.

connoisseurship (kän'ə·sur'ship) n.: expert knowledge.

impose (im·pōz') v. (used with *upon*): take advantage of.

recoiling (ri·koil'iŋ) v. used as *adj.*: moving backward, as in fear.

endeavored (en·dev'ərd) v.: tried.

obstinate (äb'stə·nət) adj.: stubborn.

succession (sək·sesh'ən) n.: series.

THE CASK OF AMONTILLADO

Edgar Allan Poe

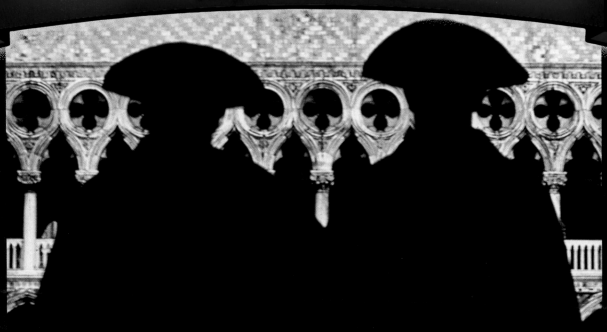

It was about dusk,
one evening during the
supreme madness of the
carnival season . . .

The thousand injuries of Fortunato I had borne as best I could; but when he ventured upon insult, I vowed revenge. You, who so well know the nature of my soul, will not suppose, however, that I gave utterance to a threat. At length I would be avenged; this was a point definitively settled—but the very definitiveness with which it was resolved <u>precluded</u> the idea of risk. I must not only punish, but punish with <u>impunity</u>. A wrong is unredressed[1] when <u>retribution</u> overtakes its redresser. It is equally unredressed when the avenger fails to make himself felt as such to him who has done the wrong.

It must be understood that neither by word nor deed had I given Fortunato cause to doubt my goodwill. I continued, as was my wont, to smile in his face, and he did not perceive that my smile *now* was at the thought of his <u>immolation</u>.

He had a weak point—this Fortunato—although in other regards he was a man to be respected and even feared. He prided himself on his <u>connoisseurship</u> in wine. Few Italians have the true virtuoso spirit. For the most part their enthusiasm is adopted to suit the time and opportunity—to practice imposture upon the British and Austrian millionaires. In painting and gemmary, Fortunato, like his countrymen, was a quack—but in the matter of old wines he was sincere. In this respect I did not differ from him materially: I was skillful in the Italian vintages myself and bought largely whenever I could.

It was about dusk, one evening during the supreme madness of the carnival season, that I encountered my friend. He accosted me with excessive warmth, for he had been drinking much. The man wore motley.[2] He had on a tight-fitting parti-striped dress, and his head was surmounted by the conical cap and bells. I was so pleased to see him that I thought I should never have done wringing his hand.

I said to him, "My dear Fortunato, you are luckily met. How remarkably well you are looking today! But I have received a pipe[3] of what passes for amontillado, and I have my doubts."

"How?" said he. "Amontillado? A pipe? Impossible! And in the middle of the carnival!"

"I have my doubts," I replied; "and I was silly enough to pay the full amontillado price without consulting you in the matter. You were not to be found, and I was fearful of losing a bargain."

"Amontillado!"

"I have my doubts."

"Amontillado!"

"And I must satisfy them."

"Amontillado!"

"As you are engaged, I am on my way to Luchesi. If anyone has a critical turn, it is he. He will tell me—"

"Luchesi cannot tell amontillado from sherry."

> **DRAWING CONCLUSIONS**
>
> 1. What does the narrator's smiling at the thought of Fortunato's death tell you about his character?

---

2. **motley** (mät′lē) *n.:* multicolored costume worn by a clown or jester.
3. **pipe** *n.:* barrel.

Vocabulary

precluded (prē·klōōd′id) *v.:* made impossible in advance; prevented.

impunity (im·pyōō′ni·tē) *n.:* freedom from punishment or harm.

retribution (re′trə·byōō′shən) *n.:* punishment.

immolation (im′ə·lā′shən) *n.:* destruction.

connoisseurship (kän′ə·sʉr′ship) *n.:* expert knowledge.

---

1. **unredressed** (un′ri·drest′) *v.* used as *adj.:* not set right or not made up for.

"And yet some fools will have it that his taste is a match for your own."

"Come, let us go."

"Whither?"

"To your vaults."[4]

"My friend, no; I will not <u>impose</u> upon your good nature. I perceive you have an engagement. Luchesi—"

"I have no engagement; come."

"My friend, no. It is not the engagement, but the severe cold with which I perceive you are afflicted. The vaults are insufferably damp. They are encrusted with niter."[5]

"Let us go, nevertheless. The cold is merely

nothing. Amontillado! You have been imposed upon. And as for Luchesi, he cannot distinguish sherry from amontillado."

Thus speaking, Fortunato possessed himself of my arm. Putting on a mask of black silk and drawing a roquelaure[6] closely about my person, I suffered him to hurry me to my *palazzo*.[7]

---

6. **roquelaure** (räk'ə·lôr') *n.:* heavy knee-length cloak.
7. *palazzo* (pä·lät'sô): Italian for "palace."

Vocabulary

impose (im·pōz') *v.* (used with *upon*): take advantage of.

---

4. **vaults** (vôlts) *n.:* storage cellars.
5. **niter** (nīt'ər) *n.:* salt deposits.

There were no attendants at home; they had absconded to make merry in honor of the time. I had told them that I should not return until the morning and had given them explicit orders not to stir from the house. These orders were sufficient, I well knew, to ensure their immediate disappearance, one and all, as soon as my back was turned.

I took from their sconces two flambeaux[8] and, giving one to Fortunato, bowed him through several suites of rooms to the archway that led into the vaults. I passed down a long and winding staircase, requesting him to be cautious as he followed. We came at length to the foot of the descent and stood together on the damp ground of the catacombs of the Montresors.

The gait of my friend was unsteady, and the bells upon his cap jingled as he strode.

"The pipe," said he.

"It is farther on," said I; "but observe the white web-work which gleams from these cavern walls."

He turned toward me, and looked into my eyes with two filmy orbs that distilled the rheum[9] of intoxication.

"Niter?" he asked, at length.

"Niter," I replied. "How long have you had that cough?"

"Ugh! ugh! ugh!—ugh! ugh! ugh!—ugh! ugh! ugh!—ugh! ugh! ugh!—ugh! ugh! ugh!"

My poor friend found it impossible to reply for many minutes.

"It is nothing," he said, at last.

"Come," I said, with decision, "we will go back; your health is precious. You are rich, respected, admired, beloved; you are happy, as once I was. You are a man to be missed. For me it is no matter. We will go back; you will be ill, and I cannot be responsible. Besides, there is Luchesi—"

"Enough," he said; "the cough is a mere nothing; it will not kill me. I shall not die of a cough."

"True—true," I replied; "and, indeed, I had no intention of alarming you unnecessarily— but you should use all proper caution. A draft of this Médoc[10] will defend us from the damps."

Here I knocked off the neck of a bottle which I drew from a long row of its fellows that lay upon the mold.

"Drink," I said, presenting him the wine.

He raised it to his lips with a leer. He paused and nodded to me familiarly, while his bells jingled.

"I drink," he said, "to the buried that repose around us."

"And I to your long life."

He again took my arm, and we proceeded.

"These vaults," he said, "are extensive."

"The Montresors," I replied, "were a great and numerous family."

"I forget your arms."[11]

"A huge human foot d'or, in a field azure; the foot crushes a serpent rampant whose fangs are embedded in the heel."[12]

"And the motto?"

"The drops of moisture trickle among the bones."

---

8. **sconces** (skän′siz) *n.:* wall fixtures that hold **flambeaux** (flam′bōz′) *n.,* candlesticks or flaming pieces of wood.
9. **rheum** (rōōm) *n.:* watery discharge.
10. **Médoc** (mā·dôk′): type of red wine.
11. **arms** *n.:* coat of arms, a group of symbols used to represent a family.
12. **foot d'or . . . heel:** The Montresor coat of arms shows a huge golden foot against a blue background, with the foot crushing a snake that is rearing up and biting the heel.

"*Nemo me impune lacessit.*"[13]

"Good!" he said.

The wine sparkled in his eyes and the bells jingled. My own fancy grew warm with the Médoc. We had passed through walls of piled bones, with casks and puncheons[14] intermingling, into the inmost recesses of the catacombs. I paused again, and this time I made bold to seize Fortunato by an arm above the elbow.

"The niter!" I said. "See, it increases. It hangs like moss upon the vaults. We are below the river's bed. The drops of moisture trickle among the bones. Come, we will go back ere it is too late. Your cough—"

"It is nothing," he said; "let us go on. But first, another draft of the Médoc."

I broke and reached him a flagon of de Grave.[15] He emptied it at a breath. His eyes flashed with a fierce light. He laughed and threw the bottle upward with a gesticulation I did not understand.

I looked at him in surprise. He repeated the movement—a grotesque one.

"You do not comprehend?" he said.

"Not I," I replied.

"Then you are not of the brotherhood."

"How?"

"You are not of the Masons."[16]

"Yes, yes," I said, "yes, yes."

"You? Impossible! A Mason?"

"A Mason," I replied.

"A sign," he said.

"It is this," I answered, producing a trowel[17] from beneath the folds of my roquelaure.

"You jest," he exclaimed, recoiling a few paces. "But let us proceed to the amontillado."

"Be it so," I said, replacing the tool beneath the cloak and again offering him my arm. He leaned upon it heavily. We continued our route in search of the amontillado. We passed through a range of low arches, descended, passed on, and, descending again, arrived at a deep crypt in which the foulness of the air caused our flambeaux rather to glow than flame.

At the most remote end of the crypt there appeared another less spacious. Its walls had been lined with human remains, piled to the vault overhead, in the fashion of the great catacombs of Paris. Three sides of this interior crypt were still ornamented in this manner. From the fourth the bones had been thrown down and lay promiscuously[18] upon the earth, forming at one point a mound of some size. Within the wall thus exposed by the displacing of the bones, we perceived a still interior recess, in depth about four feet, in width three, in height six or seven. It seemed to have been constructed for no especial use within itself, but formed merely the interval between two of the colossal supports of the roof of the catacombs and was backed by one of their

DRAWING CONCLUSIONS

3. Why might Montresor be carrying a trowel? What can you conclude about his plans?

---

13. ***Nemo me impune lacessit*** (nā'mō mā im·pōō'nä lä·ke'sit): Latin for "Nobody attacks me without punishment."
14. **puncheons** (pun'chənz) *n.:* large wine casks.
15. **flagon of de Grave:** narrow-necked bottle with a handle and sometimes a lid, containing a wine from the Graves region of France.
16. **Masons:** Freemasons, a secret society of people who believe in brotherhood, giving to the poor, and helping one another. Members use secret signs and gestures to recognize one another.

---

17. **trowel** (trou'əl) *n.:* flat tool with a pointed blade, especially used by a mason, a person who builds with stone or concrete. The Freemasons probably began as associations of stoneworkers.
18. **promiscuously** (prō·mis'kyōō·əs·lē) *adv.:* randomly; in a disorganized way.

Vocabulary

recoiling (ri·koil'iŋ) *v.* used as *adj.:* moving backward, as in fear.

circumscribing walls of solid granite.

It was in vain that Fortunato, uplifting his dull torch, endeavored to pry into the depth of the recess. Its termination the feeble light did not enable us to see.

"Proceed," I said; "herein is the amontillado. As for Luchesi—"

"He is an ignoramus," interrupted my friend, as he stepped unsteadily forward, while I followed immediately at his heels. In an instant he had reached the extremity of the niche, and finding his progress arrested by the rock, stood stupidly bewildered. A moment more and I had fettered[19] him to the granite. In its surface were two iron staples, distant from each other about two feet horizontally. From one of these depended a short chain, from the other a padlock. Throwing the links about his waist, it was but the work of a few seconds to secure it. He was too much astounded to resist. Withdrawing the

key, I stepped back from the recess.

"Pass your hand," I said, "over the wall; you cannot help feeling the niter. Indeed it is *very* damp. Once more let me *implore* you to return. No? Then I must positively leave you. But I must first render you all the little attentions in my power."

"The amontillado!" ejaculated my friend, not yet recovered from his astonishment.

"True," I replied; "the amontillado."

As I said these words, I busied myself among the pile of bones of which I have before spoken. Throwing them aside, I soon uncovered a quantity of building stone and mortar. With these materials and with the aid of my trowel, I began vigorously to wall up the entrance of the niche.

I had scarcely laid the first tier of the masonry when I discovered that the intoxication

---

19. **fettered** (fet′ərd) *v*.: chained.

Vocabulary
endeavored (en·dev′ərd) *v*.: tried.

A CLOSER LOOK
The Other Man in the Wall

On July 12, 1845, a letter appeared in a New York newspaper. The letter writer was describing his recent travels in Italy. He said that he had an amazing experience in the little town of San Giovanni when he visited the church of San Lorenzo. He was shown a niche covered with a sort of trapdoor in the wall of the church. Inside the niche was an upright human skeleton. The writer examined the skeleton and concluded that the victim had been walled in alive and suffocated. The writer supposed that the motive had been revenge. He guessed that the man had been tied securely and then walled in, brick by brick. The writer also guessed that the men involved were nobles (like Fortunato and Montresor)—no one else, he figured, could have gotten control of a church to perform the gruesome deed.

The year after this letter was published, Poe wrote his famous revenge story "The Cask of Amontillado."

Crypt of the popes. Catacomb of S. Callisto. Rome, Italy.

of Fortunato had in a great measure worn off. The earliest indication I had of this was a low moaning cry from the depth of the recess. It was *not* the cry of a drunken man. There was then a long and obstinate silence. I laid the second tier, and the third, and the fourth; and then I heard the furious vibrations of the chain. The noise lasted for several minutes, during which, that I might hearken to it with the more satisfaction, I ceased my labors and sat down upon the bones. When at last the clanking subsided, I resumed the trowel and finished without interruption the fifth, the sixth, and the seventh tier. The wall was now nearly upon a level with my breast. I again paused and, holding the flambeaux over the masonwork, threw a few feeble rays upon the figure within.

DRAWING CONCLUSIONS

4. What can you conclude about Montresor's state of mind when he stops his work to enjoy Fortunato's cries?

A succession of loud and shrill screams, bursting suddenly from the throat of the chained form, seemed to thrust me violently back. For a brief moment I hesitated—I trembled. Unsheathing my rapier,[20] I began to grope with it about the recess; but the thought of an instant reassured me. I placed my hand upon the solid fabric of the catacombs and felt satisfied. I reapproached the wall; I replied to the yells of him who clamored. I reechoed—I aided—I surpassed them in volume and in strength. I did this, and the clamorer grew still.

It was now midnight, and my task was drawing to a close. I had completed the eighth, the ninth, and the tenth tier. I had finished a portion of the last and the eleventh; there remained but a single stone to be fitted and plastered in. I struggled with its weight; I placed it partially in its destined position. But now there came from out the niche a low laugh that erected the hairs upon my head. It was succeeded by a sad voice, which I had difficulty in recognizing as that of the noble Fortunato. The voice said—

"Ha! ha! ha!—he! he! he!—a very good joke indeed—an excellent jest. We will have many a rich laugh about it at the *palazzo*—he! he! he!—over our wine—he! he! he!"

"The amontillado!" I said.

"He! he! he!—he! he! he!—yes, the amontillado. But is it not getting late? Will not they be awaiting us at the *palazzo*—the Lady Fortunato and the rest? Let us be gone."

"Yes," I said, "let us be gone."

"For the love of God, Montresor!"

"Yes," I said, "for the love of God!"

But to these words I hearkened in vain for a reply. I grew impatient. I called aloud—

"Fortunato!"

No answer. I called again—

"Fortunato!"

No answer still. I thrust a torch through the remaining aperture and let it fall within. There came forth in return only a jingling of the bells. My heart grew sick—on account of the dampness of the catacombs. I hastened to make an end of my labor. I forced the last stone into its position; I plastered it up. Against the new masonry I reerected the old rampart[21] of bones. For the half of a century no mortal has disturbed them. *In pace requiescat.*[22] ■

DRAWING CONCLUSIONS

5. Do you think Montresor's "heart grew sick" because of the dampness or for some other reason? Support your conclusion.

20. **rapier** (rā′pē·ər) *n.*: slender two-edged sword.

21. **rampart** (ram′pärt′) *n.*: wall resembling one built for protection or defense.

22. ***In pace requiescat*** (in pä′chā rā′kwē·es′kät): Latin for "May he rest in peace."

Vocabulary

obstinate (äb′stə·nət) *adj.*: stubborn.

succession (sək·sesh′ən) *n.*: series.

Meet the Writer

Edgar Allan Poe

A Haunted Life

Edgar Allan Poe (1809–1849) was the son of traveling actors. His father deserted the family, and his beautiful young mother died in a theatrical rooming house in Richmond, Virginia, before Edgar was three years old. The little boy was taken in as a foster child by the wealthy and childless Allan family of Richmond.

At first, Edgar's foster parents were pleased with his brilliant scholarship and athletic ability. But later they became angry at his moodiness and irresponsibility with money. Poe went to the University of Virginia but dropped out with heavy gambling debts. (John Allan apparently refused to

support him any longer.) Eventually Poe and his foster father split up completely, and Poe was left penniless. After several failed courtships, Poe married a thirteen-year-old cousin, Virginia Clemm, and moved to New York City. There, in 1837, they set up house, together with Virginia's mother, whom Poe fondly called Muddy.

Poe drank excessively at times, and he was always in need of money. He wrote regularly, however, and had increasing success, although his unusual poems and stories were mocked by conservative critics. "The Cask of Amontillado" was published in 1846, during a time when Poe was enduring vicious insults from critics. The story might have been Poe's way of getting even not only with hostile critics but also with his foster father. The Montresor motto is the motto of Scotland; John Allan was Scottish and, like the hated Fortunato, a businessman and a Mason.

Poe's one refuge in life was threatened when Virginia became ill with tuberculosis. (Almost 25 percent of Americans in the nineteenth century died from tuberculosis.) When she died, Poe broke down completely. Two years later he was found delirious in a tavern in Baltimore on a rainy election day. The great master of horror died a few days later.

For Independent Reading

For more tales of terror by Poe, read "The Pit and the Pendulum," in which the narrator faces heart-stopping threats to his life, and "The Tell-Tale Heart," in which a haunted man tries to convince us he's not mad. Mystery lovers will enjoy "The Gold Bug," one of Poe's tales that set the stage for the modern detective story.

Response and Analysis

Reading Check

1. What does Montresor admit is his **motive** for this crime?

2. According to Montresor, what makes a perfect crime?

3. According to Montresor, what kind of person is Fortunato?

4. How does Montresor lure Fortunato farther and farther into the catacombs?

5. What evidence suggests that Montresor has committed the perfect crime?

Thinking Critically

6. Describe the **persona** that Poe has created for Montresor. Why might Poe have chosen someone like Montresor to tell his story?

7. What **character traits** in Fortunato make him fall prey to Montresor?

8. In your opinion, what is Montresor thinking when he says, "*In pace requiescat*"? Explain your interpretation.

9. To whom could Montresor be telling his story, fifty years after the murder? What might Montresor's revelation of the truth suggest about the consequences he's suffered for his actions?

10. Montresor's **voice**—the way he speaks and his **tone**—is **ironic.** Which of Montresor's comments to Fortunato mean something different from what they seem to mean?

11. Think about whether or not Montresor is an **unreliable narrator.** Do any details suggest that he might have imagined "the thousand injuries" and the insult—or even the whole story? Can you find evidence to support Montresor's claim that Fortunato *did* in fact injure and insult him? Consider Montresor's actions, statements, and **voice.**

12. Think about Poe's decision to set his story during carnival. What is **ironic** about the **setting**? In what ways does the setting suit the plot of the story?

Extending and Evaluating

13. Is this just a gripping horror story told only for entertainment, or does it reveal some truth about people who are consumed by a desire for revenge? Explain. (Be sure to check your Quickwrite notes.) ✏

WRITING

Fortunato's Version

Suppose this story were told from Fortunato's **first-person point of view.** Write a **new beginning.** Start at the point where the two men meet at dusk, and end when they begin their journey underground. Let the reader know what Fortunato thinks of Montresor. Is he guilty of the thousand injuries and the insult that Montresor refers to? Create an individual **voice** for Fortunato (one that is different from Montresor's) by giving him a distinct tone and style of speaking. For example, is he frank, confused, or overconfident?

Crime and Punishment

Suppose the person to whom Montresor is telling his story has turned him over to the police. Montresor's lawyer will argue that he is insane. The prosecution will argue that Montresor knew exactly what he was doing and that he even planned the murder in advance. Write a **speech** for either lawyer, and argue your case before your classmates.

SKILLS FOCUS

Literary Skills
Analyze the first-person narrator and the unreliable narrator.

Reading Skills
Draw conclusions.

Writing Skills
Write a new beginning for a short story. Write a speech.

INTERNET

Projects and Activities

Keyword: LE7 9-3

After You Read Vocabulary Development

Word Maps

PRACTICE

A word map can supply several different kinds of information. It can give the word's **etymology,** or origin, by listing **root words** and **prefixes.** It can also give a definition and a sample sentence. Use a dictionary to make a word map for each word in the Word Bank. (A map of *precluded* appears below.)

Word Bank

precluded
impunity
retribution
immolation
connoisseurship
impose
recoiling
endeavored
obstinate
succession

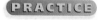

precluded

Etymology	Meaning	Sample sentence
< Latin *prae–*, "before" < Latin *claudere*, "to close"	made impossible in advance; prevented	Cara's injury precluded her entering the gymnastics meet.

Grammar Link

Dialogue—Who's Talking?

Dialogue in a story can advance the plot, reveal the thoughts of a character, or present important information to a reader. In American usage, **dialogue** is enclosed in double quotation marks (" "). Usually a new paragraph lets us know when a different person begins to speak, as in this example from "The Cask of Amontillado":

> "You do not comprehend?" he said.
> "Not I," I replied.
> "Then you are not of the brotherhood."

Most writers use **tag lines** (such as *he said* and *I replied*) to identify the speakers in a dialogue. Some writers do not always use tag lines, however. Poe, for example, has written long passages of conversation between Montresor and Fortunato in which neither speaker is directly identified. Remember that tag lines should not be enclosed in quotation marks.

PRACTICE

Look back at the dialogue beginning "Amontillado!" on page 212 and at the dialogue beginning "You do not comprehend?" on page 215.

1. Get together with a partner, and read the dialogues aloud. Use your voices to distinguish one speaker from another.

2. Now, add tag lines to Poe's dialogue. (Be sure to punctuate them correctly.) Compare your edited versions of Poe's dialogue in class.

3. Finally, look at what Poe's dialogue accomplished. What did you learn about the characters or plot from this exchange?

▶ **For more help, see Quotation Marks, 13c–j, in the Language Handbook.**

SKILLS FOCUS

Vocabulary Skills
Create word maps showing etymology, meaning, and context.

Grammar Skills
Punctuate dialogue correctly.

Four Readings About Poe's Death

Synthesizing Sources: Main Ideas and Supporting Evidence

When you research a subject, you read many different sources carefully. Then you need to **synthesize** the information, putting all the pieces together to see the big picture. Follow these steps:

- **Find the main idea.** Look for each writer's main idea, and take notes about it. To work your way through a difficult passage, **paraphrase** it—restate the passage in your own words.

- **Look for supporting evidence.** Ask yourself, "Does the writer support his or her ideas with facts, statistics, examples, anecdotes (brief real-life stories), or quotations? Does the writer use logic and reasoning to prove a point?" For help identifying the writer's main ideas and support, try making a chart.

Main Idea 1	Main Idea 2
Support 1 Support 2	Support 1 Support 2

- **Compare and contrast.** Look for similarities and differences between your sources. In particular, compare and contrast the main ideas and the types of support the authors use.

- **Make connections.** Does the information in your sources remind you of ideas that you've read about in the past—perhaps in other articles or books or even in a story or poem?

- **Put it all together.** Your last step is to put all the pieces together. To **synthesize** what you've learned, you may want to write a research report, an editorial, a speech, or a letter.

Vocabulary Development

insensible (in·sen′sə·bəl) *adj.:* not fully conscious or aware.

imposing (im·pō′ziŋ) *adj.:* large and impressive looking.

stupor (stoo′pər) *n.:* dull, half-conscious state.

spectral (spek′trəl) *adj.:* ghostly; unreal.

expired (ek·spīrd′) *v.:* died.

maligned (mə·līnd′) *v.* used as *adj.:* falsely accused of bad conduct; slandered.

belligerent (bə·lij′ər·ənt) *adj.:* angry and aggressive or ready to start a fight.

conspicuous (kən·spik′yoo·əs) *adj.:* obvious; noticeable; notable.

ascribe (ə·skrīb′) *v.:* assign or attribute something to a cause.

chronic (krän′ik) *adj.:* frequently occurring.

transmitted (trans·mit′id) *v.:* passed on.

Connecting to the Literature

The life of Edgar Allan Poe, author of "The Cask of Amontillado," is shrouded in mystery. Most scholars believe that Poe died as a result of drinking too much alcohol. According to another theory, Poe died of rabies, a disease people can get when they are bitten or scratched by an animal infected with the rabies virus. The following four selections present a debate about what killed this tragic genius.

SKILLS FOCUS

Reading Skills
Synthesize information from several sources on a single topic.

This biography traces the last few days of Poe's life, in 1849. He had just parted from Elmira Shelton, to whom he was recently engaged. Shelton lived in Richmond, Virginia, and Poe set out from there for Baltimore, Maryland, eventually planning to go to New York City. He never reached it.

Poe's Final Days

from *Edgar A. Poe: Mournful and Never-Ending Remembrance*

Kenneth Silverman

In the early morning of September 27, a Thursday, Poe began the first leg of his return to the North, setting out from Richmond for Baltimore on the 4 A.M. steamer,[1] with a trunk containing some clothing, books, and manuscripts.

No reliable evidence exists about what happened to or within Poe between that time and October 3, a week later, when a printer named Joseph Walker saw him at Gunner's Hall, a Baltimore tavern, strangely dressed and semiconscious.

It was Election Day for members of Congress, and like other local watering holes[2] the tavern served as a polling place. Poe seemed to Walker "rather the worse for wear" and "in great distress." Apparently flooded with drink, he may also have been ill from exposure. Winds and soaking rains the day before had sent Baltimoreans prematurely hunting up overcoats and seeking charcoal fires for warmth. . . . Poe managed to tell Walker that he knew Joseph Evans Snodgrass, the Baltimore editor and physician with whom he had often corresponded while living in Philadelphia. As it happened, Walker had worked as a typesetter for Snodgrass's *Saturday Visitor*. He sent Snodgrass a dire note, warning that Poe needed "immediate assistance."

When Snodgrass arrived at Gunner's Hall, he found Poe sitting in an armchair, surrounded by onlookers. Poe had a look of "vacant stupidity." He wore neither vest nor tie, his dingy trousers fit badly, his shirt was crumpled, his cheap hat soiled. Snodgrass thought he must be wearing castoff clothing, having been robbed or cheated of his own. He ordered a room for Poe at the tavern, where he might stay comfortably until his relatives in Baltimore could be notified. Just then, however, one of them arrived—Henry Herring, Poe's uncle by marriage, who somehow had also learned of his condition. A lumber dealer now nearly sixty years old, he had wed Muddy's[3] sister, and spent time with Poe

---

1. **steamer** (stēm′ər) *n.*: steamship, or ship driven by steam power.
2. **watering holes:** informal for "bars, taverns."

3. **Muddy's:** Muddy was Poe's nickname for Maria Clemm, his aunt and mother-in-law. Poe had married his cousin, Virginia Clemm.

during his early days in Baltimore and later when both families lived in Philadelphia. But he refused now to take over his care, saying that on former occasions, when drunk, Poe had been abusive and ungrateful. Instead, he suggested sending Poe to a hospital. A carriage was called for. Poe had to be carried into it, Snodgrass said—insensible, muttering.

Through the chilly wet streets Poe was driven to the hospital of Washington Medical College, set on the highest ground of Baltimore. An imposing five-story building with vaulted gothic windows, it afforded both public wards and private rooms, advertised as being spacious, well ventilated, and directed by an experienced medical staff. Admitted at five in the afternoon, Poe was given a private room, reportedly in a section reserved for cases involving drunkenness. He was attended by the resident physician, Dr. John J. Moran, who apparently had living quarters in the hospital together with his wife. Moran had received his medical degree from the University of Maryland four years earlier and was now only about twenty-six years old. But he knew the identity of his patient—a *great* man," he wrote of Poe, to whose "rarely gifted mind are we indebted for many of the brightest thoughts that adorn our literature." He as well as the medical students, nurses, and other physicians—all considered Poe, he said, "an object of unusual regard."

According to Moran and his wife, Poe reached the hospital in a stupor, unaware of who or what had brought him there. He remained thus "unconscious" until three o'clock the next morning, when he developed

> ### His face was pale and he was drenched in sweat.

a tremor[4] of the limbs and what Moran called "a busy, but not violent or active delirium."[5] His face was pale and he was drenched in sweat. He talked constantly, Moran said, addressing "spectral and imaginary objects on the walls." Apparently during Poe's delirium, his cousin Neilson Poe came to the hospital, having been contacted by Dr. Moran. A lawyer and journalist involved in Whig politics,[6] Neilson was just Poe's age. In happier circumstances Poe would not have welcomed the visit. Not only had Neilson offered Virginia[7] and Muddy a home apart from him; his cousin also, he believed, envied his literary reputation. Years before he had remarked that he considered "the little dog," as he called Neilson, the "bitterest enemy I have in the world." The physicians anyway thought it inadvisable for Neilson to see Poe at the moment, when "very excitable." Neilson sent some changes of linen and called again the next day, to find Poe's condition improved.

---

4. **tremor** (trem′ər) *n.*: involuntary trembling, especially from a physical illness.
5. **delirium** (di·lir′ē·əm) *n.*: irrational, raving behavior, often caused by high fever.
6. **Whig politics:** The Whigs were one of the two major American political parties at the time, the other being the Democrats.
7. **Virginia:** Poe's wife, Virginia Clemm. She died of tuberculosis in 1847.

Vocabulary

insensible (in·sen′sə·bəl) *adj.*: not fully conscious or aware.

imposing (im·pō′ziŋ) *adj.*: large and impressive looking.

stupor (stoo′pər) *n.*: dull, half-conscious state.

spectral (spek′trəl) *adj.*: ghostly; unreal.

Poe being quieted, Moran began questioning him about his family and about where he lived, but found his answers mostly incoherent. Poe did not know what had become of his trunk or when he had left Richmond, but said he had a wife there, as Moran soon learned was untrue. He said that his "degradation," as Moran characterized it, made him feel like sinking into the ground. Trying to rouse Poe's spirits, Moran told him he wished to contribute in every way to his comfort, and hoped Poe would soon be enjoying the company of his friends. . . .

Then Poe seemed to doze, and Moran left him briefly. On returning he found Poe violently delirious, resisting the efforts of two nurses to keep him in bed. From Moran's description, Poe seems to have raved a full day or more, through Saturday evening, October 6, when he began repeatedly calling out someone's name. It may have been that of a Baltimore family named Reynolds or, more likely, the name of his uncle-in-law Henry Herring. Moran later said that he sent for the Herring family, but that only one of Herring's two daughters came to the hospital. Poe continued deliriously calling the name until three o'clock on Sunday morning. Then his condition changed. Feeble from his exertions he seemed to rest a short time and then, Moran reported, "quietly moving his head he said '*Lord help my poor Soul*' and expired!"

The cause of Poe's death remains in doubt. Moran's account of his profuse perspiration, trembling, and hallucinations indicates

On returning he found Poe violently delirious . . .

delirium tremens, *mania à potu*.[8] Many others who had known Poe, including the professionally trained Dr. Snodgrass, also attributed his death to a lethal amount of alcohol. Moran later vigorously disputed this explanation, however, and some Baltimore newspapers gave the cause of death as "congestion of the brain" or "cerebral inflammation."[9] Although the terms were sometimes used euphemistically[10] in public announcements of deaths from disgraceful causes, such as alcoholism, they may in this case have come from the hospital staff itself. According to Moran, one of its senior physicians diagnosed Poe's condition as encephalitis, a brain inflammation, brought on by "exposure." This explanation is consistent with the prematurely wintry weather at the time, with Snodgrass's account of Poe's partly clad[11] condition, and with Elmira Shelton's recollection that on leaving Richmond Poe already had a fever. Both explanations may have been correct: Poe may have become too drunk to care about protecting himself against the wind and rain.

8. **delirium tremens, *mania à potu*:** *Delirium tremens* refers to an alcoholic state in which the victim behaves irrationally and sometimes violently, hallucinates (sees imaginary things), and trembles. *Mania à potu* is a Latin phrase meaning "madness from drinking."
9. **"congestion of the brain" or "cerebral inflammation":** These are terms for conditions of the brain caused by injury or infection.
10. **euphemistically** (yo͞o′fə·mis′tə·klē) *adv.:* in a manner meant to mask or substitute for something unpleasant or offensive.
11. **clad** (klad) *adj.:* dressed.

Vocabulary
expired (ek·spīrd′) *v.:* died.

The following newspaper article announced a new theory about Poe's death, developed by Dr. R. Michael Benitez. In response to this article, Burton R. Pollin and Robert E. Benedetto wrote a letter disputing Dr. Benitez's theory. Dr. Benitez replied by writing a letter defending his ideas. Both letters follow this article.

Poe's Death Is Rewritten as Case of Rabies, Not Telltale Alcohol

from *The New York Times*, September 15, 1996

Edgar Allan Poe did not die drunk in a gutter in Baltimore but rather had rabies, a new study suggests.

The researcher, Dr. R. Michael Benitez, a cardiologist[1] who practices a block from Poe's grave, says it is true that the writer was seen in a bar on Lombard Street in October 1849, delirious and possibly wearing somebody else's soiled clothes.

But Poe was not drunk, said Dr. Benitez, an assistant professor of medicine at the University of Maryland Medical Center. "I think Poe is much <u>maligned</u> in that respect," he added.

The writer entered Washington College Hospital comatose,[2] Dr. Benitez said, but by the next day was perspiring heavily, hallucinating, and shouting at imaginary companions. The next day, he seemed better but could not remember falling ill.

On his fourth day at the hospital, Poe again grew confused and <u>belligerent</u>, then quieted down and died.

That is a classic case of rabies, the doctor said. His study is in the September issue of *The Maryland Medical Journal.*

In the brief period when he was calm and awake, Poe refused alcohol and could drink water only with great difficulty. Rabies victims frequently exhibit hydrophobia, or fear of water, because it is painful to swallow.

There is no evidence that a rabid animal had bitten Poe. About one fourth of rabies victims reportedly cannot remember being bitten. After an infection, the symptoms can take up to a year to appear. But when the symptoms do appear, the disease is a swift and brutal killer. Most patients die in a few days.

Poe "had all the features of encephalitic[3] rabies," said Dr. Henry Wilde, who frequently treats rabies at Chulalongkorn University Hospital in Bangkok, Thailand.

Although it has been well established that Poe died in the hospital, legend has it that he

---

3. **encephalitic** (en·sef'ə·lit'ik) *adj.:* related to encephalitis, an inflammation, or swelling, of the brain.

Vocabulary

maligned (mə·līnd') *v.* used as *adj.:* falsely accused of bad conduct; slandered.

belligerent (bə·lij'ər·ənt) *adj.:* angry and aggressive or ready to start a fight.

---

1. **cardiologist** (kär'dē·äl'ə·jist) *n.:* doctor who specializes in diseases of the heart.
2. **comatose** (kō'mə·tōs') *adj.:* deeply unconscious and unable to be wakened.

The Edgar Allan Poe House and Museum in Baltimore as it appears today.

"almost everyone who has come forth with a theory has offered no proof."

Some versions have Poe unconscious under the steps of the Baltimore Museum before being taken to the hospital. Other accounts place him on planks between two barrels outside a tavern on Lombard Street. In most versions, Poe is wearing someone else's clothes, having been robbed of his suit.

Poe almost surely did not die of alcohol poisoning or withdrawal, Mr. Jerome said. The writer was so sensitive to alcohol that a glass of wine would make him violently ill for days. Poe may have had problems with alcohol as a younger man, Mr. Jerome said, but by the time he died at forty he almost always avoided it.

Dr. Benitez worked on Poe's case as part of a clinical pathologic conference. Doctors are presented with a hypothetical[6] patient and a description of the symptoms and are asked to render a diagnosis.

Dr. Benitez said that at first he did not know that he had been assigned Poe, because his patient was described only as "E. P., a writer from Richmond." But by the time he was scheduled to present his findings a few weeks later, he had figured out the mystery.

"There was a conspicuous lack in this report of things like CT scans and MRI's,"[7] the doctor said. "I started to say to myself, 'This doesn't look like it's from the 1990s.' Then it dawned on me that E. P. was Edgar Poe."

succumbed in the gutter, a victim of his debauched[4] ways.

The legend may have been fostered by his doctor, who in later years became a temperance advocate[5] and changed the details to make an object lesson of Poe's death.

The curator of the Edgar Allan Poe House and Museum in Baltimore, Jeff Jerome, said that he had heard dozens of tales but that

---

4. **debauched** (dē·bôchd′) *adj.:* characterized by extreme indulgence in pleasures.
5. **temperance advocate:** someone who believes that people should not drink alcohol.

6. **hypothetical** (hī′pə·thet′i·kəl) *adj.:* in theory; not actual.
7. **CT scans and MRI's:** medical tests that use modern technology. Both tests produce an image of a cross-section of soft tissue such as the brain.

Vocabulary
conspicuous (kən·spik′yōō·əs) *adj.:* obvious; noticeable; notable.

If Only Poe Had Succeeded When He Said Nevermore to Drink

from *The New York Times*, September 23, 1996

To the Editor:

Dr. R. Michael Benitez, an assistant professor of medicine at Maryland University Medical Center, is wrong to ascribe the death of Edgar Allan Poe to rabies through animal infection rather than to the traditionally maintained cause of alcoholism (news article, September 15).

Poe was found outside a Baltimore saloon in an alcoholic stupor on October 3, 1849, and died four days later. Dr. John J. Moran's account of his final days is given in a letter to Poe's aunt and mother-in-law, Maria Clemm, a *New York Herald* article in 1875, and a book by Moran in 1885. Supplementary accounts of Poe's alcoholic condition came from Joseph Walker, a Baltimore printer who first found him; Dr. Joseph Snodgrass, an editor well known to Poe; and two of Poe's relatives. None of these confirm Dr. Benitez's statement that "Poe was not drunk." Evidence of Poe's chronic binges is strewn through his letters, in periodic admissions of "recoveries" and promises to his wife, Virginia, and her mother to "reform."

Dr. Benitez admits the primary weakness of his theory—lack of evidence of a bite or scratch. In those days, rabies was well known as to causes and symptoms, including itching and other sensations that could affect an entire limb or side of the body. How could Moran and his staff ignore such symptoms in a patient?

And what of Poe's cat, dearly loved but left behind in the Bronx over three months earlier? Guiltless was the pet Caterina, who, uninfected and showing no sign of rabies, died of starvation when deserted by Clemm after Poe's death.

In short, there is no need to whitewash° the self-destructive behavior of this literary genius and major American poet, critic, and teller of tales.

Burton R. Pollin
Robert E. Benedetto
Bronxville, New York
September 20, 1996

The writers are, respectively, professor emeritus of English, City University of New York, and an associate film professor at the University of South Carolina.

°**whitewash** (hwīt′wôsh′) *v.:* cover up the faults or defects of something; give a favorable appearance to something.

Vocabulary
ascribe (ə·skrīb′) *v.:* assign or attribute something to a cause.
chronic (krän′ik) *adj.:* frequently occurring.

Rabies Death Theory

from *The New York Times*, September 30, 1996

To the Editor:

Contrary to a September 23 letter, I do not "admit" that the lack of bite or scratch is a weakness in my theory that Edgar Allan Poe may have died of rabies encephalitis.

Data published by the Centers for Disease Control and Prevention indicate that over the past 20 years in the United States there have been 33 reported cases of human rabies, yet only 24 percent of these victims could recall an appropriate history of animal exposure. Bat-related subtypes of rabies have been identified in 15 cases of human rabies since 1980, although patient contact of any sort with bats could be documented in only 7 of these patients.

A diagnosis is not always easy or straightforward. The incubation period[1] in humans may be as long as a year, if the inoculation[2] is small and occurs on the hand or foot. Thus the lack of evidence of a bite or scratch is not inconsistent with the diagnosis. Finally, although physicians knew how rabies was transmitted at the time of Poe's death, even at the time of Louis Pasteur's first use of a rabies "vaccine" in 1885 the causative agent, a rhabdovirus, was unknown.[3]

I was saddened to hear of the fate of Caterina, Poe's cat, yet nowhere have I suggested that Poe contracted rabies from her, although it is worth noting that there was no available vaccine for pets at that time.

R. Michael Benitez, M.D.
Baltimore, Maryland
September 26, 1996

The writer is an assistant professor of medicine at the University of Maryland Medical Center.

---

1. **incubation period:** amount of time between a person's exposure to a disease and the appearance of symptoms.
2. **inoculation** (i·näk′yə·lā′shən) *n.:* here, skin puncture from an animal bite or scratch through which a disease is passed on.
3. **even at the time of Louis Pasteur's . . . was unknown:** Louis Pasteur (1822–1895) was a French chemist who helped develop the important medical theory linking germs and disease. Pasteur developed a rabies vaccine using tissue from infected animals. Benitez is pointing out, however, that at the time of Poe's death, scientists had not isolated and identified the virus that causes rabies.

Vocabulary
transmitted (trans·mit′id) *v.:* passed on.

Reading Check

1. Make a time line of Poe's last days, based on the information in the biography "Poe's Final Days."

2. Summarize the **evidence** cited to support Dr. Benitez's theory in the article ("Poe's Death Is Rewritten as Case of Rabies, Not Telltale Alcohol").

3. According to Burton R. Pollin and Robert E. Benedetto, what is the major weakness of Dr. Benitez's theory?

SKILLS FOCUS

Reading Skills
Synthesize information from several sources on a single topic.

Test Practice

1. What is the **main idea** of the letter by Pollin and Benedetto?

   A Poe has been unjustly accused of being an alcoholic.

   B There is a great deal of evidence that Poe's death was due to alcoholism.

   C Poe's cat could not have bitten him and given him rabies.

   D Poe was a great writer, but he had human faults.

2. What is the *strongest* **evidence** Dr. Benitez presents in his letter to defend his theory?

   F Rabies has a long incubation period, and many victims do not remember being attacked by an animal.

   G There was no available vaccine for pets at the time of Poe's death.

   H During Poe's lifetime, doctors knew how rabies was passed on.

   J Louis Pasteur first used a rabies vaccine in 1885.

3. What information in the biography could support Dr. Benitez's theory that rabies caused Poe's death?

   A It had been raining, and Poe may have suffered from exposure.

   B Dr. Moran stated that Poe sweated and addressed "imaginary objects on the walls."

   C Poe was so ill that he was taken to the hospital.

   D No one knows where Poe was the week before he appeared at the tavern.

4. Which of the following statements that **contrast** the biography with Pollin and Benedetto's letter is *not* true?

   F The biography states that Dr. Moran eventually claimed Poe didn't die from drinking too much, but the letter states that Dr. Moran provided evidence for this theory.

   G Pollin and Benedetto refer to Poe's letters as evidence, but the biography does not.

   H The biography does not discuss the rabies death theory, but the letter does.

   J The letter does not refer to Joseph Walker's description of Poe, but the biography does.

   (continued)

5. Which statement is the *most* important **similarity** between the article and Dr. Benitez's letter?

   A Both inform the reader that Dr. Benitez is an assistant professor of medicine.

   B Both use statistics as support.

   C Both point out that the lack of a bite or scratch does not weaken the rabies death theory.

   D Both state that only highly skilled doctors can diagnose rabies.

6. Which of the following statements is the *best* **synthesis** of the information in these four sources?

   F Poe was a tortured genius.

   G Poe's symptoms could point to several different causes of death.

   H All theories should take into account that Poe died drunk.

   J Poe's illness would have been correctly diagnosed by modern doctors.

Constructed Response

Imagine that you are writing a biography of Poe. Write the last few paragraphs of your book, in which you tell about Poe's death. In your discussion, **synthesize** the information from the four sources by **paraphrasing** the ideas and **comparing and contrasting** the points. End your account by drawing your own **conclusions** from the information.

▶ **Use "Analyzing Nonfiction," pages 232–239, for help with this assignment.**

Vocabulary Development

Understanding Word Derivations: Useful Roots

PRACTICE

A **root** is the part of a word that establishes its core meaning. Knowing what some common roots mean will help you figure out the definitions of new words. Match each root in the chart below with a word from the Word Bank. (Note that two words share a root.) Then, define the word, and write another word with the same root.

Word Bank

insensible
imposing
stupor
spectral
expired
maligned
belligerent
conspicuous
ascribe
chronic
transmitted

Word Roots	
Latin Roots	**–spec–,** "look"
–bel–, "war"	**–spir–,** "breathe"
–mal–, "ill"	**–stup–,** "be stunned or amazed"
–mit–, "send"	
–pon–, "place"	
–scrib–, "write"	**Greek Root**
–sent–, "feel"	**–chron–,** "time"

SKILLS FOCUS

Vocabulary Skills
Understand Greek and Latin word roots.

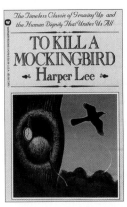

FICTION
Crisis in a Small Town

Harper Lee's *To Kill a Mockingbird* is a riveting story of race relations as viewed by a wise, plucky child. Eight-year-old Scout and her brother, Jem, learn an unforgettable lesson about courage, justice, and compassion when their father takes part in a shocking trial that will change their hometown forever. You're not likely to forget this Pulitzer Prize–winning novel.

FICTION
California Dreams

When Panchito lived in Mexico, the most excitement he ever had was hunting for chicken eggs and going to church on Sundays. Then Panchito's father moves the family to California, where jobs for migrant workers abound and the promise of an American education awaits. In Francisco Jiménez's *The Circuit,* Panchito describes his family's odyssey from one labor camp to another as they pursue the American dream.

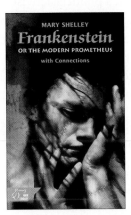

FICTION
The Monster's Revenge

Mary Shelley's classic novel, *Frankenstein,* has two narrators: Dr. Frankenstein, an obsessed scientist who creates a monster in the image of a man (and later comes to fear his creation); and the monster himself, a huge, misshapen creature who fights the men who have hurt him. Who is the real monster in this story? The answer just might surprise you.

This title is available in the HRW Library.

NONFICTION
On the Outside Looking In

Adeline Yen Mah, a young girl living in Shanghai, was a family outcast. Her father had trouble remembering her name, and her stepmother treated her no better than a servant. However, her memoir, *Chinese Cinderella,* is not about hardship alone: It also describes her friends, her aunt and grandfather, and the teachers who encouraged her talent as a writer that would one day lead Adeline into a whole new world.

Analyzing Nonfiction

Writing Assignment
Write an analytical essay in which you examine how the parts of a biography fit together to support the writer's thesis.

Earlier in this collection, you read a newspaper article, an excerpt from a book, and several letters, all about the writer Edgar Allan Poe. As you can see in these nonfiction resources, few things interest people more than other peoples' lives. We listen to friends' life stories, scan magazine articles about the lives of celebrities, and read **biographies**—nonfiction narratives that tell the life stories of famous and not-so-famous people. In this workshop you will **analyze a biography** about a person whose life you find interesting.

Prewriting

Choose a Biography

Get a Life Whose life journey would you like to follow? Think about the variety of history makers, past and present, that you could learn more about—a queen or a conquistador, a political activist or an artist. If you're interested in a particular historical period, scan a book about that period for colorful personalities. You might also explore magazines, newspapers, and the Internet to find people who are currently noteworthy or have made an impact in recent decades. Then, check to see whether there are biographies in print about them.

Analyze Character, Events, and Setting

A Closer Look Biographers combine details about character, events, and setting—the **elements of biography**—to give readers a greater understanding of their subjects. When you analyze a biography, you look at how the writer uses these elements to express his or her unique perspective, or point of view, about the person. Create a two-column **analysis log,** like the one on page 233, in which you record the details you find as you read the biography. In your log, you may **quote** the writer's *exact* words (record the page number of the quotation). You may also **paraphrase** *all* of the writer's ideas in your own words, or **summarize** only the writer's *most important* ideas in your own words.

The details you find about the character of the biography's subject, the events in his or her life, and the setting in which that person lived will point you to what the writer is saying about him or her.

- **Character** A biographer should give you a clear idea of the person's **character**—what he or she is or was like as a person. In your log,

SKILLS FOCUS

Writing Skills
Write an expository essay analyzing a biography.

take notes about what the person did, thought, felt, and said and about what others said about him or her.

- **Events** The **events** in a biography are the real-life incidents that affected the person. In your analysis log, list four to six of the most important events in the person's life. For example, look for births and deaths of people important to him or her, marriages and divorces, and successes or failures.

- **Setting** The events in the person's life take place in the context of a specific time and place—the **setting** of the biography. Write down in your log any details that relate to the living conditions of the average person of that time and place, the conditions in which the subject of the biography lived, and the historical events of the time.

TIP You may find it difficult to analyze the entire biography in great detail. Instead, you may wish to focus your analysis on one stage of the person's life: early, middle, or end.

Tying It Together After recording notes on the elements of biography—character, events, and setting—look for places in the biography where the writer **draws conclusions** about the elements' importance to the person's life. Write these conclusions in the right-hand column of your log, next to the details you've gathered. Sometimes a writer doesn't state conclusions directly. In those cases you must **infer,** or make an educated guess about, the significance of the elements. The following is part of an analysis log a student created while analyzing a biography about Edgar Allan Poe.

DO THIS

Elements of Biography	Biographer's Conclusions
Character • Although Poe's foster father (John Allan) used his influence to get Poe into West Point, Poe was court-martialed because of his bad behavior.	• Poe wanted "to use his own harm to punish John Allan" (page 65).
Events • His mother died while he was very young. • He became attached to Jane Stanard, a friend's mother, who soon died. • His chronically ill foster mother, Fanny Allan, died.	• Poe never recovered from the early death of his mother; then, the deaths of Stanard and Allan reopened these wounds.
Setting • The economy of the times forced John Allan to relocate his business and family several times. • Poe lived in the early 1800s, a time when the profession of writer was relatively new in the U.S.	• Poe didn't have a stable home life. • Poe had to take unimaginative jobs that didn't pay well.

Write and Support a Thesis Statement

The Big Idea Once you've analyzed the biography, try to determine how the conclusions fit together to form a main idea about the person. Ask yourself, "What is the biographer's point of view on this person?" Then, write a **thesis statement,** one or two sentences in which you identify the biographer's main idea about the subject of the biography. Here's the thesis statement from the analysis of the Poe biography.

In <u>Edgar A. Poe: Mournful and Never-ending Remembrance</u>, biographer Kenneth Silverman portrays Poe as a victim of circumstances.

Reference Note

For more on using **parenthetical citations,** see page 715.

Backing It Up Support for your thesis statement will come in the form of **evidence** and **elaboration.**

- **Evidence:** Gather evidence to back up your thesis by looking over your analysis log. For each of the elements of biography, select the details—the quotations, summaries, and paraphrases—that best support your thesis. Make sure the information you choose relates directly to the thesis. For each quotation, provide **parenthetical citations**—the page number (within parentheses) to indicate where you found that detail.
- **Elaboration:** Make the connections for your readers. Help them understand your analysis by explaining how the evidence supports your thesis statement. You can elaborate on individual pieces of evidence or on groups of evidence.

Organize Your Analysis

Get It Together Next, organize your analysis in a logical order. One good logical order is **order of importance,** in which you present your ideas from most important to least important, or vice versa. Decide which element includes the strongest evidence for supporting your thesis statement, and plan to discuss that element either first or last in your analysis. Discuss the strongest element first if you think it's something that will really grab your audience's attention and create a strong first impression. Discuss this element last if it's something that you'd most like your audience to remember and think about after reading your essay.

SKILLS FOCUS

Writing Skills
Write and support a thesis statement.

PRACTICE & APPLY 1 Using the information on pages 232–234, choose and analyze a biography. Gather details for each of the elements of biography; then, write a thesis statement. Support your thesis statement with evidence and elaboration. Finally, organize your analysis.

Writing

Analyzing Nonfiction

A Writer's Framework

Introduction

- Provide background information about the biography's subject.
- Introduce the biography's title and author.
- State your thesis.

Body

- Support your thesis statement with information about the elements of biography—character, events, and setting.
- Support your discussion of each element with relevant evidence.
- Elaborate on the evidence.

Conclusion

- Summarize your ideas about the elements of biography.
- Restate your thesis in different words.

A Writer's Model

The Tragic Life of Edgar Allan Poe

Edgar Allan Poe, the author of such grim and frightful tales as "The Cask of Amontillado," was a great American writer and a desperately unhappy man. In <u>Edgar A. Poe: Mournful and Never-ending Remembrance</u>, biographer Kenneth Silverman portrays Poe as a victim of circumstances. This sympathetic biography shows a man struggling unsuccessfully for love and acceptance.

Silverman suggests that Poe was a victim of the tragic events of his early life. Illness, death, abandonment, and separation seemed to plague him. Poe was not quite three years old when his mother, Eliza, died after being ill for several months, "perhaps with some infectious fever" (8). Being abandoned earlier by his father and now orphaned and separated from his brother and sister deprived Poe of a family and an inheritance. Poe was taken in, though never adopted, by John Allan, a harsh, self-made man. Allan's wife, Fanny, was "often ill and sometime absent" (20). Poe's new family was not an ideal family for emotional support. As a teenager, Poe became attached to Jane Stanard, the mother of a school friend. She soon died at the age of thirty-one. Approximately five years later, Fanny Allan passed away. According to Silverman, Poe never accepted or recovered from his mother's death; then, the deaths of Stanard and Allan reopened these old wounds. These deaths left Poe emotionally scarred.

(continued)

INTRODUCTION
Background information

Thesis statement

BODY
Element 1: Events
Evidence
Parenthetical citation
Elaboration
Evidence

Elaboration
Evidence

Biographer's conclusion
Elaboration

(continued)

Element 2:
Character

Evidence

Biographer's
conclusion

Elaboration

Biographer's
conclusion

Element 3:
Setting

Evidence

Elaboration

Evidence

Elaboration

CONCLUSION

Summary of elements
of biography

Restatement of
thesis

Poe's self-destructive character was a reaction to the events of his early years. For example, Poe asked for and received John Allan's help in gaining admission to the U.S. Military Academy. At first he did well at West Point, but after about a year, Poe stopped going to classes and was court-martialed. Silverman believes that Poe's decline began when he received the "dramatic and upsetting" news that John Allan had remarried. Silverman explains that "John Allan's marriage meant that others would now receive the attention and comforts he had looked to have himself" (63). Instead of being happy for John Allan when he remarried, Poe felt that the affection that he wanted and the inheritance that he needed from Allan would instead go to Allan's new wife and possible heirs. Silverman believes that Poe decided to quit West Point in order "to use his own harm to punish John Allan" (65).

In addition, the setting in which Poe lived also tended to make his circumstances miserable. The economy of the times forced John Allan to relocate his business and family several times. When Edgar was six and a half, the family relocated to England for five years. Much of this time Edgar spent in various boarding schools, which left him "away from his caretakers, under new and unfamiliar custodians, in a strange country, angered and frightened"(18). In early 1819, Allan's business began to fail, so the family returned to the United States, where "unsettled and financially troubled, the Allans made several moves in Richmond as Edgar grew into his teens" (23). The upheavals only worsened the stress in Poe's life. Later, as Poe began his literary career, he found it hard to make a living. In the early 1800s, the profession of writer was new. Poe had to take jobs writing unimaginative features for magazines—a task he truly hated.

Silverman shows that Poe's selfish and self-destructive behaviors are understandable. Born in a time when he could not earn a decent living by writing, shuttled around from place to place, scarred by the loss of his mother, and unloved by his foster father, Poe lived a tragic life. Edgar A. Poe: Mournful and Never-ending Remembrance makes Poe the hero—and victim—of a life as full of misery as one of the writer's own tales.

go.
hrw
.com

INTERNET

**More Writer's
Models**

Keyword: LE7 9-3

PRACTICE & APPLY 2 Refer to the framework and the Writer's Model on pages 235–236 as you write your analysis. Be sure to elaborate on all the evidence you present.

Revising

Evaluate and Revise Content, Organization, and Style

Read It Again To make sure your writing is the best it can be, read through your paper at least twice. The first time, use the guidelines below to evaluate the content and organization of your analysis. Then, in your second reading, use the guidelines on the next page to evaluate the style of your analysis.

▶ **First Reading: Content and Organization** To make sure your analysis is clear and easy to follow, use the content and organization guidelines below. Begin by asking the questions in the left-hand column. To help you answer those questions, follow the tips in the middle column. If your essay needs revision, use the revision techniques detailed in the right-hand column.

PEER REVIEW

Exchange your essay with a peer before you revise. A peer might be able to find places where you need additional evidence and elaboration to support your thesis.

Rubric: Analyzing Nonfiction

Evaluation Questions	▶ Tips	▶ Revision Techniques
❶ Does the introduction contain the title and author of the biography and a clear thesis statement?	▶ **Underline** the title and author of the biography. **Double underline** the thesis statement.	▶ If needed, **add** a thesis statement or **add** the biography's author and title to the introduction.
❷ Does the essay include information about all the elements of biography—character, events, and setting? Does the evidence support the discussion of each element?	▶ **Bracket** each element. **Put a check mark** by each piece of evidence—quotation, paraphrase, and summary.	▶ **Add** information about each element. **Replace** or **delete** any evidence that does not support the discussion of the element.
❸ Is evidence clearly explained through elaboration?	▶ **Draw an arrow** from each piece of evidence—quote, paraphrase, and summary—to its elaboration.	▶ **Elaborate** by explaining what the evidence means or why it is important.
❹ Is the organizational pattern of the analysis easy to follow?	▶ **Look back** at the elements, which you have already bracketed. If they are not organized in a logical order, revise.	▶ **Rearrange** body paragraphs into a logical order, such as order of importance.
❺ Does the conclusion summarize the elements of biography and restate the thesis?	▶ **Underline** the summary of the elements of biography. **Double underline** the restatement of the thesis.	▶ If needed, **add** sentences that summarize the elements and that restate the thesis of the analysis.

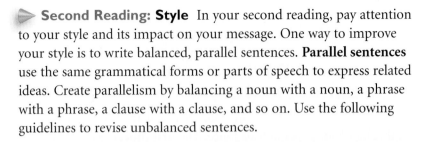

Second Reading: **Style** In your second reading, pay attention to your style and its impact on your message. One way to improve your style is to write balanced, parallel sentences. **Parallel sentences** use the same grammatical forms or parts of speech to express related ideas. Create parallelism by balancing a noun with a noun, a phrase with a phrase, a clause with a clause, and so on. Use the following guidelines to revise unbalanced sentences.

Style Guidelines

Evaluation Question	▶ Tip	▶ Revision Technique
● Are the ideas in the analysis expressed in balanced, parallel sentences?	▶ **Circle** the words *or* and *and* in all the sentences. Check to see that all items in the series joined by these words have the same grammatical form or part of speech.	▶ **Reword** sentences for parallelism. Pair nouns with nouns, phrases with phrases, clauses with clauses, and so on.

ANALYZING THE REVISION PROCESS

Study these revisions, and answer the questions that follow.

> Silverman suggests that Poe was a victim of the tragic events
>
> replace   of his early life. Illness, death, ~~abandoning,~~ *abandonment,* and separation
>
> seemed to plague him. Poe was not quite three years old when
>
> add   his mother, Eliza, died *after being ill for several months,* "perhaps with some infectious fever" (8).

Responding to the Revision Process

1. How did replacing *abandoning* with *abandonment* improve the second sentence?

2. Why did the writer add information to sentence three?

3. What does the information in parentheses tell the reader? Why is that information important?

SKILLS FOCUS

─────────────────

Writing Skills
Revise for content and style.

PRACTICE & APPLY 3 Using the rubric on page 237, revise the content and organization of your analysis. Then, use the guidelines above to revise your style. Use the example paragraph above as a model for your own revisions.

Publishing

Proofread and Publish Your Analysis

Get It Right If you want readers to take your analysis seriously, you must make sure it is free of mistakes in grammar, spelling, and punctuation. If you have time, set your analysis aside for a day or two. Having time to refresh your mind and eyes often will allow you to catch more errors. Then, carefully proofread your analysis.

Get the Word Out You've worked hard to make your analysis the best that it can be. Why be satisfied having it read by only your teacher, a couple of peer editors, or your parents? Look for a larger audience that may have an interest in reading about the person of the biography you analyzed. Try one of these ideas to share your analysis.

- Ask permission to post your analysis on a Web site dedicated to the person studied in your analysis. You may even wish to create your own site about him or her.

- Offer your analysis to local book clubs. Often an employee or a bulletin board at your local library or bookstore can direct you to a book club that would be interested in your analysis.

- Along with your classmates, gather analyses of people who have something in common, such as a group of authors or a group of current history makers. Then, create a classroom collection or display featuring information from these analyses.

Reflect on Your Analysis

Think Twice Write answers to the following questions to reflect on what you have learned in this workshop.

- What was the most interesting element of the biography you analyzed—the character of the person, the events in his or her life, or the setting? How was this element significant?

- How might you apply the analysis skills you learned in this workshop the next time you read other nonfiction works or even a novel or short story?

- Has analyzing this biography allowed you to look at the person in a different way? If so, what have you learned from his or her life story?

PRACTICE & APPLY 4 Proofread your analysis to ensure that it follows English-language conventions. Publish your analysis by using one of the ideas suggested above. Lastly, reflect on your analysis and what you have learned.

TIP Proofreading will help ensure that your analysis follows the **conventions** of standard American English. For example, your analysis might be confusing if your sentences include verbs that do not agree in number with their subjects. For more on **subject-verb agreement,** see Agreement of Subject and Verb, 2a–m, in the Language Handbook.

SKILLS FOCUS

Writing Skills
Proofread, especially for correct subject-verb agreement.

Analyzing Narrator and Voice

DIRECTIONS: Read the following selection. Then, read and respond to the questions that follow.

Snow

Julia Alvarez

Our first year in New York we rented a small apartment with a Catholic school nearby, taught by the Sisters of Charity, hefty women in long black gowns and bonnets that made them look peculiar, like dolls in mourning. I liked them a lot, especially my grandmotherly fourth-grade teacher, Sister Zoe. I had a lovely name, she said, and she had me teach the whole class how to pronounce it. *Yo-lan-da.* As the only immigrant in my class, I was put in a special seat in the first row by the window, apart from the other children, so that Sister Zoe could tutor me without disturbing them. Slowly, she enunciated the new words I was to repeat: *laundromat, cornflakes, subway, snow.*

Soon I picked up enough English to understand holocaust[1] was in the air. Sister Zoe explained to a wide-eyed classroom what was happening in Cuba. Russian missiles were being assembled, trained supposedly on New York City. President Kennedy, looking worried too, was on the television at home, explaining we might have to go to war against the Communists. At school, we had air-raid drills: An ominous bell would go off and we'd file into the hall, fall to the floor, cover our heads with our coats, and imagine our hair falling out, the bones in our

arms going soft. At home, Mami and my sisters and I said a rosary[2] for world peace. I heard new vocabulary: *nuclear bomb, radioactive fallout, bomb shelter.* Sister Zoe explained how it would happen. She drew a picture of a mushroom on the blackboard and dotted a flurry of chalk marks for the dusty fallout that would kill us all.

The months grew cold, November, December. It was dark when I got up in the morning, frosty when I followed my breath to school. One morning, as I sat at my desk daydreaming out the window, I saw dots in the air like the ones Sister Zoe had drawn—random at first, then lots and lots. I shrieked, "Bomb! Bomb!" Sister Zoe jerked around, her full black skirt ballooning as she hurried to my side. A few girls began to cry.

But then Sister Zoe's shocked look faded. "Why, Yolanda dear, that's snow!" She laughed. "Snow."

"Snow," I repeated. I looked out the window warily. All my life I had heard about the white crystals that fell out of American skies in the winter. From my desk I watched the fine powder dust the sidewalk and parked cars below. Each flake was different, Sister Zoe had said, like a person, irreplaceable and beautiful.

---

1. **holocaust** (hä′lə·kȯst′) *n.:* great or total destruction of life.

2. **rosary** (rō′zər·ē) *n.:* in the Roman Catholic religion, series of prayers counted off on a special set of beads.

SKILLS FOCUS

Pages 240–241 cover
Literary Skills
Analyze narrator (or point of view) and voice.

Collection 3: Skills Review

1. Why does Yolanda yell, "Bomb! Bomb!" when she sees snow?
   - **A** The winter landscape is bare, as if a bomb had destroyed everything.
   - **B** The snowflakes look like her teacher's pictures of the fallout from a bomb.
   - **C** New in school, she wants to gain her classmates' attention.
   - **D** She wants to show that she has understood her teacher's lessons.

2. How does the use of a **first-person narrator** affect the telling of the story?
   - **F** The reader sees events through the eyes of several characters.
   - **G** The description of events is unbiased.
   - **H** The reader is presented with Yolanda's personal view of events.
   - **J** Yolanda lies in the story.

3. Why is it important that the story is told from the **point of view** of a recent immigrant to the United States?
   - **A** Yolanda is unfamiliar with some aspects of life in the United States.
   - **B** Living in the United States makes Yolanda frightened and insecure.
   - **C** Yolanda's classmates don't explain things to her.
   - **D** Yolanda's teacher treats her unfairly.

4. What is the *best* description of the narrator's **voice** in this passage: "I saw dots in the air like the ones Sister Zoe had drawn—random at first, then lots and lots"?
   - **F** Sophisticated
   - **G** Childlike
   - **H** Hopeful
   - **J** Playful

5. What is the **tone** of the story?
   - **A** Sarcastic and superior
   - **B** Angry and suspicious
   - **C** Homesick and sad
   - **D** Innocent and sincere

6. What impression does the narrator create of Sister Zoe?
   - **F** Sister Zoe has knowingly exaggerated the danger in order to scare the children.
   - **G** Sister Zoe is a nervous, easily frightened person.
   - **H** Sister Zoe mocks Yolanda and doesn't think she's intelligent.
   - **J** A caring teacher, Sister Zoe helps her students learn.

Constructed Response

7. Suppose that Sister Zoe were the narrator of the story instead of Yolanda. What would she be able to tell you that Yolanda couldn't? How would the story be different? Support your opinions using specific examples from the story.

Test Practice

Synonyms

DIRECTIONS: Choose the *best* synonym for the underlined word in each sentence.

1. When Ulrich threatened him, Georg retorted that his men would kill Ulrich first.
   A bragged
   B replied
   C pretended
   D shouted

2. Ulrich says that his men will offer succor to Georg first.
   F help
   G food
   H advice
   J sympathy

3. Mathilde is disconsolate when she loses her friend's necklace.
   A ashamed
   B unhappy
   C angry
   D frightened

4. Mathilde talks incessantly about her desire for wealth.
   F nastily
   G unjustly
   H loudly
   J constantly

5. Recoiling at first upon seeing the trowel, Fortunato then follows Montresor into the catacombs.
   A staring
   B retreating

   C laughing
   D pausing

6. Montresor believes that Fortunato deserves retribution for insulting him.
   F imprisonment
   G payment
   H forgiveness
   J punishment

7. Struggling to break the chains, Fortunato endeavored to free himself.
   A failed
   B began
   C hoped
   D tried

8. There are several different theories that explain why Poe expired.
   F wrote
   G died
   H traveled
   J drank

9. The medical report on an unnamed patient contained conspicuous clues identifying the patient as Poe.
   A many
   B few
   C minor
   D obvious

SKILLS FOCUS

Vocabulary Skills
Understand synonyms.

Collection 3: Skills Review
Writing Skills

DIRECTIONS: The following paragraph is from a draft of a student's analysis of a biography. Read the questions below it, and choose the best answer to each question.

(1) Harold C. Livesay wrote the biography *Andrew Carnegie and the Rise of Big Business.* (2) Even though Carnegie came to the United States as a poor Scottish immigrant, he did not let his circumstances keep him down. (3) While working as a bobbin boy at the age of fourteen, "Andrew decided to learn double-entry bookkeeping and enrolled in a night school course across the river in Pittsburgh" (16). (4) He lived with his mother, father, and younger brother, Tom. (5) Carnegie never settled into a position when he thought he could climb higher. (6) His will, determining, and strength led him to become one of the most successful people in the United States.

1. Which of the following could follow sentence 1 to convey the biographer's distinctive perspective?
   A   Livesay is a biographer who writes primarily about the U.S. economy.
   B   This biography shows Carnegie's determined character.
   C   Livesay believes that Carnegie was a ruthless businessperson.
   D   Carnegie was the greatest entrepreneur of his time.

2. Which sentence, if added, would explain the details in sentence 3?
   F   Carnegie's father couldn't adapt to the market changes.
   G   Carnegie wasn't very sociable because he spent all his time working.
   H   The Carnegie family survived due to the support of friends.
   J   Young Carnegie became a model of self-improvement and determination.

3. To support the idea that Carnegie was strongly driven, the writer could
   A   quote Carnegie stating that he had "determined to make a fortune"
   B   describe the working conditions in the U.S. in the 1850s and 1860s
   C   relate details about the ten richest people in American history
   D   summarize an article that criticizes Carnegie's business ethics

4. Which sentence might the writer delete to improve the passage's organization?
   F   2
   G   3
   H   4
   J   6

5. To create parallelism in sentence 6, the writer should replace "will, determining, and strength" with
   A   will, determine, and strength
   B   will, determination, and strength
   C   will, determining, and being strong
   D   willingness, determine, and being strong

SKILLS FOCUS

Writing Skills
Write an analysis of a biography.

Collection 4

Friends and Enemies

Literary Focus:
Comparing Themes

Informational Reading Focus:
Synthesizing Sources:
Drawing Conclusions

Pierrot and Harlequin (1920) by Pablo Picasso (1881–1973). Pen and black ink with gouache on light brown paper, sheet folded in half. 10 $\frac{13}{16}$ × 8 $\frac{3}{8}$ in.

Gift of Mrs. Gilbert W. Chapman, Image ©2005 Board of Trustees, National Gallery of Art, Washington, D.C. 1981.41.2.

Elements of Literature

Theme *by* John Leggett

AN IDEA ABOUT LIFE

A story can excel in any number of ways—in the strength of its plot, in the reality of its characters, in the gracefulness of its language. But what often makes us remember a story long after we've read it is the idea on which it's built—its theme.

Revealing a Truth About Human Behavior

The **theme** of a story is the central idea, or insight, about life that it reveals. This insight is a truth about human behavior that the writer has usually discovered from experience—for example, that sometimes it is a mistake to marry for love alone or that as one grows old, death becomes less terrifying. To communicate this idea, the writer tells a story.

The theme is usually not stated directly in a story. Instead, the characters act out the theme for us. If the story works, we feel the characters' experiences so strongly that the truth revealed to them is revealed to us as well.

When the theme of a story seems fresh and true, we say, "Yes, I see what the writer means, but I hadn't quite thought of it that way before." Then we have penetrated the surface of human behavior and have seen what the writer wants us to recognize about our lives.

Although a theme is usually invisible and unstated, it can be the story's most forceful element. Themes are also important to other forms of literature, and a similar theme can be found across **genres**—in stories, novels, plays, poems, even in nonfiction. A powerful theme can be the reason that a work of literature gets to our hearts and lingers in our minds.

Universal Themes

Because a theme is a **generalization** about life or human nature and because certain experiences are common to all people everywhere, authors often express similar themes. These **universal themes** deal with such basic human concerns as good and evil, life and death, love and loss. These great themes, the ones that recur in every culture and in every period of history, shine a light on our common experiences and can help guide us through our lives.

How to Find a Story's Theme

It's not always easy to step back from a literary work and express its central idea in a sentence. Figuring out the theme, however, will help you understand a work more fully. Here are some guidelines to help you search for and state the theme of a work:

1 The theme of a work is not the same as its subject. The **subject** is simply the topic, which can be stated in a single word, such as *love*. The theme makes some revelation about the subject—for example: "Love may be more likely to bloom when we least expect it." Remember that a theme must always be an idea that can be expressed in at least one sentence.

SKILLS FOCUS

Pages 246–280 and 294–318 cover **Literary Skills** Understand theme and universal themes. Compare a theme across genres.

INTERNET

More About Theme

Keyword: LE7 9-4

2 Think about whether the main **character** changes in the course of a work or realizes something he or she hadn't known before. Often a writer expresses the theme through what a character learns.

3 Think about how the **conflict** is resolved. Conflict is central to literature, and how the conflict is resolved often provides a clue to the theme.

4 When you have finished reading a work, think about the **title**. Does it have a special meaning? Does it point to the theme? (Not all titles do.)

5 Test your statement of the theme—does it apply to the whole work, not just to parts of it?

6 Keep in mind that there is no single way to state the theme of a work. You and your classmates may express the same theme in different words, or you may even have different opinions about what the main theme is. The literary works that are richest in meaning often have more than one theme.

Thinking Critically About Theme

The wise reader makes a judgment about a writer's view of the world and doesn't accept a story's theme as valid just because it's in print. The wise reader asks, "Is this story's view of life too romantic? Is it too cynical? Is it too simple? Is it narrow-minded? Is this writer an overenthusiastic salesperson who is trying to get me to buy an idea that is false or shoddy?"

Much of popular fiction is "formula fiction," fiction written to a plan that satisfies the general preference for happy or upbeat stories over true-to-life ones. As wise readers we must learn to make our own critical judgments about the fiction we read—just as we do about the television shows we watch and the movies we see.

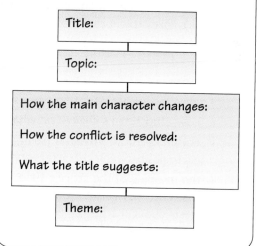

Practice

Think of a story you've read that had an impact on you. Then, use a map like the one here to help you figure out the story's **theme.** Compare your map with the ones your classmates made. Did you and any of your classmates map stories with similar themes?

Title:

Topic:

How the main character changes:

How the conflict is resolved:

What the title suggests:

Theme:

Introducing the Collection Theme

Friends and Enemies

Make the Connection

Quickwrite

Fill out a Venn diagram, like the one on the right, listing the characteristics you associate with the words *friend* and *enemy*. In the shaded area, list any qualities you think a friend and an enemy can share.

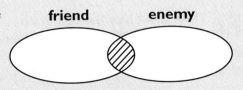

Exploring the Theme: Friends and Enemies

This collection explores the impact of friends and enemies on our lives. "The Sniper" and "Cranes" show how civil wars can blur the lines between friends and enemies. Nonfiction selections examine the divisive effects of the civil conflict in Northern Ireland. You'll also read about families who flee their political enemies in their native countries and seek new opportunities in the United States. In "Disguises," the story you are about to read, Mrs. Chen must evade enemies and find new friends in a foreign world. As you read these works, you may find other themes in them as well. Remember that a work's ability to express more than one theme can give it greater power.

Literary Focus

Theme

To develop a statement of a story's **theme,** consider

- how **characters** change or what they learn
- **conflicts**—both **internal** (struggles within characters) and **external** (struggles between characters and outside forces)—and their **resolution**
- the meaning of the story's **title**

As you read "Disguises," think about what Mrs. Chen's journey suggests about the power of friends and enemies in our lives.

Background

Many Chinese people, like Mrs. Chen, practice some form of Buddhism. According to the Buddhist belief system, people are continually reborn until they reach a divine state. Good deeds help them reach this goal. Mrs. Chen's belief system also comes from her own cultural and family traditions in which gods and goddesses, as well as demons, help determine one's fate.

Disguises

Jean Fong Kwok

On the night Mrs. Chen got lost, she was wearing a golden amulet of the goddess Kuan Yin[1] underneath her clothes, for protection. She took the subway home from the factory in Chinatown.[2] Sitting on the long seat with her feet lightly grazing the floor, she felt the weight of sleep drag her head forward, her permed curls sinking toward the small neat hands cupped politely in her lap. As the half-empty subway car lurched through the tunnel, its movement sporadically flung her head upward. She caught herself from sleep in those moments, looking about her, alarmed, only to have exhaustion fall over her again like a blanket. The swaying of the subway threw her back and forth against the hard seat, the thin fabric of her flowered pants brushed against the shopping bag full of sewing.

One . . . two . . . she had to take the subway fourteen stops to get home. The conductor's voice in English was a river of sound in her ear, noise following noise like the falling of water over rocks. Three . . . four . . .

Mrs. Chen lifted her heavy head. Five . . . six . . . the door opened and her factory supervisor strode out of the elevator with her polyester skirt flicking about her legs, stepping quickly and fastidiously, as though the clumps of fabric dust on the sewing room floor dirtied her high-heeled shoes. As she walked, she waved one wide hand in front of her mouth to clear away the dust in the air—the other gripped a wadded piece of clothing. The supervisor only came into the work area when there was a

---

1. **amulet of the goddess Kuan Yin:** An amulet is a charm worn to protect the wearer from injury or evil. Kuan Yin is the Buddhist goddess of compassion. Her name means "the one who hears the cries of the world and comes."
2. **factory in Chinatown:** Mrs. Chen works in a New York City sweatshop—a factory in which employees work long hours under difficult conditions for low pay. Chinatown is an area in lower Manhattan in New York City that has a large Chinese immigrant population.

❶ The beginning of this paragraph marks the start of a **flash-back**, a scene that interrupts the present action to show events that took place in the past. The flashback describes a **conflict** between Mrs. Chen and the factory super-visor. What does the description in this paragraph tell you about the supervisor?

problem; otherwise, she stayed in the air-conditioned offices upstairs. Mrs. Chen could feel the supervisor's presence passing through the rows of silent women bent over their Singer sewing machines; no one dared look up, their needles racing, piercing the fabric. ❶

The supervisor threaded her way through the pack of women, bright in her silver-toned suit; its light gray material stretched across her fat stomach like the skin of a snake. She stopped next to Mrs. Chen and with fingers thick with rings of jade, snapped open the garment she had been holding—a skirt. Mrs. Chen, knowing it was not her place to meet the supervisor's eyes, cautiously raised her gaze to the round collar of her shirt, while everyone about her seemed to busy themselves with their work.

"Your seams are crooked," the supervisor announced, wrenching her mouth around the crisp Cantonese words. "This is not acceptable." She always attempted to speak Cantonese, one of the so-called "sophisticated" dialects, although her accent was painfully rural.[3] She told everyone that she had been born in Hong Kong[4] where the cleanest Cantonese is spoken, but, Mrs. Chen thought, her peasant roots shone clearly through her words.

Mrs. Chen stood up.

"I am so sorry," she said, her pronunciation flawless. She knew the supervisor resented her for the breeding that meant so little in this country. She could see the skirt was one she had labored over at night, sewing between the soft breaths of her sleeping family.

"May I see it?" she asked, taking a step closer.

The supervisor held it away from her. "If this ever happens again, just one more time, you will no longer be allowed to bring work home," she said. "Please remember, Mrs. Chen, you are very new to this country—we have had much trouble with recent arrivals—and my uncle is doing you a great favor to allow you to take home extra sewing, and indeed to work here at all. I do not like to see ungrateful employees. You will, of course, not be paid for that entire bundle."

Then, before Mrs. Chen could reach for the skirt, the supervisor took one corner of it in her teeth and the other in her hands, and tore it down the seams, in half. She tossed the pieces onto Mrs. Chen's table as she turned on her heel and stalked from the room.

Mrs. Chen sank into her seat, spreading her fingers to shield her hot face. What crime have I committed, in which past life, to deserve these evil winds of fate that blow at my back,[5] she wondered. She realized that

---

3. **Cantonese . . . rural:** Cantonese is a form, or dialect, of Chinese spoken in southern China, including the city of Canton. Mrs. Chen and her supervisor both speak Cantonese, but in accents that reflect differences in their backgrounds.
4. **Hong Kong:** region in southern China with a large population.
5. **evil winds . . . back:** Some Chinese people believe the course of one's life is determined by the "good winds" and "evil winds" that blow as a person travels along the road of life.

everyone was watching her out of the corners of their eyes, pretending they had noticed nothing. No one said anything to her. The subway doors closed and her head nodded forward. ❷

The last station sped behind her. The overhead light went out, and the fluorescent flashes from the subway tunnel gleamed in the darkness behind her eyelids, pane after pane like frames of a movie.

Mrs. Chen, then just a girl named Lai Fong, was in China again. She was wearing green silk, preparing with her mother the ceremony for the seven goddesses who protected virginal maidens; it was the last time she would do this, because she was soon to be married. She bent to kneel on the cushion before the goddesses at the altar. Her mother, already kneeling, stopped her with a touch on her arm. Slowly, her mother gazed up at her, and her small rounded features, so much like Lai Fong's, were filled with grief and tenderness.

"My only daughter," she said, "before you pray with me this final time, you must remember this: It is said, one who is human must kneel only before the gods." She paused, and then said fiercely, "Never before anyone else."

The screech of the subway rang in her ears, startling her. Mrs. Chen brushed her forehead three times, to clear away painful memories. She touched the amulet of Kuan Yin hanging from the gold chain around her neck; its shape underneath her blouse reassured her. Everyone knew that pure gold protected you from evil, but even more important, the monks at Shaolin Temple[6] had "opened it to the light," so that the goddess could truly live in it, as though it were her temple. The amulet was the only part of her mother Mrs. Chen had been able to take with her when she left China. ❸

---

6. **monks at Shaolin Temple:** Monks are men who live apart from society and devote themselves to the practice of their religion—in this case, Buddhism. The Shaolin Temple is known throughout China for its religious significance to Buddhists and for the martial arts skills of its monks.

THEME AND CHARACTER

❷ The **flashback** ends in this paragraph. How does the factory supervisor act as an enemy to Mrs. Chen in this scene? What do Mrs. Chen's thoughts and actions reveal about her?

THEME AND CHARACTER

❸ The last three paragraphs include a **flashback** to Mrs. Chen's life in China. What do these paragraphs tell you about Mrs. Chen? Think in particular about her mother's advice and the amulet.

Girl kneels at an altar during a Chinese festival honoring ancestors.

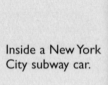

Inside a New York
City subway car.

More people filled the subway car than she had remembered. Two well-dressed black women across from her chatted, and as one laughed, the long yellow feather on her hat wiggled. A homeless man wearing a cardboard sign with English writing on it had wrapped himself around a pole near Mrs. Chen.

He gingerly peeled his hands from the pole, as if it caused him pain, and holding out his left palm, began to make his way through the car. His rancid smell, like sour milk, reached her before he did, and she tried not to breathe too deeply. Spittle clung to the sides of his mouth, suspended in droplets in his rough beard, but his lips were full and red, as though they alone had not lost their hold on life. When he stood in front of her, she studied his dirty face, and she was not afraid. It is said, she thought, we must all be beggars for one life, we only hope that that life has already passed.

She opened her change purse and pressed a quarter into his palm. She had none to spare, but in this world, she mused, the times when you are able to give are so few that when you can, you must; the gods always view compassion kindly.

"Haf nice day," Mrs. Chen said, smiling. This was one of the few English phrases she had managed to learn.

The homeless man closed his fingers around the coin, his stare not leaving her smile as though it surprised him more than the quarter. He turned to the two women sitting across from her. They had stopped talking to watch Mrs. Chen. Now, they also took out their purses and gave him some change. As the homeless man went on his way, Mrs. Chen nodded to the women and they smiled back before resuming their conversation.

Mrs. Chen settled into her seat and closed her eyes. The subway car clattered; it was as though she and the women and the homeless man were all in a carriage together, riding to the same place. But where were they going? We are the Monkey King, the monk, and their two companions, seeking enlightenment[7] on a road filled with demons and goddesses in disguise, she thought, and the voice of the English-speaking conductor sounded like her father's voice in China when he would tell her stories that she was too tired to understand. Then it seemed to her that the homeless man had put his head on her shoulder and they were resting together, sleeping, with the women across the way looking on. ❹

Suddenly, she sat up. What stop was this? This must be number fourteen! This should be the right one but why did everything seem so unfamiliar? Where should she get off? The black women were gone; there was no sign of the homeless man. Mrs. Chen grabbed her shopping bag and hurried out of the train just before the doors closed, hoping this was indeed her station. Mr. Chen always scolded her for being overly imaginative. But as she stood on the platform, she realized that she had never seen this place before.

She watched the few passengers make their way to the stairs. Then, from behind her, she heard the sound of footsteps. She panicked and fled for the exit, the shopping bag bumping against her legs. She had been mugged only a few weeks ago; she was the last one leaving the subway platform and a teenager in a leather jacket had blocked her way. He pulled out a long knife and held it in front of his body, half-hidden by the folds of his coat. His eyes horrified her. They were pale blue, blue as she'd only seen in the eyes of those blinded by cataracts[8] in China, yet this man was able to see, as if he were some sort of demon. Without a word, he gestured with his knife. She gave him her purse; he took it and ran.

---

7. **Monkey King . . . seeking enlightenment:** *The Monkey King* is a famous sixteenth-century Chinese novel about the journey of a monk and his companions to India in search of the Buddhist scriptures.
8. **cataracts** (kat′ə•rakts′) *n.:* cloudy areas that form in the lens of the eye, causing partial or complete blindness.

THEME AND TITLE

❹ Mrs. Chen imagines that she is traveling "on a road filled with demons and goddesses in disguise." Explain this image. How does it apply to her situation?

**THEME AND
CONFLICT**

5 What is Mrs. Chen's
external conflict at
this point in the story?

Mrs. Chen reached the token booth, passed it, and raced up to the street. She stood outside gulping in the cool night air, holding onto the stair rail. She looked around. No one had followed her. A desolate avenue lined with streetlamps stretched before her, the concrete buildings smothered in graffiti, interrupted by long alleys. In the distance, a dark figure walked down the block, only to quickly disappear around a corner. A skeleton of a car, windshield broken, stripped of all four wheels, loomed next to the subway entrance. She did not recognize anything. **5**

This was a terrible place. She took the amulet out of her blouse and clutched it. A low wind whistled through the avenue, setting stray pieces of litter skittering across the concrete. She went back to the token booth.

She was relieved to see the clerk, a heavy man with a gray goatee, through the murky glass; he was an official, he could help her. She went around to the front of the booth and rapped on the glass with her knuckles.

"Hello? Hello?" she said.

He was talking on the phone, and when he saw her, shifted so that his back was to her. She tapped on the booth more insistently. He waved for her to wait. She searched through her purse to find the piece of paper with her street address on it. Her son had written it out for her, just in case she got lost.

"Hello, hello," she said, her voice growing shriller.

Hunching over the phone, the clerk ignored her.

"HELLO!" she screamed.

He turned around. Mrs. Chen quickly pushed the crumpled paper toward him. He studied it, and said some words to her in English.

"No," she said, "no understand."

New York City subway scene.

> "You have to stop that crying," Mr. Chen said. His voice grew more quiet. "Listen, don't be afraid. We have to find out where you are and then we will come get you."

He repeated what he'd said, only louder. She shook her head. The man ran his fingers across the top of his puffy hair, then pointed at the receiver he was holding, like she was keeping him from something. She pressed her ear as close to the glass as she could. She tried to understand even one word of what he said, but it was just babble to her.

"Dank you," she said. "Bye bye." The man shrugged and returned to his phone conversation. ❻

She slowly climbed to the street. *Please, Kuan Yin, let me get home to my child and husband . . .* she prayed. There was a pay telephone on the corner. She walked to it as fast as she could, put down her bag, fumbled for a quarter, and dialed her home number. Her husband answered on the first ring.

"Big Brother Chen?" she said. She never called him by his first name because that would be disrespectful, even though they had been married more than ten years.[9]

"Where have you been?" he asked angrily.

"I don't know—I'm lost." She leaned against the side of the phone booth and began to sob.

"How could you be so stupid?" he yelled, as he always did when he was afraid. "Your son is here, waiting for his dinner—why don't you ever pay attention to where you're going? Where are you?"

"I don't know."

"You have to stop that crying," Mr. Chen said. His voice grew more quiet. "Listen, don't be afraid. We have to find out where you are and then we will come get you. Let me put Sonny on the line."

She wiped her eyes on her sleeve and tried to pull herself together. Her child must not know how upset she was.

His voice seemed much higher over the phone. "Mommy, where are you?"

"You have to help Mommy," she said. Sonny was only nine years old but he was as smart as the boys a grade ahead of him. He was learning English so rapidly. She described her surroundings but he did not recognize them.

---

9. **She never called . . . ten years:** In traditional Chinese society, names and titles are used to signal status. People are addressed by their first name only by those of equal or higher rank. Mrs. Chen shows Mr. Chen respect by using a title and his last name to address him.

THEME AND CHARACTER

❻ What is your opinion of the way the token booth clerk treats Mrs. Chen? What do you learn about Mrs. Chen from this scene?

"I know," Sonny said. "Can you spell the name of the street by you? Can you see the street sign?"

She found it but the word was very long. She had never been that good with the English alphabet.

"M . . . I . . . no, E . . . and then A . . . no, R . . ." she began. In the middle of her spelling, she had to put another coin in the telephone. Finally, she came up with something that Sonny thought could be the name of a street.

"But I don't know where it is," he said.

"Do you have any maps?" she asked.

"Yeah," he said. "Let me check in my geography book. That has maps."

She could hear him getting off the chair and running to his books. He was gone for a few minutes. Mrs. Chen looked at her amulet, glinting brightly against her dark blouse. She brought the golden goddess to her face and laid it against her cheek.

She heard shuffling, then Sonny came back on the phone.

"Mommy?" he said. "I can't find it. It's not in my book. I'm sorry." He started to sniffle. "When are you going to come home, Mommy?" he asked.

"Shhh . . . don't cry," she said, trying to sound calm. She could hear Mr. Chen cursing in the background. "Mommy will be fine. I will walk around and maybe I will recognize something. Just tell your father that I will call soon."

She hung up before she had to speak to Mr. Chen again. It would be more frightening to talk to her husband; he was just as helpless as she, and he would not be as easily comforted as Sonny. Her quarters were almost gone and she did not want to waste another. Perhaps she shouldn't have given one to the homeless man, she thought. What was kindness in this world? She rested her head against the telephone for a moment. *I invite the goddess Kuan Yin,* she said under her breath, *from the Shaolin Temple in the hills of Canton, to come to me now; so soon as I . . .* ❼

She felt a hand close to her ear reach for the amulet, as though it were trying to take it before she could finish her prayer. Mrs. Chen screamed and ducked at the same time. Grasping the shopping bag, she swung it in a circle, felt it hit, heard the sides rip. She hugged the bag and fled toward the subway station, hampered by its bulk. Someone seemed to race away in the opposite direction. *So soon as I call her,* she gasped, running, *so soon will she appear. . . .*

Goddess Kuan Yin on Waves. China (17th–18th century). Victoria and Albert Museum, London.

THEME AND CONFLICT

❼ Why does Mrs. Chen question her act of kindness to the homeless man earlier in the story? Explain her **internal conflict**.

As Mrs. Chen rushed to the steps, she caught a glimpse of features that looked Chinese. She skidded to a stop.

"Mister! Mister!" she shouted.

The young man turned, surprised. "Yes?" He was Chinese. He must be a student, with his thick glasses and a green bookbag slung over his narrow shoulder.

Mrs. Chen almost cried from relief. "I am lost," she said, breathing hard, "and someone just tried to take my necklace."

"My Cantonese is very bad," he said in Mandarin.[10]

"We are both Chinese," Mrs. Chen said, part in Mandarin and part in Cantonese, "please help me."

She explained the situation to him, her voice breaking—how she was lost and almost robbed, how she couldn't follow the token booth clerk, how her son and husband couldn't help her—using as much Mandarin as she remembered and filling in the rest with Cantonese. She put her bag on the ground and took out the piece of paper with her address on it. The young man listened and nodded; he seemed to understand her story. He took the slip of paper and the two of them went into the subway station. As they approached the token booth, the clerk recognized Mrs. Chen and rolled his eyes.

The young man spoke to the clerk in English and showed him her address. Then he said to Mrs. Chen, "The train you were on must have been re-routed. They probably announced the change but you did not understand. What you must do now is take the train over here for two stops and then switch . . ."

But Mrs. Chen was frantic. She clutched his arm, shaking her head.

He stopped speaking and looked at her fingers buried in his jacket. "I will go with you," he said. ❽

Mrs. Chen sighed in relief and then offered to pay for his token, but he put one in the slot as he waved her hand away. When they got on the subway, the young man took out a book and began to study, only peering at her occasionally to check that she was all right. She was too exhausted to even try to make conversation. *Kuan Yin, thank you for your aid. . . .* The student escorted her the entire way to her own station. Mrs. Chen asked him to come to her house, so she could at least give him something to eat to repay his kindness, but when she passed through the gate, he did not follow.

She turned back to him. "Thank you," she said.

The young man grinned and bowed, his schoolbag slipping off his shoulder. She bowed in response[11] but by the time she straightened, he was gone.

THEME AND CONFLICT

❽ At her moment of greatest need, Mrs. Chen meets a "friend"—a young Chinese man. How does this event lead to the **resolution** of her main **external conflict**?

---

10. **Mandarin** (man'də•rin): most widely spoken language in China.
11. **The young . . . bowed in response:** reference to the Chinese custom of bowing to express respect for another person.

When Mrs. Chen got home, Sonny threw himself at her and cried, while Mr. Chen roughly patted her on the arm. They were quiet as she told them how the young man had helped her, how he must have been sent by the gods. Mrs. Chen lit incense[12] at the altar in their kitchen to formally give thanks and noticed there were extra incense stubs in the holder—Mr. Chen had also prayed for her.

"We were afraid for you," he said. "We thought we might have lost you."

Later that night, she had to stay awake to do her work. She bent to sew the pieces of the torn skirt, joining again the severed parts with thread. ❾

---

12. **incense** (in′sens′) *n.:* substance that gives off a pleasant smell when burned. It is burned as a gesture of respect and gratitude in several religions.

THEME AND TITLE

❾ Now that you've finished the story, why do you think the author gave it the **title** "Disguises"? To answer, consider the ways in which characters in the story appear to be in disguise.

Meet the Writer
Jean Fong Kwok

A Risky Path

Jean Fong Kwok (1968–   ) was born in Hong Kong, China, and immigrated to the United States with her family when she was five years old. The youngest of seven children, she spoke no English when she entered kindergarten at a public school in Queens, New York. Kwok explains:

❝ Like most other immigrants, my family came to make a better life for themselves, and especially for the children. It was quite a difficult time for all of us. I think I had it the easiest because I was so young and I could learn English fairly quickly. ❞

Although she had always loved writing and literature, Kwok started out wanting to be an astrophysicist. She recalls, "I didn't consider being a writer to be a 'real' enough profession. It seemed too risky." She began her college career as a physics major at Harvard University, but she switched to a concentration in English and eventually received a Master of Fine Arts in fiction from Columbia University. To support herself in her quest to become a writer, Kwok worked as a teacher of English to immigrants, a math tutor, and a professional ballroom dancer. She now lives in Holland, writing, teaching, and translating texts from Dutch to English. For her, writing is a means of communicating across borders.

After You Read

Response and Analysis

Reading Check

1. Why does Mrs. Chen get lost on the subway? How does she finally get back home?

Thinking Critically

2. What **internal** and **external** conflicts does Mrs. Chen face? Are all these conflicts resolved? Explain.

3. List some religious practices and Chinese customs mentioned in this story. What do these practices and customs tell you about Mrs. Chen and the world she comes from?

4. At the end of the story, Mrs. Chen is back at home, sewing together the torn skirt. What does this final act show about her life or her character? Is this an act of defeat or one of triumph?

5. In the Venn diagram you created for your Quickwrite, you listed characteristics of friends and enemies. Now, think about the friends and enemies in this story. Which characters act like friends to Mrs. Chen? Which ones act more like enemies? Do any of these characters exhibit the qualities of both a friend and an enemy? Explain.

6. "Disguises" tells the story of one immigrant's experiences, but it's also about all of us—about the people we meet as we make our way in a sometimes confusing or unfamiliar world. What do you think this story has to say about the collection **theme** "Friends and Enemies"? To answer, consider

- Mrs. Chen's **conflicts,** both **internal** and **external,** and their **resolution**

- what Mrs. Chen learns about herself and the world

- the meaning of the **title** "Disguises"

Extending and Evaluating

7. What is your opinion of the young man's actions at the end of the story? Do you think most people would behave like the young man and go out of their way to help a stranger? Explain your response.

Exploring the Theme

Friends and Enemies

In the rest of this collection, you'll read about the role of friends and enemies in the lives of real and fictional people. As you read, consider what each work suggests about the power of friends and enemies in our lives.

SKILLS FOCUS

Literary Focus
Analyze theme, character, and conflict.

Comparing Universal Themes

Universal Ties, Universal Themes

No matter what we look like or where we come from, we are all made of the same stuff—we all have hearts and minds, feelings and thoughts. We all have hopes and fears, worries and dreams. We all experience both sorrows and joys. These universal concerns and experiences are the ties that bind us.

Writers translate these shared experiences into works of art that express **universal themes.** These themes are not restricted to literature from a particular time or place but appear over and over again. Writers, however, make these themes their own by adding their unique insights and perspectives and conveying the themes in an original way.

Divided Loyalties

We are all individuals, but we also live in communities. Sometimes our ties and needs as individuals conflict with our social responsibilities. This is particularly true during civil wars, when serving one's country can conflict with loyalty to family and friends. The next two stories concern men caught up in civil war. Read on to discover the theme each author wants to express about that experience.

Remember that the **theme** of a particular literary work is too complicated to be summed up in a single word and should be stated in a sentence. A story about war, for example, might express the following theme: "In wartime it can sometimes be difficult to distinguish the innocent from the guilty."

Reading Skills

Comparing and Contrasting Themes

After you have read and discussed each story, use a chart like the one below to help you compare and contrast the themes in the two works. Fill in comments about the characters' conflicts, motives, and decisions. The guidelines on pages 246–247 will help you state the theme of each work. Then, turn to page 280.

	"The Sniper"	"Cranes"
Main character		
Character's conflict(s)		
Character's motives		
What character learns		
How conflict(s) is resolved		
Statement of theme		

SKILLS FOCUS

Pages 260–280 cover
Literary Skills
Understand and compare universal themes.

Reading Skills
Compare and contrast themes.

Before You Read

The Sniper

Make the Connection

Quickwrite ✏️

What qualities enable people to perform well when facing heart-pounding fear or stress? Think about your own experiences or those of someone you know, as well as news stories or fiction you've read. Then, jot down your thoughts about people taking action when the stakes are high.

Literary Focus

Theme and Conflict: What's at Stake?

In many stories, particularly those involving high-stakes struggles, the **theme,** or central idea, is often revealed by the way the **conflict** in the story is resolved. "The Sniper" is such a story. It focuses for a brief but heart-stopping time on a soldier fighting in Ireland's civil war. The stakes of his conflict could not be higher: He either lives or dies. As you read, decide what idea about war the writer communicates through the sniper's experiences.

Reading Skills 📖

Making Predictions

When you read a suspenseful story like "The Sniper," you make **predictions,** or guesses, about what is going to happen: Will the main character escape the enemy? Will each new action help the main character or create new problems? How will it all end? As you read this story, keep these questions in mind. Does the writer give you any hints about the outcome?

Background

This story is set in Dublin, Ireland, in the 1920s, during a time of bitter civil war. On one side were the Republicans; they wanted all of Ireland to become a republic, totally free from British rule. On the other side were the Free Staters; they had compromised with Britain and had agreed to allow the English to continue to rule six counties in the northern province of Ulster. (For reference, see the map on page 284.)

Like all civil wars, this one tore families apart. It pitted children against parents, sister against sister, brother against brother. As the story opens, the writer immediately puts you into the war—high on a Dublin rooftop.

Vocabulary Development

beleaguered (bē·lē′gərd) v. used as *adj.*: surrounded and under attack.

ascetic (ə·set′ik) *adj.*: severe; also, self-disciplined.

fanatic (fə·nat′ik) *n.*: person whose extreme devotion to a cause is excessive or unreasonable.

ruse (rōōz) *n.*: trick.

silhouetted (sil′ə·wet′id) v. used as *adj.*: outlined.

remorse (ri·môrs′) *n.*: deep guilt.

SKILLS FOCUS

Literary Skills
Understand theme and conflict.

Pages 260–280 cover Compare universal themes.

Reading Skills
Make predictions.

go. hrw .com

INTERNET

Vocabulary Practice

Keyword: LE7 9-4

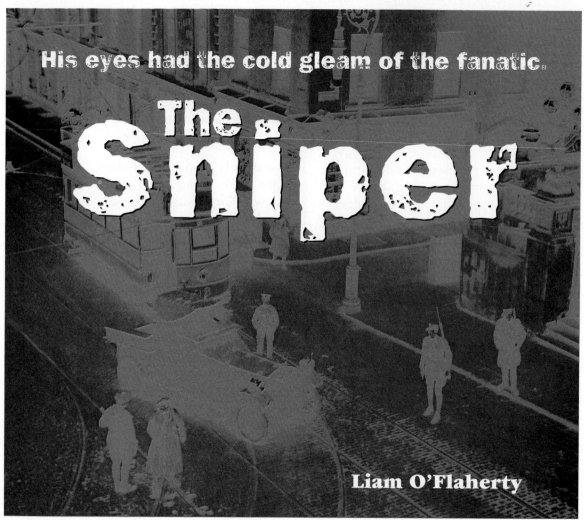

His eyes had the cold gleam of the fanatic.

The Sniper

Liam O'Flaherty

The Black and Tan—members of a British auxiliary police force—occupy a major Dublin street (November 1920).

The long June twilight faded into night. Dublin lay enveloped in darkness but for the dim light of the moon that shone through fleecy clouds, casting a pale light as of approaching dawn over the streets and the dark waters of the Liffey.[1] Around the beleaguered Four Courts[2] the heavy guns roared. Here and there through the city, machine guns and rifles broke the silence of the night, spasmodically, like dogs barking on lone farms. Republicans and Free Staters were waging civil war.

On a rooftop near O'Connell Bridge, a Republican sniper lay watching. Beside him lay his rifle and over his shoulders was slung a pair of field glasses. His face was the face of a student, thin and ascetic, but his eyes had the cold gleam of the fanatic. They were deep and thoughtful, the eyes of a man who is used to looking at death.

---

1. **Liffey:** river that runs through Dublin.
2. **Four Courts:** government buildings in Dublin.

Vocabulary

beleaguered (bē·lē′gərd) v. used as adj.: surrounded and under attack.

ascetic (ə·set′ik) adj.: severe; also, self-disciplined.

fanatic (fə·nat′ik) n.: person whose extreme devotion to a cause is excessive or unreasonable.

He was eating a sandwich hungrily. He had eaten nothing since morning. He had been too excited to eat. He finished the sandwich, and, taking a flask of whiskey from his pocket, he took a short draft. Then he returned the flask to his pocket. He paused for a moment, considering whether he should risk a smoke. It was dangerous. The flash might be seen in the darkness, and there were enemies watching. He decided to take the risk.

Placing a cigarette between his lips, he struck a match, inhaled the smoke hurriedly, and put out the light. Almost immediately, a bullet flattened itself against the parapet[3] of the roof. The sniper took another whiff and put out the cigarette. Then he swore softly and crawled away to the left.

Cautiously he raised himself and peered over the parapet. There was a flash and a bullet whizzed over his head. He dropped immediately. He had seen the flash. It came from the opposite side of the street.

He rolled over the roof to a chimney stack in the rear and slowly drew himself up behind it, until his eyes were level with the top of the parapet. There was nothing to be seen—just the dim outline of the opposite housetop against the blue sky. His enemy was under cover.

Just then an armored car came across the bridge and advanced slowly up the street. It stopped on the opposite side of the street, fifty yards ahead. The sniper could hear the dull panting of the motor. His heart beat faster. It was an enemy car. He wanted to fire, but he knew it was useless. His bullets would never pierce the steel that covered the gray monster.

Then round the corner of a side street came an old woman, her head covered by a tattered shawl. She began to talk to the man in the turret[4] of the car. She was pointing to the roof where the sniper lay. An informer.

The turret opened. A man's head and shoulders appeared, looking toward the sniper. The sniper raised his rifle and fired. The head fell heavily on the turret wall. The woman darted toward the side street. The sniper fired again. The woman whirled round and fell with a shriek into the gutter.

Suddenly from the opposite roof a shot rang out and the sniper dropped his rifle with a curse. The rifle clattered to the roof. The sniper thought the noise would wake the dead. He stooped to pick the rifle up. He couldn't lift it. His forearm was dead. "I'm hit," he muttered.

Dropping flat onto the roof, he crawled back to the parapet. With his left hand he felt the injured right forearm. The blood was oozing through the sleeve of his coat. There was no pain—just a deadened sensation, as if the arm had been cut off.

Quickly he drew his knife from his pocket, opened it on the breastwork[5] of the parapet, and ripped open the sleeve. There was a small hole where the bullet had entered. On the other side there was no hole. The bullet had lodged in the bone. It must have fractured it. He bent the arm below the wound. The arm bent back easily. He ground his teeth to overcome the pain.

Then taking out his field dressing, he ripped open the packet with his knife. He broke the neck of the iodine bottle and let the bitter fluid

There was a flash and a bullet whizzed over his head.

---

drip into the wound. A paroxysm[6] of pain swept through him. He placed the cotton wadding over the wound and wrapped the dressing over it. He tied the ends with his teeth.

Then he lay still against the parapet, and, closing his eyes, he made an effort of will to overcome the pain.

In the street beneath all was still. The armored car had retired speedily over the bridge, with the machine gunner's head hanging lifeless over the turret. The woman's corpse lay still in the gutter.

The sniper lay still for a long time nursing his wounded arm and planning escape. Morning must not find him wounded on the roof. The enemy on the opposite roof covered his escape. He must kill that enemy and he could not use his rifle. He had only a revolver to do it. Then he thought of a plan.

Taking off his cap, he placed it over the muzzle of his rifle. Then he pushed the rifle slowly upward over the parapet, until the cap was visible from the opposite side of the street. Almost immediately there was a report,[7] and a bullet pierced the center of the cap. The sniper slanted the rifle forward. The cap slipped down into the street. Then, catching the rifle in the middle, the sniper dropped his left hand over the roof and let it hang, lifelessly. After a few moments he let the rifle drop to the street. Then he sank to the roof, dragging his hand with him.

Crawling quickly to the left, he peered up at the corner of the roof. His ruse had succeeded. The other sniper, seeing the cap and rifle fall, thought that he had killed his man. He was now standing before a row of chimney pots, looking across, with his head clearly silhouetted against the western sky.

The Republican sniper smiled and lifted his revolver above the edge of the parapet. The distance was about fifty yards—a hard shot in the dim light, and his right arm was paining him like a thousand devils. He took a steady aim. His hand trembled with eagerness. Pressing his lips together, he took a deep breath through his nostrils and fired. He was almost deafened with the report and his arm shook with the recoil.

Then when the smoke cleared he peered across and uttered a cry of joy. His enemy had been hit. He was reeling over the parapet in his death agony. He struggled to keep his feet, but he was slowly falling forward, as if in a dream. The rifle fell from his grasp, hit the parapet, fell over, bounded off the pole of a barber's shop beneath, and then clattered on the pavement.

Then the dying man on the roof crumpled up and fell forward. The body turned over and over in space and hit the ground with a dull thud.

Then it lay still.

The sniper looked at his enemy falling and he shuddered. The lust of battle died in him. He became bitten by remorse. The sweat stood out in beads on his forehead. Weakened by his wound and the long summer day of fasting and watching on the roof, he revolted from the sight of the shattered mass of his dead enemy. His teeth chattered, he began to gibber to himself, cursing the war, cursing himself, cursing everybody.

He looked at the smoking revolver in his hand, and with an oath he hurled it to the roof

Morning must not find him wounded on the roof.

---

6. **paroxysm** (par′ək·siz′əm) *n*.: sudden attack; fit.
7. **report** (ri·pôrt′) *n*.: loud noise; in this case, from a gunshot.

Vocabulary

ruse (ro͞oz) *n*.: trick.

silhouetted (sil′ə·wet′id) *v*. used as *adj*.: outlined.

remorse (ri·môrs′) *n*.: deep guilt.

Irish Free State soldier keeping guard over a post office (September 1922).

at his feet. The revolver went off with the concussion and the bullet whizzed past the sniper's head. He was frightened back to his senses by the shock. His nerves steadied. The cloud of fear scattered from his mind and he laughed.

Taking the whiskey flask from his pocket, he emptied it at a draft. He felt reckless under the influence of the spirit. He decided to leave the roof now and look for his company commander, to report. Everywhere around was quiet. There was not much danger in going through the streets. He picked up his revolver and put it in his pocket. Then he crawled down through the skylight to the house underneath.

When the sniper reached the laneway on the street level, he felt a sudden curiosity as to the identity of the enemy sniper whom he had killed. He decided that he was a good shot, whoever he was. He wondered did he know him. Perhaps he had been in his own company before the split in the army. He decided to risk going over to have a look at him. He peered around the corner into O'Connell Street. In the upper part of the street there was heavy firing, but around here all was quiet.

The sniper darted across the street. A machine gun tore up the ground around him with a hail of bullets, but he escaped. He threw himself face downward beside the corpse. The machine gun stopped.

Then the sniper turned over the dead body and looked into his brother's face. ∎

Meet the Writer

Liam O'Flaherty

Soldier and Writer

Liam O'Flaherty (1896–1984) was born into a large, impoverished family on one of Ireland's rocky Aran Islands. The family faced great hardships—several of O'Flaherty's siblings died when they were quite young, and money and food were scarce. The O'Flaherty home was rich, instead, with stories. The Aran Islands have a long tradition of oral storytelling, and neighbors regularly gathered at his family's home to share tales and songs. In praise of his mother, O'Flaherty wrote:

> 66 Even when there was no food in the house, she would gather us about her at the empty hearth and weave fantastic stories. . . . 99

As a storyteller in his own right, O'Flaherty turned to the Aran Islands for inspiration, writing frequently about Irish peasant life. In his fiction he also captured the struggles of the Irish Civil War. *The Informer* (1925), his best-known novel, is a tale of betrayal set during the Irish "Troubles."

O'Flaherty himself lived during the war, and like the title character of "The Sniper," he fought on the Republican side. He participated in the Four Courts Rebellion, in which Republicans occupied Dublin's central courts of justice. The rebellion ended in failure: The courts were blown up, and the Republicans were forced to surrender. The writer responsible for the gripping, realistic detail in "The Sniper" had experienced the roar of gunfire firsthand.

Reading Check

1. Why does the sniper kill the old woman? What happens to him after he fires his weapon?

2. What does the sniper do to trick his enemy?

3. What discovery does the sniper make at the end of the story? Did you **predict** this outcome?

Thinking Critically

4. Explain the **irony** in the story's last sentence.

5. What facts are we told directly about the sniper? What can you infer about his **character**? Think, in particular, about his ability to perform in the face of fear and stress. (Refer to your Quickwrite notes for help answering.)

6. How do you think O'Flaherty wants the reader to view the sniper—is he a coldblooded killer, a soldier doing his duty, or a man caught in a tragic situation? How do the sniper's actions change your opinion of him at various moments in the story?

7. This story revolves around an **external conflict,** the sniper's life-or-death struggle. Explain the **internal conflict** the sniper also faces. How is his internal conflict resolved?

8. How would you state the **theme** of this story—that is, the point the writer is making about war, especially civil war, and friends and enemies? How do the resolutions of the story's conflicts help reveal the theme?

Extending and Evaluating

9. Do you think the story is improved by the **surprise ending,** or does the ending seem an unfair trick to make you pay attention to the story's message? Explain your answer.

WRITING

Before and After

Two important parts of this story are missing. One is the "before" narrative, telling why the two brothers ended up on opposite sides in the war. The other is the "after" narrative, describing what happens to the sniper after he discovers he has killed his brother. Write a paragraph **summarizing** what you imagine would be told in the "before" or "after" narrative.

Views from the Battlefield

Gunshots break the nighttime silence. Barbershops become battlefields. What might it be like to live in a neighborhood like the sniper's? Write a paragraph **describing** such an experience from the point of view of a teenager. For a true account of such an experience, read "Internment" on pages 288–290.

SKILLS FOCUS

Literary Skills
Analyze theme and conflict.

Reading Skills
Make predictions.

Writing Skills
Write a summary. Write a descriptive paragraph.

After You Read · Vocabulary Development

Word Knowledge: Can You Explain It?

PRACTICE 1

One way to get to know a word is to ask and answer questions about it. Write detailed answers to the following five questions. Then, write your own questions about the Word Bank words, and ask a partner to answer them.

1. What would living conditions be like in a beleaguered town?

2. What would be the first two luxuries you would give up if you decided to lead a more ascetic lifestyle?

3. What is the difference between a fanatic and a fan?

4. Think about a ruse in a story you've read or a movie you've seen. What made it particularly clever?

5. What advice would you give a friend who felt remorse for teasing a classmate?

> **Word Bank**
> beleaguered
> ascetic
> fanatic
> ruse
> remorse

Word Stories

Many words in English have interesting stories to tell. Most words come down to us from other languages with their spellings, pronunciations, and meanings altered. Some words, however, are ripped right out of the headlines, turning people's last names into new words. One such word is *boycott,* which means "refuse to deal with someone; refuse to buy, sell, or use something in order to punish a person or a group." The word comes from the name of Captain C. C. Boycott, who managed the estate of an Irish nobleman. In 1880, when the captain refused to lower the rent for tenants living on the nobleman's land, shopkeepers wouldn't sell him supplies, and people destroyed his property. The *boycott* of Captain Boycott hit the news, and a new word was born.

PRACTICE 2

> **Word Bank**
> silhouetted

In a notebook or computer file, start keeping a collection of interesting word stories. Look up *silhouette,* from the Word Bank, and write a few sentences telling the story of its origin and explaining its current meaning. As you learn about other words, add their word stories to your notebook or file. You can start now by researching *sandwich, maverick,* and *chauvinism.*

SKILLS FOCUS

Vocabulary Skills
Demonstrate word knowledge. Understand word origins.

Participial Phrases: Yes!
Dangling Participles: No!

A **participle** is a verb form that can be used as an adjective. Participles come in two varieties: **present participles** (*darkening* sky) and **past participles** (*shattered* glass). A **participial phrase** is made up of a participle and all of its modifiers and objects—for example, "*taking* off his cap" or "*weakened* by his wound."

Participles and participial phrases are economical, vivid ways of including more ideas and images in a sentence, and writers use them to avoid strings of short, choppy sentences. They are particularly good to use in action-driven writing, like that in "The Sniper." Read the following sentences aloud, and notice how much more fluid O'Flaherty's version is:

The sniper lay still for a long time. He nursed his wounded arm. He planned his escape.

O'FLAHERTY
"The sniper lay still for a long time nursing his wounded arm and planning escape."

Remember that participles and participial phrases act as adjectives and must always modify a noun or pronoun. They should be placed close to the noun or pronoun they modify. A **dangling participle** or a **dangling participial phrase** is a grammatical error that occurs when there is no word in the sentence for a participle to modify. To correct the sentence, you have to add or replace words, as in the following example:

DANGLING
Then, catching the rifle in the middle, his left hand dropped over the roof. . . .
[Who is catching the rifle?]

O'FLAHERTY (CORRECT)
"Then, catching the rifle in the middle, the *sniper* dropped his left hand over the roof. . . ."

PRACTICE 1

Identify the participial phrases in the following sentences, along with the word each one modifies. If the sentence contains a dangling participle, rewrite the sentence by adding a word or words that the participle can modify.

1. Hearing an armored car approach, his heart beat faster.

2. Wounded by the bullet, the pain was intense.

3. Hiding on a rooftop, the sniper killed three people.

4. The sniper, losing his taste for battle, threw down his gun.

5. Acting as an informer, the sniper's location was revealed.

PRACTICE 2

Take a sample of your own writing, and underline any short, choppy sentences. Then, see if you can use participles to combine some sentences. Check to see that your revised sentences don't contain any dangling participles.

▶ **For more help, see Placement of Modifiers, 5f, in the Language Handbook.**

SKILLS
FOCUS

Grammar Skills
Identify participles and participial phrases.

Before You Read

Cranes

Literary Skills
Understand theme and character.

Pages 260–280 cover Compare universal themes.

Reading Skills
Make inferences about character motivation.

go.
hrw
.com

INTERNET

Vocabulary Practice

Keyword: LE7 9-4

Make the Connection

Quickwrite ✏️

Which is worse: betraying one's duty or betraying one's friend? Imagine a situation in which you were forced to make such a choice. What issues would you weigh as you tried to make a decision? Freewrite for a few minutes about this dilemma.

Literary Focus

Theme and Character: Life Lessons

Reading a story is often like following characters on a journey. Sometimes the characters travel to a new place; other times they stay where they are. Either way, they take a journey of the heart or mind.

In the course of their journey, characters may face overwhelming obstacles or heart-rending decisions, and they learn something in the process—about themselves or others or life in general. Through what their **characters** learn, writers communicate their **theme,** or central idea.

In "Cranes," the main character travels only a short distance on foot, but the journey he takes in his heart and mind is much greater. As you read the story, think about what the main character learns and remembers during his walk. What theme does the writer convey?

Reading Skills 📖

Making Inferences About Motivation

To understand characters fully, you need to determine their **motivation,** or the reasons for their behavior. Usually writers don't make direct statements about motivation. Instead, you need to make **inferences,** or educated guesses, based on clues in the story. As you read "Cranes," think about why the main character makes certain decisions and why he behaves as he does. The questions at the open-book signs will help you make inferences.

Vocabulary Development

averted (ə·vurt′id) v. used as *adj.*: turned away.

obstruction (əb·struk′shən) n.: obstacle; barrier.

constitutes (kän′stə·tōōts′) v.: makes up; forms.

mainstay (mān′stā′) n.: principal support.

refuge (ref′yōōj) n.: shelter; protection from danger or difficulty.

Background

The conflict in this story is shaped by the civil war that took place in the early 1950s in Korea, a nation west of Japan bordering on China and Russia.

At the end of World War II, the country was divided in half, at the thirty-eighth parallel of latitude, with Soviet troops occupying the north and U.S. troops occupying the south. There had been plans to reunite the country eventually, but instead, in 1948, a Communist government was established in the north and a pro-Western government was established in the south.

In 1950, Communist troops from North Korea invaded the south. They were opposed by soldiers from South Korea, supported by United Nations (mostly U.S.) forces. Ultimately the conflict centered around the thirty-eighth parallel. During the war many villages along the thirty-eighth parallel changed hands several times between North and South Korea. "Cranes" is set in one such village.

A large number of Korean civilians and military personnel died during the war, and both North and South Korea suffered great devastation. A truce agreement was signed in 1953, the year "Cranes" was published, and the final military front line of battle became the boundary between North and South Korea. The two countries have still not achieved reunification.

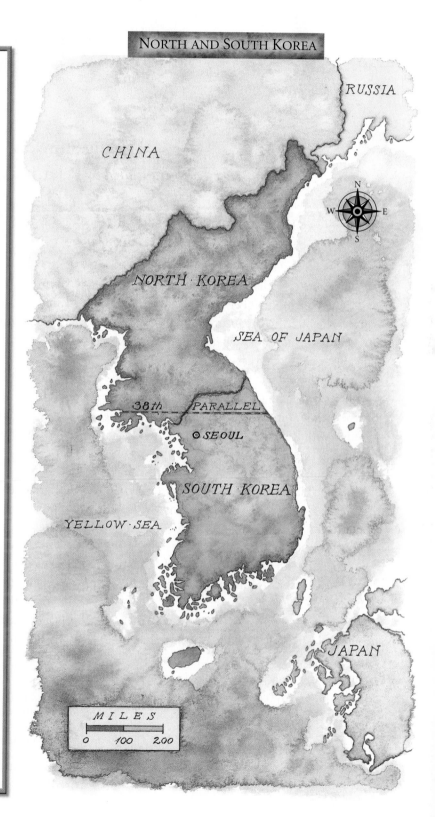

NORTH AND SOUTH KOREA

RUSSIA

CHINA

NORTH KOREA

SEA OF JAPAN

38th PARALLEL

○ SEOUL

SOUTH KOREA

YELLOW SEA

JAPAN

MILES

0   100   200

Cranes

Hwang Sunwŏn
translated by Peter H. Lee

A young man stood, tied up.

The northern village at the border of the thirty-eighth parallel[1] was snugly settled under the high, bright autumn sky.

One white gourd lay against another on the dirt floor of an empty farmhouse. The occasional village elders first put out their bamboo pipes before passing by, and the children too turned aside some distance off. Their faces were ridden with fear.

The village as a whole showed few traces of destruction from the war, but it did not seem like the same village Sŏngsam[2] had known as a boy.

At the foot of a chestnut grove on the hill behind the village he stopped and climbed a chestnut tree. Somewhere far back in his mind he heard the old man with a wen[3] shout, "You bad boy, you're climbing up my chestnut tree again!"

The old man must have passed away, for among the few village elders Sŏngsam had met, the old man was not to be found. Holding the trunk of the tree, Sŏngsam gazed at the blue sky for a while. Some chestnuts fell to the ground as the dry clusters opened of their own accord.

In front of the farmhouse that had been turned into a public peace-police office, a young man stood, tied up. He seemed to be a stranger, so Sŏngsam approached him to have a close look. He was taken aback; it was none other than his boyhood playmate, Tŏkchae.[4]

Sŏngsam asked the police officer who had come with him from Ch'ŏnt'ae[5] what it was all about. The prisoner was vice-chairman of the Farmers Communist League and had just been flushed out[6] of his hideout in his own house, Sŏngsam learned.

Sŏngsam sat down on the dirt floor and lit a cigarette.

Tŏkchae was to be escorted to Ch'ŏngdan[7] by one of the peace policemen.

After a time, Sŏngsam lit a new cigarette from the first and stood up.

"I'll take the fellow with me."

Tŏkchae, his face averted, refused to look at Sŏngsam. They left the village.

---

4. **Tŏkchae** (tək'chə').
5. **Ch'ŏnt'ae** (chən'tə').
6. **flushed out:** forced from a hiding place.
7. **Ch'ŏngdan** (chən'dän').

Vocabulary
averted (ə·vʉrt'id) v. used as *adj.*: turned away.

---

1. **northern village . . . thirty-eighth parallel:** village close to the northern border of South Korea.
2. **Sŏngsam** (səŋ'säm').
3. **wen** *n.*: harmless skin tumor.

Scenes of Daily Life by Lee Dong-Shick (1941–   ).

Sŏngsam kept on smoking, but the tobacco had no taste. He just kept drawing in the smoke and blowing it out. Then suddenly he thought that Tŏkchae too must want a puff. He thought of the days when they used to share dried gourd leaves behind walls, hidden from the adults. But today, how could he offer a cigarette to a fellow like this?

Once, when they were small, he went with Tŏkchae to steal some chestnuts from the grandpa with the wen. It was Sŏngsam's turn to go up the tree. Suddenly there came shouts from the old man. He slipped and fell to the ground. Sŏngsam got chestnut needles all over his bottom, but he kept on running. It was only when they reached a safe place where the old man could not overtake them that he turned his bottom to Tŏkchae. Plucking out those needles hurt so much that he could not keep tears from welling up in his eyes. Tŏkchae produced a fistful of chestnuts from his pocket and thrust them into Sŏngsam's. . . Sŏngsam threw away the cigarette he had just lit. Then he made up his mind not to light another while he was escorting Tŏkchae.

They reached the hill pass, the hill where he and Tŏkchae used to cut fodder for the cows until Sŏngsam had had to move near Ch'ŏnt'ae, south of the thirty-eighth parallel, two years before the liberation.

Sŏngsam felt a sudden surge of anger in spite of himself and shouted, "So how many have you killed?"

For the first time, Tŏkchae cast a quick glance at him and then turned away.

"How many did you kill, you?" he asked again.

Tŏkchae turned toward him once again and

glared. The glare grew intense and his mouth twitched.

"So you managed to kill many, eh?" Sŏngsam felt his heart becoming clear from within, as if an obstruction had been removed. "If you were vice-chairman of the Communist League, why didn't you run? You must have been lying low with a secret mission."

Tŏkchae did not answer.

"Speak up, what was your mission?"

Tŏkchae kept walking. Tŏkchae is hiding something, Sŏngsam thought. He wanted to take a good look at him, but Tŏkchae would not turn his averted face.

Fingering the revolver at his side, Sŏngsam went on: "No excuse is necessary. You are sure to be shot anyway. Why don't you tell the truth, here and now?"

"I'm not going to make any excuses. They made me vice-chairman of the league because I was one of the poorest and I was a hardworking farmer. If that constitutes a crime worthy of death, so be it. I am still what I used to be—the only thing I'm good at is digging in the soil." After a short pause, he added, "My old man is bedridden at home. He's been ill almost half a year." Tŏkchae's father was a widower, a hard-working, poor farmer who lived only for his son. Seven years ago his back had given out and his skin had become diseased.

"You married?"

"Yes," replied Tŏkchae after a while.

"To whom?"

"Shorty."

"To Shorty?" How interesting! A woman so small and plump that she knew the earth's vast-ness but not the sky's altitude. Such a cold fish! He and Tŏkchae used to tease her and make her cry. And Tŏkchae had married that girl.

"How many kids?"

Vocabulary

obstruction (əb·struk′shən) *n.*: obstacle; barrier.

constitutes (kän′stə·to͞ots′) *v.*: makes up; forms.

CHARACTER MOTIVATION

1. How is Sŏngsam's decision related to his memory of the time Tŏkchae gave him chestnuts?

CHARACTER MOTIVATION

2. What do you think motivates Sŏngsam to ask this question?

Spring Landscape by Yi Sang-Bom (1897–1972). Ink and watercolor on paper.

"The first is arriving this fall, she says."

Sŏngsam had difficulty swallowing a laugh about to explode in spite of himself. Although he had asked how many kids Tŏkchae had, he could not help wanting to burst into laughter at the image of her sitting down, with a large stomach, one span around. But he realized this was no time to laugh or joke over such matters.

"Anyway, it's strange you did not run away."

"I tried to escape. They said that once the South invaded, no man would be spared. So men between seventeen and forty were forcibly taken to the North. I thought of evacuating, even if I had to carry my father on my back. But father said no. How could the farmers leave the land behind when the crops were ready for harvest? He grew old on that farm depending on me as the prop and <u>mainstay</u> of the family. I wanted to be with him in his last moments so that I could close his eyes with my own hand. Besides, where can farmers like us go, who know only living on the land?"

L̲ast June Sŏngsam had had to take <u>refuge</u>. At night he had broken the news privately to his father. But his father had said the same thing! Where can a farmer go, leaving all the chores behind? So Sŏngsam left alone. Roaming about the strange streets and villages in the South, Sŏngsam had been haunted by thoughts of his old parents and the young children, left with all the chores. Fortunately, his family was safe then, as now.

They crossed the ridge of a hill. This time Sŏngsam walked with his face averted. The autumn sun was hot on his forehead. This was an ideal day for the harvest, he thought.

CHARACTER MOTIVATION

3. Why do you think Sŏngsam turns his face away from Tŏkchae?

W̲hen they reached the foot of the hill, Sŏngsam hesitatingly stopped. In the middle of a field he spied a group of cranes that looked like men in white clothes bending over.

Vocabulary

mainstay (mān′stā′) *n.*: principal support.

refuge (ref′yo͞oj) *n.*: shelter; protection from danger or difficulty.

Two Cranes by Chang Woo-Soung (1912–   ). Ink and watercolor on paper.

This used to be the neutralized zone along the thirty-eighth parallel. The cranes were still living here, as before, while the people were all gone.

Once, when Sŏngsam and Tŏkchae were about twelve, they had set a trap here, without the knowledge of the adults, and had caught a crane, a Tanjŏng crane. They had roped the crane, even its wings, and had paid daily visits, patting its neck and riding on its back. Then one day they overheard the neighbors whispering. Someone had come from Seoul[8] with a permit from the governor-general's office to catch cranes as specimens or something. Then and there the two boys dashed off to the field. That they would be found out and punished was no longer a weighty concern; all they worried about was the fate of their crane. Without a moment's delay, still out of breath from running, they untied the crane's feet and wings. But the bird could hardly walk. It must have been worn out from being bound.

The two held it up in the air. Then, all of a sudden, a shot was fired. The crane fluttered its wings a couple of times and came down again.

It was shot, they thought. But the next

---

8. **Seoul** (sōl): capital of South Korea.

moment, as another crane from a nearby bush fluttered its wings, the boys' crane stretched its long neck with a whoop and disappeared into the sky. For a long time the two boys could not take their eyes away from the blue sky into which their crane had soared.

CHARACTER MOTIVATION

4. Why did the boys set the bird free? Why might Sŏngsam be remembering this incident?

"Hey, why don't we stop here for a crane hunt?" Sŏngsam spoke up suddenly.

Tŏkchae was puzzled, struck dumb.

"I'll make a trap with this rope; you flush a crane over here."

Having untied Tŏkchae's hands, Sŏngsam had already started crawling among the weeds.

Tŏkchae's face turned white. "You are sure to be shot anyway"—these words flashed through his mind. Pretty soon a bullet would fly from where Sŏngsam has gone, he thought.

Some paces away, Sŏngsam quickly turned toward him.

"Hey, how come you're standing there like you're dumb? Go flush the crane!"

CHARACTER MOTIVATION

5. What is Sŏngsam's real motivation for urging Tŏkchae to flush the crane?

Only then did Tŏkchae catch on. He started crawling among the weeds.

A couple of Tanjŏng cranes soared high into the clear blue autumn sky, fluttering their huge wings. ■

Meet the Writer

Hwang Sunwŏn

The Voice of His Divided Nation

Throughout his lifetime, Hwang Sunwŏn (1915–2000) saw his beloved homeland, Korea, torn by political turmoil. That turmoil touched him deeply and greatly affected his writing.

As a small boy, Hwang saw his father imprisoned for political activities. Korea was struggling against its powerful neighbor, Japan, which had made Korea part of its empire in 1910. By the early 1940s, the Japanese had banned all writing in the Korean language, and Hwang was forced to work in secret. After World War II, when Korea was no longer under Japan's control, communism spread through the northern part of the country. Hwang and his family fled to the south, but they became refugees again when North Korea invaded South Korea at the beginning of the Korean War.

A poet in his youth, Hwang later turned his attention to writing prose, producing seven novels and gaining a reputation as a master writer of the modern Korean short story. His country's complex history is the frequent subject of his fiction, which (like "Cranes") is set in modern times as well as in the distant past. Although his work is rooted in the history and culture of his country, Hwang also explores universal themes, such as the loneliness of the individual. He is highly regarded for his insight into the hearts and minds of his characters.

Reading Check

1. What is the **setting** of the story—when and where do the events take place?

2. What was Sŏngsam's relationship with Tŏkchae when they were children?

3. For which side in the war is Sŏngsam fighting?

4. Why is Tŏkchae a prisoner? What reasons does he give for not leaving his home with his father?

Thinking Critically

5. Although Sŏngsam and Tŏkchae represent opposite sides of the war, they share similarities. Compare their **characters** and their situations.

6. What is Sŏngsam's **internal conflict** regarding Tŏkchae? How is the conflict resolved at the end of the story?

7. What does Sŏngsam recall in the two **flashbacks** to his childhood? Explain how these memories **motivate** Sŏngsam's actions in the present.

8. What does Sŏngsam learn about Tŏkchae during their walk? How does this information affect Sŏngsam's actions?

9. What is the story's **theme**—that is, what is it saying about civil war and friends and enemies?

10. In many Asian cultures the crane **symbolizes,** or represents, long life. Birds in flight often symbolize freedom. Reread the last sentence of the story, and explain how the cranes might symbolize both characters.

Extending and Evaluating

11. Do you think the ending of the story is effective? Would it be more effective if the writer directly stated what was happening or if Sŏngsam and Tŏkchae shared their thoughts with each other? Give reasons for your answer.

WRITING

The Right Choice?

Sŏngsam wrestles with divided loyalties in this story. Do you think he makes the right decision in the end? Imagine that he is on trial for letting Tŏkchae escape. Write a **speech** in which Sŏngsam defends his actions. Alternatively, compose a speech in which a prosecutor condemns Sŏngsam for his decision. Refer to your Quickwrite notes as you plan your speech.

Decisive Moments

Think up your own fictional character who faces an important decision, perhaps one that involves a moral choice, as Sŏngsam's does. Write one page in which you present the character's thoughts at the moment the decision is made. What motivates the character to make this decision?

Comparing Themes
For a writing assignment comparing the themes in "The Sniper" and "Cranes," see page 280.

After You Read Vocabulary Development

Analogies: Pairs of Related Words

Analogy questions ask you to analyze the relationship between one pair of words and then complete a second pair of words. The same relationship must be expressed in the two pairs. Follow the steps below to complete a word analogy. (For more about analogies, see page 672.)

> **Word Bank**
>
> averted
> obstruction
> constitutes
> mainstay
> refuge

MOUTH : FACE :: _____ : television

    a. entertainment   **c.** telephone

    b. living room   **d.** screen

1. Identify the relationship between the words in the first pair. In the example, the relationship is that of a part (*mouth*) to a whole (*face*).

2. Use a sentence to see the relationship in the analogy more clearly: A *mouth* is a part of a *face,* just as a _____ is a part of a *television.*

3. Select the word that completes the second pair so that it expresses the same relationship as that in the first pair. Choice d, *screen,* is correct because it refers to a part of a television.

The chart below shows some of the relationships used in analogies:

Type of Relationship	Example
Synonyms	TIRED : SLEEPY :: happy : joyous
Antonyms	RIGHT : WRONG :: few : many
Part to whole	LEAF : TREE :: kitchen : house
Member to category	EARTH : PLANET :: truck : vehicle
Object (or thing) to a characteristic of it	SUN : HOT :: desert : dry

PRACTICE 1

Complete each analogy below with the Word Bank word that fits best:

1. ANNOUNCES : DECLARES :: _____ : forms

2. SUCCEEDED : FAILED :: _____ : faced

3. SKYSCRAPER : TALL :: _____ : safe

4. CONTEST : COMPETITION :: _____ : obstacle

5. PAIL : BUCKET :: _____ : support

PRACTICE 2

Using the chart above as a reference, identify the type of relationship in each word pair:

  1. crane : bird   **3.** scream : loud   **5.** wheel : bus

  2. glass : fragile   **4.** soccer : sport

SKILLS FOCUS

Vocabulary Skills
Understand word analogies.

Writing a Comparison–Contrast Essay

Comparing Universal Themes

"The Sniper" . . . . page 262
"Cranes" . . . . page 272

Now that you have read "The Sniper" and "Cranes," you can compare and contrast their themes in an essay. When you write a **comparison-contrast essay,** you look for similarities (**comparisons**) and differences (**contrasts**) between the works.

Gather and Organize Your Information

To write your essay, use the chart on page 260 that you created to compare elements of the two stories. It will contain the basic information you need to compose your essay.

Comparison-contrast essays can be organized in two ways. One way is called the **block method,** which you will use to write this essay. The other way is the **point-by-point method,** which you will learn about on page 318.

The Block Method

When you use the block method, you discuss the *stories,* one at a time. First you write about the relevant elements of one story in the order you think most effective. Then you discuss the same elements in the other story, following the same order. The chart at the right gives an example.

Use Three-Part Structure

Most essays have three basic parts. Use this structure when you write your comparison-contrast essay:

1. In your **introduction,** tell the reader what works you will be comparing,

giving titles, authors, and any necessary background information. The introduction, usually a single paragraph, should end with a **thesis statement,** in which you state how the stories' themes are similar or different.

2. The **body** of your essay consists of paragraphs supporting your thesis statement with evidence from the stories—the information you listed in your chart.

3. In your **conclusion,** sum up your major points, and end with a new (but related) thought.

Develop Your Ideas

You should develop and **elaborate** on every general statement in your essay. Provide examples, details, or quotations to prove your thesis.

▶ **For more help writing a comparison-contrast essay, see pages 320–327.**

Block Method
Story 1: "The Sniper"
Element 1: Main character and his situation
Element 2: Character's motives and conflict(s)
Element 3: What character learns
Element 4: Resolution of conflict(s)
Element 5: Theme
Story 2: "Cranes"
Element 1: Main character and his situation
Element 2: Character's motives and conflict(s)
Element 3: What character learns
Element 4: Resolution of conflict(s)
Element 5: Theme

SKILLS FOCUS

Literary Skills
Compare universal themes.

Writing Skills
Write a comparison-contrast essay.

A Country Divided ◆ Lives in the Crossfire ◆ Internment ◆ Peace Isn't Impossible

Synthesizing Sources: Drawing Conclusions

When you research a subject, get a balanced view by using several types of sources and examining different points of view. Here are some guidelines:

- **Categorize your sources.** Is a work a **primary source**—a firsthand, or eyewitness, account? Is it a **secondary source** providing analysis of events in which the writer did not participate? (For more on primary and secondary sources, see pages 118 and 674–675.)
- **Determine the author's purpose and audience.** Was the piece written, for example, to tell a personal story, to change an unsympathetic reader's mind, or to provide background information?
- **Compare and contrast.** Write a **paraphrase** of the sources' main ideas. If your subject is controversial, do your sources agree or disagree? Compare the information in your sources, and think about what you can learn from each one. Does a source provide only objective facts or the author's feelings and thoughts? Are **facts** and **opinions** combined?
- **Connect to other sources or related topics.** Connect your resources to other works of nonfiction or fiction that you've read, perhaps ones about another time or place.
- **Synthesize.** Consider your sources as a group. How does each source contribute to your understanding of the subject? Do your sources present different opinions to give you a balanced view of the issues?

Draw conclusions from your sources and from connections to other sources you've read. What do you now understand about your subject? What do you still need to find out?

Vocabulary Development

intolerance (in·täl′ər·əns) *n.*: prejudice; hostility to other groups.

negotiations (ni·gō′shē·ā′shənz) *n.*: discussions aimed at reaching an agreement.

designate (dez′ig·nāt′) *v.*: point out; indicate.

absorb (ab·sôrb′) *v.*: take in.

reunification (rē·yoo′nə·fi′kā′shən) *n.*: joining together of things that had been divided.

divergent (dī·vur′jənt) *adj.*: separate; going in different directions.

coerced (kō·urst′) *v.*: forced.

abhor (ab·hôr′) *v.*: hate.

optimist (äp′tə·mist) *n.*: person who is always hopeful.

condone (kən·dōn′) *v.*: overlook or excuse an offense.

SKILLS FOCUS

Reading Skills
Synthesize ideas from different sources dealing with a single topic.

Connecting to the Literature

The long-standing conflicts between Catholics and Protestants in Ireland, the setting of "The Sniper" (page 262), are called the Troubles. The following selections discuss the conflict and tell what it's like to live in a place where your home is a battleground.

go.
hrw
.com

INTERNET

Interactive Reading Model

Keyword: LE7 9-4

A Country Divided

from *One Belfast Boy*

Patricia McMahon

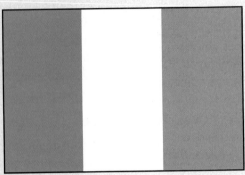

The flag of Ireland. The green is for Catholics, the orange is for Protestants, and the white symbolizes peace between them.

Around the year 1170 the king of England, Henry II, declared himself king of Ireland as well. Gradually, with great bloodshed, Ireland was brought under the control of England, or Great Britain, as England came to be known. Through the centuries, Ireland was held as a colony of the British Empire—held against the wishes of the Irish people.

There were also other people living in Ireland, however. English settlers had been going to Ireland for centuries, and beginning in 1609, James I, then king of England, offered land to Scottish settlers if they would move to Ireland and farm the land—land that was being taken from the native Irish.

To the Irish, these new arrivals came to be known as the strangers: people with a different language, a different way of life, and, most important, a different religion. For the people of Ireland were Catholic and the strangers taking over their land were Protestant. At that time in England and in much of Europe, a terrible <u>intolerance</u> existed between different religions.

The English gradually put laws into place that said Catholics could not own land, could not vote, could not be elected to public office or work for the government. Catholics were not allowed to be lawyers. They were not allowed to speak the Irish language or study Irish history or literature. They were forbidden to hold Mass. Bishops, priests, and monks[1] were forced to leave the country. By 1780 the Irish people owned only 5 percent of their own land, and in 1800 the British government passed the Act of Union, declaring Ireland part of the United Kingdom of Great Britain and Ireland.

Through the long years of British rule, the Irish fought for their freedom. They fought with what weapons they had, in rebellions great and small—rebellions that the vast British army always put down. The Irish fought with words as well as weapons. They organized and signed petitions, held massive nonviolent protests, and after Catholics

---

1. **hold Mass . . . monks:** Mass is the Catholic Church's ritual service. Bishops and priests are Catholic clergy. Monks live in religious communities governed by a set of strict rules.

Vocabulary

intolerance (in·täl′ər·əns) *n.*: prejudice; hostility to other groups.

View of damage in Dublin, Ireland, after the uprising in 1916.

regained the vote in 1829, they lobbied[2] in the English Parliament[3] for their freedom.

In 1916, during World War I, a small rebellion broke out in Dublin[4] on Easter Monday. The Irish rebels were quickly defeated. Sixteen of the leaders were shot, and many men and women were jailed, including some who had not been involved. Anger grew in Ireland. People began to join Sinn Fein, a political group working for Irish freedom. In the Irish language, Sinn Fein means "ourselves alone." Those who felt it

was necessary to fight with weapons joined the IRA—the Irish Republican Army—and fought the British army where and when they could. The outnumbered IRA, led by a man named Michael Collins, managed to inflict losses on the superior British forces. The Irish people began to believe that this time would be different, this time freedom would finally come.

But the Protestants of Ireland did not approve of the rebellion. They had lived in Ireland for generations. They owned land and businesses. And they knew who they were: They were British subjects, and they believed Ireland should remain part of the United Kingdom. They were willing to fight to keep it so. "No surrender" became

2. **lobbied** (läb′ēd) *v.:* attempted to influence public officials to do something.
3. **English Parliament:** branch of the English government with the power to make laws for the country.
4. **Dublin:** Ireland's capital.

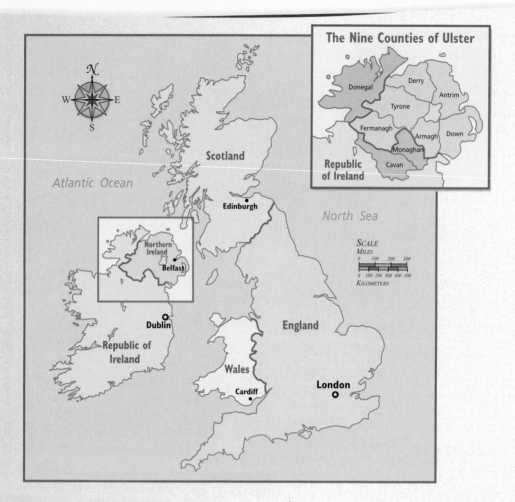

The Nine Counties of Ulster

Donegal · Derry · Antrim · Tyrone · Fermanagh · Armagh · Down · Monaghan · Cavan

Republic of Ireland

their motto. Great numbers of Protestants were living in the North; their cry was "Ulster[5] will fight, and Ulster will be right."

The damages inflicted by the Irish rebels grew, and the British government agreed in 1920 to meet with the Irish for peace talks. After difficult <u>negotiations</u>, the British agreed to the Irish demands for self-government and freedom. But they did not agree to freedom for all of Ireland. Ulster, where so many British Protestants lived, would become Northern Ireland and would become part of the United Kingdom of Great Britain and Northern Ireland. But not *all* of Ulster would become Northern

Ireland. A new border would be drawn to create a place where there would be more Protestants than Catholics. Three counties—Donegal, Cavan, and Monaghan—of the original nine making up Ulster were not included in Northern Ireland. This was the deal the British offered. If it was not accepted, the talks would be ended, and the fighting would begin again.

In Ireland, the arguments over the proposal were fierce. Some believed there should be no division of the country—no deal. Others thought it was the best deal possible at that time. They believed that

---

5. **Ulster:** name often given to the northern, predominantly Protestant, portion of Ireland.

Vocabulary

negotiations (ni·gō′shē·ā′shənz) *n.:* discussions aimed at reaching an agreement.

creating Northern Ireland was a temporary measure and Ireland would soon be re-united. In the end, Ireland took the offer. But anger over the division of the country was so strong that civil war broke out. Friends who had fought together against the British now turned on one another.

And so in 1921, while most of the Irish gained their freedom, the Catholics of Northern Ireland remained under British rule. In the new Ulster, Catholics could not vote unless they owned land, and few did. Businesses, government, public housing, and jobs were all controlled by Protestants.

In 1968, Catholics began to form civil rights organizations, inspired by the work of people like Dr. Martin Luther King, Jr., in the United States. Catholics wanted to have the same rights as Protestants. They began a series of protest marches across Northern Ireland. The government forbade the marches. Catholic demonstrators were attacked and gassed.[6] Catholic homes, neighborhoods, and churches were attacked by mobs who believed that the Catholics were not entitled to equal rights.

The Catholics began to fight back, arming themselves. The Irish Republican Army, whose numbers had dwindled since the country was divided, gained new recruits and became active again. The British army moved in to try to stop the fighting, but the battles grew worse. After fourteen unarmed protesters were killed by a British army regiment in 1972, on a day that became known as Bloody Sunday, the IRA's membership swelled. Soon the cities and towns of Northern Ireland were battlegrounds.

Both the Protestants and the Catholics made bombs, blew up buildings, and created armies. The IRA began to argue within its ranks about tactics, splitting into different groups. One group, called the Provisional IRA, or the Provos, became the present-day IRA. Both Catholics and Protestants were guilty of murder and mayhem. At one point there were as many as seven armed groups on the streets of Belfast.[7] Even the question of civil rights seemed to have been lost amidst the violence and the constant calls for revenge.

More than 3,200 people have died in the Troubles[8]—men, women, and children—Protestant and Catholic alike. They died over the question "Are we British or are we Irish?" And after all this time, there are still two very different answers to that question. The deaths have not changed this.

The habit of hating is a hard one to break. But many people believe it is worth a try. People on both sides of the walls[9] who want peace keep working to stop the fighting. In 1997, a new cease-fire went into effect. Peace talks began, which led to the signing of a peace accord in 1998. A new government for Northern Ireland was formed, intending to guarantee the rights of Catholics. Some say there will be no peace until the entire island of Ireland is united. Some say there will be no peace if that ever happens.

Although a peace accord was signed in 1998, as of 2005, peace has not been established in Northern Ireland. Both sides continue to work on resolving the conflict.

---

6. **gassed** *v.:* exposed to tear gas or some other airborne substance released in order to cause great discomfort.

7. **Belfast:** capital of Northern Ireland.
8. **More than . . . Troubles:** This figure refers to the number of deaths at the time of the book's publication, in 1999.
9. **both sides of the walls:** walls in some parts of Belfast that separate Catholics and Protestants.

Lives in the Crossfire

from *Children of "the Troubles"*

Laurel Holliday

December 20, 1976

I would love to risk sleeping some Christmas night with curtains flung back from the windows, nothing but shiny black glass between me and the stars and sky, the drizzle and the horses, but [IRA] bombs ruthlessly silence my wishes, for a while at least.

—*from the diary of Sharon Ingram, eighteen years old, Ballygawley*

28th April, 1994

I am frightened living on this street across from the Protestants. I am frightened they will come and kill us because this is the eleventh time they have shot people in our street. I don't know why they want to kill us.

—*from the diary of Bridie Murphy, eleven years old, Belfast*

From the moment children are born in Northern Ireland, they begin to live in a majority Protestant or a majority Catholic neighborhood. They go to either a Catholic or a Protestant school, and their friends are likely to be exclusively one or the other. They are taught to shop only in their "own" shops in some towns and, eventually, to socialize only in their "own" pubs. And, of course, when they die they will go to a segregated graveyard.

Amazingly, I think, to those who haven't been raised there, in Belfast even the taxis divide along religious lines, with one fleet heading to Catholic and another to Protestant neighborhoods. In some parts of the country even the sidewalks are painted to designate political/religious loyalties.

In addition to these very obvious distinctions that children need to learn in order to survive in Northern Ireland, they also absorb differences in language and perspective[1] that set them apart from one another for the rest of their lives. If you are Catholic, for example, you call Northern Ireland's second largest city Derry; if you are Protestant, it is Londonderry to you. If you are Catholic, you call the nearly three decades of the Troubles a war; if you are Protestant, you are careful to point out that there has been a terrorist uprising, not a war, in Northern Ireland.

---

1. **perspective** (pər·spek′tiv) *n.*: point of view.

Vocabulary
designate (dez′ig·nāt′) *v.*: point out; indicate.
absorb (ab·sôrb′) *v.*: take in.

In fact, even the name you call your country will be in question. If you are raised in a Catholic family wanting the reunification of Ireland, you will refer to the North of Ireland as your homeland or call it the Six Counties, rather than making it sound as if it were a separate country called Northern Ireland. And if you were raised in a Protestant environment, you will be more likely to call your country Northern Ireland or Ulster.

Not only are most children in Northern Ireland set on divergent sectarian[2] courses from birth, but from the age of seven some Protestant and Catholic children are coerced into running secret errands for terrorists and assembling and hiding their weapons.

Although the majority of people in Northern Ireland abhor the violence and take no part in it themselves, virtually every family in Northern Ireland has had members beaten, tortured, or murdered, and the country's children have been witness to it all. For this is not a private war, conducted behind closed doors, nor a war where the men go away to fight the enemy. This is an everyday, in-your-face war, where the enemy lives on the next block and speaks (almost) the same language.

Vocabulary

reunification (rē·yoo′nə·fi·kā′shən) *n*.: joining together of things that had been divided.

divergent (dī·vur′jənt) *adj*.: separate; going in different directions.

coerced (kō·urlsd′) *v*.: forced.

abhor (ab·hôr′) *v*.: hate.

---

2. **sectarian** (sek·ter′ē·ən) *adj*.: pertaining to a particular religious group.

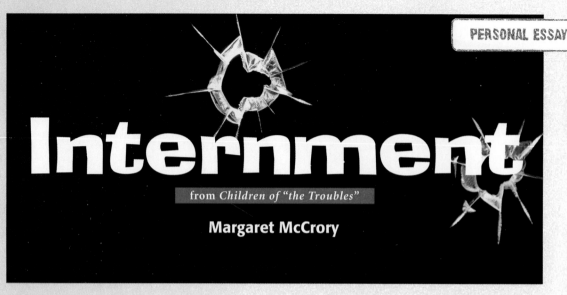

Internment

from *Children of "the Troubles"*

Margaret McCrory

Internment was a policy authorized by the British government in reaction to the violence in Northern Ireland. The policy allowed the police to jail suspected criminals without charging them with a crime or producing evidence against them. Margaret McCrory was a teenager in Belfast, and she witnessed the violent reaction to this policy.

August 9, 1971, is a day I will remember as long as I live. We were emigrating[1] to America the next day but that's not why I'll remember that date. That was the night of Internment. I was only thirteen at the time, but just thinking about that day still brings back the knotted feelings in my stomach.

I was supposed to feel excited about leaving and also sad to be saying goodbye to our friends and neighbors. But we woke up that morning to a strange silence outside. We found ourselves whispering to each other and sneaking looks out the windows. There was nothing out there at all—no people, no cars, not even the dogs were barking. It was eerie.

We felt something big was about to happen, but when? The waiting was the worst feeling I've ever felt. I don't know if we would have sensed so much tension if my mum hadn't kept repeating over and over again, "Please, Lord, get us out of here." She looked and acted like she was scared to death and I suppose some of that rubbed off on us. We were very subdued[2] all day. The funny thing was there wasn't a bite in the house, yet no one complained they were hungry.

Late afternoon, and there was still no activity outside. By this time we were all nervous wrecks. We had nothing in the house to occupy us—just a couple of mattresses and our suitcases. Hugh, who was nine, was so nervous that he made himself sick. Mum made him lie down on the mattress in the boys' room on the second floor. Eileen, eleven, was walking around like a zombie, staring straight ahead with huge eyes. She was scary. David, eight, and Maria, seven, were playing quietly on the bare floor, which was really unusual for them. Mum and I took it in turns to peek out of the windows.

---

1. **emigrating** (em′i·grāt′iŋ) *v.:* leaving a country to live in another place.

2. **subdued** (səb·dōōd′) *adj.:* quiet; reserved or restrained.

Mum had gone into the kitchen to brush[3] the floor when the shooting began. We could hear the bullets whizzing over the house and ricocheting[4] off the corrugated iron on the factory wall behind our house. The bullets smashed through the kitchen window. Mum dropped the brush and ran. To this very day she still complains about leaving a pile of dirt on the floor.

Hugh was crying upstairs and Eileen was screaming her head off. Between the deafening noise inside and the explosive noises from outside, we felt like we were in the middle of World War III. All the shooting seemed to be at the back of the house where the boys' room was so we dragged Hugh and the mattress up to the third floor where our room overlooked the front of the house. We all huddled together on the mattresses.

It was very hot but when Mum opened the window a little bit we could feel our throats begin to burn. Which meant that there was tear gas out there, and from past experience we knew what that could do to you. Your throat would begin to burn and your eyes would sting like mad. Then you would feel violently sick. It was a horrible feeling so we quickly shut the window.

The Uzis[5] were going mad out there—the noise was incredible!—and Eileen couldn't stop screaming. I was scared but I also felt excited and very curious. I really wanted to know what was going on out there so every chance I got I would sneak a look outside. I could see men with guns running up our street. They saw me and shooed me in by gesturing with their hands to get down. Mum made me sit with them on the mattresses, but Eileen's screaming was driving me mad so I finally told her that they weren't going to kill her because I was going to do it first. She quieted down to loud whimpering instead.

We could see the orange glow of petrol bombs exploding and hear the bang of plastic bullets being fired. The boys were good at recognizing the sounds because they used to collect spent cartridges after nights of violence. But this was the worst we had ever seen.

Finally Maria, David, and Hugh went to sleep. Mum had to comfort Eileen, who was scared out of her mind. There was too much going on to even think of sleep. Every so often there would be a slight lull and I would run to the window. The sky was really bright now. The barricades were burning so as to keep the soldiers out. I could see men outside shooting their guns up the avenue. They were hiding behind walls, bins, poles—anything at all. It was like watching television. When several bullets hit the wall outside our window Mum made me lie down again.

We heard people shouting for Father Murphy, our parish priest, to come and give someone the Last Rites.[6] Ten minutes later we heard shouts of "They killed Father Murphy!" "They shot him!" "Three bodies on top of each other!" Mum and I could only look at each other in shock. Father Murphy was our friend. He taught Hugh and David how to box. He had been

---

3. **brush** *v.*: sweep.
4. **ricocheting** (rik′ə·shā′iŋ) *v.* used as *adj.*: bouncing from one surface to another.
5. **Uzis** (oo̅′zēz): trademark name for submachine guns.

6. **parish priest ... the Last Rites:** The parish is the area served by one particular church and priest. In the Catholic Church the Last Rites are the final religious rituals and prayers for a person near death.

at our house only yesterday—they must be wrong.

They weren't. Ten men died that night, all from our street. Father Murphy had been shot dead while giving a man the Last Rites. And when another man went to help Father Murphy, he had been killed as well.

It was very hard lying there listening to the *rat-a-tat* of the gunfire and not think that someone else might be dead. The excitement was gone and fear and deep sadness were left. We lay there until morning when, finally, all noises stopped and we could hear our neighbors outside.

They were clustered together exchanging war stories and talking about Father Murphy. We were next on their agenda. We were never going to get out, they said, and no one was going to risk his life to get us out. I think they were a bit jealous.

Mum didn't give up. She asked everybody until one man with an old post office van said yes.

We had an awful time getting through burnt-out barricades and around overturned lorries[7]—sometimes even human barricades. After many detours we finally reached the airport to find no planes were flying that day. We were bundled into a minibus and driven to Dublin.

We were still in shock from the night before. Even after twenty-four hours with no food none of us complained that we were hungry. Every time we heard Father Murphy's name mentioned on the radio we cried our eyes out but Mum just kept repeating "Thank God we're out!" That's all she would say.

She was dead right though. Thank God we did get out.

---

7. **lorries** (lôr′ēz) *n.:* British for "trucks."

OPINION ESSAY

Peace Isn't Impossible

from *Newsweek,* June 30, 1997

George J. Mitchell

In 1997, when he wrote the essay excerpted here, George J. Mitchell was serving as chairman of the peace negotiations in Northern Ireland. He was nominated for a Nobel Peace Prize for his work. Since then he has worked to prevent international crises, including the violence in the Middle East.

Is the peace process dead? The question hangs over Northern Ireland like a heavy fog, blanketing the land with fear and anxiety.

I may be an incurable optimist, but I believe a historic opportunity to end centuries of conflict in Northern Ireland still exists. If it's not seized now, though, it may be years before we have another chance, and the failure could cost many lives on both sides.

It's worth pursuing a political settlement

Vocabulary

optimist (äp′tə·mist) *n.:* person who is always hopeful.

for one overriding reason: The overwhelming majority of people in Northern Ireland want political stability and reconciliation.[1] To give up now, to succumb[2] to despair and sectarian[3] war, would be to declare that a handful of men of violence are winners and the rest of the people are losers. That's a result I'm not prepared to accept.

During the past two years I've come to know and admire the people of Northern Ireland. They're energetic and productive. They deserve a better life than they've had. Of course, there are those who don't want anything to change, ever. They want to re-create a past that is gone forever. But their way will only guarantee never-ending conflict. It will ensure that the next half century is as full of death and fear as was the past half century. If, on the other hand, we can end the violence and people can live free of fear, then gradually the walls of division will finally come down.

I'm constantly asked by Americans concerned about Northern Ireland, "What can I do?" Here's my answer: The American people, and especially the leaders of the Irish American community, must say clearly and repeatedly that they condemn violence, that they demand its end, that they will not support those who engage in or condone violence. They must say it publicly, loudly, and forcefully. Political violence, from whatever source, is morally wrong. It's counterproductive.[4] It deepens divisions. It increases hatred. It hurts innocent people. It makes peace and reconciliation more difficult to attain. It must end.

After his election, to emphasize its importance, Prime Minister Blair[5] chose Northern Ireland for his first trip outside London. In a speech there he said: "I am ready to make one further effort to proceed with this inclusive talks process.[6] My message to Sinn Fein is clear. The settlement train is leaving. I want you on that train. But it is leaving anyway, and I will not allow it to wait for you. You cannot hold the process to ransom[7] any longer. So end the violence. Now."

So the process must and will move on. Only the outcome is in doubt. Some have said that the political talks are all that's preventing widespread war. But as the participants in those talks know better than anyone, they cannot go on indefinitely. They must either move forward or end in failure. For the people of Northern Ireland, the time for decision is now.

> It's not too late to negotiate an end to centuries of bloodshed and despair in Northern Ireland.

1. **reconciliation** (rek′ən·sil′ē·ā′shən) *n.*: bringing together to settle a conflict.
2. **succumb** (sə·kum′) *v.*: give in to.
3. **sectarian** (sek·ter′ē·ən) *adj.*: pertaining to a particular religious group.

4. **counterproductive** (kount′ər·prə·duk′tiv) *adj.*: producing results that are the opposite of what was intended.
5. **Prime Minister Blair:** Tony Blair became Britain's prime minister, or head of the government, when his Labor Party won the British national elections in 1997.
6. **inclusive talks process:** series of discussions that included representatives from all the major groups involved in the conflict.
7. **ransom** (ran′səm) *n.*: money (or another demand) paid to free someone being held prisoner. Here, Blair is saying that the peace process will not be halted by Sinn Fein's threat of violence.

Vocabulary
condone (kən·dōn′) *v.*: overlook or excuse an offense.

Reading Check

SKILLS FOCUS

Reading Skills
Synthesize ideas from different sources dealing with a single topic.

1. What caused civil war to break out in Ireland in the 1920s, according to "A Country Divided"?

2. Give two examples of how the division between Catholics and Protestants affects daily life, according to "Lives in the Crossfire."

3. Explain what happened to Father Murphy, as Margaret McCrory describes in "Internment."

4. What is George Mitchell's view of the people of Northern Ireland?

Test Practice

1. What is the **main idea** of "Lives in the Crossfire"?
   A Violence is not productive.
   B The Troubles affect the daily life of children, as well as that of adults, in Northern Ireland.
   C Most people in Northern Ireland oppose violence.
   D It is impossible to judge which side is right in the conflict.

2. What is the **purpose** of Mitchell's editorial?
   F To praise Prime Minister Blair's role in the peace talks
   G To criticize Americans for not helping to restore peace in Northern Ireland
   H To urge an end to the violence and the establishment of peace
   J To argue that the peace process is taking too long

3. Which of the following statements comparing "A Country Divided" to "Lives in the Crossfire" is *not* true?
   A Neither author expresses a bias in the selection.
   B Both include facts.

C Both are secondary sources.
   D Both explain the causes of the conflict.

4. Reading "A Country Divided" helps you understand and evaluate Mitchell's argument in "Peace Isn't Impossible" because it —
   F presents an opposing argument that shows the weaknesses of Mitchell's points
   G provides historical background for Mitchell's argument
   H explains why Tony Blair became Britain's prime minister
   J places blame for the conflict on one side

5. What do you learn from "Internment" that you *don't* learn from any of the other selections?
   A The ways Protestants and Catholics are separated in daily life
   B The feelings and thoughts of a family caught in the conflict
   C How many people have been killed during the conflict
   D The history of the conflict

6. Whose viewpoint is *not* represented in the four sources?

   F A member of the Irish Republican Army's

   G A peace negotiator's

   H Prime Minister Tony Blair's

   J A teenager's

7. Which topic is *not* related to the issues raised in these four sources?

   A Growing up in countries torn by war

   B The use of nonviolent protest to create change

   C Irish emigration to other countries in the past forty years

   D Recent changes in the daily life of the average American teenager

8. What **conclusion** can you draw from **synthesizing** the content of the selections?

   F Peace has not been established because no one is trying to achieve it.

   G The long-standing conflict has been deadly, and it has divided the Irish people.

   H The conflict is between political leaders, and it does not affect the lives of citizens.

   J If the conflict doesn't end soon, many Irish will leave the country.

Constructed Response

In a brief essay, **summarize** or **paraphrase** the main ideas in these sources about the conflict in Northern Ireland. Then, **connect** this information about the Troubles to what you may already know about civil wars in other places or times. Finally, draw a **conclusion** by giving your opinion of what future leaders can learn from these struggles.

Vocabulary Development

Word Families: Meet the Relatives

PRACTICE

Most words are members of **word families,** groups of related words that have slightly different forms and that function as different parts of speech.

For each Word Bank word, make a word-family chart like the one here, for *optimist.* Define the Word Bank word, and give its part of speech. Then, use a dictionary for help listing related words, their definitions, and their parts of speech. Write a sentence for each word in the family.

Word Bank

intolerance
negotiations
designate
absorb
reunification
divergent
coerced
abhor
optimist
condone

Word Bank Word	Sentence
optimist *n.*: person who is always hopeful	Senator Mitchell, an <u>optimist</u>, believes that peace is possible.
Related Words	**Sentences**
optimism *n.*: hopeful or cheerful viewpoint	The captain's <u>optimism</u> lifted my spirits.
optimistic *adj.*: expecting the best outcome	<u>Optimistic</u>, Amy was not discouraged.

SKILLS FOCUS

Vocabulary Skills
Create semantic charts.

Comparing a Theme Across Genres

Giving Form to Theme

Genre—the kind, or type, of literature—shapes our reactions to a work. To understand the role of genre, consider the following questions:

- **How does the choice of genre relate to the author's purpose for writing?** Nonfiction writers want their readers to *think* about issues. Fiction writers usually want readers to *experience* events with certain characters and make some discovery. Poets often want readers to *see* and *feel* something and to gain insight in the process.

- **What is the theme or the main idea, and is it stated or implied?** Authors of nonfiction generally state their main ideas. In fiction and poetry, however, themes are usually implied—you need to examine the works carefully to figure out the themes.

- **How does the writer use the characteristics of the genre to develop the theme or the main idea?** Nonfiction authors usually support their ideas with facts and examples. Fiction writers use literary elements, such as characters and conflict, to develop their themes. Poets use imagery, figurative language, and sound devices.

Examining Theme and Genre

You are about to read a short story, a poem, and a news feature about the experience of immigrants coming to the United States. As you read, ask yourself, "What insight about the immigrant experience does each work convey? What roles do friends and enemies play in the lives of immigrants? How does the choice of genre affect my response to each work?"

Reading Skills

Comparing and Contrasting a Theme Across Genres

After you have read and discussed each work, fill in a chart like the one below to compare how the genre affects the work's theme or main idea. For help stating the theme, re-read the guidelines on pages 246–247. Then, turn to page 318.

	"Liberty"	"Exile"	"An American Story"
Genre			
Author's purpose			
Theme or main idea			
How writer uses characteristics of genre to develop theme or main idea			

SKILLS FOCUS

Pages 294–318 cover

Literary Skills
Understand how genre relates to theme.

Reading Skills
Compare and contrast a theme across genres.

Liberty

Make the Connection

Quickwrite ✏

Imagine that your family is leaving home because you're all in great danger. You must leave now, and there's no chance of returning. You can take only one special belonging with you. What will it be? List your top three choices. Then, quickwrite about what you'll miss most about your home.

Literary Focus

Theme and Title: Did You Catch My Meaning?

The **title** often gives a clue to a story's **theme,** or central idea. Sometimes the title's meaning may not be clear to you until after you've read the story. Other times, as with "Liberty," the title is a familiar word or expression that brings to mind certain images or associations. By the end of the story, though, the title may take on deeper levels of meaning that help you understand the story's theme.

Reading Skills

Connecting Literature and the News

In recent decades many people have emigrated from the Dominican Republic (Julia Alvarez's birthplace) and other Caribbean and Latin American countries. They've left their homelands because of political oppression, war, or harsh living conditions.

Journalists aren't the only writers who have dealt with this topic. Many fiction writers have based their stories on the actual experiences of emigrants. In

"Liberty," Julia Alvarez tells about one young girl's experience of leaving her home, a story that could appear in today's newspaper. As you read, think about how Alvarez, through the fiction writer's craft, is able to pull us into these events in an intensely personal way. What techniques does she use?

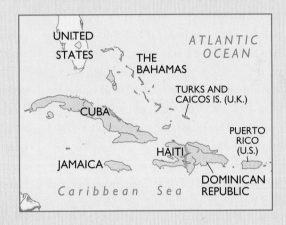

SKILLS FOCUS

Literary Skills
Understand how a story's title relates to its theme.

Reading Skills
Connect literature and the news.

INTERNET

Vocabulary Practice
•
More About Julia Alvarez
•
Keyword: LE7 9-4

Vocabulary Development

elect (ē·lekt′) v.: choose.

hyperactive (hī′pər·ak′tiv) adj.: abnormally active; very lively.

distracted (di·strakt′id) adj.: unable to concentrate on something.

putrid (pyōō′trid) adj.: offensive to the senses; disgusting.

admonitions (ad′mə·nish′ənz) n.: scoldings; warnings.

clenched (klencht) v. used as adj.: tightly closed.

inconsolable (in′kən·sōl′ə·bəl) adj.: unable to be comforted; brokenhearted.

LIBERTY

Julia Alvarez

Papi came home with a dog whose kind we had never seen before. A black-and-white-speckled electric current of energy. It was a special breed with papers, like a person with a birth certificate. Mami just kept staring at the puppy with a cross look on her face. "It looks like a mess!" she said. "Take it back."

"Mami, it is a gift!" Papi shook his head. It would be an insult to Mister Victor, who had given us the dog. The American consul[1] wanted to thank us for all we'd done for him since he'd been assigned to our country.

"If he wanted to thank us, he'd give us our visas,"[2] Mami grumbled. For a while now, my parents had been talking about going to the United States so Papi could return to school. I couldn't understand why a grown-up who could do whatever he wanted would elect to go back to a place I so much wanted to get out of.

On their faces when they talked of leaving there was a scared look I also couldn't understand.

"Those visas will come soon," Papi promised. But Mami just kept shaking her head about the dog. She had enough with four girls to take on puppies, too. Papi explained that the dog would stay at the end of the yard in a pen. He would not be allowed in the house. He would not be pooping in Mami's orchid garden. He would not be barking until late at night. "A well-behaved dog," Papi concluded. "An American dog."

The little black-and-white puppy yanked at Papi's trouser cuff with his mouth. "What shall we call you?" Papi asked him.

"Trouble," Mami suggested, kicking the puppy away. He had left Papi's trousers to come slobber on her leg.

"We will call him Liberty. Life, liberty, and the pursuit of happiness." Papi quoted the U.S.A. Constitution. "Eh, Liberty, you are a lucky sign!"

Liberty barked his little toy barks and all us kids laughed. "Trouble." Mami kept shaking her head as she walked away. Liberty trotted behind her as if he agreed that that was the better name for him.

Mami was right, too—Liberty turned out to be trouble. He ate all of Mami's orchids, and that little hyperactive baton of a tail knocked things off the low coffee table whenever Liberty climbed on the couch to leave his footprints in among the flower prints. He tore up Mami's garden looking for buried treasure. Mami screamed at Liberty and stamped her foot. "Perro sin vergüenza!"[3] But Liberty just barked back at her.

"He doesn't understand Spanish," Papi said lamely. "Maybe if you correct him in English, he'll behave better!"

---

3. **"Perro sin vergüenza!"** (per′rô sēn ver·hwen′sä): Spanish for "shameless dog."

Vocabulary

elect (ē·lekt′) v.: choose.

hyperactive (hī′pər·ak′tiv) adj.: abnormally active; very lively.

---

1. **American consul:** person appointed by the United States government to represent American interests and provide assistance to Americans living in a foreign country.
2. **visas** (vē′zəz) n.: certificates granting official approval to enter a country.

"We will call him Liberty.
Life, liberty, and the pursuit
of happiness."

tomboy, the live wire, the troublemaker, the one who was going to drive Mami to drink, the one she was going to give away to the Haitians. While the sisters dressed pretty and stayed clean in the playroom, I was out roaming the world looking for trouble. And now I had found someone to share my adventures.

"I'll take Liberty back to his pen," I offered. There was something I had figured out that Liberty had yet to learn: when to get out of Mami's way.

She didn't say yes and she didn't say no. She seemed <u>distracted</u>, as if something else was on her mind. As I led Liberty away by his col-

Mami turned on him, her slipper still in midair. Her face looked as if she'd light into him after she was done with Liberty. "Let him go be a pet in his own country if he wants instructions in English!" In recent weeks, Mami had changed her tune about going to the United States. She wanted to stay in her own country. She didn't want Mister Victor coming around our house and going off into the study with Papi to talk over important things in low, worried voices.

"All liberty involves sacrifice," Papi said in a careful voice. Liberty gave a few perky barks as if he agreed with that.

Mami glared at Papi. "I told you I don't want trouble—" She was going to say more, but her eye fell on me and she stopped herself. "Why aren't you with the others?" she scolded. It was as if I had been the one who had dug up her lily bulbs.

The truth was that after Liberty arrived, I never played with the others. It was as if I had found my double in another species. I had always been the

lar, I could see her talking to Papi. Suddenly she started to cry, and Papi held her.

"It's okay," I consoled Liberty. "Mami doesn't mean it. She really does love you. She's just nervous." It was what my father always said when Mami scolded me harshly.

At the back of the property stood Liberty's pen—a chain-link fence around a dirt square at the center of which stood a doghouse. Papi had built it when Liberty first came, a cute little house, but then he painted it a <u>putrid</u> green that reminded me of all the vegetables I didn't like. It was always a job to get Liberty to go into that pen.

Sure enough, as soon as he saw where we were headed, he took off, barking, toward the house,

Vocabulary

distracted (di·strakt′id) *adj.:* unable to concentrate on something.

putrid (pyo͞o′trid) *adj.:* offensive to the senses; disgusting.

then swerved to the front yard to our favorite spot. It was a grassy knoll[4] surrounded by a tall hibiscus hedge. At the center stood a tall, shady samán tree. From there, no one could see you up at the house. Whenever I did something wrong, this was where I hid out until the punishment winds blew over. That was where Liberty headed, and I was fast behind on his trail.

Inside the clearing I stopped short. Two strange men in dark glasses were crouched behind the hedge. The fat one had seized Liberty by the collar and was pulling so hard on it that poor Liberty was almost standing on his hind legs. When he saw me, Liberty began to bark, and the man holding him gave him a yank on the collar that made me sick to my stomach. I began to back away, but the other man grabbed my arm. "Not so fast," he said. Two little scared faces—my own—looked down at me from his glasses.

"I came for my dog," I said, on the verge of tears.

"Good thing you found him," the man said. "Give the young lady her dog," he ordered his friend, and then he turned to me. "You haven't seen us, you understand?"

I didn't understand. It was usually I who was the one lying and grown-ups telling me to tell the truth. But I nodded, relieved when the man released my arm and Liberty was back in my hands.

"It's okay, Liberty." I embraced him when I put him back in his pen. He was as sad as I was. We had both had a hard time with Mami, but this was the first time we'd come across mean and scary people. The fat man had almost broken Liberty's neck, and the other one had left his fingerprints on my arm. After I locked up the pen, I watched Liberty wander back slowly to his house and actually go inside, turn around, and stick his little head out the door. He'd always avoided that ugly doghouse before. I walked back to my own house, head down, to find my parents and tell them what I had seen.

4. **knoll** (nōl) n.: small hill.

Overnight, it seemed, Mister Victor moved in. He ate all his meals with us, stayed 'til late, and when he had to leave, someone from the embassy was left behind "to keep an eye on things." Now, when Papi and Mister Victor talked or when the tíos[5] came over, they all went down to the back of the property near Liberty's pen to talk. Mami had found some wires in the study, behind the portrait of Papi's great-grandmother fanning herself with a painted fan. The wires ran behind a screen and then out a window, where there was a little box with lots of other wires coming from different parts of the house.[6]

Mami explained that it was no longer safe to talk in the house about certain things. But the only way you knew what things those were was when Mami leveled her eyes on you as if she were pressing the off button on your mouth. She did this every time I asked her what was going on.

"Nothing," she said stiffly, and then she urged me to go outside and play. Forgotten were the admonitions to go study or I would flunk out of fifth grade. To go take a bath or the microbios[7] might kill me. To drink my milk or I would grow up stunted and with no teeth. Mami seemed absent and tense and always in tears. Papi was right—she was too nervous, poor thing.

I myself was enjoying a heyday of liberty. Several times I even got away with having one of Mister Victor's Coca-Colas for breakfast instead of my boiled milk with a beaten egg, which Liberty was able to enjoy instead.

"You love that dog, don't you?" Mister Victor asked me one day. He was standing by the pen with Papi waiting for the uncles. He had a funny

5. **tíos** (tē'ôs): Spanish for "uncles."
6. **little box . . . house:** probably a reference to a device used to listen in secretly on conversations in the house.
7. **microbios** (mē·krô'bē·ôs): Spanish for "germs."

Vocabulary
admonitions (ad'mə·nish'ənz) n.: scoldings; warnings.

accent that sounded like someone making fun of Spanish when he spoke it.

I ran Liberty through some of the little tricks I had taught him, and Mister Victor laughed. His face was full of freckles—so that it looked as if he and Liberty were kin. I had the impression that God had spilled a lot of his colors when he was making American things.

Soon the uncles arrived and the men set to talking. I wandered into the pen and sat beside Liberty with my back to the house and listened. The men were speaking in English, and I had picked up enough of it at school and in my parents' conversations to make out most of what was being said. They were planning some hunting expedition for a goat with guns to be delivered by Mister Charlie. Papi was going to have to leave the goat to the others because his tennis shoes were missing. Though I understood the words—or thought I did—none of it made sense. I knew my father did not own a pair of tennis shoes, we didn't know a Mister Charlie, and who ever heard of hunting a goat?

As Liberty and I sat there with the sun baking the tops of our heads, I had this sense that the world as I knew it was about to end. The image of the two men in mirror glasses flashed through my head. So as not to think about them, I put my arm around Liberty and buried my face in his neck.

Late one morning Mami gave my sisters and me the news. Our visa had come. Mister Victor had arranged everything, and that very night we were going to the United States of America! Wasn't that wonderful! She flashed us a bright smile, as if someone were taking her picture.

We stood together watching her, alarmed at this performance of happiness when really she looked like she wanted to cry. All morning aunts had been stopping by and planting big kisses on our foreheads and holding our faces in their hands and asking us to promise we would be very good. Until now, we hadn't a clue why they were so worked up.

Mami kept smiling her company smile. She had a little job for each of us to do. There would not be room in our bags for everything. We were to pick the one toy we wanted to take with us to the United States.

I didn't even have to think twice about my choice. It had suddenly dawned on me we were leaving, and that meant leaving *everything* behind. "I want to take Liberty."

Mami started shaking her head no. We could not take a dog into the United States of America. That was not allowed.

"Please," I begged with all my might. "Please, please, Mami, please." Repetition sometimes worked—each time you said the word, it was like giving a little push to the yes that was having a hard time rolling out of her mouth.

"I said no!" The bright smile on Mami's face had grown dimmer and dimmer. "N–O." She spelled it out for me in case I was confusing no with another word like yes. "I said a toy, and I mean a toy."

I burst into tears. I was not going to the United States unless I could take Liberty! Mami shook me by the shoulders and asked me between clenched teeth if I didn't understand we had to go to the United States or else. But all I could understand was that a world without Liberty would break my heart. I was inconsolable. Mami began to cry.

Tía[8] Mimi took me aside. She had gone to school in the States and always had her nose in a book. In spite of her poor taste in how to spend her free time, I still loved her because she had smart things to say. Like telling Mami that punishment was not the way to make kids behave. "I'm going to tell you a little secret," she offered

---

8. **tía** (tē′ä): Spanish for "aunt."

Vocabulary

clenched (klencht) *v.* used as *adj.*: tightly closed.

inconsolable (in′kən·sōl′ə·bəl) *adj.*: unable to be comforted; brokenhearted.

now. "You're going to find liberty when you get to the United States."

"Really?" I asked.

She hesitated a minute, and then she gave me a quick nod. "You'll see what I mean," she said. And then, giving me a pat on the butt, she added, "Come on, let's go pack. How about taking that wonderful book I got you on the Arabian Nights?"

Late in the night someone comes in and shakes us awake. "It's time!"

Half asleep, we put on our clothes, hands helping our arms to go into the right sleeves, buttoning us up, running a comb through our hair.

We were put to sleep hours earlier because the plane had not come in.

But now it's time.

"Go sit by the door," we are ordered, as the hands, the many hands that now seem to be in control, finish with us. We file out of the bedroom, one by one, and go sit on the bench where packages are set down when Mami comes in from shopping. There is much rushing around. Mister Victor comes by and pats us on the head like dogs. "We'll have to wait a few more minutes," he says.

In that wait, one sister has to go to the bathroom. Another wants a drink of water. I am left sitting with my baby sister, who is dozing with her head on my shoulder. I lay her head down on the bench and slip out.

Through the dark patio down the path to the back of the yard I go. Every now and then a strange figure flashes by. I have said good-bye to Liberty a dozen times already, but there is something else I have left to do.

"You're going to find liberty when you get to the United States."

Sitting on the bench, I had an image again of those two men in mirror glasses. After we are gone, they come onto the property. They smash the picture of Papi's great-grandmother fanning herself. They knock over the things on the coffee table as if they don't know any better. They throw the flowered cushions on the floor. They smash the windows. And then they come to the back of the property and they find Liberty.

Quickly, because I hear calling from the big house, I slip open the door of the pen. Liberty is all over me, wagging his tail so it beats against my legs, jumping up and licking my face.

"Get away!" I order sharply, in a voice he is not used to hearing from me. I begin walking back to the house, not looking around so as not to encourage him. I want him to run away before the gangsters come.

He doesn't understand and keeps following me.

Finally I have to resort to Mami's techniques. I kick him, softly at first, but then, when he keeps tagging behind me, I kick him hard. He whimpers and dashes away toward the front yard, disappearing in areas of darkness, then reappearing when he passes through lighted areas. At the front of the house, instead of turning toward our secret place, he keeps on going straight down the drive, through the big gates, to the world out there.

He will beat me to the United States is what I am thinking as I head back to the house. I will find Liberty there, like Tía Mimi says. But I already sense it is a different kind of liberty my aunt means. All I can do is hope that when we come back—as Mami has promised we will—my Liberty will be waiting for me here. ■

Meet the Writer

Julia Alvarez

"Magic Happened in My Life"

When Julia Alvarez (1950–   ) says, "I write stories for different reasons," she means it. Like the girl in "Liberty," she knows political terror and exile firsthand, for her family fled from the Dominican Republic when she was ten. Alvarez says she "can't shut up" about important human events. One of her novels, *In the Time of the Butterflies* (1994), is based on the true story of the 1960 murders of the three Mirabal sisters, wives of political prisoners in her homeland.

Some of her fiction, she says, is "like cupping my hands around a moth" to save it, and some stories she writes to keep her heart from breaking.

"I think of myself at ten years old, newly arrived in this country, feeling out of place, feeling that I would never belong in this

world. . . . And then, magic happened in my life. . . . An English teacher asked us to write little stories about ourselves. I began to put into words some of what my life had been like in the Dominican Republic. Stories about my gang of cousins and the smell of mangoes and the iridescent, vibrating green of hummingbirds. Since it was my own little world I was making with words, I could put what I wanted in it. . . . I could save what I didn't want to lose—memories and smells and sounds, things too precious to put anywhere else. **"**

Julia Alvarez is a writer-in-residence at Middlebury College in Vermont. Having two cultures and two languages is central to her world and writing. Two novels—*How the García Girls Lost Their Accents* (1991) and *¡Yo!* (1997)—follow four sisters who grow up in America speaking Spanglish, a mixture of Spanish and English.

"No matter what my motive is when I begin, I end up understanding myself and the world around me much better. I think that's why I like being a writer: With each revision, the world gets clearer and, ironically, though writing is so solitary, people get closer, more real. **"**

For Independent Reading

What was it really like for Julia Alvarez to find herself suddenly living in a new country—and in a new culture? To find out, read her essays in *Something to Declare*.

For additional information about Julia Alvarez, see Meet the Writer, page 308.

Reading Check

1. Sketch a map that shows the story's **setting.** Include the following elements: (a) the house, (b) the dog pen, (c) the grassy knoll and hedge, and (d) the drive and big gates. Then, make a map legend, identifying the important **events** that occur at each location.

Thinking Critically

2. What is really happening in this story? Read between the lines (the hidden wires, the American consul's visits, and so on), and explain the family's situation. Who are the family's enemies? Which people act like friends?

3. The narrator says about Liberty, "It was as if I had found my double in another species." Describe the narrator's **character.** What traits does she share with Liberty? Why does she identify with her dog and view her as a friend?

4. The word *liberty* is central to this story. You first encounter *liberty* in the **title,** but it is also the dog's name and a central concept throughout the story. Explain how the story's **theme,** or insight about life, relates to liberty.

5. Which elements of "Liberty" are characteristic of a short story as opposed to a news report? How would the account of the narrator's experiences be different if it appeared in a newspaper?

Extending and Evaluating

6. This story is told from a child's point of view. Would the story be less effective or more effective if it were told from the point of view of the mother or the father? Explain.

WRITING

Leaving It All Behind

Whether you love where you live or long to be somewhere different, moving is a jolt. As you load the last box, see the rooms suddenly bare, and take one last look at your neighborhood, memories flood in. If you've ever moved, you know how it feels to ache for the familiar. If you haven't, look around. What would break your heart to leave behind? Expand your Quickwrite notes, and in a few paragraphs, describe your thoughts about leaving it all behind. ✎

Newcomers to America

The United States was built—and continues to be built—by immigrants. How do the media cover stories about people immigrating to this country today? Write a few paragraphs **comparing** and **contrasting** reports from two different news media—a newspaper, the Internet, TV, or the radio, for example. Consider the focus and purpose of each report as well as the way in which information is presented.

▶ **Use "Comparing Media Coverage," pages 320–327, for help with this assignment.**

Group being sworn in as citizens of the United States.

SKILLS FOCUS

Literary Skills
Analyze how a story's title relates to its theme.

Reading Skills
Connect literature and the news.

Writing Skills
Write a reflective essay. Compare reports from different news media.

Using a Thesaurus to Find Synonyms

A **synonym** is a word that has the same, or nearly the same, meaning as another word. To find synonyms, writers use a **thesaurus.** Most thesauri list synonyms based on a word's different shades of meaning. Follow the cross-references given until you find the exact meaning you want to convey.

This chart shows how one student used a thesaurus to find synonyms for *admonitions*. Make a thesaurus chart for the other words in the Word Bank.

Word Bank

elect
hyperactive
distracted
putrid
admonitions
clenched
inconsolable

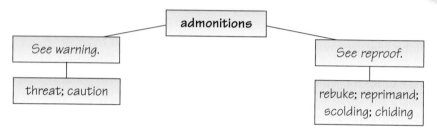

admonitions
See warning.
threat; caution
See reproof.
rebuke; reprimand; scolding; chiding

Grammar Link

Making Pronouns Clear

Inexact pronoun reference, a common mistake, causes misunderstandings. *You* always know whom you're referring to when you use *he, she,* or *they,* but your readers may have someone else in mind.

A **pronoun** should refer clearly to its **antecedent** (the noun or pronoun to which a pronoun refers). Avoid unclear, or **ambiguous,** pronoun references. These occur when a pronoun can refer to either of two antecedents. Usually you can pin down your meaning by replacing the pronoun with the noun to which it refers.

UNCLEAR
Papi and Mister Victor are fluent in two languages, but he speaks Spanish with an accent.

CLEAR
Papi and Mister Victor are fluent in two languages, but Mister Victor speaks Spanish with an accent.

CLEAR
Papi and Mister Victor, who speaks Spanish with an accent, are fluent in two languages.

PRACTICE

Reword the following sentences to correct the inexact pronoun references:

1. Papi brought home a puppy, and he caused a lot of trouble.

2. When I spotted Liberty and the strange man with the sunglasses, he looked frightened.

3. All morning, aunts stopped by to kiss the sisters because they were leaving for America.

4. Tía Mimi said that Mami was upset, and she had a secret.

▶ **For more help, see Clear Pronoun Reference, 4i, in the Language Handbook.**

SKILLS FOCUS

Vocabulary Skills
Use a thesaurus to find synonyms.

Grammar Skills
Use clear pronoun references.

Exile

Make the Connection

Quickwrite

Think about the word *exile,* and brainstorm for a few minutes about the images it calls to mind. Imagine that you have been exiled from something precious to you: a beloved place or a particular group of people. Write a few sentences about what that experience would be like.

Literary Focus

Narrative Poetry: Telling a Story Poetically

A **narrative poem** tells a story in poetic form. It has the elements of a story—a narrator, characters, a plot, and usually a setting—but it also has the characteristics of poetry. It relies heavily on imagery and figures of speech to touch your emotions and capture your imagination.

As you read the narrative poem "Exile," notice the various story elements as well as the parallels to Alvarez's short story "Liberty" (page 296). Then, think about how the poem differs from the story—or from any short story.

Theme: Comparisons Say It All

Poems, like short stories, have **themes,** or central ideas. Since poets have much less space to develop their themes than short story writers do, poets often use **metaphors** and **similes,** comparisons that connect two unlike things in an imaginative way, to help express their ideas. As you read "Exile," think about the larger meaning that swimming and a trip to the beach have. How do these comparisons help Alvarez convey the meaning of her poem?

Background

Julia Alvarez's family left their home in the Dominican Republic in 1960 because her father had become involved in a plot to overthrow Rafael Trujillo, the Dominican dictator. After Trujillo seized power in his country in 1930, the Dominican people lost many of their rights, and his opponents were frequently murdered. "Exile" begins with the speaker's family fleeing the capital city, Ciudad Trujillo (syo͞o′däd′ tro͞o·hē′yô), or Trujillo City, named in honor of the dictator in 1936. The city's original name, Santo Domingo, was restored after Trujillo was assassinated, in 1961.

The Tower of Homage, a fort that is several centuries old, stands in Santo Domingo, Dominican Republic.

SKILLS FOCUS

Literary Skills
Understand the characteristics of narrative poetry, including theme. Identify metaphors and similes.

INTERNET

More About Julia Alvarez

Keyword: LE7 9-4

Exile

Julia Alvarez

Ciudad Trujillo, New York City, 1960

The night we fled the country, Papi,
you told me we were going to the beach,
hurried me to get dressed along with the others,
while posted at a window, you looked out

5   at a curfew-darkened Ciudad Trujillo,
speaking in worried whispers to your brothers,
which car to take, who'd be willing to drive it,
what explanation to give should we be discovered . . .

On the way to the beach, you added, eyeing me.
10 The uncles fell in, chuckling phony chuckles,
What a good time she'll have learning to swim!
Back in my sisters' room Mami was packing

a hurried bag, allowing one toy apiece,
her red eyes belying° her explanation:
15 *a week at the beach so Papi can get some rest.*
She dressed us in our best dresses, party shoes.

Something was off, I knew, but I was young
and didn't think adult things could go wrong.
So as we quietly filed out of the house
20 we wouldn't see again for another decade,

I let myself lie back in the deep waters,
my arms out like Jesus' on His cross,
and instead of sinking down as I'd always done,
magically, that night, I could stay up,

---

14. belying (bē·lī′iŋ) *v.* used as *adj.:* showing to be untrue.

25 floating out, past the driveway, past the gates,
   in the black Ford, Papi grim at the wheel,
   winding through back roads, stroke by difficult stroke,
   out on the highway, heading toward the coast.

   Past the checkpoint, we raced towards the airport,
30 my sisters crying when we turned before
   the family beach house, Mami consoling,
   there was a better surprise in store for us!

   She couldn't tell, though, until . . . until we were there.
   But I had already swum ahead and guessed
35 some loss much larger than I understood,
   more danger than the deep end of the pool.

   At the dark, deserted airport we waited.
   All night in a fitful sleep, I swam.
   At dawn the plane arrived, and as we boarded,
40 Papi, you turned, your eyes scanned the horizon

   as if you were trying to sight a distant swimmer,
   your hand frantically waving her back in,
   for you knew as we stepped inside the cabin
   that a part of both of us had been set adrift.

45 Weeks later, wandering our new city, hand in hand,
   you tried to explain the wonders: escalators
   as moving belts; elevators: pulleys and ropes;
   blond hair and blue eyes: a genetic code.

   We stopped before a summery display window
50 at Macy's, *The World's Largest Department Store,*
   to admire a family outfitted for the beach:
   the handsome father, slim and sure of himself,

   so unlike you, Papi, with your thick mustache,
   your three-piece suit, your fedora hat, your accent.
55 And by his side a girl who looked like Heidi°
   in my storybook waded in colored plastic.

---

55. Heidi (hī′dē): reference to the young Swiss girl who is the
    title character in Johanna Spyri's popular children's novel.

We stood awhile, marveling at America,
both of us trying hard to feel luckier
than we felt, both of us pointing out
60   the beach pails, the shovels, the sandcastles

no wave would ever topple, the red and blue boats.
And when we backed away, we saw our reflections
superimposed,° big-eyed, dressed too formally
with all due respect as visitors to this country.

65   Or like, Papi, two swimmers looking down
at the quiet surface of our island waters,
seeing their faces right before plunging in,
eager, afraid, not yet sure of the outcome.

---

63. superimposed (soō′per·im·pōzd′) *v.* used as *adj.:* put on
top of something else.

Meet the Writer

Julia Alvarez

At Home with Words

Julia Alvarez (1950–   ) explains that she began writing as a way of acquiring a new "homeland" after her family fled from the Dominican Republic when she was ten to settle in the United States. She comments, "English, not the United States, was where I landed and sunk deep roots." As a college student she began writing seriously—and began winning awards for her poetry too. Nurturing a love of poetry in others, she has conducted poetry workshops for schoolchildren, prisoners, and senior citizens, in addition to teaching creative writing to college students.

Alvarez says of her younger self:

66 I realized that I had lost the island we had come from, but . . . I had discovered an even better world: the one words can create in a story or poem. **99**

Reading Check

1. **Summarize** the story told in this poem by filling out a **story map** like the one here:

"Exile"
Narrator:
Main characters:
Settings:
Narrator's problem:
Main events:

2. Is the speaker telling about recent events or ones that happened many years ago? Support your answer with details from the poem.

Thinking Critically

3. How would you describe the relationship between the speaker and Papi?

4. Although the speaker never names her family's enemies or the reason her family must flee Ciudad Trujillo, she vividly conveys the danger the family experiences. Choose at least three details (words, phrases, or **images**—words that appeal to our senses), and explain how they help create a feeling of danger or fear.

5. The idea of a trip to the beach grows in meaning throughout the poem. As the family flees, what is associated with the idea of going to the beach?

6. Using a **metaphor,** the speaker compares the beach scene displayed in the store window to America (line 57). Why does the scene represent America for her?

7. Once in the United States, the speaker refers to herself and her father as "visitors to this country" (line 64). What details in the poem help convey the sense that they don't fit in?

8. At the end of the poem, the speaker says that she and Papi are like "two swimmers . . . / eager, afraid, not yet sure of the outcome." What is she saying through the use of this **simile**? What feelings is she expressing?

9. How would you state the **theme** of this poem—that is, what point is the speaker making about her experience of immigrating to the United States?

10. How are the story "Liberty" and the poem "Exile" different? Consider

    • events covered

    • **setting(s)**

    • what narrator/speaker knows

    • **tone** or **mood**

Extending and Evaluating

11. Why might Alvarez have chosen to write about fleeing her home in two genres—a story and a poem? Do the story and the poem affect you differently? Explain.

WRITING

Papi's Version

Write a **poem, letter,** or **journal entry** from the point of view of Papi. Have him set down his thoughts and feelings about his family's move to the United States. Is he concerned about the speaker's safety as well as her reactions to being exiled? How does he feel when he looks in the department-store window? Check your Quickwrite notes for help capturing Papi's experience of being exiled.

After You Read | Vocabulary Development

Denotation and Connotation: Word Pictures

A word's **denotation** is its strict dictionary definition. A word's **connotations** are the feelings and associations that the word suggests. Take, for example, the word *fled* at the beginning of Alvarez's poem "Exile": "The night we fled the country . . ." The denotation of *fled*—its literal meaning—is "ran away; escaped from danger."

Why is *fled* a better word to use in this line than the synonym *ran away*? The phrase *running away* can be used in many different contexts, and it calls to mind a wide range of images or associations. For example, an untamed horse might run away from a ranch, or a person might run away from responsibility. *Fled,* on the other hand, has much more emotional power. Its connotations are more specific and include fear, panic, and confusion—associations that deepen our response to the speaker's experience.

Denotations are **objective.** They are not based on someone's individual opinions and experiences. In contrast, connotations are **subjective**—they are based on personal thoughts and feelings—and may vary from individual to individual. Over time your own associations with a word may change. For instance, the word *fled* may have new connotations for you now that you have read "Exile."

PRACTICE

For help thinking about why Alvarez used each of the underlined words rather than a synonym in the lines from "Exile" in the right column, answer the following questions about connotations. The first item is completed for you as an example.

SKILLS FOCUS

Vocabulary Skills
Identify denotations and connotations.

1. "while posted at a window, you looked out" (line 4)

   What images do you associate with *posted* that you would not associate with *standing* if it were used in this line instead?

   Answer: *Posted makes me think of a guard or soldier who is responsible for protecting others from danger.*

2. "*On the way to the beach,* you added, eyeing me." (line 9)

   In this line, what does *eyeing* tell you about Papi that the phrase *looking at* would not?

3. "The uncles fell in, chuckling phony chuckles," (line 10)

   What connotations does *phony* have that *false* does not?

4. "So as we quietly filed out of the house" (line 19)

   What connotations does *filed* have that *walked* does not? What do you associate with the action of filing out of a building?

5. "Weeks later, wandering our new city, hand in hand," (line 45)

   What connotations does *wandering* have that *exploring* does not? When you think of people wandering, what images come to mind?

6. "seeing their faces right before plunging in," (line 67)

   What connotations does *plunging* have that *diving* would not have in this line?

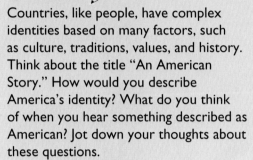
An American Story

Make the Connection

Quickwrite

Countries, like people, have complex identities based on many factors, such as culture, traditions, values, and history. Think about the title "An American Story." How would you describe America's identity? What do you think of when you hear something described as American? Jot down your thoughts about these questions.

Literary Focus

The News Feature: Read All About It

In **news reports,** journalists present information—facts, statistics, statements by other people—in a straightforward style. In **news features,** journalists also present information, but they give their reports a personal slant by including their own views and by writing in an individual style. A news feature provides a unique perspective on a current or past event. The writer's choice of subject says, in effect, "I could write about anything in the world, but I chose to write about this particular subject. Find out why."

As you read the following news feature, think about why Anthony Lewis chose to write about Viet Dinh and his family, refugees from Vietnam. What is Lewis's personal perspective in the article? What is his **main idea**?

Reading Skills

Distinguishing Between Fact and Opinion

A **fact** is something that can be proved true. An **opinion** is a personal belief or judgment that can be supported but not proved. Facts are definite, but opinions can differ greatly.

Newspapers include both fact-based and opinion-based writing. News reports are strictly factual, telling the *who, what, when, where, why,* and *how* of a particular event. Most other writing that appears in newspapers, such as editorials and movie reviews, mixes fact and opinion. As you read this news feature, fill out a two-column chart. In one column, list the main facts, and in the other, list opinions.

Facts	Opinions

Background

During the Vietnam War, which began in the 1950s and ended in 1975, South Vietnam and the United States tried unsuccessfully to prevent the Communists of North Vietnam from taking over South Vietnam.

After the war, hundreds of thousands of South Vietnamese sought escape from Vietnam—from communism and from "reeducation" camps in which political opponents were imprisoned and at times tortured or executed. Fleeing the country in small boats, many of the "boat people" perished at sea. Survivors reaching new lands were often turned away by foreign governments or confined to refugee camps that were little better than prisons. "An American Story" tells about the plight of one family of boat people.

SKILLS FOCUS

Literary Skills
Understand characteristics of news features, including the main idea.

Reading Skills
Distinguish between fact and opinion.

AN AMERICAN STORY

The family was reunited after fifteen years.

Anthony Lewis

Vietnamese boat people rescued by the cargo ship *Medicins du Monde*.

Patrick Barviel/Gamma Liaison.

Fifteen years ago this Thanksgiving weekend,[1] a ten-year-old Vietnamese boy named Viet Dinh arrived in this country as a refugee. He was with his mother, four sisters, and a brother. They had two hundred dollars, which they spent on used winter coats.

They were boat people. They had left Vietnam on a small fishing boat, which lost its engine in a storm. They drifted for days until they made it to Malaysia—swimming in at night to avoid patrol boats that had fired at them. After months in a refugee camp, they were cleared for admission to the United States and flown to Portland, Oregon.

Two members of the family were left behind in Vietnam: Viet Dinh's father, Phong Dinh, and his older sister Van Dinh, who was twenty then. She stayed behind to help their father.

Phong Dinh had been a city councilman in Vung Tau during the Saigon regime.[2] When the Communists took over in 1975, he was sent to a reeducation camp. He escaped from the camp on June 12, 1978, and was on the run when his wife and six children left.

Over the next five years, Phong Dinh tried unsuccessfully twenty-five times to get out of Vietnam by boat. He paid boatmen who never turned up or who were arrested. Finally, in 1983, he made it to the Philippines, and then to the United States.

That left the oldest child, Van Dinh. She had helped her father pay the boatmen. But it was six years before she managed to leave herself: on a boat that reached Hong Kong in August 1989.

---

1. **Fifteen years . . . weekend:** November 1978.

2. **Saigon regime:** period of time when the anti-Communist government of South Vietnam, based in the capital city of Saigon, was in power.

The family here knew that she had left Vietnam because they got a message to that effect. But for a year they did not know she was in a Hong Kong refugee camp; indeed, they did not know whether she had landed anywhere or had gone down at sea, as many boat people had.

Van Dinh was kept in the locked Hong Kong camp for three years, waiting for clearance[3] as a refugee. With her was her five-year-old son, Quan, who had a congenital heart condition.[4] That made her desperate to reach the United States, but for years she could not even get an interview with those in charge of the refugee process in Hong Kong.

At the end of 1991, Viet Dinh, then twenty-three years old, sent me an essay he had written about his sister Van's plight in Hong Kong. I forwarded it to *The New York Times* op-ed[5] page, and the editors published it in January 1992.

Last month I had another letter from Viet Dinh. It had good news about his sister. After his op-ed piece was published, other papers picked up the story. The Hong Kong authorities, feeling the pressure, finally interviewed Van Dinh—and found that she was entitled to refugee status. In September 1992, she made it to Portland. The family was reunited after fifteen years.

There is more to tell about the Dinh family, as I learned when I interviewed Viet. His parents are running a small grocery in Salem, Oregon.

---

3. **clearance** (klir´əns) *n.:* official, especially governmental, approval; in this case, permission to be released from the refugee camp.
4. **congenital heart condition:** serious heart problem that a person is born with.

5. **op-ed:** opposite the editorial (page). In a newspaper a page featuring columns and articles expressing opinions and observations.

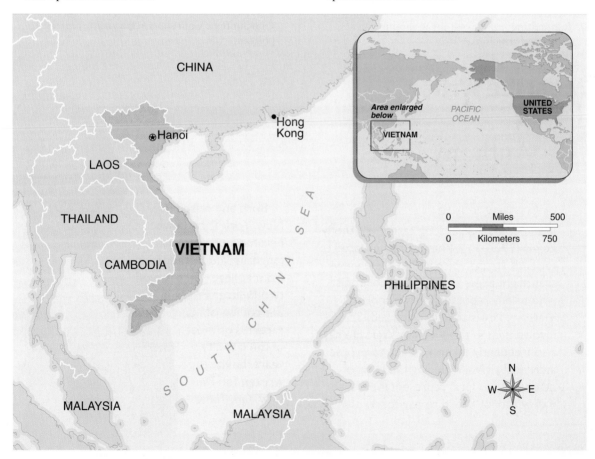

A sister, Anh, helps them. Another sister, Thu, is an accountant. Kathleen and Leanne are computer programmers. Viet's one brother, Bao, is an architect.

The child with the heart condition, Van's son Quan, has been treated in Portland. He is doing fine.

Van herself, after fourteen months in the United States, is studying at a community college in Salem and working as an assembler in an electronics plant. "After she gets her English and cultural skills together," Viet said, "I think she'd like to open a business."

It is an American story, and one that I wish members of Congress and their constituents[6] who are fulminating[7] these days about "the immigrant threat" would think about. The Dinh family is doing exactly what immigrants on the Lower East Side[8] and so many other places did in past years: struggling for themselves and making this country better.

There is no other country that has taken in so many people from so many places and cultures, and gained so much in the process. To turn away from that tradition now would do the United States great damage.

One more thing about Viet Dinh. His recent letter ended: "I graduated from the Harvard Law School in June and am now a law clerk[9] for Judge Laurence H. Silberman of the U.S. Court of Appeals in Washington. Next year I clerk for Justice Sandra Day O'Connor at the Supreme Court." ■

—from *The New York Times,*
November 26, 1993

6. **constituents** (kən·stich′ o͞o·ənts) *n.:* people represented by a particular elected official.
7. **fulminating** (ful′mə·nāt′iŋ) *v.:* shouting or expressing criticisms.

8. **Lower East Side:** area in New York City that was home to European immigrants, especially Germans and eastern Europeans, in the late nineteenth and early twentieth centuries.
9. **law clerk:** assistant to a judge or attorney. Clerking for a Supreme Court justice is a greatly respected position.

Meet the Writer

Anthony Lewis

A Strong Voice

In the course of his long career, Anthony Lewis (1927–   ) has never hesitated to raise his strong voice and express views that might anger others. As a columnist who briefly reported from Hanoi, in Vietnam, Lewis sharply criticized U.S. involvement in the Vietnam War. He has also frequently taken a stance to protect individual rights, including the right of defendants to legal representation even if they cannot afford to pay for it.

Born and raised in New York City, Lewis became a professional journalist after graduating from college. He has won two Pulitzer Prizes in the course of his career. For most of the last fifty years, he has written for *The New York Times.*

Ex-Refugee Is Nominated for Justice Post

Dena Bunis *and* Anh Do

WASHINGTON— Viet Dinh wiped tears from his eyes as a United States senator chronicled his remarkable journey from a 10-year-old fleeing Vietnam in a boat to a law professor facing a congressional panel Wednesday as a nominee for assistant attorney general.

For a young Dinh and his family it was the point of no return. They had fled Vietnam by boat in 1978. After 12 days with no food or water, they landed in a port in Malaysia, where they were met by gunfire and cast back into the South China Sea.

That night they swam ashore, sure their boat could not withstand another sea voyage. Dinh's mother, Nguyen, stayed aboard and, "wielding an ax that was almost as tall as she was," put a hole in the side of the boat to sink it so they would not be forced back to sea, Dinh said.

"That image of my mother destroying our last link to Vietnam really stands in my mind to this day as to the courage she possesses, but also the incredible lengths which my parents, like so many other people, have gone to in order to find that promise of freedom and opportunity."

"This is a spectacular American story," Senator Pete Domenici said Wednesday as he introduced Dinh. "You've got a Vietnamese scholar who just 23 years ago was a young man out on a boat at sea who could just as well have drowned, and we never would have heard from him. But because of a loving family around him, they eventually ended up American citizens."

As Domenici talked, Dinh's parents—who split their time between Garden Grove and Salem, Oregon—sat proudly next to their son. Dinh's lower lip quivered as he fought the emotion of the moment.

His journey and the patriotism for his new country came flooding back, he said, as he heard Domenici's words.

For many in the Vietnamese legal community in Orange County, Dinh is viewed as a trailblazer and risk taker.

"With his achievements, he puts the idea that a Vietnamese-American can be successful in law and on a national level," said Hao-Nhien Vu, a Garden Grove lawyer. If confirmed, Dinh will be the highest-ranking Vietnamese-American legal official in the nation. "A lot of people will be watching what he does and learning from his example."

Dinh says he's not looking beyond his new job.

"It will be in the public service," Dinh said. "I am really enamored by the institutions of government. They protect the most precious aspect of America, the promise of opportunity and freedom.

"Even when I was in the refugee camp, I knew the value of this promise."

—from *The Orange County Register,*
May 10, 2001

Viet Dinh served as assistant attorney general from 2001 to 2003. He then rejoined the faculty of Georgetown University Law Center.

Reading Check

1. Briefly summarize the key events in Viet Dinh's struggle to reach America. How old was he when he arrived in this country?

2. Why didn't Phong Dinh leave Vietnam when Viet and other members of the family fled the country?

Thinking Critically

3. How would you **characterize** the Dinh family? Think in particular about Viet Dinh, Phong Dinh, and Van Dinh. What qualities are revealed by their actions and goals?

4. List the enemies the members of the Dinh family encountered in Vietnam and on their journey to the United States. Then, think about the people who served as friends by helping Van Dinh reach this country. What did these friends do, and why do you think they tried to assist the family?

5. Lewis states that the history of the Dinh family is "an American story." What makes the story typically American? (Be sure to check your Quickwrite notes.) ✏️

6. What **opinions** does the article express? Which **facts** provide the strongest support for these opinions? 📖

7. In your own words, state the **theme,** or **main idea,** about immigrants that Lewis expresses in this news feature.

8. What does America represent for Viet Dinh and his family? Is America associated with similar or different things in "Liberty" and "Exile"? Explain.

9. In "Ex-Refugee Is Nominated for Justice Post" (see the **Connection** on page 315), Viet Dinh is presented as a role model. Based on your reading of the article and "An American Story," what do you think makes Viet Dinh a good example for other people?

Extending and Evaluating

10. Do you find Lewis's article effective and his opinions convincing? Explain.

11. Lewis's news feature is filled with **details** that leave vivid impressions in the mind of the reader. Which details had the greatest impact on you? Why?

WRITING

From Fact to Fiction

Retell part of Viet Dinh's family experience in **another genre**—a poem, song, journal entry, or short story, for example. For help getting started, think about the characteristics of the new genre. Then, decide what you need to add—or what you need to leave out—in order to tell about the experience in a new form.

In My Opinion

The United States is made up of people from many different countries and cultures, as Anthony Lewis points out. Look around your school and community, or think about our country as a whole. How have we benefited from the influence of people from many parts of the world? Write one or two paragraphs in which you explain the benefits you've observed.

> ### Comparing Themes
>
> For a writing assignment comparing the themes in "Liberty," "Exile," and "An American Story," see page 318.

SKILLS FOCUS

Literary Skills
Analyze characteristics of news features, including the main idea.

Reading Skills
Distinguish between fact and opinion.

Writing Skills
Retell a news feature in another genre. Support an opinion.

Word Origins: Borrowed Words

PRACTICE

Just as the United States is made up of people from all over the world, the English language contains many words that have come from foreign lands. For example, the words *refugee* and *regime* (in "An American Story") come from the French words *réfugié* and *régime*.

The words in the following list also come to English from other languages. For each word in the list, use a dictionary for help making a chart like the one for parachute.

- kindergarten
- plaza
- tea
- pajamas
- rodeo
- umbrella
- patio
- souvenir
- yacht

Word: *parachute*
Language of origin: French
Definition: *device made out of cloth, used to slow the fall of an object from a great height*
What you associate with the word: *safety; excitement; danger*

Grammar Link

Commas: Keeping Things Tidy

Commas keep words from running into one another like bumper cars. Here are some comma rules used in "An American Story":

1. Use commas to separate three or more items in a series.

   "He was with his mother, four sisters, and a brother."

2. When writing a date, separate the day of the month from the year with a comma. Use another comma to separate the year from the rest of the sentence.

   "He escaped from the camp on June 12, 1978, and was on the run when his wife and six children left."

   If only the month and year are given, don't separate them with a comma.

   "But it was six years before she managed to leave herself: on a boat that reached Hong Kong in August 1989."

3. Use a comma to separate the name of a city and a state or country. If the sentence continues, separate the name of the state or country from the rest of the sentence with a comma.

   "His parents are running a small grocery in Salem, Oregon."

PRACTICE

Rewrite each sentence, adding commas where necessary.

1. This article was originally published on November 26 1993.
2. Viet Dinh's father his mother and Anh all work in Salem Oregon.
3. Immigrants have made new homes in Oregon New York and other states.
4. Van Dinh arrived in Portland Oregon in September 1992.

▶ **For more help, see Commas, 12f–l, in the Language Handbook.**

Vocabulary Skills
Identify word origins of English words from foreign languages.

Grammar Skills
Use commas correctly in a series; in dates; and with cities, states, and countries.

Writing a Comparison–Contrast Essay

Comparing a Theme Across Genres

Now that you have read "Liberty," "Exile," and "An American Story," you are ready to write a comparison-contrast essay discussing how a similar topic is treated in three genres. When you write a **comparison-contrast essay,** you look for similarities (comparisons) and differences (contrasts) between the works.

Gather and Organize Your Information

The chart on page 294 that you created to show how genre shapes the theme or the main idea in each of the three selections will give you the basic information you need for your essay.

Your points in a comparison-contrast essay can be organized in two ways. For this essay, you will use the **point-by-point method.** (The **block method** was covered on page 280.)

The Point-by-Point Method

When you use the point-by-point method, you organize your essay by *ideas,* not by works (as you do in the block method). You discuss each idea, or element, in turn. The chart at the right gives an example.

Use Three-Part Structure

Use a three-part structure for your comparison-contrast essay:

- **introduction**—including background and a **thesis statement** briefly explaining how genre shapes content in the works

- **body**—including separate paragraphs for each element

- **conclusion**—summing up and adding a new thought or personal insight

Revise Your Essay

The following questions will help you revise your essay:

- Does the thesis statement clearly state the point of the essay?

- Is a point about an element in Work 1 followed by points about that element in Work 2 and Work 3?

- Have you developed and elaborated on each point?

- Is the conclusion clear and effective?

▶ **For more help writing a comparison-contrast essay, see pages 320–327.**

Point-by-Point Method
Element 1: How Genre Relates to Author's Purpose
Work 1: "Liberty"
Work 2: "Exile"
Work 3: "An American Story"
Element 2: Theme / Main Idea and Whether Stated or Implied
Work 1: "Liberty"
Work 2: "Exile"
Work 3: "An American Story"
Element 3: Genre Characteristics Used to Develop Theme / Main Idea
Work 1: "Liberty"
Work 2: "Exile"
Work 3: "An American Story"

SKILLS FOCUS

Literary Skills
Compare and contrast a theme across genres.

Writing Skills
Write a comparison-contrast essay.

FICTION

A Family Divided

To live in North Korea in 1945 is to live in a world seemingly without springtime, where each day is as grim and forbidding as winter. It is the year that the Japanese military occupies Pyongyang and begins to tear families apart, including ten-year-old Sookan's. *Year of Impossible Goodbyes* by Sook Nyul Choi is the story of one fiercely determined family that does everything in its power to be reunited, even in the face of great danger.

NONFICTION

Difficult Days

All of the Uchida family's dreams about life in California have come true: Their two daughters, Yoshiko and Keiko, enjoy all the riches of America. Their lives are happy in every respect—until that day in 1941 when Yoshiko comes home from the library and finds an eerie silence in her house. Her father is gone—sent away to an army internment camp—and the rest of her family, along with hundreds of other innocent Japanese Americans, soon joins him. Yoshiko Uchida's *Desert Exile: The Uprooting of a Japanese-American Family* is a powerful true account of a shameful chapter in our nation's history.

FICTION

Head of His Tribe

Okonkwo seems to have it all—wealth, privilege, and status within his Nigerian village. Then, in the blink of an eye, everything changes, and Okonkwo is separated from his family and sent into exile for seven years. Will his village and its tribal customs be the same when he returns? Will his family accept him? You'll find surprising answers to these questions in Chinua Achebe's classic novel *Things Fall Apart.*

This title is available in the HRW Library.

NONFICTION

The Last Great Battle

The author Bruce Catton, known for his true tales of the Civil War, considered himself more of a storyteller than a historian. You'll see why when you read his book *A Stillness at Appomattox.* Written with freshness and dramatic flair, this is a history that takes you into the hearts and minds of those who fought in the last and most devastating year of the Civil War. You'll hear the stories of hard-bitten generals and brave young soldiers, many of whom meet at the final, fateful battle at Appomattox.

This title is available in the HRW Library.

Comparing Media Coverage

Writing Assignment
Write an essay in which you compare and contrast the coverage of a single news event by two different news media.

Suppose that the event depicted in Liam O'Flaherty's "The Sniper" actually happened last week, and you saw media coverage of it—twice. The first report was on the nightly news of a major television network, and the second report you read on the Internet. The two stories were not the same, though. One was short and dramatic. The other contained more information and interviews from several people. Why, you wonder, are two reports on the same event so different?

Prewriting

Select a News Event

Topping the News Tonight As you search for a news story for your essay, look for major national and international events—it's likely you'll find more coverage about them. Watch a national news program or read a national newspaper first to select an event. Then, survey other media, such as magazines, radio programs, and Internet sites, to find additional coverage of the event. Pick an event that's interesting to you; you'll be spending a lot of time thinking about it.

Compare and Contrast Coverage

Two Horses, Different Colors The basic purpose of all responsible news organizations is to communicate information about current events, yet no two media report a news event the same way. Every news story is shaped and limited by the technology and traditions of the medium itself, as well as by the writers, editors, directors, and producers involved in creating the story.

For example, while a network news story might use dramatic video and audio to involve the viewer emotionally, the story will probably last less than a minute. Internet news, on the other hand, is usually more complex. An Internet news site can engage a viewer for a longer amount of time by allowing the viewer to move back and forth through text, audio clips, and images and to link to additional information related to the news story. By comparing how different media present the same story, you can see how different kinds of editorial decisions come across to readers, listeners, or viewers.

Answer the questions in the chart on the next page to compare the coverage of one event by two news media. Each of the boldface terms can be a specific **point of comparison** for your essay.

SKILLS FOCUS

Writing Skills
Write an essay comparing and contrasting the ways in which different news media cover the same event.

QUESTIONS TO ASK WHEN COMPARING MEDIA

Attention-getting techniques	• How are images, words, and sounds arranged to get the audience's attention?
Objectivity	• Is the main subject portrayed objectively, or is there a positive or negative slant?
	• If two people or groups are involved, does the story give the impression that one side is more honorable or honest than the other?
Complexity	• Does the story provide background information?
	• Does it help you see how this event fits into a bigger picture?
	• Does the story present multiple points of view?
	• What types of sources are interviewed?
Sequence of information	• How does the story begin and end?
	• What kinds of details make up the bulk of the story—interviews, facts, dramatic images, others?
Emotional impact	• Does the story seem to be designed to arouse a certain feeling or impression in its audience?
	• What techniques does it use to do this?

The example below shows what one student discovered when he compared the coverage of an avalanche in the French Alps by a network news program and an Internet news site. Notice that the student listed specific details and examples as he analyzed the two news stories using the points of comparison in the chart above.

TV Network News versus Internet News

Similarities

1. set up as humans vs. nature stories
2. focus on the devastation to the town and the effort to rescue skiers
3. feature interviews with local citizens and victims' families
4. inform the audience that this area of the Alps is prone to avalanches
5. show the site of the avalanche on a map of Europe

Differences

TV News

1. Begins with views of Alps, then cuts to footage of the avalanche and shots of the devastation and rescue workers. Ends with shot of heavy snowfall and warning that time is running out.

Internet News

1. Begins with a description of the avalanche and then focuses on the rescue effort. Links connect to photos of rescue workers and survivors.

(continued)

(continued)

2. Includes an interview with a rescued American couple.

3. Does not give additional sources of information.

2. Includes interviews with rescued American couple, the head of the rescue operation, and local merchants.

3. Gives links to informational sites and related stories.

Form a Thesis

What's the Point? Now that you have compared and contrasted your two media, what basic conclusion or judgment can you arrive at? Was one medium more objective, complex, or dramatic than the other? The conclusion or judgment you make based on your analysis is your **thesis.** You communicate your thesis in a **thesis statement,** a sentence or two that states the point you intend to prove to your readers. Write a thesis statement that is **clear** and **coherent.** The student comparing the stories about an avalanche wrote the following thesis statement.

| DO THIS

The online story was more complex than the network news story and depended less on emotional impact.

Organize Your Essay

Medium by Medium or Point by Point? In order for readers to understand the similarities and differences between the two reports, you will need to organize your ideas clearly. There are two basic plans you can use to organize your comparison-contrast essay.

- **Block method:** Discuss the similarities between the two stories first and then move on to the differences, or tell everything about one medium first and then move on to the second medium. The block method works best for shorter pieces with fewer comparisons.

- **Point-by-point method:** Explain how the subjects are alike and different for one point of comparison, then the next point of comparison, and so on. For example, your essay might deal first with how the stories begin, move on to discuss the sequence of information in each story, then cover each story's complexity. The point-by-point method works best for longer essays with more comparisons.

SKILLS FOCUS

Writing Skills
Establish a thesis. Organize the essay by the block method or the point-by-point method.

PRACTICE & APPLY 1 Use the instructions on the previous pages to select a news event, and analyze its coverage by two different news media. Then, write a thesis statement that communicates your conclusion about the coverage. Finally, organize the information you've gathered.

Writing

Comparing Media Coverage

A Writer's Model

The highlighted words and phrases below help the reader understand the essay's organization.

More News Is Good News

Have you ever watched a news story on network news that left you wondering, "What's the rest of the story?" I have. Just the other night I watched a story about a terrible avalanche in the French Alps. When it was over I wanted to know more, so I went to the Internet. The coverage I found on a major online news site was both similar to and different from the network news. Overall, the online story was more complex than the network news story and depended less on emotional impact.

The similarities in the two stories were obvious. Both reported the story as a human beings-versus-nature story, focusing on the awesome power of the avalanche and on the heroic efforts of rescue workers. Both featured interviews of people on the scene and informed their audiences that this area of the French Alps is prone to avalanches. Finally, both stories showed the site of the avalanche on a map of Europe.

The differences in the coverage of the avalanche by the two media were more striking. The network news story began with peaceful Alpine views, then cut to dramatic footage of the avalanche and the devastation and rescue efforts afterwards. It ended with a shot of

INTRODUCTION
Engaging opening
News event

Subjects
Thesis statement

BODY
Similarities

Differences:
1. sequence
2. attention-getting techniques

(continued)

(continued)

heavy afternoon snowfall and a warning that time was running out for victims still buried. The online news story, on the other hand, began with a brief description of the avalanche before moving on to focus on rescue efforts. The site provided links to photographs of rescue workers and survivors. The television story was much more dramatic, obviously appealing to the emotions of the viewers. The online story, by comparison, was calm and reasoned, focusing on the business at hand—the rescue.

The online story provided more background information and a wider variety of points of view than the television story. For example, the television story aired clips from an interview with a rescued American couple. The online story provided the same interview and others as well—with the head of the rescue effort and with local merchants worried about their businesses. Moreover, the online story provided links to articles on related topics such as previous avalanches in the area, their effects on the local economy, and steps taken to prevent and prepare for avalanches. The television story did not refer viewers to any other sources of information.

The online story was less dramatic and more complex than the television story. It provided more context and a wider variety of points of view. The television news coverage was no doubt influenced by the time limitations of a thirty-minute program and by a greater need to use drama and emotional impact to attract an audience. The Internet news site obviously also wants to attract an audience, but is free from the space and time limitations that restrict the television news coverage. Watching television news coverage is a good way to find out what important events have taken place on a given day, but an interested viewer may want to consider going to a reliable online news source for more complete information.

3. emotional impact

Differences in complexity

CONCLUSION
Restatement of thesis

Factors that account for differences

Idea for readers to think about

INTERNET

More Writer's Models

Keyword: LE7 9-4

PRACTICE & APPLY 2 Using the framework on page 323 and the Writer's Model above as guides, write the first draft of your essay comparing media coverage.

Revising

Revise Your Comparison-Contrast Essay

The Professional Touch For professional writers, the revision process is as important as any other phase of the writing process. Follow their example by first evaluating and revising the content and organization of your essay using the guidelines below. Then, evaluate and revise your essay's style using the guidelines in the chart on page 326.

PEER REVIEW

Exchange your essay with a peer before you revise. He or she may have ideas on how you can improve the block or point-by-point organization of your paper.

First Reading: Content and Organization Use the chart below to look for ways to improve the content and the **logic** and **coherence** of the organization of your comparison-contrast essay. As you consider the evaluation questions, take into account your essay's intended **audience,** your **purpose** for writing the essay, and the degree of **formality** required of an analytical essay such as this one. Use the tips in the middle column to help you answer the evaluation questions and the revision techniques in the last column to help you make necessary revisions.

Rubric: Comparing Media Coverage

Evaluation Questions	▶ Tips	▶ Revision Techniques
❶ Is the opening engaging? Does the introduction present the two news media and the news event?	▶ **Underline** the engaging opening. **Bracket** the introduction of the media and the news event.	▶ **Add** a startling fact, interesting quotation, or intriguing question. **Add** a sentence introducing the media and news event.
❷ Does the thesis include a conclusion about the media coverage?	▶ **Highlight** the thesis statement.	▶ If needed, **add** a thesis statement that provides a conclusion about the media coverage.
❸ Is there an obvious, easy-to-follow organizational pattern?	▶ **Label** the points of comparison. If there is no consistent pattern, revise.	▶ **Rearrange** events into point-by-point organization or block organization.
❹ Is each point of comparison adequately supported?	▶ **Put a check mark** by each detail or reference to a news story.	▶ **Add** a detail or reference, or **elaborate** to explain existing support.
❺ Does the conclusion mention factors that might account for similarities and differences? Does it remind readers of the thesis and leave them with an idea to consider?	▶ **Circle** factors that might account for similarities or differences. **Draw a line through** the sentence restating the thesis. **Double underline** the sentence with the idea for readers to consider.	▶ **Add** factors accounting for similarities or differences. **Add** a sentence restating the thesis or an idea for readers to ponder, as necessary. **Delete** material that does none of the above.

> **Second Reading: Style** Once you have revised the content and organization of your essay, you can concentrate on its style. One way to improve the style is to use transitional words and phrases, such as *next, finally,* and *most important.* **Transitional words and phrases** connect one idea to another, making your ideas easy to read and understand. Transitional words and phrases are particularly important in comparison-contrast essays, where you constantly move back and forth between the subjects or points of your essay. To help you add transitional words and phrases to your essay, use the guidelines in the chart below.

Style Guidelines

Evaluation Question	▶ Tip	▶ Revision Technique
● Does the writer use transitional words and phrases to guide the reader?	▶ **Draw a box** around transitional words and phrases such as *on the other hand, by contrast, however,* and so on.	▶ **Add** transitional words and phrases to make the points of comparison clearer to readers.

ANALYZING THE REVISION PROCESS
Study these revisions, and answer the questions that follow.

> The online story provided more background information
>
> and a wider variety of points of view than the television story.
>
> *For example,*
> add ∧The television story aired clips from an interview with a
>
> rescued American couple. The online story provided the same
>
> elaborate   interview and others as well∧ *—with the head of the rescue effort and with local merchants worried about their businesses.*

Responding to the Revision Process

1. How did adding a transitional phrase connect the ideas in the first two sentences?

2. Why do you think the writer added to the last sentence?

SKILLS FOCUS

Writing Skills
Revise for content and style.

PRACTICE & APPLY 8 Revise the content, organization, and style of your essay, using the guidelines in this section. Be sure to read through your paper twice.

Publishing

Proofread and Publish Your Essay

The Final Touch Informative and thought-provoking content that is well organized and communicated with an engaging style is the most impressive element of any essay. However, the best content can be seriously spoiled by careless errors in grammar, usage, and mechanics. Make your essay as free of such errors as you can by proofreading it carefully and correcting errors as you discover them. You might even ask a peer to help you find and correct mistakes. Once you have completed this process, make a final copy.

An Essay in Search of an Audience You've worked hard to write and polish your essay. Now, you can reap the rewards of your hard work by sharing your analysis with others. How do you find an audience? Consider the following suggestions for publication.

- Post your essay to an online site that specializes in media analysis, and ask for reader feedback.

- Form a group of three to four classmates to read and comment on each other's essays.

- E-mail your essay to the news organizations whose coverage you analyzed, and ask for their feedback.

- Adapt your essay into an oral presentation. Think about incorporating technology into your presentation so your audience can view video clips or Web pages.

Reflect on Your Essay

Food for Thought Look back and reflect on what you have learned in the process of analyzing media coverage and writing a comparison-contrast essay. Use these questions to focus your thoughts.

- How did writing this essay help you understand the editorial decisions that media professionals are required to make?

- Which of your points of comparison do you think was the strongest argument for looking to more than one source for the news of any event? Why?

- Considering your experience comparing and contrasting news media, which medium would you choose as your news source if you were forced to choose only one? Why?

PRACTICE & APPLY 4 Use the suggestions and questions on this page to proofread, publish, and reflect on your essay comparing media coverage of a news event.

> **TIP** Careful proofreading will help ensure that you have used English-language **conventions** properly. For example, check to see that you have correctly capitalized and punctuated the names of news programs or Internet news sites in your essay. For more on **capitalizing and punctuating titles,** see Capitalization, 11f, in the Language Handbook.

Writing Skills
Proofread to correct grammar, usage, and mechanics errors. Publish and reflect on the essay.

Comparing Themes

DIRECTIONS: Read the following short story and poem. Then, read and respond to the questions that follow.

Papa Who Wakes Up Tired in the Dark

Sandra Cisneros

Your *abuelito*[1] is dead, Papa says early one morning in my room. *Está muerto*,[2] and then as if he just heard the news himself, crumples like a coat and cries, my brave Papa cries. I have never seen my Papa cry and don't know what to do.

I know he will have to go away, that he will take a plane to Mexico, all the uncles and aunts will be there, and they will have a black-and-white photo taken in front of the tomb with flowers shaped like spears in a white vase because this is how they send the dead away in that country.

Because I am the oldest, my father has told me first, and now it is my turn to tell the others. I will have to explain why we can't play. I will have to tell them to be quiet today.

My Papa, his thick hands and thick shoes, who wakes up tired in the dark, who combs his hair with water, drinks his coffee, and is gone before we wake, today is sitting on my bed.

And I think if my own Papa died what would I do. I hold my Papa in my arms. I hold and hold and hold him.

---

1. ***abuelito*** (ä·bwel·ē′tō): Spanish for "grandpa."
2. ***Está muerto*** (es·tä′ mwer′tō): Spanish for "He is dead."

Those Winter Sundays

Robert Hayden

Sundays too my father got up early
and put his clothes on in the
   blueblack cold,
then with cracked hands that ached
from labor in the weekday weather
   made
5 banked fires blaze. No one ever
   thanked him.

I'd wake and hear the cold splintering,
   breaking.
When the rooms were warm, he'd call,
and slowly I would rise and dress,
fearing the chronic° angers of
   that house,

10 Speaking indifferently to him,
who had driven out the cold
and polished my good shoes as well.
What did I know, what did I know
of love's austere° and lonely offices?°

---

9. **chronic** (krän′ik) *adj.:* constant.
14. **austere** (ô·stir′) *adj.:* self-sacrificing.
   offices *n.:* services; duties.

SKILLS FOCUS

Pages 328–329 cover
Literary Skills
Compare the presentation of a theme across genres. Compare universal themes.

Collection 4: Skills Review

1. In "Papa Who Wakes Up Tired in the Dark," how does the narrator feel when she sees her father cry?
   A Guilty
   B Confused
   C Angry
   D Suspicious

2. When he was young, the speaker in "Those Winter Sundays" —
   F did not appreciate his father
   G felt grateful to his father
   H did not obey his father
   J gave orders to his father

3. Both works describe a father who wakes up early in the dark. What do these two fathers have in common?
   A Both are ambitious.
   B Both are restless and aimless.
   C Neither father wants to spend time with his family.
   D Both work hard and love their families.

4. What feeling is expressed at the end of both selections?
   F Fear or nervousness
   G Pity
   H Embarrassment
   J Love or appreciation

5. Which of the following statements about the two selections is *false*?
   A Unlike the story's narrator, the poem's speaker is an adult looking back on the past.
   B Unlike the relationship described in the poem, the parent-child relationship in the story is warm.
   C The tone of the poem, unlike the tone of the story, is regretful.
   D The poem's speaker, unlike the story's narrator, has seen his father cry.

6. Although these works are different **genres** (a story and a poem), they share each of the following elements *except* —
   F a first-person narrator or speaker
   G a repeated phrase
   H dialogue
   J an image of the father's hands

7. If Robert Hayden wanted to turn "Those Winter Sundays" into a story, he might add all of the following elements *except* —
   A a scene showing a conflict between the father and son
   B end rhyme
   C a climax to the plot
   D more characters

Constructed Response

8. In your opinion, what is the common **theme** of both selections? Provide specific examples to support your response.

Collection 4: Skills Review

Vocabulary Skills

Test Practice

Multiple-Meaning Words

DIRECTIONS: Choose the answer in which the underlined word is used in the same way it is used in the sentence from "The Sniper."

1. "Dublin lay enveloped in darkness but for the dim light of the moon that shone through fleecy clouds. . . ."
   - **A** Please light the candles on the birthday cake.
   - **B** The biography presented the author in a favorable light.
   - **C** She always dressed in light colors.
   - **D** When we go camping, we read by the light of the fire.

2. "The sniper could hear the dull panting of the motor."
   - **F** We left the party early because it was dull.
   - **G** We heard the dull roar of crowds in the distance.
   - **H** I couldn't cut the fruit with the dull knife.
   - **J** In shock after the accident, he felt dull to pain and grief.

3. "The sniper raised his rifle and fired."
   - **A** Each person fired two shots at the target.
   - **B** The supervisor fired the employee last week.
   - **C** Journalists fired questions at the mayor during the press conference.
   - **D** The speaker fired up the crowd, inspiring the audience to take action.

4. "Quickly he drew his knife from his pocket. . . ."
   - **F** The engineer drew a diagram to show how the machine worked.
   - **G** The students drew several conclusions from their survey.
   - **H** The movie star always drew large crowds wherever he went.
   - **J** I waited in suspense as my mother slowly drew a surprise from the bag.

5. "There was a flash and a bullet whizzed over his head."
   - **A** If I hurry, I can be there in a flash.
   - **B** Usually serious, my friend suddenly displayed a flash of wit.
   - **C** To enter the building, just flash your badge.
   - **D** A flash of lightning lit up the sky.

6. "Here and there through the city, machine guns and rifles broke the silence of the night. . . ."
   - **F** Her company went bankrupt, and she is broke.
   - **G** We broke away from the crowds and wandered off by ourselves.
   - **H** Chris was so upset that he broke down in tears.
   - **J** The sound of lighthearted laughter broke the tension in the room.

SKILLS FOCUS

Vocabulary Skills
Understand multiple-meaning words.

Collection 4: Skills Review

Writing Skills

Test Practice

DIRECTIONS: The following paragraph is from a draft of a student's comparison-contrast essay. Read the questions below it, and choose the best answer to each question.

(1) Recently, an online article and a newspaper article discussed wildfires in the West. (2) If you have access to the Web, you can read the online article. (3) The online article, "Western Wildfires Continue," presents a variety of information that provides an objective picture of the wildfire. (4) The newspaper article, "Local Firefighters Battle Bravely," presents a very personal look at the dangerous task of fighting wildfires. (5) Stirring photos and emotional language in the article create a strong emotional impact.

1. To present a clear, coherent thesis, which of these could the student add after sentence 1?

   A While both stories discuss wildfires in the West, the newspaper story has greater emotional impact.

   B The Web site is viewed by people worldwide, but the newspaper is read mostly locally.

   C A firefighter from my hometown has volunteered to battle the wildfires.

   D I enjoyed reading the two articles and finding out their differences.

2. Which of the following sentences would add to the ideas in sentence 3?

   F Both writers gathered some of their material from the Associated Press.

   G Too many paid advertisements surround the online story and distract the reader.

   H The newspaper article has pictures of the local firefighters hugging their families goodbye.

   J It offers links to other reports, satellite photos, and interviews with sources.

3. Which of these transitional words or phrases should the writer add to the beginning of sentence 4?

   A Meanwhile,

   B In addition,

   C On the other hand,

   D For example,

4. Which sentence should be deleted to improve the passage's organization?

   F 2

   G 3

   H 4

   J 5

5. To discuss similarities between the media, which of the following could the writer add?

   A an explanation that the newspaper article is distributed only locally

   B a statement that both articles discuss the need for more help

   C a description of the online story's graphics

   D a defense of the credibility of each source quoted in the articles

SKILLS FOCUS

Writing Skills
Write a comparison-contrast essay.

Hard Choices

Literary Focus:
**Analyzing Irony
and Ambiguity**

Informational Reading Focus:
Evaluating an Argument

INTERNET

Collection
Resources

Keyword: LE7 9-5

Crying Girl (1963) by Roy Lichtenstein (1923–1997).
Lithograph. 44.6 x 58.9 cm.
©Estate of Roy Lichtenstein.

Elements of Literature

Irony and Ambiguity *by* John Leggett
SURPRISES, TWISTS, AND MYSTERIES

Fiction, really good fiction, reflects the human experience. Good fiction is a great mirror in which we see—in ways that entertain and inform us—how the lives of others have unfolded, and so it suggests how life may unfold for ourselves.

The fiction writer who wants to bring about such a wonder must first convince the reader that the story being told is a truth. That means that we must believe in the story as a reflection of human experience. The sound of truth in a story—often described in the writing business today as "telling it like it is"—means giving the characters and events all the peculiarities of real life. These include the surprise and contrariness and uncertainty that confound us in our daily rounds—and that keep us guessing about our own futures.

Irony: Not What We Expect

Irony is the word that describes the difference between what we expect or what seems suitable and what actually happens. Imagine, for example, that the fellow we elected mayor because he ran on a platform of honesty is caught with the missing pension fund. Sometimes irony so surprises us that it is comic. The floored prizefighter lifts his head from the canvas to say, "I think I've got him worried."

Our pleasure in irony comes from our recognition that it is *true*—that life rarely fulfills our expectations and often astounds us.

We find three kinds of irony in stories. **Verbal irony**—the simplest kind—is used when someone *says* one thing but *means* the opposite. The prizefighter's comment is an example of verbal irony.

Situational irony describes an event that is not just surprising but actually contrary to what we expected. When the mayor is caught with his hand in the pension fund, we have situational irony.

A third kind of irony is **dramatic irony.** This type of irony often occurs in plays, a fact that explains how it gets its name. When *we* know what is in store for a character, but the character does *not* know, we are experiencing dramatic irony. When Joan plans a huge surprise birthday party for Fred, and Fred returns to a darkened home and wearily says, "All I want is a quiet evening," we recognize dramatic irony at work. We also feel the tug of suspense: We want to know what will happen when thirty people leap out to surprise Fred.

Ambiguity: Conflicting Interpretations

In a story, just as in actual experience, the outcome of our expectations can also be ambiguous. Irony is the reverse of what we expected; **ambiguity** offers us several conflicting consequences or meanings—and leaves us to sort them out.

In actual life we tend to have ambiguous feelings about many of our experiences. "I'm a reasonably honest person, but I never did return Rudy's watch." "Megan's a lovely girl, but she's so irresponsible." Both of these are examples of ambiguous feelings.

SKILLS FOCUS

Literary Skills
Understand irony (verbal irony, situational irony, and dramatic irony) and ambiguity.

go.hrw.com

INTERNET

More About Irony and Ambiguity
Keyword: LE7 9-5

Irony and ambiguity can apply to every aspect of storytelling. Suppose a story tells about a shy girl, Emily. Emily has bright expectations for the school dance, based upon the dress her mother is making for her and on Donald, the neighbor who will take her to the dance. If once within the gym, Donald abandons Emily and leaves her to languish alone by the water fountain, the story's ending is ironic. It is the opposite of what we would hope for and expect.

An ambiguous ending offers us a choice of outcomes. In Emily's case the storyteller might suggest that Donald's neglect actually toughened Emily for a rewarding life of research on spiders and beetles. Perhaps instead the story hints that Emily didn't really like Donald anyway and was using him to feel socially accepted. Both of these are ambiguous endings.

It's possible that the whole story—its very theme—is ironic or ambiguous, so that when you've finished and put the story aside, the *why* of the story is puzzling. Does the writer mean that Emily is happier with spiders and beetles? Is Emily really manipulative, or is she just protective of herself?

Some readers think those stories with ironic or ambiguous endings or themes are the ones we remember —because we can never be quite sure what they mean. It seems that the best stories are not the easiest ones to understand. The best stories are the ones that present life and people the way they are: complicated, unpredictable, mysterious.

Practice

Review the definition of **verbal irony**. Then, write a paragraph describing a scene between two characters. Include an ironic statement made by one character. You might take inspiration from one of the characters or situations described above.

Complete Peace

Introducing the Collection Theme

Hard Choices

Make the Connection

Quickwrite

At some point you've probably had to make a hard choice about what to do or say. Think about the choices you, or people you know, have faced in life. What factors influence our choices—our personalities, our needs and fears, or society's values, for example? Place your ideas in a cluster diagram like the one at right.

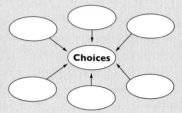

Exploring the Theme: Hard Choices

This collection centers on some of the most famous hard choices presented in literature. In the short stories "The Gift of the Magi" and "The Lady, or the Tiger?" characters must make tough choices about love and sacrifice. In Robert Frost's often-quoted poem "The Road Not Taken," the speaker reflects on the road in life he did *not* choose. You'll also read a persuasive essay in which the author argues that trial by jury is the fairest way to decide cases. "Poison," the story you're about to read, focuses on three men caught in a life-or-death situation and the hard choices they must make.

Literary Focus

Irony and Ambiguity

Writers often use irony and ambiguity to show how surprising and puzzling life can be. **Irony** is a contrast between what we expect, or what seems appropriate, and what actually happens: An "unsinkable" ocean liner goes down; the son of the police chief robs a bank. A story characterized by **ambiguity** can be interpreted in several conflicting ways. As you read "Poison," you'll probably be gripped by uncertainty—about what is going to happen and what has actually occurred.

Background

This story is set in India during the time when it was a British colony, before gaining its independence in 1947. During the long years of British rule, colonial authorities controlled India's laws, education system, army, and government, and the British people living in India enjoyed many of the privileges that came with power. Many Indians resented the control exercised by the British over their society and institutions. This simmering conflict underlies the tension in this story.

SKILLS FOCUS

Literary Skills
Understand irony and ambiguity.

POISON

Roald Dahl

It must have been around midnight when I drove home, and as I approached the gates of the bungalow I switched off the headlamps of the car so the beam wouldn't swing in through the window of the side bedroom and wake Harry Pope. But I needn't have bothered. Coming up the drive, I noticed his light was still on, so he was awake anyway—unless perhaps he'd dropped off while reading.

I parked the car and went up the five steps to the balcony, counting each step carefully in the dark so I wouldn't take an extra one which wasn't there, when I got to the top. I crossed the balcony, pushed through the screen doors into the house itself, and switched on the light in the hall. I went across to the door of Harry's room, opened it quietly, and looked in.

He was lying on the bed and I could see he was awake. But he didn't move. He didn't even turn his head toward me, but I heard him say, "Timber, Timber, come here."

He spoke slowly, whispering each word carefully, separately, and I pushed the door right open and started to go quickly across the room.

"Stop. Wait a moment, Timber." I could hardly hear what he was saying. He seemed to be straining enormously to get the words out.

"What's the matter, Harry?"

"Sshhh!" he whispered. "Sshhh! For God's sake, don't make a noise. Take your shoes off before you come nearer. *Please* do as I say, Timber."

The way he was speaking reminded me of George Barling after he got shot in the stomach, when he stood leaning against a crate containing a spare airplane engine, holding both hands on his stomach and saying things about the German pilot in just the same hoarse, straining half whisper Harry was using now.

"Quickly, Timber, but take your shoes off first."

I couldn't understand about taking off the shoes but I figured that if he was as ill as he sounded I'd better humor him, so I bent down and removed the shoes and left them in the middle of the floor. Then I went over to his bed.

"Don't touch the bed! For God's sake, don't touch the bed!" He was still speaking like he'd been shot in the stomach, and I could see him lying there on his back with a single sheet covering three quarters of his body. He was wearing a pair of pajamas with blue, brown, and white stripes, and he was sweating terribly. It was a hot night and I was sweating a little myself, but not like Harry. His whole face was wet, and the pillow around his head was sodden with moisture. It looked like a bad go of malaria[1] to me.

"What is it, Harry?"

"A krait,"[2] he said.

"A *krait!* Oh, my God! Where'd it bite you? How long ago?"

"Shut up," he whispered.

"Listen, Harry," I said, and I leaned forward and touched his shoulder. "We've got to be quick. Come on now, quickly, tell me where it bit you." He was lying there very still and tense as though he were holding on to himself hard because of sharp pain.

"I haven't been bitten," he whispered. "Not yet. It's on my stomach. Lying there asleep."

I took a quick pace backward; I couldn't help it, and I stared at his stomach or rather at the sheet that covered it. The sheet was rumpled in several places and it was impossible to tell if there was anything underneath. **❶**

"You don't really mean there's a krait lying on your stomach now?"

"I swear it."

"How did it get there?" I shouldn't have asked the question because it was easy to see he wasn't fooling. I should have told him to keep quiet.

"I was reading," Harry said, and he spoke very slowly, taking each word in turn and speaking it carefully so as not to move the muscles of his stomach. "Lying on my back reading and I felt something on my chest, behind the book. Sort of tickling. Then out of the corner of my eye I saw this little krait sliding over my pajamas. Small, about ten inches. Knew I mustn't move. Couldn't have anyway. Lay there watching it. Thought it would go over top of the sheet." Harry paused and was silent for a few moments. His eyes looked down along his body toward the place where the sheet covered his stomach, and I could see he was watching to make sure his whispering wasn't disturbing the thing that lay there.

"There was a fold in the sheet," he said, speaking more slowly than ever now and so softly I had to lean close to hear him. "See it, it's still there. It went under that. I could feel it through my pajamas, moving on my stomach. Then it stopped moving and now it's lying there in the warmth. Probably asleep. I've been waiting for you." He raised his eyes and looked at me.

THEME

❶ What is the basic situation in the story? What choices must the narrator make?

---

1. **malaria** (mə·ler′ē·ə) *n.:* infectious disease transmitted to humans by the bite of an infected mosquito. Malaria causes frequent sweats and fever.
2. **krait** (krīt) *n.:* poisonous Asian snake, usually black or dark brown with white or yellow bands.

"How long ago?"

"Hours," he whispered. "Hours and bloody hours and hours. I can't keep still much longer. I've been wanting to cough."

There was not much doubt about the truth of Harry's story. As a matter of fact it wasn't a surprising thing for a krait to do. They hang around people's houses, and they go for the warm places. The surprising thing was that Harry hadn't been bitten. The bite is quite deadly except sometimes when you catch it at once, and they kill a fair number of people each year in Bengal, mostly in the villages. ❷

"All right, Harry," I said, and now I was whispering too. "Don't move and don't talk anymore unless you have to. You know it won't bite unless it's frightened. We'll fix it in no time."

I went softly out of the room in my stocking feet and fetched a small sharp knife from the kitchen. I put it in my trouser pocket, ready to use instantly in case something went wrong while we were still thinking out a plan. If Harry coughed or moved or did something to frighten the krait and got bitten, I was going to be ready to cut the bitten place and try to suck the venom out. I came back to the bedroom and Harry was still lying there very quiet and sweating all over his face. His eyes followed me as I moved across the room to his bed, and I could see he was wondering what I'd been up to. I stood beside him, trying to think of the best thing to do.

"Harry," I said, and now when I spoke I put my mouth almost on his ear so I wouldn't have to raise my voice above the softest whisper, "I think the best thing to do is for me to draw the sheet back very, very gently. Then we could have a look first. I think I could do that without disturbing it."

"Don't be a fool." There was no expression in his voice. He spoke each word too slowly, too carefully, and too softly for that. The expression was in the eyes and around the corners of the mouth.

"Why not?"

"The light would frighten him. It's dark under there now."

"Then how about whipping the sheet back quick and brushing it off before it has time to strike?"

"Why don't you get a doctor?" Harry said. The way he looked at me told me I should have thought of that myself in the first place.

> "We've got to be quick. Come on now, quickly, tell me where it bit you."

THEME

❸ What choices do Harry and the narrator consider as they plan how to get rid of the krait?

IRONY

❹ What do you think of the way Harry reacts when the narrator informs him of Dr. Ganderbai's instructions? Why are Harry's reactions **ironic**?

"A doctor. Of course. That's it. I'll get Ganderbai." ❸

I tiptoed out to the hall, looked up Ganderbai's number in the book, lifted the phone, and told the operator to hurry.

"Doctor Ganderbai," I said. "This is Timber Woods."

"Hello, Mr. Woods. You not in bed yet?"

"Look, could you come round at once? And bring serum—for a krait bite."

"Who's been bitten?" The question came so sharply it was like a small explosion in my ear.

"No one. No one yet. But Harry Pope's in bed, and he's got one lying on his stomach—asleep under the sheet on his stomach."

For about three seconds there was silence on the line. Then speaking slowly, not like an explosion now but slowly, precisely, Ganderbai said, "Tell him to keep quite still. He is not to move or to talk. Do you understand?"

"Of course."

"I'll come at once!" He rang off and I went back to the bedroom. Harry's eyes watched me as I walked across to his bed.

"Ganderbai's coming. He said for you to lie still."

"What does he think I'm doing?"

"Look, Harry, he said no talking. Absolutely no talking. Either of us."

"Why don't you shut up, then?" When he said this, one side of his mouth started twitching with rapid little downward movements that continued for a while after he finished speaking. I took out my handkerchief and very gently I wiped the sweat off his face and neck, and I could feel the slight twitching of the muscle—the one he used for smiling—as my fingers passed over it with the handkerchief. ❹

I slipped out to the kitchen, got some ice from the icebox, rolled it up in a napkin, and began to crush it small. That business of the mouth, I didn't like that. Or the way he talked, either. I carried the ice pack back to the bedroom and laid it across Harry's forehead.

"Keep you cool."

He screwed up his eyes and drew breath sharply through his teeth. "Take it away," he whispered. "Make me cough." His smiling muscle began to twitch again.

The beam of a headlamp shone through the window as Ganderbai's car swung around to the front of the bungalow. I went out to meet him, holding the ice pack with both hands.

"How is it?" Ganderbai asked, but he didn't stop to talk; he walked on past me across the balcony and through the screen doors into the hall. "Where is he? Which room?"

He put his bag down on a chair in the hall and followed me into Harry's room. He was wearing soft-soled bedroom slippers and he walked across the floor noiselessly, delicately, like a careful cat. Harry watched him out of the sides of his eyes. When Ganderbai reached the bed he looked down at Harry and smiled, confident and reassuring, nodding his head to tell Harry it was a simple matter and he was not to worry but just to leave it to Doctor Ganderbai. Then he turned and went back to the hall and I followed him.

"First thing is to try to get some serum into him," he said, and he opened his bag and started to make preparations. "Intravenously.[3] But I must do it neatly. Don't want to make him flinch."

We went into the kitchen and he sterilized a needle. He had a hypodermic syringe in one hand and a small bottle in the other, and he stuck the needle through the rubber top of the bottle and began drawing a pale yellow liquid up into the syringe by pulling out the plunger. Then he handed the syringe to me.

"Hold that till I ask for it."

He picked up the bag and together we returned to the room. Harry's eyes were bright now and wide open. Ganderbai bent over Harry and very cautiously, like a man handling sixteenth-century lace, he rolled up the pajama sleeve to the elbow without moving the arm. I noticed he stood well away from the bed.

He whispered, "I'm going to give you an injection. Serum. Just a prick but try not to move. Don't tighten your stomach muscles. Let them go limp."

Harry looked at the syringe.

Ganderbai took a piece of red rubber tubing from his bag and slid one end under and up and around Harry's biceps; then he tied the tubing tight with a knot. He sponged a small area of the bare forearm with alcohol, handed the swab to me, and took the syringe from my hand. He held it up to the light, squinting at the calibrations,[4] squirting out some of the yellow fluid. I stood still beside him, watching. Harry was watching too and sweating all over his face so it shone like it was smeared thick with face cream melting on his skin and running down onto the pillow.

I could see the blue vein on the inside of Harry's forearm, swollen now because of the tourniquet, and then I saw the needle above the vein, Ganderbai holding the syringe almost flat against the arm, sliding the needle in sideways through the skin into the blue vein, sliding it slowly but so firmly it went in smooth as into cheese. Harry looked at the ceiling and closed his eyes and opened them again but he didn't move.

When it was finished, Ganderbai leaned forward, putting his mouth close to Harry's ear. "Now you'll be all right even if you *are* bitten. But don't move.

---

3. **intravenously** (in′trə•vē′nəs•lē) *adv.*: directly into a vein.
4. **calibrations** (kal′ə•brā′shənz) *n.*: markings on a measuring instrument.

Please don't move. I'll be back in a moment."

He picked up his bag and went out to the hall and I followed.

"Is he safe now?" I asked.

"No."

"How safe is he?"

The little Indian doctor stood there in the hall rubbing his lower lip.

"It must give some protection, mustn't it?" I asked.

He turned away and walked to the screen doors that led onto the veranda. I thought he was going through them, but he stopped this side of the doors and stood looking out into the night.

"Isn't the serum very good?" I asked.

"Unfortunately not," he answered without turning round. "It might save him. It might not. I am trying to think of something else to do." ❺

"Shall we draw the sheet back quick and brush it off before it has time to strike?"

"Never! We are not entitled to take a risk." He spoke sharply and his voice was pitched a little higher than usual.

"We can't very well leave him lying there," I said. "He's getting nervous."

"Please! Please!" he said, turning round, holding both hands up in the air. "Not so fast, please. This is not a matter to rush into baldheaded."[5] He wiped his forehead with his handkerchief and stood there, frowning, nibbling his lip.

"You see," he said at last, "there is a way to do this. You know what we must do—we must administer an anesthetic to the creature where it lies."

It was a splendid idea.

"It is not safe," he continued, "because a snake is coldblooded, and anesthetic does not work so well or so quick with such animals, but it is better than any other thing to do. We could use ether . . . chloroform . . ."[6] He was speaking slowly and trying to think the thing out while he talked.

"Which shall we use?"

"Chloroform," he said suddenly. "Ordinary chloroform. That is best. Now quick!" He took my arm and pulled me toward the balcony. "Drive to my house! By the time you get there, I will have waked up my boy on the telephone and he will show you my poisons cupboard. Here is the key of the cupboard. Take a bottle of chloroform. It has an orange label and the name is printed on it. I'll stay here in case anything happens. Be quick now, hurry! No, no, you don't need your shoes!" ❻

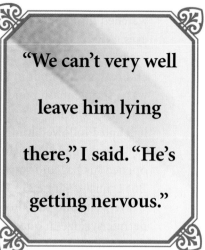

> "We can't very well leave him lying there," I said. "He's getting nervous."

---

5. **baldheaded** *adv.:* without being careful or taking precautions.
6. **ether** (ē′thər) . . . **chloroform** (klôr′ə·fôrm′): anesthetics, substances that cause loss of feeling or consciousness.

I drove fast and in about fifteen minutes I was back with the bottle of chloroform. Ganderbai came out of Harry's room and met me in the hall. "You got it?" he said. "Good, good. I've just been telling him what we are going to do. But now we must hurry. It is not easy for him in there like that all this time. I am afraid he might move."

He went back to the bedroom and I followed, carrying the bottle carefully with both hands. Harry was lying on the bed in precisely the same position as before, with the sweat pouring down his cheeks. His face was white and wet. He turned his eyes toward me, and I smiled at him and nodded confidently. He continued to look at me. I raised my thumb, giving him the okay signal. He closed his eyes. Ganderbai was squatting down by the bed, and on the floor beside him was the hollow rubber tube that he had previously used as a tourniquet, and he'd got a small paper funnel fitted into one end of the tube.

He began to pull a little piece of the sheet out from under the mattress. He was working directly in line with Harry's stomach, about eighteen inches from it, and I watched his fingers as they tugged gently at the edge of the sheet. He worked so slowly it was almost impossible to discern[7] any movement either in his fingers or in the sheet that was being pulled.

Finally he succeeded in making an opening under the sheet and he took the rubber tube and inserted one end of it in the opening so that it would slide under the sheet along the mattress toward Harry's body. I do not know how long it took him to slide that tube in a few inches. It may have been twenty minutes, it may have been forty. I never once saw the tube move. I knew it was going in because the visible part of it grew gradually shorter, but I doubted that the krait could have felt even the faintest vibration. Ganderbai himself was sweating now, large pearls of sweat standing out all over his forehead and along his upper lip. But his hands were steady, and I noticed that his eyes were watching, not the tube in his hands, but the area of crumpled sheet above Harry's stomach.

Without looking up, he held out a hand to me for the chloroform. I twisted out the ground-glass stopper and put the bottle right into his hand, not letting go till I was sure he had a good hold on it. Then he jerked his head for me to come closer, and he whispered, "Tell him I'm going to soak the mattress and that it will be very cold under his body. He must be ready for that and he must not move. Tell him now."

I bent over Harry and passed on the message.

"Why doesn't he get on with it?" Harry said.

"He's going to now, Harry. But it'll feel very cold, so be ready for it."

"Oh, get on!" For the first time he raised his voice, and Ganderbai glanced up sharply, watched him for a few seconds, then went back to his business.

---

7. **discern** (di·zʉrn′) *v.*: see; detect by looking carefully.

**THEME
AND IRONY**

❼ Describe Harry's
attitude toward Dr.
Ganderbai as he
soaks the bed with
chloroform. How
does the doctor
choose to respond?
How might someone
else in the doctor's
position react?

Ganderbai poured a few drops of chloroform into the paper funnel and waited while it ran down the tube. Then he poured some more. Then he waited again, and the heavy, sickening smell of chloroform spread out over the room, bringing with it faint unpleasant memories of white-coated nurses and white surgeons standing in a white room around a long white table. Ganderbai was pouring steadily now, and I could see the heavy vapor of the chloroform swirling slowly like smoke above the paper funnel. He paused, held the bottle up to the light, poured one more funnelful, and handed the bottle back to me. Slowly he drew out the rubber tube from under the sheet; then he stood up.

The strain of inserting the tube and pouring the chloroform must have been great, and I recollect that when Ganderbai turned and whispered to me, his voice was small and tired. "We'll give it fifteen minutes. Just to be safe."

I leaned over to tell Harry. "We're going to give it fifteen minutes, just to be safe. But it's probably done for already."

"Then why don't you look and see!" Again he spoke loudly and Ganderbai sprang round, his small brown face suddenly very angry. He had almost pure black eyes and he stared at Harry, and Harry's smiling muscle started to twitch. I took my handkerchief and wiped his wet face, trying to stroke his forehead a little for comfort as I did so. ❼

Then we stood and waited beside the bed, Ganderbai watching Harry's face all the time in a curious intense manner. The little Indian was concentrating all his willpower on keeping Harry quiet. He never once took his eyes from the patient and although he made no sound, he seemed somehow to be shouting at him all the time, saying: Now listen, you've got to listen, you're not going to go spoiling this now, d'you hear me; and Harry lay there twitching his mouth, sweating, closing his eyes, opening them, looking at me, at the sheet, at the ceiling, at me again, but never at Ganderbai. Yet somehow Ganderbai was holding him. The smell of chloroform was oppressive and it made me feel sick, but I couldn't leave the room now. I had the feeling someone was blowing up a huge balloon and I could see it was going to burst, but I couldn't look away.

At length Ganderbai turned and nodded and I knew he was ready to proceed. "You go over to the other side of the bed," he said. "We will each take one side of the sheet and draw it back together, but very slowly, please, and very quietly."

"Keep still now, Harry," I said, and I went around to the other side of the bed and took hold of the sheet. Ganderbai stood opposite me, and together we began to draw back the sheet, lifting it up clear of Harry's body, taking it back very slowly, both of us standing well away but at the same time bending forward, trying to peer underneath it. The smell of chloroform was awful. I remember trying to hold my breath, and when I couldn't do that any longer, I tried to breathe shallow so the stuff wouldn't get into my lungs.

The whole of Harry's chest was visible now, or rather the striped pajama top which covered it, and then I saw the white cord of his pajama trousers, neatly tied in a bow. A little farther and I saw a button, a mother-of-pearl button, and that was something I had never had on my pajamas, a fly button, let alone a mother-of-pearl one. This Harry, I thought, he is very refined.

It is odd how one sometimes has frivolous[8] thoughts at exciting moments, and I distinctly remember thinking about Harry being very refined when I saw that button.

Apart from the button there was nothing on his stomach.

We pulled the sheet back faster then, and when we had uncovered his legs and feet we let the sheet drop over the end of the bed onto the floor.

"Don't move," Ganderbai said, "don't move, Mr. Pope"; and he began to peer around along the side of Harry's body and under his legs.

"We must be careful," he said. "It may be anywhere. It could be up the leg of his pajamas."

When Ganderbai said this, Harry quickly raised his head from the pillow and looked down at his legs. It was the first time he had moved. Then suddenly he jumped up, stood on his bed, and shook his legs one after the other violently in the air. At that moment we both thought he had been bitten, and Ganderbai was already reaching down into his bag for a scalpel and a tourniquet[9] when Harry ceased his caperings and stood still and looked at the mattress he was standing on and shouted, "It's not there!" ❽

Ganderbai straightened up and for a moment he too looked at the mattress; then he looked up at Harry. Harry was all right. He hadn't been bitten and now he wasn't going to get bitten and he wasn't going to be killed and everything was fine. But that didn't seem to make anyone feel any better.

"Mr. Pope, you are of course *quite* sure you saw it in the first place?" There was a note of sarcasm in Ganderbai's voice that he would never have employed in ordinary circumstances. "You don't think you might possibly have been dreaming, do you, Mr. Pope?" The way Ganderbai was looking at Harry, I realized that the sarcasm was not seriously intended. He was only easing up a bit after the strain.

Harry stood on his bed in his striped pajamas, glaring at Ganderbai, and the color began to spread out over his cheeks.

"Are you telling me I'm a liar?" he shouted.

Ganderbai remained absolutely still, watching Harry. Harry took a pace forward on the bed and there was a shining look in his eyes.

"Why, you dirty little sewer rat!"

"Shut up, Harry!" I said.

"You dirty black——"

---

8. **frivolous** (friv′ə·ləs) *adj.:* silly; not as serious as the occasion requires.
9. **tourniquet** (toor′ni·kit) *n.:* bandage or other device used to put pressure on a blood vessel in order to stop the flow of blood.

IRONY AND AMBIGUITY

❽ What did you expect would happen when Dr. Ganderbai and the narrator pulled the sheet back? Were you surprised by the **ironic** turn of events?

THEME

❾ Think about what
Dr. Ganderbai and
the narrator choose
to say and not to
say at the end of
the story. How does
each man react to
Harry's outburst?

"Harry!" I called. "Shut up, Harry!" It was terrible, the things he was saying.

Ganderbai went out of the room as though neither of us was there, and I followed him and put my arm around his shoulder as he walked across the hall and out onto the balcony.

"Don't you listen to Harry," I said. "This thing's made him so he doesn't know what he's saying."

We went down the steps from the balcony to the drive and across the drive in the darkness to where his old Morris car was parked. He opened the door and got in.

"You did a wonderful job," I said. "Thank you so very much for coming."

"All he needs is a good holiday," he said quietly, without looking at me; then he started the engine and drove off. ❾

Meet the Writer
Roald Dahl

"Children Love to Be Spooked"

The British writer Roald Dahl (1916–1990) has the unusual distinction of being famous as the author of works for both adults and children. Among his best-known children's books are *James and the Giant Peach* and *Charlie and the Chocolate Factory*, both of which have been made into movies. In most of Dahl's fiction for children, the young heroes win over fearsome enemies. Responding to criticism of the violence in his children's books, Dahl said:

❝ Children love to be spooked. . . . They like a touch of the macabre as long as it's funny too. . . . And my nastiness is never gratuitous. It's retribution. Beastly people must be punished. ❞

Readers of Dahl's autobiography *Boy* understand his concern about "beastly people." During the years he spent attending British boarding schools, Dahl endured harsh discipline, including beatings, by cruel headmasters.

Like "Poison," most of Dahl's other short stories place ordinary characters in believable but bizarre situations. Many of his stories have surprise endings, some of them shockers. For another shocker, turn to "Beware of the Dog" in Collection 9.

For Independent Reading

If you'd like to read more by Dahl, check out such stories as "Dip in the Pool" in *The Best of Roald Dahl.*

After You Read

Response and Analysis

Reading Check

1. What plan does Dr. Ganderbai finally put into action to save Harry from the krait? What is the outcome of the plan?

Thinking Critically

2. Noticing Harry's mother-of-pearl button, the narrator thinks to himself that Harry "is very refined." Why is his view of Harry **ironic**?

3. Re-read the Background, which appears before the story, and then think about the importance of the story's time frame. How does the historical context help explain Harry's attitude toward Dr. Ganderbai?

4. By the end of the story, you might suspect that the **title** refers to more than the venom of the krait. What other kind of poison is the story about? (Think in particular about how Harry reacts to Dr. Ganderbai at the end of the story.)

5. Look back at the cluster diagram you made for your Quickwrite. Then, think about how the collection theme "Hard Choices" relates to the story. What choices do the narrator and Dr. Ganderbai make in the story? Why? What is your opinion of the way each chooses to act and respond?

Extending and Evaluating

6. The ending of the story is both **ironic** and **ambiguous.** Do you think there really was a krait under the sheet, or did Harry imagine that the snake was there? What evidence can you find in the text to support each conclusion? State whether you think one interpretation is stronger than the other, and explain why.

Seven-headed snake (1117 C.E.). Procession piece from the Chennakeshawa Temple in Belur, Karnataka (Mysore), India.

Exploring the Theme
Hard Choices

In the rest of this collection, you'll read about the hard choices characters and people have to make. As you read, think about the reasons for their choices. How might others, with different personalities, values, or ambitions, have chosen to act in the same situations?

SKILLS FOCUS

Literary Focus
Analyze irony and ambiguity.

Before You Read

The Gift of the Magi

Make the Connection
Quickwrite ✏️

If you could save just one item from a disaster—a fire, a flood, an earthquake—what would it be? In a few sentences, describe your most cherished possession, and tell why you treasure it. Was it a gift? If so, how does that make it especially important to you?

Literary Focus
Situational Irony: Not What We Expect

Often when we read a story, we think one thing will happen only to be surprised when something entirely different takes place. This is an example of **situational irony,** which reminds us that chance, or the unexpected, often has the last word.

    O. Henry, who wrote "The Gift of the Magi," specialized in a particular type of ironic situation: the **surprise ending.** Whether O. Henry's endings are happy or sad, they are always emotionally satisfying.

Literary Skills
Understand situational irony and the surprise ending.

Reading Skills 📖
Making Predictions: What Will Happen Next?

Why do we read? One reason is that we are curious. At the start of a story, a writer sets up a situation that raises a lot of questions. We read on because we want to know what happens.

    Read the first paragraph of this story, and then write down a **prediction.** What do you think will happen next? Stop at least twice more, and write down your predictions. As you do this, ask yourself

Reading Skills
Make predictions.

INTERNET

Vocabulary Practice
•
More About O. Henry
•
Keyword: LE7 9-5

these questions: "Is the writer keeping me in suspense? Is he succeeding in surprising me?" Keep your notes.

Background

The Magi referred to in the title of this story are the three "wise men" who, according to the Bible (Matthew 2:1–13), brought gifts of frankincense and myrrh (substances prized for their fragrance) as well as gold to the infant Jesus. Traditionally the Magi's gifts are regarded as the first Christmas presents.

Vocabulary Development

instigates (in′stə·gāts′) v.: urges on to some action, usually negative, or sets something in motion; here, gives rise to.

agile (aj′əl) adj.: moving with ease.

depreciate (dē·prē′shē·āt′) v.: make something seem less important; lower the value of.

cascade (kas·kād′) n.: waterfall.

ransacking (ran′sak′iŋ) v.: searching thoroughly.

discreet (di·skrēt′) adj.: showing good judgment in what one says or does; especially being silent or careful.

scrutiny (skrōōt″n·ē) n.: close inspection.

nimble (nim′bəl) adj.: quickly moving.

coveted (kuv′it·id) v. used as adj.: longed-for.

singed (sinjd) v. used as adj.: slightly burned.

The Gift of the Magi

O. Henry

The Magi, as you know, were wise men . . .

Hairdresser's Window (1907) by John Sloan. Oil on canvas.

One dollar and eighty-seven cents. That was all. And sixty cents of it was in pennies. Pennies saved one and two at a time by bull-dozing the grocer and the vegetable man and the butcher until one's cheeks burned with the silent imputation of parsimony[1] that such close dealing implied. Three times Della counted it. One dollar and eighty-seven cents. And the next day would be Christmas.

There was clearly nothing to do but flop down on the shabby little couch and howl. So Della did it. Which instigates the moral reflection that life is made up of sobs, sniffles, and smiles, with sniffles predominating.

While the mistress of the home is gradually subsiding from the first stage to the second, take a look at the home. A furnished flat[2] at $8 per week. It did not exactly beggar description, but it certainly had that word on the lookout for the mendicancy squad.[3]

In the vestibule[4] below was a letter box into which no letter would go, and an electric button from which no mortal finger could coax a ring. Also appertaining[5] thereunto was a card bearing the name "Mr. James Dillingham Young."

The "Dillingham" had been flung to the breeze during a former period of prosperity when its possessor was being paid $30 per week. Now, when the income was shrunk to $20, the letters of "Dillingham" looked blurred, as though they were thinking seriously of contracting to a modest and unassuming D. But whenever Mr. James Dillingham Young came home and reached his flat above, he was called Jim and greatly hugged by Mrs. James Dillingham Young, already introduced to you as Della. Which is all very good.

Della finished her cry and attended to her cheeks with the powder rag. She stood by the window and looked out dully at a gray cat walking a gray fence in a gray back yard. Tomorrow would be Christmas Day and she had only $1.87 with which to buy Jim a present. She had been saving every penny she could for months, with this result. Twenty dollars a week doesn't go far. Expenses had been greater than she had calculated. They always are. Only $1.87 to buy a present for Jim. Her Jim. Many a happy hour she had spent planning for something nice for him. Something fine and rare and sterling—something just a little bit near to being worthy of the honor of being owned by Jim.

There was a pier glass[6] between the windows of the room. Perhaps you have seen a pier glass in an $8 flat. A very thin and very agile person may, by observing his reflection in a rapid sequence of longitudinal strips, obtain a fairly accurate conception of his looks. Della, being slender, had mastered the art.

Suddenly she whirled from the window and stood before the glass. Her eyes were shining brilliantly, but her face had lost its color within twenty seconds. Rapidly she pulled down her hair and let it fall to its full length.

Now, there were two possessions of the James Dillingham Youngs in which they both took a mighty pride. One was Jim's gold watch that had been his father's and his grandfather's. The other was Della's hair. Had the Queen of Sheba lived in the flat across the air shaft,[7] Della would have let her hair hang out the window some day to dry just to

---

1. **imputation** (im′pyo͞o·tā′shən) **of parsimony** (pär′sə·mō′nē): suggestion of stinginess.
2. **flat** *n.:* apartment.
3. **mendicancy** (men′di·kən·sē) **squad:** police who arrested beggars and homeless people.
4. **vestibule** (ves′tə·byo͞ol′) *n.:* small entrance hall.
5. **appertaining** (ap′ər·tān′iŋ) *v.* used as *adj.:* belonging.

6. **pier glass** *n.:* tall mirror hung between two windows.
7. **air shaft** *n.:* narrow gap between two buildings.

Vocabulary

instigates (in′stə·gāts′) *v.:* urges on to some action, usually negative, or sets something in motion; here, gives rise to.

agile (aj′əl) *adj.:* moving with ease.

Horse-Drawn Cabs, New York (1891) by Frederick Childe Hassam. Oil pastel on canvas.

depreciate Her Majesty's jewels and gifts. Had King Solomon been the janitor, with all his treasures piled up in the basement, Jim would have pulled out his watch every time he passed, just to see him pluck at his beard from envy.

So now Della's beautiful hair fell about her rippling and shining like a cascade of brown waters. It reached below her knee and made itself almost a garment for her. And then she did it up again nervously and quickly. Once she faltered for a minute and stood still while a tear or two splashed on the worn red carpet.

On went her old brown jacket; on went her old brown hat. With a whirl of skirts and with the brilliant sparkle still in her eyes, she fluttered out the door and down the stairs to the street.

Where she stopped, the sign read: "Mme. Sofronie. Hair Goods of All Kinds." One flight up Della ran, and collected herself, panting. Madame, large, too white, chilly, hardly looked the "Sofronie."

"Will you buy my hair?" asked Della.

"I buy hair," said Madame. "Take yer hat off and let's have a sight at the looks of it."

Down rippled the brown cascade.

"Twenty dollars," said Madame, lifting the mass with a practiced hand.

"Give it to me quick," said Della.

Vocabulary

depreciate (dē·prē′shē·āt′) *v.*: make something seem less important; lower the value of.

cascade (kas·kād′) *n.*: waterfall.

Oh, and the next two hours tripped by on rosy wings. Forget the hashed metaphor. She was <u>ransacking</u> the stores for Jim's present.

She found it at last. It surely had been made for Jim and no one else. There was no other like it in any of the stores, and she had turned all of them inside out. It was a platinum fob chain,[8] simple and chaste in design, properly proclaiming its value by substance alone and not by meretricious[9] ornamentation—as all good things should do. It was even worthy of The Watch. As soon as she saw it she knew that it must be Jim's. It was like him. Quietness and value—the description applied to both. Twenty-one dollars they took from her for it, and she hurried home with the 87 cents. With that chain on his watch, Jim might be properly anxious about the time in any company. Grand as the watch was, he sometimes looked at it on the sly on account of the old leather strap that he used in place of a chain.

When Della reached home, her intoxication gave way a little to prudence and reason. She got out her curling irons and lighted the gas and went to work repairing the ravages[10] made by generosity added to love. Which is always a tremendous task, dear friends—a mammoth task.

Within forty minutes her head was covered with tiny, close-lying curls that made her look wonderfully like a truant schoolboy. She looked at her reflection in the mirror long, carefully, and critically.

"If Jim doesn't kill me," she said to herself, "before he takes a second look at me, he'll say I look like a Coney Island chorus girl. But what could I do—oh! what could I do with a dollar and eighty-seven cents?"

At 7 o'clock the coffee was made and the frying pan was on the back of the stove hot and ready to cook the chops.

Jim was never late. Della doubled the fob chain in her hand and sat on the corner of the table near the door that he always entered. Then she heard his step on the stair away down on the first flight, and she turned white for just a moment. She had a habit of saying little silent prayers about the simplest everyday things, and now she whispered: "Please God, make him think I am still pretty."

The door opened and Jim stepped in and closed it. He looked thin and very serious. Poor fellow, he was only twenty-two—and to be burdened with a family! He needed a new overcoat and he was without gloves.

Jim stepped inside the door, as immovable as a setter at the scent of quail. His eyes were fixed upon Della, and there was an expression in them that she could not read, and it terrified her. It was not anger, nor surprise, nor disapproval, nor horror, nor any of the sentiments that she had been prepared for. He simply stared at her fixedly with that peculiar expression on his face.

Della wriggled off the table and went for him.

"Jim, darling," she cried, "don't look at me that way. I had my hair cut off and sold it because I couldn't have lived through Christmas without giving you a present. It'll grow out again—you won't mind, will you? I just had to do it. My hair grows awfully fast. Say 'Merry Christmas!' Jim, and let's be happy. You don't know what a nice—what a beautiful, nice gift I've got for you."

"You've cut off your hair?" asked Jim, laboriously, as if he had not arrived at that patent[11] fact yet even after the hardest mental labor.

"Cut it off and sold it," said Della. "Don't you like me just as well, anyhow? I'm me without my hair, ain't I?"

Jim looked about the room curiously.

---

8. **fob chain:** short chain meant to be attached to a pocket watch.
9. **meretricious** (mer′ə·trish′əs) *adj.:* attractive in a cheap, flashy way.
10. **ravages** (rav′ij·iz) *n.:* terrible damage.

---

11. **patent** (pāt′′nt) *adj.:* obvious.

Vocabulary
ransacking (ran′sak′iŋ) *v.:* searching thoroughly.

The Closed Shutters by Elizabeth Nourse (c. 1860–1938). Oil on canvas.

Musée d'Orsay/Art Resource, New York.

"You say your hair is gone?" he said, with an air almost of idiocy.

"You needn't look for it," said Della. "It's sold, I tell you—sold and gone, too. It's Christmas Eve, boy. Be good to me, for it went for you. Maybe the hairs on my head were numbered," she went on with a sudden serious sweetness, "but nobody could ever count my love for you. Shall I put the chops on, Jim?"

Out of his trance Jim seemed quickly to wake. He enfolded his Della. For ten seconds let us regard with discreet scrutiny some inconsequential object in the other direction. Eight dollars a week or a million a year—what is the difference? A mathematician or a wit would give you the wrong answer. The Magi brought valuable gifts, but that was not among them. This dark assertion will be illuminated later on.

Jim drew a package from his overcoat pocket and threw it upon the table.

"Don't make any mistake, Dell," he said, "about me. I don't think there's anything in the way of a haircut or a shave or a shampoo that could make me like my girl any less. But if you'll unwrap that package, you may see why you had me going awhile at first."

White fingers and nimble tore at the string and paper. And then an ecstatic scream of joy; and then, alas! a quick feminine change to hysterical tears and wails, necessitating the immediate employment of all the comforting powers of the lord of the flat.

For there lay The Combs—the set of combs, side and back, that Della had worshiped for long in a Broadway window. Beautiful combs, pure tortoise shell, with jeweled rims—just the shade to wear in the beautiful vanished hair. They were expensive combs, she knew, and her heart had simply craved and yearned over them without the least hope of possession. And now, they were hers, but the tresses that should have adorned the coveted adornments were gone.

But she hugged them to her bosom, and at length she was able to look up with dim eyes and a smile and say: "My hair grows so fast, Jim!"

And then Della leaped up like a little singed cat and cried, "Oh, oh!"

Jim had not yet seen his beautiful present. She held it out to him eagerly upon her open palm. The dull precious metal seemed to flash with a reflection of her bright and ardent spirit.

"Isn't it a dandy, Jim? I hunted all over town to find it. You'll have to look at the time a hundred times a day now. Give me your watch. I want to see how it looks on it."

Instead of obeying, Jim tumbled down on the couch and put his hands under the back of his head and smiled.

"Dell," said he, "let's put our Christmas presents away and keep 'em a while. They're too nice to use just at present. I sold the watch to get the money to buy your combs. And now suppose you put the chops on."

The Magi, as you know, were wise men—wonderfully wise men—who brought gifts to the Babe in the manger. They invented the art of giving Christmas presents. Being wise, their gifts were no doubt wise ones, possibly bearing the privilege of exchange in case of duplication. And here I have lamely related to you the uneventful chronicle of two foolish children in a flat who most unwisely sacrificed for each other the greatest treasures of their house. But in a last word to the wise of these days, let it be said that of all who give gifts, these two were the wisest. Of all who give and receive gifts, such as they are wisest. Everywhere they are wisest. They are the Magi. ■

Vocabulary

discreet (di·skrēt′) *adj.*: showing good judgment in what one says or does; especially being silent or careful.

scrutiny (skroot′n·ē) *n.*: close inspection.

nimble (nim′bəl) *adj.*: quickly moving.

coveted (kuv′it·id) *v.* used as *adj.*: longed-for.

singed (sinjd) *v.* used as *adj.*: slightly burned.

Meet the Writer

O. Henry

He ♥ New York

O. Henry (1862–1910), whose real name was William Sydney Porter, grew up in Greensboro, North Carolina. At the age of twenty, he went to Texas, where he became a rancher, worked as a bank teller, and founded a humorous weekly called *The Rolling Stone*.

When he was accused of stealing a thousand dollars from the First National Bank of Austin, where he was a teller, Porter panicked and fled to Central America. In Honduras he traveled with the outlawed Jennings brothers and helped them spend the loot from a recent robbery. When news of his wife's illness brought him back to Austin, he was arrested, tried, and sentenced to five years in prison. Ironically, if he had not run away, Porter might have been acquitted. The bank was poorly run, and the loss of money might have been a case of mismanagement, not a crime.

Porter served only three years of his sentence. In prison he wrote more than a dozen stories and absorbed the underworld lore that he would use in stories such as "A Retrieved Reformation." He also may have found his pen name there: One of the prison guards was named Orrin Henry.

Porter left prison in 1901 and went to New York. He loved the city at once, and he wrote about it and its inhabitants for the few years remaining in his life. He once remarked:

" There are stories in everything. I've got some of my best yarns from park benches, lampposts, and newspaper stands. "

O. Henry wrote more than six hundred stories altogether—sixty-five in 1904 alone. A heavy drinker, he died of tuberculosis when he was only forty-seven. His last words were "Pull up the shades so I can see New York. I don't want to go home in the dark."

For Independent Reading

Want to read more O. Henry stories with surprising twists? Try "The Ransom of Red Chief," in which O. Henry paints a comical picture of two kidnappers who get much more than they bargain for. In "A Retrieved Reformation" an expert burglar has an unexpected change of heart.

This poem is about the love of an elderly couple—los ancianos in Spanish. As you read, consider why the poet chose these Spanish words for her title rather than their English equivalent.

Los Ancianos

Pat Mora

They hold hands
as they walk with slow steps.
Careful together they cross the plaza
both slightly stooped, bodies returning to the land,
5   he in faded khaki° and straw hat,
she wrapped in soft clothes, black
rebozo° round her head and shoulders.

Tourists in halter tops and shorts
pose by flame trees and fountains,
10   but the old couple walks step by step
on the edge.
Even in the heat, only their wrinkled
hands and faces show. They know
of moving through a crowd at their own pace.

15   I watch him help her
off the curb and I smell love
like dried flowers, old love
of holding hands with one man for fifty years.

---

5. khaki (kak′ē) *n.:* tan-colored clothing.
7. *rebozo* (re·bô′thô): Spanish for "shawl."

Reading Check

1. Suppose you are telling the story of Della and Jim to a group of your friends. Identify the two **characters,** tell what each one **wants** to do, and summarize the **main events** and the **outcome** of their story.

2. What **predictions** did you make as you read the story? Did your predictions come close to what actually happens? Check your reading notes.

Thinking Critically

3. An **ironic situation** is one that turns out to be just the opposite of what we—or the characters in the story—expect. Describe the **situational irony** in this story. What lesson about life and love do you think it teaches Della and Jim?

4. What is the real "gift" referred to in the **title**? (Notice that O. Henry uses the word *gift,* not *gifts.*)

5. A **contradiction** occurs when two statements or situations have opposite meanings. In the last paragraph of the story, the narrator first describes Della and Jim as "foolish children" who "unwisely sacrificed" their treasures for each other. The narrator then says they are "the wisest" of all who give and receive gifts. How can you explain the contradiction in the narrator's description of the characters?

6. What do you think this story, written a century ago, has to say about our consumer society today? Do you think some people equate love with money? Consider advertising, the amount of money we spend on gifts, and the value placed on having many possessions.

7. In the poem "Los Ancianos" (see the **Connection** on page 356), the elderly Hispanic couple, dressed in old clothing and walking slowly, seems to represent traditional values. In contrast, the tourists in halter tops posing for cameras seem to represent a more modern, materialistic world. What point might the poet be making by this **contrast**? Do you see any similarity between the poet's point and Della and Jim's situation? Explain.

Extending and Evaluating

8. Della's and Jim's hard choices result in O. Henry's **surprise ending.** What is your reaction to this ending? Do you enjoy this kind of **irony** in stories or movies, or does it seem contrived—a trick played on the reader? Explain your response.

WRITING

Life Goes On

The glimpse O. Henry gives us of Della and Jim is of just one brief time in their lives, early in their marriage. Provide readers with a glimpse of Della and Jim ten years later. In what ways has each character changed or stayed the same? What is each one doing? Where do they live? Write a paragraph about Della and Jim called "Life Goes On." When they are old, will they be like the couple in "Los Ancianos" (see the **Connection** on page 356)?

What It Means to Me

Imagine that you are writing a **letter** to your grandchild, telling him or her the story of a cherished possession. Explain how you got it and why it's so important to me. (Be sure to check your Quickwrite notes.)

SKILLS FOCUS

Literary Skills
Analyze situational irony and the surprise ending.

Reading Skills
Make predictions.

Writing Skills
Write a character description.
Write a letter.

go. hrw .com

INTERNET
Projects and Activities
Keyword: LE7 9-5

In Your Own Words

PRACTICE 1

How well do you understand the meaning of the Word Bank words? Try answering the following questions:

1. If a criminal <u>instigates</u> a plan to rob a bank, what does he do?

2. What might an <u>agile</u> person do on monkey bars?

3. What would <u>depreciate</u> the value of a car?

4. What would happen to a small boat that sailed into a <u>cascade</u>?

5. When might you find yourself <u>ransacking</u> your memory?

6. What does a <u>discreet</u> person do when told a secret?

7. What would a <u>scrutiny</u> of your room reveal about you?

8. When might it be particularly helpful to be <u>nimble</u>?

9. Describe something you once <u>coveted</u>.

10. If you <u>singed</u> your shirt when ironing it, what would you do with it?

Word Bank

instigates
agile
depreciate
cascade
ransacking
discreet
scrutiny
nimble
coveted
singed

Diction—Ornate or Plain?

Diction, or word choice, can make a great difference in a piece of writing. A realistic writer might use slang. A science reporter might use precise, technical language. A romantic person might want to be poetic.

O. Henry loved flowery and ornate diction. In the first paragraph he writes:

> "One's cheeks burned with the silent imputation of parsimony that such close dealing implied."

A writer who preferred a plain style might have said:

> You'd blush to think that bargaining suggested you were stingy.

PRACTICE 2

Find three ornate sentences in the story, and rewrite each of them using plain, straightforward diction, as if you were modernizing the story for today's readers. Compare your rewritten versions in class.

Writers' Tip: William Strunk, Jr., and E. B. White, the authors of a famous writing handbook called *The Elements of Style,* tell writers never to use a twenty-dollar word when a ten-cent word will do just as well. As you work on your writing, think about your **diction.** Consider the diction that is most appropriate for your characters, your setting, and your tone. Can a strong, simple word work as well as a fancy one?

SKILLS FOCUS

Vocabulary Skills
Demonstrate word knowledge. Understand diction.

PEANUTS® reprinted by permission of UFS, Inc.

The Lady, or the Tiger?

Make the Connection

Quickwrite ✏️

Did you ever have to make a choice between something that was good for you and something that was good for someone you cared about? Are you glad that you chose as you did? Jot down your thoughts about making this choice.

Literary Focus

Ambiguity: Mixed Signals

Ambiguity is a quality that allows something to be interpreted in several different —sometimes even conflicting—ways. Ambiguity adds complexity to a story. It can make fiction seem more like real life, where we often encounter people and events that are puzzling or mysterious.

An ambiguous story can linger in your mind for days or years. You might return to the story again and again, answering its questions differently each time. Ambiguity made "The Lady, or the Tiger?" an instant hit, and it has kept people trying to answer one simple—or not so simple—question for more than a century.

Reading Skills

Making Inferences About Motivation: The *Whys* and *Wherefores*

When you make an **inference** about a character's **motivation,** you make an educated guess about the character's reasons for behaving in a certain way. You base this guess on what the narrator tells you as well as on clues (such as what a character says or does) that the writer has planted in the text.

As you read "The Lady, or the Tiger?" think about the motivation of the characters—in particular, that of the king's daughter. The questions at the open-book signs will help you make inferences.

Background

During the Middle Ages an accused person's guilt or innocence was often determined by a trial by ordeal. If the person was not hurt during a physical test, it was believed the accused was saved from harm by God and was therefore innocent. Those who were injured or killed were viewed as guilty. In this story, justice is determined in a similar way.

Vocabulary Development

exuberant (eg·zōō′bər·ənt) *adj.*: elaborate; extreme; also, high-spirited.

genial (jēn′yəl) *adj.*: cheerful and friendly.

impartial (im·pär′shəl) *adj.*: fair; unbiased.

allegiance (ə·lē′jəns) *n.*: loyalty.

procured (prō·kyoord′) *v.*: gotten; obtained.

dire (dīr) *adj.*: terrible.

retribution (re′trə·byōō′shən) *n.*: punishment.

fervent (fur′vənt) *adj.*: passionate.

aspiring (ə·spīr′iŋ) *v.* used as *n.*: seeking to gain; desiring.

deliberation (di·lib′ər·ā′shən) *n.*: careful thought, especially in making a decision.

SKILLS FOCUS

Literary Skills
Understand ambiguity.

Reading Skills
Make inferences about character motivation.

go.hrw.com

INTERNET

Vocabulary Practice

Keyword: LE7 9-5

THE LADY, OR THE TIGER?

Frank R. Stockton

Proserpine (1874) by Dante Gabriel Rossetti.
Oil on canvas (125.1 cm × 61 cm).

In the very olden time, there lived a semibarbaric[1] king, whose ideas, though somewhat polished and sharpened by the progressiveness of distant Latin neighbors, were still large, florid, and untrammeled,[2] as became the half of him which was barbaric. He was a man of <u>exuberant</u> fancy, and, withal,[3] of an authority so irresistible that, at his will, he turned his varied fancies into facts. He was greatly given to self-communing; and, when he and himself agreed upon any thing, the thing was done. When every member of his domestic and political systems moved smoothly in its appointed course, his nature was bland and <u>genial</u>; but whenever there was a little hitch, and some of his orbs got out of their orbits, he was blander and more genial still, for nothing pleased him so much as to make the crooked straight, and crush down uneven places.

Among the borrowed notions by which his barbarism had become semified[4] was that of the public arena, in which, by exhibitions of manly and beastly valor, the minds of his subjects were refined and cultured.

1. **semibarbaric** (sem′ī·bär·ber′ik) *adj.:* partly uncivilized.
2. **untrammeled** (un·tram′əld) *adj.:* not restrained or kept under control.
3. **withal** (with·ôl′) *adv.:* in addition.
4. **semified:** probably an invented word suggesting "reduced in half."

Vocabulary

exuberant (eg·zōō′bər·ənt) *adj.:* elaborate; extreme; also, high-spirited.

genial (jēn′yəl) *adj.:* cheerful and friendly.

Stalking Tiger by Rosa Bonheur (1822–1899). Oil on wood.

But even here the exuberant and barbaric fancy asserted itself. The arena of the king was built, not to give the people an opportunity of hearing the rhapsodies of dying gladiators, nor to enable them to view the inevitable conclusion of a conflict between religious opinions and hungry jaws, but for purposes far better adapted to widen and develop the mental energies of the people. This vast amphitheater,[5] with its encircling galleries, its mysterious vaults, and its unseen passages, was an agent of poetic justice, in which crime was punished, or virtue rewarded, by the decrees of an impartial and incorruptible chance.

When a subject was accused of a crime of sufficient importance to interest the king, public notice was given that on an appointed day the fate of the accused person would be decided in the king's arena—a structure which well deserved its name; for, although its form and plan were borrowed from afar, its purpose emanated solely from the brain of this man, who, every barleycorn a king,[6] knew no tradition to which he owed more allegiance than pleased his fancy, and who ingrafted on every adopted form of human thought and action the rich growth of his barbaric idealism.

When all the people had assembled in the galleries, and the king, surrounded by his court, sat high up on his throne of royal state on one side of the arena, he gave a signal, a door beneath him opened, and the accused subject stepped out into the amphitheater. Directly opposite him, on the other side of the enclosed space, were two doors, exactly alike and side by side. It was the duty and the privilege of the person on trial to walk directly to these doors and open one of them. He could open either door he pleased: He was subject to no guidance or influence but that of the aforementioned impartial and incorruptible chance. If he opened the one, there came out of it a hungry tiger, the fiercest and most cruel that could be procured, which immediately sprang upon him, and tore him to pieces, as a punishment for his guilt. The

---

5. **amphitheater** (am′fə·thē′ə·tər) *n.*: round building with an open space surrounded by rows of seats.
6. **every barleycorn a king:** every bit of him a king; a barleycorn is a small unit of measure used in earlier times.

Vocabulary
impartial (im·pär′shəl) *adj.*: fair; unbiased.
allegiance (ə·lē′jəns) *n.*: loyalty.
procured (prō·kyoord′) *v.*: gotten; obtained.

moment that the case of the criminal was thus decided, doleful iron bells were clanged, great wails went up from the hired mourners posted on the outer rim of the arena, and the vast audience, with bowed heads and downcast hearts, wended slowly their homeward way, mourning greatly that one so young and fair, or so old and respected, should have merited so <u>dire</u> a fate.

But, if the accused person opened the other door, there came forth from it a lady, the most suitable to his years and station that his majesty could select among his fair subjects; and to this lady he was immediately married, as a reward of his innocence. It mattered not that he might already possess a wife and family, or that his affections might be engaged upon an object of his own selection: The king allowed no such subordinate arrangements to interfere with his great scheme of <u>retribution</u> and reward. The exercises, as in the other instance, took place immediately, and in the arena. Another door opened beneath the king, and a priest, followed by a band of choristers, and dancing maidens blowing joyous airs on golden horns and treading an epithalamic measure,[7] advanced to where the pair stood, side by side; and the wedding was promptly and cheerily solemnized. Then the gay brass bells rang forth their merry peals, the people shouted glad hurrahs, and the innocent man, preceded by children strewing flowers on his path, led his bride to his home.

This was the king's semibarbaric method of administering justice. Its perfect fairness is obvious. The criminal could not know out of which

THERE WAS
NO ESCAPE
FROM THE
JUDGMENTS
OF THE
KING'S ARENA.

door would come the lady: He opened either he pleased, without having the slightest idea whether, in the next instant, he was to be devoured or married. On some occasions the tiger came out of one door, and on some out of the other. The decisions of this tribunal[8] were not only fair, they were positively determinate:[9] The accused person was instantly punished if he found himself guilty; and, if innocent, he was rewarded on the spot, whether he liked it or not. There was no escape from the judgments of the king's arena.

The institution was a very popular one. When the people gathered together on one of the great trial days, they never knew whether they were to witness a bloody slaughter or a hilarious wedding. This element of uncertainty lent an interest to the occasion which it could not otherwise have attained. Thus, the masses were entertained and pleased, and the thinking part of the community could bring no charge of unfairness against this plan; for did not the accused person have the whole matter in his own hands?

This semibarbaric king had a daughter as blooming as his most florid fancies, and with a soul as <u>fervent</u> and imperious[10] as his own. As is

---

8. **tribunal** (trī·byoo′nəl) *n.*: court of justice.
9. **determinate** (dē·tur′mi·nit) *adj.*: final; definite.
10. **imperious** (im·pir′ē·əs) *adj.*: arrogant; self-important.

Vocabulary

dire (dīr) *adj.*: terrible.

retribution (re′trə·byoo′shən) *n.*: punishment.

fervent (fur′vənt) *adj.*: passionate.

---

7. **treading an epithalamic measure:** performing a wedding dance.

usual in such cases, she was the apple of his eye, and was loved by him above all humanity. Among his courtiers was a young man of that fineness of blood and lowness of station common to the conventional heroes of romance who love royal maidens. This royal maiden was well satisfied with her lover, for he was handsome and brave to a degree unsurpassed in all this kingdom; and she loved him with an ardor that had enough of barbarism in it to make it exceedingly warm and strong. This love affair moved on happily for many months, until one day the king happened to discover its existence. He did not hesitate nor waver in regard to his duty in the premises. The youth was immediately cast into prison, and a day was appointed for his trial in the king's arena. This, of course, was an especially important occasion; and his majesty, as well as all the people, was greatly interested in the workings and development of this trial. Never before had such a case occurred; never before had a subject dared to love the daughter of a king. In after-years such things became commonplace enough; but then they were, in no slight degree, novel and startling.

INFERRING CHARACTER MOTIVATION

2. Why doesn't the king approve of the youth's love for his daughter?

The tiger cages of the kingdom were searched for the most savage and relentless beasts, from which the fiercest monster might be selected for the arena; and the ranks of maiden youth and beauty throughout the land were carefully surveyed by competent judges, in order that the young man might have a fitting bride in case fate did not determine for him a different destiny. Of course, everybody knew that the deed with which the accused was charged had been done. He had loved the princess, and neither he, she, nor anyone else thought of denying the fact; but the king would not think of allowing any fact of this kind to interfere with the workings of the

tribunal, in which he took such great delight and satisfaction. No matter how the affair turned out, the youth would be disposed of; and the king would take an aesthetic[11] pleasure in watching the course of events, which would determine whether or not the young man had done wrong in allowing himself to love the princess.

The appointed day arrived. From far and near the people gathered, and thronged the great galleries of the arena; and crowds, unable to gain admittance, massed themselves against its outside walls. The king and his court were in their places, opposite the twin doors—those fateful portals, so terrible in their similarity.

All was ready. The signal was given. A door beneath the royal party opened, and the lover of the princess walked into the arena. Tall, beautiful, fair, his appearance was greeted with a low hum of admiration and anxiety. Half the audience had not known so grand a youth had lived among them. No wonder the princess loved him! What a terrible thing for him to be there!

As the youth advanced into the arena, he turned, as the custom was, to bow to the king: But he did not think at all of that royal personage; his eyes were fixed upon the princess, who sat to the right of her father. Had it not been for the moiety[12] of barbarism in her nature, it is probable that lady would not have been there; but her intense and fervid soul would not allow her to be absent on an occasion in which she was so terribly interested. From the moment that the decree had gone forth, that her lover should decide his fate in the king's arena, she had thought of nothing, night or day, but this great event and the various subjects connected with it. Possessed of more power, influence, and force of character than anyone who had ever before been interested in such a case, she had done what no other person had done—she had

---

11. **aesthetic** (es·thet′ik) *adj.:* relating to an appreciation for beauty.
12. **moiety** (moi′ə·tē) *n.:* half part.

possessed herself of the secret of the doors. She knew in which of the two rooms, that lay behind those doors, stood the cage of the tiger, with its open front, and in which waited the lady. Through these thick doors, heavily curtained with skins on the inside, it was impossible that any noise or suggestion should come from within to the person who should approach to raise the latch of one of them; but gold, and the power of a woman's will, had brought the secret to the princess.

INFERRING CHARACTER MOTIVATION

3. Why would the princess's barbaric half draw her to the arena, where her lover might be killed? Why would she be **motivated** to learn the secret of the doors?

And not only did she know in which room stood the lady ready to emerge, all blushing and radiant, should her door be opened, but she knew who the lady was. It was one of the fairest and loveliest of the damsels of the court who had been selected as the reward of the accused youth, should he be proved innocent of the crime of aspiring to one so far above him; and the princess hated her. Often had she seen, or imagined that she had seen, this fair creature throwing glances of admiration upon the person of her lover, and sometimes she thought these glances were perceived and even returned. Now and then she had seen them talking together; it was but for a moment or two, but much can be said in a brief space; it may have been on most unimportant topics, but how could she know that? The girl was lovely, but she had dared to raise her eyes to the loved one of the princess; and, with all the intensity of the savage blood transmitted to her through long lines of wholly barbaric ancestors, she hated the woman who blushed and trembled behind that silent door.

When her lover turned and looked at her, and his eye met hers as she sat there paler and whiter than anyone in the vast ocean of anxious faces about her, he saw, by that power of quick perception which is given to those whose souls are one, that she knew behind which door crouched the tiger, and behind which stood the lady. He had expected her to know it. He understood her nature, and his soul was assured that she would never rest until she had made plain to herself this thing, hidden to all other lookers-on, even to the king. The only hope for the youth in which there was any element of certainty was based upon the success of the princess in discovering this mystery; and the moment he looked upon her, he saw she had succeeded, as in his soul he knew she would succeed.

Then it was that his quick and anxious glance asked the question: "Which?" It was as plain to her as if he shouted it from where he stood. There was not an instant to be lost. The question was asked in a flash; it must be answered in another.

Her right arm lay on the cushioned parapet before her. She raised her hand, and made a slight, quick movement toward the right. No one but her lover saw her. Every eye but his was fixed on the man in the arena.

He turned, and with a firm and rapid step he walked across the empty space. Every heart stopped beating, every breath was held, every eye was fixed immovably upon that man. Without the slightest hesitation, he went to the door on the right, and opened it.

INFERRING CHARACTER MOTIVATION

4. Why do you think the young man trusts the princess to save his life? Do you think the princess is sure he will trust her?

N ow, the point of the story is this: Did the tiger come out of that door, or did the lady?

Vocabulary
aspiring (ə·spīr′iŋ) *v.* used as *n.*: seeking to gain; desiring.

Caracalla and Geta (1907) by Sir Lawrence Alma-Tadema.

The more we reflect upon this question, the harder it is to answer. It involves a study of the human heart which leads us through devious mazes of passion, out of which it is difficult to find our way. Think of it, fair reader, not as if the decision of the question depended upon yourself, but upon that hot-blooded, semibarbaric princess, her soul at a white heat beneath the combined fires of despair and jealousy. She had lost him, but who should have him?

How often, in her waking hours and in her dreams, had she started in wild horror, and covered her face with her hands as she thought of her lover opening the door on the other side of which waited the cruel fangs of the tiger!

But how much oftener had she seen him at the other door! How in her grievous reveries[13] had she gnashed her teeth, and torn her hair, when she saw his start of rapturous delight as he opened the door of the lady! How her soul had burned in agony when she had seen him rush to meet that woman, with her flushing cheek and sparkling eye of triumph; when she had seen him lead her forth, his whole frame kindled with the joy of recovered life; when she had heard the glad shouts from the multitudes, and the wild ringing of the happy bells; when she had seen the priest, with his joyous followers,

---

13. reveries (rev′ə·rēz) *n.:* daydreams.

advance to the couple, and make them man and wife before her very eyes; and when she had seen them walk away together upon their path of flowers, followed by the tremendous shouts of the hilarious multitude, in which her one despairing shriek was lost and drowned!

Would it not be better for him to die at once, and go to wait for her in the blessed regions of semibarbaric futurity?

And yet, that awful tiger, those shrieks, that blood!

Her decision had been indicated in an instant, but it had been made after days and nights of anguished deliberation. She had known she would be asked, she had decided what she would answer, and, without the slightest hesitation, she had moved her hand to the right.

The question of her decision is one not to be lightly considered, and it is not for me to presume to set myself up as the one person able to answer it. And so I leave it with all of you: Which came out of the opened door—the lady, or the tiger? ∎

Vocabulary
deliberation (di·lib′ər·ā′shən) *n*.: careful thought, especially in making a decision.

Meet the Writer

Frank R. Stockton

Famous Overnight

When Frank R. Stockton (1834–1902) wrote "The Lady, or the Tiger?" he never imagined that his inspired idea for a story would bring him lasting fame.

Born in Philadelphia, Stockton started out as a sickly, imaginative boy who amused himself by inventing stories. He eventually became a successful writer of works for adults and children.

In 1882, Stockton concocted a lively story, which he called "In the King's Arena," to entertain some friends at a party. *Century Magazine* published it as "The Lady, or the Tiger?" and Stockton became famous overnight. Hundreds of readers pestered him, demanding that he decide the story's outcome once and for all. Stockton did finally respond to his readers, but his answer was not the one they had hoped for.

❝If you decide which it was—the lady, or the tiger—you find out what kind of a person you are yourself.❞

Stockton was admired by his contemporaries. Near the end of his life, one critic praised him for his "inventiveness," a quality that the modern reader of "The Lady, or the Tiger?" can certainly appreciate.

After You Read Response and Analysis

Reading Check

1. How are people punished or rewarded under the king's system of justice?

2. Why is the young man put on trial in the king's arena?

3. What does the princess learn?

4. Why does the young man decide to open the door on the right?

Thinking Critically

5. How would you describe the **character** of the king and the way he rules his people? Do you think the narrator believes he is a good leader? Explain your answer.

6. **Characterize** the princess. In what ways is she similar to her father? What kind of love does she feel for the young man?

7. When the narrator says of the king's system of justice, "Its perfect fairness is obvious," he is using **verbal irony**— saying one thing but meaning something completely different. Explain what the narrator is implying in this line. Then, find another example of verbal irony in the story.

8. What do you think is behind the door the young man opens: the lady or the tiger? Consider these factors, and support your answer with evidence:

   • the **character** of the princess
   • the princess's **motivation** for directing the young man to the lady or the tiger
   • clues in the narrator's description of the princess's thoughts and behavior

   Watch for **subtleties,** or fine distinctions, which can tell you a lot about a character, even though the meaning is often implied rather than stated directly.

9. What is the **tone** of the story— the attitude expressed toward the characters and events? List one or two adjectives to describe the tone, and explain your choice of adjectives.

Extending and Evaluating

10. Why might Stockton have left the ending of his story **ambiguous**—was he trying to make a particular point or create a particular effect? Explain whether you think the ambiguous ending makes the story memorable.

WRITING

Your Verdict

Do you think most people, faced with the princess's hard choices, would save their loved one or send him or her to death? In other words, are people motivated mostly by their own desires or by concern for others? Write one or two **persuasive** paragraphs in which you defend your point of view. (Be sure to check your Quickwrite notes.)

▶ **Use "Writing a Persuasive Essay," pages 382–389, for help with this assignment.**

The End

Write a **sequel** to this story. You might decide once and for all whether the lady or the tiger is behind the door, or you might decide to make your sequel **ambiguous** in its own way. You could even invent an entirely new way of ending the story. Tell about the final events from the point of view of one of the following characters: the young man, the princess, the king, a member of the audience in the arena—or even the tiger.

SKILLS FOCUS

Literary Skills
Analyze ambiguity.

Reading Skills
Make inferences about character motivation.

Writing Skills
Write a persuasive essay.
Write a sequel.

Context Clues: Looking for Signs

Context clues are like signs that can help explain the meaning of a new word. **Context clues** can be **synonyms,** which **restate** the meaning of a word, or **antonyms,** which **contrast** with the word. They can also be **examples** or descriptive words and phrases that help **define** the word. Note how the context clues (underlined) in this sentence from "The Lady, or the Tiger?" help you understand the meaning of *dire:*

> "The moment that the case of the criminal was thus decided, . . . great wails went up from the hired mourners posted on the outer rim of the arena, and the vast audience, with bowed heads and downcast hearts, wended slowly their homeward way, mourning greatly that one . . . should have merited so **dire** a fate."

The context clues—the descriptive phrases that emphasize people's sadness—help you understand that *dire* means "terrible."

> **Word Bank**
>
> exuberant
> genial
> impartial
> allegiance
> procured
> dire
> retribution
> fervent
> aspiring
> deliberation

PRACTICE

For each sentence below, choose the Word Bank word that best completes the sentence. Then, identify the **context clues** in each sentence that helped you determine the answer.

1. The ending of the movie was predictable: The good, innocent character was rewarded whereas the evil criminal received _____.

2. The _____ referee never favored any team and was respected for making just decisions.

3. The hurricane created a _____ situation: Many families lost their homes, roads were flooded, and the town lost electricity.

4. After making a list of pros and cons, I thought about the issue for days, and finally, after much _____, I decided to move.

5. Enthusiastic and energetic, Lynette was so _____ that she always turned out to be the liveliest person in the room.

6. Eric lost his father's favorite scarf, but he _____ a similar one at a neighborhood store.

7. Practicing the violin every day, Anna hoped to play in an orchestra, and I admired her for _____ to become a professional musician.

8. The _____ student made friends easily because he was so good-natured and outgoing.

9. The soldier was suspected of being a spy even though he had shown _____ to his captain and had appeared to be patriotic.

10. Although Jamie and Jesse were twins, they were opposites in that Jamie rarely showed emotion but Jesse was always _____.

SKILLS FOCUS

Vocabulary Skills
Use context clues to understand the meaning of words.

Subject-Verb Agreement:
Interrupting Prepositional Phrases

In standard American English, verbs **agree** with their subjects in number. That is, if the subject is singular, the verb is singular; if the subject is plural, the verb is plural. Making sure that subjects and verbs agree can be tricky when **prepositional phrases** come between the subject and the verb in a sentence. Usually such phrases do not determine the number of the subject. Look at these examples from "The Lady, or the Tiger?":

"The tiger cages of the kingdom were searched for the most savage and relentless beasts. . . ." [plural subject, plural verb]

"This vast amphitheater, with its encircling galleries, its mysterious vaults, and its unseen passages, was an agent of poetic justice. . . ." [singular subject, singular verb]

When a prepositional phrase separates a subject and a verb, imagine there is a box around the interrupting words, as in the examples above. That way you'll be able to see the subject and verb as a pair, and it will be easier to decide whether the verb should be singular or plural. Remember, too, that the object of a prepositional phrase is never the subject of a sentence.

PRACTICE

In the following sentences, decide whether the verb should be singular or plural, and choose the correct form of the verb:

1. The young man, like other prisoners, (was/were) put on trial in the arena.

2. One of the most beautiful maidens (was/were) chosen to stand behind the door.

3. The princess's visions of her lover's fate (was/were) tormenting her.

4. The princess, in addition to crowds of people, (was/were) present at the trial.

5. The story, with its alternative endings, (has/have) intrigued readers for more than a century.

6. My friend, among other readers, (thinks/think) the lady was behind the door.

7. My view, unlike my classmates' opinions, (is/are) that the tiger was behind the door.

8. Our questions about the story (remains/remain) unresolved.

▶ **For more help, see Agreement of Subject and Verb, 2a–m, in the Language Handbook.**

SKILLS FOCUS

Grammar Skills
Use correct subject-verb agreement with an interrupting prepositional phrase.

A Defense of the Jury System

Evaluating an Argument: And the Verdict Is . . .

An **argument** is a series of statements designed to convince you of something. When you evaluate an author's argument, you act somewhat like a juror serving on a trial. Like a juror you need to analyze the evidence presented to you and decide whether the argument is sound. The following tips and the chart on the next page will help you determine whether an author's argument is **credible,** or believable:

1. **Understand the claim, or opinion.** First, read through the argument to make sure that you understand the matter being discussed. Identify what the author is trying to prove, which is called the **claim, or opinion.** Often the author's opinion is stated in the form of a **generalization,** or a broad statement that covers many situations. For example, the following statement is a generalization that expresses an opinion: *All jurors should be allowed to take notes during a trial.* Try to restate the author's opinion in your own words.

2. **Identify the support.** An author must provide support for a claim in order to create a persuasive argument. Here are some common types of support that authors use:

   Logical appeals. To show that their opinions are valid, authors present **reasons,** statements that explain *why* the author holds an opinion. For example, the following statement provides a reason for the author's opinion: *All jurors should be allowed to take notes during a trial because notes can help them remember important information for reaching a verdict.*

Evidence is the information that authors use to support their reasons. Every generalization, to be believable, should be backed up by evidence. There are several types of evidence:

- facts
- statistics (number facts)
- examples
- quotations from or opinions of experts

Sometimes writers use analogies, another type of logical appeal, to help them explain a point. An **analogy** is a type of comparison in which writers usually explain something complex or unfamiliar in terms of something familiar.

Emotional appeals. To win readers over to their opinions, authors sometimes appeal to readers' emotions rather than their reason. Writers, for instance, might want their readers to feel outrage over an injustice or to feel sympathy for a victim. Emotional appeals can be effective tools, but watch out for arguments that rely heavily on emotion at the expense of logic. It's usually a sign that an argument is weak. Emotional appeals include

- **loaded words** (words with strong emotional connotations)

- **anecdotes** (brief stories)

3. **Evaluate the evidence.** An argument is only as strong as its evidence. Ask yourself: "Does the evidence directly support the author's reasons? Does the author present sufficient evidence to back up generalizations and to prove the claim? Has the author loaded the argument with emotional appeals instead of providing valid evidence?"

SKILLS FOCUS

Reading Skills
Evaluate an author's argument and evidence.

INTERNET

Interactive Reading Model

Keyword: LE7 9-5

4. **Identify the author's intent.** Finally, think about why the author is making this argument. As far as you can tell, has the author carefully weighed all the evidence before arriving at an opinion? Does the author, instead, seem to be biased or prejudiced? Note how the author's **intent,** or purpose, influences the **tone** of the argument. For example, if the author wants to urge readers to take action, the tone might be strongly emotional.

5. **Create a chart.** To help you evaluate an argument, make a chart like the one shown here. Such a chart will help you see the strengths and weaknesses of an argument.

Evaluating an Author's Argument
Claim, or opinion:
Logical appeals
Reason 1: Evidence: Reason 2: Evidence:
Emotional appeals
Loaded words: Anecdotes:
Tone:

▶ **For more about persuasive writing, see "Writing a Persuasive Essay," pages 382–389, at the end of this collection.**

Vocabulary Development

irrational (i·rash′ə·nəl) *adj.*: not based on reason or logic.

superficial (soo′pər·fish′əl) *adj.*: not deep or thorough; shallow.

obscure (əb·skyoor′) *v.*: conceal; cover up.

advocates (ad′və·kāts′) *v.*: supports; argues in favor of.

conscientiously (kän′shē·en′shəs·lē) *adv.*: carefully and thoughtfully.

affluent (af′loo·ənt) *adj.*: wealthy.

Connecting to the Literature

"The Lady, or the Tiger?" describes a system of justice in which the fate of the accused is decided entirely by chance. How fair is our own system, trial by jury? Read the following persuasive essay to find out what one expert thinks.

A Defense of THE JURY SYSTEM

Thomas M. Ross, Esq.

The jury system is often attacked for delivering seemingly irrational verdicts in both criminal and civil cases.[1] Much of this criticism stems from some well-publicized verdicts that the public has felt were unjustified and unreasonable. For example, when a fast-food company was forced to pay $2.7 million in damages in a case brought by a woman who had spilled a cup of coffee on her lap, the verdict was widely ridiculed. One congressman remarked, "Most people say this doesn't make a lot of sense."

Juries are criticized for deciding cases based upon their prejudices or emotions, rather than rationally applying the law to the evidence presented in a case. They are also criticized for being incapable of understanding the complex financial and scientific issues that sometimes arise in today's court cases. For example, a jury in one case awarded a small company $35 million in damages from a communications conglomerate[2] for a patent infringement.[3] A lawyer involved in the case remarked that the jury of "unemployed laborers and housewives didn't understand that stuff." ❶

> ❶ **EVALUATING ARGUMENTS**
>
> In your own words, explain the author's two main **generalizations** in this paragraph.

People who make these criticisms, however, are very much like people who criticize voters for being irrational or ill-informed. Critics claim that many voters have only a superficial grasp of the issues and, accordingly, are easily swayed by simplistic slogans and "thirty-second sound bites"[4] that obscure the complexity of the issues. Despite these criticisms of voters, hardly anyone advocates abolishing the vote. After all, it has been said that "democracy is the worst form of government—except for all the others." The same can be said of the jury system: It's the worst system of justice—except for all the others.

Much of the criticism of the jury system is unjustified and stems from unfamiliarity with the system. When people actually serve on a jury, they usually find that the cases receiving widespread negative publicity are atypical[5]—most of their peers perform their duties conscientiously, honestly, and fairly. For example, a survey of eight hundred

---

1. **civil cases:** court cases relating to the rights and duties of individuals.
2. **conglomerate** (kən·gläm′ər·it) *n.:* large business made up of several smaller companies.
3. **patent infringement:** Patents are legal documents granting inventors exclusive rights to make and profit from their inventions. Making or using an invention without the permission of the patent owner is called patent infringement.

---

4. **sound bites** *n.:* brief, attention-getting statements, often made by politicians, that are broadcast on television and radio.
5. **atypical** (ā·tip′i·kəl) *adj.:* not typical; unusual.

Vocabulary

irrational (i·rash′ə·nəl) *adj.:* not based on reason or logic.

superficial (sōō′pər·fish′əl) *adj.:* not deep or thorough; shallow.

obscure (əb·skyoor′) *v.:* conceal; cover up.

advocates (ad′və·kāts′) *v.:* supports; argues in favor of.

conscientiously (kän′shē·en′shəs·lē) *adv.:* carefully and thoughtfully.

jurors by the *National Law Journal* in 1993 revealed that 75 percent of them would prefer to be tried by a panel of their peers rather than by a panel of judges. Even judges themselves, who observe juries daily, have confidence in most jurors. A survey of state judges in Texas found that 98 percent believed that juries do at least "moderately well" in reaching a "just and fair" verdict. Furthermore, if those judges were a party in a civil lawsuit or were accused of a crime, 60 percent said that they would rather have their civil case decided by a jury than by a judge, and 80 percent said they would rather have their criminal case decided by a jury. ②

> ② **EVALUATING EVIDENCE**
>
> What type of **evidence** is presented in this paragraph?

Some people believe that having cases decided exclusively by judges would improve our justice system. However, like jurors, judges are human beings, capable of making misjudgments. Relying on judges, instead of juries, to decide cases does not guarantee that every verdict will be considered fair by all. Furthermore, judges are not representative of society as a whole. Although more women and minority members are being appointed as judges—as more women and minority members

enter the legal profession itself—judges are still mostly Caucasian and male. Moreover, most judges, like most lawyers, generally come from middle-class and affluent backgrounds. Thus, the experiences and perspectives of women, minorities, and poor and working-class people would be underrepresented in a system in which all cases were decided by judges.

On the other hand, jurors are drawn from both sexes, all ethnic groups, all economic backgrounds, all adult ages, all religions, and all neighborhoods within a jurisdiction.[6] (Indeed, the only qualification a person needs to be a juror is the ability to be fair and impartial.) Consequently, a jury will reflect diverse viewpoints and experiences, rather than just the viewpoint and experiences of a single judge. The jury system thus helps ensure that a verdict will not be based on an individual's biases or lack of understanding of particular people's experiences.

Human beings are not perfect—we make mistakes, and sometimes we are swayed by our emotions—and that means that the jury system is also not perfect. Despite its flaws, the jury system is the best means we have for maintaining justice in a democracy. No other system guarantees that the perspectives of all citizens will be represented. ③

> ③ **EVALUATING ARGUMENTS**
>
> In your own words, state the author's main **claim,** or **opinion,** in this essay.

The author is an assistant district attorney in Kings County (Brooklyn), New York.

6. **jurisdiction** (joor´is·dik′shən) *n*.: here, geographic area under the authority of a particular court system.

Vocabulary
affluent (af′lōō·ənt) *adj*.: wealthy.

Reading Check

1. According to the first two paragraphs, why are juries frequently criticized?

2. List the advantages of having cases decided by juries instead of by judges, as described in the essay.

3. According to the author, what does the jury system guarantee that no other judicial system can guarantee?

Test Practice

1. Which statement *best* expresses the author's **claim, or opinion**?
   A   A few highly publicized cases prove that the jury system is not fair.
   B   Many judges believe that the jury system is fair.
   C   There is nothing wrong with the jury system, and it should not be replaced.
   D   Despite its problems, trial by jury is the fairest system of justice.

2. The author's comparison of the jury system to the popular vote is an example of —
   F   a fact
   G   an anecdote
   H   loaded words
   J   an analogy

3. To support his **claim,** the author relies most heavily on —
   A   reasons and facts
   B   experts' quotations
   C   anecdotes
   D   loaded words

4. What conclusion does the author want you to draw from the **statistics** he presents in the essay?
   F   Jurors and judges trust juries.
   G   More criminal cases than civil cases are decided by judges.
   H   After serving as jurors, most people feel that the jury system is not effective.
   J   Surveys are a good way to learn about the jury system.

5. Which of the following phrases from the essay is an example of **loaded language**?
   A   "simplistic slogans"
   B   "unfamiliarity with the system"
   C   "like most lawyers"
   D   "an individual's biases"

6. Which word *best* describes the **tone** of the essay?
   F   sarcastic
   G   comforting
   H   reasonable
   J   resentful

SKILLS FOCUS

Reading Skills
Evaluate an author's argument and evidence.

Constructed Response

Imagine that Ross's essay was published in your local newspaper. Write a letter to the editor in which you tell whether you think Ross's argument is **credible**. Explain your point of view by **evaluating** the **claim** and supporting **evidence** in his essay. How strong or weak do you find his argument?

Vocabulary Development

Using Contexts

PRACTICE

Each practice item below includes one of the Word Bank words used in three different **contexts**. (The first example is a quotation from the essay.) For each item, review the three examples. Then, choose the best meaning of the Word Bank word to complete the sentence in the third example.

1. "The jury system is often attacked for delivering seemingly irrational verdicts. . . . "

   Confused and panicked, he made irrational comments.

   An irrational argument is
   a. illogical
   b. predictable
   c. convincing
   d. simplistic

2. "Critics claim that many voters have only a superficial grasp of the issues. . . . "

   As she had only a superficial knowledge of the law, she consulted a legal expert.

   Someone with a superficial view of life might be called
   a. biased
   b. shallow
   c. false
   d. thorough

3. "Critics claim that many voters . . . are easily swayed by simplistic slogans and 'thirty-second sound bites' that obscure the complexity of the issues."

   On rainy days, clouds obscure the mountaintop from view.

To obscure something is to
a. highlight it
b. change it
c. exaggerate it
d. conceal it

4. "Hardly anyone advocates abolishing the vote."

   Only one candidate advocates using the plot of land for a shopping mall instead of a park.

   A politician who advocates something
   a. disagrees with it
   b. understands it
   c. prevents it
   d. supports it

5. "Most of their peers perform their duties conscientiously, honestly, and fairly."

   Sensitive and attentive, the nurse cared for her patients conscientiously.

   To do your job conscientiously means to do it
   a. independently
   b. carefully and thoughtfully
   c. with authority
   d. modestly

6. "Moreover, most judges, like most lawyers, generally come from middle-class and affluent backgrounds."

   Only affluent people shop at the elegant, expensive store.

   An affluent family is
   a. wealthy
   b. close-knit
   c. proud
   d. happy

Word Bank

irrational
superficial
obscure
advocates
conscientiously
affluent

SKILLS FOCUS

Vocabulary Skills
Use context clues to understand the meaning of words.

Before You Read

The Road Not Taken

Make the Connection

Quickwrite

Think of a choice you made that marked a turning point in your life—trying out for a sports team, signing up as a volunteer in your community, standing up for a friend. Go back to the moment when you made the choice, and imagine that you made a different one instead. Jot down notes about how you envision your life would be different if that turning point had never happened.

Literary Focus

Contradictions: Yes = No

Life is full of contradictions. A particular choice you once made might have improved your life in some ways but made it worse in others. Was it a good choice or a bad one? It was both—and it was neither. Such **contradictions**—two feelings, events, or statements that are opposites—are often captured in literature.

When you come across contradictory statements in a literary work, you might first assume that one statement is true and the other is not, or you might try to figure out which statement the writer *really* meant. However, sometimes both statements are true in some way, and the writer meant both of them.

The poet Robert Frost called "The Road Not Taken" a tricky poem. Read it several times, and try to figure out exactly what Frost's attitude is about life and the choices we make.

SKILLS FOCUS

Literary Skills
Understand contradictions.

INTERNET

More About Robert Frost

Keyword: LE7 9-5

The Road Not Taken

Robert Frost

Two roads diverged° in a yellow wood,
And sorry I could not travel both
And be one traveler, long I stood
And looked down one as far as I could
5 To where it bent in the undergrowth;

Then took the other, as just as fair,
And having perhaps the better claim,
Because it was grassy and wanted wear;
Though as for that the passing there
10 Had worn them really about the same,

And both that morning equally lay
In leaves no step had trodden black.
Oh, I kept the first for another day!
Yet knowing how way leads on to way,
15 I doubted if I should ever come back.

I shall be telling this with a sigh
Somewhere ages and ages hence:
Two roads diverged in a wood, and I—
I took the one less traveled by,
20 And that has made all the difference.

1. **diverged** (dī·vʉrjd′) *v.:* branched off in
   different directions.

Meet the Writer

Robert Frost

First Poet

Robert Frost (1874–1963), who became so strongly identified with New England, was actually born in San Francisco, California, far from the craggy northeastern countryside he celebrated. After the death of his father when Frost was a child, he and his mother moved to Lawrence, Massachusetts. Known in high school as the class poet, Frost attended college on and off, never earning a degree. To make a living, he worked as a teacher, editor, and shoemaker, and he also ran a farm, struggling all the while to get his poems published.

Frost's literary fortunes changed dramatically in 1912, when he sold his farm and moved his family to England. Several volumes of his poetry were soon published overseas, and Frost began to be recognized critically in America as well. In 1915, he came home to New England to stay, and his career in America took off. Hugely popular, he accumulated numerous awards, including four Pulitzer Prizes.

As he aged, the craggy-faced poet turned into a beloved American icon. Two years before his death he received the great honor of reciting his poem "The Gift Outright" at the inauguration of President John F. Kennedy in 1961. He was the first poet ever to read a poem at a presidential inauguration.

Frost's poetry is deeply rooted in the New England landscape. In his poems he conveys the harsh beauty of rural New England and creates vivid New England characters, often by capturing natural spoken language in his writing. However, his direct, economical style can be misleading, as in "The Road Not Taken." Frost's poems are often ironic and ambiguous, lending complexity to his work. In Frost's view,

❝Poetry provides the one permissible way of saying one thing and meaning another. . . .❞

You'll find other poems by Frost on pages 499 and 517.

Robert Frost wrote this letter to the literary editor Susan Hayes Ward.

Crossing Paths

Robert Frost

Plymouth, New Hampshire
10 February 1912

Dear Miss Ward:

Two lonely crossroads that themselves cross each other I have walked several times this winter without meeting or overtaking so much as a single person on foot or on runners. The practically unbroken condition of both for several days after a snow or a blow proves that neither is much traveled. Judge then how surprised I was the other evening as I came down one to see a man, who to my own unfamiliar eyes and in the dusk looked for all the world like myself, coming down the other, his approach to the point where our paths must intersect[1] being so timed that unless one of us pulled up we must inevitably collide. I felt as if I was going to meet my own image in a slanting mirror. Or say I felt as we slowly converged[2] on the same point with the same noiseless yet laborious strides as if we were two images about to float together with the uncrossing of someone's eyes. I verily expected to take up or absorb this other self and feel the stronger by the addition for the three-mile journey home. But I didn't go forward to the touch. I stood still in wonderment and let him pass by; and that, too, with the fatal omission of not trying to find out by a comparison of lives and immediate and remote interests what could have brought us by crossing paths to the same point in the wilderness at the same moment of nightfall. Some purpose I doubt not, if we could but have made it out. I like a coincidence almost as well as an incongruity. . . .[3]

Nonsensically yours,

---

1. **intersect** (inʹtər·sektʹ) *v.*: cross each other.
2. **converged** (kən·vurjdʹ) *v.*: moved toward each other.
3. **incongruity** (inʹkän·gro͞oʹi·tē) *n.*: something not in agreement with what is expected.

Thinking Critically

1. Why might Frost have chosen to write about roads that go through woods rather than roads that go through a garden or a wide-open plain? (Consider what woods might **symbolize,** or stand for. Think also of the expression *We're not out of the woods yet.*)

2. The speaker faces a hard choice in deciding which road to take. What do you think he means when he says that he "kept" the first road for another day (line 13)? How do we know that he realizes his choice of paths is utterly final?

3. From what the speaker says in lines 6–10, is one road really "less traveled" than the other? Explain the **contradiction** in these lines.

4. Do you think the poem's final line is meant as **verbal irony,** or is it a sincere statement? Give reasons to support your response.

5. How would you describe the **tone** of the poem—the speaker's attitude toward the subject? (Keep in mind that according to Frost, the most insightful question one could ask about the poem concerns line 16: Why the sigh?) Which words, phrases, or lines in the poem convey this tone to you?

6. Talk over your responses to Frost's letter "Crossing Paths" (see the **Connection** on page 379). What connections do you see between the poem and the incident Frost describes in the letter? What questions would you like to ask Frost? Why?

Extending and Evaluating

7. What is your opinion of the speaker's **contradiction** in lines 13–15 about having a chance to take the other road? Do you think people can ever go back and try another road? Explain your response.

WRITING

Turning Points

Write a **letter** to a friend telling about a choice you made that resulted in a turning point in your life. Explain how this choice affected your life. Are you glad that you made the choice? Do you have any regrets? Be sure to check your Quickwrite notes.

On the Road

Think of another setting and another traveler. Write a road **poem** of your own (maybe about a road taken). You can base your poem on your own experiences, or you can write about an imaginary traveler. Use vivid **images** to set the scene for your reader.

SKILLS FOCUS

Literary Skills
Interpret contradictions.

Writing Skills
Write a letter.
Write a poem.

INTERNET

Projects and Activities

Keyword: LE7 9-5

FICTION

The Secrets of Camp Green Lake

The trouble begins when Stanley is falsely accused of stealing sneakers that belong to the basketball legend Clyde Livingston, otherwise known as Sweet Feet. As punishment, Stanley is sent to Camp Green Lake, a remote juvenile detention center. There he is expected to dig enormous holes. "If you find anything interesting," says his camp counselor, "hand it over to the warden." What could possibly be interesting in a dried-up lake bed? Read Louis Sachar's suspenseful, Newbery Medal–winning novel, **Holes,** to unearth the answer.

This title is available in the HRW Library.

FICTION / NONFICTION

Wit and Wisdom

James Thurber's **My World and Welcome to It** is a collection of essays, sketches, and stories from one of America's great comic writers. Whether recording his funny observations about life abroad or complaining about the phone company, Thurber chooses his targets with gentle good humor. His combination of ironic wit and plain-spoken charm will make you feel as if you're spending the day with a favorite uncle.

FICTION

Fair Enough

What is justice? Is there more than one kind? Sharon Creeden, a storyteller and a trial attorney, takes a close look at what justice means to the world. The result is her book **Fair Is Fair: World Folktales of Justice,** an entertaining collection of myths, fables, and folklore from many lands. Creeden shows us that what's fair and just is a little more ambiguous than we might think— differing from nation to nation as well as from case to case.

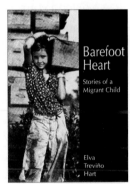

NONFICTION

Out of the Fields

Elva was a small child when her family packed up and moved from Mexico to Minnesota, hoping to earn their living as migrant laborers. Along with her brothers and sisters, Elva endures filthy living conditions and tiring work—only occasionally stealing moments to run and play barefoot in the broad, grassy fields. Then school begins, and Elva discovers that she has a special talent. What she does with this talent and the difficult decisions she has to make are beautifully outlined in Elva Treviño Hart's memoir **Barefoot Heart: Stories of a Migrant Child.**

Writing a Persuasive Essay

Writing Assignment
Write a persuasive essay on a topic about which you have a strong opinion.

As you read in his essay "A Defense of the Jury System," Thomas M. Ross has strong feelings about the jury system. What issue do you care about, and how can you get others to care about the issue, too? One way to share your views and convince others to accept them is to write persuasively. In a **persuasive essay** your goal will be to state your opinion clearly and support it with reasons and evidence.

Prewriting

Choose an Issue

A Powerful Issue   For your persuasive essay, consider **issues** that stir up strong feelings in you and in others. What situations make you and other people angry, sad, or enthusiastic? List a few issues that you really care about. Then, pick the one you have the strongest views about and the one about which you can gather enough evidence to defend your position. Keep in mind that your essay should be at least 1,500 words, so choose an issue that is interesting enough to hold readers' interest in a paper of that length.

Write an Opinion Statement

Get on Your Soapbox   You probably already know where you stand on your issue. Share your clear and well-defined **perspective** with readers by drafting an opinion statement (also known as a thesis statement). Your **opinion statement** should clearly state both the issue and your position on it. One student brainstormed the following issues and positions as he developed an opinion statement.

Issue	Position
Recycling	helps to protect our natural resources.
People who ride motorcycles	should be required to wear helmets.
Banning bicycles on sidewalks	would force riders onto unsafe streets.

SKILLS FOCUS

Writing Skills
Write a persuasive essay.

Keep your own opinion statement in mind to help you focus your ideas as you plan and draft your essay.

Consider Your Purpose and Audience

Your Readers Await You   In a persuasive essay your **purpose** is to convince readers to share your opinion or to take the action you suggest. In order to persuade your readers effectively, you must understand them. Think about your **audience** by jotting down answers to the following questions.

DO THIS

- **What will make my audience care about this issue?** Identify specific ways in which the topic affects your readers' lives.

- **What concerns might my audience have?** Consider how your issue looks from their point of view, or **bias.** For example, some readers may think that recycling is too expensive. Take this objection, or **counterclaim,** into account as you support your position.

TIP Readers' counterclaims can also be called **counterarguments.**

- **What will my audience expect from my essay?** Consider aspects of the issue about which readers might want more information. They will expect your essay to provide solid information to help them make a decision.

Gather Support for Your Position

Back It Up   To be convincing, give at least three strong **reasons** to support your opinion statement. Your reasons will tell why you believe your position is correct and may include **rhetorical devices** that appeal to your readers' logic, emotions, or ethical beliefs.

- A **logical appeal** speaks to readers' common sense and logic. Logical appeals make sense.

- An **emotional appeal** is aimed at readers' hearts. Emotional appeals speak to emotions such as fear, love, sympathy, and pride.

- An **ethical appeal** addresses readers' sense of right and wrong. Ethical appeals also rely on a reader's belief that the writer is ethical.

Here are the reasons the student writer developed.

Opinion Statement: Recycling is the best way to preserve natural resources and to reduce the costs of processing garbage.

Reasons:
1. It saves precious resources. (logical appeal)
2. It keeps us from being buried in trash. (emotional appeal)
3. It reduces the garbage we produce. (ethical appeal)

Create a chart like the one above in which you write your opinion statement and list at least three reasons to support it. As you create your chart, keep in mind that your teacher may want you to have more logical appeals than emotional or ethical appeals.

SKILLS FOCUS

Writing Skills
Identify purpose and audience. Use logical, emotional, and ethical appeals.

TIP Make sure to identify any source you quote. For more on **citing sources,** see page 715.

The Evidence Suggests . . . Provide at least two pieces of **evidence** to support each of your reasons. The following chart shows examples of the kinds of evidence you can provide to present a tightly reasoned argument. No matter which types of evidence you include, make sure your evidence is **relevant,** or clearly related to your issue. Precise, specific evidence will help readers better understand your position and will be more convincing than vague evidence.

EVIDENCE FOR PERSUASIVE APPEALS

Types of Evidence	Examples
Analogies Comparisons that show similarities between otherwise unrelated facts or ideas	We should be as concerned about the garbage problem today as they once were about finding a vaccine for polio.
Anecdotes Personal examples or stories that illustrate a point	My grandfather says the forests that once surrounded my hometown have nearly vanished.
Case studies Examples from scientific research	Government studies show that collecting and using recycled materials saves energy.
Commonly accepted beliefs Ideas that most people share	Most people think that garbage is useless and has no value.
Examples Specific instances or illustrations of a general idea	For example, recycling could help save some of the fifty thousand trees that are sacrificed every week to produce Sunday newspapers in the U.S.
Expert opinions Statements made by a recognized authority on the subject	Brenda Platt of the Institute for Local Self-Reliance says, "Studies have concluded that recycling costs less than traditional trash collection and disposal. . . ."
Facts Statements that can be proven true; some facts are in the form of statistics, or numerical information	Garbage usually goes into landfills. Of the garbage produced each year in the U.S., 42% is paper.

Plan Your Draft

Get Your Information in Order To be its most persuasive, your essay should move **smoothly and logically** from one idea to the next. Decide now how to organize the reasons that support your opinion statement. Readers will best remember ideas presented at the end of the essay and at the beginning. Therefore, you might want to put your second strongest reason in the first body paragraph and your strongest reason in the final body paragraph. Place remaining reasons in between.

SKILLS FOCUS

Writing Skills
Provide relevant evidence.
Organize the evidence.

PRACTICE & APPLY 1 Choose an issue for your persuasive essay, write an opinion statement, and gather and organize reasons and evidence to support your opinion.

Writing

Writing a Persuasive Essay

A Writer's Model

Do Something Good for the Earth

Garbage! It smells bad and looks disgusting. Most people think about trash only when they take it out. People in the United States should be thinking about garbage more, however, because they throw away 40 percent of all the garbage in the world. The solution to this problem is recycling. Recycling is the best way to preserve natural resources and to reduce the costs of processing garbage.

By recycling, we can prevent our country from being buried in trash. Much of the garbage that is now tossed out could be recycled. Of the 200 million tons of garbage that U.S. citizens produce yearly, about 42 percent is paper (from trees), 8 percent is glass, 9 percent is metal (from ore, a natural resource), 7 percent is plastic (from petroleum, a natural resource), 8 percent is food waste, and 18 percent is yard waste. Government officials estimate that 60 percent of all this trash could be recycled. Environmentalists suggest a much higher figure—as much as 70 to 90 percent.

Recycling more of our garbage can also save precious resources. My grandfather says the thick forests that once surrounded my hometown have nearly vanished. By recycling newspapers, we can rescue trees from destruction. For example, recycling could help save some of the fifty thousand trees that are sacrificed every week to produce Sunday newspapers in the United States. We can also save water and energy by

(continued)

INTRODUCTION

Attention getter
Background information

Opinion statement

BODY/ Reason 1:
Emotional appeal

Evidence: Statistics

Reason 2: Logical appeal
Evidence: Anecdote

Evidence: Example

(continued)

Evidence: Facts and statistics

recycling. Recycling paper instead of making it from trees reduces the amount of water used to make the paper by 60 percent and the amount of energy by 70 percent. Aluminum cans show the biggest savings from recycling. To produce a can from recycled aluminum takes 95 percent less energy than from ore.

Reason 3: Ethical appeal

Recycling more can reduce the mountains of garbage we produce—and reduce the costs associated with all the landfills where the garbage is dumped. Garbage does not just disappear after it is hauled away. It usually goes into landfills—many of which have created toxic pollution problems and enormous cleanup costs. People often object to recycling by saying that it costs too much. Brenda Platt of the Institute for Local Self-Reliance says, "Studies have concluded that recycling costs less than traditional trash collection and disposal when communities achieve high levels of recycling." Therefore, people should understand that recycling actually saves money by reducing waste and by eliminating the costs that go along with solid-waste disposal and landfill cleanup.

Evidence: Facts

Counterclaim addressed

Evidence: Expert opinion

CONCLUSION

Restated opinion
Summary of reasons

Much of what is thrown away now can be recycled. Anyone who loves the earth can help make it a better place by recycling. Garbage makes our shared home, this planet, less livable for the people of today and for the children of tomorrow. People have caused this garbage crisis, and only people can solve it. Do you care enough to do your part by recycling?

Call to action

go.hrw.com

INTERNET
More Writer's Models
Keyword: LE7 9-5

PRACTICE & APPLY 2 As you write the first draft of your persuasive essay, refer to the framework on page 385 and the Writer's Model above. They will help you expand and organize your ideas.

CALVIN & HOBBES ©1993 Watterson. Distributed by Universal Press Syndicate. Reprinted with permission. All rights reserved.

Revising

Evaluate and Revise Your Draft

Checking It Twice When you invest your strong feelings and
your time in writing a persuasive essay, you want to make sure that the
final product is as clear and well written as possible in order to
convince your audience. Read your essay at least twice. During the first
reading, consider your essay's content and organization. On your
second reading, focus on style, using the guidelines on page 388.

First Reading: Content and Organization Use the following
guidelines to evaluate and revise the content and organization of your
persuasive essay. Ask yourself the evaluation questions in the left-hand
column, and use the tips in the middle column to help you with your
answers. Then, use the revision techniques in the right-hand column
to make any improvements.

Rubric: Writing a Persuasive Essay

Evaluation Questions	Tips	Revision Techniques
❶ Does the introduction express a clear opinion statement?	▶ **Bracket** the opinion statement.	▶ **Add** an opinion statement that identifies the issue and states an opinion on it.
❷ Do at least three reasons support the opinion statement? Do the reasons include logical, emotional, or ethical appeals?	▶ **Underline** each reason. **Label** logical appeals with an *L*, emotional appeals with an *E*, and ethical appeals with an *H*.	▶ **Add** reasons. **Elaborate** on existing reasons so that they appeal to readers' logic, emotions, or ethics. Make sure the appeals are balanced.
❸ Do at least two pieces of evidence support each reason?	▶ **Circle** each piece of evidence, and **draw an arrow** to the reason it supports.	▶ **Add** evidence for each reason. **Rearrange** evidence so that it is in the paragraph with the reason it supports.
❹ Is the organization logical and effective?	▶ **Number** each reason with a rank (1 for strongest, and so on).	▶ **Rearrange** paragraphs to put the strongest reason first or last.
❺ Are possible reader counterclaims addressed?	▶ **Put a plus sign** by any sentence that addresses a reader counterclaim.	▶ **Add** sentences that identify and respond to reader counterclaims.
❻ Does the conclusion restate the writer's opinion? Does it include a summary of reasons or a call to action?	▶ **Put a box** around the restatement of the writer's opinion. **Highlight** the summary of reasons or the call to action.	▶ **Add** a sentence that restates the position. **Add** a summary of reasons or a call to action.

> **Second Reading: Style** The style of your persuasive essay should be formal. To maintain a serious tone, use the guidelines in the following chart to eliminate clichés in your essay. **Clichés** are over-used expressions that have lost meaning and impact. "Last but not least," "once in a blue moon," and "tough as nails" are examples of clichés. Replace clichés with original words or phrases as in the following example.

> **Cliché:** Manuel was *as busy as a bee* while he worked on his project.
> **Original words:** Manuel *worked diligently* on his project.

Style Guidelines

Evaluation Question	▶ Tip	▶ Revision Technique
● Does the essay include any worn-out, overused expressions?	▶ **Draw a line through** clichés.	▶ **Replace** each cliché with a fresh, original expression.

ANALYZING THE REVISION PROCESS
Look at these revisions, and answer the questions that follow.

replace

disappear after it is hauled away.
Garbage does not just ~~vanish into thin air.~~ It usually goes into

landfills—many of which have created toxic pollution
People often object to recycling by saying that it costs too much.
add   problems and enormous cleanup costs, Brenda Platt of the

Institute for Local Self-Reliance says, "Studies have concluded

that recycling costs less than traditional trash collection and

disposal when communities achieve high levels of recycling."

Responding to the Revision Process
1. Why did the writer replace the words *vanish into thin air* in the first sentence?

2. Why did the writer add a sentence to the paragraph?

SKILLS FOCUS

Writing Skills
Revise for content and style.

PRACTICE & APPLY 3   Read your essay once to revise its content and organization, using the guidelines on page 387. Then, revise its style, using the guidelines above.

Publishing

Proofread and Publish Your Persuasive Essay

Last Look Now that you have polished the content, organization, and style of your essay, proofread it to be sure that it is free of grammar, spelling, and punctuation errors. (For information on **proofreading,** see *The Writing Process* in the Writer's Handbook.)

Have your Say Persuasive writing is meant to be shared. Here are some ways you might share your persuasive essay with an audience.

- Send your essay to an organization with an interest in your issue or with the power to make the change you want.

- Publish your essay on a school or community Web site or on a Web site devoted to the issue you addressed. Use a graphics program to include photographs or illustrations on your Web page.

- Use a publishing program to format your essay into columns so that it looks like an article. Then, submit your article to your school newspaper or to a newspaper or magazine that publishes articles on issues such as yours.

Reflect on Your Persuasive Essay

Taking a Deeper Look To reflect on what you have learned about persuasion and how your writing skills have developed through completing this workshop, answer these questions.

- What difficulties did you have finding reasons to support your opinion or evidence to support your reasons? How did you solve these problems?

- How did addressing your readers' counterclaims or concerns help you to strengthen your persuasive argument? What did you learn about your audience and the other side of the issue from this part of the writing process?

- What revisions do you think strengthened your essay the most? Why?

  If you include your persuasive essay in a writing portfolio, attach your responses to it.

PRACTICE & APPLY Proofread your essay, checking for grammar, usage, and mechanics mistakes. Then, publish your essay, using one of the suggestions above. Finally, reflect on the skills you have used to create your persuasive essay.

TIP Proofreading your essay will help ensure that you have used the **conventions** of standard American English correctly. For example, to avoid delivering a reason that is the opposite of what you mean, check to make sure that you haven't used two negative words *(no, none, nothing, not)* in a sentence. For more on **double negatives,** see double negative, Glossary of Usage, in the Language Handbook.

COMPUTER TIP

If you have access to a computer and advanced publishing software, you can format your essay so that it looks professional. For more on **page design,** see *Designing Your Writing* in the Writer's Handbook.

SKILLS FOCUS

Writing Skills
Proofread, design, and publish the essay.

Debating an Issue

Conversations about controversial topics break down for a variety of reasons: perhaps someone is long-winded, or someone else gets angry and logic flies out the window. In a debate, however, there are rules that keep the discussion from breaking down. A **debate** is a balanced argument covering opposite sides of an issue. In a debate two teams compete to win the support of the audience.

Prepare for the Debate

Define the Proposition A debate focuses on a single, narrow issue, **the proposition.** The proposition is worded as a **resolution,** a positive statement calling for a change in the way things are. Most often, the proposition will be chosen for you and will involve a topic with equally strong arguments on both sides. Here is an example resolution one group of students used for a debate.

> *Resolved:* That Northside High School should turn an existing classroom into a computer lab.

Take Sides A traditional debate requires two teams of two people each and a chairperson.

- The **affirmative team,** which speaks first in the debate, argues for the proposition. Because this team is arguing for a change in the current state of things, it has the **burden of proof.** It is the team's task to prove why the change must be made.

- The **negative team** argues that the proposal of the affirmative side should be rejected—that things are fine the way they are.

- The **chairperson** directs the debate and ensures that all rules and time limits are followed. If a debater believes an opponent has broken the rules, he or she may appeal to the chairperson.

Participants in a debate are generally assigned to a team, without regard to how each member personally feels about the issue. You might think it would be better to argue the side of the issue you support. However, sometimes it is easier to argue for something you don't really support because you know all of the weaknesses in the case and how your opponents might approach them. Whichever side of the case you are assigned, your task is to present rational arguments that are easy to follow and understand.

SKILLS FOCUS

Listening and Speaking Skills
Debate an issue.

Research the Proposition To prepare effectively for a debate, you must research the proposition fully. Identify the **key issues**—the main differences between your position and the position of the opposing team. Key issues often involve the following questions.

- Does a problem exist?
- What is causing the problem?
- Will this proposition solve the problem?
- What will this proposition cost?

Your research should provide answers to these questions. Use the answers to develop specific **reasons** that support your side of the proposition. Reasons, even those that include **rhetorical devices,** can't stand alone. They must be supported by evidence, or **proof.** Refer to the following chart to see the four most common types of proof.

Reference Note

For more on **rhetorical devices** and **types of evidence,** see pages 383 and 384.

PROOF USED IN DEBATES

Type of Proof	Example
Specific instances—examples that illustrate a point	Many students currently attending Northside High School have so little computer experience that they can't even perform basic research tasks using the Internet.
Testimony—comments from someone who has already studied or experienced the problem	According to Sarah Jones, a former student of Northside High School, "I felt very ill prepared when I entered college because my computer skills were so far behind those of my classmates."
Facts—statements that can be proven true	The school board voted not to buy computers to be placed in the classrooms.
Statistics—facts presented as numerical information	976 students are enrolled at Northside, yet the current computer lab has space for only 30 students per class period.

To meet the standard **tests for evidence** and be appropriate for the debate, your proof must be credible, valid, and relevant to the topic you are discussing.

TESTS FOR EVIDENCE

Evidence should be . . .	That means . . .
Credible	The evidence comes from a recognized authority on the subject, a source that is not biased against or in favor of either side.
Valid	The proof clearly supports the position it claims to support.
Relevant	The proof has a close, logical relationship to the reason it supports.

Be sure to make notes on the evidence that might be used against your position as well as evidence that supports your position. If you know what proof the other team might present, you'll be better prepared to respond to their arguments. Once you've fully researched your topic, organize your evidence into these three categories:

- **Constructive arguments,** which support your side

- **Refutations,** which attack the other side

- **Rebuttals,** which reply to challenges to your side

Prepare Debate Speeches An effective structure for persuasive speeches is the **classical speech form,** in which the argument has a brief but engaging introduction, smooth transitions, a concise body, and a strong conclusion. There are two types of speeches in a debate that you'll need to organize in this manner: **constructive speeches,** delivered during the first part of the debate, and **rebuttal speeches,** delivered in response to the constructive speeches.

- **Affirmative constructive speeches** build the argument in favor of the proposition. A constructive speech for the affirmative side should present two to four reasons in support of the position. Each reason should be supported by strong evidence.

- **Negative constructive speeches** defend the way things are. They deny the existence of a problem or make the case that existing solutions are all that's needed to correct a problem. Reasons that support the argument for the negative side also need to be backed up by strong evidence.

- **Rebuttal speeches** respond to the constructive speeches. They have two objectives: refutation and rebuttal. **Refutation** means to attack the other side's argument by questioning the quantity and quality of their evidence and the logic of their reasoning. **Rebuttal** means to rebuild your argument after the other team has attacked it.

Conduct the Debate

Present Yourself When it's time for you to present your constructive and rebuttal speeches, focus on your task and speak clearly and naturally. Use your **voice, facial expressions,** and **gestures** to make your message expressive. For example, speak at a **volume** loud enough to be heard and at a **rate** that is not too fast or too slow. Make **eye contact** with your audience and with members of the other team, and use hand gestures in a natural way.

Follow the Rules The chairperson conducts the debate. He or she should state the proposition being debated and enforce the time limits for speakers and the rules of **etiquette,** or agreed-upon manners.

TIP Plan your rebuttal speeches in advance, before you hear what the other side says about your argument. The time allowed for rebuttal speeches is short, so you must focus only on the opposing team's most important points. Don't try to address every point they make.

SKILLS FOCUS

Listening and Speaking Skills
Use constructive arguments, refutations, and rebuttals. Use effective delivery techniques.

To follow debate etiquette, you should be respectful and polite and use gestures, a tone of voice, and vocabulary that are appropriate for your audience. It is traditional in debates to refer to a speaker on the other team as "my worthy opponent."

Speaking in Turn A traditional debate follows this schedule. Each team member delivers one constructive and one rebuttal speech.

TRADITIONAL DEBATE SCHEDULE

First Part: Constructive Speeches	Intermission	Second Part: Rebuttal Speeches
(10 minutes each)		(5 minutes each)
1st Affirmative Team Speaker		1st Negative Team Speaker
1st Negative Team Speaker		1st Affirmative Team Speaker
2nd Affirmative Team Speaker		2nd Negative Team Speaker
2nd Negative Team Speaker		2nd Affirmative Team Speaker

Judge a Debate

Win or Lose Unlike a football game, a debate does not always have a clear winner. Normally, in order to determine a winner, three appointed judges listen to the debate and evaluate how well each speaker met certain standards. To judge for yourself which team won a debate, answer the questions in the following chart.

QUESTIONS FOR JUDGING A DEBATE

Content	Delivery
1. Did the team prove that a significant problem does/does not exist? How thorough was the team's analysis of the problem?	**1.** Did the speakers seem confident and well prepared? Explain.
2. How did the team convince you that the proposition is/is not the best solution to solving the problem?	**2.** Did the speakers maintain eye contact and speak at an appropriate rate and volume? Explain.
3. How effectively did the team present reasons and evidence supporting the case? Was evidence credible, valid, and relevant?	**3.** Did the speakers observe proper debate etiquette? Explain.
4. How effectively did the team refute and rebut arguments made by the opposing team?	

PRACTICE & APPLY 5 Participate in a debate on a controversial proposition. First, research the proposition and prepare speeches. Then, present your speeches, following the rules of etiquette for a debate.

Analyzing Irony and Ambiguity

DIRECTIONS: Read the following fable. Then, read and respond to the questions that follow.

The Princess and the Tin Box

James Thurber

Once upon a time, in a far country, there lived a King whose daughter was the prettiest princess in the world. Her eyes were like the cornflower, her hair was sweeter than the hyacinth, and her throat made the swan look dusty.

From the time she was a year old, the Princess had been showered with presents. Her nursery looked like Cartier's[1] window. Her toys were all made of gold or platinum or diamonds or emeralds. She was not permitted to have wooden blocks or china dolls or rubber dogs or linen books, because such materials were considered cheap for the daughter of a king.

When she was seven, she was allowed to attend the wedding of her brother and throw real pearls at the bride instead of rice. Only the nightingale, with his lyre[2] of gold, was permitted to sing for the Princess. The common blackbird, with his boxwood flute, was kept out of the palace grounds. She walked in silver-and-samite[3] slippers to a sapphire-and-topaz bathroom and slept in an ivory bed inlaid with rubies.

On the day the Princess was eighteen, the King sent a royal ambassador to the courts of five neighboring kingdoms to announce that he would give his daughter's hand in marriage to the prince who brought her the gift she liked the most.

The first prince to arrive at the palace rode a swift white stallion and laid at the feet of the Princess an enormous apple made of solid gold which he had taken from a dragon who had guarded it for a thousand years. It was placed on a long ebony table set up to hold the gifts of the Princess' suitors. The second prince, who came on a gray charger, brought her a nightingale made of a thousand diamonds, and it was placed beside the golden apple. The third prince, riding on a black horse, carried a great jewel box made of platinum and sapphires, and it was placed next to the diamond nightingale. The fourth prince, astride a fiery yellow horse, gave the Princess a gigantic heart made of rubies

SKILLS
FOCUS

Pages 394–397
cover
Literary Skills
Analyze irony
and ambiguity.

---

1. **Cartier's** (kär′tē•āz): store selling expensive jewelry in New York City.
2. **lyre** (līr) *n.:* small stringed instrument.
3. **samite** (sam′īt)*n.* used as *adj.:* heavy silk fabric.

and pierced by an emerald arrow. It was placed next to the platinum-and-sapphire jewel box.

Now the fifth prince was the strongest and handsomest of all the five suitors, but he was the son of a poor king whose realm had been overrun by mice and locusts and wizards and mining engineers so that there was nothing much of value left in it. He came plodding up to the palace of the Princess on a plow horse, and he brought her a small tin box filled with mica and feldspar and hornblende[4] which he had picked up on the way.

The other princes roared with disdainful laughter when they saw the tawdry gift the fifth prince had brought to the Princess. But she examined it with great interest and squealed with delight, for all her life she had been glutted with precious stones and priceless metals, but she had never seen tin before or mica or feldspar or hornblende. The tin box was placed next to the ruby heart pierced with an emerald arrow.

"Now," the King said to his daughter, "you must select the gift you like best and marry the prince that brought it."

---

4. **mica . . . hornblende:** types of ordinary rocks.

Drawing for "The Princess and the Tin Box" (1948) by James Thurber.

The Princess smiled and walked up to the table and picked up the present she liked the most. It was the platinum-and-sapphire jewel box, the gift of the third prince.

"The way I figure it," she said, "is this. It is a very large and expensive box, and when I am married, I will meet many admirers who will give me precious gems with which to fill it to the top. Therefore, it is the most valuable of all the gifts my suitors have brought me, and I like it the best."

The Princess married the third prince that very day in the midst of great merriment and high revelry. More than a hundred thousand pearls were thrown at her and she loved it.

Moral: All those who thought that the Princess was going to select the tin box filled with worthless stones instead of one of the other gifts will kindly stay after class and write one hundred times on the blackboard, "I would rather have a hunk of aluminum silicate than a diamond necklace."

---

1. The details of the princess's life before her eighteenth birthday imply that she was —

  A raised to value only material goods

  B indifferent to the feelings of others

  C easily bored

  D not interested in getting married

2. Which adjective *best* describes the princess's **character**?

  F materialistic

  G curious

  H indecisive

  J modest

3. How are the gifts of the first four princes similar?

  A They are made from precious materials.

  B They are more valuable than anything the princess has ever been given.

  C They are useful objects.

  D They please the king more than the princess.

Collection 5: Skills Review

4. Which is the *most* important reason for expecting the princess to choose the fifth prince's gift?

   F The fifth prince is the strongest and the most handsome of the suitors.

   G His gift is not valuable.

   H She seems most impressed by his gift.

   J She feels sorry for the fifth prince because he is poor.

5. The princess's choice of the third prince's gift is an example of —

   A verbal irony

   B ambiguity

   C dramatic irony

   D situational irony

6. What **theme,** or insight about life, does the fable (and especially the moral) suggest?

   F It's impossible to understand others.

   G Some people rush to judge others.

   H Everyone really values material goods, and it is foolish to pretend otherwise.

   J People value love more than wealth.

7. Why is the moral **ironic**?

   A The reader expects the author to criticize the fifth prince for giving the princess a tin box.

   B The reader expects the author to find fault with the princess's values.

   C The reader expects the author to praise the king for thinking of his daughter's happiness.

   D The reader expects the author to express admiration for the third prince's clever gift.

8. What is the **tone** of the fable?

   F Ironic and grim

   G Ironic and sorrowful

   H Ironic and joyful

   J Ironic and humorous

Constructed Response

9. **Ambiguity** occurs in a story when there are several possible meanings or outcomes. Explain how the author's intentions could be considered ambiguous.

Collection 5: Skills Review

Vocabulary Skills

Test Practice

Synonyms

DIRECTIONS: Choose the *best* synonym for the underlined word in each sentence.

1. In "The Gift of the Magi," Jim buys Della the coveted combs that she had greatly admired.
   - A beautiful
   - B longed-for
   - C expensive
   - D unusual

2. Before Della cuts off her long, shining, wavy hair in "The Gift of the Magi," it is compared to a cascade.
   - F crown
   - G silk
   - H waterfall
   - J ribbons

3. In "The Lady, or the Tiger?" the princess's fervent nature causes her to have intense feelings of love and jealousy.
   - A sensitive
   - B unforgiving
   - C stubborn
   - D passionate

4. The king in "The Lady, or the Tiger?" believes that his system of justice is impartial because each prisoner's fate is decided entirely by chance.
   - F unbiased
   - G predictable
   - H merciful
   - J reasonable

5. In "The Lady, or the Tiger?" prisoners face the dire threat of being torn to pieces by a tiger.
   - A suspenseful
   - B unjust
   - C unexpected
   - D terrible

6. In "A Defense of the Jury System," the author advocates preserving the jury system because he feels that it's the fairest system of justice.
   - F opposes
   - G criticizes
   - H supports
   - J describes

7. In "A Defense of the Jury System," the author states that juries are criticized for having only a superficial understanding of complex issues.
   - A wrong
   - B forgetful
   - C shallow
   - D prejudiced

8. The author of "A Defense of the Jury System" says that negative publicity should not obscure the fact that most juries deliver fair verdicts.
   - F conceal
   - G reveal
   - H exaggerate
   - J suggest

SKILLS FOCUS

Vocabulary Skills
Identify synonyms.

Collection 5: Skills Review

Writing Skills

Test Practice

DIRECTIONS: Read the following paragraph from a student's persuasive essay. Then, answer the questions below it.

(1) More people should ride bicycles. (2) Using a bicycle as a means of transportation helps you to exercise each day. (3) If you ride as quick as a flash, you can burn 240 calories an hour. (4) Another reason why people should use bicycles is that riding a bicycle does not cause pollution. (5) Exhaust from cars, on the other hand, contributes to air, ground, and water pollution. (6) So get a move on for your health and the environment—dust off that old three-speed, pump up the tires, and ride to school tomorrow.

1. To help convey an opinion, the writer could revise sentence 1 to say
   A   Bicycling can be good for both you and the environment.
   B   I have two bicycles—a mountain bike and a road bike.
   C   Repairing a flat bicycle tire is easy when you know how.
   D   Many families enjoy bicycling as a hobby they can do together.

2. How might the writer of this paragraph address the concern of some readers that riding a bicycle is dangerous?
   F   by citing statistics of people who ride bicycles twice a week
   G   by comparing bicycles to cars
   H   by explaining how helmets and bike lanes have made bicycling safer
   J   by telling readers about two friends who bike to school every day

3. Which of the following sentences could be added to support the logical appeal that bicycling is a good form of exercise?
   A   Ride slowly when you begin.
   B   I prefer riding a bike to jogging.
   C   Three-mile trips are quicker by bike.
   D   Riding a bicycle tones the leg muscles.

4. How could the writer revise sentence 3 so that it conveys a serious tone?
   F   If you ride as quick as a flash, you can burn some major calories.
   G   If you ride lickety-split, you can burn 240 calories an hour.
   H   If you ride at 6 miles per hour, you can burn 240 calories in an hour.
   J   If you ride at 6 miles per hour, you can burn a whole lot of calories.

5. In a debate, which of the following sentences would the above paragraph support?
   A   *Resolved:* That bicycling is a safe form of exercise.
   B   *Resolved:* That cars cause air, ground, and water pollution.
   C   *Resolved:* That people should use bicycles as transportation.
   D   *Resolved:* That people should wear helmets while bicycling.

SKILLS FOCUS

Writing Skills
Write a persuasive essay.

Ties That Bind

Literary Focus:
Analyzing Symbolism and Allegory

Informational Reading Focus:
Synthesizing Sources: Works by One Author

INTERNET
Collection Resources
Keyword: LE7 9-6

Quilting Time (1986) by Romare Bearden.
Glass mosaic (c. 9′ 5″ × 13′ 11″).

Estate of Romare Bearden. © Romare Howard Bearden Foundation.
Licensed by VAGA, New York.

Elements of Literature

Symbolism and Allegory *by* John Malcolm Brinnin
LAYERS OF MEANING

What Symbols Stand For

A **symbol** is often an ordinary object, event, person, or animal to which we have attached extraordinary meaning and significance. We use a rectangle of dyed cloth to symbolize a country. We use a picture of a skull and crossbones to stand for poison or danger. We send red roses as a symbol of love.

Where Do Symbols Come From?

Symbols can be inherited or invented. The most familiar symbols have been inherited—that is, they have been handed down over time. For example, no one knows exactly who first thought of using the lion to symbolize power, courage, and domination. Once these qualities were associated with the animal, images of lions appeared on flags, banners, coats of arms, and castle walls, and the lion became a **public symbol,** one that shows up in art and literature even today.

People throughout history have endowed ordinary objects with meanings far beyond their simple functions: A crown symbolizes royalty; an olive branch symbolizes peace; five linked rings symbolize the Olympics.

Symbols can also be invented. You probably have a symbol for your school. Writers often take a new object, character, or event and make it the embodiment of some human concern. Some invented symbols in literature have become so widely known that they have gained the status of public

symbols. Peter Pan as the symbol of eternal childhood is an example.

Why Create Symbols?

You may ask why writers don't just come right out and say what they mean. Symbols allow writers to suggest layers and layers of meaning—possibilities that a simple, literal statement could never convey. A symbol is like a pebble cast into a pond: It sends out ever-widening ripples of meaning.

In the short story "Marigolds" (page 141), a poor woman has no beauty in her world except the dazzling marigolds that she plants around her ramshackle house. The children in the story, who are as poor as the old woman, hate the flowers and all that they stand for. In a moment of thoughtless hatred and violence, one girl destroys all the bright flowers.

Those flowers are real flowers in the story, but we also get a sense that they symbolize something else, something larger than the flowers themselves. Some readers might feel that they symbolize hope and beauty and that the children are so angry about their poverty that they want to destroy anything that expresses the beauty of another world. Other readers will have different ideas about what the marigolds stand for, but most will agree that the marigolds work on more than just a literal level in the story.

You may not be able to articulate fully what a certain symbol means, but you will find that the symbol, if it is powerful and well chosen, will speak forcefully to your emotions and to your imagination. You may also find that you will remember and think about the symbol long after you have forgotten other parts of the story's plot.

Allegory: Split-level Stories

An **allegory** is a story in which characters, settings, and actions stand for something beyond themselves. In some types of allegories, the characters and setting represent abstract ideas or moral qualities. In other types, characters and situations stand for historical figures and events.

An allegory can be read on one level for its literal, or straightforward, meaning and on a second level for its symbolic, or allegorical, meaning. Allegories are often intended to teach a moral lesson or to make a comment about goodness and vice.

Some of the most famous allegories feature characters and places whose names describe what they symbolize. In an old English play called *Everyman,* the main character is named Everyman (he stands for exactly what his name indicates). One day, Everyman is summoned by Death to give an accounting of his life. Everyman asks his friends Fellowship, Beauty, Strength, and Good Deeds to go with him to tell Death that he has led a good life. Only Good Deeds stays with him to the end. The allegory in *Everyman* doesn't get in the way of a very good story! In fact, *Everyman,* written in the 1400s, is still revived in theaters today, and it still gets good reviews.

Practice

A. Think about the great number of symbols we're surrounded by in everyday life. For starters, identify what the items below stand for. Then, see if you can explain the basis for the symbol—why is this symbol appropriate for what it stands for?

1. A snake
2. An eagle
3. Spring
4. An owl
5. A white flag

B. Here is a brief poem that works on two levels: a literal level and a symbolic level. A *fen* is a swampy place. What does the fen symbolize in this poem?

I May, I Might, I Must

If you will tell me why the fen
appears impassable, I then
will tell you why I think that I
can get across it if I try.
—Marianne Moore

Ties That Bind

Make the Connection

Quickwrite ✏️

Think about the ties that bind you to your family, friends, and community. What keeps you connected to them—love and loyalty, shared interests and experiences, or similar backgrounds, for example? What factors sometimes separate you from others? List your ideas.

Exploring the Theme: Ties That Bind

This collection centers on the rewards and responsibilities accompanying the ties that bind us to friends, family, and the global community. In the short story "The Scarlet Ibis," two brothers are bound together by love and shame. In his essay "The Grandfather," Gary Soto describes his grandfather's ties to both his family and his Mexican roots. The short story "The Golden Kite, the Silver Wind" tells the tale of two ancient cities bound together in a cycle of competition. You'll also read the views of the late scientist Albert Einstein concerning the need for nations to work together for peace. In "The Osage Orange Tree," the story you are about to read, a teenage boy arrives in a new town and finds himself tied to a girl by a mysterious, largely unspoken bond.

Literary Focus

Symbol

A **symbol** is an object, person, animal, or event that has a meaning beyond itself. Through the use of symbols, writers communicate ideas or emotions without directly stating them. One way a writer gives a symbol meaning is by having it appear in a story repeatedly. For example, an empty street that a character continually passes can come to symbolize loneliness. As you read this story, pay attention to the Osage orange tree that gives the story its title. How does the tree gain meaning through its repeated appearance in the story?

Literary Skills
Understand symbol.

Osage orange tree.

The Osage Orange Tree

William Stafford

On that first day of high school in the prairie town where the tree was, I stood in the sun by the flagpole and watched, but pretended not to watch, the others. They stood in groups and talked and knew each other, all except one—a girl though—in a faded blue dress, carrying a sack lunch and standing near the corner looking everywhere but at the crowd.

I might talk to her, I thought. But of course it was out of the question.

That first day was easier when the classes started. Some of the teachers were kind; some were frightening. Some of the students didn't care, but I listened and waited; and at the end of the day I was relieved, less conspicuous[1] from then on.

But that day was not really over. As I hurried to carry my new paper route I was thinking about how in a strange town, if you are quiet, no one notices, and some may like you, later. I was thinking about this when I reached the north edge of town where the scattering houses dwindle. Beyond them to the north lay just openness, the plains, a big swoop of nothing. There, at the last house, just as I cut across a lot and threw to the last customer, I saw the girl in the blue dress coming along the street, heading on out of town, carrying books. And she saw me.

"Hello."

"Hello."

And because we stopped we were friends. I didn't know how I could stop, but I didn't hurry on. I stood. There was nothing to do but to act as if I were walking on out too. I had three papers left in the bag, and I frantically began to fold them—box them, as we called it—for throwing. We had begun to walk and talk. The girl was timid;[2] I became more bold. Not much, but a little. ❶

"Have you gone to school here before?" I asked.

"Yes, I went here last year."

---

1. **conspicuous** (kən·spik′yoo·əs) *adj.:* noticeable.
2. **timid** (tim′id) *adj.:* shy; lacking self-confidence.

THEME

❶What do the narrator and the girl in the blue dress have in common?

Lone Cloud & Tree
(2004) by Rod Bouc
(b. 1950).
Monotype. 17¾ x
23¾ in.

Courtesy of the artist/
Keny Galleries, Ohio.

SYMBOL

❷ Note the way the
tree on the corner is
described in this para-
graph. Then, compare
the tree to the dusty
road and the gray
house by the sagging
barn. Why does the
tree seem to stand
out in this location?

A long pause. A meadowlark sitting on a fencepost hunched his wings
and flew. I kicked through the dust of the road.

I began to look ahead. Where could we possibly be walking to? I
couldn't be walking just because I wanted to be with her.

Fortunately, there was one more house, a gray house by a sagging
barn, set two hundred yards from the road.

"I thought I'd see if I could get a customer here," I said, waving toward
the house.

"That's where I live."

"Oh."

We were at the dusty car tracks that turned off the road to the house.
The girl stopped. There was a tree at that corner, a straight but little tree
with slim branches and shiny dark leaves. ❷

"I could take a paper tonight to see if my father wants to buy it."

A great relief, this. What could I have said to her parents? I held out a
paper, dropped it, picked it up, brushing off the dust. "No, here's a new
one"—a great action, putting the dusty paper in the bag over my shoulder and pulling out a fresh one. When she took the paper we stood there
a minute. The wind was coming in over the grass. She looked out with a
tranquil³ expression.

She walked away past the tree, and I hurried quickly back toward
town. Could anyone in the houses have been watching? I looked back
once. The girl was standing on the small bridge halfway in to her house.
I hurried on.

The next day at school I didn't ask her whether her father wanted to
take the paper. When the others were there I wouldn't say anything. I

---

3. tranquil (traŋˈkwəl) *adj.*: calm; peaceful.

stood with the boys. In American history the students could choose their seats, and I saw that she was too quiet and plainly dressed for many to notice her. But I crowded in with the boys, pushing one aside, scrambling for a seat by the window.

That night I came to the edge of town. Two papers were left, and I walked on out. The meadowlark was there. By some reeds in a ditch by the road a dragonfly—snake feeders, we called them—glinted. The sun was going down, and the plains were stretched out and lifted, some way, to the horizon. Could I go on up to the house? I didn't think so, but I walked on. Then, by the tree where her road turned off, she was standing. She was holding her books. More confused than ever, I stopped.

"My father will take the paper," she said.

She told me always to leave the paper at the foot of the tree. She insisted on that, saying their house was too far; and it is true that I was far off my route, a long way, a half-mile out of my territory. But I didn't think of that.

And so we were acquainted. What I remember best in that town is those evening walks to the tree. Every night—or almost every night—the girl was there. Evangeline was her name. We didn't say much. On Friday night of the first week she gave me a dime, the cost of the paper. It was a poor newspaper, by the way, cheap, sensational, unreliable. I never went up to her house. We never talked together at school. But all the time we knew each other; we just happened to meet. Every evening. ❸

There was a low place in the meadow by that corner. The fall rains made a pond there, and in the evenings sometimes ducks would be coming in—a long line with set wings down the wind, and then a turn, and a skimming glide to the water. The wind would be blowing and the grass bent down. The evenings got colder and colder. The wind was cold. As winter came on the time at the tree was dimmer, but not dark. In the winter there was snow. The pond was frozen over; all the plains were white. I had to walk down the ruts of the road and leave the paper in the crotch of the tree, sometimes, when it was cold. The wind made a sound through the black branches. But usually, even on cold evenings, Evangeline was there.

At school we played ball at noon—the boys did. And I got acquainted. I learned that Evangeline's brother was janitor at the school. A big dark boy he was—a man, middle-aged I thought at the time. He didn't ever let on that he knew me. I would see him sweeping the halls, bent down, slow. I would see him and Evangeline take their sack lunches over to the south side of the building. Once I slipped away from the ball game and went over there, but he looked at me so steadily, without moving, that I pretended to be looking for a book, and quickly went back, and got in the game, and struck out.

THEME AND SYMBOL

❸ Why do you think the narrator and Evangeline meet only at the tree? What does the tree **symbolize** at this point in the story?

THEME AND SYMBOL

❹ What does the narrator reveal in this paragraph about the time period during which he develops a bond with Evangeline?

You don't know about those winters, and especially that winter. Those were the dust years.[4] Wheat was away down in price. Everyone was poor—poor in a way that you can't understand. I made two dollars a week, or something like that, on my paper route. I could tell about working for ten cents an hour—and then not getting paid; about families that ate wheat, boiled, for their main food, and burned wheat for fuel. You don't know how it would be. All through that hard winter I carried a paper to the tree by the pond, in the evening, and gave it to Evangeline. ❹

In the cold weather Evangeline wore a heavier dress, a dark, straight, heavy dress, under a thick black coat. Outdoors she wore a knitted cap that fastened under her chin. She was dressed this way when we met and she took the paper. The reeds were broken now. The meadowlark was gone.

And then came the spring. I have forgotten to tell just how Evangeline looked. She was of medium height, and slim. Her face was pale, her forehead high, her eyes blue. Her tranquil face I remember well. I remember her watching the wind come in over the grass. Her dress was long, her feet small. I can remember her by the tree, with her books, or walking on up the road toward her house and stopping on the bridge halfway up there, but she didn't wave, and I couldn't tell whether she was watching me or not. I always looked back as I went over the rise toward town.

And I can remember her in the room at school. She came into American history one spring day, the first really warm day. She had changed from the dark heavy dress to the dull blue one of the last fall; and she had on a new belt, a gray belt, with blue stitching along the edges. As she passed in front of Jane Wright, a girl who sat on the front row, I heard Jane say to the girl beside her, "Why look at Evangeline—that old dress of hers has a new belt!"

"Stop a minute, Evangeline," Jane said, "let me see your new dress."

Evangeline stopped and looked uncertainly at Jane and blushed. "It's just made over," she said, "it's just . . . ."

"It's cute, Dear," Jane said; and as Evangeline went on Jane nudged her friend in the ribs and the friend smothered a giggle. ❺

THEME

❺ Describe Jane and her friend's attitude toward Evangeline. What separates Evangeline from her classmates?

Well, that was a good year. Commencement time came, and—along with the newspaper job—I had the task of preparing for finals and all. One thing, I wasn't a student who took part in the class play or anything like that. I was just one of the boys—twenty-fourth in line to get my diploma.

And graduation was bringing an end to my paper-carrying. My father covered a big territory in our part of the state, selling farm equipment; and we were going to move at once to a town seventy miles south. Only because of my finishing the school year had we stayed till graduation.

---

4. **dust years:** reference to a severe drought that affected the Great Plains in the early 1930s, which earned the region the name the "Dust Bowl."

The Young Apprentice (c. 1917) by Amedeo Modigliani (1884–1920).
Musée de l'Orangerie, Paris. Oil on canvas. 100 x 65 in.

THEME

❻ How does the narrator seem to feel about moving again? How do you know?

I had taught another boy my route, always leaving him at the end and walking on out, by myself, to the tree. I didn't really have to go around with him that last day, the day of graduation, but I was going anyway. ❻

At the graduation exercises, held that May afternoon, I wore my brown Sunday suit. My mother was in the audience. It was a heavy day. The girls had on new dresses. But I didn't see *her*.

I suppose that I did deserve old man Sutton's "Shhh!" as we lined up to march across the stage, but I for the first time in the year forgot my caution, and asked Jane where Evangeline was. She shrugged, and I could see for myself that she was not there.

We marched across the stage; our diplomas were ours; our parents filed out; to the strains of a march on the school organ we trailed to the hall. I unbuttoned my brown suit coat, stuffed the diploma in my pocket, and sidled out of the group and upstairs.

Evangeline's brother was emptying wastebaskets at the far end of the hall. I sauntered toward him and stopped. I didn't know what I wanted to say. Unexpectedly, he solved my problem. Stopping in his work, holding a partly empty wastebasket over the canvas sack he wore over his shoulder, he stared at me, as if almost to say something.

"I noticed that—your sister wasn't here," I said. The noise below was dwindling. The hall was quiet, an echoey place; my voice sounded terribly loud. He emptied the rest of the wastebasket and shifted easily. He was a man, in big overalls. He stared at me.

"Evangeline couldn't come," he said. He stopped, looked at me again, and said, "She stole."

"Stole?" I said. "Stole what?"

He shrugged and went toward the next wastebasket, but I followed him.

"She stole the money from her bank—the money she was to use for her graduation dress," he said. He walked stolidly on, and I stopped. He deliberately turned away as he picked up the next wastebasket. But he said something else, half to himself. "You knew her. You talked to her . . . I know." He walked away. ❼

I hurried downstairs and outside. The new carrier would have the papers almost delivered by now; so I ran up the street toward the north. I took a paper from him at the end of the street and told him to go back. I didn't pay any more attention to him.

No one was at the tree, and I turned, for the first time, up the road to the house. I walked over the bridge and on up the narrow, rutty tracks. The house was gray and lopsided. The ground of the yard was packed; nothing grew there. By the back door, the door to which the road led, there was a grayish-white place on the ground where the dishwater had been thrown. A gaunt shepherd dog trotted out growling.

THEME

❼ Why do you think Evangeline stole the money? What might her brother be thinking when he says to the narrator, "You knew her"?

And the door opened suddenly, as if someone had been watching me come up the track. A woman came out—a woman stern-faced, with a shawl over her head and a dark lumpy dress on—came out on the back porch and shouted, "Go 'way, go 'way! We don't want no papers!" She waved violently with one hand, holding the other on her shawl, at her throat. She coughed so hard that she leaned over and put her hand against one of the uprights of the porch. Her face was red. She glanced toward the barn and leaned toward me. "Go 'way!"

Behind me a meadowlark sang. Over all the plains swooped the sky. The land was drawn up somehow toward the horizon.

I stood there, half-defiant, half-ashamed. The dog continued to growl and to pace around me, stiff-legged, his tail down. The windows of the house were all blank, with blinds drawn. I couldn't say anything.

I stood a long time and then, lowering the newspaper I had held out, I stood longer, waiting, without thinking of what to do. The meadowlark bubbled over again, but I turned and walked away, looking back once or twice. The old woman continued to stand, leaning forward, her head out. She glanced at the barn, but didn't call out any more.

My heels dug into the grayish place where the dishwater had been thrown; the dog skulked along behind.

At the bridge, halfway to the road, I stopped and looked back. The dog was lying down again; the porch was empty; and the door was closed. Turning the other way, I looked toward town. Near me stood our ragged

Winter Furrows (1940) by Andrew Wyeth (b. 1917). Watercolor on paper. 21" x 29".

©Andrew Wyeth. Cedarhurst Center for the Arts. John J. and Eleanor R. Mitchell Foundation. Mt. Vernon, Illinois. Gift of John J. Parish. 1973.3.38.

The Osage Orange Tree   **411**

little tree—an Osage orange tree[5] it was. It was feebly coming into leaf, green all over the branches, among the sharp thorns. I hadn't wondered before how it grew there, all alone, in the plains country, neglected. Over our pond some ducks came slicing in. ❽

Standing there on the bridge, still holding the folded—boxed—newspaper, that worthless paper, I could see everything. I looked out along the road to town. From the bridge you could see the road going away, to where it went over the rise.

Glancing around, I flipped that last newspaper under the bridge and then bent far over and looked where it had gone. There they were—a pile of boxed newspapers, thrown in a heap, some new, some worn and weathered, by rain, by snow. ❾

---

5. **Osage orange tree:** thorny tree that thrives in hot, dry conditions. Its strong, dense wood rarely rots. Growing quickly at first, it produces a greenish-yellow fruit, shaped like an orange, that cannot be eaten.

SYMBOL

❽ How is the description of the tree in this paragraph different from earlier descriptions? How has the tree's **symbolic** meaning grown since the beginning of the story?

THEME

❾ Who threw the newspapers under the bridge? Why?

Meet the Writer
William Stafford

Landscapes of Youth

Born in Hutchinson, Kansas, of Native American heritage, William Stafford (1914–1993) moved frequently while he was growing up. His father's many jobs took the family from one small Kansas town to another. The people, animals, and landscapes of his childhood became lifelong subjects of his writing. Stafford has written that the houses in which he spent his youth were always on the outskirts of town, beyond which there were "adventure, fields forever, or rivers that wended off over the horizon, forever. And in the center of town was a library, another kind of edge out there forever, to explore."

Early in his adult life Stafford worked as a laborer in sugar-beet fields, on construction jobs, and in an oil refinery. He also spent four years in prison during World War II because of his conscientious objection to the war. Starting in 1948, Stafford taught at Lewis and Clark College in Portland, Oregon. For more than forty years he instructed and influenced several generations of students. At the same time, Stafford kept up a daily writing routine. Best known as a poet, he published more than twenty-eight collections of poetry during his lifetime. His work gained increasing acclaim for its skillful evocation of the natural world and the landscapes of the Midwest and West.

After You Read

Response and Analysis

Reading Check

1. What does Evangeline do with the money meant to be spent on her graduation dress? What are the consequences of her action?

Thinking Critically

2. What kind of person do you think the narrator is? Consider what he says and does. Then, list three or four adjectives you would use to describe his **character.**

3. The **setting**—the time and place of the story—plays a powerful role in this work. What details about the setting seem most significant to you? What **mood**—or feeling—do these details convey?

4. What do you think the Osage orange tree comes to **symbolize** for the narrator in the course of the story? To answer, consider

   • the physical descriptions of the tree

   • the tree's association with Evangeline

   • the story's setting

5. Review the description of an Osage orange tree in footnote 5. Why do you think the writer chose to use this particular type of tree as a **symbol**?

6. Think about how the collection theme "Ties That Bind" relates to this story by answering the questions below.

   • What is the tie that initially binds the narrator and Evangeline together?

   • What continues to bind the two characters together as the school year progresses?

   • The narrator tells this story during a later point in his life. Why do you think these events have remained important to him?

Extending and Evaluating

7. List the factors connecting characters to—or separating them from—others in the story. Although the story is set in the 1930s, do you think these factors play a role in our lives today? Why or why not? Be sure to check your Quickwrite notes.

Exploring the Theme
Ties That Bind

In the rest of this collection, you'll read about the various types of ties that bind people to one another. As you read, think about the reasons these ties exist and the rewards and responsibilities that come with being connected to others.

Literary Focus
Analyze symbol.

Before You Read

Make the Connection
Quickwrite

Make a list of situations that might make someone feel proud. Is pride positive or negative—can it be both? Jot down your thoughts about what it means to be proud.

Literary Focus
Symbols: Deeper Meanings

A **symbol** is an object, person, animal, or event that stands for something more than itself. We're surrounded by symbols in our everyday lives. The dove, often pictured on greeting cards, is a universal symbol of peace.

In literature, symbols add deeper levels of meaning to a work. Sometimes a symbol will be associated with a particular character. In "The Scarlet Ibis" you'll notice similarities and links between one character and a bird. These are hints that the author is making a symbolic connection between the two that can deepen your understanding of the character.

In the hands of a skillful writer, symbols have the power to move us deeply. If you're like most readers, this story about two young brothers will move you as well.

Reading Skills
Making Inferences from Details

When you notice details in a story, you're aware of the little things. Such details may seem insignificant at first, but they can develop more meaning as you read further. It's up to you to make **inferences,** or educated guesses, about what the writer wants to convey through the details.

As you read "The Scarlet Ibis," keep track of the little things—color, gesture, weather—and see what larger meanings they might point to. The questions at the open-book signs will help you.

SKILLS FOCUS

Literary Skills
Understand symbolism.

Reading Skills
Make inferences from details.

INTERNET

Vocabulary Practice

Keyword: LE7 9-6

Background

This story is set in the American South. Its climax takes place in 1918, the year World War I ended. You'll find references in the story to battles being fought far from its peaceful southern setting. As you read, think about why the author chose this setting. (See Meet the Writer on page 426.)

Vocabulary Development

sullenly (sul′ən·lē) *adv.*: resentfully; gloomily.

imminent (im′ə·nənt) *adj.*: near; about to happen.

iridescent (ir′i·des′ənt) *adj.*: rainbow-like; displaying a shifting range of colors.

serene (sə·rēn′) *adj.*: peaceful; calm.

infallibility (in·fal′ə·bil′i·tē) *n.*: inability to make a mistake.

blighted (blīt′id) *v.* used as *adj.*: suffering from conditions that destroy or prevent growth.

doggedness (dôg′id·nis) *n.*: stubbornness; persistence.

reiterated (rē·it′ə·rāt′id) *v.*: repeated.

precariously (pri·ker′ē·əs·lē) *adv.*: unsteadily; insecurely.

mar (mär) *v.*: damage; spoil.

The Scarlet Ibis

James Hurst

Doodle was just about the craziest brother a boy ever had.

It was in the clove of seasons, summer was dead but autumn had not yet been born, that the ibis lit in the bleeding tree. The flower garden was stained with rotting brown magnolia petals, and ironweeds grew rank[1] amid the purple phlox. The five o'clocks by the chimney still marked time, but the oriole nest in the elm was untenanted and rocked back and forth like an empty cradle. The last graveyard flowers were blooming, and their smell drifted across the cotton field and through every room of our house, speaking softly the names of our dead.

It's strange that all this is still so clear to me, now that that summer has long since fled and time has had its way. A grindstone stands where the bleeding tree stood, just outside the kitchen door, and now if an oriole sings in the elm, its song seems to die up in the leaves, a silvery dust. The flower garden is prim, the house a gleaming white, and the pale fence across the yard stands straight and spruce. But sometimes (like right now), as I sit in the cool, green-draped parlor, the grindstone begins to turn, and time with all its changes is ground away—and I remember Doodle.

Doodle was just about the craziest brother a boy ever had. Of course, he wasn't a crazy crazy like old Miss Leedie, who was in love with President Wilson and wrote him a letter every day, but was a nice crazy, like someone you meet in your dreams. He was born when I was six and was, from the outset, a disappointment. He seemed all head, with a tiny body which was red and shriveled like an old man's. Everybody thought he was going to die—everybody except Aunt Nicey, who had delivered him. She said he would live because he was born in a caul[2] and cauls were made from Jesus' nightgown. Daddy had Mr. Heath, the carpenter, build a little

mahogany coffin for him. But he didn't die, and when he was three months old, Mama and Daddy decided they might as well name him. They named him William Armstrong, which was like tying a big tail on a small kite. Such a name sounds good only on a tombstone.

I thought myself pretty smart at many things, like holding my breath, running, jumping, or climbing the vines in Old Woman Swamp, and I wanted more than anything else someone to race to Horsehead Landing, someone to box with, and someone to perch with in the top fork of the great pine behind the barn, where across the fields and swamps you could see the sea. I wanted a brother. But Mama, crying, told me that even if William Armstrong lived, he would never do these things with me. He might not, she sobbed, even be "all there." He might, as long as he lived, lie on the rubber sheet in the center of the bed in the front bedroom where the white

---

1. **rank** (raŋk) *adj.:* thick and wild. *Rank* also means "smelly."
2. **caul** (kôl) *n.:* membrane (thin, skinlike material) that sometimes covers a baby's head at birth.

marquisette[3] curtains billowed out in the afternoon sea breeze, rustling like palmetto fronds.[4]

It was bad enough having an invalid brother, but having one who possibly was not all there was unbearable, so I began to make plans to kill him by smothering him with a pillow. However, one afternoon as I watched him, my head poked between the iron posts of the foot of the bed, he looked straight at me and grinned. I skipped through the rooms, down the echoing halls, shouting, "Mama, he smiled. He's all there! He's all there!" and he was.

When he was two, if you laid him on his stomach, he began to try to move himself, straining terribly. The doctor said that with his weak heart this strain would probably kill him, but it didn't. Trembling, he'd push himself up, turning first red, then a soft purple, and finally collapse back onto the bed like an old worn-out doll. I can still see Mama watching him, her hand pressed tight across her mouth, her eyes wide and unblinking. But he learned to crawl (it was his third winter), and we brought him out of the front bedroom, putting him on the rug before the fireplace. For the first time he became one of us.

MAKING INFERENCES

1. What can you **infer** about the little boy from the **details** in this paragraph?

As long as he lay all the time in bed, we called him William Armstrong, even though it was formal and sounded as if we were referring to one of our ancestors, but with his creeping around on the deerskin rug and beginning to talk, something had to be done about his name. It was I who renamed him. When he crawled, he crawled backward, as if he were in reverse and couldn't change gears. If you called him, he'd turn around as if he were going in the other direction, then he'd back right up to you to be

picked up. Crawling backward made him look like a doodlebug[5] so I began to call him Doodle, and in time even Mama and Daddy thought it was a better name than William Armstrong. Only Aunt Nicey disagreed. She said caul babies should be treated with special respect since they might turn out to be saints. Renaming my brother was perhaps the kindest thing I ever did for him, because nobody expects much from someone called Doodle.

Although Doodle learned to crawl, he showed no signs of walking, but he wasn't idle. He talked so much that we all quit listening to what he said. It was about this time that Daddy built him a go-cart, and I had to pull him around. At first I just paraded him up and down the piazza,[6] but then he started crying to be taken out into the yard and it ended up by my having to lug him wherever I went. If I so much as picked up my cap, he'd start crying to go with me, and Mama would call from wherever she was, "Take Doodle with you."

He was a burden in many ways. The doctor had said that he mustn't get too excited, too hot, too cold, or too tired and that he must always be treated gently. A long list of don'ts went with him, all of which I ignored once we got out of the house. To discourage his coming with me, I'd run with him across the ends of the cotton rows and careen him around corners on two wheels. Sometimes I accidentally turned him over, but he never told Mama. His skin was very sensitive, and he had to wear a big straw hat whenever he went out. When the going got rough and he had to cling to the sides of the go-cart, the hat slipped all the way down over his ears. He was a sight. Finally, I could see I was licked. Doodle was my brother, and he was going to cling to me forever, no matter what I did, so I dragged him across the burning cotton field to share with him

---

3. **marquisette** (mär′ki·zet′) *adj.:* thin, netlike fabric.
4. **palmetto fronds:** fanlike leaves of a palm tree.

5. **doodlebug** (dood′l·bug′) *n.:* larva of a type of insect that moves backward.
6. **piazza** (pē·az′ə) *n.:* large covered porch.

the only beauty I knew, Old Woman Swamp. I pulled the go-cart through the sawtooth fern, down into the green dimness where the palmetto fronds whispered by the stream. I lifted him out and set him down in the soft rubber grass beside a tall pine. His eyes were round with wonder as he gazed about him, and his little hands began to stroke the rubber grass. Then he began to cry.

"For heaven's sake, what's the matter?" I asked, annoyed.

"It's so pretty," he said. "So pretty, pretty, pretty."

After that day Doodle and I often went down into Old Woman Swamp. I would gather wildflowers, wild violets, honeysuckle, yellow jasmine, snakeflowers, and waterlilies, and with wire grass we'd weave them into necklaces and crowns. We'd bedeck ourselves with our handiwork and loll about thus beautified, beyond the touch of the everyday world. Then when the slanted rays of the sun burned orange in the tops of the pines, we'd drop our jewels into the stream and watch them float away toward the sea.

There is within me (and with sadness I have watched it in others) a knot of cruelty borne by the stream of love, much as our blood sometimes bears the seed of our destruction, and at times I was mean to Doodle. One day I took him up to the barn loft and showed him his casket, telling him how we all had believed he would die. It was covered with a film of Paris green[7] sprinkled to kill the rats, and screech owls had built a nest inside it.

Doodle studied the mahogany box for a long time, then said, "It's not mine."

> **At times I was mean to Doodle.**

"It is," I said. "And before I'll help you down from the loft, you're going to have to touch it."

"I won't touch it," he said sullenly.

"Then I'll leave you here by yourself," I threatened, and made as if I were going down.

Doodle was frightened of being left. "Don't go leave me, Brother," he cried, and he leaned toward the coffin. His hand, trembling, reached out, and when he touched the casket, he screamed. A screech owl flapped out of the box into our faces, scaring us and covering us with Paris green. Doodle was paralyzed, so I put him on my shoulder and carried him down the ladder, and even when we were outside in the bright sunshine, he clung to me, crying, "Don't leave me. Don't leave me."

When Doodle was five years old, I was embarrassed at having a brother of that age who couldn't walk, so I set out to teach him. We were down in Old Woman Swamp and it was spring and the sick-sweet smell of bay flowers hung everywhere like a mournful song. "I'm going to teach you to walk, Doodle," I said.

He was sitting comfortably on the soft grass, leaning back against the pine. "Why?" he asked.

I hadn't expected such an answer. "So I won't have to haul you around all the time."

"I can't walk, Brother," he said.

"Who says so?" I demanded.

"Mama, the doctor—everybody."

"Oh, you can walk," I said, and I took him by the arms and stood him up. He collapsed onto the grass like a half-empty flour sack. It was as if he had no bones in his little legs.

"Don't hurt me, Brother," he warned.

---

7. **Paris green:** poisonous green powder used to kill insects.

Vocabulary
sullenly (sul′ən·lē) *adv.*: resentfully; gloomily.

"Shut up. I'm not going to hurt you. I'm going to teach you to walk." I heaved him up again, and again he collapsed.

This time he did not lift his face up out of the rubber grass. "I just can't do it. Let's make honeysuckle wreaths."

"Oh yes you can, Doodle," I said. "All you got to do is try. Now come on," and I hauled him up once more.

It seemed so hopeless from the beginning that it's a miracle I didn't give up. But all of us must have something or someone to be proud of, and Doodle had become mine. I did not know then that pride is a wonderful, terrible thing, a seed that bears two vines, life and death. Every day that summer we went to the pine beside the stream of Old Woman Swamp, and I put him on his feet at least a hundred times each afternoon. Occasionally I too became discouraged because it didn't seem as if he was trying, and I would say, "Doodle, don't you *want* to learn to walk?"

He'd nod his head, and I'd say, "Well, if you don't keep trying, you'll never learn." Then I'd paint for him a picture of us as old men, white-haired, him with a long white beard and me still pulling him around in the go-cart. This never failed to make him try again.

Finally, one day, after many weeks of practicing, he stood alone for a few seconds. When he fell, I grabbed him in my arms and hugged him, our laughter pealing through the swamp like a ringing bell. Now we knew it could be done. Hope no longer hid in the dark palmetto thicket but perched like a cardinal in the lacy toothbrush tree, brilliantly visible. "Yes, yes," I cried, and he cried it too, and the grass beneath us was soft and the smell of the swamp was sweet.

With success so <u>imminent</u>, we decided not to tell anyone until he could actually walk. Each

MAKING INFERENCES

2. What can you **infer** about the narrator from his comments about his pride and from his behavior toward Doodle?

day, barring rain, we sneaked into Old Woman Swamp, and by cotton-picking time Doodle was ready to show what he could do. He still wasn't able to walk far, but we could wait no longer. Keeping a nice secret is very hard to do, like holding your breath. We chose to reveal all on October eighth, Doodle's sixth birthday, and for weeks ahead we mooned around the house, promising everybody a most spectacular surprise. Aunt Nicey said that, after so much talk, if we produced anything less tremendous than the Resurrection,[8] she was going to be disappointed.

At breakfast on our chosen day, when Mama, Daddy, and Aunt Nicey were in the dining room, I brought Doodle to the door in the go-cart just as usual and had them turn their backs, making them cross their hearts and hope to die if they peeked. I helped Doodle up, and when he was standing alone I let them look. There wasn't a sound as Doodle walked slowly across the room and sat down at his place at the table. Then Mama began to cry and ran over to him, hugging him and kissing him. Daddy hugged him too, so I went to Aunt Nicey, who was thanks-praying in the doorway, and began to waltz her around. We danced together quite well until she came down on my big toe with her brogans,[9] hurting me so badly I thought I was crippled for life.

Doodle told them it was I who had taught him to walk, so everyone wanted to hug me, and I began to cry.

"What are you crying for?" asked Daddy, but I couldn't answer. They did not know that I did it for myself; that pride, whose slave I was, spoke to me louder than all their voices; and that Doodle walked only because I was ashamed of having a crippled brother.

---

8. Resurrection: reference to the Christian belief in the rising of Jesus from the dead after his burial.
9. brogans (brō′gənz) *n.*: heavy ankle-high shoes.

Vocabulary
imminent (im′ə·nənt) *adj.*: near; about to happen.

Within a few months Doodle had learned to walk well and his go-cart was put up in the barn loft (it's still there) beside his little mahogany coffin. Now, when we roamed off together, resting often, we never turned back until our destination had been reached, and to help pass the time, we took up lying. From the beginning Doodle was a terrible liar, and he got me in the habit. Had anyone stopped to listen to us, we would have been sent off to Dix Hill.

My lies were scary, involved, and usually pointless, but Doodle's were twice as crazy. People in his stories all had wings and flew wherever they wanted to go. His favorite lie was about a boy named Peter who had a pet peacock with a ten-foot tail. Peter wore a golden robe that glittered so brightly that when he walked through the sunflowers they turned away from the sun to face him. When Peter was ready to go to sleep, the peacock spread his magnificent tail, enfolding the boy gently like a closing go-to-sleep flower, burying him in the gloriously iridescent, rustling vortex.[10] Yes, I must admit it. Doodle could beat me lying.

Doodle and I spent lots of time thinking about our future. We decided that when we were grown, we'd live in Old Woman Swamp and pick dog's-tongue[11] for a living. Beside the stream, he planned, we'd build us a house of whispering leaves and the swamp birds would be our chickens. All day long (when we weren't gathering dog's-tongue) we'd swing through the cypresses on the rope vines, and if it rained we'd huddle beneath an umbrella tree and play stickfrog. Mama and Daddy could come and live with us if they wanted to. He even came up with the idea that he could marry Mama and I could marry Daddy. Of course, I was old enough to know this wouldn't work out, but

the picture he painted was so beautiful and serene that all I could do was whisper yes, yes.

Once I had succeeded in teaching Doodle to walk, I began to believe in my own infallibility and I prepared a terrific development program for him, unknown to Mama and Daddy, of course. I would teach him to run, to swim, to climb trees, and to fight. He, too, now believed in my infallibility, so we set the deadline for these accomplishments less than a year away, when, it had been decided, Doodle could start to school.

That winter we didn't make much progress, for I was in school and Doodle suffered from one bad cold after another. But when spring came, rich and warm, we raised our sights again. Success lay at the end of summer like a pot of gold, and our campaign got off to a good start. On hot days, Doodle and I went down to Horsehead Landing, and I gave him swimming lessons or showed him how to row a boat. Sometimes we descended into the cool greenness of Old Woman Swamp and climbed the rope vines or boxed scientifically beneath the pine where he had learned to walk. Promise hung about us like leaves, and wherever we looked, ferns unfurled and birds broke into song.

That summer, the summer of 1918, was blighted. In May and June there was no rain and the crops withered, curled up, then died under the thirsty sun. One morning in July a hurricane came out of the east, tipping over the oaks in the yard and splitting the limbs of the elm trees. That afternoon it roared back out of the west,

---

10. **vortex** (vôr′teks′) *n.:* something resembling a whirlpool.
11. **dog's-tongue** *n.:* wild vanilla.

Vocabulary

iridescent (ir′i·des′ənt) *adj.:* rainbowlike; displaying a shifting range of colors.

serene (sə·rēn′) *adj.:* peaceful; calm.

infallibility (in·fal′ə·bil′i·tē) *n.:* inability to make a mistake.

blighted (blīt′id) *v.* used as *adj.:* suffering from conditions that destroy or prevent growth.

blew the fallen oaks around, snapping their roots and tearing them out of the earth like a hawk at the entrails[12] of a chicken. Cotton bolls were wrenched from the stalks and lay like green walnuts in the valleys between the rows, while the cornfield leaned over uniformly so that the tassels touched the ground. Doodle and I followed Daddy out into the cotton field, where he stood, shoulders sagging, surveying the ruin. When his chin sank down onto his chest, we were frightened, and Doodle slipped his hand into mine. Suddenly Daddy straightened his shoulders, raised a giant knuckly fist, and with a voice that seemed to rumble out of the earth itself began cursing heaven, hell, the weather, and the Republican party.[13] Doodle and I, prodding each other and giggling, went back to the house, knowing that everything would be all right.

And during that summer, strange names were heard through the house: Château-Thierry, Amiens, Soissons, and in her blessing at the supper table, Mama once said, "And bless the Pearsons, whose boy Joe was lost in Belleau Wood."[14]

MAKING INFERENCES

3. Which **details** in the last two paragraphs show that the summer of 1918 "was blighted"? What connection can you make between the local blight and events in France?

So we came to that clove of seasons. School was only a few weeks away, and Doodle was far behind schedule. He could barely clear the ground when climbing up the rope vines, and his swimming was certainly not passable. We decided to double our efforts, to make that last drive and reach our pot of gold. I made him swim until he turned blue and row until he couldn't lift an oar. Wherever we went, I purposely walked fast, and although he kept up, his face turned red and his eyes became glazed. Once, he could go no further, so he collapsed on the ground and began to cry.

"Aw, come on, Doodle," I urged. "You can do it. Do you want to be different from everybody else when you start school?"

"Does it make any difference?"

"It certainly does," I said. "Now, come on," and I helped him up.

As we slipped through the dog days,[15] Doodle began to look feverish, and Mama felt his forehead, asking him if he felt ill. At night he didn't sleep well, and sometimes he had nightmares, crying out until I touched him and said, "Wake up, Doodle. Wake up."

It was Saturday noon, just a few days before school was to start. I should have already admitted defeat, but my pride wouldn't let me. The excitement of our program had now been gone for weeks, but still we kept on with a tired doggedness. It was too late to turn back, for we had both wandered too far into a net of expectations and had left no crumbs behind.

Daddy, Mama, Doodle, and I were seated at the dining-room table having lunch. It was a hot day, with all the windows and doors open in case a breeze should come. In the kitchen Aunt Nicey was humming softly. After a long silence, Daddy spoke. "It's so calm, I wouldn't be surprised if we had a storm this afternoon."

"I haven't heard a rain frog," said Mama, who believed in signs, as she served the bread around the table.

"I did," declared Doodle. "Down in the swamp."

"He didn't," I said contrarily.

---

12. **entrails** (en′trālz) *n.:* inner organs; guts.
13. **Republican party:** At this time most southern farmers were loyal Democrats.
14. **Château-Thierry** (sha′tō′ tē·er′ē), **Amiens** (à·myan′), **Soissons** (swä·sôn′), . . . **Belleau** (be·lô′) **Wood:** World War I battle sites in France.

---

15. **dog days** *n.:* hot days in July and August, named after the Dog Star (Sirius), which rises and sets with the sun during this period.

Vocabulary
doggedness (dôg′id·nis) *n.:* stubbornness; persistence.

"You did, eh?" said Daddy, ignoring my denial.

"I certainly did," Doodle reiterated, scowling at me over the top of his iced-tea glass, and we were quiet again.

Suddenly, from out in the yard came a strange croaking noise. Doodle stopped eating, with a piece of bread poised ready for his mouth, his eyes popped round like two blue buttons. "What's that?" he whispered.

I jumped up, knocking over my chair, and had reached the door when Mama called, "Pick up the chair, sit down again, and say excuse me."

By the time I had done this, Doodle had excused himself and had slipped out into the yard. He was looking up into the bleeding tree. "It's a great big red bird!" he called.

The bird croaked loudly again, and Mama and Daddy came out into the yard. We shaded our eyes with our hands against the hazy glare of the sun and peered up through the still leaves. On the topmost branch a bird the size of a chicken, with scarlet feathers and long legs, was perched precariously. Its wings hung down loosely, and as we watched, a feather dropped away and floated slowly down through the green leaves.

"It's not even frightened of us," Mama said.

"It looks tired," Daddy added. "Or maybe sick."

Doodle's hands were clasped at his throat, and I had never seen him stand still so long. "What is it?" he asked.

Daddy shook his head. "I don't know, maybe it's—"

At that moment the bird began to flutter, but the wings were uncoordinated, and amid much flapping and a spray of flying feathers, it tumbled down, bumping through the limbs of the bleeding tree and landing at our feet with a thud. Its long, graceful neck jerked twice into an S, then straightened out, and the bird was still. A white veil came over the eyes, and the long white

---

Vocabulary

reiterated (rē·it′ə·rāt′id) v.: repeated.

precariously (pri·ker′ē·əs·lē) adv.: unsteadily; insecurely.

beak unhinged. Its legs were crossed and its claw-like feet were delicately curved at rest. Even death did not <u>mar</u> its grace, for it lay on the earth like a broken vase of red flowers, and we stood around it, awed by its exotic beauty.

"It's dead," Mama said.

"What is it?" Doodle repeated.

"Go bring me the bird book," said Daddy.

I ran into the house and brought back the bird book. As we watched, Daddy thumbed through its pages. "It's a scarlet ibis," he said, pointing to a picture. "It lives in the tropics—South America to Florida. A storm must have brought it here."

Sadly, we all looked back at the bird. A scarlet ibis! How many miles it had traveled to die like this, in *our* yard, beneath the bleeding tree.

"Let's finish lunch," Mama said, nudging us back toward the dining room.

"I'm not hungry," said Doodle, and he knelt down beside the ibis.

"We've got peach cobbler for dessert," Mama tempted from the doorway.

Doodle remained kneeling. "I'm going to bury him."

"Don't you dare touch him," Mama warned. "There's no telling what disease he might have had."

"All right," said Doodle. "I won't."

Daddy, Mama, and I went back to the dining-room table, but we watched Doodle through the open door. He took out a piece of string from his pocket and, without touching the ibis, looped one end around its neck. Slowly, while singing softly "Shall We Gather at the River," he carried the bird around to the front yard and dug a hole in the flower garden, next to the

petunia bed. Now we were watching him through the front window, but he didn't know it. His awkwardness at digging the hole with a shovel whose handle was twice as long as he was made us laugh, and we covered our mouths with our hands so he wouldn't hear.

When Doodle came into the dining room, he found us seriously eating our cobbler. He was pale and lingered just inside the screen door. "Did you get the scarlet ibis buried?" asked Daddy.

Doodle didn't speak but nodded his head.

"Go wash your hands, and then you can have some peach cobbler," said Mama.

"I'm not hungry," he said.

"Dead birds is bad luck," said Aunt Nicey, poking her head from the kitchen door. "Specially *red* dead birds!"

As soon as I had finished eating, Doodle and I hurried off to Horsehead Landing. Time was short, and Doodle still had a long way to go if he was going to keep up with the other boys when he started school. The sun, gilded with the yellow cast of autumn, still burned fiercely, but the dark green woods through which we passed were shady and cool. When we reached the landing, Doodle said he was too tired to swim, so we got into a skiff and floated down the creek with the tide. Far off in the marsh a rail was scolding, and over on the beach locusts were singing in the myrtle trees. Doodle did not speak and kept his head turned away, letting one hand trail limply in the water.

After we had drifted a long way, I put the oars in place and made Doodle row back against the tide. Black clouds began to gather in the southwest, and he kept watching them,

MAKING INFERENCES

4. The sensory **details** in the description of the bird seem to give it extra meaning. Does the bird's struggle to fly remind you of a character in the story? What special significance might the bird have?

MAKING INFERENCES

5. Why is Doodle so fascinated by the scarlet ibis? Why does he take such pains to bury it?

Vocabulary

mar (mär) *v.*: damage; spoil.

trying to pull the oars a little faster. When we reached Horsehead Landing, lightning was playing across half the sky and thunder roared out, hiding even the sound of the sea. The sun disappeared and darkness descended, almost like night. Flocks of marsh crows flew by, heading inland to their roosting trees, and two egrets, squawking, arose from the oyster-rock shallows and careened away.

Doodle was both tired and frightened, and when he stepped from the skiff he collapsed onto the mud, sending an armada[16] of fiddler crabs rustling off into the marsh grass. I helped him up, and as he wiped the mud off his trousers, he smiled at me ashamedly. He had failed and we both knew it, so we started back home, racing the storm. We never spoke (what are the words that can solder[17] cracked pride?), but I knew he was watching me, watching for a sign of mercy. The lightning was near now, and

from fear he walked so close behind me he kept stepping on my heels. The faster I walked, the faster he walked, so I began to run. The rain was coming, roaring through the pines, and then, like a bursting Roman candle, a gum tree ahead of us was shattered by a bolt of lightning. When the deafening peal of thunder had died, and in the moment before the rain arrived, I heard Doodle, who had fallen behind, cry out, "Brother, Brother, don't leave me! Don't leave me!"

The knowledge that Doodle's and my plans had come to naught was bitter, and that streak of cruelty within me awakened. I ran as fast as I could, leaving him far behind with a wall of rain dividing us. The drops stung my face like nettles, and the wind flared the wet, glistening leaves of the bordering trees. Soon I could hear his voice no more.

I hadn't run too far before I became tired, and the flood of childish spite evanesced[18] as well. I stopped and waited for Doodle. The sound of

---

16. **armada** (är • mä′dǝ) *n.:* group. *Armada* is generally used to mean "fleet, or group, of warships."

17. **solder** (säd′ǝr) *v.:* patch or repair. *Solder* is a mixture of metals melted and used to repair metal parts.

---

18. **evanesced** (ev′ǝ • nest′) *v.:* faded away; disappeared.

rain was everywhere, but the wind had died and it fell straight down in parallel paths like ropes hanging from the sky. As I waited, I peered through the downpour, but no one came. Finally I went back and found him huddled beneath a red nightshade bush beside the road. He was sitting on the ground, his face buried in his arms, which were resting on his drawn-up knees. "Let's go, Doodle," I said.

He didn't answer, so I placed my hand on his forehead and lifted his head. Limply, he fell backward onto the earth. He had been bleeding from the mouth, and his neck and the front of his shirt were stained a brilliant red.

"Doodle! Doodle!" I cried, shaking him, but there was no answer but the ropy rain. He lay very awkwardly, with his head thrown far back, making his vermilion[19] neck appear unusually long and slim. His little legs, bent sharply at the knees, had never before seemed so fragile, so thin.

I began to weep, and the tear-blurred vision in red before me looked very familiar. "Doodle!" I screamed above the pounding storm, and threw my body to the earth above his. For a long, long time, it seemed forever, I lay there crying, sheltering my fallen scarlet ibis from the heresy[20] of rain. ■

---

19. **vermilion** (vər·mil′yən) *adj.*: bright red.

20. **heresy** (her′ə·sē) *n.*: here, mockery. *Heresy* generally means "denial of what is commonly believed to be true" or "rejection of a church's teaching."

MAKING INFERENCES

6. What do the **details** in the description of Doodle in the last two paragraphs remind you of? Explain why you think the writer makes this association.

Meet the Writer

James Hurst

Brothers at War

James Hurst (1922–   ) was born on a farm by the sea in North Carolina. Although he studied singing both in New York at the famous Juilliard School of Music and in Rome, Italy, he eventually became a banker. For thirty-four years he worked in the international department of a large bank in New York. During this time, Hurst also published some short stories, including "The Scarlet Ibis." He wants readers of "The Scarlet Ibis" to think of how the war raging among "brothers" in Europe is related to the conflict between Doodle and *his* brother. Perhaps, he reflects, people always suffer when others try to make them over in their own image.

Hurst finally retired from banking and returned to North Carolina—to New Bern, a town near his birthplace.

If There Be Sorrow

Mari Evans

If there be sorrow
let it be
for things undone . . .
undreamed
  unrealized
    unattained
to these add one;
Love withheld . . .
  . . . restrained

The Kiss (1908)
by Constantin Brancusi.

Musée National d'Art Moderne, Paris.
© 2003 Artists Rights Society (ARS),
New York/ADAGP, Paris.

Reading Check

1. Who is narrating the story?

2. When does the story about Doodle take place?

3. Why does the narrator teach Doodle to walk, and why does he cry when his family congratulates him for his effort?

4. After Doodle has learned to walk, what does his brother try to teach him to prepare him for school?

5. How does Doodle respond to the scarlet ibis and to its death?

Thinking Critically

6. Explain your opinion of the narrator's behavior at the end of the story. Is he in some way responsible for Doodle's death? Is his emotion at the very end sorrow, guilt, or something else?

7. By the end, whom do you pity more— the narrator or Doodle? Why?

8. Do you think the narrator makes any kind of discovery at the story's end, as he cradles his brother's little body?

9. In the last sentence the narrator calls his brother his "fallen scarlet ibis." In what ways could the ibis be a **symbol** for Doodle? Consider **details** about the following factors:

   • the resemblence between Doodle and the ibis

   • Doodle's identification with the bird

   • Doodle's and the ibis's struggles to survive in their worlds

   • the similarity between Doodle's and the ibis's deaths

10. In Meet the Writer (page 426), there is an indication of what Hurst thinks his famous story means. How would you state the **theme** of his story? What

truth does the story reveal about the ties that bind people together? Find passages from the story to support your response.

11. Re-read what the narrator says on page 347 about pride. Then, explain whether you think pride can lead to the kinds of sorrow that Mari Evans writes about in her poem "If There Be Sorrow" (see the **Connection** on page 427). Be sure to check your Quickwrite notes before answering.

Extending and Evaluating

12. Some people say that they will never forget "The Scarlet Ibis." Why might people find this story so memorable? Does the story and its **symbolism** appeal to your emotions? Explain.

WRITING

You Are Here

The writer creates a vivid, lush setting in "The Scarlet Ibis" by using sensory details. Choose a place, either real or imaginary, urban or rural, and **describe** it in one or two paragraphs. Use a variety of **sensory details** to help make your setting seem real.

▶ Use "Describing a Place," pages 456–463, for help with this assignment.

Doodle's Point of View

"The Scarlet Ibis" would be a very different story if it were told from Doodle's point of view. Pick a key **scene** in the story, and tell it through Doodle's eyes. You may choose to write in the first person, using Doodle's voice, or you may use a third-person-limited point of view, in which you have a narrator describe Doodle's thoughts and feelings.

SKILLS FOCUS

Literary Skills
Analyze symbolism.

Reading Skills
Make inferences from details.

Writing Skills
Describe a setting. Retell the story from a different point of view.

INTERNET

Projects and Activities

Keyword: LE7 9-6

After You Read Vocabulary Development

Word Knowledge: Own These Words

PRACTICE 1

Follow the directions in each item for using the Word Bank words.

1. Describe a moment from your childhood, using the word *sullenly*.
2. Write a headline for a newspaper article, using the word *imminent*.
3. Use the word *iridescent* in a sentence in an ad for jewelry.
4. Use the word *serene* in a sentence about the aftermath of a storm.
5. Use the word *infallibility* in a description of a person.
6. Write a sentence about a landscape, and include the word *blighted*.
7. Use the word *doggedness* in an ad for a political candidate.
8. Write an instruction from a teacher, using the word *reiterated*.
9. Write a sentence about Doodle, using the word *precariously*.
10. Write an apology, using the word *mar*.

Figurative Language—Picture This

"They named him William Armstrong, which was like tying a big tail on a small kite." How is the name William Armstrong like a big tail? This question is not a riddle. James Hurst is using a simile—the simplest form of **figurative language**—to help us understand that an impressive name is being given to frail, vulnerable Doodle. A **simile** is a comparison between two dissimilar things, using a word such as *like, as,* or *resembles*.

Here are three more sentences with similes from "The Scarlet Ibis":

1. "[The ibis] lay on the earth like a broken vase of red flowers. . . ."
2. "The sick-sweet smell of bay flowers hung everywhere like a mournful song."
3. "Success lay at the end of summer like a pot of gold. . . ."

PRACTICE 2

1. In each sentence above, locate the simile, and tell what is being compared. What exactly do the two things have in common?
2. Reword each passage using a new simile. Can you change the emotional tone of the passage by using a different comparison?
3. Highlight places in a sample of your own descriptive writing that you could make more vivid by using a simile. Rewrite each passage by adding a fresh comparison. Avoid trite, or overused, comparisons.

SKILLS FOCUS

Vocabulary Skills
Use words in context. Identify and interpret similes.

Before You Read

The Grandfather

Make the Connection

Quickwrite ✏️

Think about someone who means a great deal to you. What is this person like? Why is he or she so important to you? Write down a few sentences explaining what this person means to you.

Literary Focus

Symbols with Multiple Meanings: One Trunk, Many Branches

A wedding ring, we all know, symbolizes marriage, but what does the ocean represent? Some people might say that it symbolizes freedom and possibility; others might think it represents the frightening power of nature. Sometimes a **symbol**—an object, person, animal, or event that stands for something more than itself—has one clear-cut association (like a wedding ring). Other symbols (like the ocean) are more open-ended and may have **multiple meanings.**

Symbols in literature allow writers to suggest layers of meaning. Sometimes a symbol's meaning changes as a work unfolds. Other times a symbol represents one thing for one character and something else for another character. Symbols are also open to the reader's interpretation. In fact, they may have different shades of meaning for each of us. All of these meanings are valid as long as they are based on clues the writer plants in the text. While it may be difficult to figure out all the meanings of a symbol that operates on many levels, such a symbol can have an especially powerful appeal to our emotions and imaginations.

As you read "The Grandfather," pay special attention to what the author, Gary Soto, says about the avocado tree planted by his grandfather. Notice how the tree's meaning seems to expand as the tree itself grows over time.

Reading Skills

Main Idea: The Heart of the Matter

Many works of nonfiction are focused on a **main idea,** a central message that the writer wants to communicate to the reader. When a main idea is stated directly, you almost can't miss it. Look for it near the beginning or at the end of an essay or speech, for example. When the main idea is **implied,** or suggested, you can discover it on your own by making **inferences,** or educated guesses. You'll find clues that point to the main idea in the details included in the piece and in the type of language the writer uses. As you read "The Grandfather," try to determine what single idea lies at the heart of Soto's essay.

Vocabulary Development

gurgle (gʉr′gəl) v.: make a bubbling sound while flowing.

hovered (huv′ərd) v.: stayed suspended over something.

sulked (sulkt) v.: showed resentment and ill-humor.

meager (mē′gər) adj.: thin; small; inadequate.

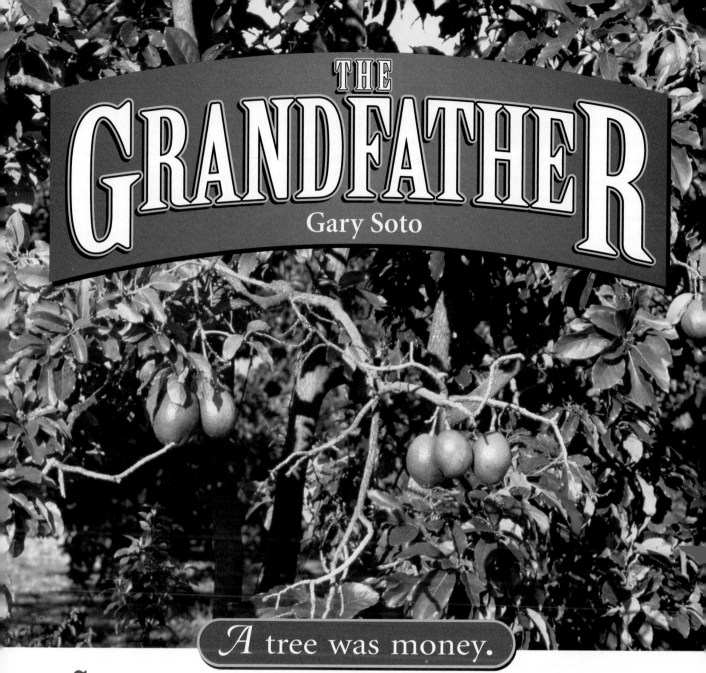

THE GRANDFATHER

Gary Soto

A tree was money.

Grandfather believed a well-rooted tree was the color of money. His money he kept hidden behind portraits of sons and daughters or taped behind the calendar of an Aztec[1] warrior. He tucked it into the sofa, his shoes and slippers, and into the tight-lipped pockets of his suits. He kept it in his soft brown wallet

that was machine tooled with "MEXICO" and a campesino[2] and donkey climbing a hill. He had climbed, too, out of Mexico, settled in Fresno[3] and worked thirty years at Sun Maid Raisin, first as a packer and later, when he was old, as a watchman with a large clock on his belt.

---

1. **Aztec** (az'tek'): of the Aztecs, a culture existing in Mexico before the Spanish conquest of the early 1500s.

2. **campesino** (käm'pe·sē'nð) *n.:* Spanish for "peasant" or "farmworker."
3. **Fresno** (frez'nō): city in central California.

After work, he sat in the backyard under the arbor,[4] watching the water gurgle in the rose-bushes that ran along the fence. A lemon tree hovered over the clothesline. Two orange trees stood near the alley. His favorite tree, the avocado, which had started in a jam jar from a seed and three toothpicks lanced in its sides, rarely bore fruit. He said it was the wind's fault, and the mayor's, who allowed office buildings so high that the haze of pollen[5] from the countryside could never find its way into the city. He sulked about this. He said that in Mexico buildings only grew so tall. You could see the moon at night, and the stars were clear points all the way to the horizon. And wind reached all the way from the sea, which was blue and clean, unlike the oily water sloshing against a San Francisco pier.

During its early years, I could leap over that tree, kick my bicycling legs over the top branch and scream my fool head off because I thought for sure I was flying. I ate fruit to keep my strength up, fuzzy peaches and branch-scuffed plums cooled in the refrigerator. From the kitchen chair he brought out in the evening, Grandpa would scold, "Hijo,[6] what's the matta with you? You gonna break it."

By the third year, the tree was as tall as I, its branches casting a meager shadow on the ground. I sat beneath the shade, scratching words in the hard dirt with a stick. I had learned "Nile"[7]

in summer school and a dirty word from my brother who wore granny sunglasses. The red ants tumbled into my letters, and I buried them, knowing that they would dig themselves back into fresh air.

A tree was money. If a lemon cost seven cents at Hanoian's Market, then Grandfather saved fistfuls of change and more because in winter the branches of his lemon tree hung heavy yellow fruit. And winter brought oranges, juicy and large as softballs. Apricots he got by the bagfuls from a son, who himself was wise for planting young. Peaches he got from a neighbor, who worked the night shift at Sun Maid Raisin. The chile plants, which also saved him from giving up his hot, sweaty quarters, were propped up with sticks to support an abundance of red fruit.

But his favorite tree was the avocado because it offered hope and the promise of more years. After work, Grandpa sat in the backyard, shirtless, tired of flagging trucks loaded with crates of raisins, and sipped glasses of ice water. His yard was neat: five trees, seven rosebushes, whose fruit were the red and white flowers he floated in bowls, and a statue of St. Francis[8] that stood in a circle of crushed rocks, arms spread out to welcome hungry sparrows.

---

8. **St. Francis:** Saint Francis of Assisi (1181?–1226), a lover of nature who was said to have preached to sparrows.

---

4. **arbor** (är′bər) *n.*: shelter made of branches or covered with vines.
5. **pollen** (päl′ən) *n.*: powdery grains from a seed plant. The fruit-bearing parts of plants must be dusted with pollen in order to produce fruit.
6. **Hijo** (ē′hô): Spanish for "child" or "son."
7. **Nile** (nīl): very long river in Africa, flowing through Egypt into the Mediterranean Sea.

Vocabulary

gurgle (gʉr′gəl) *v.*: make a bubbling sound while flowing.

hovered (huv′ərd) *v.*: stayed suspended over something.

sulked (sulkt) *v.*: showed resentment and ill-humor.

meager (mē′gər) *adj.*: thin; small; inadequate.

After ten years, the first avocado hung on a branch, but the meat was flecked with black, an omen, Grandfather thought, a warning to keep an eye on the living. Five years later, another avocado hung on a branch, larger than the first and edible when crushed with a fork into a heated tortilla. Grandfather sprinkled it with salt and laced it with a river of chile.

"It's good," he said, and let me taste.

I took a big bite, waved a hand over my tongue, and ran for the garden hose gurgling in the rosebushes. I drank long and deep, and later ate the smile from an ice cold watermelon.

Birds nested in the tree, quarreling jays with liquid eyes and cool, pulsating throats. Wasps wove a horn-shaped hive one year, but we smoked them away with swords of rolled up newspapers lit with matches. By then, the tree was tall enough for me to climb to look into the neighbor's yard. But by then I was too old for that kind of thing and went about with my brother, hair slicked back and our shades dark as oil.

After twenty years, the tree began to bear. Although Grandfather complained about how much he lost because pollen never reached the poor part of town, because at the market he had to haggle over the price of avocados, he loved that tree. It grew, as did his family, and when he died, all his sons standing on each other's shoulders, oldest to youngest, could not reach the highest branches. The wind could move the branches, but the trunk, thicker than any waist, hugged the ground. ■

Meet the Writer

Gary Soto

A California Boy

Gary Soto (1952–   ) grew up in a Mexican American family in Fresno, a city in California's San Joaquin Valley. He went to college, planning to major in geography. Then a poem—"Unwanted" by Edward Field—changed his life. The poem helped him discover the power of language. He began to see how he could reach other people by writing about his own experiences, and that's exactly what he did—and is still doing. Soto even named his first book, *The Elements of San Joaquin* (1977), after his birthplace. Much of his award-winning fiction and poetry draws on childhood memories, the everyday details of Mexican American life. As Soto puts it:

❝I tried to remain faithful to the common things of my childhood—dogs, alleys, my baseball mitt, curbs, and the fruit of the valley. . . . I wanted to give these things life.❞

For Independent Reading

If you enjoyed "The Grandfather," take a look at the book it came from: *A Summer Life*. You might also enjoy reading Soto's *Baseball in April and Other Stories* and *A Fire in My Hands*, one of his collections of poems for young adults.

Reading Check

1. How many years passed before the avocado tree produced its first fruit?

2. Why did Soto's grandfather believe that "a tree was money"?

3. Why was the avocado tree the grandfather's favorite?

Thinking Critically

4. How would you **characterize** Soto's grandfather? To answer, consider his move to California and his attitude toward his backyard and the avocado tree.

5. What differences did Soto's grandfather see between Mexico and California? How did he feel about these differences? Support your answers with evidence from the essay.

6. What do you think is the **main idea** of the essay? In other words, what point is Soto making about his grandfather and the ties that bind the family together?

7. The avocado tree is a **symbol** that has **multiple meanings** in the essay. Soto develops these meanings throughout the work, and he brings some of them together in the last paragraph. Use evidence from the essay to explain how the tree might symbolize the following people:
   • the grandfather
   • Soto
   • the grandfather's family

8. How would you describe the writer's **tone,** or attitude toward his subject? List two or three adjectives.

9. Soto's essay is filled with **imagery**—language that appeals to our senses of sight, sound, touch, taste, and smell. Choose the two or three images that most appeal to you, and explain why you think they are effective.

Extending and Evaluating

10. The essay is titled "The Grandfather," but a great deal of it focuses on the avocado tree. Do you think the essay would have been more effective if Soto had included more direct description of his grandfather and less description of the tree? Why or why not?

WRITING

VIP (Very Important Person)

Soto associates his grandfather with his backyard and, more specifically, with his avocado tree. Write a few paragraphs explaining why a particular person is important to you. Look back at your Quickwrite notes for help. Then, consider whether you associate that person with a particular place or object. If so, make that **symbolic** connection clear to your reader.

A Symbol of Your Own

Think about a natural place (such as a park or a beach) or an element of nature (such as a flower or a bird) that has symbolic meaning for you. What do you associate with this place or element? Does this **symbol** have **multiple meanings** for you? Write a paragraph or a poem in which you reveal the symbol's meaning or meanings and its appeal for you. Remember that symbols are appealing because they often carry powerful associations and affect our emotions. Try to use specific images to make your symbol vivid to your reader.

SKILLS FOCUS

Literary Skills
Analyze symbols with multiple meanings.

Reading Skills
Identify main idea.

Writing Skills
Write an explanation. Write about a symbol.

Connotations and Denotations: Ripples of Meaning

PRACTICE

The power of a word begins with its dictionary definition, its **denotation.** In addition, each word sets off ripples of feelings and associations—its **connotations.** For each Word Bank word, look back at the sentence in which the word is used, and check the word's denotation. Then, write down the connotations the word has for you. Finally, rewrite the sentence, substituting a word with different connotations, and describe how the meaning of the sentence has changed. Follow this example, for *sloshing:*

SOTO'S SENTENCE
"And wind reached all the way from the sea, which was blue and clean, unlike the oily water sloshing against a San Francisco pier."

DENOTATION: splashing about

CONNOTATIONS: splashing gently, irregularly, lazily

NEW SENTENCE
And wind reached all the way from the sea, which was blue and clean, unlike the oily water slapping against a San Francisco pier.

NEW MEANING
Now the water seems to hit the pier in a louder and more forceful, regular manner. The water seems almost angry.

Word Bank
gurgle
hovered
sulked
meager

Grammar Link

Parallel Structure: Keeping Things Balanced

"I took a big bite, waved a hand over my tongue, and ran for the garden hose gurgling in the rosebushes."

The sentence above uses a series of verbs to re-create Soto's actions when he bites into an avocado. This is an example of **parallel structure,** in which related ideas are expressed in a similar way. To create balanced sentences, a noun should be matched with a noun, an adjective with an adjective, a phrase with a phrase, a clause with a clause, and so on.

FAULTY
My favorite activities are playing baseball and to read.

PARALLEL
My favorite activities are playing baseball and reading.

PRACTICE

Complete the following sentences. Make sure that you use parallel structure.

1. The grandfather's backyard was neat, colorful, and _____.

2. The grandfather's daily routine was divided between working at Sun Maid Raisin and _____.

3. The grandfather grew heavy lemons, juicy oranges, and _____.

4. The grandfather planted the avocado tree, took care of it for many years, and _____.

5. At first, Soto could leap over the avocado tree, then he could sit in its shade, and finally _____.

▶ **For more help, see Improving Sentence Style, 10f, in the Language Handbook.**

SKILLS FOCUS

Vocabulary Skills
Identify word denotations and connotations.

Grammar Skills
Use parallel structure.

The Golden Kite, the Silver Wind

Make the Connection

Quickwrite

We compete in many aspects of our lives. Are there benefits to competition? Are there disadvantages? What happens when competition turns into hostile rivalry? Jot down your thoughts.

Literary Focus

Allegory: A Symbolic Story

An **allegory** is often written to teach a lesson. The events in an allegory can be read on two levels. They have a straightforward, surface meaning, but they also stand for something larger than themselves.

Writers of allegories tend to use simple situations, which they may exaggerate to make a point. Allegorical characters often have just one or two distinct traits that clearly show the characters' natures.

Ray Bradbury wrote "The Golden Kite, the Silver Wind" during the cold war (see Background on this page). As you read this allegory, try to figure out the lesson Bradbury wants to teach.

SKILLS FOCUS

Literary Skills
Understand allegory.

Reading Skills
Identify cause and effect.

Reading Skills

Cause and Effect: Why and What

A **cause** explains *why* something happens, and an **effect** is the *result* of something that has happened. Use these guidelines to identify cause-and-effect relationships:

- Watch for words that signal cause-and-effect relationships, such as *because, for, since, so, as a result, therefore.*
- Notice how characters or situations change. *Why* do they change? *What* event causes the change?
- Try to predict the effects of events.

INTERNET

Vocabulary
Practice
•
More About
Ray Bradbury

Keyword: LE7 9-6

Background

This story was published during the height of the cold war between the United States and the former Soviet Union. After World War II, the two nations began competing with each other for power. They never met in direct military combat, but each nation built up its nuclear arsenal, creating a dangerous situation.

In ancient China, this story's setting, sons were much more highly prized than daughters, and most women were prevented from having any public role.

Vocabulary Development

omens (ō'mənz) *n.*: things or events believed to be signs of future occurrences.

lurked (lurkt) *v.*: lay in wait, ready to attack.

portents (pôr'tents) *n.*: things that warn of events about to occur.

acclaimed (ə·klāmd') *v.*: received strong approval; applauded.

pandemonium (pan'də·mō'nē·əm) *n.*: great confusion; chaos.

spurn (spurn) *v.*: reject someone or something for being unworthy; scorn.

eclipse (i·klips') *v.*: conceal from view; overshadow.

sustain (sə·stān') *v.*: support; nourish.

monotony (mə·nät''n·ē) *n.*: lack of variety.

enduring (en·door'iŋ) *adj.*: strong and lasting.

The Golden Kite, the Silver Wind

RAY BRADBURY

*"One without
the other is nothing."*

"In the shape of a *pig*?" cried the Mandarin.[1]

"In the shape of a pig," said the messenger, and departed.

"Oh, what an evil day in an evil year," cried the Mandarin. "The town of Kwan-Si, beyond the hill, was very small in my childhood. Now it has grown so large that at last they are building a wall."

"But why should a wall two miles away make my good father sad and angry all within the hour?" asked his daughter quietly.

"They build their wall," said the Mandarin, "in the shape of a pig! Do you see? Our own city wall is built in the shape of an orange. That pig will devour us, greedily!"

---

1. **Mandarin** (man′də·rin): high-ranking government official in the Chinese Empire.

"Ah."

They both sat thinking.

Life was full of symbols and <u>omens</u>. Demons <u>lurked</u> everywhere, Death swam in the wetness of an eye, the turn of a gull's wing meant rain, a fan held *so*, the tilt of a roof, and, yes, even a city wall was of immense importance. Travelers and tourists, caravans, musicians, artists, coming upon these two towns, equally judging the <u>portents</u>, would say, "The city shaped like an orange? No! I will enter the city shaped like a pig and prosper, eating all, growing fat with good luck and prosperity!"

The Mandarin wept. "All is lost! These symbols and signs terrify. Our city will come on evil days."

Vocabulary

omens (ō′mənz) *n.:* things or events believed to be signs of future occurrences.

lurked (lʉrkt) *v.:* laid in wait, ready to attack.

portents (pôr′tents) *n.:* things that warn of events about to occur.

"Then," said the daughter, "call in your stonemasons[2] and temple builders. I will whisper from behind the silken screen and you will know the words."

The old man clapped his hands despairingly. "Ho, stonemasons! Ho, builders of towns and palaces!"

The men who knew marble and granite and onyx and quartz[3] came quickly. The Mandarin faced them most uneasily, himself waiting for a whisper from the silken screen behind his throne. At last the whisper came.

"I have called you here," said the whisper.

"I have called you here," said the Mandarin aloud, "because our city is shaped like an orange, and the vile city of Kwan-Si has this day shaped theirs like a ravenous pig—"

Here the stonemasons groaned and wept. Death rattled his cane in the outer courtyard. Poverty made a sound like a wet cough in the shadows of the room.

"And so," said the whisper, said the Mandarin, "you raisers of walls must go bearing trowels[4] and rocks and change the shape of *our* city!"

The architects and masons gasped. The Mandarin himself gasped at what he had said. The whisper whispered. The Mandarin went on: "And you will change our walls into a club which may beat the pig and drive it off!"

The stonemasons rose up, shouting. Even the Mandarin, delighted at the words from his mouth, applauded, stood down from his throne. "Quick!" he cried. "To work!"

---

2. **stonemasons** *n.:* people who build with stone.
3. **marble and granite and onyx** (än'iks) **and quartz** *n.:* high-quality stones.

4. **trowels** (trou'əlz) *n.:* tools for laying plaster or mortar.

When his men had gone, smiling and bustling, the Mandarin turned with great love to the silken screen. "Daughter," he whispered, "I will embrace you." There was no reply. He stepped around the screen, and she was gone.

Such modesty, he thought. She has slipped away and left me with a triumph, as if it were mine.

The news spread through the city; the Mandarin was <u>acclaimed</u>. Everyone carried stone to the walls. Fireworks were set off and the demons of death and poverty did not linger, as all worked together. At the end of the month the wall had been changed. It was now a mighty bludgeon[5] with which to drive pigs, boars, even lions, far away. The Mandarin slept like a happy fox every night.

"I would like to see the Mandarin of Kwan-Si when the news is learned. Such <u>pandemonium</u> and hysteria; he will likely throw himself from a mountain! A little more of that wine, oh Daughter-who-thinks-like-a-son."

But the pleasure was like a winter flower; it died swiftly. That very afternoon the messenger rushed into the courtroom. "Oh Mandarin, disease, early sorrow, avalanches, grasshopper plagues, and poisoned well water!"

The Mandarin trembled.

"The town of Kwan-Si," said the messenger, "which was built like a pig and which animal we drove away by changing our walls to a mighty stick, has now turned triumph to winter ashes. They have built their city's walls like a great bonfire to burn our stick!"

The Mandarin's heart sickened within him, like an autumn fruit upon the ancient tree. "Oh, gods! Travelers will <u>spurn</u> us. Tradesmen, reading the symbols, will turn from the stick, so easily destroyed, to the fire, which conquers all!"

"No," said a whisper like a snowflake from behind the silken screen.

"No," said the startled Mandarin.

---

5. **bludgeon** (bluj′ən) *n.*: short club.

"Tell my stonemasons," said the whisper that was a falling drop of rain, "to build our walls in the shape of a shining lake."

The Mandarin said this aloud, his heart warmed.

"And with this lake of water," said the whisper and the old man, "we will quench the fire and put it out forever!"

The city turned out in joy to learn that once again they had been saved by the magnificent Emperor of ideas. They ran to the walls and built them nearer to this new vision, singing, not as loudly as before, of course, for they were tired, and not as quickly, for since it had taken a month to rebuild the wall the first time, they had had to neglect business and crops and therefore were somewhat weaker and poorer.

There then followed a succession of horrible and wonderful days, one in another like a nest of frightening boxes.

"Oh, Emperor," cried the messenger, "Kwan-Si has rebuilt their walls to resemble a mouth with which to drink all our lake!"

"Then," said the Emperor, standing very close to his silken screen, "build our walls like a needle to sew up that mouth!"

"Emperor!" screamed the messenger. "They make their walls like a sword to break your needle!"

The Emperor held, trembling, to the silken screen. "Then shift the stones to form a scabbard to sheathe that sword!"[6]

"Mercy," wept the messenger the following morn, "they have worked all night and shaped

---

6. **scabbard . . . sword:** A scabbard is a case for a sword's blade. *To sheathe a sword* means "to put it in a case."

Vocabulary

acclaimed (ə·klāmd′) *v.*: received strong approval; applauded.

pandemonium (pan′də·mō′nē·əm) *n.*: great confusion; chaos.

spurn (spʉrn) *v.*: reject someone or something for being unworthy; scorn.

their walls like lightning which will explode and destroy that sheath!"

Sickness spread in the city like a pack of evil dogs. Shops closed. The population, working now steadily for endless months upon the changing of the walls, resembled Death himself, clattering his white bones like musical instruments in the wind. Funerals began to appear in the streets, though it was the middle of summer, a time when all should be tending and harvesting. The Mandarin fell so ill that he had his bed drawn up by the silken screen and there he lay, miserably giving his architectural orders. The voice behind the screen was weak now, too, and faint, like the wind in the eaves.

"Kwan-Si is an eagle. Then our walls must be a net for that eagle. They are a sun to burn our net. Then we build a moon to eclipse their sun!"

Like a rusted machine, the city ground to a halt.

At last the whisper behind the screen cried out:

"In the name of the gods, send for Kwan-Si!"

Upon the last day of summer the Mandarin Kwan-Si, very ill and withered away, was carried into our Mandarin's courtroom by four starving footmen. The two mandarins were propped up, facing each other. Their breaths fluttered like winter winds in their mouths. A voice said:

"Let us put an end to this."

The old men nodded.

"This cannot go on," said the faint voice. "Our people do nothing but rebuild our cities to a different shape every day, every hour. They have no time to hunt, to fish, to love, to be good to their ancestors and their ancestors' children."

"This I admit," said the mandarins of the towns of the Cage, the Moon, the Spear, the Fire, the Sword, and this, that, and other things.

"Carry us into the sunlight," said the voice.

The old men were borne out under the sun and up a little hill. In the late summer breeze a

Vocabulary
eclipse (i·klips′) v.: conceal from view; overshadow.

441

few very thin children were flying dragon kites in all the colors of the sun, and frogs and grass, the color of the sea, and the color of coins and wheat.

The first Mandarin's daughter stood by his bed.

"See," she said.

"Those are nothing but kites," said the two old men.

"But what is a kite on the ground?" she said. "It is nothing. What does it need to sustain it and make it beautiful and truly spiritual?"

"The wind, of course!" said the others.

"And what do the sky and the wind need to make *them* beautiful?"

"A kite, of course—many kites, to break the monotony, the sameness of the sky. Colored kites, flying!"

"So," said the Mandarin's daughter. "You, Kwan-Si, will make a last rebuilding of your town to resemble nothing more nor less than the wind. And we shall build like a golden kite. The wind will beautify the kite and carry it to wondrous heights. And the kite will break the sameness of the wind's existence and give it purpose and meaning. One without the other is nothing. Together, all will be beauty and cooperation and a long and enduring life."

Whereupon the two mandarins were so overjoyed that they took their first nourishment in days, momentarily were given strength, embraced, and lavished praise upon each other, called the Mandarin's daughter a boy, a man, a stone pillar, a warrior, and a true and unforgettable son. Almost immediately they parted and hurried to their towns, calling out and singing, weakly but happily.

And so, in time, the towns became the Town of the Golden Kite and the Town of the Silver Wind. And harvestings were harvested and business tended again, and the flesh returned, and disease ran off like a frightened jackal. And on every night of the year the inhabitants in the Town of the Kite could hear the good clear wind sustaining them. And those in the Town of the Wind could hear the kite singing, whispering, rising, and beautifying them.

"So be it," said the Mandarin in front of his silken screen. ■

Vocabulary

sustain (sə·stān′) *v.*: support; nourish.

monotony (mə·nät′'n·ē) *n.*: lack of variety.

enduring (en·door′iŋ) *adj.*: strong and lasting.

Meet the Writer

Ray Bradbury

Preventing the Future

When Ray Bradbury (1920–   ) was asked about predicting future events and future technological inventions in his writing, he responded, "That's not my business. My business is to prevent the future." In other words, throughout his career, Bradbury has tried to guide his readers toward a future that is more humane. Whether he is writing about the self-destructive effects of our behavior, as in "The Golden Kite, the Silver Wind," or the potentially devastating effects of our reliance on science and technology, his stories "are intended as much to instruct how to prevent dooms, as to predict them."

At age twelve, Bradbury began writing stories "long after midnight" on a toy typewriter. In his early days as a writer, he wrote about ghosts and dinosaurs, growing up in the Midwest, and going to Mars. Some of these stories ended up as highly respected "accidental novels": The Green Town, Illinois, stories became *Dandelion Wine,* and those about the Red Planet ended up as *The Martian Chronicles.*

A prolific author, Bradbury has worked in a variety of genres, writing short stories, novels, plays, film scripts, nonfiction—and poetry. Readers of "The Golden Kite, the Silver Wind"—a story filled with poetic, figurative language—will not be surprised by Bradbury's explanation of the central role that poetry has played for him:

❝ I've found inspiration for many of my short stories in other people's poetry . . . Poetry is an old love of mine, one which is central to my life. **❞**

For another story by Bradbury, see page 581.

For Independent Reading

In addition to *Dandelion Wine* and *The Martian Chronicles,* you'll enjoy reading Bradbury's *Fahrenheit 451,* a novel set in a future in which books are banned and burned (at a temperature of 451 degrees Fahrenheit).

Reading Check

1. Fill in the story's events in the proper order on a **cause-and-effect** chart like the one below. The first and last events have been filled in for you. (Use as many boxes as you need.) Then, write a sentence explaining each cause-and-effect relationship on the chart.

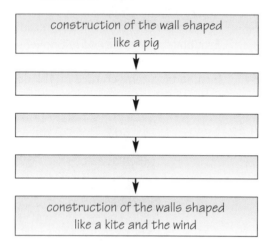

construction of the wall shaped like a pig

↓

↓

↓

construction of the walls shaped like a kite and the wind

Thinking Critically

2. What do you think **motivates** the two towns to engage in the wall-building competition? What are the negative effects of the competition on the townspeople? (Compare your answers with your Quickwrite notes.)

3. Referring to the kite and the wind, the Mandarin's daughter says, "One without the other is nothing." Explain her statement and her solution to the **conflict** between the two towns.

4. Describe the **character** of the Mandarin's daughter. For help answering, consider
   • why she offers her father advice
   • the type of advice she gives

5. How can this story be seen as an **allegory** about the cold war (see Background on page 436)? In other words, what connections do you see between events in the story and the conflict between the United States and the former Soviet Union?

6. What do you think is the **theme** of this **allegory**? That is, what lesson do you think Bradbury wanted to teach the people of his day about the ties that bind nations together?

7. Bradbury's story is filled with figures of speech. Find at least one place in the story where he uses **personification**—a kind of metaphor in which a nonhuman thing is given human characteristics—to describe poverty and death. What effect does he create by using personification in hi description?

Extending and Evaluating

8. Now that the cold war is over, do you think Bradbury's allegory still has something to teach us today? Explain your response.

WRITING

Your Version

In writing an allegory about the cold war, Bradbury chose to tell about two rival towns in ancient China. If you were writing the allegory, what situation would you describe? Pick a time, a place, and a type of conflict. Feel free to use your imagination—after all, Bradbury's townspeople build walls resembling the wind and a kite. Then, write a few paragraphs summarizing events in your **allegory.** How will you resolve the conflict so that your allegory teaches a lesson?

SKILLS FOCUS

Literary Skills
Analyze allegory.

Reading Skills
Identify cause and effect.

Writing Skills
Write a summary.

After You Read Vocabulary Development

Word Ancestors

PRACTICE 1

Like people, words have ancestors. In the English language many words are derived from Latin and Greek words (**root words**) that existed long before the English words we now use every day. Use a dictionary to research the **derivation, or origin,** of the Word Bank words. (Note that the derivation of some words may include a prefix and a root word.) Then, think of other English words that derive from the same root words. Put your information in a word map like the sample one for *ancestor* below. (For more help researching word derivations, see page 54.)

Word Bank

portents
acclaimed
sustain
monotony
enduring

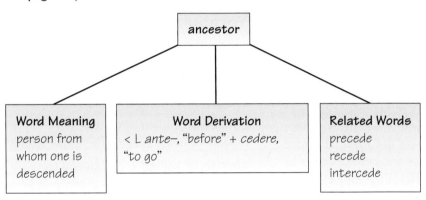

ancestor

Word Meaning	Word Derivation	Related Words
person from whom one is descended	< L *ante–*, "before" + *cedere*, "to go"	precede recede intercede

Word Knowledge: What Would Happen?

PRACTICE 2

Word Bank

omens
lurked
pandemonium
spurn
eclipse

Write one or two sentences answering the following questions. Be sure to justify your responses.

1. Would a superstitious person disregard or pay attention to omens?

2. If someone lurked near a store, was the person more likely to rob it or purchase something?

3. If pandemonium broke out during a rally, would the crowds of people be calm?

4. Would you be friendly toward people who spurn you?

5. If the moon were to eclipse the sun, would it be dark or bright outside?

SKILLS FOCUS

Vocabulary Skills
Understand word origins. Demonstrate word knowledge.

Weapons of the Spirit ◆ Letter to President Roosevelt ◆ On the Abolition of the Threat of War ◆ The Arms Race

Synthesizing Sources: Works by One Author

Sometimes authors address an important issue several times in the course of their careers. Follow these guidelines to synthesize the content of several works that express one person's ideas:

- **Paraphrase.** To understand complex ideas, **paraphrase**—restate in your own words—the points presented in your sources. A paraphrase is not a quotation, which is the author's own wording and must appear within quotation marks. Instead, a paraphrase is entirely made up of your own words. A good paraphrase covers the significant material in the source and restates ideas in the order in which they appear.

- **Compare and contrast.** Relate your sources to one another. Does the author express different opinions about the issue in your sources? If so, why have the author's views changed? If the author expresses similar views in all the sources, what is the author's **purpose** in writing about the issue each time? Is the **audience** different? Is the author covering different aspects of the issue in each source?

- **Connect.** Relate the ideas in your sources to your prior knowledge about the author or the issue. Connect your sources to other works by the author or to works about the author that you may have read.

- **Synthesize.** Finally, look at the sources as a group, and consider what they tell you about the author's views

on the issue. Keep in mind that if you look at a source in isolation or out of context, you may misinterpret the author's views or see only half the picture. By synthesizing the content of several works, you will gain a fuller understanding of the author's ideas.

Reading Skills
Synthesize information from several sources (by one author) on a single topic.

go.hrw.com

INTERNET
Interactive
Reading Model
Keyword: LE7 9-6

Vocabulary Development

eradicate (ē·rad′i·kāt′) v.: eliminate completely; get rid of.

phenomenon (fə·näm′ə·nən) n.: extraordinary thing or occurrence.

conceivable (kən·sēv′ə·bəl) adj.: capable of being imagined or understood.

abolish (ə·bäl′ish) v.: put an end to. *Abolition* is the noun form of this word.

radical (rad′i·kəl) adj.: extreme; thorough.

conviction (kən·vik′shən) n.: strong belief.

invincible (in·vin′sə·bəl) adj.: unconquerable.

inevitable (in·ev′i·tə·bəl) adj.: unavoidable; certain to happen.

vanquished (van′kwisht) v.: defeated.

renunciation (ri·nun′sē·ā′shən) n.: formal act of giving up something.

Connecting to the Literature

"The Golden Kite, the Silver Wind" is an allegory about the nuclear arms race. The following selections present Albert Einstein's views on nuclear weapons and explain his belief that nations must cooperate and work for peace.

Albert Einstein (1879–1955) is widely regarded as one of the greatest scientists of all time. Born and raised in Germany, Einstein studied physics, the science of matter and energy. Einstein, who was Jewish, escaped from Nazi Germany in 1933. He settled in the United States, where he spent the remainder of his life. Einstein was a pacifist, a person strongly opposed to war.

Weapons of the Spirit

from an interview with George Sylvester Viereck
from *Einstein on Peace*

Albert Einstein

It may not be possible in one generation to eradicate the combative instinct.[1] It is not even desirable to eradicate it entirely. Men should continue to fight, but they should fight for things worthwhile, not for imaginary geographical lines, racial prejudices, and private greed draped in the colors of patriotism. Their arms should be weapons of the spirit, not shrapnel[2] and tanks. ●

Think of what a world we could build if the power unleashed in war were applied to constructive tasks! One tenth of the energy that the various belligerents[3] spent in the World War, a fraction of the money they exploded in hand grenades and poison gas, would suffice to raise the standard of living in every country and avert the economic catastrophe of worldwide unemployment.

We must be prepared to make the same heroic sacrifices for the cause of peace that we make ungrudgingly for the cause of war. There is no task that is more important or closer to my heart.

Nothing that I can do or say will change the structure of the universe. But maybe, by raising my voice, I can help the greatest of all causes—goodwill among men and peace on earth.

—1931

> ● **PARAPHRASING**
>
> According to Einstein, what are the wrong types of battles? **Paraphrase** this paragraph.

---

1. **combative instinct:** Einstein views the tendency of human beings to fight with one another as an inborn trait.
2. **shrapnel** (shrap′nəl) *n.:* shells that explode, releasing many small metal balls.
3. **belligerents** (bə·lij′ər·ənts) *n.:* persons engaged in fighting one another.

Vocabulary
eradicate (ē·rad′i·kāt′) *v.:* eliminate completely; get rid of.

Einstein Warns President Roosevelt

During the 1930s, the Nazis built up German military power with the aim of dominating Europe. Despite Einstein's belief in pacifism, the political situation in Germany convinced him of the importance of researching the possibility of developing nuclear weapons.

At that time, scientists in the United States and Europe, like Leo Szilard, Enrico Fermi, and Frédéric Joliot-Curie, were making great strides in investigating how to create a nuclear chain reaction, which would release a tremendous amount of energy that could be used to create powerful bombs. Scientists suspected that the government of Nazi Germany was sponsoring similar experiments.

Shortly before World War II broke out, scientists persuaded Einstein to sign a letter addressed to President Franklin D. Roosevelt warning of the Nazis' research in nuclear weapons. This famous letter ultimately led to the establishment of the Manhattan Project, which developed the atomic bombs dropped on Japan in August 1945, ushering in the nuclear age.

LETTER

Letter to President Roosevelt
Albert Einstein

```
                                    Albert Einstein
                                       Old Grove Rd.
                                         Nassau Point
                                Peconic, Long Island

                                     August 2nd, 1939
```

```
F. D. Roosevelt,
President of the United States,
White House
Washington, D.C.
```

Sir:

Some recent work by E. Fermi and L. Szilard, which has been communicated to me in manuscript, leads me to expect that the element uranium may be turned into a new and important source of energy in the immediate future. Certain aspects of the situation which has arisen seem to call for watchfulness and, if necessary, quick action on the part of the Administration. I believe therefore that it is my duty to bring to your attention the following facts and recommendations:

In the course of the last four months it has been made probable--through the work of Joliot in France as well as Fermi and Szilard in

America—that it may become possible to set up a nuclear chain reaction in a large mass of uranium, by which vast amounts of power and large quantities of new radium-like elements would be generated. Now it appears almost certain that this could be achieved in the immediate future.

This new phenomenon would also lead to the construction of bombs, and it is conceivable—though much less certain—that extremely powerful bombs of a new type may thus be constructed. A single bomb of this type, carried by boat and exploded in a port, might very well destroy the whole port together with some of the surrounding territory. However, such bombs might very well prove to be too heavy for transportation by air.

The United States has only very poor ores of uranium in moderate quantities. There is some good ore in Canada and the former Czecho-slovakia while the most important source of uranium is Belgian Congo.

In view of this situation you may think it desirable to have some permanent contact maintained between the Administration and the group of physicists working on chain reactions in America. One possible way of achieving this might be for you to entrust with this task a person who has your confidence and who could perhaps serve in an inofficial capacity. His task might comprise the following:

a) to approach Government Departments, keep them informed of the further development, and put forward recommendations for Government action giving particular attention to the problem of securing a supply of uranium ore for the United States;

b) to speed up the experimental work, which is at present being carried on within the limits of the budgets of University laborato-ries, by providing funds, if such funds be required, through his contacts with private persons who are willing to make contributions for this cause, and perhaps also by obtaining the co-operation of industrial laboratories which have the necessary equipment.

I understand that Germany has actually stopped the sale of uranium from the Czechoslovakian mines which she has taken over. That she should have taken such early action might perhaps be understood on the ground that the son of the German Under-Secretary of State, von Weizsäcker, is at-tached to the Kaiser-Wilhelm-Institut in Berlin where some of the American work on uranium is now being repeated. ●

● **ANALYZING**

What is Einstein's **purpose** in writing to President Roosevelt?

Yours very truly,

A. Einstein

(Albert Einstein)

Vocabulary

phenomenon (fə·näm′ə·nən) *n.*: extraordinary thing or occurrence.

conceivable (kən·sēv′ə·bəl) *adj.*: capable of being imagined or understood.

On the Abolition of the Threat of War

from *Ideas and Opinions*

Albert Einstein

> "I made one great mistake in my life . . . when I signed the letter to President Roosevelt recommending that atom bombs be made; but there was some justification—the danger that the Germans would make them."
>
> —Albert Einstein
> November 11, 1954

My part in producing the atomic bomb consisted in a single act: I signed a letter to President Roosevelt, pressing the need for experiments on a large scale in order to explore the possibilities for the production of an atomic bomb.

I was fully aware of the terrible danger to mankind in case this attempt succeeded. But the likelihood that the Germans were working on the same problem with a chance of succeeding forced me to this step. I could do nothing else although I have always been a convinced pacifist. To my mind, to kill in war is not a whit better than to commit ordinary murder.

As long, however, as the nations are not resolved to abolish war through common actions and to solve their conflicts and protect their interests by peaceful decisions on a legal basis, they feel compelled to prepare for war. They feel obliged to prepare all possible means, even the most detestable ones, so as not to be left behind in the general armament race.[1] This road necessarily leads to war, a war which under the present conditions means universal destruction.

Under these circumstances the fight against *means* has no chance of success. Only the radical abolition of wars and of the

---

1. **armament race:** rivalry between hostile nations to build up larger and larger stores of weapons.

Vocabulary

abolish (ə·bäl′ish) *v.*: put an end to. *Abolition* is the noun form of this word.

radical (rad′i·kəl) *adj.*: extreme; thorough.

threat of war can help. This is what one has to work for. One has to be resolved not to let himself be forced to actions that run counter to this goal. This is a severe demand on an individual who is conscious[2] of his dependence on society. But it is not an impossible demand.

Gandhi,[3] the greatest political genius of our time, has pointed the way. He has shown of what sacrifices people are capable once they have found the right way. His work for the liberation of India is a living testimony[4] to the fact that a will governed by firm conviction is stronger than a seemingly invincible material power.[5]

—1952

● **PARAPHRASING**

Paraphrase this paragraph. Then, explain why Einstein calls Gandhi a political genius.

2. **conscious** (kän′shəs) *adj.:* aware.
3. **Gandhi** (gän′dē): Mohandas Gandhi (1869–1948) led the struggle for India's independence from Britain. He practiced the use of nonviolent protest to achieve political goals.

4. **testimony** (tes′tə·mō′nē) *n.:* evidence; proof.
5. **material power:** here, a nation; also, physical power.

Vocabulary
conviction (kən·vik′shən) *n.:* strong belief.
invincible (in·vin′sə·bəl) *adj.:* unconquerable.

TELEVISION INTERVIEW

Although the United States and the former Soviet Union were allies during World War II, they later became involved in a power struggle known as the cold war. The two superpowers engaged in an arms race to develop more and more powerful nuclear weapons. In 1952, the United States successfully tested the first hydrogen bomb, a weapon much more powerful than the atomic bomb. In 1953, the Soviet Union exploded its own hydrogen bomb.

The Arms Race

from *Einstein on Peace*

Albert Einstein

The arms race between the United States and the Soviet Union, initiated originally as a preventive measure, assumes hysterical proportions. On both sides, means of mass destruction are being perfected with feverish haste and behind walls of secrecy. And now the public has been advised that the production of the hydrogen bomb is the new goal which will probably be accomplished. An accelerated development toward this end has been solemnly proclaimed by the President. If these efforts should prove successful, radioactive poisoning of the atmosphere and, hence, annihilation[1] of all life on earth will have been

1. **annihilation** (ə·nī′ə·lā′shən) *n.:* absolute destruction.

brought within the range of what is technically possible. The weird aspect of this development lies in its apparently inexorable[2] character. Each step appears as the <u>inevitable</u> consequence of the one that went before. And at the end, looming ever clearer, lies general annihilation. ●

Is there any way out of this impasse[3] created by man himself? All of us, and particularly those who are responsible for the policies of the United States and the Soviet Union, must realize that, although we have <u>vanquished</u> an external enemy,[4] we have proved unable to free ourselves from the war mentality. We shall never achieve real peace as long as every step is taken with a possible future conflict in view, especially since it becomes ever clearer that such a war would spell universal annihilation. The

● **PARAPHRASING**
Einstein is describing a cause-and-effect relationship in the last three sentences of this paragraph. **Paraphrase** these sentences to explain his point.

guiding thought in all political action should therefore be: What can we do in the prevailing situation to bring about peaceful coexistence among all nations? The first goal must be to do away with mutual fear and distrust. Solemn <u>renunciation</u> of the policy of violence, not only with respect to weapons of mass destruction, is without doubt necessary.

In the last analysis the peaceful coexistence of peoples is primarily dependent upon mutual trust and, only secondarily, upon institutions such as courts of justice and the police. This holds true for nations as well as for individuals. And the basis of trust is a loyal relationship of give-and-take.

—1950

Vocabulary

inevitable (in·ev′i·tə·bəl) *adj.:* unavoidable; certain to happen.

vanquished (vaŋ′kwisht) *v.:* defeated.

renunciation (ri·nun′sē·ā′shən) *n.:* formal act of giving up something.

2. **inexorable** (in·eks′ə·rə·bəl) *adj.:* unable to be stopped.
3. **impasse** (im′pas′) *n.:* difficult situation or problem with no obvious solution.
4. **external enemy:** hostile nations. Einstein is referring to Germany, Japan, and their allies in World War II, which were defeated by the United States, Great Britain, France, the former Soviet Union, and their allies.

Reading Check

1. In "Weapons of the Spirit," what does Einstein say nations should devote their resources to, instead of preparing for war?

2. List two recommendations that Einstein makes in "Letter to President Roosevelt."

3. In "On the Abolition of the Threat of War," what reason does Einstein give for signing the letter to President Roosevelt?

4. According to Einstein in "The Arms Race," what is the first goal that must be achieved to bring about peace?

SKILLS FOCUS

Reading Skills
Synthesize information from several sources (by one author) on a single topic.

Test Practice

1. Which statement represents the *best* **paraphrase** of the first sentence of "Letter to President Roosevelt"?

   A   Some recent work by E. Fermi and L. Szilard leads me to expect that the element uranium may be turned into a new and important source of energy.

   B   There have been important scientific developments lately.

   C   The United States should investigate the possible military uses of scientific discoveries.

   D   Research by E. Fermi and L. Szilard suggests that it may soon be possible to convert uranium into a powerful new energy source.

2. Which statement *best* expresses the **main idea** of "The Arms Race"?

   F   We can't control the arms race between the United States and the Soviet Union.

   G   To prevent universal destruction, the United States and the Soviet Union must trust each other and reject violence.

   H   Individuals and the police must work to establish peace.

   J   The United States and the Soviet Union entered the arms race to protect themselves.

3. Which idea is included in *both* "On the Abolition of the Threat of War" and "The Arms Race"?

   A   Gandhi is a role model.

   B   The only part Einstein played in the creation of the atom bomb was signing a letter to President Roosevelt.

   C   The United States is working on producing a hydrogen bomb.

   D   The arms race will result in universal destruction.

4. Which selections contain ideas about war and peace that differ the *most*?

   F   "Weapons of the Spirit" and "On the Abolition of the Threat of War"

   G   "Weapons of the Spirit" and "Letter to President Roosevelt"

   H   "The Arms Race" and "On the Abolition of the Threat of War"

   J   "Weapons of the Spirit" and "The Arms Race"

5. If you read *only* "Letter to President Roosevelt," you might draw the *incorrect* conclusion that Einstein —

A felt the United States needed to protect itself

B thought the government should be aware of scientific research

C believed nuclear weapons could be dangerous

D was a firm believer in war

6. If you wanted to **connect** the content of these selections to another topic, which topic would be the *most* closely related?

F The breakup of the Soviet Union in the 1990s

G The training of physicists

H The development of nuclear arms today

J The economic policies of President Roosevelt's administration

Constructed Response

Synthesize the content of these selections by writing a paragraph summarizing Einstein's views on war. End your paragraph by **connecting** Einstein's views to the state of our world today. Does he make any statements that you think are relevant to current relationships between nations?

Vocabulary Development

Semantic Map: Charting Words

PRACTICE

Semantic mapping is a simple strategy that can help you master new words. A semantic map might include (1) a word's definition, (2) its synonyms, (3) its use in a sentence, (4) a question about the word. A sample is shown here. Make a semantic map for the other words in the Word Bank. Use a thesaurus or a dictionary to help you identify synonyms.

Word Bank

eradicate
phenomenon
conceivable
abolish
radical
conviction
invincible
inevitable
vanquished
renunciation

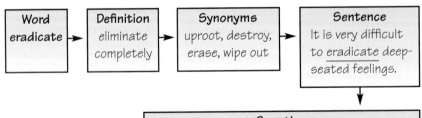

Word	Definition	Synonyms	Sentence
eradicate	eliminate completely	uproot, destroy, erase, wipe out	It is very difficult to eradicate deep-seated feelings.

Question
Why would you want to eradicate a feeling?
The feeling might be harmful to you or to others.

SKILLS FOCUS

Vocabulary Skills
Create semantic maps.

FICTION

The Prince and the Pilot

A pilot whose plane has crashed in the African desert is awakened from sleep by a strange, small voice: "Please," a boy says, "draw me a sheep!" So begins Antoine de Saint-Exupéry's timeless book, **The Little Prince.** This story of a lonely, stranded pilot and a gentle prince who has traveled to different planets—meeting a businessman, a king, a lamplighter, and a geographer—can be read as an imaginative allegory about growing up.

NONFICTION

A Study in Courage

Johnny Gunther was a tall, thin teenager with bright blue eyes and hair the color of wheat. Johnny was also kind, funny, and gifted—so gifted, in fact, that his admission to Harvard seemed guaranteed. Then tragedy struck. At age sixteen, Johnny was diagnosed with malignant brain cancer. **Death Be Not Proud,** written by his father, John Gunther, is an inspiring account of a boy who chose to live the last year of his life with dignity, hope, and humor. Once you've met Johnny Gunther, you will never forget him.

FICTION

Leap of Faith

A baseball game goes afoul for Reuven Malter when a wildly thrown ball hits him square in the eye. The pitcher is Danny Saunders—an opponent who unexpectedly becomes a friend. Reuven and Danny have much in common—their Brooklyn upbringing and their interest in their studies—but they are divided by their faiths. Danny is part of a Hasidic sect of Judaism, while Reuven belongs to a more liberal Orthodox sect. Chaim Potok's **The Chosen** is a compassionate story about tradition, tolerance, and understanding.

This title is available in the HRW Library.

NONFICTION

Stories That Hit Home

You can count on Gary Soto to offer up lively, realistic coming-of-age tales. **Living up the Street** is no exception. These stories, drawn from Soto's own experiences growing up, cover everything from joys (tomato fights, first love, and Little League games) to hardship (the sudden death of his hardworking father). Soto depicts barrio life in Fresno, California, with warmth and sympathy, sharing tales not only about himself but also about his whole community.

Describing a Place

Writing Assignment
Write an essay in which you describe a place that is both familiar and meaningful to you.

Our thoughts and feelings about a place determine our impression of it. For example, in James Hurst's short story "The Scarlet Ibis," the narrator's feelings of sadness and loss are conveyed through the descriptions of his childhood home. In this workshop you will share your personal picture of a place by writing a **descriptive essay.** This type of description, in which you express your attitude toward your subject, is called **subjective description.**

Prewriting

Choose a Place

Stake Your Claim As you search for a subject to describe, think of places that are meaningful to you in some way and that you know well. Also, think of places you can describe within a few pages. For example, you couldn't describe the entire city of San Francisco within a few pages, but you could describe the Golden Gate Bridge. Make a list of a few places that you could describe well. Choose the one place from the list that seems to stand out from the rest—the one you feel will be the most interesting for you to write about and for others to read.

Consider Purpose, Audience, and Tone

Facts or Feelings? Since you are writing a subjective description, your **purpose** is not only to describe a place, but also to share your thoughts and feelings about it. Subjective descriptions are usually written from a first-person point of view, using such pronouns as *I, me, we,* and *us.* Plan to write a description of 1,500 words.

Think about who is likely to read your essay. The **audience** you select should drive your choice of descriptive details. For example, if your intended audience is already familiar with the place you're describing, you won't include the same kinds of details that you would for an audience unfamiliar with the place.

Your purpose helps determine your **tone**—the attitude toward your subject that comes through in your writing. In a subjective description, your tone should generally be informal and conversational. Your feelings about the place you're describing will also determine your tone. For example, you might feel nostalgic, amused, or respectful about the place. Whatever tone you choose, make sure you maintain it consistently throughout your description.

SKILLS FOCUS

Writing Skills
Write a descriptive essay.

Gather Details

Do You See What I See?   You will use three kinds of details to create your description: sensory, factual, and figurative details.

● **Sensory details** are words and phrases that appeal to the five senses—sight, hearing, touch, smell, and taste. In your writing, you should try to include details from all the senses—not just sight details.

● **Factual details** include names, dates, numbers, and quotations, as well as true statements. For example, in a description of a public park, a writer might say: "About a dozen seniors meet every morning to exercise near the fountain." That statement combines a number and a fact the writer has learned.

● **Figurative details** include similes, metaphors, and examples of personification. Figurative details lose their effectiveness if they are overused, so think of them as spice to be sprinkled lightly on your description.

Be on the Lookout   To find the details you need for your essay, you can either observe directly the place you are describing or recall details from your memory. To collect secondhand details, consider doing research by reading about the place you've chosen or by interviewing other people who have been there.

Organize your sensory, factual, and figurative details in the first three rows of a chart like the one below. In the fourth row, add your thoughts and feelings about the place you're describing.

> **Reference Note**
> For more on **similes**, **metaphors**, and **personification**, see pages 504–505.

◄—————— DO THIS

Details for a description of our kitchen	
Sensory details	• pine cabinets • stepfather sings as he cooks • tangy smell of hot sauce
Factual details	• have lived in the house for 10 years • have dinner together once a week
Figurative details	The kitchen warms me like a big blanket on a winter morning.
Thoughts and feelings	• A visitor might not think our kitchen is special. • It holds special sounds, smells, and memories. • The kitchen is the place our family comes together.

Consider **shifting vantage points** as you list your details. Your vantage point is the position from which you view a place. When you look at a place from different vantage points—whether high, low, near, or far—you almost always find a different set of details.

Writing Skills
Use sensory, factual, and figurative details.

State Your Controlling Impression

Make a Statement In descriptive writing, the details you choose point to a **controlling impression,** the main idea or feeling you want to communicate about your subject. As with a thesis statement, keeping the controlling impression in mind keeps the writer focused and on track. The following diagram shows the relationship between the details in a description and the controlling impression.

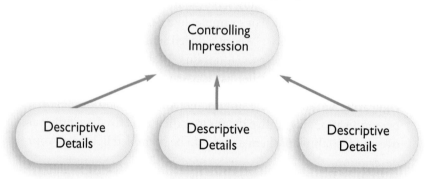

State your controlling impression for your readers. The student writing about her family's kitchen wrote the following statement of her controlling impression. Notice how it clearly conveys her **perspective,** or point of view, about the place.

> Our kitchen is a warm, welcoming place. It is the heart of our home—our place to come together.

Organize Your Details

Make Arrangements Arrange your details in an order that will make sense to your audience. For a description of a place, there are two common ways to arrange details.

- **Spatial order** organizes details according to their location. You can describe a place from top to bottom, from left to right, or from far away to close up.

- **Order of importance** arranges details from least important to most important or from most important to least important.

As you write, include words and phrases that help your readers follow your essay's organization. Spatial order signal words and phrases include *on the top, under,* and *next to.* Words and phrases that signal order of importance include *finally, most important,* and *then.*

SKILLS FOCUS

Writing Skills
Organize details around a controlling impression.

PRACTICE & APPLY 1 Using the information on these pages, choose a place to describe. Then, gather details and organize them in a logical way.

Writing

Describing a Place

A Writer's Model

The Kitchen

Great food, fellowship, and laughter are three things that come to mind right away when I think of my family's kitchen. It may seem strange to think of the kitchen as a special place, but for my family it is. We say goodbye there before school, and we say hello there when we get home. It's a place for food, of course, but it's also a place for sharing and for laughing. Our kitchen is a warm, welcoming place. It is the heart of our home—our place to come together.

A visitor seeing our kitchen for the first time might wonder why I choose to describe our kitchen as warm. The kitchen looks quite ordinary, with the usual assortment of fixtures and appliances. It has pine cabinets, a two-sided stainless-steel sink, a refrigerator/family bulletin board, and an old but sturdy stove. At the center of the room sits a butcher-block table, scuffed from years of use. That's where our family eats most meals. In short, almost any visitor would probably say it seems like a plain, ordinary kitchen.

However, the five of us in my family see that room in a different way. We've lived in the house for ten years, and for us, the kitchen is a place that holds ten years of special sounds, smells, and memories. We enjoy the sound of my stepfather singing songs from his childhood as he cooks, and the tangy smell of his special hot sauce, which never seems to leave the room entirely. We often talk in the kitchen while we

(continued)

INTRODUCTION
Attention grabber
Subject

Controlling impression

BODY
Thoughts and feelings
Sensory details

Factual details
Thoughts and feelings
Sensory details

Factual details

(continued)

prepare our mandatory once-weekly family dinner—the only time it seems we're all together at one time anymore. If it's cold outside, we might pull up our chairs around the stove, basking in its friendly heat as we talk.

Phrase signaling order of importance

Figurative detail

Thoughts and feelings

Most important, though, our kitchen is the heart of our home. It may not seem like a special place to someone else, but when I'm lonely or tired, it warms me—like a big blanket on a winter morning. It's just as important to everyone else in my family. We can't imagine a home without such a central meeting spot. Our kitchen is our place to come together and share our lives, to celebrate holidays and triumphs, to console one another over defeats and sorrows.

CONCLUSION

Summary

Restatement of controlling impression

Many people probably would not think of a kitchen as an extraordinary place. For some, it might be just a place for a sleepy kid to have a quick breakfast, for a hungry and tired parent to heat up a plate of leftovers, or for a teenager who wants a snack to make popcorn on a Friday night. However, for me and my family, our kitchen will always be a warm, wonderful place—not merely a functional place, or a place to pass through quickly on the way to somewhere else.

go.hrw.com

INTERNET

More Writer's Models

Keyword: LE7 9-6

PRACTICE & APPLY 2 Refer to the framework and Writer's Model as you write your descriptive essay. Make sure you support your controlling impression with a variety of sensory, factual, and figurative details.

Revising

Evaluate and Revise Your Draft

Double-Check It When you revise your writing, always read through your writing twice. Read your descriptive essay once for content and organization and once for style. Sometimes reading an essay aloud—to yourself, to a member of your family, or to a friend—helps you find places that need further attention. You may also get feedback on how effectively you used sensory, factual, and figurative details.

> **First Reading: Content and Organization** Use the chart below as a **think sheet** to look for ways to improve the content and organization of your descriptive essay. Respond to questions in the left-hand column. If you need help answering the questions, use the tips in the middle column. If necessary, make the changes suggested in the right-hand column.

PEER REVIEW

Exchange your descriptive essay with a classmate before you revise. Ask your classmate to make sure you have organized the details in a logical way.

Rubric: Describing a Place

Evaluation Questions	Tips	Revision Techniques
❶ Does the introduction include a statement of the controlling impression?	**Underline** the statement of the writer's perspective on the subject.	**Add** a sentence that states your perspective on the subject.
❷ Does the description include a variety of details (sensory, factual, and figurative)?	**Put an S** above sensory details, an **F** above details that show facts, and an **I** above details that make imaginative comparisons.	**Add** details that appeal to several senses. **Elaborate** with facts, such as specific dates, names, or numbers. **Add** similes, metaphors, or examples of personification.
❸ Does the description include details about the writer's thoughts and feelings?	**Put an asterisk** next to sentences that contain details about the writer's thoughts and feelings.	**Elaborate** by including your thoughts or feelings about the subject of the essay.
❹ Is the paper clearly organized using either spatial order or order of importance?	**Number** the details. Then, draw a simple map of the place described and place the numbers on it.	If you cannot see a clear pattern to the numbers, **rearrange** details so that they fall into either a clear spatial order or a clear order of importance.
❺ Does the conclusion include a summary of thoughts about the subject? Does it include a restatement of the controlling impression?	**Highlight** the sentence that summarizes the writer's thoughts about the place he or she is describing. **Bracket** the sentence that restates the controlling impression.	**Add** a sentence that summarizes your thoughts about the place you're describing. **Add** a sentence that restates the controlling impression, if necessary.

➤ **Second Reading: Style** On your second reading of your paper, your goal is to improve your essay's style. You've probably used a number of good descriptive adjectives—but have you also used unnecessarily repetitive adjectives? Using two or more adjectives that pointlessly repeat the same meaning—such as "an *old, ancient* stove," or "a *scraped* and *scuffed* cabinet"—just adds useless deadwood to your writing. Like dead limbs on a tree, these words weigh your writing down and sap it of its strength. Use the following guidelines to cut out **deadwood adjectives** so that your writing stays strong.

Style Guidelines

Evaluation Question	▸ Tip	▸ Revision Technique
● **Do some sentences contain unnecessarily repetitive adjectives?**	▸ **Circle** all pairs of adjectives (adjectives joined by a comma or by *and* or *but*). Revise any circled pair having almost the same meaning.	▸ **Cut** one of the adjectives from a pair, or **replace** one with an adjective that has a different meaning.

ANALYZING THE REVISION PROCESS
Study these revisions, and answer the questions that follow.

> replace
>
> Most important, though, our kitchen is the ~~center~~ *heart* of our
>
> home. It may not seem like a special place to someone else, but
>
> add   when I'm lonely or tired, it warms me ^*—like a big blanket on a winter morning.* It's just as important
>
> delete   ~~and significant~~ to everyone else in my family.

Responding to the Revision Process

1. Why do you think the writer changed the word *center* to *heart* in the first sentence? What is the effect of the change?

2. What type of detail did the writer add to the second sentence? Why do you think she added it?

3. How did the writer's omission of the word *significant* improve the sentence?

SKILLS FOCUS

Writing Skills
Revise for content and style.

PRACTICE & APPLY 3 Revise the content, organization, and style of your paper, using the guidelines on these two pages. Be sure to check for a variety of details.

Publishing

Proofread and Publish Your Essay

Get It Right Your paper should be as error-free as you can make it before you prepare a final copy. Check it thoroughly for grammar, usage, and mechanics errors, and correct them as you find them.

Spread the Word You've worked hard to write and polish your descriptive essay. Now you can reap the rewards of your hard work by sharing your description with readers. Try one or more of these publishing ideas.

- If your description is of a place in your community, send a copy of the description to your local newspaper.

- Publish your description as a Web page. Scan photographs of the place you described, and include them on the page. If your paper includes descriptions of sounds, record some of the sounds and create hyperlinks to sound files of the recordings.

- If any of your classmates have written descriptions that are related to your description, bind all of your descriptions together as a booklet. Give the booklet a title that summarizes the connection between the descriptions, and distribute copies of the booklet to your class.

- Videotape the place you've described in your essay. Show the videotape to an audience of your classmates as you provide a soundtrack by reading the description aloud.

Reflect on Your Essay

Decisions, Decisions Look back at the decisions you made while writing your essay. You will see that in this workshop you have practiced skills you can carry over into other writing assignments. To reflect on some of your decisions, write responses to the following questions.

- What was the best descriptive detail in your essay? Why do you think it was so effective?

- How would you use descriptive details to describe an object? to describe a person?

- If you were to describe another place, would you choose the same method of organizing your details as you used for this descriptive essay? Why or why not?

PRACTICE & APPLY 4   Proofread, publish, and reflect on your essay, using the guidelines on this page. Remember to follow the conventions of standard American English as you seek a wider distribution of your essay.

TIP Proofreading will help ensure that your essay follows the **conventions** of standard American English. For example, because first-person pronouns are common in a subjective description, check that you have used correct pronoun cases in your essay. For more on **case forms,** see Case, 4a–e, in the Language Handbook.

SKILLS FOCUS

Writing Skills
Proofread, especially for correct pronoun case.

Presenting a Description

Your listeners hear the rumble in your stomach and the buzz of conversation around you. They feel the weight of your tray as you push it toward the basket of glistening, red apples twenty feet ahead. A good **descriptive presentation**—even one that describes the cafeteria lunch line—must make your listeners see, feel, and hear what you describe. In this workshop you will have an opportunity to do just that.

Adapt Your Essay

I Spy Something In order to help your listeners see, hear, and feel the place you're describing, your presentation should include plenty of **concrete imagery**—specific details that help listeners create mental pictures of the place you are describing.

If you have limited time to speak, choose the **sensory, factual,** and **figurative details** from your written description that will be most effective in helping your audience visualize the place you are describing. If you need more details to fill the amount of time you are given, consider adding details that you might find by shifting vantage points or perspectives. By **shifting vantage points and perspectives,** you help the audience "see" the place from more than one position or from another person's viewpoint.

Get Involved Make your **point of view** and **relationship** with the place you're describing clear. Since you will be presenting a subjective description, you must show your **personal involvement** with the subject. To do that, include all of the thoughts and feelings about the place that you included in your essay. Then, consider whether you should add more information to make your thoughts and feelings about the place clear for a listening audience.

The Point Is Once you have reconsidered your details, locate the statement of your **controlling impression** in your essay's introduction. You may want to begin your presentation with this statement so that your audience is clear about your feelings early on.

Plan Your Presentation

Come to Order An **extemporaneous** presentation is one in which the speaker has practiced, but not memorized, the speech. The speaker may also use **concise note cards.** To prepare your extemporaneous presentation, write your controlling impression on

SKILLS FOCUS

Listening and Speaking Skills
Present a description.

one note card and the details that support it on separate note cards. These cards should include **summaries** that contain key words and phrases taken from your written description.

Reference Note

For more on **summarizing,** see page 711.

Should you order your details the same way as in your written description or use a different order? To answer this question you must once again consider what would be most effective for people listening to your description rather than reading it. If you use **spatial order** your audience may find it easier to create an accurate mental picture of the place. If you use **order of importance** you will emphasize to your listeners the details about the place that are most significant to you. Once you've chosen an order, number each of your note cards in the order in which you will present them.

More Than Words As you arrange your cards, watch for opportunities to incorporate **visuals,** such as props, graphs, or electronic media, into your presentation. In a presentation about a circus, for example, you might use the **occasion** to wear a red coat and carry a cane just as the ringmaster might do. In a presentation about a cave, you might want to create a slide show of the stalagmites and stalactites you describe. For best results, use the visuals that appeal to the **interests of your audience.**

Practice Your Presentation

Say It Like This Before you deliver your speech in public, try practicing in private. Keep in mind the following techniques to help you plan your delivery.

- **Verbal techniques** emphasize important details and add interest to your presentation. For example, you can change the pitch of your voice from high to low to add suspense or change the tone of your voice from serious to humorous.

- **Nonverbal techniques,** such as changing facial expressions and gestures, communicate different moods or feelings. For example, you can raise your eyebrows to show surprise or shrug your shoulders to show uncertainty.

Practice your presentation several times so that you know how to elaborate on the details from your note cards and smoothly connect those details to your visuals. Practice speaking loudly and clearly, making eye contact with audience members, and using your voice, gestures, and facial expressions to communicate your feelings.

PRACTICE & APPLY 5 Follow the instructions on these two pages to adapt the descriptive essay you wrote in the Writing Workshop for a descriptive presentation. Practice your presentation, and then deliver it to an audience.

SKILLS FOCUS

Listening and Speaking Skills
Prepare your presentation. Use appropriate verbal and nonverbal techniques.

Test Practice

Analyzing Symbolism and Allegory

DIRECTIONS: Read the following folk tale. Then, read and respond to the questions that follow.

The Happy Man's Shirt

retold by Italo Calvino

translated by George Martin

A king had an only son that he thought the world of. But this prince was always unhappy. He would spend days on end at his window staring into space.

"What on earth do you lack?" asked the king. "What's wrong with you?"

"I don't even know myself, Father."

"Are you in love? If there's a particular girl you fancy, tell me, and I'll arrange for you to marry her, no matter whether she's the daughter of the most powerful king on earth or the poorest peasant girl alive!"

"No, Father, I'm not in love."

The king tried in every way imaginable to cheer him up, but theaters, balls, concerts, and singing were all useless, and day by day the rosy hue drained from the prince's face.

The king issued a decree,[1] and from every corner of the earth came the most learned philosophers, doctors, and professors. The king showed them the prince and asked for their advice. The wise men withdrew to think, then returned to the king. "Majesty, we have given the matter close thought and we have studied the stars. Here's what you must do. Look for a happy man, a man who's happy through and through, and exchange your son's shirt for his."

That same day the king sent ambassadors to all parts of the world in search of the happy man.

A priest was taken to the king. "Are you happy?" asked the king.

"Yes, indeed, Majesty."

"Fine. How would you like to be my bishop?"[2]

"Oh, Majesty, if only it were so!"

"Away with you! Get out of my sight! I'm seeking a man who's happy just as he is, not one who's trying to better his lot."

---

1. **decree** (dē·krē′) *n.:* official order.
2. **bishop** (bish′əp) *n.:* high-ranking Christian clergyman.

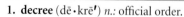

SKILLS FOCUS

Pages 466–469
cover
Literary Skills
Analyze
symbolism and
allegory.

Thus the search resumed, and before long the king was told about a neighboring king, who everybody said was a truly happy man. He had a wife as good as she was beautiful and a whole slew of children. He had conquered all his enemies, and his country was at peace. Again hopeful, the king immediately sent ambassadors to him to ask for his shirt.

The neighboring king received the ambassadors and said, "Yes, indeed, I have everything anybody could possibly want. But at the same time I worry because I'll have to die one day and leave it all. I can't sleep at night for worrying about that!" The ambassadors thought it wiser to go home without this man's shirt.

At his wit's end, the king went hunting. He fired at a hare but only wounded it, and the hare scampered away on three legs. The king pursued it, leaving the hunting party far behind him. Out in the open field he heard a man singing a refrain. The king stopped in his tracks. "Whoever sings like that is bound to be happy!" The song led him into a vineyard, where he found a young man singing and pruning the vines.

"Good day, Majesty," said the youth. "So early and already out in the country?"

"Bless you! Would you like me to take you to the capital? You will be my friend."

"Much obliged, Majesty, but I wouldn't even consider it. I wouldn't even change places with the Pope."

"Why not? Such a fine young man like you . . ."

"No, no, I tell you. I'm content with just what I have and want nothing more."

"A happy man at last!" thought the king. "Listen, young man. Do me a favor."

"With all my heart, Majesty, if I can."

"Wait just a minute," said the king, who, unable to contain his joy any

Collection 6: Skills Review

longer, ran to get his retinue.[3] "Come with me! My son is saved! My son is saved!" And he took them to the young man. "My dear lad," he began, "I'll give you whatever you want! But give me . . . give me . . ."

"What, Majesty?"

"My son is dying! Only you can save him. Come here!"

The king grabbed him and started unbuttoning the youth's jacket. All of a sudden he stopped, and his arms fell to his sides.

The happy man wore no shirt.

---

3. **retinue** (ret'n·o͞o') *n.:* assistants attending an important person.

---

1. Which pair of words *best* describes the king's feelings for his son?

- **A** Anger and frustration
- **B** Confusion and depression
- **C** Affection and irritation
- **D** Love and concern

2. The unhappy man is a prince. What might his position in life **symbolize** in the folk tale?

- **F** Respect
- **G** Pride
- **H** Material wealth
- **J** Romance

3. The wise men tell the king that his son should wear a happy man's shirt. What does wearing someone else's shirt **symbolize**?

- **A** Looking like someone else
- **B** Being like someone else
- **C** Complimenting someone
- **D** Feeling superior to someone

4. What might the character of the priest **symbolize**?

- **F** Flattery
- **G** Modesty
- **H** Ambition
- **J** Hopefulness

5. What is similar about these two **characters:** the prince and the neighboring king?

   A Both seem to have everything they could want, but neither is content.

   B Both are in love, but they are still not happy.

   C Both worry about dying, which makes them unhappy.

   D Both are sad, and neither knows why.

6. Why does the king think that the young man who sings as he works is happy?

   F He is polite.

   G He is satisfied with his life.

   H He is healthy and young.

   J He enjoys working outdoors in the country.

7. What does the happy man's lack of a shirt **symbolize**?

   A External things cannot create happiness.

   B True happiness does not exist in the real world.

   C The man will soon experience unhappiness.

   D The man does not understand what happiness is.

8. Which statement *best* expresses the **theme,** or **moral,** of the folk tale?

   F People should not rely on others to help them solve their problems.

   G It is difficult to know what other people are truly feeling.

   H True happiness must come from within you.

   J Although you may fail to attain your goals at first, you should not give up.

9. The **symbols** in this folk tale might **appeal** to us in part because they —

   A make the setting of the story vivid

   B give the narrator a distinct personality

   C contribute to the meaning and emotional impact of the story

   D provide information about the author's life

10. Which word *best* describes the **tone** of the folk tale?

   F optimistic

   G pessimistic

   H sympathetic

   J ironic

Constructed Response

11. In what way can this tale be seen as an **allegory**? Support your response using examples from the text.

Collection 6: Skills Review

Vocabulary Skills

Test Practice

Context Clues

DIRECTIONS: Use the context clues in the following passages to help you identify the meaning of the underlined vocabulary words.

1. In "The Scarlet Ibis" the summer of 1918 is blighted. Crops die because there is no rain. Then a hurricane uproots trees.
   In this passage, *blighted* means —
   A causing confusion
   B difficult to understand
   C filled with anger and resentment
   D suffering from conditions that prevent growth

2. In "The Scarlet Ibis" the narrator reveals his doggedness in his attitude toward his brother. Determined, he refuses to give up his efforts to teach his brother how to walk and swim.
   In this passage, *doggedness* means —
   F persistence
   G cruelty
   H sensitivity
   J logic

3. In "The Golden Kite, the Silver Wind" the Mandarin's plans to save his town are acclaimed at first. When he orders the wall to be redesigned, the townspeople praise him for his efforts.
   In this passage, *acclaimed* means —
   A rejected
   B criticized
   C applauded
   D mocked

4. In "The Golden Kite, the Silver Wind" the Mandarin fears that travelers will spurn the town. They won't want to visit it because they'll view the town as weak and unlucky.
   In this passage, *spurn* means —
   F attack
   G scorn
   H praise
   J discourage

5. In "On the Abolition of the Threat of War," Einstein expresses his conviction that we must end the arms race. Achieving peace was an important principle for him throughout his life.
   In this passage, *conviction* means —
   A deep guilt
   B strong belief
   C lasting doubt
   D constant worry

6. In "The Arms Race," Einstein states that a nuclear war seems inevitable. As each side continues to build up a supply of nuclear weapons, it seems certain that war will break out.
   In this passage, *inevitable* means —
   F destructive
   G unavoidable
   H unlikely
   J frightening

SKILLS FOCUS

Vocabulary Skills
Use context clues to understand word meanings.

Collection 6: Skills Review
Writing Skills

Test Practice DIRECTIONS: Read the following paragraph from a draft of a student's descriptive essay. Then, answer the questions below it.

(1) Some people enjoy extravagant theme parks; others like quiet city parks, but my favorite is the ballpark. (2) From the parking lot, I see the huge stadium looming against the sky, its brilliant flags beckoning me toward the metal entrance gates. (3) As you move into the concession area, the smell of popcorn fills your nostrils, and you can hear the muffled cheers of fans. (4) In the stands, I feel an excited tension swirl inside me as I join in the wave and hold up posters in support of my favorite player. (5) The ballpark may not have trees or roller coasters, but it thrills me every time I go.

1. If the writer wanted to add sensory details to the passage, which sentence below would be most appropriate?
   A The field is watered every night by the stadium's head groundskeeper.
   B The fans cheer when they hear the piercing *crack!* of the bat.
   C There are nine players per team.
   D As the stadium fills, I feel more and more anxious for the game to begin.

2. Which of the following sentences could be added after sentence 1 to form a stronger controlling impression?
   F At the ballpark the surroundings are just as exciting as the game itself.
   G A baseball game is no fun unless you are playing in it.
   H A baseball stadium is a very popular attraction for people of all ages.
   J Attending sporting events is a favorite pastime of many Americans.

3. Which of the sentences should be changed to first-person point of view?
   A 1   C 4
   B 3   D 5

4. Which sentence would best fit between sentences 4 and 5 to match the spatial organization of the details in the passage?
   F From my seat, I see the ballplayers spread out onto the field and run to their respective positions.
   G Most of all, I dream about being a pro baseball player.
   H You glance through the program and figure out the rankings of each player you are about to see.
   J I hope to catch a stray ball that might be knocked into the stands.

5. In an oral presentation of this description, the writer could incorporate visuals with
   A a chart of baseball statistics
   B a slide show of famous players
   C the flags and posters described
   D a graph of the concession sales

SKILLS FOCUS

Writing Skills
Write a descriptive essay.

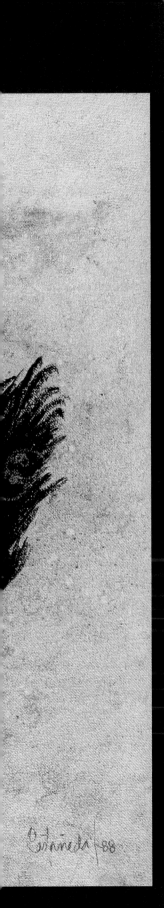

Collection 7

Imagine

Literary Focus:
Analyzing Poetry

Dialogue of Two Poets Disguised as Birds (1988) by Alfredo Castañeda. Oil on canvas (15¾″ × 19¾″).

Mary Ann Martin/Fine Art, New York.

INTERNET

Collection Resources

Keyword: LE7 9-7

Elements of Literature

Imagery *by* John Malcolm Brinnin
SEEING THINGS FRESHLY

Imagery is one of the elements that give poetry its forcefulness. Images are basically copies of things you can see. But images in poetry can do even more than help us see things. An **image** is a single word or a phrase that appeals to one of our senses. An image can help us see color or motion. Sometimes it can also help us hear a sound, smell an odor, feel texture or temperature, or even taste a sweet, sour, or salty flavor.

Suppose you were an artist and wanted to paint a picture of a house. You would emphasize certain aspects of the house. You might emphasize the age of the house by making its shingles look as worn and wrinkled and cracked as an old shoe. You might emphasize the emptiness of the house by painting curtainless windows that reflect the clouds and doors opening onto empty hallways. In each case, as an artist you would give the actual image (the house) a certain twist, a particular shading.

Poets do the same thing. Edwin Arlington Robinson in "The House on the Hill" saw an empty house and emphasized its loneliness:

Through broken walls and gray
The winds blow bleak and shrill;
They are all gone away.

Robert Frost in "The Black Cottage" saw an empty house and emphasized the new life that had moved in:

"There are bees in this wall." He struck the
    clapboards,
Fierce heads looked out; small bodies
    pivoted.
We rose to go. Sunset blazed on the
    windows.

House by the Railroad (1925) by Edward Hopper. Oil on canvas (24″ x 29″).

The Museum of Modern Art, New York. Given anonymously. Photograph © 2000 The Museum of Modern Art, New York.

Imagery is part of a poet's style. It is the product of the poet's own way of seeing the world. Just as we learn to recognize certain painters at once by noticing the colors and shapes that mark their works, so we learn to identify poets by paying attention to their imagery. Of course, the time and place in which poets live influence the kind of imagery they use. Poets who live in cities will usually draw upon the street scenes and industrial landscapes they know so well. Poets who live far from cities will usually draw their images from what they see of country life.

Imagery and Feelings

An image can be so fresh, so powerful, that it can speak to our deepest feelings. An image can be so phrased that it makes us feel joy or grief, wonder or horror, love or disgust.

Here is a poem that uses images to help us see a scene on the Great Lakes and hear the sounds made by a boat lost in the mist. Yet what readers remember most about this little poem is the way the images make them feel:

Lost
Desolate and lone
All night long on the lake
Where fog trails and mist creeps,
The whistle of a boat
Calls and cries unendingly,
Like some lost child
In tears and trouble
Hunting the harbor's breast
And the harbor's eyes.
—Carl Sandburg

The poet . . . should stop and examine what others have missed, whether it be veins on a leaf or the surge of a mob; he should hear what others miss—not just skylarks but the breath of an old man or sleet against the window; he should respond to the feel of a rusted iron railing, a cut, or a gull's feather; he should identify the variety of city smells and country odors and consider what it is that makes an unoccupied house different from one lived in; and he should taste not only food but pine gum and smog.

—Stephen Minot

Practice

To see how **images** can be drawn from all sorts of things we observe in life, create two images for each of the following categories. Have one image suggest something pleasant and the other suggest something unpleasant. Try to include images that show how a thing **looks, smells, tastes, sounds,** or **feels** to the touch.

Images	Pleasant	Unpleasant
Animal images		
Flower images		
Water images		
Sky images		
Earth images		
City images		
Country images		

Imagine

Make the Connection

Quickwrite

Look carefully at the starfish pictured on the opposite page. Now, imagine that you saw hundreds of thousands of starfish lying on a beach. What would they remind you of? Place your ideas in a cluster diagram like the one below.

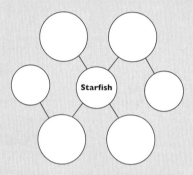

Starfish

Exploring the Theme: Imagine

The poems in this collection all show that in the imagination, nothing is impossible. You can imagine that a car is a shark, or that hands are churches, or that hope is a bird. You can imagine that the world is a stage, and we're all merely actors. In fact, some of the poets in this collection—Martín Espada, Naomi Shihab Nye, Emily Dickinson, and William Shakespeare—have imagined just those things. Like the rest of the poetry in this collection, "Starfish"—the poem you're about to read—shows how poets use language and the power of the imagination to transform personal experience and the world around them, enabling all of us to see life through new eyes.

Literary Focus

Imagery

Imagery is one of a poet's most powerful tools. An **image** is a word or phrase that appeals to one or more of our five senses: hearing, sight, touch, smell, and taste. Poets use imagery to help us share their experiences—to see what they see and hear what they hear. As you read "Starfish," note how the imagery makes you feel as if you're right there on the beach with the speaker, surrounded by starfish.

SKILLS FOCUS

Literary Skills
Understand imagery.

Starfish

Lorna Dee Cervantes

They were lovely in the quartz and jasper° sand
As if they had created terrariums with their bodies
On purpose; adding sprigs of seaweed, seashells,
White feathers, eel bones, miniature
5 Mussels, a fish jaw. Hundreds; no— ❶
Thousands of baby stars. We touched them,
Surprised to find them soft, pliant,° almost
Living in their attitudes. We would dry them, arrange them,
Form seascapes, geodesics . . .° We gathered what we could
10 In the approaching darkness. Then we left hundreds of ❷
Thousands of flawless five-fingered specimens sprawled
Along the beach as far as we could see, all massed
Together: little martyrs,° soldiers, artless° suicides
In lifelong liberation from the sea. So many
15 Splayed° hands, the tide shoveled in.

---

1. **quartz and jasper:** Quartz, a hard mineral, is the most common element in sand.
   Jasper is a reddish, yellow, or brown type of quartz.
7. **pliant** (plī′ənt) *adj.:* easily bent.
9. **geodesics** (jē′ə•des′iks) *adj.* used as *n.:* interlocking, repeating patterns.
13. **martyrs** (märt′ers) *n.:* people who choose to die rather than give up their beliefs.
13. **artless** *adj.:* simple; innocent.
15. **splayed** *v.* used as *adj.:* spread out.

THEME

❶ Terrariums are small
enclosures or contain-
ers that house plants
or animals. Why does
the speaker, seeing
the starfish in the
sand, imagine that
they have formed
terrariums with their
bodies?

IMAGERY

❷ What does the
image of the
approaching darkness
contribute to the feel-
ing of the poem?

Meet the Writer
Lorna Dee Cervantes

The Freedom of Words

Growing up in San Jose, California, Lorna Dee Cervantes (1954–   ) discovered literature by reading the books she found in the houses that her mother cleaned for a living. She was writing poetry by the age of eight and completed her first collection of poems when she was fifteen. Writing gave Cervantes, whose family is of Mexican and Native American ancestry, a sense of freedom:

66 When you grow up as I did, a Chican-India in a barrio in a Mexican neighborhood in California, you're not expected to speak. You're ignored. You're something in the periphery, emptying garbage cans or washing plates. And you're not expected to speak, much less write. 99

Cervantes has explored the Mexican American experience in her award-winning poetry, which has appeared in numerous anthologies and literary journals. (Her first book of poetry, *Emplumada,* which includes "Starfish," won an American Book Award in 1982.) She has played an important role in furthering the work of other Chicano writers by establishing a literary journal and publishing company, both called *Mango,* devoted to their work. Cervantes currently teaches at the University of Colorado at Boulder.

After You Read

Response and Analysis

Reading Check

1. Are the starfish on the beach dead or alive? Which details in the poem provide the answer?

Thinking Critically

2. To describe the starfish, Cervantes uses **images** that appeal to our senses of sight and touch. List these images in a chart like the one below. Which image do you think is the most effective? Why?

Sight	Touch

3. The speaker uses **metaphors**, or comparisons between unlike things, to describe the starfish as martyrs, soldiers, and suicides. Why do you think she makes these comparisons? What do these comparisons tell you about the way the speaker views the starfish?

4. How do you think the speaker feels about the sea? Support your answer with details from the poem. (Think, for example, about the verb "shoveled" in the poem's last line.)

5. Compare the cluster diagram you made for the Quickwrite with those of your classmates. Then, think about how the collection theme "Imagine" relates to this poem. What similarities and differences do you find between the ways Cervantes and the class described the starfish? Did Cervantes make you see the starfish in a new way? Explain.

6. Do you think this poem could be about something more than just starfish? For example, what might this poem have to say about human beings? Support your answer with details from the poem.

Extending and Evaluating

7. The beach and the sea have captured the imagination of writers and artists throughout the ages. Why do you think people are so fascinated by the sea? Which of its qualities do we find appealing or threatening?

Exploring the Theme

Imagine

In the rest of this collection, you'll read poems about a variety of subjects—fog, courage, parents, and even baseball. As you read, think about how the poets have used their imaginations to help us see ordinary things in brand-new ways.

SKILLS FOCUS

Literary Focus
Analyze imagery.

Before You Read

A Blessing

Make the Connection

Quickwrite ✏️

Close your eyes, and try to visualize something in nature. Describe what you are seeing. You could be describing something as big as the sky or as small as an ant, as soft as a rabbit or as squishy as a swamp, as . . . Well, you've got the idea. Explain how what you are describing makes you feel.

Literary Focus

Imagery

Poetry is often said to be magical. When a poem helps us see something in a new way, we sometimes feel a shiver of awe, and we say, "How did the poet do that?"

Poets create their magic by using words to excite our emotions and our imaginations. One of the ways they do that is through **imagery**—language that appeals to our senses.

Sight is the sense many people rely on most, so not surprisingly it is the most common source of imagery in poetry. Images can also appeal to our senses of **hearing, touch, smell,** and **taste.** Sometimes an image appeals to two or more senses at the same time.

All these images re-create an experience the poet wants to share with us. They give us the feeling that we're right there, a part of it all.

SKILLS FOCUS

Literary Skills
Understand sensory imagery.

A Blessing

James Wright

Just off the highway to Rochester, Minnesota,
Twilight bounds softly forth on the grass,
And the eyes of those two Indian ponies
Darken with kindness.
5   They have come gladly out of the willows
To welcome my friend and me.
We step over the barbed wire into the pasture
Where they have been grazing all day, alone.
They ripple tensely, they can hardly contain their happiness
10 That we have come.
They bow shyly as wet swans. They love each other.
There is no loneliness like theirs.
At home once more,
They begin munching the young tufts of spring in the darkness.
15 I would like to hold the slenderer one in my arms,
For she has walked over to me
And nuzzled my left hand.
She is black and white,
Her mane falls wild on her forehead,
20 And the light breeze moves me to caress her long ear
That is delicate as the skin over a girl's wrist.
Suddenly I realize
That if I stepped out of my body I would break
Into blossom.

Meet the Writer

James Wright

"We Know What He's Talking About"

Travelers who pull off I-90 at the High Forest Rest Area in Stewartville, Minnesota, may not find two ponies in a pasture. Thanks to the radio host Garrison Keillor, however, they will find a plaque engraved with the poem "A Blessing."

Keillor dedicated the plaque in 1998. A pair of horses was on hand, as were more than two hundred local high school students. One sophomore said he liked Wright's poem because it spoke "about the beauty of Minnesota. And it's so close to us; we know what he's talking about."

The Pulitzer Prize–winner James Wright (1927–1980) often wrote about the places in his life—Minnesota, where he taught college for eight years (Keillor was his student there); New York City, his home in later life; but especially Martin's Ferry, the mill town in Ohio where he grew up in a poor family during the Great Depression.

Much of Wright's poetry is dark, and it explores themes of loneliness and alienation. "A Blessing" escapes this darkness—perhaps that is the reason for its popularity. Keillor has said of the poem:

" I've seen it done in needlework, and in rye seeds glued to particle board and entered in the crop show at the state fair. I've heard it read at weddings in meadows, weddings attended by horses. . . . It is a love poem. **"**

Response and Analysis

Reading Check

1. What is the **setting** of the poem— *where* and *when* does it take place?

2. What were the ponies doing all day?

3. How do the ponies feel about the visit? How do they feel about each other?

4. Why does the speaker feel especially fond of one of the ponies?

Thinking Critically

5. Most of the **images** in this poem appeal to the senses of sight and touch. Make a two-column chart like the one here, with the headings "Sight" and "Touch." Then, list images from the poem in the appropriate columns. Some images might be listed in both columns.

Sight	Touch

6. You may have read myths in which a character is fantastically changed from one form to another. This change is called **metamorphosis.** What metamorphosis do you *see* in the last three lines of the poem? What emotion do you think the speaker is expressing there?

7. What human qualities and feelings does the speaker give to the ponies?

8. The **tone** of this poem is joyful. It expresses the pleasure that comes from springtime and love. What **images** in the poem help to create its tone?

Extending and Evaluating

9. What do you think of the **title** "A Blessing"? What does it have to do with the experience described in the poem? What other titles can you suggest for the poem?

WRITING

Capturing a Feeling

Write a **poem** or a **paragraph** that describes something in nature that you feel strongly about. You can start with an image you found for the Quickwrite on page 480, or you can come up with a new subject. Be sure to tell *where* you are as you observe your scene. Use images that appeal to the **senses** and that reveal how you feel about your subject. How does your subject **look, sound, smell, feel,** or **taste**?

Before You Read

Woman Work
Daily

Make the Connection

Quickwrite ✏

Make a list of the things that you do during an ordinary day. What is the first thing you do in the morning? What is the last thing you do before bed? What is your favorite part of the day? The following two poems tell about the things that people do every day. As you read, think about your list. How does it compare with the poems?

Literary Focus

Catalog Poem

You've probably seen the kind of catalogs that come from stores, filled with pictures of almost anything in the world you'd want to buy. Like those catalogs, a **catalog poem** brings together many different images and presents them for your attention. Unlike a retail catalog, though, a poem does not want you to part with your money; it wants you only to enter the poem and, with your imagination, share an experience with the speaker.

The repetition of images in a catalog poem creates a rolling rhythm when the poem is read aloud. Try reading the two poems that follow aloud, and see how the piling up of images creates the poems' rhythmic beat.

Woman Work
Maya Angelou

I've got the children to tend
The clothes to mend
The floor to mop
The food to shop
5   Then the chicken to fry
The baby to dry
I got company to feed
The garden to weed
I've got the shirts to press
10   The tots to dress
The cane to be cut
I gotta clean up this hut
Then see about the sick
And the cotton to pick

15   Shine on me, sunshine
Rain on me, rain
Fall softly, dewdrops
And cool my brow again.

Storm, blow me from here
20   With your fiercest wind
Let me float across the sky
'Til I can rest again.

Fall gently, snowflakes
Cover me with white
25   Cold icy kisses and
Let me rest tonight.

Sun, rain, curving sky
Mountain, oceans, leaf and stone
Star shine, moon glow
30   You're all that I can call my own.

Daily

Naomi Shihab Nye

These shriveled seeds we plant,
corn kernel, dried bean,
poke into loosened soil,
cover over with measured fingertips
5   These T-shirts we fold
into perfect white
squares
These tortillas we slice and fry to crisp strips
This rich egg scrambled in a gray clay bowl
10   This bed whose covers I straighten
smoothing edges till blue quilt fits brown blanket
and nothing hangs out
This envelope I address
so the name balances like a cloud
15   in the center of the sky
This page I type and retype
This table I dust till the scarred wood shines
This bundle of clothes I wash and hang and wash again
like flags we share, a country so close
20   no one needs to name it
The days are nouns: touch them
The hands are churches that worship the world

The Grinder (1924) by Diego Rivera. Encaustic on canvas (90 cm × 117 cm).

Courtesy Museo de Arte Moderno (INBA), Mexico City.
©1995 The Detroit Institute of Arts.
Photograph by Dirk Bakker.

Meet the Writers

Maya Angelou
Naomi Shihab Nye

Born Winner

Maya Angelou.

66 One would say of my life, 'born loser, had to be'—but it's not the truth. In the black community, however bad it looks, there's a lot of love and so much humor. **99**

Maya Angelou (1928–   ) is anything but a loser. After she left Stamps, Arkansas, she won a scholarship to the California Labor School, where she took evening classes in dance and drama. In 1954 and 1955, she toured Europe and Africa in a State Department–sponsored production of the opera *Porgy and Bess.* She later wrote and produced a ten-part television series on Africanisms in American life; wrote songs that were recorded by B. B. King; and published short stories, magazine articles, and poems. In 1992, she was asked to write a poem for the inauguration of President Bill Clinton. On Inauguration Day in 1993, Maya Angelou presented her eloquent poem "On the Pulse of Morning." Here are the final lines:

66 Here on the pulse of this new day
You may have the grace to look up and out
And into your sister's eyes,
And into your brother's face,
Your country,
And say simply
Very simply
With hope—
Good morning. **99**

Angelou is an imposing woman—six feet tall—with a gracious, formal manner. She speaks six languages fluently. Although she declares a continuing interest in exploring the character of the black woman, Angelou's focus is not narrow:

66 I speak to the black experience, but I am always talking about the human condition—about what we can endure, dream, fail at, and still survive. **99**

Noticing the World

Naomi Shihab Nye (1952–   ), born and raised in St. Louis, Missouri, has written several collections of poems, including *Red Suitcase* (1994) and *Words Under the Words: Selected Poems* (1995). Nye is also a songwriter with two albums to her credit—*Rutabaga-Roo* and *Lullaby Raft.* Many of Nye's poems are inspired by her childhood memories and by her travels, including visits to her Palestinian grandmother in Jerusalem. Nye lives in San Antonio, Texas, with her husband and her son. She regularly reads her poetry in schools, where she also runs workshops to help students find the poetry hiding in their own imaginations. She says:

66 Being alive is a common road. It's what we notice [that] makes us different. **99**

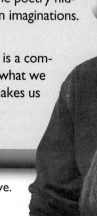

Naomi Shihab Nye.

Woman Work
Daily

Reading Check

1. Name five activities listed by the speaker of "Woman Work."

2. Name five activities listed by the speaker of "Daily."

Thinking Critically

3. What does the **catalog** of **images** in "Woman Work" tell you about the life of the speaker? Where do you think she lives? What do you learn from the images in "Daily" about the life of its speaker?

4. Both **catalog poems** list daily activities in a woman's life, but the tone of each poem is different—the speakers express different attitudes toward their lives. How would you describe the **tone** of each poem? Is it complaining? bitter? angry? resigned? accepting? loving? joyful? Is it something else? Cite details from each poem to explain the tone you hear in it.

5. The second through fifth stanzas of "Woman Work" use **apostrophe** (ə·päs′trə·fē)—they address, or speak directly to, someone or something. What things does this speaker address? What does she ask for?

6. The last two lines of "Daily" are not part of the poem's catalog; rather, they sum up the speaker's message. What do you think the poet is saying about daily work in these lines?

7. Both of these poems were written by women about their daily work. If the poems had been written by men and were called "Man Work," how might they be different?

WRITING

My Day

Expand your notes for the Quickwrite on page 484 into a **catalog poem** that lists the things you do every day. Choose images that make your day come alive for the reader. You might want to imitate the structure of one of the poems in the following ways:

- If you imitate "Woman Work," begin with *I've got* . . . Then, list the things—such as "a bus to catch"—that you have to do.

- If you imitate "Daily," begin each line with *These/This* . . . Write, for example, "This heavy backpack I carry . . ."

How do you feel about your daily work? Try to express that feeling. ✎

Woman with Basket (Mujer con Canasta) (1921) by Diego Rivera. Watercolor.

Before You Read

in Just-

Make the Connection
Quickwrite ✏️

Jot down some of the things you associate with your favorite season of the year. Think of activities, sights, smells, tastes, sounds—even special people you see during that time of year.

Literary Focus
Fresh Images

An important part of a poet's job is to find **fresh images** that help us see the world in an unusual or original way. Notice how E. E. Cummings combines *mud* with *luscious* and *puddle* with *wonderful* to make brand-new images. These images remind us how much fun it was to play in the mud and splash in puddles when we were little kids.

Literary Skills
Understand imagery, especially unusual and fresh imagery.

Meet the Writer

E. E. Cummings

Nobody-but-Himself

E. E. Cummings (1894–1962) began writing a poem a day when he was eight years old—and he kept at it until he was twenty-two. Multiply 365 poems a year by fourteen, and see what you get! Many of these poems were very short, and a lot of them weren't very good. However, if practice makes perfect, then Cummings must have been perfect—on some days anyhow.

Cummings once got a letter from a high school editor asking him what advice he had for young people who wanted to become poets. Cummings's reply tells us something about what poetry meant to him:

❝ A poet is somebody who feels, and who expresses his feeling through words. This may sound easy. It isn't . . . [because] the moment you feel, you're nobody-but-yourself. To be nobody-but-yourself—in a world which is doing its best, night and day, to make you everybody else—means to fight the hardest battle which any human being can fight; and never stop fighting. . . . If, at the end of your first ten or fifteen years of fighting and working and feeling, you find you've written one line of one poem, you'll be very lucky indeed. . . . Does this sound dismal? It isn't. It's the most wonderful life on earth. ❞

Self-Portrait by E. E. Cummings.
© Bettmann/CORBIS.

in Just-
E. E. Cummings

in Just-
spring   when the world is mud-
luscious the little
lame balloonman

5   whistles   far   and wee

and eddieandbill come
running from marbles and
piracies and it's
spring

10   when the world is puddle-wonderful

the queer
old balloonman whistles
far   and   wee
and bettyandisbel come dancing

15   from hop-scotch and jump-rope and

it's
spring
and
    the

20   goat-footed

balloonMan   whistles
far
and
wee

Eyeglasses for the Mind

Stephen King

I did the Mike Wallace radio show in New York at the CBS building. We went in and the electric eye had a case of the hiccups. The door was one of these doors where you'd step on the pad and the door would slide open. And this door was almost pitching a fit. It was jerking back and forth, not closing or opening all the way.

And my feeling about that is that somebody else would look at that and say: "Oh, that door has the hiccups." Whereas a little kid would walk up to that door and might very well shrink away from even going near it. And say: "It wants to eat me, it's alive!" Children see things from a different perspective.

And in that sense I'm childlike. I looked at the door and I thought: "Gee, that would make a good story if that thing came alive and somebody walked up to it and CHUNG!" Which is a very childish sort of fantasy.

People respond to this perspective. It doesn't really die. It atrophies[1] and lies dormant.[2] And I get paid to show people that different perspective. It's like exercising a muscle, rather than letting it go slack. But I'll tell you a funny thing. There are writers who look like children. They've used this facility so much for so long that they literally look like children.

Ray Bradbury is sixty years old and he has the face of a child. You see it in the eyes a lot of the time. Isaac Singer has the eyes of a child in that old face. They look out of that old face and they're very young.

That's why people pay writers and artists. That's the only reason we're around. We're excess baggage. I can't even fix a pipe in my house when it freezes. I am a dickey bird on the back of civilization.

I have no skill that improves the quality of life in a physical sense at all. The only thing I can do is say: "Look here, this is the way you didn't look at it before. It's just a cloud to you, but look at it, doesn't it look like an elephant?" Somebody says: "Boy! it does look like an elephant!" And for that, people pay because they've lost all of it themselves.

You know, I'm like a person who makes eyeglasses for the mind.

—1979 interview from *Feast of Fear: Conversations with Stephen King*

---

1. **atrophies** (a′trə·fēz) *v.*: wastes away.
2. **dormant** (dôr′mənt) *adj.*: inactive.

After You Read Response and Analysis

Reading Check

1. What season of the year is the **setting** for this poem? What's the weather like at that time of year?

2. List three activities that are mentioned in the poem.

3. Who is the central figure in this poem—the person who is mentioned three times?

4. What sound does this person make? Who is attracted to this sound?

Thinking Critically

5. What senses do the **images** "mud-luscious," "whistles far and wee," and "puddle-wonderful" appeal to? What impact do these images have on the poem's **mood,** or atmosphere?

6. Cummings is known for his unusual punctuation and arrangement of words. What are the children doing in the poem that matches the leaps and jumps of the words? Why might Cummings have made single words out of the names Eddie and Bill, Betty and Isbel?

7. Where does Pan, a famous goat-footed character from Greek mythology, enter this poem? Pan, who has the cloven hooves and shaggy legs of a goat, is a god of the woodlands and of merrymaking. He is usually shown playing a flute and leading shepherds in a dance. How is the balloon man like Pan?

8. According to Stephen King (see the **Connection** on page 491), what do writers do that is important? How do you interpret the title of his piece, "Eyeglasses for the Mind"? Do you think Cummings provides readers of "in Just-" with "eyeglasses for the mind"?

WRITING
What Makes It Work?

Cummings is famous for his unusual style as well as for his fresh imagery. In a few paragraphs, analyze "in Just-," paying particular attention to its **imagery, word choice, mood,** and **style** (use of punctuation and word arrangement). Explain what you think makes Cummings so popular and unique.

▶ **Use "Analyzing a Poem," pages 556–563, for help with this assignment.**

A Seasonal Salute

Stephen King recognizes the importance of seeing things with imaginative eyes (see the **Connection** on page 491). Take your turn doing that. Write a **poem** that presents **fresh images** to describe your favorite season. Your notes for the Quickwrite on page 489 should give you a start. Be sure to avoid **clichés**—overused, burned-out expressions.

You might open your poem the way Cummings does: "in Just- [your season] when the world is . . ." Play with words, punctuation, and spacing to help readers share your pleasure in this season.

LISTENING AND SPEAKING
Say It Aloud

Prepare to read "in Just-" aloud. Decide where you will pause (watch those big spaces), when you will speed up, and when you might even draw the words out, as if you were singing. Then, read the poem to a partner.

SKILLS FOCUS

Literary Skills
Analyze imagery, especially unusual and fresh imagery.

Writing Skills
Write an analysis of a poem. Write a poem containing fresh images.

Listening and Speaking Skills
Present an oral interpretation of a poem.

go. hrw .com

INTERNET

Projects and Activities

Keyword: LE7 9-7

Word Knowledge: Hunting Interesting Words

PRACTICE

Poets are always searching for words. Start your own **word bank** in which you enter unusual and interesting words. You can set your word bank up in a computer file or on index cards. To get started, leaf through an old magazine or newspaper, and choose just one page. Then, define and enter in your word bank any unusual or interesting words from the page. Map each word as shown in the chart below. Give its **meaning,** a **synonym,** and two sample sentences using the word. Use a **dictionary** and a **thesaurus** if you like.

Word: implacable
Meaning: relentless; can't be satisfied or stopped
Synonyms: inflexible, rigid
Sample sentences: • Robert is an implacable force on the student council. • We could not defeat the implacable enemy.

SKILLS FOCUS

Vocabulary Skills
Create a word bank for word study.

Before You Read

Haiku

Make the Connection

Quickwrite ✏

Pick a special day of the year. Write down what you might **hear, see, taste, smell,** or **touch** on that day. Try to find images that reveal the way you might feel at a particular moment on that special day.

Literary Focus

Haiku

Haiku, the most famous form of Japanese poetry, can capture moments of life with the speed and precision of a snapshot. While snapshots usually record only the *outside* appearance of the moments, haiku can take you *inside* to reveal an insight or truth.

To unlock the meaning of a haiku, read each word or phrase carefully. Let yourself see, hear, smell, taste, or touch each single element of the original moment. Let these **images** serve as a starting point for your own thoughts and associations. In the end you will find yourself standing inside a special moment in someone else's life—whether the experience was captured three minutes ago or three hundred years ago.

In the Japanese language a **haiku**

- has seventeen syllables—five in lines 1 and 3; seven in line 2
- presents **images** from nature and from everyday life—usually two contrasting images
- often contains a seasonal word or symbol (*kigo*)
- presents a moment of discovery or enlightenment (*satori*)

The Original Language

Here, in the original Japanese with the English translation, is Bashō's haiku from the next page. (*Ya* is a word frequently used in haiku to mean something like *Lo!* in English, which means "Look!" or "See!" Some translators indicate it with a colon, since it suggests a kind of equation.)

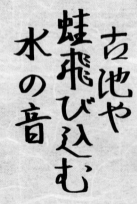

Furu	*ike*	*ya*
old	pond	:
Kawazu	*tobikomu*	
frog	jump in	
Mizu	*no*	*oto*
water	of	sound

SKILLS FOCUS

Literary Skills
Understand the characteristics of haiku.

Morning Glories (detail) (19th century) by Suzuki Kiitsu. Japanese painted screen.
Color and gold leaf on paper (6′ high × 13′ wide).

The Metropolitan Museum of Art, New York, Seymour Fund, 1954 (54.69.1).

Haiku

Get out of my road
and allow me to plant these
bamboos, Mr. Toad.
　　　　　—Miura Chora

The old pond;
A frog jumps in:
Sound of water.
—Matsuo Bashō

A morning glory
Twined round the bucket:
I will ask my neighbor for water.
　　　　　　—Chiyo

A dragonfly!
The distant hills
Reflected in his eyes.
　　　—Kobayashi Issa

Meet the Writers

Miura Chora
Chiyo
Matsuo Bashō
Kobayashi Issa

Captured Moments

Miura Chora (1729–1780), like most writers of haiku, drew his images from the ordinary objects and activities of daily life—in this case, planting bamboo shoots. In Japanese every haiku has exactly seventeen syllables, but English translators can't always achieve that. Count the number of syllables on page 495, and see if this translator has performed a miracle of translation.

Chiyo (1703–1775) is the most celebrated of the women writers of haiku. Some critics say her poems are too explicit and lack the mystery of true haiku. They want their haiku to be more subtle, indirect, and suggestive—like the classical Bashō poem on page 495. Yet Chiyo's admirers think that some people mistake haziness in haiku for profound thought.

Matsuo Bashō (1644–1694) is considered the developer of the haiku form as well as its greatest master. Bashō was a deeply spiritual man who became a Zen monk in his later years. His haiku show a zest for every speck of life—a sense that nothing in this world is unimportant.

Kobayashi Issa (1763–1827) had a very sad life. Despite his poverty and the fact that he saw all his beloved children die, Issa's extraordinarily simple poems are full of human tenderness and wry humor.

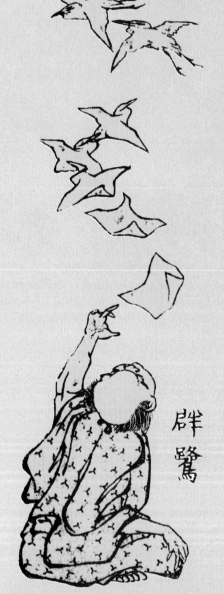

A Magician Turning Paper into Cranes (detail) (1819) from the *Manga* (a book of humorous sketches) by Katsushika Hokusai.

Asian Prints. The Metropolitan Museum of Art, New York, Rogers Fund, 1931 (JIB 81.10).

Reading Check

1. These haiku are, of course, translated. Which of the four **haiku** follow the rule of five syllables in lines 1 and 3, seven syllables in line 2?

2. Describe two **images** you see in each haiku.

3. Which haiku relies most on the sense of hearing?

Thinking Critically

4. What season of the year do you think each haiku describes? Which word or words give you a clue?

5. Haiku often balance two **contrasting images.** In Chora's haiku, for example, the toad in the road, probably resting, contrasts with the human, busy planting his bamboo. What contrasting images can you find in the other three haiku?

6. Think about the person who is speaking in each haiku. Put yourself in each person's shoes, one by one. Consider:

- In Chora's haiku, do you wait for the toad to move, or do you poke it?

- In Chiyo's haiku, do you ever use that bucket for water again?

- In Bashō's haiku, what might you be doing before the frog jumps in?

- In Issa's haiku, for how long are you able to see the hills?

WRITING

A Special-Day Haiku

Write a **haiku** celebrating the special day you made notes about for the Quickwrite on page 494. You should limit your haiku to three lines, but it is not necessary to use just seventeen syllables—unless you want a challenge! Keep in mind that a haiku usually does the following things:

- It brings two images together, usually for contrast.

- It contains a word describing the season or weather.

- It presents a moment of discovery.

Detail of frogs and a hare from the *Choju Giga* scrolls (late 12th to mid-13th century).

Burstein Collection / CORBIS.

Literary Skills
Analyze the characteristics of haiku.

Writing Skills
Write a haiku.

Once by the Pacific

Make the Connection

"Let There Be Light"

In the Bible, when God creates the universe, God says, "Let there be light" (Genesis 1:3). After each stage of creation, the Bible says, "And God saw that it was good." Keep these words in mind as you read Robert Frost's vision of an event that is the opposite of creation.

Literary Focus

Sonnet

Robert Frost loved writing sonnets because he enjoyed the challenge of fitting his thoughts into a very strict form. Here are the rules for the sonnet:

- It has fourteen lines.
- It follows a regular rhyme pattern.
- It is usually written in **iambic pentameter.**

An **iamb** is an unstressed syllable followed by a stressed one (da DAH), as in the word *before*. Writing an iambic line isn't as hard as you might think because the iamb is common in ordinary English speech:

Amanda wore her favorite pair of jeans.

Pentameter means there are five stressed syllables, or beats, in each line— *penta* is Greek for "five," and *meter* is Greek for "measure." (Occasional variations help keep the rhythm from becoming monotonous.) Here are lines from two sonnets written in iambic pentameter. Read the lines aloud to hear their beat.

Shall I compare thee to a summer's day?
—William Shakespeare

The shattered water made a misty din.
—Robert Frost

There are two traditional types of sonnet. In the **Italian,** or **Petrarchan, sonnet** the first eight lines (the **octave**) pose a problem, which is responded to in the last six lines (the **sestet**). In the **English,** or **Shakespearean, sonnet,** three four-line units are followed by a **couplet,** or two-line unit. Some modern poets, like Frost, create their own types of sonnet.

For biographies of Robert Frost, see pages 378 and 518.

SKILLS FOCUS

Literary Skills
Understand the characteristics of different types of sonnets.

**go.
hrw
.com**

INTERNET

More About Robert Frost

Keyword: LE7 9-7

Once by the Pacific

Robert Frost

The shattered water made a misty din.
Great waves looked over others coming in,
And thought of doing something to the shore
That water never did to land before.
5 The clouds were low and hairy in the skies,
Like locks blown forward in the gleam of eyes.
You could not tell, and yet it looked as if
The shore was lucky in being backed by cliff,
The cliff in being backed by continent;
10 It looked as if a night of dark intent
Was coming, and not only a night, an age.
Someone had better be prepared for rage.
There would be more than ocean-water broken
Before God's last *Put out the Light* was spoken.

Country Scene

Make the Connection

Lasting Impressions

In "Country Scene" the poet, like many other poets throughout the centuries, expresses her views about what lasts—and what doesn't last. Think about nature, your own life, and the world around you. Which things are permanent? Which things are fleeting?

Literary Focus

Lyric Poem

Robert Frost's "Once by the Pacific" (page 499) is a sonnet, which is a type of lyric poem. There are many kinds of lyric poems. In general, a **lyric poem** is a short poem that expresses a speaker's thoughts or feelings. In ancient Greece, lyric poems were sung to the music of a stringed instrument called a *lyre*. Today we call the words to all types of songs *lyrics*.

In its original Vietnamese, "Country Scene," the lyric poem that follows, is called a *lu-shih*. The English translation cannot begin to show how challenging *lu-shih* is to write. Vietnamese is a tonal language, and the tones in a poem must fall at certain places in each seven-syllable line. Every *lu-shih* poem has eight lines, with rhymes usually at the end of the first, second, fourth, sixth, and eighth lines.

While we may not be able to appreciate the complexity of this *lu-shih* poem in its English translation, we can certainly think about its message and share the beauty of its imagery.

The Original Language

Below, at the left, is "Country Scene" in its original language, Nom, which is written in an ancient Vietnamese script. Below, at the right, is a translation in modern Vietnamese. For more information about these texts, see Meet the Writer on page 502.

即景

濕　洸　頭　崇　頓　噴　湄
妬　埃　臚　特　景　蕭　踈
撑　菩　古　樹　嶒　岷　傘
屍　撮　長　江　滂　朗　詞
艦　牧　呦　唛　沔　曠　野
緰　漁　扛　鑾　壖　平　沙
鐘　埃　絗　綏　邊　箕　佐
㭲　培　鍾　情　沒　襫　詩

Tức cảnh

Thấp thoáng đầu ghềnh lún phún mưa

Đố ai vẽ được cảnh tiêu sơ

Xanh om cổ thụ chon von tán

Trắng toát tràng giang phẳng lặng tờ

Còi mục thét lừng miền khoáng dã

Lưới ngư giang gió bãi bình sa

Chuông ai đất nối bên kia tá

Ương lở chung tình một túi thơ.

SKILLS FOCUS

Literary Skills
Understand the characteristics of lyric poems.

Country Scene

Hồ Xuân Hu'o'ng

translated by John Balaban

The waterfall plunges in mist.
Who can describe this desolate scene:

the long white river sliding through
the emerald shadows of the ancient canopy

. . . a shepherd's horn echoing in the valley,
fishnets stretched to dry on sandy flats.

A bell is tolling, fading, fading
just like love. Only poetry lasts.

Meet the Writer

Hồ Xuân Hu'o'ng

The Mysterious Spring Essence

The Vietnamese poet Hồ Xuân Hu'o'ng (c. 1770s–1820s) lived in a time of political turmoil and social collapse. South Vietnam, aided by foreign powers, was at war with the north. Rulers battled for power while ordinary people struggled to stay alive through decades of chaos and destruction.

Sound familiar? It did to John Balaban, an American conscientious objector who, during another war in Vietnam two centuries later, brought medical care to wounded Vietnamese children. Along with supplies he brought a tape recorder to capture the classic poems he heard the villagers recite. Many of their favorites, they told him, had been written by the great poet Hồ Xuân Hu'o'ng, whose name means "spring essence."

Little is known about Hồ. She is thought to have been born in north central Vietnam, to the "second wife," or concubine, of a scholar. She became a concubine as well, to an official she ridiculed in a poem as Mr. Toad. At that time, Vietnamese women had little status. Yet Hồ, who often attacked male authority in her writing, earned fame and admiration instead of punishment—a mark of how deeply the people of her country loved poetry.

Today only a few dozen people know how to read Nom, the traditional Vietnamese writing system Hồ used. Balaban hopes to turn that situation around. His collection of Hồ's poetry, *Spring Essence,* includes her poems in both the modern Vietnamese and the Nom scripts next to his English translations. It is the first time the ancient script, which was originally reproduced by woodblock, has ever come off a printing press. (The Nom and modern Vietnamese texts of "Country Scene" on page 500 are reproduced from *Spring Essence.*)

Vietnamese clay plate (16th century).

Musée des Arts Asiatiques-Guimet, Paris. © Erich Lessing/Art Resource, New York.

Response and Analysis

Once by the Pacific

Reading Check

1. Where is the speaker in "Once by the Pacific" standing as he observes the ocean? What are the waves doing?

2. According to lines 10–11, what do the wild waves make the speaker think of?

3. Look at the last two lines of the **sonnet,** the concluding **couplet.** What dreadful thoughts is the speaker sharing with us there?

Thinking Critically

4. What **images** in lines 1–4 help you picture the waves—and even hear them?

5. What **images** in lines 5–6 help you picture the clouds?

6. Whose "rage" is described in line 12? What could cause that rage?

7. Look back at Make the Connection on page 498. How does the last line of the sonnet differ from God's words of creation in the Bible?

8. What do you think the **theme,** or message, of this sonnet is?

9. Look at how this poem is structured. What characteristics of a **sonnet** does it have? Is it an **Italian sonnet** or an **English sonnet,** or is it a modern variation on the sonnet form? Explain your answer.

Country Scene

Reading Check

1. What is this speaker looking at? What does she hear?

2. What does the speaker think of when she hears the bell?

Thinking Critically

3. According to this speaker, what outlasts both nature and love? In your opinion, which is more lasting—love or poetry?

4. How would you describe the **tone** of this **lyric**? Is it a pessimistic poem or a positive poem? Cite details from the poem to support your answer.

Comparing Poems

Fill out a chart like the one below to help you compare these two **lyrics:**

	Frost	Hồ
What is the speaker observing?		
What **images** create the scene?		
How does the speaker feel?		
What lesson does the speaker draw from the experience?		
What is the **tone** of the poem?		

Literary Skills
Analyze the characteristics of sonnets and lyric poems. Compare two poems.

Elements of Literature

Figures of Speech *by* John Malcolm Brinnin
SEEING CONNECTIONS

One of the ways that poets play with words is by using figurative language—expressions that put aside literal meanings in favor of imaginative connections. A **figure of speech** is always based on a comparison, and it is not literally true. If your older brother says to you, "Listen, I'm going to give you a piece of my mind," you don't say, "OK, I'll bring a plate to put it on." You understand that he is using a figure of speech, that he's going to tell you what he's *really* thinking and that it's not going to be nice.

Figurative language can be a kind of shorthand. While it can take a lot of words to express an idea in literal terms, the same idea can be communicated in-stantly by a figure of speech. Think of all the words you'd have to use to explain literally what these common expressions mean: "My heart is broken." "The check bounced." "Chill out."

Figures of Speech in Everyday Language

Many figures of speech that were once fresh and original have been completely absorbed into our everyday language. We use them without realizing that they aren't literally true. When we think about our language, in fact, we realize that figures of speech are the foundation of thousands of expressions.

When we refer to the "roof of the mouth" or the "arm of the chair" or the "foot of the bed," we are using figurative language. In each case we are imaginatively relating a part of the body to something that has nothing to do with the body.

Even the languages of science and business are based on figures of speech. Stockbrokers talk about "the market crash." Our newest technological field, computer science, has its own figures of speech in terms such as *virus, window,* and *mouse.*

Similes: "X Is Like Y"

A simile is the simplest form of figurative language. In a **simile** two dissimilar things are compared using a word such as *like, as, than,* or *resembles.* "The moon shines *like* a fifty-cent piece." "Eva's eyes are *as* glassy *as* marbles." "Lucy feels lighter *than* a grasshopper."

Here is a poet who looked at an ordinary fork and thought of a simile:

Fork
This strange thing must have crept
Right out of hell.
It resembles a bird's foot
Worn around the cannibal's neck.
As you hold it in your hand,
As you stab with it into a piece of meat,
It is possible to imagine the rest
    of the bird:
Its head which like your fist
Is large, bald, beakless, and blind.
          —Charles Simic

Metaphors: "X Is Y"

Similes are easily recognized because of their connectives (*like, as, than, resembles*): "You eat like a pig!" When the connective is omitted, we have a metaphor: "You're a pig!" A **metaphor,** then, is a comparison between two unlike things in which one thing becomes another thing without the use of a word such as *like* or *as*. The difference between a metaphor and a simile is a matter of emphasis. In a simile the two things remain separate, but in a metaphor they are united.

A metaphor can be direct or implied. A **direct metaphor** directly compares the two things using a verb such as *is*. An **implied metaphor** implies or suggests the comparison between the two things without stating it directly. If we say, "The city is a sleeping woman," we are using a direct metaphor. If we say, "The city sleeps peacefully," we use an implied metaphor. Both metaphors identify a city that has its lights out with a person who has fallen into the darkness of sleep.

Metaphor is the most flexible type of figurative language. It is a means by which all experience can be imaginatively connected.

Personification: Making the World Human

Personification is a special kind of metaphor in which human qualities are given to something that is not human—an animal, an object, or even an idea. Explain the personification you find in each of these headlines:

- Every Computer "Whispers" Its Secrets
- China Now a Struggling Giant
- White House Digs In Its Heels on Budget Issue

When we say that a cough is stubborn or a computer is user-friendly or love is blind, we are using a kind of personification. Personification is yet another example of how we use our imaginations to give meaning to the whole nonhuman world.

Reprinted with special permission of King Features Syndicate.

Practice

Figures of speech are widely used. Look through a newspaper or magazine, including the advertisements, and gather at least six figures of speech. Look for examples of **similes, metaphors,** and **personification.**

Tiburón

Make the Connection

Quickwrite

Think of something manufactured. It can be something large, like a snowmobile or a jet plane, or something small, like a pencil sharpener or a cell phone. Jot down some notes about how this item **looks, sounds,** and **smells** (if it has a smell) and what it **feels** like. Does it remind you of anything?

Literary Focus

SKILLS FOCUS

Literary Skills
Understand similes.

Similes

When you compare two *unlike* things using a specific word of comparison such as *like, as,* or *resembles,* you are using a **simile.** A simile is much more imaginative than a simple, literal comparison. If you say, "That car is as red as an apple," you are expressing a simple comparison. It is a literal truth that the color of the apple and the color of the car are similar. If, however, you say, "That car is as sweet and delicious as an apple," you are using a simile. The car cannot be bitten into as an apple can, and it certainly would not taste delicious if you could eat it. What the simile does is communicate to us how much you love that red car.

The following poem is based on one simile. The simile is first suggested in the title, which means "shark" in Spanish.

Tiburón

Martín Espada

East 116th
and a long red car
stalled with the hood up
roaring salsa
5   like a prize shark
mouth yanked open
and down in the stomach
the radio
of the last fisherman
10   still tuned
to his lucky station

Meet the Writer

Martín Espada

"You Can't Tell a Poet to Shut Up"

Lots of poets earn their living by teaching English at a college, as Martín Espada (1957–   ) does. Not many others have also worked as a gas-station attendant, nightclub bouncer, monkey caretaker in a laboratory, radio journalist in Nicaragua, encyclopedia salesperson, and lawyer.

Martín Espada was born and raised in Brooklyn, New York, the son of Puerto Rican parents. He dropped out of college, discouraged by literature classes that taught only works by white male authors. Then a friend introduced him to Latin American revolutionary poetry, and he realized that his kind of writing—politically charged as well as deeply personal—did have its own tradition. He

completed college, and he went on to law school. As both a lawyer and a poet he tries to speak for those who cannot speak for themselves.

Espada's poems often cause controversy, but he always speaks his mind. He says,

❝The worst thing you can say to a poet is 'Don't say that.' You can't tell a poet to shut up. That just makes us want to say it all the more. ❞

After You Read   Response and Analysis

Reading Check

1. Describe the scene in the poem.
2. Where does the salsa music come from?

Thinking Critically

3. Think about the **images** in this poem. What can you see? hear?
4. This poem is based on a **simile** comparing a car to a shark. In what ways is this car like a shark?
5. What do you think has happened to the "last fisherman"? Why is his station "lucky"?

WRITING

It Looks Like ...

Write a **poem** about the manufactured item you described in your Quickwrite notes. Use at least one **simile** that compares your subject to something that is alive. Include **images** that appeal to at least two senses. Will you title your poem after the subject of your poem ("A Long Red Car") or after the living thing you compare it to ("Shark")?

SKILLS FOCUS

Literary Skills
Analyze similes.

Writing Skills
Write a poem containing similes and images.

Before You Read

Folding Won Tons In

Make the Connection

Quickwrite

Think of something that another person taught you to do, such as dance, mow the lawn, rock climb, play a game, surf the Internet, build a campfire, or cook a special food. Then, list all the words and phrases you can think of that are associated with that activity. If you choose cooking a special food, for instance, you might start with *winter night, Dad, radio playing, sausage, sizzling onions, pasta.*

Literary Focus

Figurative Language

Images can be created by using both literal language (such as "mud-luscious" from "in Just-" on page 490) and figurative language. **Figurative language** is language that is based on imaginative comparisons and is not literally true. Two kinds of figurative language are **similes,** comparisons using a word such as *like* or *as,* and **metaphors,** comparisons that do not use *like* or *as.* "The road was a ribbon of moonlight" is a famous metaphor from a poem called "The Highwayman." If that poem's author had written, "The road was *like* a ribbon of moonlight," he would have written a simile. Both of those figures of speech help put pictures in readers' minds.

Reading Skills

Reading a Poem

When you're reading poetry, keep the following strategies in mind:

- Look for punctuation telling you where sentences begin and end. Most poems are written in full sentences.

- If lines of a poem are difficult to understand, look for the subject, verb, and object (if there is one) of each sentence. Try to decide what words the clauses and phrases modify.

- Do not make a full stop at the end of a line if there is no period, question mark, exclamation point, comma, colon, semicolon, or dash there. If a line has no punctuation at its end, read on to the next line to complete the sense of the sentence. A line of poetry without punctuation at its end is called a **run-on line.** A line of poetry that has punctuation at its end is called an **end-stopped line.**

- Read the poem aloud. The sound of a poem is very important to its meaning. Then, read the poem a second or a third time. Each time you read a poem, you'll get more meaning—and probably more pleasure—from it.

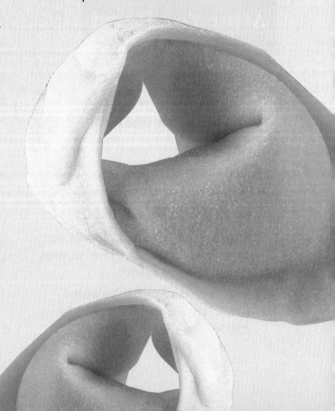

SKILLS FOCUS

Literary Skills
Identify figurative language, including similes and metaphors.

Reading Skills
Use strategies for reading a poem.

Folding Won Tons In

Abraham Chang

I've seasoned the pork as I imagine my mother
     would—
sesame oil, ginger, pepper,
scallions chopped imperfectly.
Sheets of doughy skin,
5 I only have the skill
to buy.

Thumb and forefinger peel
each tender, white scrap of noodle
from the clinging stack.
10 I pat their centers pink
with fragrant spoonfuls
the color of the fat sun in October.

Mimicking from memory:
A twist, a tuck, a folding over—
15 a finger lick of water to seal
my misshapen flowers.

My hands powderdusted;
acquainted with each new blossom.
I line them up
20 like newborns huddled
together, waiting to be fed
to their distant fathers.

The soup bubbles to overflowing,
I slide the dumplings in
25 and stir them in their dizzy descent.

Drowned, swollen,
and glistening; steam hidden
for an instant—

I set them on the table
30 and decide how many
I will save
for one more day.

Meet the Writer

Abraham Chang

Filled with Memories

Abraham Chang (1976–   ) is a "replanted" New Yorker. This young poet was born and raised in New York City, but he spent his college years in Boston and abroad. In 1998, after receiving an Academy of American Poets Prize, Chang returned to New York to attend a master's program in creative writing at New York University. There he worked with several award-winning poets, including Galway Kinnell, Sharon Olds, Donald Hall, and his mentor, Philip Levine.

For Chang's reflection on his poem, see the Connection on page 510.

After You Read

On "Folding Won Tons In"

Abraham Chang

The poem was based on my attempt at making won-ton soup while I was living by myself for the first time. I felt powerful but also a bit anxious at the prospect of being alone in the "real world." I had just returned to New York for graduate school, and I was living in my grandparents' former apartment. I was left to care for this place that had been in our family for over two decades. The apartment felt different, mainly because I was different. The place was "my own" now, but it was filled with the memories of growing up there. The crayon drawings that I had scribbled inside closet doors as a kid still remained, but here I was—in my early twenties, feeling like a new creation and figuring out what it meant to be independent.

I tried my best to remember how my mother used to make dumplings; the recipe and technique were much more difficult than I thought they would be. I couldn't get it exactly right—I couldn't make the skins; I couldn't get the spices or ingredients in the right proportions. But I was determined to do this by myself, so I chopped and mixed and shaped those won tons with my own hands. I "folded" the memories of my family's customs and culture, my anxiety, and my new independence into those won tons, and I nourished myself in more ways than one. They were nowhere near perfect, but they expressed what I was going through at the time: how I cherished my past, kept my focus on the present, and stirred hope for my future by creating something for myself—even if it was only dinner.

Response and Analysis

Reading Check

1. List all the steps the speaker follows as he makes the won tons.

2. What does the speaker do with the won tons after they're made?

Thinking Critically

3. Imagine that you are the poet. Which **image**—a word or phrase that appeals to your senses—in this poem would you feel most pleased with? Why does it especially please you?

4. This poem is full of **figures of speech** that create vivid images. List the figures of speech—all the things that the won tons are compared to. How does the speaker feel about his won-ton soup?

5. Read the first stanza aloud, paying attention to the **end-stopped lines** and the **run-on line.** What is the subject of the sentence that begins on line 4?

WRITING

Remembering the Lesson

Starting with the notes you jotted down for your Quickwrite on page 508, write a **poem** in which you describe the "lesson" you learned. Does your lesson have a special meaning, like that described by Chang (see the *Connection* at the left)?

Take your readers *inside* the experience. Choose **figures of speech** and **images** that help them feel that they are experiencing the lesson with you. Be sure to read your lines aloud so that you can hear the way they sound.

SKILLS FOCUS

Literary Skills
Analyze figures of speech, including similes and metaphors.

Reading Skills
Use strategies for reading a poem.

Writing Skills
Write a poem with figures of speech and images.

"Hope" is the thing with feathers

Make the Connection

Quickwrite ✏️

Think of an emotion or a state of mind. You might choose feelings like grief, joy, anger, dreaminess, selfishness, or ambition. Then, jot down three metaphors in which you identify your subject with something else. Open like this: "Joy is . . ."

Literary Focus

Extended Metaphor

This famous poem is built around a **metaphor** that is carried throughout the entire work. Emily Dickinson states her metaphor in the first line: "Hope," she says, is the "thing with feathers." Notice all the ways she imagines how the gift of hope is like a bird ("the thing with feathers"). When a metaphor is developed over several lines or even through an entire poem like this, it is called an **extended metaphor.**

Bird Singing in the Moonlight (1938–1939) by Morris Graves. Tempera and watercolor on mulberry paper (26 ³/₄″ × 30 ¹/₈″).
The Museum of Modern Art, New York. Purchase. Photograph © 1997 The Museum of Modern Art, New York.

"Hope" is the thing with feathers

Emily Dickinson

"Hope" is the thing with feathers—
That perches in the soul—
And sings the tune without the words—
And never stops—at all—

5　And sweetest—in the Gale—is heard—
And sore must be the storm—
That could abash the little Bird
That kept so many warm—

I've heard it in the chillest land—
10　And on the strangest Sea—
Yet, never, in Extremity,
It asked a crumb—of Me.

Literary Skills
Understand extended metaphors.

INTERNET

More About Emily Dickinson

Keyword: LE7 9-7

Before You Read

Internment

Make the Connection

Branded

Imagine a situation in which you feel "disrespected," treated as less than the person that you know you are. How might you feel in that situation?

Literary Focus

Diction

Diction is a writer's choice of words. In all writing, but especially in poetry, every word counts, so poets choose their words very carefully. Poems rarely appear fully formed and perfect in a poet's head. Instead, they are developed painstakingly, through many revisions. Poets work hard to find words that have the exact meanings and connotations (or associations) that they want to convey.

Denotation and Connotation

Words are not as simple as they look sitting on a page. Words often have many meanings and represent complicated ideas. First there are the literal meanings of words—the definitions found in a dictionary. These are called **denotations.** Then there are the **connotations**—all the associations and emotions that have come to be attached to a word.

For example, in the poem that follows, the poet uses the word *barracks*. Dictionaries say that this word means "large, simple buildings providing temporary housing for people, often soldiers." That's the denotation of the word. What associations and emotions come to mind when you hear the word *barracks*, though? The connotations of the word might include *cold, bare, ugly, lonely, homesick*. In order to

appreciate the full meaning of a poem, pay attention to the writer's **diction,** or word choice. Did the poet choose some words with very specific connotations? How can you explain the choice?

Background

On December 8, 1941, the day after Japan attacked Pearl Harbor, the United States entered World War II. Early in 1942, the U.S. government sent notices to thousands of Japanese Americans living on the West Coast, requiring them to report to relocation centers, where they were assigned to internment camps in inland areas. The Japanese Americans had committed no crime, and most of them were American citizens, but an executive order signed by the president made it legal for the government to imprison them in these camps. While many Nisei (second-generation Japanese Americans) served heroically in the United States armed forces, more than 110,000 of their family members were confined behind barbed wire until 1946, after World War II had already ended. When these people returned to their homes, many of them found that their property had been stolen. After forty years the U.S. government formally apologized, and it paid a small compensation to the Americans who had been interned in the camps.

Internment

Juliet S. Kono

Corralled, they are herded inland
from Santa Rosa.
After the long train ride
on the Santa Fe,
5   the physical exam,
the delousing with DDT,
the branding of her indignation,
she falls asleep.

Days later, she awakens
10   in an unfamiliar barracks—
Crystal City, Texas—
on land once a pasture.
Not wanting to,
not meaning to see beauty
15   in this stark landscape,
she sees, nonetheless,
through her tears—
on the double row
of barbed wire fencing
20   which holds them in
like stolid cattle—
dewdrops, impaled
and golden.

A Japanese American mother carries her sleeping daughter
during the relocation from Bainbridge Island, Washington,
to internment camps in 1942.

© Seattle Post-Intelligencer Collection; Museum of History and
Industry/CORBIS.

Meet the Writers

Emily Dickinson
Juliet S. Kono

She Knows Poetry

Unlike most people today, **Emily Dickinson** (1830–1886) was born, lived most of her life, and died in the same house. From the time she was twenty-six, she rarely went out of that house in Amherst, Massachusetts. Yet for the next thirty years she traveled to the ends of the earth and the universe—in her imagination. She jotted down poems in the margins of newspapers, on brown paper bags, and even on the insides of envelopes.

Dickinson also wrote many letters. In one of them, she defined poetry:

66 If I read a book and it makes my whole body so cold no fire can ever warm me, I know it is poetry. If I feel physically as if the top of my head were taken off, I know that it is poetry. These are the only ways I know it. 99

A famous editor, T. W. Higginson, once asked Emily Dickinson for a photograph of herself. In her reply the poet created a photograph in words.

66 Could you believe me—without? I had no portrait, now, but am small, like the Wren, and my Hair is bold, like the Chestnut Bur—and my eyes like the Sherry in the Glass, that the Guest leaves. 99

While she was alive, only seven of her poems were published—all anonymously. Dickinson died not knowing that she would be recognized as one of the greatest poets who ever wrote in English.

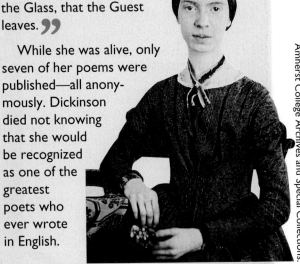

Emily Dickinson.

"They Just Love It When I Misspell Something"

The poet and college teacher **Juliet Kono** (1943–   ) writes when her students write. She says,

66 They like to listen and see these first drafts because they can see how raw and 'chicken scratch' even my work can be. They just love it when I misspell something or if the ideas do not flow. They like it even better when they suggest something and my piece gets better. 99

Kono was born and raised in Hilo, on the Big Island of Hawaii. As a young girl she and her Japanese American family survived a thirty-foot-high tsunami, a tidal wave that swept away their house and car and killed 159 people. "My mother carried my sister on her back," she says, "and my Aunt Dot held me, as she says, under her arm like a suckling pig." This extraordinary experience turns up in many of her poems, collected in the books *Hilo Rains* and *Tsunami Years*.

"Hope" is the thing . . .

Reading Check

1. Dickinson uses a **metaphor** that compares hope to a bird. Where does the bird perch? Under what conditions has the speaker heard it sing?

2. What does hope (or the bird) ask for in return for its song?

Thinking Critically

3. A gale is a strong wind. What do you think the "gale" **symbolizes,** or stands for, in this poem?

4. Think of all the ways Dickinson **extends** the **metaphor.** How is hope's song endless? How does it keep you warm?

5. How do you interpret what the speaker says about hope in the last stanza?

Internment

Reading Check

1. In the first stanza, what events happen to the girl before she falls asleep?

2. Describe the place where she finds herself upon waking.

Thinking Critically

3. What words in the first stanza have **connotations** that suggest that Kono is comparing the imprisoned travelers to cattle? Find the **simile** in the second stanza that restates this comparison. How do these words help you to understand the girl's feelings?

4. In Kono's poem, what does the girl see that she considers beautiful? Why is she reluctant to find beauty in her situation?

5. Look at the poet's **diction,** or word choice, in line 22. What **connotations,** or associations, do you have with the verb *impaled*? What other words could the poet have used to describe how the dewdrop is fixed on the barbed wire?

6. What could the dewdrops in Kono's poem **symbolize,** or stand for? (Consider the significance of the fact that the fragile dewdrops are "impaled" on the barbed wire but are still "golden.")

Comparing Poems

After reading Dickinson's poem, a sixteen-year-old student in California wrote:

> It reminds me that although bad things happen and I feel lonely and alone, hope is there protecting me.

Do you think the speaker in Kono's poem has a similar feeling? In what ways might Dickinson's and Kono's poems address the same thoughts and feelings?

WRITING

With Metaphors

Like Dickinson, write a **poem** in which you compare an emotion to something else, perhaps something in the world of nature. You might find ideas in your Quickwrite on page 511. Begin your first line with a **metaphor,** and extend it in the poem as far as you can.

Text Reformulation

When you **reformulate** a text, you rewrite it using a different format. For example, you could reformulate the poem "Internment" as a news article or an interview. Try it. You will find that when you reformulate a poem, you come to understand it very well.

SKILLS FOCUS

Literary Skills
Analyze extended metaphor. Analyze diction and connotations. Compare poems.

Writing Skills
Write a poem using an extended metaphor. Reformulate a poem.

Fog
Fire and Ice

Make the Connection
Quickwrite

The titles of these two poems cite three natural conditions: fog, fire, and ice. What thoughts and pictures come into your mind when you hear those words? What do you associate with each word? Jot down your ideas.

Literary Focus
Implied Metaphor

By now you know that **figures of speech** compare one thing to another, very different thing.

A **simile** expresses the comparison by using a word such as *like, as, than,* or *resembles:*

The moon looks like a balloon.

A **direct metaphor** tells us directly that one thing *is* something else:

The moon is a balloon.

An **implied metaphor,** however, does not tell us directly that one thing is something else. Instead, it *suggests* the comparison:

Without a string, the moon drifts across the sky.

The following poems are two of the shortest that Carl Sandburg and Robert Frost ever wrote. As you read the poems, use your powers of inference to figure out the implied metaphor in each one.

SKILLS FOCUS

Literary Skills
Understand implied metaphors.

INTERNET

More About Robert Frost

Keyword: LE7 9-7

Fog
Carl Sandburg

The fog comes
on little cat feet.

It sits looking
over harbor and city
on silent haunches
and then moves on.

Fire and Ice

Robert Frost

Some say the world will end in fire,
Some say in ice.
From what I've tasted of desire
I hold with those who favor fire.
But if it had to perish twice,
I think I know enough of hate
To say that for destruction ice
Is also great
And would suffice.

The Polar Sea (1824) by Caspar David Friedrich.
Hamburg Kunsthalle, Hamburg, Germany.

Meet the Writers

Carl Sandburg
Robert Frost

Sandburg on Poetry

Carl Sandburg (1878–1967) wrote a poem called "Ten Definitions of Poetry." Here are three of the definitions:

> " Poetry is a search for syllables to shoot at the barriers of the unknown and the unknowable. . . .
>
> Poetry is the synthesis of hyacinths and biscuits. . . .
>
> Poetry is the opening and closing of a door, leaving those who look through to guess about what is seen during a moment. "

Sandburg, the son of Swedish immigrants, was born in Galesburg, Illinois. Between the ages of thirteen and nineteen, he worked on a milk wagon, in a barbershop, at a theater, in a brickyard, and as a hotel dishwasher and a harvest hand.

Carl Sandburg.

He became known as the poet of Chicago in the days when that city was the expanding center of steel mills, stockyards, and railroads. Though he was unknown to the poetry world until he was thirty-six, Sandburg's name was a household word by the time he died. His sometimes tough, often tender poems about nature and the American people—especially working-class people—were loved by millions.

Frost on Poetry

New England, where **Robert Frost** (1874–1963) lived most of his life, still bears the scars of the Ice Age glacier that stripped the land bare and buried everything in its path. Enormous boulders litter the landscape where the glacier dropped them many thousands of years ago. Indeed, Frost had only to look out his farmhouse window to see the destructive effects of ice—and he had only to take a short walk to find the charred

Robert Frost.

clearings left by lightning fires. Then, like all human beings, he had only to look inside himself to discover the destructive forces of desire and hate.

In his essay "The Figure a Poem Makes," Frost talks about poetry:

> " [A poem] . . . begins in delight and ends in wisdom . . . a clarification of life—not necessarily a great clarification, such as sects and cults are founded on, but in a momentary stay against confusion. "

Late in his life, Robert Frost played an important role on the national stage when he recited one of his poems at John F. Kennedy's inauguration as president in 1961.

For another biography of Frost, see page 378.

Fog

Reading Check

1. What animal does Sandburg compare the fog to, and how do you know?
2. What parts of the animal's body does he mention?
3. What does this animal do?

Thinking Critically

4. What qualities does fog share with the animal in Sandburg's poem? Could fog also be compared to an elephant? a snake? a dog?

Fire and Ice

Reading Check

1. According to the speaker in "Fire and Ice," what disagreement do some people have about how the world will end?
2. Which side of the argument does the speaker agree with?

Thinking Critically

3. How could the world end in fire?
4. How could the world end in ice?
5. How would you define *desire* as Frost uses the word in his poem? How is desire like fire? How could desire bring on the end of the world?
6. Why would the speaker feel that hate and ice have something in common? How could hate cause the destruction of the world?

Comparing Poems

Now that you have read these two poems, go back to your Quickwrite notes for page 516. How have your ideas about fog, fire, and ice changed? How has the poets' use of **metaphor** changed the thoughts, images, and emotions you associate with those words? (You can gather your ideas in a chart like the one below.) Which poem do you find more powerful? Which do you think you will remember longer? Why?

	Fog	Fire	Ice
Old associations			
Poet's metaphors			
New associations			

WRITING

The Heat Wave Comes In . . .

Write a **poem** in the style of Sandburg's in which you compare a force of nature to an animal. Extend your metaphor as far as it will go, without forcing it. You can use a **direct metaphor:** " . . . is . . . ," or you can use an **implied metaphor,** as Sandburg does.

Your Opinion

Fire and ice are two extremes of nature. Either force could put an end to all living things. Desire and hate are two human emotions; we can be consumed by desire and hardened by hate. Which emotion—desire or hate—do you feel is more destructive? (Think in terms of an individual's life as well as the life of the world.) Write a paragraph explaining your opinion.

SKILLS FOCUS

Literary Skills
Analyze implied metaphors. Compare poems.

Writing Skills
Write a poem containing a metaphor. Write a paragraph supporting an opinion.

INTERNET

Projects and Activities

Keyword: LE7 9-7

The Seven Ages of Man

SKILLS FOCUS

Literary Skills
Understand extended metaphors.

INTERNET

More About William Shakespeare

Keyword: LE7 9-7

Make the Connection

Quickwrite 🖉

Seven acts—that's how long this poet imagines the play of your life is going to be. According to Jaques (pronounced jā'kwēz), a character in Shakespeare's comedy *As You Like It*, you're now in the middle of the second act of your life. Before you read what he predicts about the rest of your life, try to second-guess him. Write down what you think are the seven stages of a person's life.

Literary Focus

Extended Metaphor

In *As You Like It*, Jaques makes a speech that is considered one of the finest examples of extended metaphor ever written.

An **extended metaphor** is a comparison developed over several lines of writing. (In the play, Jaques's speech is a **monologue**—a long speech delivered by a single character. Here it is presented as a separate poem.)

Jaques opens with the famous metaphor: "All the world's a stage." As he goes on, Jaques extends that metaphor to compare the stages of our lives to seven acts, with seven different roles all played by the same actor. In the play, Jaques is a moody character. See if you think this speech reflects his gloomy outlook on life.

For a biography of William Shakespeare, see page 890.

The Seven Ages of Man
William Shakespeare

                    All the world's a stage,
        And all the men and women merely players;
        They have their exits and their entrances,
        And one man in his time plays many parts,
5   His acts being seven ages. At first the infant,
        Mewling and puking in the nurse's arms;
        And then the whining schoolboy, with his satchel
        And shining morning face, creeping like snail
        Unwillingly to school. And then the lover,
10   Sighing like furnace, with a woeful ballad
        Made to his mistress' eyebrow. Then a soldier,
        Full of strange oaths, and bearded like the pard,°
        Jealous in honor, sudden and quick in quarrel,
        Seeking the bubble reputation

12. pard (pärd) *n.:* leopard.

First Steps by Vincent van Gogh (1853–1890), after Millet. Oil on canvas (28½″ × 35⅞″).

15   Even in the cannon's mouth. And then the justice,°
    In fair round belly with good capon° lined,
    With eyes severe and beard of formal cut,
    Full of wise saws° and modern instances;
    And so he plays his part. The sixth age shifts
20   Into the lean and slippered pantaloon,°
    With spectacles on nose and pouch on side;
    His youthful hose,° well saved, a world too wide
    For his shrunk shank; and his big manly voice,
    Turning again toward childish treble, pipes
25   And whistles in his sound. Last scene of all,
    That ends this strange eventful history,
    Is second childishness and mere oblivion,
    Sans° teeth, sans eyes, sans taste, sans everything.

15. justice *n.:* judge.
16. capon (kā′pän′) *n.:* fat chicken.

18. saws (sôz) *n.:* old sayings.

20. pantaloon (pan′tə·lōon′) *n.:* silly old man.

22. hose (hōz) *n.:* stockings.

28. sans (sanz) *prep.:* without.

Reading Check

1. In Shakespeare's famous **metaphor** that compares the world to a stage, what does he compare men and women to?

2. Shakespeare uses an **extended metaphor** when he has Jaques describe a person's life as though it were a play made up of seven acts. Name those seven acts.

Thinking Critically

3. In this **monologue,** what **images** help you picture childhood (the first two acts) as Jaques sees it? What **simile** describes the schoolboy's attitude toward school? How do you think Jaques feels about infants and schoolboys?

4. If the justice's belly is lined "with good capon," what do we know about him? What details make the judge seem like a ridiculous character?

5. According to Jaques, what physical and mental changes take place when a man reaches the sixth and seventh ages? Does he make old age seem dignified or silly? What do you think of Jaques's view of old age?

6. Shakespeare's famous lines were written more than four hundred years ago. Of the seven ages of man that he characterizes, which do you think remain true to life today? Have any changed? (Be sure to check your Quickwrite notes.) ✎

WRITING

The Seven Ages of Woman

Shakespeare wrote about the seven ages of man. Write your own **poem**—or a paragraph—focusing on the seven ages of woman. Begin with the **metaphor** of life as a stage, and extend it as far as you can. Start with the infant, and describe seven ages. What attitude will you take toward the stages of a woman's life?

This Is What It Says

When you **paraphrase** a text, you re-state it in your own words. Write a paraphrase of Jaques's speech. Explain his comparisons in your own words. Here is a possible paraphrase of lines 1–2: "The whole world can be compared to a stage, and all the people in the world can be compared to actors on that stage."

Vocabulary Development

Multiple Meanings

PRACTICE

The common words in boldface below have multiple meanings. Each word is used at least once by Jaques. Find where he uses each word, examine its **context,** and then create a word map for each word like the one here. The footnotes will help you.

strange   **fair**   **saws**   **hose**

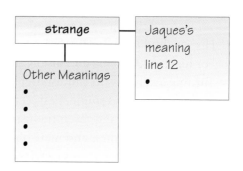

INTERNET

Projects and Activities

Keyword: LE7 9-7

Before You Read

Women

Make the Connection

Quickwrite ✏️

Make notes about people whom you consider heroes because they helped you become the person you are today. You'll probably think of relatives, friends, or teachers, but you might also include people you've never met—people in the news or people from the past, for instance. What makes these people heroes to you?

Literary Focus

Tone

Tone is a writer's or speaker's attitude toward a subject or toward an audience. You know from your own life how important it is to be sensitive to tone. If you're talking to a friend, for example, and you misread tone of sarcasm for a tone of sincerity, you've made a big mistake. In speech, and body language help to convey tone. In writing, however, tone can be revealed only by an author's choice of words, or **diction.**

You've read poems in this book that reveal many tones, from cynical to sincere to playful. In the following poem, what tone does the poet take toward her subject?

SKILLS FOCUS

Literary Skills
Understand tone and diction.

INTERNET

More About Alice Walker

Keyword: LE7 9-7

Rosa Parks's refusal to give up her seat to a white man prompted the Montgomery bus boycott in 1955.

John H. Glenn, Jr., became the first American to orbit the earth in 1962.

Blind, deaf, and mute by the age of two, Helen Keller eventually became a world-famous author and activist.

Women

Alice Walker

They were women then
My mama's generation
Husky of voice—stout of
Step
5 With fists as well as
Hands
How they battered down
Doors
And ironed
10 Starched white
Shirts
How they led
Armies
Headragged generals
15 Across mined
Fields
Booby-trapped
Ditches
To discover books
20 Desks
A place for us
How they knew what we
Must know
Without knowing a page
25 Of it
Themselves.

Meet the Writer

Alice Walker

"I Had Terrific Teachers"

Alice Walker (1944–   ) is a poet, novelist, short story writer, and essayist. She is best known for her novel *The Color Purple,* which won a Pulitzer Prize in 1983. Walker was born in Eatonton, a small town in Georgia. She was the youngest of eight children. Her father was a sharecropper, and her mother was a maid.

Walker says that "Women" is for her mother, one of several important people in her life:

❝I also had terrific teachers. When I was four and my mother had to go work in the fields, my first-grade teacher let me start in her class. Right on through grammar school and high school and college, there was one—sometimes even two—teachers who saved me from feeling alone, from worrying that the world I was stretching to find might not even exist . . .

My teachers lent me books: *Jane Eyre* was my friend for a long time. Books became my world, because the world I was in was very hard. My mother was working as a maid, so she was away from six-thirty in the morning until after dark. . . . I was supposed to take care of the house and do the cooking. I was twelve, coming home to an empty house and cleaning and fixing dinner—for people who didn't really appreciate the struggle it was to fix it. I missed my mother very much.❞

After You Read   Response and Analysis

Reading Check

1. What generation of women does the speaker describe?

2. List three things that these women tried to obtain for their children.

3. How did they go about obtaining what they knew their children needed?

Thinking Critically

4. In lines 12–18, Walker uses an **implied metaphor,** suggesting rather than stating a comparison. What does she compare the women to?

5. Think about the **historical context** of this poem. What "doors" did these women have to batter down? What do you think the "mined fields" and "booby-trapped ditches" stand for?

6. What do you think these women *knew* their children had to know?

7. What is the speaker's **tone,** her attitude toward these women? What words or phrases in the poem help you identify the speaker's tone?

WRITING

Celebrate Heroes

How would you describe the heroic women and men of today? What do they struggle for? What obstacles do they face? Write a paragraph describing these people. (Check your Quickwrite notes.) ✏️

Before You Read

Boy at the Window

Make the Connection

A Cold Winter Night

What do you think children fear? What makes children feel safe? When a child looks out the window on a cold winter night, what might he or she be thinking?

Literary Focus

Personification

Personification is a type of figurative language in which the writer speaks of something nonhuman as if it had human qualities. If you say, "The sun smiled down on us," you are personifying the sun, which can't really smile at all. If you say, "Time is a thief," you are personifying time, which isn't able to rob us of our valuables at all. In "Once by the Pacific" (see page 499), Robert Frost personifies waves when he writes:

> Great waves looked over others
>   coming in,
> And thought of doing something to
>   the shore
> That water never did to land before.

Waves don't have eyes; they can't "look." Nor do waves have brains; they can't "think." By personifying the great waves, Frost helps us see the stormy ocean as a kind of dangerous monster.

SKILLS FOCUS

Literary Skills
Understand personification.

Boy at the Window

Richard Wilbur

Seeing the snowman standing all alone
In dusk and cold is more than he can bear.
The small boy weeps to hear the wind prepare
A night of gnashings° and enormous moan.
His tearful sight can hardly reach to where
The pale-faced figure with bitumen° eyes
Returns him such a god-forsaken stare
As outcast Adam gave to Paradise.°

The man of snow is, nonetheless, content,
Having no wish to go inside and die.
Still, he is moved to see the youngster cry.
Though frozen water is his element,
He melts enough to drop from one soft eye
A trickle of the purest rain, a tear
For the child at the bright pane surrounded by
Such warmth, such light, such love, and so much fear.

---

4. **gnashings** (nash′iŋz) *n.:* grinding of teeth, as in anger.
6. **bitumen** (bi·tōō′mən) *n.:* coal.
8. **outcast . . . Paradise:** reference to the biblical account of
   Adam and Eve's expulsion from Paradise.

Meet the Writer

Richard Wilbur

A Model Poet

When the two-time Pulitzer Prize–winner and national poet laureate Richard Wilbur (1921–   ) first appeared before the American public, he was standing on a can of beans. Wilbur's father worked as a commercial artist in New York City, and he used his son as a model for the advertisements he drew. "Often I posed as a child flushed with health because he was taking the right vitamins," Wilbur says, or as "a child running excitedly home from the grocery with the right cereal."

Young Richard wasn't just another handsome face. When he was only eight, he sold his first poem (about owls and nightingales) to a children's magazine for one dollar. He went on to college and other adventures—one Depression summer he lived as a teenage hobo, jumping freight trains and traveling through nearly every state in the country. He returned to writing poetry at an unlikely moment: in a World War II foxhole, with enemy artillery falling all around him.

Back home from the war, he stuffed his writing in a desk drawer and started graduate school. Then one day an editor friend came to visit, and Wilbur's wife mentioned the poems in his desk. "He took them home to his apartment," Wilbur says, "reappeared an hour later, kissed me on both cheeks"—the friend was European—"and declared me a poet. And then he sent the things off to New York."

Wilbur's work was an immediate success. Readers enjoyed his wit, his skill with words, and the way he focused on the details of the world around him. "I was always averse to high-minded abstract talk," he says; he prefers "poetry of close observation . . . poetry that acknowledges the importance of things however small." As small as a drop of water trickling down a snowman's cheek?

Reading Check

1. The first stanza focuses on the boy. Where is he?

2. Why does the boy feel so sad that he weeps?

3. The second stanza focuses on the snowman. Why is the "man of snow" content?

4. What word in the last line reveals why the snowman feels so sad for the boy that *he* weeps?

Thinking Critically

5. Which words in line 4 **personify** the weather conditions as a threatening person or animal? What words might a television weather reporter use to describe the same conditions?

6. What details in the poem **personify,** or give human qualities to, the snowman?

7. In line 8, the poet **alludes,** or refers, to the biblical account of Adam and Eve's expulsion from Paradise. Why does the poet compare the snowman to Adam? What does the expression "god-forsaken" mean?

8. The boy and the snowman cry for each other. In the poem, who actually has more reason to feel sorry for the other? In what ways is this **ironic**— just the opposite of what we might expect the situation to be?

9. What do you think this poem is saying about fear, pity, and sympathy?

WRITING

Analyzing a Poem

Many readers are moved by "Boy at the Window." In a brief **essay,** analyze what makes the poem effective. Consider elements like **figurative language, imagery, tone,** and **theme.** Pay particular attention to the poem's use of **personification.**

▶ Use "Analyzing a Poem," pages 556–563, for help with this assignment.

LISTENING AND SPEAKING

Oral Presentation

Prepare this poem for **oral presentation.** You might have two speakers: one for the first verse (the boy's point of view) and one for the second (the snowman's point of view). Before you present the poem, note when you will pause at the end of a line because a mark of punctuation (a period or a comma) tells you to and when you will read on to the next line to complete the meaning of the phrase or sentence. This poem was written with great care for the way it sounds. Where do you find the poem's rhyming words?

SKILLS
FOCUS

Literary Skills
Analyze personification.

Writing Skills
Write an analysis of a poem.

Listening and Speaking Skills
Prepare a poem for oral presentation.

Elements of Literature

The Sounds of Poetry *by* John Malcolm Brinnin
RHYME, RHYTHM, AND MORE

Make It Rhyme

Everyone loves rhyme—even babies respond to rhyme, so the first books read to you were probably written in rhyme. **Rhyme** is the repetition of the sound of the stressed vowel and any sounds that follow it in words that are close together in a poem: *nails* and *whales; material* and *cereal; icicle* and *bicycle.*

Until very recently rhyme was considered essential to poetry, but for poets today its use is a matter of choice. Modern poets who use rhyme feel that it helps make a poem sing. It enhances the music of a poem by adding chiming sounds. A regular pattern of end rhyme, or **rhyme scheme,** defines the shape of a poem and holds it together.

Many poets feel that just about all the words in the English language that can be rhymed were used long ago. The contemporary poet who writes in rhyme may have to repeat rhymes that have echoed down the centuries.

Approximate Rhyme: Not Quite Exact

Some poets solve the problem of creating new rhymes by using **approximate rhyme**—that is, words that repeat some sounds but are not exact echoes. Approximate rhymes are also called *half rhymes, off rhymes, slant rhymes,* or—by readers who dislike them—*imperfect rhymes.* In any case, they are substitutes for **exact rhymes** like *moon* and *June* or *hollow* and *follow.* Instead of being an exact echo, approximate rhyme is a partial echo: *moon* and *morn; hollow* and *mellow.*

Internal Rhyme Versus End Rhyme: Chimes Inside and Out

Rhymes usually occur at the ends of lines. This type of rhyme is called **end rhyme.** The rhyming words are seldom spaced more than four lines apart—if the interval is longer than that, the chiming sound cannot be clearly heard. Rhyme can also occur inside the lines. This is called **internal rhyme.** Here are some lines from "The Raven" by Edgar Allan Poe in which two internal rhymes (*remember* and *ember*) chime with *December:*

Ah, distinctly I remember it was in the
    bleak December;
And each separate dying ember wrought
    its ghost upon the floor.

You've Got Rhythm

As long as your heart is beating, you've got rhythm. Musicians and poets, perhaps in imitation of that heartbeat, create rhythm in their compositions. **Rhythm** is a musical quality based on repetition.

Meter: A Pattern of Stressed Syllables

A common form of rhythm is **meter,** a regular pattern of stressed and unstressed syllables in each line. The poem on the next page by Robert Frost is written in meter. The stressed syllables are marked ´; the unstressed syllables are marked ˘. Read the poem aloud to feel its steady beat.

SKILLS FOCUS

Literary Skills
Understand rhyme, rhythm, meter, free verse, onomatopoeia, and alliteration.

go.hrw.com

INTERNET
More About the Sounds of Poetry
Keyword: LE7 9-7

Dust of Snow

The way a crow

Shook down on me

The dust of snow

From a hemlock tree

Has given my heart
A change of mood
And saved some part
Of a day I had rued.
—Robert Frost

Frost wrote his poem mostly in iambs. An **iamb** (ī'amb') is an unstressed syllable followed by a stressed syllable (da DAH). An iamb is one kind of poetic foot. A **foot** usually consists of one stressed syllable and one or more unstressed syllables.

English poetry has other kinds of feet. A **trochee** (trō'kē) is a stressed syllable followed by an unstressed syllable (DAH da); it is the opposite of an iamb. This line from Poe's "The Raven" uses trochees:

Once upon a midnight dreary

An **anapest** (an'ə·pest') is two unstressed syllables followed by a stressed syllable (da da DAH). Here is a line from Byron's poem "The Destruction of Sennacherib" that uses anapests:

The Assyrian came down like
   the wolf on the fold

A **dactyl** (dak'təl) is one stressed syllable followed by two unstressed syllables (DAH da da). Here is the beginning of a nursery rhyme that uses dactyls:

Hickory, dickory, dock

A **spondee** (spän'dē) is two stressed syllables (DAH DAH). Here are some lines from "We Real Cool" by Gwendolyn Brooks that use spondees:

We real cool. We

Left school. We

Lurk late. . . .

When you analyze a poem to show its meter, you are **scanning** the poem. Scanning is a way of taking a poem apart to see how the poet has created its music.

Free Verse Isn't Free

Until the nineteenth century almost all poetry in English used a strict rhyme scheme and meter pattern. Eventually, however, poets began to abandon the old poetic rules to write **free verse,** which does not follow a regular pattern of rhyme and meter. This kind of poetry sometimes sounds similar to prose or to everyday spoken language.

Free verse is free only in the sense that it is liberated from formal rules. Poets writing free verse still pay close attention to the sound and rhythm of their lines— to the rhythmic rise and fall of the voice, to pauses, and to the balance between long and short phrases. Rhythm is also created in free verse by the repetition of words or even lines.

The poem on the next page by David Ignatow is written in free verse. You'll notice how close to ordinary spoken language it sounds at first. But then you'll notice how the rhythm of the poem imitates the rhythm of a bagel rolling—the words come faster and faster—and at the end the reader feels as "strangely happy" as the speaker of the poem.

(continued)

POETRY IN MOTION

The Bagel

David Ignatow

I stopped to pick up the bagel
rolling away in the wind,
annoyed with myself
for having dropped it
as it were a portent.
Faster and faster it rolled,
with me running after it

bent low, gritting my teeth,
and I found myself doubled over
and rolling down the street
head over heels, one complete somersault
after another like a bagel
and strangely happy with myself.

New York City Transit

This poem, along with many others, has appeared in New York City subway cars and on buses as part of a program called Poetry in Motion.

Other Sounds Singing

Rhyme and rhythm are not the only ways to create the sounds of poetry. Two other important techniques are **onomatopoeia** (än′ō·mat′ō·pē′ə) and **alliteration** (ə·lit′ər·ā′shən). The names may be difficult to say, but the techniques are easy to learn and use.

Onomatopoeia: Imitating Sounds

Onomatopoeia is the use of words that sound like what they mean. We use onomatopoeia when we say a cannon "booms" or bacon "sizzles." The words can echo a natural sound (*hiss, slap, rumble, snarl, moan*) or a mechanical sound (*whack, clickety-clack, putt-putt, toot*).

Alliteration: Repeating Sounds

Alliteration is the repetition of the same consonant sound in several words, usually at the beginnings of the words: *fragrant flowers, hot and heavy, dog days*. Alliteration can also be the repetition of similar but not identical sounds: a series of *p*'s and *b*'s or *s*'s and *z*'s. The repetition of vowel sounds is called **assonance.**

Alliteration and onomatopoeia can sometimes be used together to echo sounds. Here is another example from "The Raven":

The silken sad uncertain rustling of each
purple curtain

The alliteration of "silken sad uncertain" and the onomatopoeia of "rustling" combine to imitate the sound that wind makes blowing past heavy silk draperies.

Practice

Find elements of poetry in the world around you:

1. List ten names. Which syllables are stressed? Which are not stressed? What "tunes" do the names make?

2. Collect some political slogans with **rhyme** and **alliteration** in them.

3. Think of two **exact rhymes** and two **approximate rhymes** to go with these words: *ocean, wash, warm, beard, power.*

4. Describe the following scenes, using **onomatopoeia:**
   - a rainy, windy night
   - a cat munching on dry cat food

I Wandered Lonely as a Cloud

Make the Connection

Quickwrite ✏️

Recall a scene you once saw that made a strong impression on you. Perhaps it was the earth seen from a plane window, the ocean just before a storm, the desert at night, or a sky filled with migrating birds. Close your eyes, and be there again. Make notes about what you see.

Literary Focus

Rhythm and Meter

Rhythm, or the repetition of sound patterns, is what gives poems their musical quality. William Wordsworth, like most poets of his time, created rhythm by arranging his words so that the lines repeat a regular pattern of stressed and unstressed syllables. This regular pattern is called **meter.** You can hear meter just as you can hear the steady beat of a heart.

When you **scan** a poem to describe its meter, you mark the stressed syllables with the symbol ′ and the unstressed syllables with the symbol ˘.

Scanning a poem requires you to read the poem aloud. As you read Wordsworth's famous poem, listen for its beat. What syllables do you stress?

Background

This poem captures with enormous precision a special moment that occurred two hundred years ago—on April 15, 1802, to be precise. We *can* be precise because there was another witness to that miracle—the poet's sister, Dorothy, also a wonderful writer—who captured the very same scene in her journal.

SKILLS FOCUS

Literary Skills
Understand rhythm and meter.

I Wandered Lonely as a Cloud

William Wordsworth

I wandered lonely as a cloud
That floats on high o'er vales and hills,
When all at once I saw a crowd,
A host, of golden daffodils,
5 Beside the lake, beneath the trees,
Fluttering and dancing in the breeze.

Continuous as the stars that shine
And twinkle on the Milky Way,
They stretched in never-ending line
10 Along the margin of a bay;
Ten thousand saw I at a glance,
Tossing their heads in sprightly dance.

The waves beside them danced, but they
Outdid the sparkling waves in glee;
15 A poet could not but be gay,
In such a jocund° company;
I gazed—and gazed—but little thought
What wealth the show to me had brought:

For oft, when on my couch I lie
20 In vacant or in pensive mood,
They flash upon that inward eye
Which is the bliss of solitude;
And then my heart with pleasure fills,
And dances with the daffodils.

---

16. jocund (jäk′ənd) *adj.*: merry.

Meet the Writer

William Wordsworth

Nature: The Best Teacher

The English Romantic poet William Wordsworth (1770–1850) believed that nature is the best teacher. He also believed that uneducated people who live close to nature have at least as much to teach us as sages, or wise people.

> One impulse from a vernal wood
> May teach you more of man,
> Of moral evil and of good,
> Than all the sages can.

Wordsworth's mother died when he was seven. Six years later his father was also dead. Wordsworth had started writing poems by the age of fifteen. When he was twenty-eight, he and his close friend Samuel Taylor Coleridge published a collection of poems called *Lyrical Ballads*. This slim book contained only twenty-four poems, all very different from the fancy, aristocratic poetry that most poets then wrote. Wordsworth and Coleridge used simple people and ordinary experiences as their subjects. They used common speech. They said that the human mind is intimately related to the workings of the natural world. They said that God is revealed in the laws and forces of nature.

According to Wordsworth, poetry begins when we get in touch with a memory and relive the experience:

William Wordsworth (1842) by B. R. Haydon.
By Courtesy of the National Portrait Gallery, London.

> Poetry is the spontaneous overflow of powerful feelings: It takes its origin from emotion recollected in tranquillity.

By "tranquillity," Wordsworth means that it's better to write about an experience later than when you're right in the middle of it. Of course, you can still take notes, as Wordsworth and his sister, Dorothy, regularly did. Then you can take your time to relive what you experienced and put it down on paper just the way you want to.

I Never Saw Daffodils So Beautiful

Dorothy Wordsworth

April 15, 1802: . . . The wind seized our breath. The lake was rough. There was a boat by itself floating in the middle of the bay below Water Millock. We rested again in the Water Millock Lane. The hawthorns are black and green, the birches here and there greenish, but there is yet more of purple to be seen on the twigs. We got over into a field to avoid some cows—people working. A few primroses by the roadside—wood sorrel flower, the anemone, scentless violets, strawberries, and that starry, yellow flower which Mrs. C. calls pile wort. When we were in the woods beyond Gowbarrow Park, we saw a few daffodils close to the waterside. We fancied that the lake had floated the seeds ashore, and that the little colony had so sprung up. But as we went along there were more and yet more; and at last, under the boughs of the trees, we saw that there was a long belt of them along the shore, about the breadth of a country turnpike road. I never saw daffodils so beautiful. They grew along the mossy stones about and about them; some rested their heads upon these stones as on a pillow for weariness; and the rest tossed and reeled and danced, and seemed as if they verily laughed with the wind that blew upon them over the lake, they looked so gay, ever glancing, ever changing. This wind blew directly over the lake to them. There was here and there a little knot, and a few stragglers a few yards higher up; but they were so few as not to disturb the simplicity, unity, and life of that one busy highway. We rested again and again. The bays were stormy, and we heard the waves at different distances, and in the middle of the water. Rain came on—we were wet when we reached Luff's. . . .

After You Read Response and Analysis

Reading Check

1. What is the **speaker's** mood at the beginning of the poem?

2. As the speaker wanders, what does he see "all at once"?

3. How does the speaker's mood change that day because of what he sees?

4. How does the memory of what he saw affect him later?

Thinking Critically

5. What **simile** does the speaker use to describe his loneliness?

6. Which words in the poem **personify** the daffodils, or make them seem like people—even friends and companions—to the lonely speaker? Which words in Dorothy Wordsworth's journal entry (see the **Connection** on page 535) also personify the daffodils?

7. The word *wealth* can mean many different things. What kind of wealth is the speaker referring to in line 18? Name other ways people can get that kind of wealth.

8. How would you explain the "inward eye" in line 21 of the poem?

9. **Scan** the first four lines of "I Wandered Lonely as a Cloud" to show the poem's **meter.** Mark each stressed syllable ′ and each unstressed syllable ˘. How does the meter affect the sound of the poem?

Literary Skills
Analyze rhythm and meter.

Writing Skills
Write a description.
Write a comparison.

WRITING

Be There Again

Write a **description**—in prose or poetry—of the scene you visualized for your Quickwrite notes. Ask yourself, "What time of year is it? What time of day is it? Is anybody with me? What do I see? What does the scene remind me of? How has the scene affected me?"

Journal and Poem

Write at least one paragraph **comparing** Dorothy Wordsworth's journal entry (see the **Connection** on page 535) with her brother's poem. Before you write, make a chart like the one here to identify how the journal compares with the poem:

	Journal Entry
Details not in poem	
Details that contradict poem	
Figurative language similar to that in poem	
Figurative language different from that in poem	
Lesson drawn from experience (if any)	

The Courage That My Mother Had

Make the Connection

Quickwrite ✏️

Is there something in your family that you would like to inherit? It could be something material, like a picture. (In this poem the speaker has inherited a brooch, or large decorative pin, from her mother.) It could also be a wonderful quality or talent —like the ability to play the piano. Jot down your thoughts.

Literary Focus

Rhyme

Rhyme is often the first thing we notice about a poem. We all know rhyme when we hear it; **rhyme** is the repetition of accented vowel sounds, and all sounds following them, in words that are close together: *raid/evade; funny/money.*

Rhymes usually come at the end of a line of poetry. When these **end rhymes** fall in a pattern, it is called a **rhyme scheme.** A rhyme scheme is indicated using different letters of the alphabet, beginning with *a,* for each new rhyme at the end of a line. Here is how the rhyme scheme of this old children's rhyme is indicated:

Little Miss Muffet	*a*
Sat on a tuffet	*a*
Eating her curds and whey.	*b*
Along came a spider	*c*
Who sat down beside her	*c*
And frightened Miss Muffet away.	*b*

The rhyme scheme of Miss Muffet's poem is *aabccb.*

Listen for the rhymes in Millay's poem. What pattern do they make?

SKILLS FOCUS

Literary Skills
Understand rhyme.

The Courage That My Mother Had

Edna St. Vincent Millay

The courage that my mother had
Went with her, and is with her still:
Rock from New England quarried;
Now granite in a granite hill.

5　The golden brooch my mother wore
She left behind for me to wear;
I have no thing I treasure more:
Yet, it is something I could spare.

Oh, if instead she'd left to me
10　The thing she took into the grave!—
That courage like a rock, which she
Has no more need of, and I have.

Meet the Writer

Edna St. Vincent Millay

Family Ties

Edna St. Vincent Millay (1892–1950) was born and grew up in Rockland, Maine. She started writing poetry as a child. Millay wrote "Renascence" (ri·nas'əns), one of her most famous poems, when she was only nineteen, and she published her first book of poetry the year she graduated from Vassar College.

As you might have guessed from "The Courage That My Mother Had," the strength of women is an important theme in Millay's writing. Millay worshiped her mother, a strong New Englander who worked as a nurse to support her three daughters after their father deserted the family.

After You Read   Response and Analysis

Reading Check

1. What has the mother left her daughter?
2. Where is the mother now?
3. What does the daughter wish her mother had left her?

Thinking Critically

4. What **metaphor** in line 3, later expressed as a **simile** in line 11, does Millay use to describe her mother's courage? What does her comparison suggest to you about Millay's view of courage?
5. Like all **lyric poems** this one expresses a strong emotion. How would you describe this feeling?
6. Describe the **rhyme scheme** in this poem by using letters from the alphabet to indicate each end rhyme. Which pairs of words are **approximate rhymes**?
7. Where do you think the quality of courage comes from? Is courage something that can be passed on from one person to another? Can it be learned? Give reasons for your answer.

WRITING

Passing It On

Expand your Quickwrite notes by writing a paragraph describing the material possession, personal quality, or talent that you'd most like to inherit from your family. Try to find a **metaphor** for the possession, quality, or talent that shows how you feel about it.

Before You Read

Ballad of Birmingham

Make the Connection

Quickwrite ✏️

Think of an event that has taken place in your lifetime that tells a story. Jot down your ideas. Now imagine your story as a song. What type of song would it be?

Literary Focus

Ballad

A **ballad** is a song that tells a story, often a story about love, death, or betrayal. Ballads can be sad or humorous. They tell their stories using a steady **rhythm** and a simple pattern of **rhymes,** which make them easy to memorize. A typical ballad uses **repetition,** often in the form of a **refrain**—a phrase or a stanza that is repeated throughout the work, usually at the end of each verse.

Ballads have been popular since the Middle Ages, and in the twenty-first century the form is still alive and well. Old **folk ballads,** which were composed by unknown singers and passed along orally for many years before being written down, are still sung today. Singers writing new ballads today have a rich tradition to draw on. **Literary ballads,** like the one that follows, are written in imitation of the old ballads.

Every ballad, old or new, tells a tale that can be as gripping as a front-page newspaper story. Dudley Randall wrote his ballad in response to the tragic events that made headlines on September 15, 1963. In the midst of the struggle for civil rights for African Americans, a bomb exploded in a church in Birmingham, Alabama. Four teenage girls were killed.

Like many of the traditional ballads, this one uses dialogue to tell a story.

The Sixteenth Street Baptist Church in 1964, after damaged parts were rebuilt with gifts from around the world.

SKILLS FOCUS

Literary Skills
Understand the characteristics of ballads.

Ballad of Birmingham
(On the bombing of a church in Birmingham, Alabama, 1963)

Dudley Randall

"Mother dear, may I go downtown
Instead of out to play,
And march the streets of Birmingham
In a Freedom March today?"

5   "No, baby, no, you may not go,
For the dogs are fierce and wild,
And clubs and hoses, guns and jails
Aren't good for a little child."

"But, mother, I won't be alone.
10   Other children will go with me,
And march the streets of Birmingham
To make our country free."

"No, baby, no, you may not go,
For I fear those guns will fire.
15   But you may go to church instead
And sing in the children's choir."

She has combed and brushed her
    night-dark hair,
And bathed rose-petal sweet,
And drawn white gloves on her small
    brown hands,
20   And white shoes on her feet.

The mother smiled to know her child
Was in the sacred place,
But that smile was the last smile
To come upon her face.

25   For when she heard the explosion,
Her eyes grew wet and wild.
She raced through the streets of Birmingham
Calling for her child.

She clawed through bits of glass and brick,
30   Then lifted out a shoe.
"O, here's the shoe my baby wore,
But, baby, where are you?"

The Migration Series (1940–1941), Panel 54, by Jacob Lawrence. Tempera on gesso on composition board (12″ × 18″). "For the migrants the church was the center of life." (Text and title revised by the artist 1993.)
The Museum of Modern Art, New York. Gift of Mrs. David M. Levy.

Meet the Writer

Dudley Randall

"I Liked the Feel of Those Books"

The newsboys hawking the *Detroit Free Press* always sold as many copies as they could. One morning, though, one of the boys, Dudley Randall (1914–2000), had a special reason to persuade folks to buy a paper: He'd published his first poem in it.

No one who knew the Randalls would have been surprised to see thirteen-year-old Dudley's name in print. His father, a minister, loved to recite poems and often used them in his sermons. "There were a lot of books around the house," Randall recalled, including beautifully bound volumes of poetry by Alfred, Lord Tennyson and Robert Browning. "I liked the feel of those books."

After serving in the army during World War II, Randall devoted himself to the books he loved. He worked his way through college and graduate school, and he became a university librarian as well as a poet. Then, in 1965, he started his own publishing company, Broadside Press, "so black people could speak to and for their people."

"Ballad of Birmingham" was the first poem Broadside Press published. (It was an actual broadside—a large poster with the poem printed on it.) Randall poured his time, energy, and money into the publishing venture. At first he ran the press from his home; later he moved to a small building next door. A friend recalled, "I would often walk in and see him doing everything from writing invoices and packing boxes to sweeping the floor."

Many outstanding poets of the time sent their work to Broadside: Alice Walker, Gwendolyn Brooks, Robert Hayden, Nikki Giovanni, Amiri Baraka (Leroi Jones), Audre Lorde, Etheridge Knight, and dozens more. Randall encouraged and supported African American writers, and they in turn saw Broadside Press as their own.

The History Behind the Ballad

Taylor Branch

The following account is from Parting the Waters, *a book that won the Pulitzer Prize in history in 1989.*

That Sunday was the annual Youth Day at the Sixteenth Street Baptist Church. Mamie H. Grier, superintendent of the Sunday school, stopped in at the basement ladies' room to find four young girls who had left Bible classes early and were talking excitedly about the beginning of the school year. All four were dressed in white from head to toe, as this was their day to run the main service for the adults at eleven o'clock. Grier urged them to hurry along and then went upstairs to sit in on her own women's Sunday-school class. They were engaged in a lively debate on the lesson topic, "The Love That Forgives," when a loud earthquake shook the entire church and showered the classroom with plaster and debris. Grier's first thought was that it was like a ticker-tape parade. Maxine McNair, a schoolteacher sitting next to her, reflexively went stiff and was the only one to speak. "Oh, my goodness!" she said. She escaped with Grier, but the stairs down to the basement were blocked and the large stone staircase on the outside literally had vanished. They stumbled through the church to the front door and then made their way around outside through the gathering noise of moans and sirens. A hysterical church member shouted to Grier that her husband had already gone to the hospital in the first ambulance. McNair searched desperately for her only child until finally she came upon a sobbing old man and screamed, "Daddy, I can't find Denise!" The man helplessly replied, "She's dead, baby. I've got one of her shoes." He held a girl's white dress shoe, and the look on his daughter's face made him scream out, "I'd like to blow the whole town up!"

The windows of the Sixteenth Street Baptist Church, where four young girls were killed.

After You Read Response and Analysis

Reading Check

1. Who are the two people who speak in this ballad?

2. What does the younger person ask permission to do? Why does the older person say no?

3. What happens that day in the church?

4. What does the older person find after clawing through glass and brick?

Thinking Critically

5. This ballad's emotional effect is based in part on **dramatic irony,** which occurs when the reader knows something that a character does not know. What does the reader know that the mother in the ballad doesn't know? Explain why the mother's refusing to let her child join a demonstration and sending her to church instead is a powerful example of dramatic irony.

6. Find and explain an example of **irony** (the contrast between what is expected or considered appropriate and what actually happens) in "The History Behind the Ballad," Taylor Branch's historical account of the church bombing (see the **Connection** on page 542).

7. This ballad does not have a refrain, but it does contain **repetition.** Which two lines are repeated? What does the repetition of the words *baby, child,* and *children* add to the emotional effect of the poem?

8. Like many folk ballads this **literary ballad** is written in four-line stanzas with **end rhymes.** Which lines rhyme in every stanza of this ballad?

9. Read the ballad aloud, paying special attention to its **rhythm** and **end rhyme.** How would you describe the sound of the ballad?

WRITING

Recasting the News

Go back to your Quickwrite notes. Turn one of the subjects on your list into a **ballad.** If you want a challenge, try to find rhyming words to end either lines 1 and 3 or lines 2 and 4. You might want to imitate the style of Randall's ballad and use **dialogue** to tell your story.

Poetry and History

In a short essay, **compare** and **contrast** Randall's ballad with Branch's historical account (see the **Connection** on page 542). Although the authors use very different forms to tell the same story, what similarities do you see between the two works? Consider, for example, the use of **descriptive details, dialogue,** and **irony.** What are the key differences between the two works? Conclude by explaining whether the ballad or the historical account seems most powerful to you.

> ▶ **For help writing a comparison-contrast essay, see pages 280 and 318.**

	Ballad	Historical Account
Descriptive details		
Dialogue		
Irony		
Impact on me		

SKILLS FOCUS

Literary Skills
Analyze the characteristics of ballads.

Writing Skills
Write a ballad.
Write a comparison-contrast essay.

The Gift

Make the Connection

Quickwrite

Try to recall a time when a parent, a teacher, or a friend did something special for you that you would like to be able to do for others someday. (Maybe you have already done it.) Write down what you remember about that person's actions and your feelings about them.

Literary Focus

Free Verse

Free verse is poetry that does not adhere to strict patterns of rhyme and meter. No rhyme scheme. No regular meter. No rules about line length and stanzas to worry about. What could be easier to write than free verse?

You have probably learned by now that writing anything well is not easy—especially poetry. A free-verse poem may not have rhyme and meter, but it does have clearly focused images, original figures of speech, and words chosen carefully for both what they mean and what they suggest.

Free verse also has rhythm. The **rhythm** in free verse comes from the natural rise and fall of the voice, from pauses, and from the balance between long and short lines. Rhythm also comes from the repetition of sounds, words, phrases, and even entire lines.

Read "The Gift" aloud, watching for punctuation marks. Pause briefly at commas. Make full stops at periods. Let your voice rise and fall in a natural way, like the voice of an oral storyteller. Do you feel the poem's rhythm?

SKILLS FOCUS

Literary Skills
Understand the characteristics of free verse.

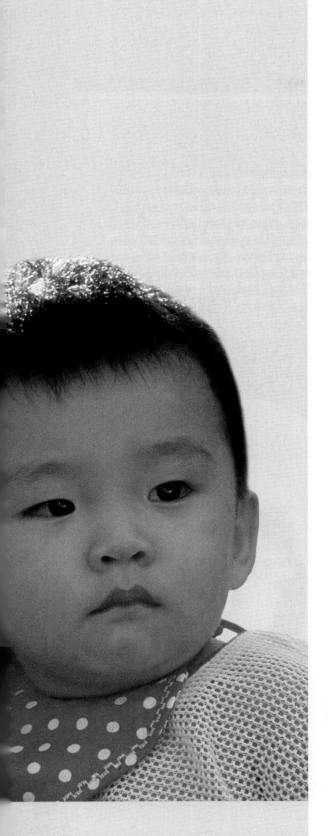

The Gift

Li-Young Lee

To pull the metal splinter from my palm
my father recited a story in a low voice.
I watched his lovely face and not the blade.
Before the story ended he'd removed
5   the iron sliver I thought I'd die from.

I can't remember the tale
but hear his voice still, a well
of dark water, a prayer.
And I recall his hands,
10   two measures of tenderness
he laid against my face,
the flames of discipline
he raised above my head.

Had you entered that afternoon
15   you would have thought you saw a man
planting something in a boy's palm,
a silver tear, a tiny flame.
Had you followed that boy
you would have arrived here,
20   where I bend over my wife's right hand.

Look how I shave her thumbnail down
so carefully she feels no pain.
Watch as I lift the splinter out.
I was seven when my father
25   took my hand like this,
and I did not hold that shard
between my fingers and think,
Metal that will bury me,
christen it Little Assassin,
30   Ore Going Deep for My Heart.
And I did not lift up my wound and cry,
Death visited here!
I did what a child does
when he's given something to keep.
35   I kissed my father.

Meet the Writer

Li-Young Lee

"The Winged Seed"

The great-grandfather of Li-Young Lee (1957–   ) was the first president of the Republic of China. His father, on whom the character in "The Gift" is based, was the personal physician to the revolutionary leader Mao Tse-tung. In the 1950s, the family fled the political turmoil in China when the Communist People's Republic was established. They went first to Indonesia, and Li-Young Lee was born in Jakarta. There his father was thrown into jail by the corrupt dictator Sukarno. His father spent nineteen months in prison, seventeen of them in a leper colony. When the family fled again, they went to Hong Kong. When Lee was six, they arrived in the United States, where his father became a Presbyterian minister.

Lee has recorded his family's history in *The Winged Seed: A Remembrance* (1995). His first book of poems, *Rose,* won the 1986 Delmore Schwartz Memorial Poetry Award, and a second book, *The City in Which I Love You,* was the 1990 Lamont Poetry Selection of the Academy of American Poets.

Lee, who now lives in Chicago with his family, has said about his writing:

❝I know I am not a poet. How do I know this? Because I know a poet when I read one. There are living poets in the world today. I am not one of them. But I want to be one, and I know only of one path: serious and passionate apprenticeship, which involves a strange combination of awe and argument, with the Masters.

Other than this, I don't know anything about poetry, though if space permitted, I could go on earnestly, and to the boredom and horror of everyone, about all those things I don't know. **❞**

Reading Check

1. What does the **speaker** of the poem remember about his father when he removed a splinter from the speaker's hand?

2. Later in the poem, whose splinter does the speaker remove?

3. What was the speaker given to keep? What did the speaker give his father in return?

Thinking Critically

4. In the first stanza, why do you think the father recited a story to his son?

5. Throughout the poem, Lee uses precise **images.** List at least four images that appeal to your senses of sight, hearing, and touch and therefore help you imagine what happened to the little boy and to the speaker's wife.

6. In the second stanza, what **metaphors** does the speaker use to describe his father's voice? What metaphor describes his father's hands? What do these figures of speech reveal about the speaker's feelings toward his father?

7. In the third stanza, whom do you think the speaker is talking to when he says "you"? What scene is taking place in the present?

8. What does the speaker say he *didn't* do with the shard, or piece of metal, in his hand? Why, instead, did he kiss his father?

9. How is the speaker's behavior in the present, described in the third and fourth stanzas, similar to his father's behavior in the first two stanzas?

10. Read the poem aloud, and listen to the sounds it creates. The poet is so skillful that we hardly notice his technique—but it is there. In line 1, what sounds are **alliterated**? What **sentence pattern** is repeated in the third stanza? What pattern is repeated in the fourth stanza? What initial sound is **alliterated** in line 17?

Extending and Evaluating

11. In lines 26–32, the poem has a brief but intense change in tone. What is the **tone,** or the speaker's attitude, in these lines, and how does it differ from the tone in the rest of the poem? List words that help create the tone in this section. Then, explain whether you find these lines distracting. Why might the poet have included them?

WRITING

A Gift to You

Write a **free-verse poem** about a gift you received. The gift could have come in the form of advice or in the form of an experience in which you learned something valuable, such as the one you described in your Quickwrite notes. Use **images** and **figures of speech** to show how you feel about the person who gave you the gift. Try to repeat sentence patterns to create **rhythm.** Read the lines of your poem over, revising them until you're pleased with the way they sound. Can you feel the rhythm?

Analyzing Free Verse

Write a few paragraphs analyzing the strategies Li-Young Lee uses in "The Gift" to create verbal music. Look specifically for the **repetition** of words and **alliteration.** Discuss the ways he creates a natural rhythm in his poem.

▶ **Use "Analyzing a Poem," pages 556–563, for help with this assignment.**

SKILLS FOCUS

Literary Skills
Analyze the characteristics of free verse.

Writing Skills
Write a free-verse poem.
Write an analysis of a free-verse poem.

Legal Alien/Extranjera legal

Make the Connection

Quickwrite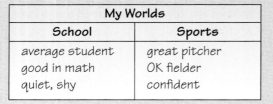

Think of all the worlds you belong to: the worlds of home, family, school, sports, and friends, for example. Make a chart like the one here, in which you list at least three ways you feel or behave in *two* of your worlds:

My Worlds	
School	Sports
average student	great pitcher
good in math	OK fielder
quiet, shy	confident

Literary Focus

Speaker

Poets can imagine anyone or anything as their **speaker,** the voice talking to us in a poem. The speaker is often the poet— but not always. The poet may assume a persona, or mask, and speak as someone much younger or older than himself or herself. Sometimes the speaker is an animal or even an object that doesn't have the power of speech in real life.

The choice of a speaker affects a poem's **tone,** the attitude expressed toward its subject or audience. The speaker's tone and his or her style of speaking create the speaker's **voice.**

As you read a poem, listen carefully to the voice. Do you hear the formal, somber voice of an older man reflecting on his life? Do you hear the excited chatter of a young child? Often the speaker's identity and voice are keys to the meaning of a poem.

As you start to read Pat Mora's poem, ask yourself, "Who's talking to me?" Keep in mind that a legal alien is a person from another country who enters the United States through legal channels.

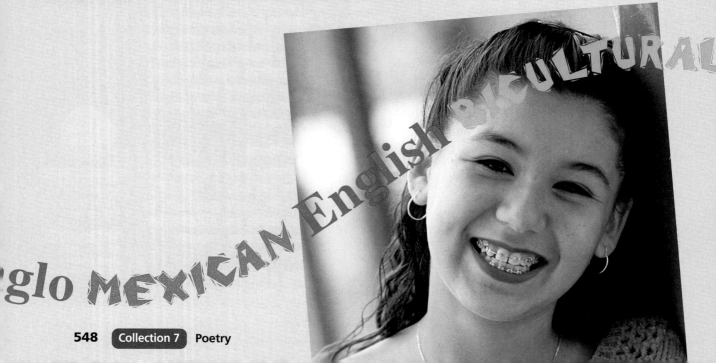

Legal Alien

Pat Mora

Bi-lingual, Bi-cultural,
able to slip from "How's life?"
to *"Me'stan volviendo loca,"*°
able to sit in a paneled office
5 drafting memos in smooth English,
able to order in fluent Spanish
at a Mexican restaurant,
American but hyphenated,
viewed by Anglos as perhaps exotic,
10 perhaps inferior, definitely different,
viewed by Mexicans as alien
(their eyes say, "You may speak
Spanish but you're not like me"),
an American to Mexicans
15 a Mexican to Americans
a handy token
sliding back and forth
between the fringes of both worlds
by smiling
20 by masking the discomfort
of being pre-judged
Bi-laterally.°

---

3. *Me'stan ... loca* (me·stän′ vōl·vē·en′ dō lō′cä):
  Spanish for "They're driving me crazy."
22. **Bi-laterally** (bī · lat′ər · əl · ē) *adv.:* by both sides.
  (Mora has added a hyphen to this word.)

Extranjera legal

Pat Mora

Bi-lingüe, bi-cultural,
capaz de deslizarse de *"How's life?"*
a "Me'stan volviendo loca,"
capaz de ocupar un despacho bien apuntado,
5 redactando memorandums en inglés liso,
capaz de ordenar la cena en español fluido
en restaurante mexicano,
americana pero con guión,
vista por los anglos como exótica,
10 quizás inferior, obviamente distinta,
vista por mexicanos como extranjera
(sus ojos dicen "Hablas español
pero no eres como yo"),
americana para mexicanos
15 mexicana para americanos
una ficha servible
pasando de un lado al otro
de los márgenes de dos mundos
sonriéndome
20 disfrazando la incomodidad
del pre-juicio
bi-lateralmente.

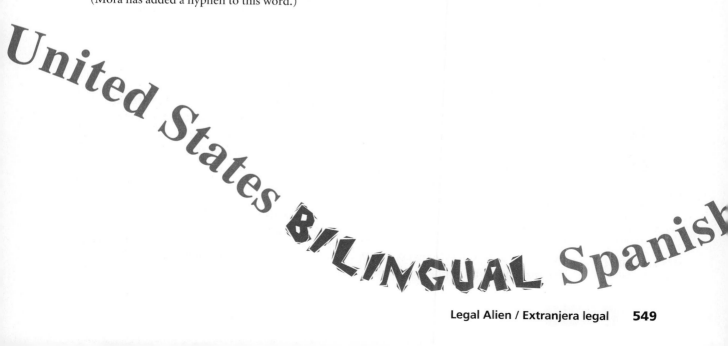

Meet the Writer

Pat Mora

Beyond Borders

Pat Mora (1942–   ) maintains that people's identities grow out of all the worlds they inhabit—the ones they inherit from the past as well as the ones they encounter as they go through life. Born and raised in the border town of El Paso, Texas, Mora has spent her life observing the interactions between Mexican and Anglo cultures. While never denying the painful side of bicultural existence, Mora stresses the harmonies between the cultures—harmonies that are the result of centuries of shared living. She finds the differences among people less important than the things all cultures share—marrying, raising children, working, growing old, and dying.

The poem "Legal Alien" is from *Chants* (1984), Mora's first book of poems. Her other books include *Communion* (1991), a book of poems, and *House of Houses* (1997), a memoir of her family.

After You Read   Response and Analysis

Reading Check

1. According to the speaker, how do Americans view her?

2. Why does the speaker believe that Mexicans view her as "alien"?

3. What does her smile "mask," or hide?

Thinking Critically

4. Who do you think the **speaker** of "Legal Alien" is? How do you know?

5. What does the speaker mean when she says, "American but hyphenated"? Who could say they are unhyphenated Americans? In the great "melting pot" of cultures that is America, why might "hyphenated Americans" feel proud of their two heritages?

6. In line 16, the speaker uses a **metaphor** in which she compares herself to a token. However, *token* is a word with multiple meanings. What different meanings of *token* is the poet suggesting?

7. Read the poem aloud, and listen carefully to how the speaker expresses her thoughts. How would you describe the **voice** of the **persona**? To answer, consider her **tone** and her style of speaking.

WRITING

Your Worlds

Use the notes you made for the Quickwrite on page 548 as the basis for a **poem** about the worlds you live in. You might want to use this framework:

> In the world of . . . ,
> I am . . .
>
> In the world of . . . ,
> I am . . .
>
> Some people think I'm . . . ,
> But I am really . . .

The Base Stealer
American Hero

Make the Connection

Quickwrite 🖉

Take a few minutes to imagine that you're a sports hero. You pick the sport—one that you've played or one that you've watched a lot. Imagine that you're at the critical point in an important game. The pressure's on. You go into action. Jot down what happens and what you are feeling.

Literary Focus

Sound and Sense

Baseball games, basketball games, football games, hockey games—all are exciting because they are like stories: They have a beginning, a middle, and an end, and they contain action and tension. When poets tackle sports, they use elements of poetry

to try to re-create the excitement—and even the beauty—of the game.

One of the poems that follows is about a base stealer. The base stealer is modeled on Jackie Robinson, who played mostly second base for the Brooklyn Dodgers from 1947 to 1956. (For an essay about Robinson, see page 844.) The other poem is about an unnamed basketball player whose slam-dunk wins the game. The poets use sentence structure, alliteration, and onomatopoeia to help us see and hear what happens on the court and on the field.

Poets sometimes use **sentence structure** to reflect the meaning of a line of poetry. To describe a short, quick action, a poet might place just one short sentence in a line of a poem. To describe a long, continuous action, a poet might continue the description for several lines. As you read "The Base Stealer," listen to how the poet uses sentence structure to reflect the actions described in the poem.

Alliteration is the repetition of consonant sounds in several words, usually at the beginnings of the words. The sentence *Harry hurried home for a hamburger* uses alliteration. Advertisers make use of alliteration all the time because they know it is pleasing to our ears.

Onomatopoeia is the use of a word whose sound imitates or suggests its meaning (*clang, honk, meow*). One television sportscaster became famous for his use of onomatopoeia when he said "swish" every time a player made a basket. You'll find more examples of onomatopoeia in "American Hero."

SKILLS FOCUS

Literary Skills
Understand alliteration, onomatopoeia, and sentence structure.

Jackie Robinson slides into home plate.

The Base Stealer
Robert Francis

Poised between going on and back, pulled
Both ways taut like a tightrope-walker,
Fingertips pointing the opposites,
Now bouncing tiptoe like a dropped ball
5 Or a kid skipping rope, come on, come on,
Running a scattering of steps sidewise,
How he teeters, skitters, tingles, teases,
Taunts them, hovers like an ecstatic bird,
He's only flirting, crowd him, crowd him,
10 Delicate, delicate, delicate, delicate—now!

American Hero
Essex Hemphill

I have nothing to lose tonight.
All my men surround me, panting,
as I spin the ball above our heads
on my middle finger.
5 It's a shimmering club light
and I'm dancing, slick in my sweat.
Squinting, I aim at the hole
fifty feet away. I let the tension go.
Shoot for the net. Choke it.
10 I never hear the ball
slap the backboard. I slam it
through the net. The crowd goes wild
for our win. I scored
thirty-two points this game
15 and they love me for it.
Everyone hollering
is a friend tonight.
But there are towns,
certain neighborhoods
20 where I'd be hard pressed
to hear them cheer
if I move on the block.

Meet the Writers

Robert Francis
Essex Hemphill

A One-man Show

Robert Francis (1901–1987) liked to do things for himself. He lived alone in a cottage on the outskirts of Amherst, Massachusetts, baking his own bread, growing his own vegetables, and walking seven miles round-trip to town for groceries and library books because he didn't earn enough money from his writing to buy a car.

When publishers rejected his fourth collection of poems, Francis paid a printer to run copies labeled "Published by the Author." When the volume failed to draw attention, he went one step further: He wrote a negative review of his own book ("The subjects, for the most part, are most unpoetic . . . Strange as anything else are, if you please, two baseball poems."), and he sent it to the local newspaper under an assumed name, hoping someone would write in to defend him. No one did. So Francis wrote another letter criticizing the first. Unfortunately, the paper did not print the second letter. Eventually Francis found many publishers for his writings.

Francis once said,

66 Poetry is at its best when it provides enjoyable excitement and when that excitement comes as much from what the poet makes of words as from what he says in words. Poetry at its best is a highly skilled game a poet plays with life and language, a game that the reader can follow play by play. . . . 99

"Take Care of Your Blessings"

When **Essex Hemphill** (1957–1995) said goodbye to friends, he used to add, "Take care of your blessings." He believed that everyone has special gifts that need to be nurtured and used to the fullest. "Our blessings," he said, "are only as good to us as we are to them."

Hemphill found one of his blessings when he was fourteen. Feeling out of place in his working-class neighborhood in Washington, D.C., he turned to writing as a way to explore who he really was. "Tablets, journals, those became my confidants," he said.

As a student at the University of Maryland, he made friends with a group of local African American poets (one recalls him as "a young brother with a big heart"), and he discovered another blessing—a talent for performance. Hemphill loved to read his poems aloud. He said that "poetry doesn't solely live on the page. Poetry is meant to be heard."

Before his tragic death at thirty-eight, Hemphill had become widely known as a writer, editor, and activist. He said,

66 I'm part of a generation that is making it possible for the young to feel empowered earlier . . . I know long after I'm gone, the space I'm carving out will help other voices come through. 99

The Base Stealer
American Hero

Reading Check

1. In the first four lines of "The Base Stealer," what is the character's situation? What is he doing?

2. List at least three verbs that describe what the player in "American Hero" is doing before the crowd goes wild in line 12.

Literary Skills
Analyze alliteration, onomatopoeia, and sentence structure.

Writing Skills
Write a free-verse poem.

INTERNET

Projects and Activities

Keyword: LE7 9-7

Thinking Critically

3. Find three lines in "The Base Stealer" that use **alliteration** to describe the base stealer's actions. Where is alliteration used in "American Hero" to describe the basketball player and his game? Read the lines in both poems aloud, and explain the effects created by the repeated sounds.

4. Find at least three examples of **onomatopoeia** in "American Hero." How do those words contribute to the poem's appeal?

5. Notice how the **sentence structure** in "The Base Stealer" suggests motion and helps to convey the actions being described. How does the sentence structure in lines 1–2 reflect the meaning of those lines? Why do you think Francis lists four verbs in line 7? Find two different commands that Francis repeats to make us feel part of the crowd cheering the player on.

6. Find three **similes** in "The Base Stealer" that compare the movements of the base stealer to other movements.

7. Read "American Hero" aloud to hear how the short sentences re-create the tension of a basketball game. Which part of speech—noun, verb, adjective, or adverb—is emphasized the most in these sentences? Why?

8. Both of these poems are about sports. Which poem also has a serious message, and what is it? How does that poem's title create a sense of **irony**—a sense that the title does not mean exactly what it says?

WRITING

Poetry in Sports

Review your Quickwrite notes. Then, write a **free-verse poem** about the turning point of a game that you've played or watched or imagined. Make yourself the hero. Use short sentences and alliteration to help re-create fast-paced action.

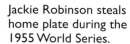

Jackie Robinson steals home plate during the 1955 World Series.

POETRY

Distant Times and Remote Places

Ever read any African chants, European lullabies, or Native American myths set to verse? If you'd like to, *Talking to the Sun* is the place to start. Poems covering almost all aspects of life and nature—including the sky, sand, flowers, animals, forests, and love—are arranged by topic. Works by such poets as Langston Hughes, Edna St. Vincent Millay, and William Shakespeare are represented alongside tribal hymns and American folk songs. This beautiful collection is enhanced by artwork from New York's Metropolitan Museum of Art.

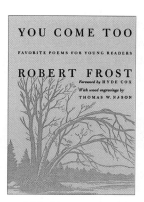

POETRY

Almost There

Discover some of the best of Robert Frost's poetry in *You Come Too.* In this collection for readers of all ages, you'll encounter poems like "Christmas Tree," "Hyla Brook," and his famous, inviting title poem. Frost brings to life the trees, mountains, cliffs, dirt roads, old fences, grassy fields, and abandoned houses of his beloved New England. Reading his work, you'll have the sense that you are there—deep in the woods or at the edge of a babbling brook.

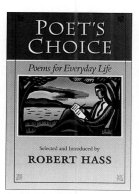

POETRY

From the Morning Papers

"Poet's Choice" was a weekly newspaper column designed to add poetry to your morning cereal. The poet Robert Hass chose one poem each week to appear in twenty-five major American newspapers. Each poem addressed a different subject, from the changing of the seasons to the celebration of a holiday to the death of a great writer. Hass has collected these poems in one volume, *Poet's Choice: Poems for Everyday Life.*

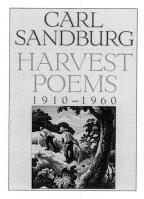

POETRY

Man of the People

Carl Sandburg, a poet known for his direct, conversational style, wanted to celebrate the simple things in life. He also wanted to pay tribute to the unsung heroes of our country. Reading his collection *Harvest Poems: 1910–1960* is like sifting through snapshots of the everyday people—waitresses, farmers, mothers, and children—who represent the heart of America. This collection includes all of his most popular poems, including "Chicago" and selections from his book *The People, Yes.*

Analyzing a Poem

Writing Assignment
Write a response to literature in which you analyze the literary elements of a poem.

In this collection, you've focused on two important elements of literature—imagery and figurative language. In this Writing Workshop you'll write an **analysis of a poem** in which you examine the poem's elements to discover how those elements combine to convey the poem's theme and overall effect.

Prewriting

Choose and Analyze a Poem

So Many Options The poem you select for analysis should be just right: not so short that it contains too little to examine, nor so long that you can't cover it in detail in an essay of 1,500 words. Poems of ten to twenty lines that are rich in meaning are often suited to analyses of that length. To find a poem to analyze, re-read poems you have enjoyed before; ask for recommendations from your teacher, a librarian, family members, and friends; or look for collections of poems in your school or community library or on the Internet.

The Poet's Tools To analyze the poem you've selected, you'll need to re-read it several times. As you re-read, pay close attention to the poem's **literary elements.** Careful analysis of the elements used in a particular work will make you aware of how the poet uses those elements to shape meaning and create certain effects. The following chart lists some common literary elements found in poetry and gives questions to help you analyze them.

LITERARY ELEMENTS	
Element	**Analysis Questions**
Speaker: the voice talking in the poem; the narrator of the poem (not necessarily the poet)	Who is speaking in the poem? Is the speaker the poet or a character created by the poet?
Theme: the meaning, or main idea, of the poem, usually involving some insight into human existence	Does the poem examine some common life experience or problem? Does it suggest solutions or answers?
Tone: the poet's attitude toward the subject, the audience, or a character	What is the poet's attitude toward the subject (sarcastic, respectful)? the audience (friendly, hostile)? the characters (sympathetic, cruel)?

(continued)

Stylistic devices: the techniques the poet uses to control language to create certain effects	How does **diction,** the poet's choice of key words, influence the poem's meaning? Does the poet use **figurative language,** such as **metaphors** and **similes,** to make imaginative comparisons? What **sound devices,** such as **rhythm, rhyme,** and **repetition,** does the poet use? What effects do they have on the poem?

Identify one or more **key literary elements** that are essential to understanding the poem's theme. Below you will find an analysis log one student created while analyzing the poem "A Dream Deferred" by Langston Hughes. It shows the poem and some of the student's notes on the poem's stylistic devices—what he determined to be the key literary element.

 **DO THIS**

ANALYSIS LOG

1	What happens to a dream deferred?	Line 1	DICTION: "dream" = hope, aspiration for the future. "defer" = to delay temporarily, to give in to someone else.
2	Does it dry up	Lines 2–3	SIMILE: Deferred dream shrivels.
3	like a raisin in the sun?	Lines 4–5	SIMILE: Deferred dream becomes diseased, infected.
4	Or fester like a sore—		
5	And then run?	Line 6	SIMILE: Deferred dream stinks of decay.
6	Does it stink like rotten meat?	Lines 7–8	SIMILE: Deferred dream is sickeningly sweet.
7	Or crust and sugar over—	Lines 9–10	SIMILE: Deferred dream is a burden; it weighs the dreamer down.
8	like a syrupy sweet?		
9	Maybe it just sags	Line 11	METAPHOR: Deferred dream is a bomb that explodes and destroys.
10	like a heavy load.		Possible THEME: A dream deferred causes destruction. This is the answer to the poem's question.
11	Or does it explode?		

Write Your Thesis

The Key Point Now, summarize your main idea about the poem in a coherent **thesis statement**—one or two sentences that make the focus of your analysis clear to your audience. The student analyzing "A Dream Deferred" wrote the following thesis statement while prewriting. He later fine-tuned it to better fit the introduction to his analysis.

> In "A Dream Deferred," Langston Hughes uses the stylistic devices of diction, figurative language, and sound to show that keeping people from achieving their dreams can have destructive consequences.

 SKILLS FOCUS

Writing Skills
Write an analysis of a poem. Establish a thesis statement.

Gather Supporting Evidence

The Poem as Witness An analysis of a poem should contain accurate **references** to the poem. These references—quotations from the poem and details restated in your own words—will support the thesis. Each reference should be followed by **elaboration:** an explanation of how the quotation or detail supports your thesis. Elaboration shows you have a good grasp of the poem's **significant ideas** and enables you to address the poem's **ambiguities, nuances,** and **complexities.**

- **Ambiguities** are lines or words that lend themselves to more than one interpretation.

- **Nuances** are changes in tone or meaning. For example, a poem might start with a light tone and then turn more serious.

- **Complexities** result when a poem is rich in meaning but difficult to interpret. For example, a poem may discuss problems that don't have simple solutions, or ask questions that don't have easy answers.

Below is the beginning of a chart one student created to show the references and the elaboration he will include in his analysis.

Literary Element	Detail or Quotation	Elaboration
Stylistic device: Diction	"What happens to a dream deferred?" (1)	A dream can be a hope or an aspiration for the future. <u>Defer</u> is an ambiguous word. It can mean "to delay" or "to give in to what someone else wants."
Stylistic device: Simile	"Does it dry up /like a raisin in the sun?" (2–3)	This is a complex image. The reader is meant to think of the dried and wrinkled raisin in contrast to the fat, juicy grape that the dream once was, before it dried up.

Organize Your Analysis

Putting Things in Order Before beginning your first draft, put your ideas in order. You might arrange your analysis by **order of importance,** beginning or ending with the key literary element most important to the poem's theme and effect. You might also arrange your analysis by discussing the key literary elements in the order in which they appear in the poem.

SKILLS FOCUS

Writing Skills
Support ideas with references to the poem. Arrange ideas in their order of importance.

PRACTICE & APPLY 1 Using the instructions on pages 556–557, choose and analyze a poem. Then, decide on the poem's key literary elements, write a thesis statement, and gather evidence to support the thesis. Organize your analysis.

Writing

Analyzing a Poem

A Writer's Framework

Introduction

- Grab readers' attention by relating the poem's meaning to experiences people have in common.
- Introduce the poem's title and author.
- State your thesis, including the key elements and theme you will discuss.

Body

- Organize the key literary elements by order of importance or in the order in which they appear in the poem.
- Discuss each key literary element.
- Provide references for each key element, and elaborate on each key element.

Conclusion

- Remind readers of your thesis by restating it.
- Summarize your main points.
- Show how the poem relates to broader themes in life.

A Writer's Model

Stylistic Devices in "A Dream Deferred"

What is life worth without dreams and the hope that those dreams can come true someday? What happens when the achievement of a dream is postponed—again and again? In "A Dream Deferred," Langston Hughes answers these questions by using the stylistic devices of diction, figurative language, and sound to show that keeping people from achieving their dreams can have destructive consequences.

Hughes starts with a question to get his readers thinking about his message: "What happens to a dream deferred?" (line 1). His diction here is important. He uses the word "dream" to mean a hope for or vision of a better future. He chooses the word defer for its two meanings. It can mean both "to put something off until sometime in the future" and "to give in to what someone else wants." Hughes uses the word in both ways: Someone else postpones the dream, but the dreamer gives in to the delay. The question then is, "How long will the dreamer accept the postponement of his or her dream?"

In the next part of the poem, Hughes answers this basic question about deferred dreams with a series of similes written as questions. The first simile asks if a deferred dream dries up "like a raisin in the sun" (3). The image of the dried and wrinkled raisin contrasts with the fat, juicy grape the dream once was. The images created by the following three similes are worse. Does the deferred dream "fester like

INTRODUCTION
Attention-getting opener

Thesis (with title and author)

BODY
First stylistic device: diction

Ambiguity explained

Second stylistic device: figurative language

Complexities explained

(continued)

(continued)

Similes

a sore— / And then run?" (4–5) or "stink like rotten meat?" (6) or "crust and sugar over— / like a syrupy sweet?" (7–8)? The images in these similes seem to say that if a dream is postponed, it rots or spoils or infects the dreamer. The last simile is not a question but a guess. "Maybe" a deferred dream "just sags / like a heavy load." (9–10). This simile makes the deferred dream seem like a heavy burden carried on the dreamer's back, making him or her bow under its weight. All of these similes suggest that a deferred dream becomes something terrible.

Metaphor

Ambiguity explained

In the poem's last line, Hughes uses another piece of figurative language, a metaphor—"Or does it explode?" (11)—to address his message. He emphasizes the metaphor even more by using different print from the rest of the poem. He seems to be saying that this is exactly what happens: a deferred dream is a bomb that finally explodes. He might also mean that it is not the dream but the dreamer that explodes—in anger.

Third stylistic device: sound

Rhyme
Nuance explained

Rhythm

Nuance explained

The sound of the poem intensifies its meaning even more. Like a piece of jazz music, the poem uses rhyme and short bursts of rhythm. The rhymes—"sun/run," "meat/sweet," and "load/explode"—pull the ideas behind the similes and the metaphor together, repeating and building up the importance of the ideas like a series of notes repeated in music. Similarly, just as pauses in music provide dynamic rhythms, the lines in the poem have pauses between them, shown by the use of dashes and the skipped lines that set off the central section. The last important question of the poem, asked after a skipped-line pause, is like a final drumbeat that ends a piece of jazz music.

CONCLUSION
Restatement of thesis

Summary of main points

Just what does happen when the achievement of a dream is postponed again and again? Hughes uses the stylistic devices of diction, figurative language, and sound to tell his readers what might happen to a deferred dream. The word "deferred" hints that the dreamer might not always accept the postponement of his or her dream. The five similes seem to say that only the dreamer is hurt. In the final metaphor, however, the deferred dream is a bomb that will eventually explode and hurt many people. Hughes ties the poem together with jazzy rhyme and rhythm. "A Dream Deferred" carries an idea we should all consider— not to let our own dreams become deferred, and not to block others in their quests to follow their own dreams.

Relation to broader themes in life

INTERNET

More Writer's Models

Keyword: LE7 9-7

PRACTICE & APPLY 2 Now it is your turn to write an analysis. Use the framework on page 559 and the Writer's Model as guidelines while you write the first draft of your analysis of a poem.

Revising

Evaluate and Revise Your Draft

Rework and Refine Poets write and rewrite their poems, changing words and phrases until they find exactly the right meaning that rests in exactly the right words. As a writer, you may find that your first draft also may need a rewrite or two. To make your analysis of a poem as clear, precise, and effective as it can be, review your paper. Evaluate and revise the content and organization of your analysis first. Then, evaluate and revise its style.

> **PEER REVIEW**
>
> Before you revise, ask a classmate to read your analysis and the poem you analyzed. He or she may offer you more ideas about how the key literary elements you identified influence the poem.

First Reading: Content and Organization The following chart will help you evaluate and revise your analysis. Answer the questions in the first column, check the tips in the second column, and look at the third column for suggestions.

Rubric: Analyzing a Poem

Evaluation Questions	▶ Tips	▶ Revision Techniques
❶ Does the introduction mention the poem's title and author? Does it include a clear thesis statement that names the key elements and the poem's theme?	**Circle** the poet, title, and thesis statement. **Put a check mark** next to the key elements and theme in the thesis statement.	**Add** a sentence that names the poem's title and author. **Add** a clear thesis statement that names the key elements and the theme.
❷ Does each body paragraph discuss a key literary element that supports the thesis?	**Bracket** the key literary element in each body paragraph.	**Replace** body paragraphs that don't address key elements.
❸ Is each key literary element supported with references to the poem? Does the writer explain each reference?	**Highlight** quotations or restated details from the poem, and **draw an arrow** to their explanations.	**Add** quotations or restated details. **Elaborate** by explaining how the quotations and details support the thesis.
❹ Is the analysis organized by order of importance or in the order that the key elements appear in the poem?	**Number** the body paragraphs. If the numbers do not reflect an appropriate sequence, revise.	**Rearrange** the body paragraphs in the order of importance or in the order the key elements appear in the poem.
❺ Does the conclusion effectively remind readers of the thesis and summarize the main points? Does it show how the poem relates to broader themes in life?	**Underline** the sentence in the conclusion that restates the thesis. **Put a star** beside the sentences that summarize the main points. **Put two stars** by the sentences that relate the poem to broader themes.	If necessary, **add** a sentence restating the thesis. **Add** sentences that summarize the main points and that relate the poem to broader themes.

▷ **Second Reading: Style** In your second reading, pay attention to your writing style and its impact on your tone. Sentences with wordy, unnecessary clauses can create a **tone** that intimidates readers. For example, note how clumsy the following sentence is: "What transpires when the achievement of what a person creates in the mind's eye, what the person desires in reality, is postponed, and that postponement happens repeatedly?" Now, compare the stiff formality of that sentence to its rewrite: "What happens when the achievement of a dream is postponed—again and again?" Eliminating the unnecessary clauses improved the tone. Your analysis's tone should be knowledgeable yet friendly, not intimidating. Use the following guidelines to help you cut down on wordiness.

Style Guidelines

Evaluation Question	▷ **Tip**	▷ **Revision Technique**
● Does the analysis contain wordy sentences with unnecessary clauses?	▷ **Double underline** clauses beginning with *which is, which are, that is, that are, who is,* and *who are.*	▷ **Reduce** half of these clauses to participles or participial phrases by **deleting** the pronouns *who, which,* or *that* and the *be* verb. If necessary, **rearrange** the remaining words.

ANALYZING THE REVISION PROCESS

Study these revisions, and answer the questions that follow.

> In "A Dream Deferred," Langston Hughes answers these ques-
>
> *the stylistic devices of diction, figurative language, and sound*
>
> **replace**   tions by using ~~different elements~~ to show that keeping people
>
>   *destructive*
>
> **rearrange/delete**   from achieving their dreams can have ⌃consequences⊙ ~~that are~~
>
> **delete**   ~~destructive.~~ ✓

Responding to the Revision Process

1. How do the writer's revisions improve the thesis statement?
2. Why do you think the writer reworded the end of the sentence?

SKILLS FOCUS

Writing Skills
Revise for content and style.

 PRACTICE & APPLY ③   Revise the content, organization, and style of your analysis by using the preceding guidelines and those on page 561. Look at the Writer's Model on page 559 and the revisions shown in the example above as models for your own revisions.

Publishing

Proofread and Publish Your Analysis

The Finishing Touches Avoid letting minor mistakes in your final draft distract readers or discredit your ideas. **Proofread** your paper carefully to eliminate any errors in grammar, usage, and mechanics. Even a few errors in your analysis can damage its effectiveness.

Sharing Your Work After you've done all the hard work of analyzing a poem and putting your insights onto paper, it would be a shame to have only your teacher and a small number of classmates read your analysis. Here are some suggestions on how you might share your analysis of a poem with a larger audience.

- Ask an older sibling or relative who has taken high school or college literature classes to read and critique your analysis.

- Submit your analysis to your school's literary magazine.

- Post your analysis to a teen literary magazine on the Internet, or find a Web site devoted to the writer of the poem you analyzed and inquire as to whether you could post your analysis to the site.

- Organize a poetry night at your school. Read aloud the poems you and your classmates have analyzed. Select several analyses of the poetry to read, also.

Reflect on Your Analysis

Relive the Experience Write brief responses to the following questions to reflect on what you have learned in this workshop. Recognizing your strengths and weaknesses can help you improve future writing.

- How did writing this paper change your feelings about the poem you selected? How did your understanding of the poem change after you performed an in-depth analysis of it?

- Was the tone of your analysis knowledgeable yet friendly? How might you adjust your tone if you were writing this analysis for a different audience, for example, a class of sixth-graders?

- What new techniques or ideas about analyzing poetry did you learn in this workshop? How could you apply them to analyzing other forms of literature?

PRACTICE & APPLY 4 Proofread your analysis carefully, and eliminate any errors you find. Select one or two publishing options to get your analysis out to a larger audience. Finally, answer the preceding reflection questions.

> **TIP** Proofreading will help ensure that your essay follows the **conventions** of standard American English. For example, you should make sure that you have correctly punctuated the quotations in your analysis. For more on **punctuating quotations,** see Quotation Marks, 13f, in the Language Handbook.

SKILLS FOCUS

Writing Skills
Proofread, especially for correct punctuation of quotations. Publish and reflect on the essay.

Presenting a Poem

Speaking Assignment
Deliver an oral interpretation of a poem to an audience.

Long before paper was invented, there was a tradition of poems being spoken aloud in order to pass on the important cultural events of a people. Many of us would agree that poetry—with its distinctive rhymes, rhythms, and imagery—lends itself to being heard, not just being read silently. Presenting a poem orally is another way to help others fully appreciate a poem's message and effects. It can also deepen your own understanding as you bring the poem dramatically to life.

Preparing to Read Aloud

Think It Over Your first step in preparing to read a poem aloud to an audience is to build your private, personal understanding of the poem.

- **Make a Choice** As you worked through the collection, you may have already found a poem that you feel strongly about. If you still haven't found a poem that's right for you, read aloud several from this collection again to see which one you'd most enjoy reading in public.

- **Shape Your Interpretations** Make a copy of the poem, and use it as a working script. Underline the parts you find most dramatic—**words, images, sounds, rhythms,** and **figures of speech.** Note places where you want to go slowly, speed up, or pause. Be sure to note which lines do not end with a punctuation mark. This means that you don't come to a full pause: You read on to the next line to complete the thought.

- **Get to Know the Speaker** Make notes describing the speaker of the poem. Is the speaker a particular age? How does the speaker feel in the poem? Do his or her feelings change as the poem goes on?

- **Get an Attitude!** What will your own tone, or attitude, be? Thoughtful? Serious? Sarcastic? How will you use your voice to convey your tone? Your tone should convey that of the poem.

SKILLS FOCUS

Listening and Speaking Skills
Present an oral interpretation of a poem.

Rehearse Your Presentation

Memorizing (or Not) You may or may not decide to memorize your poem. Even if you plan to hold and look at a copy of the poem throughout your reading, you should be extremely familiar with it. Should you choose to memorize your poem, this secret will help you: Thoroughly understanding a text makes it much easier to memorize.

Practice, Practice, Practice You'll give a more effective presentation if you've rehearsed it several times. To increase the effectiveness of your delivery, practice using the following **verbal** and **nonverbal techniques** as you rehearse.

GUIDELINES TO IMPROVE DELIVERY

Verbal Techniques

Diction: In speaking, diction refers to the clarity of your pronunciation. Always speak clearly and carefully so that your listeners can understand you.

Emphasis: Stress key words or phrases in your presentation by saying them with a different volume or tone than you have been using.

Pauses: Use pauses—small silences in your presentation—to help listeners understand the meaning of the poem.

Nonverbal Techniques

Eye contact: Look directly into the eyes of as many audience members as you can. Eye contact communicates confidence and sincerity.

Facial expressions: Be relaxed and natural, using a smile, a grimace, or a raised eyebrow to convey the meaning of the poem.

Gestures: Don't be stiff or fidget; make relaxed and natural gestures with your head, hands, and arms as you speak. Move around a bit, rather than being rooted in one place.

Present Your Poem

A Lasting Impression Make a clean copy of the poem. Across the top, write your finished version of the following sentence that begins "If the audience gets just one single impression. . . ." Add any final important interpretive and performance notes. This is your script.

PRACTICE & APPLY 5 Try reading your poem aloud to friends. Prepare notes for your presentation based on their feedback. Practice verbal and nonverbal techniques. Then, deliver your poem.

SKILLS FOCUS

Listening and Speaking Skills
Use appropriate verbal and nonverbal techniques.

Analyzing Poetry

DIRECTIONS: Read the following poem. Then, read and respond to the questions that follow.

The Girl Who Loved the Sky

Anita Endrezze

Outside the second-grade room,
the jacaranda tree blossomed
into purple lanterns, the papery petals
drifted, darkening the windows.
5   Inside, the room smelled like glue.
The desks were made of yellowed wood,
the tops littered with eraser rubbings,
rulers, and big fat pencils.
Colored chalk meant special days.
10   The walls were covered with precise
bright tulips and charts with shiny stars
by certain names. There, I learned
how to make butter by shaking a jar
until the pale cream clotted
15   into one sweet mass. There, I learned
that numbers were fractious° beasts
with dens like dim zeros. And there,
I met a blind girl who thought the sky
tasted like cold metal when it rained
20   and whose eyes were always covered
with the bruised petals of her lids.
She loved the formless sky, defined
only by sounds, or the cool umbrellas
of clouds. On hot, still days
25   we listened to the sky falling
like chalk dust. We heard the noon
whistle of the pig-mash factory,
smelled the sourness of homebound men.
I had no father; she had no eyes;
30   we were best friends. The other girls
drew shaky hopscotch squares
on the dusty asphalt, talked about

---

16. fractious (frak′shəs) *adj.:* hard to manage; rebellious.

Pages 566–568
cover
Literary Skills
Understand
characteristics of
poetry, including
imagery,
figurative
language, and
sound effects.

pajama parties, weekend cookouts,
and parents who bought sleek-finned cars.

35 Alone, we sat in the canvas swings,
our shoes digging into the sand, then pushing,
until we flew high over their heads,
our hands streaked with red rust
from the chains that kept us safe.

40 I was born blind, she said, an act of nature.
Sure, I thought, like birds born
without wings, trees without roots.
I didn't understand. The day she moved
I saw the world clearly; the sky

45 backed away from me like a departing father.
I sat under the jacaranda, catching
the petals in my palm, enclosing them
until my fist was another lantern
hiding a small and bitter flame.

---

1. The **speaker** in this poem is —

  A a blind woman looking back at her lonely childhood

  B a popular girl in second grade

  C a girl who felt like an outsider

  D a child who grew up feeling uneasy in the natural world

2. In line 35, "Alone, we sat in the canvas swings," the poet uses the word *alone* to convey that the speaker and the blind girl —

  F have lost their parents

  G are separated from their classmates

  H are not supervised by their teacher

  J are independent, self-confident children

3. The poet uses the word *papery* in the **image** "the papery petals/drifted" (lines 3–4) to show that the petals are —

  A white

  B stiff

  C lightweight

  D heavy

(continued)

Collection 7: Skills Review

4. An example of **metaphor** in this poem is —

  F "the pale cream clotted" (line 14)

  G "The walls were covered with precise/bright tulips" (lines 10–11)

  H "I saw the world clearly" (line 4)

  J "my fist was another lantern" (line 48)

5. An example of **implied metaphor** is —

  A "The desks were made of yellowed wood,/the tops littered with eraser rubbings" (lines 6–7)

  B "and whose eyes were always covered/with the bruised petals of her lids" (lines 20–21)

  C "dens like dim zeros" (line 17)

  D "the jacaranda tree blossomed" (line 2)

6. Which phrase does *not* include **alliteration**?

  F "our hands streaked with red rust" (line 38)

  G "the cool umbrellas/of clouds" (lines 23–24)

  H "whistle of the pig-mash factory" (line 27)

  J "birds born/without wings" (lines 41–42)

7. "The sky/backed away from me like a departing father" (lines 44–45) is an example of **simile** and —

  A rhyme

  B metaphor

  C onomatopoeia

  D personification

8. This poem is a —

  F sonnet

  G haiku

  H ballad

  J free-verse poem

9. Why does the speaker say, "the sky/backed away from me like a departing father" (lines 44–45)?

  A She is describing an approaching storm.

  B The blind girl loves the sky, and the speaker feels that the girl's leaving is like the loss of her father.

  C She is swinging and feeling sad as she thinks about her father.

  D She thinks her friend's blindness is unnatural, like a sky that moves away from you.

Constructed Response

10. Describe the speaker's **tone** in this poem. Cite specific lines or words to support your opinion.

Collection 7: Skills Review
Writing Skills

Test Practice

DIRECTIONS: Read the following paragraph from a draft of a student's analysis of a poem. Then, answer the questions below it.

(1) In "The Seven Ages of Man," a poem that was written by William Shakespeare, Shakespeare uses figurative language to talk about human nature in a satire. (2) The poem is actually from a speech by Jaques in Shakespeare's comedy *As You Like It.* (3) The metaphor "All the world's a stage / And all the men and women merely players" in the first two lines compares life to a play. (4) Shakespeare also uses similes to make human life seem simple.

1. How could the tone and wordiness of sentence 1 be corrected?

   A "The Seven Ages of Man" is a poem by Shakespeare that uses language that is figurative.

   B Shakespeare wrote "The Seven Ages of Man" and uses figurative language to poke fun at human nature.

   C Shakespeare, with figurative language, ridicules human nature in "The Seven Ages of Man."

   D Shakespeare's "The Seven Ages of Man" uses figurative language to satirize human nature.

2. To support the statement that Shakespeare uses similes, the student could

   F refer to several specific similes within the poem

   G quote similes from another of Shakespeare's works

   H show examples of Shakespeare's metaphors in the poem

   J rewrite Shakespeare's similes to be more familiar to modern audiences

3. Which sentence could be added to develop the reference in sentence 3?

   A The words "merely players" suggest that people simply perform the roles they are given.

   B This is a good metaphor because Shakespeare knew about stages.

   C Later, Shakespeare compares humans to leopards to show that both are simple beasts.

   D Although this line refers to women, the "seven ages" apply only to men.

4. To improve the passage's organization, which sentence should be moved?

   F 1 **H** 3
   G 2 **J** 4

5. To present this passage as part of an oral literary presentation, the student could

   A avoid distractions by not looking at the audience

   B use verbal techniques to stress key ideas or points

   C tell a series of jokes to entertain the audience

   D pause after each sentence to ensure the information sinks in

SKILLS FOCUS

Writing Skills
Write an analysis of a poem.

Collection 8

Crossing Borders

Literary Focus:
Literary Criticism:
Evaluating Style

Informational Reading Focus:
Evaluating Arguments:
Pro and Con

Paris Through the Window (1913) by Marc Chagall.
Oil on canvas (53½″ × 55¾″).

The Solomon R. Guggenheim Museum, New York.
Gift, Solomon R. Guggenheim, 1937 (37.438).

INTERNET

Collection
Resources

Keyword: LE7 9-8

Elements of Literature

Evaluating Style *by* Kylene Beers
THE WRITER'S PERSONAL STAMP

Here are two questions you might be asked about style:

> **1. What kind of music do you like?**
>
> a. I'm a boot-stomping, line-dancing, country-and-western fan.
>
> b. I live for the beat of a rock-and-roll band.
>
> c. I never listen to any music composed after 1890.
>
> **2. How does the inside of your locker look?**
>
> a. Neat. Inside of door is decorated. Books are all lined up.
>
> b. Might have been neat once, but I really can't remember.
>
> c. I have a locker?

The way you answered each question reveals a little about who you are and what your personal style is. Just as your style emerges through what you say and do, a writer's **style** emerges through the way he or she uses words to recreate an experience.

Diction: It's the Way You Say It

Style in writing is revealed chiefly through word choice, or **diction,** and through **sentence patterns.** Some authors write in informal English or even in slang. Others use formal English. While some writers might say, "He could never have done that of which he is accused," others might prefer the less formal "He couldn't have done it."

Some writers use elegant, multisyllabic words; others prefer short, everyday words—*home* instead of *abode; sleepy* instead of *somnolent.*

Some writers like to use **figures of speech:** "The eerie sound pulled me down the hall as if I were a dog on a leash." Others prefer to stick with the literal: "I walked down the hall, trying to trace the eerie sound."

Some writers use short, punchy sentences; others use long, complex ones. The choice depends on the topic and the effects writers want to create.

Here are two paragraphs by two writers. Read each passage, and note their different styles. Which style is more formal? Which is more modern? What details are you basing your answers on?

Restless, shifting, fugacious as time itself is a certain vast bulk of the population of the red brick district of the lower West Side. Homeless, they have a hundred homes. They flit from furnished room to furnished room, transients forever—transients in abode, transients in heart and mind.

—from "The Furnished Room" by O. Henry

But Easter's early morning sun had shown the dress to be a plain ugly cut-down from a white woman's once-was-purple throwaway. It was old-lady-long too, but it didn't hide my skinny legs, which had been greased with Blue Seal Vaseline and powdered with the Arkansas red clay.

—from *I Know Why the Caged Bird Sings* by Maya Angelou

Tone: It's an Attitude

Another element of style is **tone,** a writer's attitude toward a subject, a character, or the audience. Tone isn't only what you say but also *how* you say it. A writer creates tone through word choice.

Read the following sentence from Charles Dickens's description of Uriah Heep, a character in *David Copperfield.* What details reveal how Dickens feels about Uriah? What is Dickens's tone?

I observed that he had not such a thing as a smile about him, and that he could only widen his mouth and make two hard creases down his cheeks, one on each side, to stand for one.

Tone can also be revealed in the way a writer handles plot and **theme.** If a writer provides a happy ending to a conflict, the story might convey a romantic, positive, or hopeful theme. There is a possibility, this writer seems to say, that life will reward us with great joys. But what if all a writer's characters come to tragic or disappointing ends? Then you might determine that the writer is pessimistic, that he or she feels that life, in the long run, is unfulfilling.

Mood: An Emotional Atmosphere

Mood is the feeling a story evokes. Mood is also created by diction and figures of speech. Many writers are famous for their ability to evoke particular moods. Read this description from Edgar Allan Poe's "The Fall of the House of Usher." What is the mood in this passage? Which words create that mood?

During the whole of a dull, dark, and soundless day in the autumn of the year, when the clouds hung oppressively low in the heavens, I had been passing alone, on horseback, through a singularly dreary tract of country; and at length found myself, as the shades of evening drew on, within view of the melancholy House of Usher.

How to Talk About Style: The Vocabulary of Criticism

Literary critics often focus on style. They evaluate how well a writer uses language, sets a mood, and establishes tone. As you take on the role of a literary critic, you might find the following words helpful in describing **tone** and **mood:**

Words for Tone		
admiring	comic	sarcastic
affectionate	forgiving	serious
bitter	mocking	vengeful

Words for Mood		
eerie	joyful	peaceful
gloomy	mysterious	sad

Practice

Choose one of these topics: tests, friends, school lunches. Then, write about it twice. Write one paragraph in the **formal** style you would use in a research paper. Write the other in the **informal** style you would use when talking with friends.

Introducing the Collection Theme

Crossing Borders

Make the Connection

Quickwrite 🖉

Life is filled with borders—geographical, cultural, social, even historical, for example. What kinds of borders exist in your life and the world around you? What can happen when you cross one of these borders? Jot down your thoughts.

Exploring the Theme: Crossing Borders

As the selections in this collection reveal, when you cross a border, a life-changing discovery or event can take place. In the short story "A Sound of Thunder," devastating consequences occur when time travelers cross the border between the present and the past. "To Da-duh, in Memoriam" and "How to Eat a Guava" explore the effects of crossing geographical and cultural borders. You'll also read two opposing arguments in which the authors examine the borders separating humans from nature and explore our impact on the environment. In "Caline," the story you're about to read, a girl's journey to a new world leads to an unexpected discovery.

Literary Focus

Style

Style refers to the many ways writers use language. For example, writers can create a distinctive style through their choice of **sentence structure** (long, complex sentences or short, simple ones). The way writers use **imagery**—words or phrases that appeal to one or more of our senses—also shapes their style. **Mood**—the feeling a story evokes—is part of a writer's style as well. As you read "Caline," think about how Chopin's style enables her to create a very brief story that packs a powerful punch.

Background

"Caline" takes place in Louisiana during the 1800s. There are two settings in the story: the log cabin and farm where Caline lives with her parents and the city of New Orleans. Caline and her family are Acadians, descendants of the French people who were forced out of eastern Canada by the British in the 1750s. At the time in which this story is set, the Acadians in Louisiana spoke a dialect of French and, in general, kept to their old ways. Today, the descendants of the Acadians in Louisiana are called Cajuns.

Caline

Kate Chopin

The sun was just far enough in the west to send inviting shadows. In the center of a small field, and in the shade of a haystack which was there, a girl lay sleeping. She had slept long and soundly, when something awoke her as suddenly as if it had been a blow. She opened her eyes and stared a moment up in the cloudless sky. She yawned and stretched her long brown legs and arms, lazily. Then she arose, never minding the bits of straw that clung to her black hair, to her red bodice,[1] and the blue cotonade[2] skirt that did not reach her naked ankles. ❶

The log cabin in which she dwelt with her parents was just outside the enclosure in which she had been sleeping. Beyond was a small clearing that did duty as a cotton field. All else was dense wood, except the long stretch that curved round the brow of the hill, and in which glittered the steel rails of the Texas and Pacific road. ❷

When Caline emerged from the shadow she saw a long train of passenger coaches standing in view, where they must have stopped abruptly. It was that sudden stopping which had awakened her; for such a thing had not happened before within her recollection, and she looked stupid, at first, with astonishment. There seemed to be something wrong with the engine; and some of the passengers who dismounted went forward to investigate the trouble. Others came strolling along in the direction of the cabin, where Caline stood under an old gnarled mulberry tree, staring. Her father had halted his mule at the end of the cotton row, and stood staring also, leaning upon his plow.

There were ladies in the party. They walked awkwardly in their high-heeled boots over the rough, uneven ground, and held up their skirts mincingly.[3] They twirled parasols[4] over their shoulders, and laughed immoderately at the funny things which their masculine companions were saying.

---

1. **bodice** (bäd′is) *n.*: fitted upper part of a dress.
2. **cotonade** (kät′un·ād′) *n.* used as *adj.*: coarse cotton fabric.
3. **mincingly** (min′siŋ·lē) *adv.*: done in an elegant or dainty manner to impress people.
4. **parasols** (par′ə·sôlz′) *n.*: lightweight umbrellas that provide protection from the sun.

STYLE

❶ What **images** in this paragraph help you visualize the girl and the scene?

STYLE

❷ How does the **image** of the steel rails contrast with the other images Chopin uses in this paragraph to describe the setting?

Cabin in the Cotton (before 1937) by Horace Pippin (1888–1946). Oil on panel. 46 x 84 cm.

In memory of Frances W. Pick from her children Thomas F. Pick and Mary P. Hines. 1990.417. Reproduction ©The Art Institute of Chicago.

THEME

❸ How are the ladies who had been riding on the train different from Caline? What creates a boundary between them?

THEME AND STYLE

❹ In one simple sentence, Chopin tells us how Caline is affected by her encounter with the train passengers. What is that sentence? How would you interpret its meaning?

They tried to talk to Caline, but could not understand the French patois[5] with which she answered them. ❸

One of the men—a pleasant-faced youngster—drew a sketch book from his pocket and began to make a picture of the girl. She stayed motionless, her hands behind her, and her wide eyes fixed earnestly upon him.

Before he had finished there was a summons from the train; and all went scampering hurriedly away. The engine screeched, it sent a few lazy puffs into the still air, and in another moment or two had vanished, bearing its human cargo with it.

Caline could not feel the same after that. She looked with new and strange interest upon the trains of cars that passed so swiftly back and forth across her vision, each day; and wondered whence these people came, and whither they were going. ❹

Her mother and father could not tell her, except to say that they came from "loin là bas,"[6] and were going "Djieu sait é où."[7]

One day she walked miles down the track to talk with the old flagman,[8] who stayed down there by the big water tank. Yes, he knew. Those people came from the great cities in the north, and were going to the city in the south. He knew all about the city; it was a grand place. He had lived there once. His sister lived there now; and she

---

5. **patois** (pa′twä′) *n.*: form of a language that differs from the accepted standard; dialect.
6. **loin là bas:** French dialect for "far away; over there."
7. **Djieu sait é où:** French dialect for "God knows where."
8. **flagman** *n.*: years ago, a man who signaled a train with a flag or lantern.

would be glad enough to have so fine a girl as Caline to help her cook and scrub, and tend the babies. And he thought Caline might earn as much as five dollars a month, in the city.

So she went; in a new cotonade, and her Sunday shoes; with a sacredly guarded scrawl that the flagman sent to his sister.

The woman lived in a tiny, stuccoed house, with green blinds, and three wooden steps leading down to the banquette.[9] There seemed to be hundreds like it along the street. Over the house tops loomed the tall masts of ships, and the hum of the French market could be heard on a still morning.

Caline was at first bewildered.[10] She had to readjust all her preconceptions to fit the reality of it. The flagman's sister was a kind and gentle task-mistress. At the end of a week or two she wanted to know how the girl liked it all. Caline liked it very well, for it was pleasant, on Sunday afternoons, to stroll with the children under the great, solemn sugar sheds; or to sit upon the compressed cotton bales, watching the stately steamers, the graceful boats, and noisy little tugs that plied the waters of the Mississippi. And it filled her

---

9. **banquette** (ban·ket') *n.:* Southern term for "sidewalk."
10. **bewildered** (bē·wil'dərd) *v.* used as *adj.:* hopelessly confused; puzzled.

New Orleans, 1844, The Levee (detail) by Currier & Ives. Lithograph.

The Granger Collection, New York.

THEME

❺ At this point, what are Caline's reactions to crossing the border into the city?

STYLE

❻ How would you define the **mood** in this paragraph? Which details help create that mood?

with agreeable excitement to go to the French market, where the handsome Gascon[11] butchers were eager to present their compliments and little Sunday bouquets to the pretty Acadian girl; and to throw fistfuls of *lagniappe*[12] into her basket. ❺

When the woman asked her again after another week if she were still pleased, she was not so sure. And again when she questioned Caline the girl turned away, and went to sit behind the big, yellow cistern,[13] to cry unobserved. For she knew now that it was not the great city and its crowds of people she had so eagerly sought; but the pleasant-faced boy, who had made her picture that day under the mulberry tree. ❻

---

11. **Gascon** (gas′kən): from Gascony, in southwestern France.
12. **lagniappe** (lan•yap′) *n.:* Southern term for "small present."
13. **cistern** (sis′tərn) *n.:* large container or tank for holding water.

Meet the Writer
Kate Chopin

The Missouri Historical Society, St. Louis, Missouri.

Writing Across Borders

The vastly different worlds portrayed in "Caline" are ones that Kate Chopin (c. 1850–1904) knew well. Chopin was born in St. Louis, Missouri. Her father, an Irish immigrant who became a successful merchant, died in a Pacific Railroad train accident when she was a young child. Her mother was an upper-class French Creole (a descendant of French settlers), and Chopin, as a teenager, was greatly admired in St. Louis's high society.

Once married, Chopin first lived in New Orleans, where she participated in the city's cultural life. She and her French Creole husband then moved to his family's plantations in northwestern Louisiana—in a small town consisting of six hundred or seven hundred people and one street surrounded by fields. Eventually, Chopin drew on these worlds for the subjects of her fiction.

Chopin began writing after the death of her husband. Moving back to St. Louis and raising six children, she could find only one or two days a week to work, but she produced three novels and more than one hundred short stories. In her lifetime she was praised for her depiction of Louisiana life but harshly criticized for her exploration of love, marriage, and women's roles, especially in her novel *The Awakening* (1899). It wasn't until the 1970s that *The Awakening* was recognized as a major American novel and Chopin's reputation as an important writer was secured.

After You Read

Response and Analysis

Reading Check

1. Why does Caline talk to the flagman? What action does she take as a result of the conversation?

Thinking Critically

2. Although she does not provide a lot of information about Caline, Chopin brings the character to life for the reader. Think about Caline's appearance, her thoughts, and her actions. Then, **characterize** her. Use examples from the story to support your points.

3. Review your Quickwrite notes, and then think about how the collection theme "Crossing Borders" relates to this story. What kinds of borders exist in the story? What does Caline discover when these borders are crossed?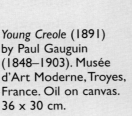

Literary Criticism

4. Through the use of **images** that appeal to our senses of sight and hearing, Chopin skillfully contrasts the city of New Orleans with Caline's home in the country. For each location, list at least four images in a chart like the one at right. Then, explain what these images tell you about the differences between the two locations.

5. To make her point in this story, Chopin gives the reader only a few choice details about the characters, settings, and events. Do you find her **style** effective, or do you wish she had given you more details? (For example, do you wish she had told you more about the "pleasant-faced" boy?) Explain your response.

Exploring the Theme
Crossing Borders

The rest of the selections in this collection center on the crossing of borders. As you read, think about the types of borders that are crossed and the ways life can change as a result.

Images	
Country	**City**

Young Creole (1891) by Paul Gauguin (1848–1903). Musée d'Art Moderne, Troyes, France. Oil on canvas. 36 x 30 cm.

SKILLS FOCUS

Literary Focus
Analyze elements of style, including sentence structure, imagery, and mood.

Caline **579**

A Sound of Thunder

Make the Connection

Quickwrite ✏️

"A Sound of Thunder" is a story about time travel. Jot down some thoughts about where you'd go if you could travel through time. Would you choose the past or the future as your destination? Would you stay in the region where you live, or would you go someplace else? How would traveling through time affect your life?

Literary Focus

Style: Figurative Language and Mood

Ray Bradbury tells this science fiction story in a lush style. In a literary work, **style** refers to the particular way a writer uses language. Style is largely created through **diction,** or word choice, and sentence patterns.

Bradbury's style owes much to vivid **images** and imaginative **figurative language.** (For more about figurative language—similes, metaphors, and personification—see pages 504–505.) These elements help him create one of the most exotic **settings** you will ever enter—a setting with a prehistoric creature whose "armored flesh glittered like a thousand green coins"—and a minor setting placed far into the future.

Setting and figurative language help to shape a story's **mood,** the feeling or the atmosphere it evokes. For example, the night sky might be a soft blanket or an icy lake—each metaphor suggests a different mood. Notice how Bradbury's language propels you into a frightening, exotic world—where anything can happen.

Reading Skills

Cause and Effect: Chain Reaction

The events in a plot are interconnected, like links in a chain: One event causes another event, which causes another event, and so on. When you read, ask, "Why do these events happen? How do they affect the plot or the characters?" This story is very much *about* causes and effects. The questions at the open-book signs will help you examine them.

Vocabulary Development

annihilate (ə·nī′ə·lāt′) *v.*: destroy; wipe out.

expendable (ek·spen′də·bəl) *adj.*: worth sacrificing to gain an objective.

depression (dē·presh′ən) *n.*: major economic downturn. (*Depression* also means "sadness.")

paradox (par′ə·däks′) *n.*: something that has or seems to have contradictory qualities.

delirium (di·lir′ē·əm) *n.*: extreme mental disturbance, often accompanied by hallucinations (seeing things that are not there).

resilient (ri·zil′yənt) *adj.*: able to return to its original shape quickly after being stretched or compressed; elastic.

remit (ri·mit′) *v.*: return payment.

revoke (ri·vōk′) *v.*: cancel; withdraw.

primeval (prī·mē′vəl) *adj.*: primitive; of the earliest times.

subliminal (sub·lim′ə·nəl) *adj.*: below the level of awareness.

A SOUND OF THUNDER

Ray Bradbury

"Does this safari guarantee I come back alive?"

The sign on the wall seemed to quaver under a film of sliding warm water. Eckels felt his eyelids blink over his stare, and the sign burned in this momentary darkness:

TIME SAFARI, INC.

Safaris to any
year in the past.
You name the animal.
We take you there.
You shoot it.

A warm phlegm gathered in Eckels's throat; he swallowed and pushed it down. The muscles around his mouth formed a smile as he put his hand slowly out upon the air, and in that hand waved a check for ten thousand dollars to the man behind the desk.

"Does this safari guarantee I come back alive?"

"We guarantee nothing," said the official, "except the dinosaurs." He turned. "This is Mr. Travis, your Safari Guide in the Past. He'll tell you what and where to shoot. If he says no shooting, no shooting. If you disobey instructions, there's a stiff penalty of another ten thousand dollars, plus possible government action, on your return."

Eckels glanced across the vast office at a mass and tangle, a snaking and humming of wires and steel boxes, at an aurora[1] that flickered now orange, now silver, now blue. There was a sound like a gigantic bonfire burning all of Time, all the years and all the parchment calendars, all the hours piled high and set aflame.

A touch of the hand and this burning would, on the instant, beautifully reverse itself. Eckels remembered the wording in the advertisements to the letter. Out of chars and ashes, out of dust and coals, like golden salamanders, the old years, the green years, might leap; roses sweeten the air, white hair turn Irish-black, wrinkles vanish; all, everything fly back to seed, flee death, rush down to their beginnings, suns rise in western skies and set in glorious easts, moons eat themselves opposite to the custom, all and everything cupping one in another like Chinese boxes,[2] rabbits into hats, all and everything returning to the fresh death, the seed death, the green death, to the time before the beginning. A touch of a hand might do it, the merest touch of a hand.

STYLE

1. Find at least three examples of **figurative language** (similes, metaphors, and personification) in the previous two paragraphs.

"Unbelievable." Eckels breathed, the light of the Machine on his thin face. "A real Time Machine." He shook his head. "Makes you think. If the election had gone badly yesterday, I might be here now running away from the results. Thank God Keith won. He'll make a fine President of the United States."

"Yes," said the man behind the desk. "We're lucky. If Deutscher had gotten in, we'd have the worst kind of dictatorship. There's an anti-everything man for you, a militarist, anti-Christ, anti-human, anti-intellectual. People called us up, you know, joking but not joking. Said if Deutscher became President they wanted to go live in 1492. Of course it's not our business to conduct Escapes, but to form Safaris. Anyway, Keith's President now. All you got to worry about is—"

"Shooting my dinosaur," Eckels finished it for him.

"A *Tyrannosaurus rex*. The Tyrant Lizard, the most incredible monster in history. Sign

---

1. **aurora** (ô·rôr′ə) *n.:* Bradbury is comparing the glow coming from the time machine to an aurora, a colorful display of light that appears at night in the skies near the North and South Poles.

2. **Chinese boxes**: set of boxes, each of which fits into the next-largest one.

this release. Anything happens to you, we're not responsible. Those dinosaurs are hungry."

Eckels flushed angrily. "Trying to scare me!"

"Frankly, yes. We don't want anyone going who'll panic at the first shot. Six Safari leaders were killed last year, and a dozen hunters. We're here to give you the severest thrill a *real* hunter ever asked for. Traveling you back sixty million years to bag the biggest game in all of Time. Your personal check's still there. Tear it up."

Mr. Eckels looked at the check. His fingers twitched.

"Good luck," said the man behind the desk. "Mr. Travis, he's all yours."

They moved silently across the room, taking their guns with them, toward the Machine, toward the silver metal and the roaring light.

First a day and then a night and then a day and then a night, then it was day-night-day-night-day. A week, a month, a year, a decade! A.D. 2055. A.D. 2019. 1999! 1957! Gone! The Machine roared.

They put on their oxygen helmets and tested the intercoms.

Eckels swayed on the padded seat, his face pale, his jaw stiff. He felt the trembling in his arms, and he looked down and found his hands tight on the new rifle. There were four other men in the Machine. Travis, the Safari Leader; his assistant, Lesperance; and two other hunters, Billings and Kramer. They sat looking at each other, and the years blazed around them.

"Can these guns get a dinosaur cold?" Eckels felt his mouth saying.

"If you hit them right," said Travis on the helmet radio. "Some dinosaurs have two brains, one in the head, another far down the spinal column. We stay away from those. That's stretching luck. Put your first two shots into the eyes, if you can, blind them, and go back into the brain."

The Machine howled. Time was a film run backward. Suns fled and ten million moons fled after them. "Think," said Eckels. "Every hunter that ever lived would envy us today. This makes Africa seem like Illinois."

The Machine slowed; its scream fell to a murmur. The Machine stopped.

The sun stopped in the sky.

The fog that had enveloped the Machine blew away and they were in an old time, a very old time indeed, three hunters and two Safari Heads with their blue metal guns across their knees.

"Christ isn't born yet," said Travis. "Moses has not gone to the mountain to talk with God. The Pyramids are still in the earth, waiting to be cut out and put up. *Remember* that. Alexander, Caesar, Napoleon, Hitler—none of them exists."

The men nodded.

"That"—Mr. Travis pointed—"is the jungle of sixty million two thousand and fifty-five years before President Keith."

He indicated a metal path that struck off into green wilderness, over streaming swamp, among giant ferns and palms.

"And that," he said, "is the Path, laid by Time Safari for your use. It floats six inches above the earth. Doesn't touch so much as one grass blade, flower, or tree. It's an anti-gravity metal. Its purpose is to keep you from touching this world of the Past in any way. Stay on the Path. Don't go off it. I repeat. *Don't go off.* For *any* reason! If you fall off, there's a penalty. And don't shoot any animal we don't okay."

"Why?" asked Eckels.

They sat in the ancient wilderness. Far birds' cries blew on a wind, and the smell of tar and an old salt sea, moist grasses, and flowers the color of blood.

"We don't want to change the Future. We don't belong here in the Past. The government doesn't *like* us here. We have to pay big graft[3] to keep our franchise. A Time Machine is finicky business. Not knowing it, we might kill an important animal, a small bird, a roach, a flower even, thus destroying an important link in a growing species."

"That's not clear," said Eckels.

"All right," Travis continued, "say we accidentally kill one mouse here. That means all the future families of this one particular mouse are destroyed, right?"

"Right."

"And all the families of the families of the families of that one mouse! With a stamp of your foot, you annihilate first one, then a dozen,

---

3. graft *n.:* bribes.

Vocabulary
annihilate (ə·nī′ə·lāt′) *v.:* destroy; wipe out.

then a thousand, a million, a *billion* possible mice!"

"So they're dead," said Eckels. "So what?"

"So what?" Travis snorted quietly. "Well, what about the foxes that'll need those mice to survive? For want of ten mice, a fox dies. For want of ten foxes, a lion starves. For want of a lion, all manner of insects, vultures, infinite billions of life forms are thrown into chaos and destruction. Eventually it all boils down to this: Fifty-nine million years later, a cave man, one of a dozen in the *entire world,* goes hunting wild boar or saber-toothed tiger for food. But you, friend, have *stepped* on all the tigers in that region. By stepping on *one* single mouse. So the cave man starves. And the cave man, please note, is not just *any* <u>expendable</u> man, no! He is an *entire future nation.* From his loins would have sprung ten sons. From *their* loins one hundred sons, and thus onward to a civilization. Destroy this one man, and you destroy a race, a people, an entire history of life. It is comparable to slaying some of Adam's grandchildren. The stomp of your foot, on one mouse, could start an earthquake, the effects of which could shake our earth and destinies down through Time, to their very foundations. With the death of that one cave man, a billion others yet unborn are throttled in the womb. Perhaps Rome never rises on its seven hills. Perhaps Europe is forever a dark forest, and only Asia waxes healthy and teeming.[4] Step on a mouse and you crush the Pyramids. Step on a mouse and you leave your print, like a Grand Canyon, across Eternity. Queen Elizabeth might never be born, Washington might not cross the Delaware, there might never be a United States at all. So be careful. Stay on the Path. *Never* step off!"

CAUSE AND EFFECT

2. In this cause-and-effect chain, what small **cause** leads to what enormous **effect**?

---

4. **teeming** (tēm′iŋ) *adj.:* swarming; overflowing.

"I see," said Eckels. "Then it wouldn't pay for us even to touch the *grass*?"

"Correct. Crushing certain plants could add up infinitesimally.[5] A little error here would multiply in sixty million years, all out of proportion. Of course maybe our theory is wrong. Maybe Time *can't* be changed by us. Or maybe it can be changed only in little subtle ways. A dead mouse here makes an insect imbalance there, a population disproportion later, a bad harvest further on, a <u>depression</u>, mass starvation, and, finally, a change in *social* temperament in far-flung countries. Something much more subtle, like that. Perhaps only a soft breath, a whisper, a hair, pollen on the air, such a slight, slight change that unless you looked close you wouldn't see it. Who knows? Who really can say he knows? We don't know. We're guessing. But until we do know for certain whether our messing around in Time *can* make a big roar or a little rustle in history, we're being careful. This Machine, this Path, your clothing and bodies, were sterilized, as you know, before the journey. We wear these oxygen helmets so we can't introduce our bacteria into an ancient atmosphere."

"How do we know which animals to shoot?"

"They're marked with red paint," said Travis. "Today, before our journey, we sent Lesperance here back with the Machine. He came to this particular era and followed certain animals."

"Studying them?"

"Right," said Lesperance. "I track them through their entire existence, noting which of them lives longest. Very few. How many times they mate. Not often. Life's short. When I find one that's going to die when a tree falls on him,

---

5. **infinitesimally** (in′fin·i·tes′i·məl·ē) *adv.:* in amounts too small to be measured.

Vocabulary

expendable (ek·spen′də·bəl) *adj.:* worth sacrificing to gain an objective.

depression (dē·presh′ən) *n.:* major economic downturn. (*Depression* also means "sadness.")

or one that drowns in a tar pit, I note the exact hour, minute, and second. I shoot a paint bomb. It leaves a red patch on his side. We can't miss it. Then I correlate our arrival in the Past so that we meet the Monster not more than two minutes before he would have died anyway. This way, we kill only animals with no future, that are never going to mate again. You see how *careful* we are?"

"But if you came back this morning in Time," said Eckels eagerly, "you must've bumped into *us*, our Safari! How did it turn out? Was it successful? Did all of us get through —alive?"

Travis and Lesperance gave each other a look.

"That'd be a paradox," said the latter. "Time doesn't permit that sort of mess—a man meeting himself. When such occasions threaten, Time steps aside. Like an airplane hitting an air pocket. You felt the Machine jump just before we stopped? That was us passing ourselves on the way back to the Future. We saw nothing. There's no way of telling *if* this expedition was a success, *if we* got our monster, or whether all of us— meaning *you*, Mr. Eckels—got out alive."

Eckels smiled palely.

"Cut that," said Travis sharply. "Everyone on his feet!"

They were ready to leave the Machine.

The jungle was high and the jungle was broad and the jungle was the entire world forever and forever. Sounds like music and sounds like flying tents filled the sky, and those were pterodactyls soaring with cavernous gray wings, gigantic bats of delirium and night fever. Eckels, balanced on the narrow Path, aimed his rifle playfully.

"Stop that!" said Travis. "Don't even aim for fun, blast you! If your guns should go off—"

Eckels flushed.

"Where's our *Tyrannosaurus*?"

Lesperance checked his wristwatch. "Up ahead. We'll bisect his trail in sixty seconds. Look for the red paint! Don't shoot till we give the word. Stay on the Path. *Stay on the Path!*"

They moved forward in the wind of morning.

"Strange," murmured Eckels. "Up ahead, sixty million years, Election Day over. Keith made President. Everyone celebrating. And here we are, a million years lost, and they don't exist. The things we worried about for months, a lifetime, not even born or thought of yet."

"Safety catches off, everyone!" ordered Travis. "You, first shot, Eckels. Second, Billings. Third, Kramer."

"I've hunted tiger, wild boar, buffalo, elephant, but now, this is *it*," said Eckels. "I'm shaking like a kid."

Vocabulary

paradox (par′ə·däks′) *n.*: something that has or seems to have contradictory qualities.

delirium (di·lir′ē·əm) *n.*: extreme mental disturbance, often accompanied by hallucinations (seeing things that are not there).

"Ah," said Travis.

Everyone stopped.

Travis raised his hand. "Ahead," he whispered. "In the mist. There he is. There's His Royal Majesty now."

The jungle was wide and full of twitterings, rustlings, murmurs, and sighs.

Suddenly it all ceased, as if someone had shut a door.

Silence.

A sound of thunder.

Out of the mist, one hundred yards away, came *Tyrannosaurus rex*.

"It," whispered Eckels. "It . . ."

"Sh!"

It came on great oiled, resilient, striding legs. It towered thirty feet above half of the trees, a great evil god, folding its delicate watchmaker's claws close to its oily reptilian chest. Each lower leg was a piston, a thousand pounds of white bone, sunk in thick ropes of muscle, sheathed over in a gleam of pebbled skin like the mail[6] of a terrible warrior. Each thigh was a ton of meat, ivory, and steel mesh. And from the great breathing cage of the upper body those two delicate arms dangled out front, arms with hands which might pick up and examine men like toys, while the snake neck coiled. And the head itself, a ton of sculptured stone, lifted easily upon the sky. Its mouth gaped, exposing a fence of teeth like daggers. Its eyes rolled, ostrich eggs, empty of all expression save hunger. It closed its mouth in a death grin. It ran, its pelvic bones crushing aside trees and bushes, its taloned feet clawing damp earth, leaving prints six inches deep wherever it settled its weight. It ran with a gliding ballet step, far too poised and balanced for its ten tons. It moved into a sunlit arena warily, its beautifully reptilian hands feeling the air.

> **STYLE**
>
> **3.** What **descriptive details** and **figures of speech** make the dinosaur seem terrifying?

6. **mail** *n.*: here, flexible metal armor.

"Why, why," Eckels twitched his mouth. "It could reach up and grab the moon."

"Sh!" Travis jerked angrily. "He hasn't seen us yet."

"It can't be killed." Eckels pronounced this verdict quietly, as if there could be no argument. He had weighed the evidence and this was his considered opinion. The rifle in his hands seemed a cap gun. "We were fools to come. This is impossible."

"Shut up!" hissed Travis.

"Nightmare."

"Turn around," commanded Travis. "Walk quietly to the Machine. We'll remit one half your fee."

"I didn't realize it would be this *big*," said Eckels. "I miscalculated, that's all. And now I want out."

"It *sees* us!"

"There's the red paint on its chest!"

The Tyrant Lizard raised itself. Its armored flesh glittered like a thousand green coins. The coins, crusted with slime, steamed. In the slime, tiny insects wriggled, so that the entire body seemed to twitch and undulate,[7] even while the monster itself did not move. It exhaled. The stink of raw flesh blew down the wilderness.

"Get me out of here," said Eckels. "It was never like this before. I was always sure I'd come through alive. I had good guides, good safaris, and safety. This time, I figured wrong. I've met my match and admit it. This is too much for me to get hold of."

"Don't run," said Lesperance. "Turn around. Hide in the Machine."

"Yes." Eckels seemed to be numb. He looked

7. **undulate** (un′jə ·lāt′) *v.*: move in waves.

Vocabulary

resilient (ri·zil′yənt) *adj.*: able to return to its original shape quickly after being stretched or compressed; elastic.

remit (ri·mit′) *v.*: return payment.

at his feet as if trying to make them move. He gave a grunt of helplessness.

"Eckels!"

He took a few steps, blinking, shuffling.

"Not *that* way!"

The Monster, at the first motion, lunged forward with a terrible scream. It covered one hundred yards in six seconds. The rifles jerked up and blazed fire. A windstorm from the beast's mouth engulfed them in the stench of slime and old blood. The Monster roared, teeth glittering with sun.

Eckels, not looking back, walked blindly to the edge of the Path, his gun limp in his arms, stepped off the Path, and walked, not knowing it, in the jungle. His feet sank into green moss. His legs moved him, and he felt alone and remote from the events behind.

The rifles cracked again. Their sound was lost in shriek and lizard thunder. The great level of the reptile's tail swung up, lashed sideways. Trees exploded in clouds of leaf and branch. The Monster twitched its jeweler's hands down to fondle at the men, to twist them in half, to crush them like berries, to cram them into its teeth and its screaming throat. Its boulder-stone eyes leveled with the men. They saw themselves mirrored. They fired at the metallic eyelids and the blazing black iris.

Like a stone idol, like a mountain avalanche, *Tyrannosaurus* fell. Thundering, it clutched trees, pulled them with it. It wrenched and tore the metal Path. The men flung themselves back and away. The body hit, ten tons of cold flesh and stone. The guns fired. The Monster lashed its armored tail, twitched its snake jaws, and lay still. A fount of blood spurted from its throat. Somewhere inside, a sac of fluids burst. Sickening gushes drenched the hunters. They stood, red and glistening.

The thunder faded.

The jungle was silent. After the avalanche, a green peace. After the nightmare, morning.

A CLOSER LOOK

How Did They Disappear?

What caused the extinction of the dinosaurs? How could such a dominant, thriving population disappear? Scientists have wondered whether their extinction was the result of a gradual decline or a sudden catastrophe. Now some geologists think they've found the answer—in rocks.

Geologists know the secret of time travel: They know that layers—or sediments—of rock can reveal the history of the earth. It is in these layers that a team of scientists from the University of California at Berkeley found evidence indicating that the dinosaurs were wiped out after an asteroid or a comet—nobody knows which it was—slammed into the earth 65 million years ago. It's a theory that combines some of science fiction's favorite subjects: time travel, asteroids, and dinosaurs.

The rocks tell the story. All over the world the sediment that forms the boundary between the age of the dinosaurs and the age following their extinction contains deposits of iridium, a mineral that is extremely rare on earth but common in outer space. Some scientists believe that the iridium was deposited when a huge asteroid or a comet—about six miles across—struck the earth.

Scientists even believe that they have discovered the site where the comet or asteroid hit, in Chicxulub (chek′shoo·loob′), on the coast of the Yucatán Peninsula in Mexico. The proof is in the rocks, which contain not just deposits of iridium but also all the other right minerals and chemicals to prove the theory.

Billings and Kramer sat on the pathway and threw up. Travis and Lesperance stood with smoking rifles, cursing steadily.

In the Time Machine, on his face, Eckels lay shivering. He had found his way back to the Path, climbed into the Machine.

Travis came walking, glanced at Eckels, took cotton gauze from a metal box, and returned to the others, who were sitting on the Path.

"Clean up."

They wiped the blood from their helmets. They began to curse too. The Monster lay, a hill of solid flesh. Within, you could hear the sighs and murmurs as the furthest chambers of it died, the organs malfunctioning, liquids running a final instant from pocket to sac to spleen, everything shutting off, closing up forever. It was like standing by a wrecked locomotive or a steam shovel at quitting time, all valves being released or levered tight. Bones cracked; the tonnage of its own flesh, off balance, dead weight, snapped the delicate forearms, caught underneath. The meat settled, quivering.

Another cracking sound. Overhead, a gigantic tree branch broke from its heavy mooring, fell. It crashed upon the dead beast with finality.

"There." Lesperance checked his watch. "Right on time. That's the giant tree that was scheduled to fall and kill this animal originally." He glanced at the two hunters. "You want the trophy picture?"

"What?"

"We can't take a trophy back to the Future. The body has to stay right here where it would have died originally, so the insects, birds, and bacteria can get at it, as they were intended to. Everything in balance. The body stays. But we *can* take a picture of you standing near it."

The two men tried to think, but gave up, shaking their heads.

CAUSE AND EFFECT

4. Why doesn't the hunters' killing the dinosaur affect the future?

The impact would have caused massive fires, tidal waves, and floods, but the dust created by the impact—composed of iridium and other minerals—caused even bigger problems. The dust blocked the sunlight; the earth became cool and dark, plants died, and the food chain was devastated. Eventually the dust settled, but then a greenhouse effect set in, creating temperatures too high to support most life forms. Almost all life on earth vanished. The 150-million-year reign of the dinosaurs had reached its catastrophic end.

They let themselves be led along the metal Path. They sank wearily into the Machine cushions. They gazed back at the ruined Monster, the stagnating mound, where already strange reptilian birds and golden insects were busy at the steaming armor.

A sound on the floor of the Time Machine stiffened them. Eckels sat there, shivering.

"I'm sorry," he said at last.

"Get up!" cried Travis.

Eckels got up.

"Go out on that Path alone," said Travis. He had his rifle pointed. "You're not coming back in the Machine. We're leaving you here!"

Lesperance seized Travis's arm. "Wait—"

"Stay out of this!" Travis shook his hand away. "This fool nearly killed us. But it isn't *that* so much, no. It's his *shoes*! Look at them! He ran off the Path. That *ruins* us! We'll forfeit! Thousands of dollars of insurance! We guarantee no one leaves the Path. He left it. Oh, the fool! I'll have to report to the government. They might <u>revoke</u> our license to travel. Who knows *what* he's done to Time, to History!"

"Take it easy, all he did was kick up some dirt."

"How do we *know*?" cried Travis. "We don't know anything! It's all a mystery! Get out of here, Eckels!"

Eckels fumbled his shirt. "I'll pay anything. A hundred thousand dollars!"

Travis glared at Eckels's checkbook and spat. "Go out there. The Monster's next to the Path. Stick your arms up to your elbows in his mouth. Then you can come back with us."

"That's unreasonable!"

"The Monster's dead, you idiot. The bullets! The bullets can't be left behind. They don't belong in the Past; they might change anything. Here's my knife. Dig them out!"

The jungle was alive again, full of the old tremorings and bird cries. Eckels turned slowly to regard the <u>primeval</u> garbage dump, that

hill of nightmares and terror. After a long time, like a sleepwalker he shuffled out along the Path.

He returned, shuddering, five minutes later, his arms soaked and red to the elbows. He held out his hands. Each held a number of steel bullets. Then he fell. He lay where he fell, not moving.

"You didn't have to make him do that," said Lesperance.

"Didn't I? It's too early to tell." Travis nudged the still body. "He'll live. Next time he won't go hunting game like this. Okay." He jerked his thumb wearily at Lesperance. "Switch on. Let's go home."

1492. 1776. 1812.

They cleaned their hands and faces. They changed their caking shirts and pants. Eckels was up and around again, not speaking. Travis glared at him for a full ten minutes.

"Don't look at me," cried Eckels. "I haven't done anything."

"Who can tell?"

"Just ran off the Path, that's all, a little mud on my shoes—what do you want me to do—get down and pray?"

"We might need it. I'm warning you, Eckels, I might kill you yet. I've got my gun ready."

"I'm innocent. I've done nothing!"

1999. 2000. 2055.

The Machine stopped.

"Get out," said Travis.

The room was there as they had left it. But not the same as they had left it. The same man sat behind the same desk. But the same man did not quite sit behind the same desk.

Travis looked around swiftly. "Everything okay here?" he snapped.

Vocabulary

revoke (ri·vōk′) *v*.: cancel; withdraw.

primeval (prī·mē′vəl) *adj*.: primitive; of the earliest times.

"Fine. Welcome home!"

Travis did not relax. He seemed to be looking at the very atoms of the air itself, at the way the sun poured through the one high window.

"Okay, Eckels, get out. Don't ever come back."

Eckels could not move.

"You heard me," said Travis. "What're you *staring* at?"

Eckels stood smelling of the air, and there was a thing to the air, a chemical taint so subtle, so slight, that only a faint cry of his <u>subliminal</u> senses warned him it was there. The colors, white, gray, blue, orange, in the wall, in the furniture, in the sky beyond the window, were . . . were . . . And there was a *feel*. His flesh twitched. His hands twitched. He stood drinking the oddness with the pores of his body. Somewhere, someone must have been screaming one of those whistles that only a dog can hear. His body screamed silence in return. Beyond this room, beyond this wall, beyond this man who was not quite the same man seated at this desk that was not quite the same desk . . . lay an entire world of streets and people. What sort of world it was now, there was no telling. He could feel them moving there, beyond the walls, almost, like so many chess pieces blown in a dry wind. . . .

But the immediate thing was the sign painted on the office wall, the same sign he had read earlier today on first entering.

Somehow, the sign had changed:

TYME SEFARI INC.
Sefaris tu any yeer en the past.

Yu naim the animall.
Wee taekyuthair.

Yu shoot itt.

Eckels felt himself fall into a chair. He fumbled crazily at the thick slime on his boots. He held up a clod of dirt, trembling, "No, it *can't* be. Not a *little* thing like that. No!"

Embedded in the mud, glistening green and gold and black, was a butterfly, very beautiful and very dead.

"Not a little thing like *that*! Not a butterfly!" cried Eckels.

It fell to the floor, an exquisite thing, a small thing that could upset balances and knock down a line of small dominoes and then big dominoes and then gigantic dominoes, all down the years across Time. Eckels's mind whirled. It *couldn't* change things. Killing one butterfly couldn't be *that* important! Could it?

His face was cold. His mouth trembled, asking: "Who—who won the presidential election yesterday?"

The man behind the desk laughed. "You joking? You know very well. Deutscher, of course! Who else? Not that fool weakling Keith. We got an iron man now, a man with guts!" The official stopped. "What's wrong?"

Eckels moaned. He dropped to his knees. He scrabbled at the golden butterfly with shaking fingers. "Can't we," he pleaded to the world, to himself, to the officials, to the Machine, "can't we take it *back*, can't we *make* it alive again? Can't we start over? Can't we—"

He did not move. Eyes shut, he waited, shivering. He heard Travis breathe loud in the room; he heard Travis shift his rifle, click the safety catch, and raise the weapon.

There was a sound of thunder. ∎

Vocabulary

subliminal (sub·lim′ə·nəl) *adj.:* below the level of awareness.

Meet the Writer

Ray Bradbury

Teller of Tales

Ray Bradbury (1920–   ) calls himself a teller of tales and a magic realist. He also claims to remember everything—every book he's read, every movie he's seen, all the events of his life back to and including his birth, in Waukegan, Illinois, on August 22, 1920. All those memories and a big imagination are the materials for the fiction and poetry he's been publishing for more than fifty years. Bradbury gives credit for his writing to his boyhood self:

66 I don't know if I believe in previous lives; I'm not sure I can live forever. But that young boy believed in both, and I have let him have his head. He has written my stories and books for me. **99**

Bradbury's work is full of childhood imaginings, fantasies, and night-mares—portraits of Venus and Mars, time travel, ageless children, never-ending rains—but Bradbury the grown-up is a concerned citizen. His fantasy stories are often warnings against blind faith in science, but they're optimistic. By giving strange twists to everyday objects and events, Bradbury

challenges his readers to look at them as if for the first time. As a writer he lets readers see science through the excited eyes of children, but he also informs, suggesting ways we might use technology more responsibly.

For another Bradbury story, see page 437.

from Jurassic Park
Michael Crichton

In Michael Crichton's novel Jurassic Park *(1990), John Hammond, a rich corporate executive, hires a team of scientists to clone dinosaurs from DNA, and he succeeds in bringing the giant reptiles back from extinction. Hammond populates an island reserve, Jurassic Park, with his clones, letting them roam on lands surrounded by electric fences. He plans to have visitors pay to view the monstrous creatures, using Land Cruisers that run on electric tracks throughout the reserve. Just before the park's scheduled opening, something goes seriously wrong: A park employee's attempt to enter an off-limits laboratory automatically shuts down portions of the park's electricity. As a result, the power feeding the fences and the tracks fails. The dinosaurs are loose.*

As this excerpt opens, the Land Cruisers stop. Inside one are two visiting scientists, Dr. Malcolm and Dr. Grant; in the other are Hammond's grandchildren, Tim and his sister, Lex. A tyrannosaur approaches.

The huge head raised back up, jaws open, and then stopped by the side windows. In the glare of lightning, they saw the beady, expressionless reptile eye moving in the socket.

It was looking in the car.

His sister's breath came in ragged, frightened gasps. He reached out and squeezed her arm, hoping she would stay quiet. The dinosaur continued to stare for a long time through the side window. Perhaps the dinosaur couldn't really see them, he thought. Finally the head lifted up, out of view again.

"Timmy . . . ," Lex whispered.

"It's okay," Tim whispered. "I don't think it saw us."

He was looking back toward Dr. Grant when a jolting impact rocked the Land Cruiser and shattered the windshield in a spider web as the tyrannosaur's head crashed against the hood of the Land Cruiser. Tim was knocked flat on the seat. The night-vision goggles slid off his forehead.

He got back up quickly, blinking in the darkness, his mouth warm with blood.

"Lex?"

He couldn't see his sister anywhere.

The tyrannosaur stood near the front of the Land Cruiser, its chest moving as it breathed, the forelimbs making clawing movements in the air.

"Lex!" Tim whispered. Then he heard her groan. She was lying somewhere on the floor under the front seat.

Then the huge head came down, entirely blocking the shattered windshield. The tyrannosaur banged again on the front hood of the Land Cruiser. Tim grabbed the seat as the car rocked on its wheels. The tyrannosaur banged down twice more, denting the metal.

Then it moved around the side of the car. The big raised tail blocked his view out of all the side windows. At the back, the animal snorted, a deep rumbling growl that blended with the thunder. It sank its jaws into the spare tire mounted on the back of the Land Cruiser and, in a single headshake, tore it away. The rear of the car lifted into the air for a moment; then it thumped down with a muddy splash.

"Tim!" Dr. Grant said. "Tim, are you there?"

Tim grabbed the radio. "We're okay," he said. There was a shrill metallic scrape as claws raked the roof of the car. Tim's heart was pounding in his chest. He couldn't see anything out of the windows on the right side except pebbled leathery flesh. The tyrannosaur was leaning against the car, which rocked back and forth with each breath, the springs and metal creaking loudly.

Lex groaned again. Tim put down the radio and started to crawl over into the front seat. The tyrannosaur roared and the metal roof dented downward. Tim felt a sharp pain in his head and tumbled to the floor, onto the transmission hump. He found himself lying alongside Lex, and he was shocked to see that the whole side of her head was covered in blood. She looked unconscious.

There was another jolting impact, and pieces of glass fell all around him. Tim felt rain. He looked up and saw that the front windshield had broken out. There was just a jagged rim of glass and, beyond, the big head of the dinosaur.

Looking down at him.

Tim felt a sudden chill and then the head rushed forward toward him, the jaws open. There was the squeal of metal against teeth, and he felt the hot stinking breath of the animal, and a thick tongue stuck into the car through the windshield opening. The tongue slapped wetly around inside the car—he felt the hot lather of dinosaur saliva—and the tyrannosaur roared—a deafening sound inside the car—

The head pulled away abruptly.

Tim scrambled up, avoiding the dent in the roof. There was still room to sit on the front seat by the passenger door. The tyrannosaur stood in the rain near the front fender. It seemed confused by what had happened to it. Blood dripped freely from its jaws.

The tyrannosaur looked at Tim, cocking its head to stare with one big eye. The head moved close to the car, sideways, and peered in. Blood splattered on the dented hood of the Land Cruiser, mixing with the rain.

It can't get to me, Tim thought. It's too big.

Then the head pulled away, and in the flare of lightning he saw the hind leg lift up. And the world tilted crazily as the Land Cruiser slammed over on its side, the windows splatting in the mud. He saw Lex fall helplessly against the side window, and he fell down beside her, banging his head. Tim felt dizzy. Then the tyran-nosaur's jaws clamped onto the window frame, and the whole Land Cruiser was lifted up into the air and shaken.

"Timmy!" Lex shrieked so near to his ear that it hurt. She was sud-denly awake, and he grabbed her as the tyrannosaur crashed the car down again. Tim felt a stabbing pain in his side, and his sister fell on top of him. The car went up again, tilting crazily. Lex shouted *"Timmy!"* and he saw the door give way be-neath her, and she fell out of the car into the mud, but Tim couldn't answer because in the next instant everything swung crazily—he saw the trunks of the palm trees sliding downward past him—moving sideways through the air—he glimpsed the ground very far below—the hot roar of the tyrannosaur—the blazing eye—the tops of the palm trees—

And then, with a metallic scraping shriek, the car fell from the tyran-nosaur's jaws, a sickening fall, and Tim's stomach heaved in the moment before the world became totally black, and silent.

Reading Check

1. Fill in a **cause-and-effect** chart like the one here to show the sequence of events in the story. The first and the last event are already filled in. Add other boxes as you need them to include all the main events.

> Eckels signs up for a safari to the past.

↓

↓

> We hear "a sound of thunder."

Thinking Critically

SKILLS FOCUS

Literary Skills
Analyze elements of style, including figurative language and mood.

Reading Skills
Understand cause-and-effect relationships.

Writing Skills
Write a descriptive essay.

2. Identify the steps in the chain of **causes and effects** that Travis says would occur if a time traveler accidentally killed even one mouse (see pages 584–585). Do you think his theory might really be accurate? Explain.

3. When the time travelers, crossing the border between the past and the present, return to the world of 2055, how has that **setting** changed? What details reveal the changes?

4. What happens to Eckels at the end of the story? What is the **cause** of the final event?

5. What different meanings can you give for the story's **title**?

6. Do you think Bradbury's **purpose** is to entertain, or does his story have a serious **theme,** or message? Explain. Consider the same question for the *Jurassic Park* excerpt (see the **Connection** on page 593).

Extending and Evaluating

7. There's no doubt that Bradbury has written what critics would call a blockbuster story. Now, take it apart. Do you find flaws in its logic? Work in teams, and share your findings. Be sure to consider this question: Do flaws in the story (if any) lessen your enjoyment of it?

Literary Criticism

8. Bradbury's writing **style** is full of vivid descriptions and **images.** What descriptive details help you see, hear, and smell Bradbury's prehistoric swamp?

9. How would you describe the **mood** of Bradbury's story? How do elements of his **style** such as **figurative language** help to create that mood?

10. Bradbury's story has an exciting adventure plot, which could have been related in simple concrete language without **figures of speech.** What might the story have gained if it had been written in such a **style**? What might it have lost?

WRITING

Excursions in Time

Imagine that you're entering an essay contest in which the grand prize is a time-travel journey. Write a brief **essay** telling exactly where you'd go, to what point in time (select a year in the future or the past), and why. Describe what you imagine you will see when you arrive. What do you want to accomplish when you reach your destination? (Check your Quickwrite notes for ideas.)

go. hrw .com

INTERNET

Projects and Activities

Keyword: LE7 9-8

Prefixes and Root Words: Keys to Meaning

PRACTICE

Knowing the meanings of some Greek and Latin **prefixes** and **root words** can help you decipher the meanings of many English words. Use a dictionary to look up the **etymology** (word origin) of each Word Bank word. Then, make a chart like the one here for each word (skip *expendable*). (Most, but not all, of the words begin with a prefix.)

expendable
Meaning: worth sacrificing to gain an objective
Prefix: Latin *ex–,* "out"
Root word: Latin *pendere,* "to weigh"
Words with same root word or prefix: expenditure, expense, exclude
Sentence: No member of the crew was <u>expendable</u>.

Word Bank

annihilate
expendable
depression
paradox
delirium
resilient
remit
revoke
primeval
subliminal

Grammar Link

Verbs Play Active and Passive Roles

Like people, **action verbs** have voices. A verb in the **active voice** expresses an action performed *by* its subject.

> Ray Bradbury <u>wrote</u> "A Sound of Thunder."
> "Mr. Eckels <u>looked</u> at the check."

A verb in the **passive voice** expresses an action done *to* its subject. (Hint: A passive-voice verb always includes a form of *be* and the past participle of the verb.)

> "A Sound of Thunder" <u>was written</u> by Ray Bradbury.
> "'Six safari leaders <u>were killed</u> last year. . . .'"

The active voice is strong and direct. A verb in the passive voice sounds weak partly because it needs a helping verb.

The passive voice is useful when a writer doesn't know who or what performed an action (*My bicycle was stolen*) or when a writer doesn't want readers to know who performed an action (*The TV was left on*).

PRACTICE

Rewrite each sentence, changing the verb from the passive voice to the active voice. Notice how the active voice results in shorter, more vigorous sentences.

1. The idea of hunting the dinosaur was abandoned by Eckels.

2. The dinosaur's footsteps could be heard and felt by the hunters.

3. The silence was shattered by the dinosaur's scream.

4. This story has been reviewed favorably by most students.

▶ **For more help, see Active and Passive Voice, 3f–g, in the Language Handbook.**

SKILLS FOCUS

Vocabulary Skills
Understand Greek and Latin prefixes and root words.

Grammar Skills
Use verbs in the active and passive voices.

Rising Tides ◆ An Arctic Floe of Climate Questions

Evaluating Arguments: Pro and Con

When you read or listen to opposing views on an important issue, how can you decide which side to believe?

1. **Understand the arguments.** Begin by making sure that you understand the issue and the **opinion,** or **claim,** presented in each argument. It helps to **paraphrase** the arguments, using your own words.

2. **Identify the support.** Start by identifying the **logical appeals**—the **reasons** why the writer holds that opinion—and the **evidence** given to back up each reason. The evidence may consist of the following items:

   - **facts** (statements that can be verified objectively)
   - **statistics** (numerical facts)
   - **examples**
   - **comments from experts**

   To what extent has the author also used **emotional appeals,** such as **loaded words** and **anecdotes** (colorful or emotional stories)?

Who Is More Persuasive?

You can create a chart like the one on the next page to help you evaluate the **credibility** of each argument. To decide which argument is stronger and why, consider these questions:

1. **Is the argument logical?** Do the **reasons** make sense, and are they relevant to the issue? Learn to recognize these common **fallacies,** or errors in logical thinking:

   - **Circular reasoning.** Watch out for statements that look like reasons or conclusions but simply restate an author's opinion.

     "After-school sports are essential because they're a necessary part of school activities."

   - **False cause and effect.** Just because one event happens *after* another event, the first event did not necessarily *cause* the second event. The two events may be (and often are) totally unrelated.

     "When after-school sports were dropped at Adams High School, the dropout rate increased."

   - **Hasty generalization.** A **generalization** is a broad statement. An author can't generalize about everyone or everything based on one or two cases. An author must examine many cases before he or she can make a **valid** (true) generalization.

     "Everyone agrees that dropping after-school sports is a bad idea. I know because I asked my friend Chad, and he agrees with me."

   - **Attacking the person.** A good argument stays focused on an issue and on an opponent's argument— not on an opponent's character or judgment.

     "Mr. McAloo, who proposed cutting after-school sports, is a mean, stingy person."

2. **How comprehensive is the support?** Does the writer provide reasons and sufficient **evidence** to support every generalization? An

unsupported generalization seriously weakens an argument.

3. **Does the writer deal with opposing evidence?** To strengthen his or her argument, does the writer discuss opposing evidence to anticipate objections? Dealing with the opponent's viewpoint is important when an issue is a controversial one about which many people have clear **pro** (for) or **con** (against) views.

4. **Is the structure effective?** A good writer carefully structures an argument to be most persuasive. Readers generally remember the beginning and the end of a piece most clearly, so an effective technique is to put the strongest reasons in those positions. (Writers also commonly structure arguments using **comparison and contrast** and **cause and effect**.)

5. **What is the author's intent?** Is the writer's purpose clear throughout? Often the writer's goal is just to change your thinking, but sometimes it is a **call to action,** asking you to go out and *do* something. Are you being asked to change your behavior in any way? to write a letter? to offer your help? Do there seem to be hidden agendas in the writer's argument?

6. **What is the tone?** An author's intent directly affects a work's **tone,** a writer's attitude toward his or her subject or audience. If the intent is to persuade, look for a tone that is serious, calm, and reasonable. You should question the credibility of the argument if the author uses a humorous, angry, or highly emotional tone or if the author exaggerates or tries to make light of various issues.

Answering all of these questions will help you evaluate the strengths and weaknesses of opposing arguments.

Evaluating Arguments	Piece 1 Pro	Piece 2 Con
Claim		
Logical appeals		
Emotional appeals		
Tone		
Author's intent		
Credibility		

Vocabulary Development

receding (ri·sēd′iŋ) *v.:* moving back; becoming less.

catastrophic (kat′ə·sträf′ik) *adj.:* disastrous.

implications (im′pli·kā′shənz) *n.:* possible connections or consequences.

indiscriminate (in′di·skrim′i·nit) *adj.:* careless.

deficient (dē·fish′ənt) *adj.:* lacking.

equitable (ek′wit·ə·bəl) *adj.:* fair; just.

demise (dē·mīz′) *n.:* death; end.

ominous (äm′ə·nəs) *adj.:* threatening.

impending (im·pend′iŋ) *v.* used as *adj.:* about to happen.

ignorance (ig′nə·rəns) *n.:* lack of knowledge.

Connecting to the Literature

"A Sound of Thunder" and the *Jurassic Park* excerpt depict a future in which humans tamper with their environment—with disastrous results. The following articles take different positions on the impact humans have on the environment today.

The following two opinion articles, "Rising Tides" by Bob Herbert and "An Arctic Floe of Climate Questions" by Robert Cooke, present opposing views on global warming. Most scientists believe that we have altered the earth's atmosphere by releasing huge amounts of carbon dioxide and other greenhouse gases from our factories and cars. These gases trap heat in the earth's lower atmosphere and increase the earth's average temperatures, causing global warming. Some people, however, question whether our current global warming reflects a permanent change in our climate.

Rising Tides

from *The New York Times*, February 22, 2001

Bob Herbert

The easiest approach for the time being is to pretend it's not happening. It's better for the nerves in the short run . . . than to acknowledge that the majestic ice cap atop Mount Kilimanjaro,[1] which seemed for so long to be an almost permanent feature of the planet, will vanish in less than 15 years.

It's February and it's cold in New York, which can help us maintain the fiction that the planet is not warming at a scary rate. But the snows are disappearing from Kilimanjaro, and a few years ago scientists were astonished when a mammoth[2] fragment of the Larsen Ice Shelf at the edge of the Antarctic Peninsula[3] collapsed like a window shattered by a rock. The fragment had measured 48 miles by 22 miles and was hundreds of feet thick. It eventually disappeared. ❶

Many strange things are happening. The seasons are changing, rainstorms are becoming more intense, sea levels are rising, mighty glaciers are receding, the permafrost (by definition, the *permanently* frozen subsoil in the polar regions) is thawing, trees are flowering earlier, insects are emerging sooner, and so on.

Global warming is not coming, it's here. ❷

There are likely to be some beneficial results in some areas from the warming, such as longer growing seasons and increased crop yields in certain

---

1. **Mount Kilimanjaro** (kil′ə·män·jär′ō): highest mountain in Africa (19,340 feet), located in Tanzania.
2. **mammoth** (mam′əth) *adj.:* enormous.
3. **Antarctic Peninsula** (ant·ärk′tik pə·nin′sə·lə): narrow body of land (about eight hundred miles long) extending from Antarctica toward South America. The icy continent of Antarctica is a landmass surrounding the South Pole.

❶ **EMOTIONAL APPEALS**

What **loaded words** can you find in this paragraph?

❷ **EVALUATING AN ARGUMENT**

What is the author's main **claim** so far? What **evidence** supports that claim?

Vocabulary
receding (ri·sēd′iŋ) *v.:* moving back; becoming less.

An African elephant roams in a meadow by Mount Kilimanjaro.

mid-latitude regions,[4] and a decline in deaths related to extreme cold. But over all, the effects of this sharp and accelerating and largely artificial warming of the planet—including the consequences of such extreme events as droughts, floods, heat waves, avalanches, and tropical storms—are potentially <u>catastrophic</u>.

The Intergovernmental Panel on Climate Change, in a report released Tuesday in Geneva,[5] said, "More people are projected to be harmed than benefited by climate change, even for global mean temperature increases[6] of less than a few degrees centigrade."

The report also discussed an issue that has profound policy and ethical[7] <u>implications</u>.

The worst effects of global warming will probably not be felt by those most responsible for the pollution of the atmosphere by heat-trapping greenhouse gases. The great industrial societies, which have benefited so long from the rapacious devouring of resources[8] and the <u>indiscriminate</u> release of pollutants, are also the societies best positioned to cope with the treacherous forces of global warming.

As the panel noted in its report, "The ability of human systems to adapt to and cope with climate change depends on such factors as wealth, technology, education,

8. **rapacious devouring of resources:** greedy using up of natural resources.

4. **mid-latitude regions:** areas of the world with moderate temperatures.
5. **Geneva** (jə·nē′və): city in southwest Switzerland.
6. **global mean temperature increases:** increases in average temperatures all over the world.
7. **ethical** (eth′i·kəl) *adj.:* moral; relating to principles of what's right and just.

Vocabulary
catastrophic (kat′ə·sträf′ik) *adj.:* disastrous.
implications (im′pli·kā′shənz) *n.:* possible connections or consequences.
indiscriminate (in′di·skrim′i·nit) *adj.:* careless.

information, skills, infrastructure,[9] access to resources, and management capabilities."

Developing countries, deficient in those areas, are doomed to suffer disproportion-ately[10] from the warming of the planet. "The effects of climate change," the panel said, "are expected to be greatest in develop-ing countries in terms of loss of life and relative effects on investment and the economy." ❸

❸ **EVALUATING AN ARGUMENT**

Paraphrase the **generalization** that the author makes in this paragraph.

Despite the powerful and increasing evi-dence of the role of carbon dioxide and other greenhouse gases in the warming of the earth, the concentrations of those gases in the atmosphere are expected to increase, not decrease, over the next several decades. Government leaders are not responding to the problem with the sense of urgency that is called for.

Carbon dioxide doesn't just float away in a day or two. It remains in the atmosphere for more than 100 years. The consequences of our failure to act will last for centuries.

Americans have a special responsibility here. The United States is the mightiest nation on the planet and the greatest con-tributor to the industrial component of global warming.[11] The nation is wealthy and

at peace. A mature approach would require certain sacrifices designed to provide a better environment for future genera-tions of Americans and a more equitable relationship with neighbors around the world. ❹

❹ **AUTHOR'S INTENT**

What is the **call to action** here? What does the author want Americans to do?

But that's only one approach. Another is to just ignore the problem and continue to feast like gluttons[12] at the table of the world's resources. That will work for a while. Why not? All you have to do is convince yourself that damaging the planet is some-body else's problem.

---

12. **gluttons** (glut′nz) *n.:* persons who greedily eat too much.

Vocabulary
deficient (dē·fish′ənt) *adj.:* lacking.
equitable (ek′wit·ə·bəl) *adj.:* fair; just.

This aerial view shows the Brunt Ice Shelf in Antarctica.

---

9. **infrastructure** (in′frə·struk′chər) *n.:* basic installations such as roads, schools, power plants, and transportation and communication systems needed to support a modern, developed society.
10. **disproportionately** (dis′prə·pôr′shə·nət·lē) *adv.:* not in fair balance; here, to an excessive degree.
11. **industrial component of global warming:** the release of pollutants during the manufacturing process, which increases the overall warming of the earth.

An Arctic Floe of Climate Questions

from *Newsday,* April 18, 2001

Robert Cooke

Recent reports of the North Pole's demise are, to borrow from Mark Twain, "exaggerated."[1] ❶

Although the blanket of floating ice that usually covers the North Pole was found last summer to be gone—there was just open water—climate specialists say that's not such a big deal. As the ice shifts, leads, or channels of water, open up, and ice-free areas called polynyas form.

Eventually, the ice moves and such gaps close.

But some alarm bells did ring, because there is growing concern that we humans are fouling things up through our burning of gas, oil, and coal, which releases so-called greenhouse gases such as carbon dioxide into the air. These gases, which trap heat, may be causing the whole world's temperature to steadily creep higher and higher. And an absence of ice at the North Pole seemed like one more ominous sign of impending trouble. ❷

> ❶ **EVALUATING AN ARGUMENT**
>
> From this first sentence, what can we anticipate the author's **opinion,** or **claim,** will be?

> ❷ **EVALUATING AN ARGUMENT**
>
> Explain how the author addresses **opposing arguments** here.

Temperature records also show, clearly, that globally temperatures have gone up by about 3 degrees Fahrenheit in the past 150 years, or since temperatures have been recorded. And, perhaps coincidentally, the last few years have been the warmest on record, accentuating[2] concerns. One scenario[3] suggests that the greatest impact from warming will be apparent at high latitudes near the poles.[4]

A recent University of Wisconsin study has shown that in the Northern Hemisphere[5] many of the rivers and lakes that freeze are doing so later—by 8.7 days—than they did more than a century ago. Also, "ice-out," or breakup, is occurring about 9.8 days sooner. This suggests that winters are now a bit shorter.

What people need to know, however, is that the global weather equation is enormously complex, and no one knows exactly how to work it out. A few years with extra-hot

---

1. **Recent reports . . . "exaggerated":** reference to an 1897 cable sent by the American humorist Mark Twain (1835–1910) to a journalist in response to rumors of Twain's death, often quoted as "The reports of my death are greatly exaggerated."

2. **accentuating** (ak·sen′cho͞o·āt′iŋ) *v.* used as *adj.:* heightening; emphasizing.
3. **scenario** (sə·ner′ē·ō′) *n.:* outline of events, real or imagined.
4. **poles** *n.:* regions around the North and South Poles.
5. **Northern Hemisphere:** the half of the earth north of the equator.

Vocabulary

demise (dē·mīz′) *n.:* death; end.

ominous (äm′ə·nəs) *adj.:* threatening.

impending (im·pend′iŋ) *v.* used as *adj.:* about to happen.

summers or an episode of ice shrinking at the poles does not make a disaster. Such things could be normal fluctuations[6] in a very changeable system. ❸

The reason it's so hard to find answers is, in part, a matter of ignorance. Only in the past half-century have instruments begun to be set out at sea and on land to monitor[7] what's actually happening. And only since about 1972 have orbiting satellites[8] been able to even roughly track what's happening to ice at the poles. Because there is no reliable, long-term history of climate variability,[9] we can't know whether what seems unusual now is actually unusual in global climate. Tests in sediments[10] and ice cores show that the world's temperature has been higher in the past and, of course, sometimes lower during ice ages.

What recent data have suggested is that ice in the Arctic has been thinning, and the extent or area of sea ice has shrunk by a measurable degree. On the other hand, there's substantial disagreement among scientists there too. Measurements taken by submarines under the ice are being debated; some experts think the ice has thinned, others think it hasn't. In any case, the submarines have been cruising beneath the ice cap for less than 50 years.

Still, "if you look at the records, it seems that since 1972, when satellite observations began, there has definitely been a significant decrease in sea ice. It's a statistically significant decrease and that is pretty well accepted," said climatologist[11] Mark Serreze, at the University of Colorado.

But, he added, "the problem is that when you look at what the sea ice is doing, it's not just temperature that governs what the ice is doing. The winds are involved in blowing it around." So a large storm is capable of moving the ice, breaking it up and opening a polynya, an open sea area, at the North Pole. ❹

"These are known to exist, even at the pole," said George Kukla, a paleoclimatologist[12] at Columbia University's Lamont Doherty Earth Observatory.

"From what I understand, in the past 20 years we've been observing a trend in the thinning of the ice and a decrease in the area covered by ice," Kukla said.

"But according to comparisons, it doesn't seem to be reaching the situation [seen] in the 1940s and 1950s, when there was relatively little ice in that area," Kukla said. "So we can't say it is something that was unprecedented."[13] ❺

❸ **EVALUATING AN ARGUMENT**

What is the author's main **claim**?

❹ **EVALUATING EVIDENCE**

What type of **evidence** does the author present in the last two paragraphs?

❺ **EVALUATING EVIDENCE**

Paraphrase the quotations in the last two paragraphs. Why might the author have chosen to end his article with this **expert's opinion**?

---

6. **fluctuations** (fluk′choo·ā′·shənz) *n.:* temporary increases and decreases.
7. **monitor** (män′i·tər) *v.:* check on; observe.
8. **orbiting satellites:** artificial, unmanned spacecraft that circle the earth, transmitting images and data from space.
9. **variability** (ver′ē·ə·bil′ə·tē) *n.:* changeability.
10. **sediments** (sed′ə·mənts) *n.:* soil, rock, and other solids deposited by water or wind.

11. **climatologist** (klī′mə·täl′ə·jist) *n.:* scientist who studies climate and its effects.
12. **paleoclimatologist** (pā′ lē·ō·klī′mə·täl′ə·jist) *n.:* scientist who studies earth's ancient, prehistoric climates.
13. **unprecedented** (un·pres′ə·den′tid) *adj.:* never happening before.

Vocabulary
ignorance (ig′nə·rəns) *n.:* lack of knowledge.

Reading Check

1. Name six effects of global warming mentioned in "Rising Tides."

2. What two opposing approaches to global warming does Herbert say Americans can take?

3. According to Cooke's article, what do temperature records show for the "last few years"?

4. According to Cooke, what do people need to know about the "global weather equation"?

SKILLS FOCUS

Reading Skills
Evaluate the credibility of opposing arguments.

Test Practice

1. The two writers have opposing views about —
   A the causes of global warming
   B whether we are now experiencing serious global warming
   C the ability of people to adapt to climate changes
   D the impact of global warming on developing nations

2. In "Rising Tides," to support his **claim** that global warming is already here, Herbert cites many —
   F facts about weather-related changes
   G facts about the world's population
   H anecdotes about weather
   J quotations from experts

3. Herbert supports his statement that the effects of global warming will be more disastrous for developing nations by using —
   A his personal observations
   B quotations from a panel of experts
   C a number of emotional appeals
   D an anecdote

4. In the last paragraph of "Rising Tides," Herbert's **tone** is —
   F sympathetic

   G serious
   H humorous
   J ironic

5. What is Cooke's **intent** in writing his article "An Arctic Floe of Climate Questions"?
   A To prove that global warming has really begun
   B To reassure his audience that global warming, even if it occurs, poses no threat to life as we know it
   C To present what he feels is a balanced view of the likelihood of global warming
   D To warn his audience about the possibility of global warming and its terrible consequences

6. In the second half of his article, Cooke uses the **example** of shrinking Arctic ice to show that —
   F data collected by submarines is unreliable
   G global warming is a highly emotional issue
   H scientists have been measuring the ice for hundreds of years
   J scientists disagree about the meaning of the data

7. Which of the following items contains an **emotional appeal**?

A Herbert's statement: "Carbon dioxide . . . remains in the atmosphere for more than 100 years."

B Herbert's statement: "The United States is the mightiest nation on the planet. . . ."

C Cooke's statement: "As the ice shifts, leads, or channels of water, open up. . . ."

D Cooke's statement: "Eventually, the ice moves and such gaps close."

Constructed Response

Write a brief essay in which you **evaluate** the **credibility** of the two arguments. What is the author's **intent** in each case? What is each writer's **opinion, or claim**? Is each argument logical and convincing? How strong and comprehensive is the **evidence** and other support each writer presents in his argument? Whose view—Herbert's or Cooke's—do you find more credible and persuasive? (A chart like the one below will help you organize your ideas.)

	Herbert	Cooke
Writer's intent		
Writer's opinion, or claim		
Evidence and other support		
Credibility of argument		

Vocabulary Development

Word Knowledge: What If?

PRACTICE

Demonstrate your understanding of the Word Bank words by listing at least two possible outcomes for each of the following situations:

1. What if you noticed that your hairline was <u>receding</u>?
2. What if you heard that a <u>catastrophic</u> storm was approaching?
3. What if you had to explain the <u>implications</u> of your report card?
4. What if you painted your room in an <u>indiscriminate</u> way?
5. What if you decided your physical strength was <u>deficient</u>?
6. What if the distribution of household chores in your family became more <u>equitable</u>?
7. What if you heard a rumor about the <u>demise</u> of your favorite television program?
8. What if you noticed someone approaching you with an <u>ominous</u> look?
9. What if you faced an <u>impending</u> move to another state?
10. What if your <u>ignorance</u> prevented you from doing well on your history test?

Word Bank

receding
catastrophic
implications
indiscriminate
deficient
equitable
demise
ominous
impending
ignorance

SKILLS FOCUS

Vocabulary Skills
Demonstrate word knowledge.

To Da-duh, in Memoriam

Make the Connection

Quickwrite ✏️

Do you consider yourself a city slicker or a country bumpkin? Make a list of things you associate with life in the country. Then, make a list of things you associate with city life. Save your lists.

Literary Focus

Diction and Sentence Patterns: A Matter of Style

Style refers to the way a writer uses language. **Diction,** a writer's choice of words, is an important element of style. Writers must decide whether to use a plain word (*upset*) or a complex one (*distraught*). They must choose between words with different **connotations,** the emotions and associations suggested by words (*crawl* or *creep*).

Sometimes a writer's diction is distinguished by his or her use of **dialect,** the way of speaking characteristic of a particular region or group of people. Paule Marshall brings her grandmother to life by reproducing her rhythmic Barbados dialect.

Another element of style is **sentence structure.** Some writers use short, punchy sentences. Others use long, rhythmic sentences. Finally, **figures of speech,** or unusual comparisons, make a writer's style more descriptive.

As you read this story, think about how you would describe Marshall's style.

Reading Skills 📖

Visualizing the Story

This story presents a series of striking images that help you imagine an unfamiliar setting and an unusual character. The story will be easier to read if you try **visualizing** it—seeing the story happen in your mind as if it were a movie. The questions at the open-book signs will help you.

Background

This story is set in Barbados, a tropical island in the Caribbean that was a British colony for almost 340 years before gaining its independence in 1966. The rich culture of Barbados is the product of English, African, and Caribbean influences. Most of today's Barbadians are descendants of Africans who were slaves on British-owned sugar plantations.

Vocabulary Development

unrelenting (un·ri·len′tiŋ) *adj.*: not letting up or weakening.

formidable (fôr′mə·də·bəl) *adj.*: impressive; causing fear or dread.

reproved (ri·pro͞ovd′) *v.*: disapproved of.

truculent (truk′yo͞o·lənt) *adj.*: fierce.

decrepit (dē·krep′it) *adj.*: falling apart.

admonished (ad·män′isht) *v.*: scolded mildly.

perennial (pə·ren′ē·əl) *adj.*: year-round; continual.

austere (ô·stir′) *adj.*: very plain; severe.

protracted (prō·trakt′id) *adj.*: extended.

menacing (men′əs·iŋ) *v.* used as *adj.*: threatening.

Literary Skills
Understand elements of style, including diction and sentence structure.

Reading Skills
Visualize the story.

INTERNET

Vocabulary Practice

Keyword: LE7 9-8

Family (1955) by Charles H. Alston. Oil on canvas (48¼″ × 35¾″).

To Da-duh,

in Memoriam

Paule Marshall

Da-duh stared at me as if I were a creature from Mars . . .

". . . Oh Nana! all of you is not involved in this evil business Death,
Nor all of us in life."

—from "At My Grandmother's Grave"
by Lebert Bethune

I did not see her at first I remember. For not only was it dark inside the
crowded disembarkation shed[1] in spite of the daylight flooding in from outside, but standing there waiting for her with my mother and sister I was still somewhat blinded from the sheen of tropical sunlight on the water of the bay which we
had just crossed in the landing boat, leaving behind us the ship that had brought us
from New York lying in the offing.[2] Besides, being only nine years of age at the
time and knowing nothing of islands I was busy attending to the alien sights and
sounds of Barbados, the unfamiliar smells.

---

1. **disembarkation shed:** place where passengers wait or assemble after leaving a ship or plane.
2. **in the offing:** at some distance but in sight.

Sharecropper (1970) by Elizabeth Catlett. Woodcut.

sweep past us out the doorway which opened onto the sea and like Christ walk upon the water!), she was caught between the sunlight at her end of the building and the darkness inside—and for a moment she appeared to contain them both: the light in the long severe old-fashioned white dress she wore which brought the sense of a past that was still alive into our bustling present and in the snatch of white at her eye; the darkness in her black high-top shoes and in her face which was visible now that she was closer.

It was as stark and fleshless as a death mask, that face. The maggots might have already done their work, leaving only the framework of bone beneath the ruined skin and deep wells at the temple and jaw. But her eyes were alive, unnervingly so for one so old, with a sharp light that flicked out of the dim clouded depths like a lizard's tongue to snap up all in her view. Those eyes betrayed a child's curiosity about the world, and I wondered vaguely seeing them, and seeing the way the bodice of her ancient dress had collapsed in on her flat chest (what had happened to her breasts?), whether she might not be some kind of child at the same time that she was a woman, with

I did not see her, but I was alerted to her approach by my mother's hand which suddenly tightened around mine, and looking up I traced her gaze through the gloom in the shed until I finally made out the small, purposeful, painfully erect figure of the old woman headed our way.

Her face was drowned in the shadow of an ugly rolled-brim brown felt hat, but the details of her slight body and of the struggle taking place within it were clear enough—an intense, unrelenting struggle between her back which was beginning to bend ever so slightly under the weight of her eighty-odd years and the rest of her which sought to deny those years and hold that back straight, keep it in line. Moving swiftly toward us (so swiftly it seemed she did not intend stopping when she reached us but would

Vocabulary

unrelenting (un·ri·len'tiŋ) *adj.*: not letting up or weakening.

fourteen children, my mother included, to prove it. Perhaps she was both, both child and woman, darkness and light, past and present, life and death—all the opposites contained and reconciled in her.

VISUALIZING

1. Pause for a few seconds. Describe how you **visualize** Da-duh.

"My Da-duh," my mother said formally and stepped forward. The name sounded like thunder fading softly in the distance.

"Child," Da-duh said, and her tone, her quick scrutiny of my mother, the brief embrace in which they appeared to shy from each other rather than touch, wiped out the fifteen years my mother had been away and restored the old relationship. My mother, who was such a formidable figure in my eyes, had suddenly with a word been reduced to my status.

"Yes, God is good," Da-duh said with a nod that was like a tic. "He has spared me to see my child again."

We were led forward then, apologetically because not only did Da-duh prefer boys but she also liked her grandchildren to be "white," that is, fair-skinned; and we had, I was to discover, a number of cousins, the outside children of white estate managers and the like, who qualified. We, though, were as black as she.

My sister being the oldest was presented first. "This one takes after the father," my mother said and waited to be reproved.

Frowning, Da-duh tilted my sister's face toward the light. But her frown soon gave way to a grudging smile, for my sister with her large mild eyes and little broad winged nose, with our father's high-cheeked Barbadian cast to her face, was pretty.

"She's goin' be lucky," Da-duh said and patted her once on the cheek. "Any girl child that takes after the father does be lucky."

She turned then to me. But oddly enough she did not touch me. Instead leaning close, she peered hard at me, and then quickly drew back. I thought I saw her hand start up as though to shield her eyes. It was almost as if she saw not only me, a thin truculent child who it was said took after no one but myself, but something in me which for some reason she found disturbing, even threatening. We looked silently at each other for a long time there in the noisy shed, our gaze locked. She was the first to look away.

VISUALIZING

2. Pause and think about what you see happening here. What do the details suggest about the way Da-duh regards her granddaughter?

"But Adry," she said to my mother and her laugh was cracked, thin, apprehensive. "Where did you get this one here with this fierce look?"

"We don't know where she came out of, my Da-duh," my mother said, laughing also. Even I smiled to myself. After all I had won the encounter. Da-duh had recognized my small strength—and this was all I ever asked of the adults in my life then.

"Come, soul," Da-duh said and took my hand. "You must be one of those New York terrors you hear so much about."

She led us, me at her side and my sister and mother behind, out of the shed into the sunlight that was like a bright driving summer rain and over to a group of people clustered beside a decrepit lorry.[3] They were our relatives, most of them from St. Andrews although Da-duh herself lived in St. Thomas, the women wearing bright print dresses, the colors vivid against their darkness, the men rusty black suits that encased

---

3. **lorry** (lôr′ē) *n.*: British for "truck."

Vocabulary

formidable (fôr′mə·də·bəl) *adj.*: impressive; causing fear or dread.

reproved (ri·prōōvd′) *v.*: disapproved of.

truculent (truk′yōō·lənt) *adj.*: fierce.

decrepit (dē·krep′it) *adj.*: falling apart.

them like straitjackets. Da-duh, holding fast to my hand, became my anchor as they circled round us like a nervous sea, exclaiming, touching us with their calloused hands, embracing us shyly. They laughed in awed bursts: "But look Adry got big-big children!" / "And see the nice things they wearing, wristwatch and all!" / "I tell you, Adry has done all right for herself in New York. . . ."

Da-duh, ashamed at their wonder, embarrassed for them, <u>admonished</u> them the while. . . . She said, "Why you all got to get on like you never saw people from 'Away' before? You would think New York is the only place in the world to hear wunna. That's why I don't like to go anyplace with you St. Andrews people, you know. You all ain't been colonized."

We were in the back of the lorry finally, packed in among the barrels of ham, flour, cornmeal, and rice and the trunks of clothes that my mother had brought as gifts. We made our way slowly through Bridgetown's clogged streets, part of a funereal procession of cars and open-sided buses, bicycles and donkey carts. The dim little limestone shops and offices along the way marched with us, at the same mournful pace, toward the same grave ceremony—as did the people, the women balancing huge baskets on top their heads as if they were no more than hats they wore to shade them from the sun. Looking over the edge of the lorry I watched as their feet slurred the dust. I listened, and their voices, raw and loud and dissonant[4] in the heat, seemed to be grappling with each other high overhead.

Da-duh sat on a trunk in our midst, a monarch amid her court. She still held my hand, but it was different now. I had suddenly become her anchor, for I felt her fear of the lorry with its

---

4. **dissonant** (dis′ə·nənt) *adj.:* lacking harmony; clashing.

Vocabulary
admonished (ad·män′isht) *v.:* scolded mildly.

Landscape with Royal Palms (1977) by Roosevelt. Oil on wood panel (21.1″ × 14″).

asthmatic motor (a fear and distrust, I later learned, she held of all machines) beating like a pulse in her rough palm.

As soon as we left Bridgetown behind though, she relaxed, and while the others around us talked she gazed at the canes[5] standing tall on either side of the winding marl road. "C'dear," she said softly to herself after a time. "The canes this side are pretty enough."

They were too much for me. I thought of them as giant weeds that had overrun the island, leaving scarcely any room for the small tottering houses of sun-bleached pine we passed or the people, dark streaks as our lorry hurtled by. I suddenly feared that we were journeying, unaware that we were, toward some dangerous place where the canes, grown as high and thick as a forest, would close in on us and run us through with their stiletto blades. I longed then for the familiar: for the street in Brooklyn where I lived, for my father who had refused to accompany us ("Blowing out good money on foolishness," he had said of the trip), for a game of tag with my friends under the chestnut tree outside our aging brownstone house.

"Yes, but wait till you see St. Thomas canes," Da-duh was saying to me. "They's canes father, bo," she gave a proud arrogant nod. "Tomorrow, God willing, I goin' take you out in the ground and show them to you."

True to her word Da-duh took me with her the following day out into the ground. It was a fairly large plot adjoining her weathered board-and-shingle house and consisting of a small orchard, a good-sized cane piece, and behind the canes, where the land sloped abruptly down, a gully. She had purchased it with Panama money sent by her eldest son, my uncle Joseph, who had died work-

ing on the canal. We entered the ground along a trail no wider than her body and as devious and complex as her reasons for showing me her land. Da-duh strode briskly ahead, her slight form filled out this morning by the layers of sacking petticoats she wore under her working dress to protect her against the damp. A fresh white cloth, elaborately arranged around her head, added to her height, and lent her a vain, almost roguish[6] air.

Her pace slowed once we reached the orchard, and glancing back at me occasionally over her shoulder, she pointed out the various trees.

"This here is a breadfruit," she said. "That one yonder is a papaw. Here's a guava. This is a mango. I know you don't have anything like these in New York. Here's a sugar apple." (The fruit looked more like artichokes than apples to me.) "This one bears limes. . . ." She went on for some time, intoning the names of the trees as though they were those of her gods. Finally, turning to me, she said, "I know you don't have anything this nice where you come from." Then, as I hesitated: "I said I know you don't have anything this nice where you come from. . . ."

"No," I said and my world did seem suddenly lacking.

Da-duh nodded and passed on. The orchard ended and we were on the narrow cart road that led through the cane piece, the canes clashing like swords above my cowering head. Again she turned and her thin muscular arms spread wide, her dim gaze embracing the small field of canes, she said— and her voice almost broke under the weight of her pride, "Tell me, have you got anything like these in that place where you were born?"

"No."

> "I know you don't have anything like these in New York."

---

5. **canes** *n.*: tall stems of sugar-cane plants.

6. **roguish** (rō′gish) *adj.*: mischievous.

"I din' think so. I bet you don't even know that these canes here and the sugar you eat is one and the same thing. That they does throw the canes into some machine at the factory and squeeze out all the little life in them to make sugar for you all so in New York to eat. I bet you don't know that."

"I've got two cavities and I'm not allowed to eat a lot of sugar."

But Da-duh didn't hear me. She had turned with an inexplicably angry motion and was making her way rapidly out of the canes and down the slope at the edge of the field which led to the gully below. Following her apprehensively down the incline amid a stand of banana plants whose leaves flapped like elephants' ears in the wind, I found myself in the middle of a small tropical wood—a place dense and damp and gloomy and tremulous with the fitful play of light and shadow as the leaves high above moved against the sun that was almost hidden from view. It was a violent place, the tangled foliage fighting each other for a chance at the sunlight, the branches of the trees locked in what seemed an immemorial struggle, one both necessary and inevitable. But despite the violence, it was pleasant, almost peaceful in the gully, and beneath the thick undergrowth the earth smelled like spring.

VISUALIZING

3. Describe two pictures that this description of the wood puts in your mind.

This time Da-duh didn't even bother to ask her usual question, but simply turned and waited for me to speak.

"No," I said, my head bowed. "We don't have anything like this in New York."

"Ah," she cried, her triumph complete. "I din' think so. Why, I've heard that's a place where you can walk till you near drop and never see a tree."

"We've got a chestnut tree in front of our house," I said.

"Does it bear?" She waited. "I ask you, does it bear?"

"Not anymore," I muttered. "It used to, but not anymore."

She gave the nod that was like a nervous twitch. "You see," she said. "Nothing can bear there." Then, secure behind her scorn, she added, "But tell me, what's this snow like that you hear so much about?"

Looking up, I studied her closely, sensing my chance, and then I told her, describing at length and with as much drama as I could summon not only what snow in the city was like, but what it would be like here, in her perennial summer kingdom.

". . . And you see all these trees you got here," I said. "Well, they'd be bare. No leaves, no fruit, nothing. They'd be covered in snow. You see your canes. They'd be buried under tons of snow. The snow would be higher than your head, higher than your house, and you wouldn't be able to come down into this here gully because it would be snowed under. . . ."

She searched my face for the lie, still scornful but intrigued. "What a thing, huh?" she said finally, whispering it softly to herself.

"And when it snows you couldn't dress like you are now," I said. "Oh no, you'd freeze to death. You'd have to wear a hat and gloves and galoshes and earmuffs so your ears wouldn't freeze and drop off, and a heavy coat. I've got a Shirley Temple[7] coat with fur on the collar. I can dance. You wanna see?"

Before she could answer I began, with a dance called the Truck which was popular back then in the 1930s. My right forefinger waving, I trucked around the nearby trees and around Da-duh's awed and rigid form. After the Truck I did the Suzy-Q, my lean hips swishing, my sneakers sidling zigzag over the ground. "I can sing," I

---

7. **Shirley Temple:** child movie star popular during the 1930s.

Vocabulary
perennial (pə·ren′ē·əl) *adj.:* year-round; continual.

said and did so, starting with "I'm Gonna Sit Right Down and Write Myself a Letter," then without pausing, "Tea for Two," and ending with "I Found a Million Dollar Baby in a Five and Ten Cent Store."

For long moments afterwards Da-duh stared at me as if I were a creature from Mars, an emissary from some world she did not know but which intrigued her and whose power she both felt and feared. Yet something about my performance must have pleased her, because bending down she slowly lifted her long skirt and then, one by one, the layers of petticoats until she came to a drawstring purse dangling at the end of a long strip of cloth tied round her waist. Opening the purse she handed me a penny. "Here," she said half-smiling against her will. "Take this to buy yourself a sweet at the shop up the road. There's nothing to be done with you, soul."

From then on, whenever I wasn't taken to visit relatives, I accompanied Da-duh out into the ground, and alone with her amid the canes or down in the gully I told her about New York. It always began with some slighting remark on her part: "I know they don't have anything this nice where you come from," or "Tell me, I hear those foolish people in New York does do such and such. . . ." But as I answered, recreating my towering world of steel and concrete and machines for her, building the city out of words, I would feel her give way. I came to know the signs of her surrender: the total stillness that would come over her little hard dry form, the probing gaze that like a surgeon's knife sought to cut through my skull to get at the images there, to see if I were lying; above all, her fear, a fear nameless and profound, the same one I had felt beating in the palm of her hand that day in the lorry.

Over the weeks I told her about refrigerators, radios, gas stoves, elevators, trolley cars, wringer washing machines, movies, airplanes, the cyclone at Coney Island,[8] subways, toasters, electric lights: "At night, see, all you have to do is flip this little switch on the wall and all the lights in the house go on. Just like that. Like magic. It's like turning on the sun at night."

"But tell me," she said to me once with a faint mocking smile, "do the white people have all these things too or it's only the people looking like us?"

I laughed. "What d'ya mean," I said. "The white people have even better." Then: "I beat up a white girl in my class last term."

"Beating up white people!" Her tone was incredulous.[9]

"How you mean!" I said, using an expression of hers. "She called me a name."

For some reason Da-duh could not quite get over this and repeated in the same hushed, shocked voice, "Beating up white people now! Oh, the lord, the world's changing up so I can scarce recognize it anymore."

One morning toward the end of our stay, Da-duh led me into a part of the gully that we had never visited before, an area darker and more thickly overgrown than the rest, almost impenetrable. There in a small clearing amid the dense bush, she stopped before an incredibly tall royal palm which rose cleanly out of the ground, and drawing the eye up with it, soared high above the trees around it into the sky. It appeared to be touching the blue dome of sky, to

> "We've got buildings hundreds of times this tall in New York."

---

8. **cyclone at Coney Island:** roller-coaster ride in an amusement park in Brooklyn, New York.
9. **incredulous** (in·krej′ oo ·ləs) *adj.:* unbelieving; doubting.

A Garden in Nassau (1885) by Winslow Homer. Watercolor, gouache, and pencil on paper.

be flaunting[10] its dark crown of fronds right in the blinding white face of the late morning sun.

Da-duh watched me a long time before she spoke, and then she said very quietly, "All right, now, tell me if you've got anything this tall in that place you're from."

I almost wished, seeing her face, that I could have said no. "Yes," I said. "We've got buildings hundreds of times this tall in New York. There's one called the Empire State Building that's the tallest in the world. My class visited it last year and I went all the way to the top. It's got over a hundred floors. I can't describe how tall it is. Wait a minute. What's the name of that hill I went to visit the other day, where they have the police station?"

"You mean Bissex?"

"Yes, Bissex. Well, the Empire State Building is way taller than that."

"You're lying now!" she shouted, trembling with rage. Her hand lifted to strike me.

"No, I'm not," I said. "It really is, if you don't believe me I'll send you a picture postcard of it soon as I get back home so you can see for yourself. But it's way taller than Bissex."

All the fight went out of her at that. The hand poised to strike me fell limp to her side, and as she stared at me, seeing not me but the building that was taller than the highest hill she knew, the small stubborn light in her eyes (it was the same amber as the flame in the kerosene lamp she lit at dusk) began to fail. Finally, with a vague gesture that even in the midst of her defeat still tried to dismiss me and my world, she turned and started back through the gully, walking slowly, her steps groping and uncertain, as if she were suddenly

---

10. flaunting (flônt′iŋ) *v.*: showing off proudly or disrespectfully.

Enclosed Field with Rising Sun (1889) by Vincent van Gogh. Oil on canvas. (71 cm × 90.5 cm)

© Francis G. Mayer/CORBIS

no longer sure of the way, while I followed triumphant yet strangely saddened behind.

The next morning I found her dressed for our morning walk but stretched out on the Berbice chair in the tiny drawing room where she sometimes napped during the afternoon heat, her face turned to the window beside her. She appeared thinner and suddenly indescribably old.

"My Da-duh," I said.

"Yes, nuh," she said. Her voice was listless and the face she slowly turned my way was, now that I think back on it, like a Benin mask,[11] the features drawn and almost distorted by an ancient abstract sorrow.

"Don't you feel well?" I asked.

"Girl, I don't know."

"My Da-duh, I goin' boil you some bush tea," my aunt, Da-duh's youngest child, who lived with her, called from the shed-roof kitchen.

"Who tell you I need bush tea?" she cried, her voice assuming for a moment its old authority. "You can't even rest nowadays without some malicious person looking for you to be dead. Come girl," she motioned me to a place beside her on the old-fashioned lounge chair, "give us a tune."

I sang for her until breakfast at eleven, all my brash irreverent Tin Pan Alley songs,[12] and then just before noon we went out into the ground. But it was a short, dispirited walk. Da-duh didn't

11. **Benin mask:** reference to the beautiful ivory-and-wood masks carved in the West African kingdom of Benin, which flourished from the fourteenth to the seventeenth centuries.

12. **Tin Pan Alley songs:** Tin Pan Alley is a district in New York City, associated since the late nineteenth century with popular songwriters. Tin Pan Alley songs were "brash" (bold) and "irreverent" (mocking; disrespectful).

even notice that the mangoes were beginning to ripen and would have to be picked before the village boys got to them. And when she paused occasionally and looked out across the canes or up at her trees, it wasn't as if she were seeing them but something else. Some huge, monolithic[13] shape had imposed itself, it seemed, between her and the land, obstructing her vision. Returning to the house she slept the entire afternoon on the Berbice chair.

She remained like this until we left, languishing[14] away the mornings on the chair at the window gazing out at the land as if it were already doomed; then, at noon, taking the brief stroll with me through the ground during which she seldom spoke, and afterwards returning home to sleep till almost dusk sometimes.

On the day of our departure she put on the austere, ankle-length white dress, the black shoes and brown felt hat (her town clothes she called them), but she did not go with us to town. She saw us off on the road outside her house and in the midst of my mother's tearful protracted farewell, she leaned down and whispered in my ear, "Girl, you're not to forget now to send me the picture of that building, you hear."

By the time I mailed her the large colored picture postcard of the Empire State Building, she was dead. She died during the famous '37 strike,[15] which began shortly after we left. On the day of her death England sent planes flying low over the island in a show of force—so low, according to my aunt's letter, that the downdraft from them shook the ripened mangoes from the trees in Da-duh's orchard. Frightened, everyone in the village fled into the canes.

Except Da-duh. She remained in the house at the window so my aunt said, watching as the planes came swooping and screaming like monstrous birds down over the village, over her house, rattling her trees and flattening the young canes in her field. It must have seemed to her lying there that they did not intend pulling out of their dive, but like the hardback beetles which hurled themselves with suicidal force against the walls of the house at night, those menacing silver shapes would hurl themselves in an ecstasy of self-immolation[16] onto the land, destroying it utterly.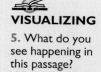

VISUALIZING

5. What do you see happening in this passage? Which details create the most vivid pictures?

When the planes finally left and the villagers returned, they found her dead on the Berbice chair at the window.

She died and I lived, but always, to this day even, within the shadow of her death. For a brief period after I was grown I went to live alone, like one doing penance,[17] in a loft above a noisy factory in downtown New York and there painted seas of sugar cane and huge, swirling van Gogh[18] suns and palm trees striding like brightly-plumed Tutsi[19] warriors across a tropical landscape, while the thunderous tread of the machines downstairs jarred the floor beneath my easel, mocking my efforts. ■

---

13. **monolithic** (män′ə·lith′ik) *adj.:* like a single large block of stone.
14. **languishing** (laŋ′gwish·iŋ) *adj.:* losing strength and energy; here, lying stretched out, without much energy.
15. **famous '37 strike:** Political factors and economic hardships led Barbadian workers to riot against the British in 1937.

---

16. **self-immolation** (self·im′ə·lā′shən) *n.:* violent self-destruction, usually by fire.
17. **penance** (pen′əns) *n.:* action done to make up for wrong behavior.
18. **van Gogh:** Dutch artist Vincent van Gogh (1853–1890) painted suns that seemed to roll through skies filled with swirling colors.
19. **Tutsi** (too͞t′sē): Watusi (or Watutsi), a people of Burundi and Rwanda, in central Africa.

Vocabulary

austere (ô·stir′) *adj.:* very plain; severe.

protracted (prō·trakt′id) *adj.:* extended.

menacing (men′əs·iŋ) *v.* used as *adj.:* threatening.

Meet the Writer

Paule Marshall

"I Am . . . an Unabashed Ancestor Worshipper"

Paule Marshall (1929–   ) calls this story the "most autobiographical" of her works. The Latin words *in memoriam* in the title mean "in memory of." The story is written in memory of Marshall's grandmother, who was called Da-duh by her family. Marshall based her story on a yearlong visit she made when she was nine to see her grandmother in Barbados. While she was there, she sensed "a subtle kind of power struggle" between her and her grandmother.

“ It was as if we both knew, at a level beyond words, that I had come into the world not only to love her and to continue her line but to take her very life in order that I might live. ”

Marshall adds that she has based other characters on her grandmother:

“ She's an ancestor figure, symbolic for me of the long line of black women and men—African and New World—who made my being possible, and whose spirit I believe continues to animate my life and work. I wish to acknowledge and celebrate them. I am . . . an unabashed ancestor worshipper. ”

Marshall was born in Brooklyn, New York, and she grew up among people who had emigrated from Caribbean islands like Barbados to the United States. Her writings have always reflected her background, which combines African American and Caribbean influences.

After graduating from college, Marshall found work as a journalist, and she began writing her first novel, *Brown Girl, Brownstones*. Her fiction focuses on the links among all the different African cultures in the Western Hemisphere.

After You Read   Response and Analysis

Reading Check

1. When Da-duh takes the narrator "out into the ground," what question does the old woman repeatedly ask?

2. What causes "all the fight" to go out of Da-duh?

3. What happens to Da-duh on the day that British planes fly over her house?

Thinking Critically

4. What types of borders does the narrator cross when she visits her grandmother? Explain the conflict that develops between the two characters as a result. How is their competition finally resolved?

5. Why is Da-duh so frightened by the narrator's stories about New York?

6. Why, once her grandmother is defeated, does the narrator feel "triumphant yet strangely saddened"?

7. Why does the narrator live "within the shadow" of Da-duh's death? Why is it significant that the factory machines mock her efforts to paint sugar cane, suns, and palm trees?

8. Consider what the story says about the following conflicts. Then, state what you think is the story's **theme.** (Check your Quickwrite notes.)

   • youth versus old age
   • colonial rule versus independence
   • urban life versus rural life

9. Which scene is most vivid in your mind? How does the writer's **style** help you **visualize** the scene?

Literary Criticism

10. Marshall describes her own relationship with her grandmother as "close, affectionate yet rivalrous." Using evidence from the story, show how the relationship between the **narrator** and Da-duh reflects the author's relationship with her grandmother. (See Meet the Writer on page 620.)

11. Look back at your statement of the story's theme (question 8). Find examples of specific words (**diction**) or **figures of speech** that help convey that **theme.** (For example, what might the author's comparison of the British planes to "monstrous birds" at the end of the story tell you about the conflict between colonies and the nations that rule them?)

12. How would you describe the story's **mood**—the feeling evoked by the setting? Give examples to show how the author's **diction** and **figures of speech** help create that mood.

WRITING

Analyzing a Story: It's Got Style

How would you describe Paule Marshall's **style**? Is it poetic, suspenseful, realistic, or fanciful, for example? Consider her **diction,** especially her use of **dialect,** her **figures of speech,** and her sentence structure. Then, write a few paragraphs analyzing Marshall's style. Before you write, gather examples from the story to support your points. Place your examples in a chart like the one below:

Elements of Style	Examples from Story
Descriptive words	
Dialect	
Figures of speech	
Sentence structure	

▶ Use "Analyzing a Short Story," pages 630–637, for help with this assignment.

SKILLS FOCUS

Literary Skills
Analyze elements of style, including diction and figures of speech.

Reading Skills
Visualize the story.

Writing Skills
Analyze a story's style.

Word Mapping

PRACTICE 1

The following word map for *unrelenting* shows its meaning, related words, and examples of things or situations that can be unrelenting. Make a similar map for each of the remaining Word Bank words. Be sure to compare your word maps with those of a partner.

Word Bank

unrelenting
formidable
reproved
truculent
decrepit
admonished
perennial
austere
protracted
menacing

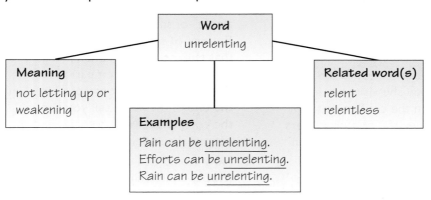

Word
unrelenting

Meaning
not letting up or weakening

Examples
Pain can be unrelenting.
Efforts can be unrelenting.
Rain can be unrelenting.

Related word(s)
relent
relentless

Denotation and Connotation: Fine-tuning

All words have **denotations**—literal meanings. Some words also have **connotations**—emotions and associations that have come to be attached to them. The words *cheap, inexpensive*, and *reasonable*, for ex-ample, all mean "not costly." However, *cheap* has negative connotations, whereas *inexpensive* and *reasonable* do not. *Cheap* suggests that something is not worth very much. The phrase "cheap sweater" suggests that a sweater is not well made or that it's of poor quality.

Paule Marshall's **diction** is characterized by her use of words with rich connotations, which add emotional depth to her writing. When you write, think carefully about the connotations of the words you use—doing so can make your writing more vivid and complex.

PRACTICE 2

For help thinking about the connotations of the words that Marshall uses, answer the following questions:

1. The narrator describes the sights of Barbados as "alien." What do you associate with *alien* that you don't associate with *strange*?

2. Da-duh notices the narrator's "fierce" look. How is a fierce look different from a cruel look?

3. Marshall says that sugar-cane plants "overrun" the island. What does *overrun* suggest that *cover* doesn't?

4. The procession of cars, buses, bicycles, and donkey carts leaving Bridgetown is called "funereal." What does *funereal* suggest that *solemn* doesn't?

5. Marshall describes the British planes as looking like "monstrous birds." What images does *monstrous* call to mind that aren't suggested by *large* or *huge*?

SKILLS FOCUS

Vocabulary Skills
Create semantic maps. Understand word denotations and connotations.

Before You Read

How to Eat a Guava

Make the Connection

Quickwrite ✏️

What is your absolutely favorite food? Think about eating that food, and write down all the sensations you experience while eating it. Do you associate that food with a certain time or place in your life or with certain experiences? Make a list of all the memories and feelings you connect with your favorite food.

Literary Focus

Style: Diction and Imagery

An important element of an author's style is **diction,** or word choice, and an important element of diction is imagery. **Imagery** is language that appeals to one or more of our senses—sight, sound, taste, touch, and smell. An image can help to re-create a place, a thing, or a person. Images give printed words on a page the glow and hum of real life.

In "How to Eat a Guava," Esmeralda Santiago takes a relatively simple subject —the eating of a tropical fruit—and turns it into a feast for all the senses. If you have eaten a guava, see how well her imagery re-creates the experience for you. If, on the other hand, this is your introduction to the guava—enjoy!

Tone: An Attitude

Diction and imagery have a powerful effect on creating tone in a piece of writing. **Tone** is a writer's attitude toward a subject. Since tone can be difficult to identify, it's helpful to think of a tone as "an attitude," which might be positive or negative, joyful or sorrowful, serious or humorous. A writer's tone can usually be expressed in a single word. As you read this excerpt from Santiago's memoir, you'll notice that her vivid imagery conveys an attitude about the guavas of her youth in Puerto Rico. What tone does Santiago create?

Background

The author of "How to Eat a Guava" comes from Puerto Rico, a Caribbean island where guavas and other tropical fruits grow in abundance. Located about one thousand miles southeast of Florida, Puerto Rico is a commonwealth of the United States, and its inhabitants are U.S. citizens. Spanish is the chief language of Puerto Rico, reflecting its long history as a Spanish colony; English is its other official language.

SKILLS FOCUS

Literary Skills
Understand elements of style, including diction, imagery, and tone.

INTERNET

More About Esmeralda Santiago

Keyword: LE7 9-8

How to Eat a Guava

from When I Was Puerto Rican
Esmeralda Santiago

> "You grimace, your eyes water,
> and your cheeks disappear as your
> lips purse into a tight ○ ."

Barco que no anda, no llega a puerto.
A ship that doesn't sail, never reaches port.

There are guavas at the Shop & Save. I pick one the size of a tennis ball and finger the prickly stem end. It feels familiarly bumpy and firm. The guava is not quite ripe; the skin is still a dark green. I smell it and imagine a pale pink center, the seeds tightly embedded in the flesh.

A ripe guava is yellow, although some varieties have a pink tinge. The skin is thick, firm, and sweet. Its heart is bright pink and almost solid with seeds. The most delicious part of the guava surrounds the tiny seeds. If you don't know how to eat a guava, the seeds end up in the crevices between your teeth.

When you bite into a ripe guava, your teeth must grip the bumpy surface and sink into the thick edible skin without hitting the center. It takes experience to do this, as it's quite tricky to determine how far beyond the skin the seeds begin.

Some years, when the rains have been plentiful and the nights cool, you can bite into a guava and not find many seeds. The guava bushes grow close to the ground, their branches laden with green then yellow fruit that seem to ripen overnight. These guavas are large and juicy, almost seedless, their roundness enticing you to have one more, just one more, because next year the rains may not come.

As children, we didn't always wait for the fruit to ripen. We raided the bushes as soon as the guavas were large enough to bend the branch.

A green guava is sour and hard. You bite into it at its widest point, because it's easier to grasp with your teeth. You hear the skin, meat, and seeds crunching inside your head, while the inside of your mouth explodes in little spurts of sour.

You grimace, your eyes water, and your cheeks disappear as your lips purse into a tight O. But you have another and then another, enjoying the crunchy sounds, the acid taste, the gritty texture of the unripe center. At night, your mother makes you drink castor oil,° which she says tastes better than a green guava. That's when you know for sure that you're a child and she has stopped being one.

I had my last guava the day we left Puerto Rico. It was large and juicy, almost red in the center, and so fragrant that I didn't want to eat it because I would lose the smell. All the way to the airport I scratched at it with my teeth, making little dents in the skin, chewing small pieces with my front teeth, so that I could feel the texture against my tongue, the tiny pink pellets of sweet.

Today, I stand before a stack of dark green guavas, each perfectly round and hard, each $1.59. The one in my hand is tempting. It smells faintly of late summer afternoons and hopscotch under the mango tree. But this is autumn in New York, and I'm no longer a child.

The guava joins its sisters under the harsh fluorescent lights of the exotic fruit display. I push my cart away, toward the apples and pears of my adulthood, their nearly seedless ripeness predictable and bittersweet. ∎

° **castor oil** *n.:* yellow or colorless oil made from castor beans, used as a home remedy for digestive problems.

Meet the Writer

Esmeralda Santiago

Between Two Worlds

Esmeralda Santiago (1948–   ) grew up in Puerto Rico, the eldest of eleven children. At the age of thirteen, she moved to New York City with her mother, her brothers, and her sisters. Living in Puerto Rico and in New York, she says, has to some extent made her feel that she doesn't quite fit into either culture—a feeling she highlights in the title of her memoir, *When I Was Puerto Rican*. In a note to readers of the book she writes:

❝ When I returned to Puerto Rico after living in New York for seven years, I was told I was no longer Puerto Rican because my Spanish was rusty, my gaze too direct, my personality too assertive. . . . Yet, in the United States, my darkness, my accented speech, my frequent lapses into confused silence between English and Spanish identified me as foreign, non-American. In writing the book I wanted to get back to that feeling of Puertoricanness I had before I came here. Its title reflects who I was then, and asks, who am I today? ❞

After graduating from Harvard University, Santiago earned a master's degree from Sarah Lawrence College. She currently lives in Westchester County, New York. Now, after years of struggling with not being entirely at home in her two cultures, Santiago says she defines *home* "as the place where I am."

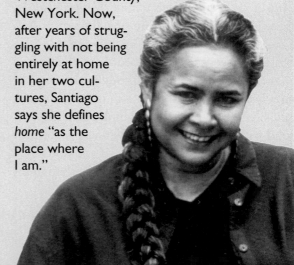

The Tropics in New York

Claude McKay

Bananas ripe and green, and ginger-root,
    Cocoa in pods and alligator pears,°
And tangerines and mangoes and grape fruit,
    Fit for the highest prize at parish° fairs,

5 Set in the window, bringing memories
    Of fruit-trees laden by low-singing rills,°
And dewy dawns, and mystical blue skies
    In benediction° over nun-like hills.

My eyes grew dim, and I could no more gaze;
10 A wave of longing through my body swept,
And, hungry for the old, familiar ways,
    I turned aside and bowed my head and wept.

---

2. alligator pears: avocados.
4. parish (par′ish) *n.*: church district; here, county.
6. rills *n.*: small streams.
8. benediction (ben′ə · dik′shən) *n.*: blessing.

Reading Check

1. Why do you have to be careful when you bite into a ripe guava?

2. Where is Santiago living at the time of the incident at the Shop & Save?

3. At the end, what does the author do with the guava in her hand?

Thinking Critically

4. What memories does Santiago associate with the guavas she ate in her youth in Puerto Rico? What do her recollections reveal about her feelings about her youth and her homeland?

5. At the end of the piece, what can you **infer** from the fact that Santiago heads toward the apples and pears? Why do you think she doesn't eat guavas anymore?

Literary Criticism

6. **Compare and contrast** Santiago's **images** of a ripe guava and a green one. List words and phrases that she uses to describe each one. Which senses does she emphasize? Make a chart like the one here to organize your thoughts:

	Ripe	Green
Sight		
Taste		
Smell		
Touch		
Sound		

7. How would you identify the **tone** of the essay until the point when Santiago describes having her last guava? Look carefully at the **diction,** especially the **imagery.** Find words and phrases that help to create the tone.

8. How would you describe the **tone** at the end of the piece? Has it changed? What words help create the tone at the end?

9. On the surface, Santiago's description of eating a guava is pure sensation. However, her description is also a way of communicating some serious ideas about time, crossing borders, growing up, and home. What **theme** do you think Santiago expresses through the **imagery** in "How to Eat a Guava"?

WRITING

Tasty Time Remembered

Choose a particular food memory—eating pumpkin pie at Thanksgiving, for example—and write a paragraph in which you share the experience with your readers. Be sure to use **sensory details.** (Check your Quickwrite notes.)

Comparing Literature

In a paragraph or two, **compare and contrast** Santiago's memoir "How to Eat a Guava" with McKay's poem "The Tropics in New York" (see the **Connection** on page 627), two pieces about tropical fruit. Consider the following factors: the **imagery** used; the situation described; the writer's or speaker's memories; the **tone,** or the attitude, of the piece. Be sure to consider ways in which the memoir and poem may differ. Use a chart like the one here to organize your ideas:

	"How to Eat a Guava"	"The Tropics in New York"
Imagery		
Situation		
Memories		
Tone		

SKILLS FOCUS

Literary Skills
Analyze elements of style, including diction, imagery, and tone.

Writing Skills
Write a descriptive paragraph. Compare and contrast a memoir with a poem.

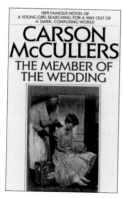

FICTION

Belonging

Twelve-year-old Frankie Addams is filled with contradictions. She wants to be accepted for who she is—and she wants to change into somebody different. She wants to be treated as a grown-up—and she wants to remain a child forever. Most of all, she wants a sense of belonging. When Frankie's older brother announces his engagement, a wave of excitement passes through her sleepy Georgian town. No one is more excited than Frankie, who sees the wedding as her chance to become a "we." You can find out what happens to Frankie by reading **The Member of the Wedding** by Carson McCullers.

FICTION

A Part of the Family

In Seoul, Korea, there is a season known as *changma*, the rainy season. For eleven-year-old Junehee and her family, the season of *changma* brings more than the usual rainfall—it brings Pyungsoo, a young boy orphaned by a mudslide. When the strange, quiet boy joins her household, Junehee does not welcome him at first. Then, as her parents' marriage begins to disintegrate—in part because of Pyungsoo's arrival—Junehee turns to the friendless boy for comfort. **The Long Season of Rain** by Helen Kim is the story of two "siblings" brought together at first by fate and then by love.

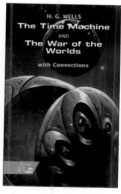

FICTION

Other Worlds

One of H. G. Wells's most inspired creations is a character known as the Time Traveler, the inventor of the Time Machine. This machine propels him from Victorian England thousands of years into the future, where he lands at the heart of a conflict between good and evil. Another of Wells's stories—one about a nightmarish invasion from Mars—is so convincing that it created a panic in America when the actor Orson Welles read it aloud in a radio broadcast in 1938. Take your own journey into worlds beyond with Wells's **The Time Machine** and **The War of the Worlds**.

These titles are available in the HRW Library.

NONFICTION

Writer at Work

In Alice Walker's **In Search of Our Mothers' Gardens** you'll meet the writer—up close and personal. This collection of essays, articles, reviews, and speeches covers a wide range of topics. You'll read moving tributes to famous African American writers such as Langston Hughes and Zora Neale Hurston, and you'll learn about Walker's own writing process as well. The collection also includes an autobiographical piece about the author's childhood injury and one about her experiences as a civil rights activist during the 1960s.

Analyzing a Short Story

Writing Assignment
Write a response to literature in which you analyze the literary elements in a short story.

Did the short stories you read earlier in this collection—"A Sound of Thunder" and "To Da-Duh, in Memoriam"—make a deep impression on you? Some stories can create a variety of emotions in their readers: tingling excitement, gut-wrenching fear, profound sadness, or exceptional delight. How do authors create such intense feelings in their readers? You can better understand the effects a story causes if you write an **analysis** of it.

Prewriting

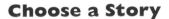

Choose a Story

It's Up To You   Since you'll be putting a lot of time and thought into your short story analysis, be sure to find a short story that interests you. To find a good short story:

- look for stories by an author whose work you have enjoyed in the past
- ask your friends, parents, or teachers to recommend a short story
- scan short story collections at your school or community library

Analyze Literary Elements

Take Two   Begin by reading the story to get an overall impression of it. Then, go back and take a closer look at the literary elements to **grasp the significant ideas** in the story. You are probably familiar with the basic literary elements of character, plot, and setting. To analyze these elements, ask yourself these questions.

- **Character**—What are the major characters like? What motivates them? Do any of them change? If so, how?

- **Plot**—What conflict or problem do the characters face? How is the conflict resolved? Does the resolution make sense?

- **Setting**—Where and when does the story take place? Does the setting affect the story's plot or characters? If so, how?

   The story may include additional literary elements such as those listed in the chart on the next page. Read the description of each element, and jot down answers to the questions in the right-hand column as you begin to look deeper into the short story.

SKILLS FOCUS

Writing Skills
Write an analysis of a short story.

LITERARY ELEMENTS

Description	Analysis Questions
Mood is the dominant feeling created in the story.	• Is the mood tense? hectic? happy and fun? frightening? quiet and calm? • What helps to create the story's mood?
Point of view is the vantage point or angle from which the narrator tells the story.	• Is the narrator of the story a character in the story (first-person point of view), or is he or she outside of the story (third-person point of view)? • How does the point of view affect your understanding of the story?
Stylistic devices are the language techniques the author uses to create certain effects.	• How does the author's word choice, or **diction,** influence the story's meaning? • What **metaphors, similes,** or examples of **personification** does the author use to prompt you to look at things differently?
Symbolism is the use of an object, person, or event to represent something beyond itself.	• Is a specific object closely related to a character or event? • Does one character or one event represent an abstract idea, such as bravery, greed, or education?
Theme is the main idea the story reveals or suggests about life or human nature.	• What common life experience or problem does the story examine? • How do the other elements in the story work together to reveal the theme?

Write a Thesis Statement

Focus In   Select the element you think has the most influence on the story. This will be the **focus element** of your analysis. To do this, ask yourself, "Why do I like this story?" and "What makes this story successful?" For example, a student analyzing "The Scarlet Ibis" (page 415) decided that mood is the element that gives that story its impact.

Next, think about what the author does to create the focus element or make it effective. You may notice that other elements work together to develop the focus element. The student writing about "The Scarlet Ibis" decided that diction, point of view, and symbolism all contribute to the mood of the story. He will develop a **key point,** or main idea, about each of these elements to support his discussion of mood.

Finally, write a **thesis statement** that identifies both the focus element and the key points about it. The student wrote the following draft of a thesis statement for his analysis of "The Scarlet Ibis."

In "The Scarlet Ibis," James Hurst uses diction, point of view, and symbolism to create a mood of tragedy, sadness, and loss.

TIP   You may find that two or more elements contribute equally to the story's impact. If so, try to focus your essay equally on each element. Be sure you have enough time and space to create an in-depth analysis of each element.

SKILLS FOCUS

Writing Skills
Establish a thesis statement.

Support Your Thesis Statement

DO THIS

What's the Point? To support your key points, gather **evidence** by taking notes on details from the short story. Evidence comes in three forms:

- **Direct quotation:** Exact words from the short story, set within quotation marks.

- **Paraphrase:** A restatement of all the author's ideas in your own words.

- **Summary:** A condensed restatement of the author's most important ideas.

It's not enough just to present evidence. **Elaborate** on the evidence you've included by explaining what it means and how it supports your key points. You can use elaboration to clarify and explain any ambiguities, nuances, and complexities you find in the story. **Ambiguities** are words, sentences, or passages that lend themselves to more than one interpretation. **Nuances** are changes in tone or meaning. **Complexities** result when a story is rich in meaning but difficult to interpret. (The Writer's Model on page 633 contains examples of a nuance and a complexity.)

Here is how one student supported a key point with evidence from the story and with elaboration.

Key point	Supporting evidence	Elaboration
The author uses the stylistic device of diction to help create the mood.	The narrator describes the flowers around his childhood home as "rotting brown magnolia petals" and "graveyard flowers."	This description refers to the aspects of nature with words that remind the reader of death. Hurst is creating an atmosphere of approaching tragedy.

Organize Your Analysis

Line It Up Next, you must organize your analysis. One way to organize the information is **chronologically,** in the order that the key points appear in the story. Another way is to arrange the information by **order of importance**—presenting the analysis of the most important point either first, to create a strong first impression, or last, to end your analysis on a strong note. Use order of importance if one key point is clearly more important than the others.

SKILLS FOCUS

Writing Skills
Support the thesis statement. Arrange ideas logically and effectively.

PRACTICE & APPLY 1 Choose a short story and analyze the literary elements in it. Choose a focus element and develop key points about it. Write a thesis, select strong supporting evidence, and organize the ideas for your analysis.

Writing

Analyzing a Short Story

A Writer's Framework

Introduction

- Grab readers' attention by relating an anecdote or by asking a question.
- Identify the story's author and title.
- State your thesis, presenting the focus element and key points.

Body

- Discuss one key point in each paragraph.
- Support each key point with evidence from the text.
- Elaborate by explaining how evidence supports each key point.

Conclusion

- Restate your thesis in a fresh way.
- Summarize your key points.
- End with a thoughtful comment that connects your analysis to real life.

A Writer's Model

Birds of a Feather Fall Together

When you pass an abandoned mansion, do you see a creepy haunted house or an intriguing historical home? Your view of the mansion depends on its atmosphere—the mood surrounding it. The same can be said of a short story—a story's mood influences the reader's feelings about the story itself. In "The Scarlet Ibis," James Hurst uses diction, point of view, and symbolism to create a mood of tragedy, sadness, and loss.

Throughout the story, the author creates the mood through diction, a stylistic device. In the first paragraph, the narrator describes the flowers around his childhood home as "rotting brown magnolia petals" and "graveyard flowers." He describes an abandoned bird's nest as "an empty cradle." Even the scent of the flowers that surround him is described as "speaking softly the names of our dead." This complex description refers to the aspects of nature with words that remind the reader of death. Hurst is creating an atmosphere of approaching tragedy. Because the story revolves around the relationship between the narrator and his frail brother, Doodle, the mood makes the reader worry about Doodle's future.

The point of view from which the story is told also influences its mood. Everything the reader knows about the relationship between the brothers comes directly from the first-person point of view of the

(continued)

INTRODUCTION

Title and author
Thesis statement

BODY
Key point: diction
Direct quotation

Elaboration

Key point: point of view

(continued)

narrator. The narrator is an older person looking back to his past to tell the story of his brother, for whose death he feels responsible. The narrator confesses both his positive and negative feelings for his brother. In his first description of Doodle, he refers to his brother as "nice crazy, like someone you meet in your dreams" and yet also as "a disappointment." The narrator loves his brother, but is disappointed in him because of his physical disabilities. This mixture of disappointment and love had fueled the narrator's actions towards his brother, and now he feels grief and guilt over the results.

The most direct way readers understand the story's mood is through the symbol of the scarlet ibis. With its arrival the mood in the short story becomes gloomier. A storm has blown the bird out of its natural place into the bleeding tree in the narrator's front yard. His family is fascinated by it until the dying bird falls to the ground, its "long, graceful neck" straightening and its feet curling underneath its body. When Doodle dies a short time later, probably from exhaustion and heart failure after his brother abandons him, his limp neck looks "unusually long and slim," and his legs are "bent sharply at the knees." The blood from Doodle's mouth colors his neck and shirt red like the bird's feathers. The connection between the ibis and Doodle becomes even clearer as the narrator cries over his brother, referring to him as "my fallen scarlet ibis." Doodle, like the bird, is a rare and fragile creature who could not survive the harshness of life. The symbolic relationship between the ibis and Doodle creates sympathy and compassion for the frail boy and helps the reader understand why the narrator suffers grief and guilt over Doodle's death.

In "The Scarlet Ibis," the author uses diction, point of view, and symbolism to create a gloomy, somber mood. Through diction, Hurst gives us an overwhelming sense that something sad is going to happen. Through point of view, we come to understand how the narrator's conflicted feelings about his deceased brother have brought him grief and guilt. Finally, through symbolism, we see the tragic fate of fragile creatures in our harsh world. By presenting this complex relationship, James Hurst helps all readers better explore their own feelings about love and cruelty and about loyalty and loss.

Sidebar annotations (left margin):

Complexity

Direct quotation
Elaboration

Key point: symbolism
Nuance
Paraphrase

Direct quotation

Elaboration

Direct quotation

CONCLUSION
Restatement of thesis

Summary of points

Final comment

INTERNET
More Writer's Models
Keyword: LE7 9-8

PRACTICE & APPLY 2 Write the first draft of your analysis of the short story you have examined. Use the framework on page 633 and the Writer's Model above as guides.

Revising

Evaluate and Revise Your Draft

Once Is Not Enough Reading over your draft just once is not enough. Carefully read your analysis at least twice. First, evaluate and revise the content and organization of your essay by using the guidelines in the chart below. Then, on your second reading, use the guidelines in the chart on the next page to improve the style of the writing in your analysis.

PEER REVIEW

Exchange your analysis with a peer before you revise. He or she can help you make sure that your key points are adequately supported by direct quotations, paraphrases, and summaries.

➤ **First Reading: Content and Organization** Use the chart below to help you evaluate and revise the content and organization of your short story analysis. Ask yourself the questions in the column to the left. If you need help answering the questions, use the tips in the middle column. If you need to revise, use the techniques in the column to the right.

Rubric: Analyzing a Short Story

Evaluation Questions	▶ Tips	▶ Revision Techniques
❶ Does the introduction grab the reader's attention and name the author and title of the story?	▶ **Put a check mark** by the sentences that capture the reader's interest. **Highlight** the title and the author in the introduction.	▶ **Add** sentences that will capture the reader's interest. **Add** the story's title or the author's name to the introduction.
❷ Does the thesis list the focus element and key points the analysis will discuss?	▶ **Draw a wavy line** under the focus element. **Put a star** beside the key points.	▶ **Add** specific information about the focus element and key points the analysis will cover.
❸ Does each body paragraph discuss one key point?	▶ **Number** each key point. Be sure that each paragraph covers only one key point.	▶ **Rearrange** key points so that only one is discussed in each body paragraph.
❹ Are the key points supported with evidence from the text and with elaboration?	▶ **Underline** the supporting evidence for each key point, and **double underline** the elaboration that explains the evidence.	▶ **Add** evidence to support each key point. **Elaborate** by explaining how evidence supports each key point.
❺ Does the conclusion restate the thesis and summarize the key points? Does it end with a final comment that relates the analysis to real life?	▶ **Highlight** the restated thesis. **Bracket** the summary of the key points, and **double bracket** the final comment.	▶ **Add** a restatement of the thesis and a summary of key points. **Add** a thoughtful final comment that connects the analysis to real life.

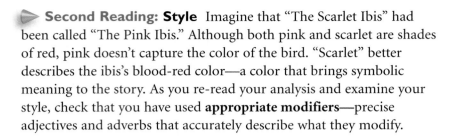

Second Reading: **Style** Imagine that "The Scarlet Ibis" had been called "The Pink Ibis." Although both pink and scarlet are shades of red, pink doesn't capture the color of the bird. "Scarlet" better describes the ibis's blood-red color—a color that brings symbolic meaning to the story. As you re-read your analysis and examine your style, check that you have used **appropriate modifiers**—precise adjectives and adverbs that accurately describe what they modify.

Style Guidelines

Evaluation Question	▶ Tip	▶ Revision Technique
● Do all adjectives and adverbs precisely describe the words or word groups they are supposed to modify?	▶ **Circle** all adjectives and adverbs in your analysis.	▶ **Replace** adjectives and adverbs that are inaccurate or weak with precise and accurate ones.

ANALYZING THE REVISION PROCESS

Study these revisions, and answer the questions that follow.

> The connection between the ibis and Doodle becomes even
>
> clearer as the narrator cries over his brother, referring to
>
> him as "my fallen scarlet ibis." Doodle, like the bird, is a rare
>
> *fragile*   *who could not survive the harshness of life.*
> replace/elaborate   and ~~weak~~ creature. The symbolic relationship between the ibis
>
> *frail*
> replace   and Doodle creates sympathy and compassion for the ~~weak~~
>
> *and helps the reader understand why the narrator suffers*
> elaborate   boy, *grief and guilt over Doodle's death.*

Responding to the Revision Process

1. How does replacing *weak* with *fragile* and *frail* change the meaning of this passage?

2. How does the elaboration in this section add to the reader's understanding of the story?

SKILLS FOCUS

Writing Skills
Revise for content and style.

PRACTICE & APPLY 3 Use the guidelines on page 635 to help you evaluate and revise the content and organization of the first draft of your analysis. Then, use the style guidelines above for further revisions. Finally, examine the revisions in the paragraph above as a model for your own revisions.

Publishing

Proofread and Publish Your Analysis

Look Carefully   Before you publish your short story analysis, make sure it is error-free. If you have too many errors in your analysis, your readers may not take your ideas seriously. Read over it several times, looking for mistakes in grammar, usage, and mechanics. To make sure you catch every error, have a classmate proofread your analysis, too.

Show It Off   Once you know your analysis is error-free, it's time to share it with its intended audience. Here are a few ways to get your work before the public.

- Form a literary club with your friends. Take turns sharing your literary analyses at your meetings.

- Submit your short story analysis to a Web site dedicated to student publishing. Also, look for online book stores that encourage readers to submit analyses and reviews.

- Compile your class's short story analyses into a booklet. Ask your school librarian to add it to your school library. Also, ask your librarian to index your compilation on the library database as a reference tool for other students.

- Deliver your short story analysis as an oral response to literature. For more on **presenting a literary response,** see page 564.

Reflect on Your Analysis

Thinking Back   Take time to think about writing your short story analysis. The questions below can help you think about what you learned as you wrote your literary analysis.

- How did you choose the story you analyzed? Would this process help you choose other stories to read informally? Why or why not?

- What did you find easy or difficult about writing an analysis? Why?

- Did you enjoy the story more or less after you analyzed it in depth? Explain your answer.

PRACTICE & APPLY 4   First, proofread your analysis. Then, consider your publishing options, and follow through on the one you think is most appropriate. Finally, reflect upon what you have learned in this workshop by answering the questions above.

TIP   Proofreading will help ensure that your essay follows the **conventions** of standard American English. For example, you most likely used pronouns at times to stand in for characters' names. Your reader may get confused if your pronouns' antecedents are not clear. Correct all inexact pronoun references in your analysis. For more on **clear pronoun reference,** see Clear Pronoun Reference, 4i, in the Language Handbook.

SKILLS FOCUS

Writing Skills
Proofread, especially for clear pronoun reference.

Literary Criticism: Evaluating Style

DIRECTIONS: Read the following story. Then, read and respond to the questions that follow.

Salvador Late or Early

Sandra Cisneros

Salvador with eyes the color of caterpillar, Salvador of the crooked hair and crooked teeth, Salvador whose name the teacher cannot remember, is a boy who is no one's friend, runs along somewhere in that vague direction where homes are the color of bad weather, lives behind a raw wood doorway, shakes the sleepy brothers awake, ties their shoes, combs their hair with water, feeds them milk and cornflakes from a tin cup in the dim dark of the morning.

Salvador, late or early, sooner or later arrives with the string of younger brothers ready. Helps his mama, who is busy with the business of the baby. Tugs the arms of Cecilio, Arturito, makes them hurry, because today, like yesterday, Arturito has dropped the cigar box of crayons, has let go the hundred little fingers of red, green, yellow, blue, and nub of black sticks that tumble and spill over and beyond the asphalt puddles until the crossing-guard lady holds back the blur of traffic for Salvador to collect them again.

Salvador inside that wrinkled shirt, inside the throat that must clear itself and apologize each time it speaks, inside that forty-pound body of boy with its geography of scars, its history of hurt, limbs stuffed with feathers and rags, in what part of the eyes, in what part of the heart, in that cage of the chest where something throbs with both fists and knows only what Salvador knows, inside that body too small to contain the hundred balloons of happiness, the single guitar of grief, is a boy like any other disappearing out the door, beside the schoolyard gate, where he has told his brothers they must wait. Collects the hands of Cecilio and Arturito, scuttles off dodging the many schoolyard colors, the elbows and wrists crisscrossing, the several shoes running. Grows small and smaller to the eye, dissolves into the bright horizon, flutters in the air before disappearing like a memory of kites.

SKILLS FOCUS

Pages 638–639
cover
Literary Skills
Evaluate
elements of
style, including
diction,
figurative
language, tone,
and mood.

1. Cisneros's **diction** in the phrase "Salvador inside that wrinkled shirt" helps you understand that Salvador is —
   A wearing someone else's clothes
   B too big for his shirt
   C too busy to care about his appearance
   D irresponsible and undependable

2. One characteristic of Cisneros's **diction** in this piece is her use of verbs to describe Salvador. What do these verbs tell you about his **character**?
   F He is indecisive.
   G He is seldom at rest.
   H He is confident.
   J He takes advantage of opportunities.

3. Cisneros uses a **simile** comparing Salvador to "a memory of kites" to show that he —
   A is not forgotten
   B is lively and cheerful
   C leaves a fleeting impression
   D moves swiftly

4. Which word *best* describes the **mood** Cisneros creates through her description of the homes and the morning in the first paragraph?
   F gloomy
   G suspenseful
   H hopeful
   J terrifying

5. Which of the following is the *best* expression of the selection's **theme**?
   A Children like Salvador will eventually triumph over the many obstacles in their lives and find happiness.
   B There are children like Salvador whose difficult life and small acts of courage go almost unnoticed.
   C In many families the oldest child often takes responsibility for younger siblings.
   D Although children may seem different on the outside, they are actually similar.

6. Which word *best* describes the **tone** the author creates through her description of Salvador?
   F sympathetic
   G mocking
   H bitter
   J objective

7. Cisneros's **style** in this selection is characterized by her use of —
   A ambiguity and contradiction
   B dialogue and symbolism
   C repetition and irony
   D imagery and long sentences

Constructed Response

8. List five ways that the author describes Salvador. Then, write down one way that you would describe him.

Collection 8: Skills Review

Vocabulary Skills

Context Clues

DIRECTIONS: Use the context clues in the following passages for help identifying the meaning of the underlined Vocabulary words.

1. In "A Sound of Thunder," Travis warns Eckels to stay on the path so that he doesn't accidentally annihilate a whole race of people. By killing just one mouse, Eckels could prevent the birth of a billion people.

   In this passage, *annihilate* means —

   A meet

   B destroy

   C frighten

   D discourage

2. In "A Sound of Thunder," Eckels travels to the past and enters a primeval world. Dinosaurs rule the earth, and there is no evidence of human civilization.

   In this passage, *primeval* means —

   F primitive

   G better

   H familiar

   J forgotten

3. In "Rising Tides," Bob Herbert argues that the effects of global warming could be catastrophic. As the world grows warmer and the oceans rise, there could be widespread destruction and loss of life.

   In this passage, *catastrophic* means —

   A mysterious

   B disastrous

   C immediate

   D prevented

4. In "An Arctic Floe of Climate Questions," Robert Cooke discusses our ignorance about climate changes. We do not know if warmer temperatures, which seem unusual to us now, are actually typical of long-term weather patterns.

   In this passage, *ignorance* means —

   F warnings

   G neglect

   H desire to prevent

   J lack of knowledge

5. In "To Da-duh, in Memoriam," Da-duh is a formidable woman. Her adult daughter greets her like an obedient child, for Da-duh commands respect from everyone.

   In this passage, *formidable* means —

   A frail

   B motherly

   C impressive

   D sensitive

6. In "To Da-duh, in Memoriam," Da-duh dresses in an austere manner. Her plain, simple clothes suit her strong, proud personality and her old-fashioned way of life.

   In this passage, *austere* means —

   F elegant

   G shabby

   H ugly

   J severe

SKILLS FOCUS

Vocabulary Skills
Use context clues to understand the meanings of words.

Collection 8: Skills Review
Writing Skills

DIRECTIONS: Read the following paragraph from a draft of a student's analysis of a short story. Then, answer the questions below it.

(1) In "A Sound of Thunder," Ray Bradbury uses similes to create a frightening tone that alerts readers to the dangers of toying with nature. (2) After traveling back in time for a prehistoric safari, a group of silly men shoots a Tyrannosaurus rex. (3) The dinosaur falls "[l]ike a stone idol," and the men stare in awe "like [they were] standing by a wrecked locomotive." (4) Bradbury also uses diction in his short story. (5) When Travis describes the consequences of killing animals before their time, he says, "Step on a mouse, and you leave your print, like a Grand Canyon, across Eternity."

1. To support the idea that Bradbury's use of similes creates a frightening tone, the student could also
   A explain the definition of tone
   B provide a paraphrase of another passage that includes a simile
   C give examples of various stylistic devices that appear in the story
   D tell another one of Bradbury's stories

2. Which sentence could be added to elaborate on the direct quotations in sentence 3?
   F The men are uncaring when they kill the dinosaur, and hunting only makes them want to kill even bigger animals.
   G The similes show that nature is more powerful than humans.
   H These similes give the impression that the death of the dinosaur has a greater impact than expected.
   J The men have to be careful to stay on the anti-gravity path so that they do not disturb anything from the past.

3. Which of the following words would be the best replacement for the weak modifier *silly* in sentence 2?
   A foolish   C angry
   B stupid   D adventuresome

4. To demonstrate an understanding of the short story, the writer could add which of the following sentences as a conclusion?
   F If the humans in this story hadn't been so careless, everything would have worked out fine.
   G The similes demonstrate humans' dangerous potential to alter the past, and worse, the future.
   H Greed ultimately costs one safari hunter his life.
   J The stylistic devices create a suspenseful mood throughout the story.

5. Which sentence should be moved to another paragraph in order to improve the passage's organization?
   A 1   C 4
   B 3   D 5

SKILLS FOCUS

Writing Skills
Write an analysis of a short story.

Turning Points

Literary Focus:
Literary Criticism:
Using Biographical and
Historical Approaches

Informational
Reading Focus:
Using Primary and
Secondary Sources

INTERNET

Collection
Resources

Keyword: LE7 9-9

Moonwalk (1987) by Andy Warhol (1928–1987). Silkscreen. 38 x 28 in.

Image ©Andy Warhol Foundation/CORBIS. Artwork ©The Andy Warhol Foundation for the Visual Arts/CORBIS. Courtesy Ronald Feldman Fine Arts, New York.

Elements of Literature

Literary Roots *by* Kylene Beers
THE WRITER'S LIFE AND TIMES

Once upon a time not too long ago, a hard drive meant a long trip in a car with too many children and not enough air conditioning. A mouse scared you, and a desktop was the top of your desk. You needed waves to surf, a speedy car to be an instant messenger, and a pencil to draw. As times change, our world and the language we use to describe it change too.

When and Where Are Important

Without doubt, our **historical setting**—the time and the place—affects our language and our vision of the world. Historical setting also has an impact on the way people write and what they write about. Read the following few lines:

> That man over there say
>   a woman needs to be helped into carriages
> and lifted over ditches
>   and to have the best place everywhere.
> Nobody ever helped me into carriages
>   or over mud puddles
>   or gives me a best place. . . .
> —from "Ain't I a Woman?"
> Sojourner Truth

Pause now, and ask yourself, "Who are the people in this text? What's the situation? Is the speaker male or female? angry or happy? frustrated or content? Why is the speaker saying this?"

Now here's a little historical background: This is the first part of a speech given at a women's rights convention in Akron, Ohio, in 1851. Unfortunately, there is no exact copy of the speech in existence today. It has been adapted here in the form of a poem. The speaker is a woman. She is responding to other speakers—all men—who are explaining why women shouldn't have the same rights as men.

Read the lines again, and ask yourself more questions: "What do the details about how a woman should be treated ('helped into carriages and lifted over ditches') tell me? What might a man say today about how to treat a woman?" Understanding the historical setting of this speech helps us grasp the issues that were important at the time it was given.

The Writer's Life Experience Is Important

Now let's add another dimension—a **biographical** one—to our discussion by focusing on the author, Sojourner Truth. Not only was Sojourner Truth a woman, but she was also an African American woman. Think about the time—1851. At that time in America, most African Americans were held as slaves. Sojourner Truth, however, had gained her freedom and changed her name. The word *sojourner* means "traveler; person on a journey." Suddenly the speaker's name, meaning "traveler on a journey toward truth," adds to what we know about her.

Read the text one more time, and answer those original questions again:

1. Who are the people in this text?
2. What's the situation?
3. Is the speaker male or female? angry or happy? frustrated or content?
4. Why is the speaker saying this?

SKILLS FOCUS

Literary Skills
Understand biographical and historical approaches to literary works.

You'll probably find that your answers, now that you know the historical setting and some biographical information about the author, have a fuller meaning.

Put It All Together

Read more of what Sojourner Truth said:

> Look at me
> Look at my arm!
> I have plowed and planted
> and gathered into barns
> and no man could head me. . . .
> And ain't I a woman? . . .
> that little man in black there say
> a woman can't have as much rights as
> a man
> cause Christ wasn't a woman
> Where did your Christ come from?
> From God and a woman!
> Man had nothing to do with him!
> If the first woman God ever made
> was strong enough to turn the world
> upside down, all alone
> together women ought to be able to
> turn it
> rightside up again.

We can see the issue of women's rights emerging in this part of the speech as well. Look carefully at the phrase "that little man in black there," above. Who is this man? Look at his argument against women having the same rights as men. He's offering a religious justification for his views. Is the "man in black" a clergyman? Again, understanding the historical context helps us see an issue of the time—the conflict between men and women and the use of religious justifications for some laws that gave men more rights than women. Sojourner Truth also discusses her own experience in this speech. Understanding a writer's life, including his or her attitudes, heritage, and traditions, adds meaning to what we are reading.

Don't Jump to Conclusions

Remember, however, that an author's life is not always mirrored in a text. Ray Bradbury, for example, has written some famous stories about Mars, but Bradbury is from Waukegan, Illinois, and he is certainly not a Martian. However, a close look at Bradbury's work shows concern for some issues specific to our time, such as the conflict between personal freedom and technology.

Practice

Working with a partner or in a small group, make a list of some short stories or novels you've read that have a **historical setting.** Then, jot down notes about each work, using a chart like the one below. Be sure to compare your findings with those of your classmates.

Title of story or novel:
When was the work written?
What is the writer's background?
What issues of the writer's time are reflected in the work?

Turning Points

Make the Connection

Quickwrite 🖉

The turning points in our lives often hinge on important choices. For example, we might have to choose between taking a risk and playing it safe. List the types of choices you, people you know, or even fictional characters have faced at key moments in life. Save your list.

Exploring the Theme: Turning Points

The turning points in our lives often result from personal experiences as well as historical forces. In the story "American History," a teenager learns about friendship and prejudice on the day President John F. Kennedy was shot. Several nonfiction selections explore how President Kennedy's assassination was a turning point for Americans. In the story "Beware of the Dog," a fighter pilot's life is on the line. In "The Old Demon" the main character makes a decision from which there's no turning back.

Literary Focus

Biographical and Historical Approaches

Sometimes writers draw on their lives or on the historical period in which they live to create fictional stories. Through the power of the imagination, writers transform real-life people, events, and places—sometimes in surprising ways. Pay careful attention to the **historical** and **biographical** information accompanying "The Old Demon." Think about the connections between the writer's life and times and the events in the story.

Background

This story takes place in China during the Chinese-Japanese War, which began in 1937, during which the Chinese and Japanese struggled for control of the Chinese mainland. In 1938, in an effort to stop the Japanese invasion, the head of the Chinese government ordered the flooding of the Huang Ho River, also known as the Yellow River. Hundreds of thousands of Chinese died as a result, and the flooding failed to stop the Japanese troops. Japan surrendered in 1945 after becoming involved in World War II.

Literary Skills
Understand biographical and historical approaches to literary works.

The Old Demon

Pearl S. Buck

Old Mrs. Wang knew of course that there was a war. Everybody had
known for a long time that there was war going on and that Japanese
were killing Chinese. But still it was not real and no more than hearsay[1]
since none of the Wangs had been killed. The Village of Three Mile Wangs
on the flat banks of the Yellow River, which was old Mrs. Wang's clan village, had never even seen a Japanese. This was how they came to be talking
about Japanese at all.

It was evening and early summer, and after her supper Mrs. Wang had
climbed the dike steps,[2] as she did every day, to see how high the river had
risen. She was much more afraid of the river than of the Japanese. She knew
what the river would do. And one by one the villagers had followed her up
the dike, and now they stood staring down at the malicious yellow water,
curling along like a lot of snakes, and biting at the high dike banks. ❶

"I never saw it as high as this so early," Mrs. Wang said. She sat down
on a bamboo stool that her grandson, Little Pig, had brought for her, and
spat into the water.

"It's worse than the Japanese, this old devil of a river," Little Pig said
recklessly.

"Fool!" Mrs. Wang said quickly. "The river god will hear you. Talk
about something else."

So they had gone on talking about the Japanese. . . . How, for instance,
asked Wang, the baker, who was old Mrs. Wang's nephew twice removed,
would they know the Japanese when they saw them?

Mrs. Wang at this point said positively, "You'll know them. I once saw a
foreigner. He was taller than the eaves of my house and he had mud-
colored hair and eyes the color of a fish's eyes. Anyone who does not look
like us—that is a Japanese."

Everybody listened to her since she was the oldest woman in the village
and whatever she said settled something.

Then Little Pig spoke up in his disconcerting way. "You can't see them,
Grandmother. They hide up in the sky in airplanes."

**HISTORICAL
APPROACH**

❶ Why is Mrs. Wang
more afraid of the
river than of the
Japanese?

---

1. **hearsay** (hir'sā') *n.*: rumor; gossip.
2. **dike steps** *n.*: A dike is a wall of earth or rock built to prevent flooding.

Landscape (detail) (1795) by Cai Jia (1730–1782). Ink and color on paper. 12 x 10 in.

HISTORICAL APPROACH

② Why does Mrs. Wang say that she doesn't believe in the Japanese?

Mrs. Wang did not answer immediately. Once she would have said positively, "I shall not believe in an airplane until I see it." But so many things had been true which she had not believed—the Empress, for instance, whom she had not believed dead, was dead. The Republic,[3] again, she had not believed in because she did not know what it was. She still did not know, but they had said for a long time there had been one. So now she merely stared quietly about the dike where they all sat around her. It was very pleasant and cool, and she felt nothing mattered if the river did not rise to flood.

"I don't believe in the Japanese," she said flatly. **②**

They laughed at her a little, but no one spoke. Someone lit her pipe—it was Little Pig's wife, who was her favorite, and she smoked it.

"Sing, Little Pig!" someone called.

So Little Pig began to sing an old song in a high, quavering voice, and old Mrs. Wang listened and forgot the Japanese. The evening was beautiful, the sky so clear and still that the willows overhanging the dike were reflected even in the muddy water. Everything was at peace. The thirty-odd houses which made up the village straggled along beneath them. Nothing could break this peace. After all, the Japanese were only human beings.

"I doubt those airplanes," she said mildly to Little Pig when he stopped singing.

But without answering her, he went on to another song.

Year in and year out she had spent the summer evenings like this on the dike. The first time she was seventeen and a bride, and her husband had shouted to her to come out of the house and up the dike, and she had come, blushing and twisting her hands together, to hide among the women while the men roared at her and made jokes about her. All the same, they had liked her. "A pretty piece of meat in your bowl," they had said to her

---

3. **Republic:** The Revolution of 1911 overthrew the dynasty that had ruled China since 1644. The republic established by the revolution lasted until 1949.

husband. "Feet a trifle big,"[4] he had answered deprecatingly.[5] But she could see he was pleased, and so gradually her shyness went away.

He, poor man, had been drowned in a flood when he was still young. ❸ And it had taken her years to get him prayed out of Buddhist purgatory.[6] Finally she had grown tired of it, what with the child and the land all on her back, and so when the priest said coaxingly, "Another ten pieces of silver and he'll be out entirely," she asked, "What's he got in there yet?"

"Only his right hand," the priest said, encouraging her.

Well, then, her patience broke. Ten dollars! It would feed them for the winter. Besides, she had had to hire labor for her share of repairing the dike, too, so there would be no more floods.

"If it's only one hand, he can pull himself out," she said firmly.

She often wondered if he had, poor silly fellow. As like as not, she had often thought gloomily in the night, he was still lying there, waiting for her to do something about it. That was the sort of man he was. Well, some day, perhaps, when Little Pig's wife had had the first baby safely and she had a little extra, she might go back to finish him out of purgatory. There was no real hurry, though. . . .

"Grandmother, you must go in," Little Pig's wife's soft voice said. "There is a mist rising from the river now that the sun is gone."

"Yes, I suppose I must," old Mrs. Wang agreed. She gazed at the river a moment. That river—it was full of good and evil together. It would water the fields when it was curbed and checked, but then if an inch were allowed it, it crashed through like a roaring dragon. That was how her husband had been swept away—careless, he was, about his bit of the dike. He was always going to mend it, always going to pile more earth on top of it, and then in a night the river rose and broke through. He had run out of the house, and she had climbed on the roof with the child and had saved herself and it while he was drowned. Well, they had pushed the river back again behind its dikes, and it had stayed there this time. Every day she herself walked up and down the length of the dike for which the village was responsible and examined it. The men laughed and said, "If anything is wrong with the dikes, Granny will tell us." ❹

It had never occurred to any of them to move the village away from the river. The Wangs had lived there for generations, and some had always escaped the floods and had fought the river more fiercely than ever afterward.

Little Pig suddenly stopped singing.

"The moon is coming up!" he cried. "That's not good. Airplanes come out on moonlight nights."

---

4. **feet a trifle big:** Certain upper-class Chinese women used to have their feet bound from an early age to make them smaller. Small feet were considered attractive, and they indicated that the women did not have to work.
5. **deprecatingly** (dep′rə·kāt·iŋ·lē) *adv.:* in a disapproving, disrespectful manner.
6. **Buddhist purgatory:** in the Buddhist religion, the state in which the dead are purified before they can achieve nirvana, a state of perfect freedom and bliss.

THEME

❸ What does the death of Mrs. Wang's husband reveal about the river?

THEME

❹ Why does Mrs. Wang view the river as both good and evil?

**HISTORICAL
APPROACH**

❺ What do the last
two paragraphs tell
you about how the
Chinese regard people
who have reached
an advanced age?

THEME

❻ The bombing of
the village marks a
turning point for Mrs.
Wang. Why doesn't
she run? Why does
she tell Little Pig's
wife to leave her?

"Where do you learn all this about airplanes?" old Mrs. Wang exclaimed. "It is tiresome to me," she added, so severely that no one spoke. In this silence, leaning upon the arm of Little Pig's wife, she descended slowly the earthen steps which led down into the village, using her long pipe in the other hand as a walking stick. Behind her the villagers came down, one by one, to bed. No one moved before she did, but none stayed long after her.

And in her own bed at last, behind the blue cotton mosquito curtains which Little Pig's wife fastened securely, she fell peacefully asleep. She had lain awake a little while thinking about the Japanese and wondering why they wanted to fight. Only very coarse persons wanted wars. In her mind she saw large coarse persons. If they came one must wheedle them, she thought, invite them to drink tea, and explain to them, reasonably— only why should they come to a peaceful farming village . . . ? ❺

So she was not in the least prepared for Little Pig's wife screaming at her that the Japanese had come. She sat up in bed muttering, "The tea bowls—the tea—"

"Grandmother, there's no time!" Little Pig's wife screamed. "They're here—they're here!"

"Where?" old Mrs. Wang cried, now awake.

"In the sky!" Little Pig's wife wailed.

They had all run out at that, into the clear early dawn, and gazed up. There, like wild geese flying in autumn, were great birdlike shapes.

"But what are they?" old Mrs. Wang cried.

And then, like a silver egg dropping, something drifted straight down and fell at the far end of the village in a field. A fountain of earth flew up, and they all ran to see it. There was a hole thirty feet across, as big as a pond. They were so astonished they could not speak, and then, before anyone could say anything, another and another egg began to fall and everybody was running, running . . .

Everybody, that is, but Mrs. Wang. When Little Pig's wife seized her hand to drag her along, old Mrs. Wang pulled away and sat down against the bank of the dike.

"I can't run," she remarked. "I haven't run in seventy years, since before my feet were bound. You go on. Where's Little Pig?" She looked around. Little Pig was already gone. "Like his grandfather," she remarked, "always the first to run."

But Little Pig's wife would not leave her, not, that is, until old Mrs. Wang reminded her that it was her duty.

"If Little Pig is dead," she said, "then it is necessary that his son be born alive." And when the girl still hesitated, she struck at her gently with her pipe. "Go on—go on," she exclaimed.

So unwillingly, because now they could scarcely hear each other speak for the roar of the dipping planes, Little Pig's wife went on with the others. ❻

Beneficent Rain (detail #5)
(Yuan Dynasty) by
Chang Yu-ts'ai.
Handscroll. Ink on silk.
10⅝ in. high x 106¾ in.
long.
The Metropolitan Museum of
Art. Gift of Douglas Dillon, 1985.
(1985.277.2). Photograph by
Malcolm Varon. Photograph
©1991 The Metropolitan
Museum of Art.

By now, although only a few minutes had passed, the village was in ruins and the straw roofs and wooden beams were blazing. Everybody was gone. As they passed they had shrieked at old Mrs. Wang to come on, and she had called back pleasantly:

"I'm coming—I'm coming!"

But she did not go. She sat quite alone watching now what was an extraordinary spectacle. For soon other planes came, from where she did not know, but they attacked the first ones. The sun came up over the fields of ripening wheat, and in the clear summery air the planes wheeled and darted and spat at each other. When this was over, she thought, she would go back into the village and see if anything was left. Here and there a wall stood, supporting a roof. She could not see her own house from here. But she was not unused to war. Once bandits had looted their village, and houses had been burned then, too. Well, now it had happened again. Burning houses one could see often, but not this darting silvery shining battle in the air. She understood none of it—not what those things were, nor how they stayed up in the sky. She simply sat, growing hungry, and watching.

"I'd like to see one close," she said aloud. And at that moment, as though in answer, one of them pointed suddenly downward, and, wheeling and twisting as though it were wounded, it fell head down in a field which Little Pig had plowed only yesterday for soybeans. And in an instant the sky was empty again, and there was only this wounded thing on the ground and herself.

She hoisted[7] herself carefully from the earth. At her age she need be afraid of nothing. She could, she decided, go and see what it was. So, leaning on her bamboo pipe, she made her way slowly across the fields. Behind her in the sudden stillness two or three village dogs appeared and followed, creeping close to her in their terror. When they drew near to the fallen plane, they barked furiously. Then she hit them with her pipe.

"Be quiet," she scolded, "there's already been noise enough to split my ears!"

She tapped the airplane.

"Metal," she told the dogs. "Silver, doubtless," she added. Melted up, it would make them all rich.

She walked around it, examining it closely. What made it fly? It seemed dead. Nothing moved or made a sound within it. Then, coming to the side to which it tipped, she saw a young man in it, slumped into a heap in a little seat. The dogs growled, but she struck at them again and they fell back. ❼

"Are you dead?" she inquired politely.

The young man moved a little at her voice, but did not speak. She drew nearer and peered into the hole in which he sat. His side was bleeding.

"Wounded!" she exclaimed. She took his wrist. It was warm, but inert,[8] and when she let it go, it dropped against the side of the hole. She stared at him. He had black hair and a dark skin like a Chinese and still he did not look like a Chinese.

"He must be a Southerner," she thought. Well, the chief thing was, he was alive.

"You had better come out," she remarked. "I'll put some herb plaster[9] on your side."

The young man muttered something dully.

"What did you say?" she asked. But he did not say it again.

"I am still quite strong," she decided after a moment. So she reached in and seized him about the waist and pulled him out slowly, panting a good deal. Fortunately he was rather a little fellow and very light. When she had him on the ground, he seemed to find his feet; and he stood shakily and clung to her, and she held him up.

"Now if you can walk to my house," she said, "I'll see if it is there."

Then he said something, quite clearly. She listened and could not understand a word of it. She pulled away from him and stared.

"What's that?" she asked.

He pointed at the dogs. They were standing growling, their ruffs up. Then he spoke again, and as he spoke he crumpled to the ground. The dogs fell on him, so that she had to beat them off with her hands.

"Get away!" she shouted. "Who told *you* to kill him?"

HISTORICAL
APPROACH

❼ Who do you
predict the young
man is?

---

7. **hoisted** (hoist′id) *v.*: raised; lifted.
8. **inert** (in•urt′) *adj.*: unable to move.
9. **plaster** *n.*: pastelike mixture applied to the body to heal wounds.

And then, when they had slunk back, she heaved him somehow onto her back; and, trembling, half carrying, half pulling him, she dragged him to the ruined village and laid him in the street while she went to find her house, taking the dogs with her.

Her house was quite gone. She found the place easily enough. This was where it should be, opposite the water gate into the dike. She had always watched that gate herself. Miraculously it was not injured now, nor was the dike broken. It would be easy enough to rebuild the house. Only, for the present, it was gone.

So she went back to the young man. He was lying as she had left him, propped against the dike, panting and very pale. He had opened his coat and he had a little bag from which he was taking out strips of cloth and a bottle of something. And again he spoke, and again she understood nothing. Then he made signs and she saw it was water he wanted, so she took up a broken pot from one of many blown about the street, and, going up the dike, she filled it with river water and brought it down again and washed his wound, and she tore off the strips he made from the rolls of bandaging. He knew how to put the cloth over the gaping wound and he made signs to her, and she followed these signs. All the time he was trying to tell her something, but she could understand nothing. ❽

"You must be from the South, sir," she said. It was easy to see that he had education. He looked very clever. "I have heard your language is different from ours." She laughed a little to put him at his ease, but he only stared at her somberly with dull eyes. So she said brightly, "Now if I could find something for us to eat, it would be nice."

He did not answer. Indeed he lay back, panting still more heavily, and stared into space as though she had not spoken.

"You would be better with food," she went on. "And so would I," she added. She was beginning to feel unbearably hungry.

It occurred to her that in Wang the baker's shop there might be some bread. Even if it were dusty with fallen mortar, it would still be bread. She would go and see. But before she went she moved the soldier a little so that he lay in the edge of shadow cast by a willow tree

HISTORICAL APPROACH

❽ How does Mrs. Wang treat the young man? What is your view of her behavior during wartime?

The Power (1992) by Hsu Soo Ming (20th century).

that grew in the bank of the dike. Then she went to the baker's shop. The dogs were gone.

The baker's shop was, like everything else, in ruins. No one was there. At first she saw nothing but the mass of crumpled earthen walls. But then she remembered that the oven was just inside the door, and the door frame still stood erect, supporting one end of the roof. She stood in this frame, and, running her hand in underneath the fallen roof inside, she felt the wooden cover of the iron caldron. Under this there might be steamed bread. She worked her arm delicately and carefully in. It took quite a long time, but, even so, clouds of lime and dust almost choked her. Nevertheless she was right. She squeezed her hand under the cover and felt the firm smooth skin of the big steamed bread rolls, and one by one she drew out four.

"It's hard to kill an old thing like me," she remarked cheerfully to no one, and she began to eat one of the rolls as she walked back. If she had a bit of garlic and a bowl of tea—but one couldn't have everything in these times.

It was at this moment that she heard voices. When she came in sight of the soldier, she saw surrounding him a crowd of other soldiers, who had apparently come from nowhere. They were staring down at the wounded soldier, whose eyes were now closed.

"Where did you get this Japanese, Old Mother?" they shouted at her.

"What Japanese?" she asked, coming to them.

"This one!" they shouted.

"Is he a Japanese?" she cried in the greatest astonishment. "But he looks like us—his eyes are black, his skin—"

"Japanese!" one of them shouted at her.

"Well," she said quietly, "he dropped out of the sky."

"Give me that bread!" another shouted.

"Take it," she said, "all except this one for him."

"A Japanese monkey eat good bread?" the soldier shouted.

"I suppose he is hungry also," old Mrs. Wang replied. She began to dislike these men. But then, she had always disliked soldiers.

"I wish you would go away," she said. "What are you doing here? Our village has always been peaceful."

"It certainly looks very peaceful now," one of the men said, grinning, "as peaceful as a grave. Do you know who did that, Old Mother? The Japanese!"

"I suppose so," she agreed. Then she asked, "Why? That's what I don't understand."

"Why? Because they want our land, that's why!"

"Our land!" she repeated. "Why, they can't have our land!"

"Never!" they shouted. ❾

But all this time while they were talking and chewing the bread they had divided among themselves, they were watching the eastern horizon.

"Why do you keep looking east?" old Mrs. Wang now asked.

THEME AND HISTORICAL APPROACH

❾ What new understanding has Mrs. Wang gained about the war?

"The Japanese are coming from there," the man replied who had taken the bread.

"Are you running away from them?" she asked, surprised.

"There are only a handful of us," he said apologetically.

"We were left to guard a village—Pao An, in the county of—"

"I know that village," old Mrs. Wang interrupted. "You needn't tell me. I was a girl there. How is the old Pao who keeps the teashop in the main street? He's my brother."

"Everybody is dead there," the man replied. "The Japanese have taken it—a great army of men came with their foreign guns and tanks, so what could we do?"

"Of course, only run," she agreed. Nevertheless she felt dazed and sick. So he was dead, that one brother she had left! She was now the last of her father's family. ❿

But the soldiers were straggling away again leaving her alone.

"They'll be coming, those little black dwarfs," they were saying. "We'd best go on."

Nevertheless, one lingered a moment, the one who had taken the bread, to stare down at the young wounded man, who lay with his eyes shut, not having moved at all.

"Is he dead?" he inquired. Then, before Mrs. Wang could answer, he pulled a short knife out of his belt. "Dead or not, I'll give him a punch or two with this—"

But old Mrs. Wang pushed his arm away.

"No, you won't," she said with authority. "If he is dead, then there is no use in sending him into purgatory all in pieces. I am a good Buddhist myself."

The man laughed. "Oh well, he is dead," he answered; and then, seeing his comrades already at a distance, he ran after them.

A Japanese, was he? Old Mrs. Wang, left alone with this inert figure, looked at him tentatively. He was very young, she could see, now that his eyes were closed. His hand, limp in unconsciousness,[10] looked like a boy's hand, unformed and still growing. She felt his wrist but could discern no pulse. She leaned over him and held to his lips the half of her roll which she had not eaten.

"Eat," she said very loudly and distinctly. "Bread!"

But there was no answer. Evidently he was dead. He must have died while she was getting the bread out of the oven.

There was nothing to do then but to finish the bread herself. And when that was done, she wondered if she ought not to follow after Little Pig and his wife and all the villagers. The sun was mounting and it was growing hot. If she were going, she had better go. But first she would climb the dike and see what the direction was. They had gone straight

---

10. **unconsciousness** (un·kän′shəs·nes) *n.*: state of being unaware.

THEME

❿ How does the news of her brother's death mark a turning point for Mrs. Wang?

west, and as far as eye could look westward was a great plain. She might even see a good-sized crowd miles away. Anyway, she could see the next village, and they might all be there. ⓫

So she climbed the dike slowly, getting very hot. There was a slight breeze on top of the dike and it felt good. She was shocked to see the river very near the top of the dike. Why, it had risen in the last hour!

"You old demon!" she said severely. Let the river god hear it if he liked. He was evil, that he was—so to threaten flood when there had been all this other trouble.

She stooped and bathed her cheeks and her wrists. The water was quite cold, as though with fresh rains somewhere. Then she stood up and gazed around her. To the west there was nothing except in the far distance the soldiers still half-running, and beyond them the blur of the next village, which stood on a long rise of ground. She had better set out for that village. Doubtless Little Pig and his wife were there waiting for her.

Just as she was about to climb down and start out, she saw something on the eastern horizon. It was at first only an immense cloud of dust. But, as she stared at it, very quickly it became a lot of black dots and shining spots. Then she saw what it was. It was a lot of men—an army. Instantly she knew what army.

"That's the Japanese," she thought. Yes, above them were the buzzing silver planes. They circled about, seeming to search for someone.

"I don't know who you're looking for," she muttered, "unless it's me and Little Pig and his wife. We're the only ones left. You've already killed my brother Pao."

She had almost forgotten that Pao was dead. Now she remembered it acutely. He had such a nice shop—always clean, and the tea good and the best meat dumplings to be had and the price always the same. Pao was a good man. Besides, what about his wife and his seven children? Doubtless they were all killed, too. Now these Japanese were looking for her. It occurred to her that on the dike she could easily be seen. So she clambered hastily down.

It was when she was about halfway down that she thought of the water gate. This old river—it had been a curse to them since time began. Why should it not make up a little now for all the wickedness it had done? It was plotting wickedness again, trying to steal over its banks. Well, why not? She wavered a moment. It was a pity, of course, that the young dead Japanese would be swept into the flood. He was a nice-looking boy, and she had saved him from being stabbed. It was not quite the same as saving his life, of course, but still it was a little the same. If he had been alive, he would have been saved. She went over to him and tugged at him until he lay well near the top of the bank. Then she went down again. ⓬

THEME

⓫ What choice does Mrs. Wang now face?

THEME

⓬ What do you think Mrs. Wang is imagining the river could do? How could the river "make up" for its wickedness?

She knew perfectly how to open the water gate. Any child knew how to open the sluice[11] for crops. But she knew also how to swing open the whole gate. The question was, could she open it quickly enough to get out of the way?

"I'm only one old woman," she muttered. She hesitated a second more. Well, it would be a pity not to see what sort of a baby Little Pig's wife would have, but one could not see everything. She had seen a great deal in this life. There was an end to what one could see, anyway.

She glanced again to the east. There were the Japanese coming across the plain. They were a long clear line of black, dotted with thousands of glittering points. If she opened this gate, the impetuous water would roar toward them, rushing into the plains, rolling into a wide lake, drowning them, maybe. Certainly they could not keep on marching nearer and nearer to her and to Little Pig and his wife who were waiting for her. Well, Little Pig and his wife—they would wonder about her—but they would never dream of this. It would make a good story—she would have enjoyed telling it.

She turned resolutely[12] to the gate. Well, some people fought with airplanes and some with guns, but you could fight with a river, too, if it were a wicked one like this one. She wrenched out a huge wooden pin. It was slippery with silvery green moss. The rill[13] of water burst into a strong jet. When she wrenched one more pin, the rest would give way themselves. She began pulling at it, and felt it slip a little from its hole.

"I might be able to get myself out of purgatory with this," she thought, "and maybe they'll let me have that old man of mine, too. What's a hand of his to all this? Then we'll—"

---

11. **sluice** (slo͞os) *n.:* artificial channel or passage for water with a gate or valve at one end to regulate the flow of water.
12. **resolutely** (rez′ə·lo͞ot′lē′) *adv.:* in a firm, determined manner.
13. **rill** *n.:* little brook or stream.

The pin slipped away suddenly, and the gate burst flat against her and knocked her breath away. She had only time to gasp, to the river:

"Come on, you old demon!"

Then she felt it seize her and lift her up to the sky. It was beneath her and around her. It rolled her joyfully hither and thither, and then, holding her close and enfolded, it went rushing against the enemy. **⑬**

Introducing the Collection Theme

THEME

⑬ What happens to Mrs. Wang at the end of the story?

Meet the Writer
Pearl S. Buck

At Home in Two Worlds

Although Pearl S. Buck (1892–1973) was born in West Virginia, she was as familiar with China as she was with her native country. When she was only a few months old, her parents took the family back to China, where they had worked as missionaries, and Buck spent most of the next forty years there.

Learning to speak Chinese before English, Buck grew up bilingual, and she became, in her own words, "mentally bifocal"—able to appreciate two vastly different cultures. She was educated by her mother and a Chinese tutor before being sent to a Chinese boarding school. After attending college in the United States, she returned to China, where she settled with her first husband. Buck lived with her family in towns and cities along the Yangtze River, and for three years she and her husband made their home in a poor farming village. She absorbed the Chinese culture, and her knowledge of the land and its people fueled her writing.

In 1927, Buck felt the full force of the conflict in China between the Nationalists, the Communists, and the warlords. She and her husband were living in Nanking when the city was invaded. Ten minutes after they fled their home, it was burned to the ground, and the manuscript of Buck's first novel was destroyed in the flames.

Buck threw herself back into writing, and by 1931, she had published her moving account of Chinese peasant life, *The Good Earth*. This novel was on the bestseller list for twenty-one months, received a Pulitzer Prize, became both a play and a hit movie, and has been translated into more than thirty languages. Buck's enormous literary output earned her the Nobel Prize in literature in 1938.

After You Read

Response and Analysis

Reading Check

1. What threat do the Japanese pose to the Chinese villagers? How does Mrs. Wang use the river as a weapon against the Japanese army?

Thinking Critically

2. Why does Mrs. Wang continue to help the pilot even after she learns that he is Japanese? After trying to save the pilot, why does she decide to fight the Japanese army?

3. Explain why you think the river is compared to a snake and the devil in the course of the story. Do you think "The Old Demon" is an appropriate **title** for the story? Why or why not?

4. In your opinion, what does this story reveal about war and its effects on people? Support your answer with examples from the story.

5. Look back at your Quickwrite notes. Then, think about how the collection theme "Turning Points" relates to this story. Why does Mrs. Wang choose to give up her own life and open the water gate? How do you think the writer wants us to feel about her death?—Is it tragic or triumphant? Cite details from the story to support your interpretation.

Exploring the Theme
Turning Points

The rest of the selections in this collection focus on various types of turning points in life. As you read, think about the causes and effects of each turning point.

Literary Criticism

6. Review the Background, which appears before the story. How does knowing the **historical** information about the flooding of the Yellow River affect your view of Mrs. Wang and her actions?

7. Review the **biographical** information in Meet the Writer on the previous page. In what ways do you think Pearl S. Buck drew on her personal experiences to write "The Old Demon"? Support your ideas with examples from Meet the Writer and the story.

SKILLS FOCUS

Literary Focus
Analyze a literary work using biographical and historical approaches.

The Old Demon **659**

Before You Read

American History

Make the Connection

Quickwrite ✏️

List moments in your life that you'll always remember. Your list might include events that have historical significance as well as personal importance. Jot down notes explaining why each event is memorable.

Literary Focus

Biographical and Historical Approach: The Roots of Literature

Where do writers get ideas for their works? Sometimes they turn to their own lives because they want to share an insight they've gained. Although names and details may be changed, these works reveal something about their authors, such as their childhoods, heritages, or beliefs.

Other times the **themes** and issues of a literary work are related to the **historical period** in which its writer is living. These issues may be central to the work, or they may provide background for the characters' lives.

The title "American History" hints that the personal experiences of Elena, the main character, are related in some way to life in this country. Meet the Writer (page 668) and the personal essay "Volar" (see the **Connection** on page 669) show that Elena's experiences also reflect those of the author. As you read, consider how the life and times of the author shape her story.

Reading Skills 📖

Summarizing: The Big Picture

When you finish a story, you should pause to summarize what happens. For help focusing on a story's most important elements, review who the main characters are and what happens to them.

SKILLS FOCUS

Literary Skills
Understand biographical and historical approaches to literary works.

Reading Skills
Summarize a story.

INTERNET

Vocabulary Practice
•
More About Judith Ortiz Cofer
•
Keyword: LE7 9-9

Background

President John F. Kennedy was assassinated on November 22, 1963, while riding in a motorcade in Dallas, Texas. That unforgettable day has become an important part of the way we view ourselves as a nation. Even today people from all walks of life share stories about where they were and what they were doing when Kennedy was killed. (For more about Kennedy, see pages 676–683.)

Vocabulary Development

literally (lit′ər·əl·ē) *adv.*: actually; in fact.

discreet (di·skrēt′) *adj.*: careful; showing good judgment.

linger (liŋ′gər) *v.*: continue to stay; be reluctant to leave.

infatuated (in·fach′ōō·āt′id) *adj.*: carried away by shallow or foolish love.

vigilant (vij′ə·lənt) *adj.*: watchful.

enthralled (en·thrôld′) *v.*: fascinated.

elation (ē·lā′shən) *n.*: great joy.

distraught (di·strôt′) *adj.*: deeply troubled, as with worry or grief.

dilapidated (də·lap′ə·dāt′id) *adj.*: in poor condition; shabby and neglected.

solace (säl′is) *n.*: comfort; easing of grief.

AMERICAN HISTORY

Judith Ortiz Cofer

"Listen," he repeated, "something awful has happened."

Teach Our Children (1990) by Juan Sanchez. Oil and mixed media on canvas.

Collection of the Museum of Tourism, San Juan, Puerto Rico.

I once read in a "Ripley's Believe It or Not" column that Paterson, New Jersey, is the place where the Straight and Narrow (streets) intersect. The Puerto Rican tenement known as El Building was one block up on Straight. It was, in fact, the corner of Straight and Market; not "at" the corner, but *the* corner. At almost any hour of the day, El Building was like a monstrous jukebox, blasting out salsas[1] from open windows as the residents, mostly new immigrants just up from the island, tried to drown out whatever they were currently enduring with loud music. But the day President Kennedy was shot, there was a profound silence in El Building; even the abusive tongues of viragoes,[2] the cursing of the unemployed, and the screeching of small children had been somehow muted. President Kennedy was a saint to these people. In fact, soon his photograph would be hung alongside the Sacred Heart and over the spiritist altars[3] that many women kept in their apartments. He would become part of

---

1. **salsas** (säl′səz) *n:* lively dance music from Latin America.

2. **viragoes** (vi·rä′gōz) *n.:* quarrelsome women.
3. **the Sacred Heart . . . altars:** The Sacred Heart is an image depicting the wounded heart of Jesus, often encircled by a crown of thorns. "Spiritist altars" most likely refers to memorials for dead relatives.

the hierarchy of martyrs[4] they prayed to for favors that only one who had died for a cause would understand.

On the day that President Kennedy was shot, my ninth-grade class had been out in the fenced playground of Public School Number 13. We had been given "free" exercise time and had been ordered by our PE teacher, Mr. DePalma, to "keep moving." That meant that the girls should jump rope and the boys toss basketballs through a hoop at the far end of the yard. He in the meantime would "keep an eye" on us from just inside the building.

It was a cold gray day in Paterson. The kind that warns of early snow. I was miserable, since I had forgotten my gloves and my knuckles were turning red and raw from the jump rope. I was also taking a lot of abuse from the black girls for not turning the rope hard and fast enough for them.

"Hey, Skinny Bones, pump it, girl. Ain't you got no energy today?" Gail, the biggest of the black girls who had the other end of the rope yelled, "Didn't you eat your rice and beans and pork chops for breakfast today?"

The other girls picked up the "pork chop" and made it into a refrain: "Pork chop, pork chop, did you eat your pork chop?" They entered the double ropes in pairs and exited without tripping or missing a beat. I felt a burning on my cheeks and then my glasses fogged up so that I could not manage to coordinate the jump rope with Gail. The chill was doing to me what it always did: entering my bones, making me cry, humiliating me. I hated the city, especially in winter. I hated Public School Number 13. I hated my skinny, flat-chested body, and I envied the black girls, who could jump rope so fast that their legs became a blur. They always seemed to be warm, while I froze.

---

4. **hierarchy** (hī′ər·är′kē) **of martyrs** (märt′ərz): *Hierarchy* means "ranking in order of importance." Martyrs are people who have suffered or died rather than give up their faith or principles.

There was only one source of beauty and light for me that school year—the only thing I had anticipated at the start of the semester. That was seeing Eugene. In August, Eugene and his family had moved into the only house on the block that had a yard and trees. I could see his place from my window in El Building. In fact, if I sat on the fire escape I was literally suspended above Eugene's backyard. It was my favorite spot to read my library books in the summer. Until that August the house had been occupied by an old Jewish couple. Over the years I had become part of their family, without their knowing it, of course. I had a view of their kitchen and their backyard, and though I could not hear what they said, I knew when they were arguing, when one of them was sick, and many other things. I knew all this by watching them at mealtimes. I could see their kitchen table, the sink, and the stove. During good times, he sat at the table and read his newspapers while she fixed the meals. If they argued, he would leave and the old woman would sit and stare at nothing for a long time. When one of them was sick, the other would come and get things from the kitchen and carry them out on a tray. The old man had died in June. The last week of school I had not seen him at the table at all. Then one day I saw that there was a crowd in the kitchen. The old woman had finally emerged from the house on the arm of a stocky middle-aged woman, whom I had seen there a few times before, maybe her daughter. Then a man had carried out suitcases. The house had stood empty for weeks. I had had to resist the temptation to climb down into the yard and water the flowers the old lady had taken such good care of.

By the time Eugene's family moved in, the yard was a tangled mass of weeds. The father had spent several days mowing, and when he finished, from where I sat I didn't see the red,

Vocabulary
literally (lit′ər·əl·ē) *adv.*: actually; in fact.

yellow, and purple clusters that meant flowers to me. I didn't see this family sit down at the kitchen table together. It was just the mother, a redheaded, tall woman who wore a white uniform—a nurse's, I guessed it was; the father was gone before I got up in the morning and was never there at dinner time. I only saw him on weekends, when they sometimes sat on lawn chairs under the oak tree, each hidden behind a section of the newspaper; and there was Eugene. He was tall and blond, and he wore glasses. I liked him right away because he sat at the kitchen table and read books for hours. That summer, before we had even spoken one word to each other, I kept him company on my fire escape.

Once school started, I looked for him in all my classes, but PS 13 was a huge, overpopulated place and it took me days and many discreet questions to discover that Eugene was in honors classes for all his subjects, classes that were not open to me because English was not my first language, though I was a straight-A student. After much maneuvering I managed to "run into him" in the hallway where his locker was—on the other side of the building from mine—and in study hall at the library, where he first seemed to notice me but did not speak, and finally, on the way home after school one day when I decided to approach him directly, though my stomach was doing somersaults.

I was ready for rejection, snobbery, the worst. But when I came up to him, practically panting in my nervousness, and blurted out: "You're Eugene. Right?" he smiled, pushed his glasses up on his nose, and nodded. I saw then that he was blushing deeply. Eugene liked me, but he was shy. I did most of the talking that day. He nodded and smiled a lot. In the weeks that followed, we walked home together. He would linger at the corner of El Building for a few minutes, then walk down to his two-story house. It was not until Eugene moved into that house that I noticed that El Building blocked most of the

Untitled (1992) by Juan Sanchez.
Mixed media on paper.

sun and that the only spot that got a little sunlight during the day was the tiny square of earth the old woman had planted with flowers.

I did not tell Eugene that I could see inside his kitchen from my bedroom. I felt dishonest, but I liked my secret sharing of his evenings, especially now that I knew what he was reading since we chose our books together at the school library.

One day my mother came into my room as I was sitting on the windowsill staring out. In her abrupt way she said: "Elena, you are acting 'moony.'" "Enamorada" was what she really said, that is—like a girl stupidly infatuated. Since I had turned fourteen . . . , my mother had been

Vocabulary

discreet (di·skrēt′) *adj.*: careful; showing good judgment.

linger (liŋ′gər) *v.*: continue to stay; be reluctant to leave.

infatuated (in·fach′o͞o·āt′id) *adj.*: carried away by shallow or foolish love.

more vigilant than ever. She acted as if I was going to go crazy or explode or something if she didn't watch me and nag me all the time about being a señorita[5] now. She kept talking about virtue, morality, and other subjects that did not interest me in the least. My mother was unhappy in Paterson, but my father had a good job at the bluejeans factory in Passaic and soon, he kept assuring us, we would be moving to our own house there. Every Sunday we drove out to the suburbs of Paterson, Clifton, and Passaic, out to where people mowed grass on Sundays in the summer and where children made snowmen in the winter from pure white snow, not like the gray slush of Paterson, which seemed to fall from the sky in that hue. I had learned to listen to my parents' dreams, which were spoken in Spanish, as fairy tales, like the stories about life in the island paradise of Puerto Rico before I was born. I had been to the island once as a little girl, to Grandmother's funeral, and all I remembered was wailing women in black, my mother becoming hysterical and being given a pill that made her sleep two days, and me feeling lost in a crowd of strangers all claiming to be my aunts, uncles, and cousins. I had actually been glad to return to the city. We had not been back there since then, though my parents talked constantly about buying a house on the beach someday, retiring on the island—that was a common topic among the residents of El Building. As for me, I was going to go to college and become a teacher.

But after meeting Eugene I began to think of the present more than of the future. What I wanted now was to enter that house I had watched for so many years. I wanted to see the other rooms where the old people had lived and where the boy spent his time. Most of all I wanted to sit at the kitchen table with Eugene like two adults, like the old man and his wife had done, maybe drink some coffee and talk about

books. I had started reading *Gone with the Wind.* I was enthralled by it, with the daring and the passion of the beautiful girl living in a mansion, and with her devoted parents and the slaves who did everything for them. I didn't believe such a world had ever really existed, and I wanted to ask Eugene some questions since he and his parents, he had told me, had come up from Georgia, the same place where the novel was set. His father worked for a company that had transferred him to Paterson. His mother was very unhappy, Eugene said, in his beautiful voice that rose and fell over words in a strange, lilting way. The kids at school called him "the Hick" and made fun of the way he talked. I knew I was his only friend so far, and I liked that, though I felt sad for him sometimes. "Skinny Bones and the Hick" was what they called us at school when we were seen together.

The day Mr. DePalma came out into the cold and asked us to line up in front of him was the day that President Kennedy was shot. Mr. DePalma, a short, muscular man with slicked-down black hair, was the science teacher, PE coach, and disciplinarian at PS 13. He was the teacher to whose homeroom you got assigned if you were a troublemaker, and the man called out to break up playground fights and to escort violently angry teenagers to the office. And Mr. DePalma was the man who called your parents in for "a conference."

That day, he stood in front of two rows of mostly black and Puerto Rican kids, brittle from their efforts to "keep moving" on a November day that was turning bitter cold. Mr. DePalma, to our complete shock, was crying. Not just silent adult tears, but really sobbing. There were a few titters from the back of the line where I stood shivering.

---

5. señorita (se′nyô·rē′tä) *n.:* Spanish for "unmarried woman."

Vocabulary
vigilant (vij′ə·lənt) *adj.:* watchful.
enthralled (en·thrôld′) *v.:* fascinated.

"Listen," Mr. DePalma raised his arms over his head as if he were about to conduct an orchestra. His voice broke, and he covered his face with his hands. His barrel chest was heaving. Someone giggled behind me.

"Listen," he repeated, "something awful has happened." A strange gurgling came from his throat, and he turned around and spat on the cement behind him.

"Gross," someone said, and there was a lot of laughter.

"The president is dead, you idiots. I should have known that wouldn't mean anything to a bunch of losers like you kids. Go home." He was shrieking now. No one moved for a minute or two, but then a big girl let out a "Yeah!" and ran to get her books piled up with the others against the brick wall of the school building. The others followed in a mad scramble to get to their things before somebody caught on. It was still an hour to the dismissal bell.

A little scared, I headed for El Building. There was an eerie feeling on the streets. I looked into Mario's drugstore, a favorite hangout for the high school crowd, but there were only a couple of old Jewish men at the soda bar talking with the short-order cook in tones that sounded almost angry, but they were keeping their voices low. Even the traffic on one of the busiest intersections in Paterson—Straight Street and Park Avenue—seemed to be moving slower. There were no horns blasting that day. At El Building, the usual little group of unemployed men was not hanging out on the front stoop making it difficult for women to enter the front door. No music spilled out from open doors in the hallway. When I walked into our apartment, I found my mother sitting in front of the grainy picture of the television set.

Retroactive I (1964) by Robert Rauschenberg. Oil on canvas (84″ × 60″).

She looked up at me with a tear-streaked face and just said: "Dios mío,"[6] turning back to the set as if it were pulling at her eyes. I went into my room.

Though I wanted to feel the right thing about President Kennedy's death, I could not fight the feeling of <u>elation</u> that stirred in my chest. Today was the day I was to visit Eugene in his house. He had asked me to come over

---

6. **dios mío** (dē′ōs mē′ō): Spanish for "Oh, my God."

Vocabulary
elation (ē·lā′shən) *n.*: great joy.

after school to study for an American history test with him. We had also planned to walk to the public library together. I looked down into his yard. The oak tree was bare of leaves and the ground looked gray with ice. The light through the large kitchen window of his house told me that El Building blocked the sun to such an extent that they had to turn lights on in the middle of the day. I felt ashamed about it. But the white kitchen table with the lamp hanging just above it looked cozy and inviting. I would soon sit there, across from Eugene, and I would tell him about my perch just above his house. Maybe I should.

In the next thirty minutes I changed clothes, put on a little pink lipstick, and got my books together. Then I went in to tell my mother that I was going to a friend's house to study. I did not expect her reaction.

"You are going out *today*?" The way she said "today" sounded as if a storm warning had been issued. It was said in utter disbelief. Before I could answer, she came toward me and held my elbows as I clutched my books.

"Hija,[7] the president has been killed. We must show respect. He was a great man. Come to church with me tonight."

She tried to embrace me, but my books were in the way. My first impulse was to comfort her, she seemed so distraught, but I had to meet Eugene in fifteen minutes.

"I have a test to study for, Mama. I will be home by eight."

"You are forgetting who you are, Niña.[8] I have seen you staring down at that boy's house. You are heading for humiliation and pain." My mother said this in Spanish and in a resigned tone that surprised me, as if she had no intention of stopping me from "heading for humiliation and pain." I started for the door. She sat in front of the TV holding a white handkerchief to her face.

I walked out to the street and around the chain-link fence that separated El Building from Eugene's house. The yard was neatly edged around the little walk that led to the door. It always amazed me how Paterson, the inner core of the city, had no apparent logic to its architecture. Small, neat single residences like this one could be found right next to huge, dilapidated apartment buildings like El Building. My guess was that the little houses had been there first, then the immigrants had come in droves, and the monstrosities had been raised for them—the Italians, the Irish, the Jews, and now us, the Puerto Ricans and the blacks. The door was painted a deep green: verde, the color of hope. I had heard my mother say it: verde-esperanza.

I knocked softly. A few suspenseful moments later the door opened just a crack. The red, swollen face of a woman appeared. She had a halo of red hair floating over a delicate ivory face—the face of a doll—with freckles on the nose. Her smudged eye makeup made her look unreal to me, like a mannequin[9] seen through a warped store window.

"What do you want?" Her voice was tiny and sweet sounding, like a little girl's, but her tone was not friendly.

"I'm Eugene's friend. He asked me over. To study." I thrust out my books, a silly gesture that embarrassed me almost immediately.

"You live there?" She pointed up to El Building, which looked particularly ugly, like a gray prison, with its many dirty windows and rusty fire escapes. The woman had stepped halfway out and I could see that she wore a white nurse's uniform with "St. Joseph's Hospital" on the name tag.

---

9. **mannequin** (man**ʹ**ə‧kin) *n.*: life-size model of a person.

Vocabulary

distraught (di‧strôt**ʹ**) *adj.*: deeply troubled, as with worry or grief.

dilapidated (də‧lap**ʹ**ə‧dāt**ʹ**id) *adj.*: in poor condition; shabby and neglected.

---

7. **hija** (ē**ʹ**hä) *n.*: Spanish for "daughter."
8. **niña** (nē**ʹ**nyä) *n.*: Spanish for "girl."

Untitled (1993) by Juan Sanchez.
Mixed media on paper.

Originally commissioned for the Center for Puerto Rican Studies at Hunter College, New York.

"Yes. I do."

She looked intently at me for a couple of heartbeats, then said as if to herself, "I don't know how you people do it." Then directly to me: "Listen. Honey. Eugene doesn't want to study with you. He is a smart boy. Doesn't need help. You understand me. I am truly sorry if he told you you could come over. He cannot study with you. It's nothing personal. You understand? We won't be in this place much longer, no need for him to get close to people—it'll just make it harder for him later. Run back home now."

I couldn't move. I just stood there in shock at hearing these things said to me in such a honey-drenched voice. I had never heard an accent like hers, except for Eugene's softer version. It was as if she were singing me a little song.

"What's wrong? Didn't you hear what I said?" She seemed very angry, and I finally snapped out of my trance. I turned away from the green door and heard her close it gently.

Our apartment was empty when I got home. My mother was in someone else's kitchen, seeking the solace she needed. Father would come in from his late shift at midnight. I would hear them talking softly in the kitchen for hours that night. They would not discuss their dreams for the future, or life in Puerto Rico, as they often did; that night they would talk sadly about the young widow and her two children, as if they were family. For the next few days, we would observe luto in our apartment; that is, we would practice restraint and silence—no loud music or laughter. Some of the women of El Building would wear black for weeks.

That night, I lay in my bed trying to feel the right thing for our dead president. But the tears that came up from a deep source inside me were strictly for me. When my mother came to the door, I pretended to be sleeping. Sometime during the night, I saw from my bed the streetlight come on. It had a pink halo around it. I went to my window and pressed my face to the cool glass. Looking up at the light, I could see the white snow falling like a lace veil over its face. I did not look down to see it turning gray as it touched the ground below. ∎

Vocabulary

solace (säl′is) *n.*: comfort; easing of grief.

Meet the Writer

Judith Ortiz Cofer

"The Human Experience"

Judith Ortiz Cofer (1952–   ) was born in Puerto Rico, but her family moved to the mainland United States when she was a toddler. In her autobiography, *Silent Dancing: A Partial Remembrance of a Puerto Rican Childhood,* Cofer explains that her family moved to Paterson, New Jersey—to a large apartment building that was known as El Building (like Elena's home in "American History"). Cofer says that her "memories of life in Paterson during those first few years are in shades of gray." Her father had encountered prejudice while looking for an apartment, but in El Building the family joined a community of fellow Puerto Rican immigrants. Cofer says of her early home:

> 66 The walls were thin, and voices speaking and arguing in Spanish could be heard all day. Salsas blasted out of radios turned on early in the morning and left on for company. Women seemed to cook rice and beans perpetually—the strong aroma of red kidney beans boiling permeated the hallways. 99

It was a challenge for Cofer to master English in her new home, but she achieved her goal. She earned a master's degree, and she attended Oxford University in England, where she received recognition as a Scholar of the English-Speaking Union. She has taught English at colleges in Florida and Georgia, and she has published several books of poetry, as well as fiction and nonfiction.

Cofer's stories often reflect the issues of her time. However, she explains that this does not make her a "political writer":

> 66 I am not a political writer in that I never take an issue and write a story about it. The people in my stories deal with political issues but only in accordance with the needs of their personal lives. My politics are imbedded in my work as part of the human experience. A story like 'American History' . . . takes place on the day Kennedy was shot. The girl in the story wants to feel the right way about the president's death, but she's in love and she can't help thinking about this boy. Yet she is faced at the end of the story with a political situation. The mother of the boy she loves rejects her because she's Puerto Rican. The story doesn't end with a speech on prejudice but with the heartbreak of a girl still unable to comprehend that it all comes together and affects her life: the death of a president, life in America, prejudice, the plight of the immigrant. 99

For Independent Reading

If you want to read more by and about Cofer, try *Silent Dancing: A Partial Remembrance of a Puerto Rican Childhood*, her award-winning collection of autobiographical essays and poems.

Volar

Judith Ortiz Cofer

At twelve I was an avid consumer of comic books—*Supergirl* being my favorite. I spent my allowance of a quarter a day on two twelve-cent comic books or a double issue for twenty-five. I had a stack of *Legion of Super Heroes* and *Supergirl* comic books in my bedroom closet that was as tall as I. I had a recurring dream in those days: that I had long blond hair and could fly. In my dream I climbed the stairs to the top of our apartment building as myself, but as I went up each flight, changes would be taking place. Step by step I would fill out: my legs would grow long, my arms harden into steel, and my hair would magically go straight and turn a golden color. . . . Supergirl had to be aerodynamic.[1] Sleek and hard as a supersonic missile. Once on the roof, my parents safely asleep in their beds, I would get on tip-toe, arms outstretched in the position for flight and jump out my fifty-story-high window into the black lake of the sky. From up there, over the rooftops, I could see everything, even beyond the few blocks of our barrio;[2] with my

X-ray vision I could look inside the homes of people who interested me. Once I saw our landlord, whom I knew my parents feared, sitting in a treasure-room dressed in an ermine coat and a large gold crown. He sat on the floor counting his dollar bills. I played a trick on him. Going up to his building's chimney, I blew a little puff of my super-breath into his fireplace, scattering his stacks of money so that he had to start counting all over again. I could more or less program my Supergirl dreams in those days by focusing on the object of my current obsession. This way I "saw" into the private lives of my neighbors, my teachers, and in the last days of my childish fantasy and the beginning of adolescence, into the secret room of the boys I liked. In the mornings I'd wake up in my tiny bedroom with the incongruous[3]— at least in our tiny apartment —white "princess" furniture my mother had chosen for me, and find myself back in my body: my tight curls still clinging to my head, skinny arms and legs and flat chest unchanged.

(continued)

1. **aerodynamic** (er′ō·dī·nam′ik) *adj.:* having characteristics that easily enable flight.
2. **barrio** (bär′ē·ō) *n.:* area of a city inhabited by people who speak Spanish.
3. **incongruous** (in·kän′grōō·əs) *adj.:* lacking harmony; not fitting in.

In the kitchen my mother and father would be talking softly over a *café con leche*.[4] She would come "wake me" exactly forty-five minutes after they had gotten up. It was their time together at the beginning of each day and even at an early age I could feel their disappointment if I interrupted them by getting up too early. So I would stay in my bed recalling my dreams of flight, perhaps planning my next flight. In the kitchen they would be discussing events in the barrio. Actually, he would be carrying that part of the conversation; when it was her turn to speak she would, more often than not, try shifting the topic toward her desire to see her *familia*[5] on the Island: *How about a vacation in Puerto Rico together this year, Querido?*[6] *We could rent a car, go to the beach. We could . . .* And he would answer patiently, gently, *Mi amor,*[7] *do*

you know how much it would cost for all of us to fly there? It is not possible for me to take the time off . . . Mi vida,[8] *please understand. . . .* And I knew that soon she would rise from the table. Not abruptly. She would light a cigarette and look out the kitchen window. The view was of a dismal alley that was littered with refuse thrown from windows. The space was too narrow for anyone larger than a skinny child to enter safely, so it was never cleaned. My mother would check the time on the clock over her sink, the one with a prayer for patience and grace written in Spanish. A birthday gift. She would see that it was time to wake me. She'd sigh deeply and say the same thing the view from her kitchen window always inspired her to say: *Ay, si yo pudiera volar.*[9]

---

4. *café con leche* (kä·fä′ kän·lä′chä): Spanish for "coffee with hot milk."
5. *familia* (fä·mē′ lyä) *n.*: Spanish for "family.
6. *querido* (ke·rē′ dō) *n.:* Spanish for "dear."
7. *mi amor* (mē ä·mor′): Spanish for "my love."

8. *mi vida* (mē vē′dä): Spanish for "my life"; used as an affectionate term for a loved one.
9. *Ay, si yo pudiera volar* (ī sē yō pōōd·yē′rä vō·lär′): Spanish for "Oh, if only I could fly."

After You Read — Response and Analysis

Reading Check

1. **Summarize** the story by identifying the main **characters** and describing the **setting** and main **events.** In your summary, answer the following questions:
   - How do Elena and Eugene know each other?
   - What is El Building, and where is it?
   - What happened in the United States on November 22, 1963?
   - What happens to Elena on November 22, 1963?

Thinking Critically

2. Eugene, nicknamed "the Hick," and Elena, nicknamed "Skinny Bones," come from very different cultures, yet they have some things in common. What are they?

3. Why is Elena turned away from Eugene's house?

4. Re-read the last sentence in the story. Why doesn't Elena want to see the snow turning gray? What does this statement reveal about Elena's character—about how she faces a loss in her life?

Literary Criticism

5. The story takes place on a day of great **historical** importance. How do Elena's family and community react to the death of President Kennedy? What **conflict** does Elena experience concerning her own reaction to the president's death?

6. Answer the questions in each of the following bulleted items. Doing so will help you figure out the story's **theme.**

   - President Kennedy was committed to eliminating prejudice and establishing equal rights for all Americans. How does Elena encounter prejudice in the story?
   - President Kennedy's assassination is often described as a turning point in American history. His death marked a loss of innocence in this country—that is, the discovery that dreams can be destroyed in one horrible moment. In what way does Elena make such a discovery?
   - Review Cofer's discussion of the story in Meet the Writer on page 668. How do Elena's personal situation and the political issues of the time come together at the end of the story?
   - Now, considering your answers to the previous questions, state the **theme** of the story. How does the **title** relate to the theme?

7. How are Cofer's feelings and attitudes when she was young, as described in "Volar" (see the **Connection** on page 669), reflected in the character of Elena in "American History"? What similarities do you see between Cofer's parents in the essay and Elena's parents in the story?

WRITING

"I Will Never Forget"

Review your Quickwrite notes, and choose one memorable moment on your list. Write one or two paragraphs explaining why the event had a significant impact on you. Did you gain a particular insight from the event? Did it affect you emotionally? Did it change your life in some way? Use specific details to make the meaning of the event clear.

SKILLS FOCUS

Literary Skills
Analyze a literary work using biographical and historical approaches.

Reading Skills
Summarize a story.

Writing Skills
Write an explanatory paragraph.

go.
hrw
.com

INTERNET
Projects and Activities
Keyword: LE7 9-9

Analogies: Word Pairs

In an **analogy** the same relationship must be expressed in two pairs of words. Follow this example for completing analogies:

TERRIFIED : AFRAID :: hot : _____

a. cold   **b.** warm   **c.** dry   **d.** thirsty

1. The relationship between the first pair of words is one of degree. *Terrified* describes a more intense, overwhelming type of fear than the word *afraid* implies.

2. In the second pair, *hot* refers to having a high temperature. The one word choice that indicates less intense heat is *warm*.

The following chart shows some relationships used in analogies. (For more information about analogies, see page 279.)

Type of Relationship	Example
Synonyms	HELP : AID :: speak : talk
Degree	DISAPPOINTED : HEARTBROKEN :: pretty : beautiful
Object (or thing) to a characteristic of it	APPLE : CRISP :: lemon : sour
Cause and effect	COLD : SHIVER :: happiness : smile
Object to function	SCALE : WEIGH :: knife : cut
Worker to tool	CARPENTER : SAW :: firefighter : hose
Performer to action	CLOWN : JUGGLE :: pitcher : throw

PRACTICE 1

Complete each analogy below with the Word Bank word that fits best:

1. LABOR : FATIGUE :: victory : _____
2. DAMP : WET :: worried : _____
3. PIN : SHARP :: shack : _____
4. HONESTLY : TRUTHFULLY :: actually : _____
5. CHILLY : FREEZING :: attracted : _____
6. LOYAL : FAITHFUL :: careful : _____
7. AMUSING : HILARIOUS :: interested : _____
8. ARTIST : CREATIVE :: guard : _____
9. WRITER : AUTHOR :: comfort : _____
10. ADMIT : CONFESS :: stay : _____

PRACTICE 2

Using the chart above as a reference, identify the type of relationship in each word pair below:

1. photographer : camera
2. fan : cool
3. mayor : govern
4. ballerina : dance
5. farmer : plow

SKILLS FOCUS

Vocabulary Skills
Complete word analogies.

Adverb Clauses

To avoid writing a series of short, choppy sentences and to show relationships between ideas, writers use adverb clauses.

An **adverb clause** is a subordinate clause that tells *where, when, how, why, to what extent,* or *under what conditions* an action occurs. Throughout her story, Cofer uses adverb clauses (underlined below) and a variety of subordinating conjunctions (boldface below) to make the relationships between her ideas clear. The first item in each pair shows how a passage from Cofer's story would have looked if she had not put one of her ideas in a subordinate clause.

1. I sat on the fire escape. In fact, I was literally suspended above Eugene's backyard.

   COFER: "In fact, **if** I sat on the fire escape I was literally suspended above Eugene's backyard." [Subordinate clause tells *under what conditions.*]

2. He sat at the kitchen table and read books for hours. I liked him right away.

   COFER: "I liked him right away **because** he sat at the kitchen table and read books for hours." [Subordinate clause tells *why.*]

3. I got home. Our apartment was empty.

   COFER: "Our apartment was empty **when** I got home." [Subordinate clause tells *when.*]

Remember to use **commas,** where appropriate, when you combine two sentences using an adverb clause. Place a comma after an introductory adverb clause. An adverb clause in the middle or at the end of a sentence is generally not set off by a comma. The box in the next column lists some of the most widely used subordinating conjunctions:

Subordinating Conjunctions

after	before	until
although	once	when
as	since	where
because	though	while

PRACTICE

Combine each pair of sentences by turning one of them into an adverb clause. Refer to the list of subordinating conjunctions above to help you rewrite the sentences. Use commas where appropriate.

1. President Kennedy was killed on November 22, 1963. The whole world mourned.

2. The students were in the yard. The girls jumped rope and the boys played basketball.

3. The gym teacher was a tough man. He cried openly about President Kennedy's death.

4. Elena's old neighbor died. His wife moved away.

5. The other girls made fun of Elena. She was different from them.

6. Elena felt alone and unhappy. Eugene moved into her neighborhood.

7. Elena watched Eugene from her fire escape. He sat in his kitchen reading library books.

8. Elena went to Eugene's house. Her mother tried to persuade her to stay home.

9. Elena felt sad at the end of the story. Her friendship with Eugene was over.

10. Elena looked out her window. Snow fell softly to the ground.

▶ **For more help, see Kinds of Clauses, 7e, in the Language Handbook.**

SKILLS FOCUS

Grammar Skills
Understand and use adverb clauses.

A Warm, Clear Day in Dallas ◆ Address to Congress, November 27, 1963 ◆ Students React to President Kennedy's Death

Primary and Secondary Sources: Through Whose Eyes?

When you do research, you use sources that fall into two main categories: primary sources and secondary sources.

- A **primary source** is a firsthand account, such as a speech, an autobiography, or a letter. A primary source is useful because it directly expresses the thoughts and feelings of a writer, and it may include details that only an eyewitness can provide. Remember, though, that a primary source expresses the viewpoint of only one person, who may be biased or whose knowledge may be limited.

- A **secondary source** is a secondhand account. Authors of secondary sources, such as history books, biographies, and textbooks, summarize or analyze events in which they did not participate. Most magazine and newspaper articles are secondary sources, unless they are eyewitness reports, editorials, or opinion pieces. (Note that a historian would consider any newspaper or magazine article from the past to be a primary-source document from a particular historical period.)

Some types of secondary sources, such as encyclopedias, are more objective than primary sources because they are based on several different viewpoints. Secondary sources can also give you a broader view of a subject than primary sources might provide.

The following chart lists some types of primary and secondary sources:

Primary Sources	Secondary Sources
Diaries	Encyclopedia articles
Autobiographies	Biographies
Letters	Reference books
Personal essays	History books
Speeches	Textbooks
Interviews	Most newspaper articles
Oral histories	Most magazine articles
Editorials	Literary criticism
Eyewitness news reports	
Literary works	
Public documents	

Using the Sources

To get the most out of using primary and secondary sources, follow these steps:

1. **Analyze.** First, determine whether your resources are primary or secondary sources. Examine what the authors say, why they say it, and how they express themselves.

   - Ask yourself, "Who is the author?" (For example, is the author a historian or a participant in an event?)

   - Also ask, "What is the **main idea** of the work? How does the author support the main idea?"

   - Determine the author's **purpose** and **audience.** For example, is the author writing to inform the general public, to describe an experience to a friend, or to persuade a group of senators to take action?

SKILLS FOCUS

Reading Skills
Understand and use primary and secondary sources.

go.hrw.com

INTERNET

Interactive Reading Model

Keyword: LE7 9-9

- Describe the author's **tone** (attitude toward the subject) and writing **style**. In a speech, for example, an author might use a formal style and express opinions in a confident, uplifting tone. However, when writing about the same subject in a diary entry, an author might use an informal style and express doubts or worries in a cautious, concerned tone. Keep in mind that the tone and style of a work are affected by an author's audience and purpose.

2. **Evaluate.** First, determine whether points in your sources are objective **facts** (which can be proved) or subjective **opinions** (which cannot be proved). Both primary and secondary sources usually include a mixture of facts and opinions. Then, evaluate whether the facts and opinions are **credible,** or reliable. Follow these guidelines:

   - Verify that **facts** are **accurate** by checking other sources. Remember to note when each source was written. Do your sources present the latest findings?

   - Decide whether you think **opinions** are **valid** by considering whether you trust the authors and the experts or eyewitnesses who are quoted in your sources. Ask yourself, "Do these people know the subject well? Are they **biased,** or prejudiced, in some way?"

   - Consider how an author's **purpose** and **audience** affect the way that he or she presents facts and opinions. Watch out for sources that present opinions as if they were objective facts.

3. **Elaborate.** Draw connections between what you've learned from your sources and your prior knowledge of the subject. Do further research, or discuss your own opinions about the subject.

Vocabulary Development

denouncing (dē·noʊns′iŋ) v. used as adj.: accusing publicly; condemning.

virtuous (vʉr′chōō·əs) adj.: good and moral; honorable.

controversial (kän′trə·vʉr′shəl) adj.: stirring up disagreement between groups holding opposing views.

conspiracy (kən·spir′ə·sē) n.: secret, often unlawful plan carried out by a group.

immortal (i·môrt′l) adj.: lasting or living forever.

vitalized (vīt′l·īzd′) v.: given life to; energized.

resolve (ri·zälv′) n.: strength of purpose; determination.

tolerance (täl′ər·əns) n.: respect for others who differ from you; freedom from prejudice.

bigotry (big′ə·trē) n.: strong prejudice against a particular group of people.

defiant (dē·fī′ənt) adj.: openly and boldly resisting or opposing.

Connecting to the Literature

In "American History," Elena's family and community are devastated by the assassination of President John F. Kennedy. The following selections tell what President Kennedy meant to our nation and to individual Americans as well.

SECONDARY SOURCE

A Warm, Clear Day in Dallas

from *John F. Kennedy*

Marta Randall

The Texas School Book Depository Building.

On November 22, 1963, at 12:30 in the afternoon, a man with a rifle crouched behind a window in the Texas School Book Depository above Dealey Plaza in Dallas, Texas. ❶

❶ EVALUATE

Why is this an effective first sentence for a historical account?

It was a clear, brilliant autumn day, and the crowds in the street below cheered and waved as President John F. Kennedy's limousine passed by. The president and his wife, Jacqueline, smiled and waved back; earlier the president had stopped the motorcade[1] twice, once to shake hands with a little girl, and a second time to greet a Catholic nun and her group of

schoolchildren. During both of these stops, the Secret Service worked frantically to keep the crowd at a distance. Dallas, with a murder rate twice the national average and a vocal and hostile anti-Kennedy element, was not a safe city. Just a day earlier the city had been covered with hate posters and leaflets[2] denouncing the president. That morning's *Dallas News* had carried a full-page advertisement criticizing Kennedy for his abandonment of the Constitution and softness toward Moscow and communism.[3] But this afternoon the crowd seemed friendly, and the president wanted to be close to the people, to touch their hands and talk with them.

The motorcade entered Main Street and approached Dealey Plaza. Texas Governor

---

1. **motorcade** (mōt′ər·kād′) *n.*: procession of cars or other vehicles, usually to escort an important person.

2. **leaflets** (lēf′lits) *n.*: printed material distributed to the public, often used to spread the views of a particular group.

3. **Moscow and communism:** Moscow is the capital of Russia, formerly the Soviet Union. Kennedy was president during a tense stage in the cold war, the bitter rivalry between the United States and its allies (supporters of democracy and capitalism) and the Soviet Union and its allies (supporters of communism).

Vocabulary

denouncing (dē·nɑuns′iŋ) *v.* used as *adj.*: accusing publicly; condemning.

President Kennedy and Mrs. Kennedy smile at the crowds lining their motorcade route in Dallas, Texas, on November 22, 1963.

John Connally and his wife, Nellie, were riding in the limousine with the president, and Mrs. Connally said, "Mr. President, you can't say Dallas doesn't love you." The president waved at the crowd and said, "That's obvious." It seemed to be true.

John F. Kennedy had been president for a little more than a thousand days, and in that time he had brought the country through crises that shook the world. From the early humiliation of a badly planned and disastrous invasion of Cuba, he had gone on to challenge the nuclear might of the Soviet Union over missile bases in Cuba, confronted the Soviet Union over the explosive issue of the Berlin Wall,[4] founded an Alliance for Progress that knit together the United States and Latin America, committed the United States to outer space exploration, and signed a nuclear test ban treaty with the Soviet Union and other countries. Perhaps the most important of his achievements was his support for civil rights and his effort to move the United States away from racial segregation and toward freedom and equal rights for all Americans. Kennedy called his program "the New Frontier"; he emphasized fresh solutions to the new, increasingly complex problems faced by the United States. Though he demanded hard work from himself, his staff, and all Americans, his youth, intellectual vigor,[5] and spirit of practical optimism imbued[6] many Americans with

---

4. **Berlin Wall:** In 1961, the Communist government in East Germany constructed a wall dividing East and West Berlin to prevent people living in East Germany from fleeing to West Germany (a Western-style democracy). The Berlin Wall was opened in 1989.

5. **intellectual vigor:** strong mental ability; high intelligence.
6. **imbued** (im·byo͞od′) *v.:* inspired; filled with.

the belief that real progress could be made toward creating a better, more just society. Some people compared the Kennedy White House with Camelot, the idyllic court of King Arthur, the legendary Celtic king,[7] where for "one brief, shining moment" the strongest and most virtuous knights had gathered. ②

> **② EVALUATE**
> List four **facts** contained in this paragraph. Then, find one **opinion.**

Not everyone was pleased with Kennedy and his administration, and segregation and U.S.-Soviet relations were both controversial subjects in Texas. But as the motorcade rolled on, the president was not worried. As he passed out of sight of the people in Dealey Plaza, the man in the sixth-floor window of the Texas School Book Depository aimed his rifle and fired.

Kennedy was hit first in the throat; the second bullet shattered his skull. Governor Connally was shot through the back. Jacqueline Kennedy cried, "Oh no, no . . . Oh, my God, they have shot my husband," and held the president tightly. As the two women cradled their husbands, the limousine pulled out of the motorcade and rushed to Parkland Hospital. Mrs. Connally later recalled, ". . . we must have been a horrible sight flying down the freeway with those dying men in our arms. There was no screaming in that horrible car. It was just a silent, terrible drive."

At one o'clock, the president was pronounced dead; an hour and a half later,

aboard Air Force One,[8] Vice President Lyndon Johnson was sworn in as the 36th president of the United States. Jacqueline Kennedy stood beside him, still wearing her blood-soaked suit.

At 2:15 that afternoon, a young man named Lee Harvey Oswald was arrested for the murder of John Kennedy; two days later, on national television, Oswald was shot to death by a Dallas nightclub owner named Jack Ruby. One of President Johnson's first acts in office was to create a commission[9] headed by Earl Warren, chief justice of the Supreme Court, to investigate Kennedy's assassination. Despite the commission's finding that Oswald worked alone in killing the president, many people still believe that the assassination was the result of a conspiracy. It is likely that there will never be an explanation that satisfies everyone. ③

> **③ EVALUATE**
> What **opinion** does the author express in this paragraph?

John Kennedy was buried in Arlington National Cemetery on November 25, 1963. Leaders from 92 countries attended the funeral and millions of people lined the route. Jacqueline lit an eternal flame over his grave while his two young children looked on.

---

8. **Air Force One:** airplane on which the president of the United States travels.
9. **commission** (kə·mish′ən) *n.:* group of people officially appointed to perform a duty.

Vocabulary

virtuous (vʉr′chōō·əs) *adj.:* good and moral; honorable.

controversial (kän′trə·vʉr′shəl) *adj.:* stirring up disagreement between groups holding opposing views.

conspiracy (kən·spir′ə·sē) *n.:* secret, often unlawful plan carried out by a group.

---

7. **Camelot . . . Celtic king:** According to legend, Arthur was a noble, brave king of Britain and the leader of the knights of the Round Table in the sixth century. Camelot has come to symbolize the glories of his rule.

Historian Herbert S. Parmet has written: "Few deaths have ever shocked so much of the world." People everywhere reacted with disbelief, shock, and grief. Jimmy Carter, a Georgia farmer who later became president of the United States, said, "I wept openly for the first time in ten years, for the first time since my own father died." Businesses and schools closed as American daily life virtually came to a halt. For four days, until the president was buried, people huddled around television sets and radios in grief and disbelief. In Copenhagen, Denmark, thousands of people brought flowers to the U.S. Embassy, so many that by the next morning the building was surrounded by flowers six feet deep. In West Berlin, people placed lit candles in darkened windows. Almost any American born before 1957 can remember where she or he was the day John Kennedy died. ❹

❹ **ANALYZE**

How would you describe the author's **purpose** in this **secondary source**? Is the **tone** of the piece generally objective or subjective?

Jacqueline Kennedy and her children, Caroline and John, along with other members of the Kennedy family, at the funeral of President John F. Kennedy.

SPEECH

Immediately after President Kennedy's death, Vice President Lyndon B. Johnson was sworn in as the new president. Five days later Johnson made the following speech to a joint session of the House of Representatives and the Senate.

Address to Congress
November 27, 1963

from "Address Before a Joint Session of the Congress"

Lyndon B. Johnson

Mr. Speaker, Mr. President, Members of the House, Members of the Senate, my fellow Americans:

All I have I would have given gladly not to be standing here today.

The greatest leader of our time has been struck down by the foulest deed of our time. Today John Fitzgerald Kennedy lives on in the immortal words and works that he left behind. He lives on in the mind and memories of mankind. He lives on in the hearts of his countrymen. ❶

No words are sad enough to express our sense of loss. No words are strong enough to express our determination to continue the forward thrust of America that he began.

The dream of conquering the vastness of space—the dream of partnership across the Atlantic—and across the Pacific as well—the dream of a Peace Corps[1] in less developed nations—the dream of education for all of our children—the dream of jobs for all who seek them and need them—the dream of care for our elderly—the dream of an all-out attack on mental illness—and above all, the dream of equal rights for all Americans, whatever their race or color—these and other American dreams have been vitalized by his drive and by his dedication.

And now the ideas and the ideals which he so nobly represented must and will be translated into effective action.

On the 20th day of January, in 1961, John F. Kennedy told his countrymen that our national work would not be finished "in the first thousand days, nor in the life of this administration, nor even perhaps in our lifetime on this planet. But," he said, "let us begin."

Today, in this moment of new resolve, I would say to all my fellow Americans, let us continue.

> ❶ **ANALYZE**
>
> What is the **tone** of this paragraph? How does Johnson's repetition of the phrase "lives on" contribute to the tone?

---

1. **Peace Corps:** U.S. agency, established in 1961, that sends volunteers abroad to assist people in underdeveloped areas.

Vocabulary
immortal (i·môrt′'l) *adj.:* lasting or living forever.
vitalized (vīt′'l·īzd′) *v.:* given life to; energized.
resolve (ri·zälv′) *n.:* strength of purpose; determination.

President Johnson addressing Congress on November 27, 1963.

This is our challenge—not to hesitate, not to pause, not to turn about and linger over this evil moment, but to continue on our course so that we may fulfill the destiny that history has set for us. Our most immediate tasks are here on this Hill.[2]

First, no memorial oration or eulogy[3] could more eloquently honor President Kennedy's memory than the earliest possible passage of the civil rights bill for which he fought so long. We have talked long enough in this country about equal rights. We have talked for one hundred years or more. It is time now to write the next collection, and to write it in the books of law.

2. **Hill:** Capitol Hill in Washington, D.C., where Congress meets and where Johnson was giving the speech.
3. **oration** (ō·rā'shən) **or eulogy** (yōō'lə·jē): *oration* means "formal speech"; *eulogy* means "speech praising someone who has died."

We meet in grief, but let us also meet in renewed dedication and renewed vigor. Let us meet in action, in tolerance, and in mutual understanding. John Kennedy's death commands what his life conveyed—that America must move forward. The time has come for Americans of all races and creeds[4] and political beliefs to understand and to respect one another. So let us put an end to the teaching and the preaching of hate and evil and violence. Let us turn away from the fanatics[5] of the far left and the far right, from the apostles[6] of bitterness and bigotry, from those defiant of law, and those who pour venom[7] into our nation's bloodstream. ❷

I profoundly hope that the tragedy and the torment of these terrible days will bind us together in new fellowship, making us one people in our hour of sorrow. So let us here highly resolve that John Fitzgerald Kennedy did not live—or die—in vain.

❷ **ANALYZE**

In this paragraph, what is Johnson urging his audience to do? What is his **tone** here?

4. **creeds** (krēdz) *n.:* religious beliefs.
5. **fanatics** (fə·nat'iks) *n.:* people whose extreme devotion to a cause is excessive or unreasonable.
6. **apostles** (ə·päs'əls) *n.:* people sent forth to spread a view or belief.
7. **venom** (ven'əm) *n.:* poison.

Vocabulary

tolerance (täl'ər·əns) *n.:* respect for others who differ from you; freedom from prejudice.

bigotry (big'ə·trē) *n.:* strong prejudice against a particular group of people.

defiant (dē·fi'ənt) *adj.:* openly and boldly resisting or opposing.

The following personal essays were written by students two months after President Kennedy was assassinated. The essays appear here exactly as the students wrote them and include some spelling and grammatical errors.

Students React to President Kennedy's Death

from *Children and the Death of a President*

Girl Age Twelve, Grade Seven

How I felt about President Kennedy's Assassination.

When I found out about President Kennedy's assassination I was full of sorrow and I was very worried.

When this drastic event took place I was sorry because I did not think anybody could stoop to such a low thing to do as murder. When I heard that our President was dead, I just could not believe it. I felt just like crying. To think that our President was dead, struck down by an assassin's bullet, made me burn up inside.

I was worried about our country. Maybe it was just for a little while but I was worried because for a while we did not have a President. Some question kept flashing through my mind. What was to become of our country? Why should anybody do such a thing? Would Lindin Baynes Johnson be as good a president as the late President Kennedy? These are questions to be answered in the future. Maybe not even then.

I wish President Kennedy was not taken away from the world, his family and his country.

Girl Age Fourteen, Grade Eight

What I Remmember About the Weekend President Kennedy Was Assassinated.

It was a sunny and beautiful day, November 22, 1963. The air was chilled with a slight breeze, but there wasn't a cloud in the sky. For almost everyone on the earth there was no anxiety or fear of and unexpected tradgedy. It was a normal Friday and everyone went about their business as usual, but, the day was brought to an abrupt standstill.

Our class was in math our sixth period class. We were in the middle of the test when a neighboring teacher came in and handed our math teacher a note. A sudden expression of horror filled her face. She followed the other teacher into the hall, leaving us unattended. I began to feel uneasy and quite nervous when the teacher returned. She had a look of utter disbelief and shock on her face. At once the thought of another World War came into my head. I got very fidgety and was distracted from my work on the test.

The eternal flame at the John F. Kennedy Memorial in Arlington, Virginia.

For the next five minutes or so she just sat staring into space. Then she stood up and kind of moped around the classroom watching us. Almost immediately after she stood up the test was discontinued. There was a piercing silence in the room as we passed forward our papers. I think we all knew something was wrong. Then she told us the horrible and tradgedy filled event. "The President had been killed." I was standing almost frozen stiff with shock and disbelief. Presently I began to move again and I found my seat. The school was dismissed very shortly. We all moved in silence back to our homeroom where we gathered our books and coats. The halls in school were never so quiet. We went home and tried to console ourselves but it was too much. Most of us cried. I shed one tear I couldn't allow myself to cry although I certainly felt like it. ●

●**ANALYZE**
Review the title and the first two paragraphs of this essay. What are the first two clues that this is a **primary source**?

That whole weekend you were glued to the television. It showed from the tragic moment until his casket was lowered into the ground. I never felt so empty in all my life. I felt as if he was one of the family. Never could such a thing happen I said to myself. It's just impossible.

I'm Catholic so Monday night our church had a Mass said for him. When I walked into church and saw the imposter casket° sitting in the middle of the isle I almost died. My sunk to my knees.

From that Black day to this day I still can't bring myself to really believe deeply inside my heart what had happened that day President Kennedy was assassinated.

° **Mass . . . imposter casket:** Mass is the traditional church service of worship for Roman Catholics. In most funeral masses the casket holding the body of the dead person remains in front of the congregation during the service. Here an empty casket symbolized Kennedy's death.

Reading Check

SKILLS FOCUS

Reading Skills
Analyze primary and secondary sources.

1. Explain how President Kennedy died, as recounted in "A Warm, Clear Day in Dallas." Then, list two important events that occurred in the first hours after his death.

2. According to his speech, what does President Johnson think would be the best way to honor President Kennedy's memory?

3. What concerns does the twelve-year-old girl express in her personal essay?

Test Practice

1. Which statement represents the *most* accurate **evaluation** of "A Warm, Clear Day in Dallas"?

   A The author includes many more opinions than facts in the selection.

   B The author does not support her statement "People everywhere reacted with disbelief, shock, and grief" to the news of President Kennedy's death.

   C The author presents both facts and opinions in her account of Kennedy's assassination.

   D The author includes quotations from people who seem unreliable.

2. The **purpose** of President Johnson's speech was to —

   F tell how much he mourned the loss of Kennedy

   G convey that he would be a better president than Kennedy was

   H describe his outrage over violent, evil acts

   J express his commitment to pursuing Kennedy's goals for the country

3. Why is Johnson's speech appropriate for his **audience,** members of Congress?

   A He discusses the need to turn ideas into actions, and his audience makes laws for the country.

   B Only his audience, the country's political leaders, could help Americans keep Kennedy's memory alive.

   C His audience, who worked closely with Kennedy, was especially affected by his death and would agree with Johnson's views.

   D Using Kennedy as a model, he wants to tell his audience how to become better leaders.

4. Which statement in the fourteen-year-old's personal essay *cannot* be **verified** with information from "A Warm, Clear Day in Dallas"?

   F "That whole weekend you were glued to the television."

   G "It was a sunny and beautiful day, November 22, 1963."

   H "It was a normal Friday and everyone went about their business as usual. . . ."

   J "The school was dismissed very shortly."

5. Which of the following statements describing a **difference** between "A Warm, Clear Day in Dallas" and Johnson's speech is *true*?

   A One can learn about the views of an individual person only from Johnson's speech.

   B "A Warm, Clear Day in Dallas" is more objective than Johnson's speech.

   C Only Johnson's speech describes Kennedy's commitment to civil rights.

   D Only "A Warm, Clear Day in Dallas" discusses Kennedy's dedication to improving society.

6. Which statement can be supported by **facts** or **opinions** in *all* of the selections?

   F President Kennedy's untimely death was a tragedy from which the United States has never recovered.

   G Millions of people, adults as well as children, were deeply saddened by President Kennedy's death.

   H There will always be some people who believe that President Kennedy was not killed by a lone gunman.

   J President Kennedy has come to be admired more in death than he was in life.

Constructed Response

Extend the information in these selections by doing your own original research. Ask two adults whom you know well to describe what they remember about the day President Kennedy was shot. Then, write one or two paragraphs in which you **elaborate** on the ideas in the selections, using your new **primary-source** information. Does your research support the information and the ideas in the selections, or does it offer a different perspective?

Vocabulary Development

Word Knowledge: What's the Difference?

PRACTICE

Answer each of the following questions by explaining the differences in meaning between the two words. The two words may be **antonyms** (opposites) or **synonyms** with different **connotations** (associations), or they may be different in other ways.

 1. What's the difference between *denouncing* and *criticizing*?

 2. What's the difference between *virtuous* and *immoral*?

 3. What's the difference between *controversial* and *contradictory*?

 4. What's the difference between *conspiracy* and *plan*?

 5. What's the difference between *immortal* and *mortal*?

 6. What's the difference between *vitalized* and *weakened*?

 7. What's the difference between *resolve* and *desire*?

 8. What's the difference between *tolerance* and *bigotry*?

 9. What's the difference between *defiant* and *uncooperative*?

> **Word Bank**
>
> denouncing
> virtuous
> controversial
> conspiracy
> immortal
> vitalized
> resolve
> tolerance
> bigotry
> defiant

SKILLS FOCUS

Vocabulary Skills
Clarify word meanings.

Before You Read

Beware of the Dog

Make the Connection

Quickwrite

There's an old saying, "Appearances can be deceiving." Have you ever been misled by the appearance of someone or something? List some situations in which people might be deceived. Why might they be misled? How might they discover that their initial impressions were wrong? Jot down your responses.

Literary Focus

Understanding Historical Setting

Usually when a writer sets a story in a distinct **historical period,** the story's **conflicts** reflect the conflicts faced by the people living in that particular time and place.

Many works of fiction are driven by the high-stakes struggles of actual wars. Roald Dahl's "Beware of the Dog" tells the story of a British fighter pilot during World War II. As you read this story, remember its historical setting. Keep in mind that every breath the pilot takes, every thought he has, is influenced by the fact that his country is at war, and he is fighting for his life.

Literary Skills
Understand historical setting.

Reading Skills
Make inferences.

go.
hrw
.com

INTERNET

Vocabulary Practice
•
More About Roald Dahl
•
Keyword: LE7 9-9

Reading Skills

Making Inferences: Telltale Signs

When you make an **inference,** you make an educated guess about something. Some stories contain telltale signs or hints that something may be going on that the writer is not spelling out for you. In such cases, as in "Beware of the Dog," it's your job to infer what those hints might mean, using your experience and imagination. As you read this story, the questions at the open-book signs will help you make inferences.

Background

World War II began when Germany invaded Poland, in 1939, prompting Great Britain and France to declare war on Germany. France surrendered to Germany in 1940, and it was occupied by the German army until it was liberated by Allied forces, in 1944. The war finally ended on September 2, 1945.

This story is told from the vantage point of a British fighter pilot, probably after the Battle of Britain (1940). As the story opens, the pilot is trying to get back home after a bombing mission against German targets somewhere in Europe.

Vocabulary Development

undulating (un′jə·lāt′iŋ) v. used as *adj.*: moving in waves.

giddy (gid′ē) *adj.*: dizzy.

unconscious (un·kän′shəs) *adj.*: not awake and alert.

idly (īd′lē) *adv.*: without aim or purpose.

delirious (di·lir′ē·əs) *adj.*: temporarily confused and seeing imaginary things, often because of injury or fever.

obsession (əb·sesh′ən) *n.*: persistent idea or desire that consumes a person's attention.

hoisted (hoist′id) *v.*: lifted or pulled up.

beckoned (bek′ənd) *v.*: gestured or signaled to request someone to approach or follow.

BEWARE OF THE DOG

Roald Dahl

Something had occurred to him; something so fantastic and absurd...

own below there was only a vast white undulating sea of cloud. Above there was the sun, and the sun was white like the clouds, because it is never yellow when one looks at it from high in the air.

He was flying the Spitfire.[1] His right hand was on the stick and he was working the rudder bar[2] with his left leg alone. It was quite easy. The machine was flying well. He knew what he was doing.

Everything is fine, he thought. I'm doing all right. I'm doing nicely. I know my way home. I'll be there in half an hour. When I land, I shall taxi in and switch off my engine and I shall say, help me to get out, will you. I shall make my voice sound ordinary and natural and none of them will take any notice. Then I shall say, someone help me to get out. I can't do it alone because I've lost one of my legs. They'll all laugh and think that I'm joking and I shall say, all right, come and have a look. . . . Then Yorky will climb up on to the wing and look inside. He'll probably be sick because of all the blood and the mess. I shall laugh and say, for God's sake, help me get out.

He glanced down again at his right leg. There was not much of it left. The cannon shell had taken him on the thigh, just above the knee, and now there was nothing but a great mess and a lot of blood. But there was no pain. When he looked down, he felt as though he were seeing something that did not belong to him. It had nothing to do with him. It was just a mess which happened to be there in the cockpit; something strange and unusual and rather interesting. It was like finding a dead cat on the sofa.

He really felt fine, and because he still felt fine, he felt excited and unafraid.

I won't even bother to call up on the radio for the bloodwagon, he thought. It isn't necessary. And when I land, I'll sit there quite normally

and say, some of you fellows come and help me out, will you, because I've lost one of my legs. That will be funny. I'll laugh a little while I'm saying it; I'll say it calmly and slowly, and they'll think I'm joking. When Yorky comes up on to the wing and gets sick, I'll say, Yorky . . . have you fixed my car yet. Then when I get out, I'll make my report. Later I'll go up to London and see Bluey. I'll say, Bluey I've got a surprise for you. I lost a leg today. But I don't mind so long as you don't. It doesn't even hurt. We'll go everywhere in cars. I always hated walking except when I walked down the street of the coppersmiths in Baghdad,[3] but I could go in a rickshaw.[4] I could go home and chop wood, but the head always flies off the ax. Hot water, that's what it needs; put it in the bath and make the handle swell. I chopped lots of wood last time I went home and I put the ax in the bath . . .

MAKING INFERENCES

1. What can you **infer** about the pilot's condition from the way his thoughts are wandering?

Then he saw the sun shining on the engine cowling[5] of his machine. He saw the sun shining on the rivets in the metal, and he remembered the airplane and he remembered where he was. He realized that he was no longer feeling good; that he was sick and giddy. His head kept falling forward on to his chest because his neck seemed no longer to have any strength. But he knew that he was flying the Spitfire. He could feel the handle of the stick between the fingers of his right hand.

I'm going to pass out, he thought. Any moment now I'm going to pass out.

---

1. **Spitfire:** British fighter plane used in World War II.
2. **stick . . . rudder bar:** "Stick" refers to the plane's joystick, which controls its movement up or down. The rudder bar helps control movement to the right or the left.

3. **Baghdad** (bag′dad′): capital of Iraq.
4. **rickshaw** n.: small, two-wheeled carriage, pulled by a person.
5. **cowling** n.: metal covering of an airplane engine.

Vocabulary

undulating (un′jə·lāt′iŋ) v. used as adj.: moving in waves.

giddy (gid′ē) adj.: dizzy.

British Spitfire, the famous fighter plane used in the Battle of Britain. (A Spitfire is also shown in the photograph on page 687.)

He looked at his altimeter.[6] Twenty-one thousand. To test himself he tried to read the hundreds as well as the thousands. Twenty-one thousand and what? As he looked, the dial became blurred and he could not even see the needle. He knew then that he must bail out;[7] that there was not a second to lose, otherwise he would become <u>unconscious</u>. Quickly, frantically, he tried to slide back the hood with his left hand, but he had not the strength. For a second he took his right hand off the stick and with both hands he managed to push the hood back. The rush of cold air on his face seemed to help. He had a moment of great clearness. His actions became orderly and precise. That is what happens with a good pilot. He took some quick deep breaths from his oxygen mask, and as he did so, he looked out over the side of the

---

6. **altimeter** (al·tim′ət·ər) *n.*: instrument that measures altitude, or height.
7. **bail out** *v.*: parachute out of an airplane in an emergency.

Vocabulary
unconscious (un·kän′shəs) *adj.*: not awake and alert.

cockpit. Down below there was only a vast white sea of cloud and he realized that he did not know where he was.

It'll be the Channel,[8] he thought. I'm sure to fall in the drink.[9]

He throttled back,[10] pulled off his helmet, undid his straps, and pushed the stick hard over to the left. The Spitfire dipped its port[11] wing and turned smoothly over on to its back. The pilot fell out.

As he fell, he opened his eyes, because he knew that he must not pass out before he had pulled the cord. On one side he saw the sun; on the other he saw the whiteness of the clouds, and as he fell, as he somersaulted in the air, the white clouds chased the sun and the sun chased the clouds. They chased each other in a small circle; they ran faster and faster and there was the sun and the clouds and the clouds and the sun, and the clouds came nearer until suddenly there was no longer any sun but only a great whiteness. The whole world was white and there was nothing in it. It was so white that sometimes it looked black, and after a time it was either white or black, but mostly it was white. He watched it as it turned from white to black, then back to white again, and the white stayed for a long time, but the black lasted only for a few seconds. He got into the habit of going to sleep during the white periods, of waking up just in time to see the world when it was black. The black was very quick. Sometimes it was only a flash, a flash of black lightning. The white was slow and in the slowness of it, he always dozed off.

One day, when it was white, he put out a hand and he touched something. He took it between his fingers and crumpled it. For a time he lay there, idly letting the tips of his fingers play with

the thing which they had touched. Then slowly he opened his eyes, looked down at his hand, and saw that he was holding something which was white. It was the edge of a sheet. He knew it was a sheet because he could see the texture of the material and the stitchings on the hem. He screwed up his eyes and opened them again quickly. This time he saw the room. He saw the bed in which he was lying: He saw the gray walls and the door and the green curtains over the window. There were some roses on the table by his bed.

Then he saw the basin on the table near the roses. It was a white enamel basin and beside it there was a small medicine glass.

This is a hospital, he thought. I am in a hospital. But he could remember nothing. He lay back on his pillow, looking at the ceiling and wondering what had happened. He was gazing at the smooth grayness of the ceiling which was so clean and gray, and then suddenly he saw a fly walking upon it. The sight of this fly, the suddenness of seeing this small black speck on a sea of gray, brushed the surface of his brain, and quickly, in that second, he remembered everything. He remembered the Spitfire and he remembered the altimeter showing twenty-one thousand feet. He remembered the pushing back of the hood with both hands and he remembered the bailing out. He remembered his leg.

It seemed all right now. He looked down at the end of the bed, but he could not tell. He put one hand underneath the bedclothes and felt for his knees. He found one of them, but when he felt for the other, his hand touched something which was soft and covered in bandages.

Just then the door opened and a nurse came in. "Hello," she said. "So you've waked up at last."

MAKING INFERENCES

2. Look carefully at the description in the last two paragraphs. Where do you think the pilot is?

---

8. **Channel:** English Channel, the narrow body of water separating England and France.
9. **fall in the drink:** British expression meaning "fall into the water."
10. **throttled back:** reduced the speed of an airplane.
11. **port** *adj.:* left, on a ship or an airplane.

Vocabulary
idly (īd′′lē) *adv.:* without aim or purpose.

She was not good-looking, but she was large and clean. She was between thirty and forty and she had fair hair. More than that he did not notice.

"Where am I?"

"You're a lucky fellow. You landed in a wood near the beach. You're in Brighton.[12] They brought you in two days ago, and now you're all fixed up. You look fine."

"I've lost a leg," he said.

"That's nothing. We'll get you another one. Now you must go to sleep. The doctor will be coming to see you in about an hour." She picked up the basin and the medicine glass and went out.

But he did not sleep. He wanted to keep his eyes open because he was frightened that if he shut them again everything would go away. He lay looking at the ceiling. The fly was still there. It was very energetic. It would run forward very fast for a few inches, then it would stop. Then it would run forward again, stop, run forward, and every now and then it would take off and buzz around viciously in small circles. It always landed back in the same place on the ceiling and started running and stopping all over again. He watched it for so long that after a while it was no longer a fly, but only a black speck upon a sea of gray, and he was still watching it when the nurse opened the door, and stood aside while the doctor came in. He was an army doctor, a major, and he had some last war ribbons on his chest. He was bald and small, but he had a cheerful face and kind eyes.

"Well, well," he said. "So you've decided to wake up at last. How are you feeling?"

"I feel all right."

"That's the stuff. You'll be up and about in no time."

The doctor took his wrist to feel his pulse.

"By the way," he said, "some of the lads from your squadron[13] were ringing up[14] and asking about you. They wanted to come along and see you, but I said that they'd better wait a day or two. Told them you were all right and that they could come and see you a little later on. Just lie quiet and take it easy for a bit. Got something to read?" He glanced at the table with the roses. "No. Well, nurse will look after you. She'll get you anything you want." With that he waved his hands and went out, followed by the large clean nurse.

When they had gone, he lay back and looked at the ceiling again. The fly was still there and as he lay watching it he heard the noise of an airplane in the distance. He lay listening to the sound of its engines. It was a long way away. I wonder what it is, he thought. Let me see if I can place it. Suddenly he jerked his head sharply to one side. Anyone who has been bombed can tell the noise of a Junkers 88. They can tell most other German bombers for that matter, but especially a Junkers 88. The engines seem to sing a duet. There is a deep vibrating bass voice and with it there is a high-pitched tenor. It is the singing of the tenor which makes the sound of a Ju-88 something which one cannot mistake.

He lay listening to the noise and felt quite certain about what it was. But where were the sirens and where the guns? That German pilot certainly had a nerve coming near Brighton alone in daylight.

The aircraft was always far away and soon the noise faded away into the distance. Later on there was another. This one, too, was far away, but there was the same deep undulating bass and the high swinging tenor and there was no mistaking it. He had heard that noise every day during the Battle.[15]

---

12. **Brighton** (brīt′′n): English city on the English Channel.

13. **squadron** (skwäd′rən) *n.:* military unit.
14. **ringing up:** British expression meaning "telephoning."
15. **Battle:** Battle of Britain (1940), in which Germany tried to conquer Great Britain. The Germans launched heavy air attacks, but they could not defeat Britain's Royal Air Force.

An area in London hit by German bombs during an air raid in 1940.

He was puzzled. There was a bell on the table by the bed. He reached out his hand and rang it. He heard the noise of footsteps down the corridor. The nurse came in.

"Nurse, what were those airplanes?"

"I'm sure I don't know. I didn't hear them. Probably fighters or bombers. I expect they were returning from France. Why, what's the matter?"

"They were Ju-88s. I'm sure they were Ju-88s. I know the sound of the engines. There were two of them. What were they doing over here?"

The nurse came up to the side of his bed and began to straighten out the sheets and tuck them in under the mattress.

"Gracious me, what things you imagine. You mustn't worry about a thing like that. Would you like me to get you something to read?"

"No, thank you."

She patted his pillow and brushed back the hair from his forehead with her hand.

"They never come over in daylight any longer. You know that. They were probably Lancasters or Flying Fortresses."[16]

"Nurse."

"Yes."

"Could I have a cigarette?"

"Why certainly you can."

She went out and came back almost at once with a packet of Players and some matches. She handed one to him and when he had put it in his mouth, she struck a match and lit it.

"If you want me again," she said, "just ring the bell," and she went out.

_____

16. **Lancasters or Flying Fortresses:** Lancasters are British heavy bombers; Flying Fortresses are American heavy bombers.

MAKING INFERENCES

3. If the planes are German bombers, what might that signify? What can you **infer** about the nurse from her responses to the pilot's questions about the planes?

Once toward evening he heard the noise of another aircraft. It was far away, but even so he knew that it was a single-engined machine. It was going fast; he could tell that. He could not place it. It wasn't a Spit, and it wasn't a Hurricane.[17] It did not sound like an American engine either. They make more noise. He did not know what it was, and it worried him greatly. Perhaps I am very ill, he thought. Perhaps I am imagining things. Perhaps I am a little delirious. I simply do not know what to think.

That evening the nurse came in with a basin of hot water and began to wash him.

"Well," she said, "I hope you don't think that we're being bombed."

She had taken off his pajama top and was soaping his right arm with a flannel.[18] He did not answer.

She rinsed the flannel in the water, rubbed more soap on it, and began to wash his chest.

"You're looking fine this evening," she said. "They operated on you as soon as you came in. They did a marvelous job. You'll be all right. I've got a brother in the RAF,"[19] she added. "Flying bombers."

He said, "I went to school in Brighton."

She looked up quickly. "Well, that's fine," she said. "I expect you'll know some people in the town."

"Yes," he said, "I know quite a few."

She had finished washing his chest and arms. Now she turned back the bedclothes so that his left leg was uncovered. She did it in such a way that his bandaged stump remained under the sheets. She undid the cord of his pajama trousers and took them off. There was no trouble because they had cut off the right trouser leg so that it could not interfere with the bandages. She began to wash his left leg and the rest of his body. This was the first time he had had a bed bath and he was embarrassed. She laid a towel under his leg and began washing his foot with the flannel. She said, "This wretched soap won't lather at all. It's the water. It's as hard as nails."

He said, "None of the soap is very good now and, of course, with hard water[20] it's hopeless." As he said it, he remembered something. He remembered the baths which he used to take at school in Brighton, in the long stone-floored bathroom which had four baths in a row. He remembered how the water was so soft that you had to take a shower afterward to get all the soap off your body, and he remembered how the foam used to float on the surface of the water, so that you could not see your legs underneath. He remembered that sometimes they were given calcium tablets because the school doctor used to say that soft water was bad for the teeth.

"In Brighton," he said, "the water isn't . . ."

He did not finish the sentence. Something had occurred to him; something so fantastic and absurd that for a moment he felt like telling the nurse about it and having a good laugh.

She looked up. "The water isn't what?" she said.

"Nothing," he answered. "I was dreaming."

She rinsed the flannel in the basin, wiped the soap off his leg, and dried him with a towel.

"It's nice to be washed," he said. "I feel better." He was feeling his face with his hand. "I need a shave."

---

17. **Hurricane:** type of British fighter plane.
18. **flannel** *n.:* piece of soft woolen fabric; here, used as a washcloth.
19. **RAF:** abbreviation for Royal Air Force, Great Britain's air force.
20. **hard water:** water that contains minerals that prevent soap from making a good lather.

Vocabulary
delirious (di·lir′ē·əs) *adj.:* temporarily confused and seeing imaginary things, often because of injury or fever.

"We'll do that tomorrow," she said. "Perhaps you can do it yourself then."

That night he could not sleep. He lay awake thinking of the Junkers 88s and of the hardness of the water. He could think of nothing else. They were Ju-88s, he said to himself. I know they were. And yet it is not possible, because they would not be flying around so low over here in broad daylight. I know that it is true and yet I know that it is impossible. Perhaps I am ill. Perhaps I am behaving like a fool and do not know what I am doing or saying. Perhaps I am delirious. For a long time he lay awake thinking these things, and once he sat up in bed and said aloud, "I will prove that I am not crazy. I will make a little speech about something complicated and intellectual. I will talk about what to do with Germany after the war." But before he had time to begin, he was asleep.

He woke just as the first light of day was showing through the slit in the curtains over the window. The room was still dark, but he could tell that it was already beginning to get light outside. He lay looking at the gray light which was showing through the slit in the curtain and as he lay there he remembered the day before. He remembered the Junkers 88s and the hardness of the water; he remembered the large pleasant nurse and the kind doctor, and now a small grain of doubt took root in his mind and it began to grow.

He looked around the room. The nurse had taken the roses out the night before. There was nothing except the table with a packet of cigarettes, a box of matches, and an ashtray. The room was bare. It was no longer warm or friendly. It was not even comfortable. It was cold and empty and very quiet.

Slowly the grain of doubt grew, and with it came fear, a light, dancing fear that warned but did not frighten; the kind of fear that one gets not because one is afraid, but because one feels that there is something wrong. Quickly the doubt and the fear grew so that he became restless and angry, and when he touched his forehead with his hand, he found that it was damp with sweat. He knew then that he must do something; that he must find some way of proving to himself that he was either right or wrong, and he looked up and saw again the window and the green curtains. From where he lay, that window was right in front of him, but it was fully ten yards away. Somehow he must reach it and look out. The idea became an obsession with him and soon he could think of nothing except the window. But what about his leg? He put his hand underneath the bedclothes and felt the thick bandaged stump which was all that was left on the right-hand side. It seemed all right. It didn't hurt. But it would not be easy.

He sat up. Then he pushed the bedclothes aside and put his left leg on the floor. Slowly, carefully, he swung his body over until he had both hands on the floor as well; then he was out of bed, kneeling on the carpet. He looked at the stump. It was very short and thick, covered with bandages. It was beginning to hurt and he could feel it throbbing. He wanted to collapse, lie down on the carpet, and do nothing, but he knew that he must go on.

With two arms and one leg, he crawled over toward the window. He would reach forward as far as he could with his arms, then he would give a little jump and slide his left leg along after them. Each time he did it, it jarred his wound so that he gave a soft grunt of pain, but he continued to crawl across the floor on two hands and one knee. When he got to the window, he reached up, and one at a time he placed both hands on the sill. Slowly he raised himself up until he was standing on his left leg. Then quickly he pushed aside the curtains and looked out.

Vocabulary

obsession (əb·sesh′ən) *n.*: persistent idea or desire that consumes a person's attention.

He saw a small house with a gray tiled roof standing alone beside a narrow lane, and immediately behind it there was a plowed field. In front of the house there was an untidy garden, and there was a green hedge separating the garden from the lane. He was looking at the hedge when he saw the sign. It was just a piece of board nailed to the top of a short pole, and because the hedge had not been trimmed for a long time, the branches had grown out around the sign so that it seemed almost as though it had been placed in the middle of the hedge. There was something written on the board with white paint. He pressed his head against the glass of the window, trying to read what it said. The first letter was a *G*, he could see that. The second was an *A*, and the third was an *R*. One after another he managed to see what the letters were. There were three words, and slowly he spelled the letters out aloud to himself as he managed to read them.

G-A-R-D-E A-U C-H-I-E-N, *Garde au chien.*[21] That is what it said.

He stood there balancing on one leg and holding tightly to the edges of the windowsill with his hands, staring at the sign and at the whitewashed lettering of the words. For a moment he could think of nothing at all. He stood there looking at the sign, repeating the words over and over to himself. Slowly he began to realize the full meaning of the thing. He looked up at the cottage and at the plowed field. He looked at the small orchard on the left of the cottage and he looked at the green countryside beyond. "So this is France," he said. "I am in France."

MAKING INFERENCES

5. Why does the pilot conclude that he is in France?

---

21. *Garde au chien* (gärd ō shyen): French for "Beware of the dog."

Now the throbbing in his right thigh was very great. It felt as though someone was pounding the end of his stump with a hammer and suddenly the pain became so intense that it affected his head. For a moment he thought he was going to fall. Quickly he knelt down again, crawled back to the bed, and hoisted himself in. He pulled the bedclothes over himself and lay back on the pillow, exhausted. He could still think of nothing at all except the small sign by the hedge and the plowed field and the orchard. It was the words on the sign that he could not forget.

> There was something a little uneasy about her eyes.

It was some time before the nurse came in. She came carrying a basin of hot water and she said, "Good morning, how are you today?"

He said, "Good morning, nurse."

The pain was still great under the bandages, but he did not wish to tell this woman anything. He looked at her as she busied herself with getting the washing things ready. He looked at her more carefully now. Her hair was very fair. She was tall and big-boned and her face seemed pleasant. But there was something a little uneasy about her eyes. They were never still. They never looked at anything for more than a moment and they moved too quickly from one place to another in the room. There was something about her movements also. They were too sharp and nervous to go well with the casual manner in which she spoke.

She set down the basin, took off his pajama top, and began to wash him.

"Did you sleep well?"

"Yes."

"Good," she said. She was washing his arms and his chest.

"I believe there's someone coming down to see you from the Air Ministry after breakfast," she went on. "They want a report or something.

I expect you know all about it. How you got shot down and all that. I won't let him stay long, so don't worry."

He did not answer. She finished washing him and gave him a toothbrush and some tooth powder. He brushed his teeth, rinsed his mouth, and spat the water out into the basin.

Later she brought him his breakfast on a tray, but he did not want to eat. He was still feeling weak and sick and he wished only to lie still and think about what had happened. And there was a sentence running through his head. It was a sentence which Johnny, the intelligence officer of his squadron, always repeated to the pilots every day before they went out. He could see Johnny now, leaning against the wall of the dispersal hut with his pipe in his hand, saying, "And if they get you, don't forget, just your name, rank, and number. Nothing else. For God's sake, say nothing else."

📖

MAKING INFERENCES

6. Why might the pilot now recall the sentence Johnny used to repeat to the pilots every day?

"There you are," she said as she put the tray on his lap. "I've got you an egg. Can you manage all right?"

"Yes."

She stood beside the bed. "Are you feeling all right?"

"Yes."

"Good. If you want another egg, I might be able to get you one."

"This is all right."

"Well, just ring the bell if you want any more." And she went out.

Vocabulary
hoisted (hoist′id) v.: lifted or pulled up.

He had just finished eating, when the nurse came in again.

She said, "Wing Commander Roberts is here. I've told him that he can only stay for a few minutes."

She beckoned with her hand and the wing commander came in.

"Sorry to bother you like this," he said.

He was an ordinary RAF officer, dressed in a uniform which was a little shabby. He wore wings and a DFC.[22] He was fairly tall and thin with plenty of black hair. His teeth, which were irregular and widely spaced, stuck out a little even when he closed his mouth. As he spoke, he took a printed form and a pencil from his pocket and he pulled up a chair and sat down.

"How are you feeling?"

There was no answer.

---

22. **wings and a DFC:** Wings are an emblem worn by the pilot and the crew of an aircraft. DFC stands for Distinguished Flying Cross, a medal awarded to officers of the Royal Air Force for distinguished conduct in combat.

"Tough luck about your leg. I know how you feel. I hear you put up a fine show before they got you."

The man in the bed was lying quite still, watching the man in the chair.

The man in the chair said, "Well, let's get this stuff over. I'm afraid you'll have to answer a few questions so that I can fill in this combat report. Let me see now, first of all, what was your squadron?"

The man in the bed did not move. He looked straight at the wing commander and he said, "My name is Peter Williamson. My rank is squadron leader and my number is nine seven two four five seven." ■

MAKING INFERENCES

7. What can you **infer** from the pilot's answer to the wing commander's question at the end of the story? What has the pilot realized?

Vocabulary

beckoned (bek′ənd) *v.*: gestured or signaled to request someone to approach or follow.

Meet the Writer

Roald Dahl

A Dragon to Be Slain

"Beware of the Dog" appeared in *Over to You: Ten Stories of Flyers and Flying*, the first collection of stories published by Roald (roo′ôl) Dahl (1916–1990). Reviewing the collection, one critic commented, "This, one never doubts, is the way British pilots talked, felt, acted."

In his fiction, Dahl was able to capture the life of flying because he himself had been a flier. Dahl was born in Wales of Norwegian parents. When World War II began, he joined Great Britain's Royal Air Force and became a fighter pilot. Dahl suffered grave injuries when his plane crashed in 1940. Although a widely circulated story states that Dahl's plane was shot down by enemy fire, his crash actually occurred because he was given the wrong information about the location of an airfield. In his autobiography, *Going Solo*, Dahl explains what happened when he was forced to make an emergency landing in the desert once his fuel supply ran low:

"My undercarriage hit a boulder and collapsed completely and the Gladiator buried its nose in the sand at what must have been about seventy-five miles an hour.

My injuries in that bust-up came from my head being thrown forward violently against the reflector-sight when the plane hit the ground (in spite of the fact that I was strapped tightly, as always, into the cockpit), and apart from the skull fracture, the blow pushed my nose in and knocked out a few teeth and blinded me completely for days to come.

It is odd that I can remember very clearly quite a few of the things that followed seconds after the crash. Obviously I was unconscious for some moments, but I must have recovered my senses very quickly because I can remember hearing a mighty *whoosh* as the petrol tank in the port wing exploded, followed almost at once by another mighty *whoosh* as the starboard tank went up in flames. I could see nothing at all, and I felt no pain. All I wanted was to go gently off to sleep and to hell with the flames. But soon a tremendous heat around my legs galvanized my soggy brain into action. With great difficulty I managed to undo first my seat-straps and then the straps of my parachute, and I can even remember the desperate effort it took to push myself upright in the cockpit and roll out headfirst on to the sand below."

Dahl dragged himself away from the burning plane—and then he collapsed. He was later told that the flames from his plane lit up the desert for miles. When British soldiers set out to investigate the crash site, they were astonished to find Dahl's "still-breathing body."

Dahl lived to fly—and be injured—again. He was eventually encouraged to write about his military adventures. The story of his military experiences marked the beginning of Dahl's career as a writer.

At first, Dahl mostly wrote fiction for adults, specializing in stories with a surprising twist. After his own children were born, he began to write children's stories and novels, and these works—such as *Charlie and the Chocolate Factory*—made him famous.

As a child and an adult, Dahl experienced many personal tragedies. His life was not easy, but as one person put it, "He fought misfortune as if it was a dragon to be slain."

For Independent Reading

For more gripping adventures about the lives of pilots, read Dahl's autobiography, *Going Solo*, and his short story collection *Over to You: Ten Stories of Flyers and Flying*.

Ernie Pyle (1900–1945) was an award-winning American journalist and war correspondent who covered World War II. In the following report he describes the courage of a British pilot whose plane was shot down.

Wounded and Trapped

Ernie Pyle

A World War II RAF pilot.

ON THE WESTERN FRONT—(by wireless)— We ran to the wrecked British plane, lying there upside down, and dropped on our hands and knees and peeked through a tiny hole in the side.

A man lay on his back in the small space of the upside-down cockpit. His feet disappeared somewhere in the jumble of dials and rubber pedals above him. His shirt was open and his chest was bare to the waist. He was smoking a cigarette.

He turned his eyes toward me when I peeked in, and he said in a typical British manner of offhand friendliness, "Oh, hello."

"Are you all right," I asked, stupidly.

He answered, "Yes, quite. Now that you chaps are here."

I asked him how long he had been trapped in the wrecked plane. He said he didn't know for sure as he had got mixed up about the passage of time. But he did know the date of the month he was shot down. He told me the date. And I said out loud, "Good God!"

For, wounded and trapped, he had been lying there for eight days!

His left leg was broken and punctured by an ack-ack burst. His back was terribly burned by raw gasoline that had spilled. The foot of his injured leg was pinned rigidly under the rudder bar.

His space was so small he couldn't squirm around to relieve his own weight from his paining back. He couldn't straighten out his legs, which were bent above him. He couldn't see out of his little prison. He had not had a bite to eat or a drop of water. All this for eight days and nights.

Yet when we found him, his physical condition was strong, and his mind was as calm and rational as though he were sitting in a London club. He was in agony, yet in his correct Oxford accent he even apologized for taking up our time to get him out.

The American soldiers of our rescue party cussed as they worked, cussed with open admiration for this British flier's greatness of heart which had kept him alive and sane through his lonely and gradually hope-dimming ordeal.

One of them said, "These Limies[1] have got guts!"

It took us almost an hour to get him out. We don't know whether he will live or not, but he has a chance. During the hour we were ripping the plane open to make a hole, he talked to us. And here, in the best nutshell I can devise from the conversation of a brave man whom you didn't want to badger with trivial questions, is what happened—

He was an RAF flight lieutenant, piloting a night fighter. Over a certain area the Germans began letting him have it from the ground with machine-gun fire.

The first hit knocked out his motor. He was too low to jump, so—foolishly, he said—he turned on his lights to try a crash landing. Then they really poured it on him. The second hit got him in the leg. And a third bullet cut right across the balls of his right-hand forefingers, clipping every one of them to the bone.

He left his wheels up, and the plane's belly hit the ground going uphill on a slight slope. We could see the groove it had dug for about 50 yards. Then it flopped, tail over nose, onto its back. The pilot was absolutely sealed into the upside-down cockpit.

"That's all I remember for a while," he told us. "When I came to, they were shelling all around me."

Thus began the eight days. He had crashed right between the Germans and Americans in a sort of pastoral[2] no man's land.[3]

For days afterwards the field in which he lay surged back and forth between German hands and ours.

His pasture was pocked with hundreds of shell craters. Many of them were only yards away. One was right at the end of his wing. The metal sides of the plane were speckled with hundreds of shrapnel holes.

He lay there, trapped in the midst of this inferno of explosions. The fields around him gradually became littered with dead. At last American strength pushed the Germans back, and silence came. But no help. Because, you see, it was in that vacuum behind the battle, and only a few people were left.

The days passed. He thirsted terribly. He slept some; part of the time he was unconscious; part of the time he undoubtedly was delirious. But he never gave up hope.

After we had finally got him out, he said as he lay on the stretcher under a wing, "Is it possible that I've been out of this plane since I crashed?"

Everybody chuckled. The doctor who had arrived said, "Not the remotest possibility. You were sealed in there and it took men with tools half an hour to make an opening. And your leg was broken and your foot was pinned there. No, you haven't been out."

"I didn't think it was possible," the pilot said, "and yet it seems in my mind that I was out once and back in again."

That little memory of delirium was the only word said by that remarkable man in the whole hour of his rescue that wasn't as dispassionate and matter-of-fact as though he had been sitting comfortably at the end of the day in front of his own fireplace.

—Scripps-Howard wire copy,
August 22, 1944

---

1. **Limies** (līm′ēz): slang for "English sailors" or, sometimes, "English soldiers."
2. **pastoral** (pas′tər·əl) *adj.*: rural.
3. **no man's land:** unoccupied area separating opposing armies.

Reading Check

1. Describe the situation as the story opens. Who is the **main character,** what is he doing, and what has just happened to him?

2. Where does the nurse tell the pilot he is?

3. What does the wing commander ask the pilot at the end of the story? What is the pilot's response?

Thinking Critically

4. Summarize the clues in the story and the **inferences** you made that helped you understand the pilot's situation.

5. What do the people working in the hospital do and say to create the appearance that the pilot is in England? How does the pilot figure out that he has been deceived? Find the moment that marks a turning point in his understanding of his situation. (Be sure to check your Quickwrite notes.)

6. Describe the **character** of the pilot. Consider
   - his reactions to his situation at the beginning of the story
   - his attempt to get to the window
   - his responses to the nurse and the wing commander at the end of the story

7. For the **title** of his story, Dahl chose the wording of a common sign. What other meanings, in addition to its literal one, might this title have? (Hint: Figuratively speaking, who is the dog? Who must beware, and why?)

8. This story grips the reader from the start. How does Dahl create **suspense** in the story? Give examples from the text.

Literary Criticism

9. Describe the **conflicts** the pilot faces in the course of the story. How does each conflict reflect the issues or themes of the story's **historical period?**

10. "Wounded and Trapped" (see the **Connection** on page 701) is about a real World War II fighter pilot. What similarities can you find between the situation of Dahl's fictional pilot and the real pilot's situation during this **historical period?**

11. How might Dahl have drawn on his own experiences as a fighter pilot when writing this story? Review the biographical information in Meet the Writer (see pages 699–700) to help you answer, and point to specific places in the story as examples.

WRITING

Research Paper

Select a topic related to World War II that you would like to know more about. Keep your topic limited so that you can explore it in a short **research paper** ("the Battle of Britain," for example, instead of "World War II aviation battles"). Make a list of questions that you want to answer, and identify sources that you could use to research your topic. Take notes as you read your sources, and then organize your information into a short report. Be sure to credit your sources.

▶ **Use "Writing a Research Paper," pages 706–725, for help with this assignment.**

SKILLS FOCUS

Literary Skills
Analyze historical setting.

Reading Skills
Make inferences.

Writing Skills
Write a research paper.

After You Read　Vocabulary Development

Semantic Map

For each Word Bank word, make a **semantic map** like the one below for *undulating*. First, define the word. Then, write at least two questions about the word, and answer them. You'll have to make up different questions for each word. Compare your maps with those of your classmates.

Word Bank

undulating
giddy
unconscious
idly
delirious
obsession
hoisted
beckoned

undulating: moving in waves

What can be described as undulating?

• a flag in a breeze
• long, wavy hair
• a wheat field on a windy day

What would you *not* describe as undulating?

• a falling rock
• a bouncing ball
• a high-speed train

Jargon: Working Words

When is a *nose* not as plain as the thing in the middle of your face? When it's actually the front of an airplane. This use of the word *nose* is an example of **jargon,** the specialized words, or **technical vocabulary,** used by people who hold particular jobs or who have particular interests. Newspaper reporters, chefs, and basketball players, for example, all have their own specialized vocabulary. In "Beware of the Dog," Dahl uses the jargon of pilots to make his story as specific and realistic as possible.

Many jargon words have no meaning outside their specialized field. Often, however, words can take on a specialized meaning in a particular field while still maintaining other, more common meanings. For each example of jargon listed in the box below, fill out a chart like the one for *taxi* at the right. Use a dictionary and the footnotes in the story to help you complete your charts.

| stick | throttled | wings |
| bail out | port | |

taxi
Sentence in story: "When I land, I shall taxi in and switch off my engine. . . ."
Meaning in story: move slowly along the ground after landing
Other meaning: travel in a taxicab
Sample sentence for other meaning: We taxied from the train station to our hotel.

SKILLS FOCUS

Vocabulary Skills
Create semantic maps.
Understand jargon, or technical vocabulary.

FICTION
America Has Many Streets

Reading the stories in *America Street* is like taking a walk through fourteen American neighborhoods—each with its own distinct character. On one street, Toni Cade Bambara will introduce you to Squeaky, who's absolutely determined to win the neighborhood race. On another street you'll meet Grace Paley's Shirley, who's memorizing lines for her first school play. Duane Big Eagle will take you to Raoul's neighborhood, where Raoul is boarding a train in search of his mysterious medicine-woman aunt. Why not go for a walk and meet your neighbors?

FICTION
Fateful Storm

War, romance, typhoons, and an edge-of-your-seat courtroom drama are interwoven in the novel *The Caine Mutiny.* When the behavior of the captain aboard the USS *Caine* threatens the ship and its crew, a mutiny takes place. Although the lieutenant responsible for the mutiny is court-martialed (taken to court for breaking military law), the character of the captain is really on trial. Herman Wouk won a Pulitzer Prize for this novel, which was partly inspired by his own U.S. Navy experiences during World War II.

NONFICTION
A Survivor's Story

The Endless Steppe by Esther Hautzig is a true account of a family taken captive during World War II. Ten-year-old Esther and her family—like many other innocent Polish Jews—are arrested in their home, crowded onto a train car usually used to transport cattle, and sent to a Russian-owned labor camp in frigid Siberia. Whether describing harsh winds and hunger or her family's love for one another, Esther Hautzig shows spirit, courage, and faith—she'll remind you of Anne Frank.

NONFICTION
Taking Her Place

Charlayne Hunter-Gault was the first African American woman to attend the University of Georgia. As you'll see in her autobiography, *In My Place,* being the first wasn't easy. After the triumph of being admitted to the university came the pain of prejudice. Some of her classmates and professors didn't want her at the school, and she had to fight for her civil rights. Hunter-Gault explains why her struggle was worth it.

Writing a Research Paper

Writing Assignment
Write a research paper in which you present documented evidence that supports a thesis.

Suppose that after reading "American History" earlier in this collection, you found yourself wanting to know more about Puerto Rico or the assassination of President John F. Kennedy. It's not unusual for new subjects to grab your interest and make you want to learn more. Whether it's learning the history that leads to current events, discovering the truth behind the latest urban legend, or exploring the background of a story you've just read, asking questions and finding the answers help feed your interest. Writing a research paper about a topic that interests you works much the same way. You begin by asking questions and tracking down the answers; then, you tell others about your new knowledge by writing a paper.

Prewriting

Select a Topic

A Need to Know With so many topics you can research, where will you start? First, consider the task you will be undertaking—researching and writing a paper of at least 1,500 words. Because you'll be spending a lot of time and energy on this task, the topic of your research paper should be something that interests you and will also interest others. Here are ways to generate ideas for a topic if you don't already have one in mind.

- **Follow current events.** Consider any topic on the news that catches your attention, such as legislation affecting teenagers or a new scientific breakthrough.

- **Dream up a vacation.** Look over maps or visit Web sites for a location you'd like to visit. Learn all you can about the people, geography, and attractions in the area.

- **Make a list of your personal interests.** Consider hobbies, sports, music, or other interests you already have. Use your research paper as a way to learn more about one of your pastimes or to get involved in a new area of interest.

- **Think about historical or literary figures.** You've learned about many interesting people in this class and in others. Which historical or literary figure interests you?

SKILLS FOCUS

Writing Skills
Write a research paper.

Form a Research Question

In a Nutshell Once you've thought of a topic, consider what you want and need to know about it. Develop one question that will focus your project and keep you on track as you gather information. This **research question** should ask exactly what you want to find out from your research. To get started, ask yourself the questions shown in the left column of the chart below. One writer's responses are shown to the right as an example. Notice that the writer's research question cannot be answered with a single word.

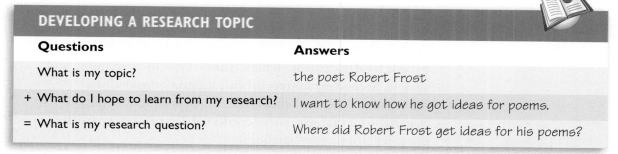

DEVELOPING A RESEARCH TOPIC

Questions	Answers
What is my topic?	the poet Robert Frost
+ What do I hope to learn from my research?	I want to know how he got ideas for poems.
= What is my research question?	Where did Robert Frost get ideas for his poems?

From One Come Many Next, let your research question lead you to form several related, more-detailed questions. These detailed questions, in turn, will help you find the specific evidence you need for your paper. The student writer broke up his research question into the following three detailed questions.

—Did Frost base any poems on actual events from his life?
—Did Frost write about the places where he lived?
—Did Frost ever explain where he got the ideas for his poems?

Identify Purpose and Audience

Why Write? Before you head to the library or hit the Internet, think about why you are researching this topic and who will be reading about your findings. The **purpose** of your research paper is to uncover information from various sources. You'll **synthesize,** or combine, the information you gather from multiple sources, draw conclusions based on your research, and inform others about your findings.

Who Will Read It? The others that you'll inform are your **audience**—consisting of your classmates, your teacher, and anyone else with whom you wish to share your research. For your audience to understand you, you must first understand them. Ask yourself the following questions about your audience so you can tailor your research to anticipate and address their wants and needs.

SKILLS FOCUS

Writing Skills
Develop a research question. Consider your purpose and audience.

TIP Add the questions you think your audience will expect you to answer to the list of detailed questions you created on page 707.

- What information will my readers already have about my topic?
- What questions will they expect me to answer about it?
- How can I clear up potential misunderstandings or biases they might have?
- What unfamiliar terms or technical notations will I need to define for my readers?

Find Sources

A Wealth of Information Where will you find the answers to your research questions? You'll need to gather information from both primary and secondary sources. **Primary sources** contain original, firsthand information that is unfiltered and unedited. Primary sources include legal documents, letters, diaries, eyewitness accounts, and surveys. **Secondary sources** provide indirect or secondhand information. They are other people's interpretations of primary material—for example, encyclopedia entries, newspaper articles, documentaries, and biographies.

Let's Get Started Begin your search at your school library, but also plan on visiting your community library and any college or university libraries in your area. Although your search might start at a library, it certainly should not end there. Check out community resources that might be valuable sources, such as various local, state, and national government agencies, as well as electronic media. The charts below and on the next page list resources that might be available in your area libraries and in your community, along with the sources or types of information they provide.

LIBRARY RESOURCES	
Resource	**Source or Type of Information**
Card catalog or online catalog	books listed by title, author, and subject; in some libraries this catalog also lists audiovisual materials—videotapes, records, CDs, audiotapes, filmstrips, and films
Readers' Guide to Periodical Literature	articles in magazines and journals
Microfilm, microfiche, or online databases	encyclopedias (electronic or print), biographical references, atlases, almanacs
General and specialized reference books or CD-ROMs	indexes to major newspapers such as *The New York Times*, back issues of newspapers
World Wide Web and online services	articles, interviews, bibliographies, pictures, videos, sound recordings; access to the Library of Congress and other libraries

COMMUNITY RESOURCES

Resource	Source or Type of Information
Local, state, and national government agencies	voting records, recent or pending legislation, experts on state and federal government
Local newspaper offices	accounts of events of local interest, historical information on city or area
Museums, historical societies, service groups	historical events, scientific achievements, art and artists, special exhibits, and experts
Video stores, audiotape rental stores	documentary and instructional videotapes and audiotapes

TIP Consider **interviewing experts** in the subject areas you are researching. Experts can be valuable primary sources, and often they can direct you to other useful sources. Be sure to arrive at the interview on time with relevant questions prepared in advance. Take careful notes of the responses to your questions. Conduct yourself in a mature and respectful way, speaking courteously and sensitively to the person you are interviewing—this person is providing you with priceless help. Finally, compile the most useful responses while they're fresh in your mind so you can accurately report them.

Evaluate Sources

A Source to Trust? Just as members of a jury have to decide which witnesses are **credible,** or believable, and which are not, you have to determine the extent to which you can trust your sources of information. Here are some questions you can use to put them to the test.

1. **Is the source up-to-date?** Information is generated so quickly now that it is easy to find current material. If information on your topic is constantly changing, be sure that your sources are up-to-date.

2. **Does the source seem factual?** Check its information against your own knowledge and against other sources. If you find a **discrepancy,** or difference, between sources, check additional sources to determine which information is most accurate or most useful. For example, one writer might state that Robert Frost quit college and never graduated. However, another writer might give an explanation: Frost left college to help his wife, who was having difficulties with her pregnancy.

3. **Does the source provide explanations?** Look for explanations that might help you and your readers understand the **complexities** of the topic. For example, even though many of Frost's poems deal with nature, they may have several interpretations. By explaining the interpretations, you may help your audience gain insight into Frost's poems.

Writing Skills
Interview experts. Evaluate sources.

4. **Do the sources cover different perspectives?** Some sources may be biased, or slanted, toward one point of view. Therefore, you may find that different sources present varying **perspectives** on the same subject. For example, a short biography included in a book of Robert Frost's poetry might be entirely positive about the poet and mention only his awards. However, a newspaper critic who is reviewing the book might mention negative aspects of Frost's writing. It is important to include in your research all relevant perspectives concerning any controversial or strongly slanted information.

Prepare Source Cards

Keeping Track of Everything Since your paper will include a *Works Cited* list, a list of all the sources you use in your paper, you need a way to keep track of all your information. One way is to write information about each source on a 3- x 5-inch index card and number each card. If you keep track of your sources on a computer, create a separate file or record for each source. Keeping your source files or records separate will ensure that you don't get confused about where a piece of information came from.

The following chart tells you the information you need to record for each type of source. Pay close attention to the punctuation used in each type of record. The listings follow the **Modern Language Association (MLA)** format. Your teacher may ask you to use a different format, such as that of *The Chicago Manual of Style.* Be sure you know which format your teacher requires. Noting source information in the correct format now will make it easier for you to create your *Works Cited* list later.

TIP Make a card for each source you consult in your research. You may later discover that you need to re-examine sources that you didn't use initially.

Reference Note

For more on *Works Cited* lists, see pages 716 and 722.

GUIDELINES FOR RECORDING SOURCE INFORMATION

1. **Book with One Author.** Write author's name, last name first; book title; place of publication; name of publishing company; and year of publication.

   Parini, Jay. <u>Robert Frost: A Life</u>. New York: Henry Holt and Company, 1999.

2. **Book with More Than One Author.** Write first author's name, last name first; then list other authors, first name first. Record other information as for a book with one author.

   Thompson, Lawrance, and R. H. Winnick. <u>Robert Frost: The Later Years, 1938–1963</u>. New York: Holt, Rinehart and Winston, 1976.

3. **Magazine or Newspaper Article.** Write author's name, last name first; article title; magazine or newspaper name; day, month, and year of publication; edition; and beginning page number. For magazine articles, also list the end page number. For newspaper articles, indicate the section as part of the page number. If no author is listed, start with the article title.

   "A Lover's Quarrel With the World." <u>Time</u> 8 Feb. 1963: 84.

(continued)

4. Encyclopedia Article. Write author's name, last name first; article title; encyclopedia name; edition number, followed by the abbreviation *ed.;* and year of publication. If no author is listed, start with article title.

Costello, Bonnie. "Frost, Robert Lee." <u>The World Book Encyclopedia</u>. 2000 ed. 2000.

5. Radio or Television Program. Write episode or segment title; program name; series title (if any); network name; local station call letters and city (if any); and day, month, and year of broadcast.

"Poet Laureate Reads an Ode to Spring." <u>All Things Considered</u>. National Public Radio. 21 Apr. 1996.

6. Film, Audio, or Video. Write title; director (first name first); distributor; and year of release. When citing an audio or video recording, include the original release date (if relevant) and the medium (for example, audiocassette, videocassette, DVD) before the distributor.

<u>Understanding Literature and Life: Drama, Poetry, and Narrative: Part IIb: Poetry</u>. Arnold Weinstein. Audiocassette. The Teaching Company, 1997.

7. Personal or Telephone Interview. Write interviewee's last name, then first name; interview type (personal or telephone); and day, month, and year of interview.

Thompson, Carole. Telephone and e-mail interviews. 12 May 2002.

8. Portable database. Write author's name, last name first; title of document, article, or part of work; database title; publication medium (for example, CD-ROM, diskette, or magnetic tape); edition, release, or version; place of publication (if known), name of publisher, and date of publication.

Greiner, Donald J. "Robert (Lee) Frost." <u>Dictionary of Literary Biography, Volume 54: American Poets, 1880–1945, Third Series</u>. CD-ROM. 1987 ed. Gale Group, 2001.

9. Online sources. Write author's name, last name first (if listed); title of document; title of database or site; date of electronic publication (if available); name of sponsoring institution; date information was accessed; <URL> [or] name of online service.

"Ripton, Vermont." <u>The Friends of Robert Frost</u>. The Friends of Robert Frost. 23 May 2002 <http://www.frostfriends.org/ripton.html>.

Take Notes

The Researcher's Best Friend Take **accurate and coherent notes** of information and ideas you find in your sources. You'll use these facts and details as evidence to support your thesis. Note specific data, facts, and ideas that seem significant and will provide valuable support to answer your questions. Take notes on each piece of information by using one of the following methods.

- **Quote** the information directly, writing the author's exact words.

- **Paraphrase** the information by restating all of the author's ideas in your own words.

- **Summarize** the information by briefly restating only the author's main idea and most important details.

Writing Skills
Use appropriate documentation for sources.

TIP If you choose to make notes on your computer, record the information from each source in a separate file.

Write your direct quotations, paraphrases, and summaries on **note cards.** In the upper left-hand corner of each card, write a key word or phrase as the heading for the card so that you can tell at a glance what the note is about. In the upper right-hand corner, write the number (from your source cards) of the source where you found the information. Then, write the text of the note. Finally, in the bottom right-hand corner, record the page number when appropriate. Here are sample note cards that show a direct quotation, a paraphrase, and a summary of information a student found in the book *Robert Frost: The Later Years 1938–1963.*

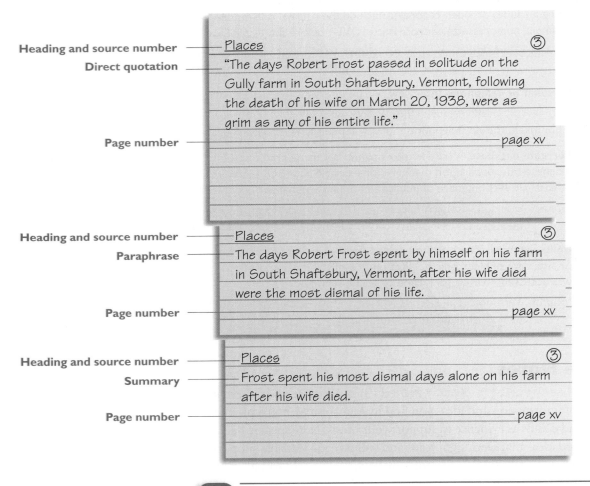

Heading and source number — Places ③
Direct quotation — "The days Robert Frost passed in solitude on the Gully farm in South Shaftsbury, Vermont, following the death of his wife on March 20, 1938, were as grim as any of his entire life."
Page number — page xv

Heading and source number — Places ③
Paraphrase — The days Robert Frost spent by himself on his farm in South Shaftsbury, Vermont, after his wife died were the most dismal of his life.
Page number — page xv

Heading and source number — Places ③
Summary — Frost spent his most dismal days alone on his farm after his wife died.
Page number — page xv

SKILLS FOCUS

Writing Skills
Take notes. Develop main ideas.

TIP A variety of types of evidence will hold your readers' interest while developing the main points in your paper. In addition to facts and details, note these types of evidence, if they're relevant to your research questions.

- **scenarios:** general descriptions of potential events or common situations
- **commonly held beliefs:** broad ideas that most people accept
- **hypotheses:** educated guesses about causes or outcomes
- **definitions:** objective explanations of unfamiliar terms

Write a Thesis Statement

The Bottom Line Your **thesis** is the main idea of your report and the answer to your original research question. Through research, the writer who began with the research question *Where did Robert Frost get ideas for his poems?* found that Frost was inspired by the places where he lived and the natural areas nearby. To state his thesis, he turned his research question into a statement and added information that answered the question. Below is his preliminary thesis statement. As you will see in the Writer's Model on page 718, the writer later fine-tuned his thesis statement to fit the focus of his final draft.

> Robert Frost got many of the ideas for his poems from the places where he lived and the natural areas nearby.

What Tone of Voice? Since you want your readers to take your ideas seriously, be sure that your thesis statement has a formal tone that reflects confidence in what you say. Use this **formal tone** throughout your paper. That means you should avoid slang words, contractions, and first-person pronouns, such as *I* or *we,* and you should use correct grammar. Use technical terms where appropriate, defining or thoroughly explaining them for readers.

Organize Information and Develop an Outline

Get It Together Next you'll need to organize the information you've gathered. Begin by reviewing your note cards and sorting them into groups with similar headings. If a group doesn't have enough note cards to provide adequate support for its heading, you may decide to omit that group or to do additional research for more support.

DO THIS

Organize the groups of cards in the order in which you will present them in the paper. Choose the organizational method below that best fits your topic.

- **Chronological order** presents events in the order that they happened.

- **Logical order** groups related ideas together—explaining the parts of a whole or comparing two subjects, for example.

- **Order of importance** places the most important ideas first and moves to the least important (or vice versa).

You can combine orders in your report if doing so will make your information clearer. For example, you could arrange your main points in logical order but organize the support for those points chronologically.

Writing Skills
Establish a coherent thesis statement.

Pick a Card   After sorting your note cards, it's time to create an outline of your ideas. An outline for a writing project is like a traveler's map. Good outlines and good maps give guidance and keep people going in the right direction but also leave them free to change their plans. Your outline will include the answers to your detailed questions and the important facts and details that support those answers.

Begin outlining by creating an early plan based on your sorted note cards. This early plan, or **informal outline,** should include the major headings and broad categories of support from your notes. Here is a student's early plan for his report on Robert Frost:

Thesis: Frost's poetry inspired by places where he lived, nature
   Early life (San Francisco, aunt's farm)
   Places he lived as an adult (Derry and other farms, England)
   Natural areas (poems inspired by nature walks)
Conclusion: Frost's importance

You will use your informal outline as a guide to create a more detailed **formal outline.** In a formal outline, you plan the arrangement of more specific information from your notes and show the hierarchy of ideas using a formal structure. As you create your formal outline, use numerals and letters to identify main points (headings), supporting ideas (subheadings), and details (facts and examples). This format is shown in the following student outline:

I. Introduction
   A. Thesis statement: Robert Frost got many of the ideas for his poems from the places where he lived and natural areas nearby.
   B. Background information
II. Body
   A. Early life
      1. San Francisco
         a. "Once by the Pacific"
         b. "At Woodward's Gardens"
      2. Aunt's farm
   B. Adulthood—Places he lived
      1. Background information
      2. Farm in Derry
         a. Description
         b. "Mending Wall"

SKILLS FOCUS

Writing Skills
Create an outline.

3. England
    a. Reasons for move
    b. Accomplishments
4. Return to U.S.
    a. Newfound fame
    b. "Directive"
    c. Reputation
  C. Adulthood—Nature
    1. Nature walks
    2. "Stopping by Woods on a Snowy Evening"
    3. Robert Frost Trail
III. Conclusion
  A. Restatement of thesis
  B. Obituary quote
  C. Frost's impact

Document Sources

Where Credit Is Due In a research paper, you use information and ideas that you obtained from outside sources. Give credit to these sources by citing them in the body of your paper and by listing them at the end of your finished paper—by doing so, you'll avoid the serious academic offense of plagiarism, or claiming someone else's words or ideas as your own.

Citing Sources in the Body When you are writing the body of your report, you must decide what to give credit for and how to give it.

- **What to credit:** If the same information can be found in several easy-to-find sources, it is considered common knowledge. You do not have to document it. For example, it is common knowledge that Robert Frost was an American poet. However, any information that you obtain from outside sources that is not common knowledge must be documented.

- **How to credit:** There are several ways to give credit. One of the most widely used methods is **parenthetical citation.** In this workshop you'll see examples of the parenthetical citation format recommended by the Modern Language Association (MLA). When using parenthetical citations, you should place each citation as close as possible to the information it documents. In most cases you will insert the citation in parentheses before the end punctuation of the sentence in which you have used someone else's words or ideas. Parenthetical citations should be brief so as not to interrupt the flow of the sentences. The chart on the next page tells the information you will need to cite for different sources.

Writing Skills
Use appropriate documentation for sources.

Include a *Works Cited* List At the end of your research paper, you'll include a *Works Cited* list that identifies all the print and nonprint sources used in your paper. If you use only print sources in your paper, you can title your list of sources "Bibliography." You provide this list to help readers learn more about your topic. Be sure your citations are accurate; imagine the trouble your readers would have looking for your sources if one or more elements were missing from a citation.

SKILLS FOCUS

Writing Skills
Use appropriate documentation for sources.

TIP Before drafting, find out your teacher's formatting requirements. For example, you may need to number every page except the first one in the top right-hand corner or include a footer with your name. You'll also need to prepare a separate title page that includes your name, the date, the title of your report, and the teacher's name. If you take care of details such as these now, you won't have to worry about them when you're preparing your final draft.

Integrate Quotations

Straight from the Horse's Mouth Look back at the direct quotations you have in your notes. While quotations make your paper more credible, too many can make your paper choppy and difficult to read. Directly quote a source only when you can't more effectively summarize or paraphrase an idea. Synthesize the ideas in each quotation you use by connecting the quoted words with your own thoughts or by providing your own interpretation of the quotation.

Be careful when inserting quotations that you don't interrupt the paper's flow of ideas. The chart below shows examples of ways to integrate quotations into your paper once you begin writing. The examples are from a newspaper article you can find in the *Works Cited* list on page 722.

INTEGRATING QUOTATIONS

Type of Quotation	Directions	Example
phrase or clause	Place the quotation within your own sentence, and enclose it in quotation marks.	Frost's images of New England were considered part of "a great American tradition" ("Robert Frost Dies" 5).
short quotation (four lines or less)	Introduce the quotation with your own words, then place it within quotation marks.	One newspaper account of Robert Frost's death says, "he exemplified a great American tradition with his superb, almost angular verses written out of the New England scene" ("Robert Frost Dies" 5).
long quotation (more than four lines)	Introduce the quotation in your own words, followed by a colon. Indent each line ten spaces from the left margin, or one inch if you are using a computer. Do not use quotation marks. Place the parenthetical citation *after* the end punctuation.	In the account of Robert Frost's death in *The New York Times,* the writer chose Frost's images of New England farms and nature to leave a final impression of the poet on his readers: To countless persons who had never seen New Hampshire birches in the snow or caressed a perfect ax he exemplified a great American tradition with his superb, almost angular verses written out of the New England scene. ("Robert Frost Dies" 5)

PRACTICE & APPLY 1 Use the preceding prewriting information to plan your research paper. First, choose a topic and develop research questions. As you research, create source cards and note cards. Then, develop a thesis and form an outline.

Writing

Writing a Research Paper

A Writer's Framework

Introduction

- Capture your readers' attention with a question, anecdote, or interesting fact.
- Supply readers with background information on your topic.
- Include a clear thesis statement that gives the answer to your original research question.

Body

- Develop each main point from your outline in a separate body paragraph.
- Support each main point with evidence—facts and details in the form of smoothly integrated direct quotations, paraphrases, and summaries.
- Arrange your main points and evidence in a logical order.

Conclusion

- Remind readers of your thesis by restating it in different words.
- Leave your readers with a closing thought—an idea or point to ponder.

A Writer's Model

INTRODUCTION

Source with one author

Background information

Source with no author listed

Thesis statement

BODY
First main point

A Walk with Frost

As a high school boy walked home from school in Lawrence, Massachusetts, in 1890, a few lines of poetry about the conquest of Mexico unexpectedly popped into his head. He wrote them down and submitted them to his school paper, where the finished poem was published (Parini 25). No one who read the poem could have possibly known that this boy, Robert Frost, would eventually become "the most popular American poet of his time" (Costello 543).

Frost's popularity and widespread fame did not come early or easily. He spent almost forty years soaking up the sights and sounds of life around him before publishing his first book of poetry ("Lover's Quarrel" 84). Those forty years, however, created memories and experiences that would shape his writing for the remaining forty-five years of his life. Looking back on the sum of his work, readers should see that Robert Frost found much of the inspiration for his poetry from the places where he lived and the natural areas nearby.

This inspiration began where Frost's life began—in San Francisco. The Frost family took many trips to local parks and beaches, including the Cliff House beach, where Frost walked with his father near the pounding surf. This sparked a poem called "Once by

(continued)

---

the Pacific" (Parini 14). As a boy, with his sister, Jeanie, and his parents, Will and Isabelle, he often visited a zoo in a Victorian park called Woodward's Gardens. This park became the setting for his poem "At Woodward's Gardens," in which a boy teases two monkeys with a magnifying glass and the monkeys snatch it from him (Untermeyer 35).

When Frost was only eleven, his father died, leaving the family penniless. His mother returned with her children to her home state of Massachusetts, where her family could take them in (Parini 19). Frost spent many happy days at his aunt's farm, where he learned to love farming and formed the basis for many of the images found in his poetry (Parini 22). He finished high school as co-valedictorian of his class.

As an adult, Frost continued finding inspiration in farming and nature. After briefly attending Dartmouth College, he taught school to help his mother and rented his first farm in 1893. He later tried his hand at journalism, married his high school sweetheart, and briefly attended Harvard University, leaving Harvard to help his wife during a difficult pregnancy.

Life changed for Frost when he was able to buy a larger, more beautiful farm in Derry, New Hampshire. The farm in Derry was a lovely place with an apple orchard and a brook running along the property. This farm and this time of Frost's life eventually provided experiences and images for much of his poetry. Frost himself once commented, "There was something about the experience at Derry which stayed in my mind, and was tapped for poetry in the years that came after" (qtd. in Parini 73).

The Derry farm was the inspiration of several of Frost's most well-known poems, including "Mending Wall," in which two neighbors repair the wall between their properties:

> Something there is that doesn't love a wall,
> That sends the frozen-ground-swell under it,
> And spills the upper boulders in the sun;
> And makes gaps even two can pass abreast. (lines 1–4)

The actual wall that needed mending is still located at the Derry farm, which is open to the public as a museum filled with Frost memorabilia ("Derry").

The Frosts spent eleven simple and pleasant years on the Derry farm. In 1912, however, Frost made the risky decision to sell the farm and move to England. He wanted a new adventure that would

Second main point
Summary

Short quotation

Indirect source

Long quotation

Online source

Phrase/quotation

Source with two authors

Summary

Paraphrase

Short quotation

Third main point

give him "peace to write, the excitement of change" (Parini 113). While he had managed to publish a few poems, he felt he had the ability to write great poetry and to "realize his childhood dream of achieving honor and glory as a poet" (Thompson and Winnick xvi). England turned out to provide the inspiration Frost needed. Within a few months of his family's move, Frost had published his first book, *A Boy's Will,* and was working on a second. During his two years in England, he made many important literary friends and began to believe he would actually be able to make his way as a poet. World War II was brewing, however, and the Frosts quickly made their escape back to America ("England").

Frost returned home to unexpected fame. The two books he completed while in England were widely available and well-reviewed. Suddenly Frost was considered at the forefront of "the new era in American poetry" (qtd. in Untermeyer xxii). Despite this success, he settled back into his familiar way of life, buying a farm in New Hampshire. As before, he supported his family through the combination of farming and teaching. At last, though, his talents were being recognized by editors and reviewers (Parini 160).

Frost's love of farms remained, even though he could not make a living at it (Parini 173). He continued writing poems with imagery and settings he knew well, including many poems with what was becoming Frost's trademark—the voice of the New England farmer. Among these was "Directive," which describes with great sadness an abandoned farmhouse: "There is a house that is no more a house/Upon a farm that is no more a farm" (qtd. in Parini 361). According to biographer Jay Parini, the landscape Frost describes serves as "a map of his inner landscape," whose sorrow he then can leave behind (361).

As his reputation grew, Frost began lecturing at many colleges and universities, cementing his reputation as a farmer-poet (Thompson and Winnick xvii). This carefully crafted image lasted right up to one of his last poems, still about a farm, called "A Cabin in the Clearing" ("Ripton").

Along with his love of farms, Frost was fond of nature. One of his favorite pastimes throughout his life was walking in woods or along nature trails, which he called "botanizing" walks ("Ripton"). Two of his most quoted poems are about traveling alone in a natural setting—"Stopping by Woods on a Snowy Evening" and "The Road Not Taken." Both poems sparked lively debates about whether Frost's

(continued)

message was simple or complex. In "Stopping by Woods on a Snowy Evening," for example, there are many interpretations to these lines:

> The woods are lovely, dark and deep,
> But I have promises to keep,
> And miles to go before I sleep,
> And miles to go before I sleep. (lines 13–16)

Some people argue that the last lines simply mean the traveler has a long way to go before getting home. Others take a more complex view that "travelers in life" often do not know where they are going. During public readings of the poem, Frost would not say what he really meant, but that he wanted to leave the interpretation open to the listener (Parini 213).

Frost's love of nature is so tied to his poetry that many of the places dedicated to his memory follow the themes of his poems and continue to inspire other nature lovers. According to the president of The Friends of Robert Frost, the Green Mountain National Forest has a Robert Frost Trail along scenic paths where visitors can stop and read plaques inscribed with poems. One such plaque displays the poem "A Winter Eden" and stands near a swamp much like the one described in the poem. At one spot, walkers arrive at a fork in a path where they can consider the words of "The Road Not Taken" (Carole Thompson).

The boy who was first inspired to write poetry by an account of the conquest of Mexico had earned a reputation as the poetic voice of the common farmer through imagery inspired by his surroundings. The young man who had subsisted on farming and teaching came to be considered "America's best-known and best-loved poet" (Thompson and Winnick xvi). In the account of Robert Frost's death in *The New York Times,* the writer chose Frost's images of New England farms and nature to leave his readers with a final impression:

> To countless persons who had never seen New
> Hampshire birches in the snow or caressed a perfect
> ax he exemplified a great American tradition with his
> superb, almost angular verses written out of the New
> England scene. ("Robert Frost Dies" 5)

Frost certainly succeeded in his aim to "lodge a few poems where they can't be gotten rid of easily" (Parini xi). With four Pulitzer prizes, countless honorary degrees, and poetry that has been read all over the world, Robert Frost found his honor and glory in writing poetry, just as he always knew he would.

Complexity explained

Interview

CONCLUSION
Restatement of thesis

Concluding thought

(continued)

TIP Generally, research papers and their *Works Cited* lists are double-spaced. They are shown here single-spaced because of limited room. See *go.hrw.com* for a double-spaced model of a research paper.

(continued)

Works Cited

Costello, Bonnie. "Frost, Robert Lee." <u>The World Book Encyclopedia</u>. 2000 ed. 2000.

"Derry, New Hampshire." <u>The Friends of Robert Frost</u>. The Friends of Robert Frost. 23 May 2002 <http://www. frostfriends.org/ derry.html>.

"England." <u>The Friends of Robert Frost</u>. The Friends of Robert Frost. 23 May 2002 <http://www.frostfriends.org/ england.html>.

"A Lover's Quarrel With the World." <u>Time</u> 8 Feb. 1963: 84.

Parini, Jay. <u>Robert Frost: A Life</u>. New York: Henry Holt and Company, 1999.

"Robert Frost Dies at 88; Kennedy Leads in Tribute." <u>New York Times</u> 30 Jan. 1963. Western ed.: 1+.

"Ripton, Vermont." <u>The Friends of Robert Frost</u>. The Friends of Robert Frost. 23 May 2002 <http://www.frostfriends.org/ ripton.html>.

Thompson, Carole. Telephone and e-mail interviews. 12 May 2002.

Thompson, Lawrance, and R. H. Winnick. <u>Robert Frost: The Later Years, 1938–1963</u>. New York: Holt, Rinehart and Winston, 1976.

Untermeyer, Louis, ed. <u>The Road Not Taken</u>. New York: Holt, Rinehart and Winston, 1962.

INTERNET

More Writer's Models

Keyword: LE7 9-9

PRACTICE & APPLY 2 Write the first draft of your research paper and *Works Cited* list. Look back at the framework on page 718 to make sure you include all the essential elements of a research paper. Also, use the Writer's Model and its annotations as guides for writing your own paper. Be sure to smoothly integrate any direct quotations, and use a variety of quotations, paraphrases, and summaries from your sources. Include parenthetical citations to document your sources for all of these types of information.

Revising

Evaluate and Revise Your Draft

Touch-up or Major Overhaul? Many famous writers revise their works several times. Sometimes they even revise works that have already been published. Very few writers get it just right the first time. To refine your own writing, you should read through your paper at least twice. First, evaluate the content and organization using the following guidelines. Then, use the guidelines on the next page to revise your essay for style.

PEER REVIEW

Ask a peer to read your paper before you begin revising. He or she may be able to point out places where you need more evidence to support a main point.

▶ **First Reading: Content and Organization** The following chart should help you evaluate and revise the content and organization of your draft. Ask yourself the questions in the left-hand column. If you need help answering them, use the tips in the middle column. Then, make the changes suggested in the right-hand column.

Rubric: Writing a Research Paper

Evaluation Questions	▶ Tips	▶ Revision Techniques
❶ Is the thesis clearly stated? Does it seem to answer a specific research question?	▶ **Underline** the thesis statement. **Draw a box** around the part that answers a specific research question.	▶ **Add** a thesis statement or **replace** an existing statement with one that clearly answers the research question.
❷ Is each main point well supported with evidence—facts and details in the form of direct quotations, summaries, and paraphrases?	▶ **Highlight** each main point with a different colored marker. Then, **highlight** evidence with the color of its corresponding main point.	▶ **Add** additional evidence for any main points that have too little support.
❸ Are direct quotations smoothly integrated into the paper?	▶ **Draw an arrow** from each direct quotation to the words that introduce the quotation.	▶ **Reword** the text around quotations so that the flow of ideas is not disrupted.
❹ Are all sources given proper credit?	▶ **Look back** at all highlighted direct quotations, paraphrases, and summaries. **Place check marks** by their parenthetical citations.	▶ **Add** parenthetical citations for direct quotations, paraphrases, or summaries from sources.
❺ Does the conclusion restate the thesis and give the readers a closing thought?	▶ **Underline** the restatement of the thesis. **Put a wavy line** under the closing thought.	▶ **Add** a restatement of the thesis. **Elaborate** on the ideas in the essay by leaving readers with an idea or point to ponder.

Second Reading: Style In your second reading, look at your sentence style. Since your research paper is so full of information, you don't want to risk losing your readers' attention. Starting many sentences with phrases like *there is* and *there was* can make your research paper monotonous to readers and cause their attention to fade. Instead of overusing these tired sentence structures, add variety to your sentence beginnings by starting with your subject and following it with a lively verb. The following style guidelines will help.

editor in charge

Style Guidelines

Evaluation Question	Tip	Revision Technique
Do many sentences begin with the words *there is, there was, there are,* or *there were?*	**Double underline** each sentence that begins this way. If you have more than two or three in your entire paper, revise.	**Rearrange** the sentence so that the subject comes first. Then, **replace** *is, are, was,* or *were* with a more lively verb.

ANALYZING THE REVISION PROCESS

Study these revisions, and answer the questions that follow.

> This inspiration began where Frost's life began—in San Francisco. ~~There were~~ The Frost family took many trips to local parks and beaches, including the Cliff House beach, where Frost walked with his father near the pounding surf. This sparked a poem called "Once by the Pacific~~."~~ (Parini 14).

replace

add

Responding to the Revision Process

1. Why did the writer revise the beginning of the second sentence?
2. Why did the writer add the parenthetical citation to the last sentence? What does the citation tell the reader about the information in that sentence?

SKILLS FOCUS

Writing Skills
Revise for content and style.

PRACTICE & APPLY 3 Revise the content, organization, and style of your research paper by using the charts on the last two pages to guide you. Look at the revisions in the paragraph above as a model for your own revisions.

Publishing

Proofread and Publish Your Essay

A Fine-toothed Comb Before you prepare the final copy of your research paper, make sure it's free of grammar, spelling, and punctuation errors. Particularly, watch for errors in documenting your sources. Compare the format of your entries in the *Works Cited* list against the MLA format guidelines shown on pages 710–711. Double check that the information in your parenthetical citations matches the information you give in your *Works Cited* list.

Share the Wealth Once you've corrected any errors, make sure your final draft meets your teacher's manuscript requirements. Include a correctly formatted title page, and use pagination, spacing, and margins appropriate to a research report. Now that you've spent so much time and energy researching and writing your paper, consider how you can share what you've learned with a larger audience. Here are some suggestions:

- Locate a group or organization that would have a special interest in your research. For example, organizations of Frost fans might be interested in publishing all or parts of the Writer's Model on page 718.

- Collect other research papers from your class for a special display at your school or in your classroom. Using advanced publishing software and graphics software, polish the design of your papers to heighten their appeal.

- Send a copy of your paper to any professional you may have interviewed. For example, the writer of the Frost paper might mail a copy to the Frost organization president whom he interviewed.

Reflect on Your Essay

Give It Some Thought Writing short responses to the following questions will help you build on what you've learned in this workshop.

- What difficulties did you encounter while writing this paper? How might you avoid these problems when writing future research reports?

- How might you use the research skills you've acquired in this workshop in your other classes?

- What discoveries did you make about the topic and about yourself as a writer while completing this workshop?

PRACTICE & APPLY 4 Proofread your research paper, and consider all your publishing options. Plan and carry out the publishing option or options that most appeal to you. Then, answer the reflection questions above.

TIP Proofreading helps ensure that your essay follows the **conventions** of standard American English. For example, because you are presenting so much information on your topic, you may have a tendency to merge two complete sentences into one run-on sentence. Proofread your paper to make sure that it's free of run-on sentences. For more on **run-on sentences,** see Run-on Sentences, 9b, in the Language Handbook.

COMPUTER TIP

For information on creating an appealing document design using computer software, see Designing Your Writing in the Writer's Handbook.

SKILLS FOCUS

Writing Skills
Proofread, especially to correct run-on sentences.

Presenting Research

Speaking Assignment
Adapt the information from a written research report to effectively deliver it in an oral presentation.

All day long you listen—to teachers, to other students, to your parents. Everybody has information that you need to hear. What do you do when it's your turn to speak? How do you share information—like the contents of a research paper—effectively? This workshop explains how to share your research in an **oral presentation.**

Adapt Your Research Paper

Similar but Different The information in your oral presentation will likely be the same as the information in your paper. You will, though, need to adapt your written ideas so you can deliver them effectively orally. To start, consider the following suggestions.

Shorten and Simplify Make your points directly, keeping your words and sentences simple to make sure that listeners don't get lost. Plan to use standard American English and avoid slang. If you must use certain unfamiliar words, technical terms, or notations, be sure you define and explain them carefully and clearly.

Give Previews and Repeat Yourself Break the information in your presentation into small units; then, prepare a one- or two-sentence preview of each section to let listeners know what to expect. At the end of each section sum up the ideas you have given. Obvious previews and repetition help listeners absorb and remember information.

Drop Clues Listeners need to know where you are leading them. Help them by presenting your ideas in a logical, easy-to-follow order. Do not stray too far from the simplest, most straightforward uses of chronological order or order of importance. Insert transitional words and phrases, such as *first, second, next, most important,* and *finally,* to help make the organization of your ideas crystal clear.

Anticipate Your Listeners' Reactions Be prepared to deal with listeners who may misunderstand you or have a bias against your ideas. You should be able to restate or paraphrase information if your listeners look confused. Handle doubters by referring to your facts. Remember to respect their ideas, but also express confidence and defend the research you have gathered.

Mapping Your Course As you review your material for adaptation, make sure that you maintain a strong basic presentation structure of introduction, body, and conclusion. Use the chart on the next page to plan the content of each section.

Listening and Speaking Skills
Present a research report.

ORGANIZING SPEECH CONTENT

Introduction	• Plan to grab your listeners' attention with a startling statement, an interesting and relevant anecdote, or a connection to the interests of the listeners. • Consider incorporating your original research question into your introduction.
Body	• Support your thesis with only the most relevant and significant evidence from your paper. • Use ideas from both primary and secondary sources to show listeners that you've considered all important ideas and perspectives. • Keep your ideas logically organized in either chronological order or order of importance. • Add to your credibility by telling where your information came from. Smoothly introduce source information by saying something like "Biologist Kim Griffith suggests that . . ."
Conclusion	• Summarize your main points. • Pose an interesting thought or question to keep your listeners thinking about the ideas you've presented after you're finished.

Prepare for Delivery

In the Spotlight   In an oral presentation, preparing your content is only half the battle. Now, you must prepare to stand before an audience and say your ideas aloud. Practice communicating your ideas effectively, using verbal and nonverbal techniques.

Show 'Em!   Consider using the technology available at your school to include **visuals**—such as charts, maps, or graphs—to enhance the appeal and clarity of your presentation. Short video clips and graphics shown on a television or an overhead projector can help you express ideas more effectively. For example, rather than simply reporting responses from an interview you've conducted, why not videotape the interview and show the most relevant segments of it to your audience? Also, consider using **props** in your presentation. For example, a speaker could enhance a presentation about Japanese culture by wearing a kimono. Whatever audiovisual support you use, be sure that it is relevant and easy to understand.

PRACTICE & APPLY 5   Adapt the information from your research paper for an oral presentation. Practice your verbal and nonverbal techniques; then, deliver your presentation to an audience.

Reference Note
For information on **verbal and nonverbal delivery techniques,** see page 87.

SKILLS FOCUS

Listening and Speaking Skills
Organize the speech. Use visual aids.

Test Practice

Using Primary and Secondary Sources

DIRECTIONS: Read the following encyclopedia article and personal recollection. Then, read and respond to the questions that follow.

Kennedy's Assassination

Eric Sevareid

John F. Kennedy was shot to death by an assassin on November 22, 1963, as he rode through the streets of Dallas, Texas. His death continued the unhappy coincidence that, since William H. Harrison, every American president elected in a year ending in "0" had died while in office. These presidents and the years of election were Harrison (1840), Abraham Lincoln (1860), James A. Garfield (1880), William McKinley (1900), Warren G. Harding (1920), and Franklin D. Roosevelt (1940). Only one president elected in a year ending in "0" has not died in office. That president was Ronald Reagan, who was elected in 1980. Kennedy was succeeded by Lyndon B. Johnson, the first Southerner to become president since Andrew Johnson succeeded Lincoln when Lincoln was assassinated in 1865.

The new president. Television and radio flashed the news of the shooting to a shocked world. Vice President Johnson raced to the hospital and remained until Kennedy died. Then, he went to the airport where the presidential plane waited. Mrs. Kennedy and the coffin holding her husband's body arrived later. At 2:39 P.M., U.S. District Judge Sarah T. Hughes administered the oath of office to Johnson, who became the 36th president of the United States. As Johnson took the oath in the airplane, he was flanked by his wife and by Mrs. Kennedy.

Then the plane carrying the new chief executive and his wife, the body of the dead president, and the late president's widow returned to Washington. When the plane arrived, Johnson told the nation: "This is a sad time for all people. We have suffered a loss that cannot be weighed. . . ."

The world mourns. The sudden death of the young and vigorous American president shocked the world. Kennedy's body was brought back to the White House and placed in the East Room for 24 hours. On the Sunday after the assassination, the president's flag-draped coffin was carried to the Capitol Rotunda to lie in state.° Throughout the day and night, hundreds

SKILLS
FOCUS

Pages 728–731
cover
Reading Skills
Analyze primary
and secondary
sources.

°**Capitol Rotunda to lie in state:** The Capitol Rotunda is the round room beneath the dome of the Capitol, the building in which the U.S. Congress meets in Washington, D.C. *Lie in state* means "be displayed to the public before burial."

of thousands of people filed past the guarded casket. Representatives from over 90 countries attended the funeral on November 25.

Kennedy was buried with full military honors at Arlington National Cemetery across the Potomac River from Washington, D.C. At the close of the funeral service, Mrs. Kennedy lighted an "eternal flame" to burn over the president's grave. In one of his first acts, President Johnson named the National Aeronautics and Space Administration installation in Florida the John F. Kennedy Space Center.

Other public buildings and geographical sites throughout the world were named for President Kennedy. Congress voted funds for the John F. Kennedy Center for the Performing Arts in Washington, D.C. Great Britain made one acre of ground permanent United States territory as part of a Kennedy memorial at Runnymede. In 1979, the John F. Kennedy Library opened in Boston.

—from "John Fitzgerald Kennedy," *The World Book Encyclopedia* (2001)

For Me, It Was a Dramatic Day
Pierre Salinger

Pierre Salinger, President Kennedy's press secretary, remembers where he was and how he felt when he heard the news of Kennedy's assassination.

For me, it was a dramatic day. I had left the White House on November 19 to accompany six members of JFK's cabinet[1] to an economic conference in Tokyo. President Kennedy had asked me to join the trip to organize his visit to Tokyo, planned for February 1964. This would have been the first visit by an American president to Japan since the end of World War II.

We stopped in Honolulu[2] for three days for an important meeting on the Vietnam crisis. Early in the morning of November 22, the White

---

1. **cabinet** *n.:* The president's cabinet includes the heads of the various departments of the executive branch, such as the departments of State, Treasury, and Defense.
2. **Honolulu** (hän′ə·lōō′lōō): capital of Hawaii.

House plane headed for Tokyo. I was in the back of the plane reading the economic papers when suddenly somebody came and told me the six cabinet secretaries had to see me. They were in the office in the front of the plane. When I walked in, it was grim. They handed me a wire bulletin[3] saying Kennedy had been shot.

The plane turned around and headed back to Honolulu, and I was instructed to take over the communications system to the White House and find out what had happened. When I connected with the White House, there was total confusion. For many minutes nothing was coming through clearly. About a half hour after the plane had turned around, I heard in my ear: "Wayside. Standby." Wayside was my code name. About every thirty seconds for the next five minutes, I heard the same thing. Then suddenly came a new message. "Wayside. Lancer is dead." Lancer was the code name for President Kennedy.

I was destroyed. I so admired and liked JFK. I had a feeling that not only was he lost, but that my life was lost.

When we reached Washington, a car took me to the White House. JFK's body had just arrived in the East Room and there was a short prayer service. Jackie Kennedy came up to me after the prayer and said I had had a terrible day and should sleep in the White House.

I went upstairs where I talked with colleagues like Ken O'Donnell and Larry O'Brien until five in the morning. Finally, I went to sleep.

At 7 A.M. the phone rang. I heard the operator say: "Mr. Salinger, the president wants to talk to you." For an instant, I thought I'd had a nightmare. Then, on the phone I heard: "Pierre, this is Lyndon."[4] It was over. It was now clear to me that Kennedy was dead.

—from *Where Were You When President Kennedy Was Shot?*

---

3. **wire bulletin:** news bulletin from a wire service, an organization that transmits news stories to newspapers and radio and television stations by telegraph or electronic means.
4. **Lyndon:** Lyndon B. Johnson, Kennedy's vice president, who became president after Kennedy was killed.

1. Why is "Kennedy's Assassination" a valuable source for research?

   A It is written for an audience made up of experts.

   B Its purpose is to show why Kennedy was a great president.

   C It reveals Lyndon B. Johnson's opinion of the assassination.

   D It presents a factual, historical perspective on the assassination and its aftermath.

2. What is the **tone** of "Kennedy's Assassination"?

   F dramatic

   G objective

   H sorrowful

   J enraged

3. Which statement is the *most* accurate **evaluation** of "For Me, It Was a Dramatic Day"?

   A It is a primary source because it is a firsthand account of one person's experiences.

   B It is a secondary source because the author did not actually witness the assassination.

   C It is a secondary source because it is a strictly factual description of an event.

   D It is a primary source because it includes only opinions and no facts.

4. The **purpose** of "For Me, It Was a Dramatic Day" is to —

   F reveal the author's sense of shock and loss at the news of Kennedy's death

   G show that Lyndon B. Johnson effectively took control of the country

   H warn that the government could easily be thrown into confusion

   J emphasize the author's personal relationship with Kennedy and his family

5. Which point in "For Me, It Was a Dramatic Day" can be **verified** by reading "Kennedy's Assassination"?

   A Kennedy's code name was Lancer.

   B Kennedy had planned to visit Japan.

   C Kennedy's body was placed in the East Room in the White House.

   D Pierre Salinger communicated with the White House about Kennedy's death.

Constructed Response

6. Examine the two sources, "Kennedy's Assassination" and "For Me, It Was a Dramatic Day," and explain how they differ. How might each source be used in a research paper about John F. Kennedy's assassination?

Collection 9: Skills Review

Vocabulary Skills

Synonyms

DIRECTIONS: Choose the *best* synonym for the underlined word in each sentence.

1. In "American History," Elena's mother is vigilant in making sure that Elena's behavior is appropriate for a young lady.
   A   harsh
   B   forgiving
   C   irresponsible
   D   watchful

2. Elena loves to read, and she is enthralled by one novel in particular.
   F   enraged
   G   fascinated
   H   bored
   J   educated

3. Elena's mother visits a neighbor, seeking solace after the assassination of President Kennedy.
   A   entertainment
   B   knowledge
   C   comfort
   D   pity

4. In "A Warm, Clear Day in Dallas" the author states that some people were denouncing the president before his assassination.
   F   condemning
   G   praising
   H   warning
   J   mocking

5. In his speech, President Johnson explains his resolve to continue the work begun by President Kennedy.
   A   dream
   B   doubts
   C   refusal
   D   determination

6. In "Beware of the Dog" the pilot, feeling giddy from his injury, fears that he will pass out.
   F   threatened
   G   dizzy
   H   numb
   J   distressed

7. After he looked out the window, the pilot hoisted himself back onto his bed.
   A   rolled
   B   lifted
   C   slid
   D   threw

8. The nurse beckoned to the wing commander to indicate that he could enter the pilot's hospital room.
   F   gestured
   G   wrote
   H   shouted
   J   whispered

SKILLS FOCUS

Vocabulary Skills
Identify synonyms.

Test Practice

DIRECTIONS: Read the following paragraph from a draft of a student's research paper. Then, answer the questions below it.

(1) The introduction of the first commercially produced radios, in 1920, altered the way people learned about world events. (2) For the first time in history, everyone could receive the same information simultaneously. (3) In the 1920s, sociologists Robert and Helen Lynd said, "With but little equipment one can call the life of the rest of the world from the air. . . ." (4) Live coverage gave news events an immediacy far greater than the newspapers could provide. (5) My great-grandfather told me that each night his family listened to radio news programs. (6) In fact, according to the researcher Phyllis Stark, most people first learned of historic events from the radio.

1. To improve the coherence of this paragraph, which sentence could be deleted?
   A 2
   B 3
   C 5
   D 6

2. If the student wanted to add a quotation from a primary source, which of these sources would be appropriate?
   F the autobiography of an early radio pioneer
   G an analysis of statistics on early radio audiences
   H a Web site dedicated to a famous radio star
   J a documentary on popular music in the 1920s

3. To show a different perspective on this topic, the next paragraph could discuss
   A a short history of the rise of television
   B an excerpt from a radio transcript of the attack on Pearl Harbor
   C a discussion of the negative impact radio had on newspapers
   D a list of other inventions from the 1920s that changed the world

4. To credit the source of the quotation in sentence 3, the student could
   F insert the title of the source name in the margin
   G include a parenthetical citation at the end of the quotation
   H take credit for the information as an original thought
   J include a parenthetical citation at the end of the paragraph

5. If the student were presenting the report orally, how could she help the audience understand the topic?
   A play relaxing music in the background to soothe her audience
   B bring a map of Pearl Harbor, Hawaii
   C bring an example of a radio recording from the 1920s
   D read directly from the paper to avoid forgetting important ideas

SKILLS FOCUS

Writing Skills
Write a research paper.

Collection 10

Heroes and Monsters

Literary Focus:
Analyzing Epic and Myth

Informational
Reading Focus:
**Evaluating an Argument:
Intent and Tone**

INTERNET

Collection
Resources

Keyword: LE7 9-10

Ulysses and the Sirens. Detail from a mosaic
(4th century A.D.).

Introducing the Collection Theme

Heroes and Monsters

Make the Connection

Quickwrite ✎

Throughout the ages, people have looked up to heroes. Make a list of your favorite heroes from stories, movies, or video games. (Don't forget about *Star Wars* and *The Lord of the Rings*.) Explain whom or what these heroes battle against. Who usually wins? Why? Jot down your thoughts.

Exploring the Theme: Heroes and Monsters

Heroes battling monsters—that's the focus of this collection. In the *Odyssey* the famous Greek hero Odysseus must overcome monsters and rivals on his long journey home from fighting the Trojan War. The Norse myth "The Fenris Wolf" describes the gods' struggle to control the monstrous beast named in the title. You'll also read about everyday heroes and their acts of courage and compassion. The selection you're about to read offers interesting insights into good and evil and the heroes and monsters of ancient Greek myths.

Literary Focus

Heroes and Conflict

Heroes in **epics** (long narrative poems) and **myths** (traditional stories that usually explain a belief or a natural phenomenon) are often courageous, strong, clever, and persistent. They reveal their heroism in the course of facing **external conflicts,** or struggles between characters and outside forces. These forces come in many forms— as monsters that heroes must overcome or outwit or as hardships or tests they must endure, for example. As you read this selection, think about how these grand conflicts between good and evil have set the pattern for stories told throughout the ages.

Literary Skills
Understand heroic characters and external conflicts in epics and myths.

from HEROES & MONSTERS OF GREEK MYTH

Bernard Evslin, Dorothy Evslin, *and* Ned Hoopes

In Greek mythology, heroes and monsters alike are spawned[1] by the gods. The Gorgons[2] are granddaughters of Rhea, mother of Zeus,[3] which makes them cousins of their arch-enemy, Perseus.[4] In other words, both good and evil come from the gods. Good is the divine energy expressing itself through men of high deeds. Evil is the same energy, twisted. When hero confronts monster in these myths, there is apt to be a family quarrel. . . . ❶

The birth of the monster is attended by rage, and that is what makes him monstrous, the wrath of a god—or, more often, a goddess—carving a dangerous, ugly form for itself out of living flesh.

These tales are drenched in sunlight, and this sunlight is more than weather; it is a moral quality. Heroes love to cavort in the open air, to fly, to cleave the burning sea, to race on the hills, to hunt over the fields. But monsters belong to darkness. The Gorgons live where it is always winter. Cerberus, the three-headed dog, guards the gate of dark Tartarus.[5] Scylla and Echidne, those dread serpent-women, lurk in a sea-cave waiting to make shipwrecks, to catch sailors and crack their bones. The Minotaur[6] howls in a maze of shadows. All monsters wait in darkness; and when heroes hunt them, they must come in out of the sun. The ordeal starts right there.

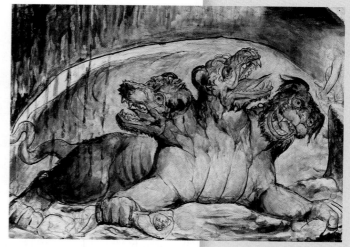

Cerberus (1824–1827) by William Blake (1757–1827). Pen, ink, watercolor over pencil and black chalk.

---

1. **spawned** *v.:* produced.
2. **Gorgons** (gôr′gənz): three female monsters whose glance turns men into stone.
3. **Zeus** (zo͞os): highest of the Greek gods; ruler of the heavens and earth.
4. **Perseus** (pʉr′sē•əs): son of Zeus and Danaë, a mortal woman. Perseus becomes a celebrated hero when he beheads Medusa, one of the Gorgons.
5. **Tartarus** (tär′tə•rəs): part of the underworld, the world of the dead.
6. **Minotaur** (min′ə•tôr′): creature, half human and half bull, that is imprisoned in a labyrinth, or maze, and killed by the hero Theseus.

THEME AND CONFLICT

❷ Who or what represents "the powers of Light" and "the powers of Darkness" in the **conflict** between these forces?

So we see a great religious theme: the eternal struggle between the powers of Light and the powers of Darkness embodied in these simple stories in a way that has branded itself on man's consciousness forever. ❷

Meet the Writers
Bernard Evslin, Dorothy Evslin, *and* Ned Hoopes

Masters of Myths

Bernard Evslin (1922–1993) is known for his many works about mythology, including the award-winning children's book *Hercules* (1984) and a series of books about monsters in Greek mythology. Dorothy Evslin (1923–   ) collaborated with her husband on mythology projects. She has taught English at the college level and has written for newspapers and magazines. Ned Hoopes (1932–1984) taught at the high school and college level and edited collections of stories, including *Incredible Tales by Saki* (1966) and *Surprises: 20 Stories by O. Henry* (1966).

After You Read

Response and Analysis

Reading Check

1. Which places are associated with heroes, and which are associated with monsters? Where do the struggles between heroes and monsters take place?

Thinking Critically

2. Why do the writers say that the **conflict** between a hero and a monster is usually "a family quarrel"?

3. Explain what the writers mean when they say that "sunlight is more than weather; it is a moral quality."

4. Think about what this selection has to say about the collection theme "Heroes and Monsters." What makes the heroes of Greek myths heroic? What makes the monsters monstrous? What do their **conflicts** represent?

Extending and Evaluating

5. Look back at your Quickwrite notes. What similarities and differences do you see between the heroes and battles you noted and the Greek heroes and **conflicts** described in this selection? In what ways are all these stories—ancient and contemporary—about the struggle between "the powers of Light and the powers of Darkness"?

Scylla and Charybdis (1977)
by Romare Bearden
(1914–1988). Watercolor.
14¹/₂ x 15³/₄ in.
Art ©Romare Bearden
Foundation/Licensed by VAGA,
New York, NY.

Exploring the Theme
Heroes and Monsters

In the rest of this collection, you'll read about heroes and monsters in epics and myths, as well as real-life heroes of today. As you read, think about what each work has to say about the characteristics we value in heroes.

SKILLS FOCUS

Literary Focus
Analyze heroic characters and external conflicts in epics and myths.

An Introduction to the
ODYSSEY

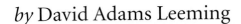

by David Adams Leeming

These battles might have taken place as early as 1200 B.C.—a time that was at least as long ago for Homer's audience as the Pilgrims' landing at Plymouth Rock is for us.

Almost three thousand years ago, people who lived in the starkly beautiful part of the world we now call Greece were telling stories about a great war. The person credited with later gathering all these stories together and telling them as one unified epic is a man named Homer (*Homēros,* in Greek). Homer's great war stories are called, in English, the *Iliad* and the *Odyssey.* (In Greek, the *Iliad* is *Ilias* and the *Odyssey* is *Odysseia.*)

Homer's stories probably can be traced to historical struggles for control of the waterway leading from the Aegean Sea to the Sea of Marmara and the Black Sea. These battles might have taken place as early as 1200 B.C.—a time that was at least as long ago for Homer's audience as the Pilgrims' landing at Plymouth Rock is for us.

Homer's first epic was the *Iliad,* which tells of a ten-year war fought on the plains outside the walls of a great city called Troy (also known as Ilion). The ruins of Troy can still be seen in western Turkey. In Homer's story the Trojan War was fought between the people of Troy and an alliance of Greek kings (at that time each island and area of the Greek mainland had its own king). The *Iliad* tells us that the cause of the war was sexual jealousy: The world's most beautiful woman, Helen, abandoned her husband, Menelaus, a Greek king, and ran off with Paris, a prince of Troy. (See "The Beautiful Helen," page 129.)

The *Odyssey,* Homer's second epic, is the story of the attempt of one Greek soldier, Odysseus, to get home after the Trojan War. All epic poems in the Western world owe something to the basic patterns established by these two stories.

EPICS AND VALUES

Epics are long narrative poems that tell of the adventures of heroes who in some way embody the values of their civilizations. The Greeks for centuries used the *Iliad* and the *Odyssey* in schools to teach Greek virtues. So it is not surprising that later cultures that admired the Homeric epics created their own epics, imitating Homer's style but conveying their own value systems.

SKILLS FOCUS

Pages 740–746 cover
Literary Skills
Understand characteristics of epic poetry. Understand the way a work of literature is related to the themes and issues of its historical period.

Still, for all the epics written since Homer's time and for all the ones composed before it, when people in the Western world think of the word *epic*, they think primarily of the *Iliad* and the *Odyssey*. Rome's *Aeneid*, France's *Song of Roland*, Italy's *The Divine Comedy*, the ancient Mesopotamian tale of Gilgamesh, India's *Mahabharata* and *Ramayana*, Mali's *Sundiata*—all are great stories in the epic tradition. But Homer's epics are at the heart of the epic tradition.

The *Iliad* is the primary model for the epic of war. The *Odyssey* is the model for the epic of the long journey. The theme of the journey has been basic in Western literature—it is found in fairy tales, in such novels as *The Incredible Journey, Moby-Dick,* and *The Hobbit,* and in such movies as *The Wizard of Oz* and *Star Wars.* Thus, the *Odyssey* has been the more widely read of Homer's two great stories.

THE WAR-STORY BACKGROUND: VIOLENCE AND BRUTALITY

The background for Odysseus's story is found in the *Iliad,* which is set in the tenth and final year of the Trojan War. According to the *Iliad,* the Greeks attacked Troy to avenge the insult suffered by Menelaus, king of Sparta, when his wife, Helen, ran off with Paris, a young prince of Troy. The Greek kings banded together under the leadership of Agamemnon,

The blind poet Homer. Detail from statue found near Naples (probably 2nd century A.D.).
British Museum, London.

Home to Ithaca (1977) from the *Odysseus Collages* by Romare Bearden. Collage on board (14″ × 22¾″).
Estate of Romare Bearden. © Romare Howard Bearden Foundation. Licensed by VAGA, New York.

the brother of Menelaus. In a thousand ships, they sailed across the Aegean Sea and laid siege to the walled city of Troy.

The audience of the *Odyssey* would have known this war story. Listeners would have known that the Greeks were eventually victorious—that they gained entrance to Troy, reduced the city to smoldering ruins, and butchered all the inhabitants, except for those they took as slaves back to Greece. They would have known all about the greatest of the Greek warriors, Achilles, who died young in the final year of the war. The audience would probably have heard other epic poems (now lost) that told of the homecomings of the various Greek heroes who survived the war. They would especially have known about the homecoming of Agamemnon, the leader of the Greek forces, who was murdered by his unfaithful wife when he returned from Troy.

Finally, Homer's listeners might well have been particularly fascinated by another homecoming story—this one about a somewhat unusual hero, known as much for his brain as for his brawn. In fact, many legends had already grown up around this hero, whose name was Odysseus. He was the subject of Homer's new epic, the *Odyssey*.

ODYSSEUS: A HERO IN TROUBLE

In Homer's day, heroes were thought of as a special class of aristocrats. They were placed somewhere between the gods and ordinary human beings. Heroes experienced pain and death, but they were always sure of themselves, always "on top of the world."

Odysseus is different. He is a hero in trouble. We can relate to Odysseus because like him we also face a world of difficult choices. Like Odysseus we have to cope with unfair authority figures. Like him we have to work very hard to get what we want.

The *Odyssey* is a story marked by melancholy and a feeling of postwar disillusionment. Odysseus was a great soldier in the war, but his war record is not of interest to the monsters that populate the world of his wanderings. Even the people of his home island, Ithaca, seem to lack respect for him. It is as if society were saying to the returning hero, "You were a great soldier once—or so they say—but times have changed. This is a difficult world, and we have more important things to think about than your record."

In the years before the great war, Odysseus had married the beautiful and ever-faithful Penelope, one of several very strong women in the man's world of the Greek epic. (One critic, Robert Graves, was so impressed by the unusual importance of women and home and hearth in the *Odyssey* that he believed Homer must have been a woman.)

Penelope and Odysseus had one son, Telemachus (tə·lem′ə·kəs). He was still a toddler when Odysseus was called by Agamemnon and

The *Odyssey* is a story marked by melancholy and a feeling of postwar disillusionment.

One critic, Robert Graves, was so impressed by the unusual importance of women and home and hearth in the *Odyssey* that he believed Homer must have been a woman.

Menelaus to join them in the war against Troy. But Odysseus was a homebody. He preferred not to go to war, especially a war fought for an unfaithful woman. Even though he was obligated under a treaty to go, Odysseus tried draft-dodging. It is said that when Agamemnon and Menelaus came to fetch him, he pretended to be insane and acted as if he did not recognize his visitors. Instead of entertaining them, he dressed as a peasant and began plowing a field and sowing it with salt. But the "draft board" was smarter than Odysseus. They threw his baby, Telemachus, in front of his oncoming plow. Odysseus revealed his sanity by quickly turning the plow aside to avoid running over his son.

THE WOODEN-HORSE TRICK

Once in Troy, Odysseus performed extremely well as a soldier and commander. It was he, for example, who thought of the famous wooden-horse trick that would lead to the downfall of Troy. For ten years the Greeks had been fighting the Trojans, but they were fighting outside Troy's massive walls. They had been unable to break through the walls and enter the city. Odysseus's plan was to build an enormous wooden horse and hide a few Greek soldiers inside its hollow belly. After the horse was built, the Greeks pushed it up to the gates of Troy and withdrew their armies, so that their camp appeared to be abandoned. Thinking that the Greeks had given up the fight and that the horse was a peace offering, the Trojans brought the horse into their city. That night the Greeks hidden inside the hollow belly came out, opened the gates of Troy to the whole Greek army, and began the battle that was to win the war.

Trojan Horse (16th century) by Niccolò dell' Abbate. Tempera on panel.
Galleria Estense, Modena, Italy.

THE ANCIENT WORLD AND OURS

The world of Odysseus was harsh, a world familiar with violence. In a certain sense, Odysseus and his men act like pirates on their journey home. They think nothing of entering a town and carrying off all its worldly goods. The "worldly goods" in an ancient city might have been only pots and pans and cattle and sheep. The "palaces" the Greeks raided might have been little more than elaborate mud and stone farmhouses. Yet, in the struggles of Odysseus, Penelope, and Telemachus in their "primitive" society that had little in common with the high Athenian culture that would develop several centuries later, there is something that has a great deal to do with us.

A SEARCH FOR THEIR PLACES IN LIFE

Odysseus and his family are people searching for the right relationships with one another and with the people around them. They want to find their proper places in life. It is this **theme** that sets the tone for the *Odyssey* and determines the unusual way in which the poem is structured.

Instead of beginning at the beginning with Odysseus's departure from Troy, the story begins with his son, Telemachus. Telemachus is now twenty years old. He is threatened by rude, powerful men swarming about his own home, pressuring his mother to marry one of them. These men are bent on robbing Telemachus of his inheritance. Telemachus is a young man who needs his father, the one person who can put things right at home.

Meanwhile, we hear that his father is stranded on an island, longing to find a way to get back to his wife, child, and home. It is ten years since Odysseus sailed from Troy, twenty years since he left Ithaca to fight in Troy. While Telemachus is in search of his father, Odysseus is in search of a way out of what we might today call his midlife crisis. He is searching for inner peace, for a way to reestablish a natural balance in his life. The quests of father and son provide a framework for the poem and bring us into it as well—because we all are in search of our real identities, our true selves.

RELATIONSHIPS WITH THE GODS

This brings us to mythic and religious questions in the *Odyssey*. **Myths** are traditional stories, rooted in a particular culture, that usually explain a belief, a ritual, or a mysterious natural phenomenon. Myths are essentially religious because they are concerned with the relationship between human beings and the unknown or spiritual realm.

As you will see, Homer is always concerned with the relationship between humans and gods. Homer is religious: For him, the gods control all things. Athena, the goddess of wisdom, is always at the side of Odysseus. This is appropriate, because Odysseus is known for his mental abilities. Thus, in Homer's stories a god can be an **alter ego,** a reflection of a hero's best or worst qualities. The god who works against Odysseus is Poseidon, the god of the sea, who is known for arrogance and a certain brutishness. Odysseus himself can be violent and cruel, just as Poseidon is.

WHO WAS HOMER?

No one knows for sure who Homer was. The later Greeks believed he was a blind minstrel, or singer, who came from the island of Chios.

O dysseus and his family are people searching for the right relationships with one another and with the people around them.

O dysseus is in search of a way out of what we might today call his midlife crisis.

S ome scholars think Homer was just a legend. But scholars have also argued about whether a man called Shakespeare ever existed. It is almost as if they were saying that Homer and Shakespeare are too good to be true.

Some scholars feel there must have been two Homers; some think he was just a legend. But scholars have also argued about whether a man called Shakespeare ever existed. It is almost as if they were saying that Homer and Shakespeare are too good to be true. On the whole, it seems sensible to take the word of the Greeks themselves. We can at least accept the existence of Homer as a model for a class of wandering bards or minstrels later called rhapsodes (rap**'**sōdz′).

These **rhapsodes,** or "singers of tales," were the historians and entertainers as well as the mythmakers of their time. There was probably no written history in Homer's day. There were certainly no movies and no television, and the Greeks had nothing like a Bible or a book of religious stories. So it was that the minstrels traveled about from community to community singing of recent events or of the doings of heroes, gods, and goddesses. It is as if the author of the Book of Kings in the Bible, the writer of a history of World War II, and a famous pop singer were combined in one person. The people in Homer's day saw no conflict among religion, history, and good fun.

HOW WERE THE EPICS TOLD?

Scholars have found that oral epic poets are still composing today in Eastern Europe and other parts of the world. These scholars suggest that stories like the *Iliad* and the *Odyssey* were originally told aloud by people who could not read and write. The stories followed a basic story line, but most of the actual words were improvised—made up on the spot—in a way that fit a particular rhythm or meter. The singers of these stories had to be very talented, and they had to work very hard. They also needed an audience that could listen closely.

We can see from this why there is so much repetition in the Homeric epics. The oral storyteller, in fact, had a store of formulas ready in his memory. He knew formulas for describing the arrival and greeting of guests, the eating of meals, and the taking of baths. He knew formulas for describing the sea (it is "wine-dark") and for describing Athena (she is "gray-eyed Athena").

Formulas such as these had another advantage: they gave the singer and his audience some breathing time. The audience could relax for a moment and enjoy a familiar and memorable passage, while the singer could think ahead to the next part of his story.

When we think about the audience that listened to these stories, we can also understand the value of the extended comparisons that we today call **Homeric** or **epic similes.** These similes compare heroic or epic events to simple and easily understandable everyday events—

Singer with lyre. Bronze statue from the Minoan period.
Archaeological Museum, Heraklion, Crete.

The oral storyteller, in fact, had a store of formulas ready in his memory. He knew formulas for describing the arrival and greeting of guests, the eating of meals, and the taking of baths.

events the audience would recognize instantly. For example, at one point in the *Iliad,* Athena prevents an arrow from striking Menelaus. The singer compares the goddess's actions to an action that would have been familiar to every listener:

> She brushed it away from his skin as lightly as when a mother
> Brushes a fly away from her child who is lying in sweet sleep.

Epic poets such as Homer would come to a city and would go through a part of their repertory while there. A story as long as the *Odyssey* (11,300 lines) could not be told at one sitting. We have to assume that if the singer had only a few days in a town, he would summarize some of his story and sing the rest in detail, in as many sittings as he had time for.

This is exactly what will happen in the selections from the *Odyssey* that are presented here. We'll assume that Homer wants to get his story told to us, but that his time is limited. We'll also assume that the audience, before retiring at the end of each performance, wants to talk about the stories they've just heard. You are now part of that audience.

A LIVE PERFORMANCE

What was it like to hear a live performance of the *Odyssey*? We can guess what it was like because there are many instances in the epic itself in which traveling singers appear and sing their tales. In the court of the Phaeacian king, Alcinous (al·sin′ō·əs), in Book 8, for instance, there is a particularly wonderful singer who must make us wonder if the blind Homer is talking about himself. Let's picture the setting of a performance before we start the story.

Imagine a large hall full of people who are freshly bathed, rubbed with fine oils, and draped in clean tunics. Imagine the smell of meat being cooked over charcoal, the sound of voices. Imagine wine being freely poured, the flickering reflections of the great cooking fires, and the torches that light the room. A certain anticipation hangs in the air. It is said that the blind minstrel Homer is in the city and that he has new stories about that long war in Troy. Will he appear and entertain tonight?

> Imagine a large hall full of people who are freshly bathed, rubbed with fine oils, and draped in clean tunics. Imagine the smell of meat being cooked over charcoal, the sound of voices. Imagine wine being freely poured, the flickering reflections of the great cooking fires, and the torches that light the room.

Ruins of an amphitheater at the temple of Hephaestus in Athens.

PEOPLE AND PLACES IN THE ODYSSEY

The following cast of characters lists some of those who take part in the sections of the *Odyssey* included in this book. Note that the Greeks in the *Odyssey* are often referred to as **Achaeans** (ə·kē'ənz) or **Argives** (är'gīvz'). *Achaeans* is the most general term, which also includes the people of Ithaca, the island off the west coast of Greece where Odysseus ruled. The word *Achaeans* is taken from the name of an ancient part of northeastern Greece called Achaea. The name *Argives* usually refers to the Greeks who went to fight at Troy.

Penelope by John Roddam Spencer Stanhope.

THE WANDERINGS: CHARACTERS AND PLACES

Aeaea (ē·ē'ə): home of Circe, the enchantress and goddess.

Alcinous (al·sin'ō·əs): king of Phaeacia. Odysseus tells the story of his adventures to Alcinous's court.

Calypso (kə·lip'sō): beautiful nymph goddess who keeps Odysseus on her island for seven years.

Circe hands the magic potion to Odysseus. Detail from a lecythus, a vase used for oils and ointments (5th century B.C.).

Charybdis (kə·rib'dis): female monster who sucks in water three times a day to form a deadly whirlpool. (Scholars believe the character is based on a real whirlpool in the Strait of Messina.)

Cicones (si·kō'nēz'): people living on the southwestern coast of Thrace who battled Odysseus and his men on their journey.

Circe (sʉr'sē): enchantress and goddess who turns Odysseus's men into swine.

Cyclops: See **Polyphemus**, below.

Erebus (er'ə·bəs): dark area of the underworld where the dead reside.

Eurylochus (yoō·ril'ə·kəs): a member of Odysseus's loyal crew.

Lotus Eaters: people who feed Odysseus's men lotus plants to make them forget Ithaca.

Phaeacia (fē·ā'shə): island kingdom ruled by King Alcinous. The Phaeacians are shipbuilders and traders.

Polyphemus (päl'i·fē'məs): son of the sea god Poseidon and blinded by Odysseus. Polyphemus is a **Cyclops** (sī'kläps'), one of a race of brutish one-eyed giants, the **Cyclopes** (sī·klō'pēz'), who live solitary lives as shepherds, supposedly on the island now known as Sicily.

Poseidon. Detail from a bronze statue.
(5th century B.C.).

Scylla (sil'ə): female monster with six serpent heads, each head having a triple row of fangs. (Scholars believe this character is based on a dangerous rock in the Strait of Messina.)

Sirens: sea nymphs whose beautiful and mysterious music lures sailors to steer their ships toward dangerous rocks.

Teiresias (tī·rē′sē·əs): famous blind prophet from the city of Thebes. Odysseus meets him in the Land of the Dead.

Thrinakia (thri·nā′kē·ə): island where the sun god Helios keeps his cattle.

ITHACA: THE PEOPLE AT HOME

Antinous (an·tin′ō·əs): one of Penelope's main suitors; an arrogant and mean young noble from Ithaca.

Eumaeus (yōō·mē′əs): swineherd, one of Odysseus's loyal servants.

Eurycleia (yōō′ri·klē′yə): Odysseus's old nurse.

Eurymachus (yōō·rim′ə·kəs): suitor of Penelope.

Eurynome (yōō·rin′ə·mē): Penelope's housekeeper.

Penelope (pə·nel′ə·pē): Odysseus's faithful wife.

Philoeteus (fi·lē′shē·əs): cowherd, one of Odysseus's loyal servants.

Telemachus (tə·lem′ə·kəs): Odysseus's son.

THE GODS

Apollo (ə·päl′ō): god of poetry, music, prophecy, medicine, and archery.

Athena (ə·thē′nə): favorite daughter of Zeus; the great goddess of wisdom as well as war and peace. She favored the Greeks during the Trojan War. She is often called Pallas Athena.

Cronus (krō′nəs): Titan (giant god) who ruled the universe until his son Zeus overthrew him.

Helios (hē′lē·äs′): sun god.

Hephaestus (hē·fes′təs): god of metalworking.

Hermes (hʉr′mēz′): messenger god.

Poseidon (pō·sī′dən): god of the sea; brother of Zeus. Poseidon is called Earth Shaker because he is believed to cause earthquakes. He is an enemy of Odysseus.

Zeus (zōōs): the most powerful god. His home is on Olympus.

Athena mourning the death of Achilles at Troy. Detail from a marble stele, or pillar.

Before You Read

from the Odyssey, Part One

Make the Connection

Quickwrite ✏️

What makes a hero? Write down the names of people, real or fictional, whom you consider heroic. Then, list character traits that you think a hero should have. Are these traits universal, or do they reflect only our own culture? Add to your notes as you read the *Odyssey*.

Literary Focus

Heroes at Large

We admire them in books and movies, on TV shows, and in the news, and if we look closely, even in our own lives. They're our heroes—real or fictional.

In fiction, as in real life, heroes often set off on a journey that we're all on: the quest to discover who we are and what we can do. Encountering challenges and dangers, heroic characters face **external conflicts** —struggles with other characters (these are often **subordinate characters** who play a secondary role in the story) or with the forces of nature.

Whether heroes fail or succeed on their journeys, they do it on a grand scale, giving us new perspectives on our own lives. As you read these tales of Odysseus's wanderings, think about how he overcomes his conflicts. What makes him heroic?

Reading Skills 📖

Monitor Your Comprehension

As you read this epic, stop now and then to ask yourself questions and to sum up what you've read. Ask:

- What has happened so far?

- Why did it happen?
- What are the important events in this episode?
- When do the events take place?
- What might happen next?
- Can I visualize what is being described?
- What is my evaluation of the characters' decisions and actions?
- What connections can I make between what I've read and my own life?

The questions at the open-book signs will help you monitor your comprehension. If you can't answer the questions, go back through the text to find the answers.

Vocabulary Development

adversity (ad·vur′sə·tē) *n.*: hardship; great misfortune.

formidable (fôr′mə·də·bəl) *adj.*: awe-inspiring by reason of excellence; strikingly impressive.

ravage (rav′ij) *v.*: destroy violently; ruin.

profusion (prō·fyo͞o′zhən) *n.*: large supply; abundance.

adversary (ad′vər·ser′ē) *n.*: enemy; opponent.

rancor (raŋ′kər) *n.*: bitter hatred; ill will.

abominably (ə·bäm′ə·nə·blē) *adv.*: in an extremely unpleasant or disgusting manner.

ardor (är′dər) *n.*: passion; enthusiasm.

tumult (to͞o′mult) *n.*: commotion; uproar; confusion.

restitution (res′tə·to͞o′shən) *n.*: compensation; repayment.

SKILLS FOCUS

Literary Skills
Understand characteristics of epic poetry, including heroes and their external conflicts.

Reading Skills
Monitor your comprehension.

go.
hrw
.com

INTERNET

Vocabulary Practice

●

More About Homer

●

Keyword: LE7 9-10

from the ODYSSEY

Homer

translated by Robert Fitzgerald

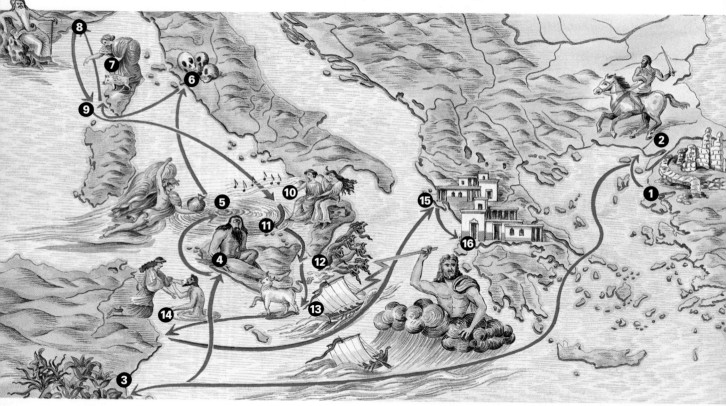

① *Troy*
② *Cicones*
③ *Lotus Eaters*
④ *Cyclops*
⑤ *Island of Aeolia*
⑥ *Laestrygonians*
⑦ *Circe*
⑧ *Teiresias and the Land of the Dead*
⑨ *Circe*
⑩ *Sirens*
⑪ *Charybdis*
⑫ *Scylla*
⑬ *Thrinakia*
⑭ *Calypso*
⑮ *Phaeacia*
⑯ *Ithaca*

TELL THE STORY

Homer opens with an invocation, or prayer, asking the Muse° to help him sing his tale. Notice how the singer gives his listeners hints about how his story is to end.

Sing in me, Muse, and through me tell the story
of that man skilled in all ways of contending,°
the wanderer, harried for years on end,
after he plundered the stronghold
on the proud height of Troy.

5   He saw the townlands
and learned the minds of many distant men,
and weathered many bitter nights and days
in his deep heart at sea, while he fought only
to save his life, to bring his shipmates home.

10 But not by will nor valor could he save them,
for their own recklessness destroyed them all—
children and fools, they killed and feasted on
the cattle of Lord Helios, the Sun,
and he who moves all day through heaven

15 took from their eyes the dawn of their return.

Of these adventures, Muse, daughter of Zeus,
tell us in our time, lift the great song again.
Begin when all the rest who left behind them
headlong death in battle or at sea

20 had long ago returned, while he alone still hungered
for home and wife. Her ladyship Calypso
clung to him in her sea-hollowed caves—
a nymph, immortal and most beautiful,
who craved him for her own.

                    And when long years and seasons

25 wheeling brought around that point of time
ordained for him to make his passage homeward,
trials and dangers, even so, attended him
even in Ithaca, near those he loved.
Yet all the gods had pitied Lord Odysseus,

30 all but Poseidon, raging cold and rough
against the brave king till he came ashore
at last on his own land. . . .

                        (*from* Book 1)

°The Greeks believed that there were nine Muses, daughters of Zeus, the chief god. The Muses inspired people to produce music, poetry, dance, and all the other arts.

2. contending (kən·tend′iŋ) *v.* used as *n.*: fighting; dealing with difficulties.

Oral presentation.
1–32. Read this prayer to the Muse aloud. (You and a partner could read it as a chorus, or you could alternate with single voices.) What does Homer tell you about the hero and about what is going to happen to him?

PART ONE: THE WANDERINGS

CALYPSO, THE SWEET NYMPH

*Books 1–4 of the epic tell about Odysseus's son, Telemachus. Telemachus has been
searching the Mediterranean world for his father, who has never returned from the
ten-year Trojan War. (Today, Odysseus would be listed as missing in action.)*

*When we first meet Odysseus, in Book 5 of the epic, he is a prisoner of the beau-
tiful goddess Calypso. The old soldier is in despair: He has spent ten years (seven of
them as Calypso's not entirely unwilling captive) trying to get home.*

*The goddess Athena has supported and helped Odysseus on his long journey.
Now she begs her father, Zeus, to help her favorite, and Zeus agrees. He sends the
messenger god Hermes to Calypso's island to order Odysseus released. Although
Calypso is not described as evil, her seductive charms—even her promises of im-
mortality for Odysseus—threaten to keep the hero away from his wife, Penelope.*

    No words were lost on Hermes the Wayfinder
    who bent to tie his beautiful sandals on,
35   ambrosial,° golden, that carry him over water
    or over endless land in a swish of the wind,
    and took the wand with which he charms asleep—
    or when he wills, awake—the eyes of men.
    So wand in hand he paced into the air,
40   shot from Pieria° down, down to sea level,
    and veered to skim the swell. A gull patrolling
    between the wave crests of the desolate sea
    will dip to catch a fish, and douse his wings;
    no higher above the whitecaps Hermes flew
45   until the distant island lay ahead,
    then rising shoreward from the violet ocean
    he stepped up to the cave. Divine Calypso,
    the mistress of the isle, was now at home.
    Upon her hearthstone a great fire blazing
50   scented the farthest shores with cedar smoke
    and smoke of thyme, and singing high and low
    in her sweet voice, before her loom aweaving,
    she passed her golden shuttle to and fro.
    A deep wood grew outside, with summer leaves
55   of alder and black poplar, pungent cypress.
    Ornate birds here rested their stretched wings—
    horned owls, falcons, cormorants—long-tongued
    beachcombing birds, and followers of the sea.
    Around the smooth-walled cave a crooking vine
60   held purple clusters under ply° of green;

35. ambrosial (am·brō′zhəl) *adj.:* fit
for the gods; divine. Nectar and ambrosia are the drink and food that
kept the gods immortal.

40. Pieria (pī·ir′ē·ə): place in
central Greece not far from Olympus;
a favorite spot of Hermes'.

Man with a headband. Detail from
a bronze statue (c. 460–450 B.C.).

60. ply (plī) *n.:* twisted strands.

and four springs, bubbling up near one another
shallow and clear, took channels here and there
through beds of violets and tender parsley.
Even a god who found this place
65   would gaze, and feel his heart beat with delight:
so Hermes did; but when he had gazed his fill
he entered the wide cave. Now face-to-face
the magical Calypso recognized him,
as all immortal gods know one another
70   on sight—though seeming strangers, far from home.
But he saw nothing of the great Odysseus,
who sat apart, as a thousand times before,
and racked his own heart groaning, with eyes wet
scanning the bare horizon of the sea. . . .

Hermes tells Calypso that she must give up Odysseus forever.
Now we are directly introduced to Odysseus. Notice what this
great warrior is doing when we first meet him.

75   The strong god glittering left her as he spoke,
and now her ladyship, having given heed
to Zeus's mandate, went to find Odysseus
in his stone seat to seaward—tear on tear
brimming his eyes. The sweet days of his lifetime
80   were running out in anguish over his exile,
for long ago the nymph had ceased to please.
Though he fought shy of her and her desire,
he lay with her each night, for she compelled him.
But when day came he sat on the rocky shore
85   and broke his own heart groaning, with eyes wet
scanning the bare horizon of the sea.
Now she stood near him in her beauty, saying:

"O forlorn man, be still.
Here you need grieve no more; you need not feel
90   your life consumed here; I have pondered it,
and I shall help you go. . . ."

Calypso promises Odysseus a raft and provisions to help him
homeward without harm—provided the gods wish it. Now
Odysseus and Calypso say goodbye.

Swiftly she turned and led him to her cave,
and they went in, the mortal and immortal.
He took the chair left empty now by Hermes,

33–66. *There is a great deal of nature* **imagery** *in this episode. Jot down some of the images that help you see Hermes' flight. What images describing Calypso's island appeal to your senses of sight, hearing, and smell? How does the natural beauty of Calypso's island compare with the reality of Odysseus's situation?*

Hermes. Bronze statue
(5th century B.C.).

National Archaeological Museum, Athens.

88–91. *Zeus ordered Calypso to free Odysseus, but the nymph claims that the idea is her own. Why do you think she does this? What is your opinion of her deception?*

95 where the divine Calypso placed before him
    victuals and drink of men; then she sat down
    facing Odysseus, while her serving maids
    brought nectar and ambrosia to her side.
    Then each one's hands went out on each one's feast
100 until they had had their pleasure; and she said:

    "Son of Laertes,° versatile Odysseus,
    after these years with me, you still desire
    your old home? Even so, I wish you well.
    If you could see it all, before you go—
105 all the adversity you face at sea—
    you would stay here, and guard this house, and be
    immortal—though you wanted her forever,
    that bride for whom you pine each day.
    Can I be less desirable than she is?
110 Less interesting? Less beautiful? Can mortals
    compare with goddesses in grace and form?"

    To this the strategist Odysseus answered:

    "My lady goddess, there is no cause for anger.
    My quiet Penelope—how well I know—
115 would seem a shade before your majesty,
    death and old age being unknown to you,
    while she must die. Yet, it is true, each day
    I long for home, long for the sight of home. . . ."

So Odysseus builds the raft and sets sail. But the sea god Poseidon is by no means ready to allow an easy passage over his watery domain. He raises a storm and destroys the raft. It is only with the help of Athena and a sea nymph that Odysseus arrives, broken and battered, on the island of Scheria (skē'rē·ə). There he hides himself in a pile of leaves and falls into a deep sleep.

    A man in a distant field, no hearth fires near,
120 will hide a fresh brand° in his bed of embers
    to keep a spark alive for the next day;
    so in the leaves Odysseus hid himself,
    while over him Athena showered sleep
    that his distress should end, and soon, soon.
125 In quiet sleep she sealed his cherished eyes.

                                        (*from* Book 5)

101. Laertes (lā·ʉr'tēz').

Calypso and Odysseus. Detail from a red-figured vase (5th century B.C.).

101–118. *According to Calypso, what would Odysseus gain by staying with her? What does Odysseus's response tell you about his feelings for his wife? How has Odysseus managed to say no to Calypso and still not offend her?*

120. fresh brand: burning stick.

Vocabulary
adversity (ad·vʉr'sə·tē) *n.*: hardship; great misfortune.

Calypso

Suzanne Vega

My name is Calypso
And I have lived alone
I live on an island
And I waken to the dawn
5 A long time ago
I watched him struggle with the sea
I knew that he was drowning
And I brought him into me
Now today
10 Come morning light
He sails away
After one last night
I let him go.

My name is Calypso
15 My garden overflows
Thick and wild and hidden
Is the sweetness there that grows
My hair it blows long
As I sing into the wind
20 I tell of nights
Where I could taste the salt on his skin

Salt of the waves
And of tears
And though he pulled away
25 I kept him here for years
I let him go.

My name is Calypso
I have let him go
In the dawn he sails away
30 To be gone forever more
And the waves will take him in again
But he'll know their ways now
I will stand upon the shore
With a clean heart
35 And my song in the wind
The sand will sting my feet
And the sky will burn
It's a lonely time ahead
I do not ask him to return
40 I let him go
I let him go.

The Departure of Ulysses from the Isle of Calypso (1848–1849) by Samuel Palmer.

The Whitworth Art Gallery, the University of Manchester.

"I am Laertes' son. . . ."

Odysseus is found by the daughter of Alcinous, king of the Phaeacians. That evening he is a guest at court (Books 6–8).

To the ancient people of Greece and Asia Minor, all guests were godsent. They had to be treated with great courtesy before they could be asked to identify themselves and state their business. That night, at the banquet, the stranger who was washed up on the beach is seated in the guest's place of honor. A minstrel, or singer, is called, and the mystery guest gives him a gift of pork, crisp with fat, and requests a song about Troy. In effect, Odysseus is asking for a song about himself.

Odysseus weeps as the minstrel's song reminds him of all his companions, who will never see their homes again. Now Odysseus is asked by the king to identify himself. It is here that he begins the story of his journey.

Now this was the reply Odysseus made: . . .

"I am Laertes' son, Odysseus.

                       Men hold me
formidable for guile in peace and war:
this fame has gone abroad to the sky's rim.

130   My home is on the peaked seamark of Ithaca
under Mount Neion's windblown robe of leaves,
in sight of other islands—Doulikhion,
Same, wooded Zakynthos—Ithaca
being most lofty in that coastal sea,

135   and northwest, while the rest lie east and south.
A rocky isle, but good for a boy's training;
I shall not see on earth a place more dear,
though I have been detained long by Calypso,
loveliest among goddesses, who held me

140   in her smooth caves, to be her heart's delight,
as Circe of Aeaea, the enchantress,
desired me, and detained me in her hall.
But in my heart I never gave consent.
Where shall a man find sweetness to surpass

145   his own home and his parents? In far lands
he shall not, though he find a house of gold.

What of my sailing, then, from Troy?

                      What of those years
of rough adventure, weathered under Zeus?

εἴμ' Ὀδυσεὺς Λαερτιάδης,
ὃς πᾶσι δόλοισιν
ἀνθρώποισι μέλω, καί
μευ κλέος οὐρανὸν
ἵκει. ναιετάω δ'
Ἰθάκην εὐδείελον·
ἐν δ' ὄρος αὐτῇ,
Νήριτον εἰνοσίφυλλον
ἀριπρεπές· ἀμφὶ δὲ
νῆσοι πολλαὶ
ναιετάουσι μάλα
σχεδὸν ἀλλήλῃσι,
Δουλίχιόν τε Σάμη
τε καὶ ὑλήεσσα
Ζάκυνθος.

The passage beginning "I am Laertes' son" in Greek.

Vocabulary
formidable (fôr′mə·də·bəl) *adj.*: awe-inspiring by reason of excellence; strikingly impressive.

The wind that carried west from Ilion°
150   brought me to Ismaros, on the far shore,
        a strongpoint on the coast of the Cicones.
        I stormed that place and killed the men who fought.
        Plunder we took, and we enslaved the women,
        to make division, equal shares to all—
155   but on the spot I told them: 'Back, and quickly!
        Out to sea again!' My men were mutinous,
        fools, on stores of wine. Sheep after sheep
        they butchered by the surf, and shambling cattle,
        feasting—while fugitives went inland, running
160   to call to arms the main force of Cicones.
        This was an army, trained to fight on horseback
        or, where the ground required, on foot. They came
        with dawn over that terrain like the leaves
        and blades of spring. So doom appeared to us,
165   dark word of Zeus for us, our evil days.
        My men stood up and made a fight of it—
        backed on the ships, with lances kept in play,
        from bright morning through the blaze of noon
        holding our beach, although so far outnumbered;
170   but when the sun passed toward unyoking time,
        then the Achaeans, one by one, gave way.
        Six benches were left empty in every ship
        that evening when we pulled away from death.
        And this new grief we bore with us to sea:
175   our precious lives we had, but not our friends.
        No ship made sail next day until some shipmate
        had raised a cry, three times, for each poor ghost
        unfleshed by the Cicones on that field.
        Now Zeus the lord of cloud roused in the north
180   a storm against the ships, and driving veils
        of squall moved down like night on land and sea.
        The bows went plunging at the gust; sails
        cracked and lashed out strips in the big wind.
        We saw death in that fury, dropped the yards,°
185   unshipped the oars, and pulled for the nearest lee:°
        then two long days and nights we lay offshore
        worn out and sick at heart, tasting our grief,
        until a third Dawn came with ringlets shining.
        Then we put up our masts, hauled sail, and rested,
190   letting the steersmen and the breeze take over.

149. Ilion (il′ē·än′): another name for Troy.

152–160. *What do you think of the way Odysseus and his men behave toward the Cicones? Do armies behave like this in modern times?*

184. yards (yärdz) *n.:* rods supporting the sails.
185. lee (lē) *n.:* place of shelter from the wind.

I might have made it safely home, that time,
but as I came round Malea the current
took me out to sea, and from the north
a fresh gale drove me on, past Cythera.°
195   Nine days I drifted on the teeming sea
before dangerous high winds."

                                   (*from* Book 9)

194. Cythera (si·thir'ə).

THE LOTUS EATERS

                              "Upon the tenth
      we came to the coastline of the Lotus Eaters,
      who live upon that flower. We landed there
200   to take on water. All ships' companies
      mustered° alongside for the midday meal.
      Then I sent out two picked men and a runner
      to learn what race of men that land sustained.
      They fell in, soon enough, with Lotus Eaters,
205   who showed no will to do us harm, only
      offering the sweet Lotus to our friends—
      but those who ate this honeyed plant, the Lotus,
      never cared to report, nor to return:
      they longed to stay forever, browsing on
210   that native bloom, forgetful of their homeland.
      I drove them, all three wailing, to the ships,
      tied them down under their rowing benches,
      and called the rest: 'All hands aboard;
      come, clear the beach and no one taste
215   the Lotus, or you lose your hope of home.'
      Filing in to their places by the rowlocks
      my oarsmen dipped their long oars in the surf,
      and we moved out again on our seafaring. . . ."

                                   (*from* Book 9)

201. mustered (mus'tərd) *v.:*
gathered; assembled.

204–215. *Why does
Odysseus tie down the three men?
What does this action tell you about
him?*

A CLOSER LOOK

Troy: It Casts a Spell

The ancient Greeks and Romans had no doubt that the Trojan War really happened. They believed it took place around 1200 B.C. The Greek historian Thucydides (c. 460–c. 400 B.C.) believed that the real causes of the war were economic and political—he rejected Homer's story of Helen's abduction and the vengeance taken on Troy by the Greeks. By the middle of the nineteenth century, however, most historians had dismissed the Trojan War as a legend.

Enter Heinrich Schliemann (1822–1890). Schliemann was a wealthy German merchant who turned archaeologist when he was middle-aged and archaeology was in its infancy. Armed with a well-thumbed copy of Homer's *Iliad,* Schliemann arrived in northwestern Turkey in 1871. A few miles from the Dardanelles, the narrow and windy sea lane that divides Europe from Asia, Schliemann began excavations at a small hill called Hissarlik, perched about a hundred feet above a wide plain.

After five long years, Schliemann made an electrifying discovery. He unearthed gold cups, bracelets, and a spectacular gold headdress. Homer had called Troy "rich in gold," and Schliemann now told the world he had found the treasure of Priam, the last king of Troy. (The gold's eventful history was not over. Schliemann took the treasure to Berlin, where it disappeared at the end of World War II. "Priam's gold" surfaced again in 1993 in Moscow's Pushkin Museum.)

Schliemann went on to excavate Mycenae, the home of King Agamemnon in Greece. There he also found treasure.

Despite his successes, he was plagued by doubts about whether he had really found Troy. The level, or stratum, where the gold was discovered seemed too ancient to date from the traditional time of the Trojan War.

We now know that Schliemann's treasure came from a stratum (called Troy II) that dated back to a thousand years before the Trojan War. Another level (Troy VIIA) showed violent destruction by fire around 1200 B.C. Could this have been Homer's Troy? During the 1930s, another team of archaeologists (this time from the United States) thought so. Despite the inconsistencies that remain, the hill of Hissarlik is now widely accepted as the most likely location of the Trojan War.

In the 1990s, a fifteen-year archaeological project began in Turkey, directed by Professor Manfred Korfmann from the University of Tübingen in Germany. Whatever Korfmann and his international team of seventy scientists and ninety local workers discover, their presence at Troy in the third millennium is powerful proof that this ancient war still casts a spell.

In his next adventure, Odysseus describes his encounter with the Cyclops named Polyphemus, Poseidon's one-eyed monster son. Polyphemus may represent the brute forces that any hero must overcome before he can reach home. Now Odysseus must rely on the special intelligence associated with his name. Odysseus is the cleverest of the Greek heroes because he is guided by the goddess of wisdom, Athena.

It is Odysseus's famed curiosity that leads him to the Cyclops's cave and that makes him insist on waiting for the barbaric giant.

Odysseus is still speaking to the court of King Alcinous.

> "We lit a fire, burnt an offering,
> 220   and took some cheese to eat; then sat in silence
> around the embers, waiting. When he came
> he had a load of dry boughs on his shoulder
> to stoke his fire at suppertime. He dumped it
> with a great crash into that hollow cave,
> 225   and we all scattered fast to the far wall.
> Then over the broad cavern floor he ushered
> the ewes he meant to milk. He left his rams

The Cyclops (detail) (late 19th or early 20th century) by Odilon Redon.

and he-goats in the yard outside, and swung
high overhead a slab of solid rock
230 to close the cave. Two dozen four-wheeled wagons,
with heaving wagon teams, could not have stirred
the tonnage of that rock from where he wedged it
over the doorsill. Next he took his seat
and milked his bleating ewes. A practiced job
235 he made of it, giving each ewe her suckling;
thickened his milk, then, into curds and whey,
sieved out the curds to drip in withy baskets,°
and poured the whey to stand in bowls
cooling until he drank it for his supper.
240 When all these chores were done, he poked the fire,
heaping on brushwood. In the glare he saw us.

'Strangers,' he said, 'who are you? And where from?
What brings you here by seaways—a fair traffic?
Or are you wandering rogues, who cast your lives
245 like dice, and ravage other folk by sea?'

We felt a pressure on our hearts, in dread
of that deep rumble and that mighty man.
But all the same I spoke up in reply:

'We are from Troy, Achaeans, blown off course
250 by shifting gales on the Great South Sea;
homeward bound, but taking routes and ways
uncommon; so the will of Zeus would have it.
We served under Agamemnon,° son of Atreus°—
the whole world knows what city
255 he laid waste, what armies he destroyed.
It was our luck to come here; here we stand,
beholden for your help, or any gifts
you give—as custom is to honor strangers.
We would entreat you, great Sir, have a care
260 for the gods' courtesy; Zeus will avenge
the unoffending guest.'

He answered this
from his brute chest, unmoved:

'You are a ninny,
or else you come from the other end of nowhere,
telling me, mind the gods! We Cyclopes

---

237. withy baskets: baskets made from willow twigs.

253. Agamemnon (ag′ə·mem′nän′). **Atreus** (ā′trē·əs).

Vocabulary
ravage (rav′ij) v.: destroy violently; ruin.

Ulysses and His Companions on the Island of the Cyclops (16th century) by Pellegrino Tibaldi.

Palazzo Poggi, Bologna, Italy.

265　care not a whistle for your thundering Zeus
　　or all the gods in bliss; we have more force by far.
　　I would not let you go for fear of Zeus—
　　you or your friends—unless I had a whim to.
　　Tell me, where was it, now, you left your ship—
270　around the point, or down the shore, I wonder?'

　　He thought he'd find out, but I saw through this,
　　and answered with a ready lie:

　　　　　　　　　　　　　　　　　　　　'My ship?

　　Poseidon Lord, who sets the earth atremble,
　　broke it up on the rocks at your land's end.
275　A wind from seaward served him, drove us there.
　　We are survivors, these good men and I.'

　　Neither reply nor pity came from him,
　　but in one stride he clutched at my companions
　　and caught two in his hands like squirming puppies
280　to beat their brains out, spattering the floor.
　　Then he dismembered them and made his meal,
　　gaping and crunching like a mountain lion—
　　everything: innards, flesh, and marrow bones.
　　We cried aloud, lifting our hands to Zeus,
285　powerless, looking on at this, appalled;
　　but Cyclops went on filling up his belly
　　with manflesh and great gulps of whey,
　　then lay down like a mast among his sheep.
　　My heart beat high now at the chance of action,
290　and drawing the sharp sword from my hip I went
　　along his flank to stab him where the midriff
　　holds the liver. I had touched the spot
　　when sudden fear stayed me: if I killed him
　　we perished there as well, for we could never
295　move his ponderous doorway slab aside.
　　So we were left to groan and wait for morning.

　　When the young Dawn with fingertips of rose
　　lit up the world, the Cyclops built a fire
　　and milked his handsome ewes, all in due order,
300　putting the sucklings to the mothers. Then,
　　his chores being all dispatched, he caught
　　another brace° of men to make his breakfast,
　　and whisked away his great door slab
　　to let his sheep go through—but he, behind,
305　reset the stone as one would cap a quiver.°

The Cyclops Polyphemus. Detail from a marble statue (2nd century B.C.).

Museum of Fine Arts, Boston.

289–295. *Why doesn't Odysseus kill the Cyclops at this moment? What factors must Odysseus consider in devising a successful plan of escape?*

302. brace (brās) *n.:* pair.

305. quiver (kwiv'ər) *n.:* case for arrows.

There was a din of whistling as the Cyclops
rounded his flock to higher ground, then stillness.
And now I pondered how to hurt him worst,
if but Athena granted what I prayed for.
310 Here are the means I thought would serve my turn:

a club, or staff, lay there along the fold—
an olive tree, felled green and left to season
for Cyclops' hand. And it was like a mast
a lugger° of twenty oars, broad in the beam—
315 a deep-seagoing craft—might carry:
so long, so big around, it seemed. Now I
chopped out a six-foot section of this pole
and set it down before my men, who scraped it;
and when they had it smooth, I hewed again
320 to make a stake with pointed end. I held this
in the fire's heart and turned it, toughening it,
then hid it, well back in the cavern, under
one of the dung piles in profusion there.
Now came the time to toss for it: who ventured
325 along with me? Whose hand could bear to thrust
and grind that spike in Cyclops' eye, when mild
sleep had mastered him? As luck would have it,
the men I would have chosen won the toss—
four strong men, and I made five as captain.

330 At evening came the shepherd with his flock,
his woolly flock. The rams as well, this time,
entered the cave: by some sheepherding whim—
or a god's bidding—none were left outside.
He hefted his great boulder into place
335 and sat him down to milk the bleating ewes
in proper order, put the lambs to suck,
and swiftly ran through all his evening chores.
Then he caught two more men and feasted on them.
My moment was at hand, and I went forward
340 holding an ivy bowl of my dark drink,
looking up, saying:

                              'Cyclops, try some wine.
Here's liquor to wash down your scraps of men.
Taste it, and see the kind of drink we carried

314. lugger (lug'ər) *n.:* type of sailboat.

Odysseus handing the drink to Polyphemus. Relief on a Grecian marble sarcophagus (1st century A.D.).
Museo Archeologico Nazionale, Naples, Italy.

Vocabulary
profusion (prō·fyoo'zhən) *n.:* large supply; abundance.

under our planks. I meant it for an offering
345 if you would help us home. But you are mad,
unbearable, a bloody monster! After this,
will any other traveler come to see you?'

He seized and drained the bowl, and it went down
so fiery and smooth he called for more:

350 'Give me another, thank you kindly. Tell me,
how are you called? I'll make a gift will please you.
Even Cyclopes know the wine grapes grow
out of grassland and loam in heaven's rain,
but here's a bit of nectar and ambrosia!'

355 Three bowls I brought him, and he poured them down.
I saw the fuddle and flush come over him,
then I sang out in cordial tones:

        'Cyclops,
you ask my honorable name? Remember
the gift you promised me, and I shall tell you.
360 My name is Nohbdy: mother, father, and friends,
everyone calls me Nohbdy.'

        And he said:
'Nohbdy's my meat, then, after I eat his friends.
Others come first. There's a noble gift, now.'

Even as he spoke, he reeled and tumbled backward,
365 his great head lolling to one side; and sleep
took him like any creature. Drunk, hiccuping,
he dribbled streams of liquor and bits of men.

Now, by the gods, I drove my big hand spike
deep in the embers, charring it again,
370 and cheered my men along with battle talk
to keep their courage up: no quitting now.
The pike of olive, green though it had been,
reddened and glowed as if about to catch.
I drew it from the coals and my four fellows
375 gave me a hand, lugging it near the Cyclops
as more than natural force nerved them; straight
forward they sprinted, lifted it, and rammed it
deep in his crater eye, and I leaned on it
turning it as a shipwright turns a drill
380 in planking, having men below to swing
the two-handled strap that spins it in the groove.
So with our brand we bored that great eye socket

Odysseus and three companions
blinding Polyphemus. Detail from a
Cyrenean cup (6th century B.C.).
Bibliothèque Nationale, Paris.

while blood ran out around the red-hot bar.
Eyelid and lash were seared; the pierced ball
hissed broiling, and the roots popped.

385   In a smithy°
one sees a white-hot axhead or an adze°
plunged and wrung in a cold tub, screeching steam—
the way they make soft iron hale and hard—
just so that eyeball hissed around the spike.
390   The Cyclops bellowed and the rock roared round him,
and we fell back in fear. Clawing his face
he tugged the bloody spike out of his eye,
threw it away, and his wild hands went groping;
then he set up a howl for Cyclopes
395   who lived in caves on windy peaks nearby.
Some heard him; and they came by divers° ways
to clump around outside and call:

                                           'What ails you,
Polyphemus? Why do you cry so sore
in the starry night? You will not let us sleep.
400   Sure no man's driving off your flock? No man
has tricked you, ruined you?'

                                           Out of the cave
the mammoth Polyphemus roared in answer:

'Nohbdy, Nohbdy's tricked me. Nohbdy's ruined me!'

To this rough shout they made a sage° reply:

405   'Ah well, if nobody has played you foul
there in your lonely bed, we are no use in pain
given by great Zeus. Let it be your father,
Poseidon Lord, to whom you pray.'

                                           So saying
they trailed away. And I was filled with laughter
410   to see how like a charm the name deceived them.
Now Cyclops, wheezing as the pain came on him,
fumbled to wrench away the great doorstone
and squatted in the breach with arms thrown wide
for any silly beast or man who bolted—
415   hoping somehow I might be such a fool.
But I kept thinking how to win the game:
death sat there huge; how could we slip away?
I drew on all my wits, and ran through tactics,
reasoning as a man will for dear life,

385. smithy (smith′ē) *n.*: black-smith's shop, where iron tools are made.
386. adze (adz) *n.*: axlike tool with a long, curved blade.

396. divers (dī′vərz) *adj.*: diverse; various.

404. sage (sāj) *adj.*: wise.

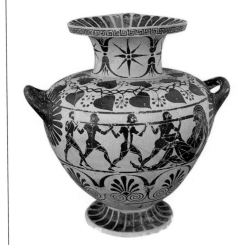

Odysseus and his men blinding the Cyclops. Hydria, or water jar (530–510 B.C.).
Collection Villa Guilia, Rome.

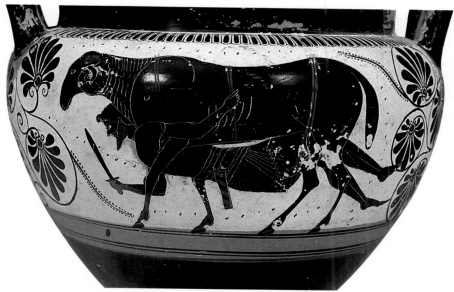

Odysseus escaping the cave of Polyphemus under the belly of the ram. Detail from a krater, a vessel for holding wine (c. 510 B.C.).

Badisches Landesmuseum, Karlsruhe, Germany.

420   until a trick came—and it pleased me well.
The Cyclops' rams were handsome, fat, with heavy
fleeces, a dark violet.

                                       Three abreast

I tied them silently together, twining
cords of willow from the ogre's bed;
425   then slung a man under each middle one
to ride there safely, shielded left and right.
So three sheep could convey each man. I took
the woolliest ram, the choicest of the flock,
and hung myself under his kinky belly,
430   pulled up tight, with fingers twisted deep
in sheepskin ringlets for an iron grip.
So, breathing hard, we waited until morning.

When Dawn spread out her fingertips of rose
the rams began to stir, moving for pasture,
435   and peals of bleating echoed round the pens
where dams with udders full called for a milking.
Blinded, and sick with pain from his head wound,
the master stroked each ram, then let it pass,
but my men riding on the pectoral fleece°
440   the giant's blind hands blundering never found.
Last of them all my ram, the leader, came,

439. pectoral fleece: wool on an animal's chest.

weighted by wool and me with my meditations.
The Cyclops patted him, and then he said:

'Sweet cousin ram, why lag behind the rest
445   in the night cave? You never linger so,
but graze before them all, and go afar
to crop sweet grass, and take your stately way
leading along the streams, until at evening
you run to be the first one in the fold.
450   Why, now, so far behind? Can you be grieving
over your Master's eye? That carrion rogue°
and his accurst companions burnt it out
when he had conquered all my wits with wine.
Nohbdy will not get out alive, I swear.
455   Oh, had you brain and voice to tell
where he may be now, dodging all my fury!
Bashed by this hand and bashed on this rock wall
his brains would strew the floor, and I should have
rest from the outrage Nohbdy worked upon me.'

460   He sent us into the open, then. Close by,
I dropped and rolled clear of the ram's belly,
going this way and that to untie the men.
With many glances back, we rounded up
his fat, stiff-legged sheep to take aboard,
465   and drove them down to where the good ship lay.
We saw, as we came near, our fellows' faces
shining; then we saw them turn to grief
tallying those who had not fled from death.
I hushed them, jerking head and eyebrows up,
470   and in a low voice told them: 'Load this herd;
move fast, and put the ship's head toward the breakers.'
They all pitched in at loading, then embarked
and struck their oars into the sea. Far out,
as far offshore as shouted words would carry,
475   I sent a few back to the adversary:

'O Cyclops! Would you feast on my companions?
Puny, am I, in a Caveman's hands?
How do you like the beating that we gave you,
you damned cannibal? Eater of guests
480   under your roof! Zeus and the gods have paid you!'

Vocabulary
adversary (ad′vər·ser′ē) *n.*: enemy; opponent.

📖 **421–442.** *Explain Odysseus's trick. What do you **visualize** happening in this scene?*

451. carrion rogue: rotten scoundrel. *Carrion* is decaying flesh.

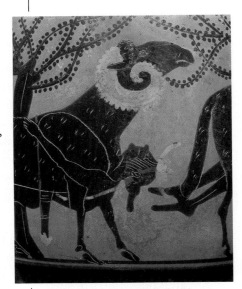

Odysseus escaping under the ram. Detail from a black-figured convex lecythus (c. 590 B.C.), by the Ambush Vase Painter.

Staatliche Antikensammlung, Munich, Germany.

The blind thing in his doubled fury broke
a hilltop in his hands and heaved it after us.
Ahead of our black prow it struck and sank
whelmed in a spuming geyser, a giant wave
485   that washed the ship stern foremost back to shore.
I got the longest boathook out and stood
fending us off, with furious nods to all
to put their backs into a racing stroke—
row, row or perish. So the long oars bent
490   kicking the foam sternward, making head
until we drew away, and twice as far.
Now when I cupped my hands I heard the crew
in low voices protesting:

                            'Godsake, Captain!
Why bait the beast again? Let him alone!'

495   'That tidal wave he made on the first throw
all but beached us.'

                     'All but stove us in!'

'Give him our bearing with your trumpeting,
he'll get the range and lob° a boulder.'

                              'Aye
He'll smash our timbers and our heads together!'

500   I would not heed them in my glorying spirit,
but let my anger flare and yelled:

                           'Cyclops,
if ever mortal man inquire
how you were put to shame and blinded, tell him
Odysseus, raider of cities, took your eye:
505   Laertes' son, whose home's on Ithaca!'

At this he gave a mighty sob and rumbled:

'Now comes the weird° upon me, spoken of old.
A wizard, grand and wondrous, lived here—Telemus,°
a son of Eurymus;° great length of days
510   he had in wizardry among the Cyclopes,
and these things he foretold for time to come:
my great eye lost, and at Odysseus' hands.
Always I had in mind some giant, armed
in giant force, would come against me here.
515   But this, but you—small, pitiful, and twiggy—

498. lob (läb) *v.*: toss.

507. weird (wird) *n.*: fate.
508. Telemus (tel**′**ə·məs).
509. Eurymus (yo͞o**′**rē·məs).

you put me down with wine, you blinded me.
Come back, Odysseus, and I'll treat you well,
praying the god of earthquake to befriend you—
his son I am, for he by his avowal
520 fathered me, and, if he will, he may
heal me of this black wound—he and no other
of all the happy gods or mortal men.'

Few words I shouted in reply to him:

'If I could take your life I would and take
525 your time away, and hurl you down to hell!
The god of earthquake could not heal you there!'

At this he stretched his hands out in his darkness
toward the sky of stars, and prayed Poseidon:

'O hear me, lord, blue girdler of the islands,
530 if I am thine indeed, and thou art father:
grant that Odysseus, raider of cities, never
see his home: Laertes' son, I mean,
who kept his hall on Ithaca. Should destiny
intend that he shall see his roof again
535 among his family in his fatherland,
far be that day, and dark the years between.
Let him lose all companions, and return
under strange sail to bitter days at home.' . . ."

(*from* Book 9)

*Here we will imagine that Homer stops reciting for the night. The
blind poet might take a glass of wine before turning in. The listeners
would go off to various corners of the local nobleman's house. They
might discuss highlights of the poet's tale among themselves and
look forward to the next evening's installment.*

Polyphemus. Terra-cotta head
(4th century B.C.).

Louvre, Paris, France.

538. *Take a few minutes to
list what you think are the highlights of Odysseus's journey so far.
What questions do you have?
What do you think will happen
next?*

Read **"Welcome: A
Religious Duty"** *on page 771.
Then, as you continue reading
the story, trace the ways Homer
repeatedly dramatizes the importance of mutual respect among
people. Think about your own
ideas of hospitality today—what
are the customs in your family
and neighborhood? What are the
customs in American society as a
whole?*

A CLOSER LOOK

Welcome: A Religious Duty

Today's visitors to Greece are often struck by the generous hospitality of its people. An ancient tradition lies behind the traveler's welcome in Greece—and it is a tradition that was fundamentally religious before it became a part of social custom.

Zeus, the king of the gods, demanded that strangers be treated graciously. Hosts had a religious duty to welcome strangers, and guests had a responsibility to respect hosts. The close interconnections and mutual respect in this host-guest relationship are reflected in the fact that the word *xenos* (zen′ōs) in ancient Greek can mean both "host" and "guest." The relationship is often symbolized in the *Odyssey* by the presentation of gifts. Alcinous, the king of the Phaeacians, for example, gives Odysseus a magically swift ship in which to sail home.

What happens when the host-guest relationship is abused or otherwise breaks down? In Homer's epic songs about the Trojan War, the *Iliad* and the *Odyssey*, the customs of hospitality are violated at least three times. The first occasion caused the war itself: Paris, prince of Troy, ran off with the beautiful Helen from Sparta while he was the guest of Helen's husband, Menelaus. For the Greeks this insult to *xenia* (hospitality) was at least as serious as Helen's unfaithfulness, and it meant that Zeus would, in the end, allow the Greeks to triumph in the long war.

The second example of violated hospitality has its humorous and ironic side.

In the *Odyssey* the Cyclops is monstrous not only because of his huge size and brutish appearance. He is set apart from civilized beings precisely because of his barbaric outlook on *xenia*. When Odysseus begs the Cyclops for hospitality and warns that Zeus will avenge an injured guest, the Cyclops replies that he and his kind "care not a whistle for . . . Zeus" (line 265). With dark humor the Cyclops uses the word *xeineion* (Greek for "guest-gift" or "noble gift") when he tells Odysseus that he will have the privilege of being eaten last (lines 362–363). The poetic justice of the Cyclops's blinding would not be lost on Homer's Greek audience.

The final example of a breach in the law of hospitality underlies the entire plot structure of the *Odyssey*: Back in Ithaca, year after year the suitors abuse the hospitality of Odysseus—an absent "host"—and threaten to take away his wife. The bloody vengeance that Odysseus wreaks on these suitors should be understood in the context of their outrageous violation of religious law. The suitors have turned hospitality into a crude mockery. Perhaps it is not accidental that Odysseus invokes the host-guest relationship just before the battle, when he quietly gives his son, Telemachus, the signal to fight (lines 1208–1209):

"Telemachus, the stranger [*xeinos*] you welcomed in your hall has not disgraced you."

The Cyclops in the Ocean
Nikki Giovanni

Moving slowly . . . against time . . . patiently majestic . . .
the cyclops . . . in the ocean . . . meets no Ulysses . . .

Through the night . . . he sighs . . . throbbing against the
shore . . . declaring . . . for the adventure . . .

5 A wall of gray . . . gathered by a slow touch . . . slash and
slither . . . through the waiting screens . . . separating into
nodules . . . making my panes . . . accept the touch . . .

Not content . . . to watch my frightened gaze . . . he clamors
beneath the sash . . . dancing on my sill . . .

10 Certain to die . . . when the sun . . . returns . . .

Tropical Storm Dennis
August 15–18, 1981, Florida

THE ENCHANTRESS CIRCE

After sailing from the Cyclops's island, Odysseus and his men land on the island of Aeolia. There the wind king, Aeolus (ē'ə·ləs), does Odysseus a favor. He puts all the stormy winds in a bag so that they will not harm the Ithacans. The bull's-hide bag containing the winds is wedged under Odysseus's afterdeck. During the voyage, when the curious and suspicious sailors open the bag, thinking it contains treasure, the evil winds roar up into hurricanes that blow the ships back to Aeolia. Aeolus drives them away again.

On the island of the Laestrygonians (les·trig·ō'nē·ənz), gigantic cannibals, all the ships but one are destroyed and their crews devoured. Odysseus's ship escapes and lands on Aeaea, the home of the enchantress and goddess Circe. Here a party of twenty-three men, led by Eurylochus, goes off to explore the island. Odysseus is still telling his story to Alcinous and his court.

"In the wild wood they found an open glade,
540   around a smooth stone house—the hall of Circe—
and wolves and mountain lions lay there, mild
in her soft spell, fed on her drug of evil.
None would attack—oh, it was strange, I tell you—
but switching their long tails they faced our men
545   like hounds, who look up when their master comes
with tidbits for them—as he will—from table.
Humbly those wolves and lions with mighty paws
fawned on our men—who met their yellow eyes
and feared them.

               In the entranceway they stayed
550   to listen there: inside her quiet house
they heard the goddess Circe.

                      Low she sang
in her beguiling voice, while on her loom
she wove ambrosial fabric sheer and bright,
by that craft known to the goddesses of heaven.
555   No one would speak, until Polites°—most
faithful and likable of my officers—said:

'Dear friends, no need for stealth:° here's a young weaver
singing a pretty song to set the air
atingle on these lawns and paven courts.
560   Goddess she is, or lady. Shall we greet her?'

So reassured, they all cried out together,
and she came swiftly to the shining doors
to call them in. All but Eurylochus—
who feared a snare—the innocents went after her.

Pigs, swineherd, and Odysseus by the Pig Painter. Pelike, or jar (470–460 B.C.).

Fitzwilliam Museum, University of Cambridge.

555. Polites (pō·lī'tēz').

557. stealth (stelth) *n.:* sneaky behavior.

Circe offers the magic potion to Odysseus. Detail from Greek vase from Thebes.

British Museum, London.

565 On thrones she seated them, and lounging chairs,
while she prepared a meal of cheese and barley
and amber honey mixed with Pramnian wine,°
adding her own vile pinch, to make them lose
desire or thought of our dear fatherland.
570 Scarce had they drunk when she flew after them
with her long stick and shut them in a pigsty—
bodies, voices, heads, and bristles, all
swinish now, though minds were still unchanged.
So, squealing, in they went. And Circe tossed them
575 acorns, mast,° and cornel berries—fodder
for hogs who rut and slumber on the earth.

Down to the ship Eurylochus came running
to cry alarm, foul magic doomed his men!
But working with dry lips to speak a word
580 he could not, being so shaken; blinding tears
welled in his eyes; foreboding filled his heart.
When we were frantic questioning him, at last
we heard the tale: our friends were gone. . . .”

(*from* Book 10)

567. Pramnian wine: strong wine from Mount Pramnos in ancient Greece.

575. mast *n.:* various kinds of nuts used as food for hogs.

549–583. *Note your responses to this horrible experience. What have the men done to deserve being turned into pigs? How does Circe violate the laws of hospitality?*

Odysseus leaves the ship and rushes to Circe's hall. The god Hermes stops him to give him a plant that will weaken Circe's power. (Homer calls it a moly; it might have been a kind of garlic.) Protected by the plant's magic, Odysseus resists Circe's sorcery. The goddess, realizing she has met her match, frees Odysseus's men. Now Circe, "loveliest of all immortals," persuades Odysseus to stay with her. Odysseus shares her meat and wine, and she restores his heart. After many seasons of feasting and other pleasures, Odysseus and his men beg Circe to help them return home.

She responds to their pleas with the command that Odysseus alone descend to the Land of the Dead, "the cold homes of Death and pale Persephone," queen of the underworld. There Odysseus must seek the wisdom of the blind prophet Teiresias.

Odysseus pursuing Circe.
Greek vase.
Louvre, Paris, France.

THE LAND OF THE DEAD

In the Land of the Dead, Odysseus seeks to learn his destiny. The source of his information is Teiresias, the famous blind prophet from the city of Thebes. The prophet's lack of external sight suggests the presence of true insight. Circe has told Odysseus exactly what rites he must perform to bring Teiresias up from the dead. Odysseus continues telling his story to Alcinous's court.

"Then I addressed the blurred and breathless dead,
585   vowing to slaughter my best heifer for them
        before she calved, at home in Ithaca,
        and burn the choice bits on the altar fire;
        as for Teiresias, I swore to sacrifice
        a black lamb, handsomest of all our flock.
590   Thus to assuage the nations of the dead
        I pledged these rites, then slashed the lamb and ewe,
        letting their black blood stream into the well pit.
        Now the souls gathered, stirring out of Erebus,
        brides and young men, and men grown old in pain,
595   and tender girls whose hearts were new to grief;
        many were there, too, torn by brazen lanceheads,
        battle-slain, bearing still their bloody gear.

From every side they came and sought the pit
with rustling cries; and I grew sick with fear.
600 But presently I gave command to my officers
to flay° those sheep the bronze cut down, and make
burnt offerings of flesh to the gods below—
to sovereign Death, to pale Persephone.°
Meanwhile I crouched with my drawn sword to keep
605 the surging phantoms from the bloody pit
till I should know the presence of Teiresias. . . .

Soon from the dark that prince of Thebes came forward
bearing a golden staff; and he addressed me:

'Son of Laertes and the gods of old,
610 Odysseus, master of landways and seaways,
why leave the blazing sun, O man of woe,
to see the cold dead and the joyless region?
Stand clear, put up your sword;
let me but taste of blood, I shall speak true.'

615 At this I stepped aside, and in the scabbard
let my long sword ring home to the pommel silver,
as he bent down to the somber blood. Then spoke
the prince of those with gift of speech:
                                        'Great captain,
a fair wind and the honey lights of home
620 are all you seek. But anguish lies ahead;

601. flay (flā) *v.:* strip the skin from.

603. Persephone (pər·sef′ə·nē).

Persephone, queen of
the underworld, with her
husband, Hades
(4th century B.C.).
British Museum, London.

the god who thunders on the land prepares it,
not to be shaken from your track, implacable,°
in rancor for the son whose eye you blinded.
One narrow strait may take you through his blows:
625   denial of yourself, restraint of shipmates.
When you make landfall on Thrinakia first
and quit the violet sea, dark on the land
you'll find the grazing herds of Helios
by whom all things are seen, all speech is known.
630   Avoid those kine,° hold fast to your intent,
and hard seafaring brings you all to Ithaca.
But if you raid the beeves,° I see destruction
for ship and crew. Though you survive alone,
bereft of all companions, lost for years,
635   under strange sail shall you come home, to find
your own house filled with trouble: insolent men
eating your livestock as they court your lady.
Aye, you shall make those men atone in blood!
But after you have dealt out death—in open
640   combat or by stealth—to all the suitors,
go overland on foot, and take an oar,
until one day you come where men have lived
with meat unsalted, never known the sea,
nor seen seagoing ships, with crimson bows
645   and oars that fledge light hulls for dipping flight.
The spot will soon be plain to you, and I
can tell you how: some passerby will say,
"What winnowing fan° is that upon your shoulder?"
Halt, and implant your smooth oar in the turf
650   and make fair sacrifice to Lord Poseidon:
a ram, a bull, a great buck boar; turn back,
and carry out pure hecatombs° at home
to all wide heaven's lords, the undying gods,
to each in order. Then a seaborne death
655   soft as this hand of mist will come upon you
when you are wearied out with rich old age,
your countryfolk in blessed peace around you.
And all this shall be just as I foretell.' . . ."

(*from* Book 11)

Vocabulary
rancor (raŋ′kər) *n.:* bitter hatred; ill will.

622. implacable (im·plak′ə·bəl)
adj.: unyielding; merciless.

630. kine (kīn) *n.:* old term for
"cattle."

632. beeves *n.:* another old term for
"cattle."

648. winnowing fan: device used to
remove the useless dry outer covering
from grain. (These people would
never have seen an oar.)

652. hecatombs (hek′ə·tōmz′) *n.:*
sacrifices of one hundred cattle at a
time to the gods. In Greek, *hekaton*
means "one hundred."

618–658. *What prophecy
does Odysseus receive? Take notes on
how you might film this important
scene in the underworld. How many
actors would you need? What props
would you use? You might sketch the
scene as you* **visualize** *it.*

THE SIRENS; SCYLLA AND CHARYBDIS

Odysseus and his men return to Circe's island, where Circe warns Odysseus of the perils that await him. In the following passage, Odysseus, quoting Circe, is still speaking at Alcinous's court.

>   "'Listen with care
> 660   to this, now, and a god will arm your mind.
> Square in your ship's path are Sirens, crying
> beauty to bewitch men coasting by;
> woe to the innocent who hears that sound!
> He will not see his lady nor his children
> 665   in joy, crowding about him, home from sea;
> the Sirens will sing his mind away
> on their sweet meadow lolling. There are bones
> of dead men rotting in a pile beside them
> and flayed skins shrivel around the spot.
>   Steer wide;
> 670   keep well to seaward; plug your oarsmen's ears
> with beeswax kneaded soft; none of the rest
> should hear that song.
>
>   But if you wish to listen,
> let the men tie you in the lugger, hand
> and foot, back to the mast, lashed to the mast,
> 675   so you may hear those Harpies'° thrilling voices;
> shout as you will, begging to be untied,
> your crew must only twist more line around you
> and keep their stroke up, till the singers fade. . . .'"

The next peril lies between two headlands. Circe continues her warning.

> "'. . . That is the den of Scylla, where she yaps
> 680   abominably, a newborn whelp's° cry,
> though she is huge and monstrous. God or man,
> no one could look on her in joy. Her legs—
> and there are twelve—are like great tentacles,
> unjointed, and upon her serpent necks
> 685   are borne six heads like nightmares of ferocity,
> with triple serried° rows of fangs and deep
> gullets of black death. Half her length, she sways
> her heads in air, outside her horrid cleft,

675. Harpies (här′pēz): monsters, half bird and half woman, who are greedy for victims.

680. whelp's (hwelps) *n.:* puppy's.

686. serried (ser′ēd) *adj.:* crowded together; densely packed.

Vocabulary
abominably (ə·bäm′ə·nə·blē) *adv.:* in an extremely unpleasant or disgusting manner.

	hunting the sea around that promontory°
690	for dolphins, dogfish, or what bigger game
	thundering Amphitrite° feeds in thousands.
	And no ship's company can claim
	to have passed her without loss and grief; she takes,
	from every ship, one man for every gullet.
695	The opposite point seems more a tongue of land
	you'd touch with a good bowshot, at the narrows.
	A great wild fig, a shaggy mass of leaves,
	grows on it, and Charybdis lurks below
	to swallow down the dark sea tide. Three times
700	from dawn to dusk she spews it up
	and sucks it down again three times, a whirling
	maelstrom;° if you come upon her then
	the god who makes earth tremble could not save you.
	No, hug the cliff of Scylla, take your ship
705	through on a racing stroke. Better to mourn
	six men than lose them all, and the ship, too. . . .

689. promontory (präm′ən·tôr′ē) *n.*: high area of land that juts out into a body of water.

691. Amphitrite (am′fi·trīt′ē): goddess of the sea and wife of Poseidon.

702. maelstrom (māl′strəm) *n.*: large, violent whirlpool.

The Sirens (c. 1875) by Sir Edward Burne-Jones.

Then you will coast Thrinakia, the island
where Helios's cattle graze, fine herds, and flocks
of goodly sheep. The herds and flocks are seven,
with fifty beasts in each.

710 No lambs are dropped,
or calves, and these fat cattle never die. . . .

Now give those kine a wide berth, keep your thoughts
intent upon your course for home,
and hard seafaring brings you all to Ithaca.
715 But if you raid the beeves, I see destruction
for ship and crew. . . .'"

*The Ithacans set off. Odysseus does not tell his men of Circe's last
prophecy—that he will be the only survivor of their long journey.
Still speaking to Alcinous's court, Odysseus continues his tale.*

"The crew being now silent before me, I
addressed them, sore at heart:

'Dear friends,
more than one man, or two, should know those things
720 Circe foresaw for us and shared with me,
so let me tell her forecast: then we die
with our eyes open, if we are going to die,
or know what death we baffle if we can. Sirens
weaving a haunting song over the sea
725 we are to shun, she said, and their green shore
all sweet with clover; yet she urged that I
alone should listen to their song. Therefore
you are to tie me up, tight as a splint,
erect along the mast, lashed to the mast,
730 and if I shout and beg to be untied,
take more turns of the rope to muffle me.'

I rather dwelt on this part of the forecast,
while our good ship made time, bound outward down
the wind for the strange island of Sirens.
735 Then all at once the wind fell, and a calm
came over all the sea, as though some power
lulled the swell.
The crew were on their feet
briskly, to furl the sail, and stow it; then,
each in place, they poised the smooth oar blades
740 and sent the white foam scudding by. I carved
a massive cake of beeswax into bits

659–716. *According to
Circe, what dangers lie ahead for
Odysseus and his crew? List the
dangers in order from least severe
to most severe, and give your
reasons for placing the threats in
this order.*

*Circe Pouring Poison into a Vase and Awaiting
the Arrival of Ulysses (19th century)
by Sir Edward Burne-Jones.*

The Bridgeman Art Library.

and rolled them in my hands until they softened—
no long task, for a burning heat came down
from Helios, lord of high noon. Going forward
745   I carried wax along the line, and laid it
thick on their ears. They tied me up, then, plumb°
amidships, back to the mast, lashed to the mast,
and took themselves again to rowing. Soon,
as we came smartly within hailing distance,
750   the two Sirens, noting our fast ship
off their point, made ready, and they sang. . . .

The lovely voices in <u>ardor</u> appealing over the water
made me crave to listen, and I tried to say
'Untie me!' to the crew, jerking my brows;
755   but they bent steady to the oars. Then Perimedes°
got to his feet, he and Eurylochus,
and passed more line about, to hold me still.
So all rowed on, until the Sirens
dropped under the sea rim, and their singing
dwindled away.
760   My faithful company
rested on their oars now, peeling off
the wax that I had laid thick on their ears;
then set me free.
                   But scarcely had that island
faded in blue air when I saw smoke
765   and white water, with sound of waves in <u>tumult</u>—
a sound the men heard, and it terrified them.
Oars flew from their hands; the blades went knocking
wild alongside till the ship lost way,
with no oar blades to drive her through the water.

746. plumb (plum) *adv.:* vertically.

755. Perimedes (per·i·mē'dēz').

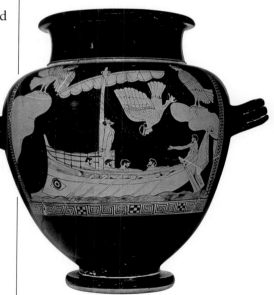

Odysseus and the Sirens, Athenian red-figure stamnos vase by the Siren Painter, late Archaic, c. 490 B.C. (earthenware).
British Museum, London, UK.

Vocabulary
ardor (är'dər) *n.:* passion; enthusiasm.
tumult (too'mult) *n.:* commotion; uproar; confusion.

770 Well, I walked up and down from bow to stern,
     trying to put heart into them, standing over
     every oarsman, saying gently,
                                                  'Friends,
     have we never been in danger before this?
     More fearsome, is it now, than when the Cyclops
775 penned us in his cave? What power he had!
     Did I not keep my nerve, and use my wits
     to find a way out for us?
                                        Now I say

     by hook or crook this peril too shall be
     something that we remember.
                                        Heads up, lads!

780 We must obey the orders as I give them.
     Get the oar shafts in your hands, and lie back
     hard on your benches; hit these breaking seas.
     Zeus help us pull away before we founder.°

     You at the tiller, listen, and take in
785 all that I say—the rudders are your duty;
     keep her out of the combers° and the smoke;
     steer for that headland; watch the drift, or we
     fetch up in the smother,° and you drown us.'

     That was all, and it brought them round to action.
790 But as I sent them on toward Scylla, I
     told them nothing, as they could do nothing.
     They would have dropped their oars again, in panic,
     to roll for cover under the decking. Circe's
     bidding against arms had slipped my mind,
795 so I tied on my cuirass° and took up
     two heavy spears, then made my way along
     to the foredeck—thinking to see her first from there,
     the monster of the gray rock, harboring
     torment for my friends. I strained my eyes
800 upon that cliffside veiled in cloud, but nowhere
     could I catch sight of her.
                                        And all this time,
     in travail,° sobbing, gaining on the current,
     we rowed into the strait—Scylla to port
     and on our starboard beam Charybdis, dire
805 gorge° of the salt sea tide. By heaven! when she
     vomited, all the sea was like a caldron
     seething over intense fire, when the mixture
     suddenly heaves and rises.

Scylla. Greek bronze.
National Archaeological Museum, Athens.

783. founder (foun′dər) v.: sink.

786. combers (kōm′ərz) n.: large waves.

788. smother (smu*th*′ər) n.: commotion; violent action or disorder.

770–793. *Think about what kind of leader Odysseus is. What does he tell his men, to reassure them? What does he decide not to tell them? Why?*

795. cuirass (kwi·ras′) n.: armor for the breast and back.

802. travail (trə·vāl′) n.: hard, exhausting work or effort; tiring labor.

805. gorge (gôrj) n.: throat and jaws of a greedy, all-devouring being.

The shot spume
soared to the landside heights, and fell like rain.

810 But when she swallowed the sea water down
we saw the funnel of the maelstrom, heard
the rock bellowing all around, and dark
sand raged on the bottom far below.
My men all blanched° against the gloom, our eyes
815 were fixed upon that yawning mouth in fear
of being devoured.

Then Scylla made her strike,
whisking six of my best men from the ship.

I happened to glance aft at ship and oarsmen
and caught sight of their arms and legs, dangling
820 high overhead. Voices came down to me
in anguish, calling my name for the last time.

A man surf-casting on a point of rock
for bass or mackerel, whipping his long rod
to drop the sinker and the bait far out,
825 will hook a fish and rip it from the surface
to dangle wriggling through the air;

so these
were borne aloft in spasms toward the cliff.

She ate them as they shrieked there, in her den,
in the dire grapple,° reaching still for me—
830 and deathly pity ran me through
at that sight—far the worst I ever suffered
questing the passes of the strange sea.

We rowed on.
The Rocks were now behind; Charybdis, too,
and Scylla dropped astern.

Then we were coasting
835 the noble island of the god, where grazed
those cattle with wide brows, and bounteous flocks
of Helios, lord of noon, who rides high heaven.
From the black ship, far still at sea, I heard
the lowing of the cattle winding home
840 and sheep bleating; and heard, too, in my heart
the words of blind Teiresias of Thebes
and Circe of Aeaea: both forbade me
the island of the world's delight, the Sun. . . ."

(*from* Book 12)

814. blanched (blancht) *v.*: grew pale.

829. dire grapple: terrible struggle.

843. *Suppose you wanted to write a **screenplay** dramatizing this famous part of the* Odyssey—*the crew's struggle against the Sirens and against Scylla and Charybdis. Who would be your main characters? How would you use music and visuals—especially in the Sirens scene? Write down your ideas about filming the epic.*

Odysseus urges his exhausted crew to bypass Thrinakia, the island of the sun god, Helios. When the men insist on landing, Odysseus makes them swear not to touch the god's cattle. Odysseus is still speaking to Alcinous's court.

"In the small hours of the third watch, when stars
845   that shone out in the first dusk of evening
had gone down to their setting, a giant wind
blew from heaven, and clouds driven by Zeus
shrouded land and sea in a night of storm;
so, just as Dawn with fingertips of rose
850   touched the windy world, we dragged our ship
to cover in a grotto, a sea cave
where nymphs had chairs of rock and sanded floors.
I mustered all the crew and said:

                  'Old shipmates,
our stores are in the ship's hold, food and drink;
855   the cattle here are not for our provision,
or we pay dearly for it.

                     Fierce the god is
who cherishes these heifers and these sheep:
Helios; and no man avoids his eye.'

To this my fighters nodded. Yes. But now
860   we had a month of onshore gales, blowing
day in, day out—south winds, or south by east.
As long as bread and good red wine remained
to keep the men up, and appease their craving,
they would not touch the cattle. But in the end,
865   when all the barley in the ship was gone,
hunger drove them to scour the wild shore
with angling hooks, for fishes and sea fowl,

The Companions of Ulysses Slaying the Cattle of the Sun God Helios (16th century) by Pellegrino Tibaldi.
Palazzo Poggi, Bologna, Italy.

whatever fell into their hands; and lean days
wore their bellies thin.

                       The storms continued.

870 So one day I withdrew to the interior
to pray the gods in solitude, for hope
that one might show me some way of salvation.
Slipping away, I struck across the island
to a sheltered spot, out of the driving gale.

875 I washed my hands there, and made supplication°
to the gods who own Olympus, all the gods—
but they, for answer, only closed my eyes
under slow drops of sleep.

                 Now on the shore Eurylochus
made his insidious° plea:

                       'Comrades,' he said,

880 'You've gone through everything; listen to what I say.
All deaths are hateful to us, mortal wretches,
but famine is the most pitiful, the worst
end that a man can come to.

                     Will you fight it?
Come, we'll cut out the noblest of these cattle

885 for sacrifice to the gods who own the sky;
and once at home, in the old country of Ithaca,
if ever that day comes—
we'll build a costly temple and adorn it
with every beauty for the Lord of Noon.

890 But if he flares up over his heifers lost,
wishing our ship destroyed, and if the gods
make cause with him, why, then I say: Better
open your lungs to a big sea once for all
than waste to skin and bones on a lonely island!'

895 Thus Eurylochus; and they murmured 'Aye!'
trooping away at once to round up heifers.
Now, that day tranquil cattle with broad brows
were grazing near, and soon the men drew up
around their chosen beasts in ceremony.

900 They plucked the leaves that shone on a tall oak—
having no barley meal—to strew° the victims,
performed the prayers and ritual, knifed the kine
and flayed each carcass, cutting thighbones free
to wrap in double folds of fat. These offerings,

905 with strips of meat, were laid upon the fire.
Then, as they had no wine, they made libation°

875. supplication (sup′lə·kā′shən)
n.: humble requests; prayers.

879. insidious (in·sid′ē·əs) *adj.*:
treacherous; more dangerous than
is apparent.

878–894. *What is Eurylochus's "insidious plea"? If you
were a member of the crew, would
you be swayed by this argument, or
would you heed Odysseus's warning?
Do you think murdering the cattle is
justified, or is it an offense against
the god Helios?*

901. strew (strōō) *v.*: scatter about.

906. libation (lī·bā′shən) *n.*:
offering of wine or oil to the gods.

with clear spring water, broiling the entrails° first;
and when the bones were burnt and tripes° shared,
they spitted the carved meat.

907. **entrails** (en′trālz) *n.:* intestines;
guts.
908. **tripes** (trīps) *n.:* stomach parts.

                                   Just then my slumber
910   left me in a rush, my eyes opened,
      and I went down the seaward path. No sooner
      had I caught sight of our black hull, than savory
      odors of burnt fat eddied around me;
      grief took hold of me, and I cried aloud:

915   'O Father Zeus and gods in bliss forever,
      you made me sleep away this day of mischief!
      O cruel drowsing, in the evil hour!
      Here they sat, and a great work they contrived.'

      Lampetia° in her long gown meanwhile
920   had borne swift word to the Overlord of Noon:

      'They have killed your kine.'

                                   And the Lord Helios
      burst into angry speech amid the immortals:

      'O Father Zeus and gods in bliss forever,
      punish Odysseus' men! So overweening,°
925   now they have killed my peaceful kine, my joy
      at morning when I climbed the sky of stars,
      and evening, when I bore westward from heaven.
      Restitution or penalty they shall pay—
      and pay in full—or I go down forever
930   to light the dead men in the underworld.' . . ."

                                   (*from* Book 12)

919. **Lampetia** (lam·pē′shē·ə):
daughter of Helios. Lampetia
guarded her father's herds of cattle.

924. **overweening** (o′vər·wēn′iŋ)
adj.: excessively proud.

921–930. *What exactly has
happened to cause the god's fury?*

*When Odysseus and his men set sail again, they are punished with
death—a thunderbolt from Zeus destroys their boat, and all the
men drown. Only Odysseus survives. Exhausted and nearly
drowned, he makes his way to Calypso's island, where we met him
originally, in Book 5.*

*Odysseus has brought us up to date. He can now rest and enjoy
the comforts of Alcinous's court—but not for long. Ahead lies his
most difficult task—reclaiming his own kingdom.*

*At this moment of suspense, Homer might have put aside his
harp until the next night.*

Zeus seated on his throne, holding
thunderbolts. Bronze statuette
found on Mount Lyceum (6th century B.C.).

National Archaeological Museum, Athens.

Vocabulary
restitution (res′tə·tōo′shən) *n.:* compensation; repayment.

from the Odyssey, Part One

Reading Check

1. In a chart like the one below, **summarize** the **external conflict** and its **resolution** in each episode.

Adventure	Summary
Calypso	
Lotus Eaters	
Cyclops	
Circe	
Sirens; Scylla and Charybdis	
Cattle of the Sun God	

2. What does Odysseus learn about his future from blind Teiresias in the Land of the Dead?

Thinking Critically

3. "Nobody" in Greek is *outis,* which sounds like *Odysseus.* In his **conflict** with the Cyclops, how does Odysseus overcome the monster through a clever use of language? What curse at the end of this adventure **foreshadows** trouble?

4. What conclusions about the deceptive nature of beauty can you draw from the Circe episode?

5. Book 5 of the *Odyssey* focuses on Odysseus's captivity on Calypso's island. Suzanne Vega (see the **Connection** on page 755) expresses Calypso's view of the affair. How does her song compare with Homer's story? Whom do you sympathize with—Odysseus or Calypso?

6. From what you've observed of Odysseus, how would you describe what the Greeks valued in a hero? Do we value these same traits today? Check your Quickwrite notes for page 749.

Extending and Evaluating

7. How many of the monsters or threats to Odysseus in this part of the epic are female? What do you think of the way women are portrayed so far?

WRITING

It's Alive!

In "The Cyclops in the Ocean" (see the **Connection** on page 772), the modern poet Nikki Giovanni **personifies** a tropical storm—that is, she describes the storm as if it were a living creature. Write a paragraph personifying some other violent force of nature. Describe how it looks and sounds and what it does with its victims.

Cause and Effect

Characters in the *Odyssey* often use cause-and-effect arguments when they try to **persuade.** For example, when Odysseus asks the Cyclops for help, he warns the Cyclops of the effects of offending the gods by harming a guest. Calypso tries to persuade Odysseus to remain with her by mentioning the effects he will suffer if he leaves her. Choose one argument from the epic, and describe why it is persuasive or how you think it could be strengthened.

▶ **Use "Persuading with Cause and Effect," pages 834–841, for help with this assignment.**

SKILLS FOCUS

Literary Skills
Analyze characteristics of epic poetry, including heroes and their external conflicts.

Reading Skills
Monitor your comprehension.

Writing Skills
Write a paragraph with personification. Analyze a persuasive argument.

INTERNET

Projects and Activities

Keyword: LE7 9-10

After You Read   Vocabulary Development

Semantic Mapping

PRACTICE 1

With a partner, create a semantic map for each Word Bank word. Make up questions about each word, and provide your own answers. A sample map is done for *formidable*. Compare your maps in class.

Who is formidable in the *Odyssey*?
• Odysseus   • the gods

Do I want to be called formidable?
• Yes, I'd like to be formidable as a center forward.

formidable

What have I seen that is formidable?
• Josh on football field
• Emma in math class
• volcano

What is not formidable?
• ant
• baby
• peaceful pond

Figures of Speech—Homeric Similes

In a **figure of speech,** a writer compares one thing to something else, something quite different from it in all but a few important ways. For example, Homer compares the army of the Cicones to "the leaves and blades of spring" (lines 163–164). He is saying that enemy soldiers suddenly appeared everywhere, as green grass and leaves do in spring. The comparison is surprising because a fierce army seems very different from the tender leaves and grass of spring.

The **Homeric simile** (also called **epic simile**) is an extended comparison between something that the audience cannot have seen (such as Odysseus boring out the Cyclops's eye) and something ordinary that they would know (such as a shipbuilder drilling a plank; see lines 379–381 on page 765).

PRACTICE 2

1. Re-read lines 822–827 on page 783. Explain how this Homeric simile brings the audience into the story by comparing a strange, unfamiliar occurrence to something familiar.

2. Make up three Homeric similes of your own, in which you compare something strange or unfamiliar to something ordinary and familiar. (Remember that a simile makes a comparison using a word such as *like, as,* or *resembles*.) You might consider describing one of the following things:

   • a space launch

   • the surface of the moon

   • something you see through a microscope

SKILLS FOCUS

Vocabulary Skills
Create semantic maps. Analyze Homeric (epic) similes.

Before You Read

from the Odyssey, Part Two

Make the Connection

Quickwrite ✏

Imagine that someone has been absent
from home for many years. What might
that person think or feel upon returning
home? Make a list of possible reactions,
and save your notes.

Literary Focus

Living Characters

Odysseus is brave and clever. Penelope is
faithful—and clever, too. Circe is lovely
and bewitching. Homer has depicted his
characters—mortals, gods, goddesses,
and monsters alike—with bold, vivid
strokes.

Storytellers reveal **character traits**
in many ways. As you read, look carefully
at what characters *say* and *do* and *think*.
Note how they *interact* and how they are
described. Then, think about what all this
information tells you. Is a character
noble or evil? wise or foolish? arrogant
or humble? Does the character possess
a combination of both positive and negative traits?

Part Two of the *Odyssey* contains the
climax of the epic. Suspenseful and exciting, it is also deeply moving, as Odysseus
returns home to Ithaca and is reunited
with his wife, Penelope. As you read,
think about what these characters are like
and why they have lived in the imagination
of readers for centuries.

Vocabulary Development

candor (kan′dər) *n.*: honesty; frankness.

disdainful (dis·dān′fəl) *adj.*: scornful;
regarding someone as beneath you.

adorn (ə·dôrn′) *v.*: add beauty to;
decorate.

revelry (rev′əl·rē) *n.*: merrymaking;
festivity.

glowered (glou′ərd) *v.*: glared; stared
angrily.

avails (ə·vālz′) *v.*: is of use; helps.

lavished (lav′isht) *v.*: gave generously.

aloof (ə·lo͞of′) *adj.*: at a distance;
unfriendly.

pliant (plī′ənt) *adj.*: flexible.

tremulous (trem′yo͞o·ləs) *adj.*:
trembling; shaking.

SKILLS
FOCUS

Literary Skills
Understand
characteristics
of epic poetry,
including
character traits.

INTERNET

Vocabulary
Practice
•
More About
Homer

Keyword: LE7 9-10

PART TWO: COMING HOME

In Book 13, Odysseus, laden with gifts, is returned in secret to Ithaca in one of the magically swift Phaeacian ships. In Ithaca, Athena appears to the hero. Because his home is full of enemies, she advises him to proceed disguised as a beggar. Now Odysseus must succeed not only by physical power but also by intelligence.

In Book 14, Odysseus, in his beggar's disguise, finds his way to the hut of Eumaeus, his old and trusty swineherd. Eumaeus is the very image of faithfulness in a servant—a quality much admired by Homer's society. The introduction of members of the so-called servant class as important actors is unusual in epic poetry, and it indicates Homer's originality. Odysseus is politely entertained by Eumaeus, but the king remains disguised from his old servant.

In Book 15, Athena appears to Odysseus's son, Telemachus. The young man has gone to Pylos and Sparta to talk to old comrades of his father's to try to discover if Odysseus is alive or dead. Athena advises him to return to Ithaca. His home—the palace of Odysseus—has been overrun by his mother's suitors. These arrogant men are spending money from Telemachus's inheritance on feasting and drinking, and they are demanding that his mother, Penelope, take one of them as a husband. Athena warns Telemachus that the suitors plan to ambush him. Telemachus boards a ship for home, lands secretly on Ithaca, and heads toward the hut of the swineherd.

As father and son move closer and closer together, the suspense becomes great. Now Homer is ready to recount what could be the most dramatic moment in the epic. Remember that Odysseus has not seen his son for twenty years. Telemachus has been away from Ithaca for a year.

Penelope at Her Loom (detail), from *The Story of Virtuous Women* series (c. 1480–1483). Wool tapestry.

But there were two men in the mountain hut—
Odysseus and the swineherd. At first light
blowing their fire up, they cooked their breakfast
and sent their lads out, driving herds to root
in the tall timber.

935   When Telemachus came,
the wolfish troop of watchdogs only fawned on him
as he advanced. Odysseus heard them go
and heard the light crunch of a man's footfall—
at which he turned quickly to say:

                        "Eumaeus,
940   here is one of your crew come back, or maybe
another friend: the dogs are out there snuffling
belly down; not one has even growled.
I can hear footsteps—"

                 But before he finished
his tall son stood at the door.

                   The swineherd
945   rose in surprise, letting a bowl and jug
tumble from his fingers. Going forward,
he kissed the young man's head, his shining eyes
and both hands, while his own tears brimmed and fell.
Think of a man whose dear and only son,
950   born to him in exile, reared with labor,
has lived ten years abroad and now returns:
how would that man embrace his son! Just so
the herdsman clapped his arms around Telemachus
and covered him with kisses—for he knew
955   the lad had got away from death. He said:

"Light of my days, Telemachus,
you made it back! When you took ship for Pylos°
I never thought to see you here again.
Come in, dear child, and let me feast my eyes;
960   here you are, home from the distant places!
How rarely, anyway, you visit us,
your own men, and your own woods and pastures!
Always in the town, a man would think
you loved the suitors' company, those dogs!"

Odysseus and Telemachus.
Mosaic (1st century A.D.)
(31.5 cm wide).
Kunsthistorisches Museum,
Vienna, Austria.

957. Pylos (pī′lōs): home of Nestor,
one of Odysseus's fellow soldiers in
the Trojan War. Telemachus had gone
to see if Nestor knew anything about
Odysseus's whereabouts.

965 Telemachus with his clear <u>candor</u> said:

"I am with you, Uncle.° See now, I have come
because I wanted to see you first, to hear from you
if Mother stayed at home—or is she married
off to someone, and Odysseus' bed
970 left empty for some gloomy spider's weaving?"
Gently the forester replied to this:

"At home indeed your mother is, poor lady
still in the women's hall. Her nights and days
are wearied out with grieving."

Stepping back
975 he took the bronze-shod lance, and the young prince
entered the cabin over the worn door stone.
Odysseus moved aside, yielding his couch,
but from across the room Telemachus checked him:

"Friend, sit down; we'll find another chair
980 in our own hut. Here is the man to make one!"

The swineherd, when the quiet man sank down,
built a new pile of evergreens and fleeces—
a couch for the dear son of great Odysseus—
then gave them trenchers° of good meat, left over
985 from the roast pork of yesterday, and heaped up
willow baskets full of bread, and mixed
an ivy bowl of honey-hearted wine.
Then he in turn sat down, facing Odysseus,
their hands went out upon the meat and drink
990 as they fell to, ridding themselves of hunger. . . .

Not realizing that the stranger is his father, Telemachus tries to protect him as best he can. He says that the beggar cannot stay in the palace hall because he will be abused by the drunken suitors.

The swineherd is sent to Penelope with news of her son's return. Now even Athena cannot stand the suspense any longer. She turns to Odysseus, who is still in beggar's rags:

. . . She tipped her golden wand upon the man,
making his cloak pure white, and the knit tunic
fresh around him. Lithe° and young she made him,

966. Uncle: here, a term of affection.

The return of Odysseus. Terracotta relief believed to be from the island of Melos (first half of the 5th century B.C.).

The Metropolitan Museum of Art, New York. Fletcher Fund, 1930 (30.11.9). Photograph ©1982 The Metropolitan Museum of Art.

984. trenchers (tren′chərz) *n.*: wooden platters.

974–990. *Who is still in disguise in this scene? How does the ancient Greeks' regard for hospitality affect the way the other characters treat him? What do you think each character is feeling and thinking as he eats?*

993. lithe (līth) *adj.*: limber.

Vocabulary
candor (kan′dər) *n.*: honesty; frankness.

995 ruddy with sun, his jawline clean, the beard
no longer gray upon his chin. And she
withdrew when she had done.

Then Lord Odysseus
reappeared—and his son was thunderstruck.
Fear in his eyes, he looked down and away
as though it were a god, and whispered:

"Stranger,
1000 you are no longer what you were just now!
Your cloak is new; even your skin! You are
one of the gods who rule the sweep of heaven!
Be kind to us, we'll make you fair oblation°
and gifts of hammered gold. Have mercy on us!"

1005 The noble and enduring man replied:

"No god. Why take me for a god? No, no.
I am that father whom your boyhood lacked
and suffered pain for lack of. I am he."

Held back too long, the tears ran down his cheeks
as he embraced his son.

1010 Only Telemachus,
uncomprehending, wild
with incredulity,° cried out:

"You cannot
be my father Odysseus! Meddling spirits
conceived this trick to twist the knife in me!
1015 No man of woman born could work these wonders
by his own craft, unless a god came into it
with ease to turn him young or old at will.
I swear you were in rags and old,
and here you stand like one of the immortals!"

1020 Odysseus brought his ranging mind to bear
and said:

"This is not princely, to be swept
away by wonder at your father's presence.
No other Odysseus will ever come,
for he and I are one, the same; his bitter
1025 fortune and his wanderings are mine.
Twenty years gone, and I am back again
on my own island. . . ."

Then, throwing
his arms around this marvel of a father,
Telemachus began to weep. Salt tears

Telemachus Sees His Father (1875).
Lithograph by Friedrich Preller the
Elder.

Archiv f.Kunst and Geschichte, Berlin.

1030

rose from the wells of longing in both men,
and cries burst from both as keen and fluttering
as those of the great taloned hawk,
whose nestlings° farmers take before they fly.
So helplessly they cried, pouring out tears,
and might have gone on weeping so till sundown. . . .

(from Book 16)

1033. nestlings (nest′liŋz) *n.:* young birds that are not ready to leave the nest.

1005–1035. *Which part of this recognition scene between father and son do you find most moving or most dramatic? Sum up the problems that now face father and son in the palace at Ithaca.*

THE BEGGAR AND THE FAITHFUL DOG

Telemachus returns to the family compound and is greeted tearfully by his mother, Penelope, and his old nurse, Eurycleia. A soothsayer has told his mother that Odysseus is alive and in Ithaca. However, Telemachus does not report that he has seen his father. The suspense builds as Odysseus, once again disguised as a beggar, returns to his home, accompanied only by the swineherd. He has been away for twenty years. Only one creature recognizes him.

While he spoke

an old hound, lying near, pricked up his ears
and lifted up his muzzle. This was Argos,
trained as a puppy by Odysseus,
but never taken on a hunt before
his master sailed for Troy. The young men, afterward,
hunted wild goats with him, and hare, and deer,
but he had grown old in his master's absence.
Treated as rubbish now, he lay at last
upon a mass of dung before the gates—
manure of mules and cows, piled there until
field hands could spread it on the king's estate.
Abandoned there, and half destroyed with flies,
old Argos lay.

But when he knew he heard

Odysseus' voice nearby, he did his best
to wag his tail, nose down, with flattened ears,
having no strength to move nearer his master.
And the man looked away,
wiping a salt tear from his cheek; but he
hid this from Eumaeus. Then he said:

"I marvel that they leave this hound to lie
here on the dung pile;
he would have been a fine dog, from the look of him,

Laconian hound scratching his head. Detail from an Attic red-figured ceramic scyphus, or drinking cup, by the Euergides Painter (c. 500 B.C.).
Ashmolean Museum, Oxford, England.

1060   though I can't say as to his power and speed
when he was young. You find the same good build
in house dogs, table dogs landowners keep
all for style."

                     And you replied, Eumaeus:

"A hunter owned him—but the man is dead
in some far place. If this old hound could show
1065   the form he had when Lord Odysseus left him,
going to Troy, you'd see him swift and strong.
He never shrank from any savage thing
he'd brought to bay in the deep woods; on the scent
no other dog kept up with him. Now misery
1070   has him in leash. His owner died abroad,
and here the women slaves will take no care of him.
You know how servants are: without a master
they have no will to labor, or excel.
For Zeus who views the wide world takes away
1075   half the manhood of a man, that day
he goes into captivity and slavery."

Eumaeus crossed the court and went straight forward
into the megaron° among the suitors;
but death and darkness in that instant closed
1080   the eyes of Argos, who had seen his master,
Odysseus, after twenty years. . . .

                     (*from* Book 17)

1044–1071. *Here again we
hear about people who mock the
sacred laws of respect and hospitality. In showing us how the old dog
is treated, what is Homer telling us
about conditions in Ithaca?*

1078. megaron (meg′ə · rän) *n.:* great
hall or central room.

The Epic Continues

In the hall the "beggar" is taunted by the evil suitors, but Penelope supports him. She has learned that the ragged stranger claims to have news of her husband. Unaware of who the beggar is, she invites him to visit her later in the night to talk about Odysseus.

In Book 18, Penelope appears among the suitors and reproaches Telemachus for allowing the stranger to be abused. She certainly must have warmed her husband's heart by doing this and by singing the praises of her lost Odysseus.

In Book 19, the suitors depart for the night, and Odysseus and Telemachus discuss their strategy. The clever hero goes as appointed to Penelope with the idea of testing her and her maids. (Some of the maids have not been loyal to the household and have been involved with the suitors.) The faithful wife receives her disguised husband. We can imagine the tension Homer's audience must have felt. Would Odysseus be recognized?

The "beggar" spins a yarn about his origins, pretending that he has met Odysseus on his travels. He cannot resist praising the lost hero, and he does so successfully enough to bring tears to Penelope's eyes. We can be sure that this does not displease her husband.

The storytelling beggar reveals that he has heard that Odysseus is alive and is even now sailing for home. Penelope calls for the old nurse and asks her to wash the guest's feet—a sign of respect and honor. As Eurycleia does so, she recognizes Odysseus from a scar on his leg.

Quickly Odysseus swears the old nurse to secrecy. Meanwhile, Athena has cast a spell on Penelope so that she has taken no notice of this recognition scene. Penelope adds to the suspense by deciding on a test for the suitors on the next day. Without realizing it, she has now given Odysseus a way to defeat the men who threaten his wife and kingdom.

In Book 20, Odysseus, brooding over the shameless behavior of the maidservants and the suitors, longs to destroy his enemies but fears the revenge of their friends. Athena reassures him. Odysseus is told that the suitors will die.

Odysseus is recognized by Eurycleia. Detail from a scyphus, a drinking cup.
Museo Archeologico, Chiusi, Italy.

Penelope to Ulysses

Penelope, distressed by the suitors' demands that she marry one of them, plays a trick on them. She has told them that she is weaving a shroud (a cloth used to wrap a body for burial) for Laertes, her father-in-law. She promises that she will choose a husband when she has completed the work. "So every day I wove on the great loom, but every night by torchlight I unwove it. . . ." With this simple trick she has deceived her suitors for three years. What do this trick and this poem reveal about Penelope? As you read the Odyssey, *look for places where she displays these same traits.*

Like a spider committing suicide
each night I unweave the web of my day.
I have no peace.
About me the insistent buzz of flies
5   drones louder every day.
I am starving.
I watch them, always, unblinking stare.
All my dwindling will
I use in not moving, not trying, unweaving.
10 I pull in my empty nets
eating myself, waiting.

—Meredith Schwartz
    Highland Park High School
    Highland Park, New Jersey

An Ancient Gesture
Edna St. Vincent Millay

I thought, as I wiped my eyes on the corner of my apron:
Penelope did this too.
And more than once: you can't keep weaving all day
And undoing it all through the night;
5   Your arms get tired, and the back of your neck gets tight;
And along towards morning, when you think it will never be light,
And your husband has been gone, and you don't know where, for years,
Suddenly you burst into tears;
There is simply nothing else to do.

10 And I thought, as I wiped my eyes on the corner of my apron:
This is an ancient gesture, authentic, antique,
In the very best tradition, classic, Greek;
Ulysses did this too.
But only as a gesture,—a gesture which implied
15 To the assembled throng that he was much too moved to speak.
He learned it from Penelope . . .
Penelope, who really cried.

Penelope with the Suitors (c. 1509) by Pínturicchio.

THE TEST OF THE GREAT BOW

In Book 21, Penelope, like many unwilling princesses of myth and fairy tale, proposes an impossible task for those who wish to marry her. By so doing, she causes the bloody events that lead to the restoration of her husband. The test involves stringing Odysseus's huge bow, an impossible feat for anyone except Odysseus himself. Odysseus had left his bow home in Ithaca twenty years earlier.

Now the queen reached the storeroom door and halted.
Here was an oaken sill, cut long ago
and sanded clean and bedded true. Foursquare
1085   the doorjambs and the shining doors were set
by the careful builder. Penelope untied the strap
around the curving handle, pushed her hook
into the slit, aimed at the bolts inside,
and shot them back. Then came a rasping sound
1090   as those bright doors the key had sprung gave way—
a bellow like a bull's vaunt° in a meadow—

1091. vaunt (vônt) *n.:* boast.

followed by her light footfall entering
over the plank floor. Herb-scented robes
lay there in chests, but the lady's milk-white arms
1095   went up to lift the bow down from a peg
in its own polished bow case.

Now Penelope
sank down, holding the weapon on her knees,
and drew her husband's great bow out, and sobbed
and bit her lip and let the salt tears flow.
1100   Then back she went to face the crowded hall
tremendous bow in hand, and on her shoulder hung
the quiver spiked with coughing death. Behind, her
maids bore a basket full of ax heads, bronze
and iron implements for the master's game.
1105   Thus in her beauty she approached the suitors,
and near a pillar of the solid roof
she paused, her shining veil across her cheeks,
her maids on either hand and still,
then spoke to the banqueters:

"My lords, hear me:
1110   suitors indeed, you recommended this house
to feast and drink in, day and night, my husband
being long gone, long out of mind. You found
no justification for yourselves—none
except your lust to marry me. Stand up, then:
1115   we now declare a contest for that prize.
Here is my lord Odysseus' hunting bow.
Bend and string it if you can. Who sends an arrow
through iron ax-helve sockets,° twelve in line?
I join my life with his, and leave this place, my home,
1120   my rich and beautiful bridal house, forever
to be remembered, though I dream it only." . . .

*Many of the suitors boldly try the bow, but not one man can even
bend it enough to string it.*

Two men had meanwhile left the hall:
swineherd and cowherd, in companionship,
one downcast as the other. But Odysseus
1125   followed them outdoors, outside the court,
and coming up said gently:

"You, herdsman,
and you, too, swineherd, I could say a thing to you,
or should I keep it dark?

Odysseus slaying the suitors. Detail from an Attic red-figured scyphus, or drinking cup, by the Penelope Painter, from Tarquinii, an ancient city in central Italy (c. 440 B.C.).
Antikensammlung Staatliche Museen zu Berlin Preussischer Kulturbesitz.

1118. ax-helve sockets: An ax helve is an ax handle; a socket is a hollow piece lined with iron at the end of the handle. Shooting an arrow through a line of ax-helve sockets would be a task possible only for a superhero like Odysseus.

No, no; speak,
my heart tells me. Would you be men enough
1130   to stand by Odysseus if he came back?
Suppose he dropped out of a clear sky, as I did?
Suppose some god should bring him?
Would you bear arms for him, or for the suitors?"

The cowherd said:

                "Ah, let the master come!
1135   Father Zeus, grant our old wish! Some courier°
guide him back! Then judge what stuff is in me
and how I manage arms!"

              Likewise Eumaeus

fell to praying all heaven for his return,
so that Odysseus, sure at least of these,
told them:

1140   "I am at home, for I am he.
I bore adversities, but in the twentieth year
I am ashore in my own land. I find
the two of you, alone among my people,
longed for my coming. Prayers I never heard
1145   except your own that I might come again.
So now what is in store for you I'll tell you:
If Zeus brings down the suitors by my hand
I promise marriages to both, and cattle,
and houses built near mine. And you shall be
1150   brothers-in-arms of my Telemachus.
Here, let me show you something else, a sign
that I am he, that you can trust me, look:
this old scar from the tusk wound that I got
boar hunting on Parnassus°— . . ."
                    Shifting his rags
1155   he bared the long gash. Both men looked, and knew
and threw their arms around the old soldier, weeping,
kissing his head and shoulders. He as well
took each man's head and hands to kiss, then said—
to cut it short, else they might weep till dark—

1160   "Break off, no more of this.
Anyone at the door could see and tell them.
Drift back in, but separately at intervals
after me.
              Now listen to your orders:

1135. courier (ko͞or′ē·ər) *n.*: guide or messenger.

📖 **1122–1140.** *How does Odysseus test the loyalty of the swineherd and the cowherd? How do they prove that they can be trusted?*

1154. Parnassus (pär·nas′əs): As a young man, Odysseus had gone hunting on Parnassus, his mother's home, and was gored above the knee by a boar.

1165   when the time comes, those gentlemen, to a man,
        will be dead against giving me bow or quiver.
        Defy them. Eumaeus, bring the bow
        and put it in my hands there at the door.
        Tell the women to lock their own door tight.
        Tell them if someone hears the shock of arms
1170   or groans of men, in hall or court, not one
        must show her face, but keep still at her weaving.
        Philoeteus, run to the outer gate and lock it.
        Throw the crossbar and lash it." . . .

*Now Odysseus, still in his beggar's clothes, asks to try the bow. The
suitors refuse to allow a mere beggar to try where they have failed,
but Penelope insists that the stranger be given his chance. The suspense is very great—by this act, Penelope has accepted her husband
as a suitor.*

*Eumaeus, the swineherd, hands Odysseus the bow and tells the
nurse to retire with Penelope and the maids to the family chambers
(the harem) and to bolt the doors. Odysseus had earlier told
Telemachus to remove the suitors' weapons from the great hall.
Now he takes the bow.*

                            And Odysseus took his time,
1175   turning the bow, tapping it, every inch,
        for borings that termites might have made
        while the master of the weapon was abroad.
        The suitors were now watching him, and some
        jested among themselves:

                                    "A bow lover!"

        "Dealer in old bows!"

1180   "Maybe he has one like it
        at home!"

                        "Or has an itch to make one for himself."

        "See how he handles it, the sly old buzzard!"

        And one <u>disdainful</u> suitor added this:

        "May his fortune grow an inch for every inch he bends it!"

1185   But the man skilled in all ways of contending,
        satisfied by the great bow's look and heft,

1174–1220. *As you read
this scene, make notes about how
you **visualize** it. Where are various characters placed? How are
they reacting? It might help to
draw a picture of the great hall
and indicate where various actions
take place.*

Vocabulary
disdainful (dis·dān′fəl) *adj.:* scornful; regarding someone as
   beneath you.

like a musician, like a harper, when
with quiet hand upon his instrument
he draws between his thumb and forefinger
1190 a sweet new string upon a peg: so effortlessly
Odysseus in one motion strung the bow.
Then slid his right hand down the cord and plucked it,
so the taut gut vibrating hummed and sang
a swallow's note.

In the hushed hall it smote the suitors
1195 and all their faces changed. Then Zeus thundered
overhead, one loud crack for a sign.
And Odysseus laughed within him that the son
of crooked-minded Cronus° had flung that omen down.
He picked one ready arrow from his table
1200 where it lay bare: the rest were waiting still
in the quiver for the young men's turn to come.
He nocked° it, let it rest across the handgrip,
and drew the string and grooved butt of the arrow,
aiming from where he sat upon the stool.

Now flashed
1205 arrow from twanging bow clean as a whistle
through every socket ring, and grazed not one,
to thud with heavy brazen head beyond.

Then quietly
Odysseus said:

"Telemachus, the stranger
you welcomed in your hall has not disgraced you.
1210 I did not miss, neither did I take all day
stringing the bow. My hand and eye are sound,
not so contemptible as the young men say.
The hour has come to cook their lordships' mutton—
supper by daylight. Other amusements later,
1215 with song and harping that adorn a feast."

He dropped his eyes and nodded, and the prince
Telemachus, true son of King Odysseus,
belted his sword on, clapped hand to his spear,
and with a clink and glitter of keen bronze
1220 stood by his chair, in the forefront near his father.

(*from* Book 21)

1198. Cronus (krō′nəs): father of
Zeus, called crooked-minded because
of his schemes to destroy his children.

1202. nocked (näkt) *v.:* fitted to the
bowstring.

*1220. What do you pre-
dict will happen next? Review the
episode, looking for clues in what
Odysseus says and does.*

Vocabulary
adorn (ə·dôrn′) *v.:* add beauty to; decorate.

DEATH AT THE PALACE

The climax of the story is here, in Book 22. Although Odysseus is ready to reclaim his rightful kingdom, he must first confront more than a hundred hostile suitors. The first one he turns to is Antinous. All through the story, Antinous has been the meanest of the suitors and their ringleader. He hit Odysseus with a stool when the hero appeared in the hall as a beggar, and he ridiculed the disguised king by calling him a bleary vagabond, a pest, and a tramp.

Now shrugging off his rags the wiliest fighter of the islands
leapt and stood on the broad doorsill, his own bow in his
    hand.
He poured out at his feet a rain of arrows from the quiver
and spoke to the crowd:

       "So much for that. Your clean-cut game is over.
1225   Now watch me hit a target that no man has hit before,
if I can make this shot. Help me, Apollo."°

He drew to his fist the cruel head of an arrow for Antinous
just as the young man leaned to lift his beautiful drinking
    cup,
embossed, two-handled, golden: the cup was in his fingers,
1230   the wine was even at his lips, and did he dream of death?
How could he? In that <u>revelry</u> amid his throng of friends
who would imagine a single foe—though a strong foe
    indeed—
could dare to bring death's pain on him and darkness on
    his eyes?
Odysseus' arrow hit him under the chin
1235   and punched up to the feathers through his throat.

Backward and down he went, letting the wine cup fall
from his shocked hand. Like pipes his nostrils jetted
crimson runnels,° a river of mortal red,
and one last kick upset his table
1240   knocking the bread and meat to soak in dusty blood.
Now as they craned to see their champion where he lay
the suitors jostled in uproar down the hall,
everyone on his feet. Wildly they turned and scanned
the walls in the long room for arms; but not a shield,

1221–1303. *As you read this action scene, imagine it as a film. After you finish reading, choose one part of the scene, and sketch it in your notebook. Make a list of the props you would need if you were filming the battle.*

1226. Help me, Apollo: Odysseus prays to Apollo because this particular day is one of the god's feast days. Apollo is also the god of archery.

1238. runnels (run'əlz) *n.:* streams.

Vocabulary
revelry (rev'əl·rē) *n.:* merrymaking; festivity.

1245　not a good ashen spear was there for a man to take and
　　　　　　throw.
　　　All they could do was yell in outrage at Odysseus:

"Foul! to shoot at a man! That was your last shot!"

"Your own throat will be slit for this!"

　　　　　　　　　"Our finest lad is down!

You killed the best on Ithaca."

　　　　　　　　"Buzzards will tear your eyes out!"

1250　For they imagined as they wished—that it was a wild shot,
　　　an unintended killing—fools, not to comprehend
　　　they were already in the grip of death.
　　　But glaring under his brows Odysseus answered:

　　　"You yellow dogs, you thought I'd never make it
1255　home from the land of Troy. You took my house to plunder,
　　　twisted my maids to serve your beds. You dared
　　　bid for my wife while I was still alive.
　　　Contempt was all you had for the gods who rule wide
　　　　　　heaven,
　　　contempt for what men say of you hereafter.
1260　Your last hour has come. You die in blood."

　　　As they all took this in, sickly green fear
　　　pulled at their entrails, and their eyes flickered
　　　looking for some hatch or hideaway from death.
　　　Eurymachus alone could speak. He said:

1265　"If you are Odysseus of Ithaca come back,
　　　all that you say these men have done is true.
　　　Rash actions, many here, more in the countryside.
　　　But here he lies, the man who caused them all.
　　　Antinous was the ringleader, he whipped us on
1270　to do these things. He cared less for a marriage
　　　than for the power Cronion° has denied him
　　　as king of Ithaca. For that
　　　he tried to trap your son and would have killed him.
　　　He is dead now and has his portion. Spare
1275　your own people. As for ourselves, we'll make
　　　restitution of wine and meat consumed,
　　　and add, each one, a tithe of twenty oxen
　　　with gifts of bronze and gold to warm your heart.
　　　Meanwhile we cannot blame you for your anger."

Suitor hiding behind a table: The return
of Odysseus. Limestone relief from
Turkey (380 B.C.).
Kunsthistorisches Museum,
Vienna, Austria.

1271. Cronion (krō′nē·ən): another
name for Zeus, meaning "son of
Cronus."

1280   Odysseus glowered under his black brows
and said:

> "Not for the whole treasure of your fathers,
> all you enjoy, lands, flocks, or any gold
> put up by others, would I hold my hand.
> There will be killing till the score is paid.

1285   You forced yourselves upon this house. Fight your way out,
or run for it, if you think you'll escape death.
I doubt one man of you skins by." . . .

*Telemachus joins his father in the fight. They are helped by the
swineherd and cowherd. Now the suitors, trapped in the hall without weapons, are struck right and left by arrows, and many of them
lie dying on the floor.*

Ulysses Slaying the Suitors (detail)
(1802) by Henry Fuseli.
© 2003 Kunsthaus Zurich.

1295. eyries (er**′**ēz) *n.:* nests built in
high places.

    At this moment that unmanning thundercloud,
the aegis, Athena's shield,
took form aloft in the great hall.

1290   And the suitors mad with fear
at her great sign stampeded like stung cattle by a river
when the dread shimmering gadfly strikes in summer,
in the flowering season, in the long-drawn days.
After them the attackers wheeled, as terrible as falcons
from eyries° in the mountains veering over and diving

1295   down
with talons wide unsheathed on flights of birds,
who cower down the sky in chutes and bursts along the
         valley—
but the pouncing falcons grip their prey, no frantic wing
         avails,
and farmers love to watch those beakèd hunters.

1300   So these now fell upon the suitors in that hall,
turning, turning to strike and strike again,
while torn men moaned at death, and blood ran smoking
over the whole floor. . . .

                                 (*from* Book 22)

*1221–1303. How does this
bloody episode relate to the epic's
theme about the value of hospitality and about what happens to
people who mock divine laws?*

Vocabulary
glowered (glou**′**ərd) *v.:* glared; stared angrily.
avails (ə·vālz**′**) *v.:* is of use; helps.

ODYSSEUS AND PENELOPE

*Odysseus now calls forth the maids who have betrayed his household by associat-
ing with the suitors. He orders them to clean up the house and dispose of the dead.
Telemachus then "pays" them by hanging them in the courtyard.*

*Eurycleia tells Penelope about the return of Odysseus and the defeat of the suit-
ors. The faithful wife—the perfect mate for the wily Odysseus—suspects a trick
from the gods. She decides to test the stranger who claims to be her husband.*

Crossing the doorsill she sat down at once
1305 in firelight, against the nearest wall,
across the room from the lord Odysseus.

           There

leaning against a pillar, sat the man
and never lifted up his eyes, but only waited
for what his wife would say when she had seen him.
1310 And she, for a long time, sat deathly still
in wonderment—for sometimes as she gazed
she found him—yes, clearly—like her husband,
but sometimes blood and rags were all she saw.
Telemachus's voice came to her ears:

           "Mother,

1315 cruel mother, do you feel nothing,
drawing yourself apart this way from Father?
Will you not sit with him and talk and question him?
What other woman could remain so cold?
Who shuns her lord, and he come back to her
1320 from wars and wandering, after twenty years?
Your heart is hard as flint and never changes!"

Penelope answered:

        "I am stunned, child.
I cannot speak to him. I cannot question him.
I cannot keep my eyes upon his face.
1325 If really he is Odysseus, truly home,
beyond all doubt we two shall know each other
better than you or anyone. There are
secret signs we know, we two."

           A smile

came now to the lips of the patient hero, Odysseus,
1330 who turned to Telemachus and said:

"Peace: let your mother test me at her leisure.
Before long she will see and know me best.

Penelope (1878) by Anthony
Frederick Augustus Sandys.
Colored chalk on paper.
Cecil Higgins Art Gallery, Bedford,
Bedfordshire, England.

> **1304.** *Make notes about
> Penelope as you read this episode.
> What might she be thinking?*

These tatters, dirt—all that I'm caked with now—
make her look hard at me and doubt me still. . . ."

*Odysseus orders Telemachus, the swineherd, and the cowherd to
bathe and put on fresh clothing.*

1335   Greathearted Odysseus, home at last,
        was being bathed now by Eurynome
        and rubbed with golden oil, and clothed again
        in a fresh tunic and a cloak. Athena
        lent him beauty, head to foot. She made him
1340   taller, and massive, too, with crisping hair
        in curls like petals of wild hyacinth
        but all red-golden. Think of gold infused
        on silver by a craftsman, whose fine art
        Hephaestus taught him, or Athena: one
1345   whose work moves to delight: just so she lavished
        beauty over Odysseus' head and shoulders.
        He sat then in the same chair by the pillar,
        facing his silent wife, and said:

                              "Strange woman,
        the immortals of Olympus made you hard,
1350   harder than any. Who else in the world
        would keep aloof as you do from her husband
        if he returned to her from years of trouble,
        cast on his own land in the twentieth year?

        Nurse, make up a bed for me to sleep on.
        Her heart is iron in her breast."

1355   Penelope
        spoke to Odysseus now. She said:

                              "Strange man,
        if man you are . . . This is no pride on my part
        nor scorn for you—not even wonder, merely.
        I know so well how you—how he—appeared
1360   boarding the ship for Troy. But all the same . . .

        Make up his bed for him, Eurycleia.
        Place it outside the bedchamber my lord
        built with his own hands. Pile the big bed
        with fleeces, rugs, and sheets of purest linen."

Penelope by John Roddam Spencer
Stanhope.
The De Morgan Foundation, London, UK.

Vocabulary
lavished (lav′isht) *v.:* gave generously.
aloof (ə·lōōf′) *adj.:* at a distance; unfriendly.

1365   With this she tried him to the breaking point,
and he turned on her in a flash, raging:

"Woman, by heaven you've stung me now!
Who dared to move my bed?
No builder had the skill for that—unless
1370   a god came down to turn the trick. No mortal
in his best days could budge it with a crowbar.
There is our pact and pledge, our secret sign,
built into that bed—my handiwork
and no one else's!

                          An old trunk of olive
1375   grew like a pillar on the building plot,
and I laid out our bedroom round that tree,
lined up the stone walls, built the walls and roof,
gave it a doorway and smooth-fitting doors.
Then I lopped off the silvery leaves and branches,
1380   hewed and shaped the stump from the roots up
into a bedpost, drilled it, let it serve
as model for the rest, I planed them all,
inlaid them all with silver, gold, and ivory,
and stretched a bed between—a <u>pliant</u> web
of oxhide thongs dyed crimson.

1385   There's our sign!
I know no more. Could someone else's hand
have sawn that trunk and dragged the frame away?"

Their secret! as she heard it told, her knees
grew <u>tremulous</u> and weak, her heart failed her.
1390   With eyes brimming tears she ran to him,
throwing her arms around his neck, and kissed him,
murmuring:

                "Do not rage at me, Odysseus!
No one ever matched your caution! Think
what difficulty the gods gave: they denied us
1395   life together in our prime and flowering years,
kept us from crossing into age together.
Forgive me, don't be angry. I could not
welcome you with love on sight! I armed myself
long ago against the frauds of men,
1400   impostors who might come—and all those many

> 📖 **1374–1384.** *This description of Odysseus and Penelope's bed is famous—and complex.* **Paraphrase** *Odysseus's description of the bed. What characteristics of the bed suggest the strength and endurance of their love?*

Vocabulary

pliant (plī′ənt) *adj.:* flexible.

tremulous (trem′yoo·ləs) *adj.:* trembling; shaking.

whose underhanded ways bring evil on! . . .
But here and now, what sign could be so clear
as this of our own bed?
No other man has ever laid eyes on it—
1405   only my own slave, Actoris, that my father
sent with me as a gift—she kept our door.
You make my stiff heart know that I am yours."

Now from his breast into his eyes the ache
of longing mounted, and he wept at last,
1410   his dear wife, clear and faithful, in his arms,
longed for
        as the sun-warmed earth is longed for by a swimmer
spent in rough water where his ship went down
under Poseidon's blows, gale winds and tons of sea.
Few men can keep alive through a big surf
1415   to crawl, clotted with brine, on kindly beaches
in joy, in joy, knowing the abyss behind:
and so she too rejoiced, her gaze upon her husband,
her white arms round him pressed, as though forever. . . .

(*from* Book 23)

1408–1418. *The journey ends with an embrace. What* **simile** *helps you understand the joy Odysseus feels in the arms of his wife?*

Penelope and Her Suitors (1912) by J. W. Waterhouse.

Ulysses Deriding Polyphem (detail) (19th century) by J.M.W. Turner. Oil on canvas.
Tate Gallery, London.

Ithaka

C. P. Cavafy

translated by Edmund Keeley
and Philip Sherrard

When you set out for Ithaka,
pray that your road's a long one,
full of adventure, full of discovery.
Laistrygonians, Cyclops,
5   angry Poseidon—don't be scared of them:
you won't find things like that on your way
as long as your thoughts are exalted,
as long as a rare excitement
stirs your spirit and your body.
10 Laistrygonians, Cyclops,
wild Poseidon—you won't encounter them
unless you bring them along inside you,
unless your soul raises them up in front of you.

Pray that your road's a long one.
15 May there be many a summer morning when—
full of gratitude, full of joy—
you come into harbors seen for the first time;
may you stop at Phoenician trading centers
and buy fine things,
20 mother-of-pearl and coral, amber and ebony,
sensual perfumes of every kind,
as many sensual perfumes as you can;
may you visit numerous Egyptian cities
to fill yourself with learning from the wise.

25 Keep Ithaka always in mind.
Arriving there is what you're destined for.
But don't hurry the journey at all.
Better if it goes on for years
so you're old by the time you reach the island,
30 wealthy with all you've gained on the way,
not expecting Ithaka to make you rich.
Ithaka gave you the marvelous journey.
Without her you wouldn't have set out.
She hasn't anything else to give.

35 And if you find her poor, Ithaka won't have
        fooled you.
Wise as you'll have become, and so
        experienced,
you'll have understood by then what an
        Ithaka means.

The Sea Call

Nikos Kazantzakis

translated by Kimon Friar

When Odysseus meets Teiresias in the underworld, the prophet tells him that he will reach home but will then take yet another journey to a land where people live who know nothing of the sea. (See pages 776–777.) In this excerpt from a modern sequel to the Odyssey *by the twentieth-century Greek poet Nikos Kazantzakis, Odysseus has returned to Ithaca. Sitting by the hearth with his family, his eyes alight with excitement, he relates his adventures. But then . . .*

Odysseus sealed his bitter lips and spoke no more,
but watched the glowering fire fade, the withering flames,
the ash that spread like powder on the dying coals,
then turned, glanced at his wife, gazed on his son and father,
5 and suddenly shook with fear and sighed, for now he knew
that even his native land was a sweet mask of Death.
Like a wild beast snared in a net, his eyes rolled round
and tumbled down his deep eye-sockets, green and bloodshot.
His tribal palace seemed a narrow shepherd's pen,
10 his wife a small and wrinkled old housekeeping crone,
his son an eighty-year-old drudge who, trembling, weighed
with care to find what's just, unjust, dishonest, honest,
as though all life were prudence, as though fire were just,
and logic the highest good of eagle-mounting man!
15 The heart-embattled athlete laughed, dashed to his feet,
and his home's sweetness, suddenly, his longed-for land,
the twelve gods, ancient virtue by his honored hearth,
his son—all seemed opposed now to his high descent.
The fire dwindled and died away, and the four heads
20 and his son's smooth-skinned calves with tender softness glowed
till in the trembling hush Penelope's wan cries
broke in despair like water flowing down a wall.
Her son dashed and stood upright by his mother's throne,
touched gently with a mute compassion her white arm,
25 then gazed upon his father in the dim light, and shuddered,
for in the last resplendence of the falling fire
he could discern the unmoving eyes flash yellow, blue,
and crimson, though the dark had swallowed the wild body.
With silent strides Odysseus then shot back the bolt,
30 passed lightly through the courtyard and sped down the street.
Some saw him take the graveyard's zigzag mountain path,
some saw him leap on rocks that edged the savage shore,
some visionaries saw him in the dead of night
swimming and talking secretly with the sea-demons,
35 but only a small boy saw him in a lonely dream
sit crouched and weeping by the dark sea's foaming edge.

from the Odyssey, Part Two

Reading Check

1. Describe Argos's condition when Odysseus sees him.

2. What is the contest of the bow, and how will Penelope reward the winner?

3. Just before trying the bow, Odysseus reveals himself to two people. Who are they? Why does he confide in them?

4. List at least five images or events from Odysseus's battle with the suitors.

5. How does Penelope test Odysseus after the battle?

Thinking Critically

6. What **Homeric simile** in lines 1031–1033 describes the feelings of Odysseus and his son as they embrace after twenty years? How would you describe exactly what the father and his son are feeling here?

7. **Situational irony** occurs when what happens is different from what we expect. Why is it ironic that Odysseus returns to his kingdom dressed as a beggar?

8. **Dramatic irony** refers to a situation in which readers know more than the characters know. Where in the scene in the swineherd's hut is there dramatic irony?

9. In epics it is rare for heroes to have relationships with ordinary people, but in the *Odyssey*, servants play important roles. How does Odysseus treat Eumaeus and the cowherd? What values might Homer be trying to teach through that treatment?

10. What **character traits** does Penelope reveal in her interactions with Odysseus disguised as a beggar?

11. What does the interaction between Odysseus and Penelope in lines 1348–1418 tell you about their relationship? Calypso wondered what it was about Penelope that drew Odysseus homeward (see page 754). Now that you've met Penelope, how would you answer Calypso?

12. The *Odyssey* is many centuries old. Do you think the feelings and needs shown by the people in the *Odyssey* are shared by people today? Which feelings does the speaker in "An Ancient Gesture" identify with (see the **Connection** on page 797)? Which experiences or people in this story did you identify with most? Why?

13. Suppose a modern general, like Odysseus, had fought a war for ten years and was missing for another ten years. What emotions might he (or she) have experienced upon returning home? What changes might he (or she) have found at home after twenty years? (Check your Quickwrite notes for page 789.)

14. In "Ithaka" (see the **Connection** on page 811), a modern Greek poet uses Ithaka as a **symbol,** a place that functions as itself in the poem but also stands for something beyond itself. Explain what you think "arriving in Ithaka" could mean for all of us.

Extending and Evaluating

15. Do you think Odysseus's revenge on the suitors and maids is excessive or too brutal? Explore this question from Odysseus's viewpoint (remember that he is the rightful king) and from your own modern viewpoint.

SKILLS FOCUS

Literary Skills
Analyze characteristics of epic poetry, including character traits.

Writing Skills
Discuss the hero's character traits in a brief essay. Write a continuation of the story. Write a story plan. Write a movie proposal. Discuss how the epic relates to life today in a brief essay.

WRITING

Choose from among the following assignments to respond to the *Odyssey:*

1. Noble or Not?

In a brief **essay,** discuss at least four of Odysseus's **character traits.** Find situations in the epic that reveal each trait. In your final paragraph, sum up your opinion of Odysseus's character. Do you think he is totally admirable? To what extent would he be considered a hero today?

2. Prophetic Puzzler

In Part One, lines 639–658 (page 777), Teiresias makes a famous prophecy: Odysseus will take off on yet another journey after he returns home. (For part of one writer's extension of the *Odyssey,* see "The Sea Call," the **Connection** on page 812.) What do you think happens to Odysseus after he takes back his kingdom? Write your own continuation of Odysseus's story based on Teiresias's prophecy.

3. Her Odyssey

Write a **story plan** showing how an odyssey could have a woman as its voyaging hero. You may set your story in any time and place, from Odysseus's Greece to your hometown today to a distant galaxy in the future. Consider these points in your plan:

- occupation of the hero; her reason for being away from home; her situation at home
- trials of her journey; how she deals with the "monsters" she meets
- what happens when she returns home

4. And Now—The Movie

Write a **proposal** in which you suggest ways that the *Odyssey* could be made into a movie—set in contemporary times. In your proposal, written for the people who will produce the movie, you will have to explain how you would modernize the *Odyssey.*

Write two or three paragraphs. Use a chart like the one below to organize your ideas:

1200 B.C.		Today
a.	Trojan War as a background	**a.**
b.	Hero is soldier who fought in war	**b.**
c.	Hero journeys home around Mediterranean and down to the underworld	**c.**
d.	Hero uses ships with oars and sails	**d.**
e.	Hero meets Lotus Eaters, Sirens, Scylla, and Charybdis	**e.**
f.	Hero is tempted by Circe and Calypso	**f.**
g.	Fortune hunters at home hound hero's wife	**g.**
h.	Hero's son is insulted	**h.**
i.	*Gods dominate the action*	**i.**

5. Timeless Messages

A work of literature becomes important to us when we feel that it relates to our lives. In a brief **essay,** discuss at least three ways in which the *Odyssey* relates to life today. You might consider what it says about these values:

- courtesy and respect for all groups of people
- courage, trust, and discipline
- loyalty to family and community
- obedience to law—human or divine

After You Read | Vocabulary Development

Synonyms

PRACTICE 1

Synonyms are words with similar meanings, such as *beast* and *monster*. You have to use synonyms with care since they do not always mean exactly the same thing. Create a chart like the one here, listing synonyms for each Word Bank word. Can you substitute the synonyms in the original sentence?

candor
Original Sentence: "Telemachus with his clear candor said . . ."
Synonyms: honesty, frankness, fairness, impartiality
Response to Substitutions: Here, *candor* describes a way of expressing oneself. *Frankness* works best. *Honesty* could also apply. Judgment is not involved, so *fairness* and *impartiality* don't work.

Epithets

An **epithet** (ep′ə·thet′) is an adjective or phrase used to characterize someone. *Catherine the Great* and *baby boomers* are epithets used to characterize an empress and a generation. Homer uses epithets as formulas to characterize places and people. The epithet "faithful Penelope" instantly reminds us of Penelope's outstanding character trait.

A Famous Epithet Mystery

One of Homer's famous epithets is "the wine-dark sea." Since wine is red or white or yellowish, and the sea is none of these hues, the description is puzzling. Some say that the ancient Greeks diluted their wine with water and that the alkali in the water changed the color of the wine from red to blue. Others think the sea was covered with red algae. Robert Fitzgerald, the great translator of the *Odyssey*, thought about the question when he was sailing on the Aegean Sea:

> "The contrast of the bare arid baked land against the sea gave the sea such a richness of hue that I felt as though we were sailing through a bowl of dye. The depth of hue of the water was like the depth of hue of a good red wine."

PRACTICE 2

1. Odysseus is called "versatile Odysseus," "wily Odysseus," "the strategist," and "the noble and enduring man." What does each underlined word mean?

2. Telemachus is called "clearheaded Telemachus." How would you define *clearheaded*? What is its opposite?

3. Dawn is described as "rosy-fingered." What does this epithet help you see?

4. Make up your own epithets for these characters: the Cyclops, Circe, Argos, Penelope, and the suitors.

SKILLS FOCUS

Vocabulary Skills
Understand synonyms.
Understand epithets.

Words from Greek and Roman Myths

Myths are stories associated with a particular society that are essentially religious. Myths often explain the mysteries of nature, the origins of rituals, and the relationships between gods and humans. Myths taught Homer's audiences important lessons about religion and conduct.

The Greek and Roman myths live on in the English language, as the charts below show. As we read the *Iliad* and the *Odyssey*, we come across names of gods, goddesses, mythical heroes, human heroes—and monsters and villains. Many English words have their origins in these names. For example, a long, difficult journey in search of something of value is called an *odyssey*, whether it be Alex Haley's odyssey in search of his African roots or a scientist's odyssey in search of the secrets of DNA.

Names from Greek and Roman Myths (and English Words That Derive from Them)			
Name	**English Word**	**Name**	**English Word**
aegis	aegis	Muses	museum; music
Ceres	cereal	Narcissus	narcissistic
Hector	hector	Olympia	Olympics
Jove	jovial	Siren	siren
Mars	martial	Tantalus	tantalize
Mentor	mentor	Titans	titanic
Mercury	mercury	Vulcan	volcano; vulcanize

Planets Named for Gods from Greek and Roman Myths	
Mercury	Saturn
Venus	Uranus
Mars	Neptune
Jupiter	Pluto

NASA Expeditions Named for Gods from Greek and Roman Myths	
Apollo	Mercury

PRACTICE 1

Read the following information, and answer the questions about words derived from the Greek myths and epics. To help you answer, look up the underlined words in a good dictionary.

1. Homer opens his epic poems with a prayer to the **Muse.** In mythology the nine Muses were goddesses who inspired people working in the arts and sciences. One word derived from the name Muse is *music.*

   How is the meaning of our word museum related to the Muses?

2. The **Sirens** were island creatures with enchanting female voices who lured sailors to steer their ships toward dangerous rocks.

   Why do you think the horn of an ambulance is called a siren?

3. The **aegis** (ē′jis) was the great shield of Zeus, king of the gods. Anyone who acted "under the aegis" had Zeus's power and support. Athena later carried the aegis (see the *Odyssey,* line 1289).

   What do we mean today when we say we live under the aegis of the Constitution?

SKILLS FOCUS

Vocabulary Skills
Understand words from Greek and Roman myths.

4. **Hector,** the oldest of Priam's sons in the *Iliad,* was the bravest Trojan hero, a great leader who loved his family. Hector didn't deserve the meaning that his name took on during the seventeenth century. The word *hector* came to be associated with the unpleasant act of bullying.

What do children do when they hector *others to get what they want?*

5. **Tantalus,** a mortal son of Zeus, was punished in Hades for having revealed his father's secrets. There he is forced to stand in water, with luscious fruit dangling over his head. Whenever he tries to drink the water or eat the fruit, he cannot reach them.

How is the word tantalize *related to Tantalus?*

6. **Narcissus,** son of a river god, was a handsome youth who was cold to all who loved him. To punish him, the gods doomed him to fall in love with his own reflection in the water. When Narcissus tried to embrace his beloved, the reflection in the water disappeared. After Narcissus died from grief, he was changed into a flower, which we call narcissus.

What kind of teenager might be called narcissistic?

PRACTICE 2

The ancient Romans adopted many Greek myths, but they changed Greek names to Latin ones. Read the following information about words derived from Roman myths, and answer the questions. Check your answers by looking up each underlined word in a good dictionary.

1. **Jove** was another name for the Roman god Jupiter (the Greek god Zeus). According to those who believe the stars and planets influence our lives, people who are born under the sign of the planet Jupiter are jovial.

Why is it fun to have a jovial *guest at your party?*

2. **Mars** was the Roman god of war (the Greek god Ares). To the Romans he was second in importance to Jove. The third month of the year is named in his honor, as is the fourth planet from the sun.

What happens when a peace-loving nation becomes martial?

3. **Vulcan** was the Roman god of fire and metalworking. A blacksmith, he created beautiful things and instruments of war. He lived under various mountains. When he worked, smoke and fire came out of the mountain.

How is our word volcano *related to Vulcan?*

4. **Ceres** was the Roman goddess of corn and grain, who also controlled fertility and the harvest. After Pluto (his Greek name was Hades) kidnapped her daughter, Proserpina (the Greek Persephone), Ceres was so stricken with grief that she caused crops to stop growing and let the earth become barren. When Proserpina, goddess of springtime, returns to Ceres for six months each year, the earth bears fruit again.

Why might people have given the name cereal *to a breakfast food?*

PRACTICE 3

Why are these names, based on the names of Greek and Roman gods and goddesses, appropriate?

1. Vulcan's Forge—a blacksmith shop

2. Mercury's Messengers—a delivery service

3. Ceres' Place—a vegetarian cafe

Where I Find My Heroes ◆ Heroes with Solid Feet

Evaluating an Author's Argument: Intent and Tone

Arguments can appeal to both our hearts and our minds—to both emotion and reason. Writers make **appeals to reason,** or **logic,** by supporting their opinions with objective evidence (such as facts and statistics). In contrast, **emotional appeals** (such as anecdotes and loaded words) can win readers' hearts, even though they do not offer objective evidence.

1. **What's the intent?** The author's **intent,** or **purpose,** determines which mix of logical and emotional appeals is appropriate. For example, a writer trying to convince us of the dangers of drunk driving would use an argument based mostly on **logical appeals.** A reliance on emotional appeals would suggest that the writer was unable to back up his or her ideas with hard evidence.

   However, a writer who wants us to see a personal, subjective issue—such as honor or love—in a new light would probably not use facts and statistics, which could seem cold and unfeeling. Instead, he or she would probably appeal more to our hearts than our minds, using the following **emotional appeals:**

   Anecdotes. Brief, often colorful stories that personalize an issue, anecdotes put a human face on cold facts. For example, a story about one firefighter's heroic rescue of a child is more powerful than statistics showing the number of lives saved by firefighters.

   Loaded words. Words like *hero, evil, victim,* and *freedom* have strong positive or negative **connotations,** or emotional associations. Loaded words work on our feelings. Writers must avoid overusing them because readers sense when their feelings are being manipulated.

2. **What's the tone?** The author's intent has a direct impact on **tone.** A serious subject demands a sober, objective tone. An attempt to inspire requires an uplifting, encouraging tone. A desire to entertain requires a humorous tone.

   Tone is created primarily through the author's choice of words. In addition to **loaded language, sensory images** and **figurative language** also contribute to tone by painting vivid pictures in readers' minds.

   As you read the following arguments, note each author's tone and the way he supports his argument.

Vocabulary Development

advocate (ad′və·kit) *n.:* supporter.

defers (dē·furz′) *v.:* delays; puts off.

emaciated (ē·mā′shē·āt′id) *adj.:* extremely thin; wasted away.

annihilate (ə·nī′ə·lāt′) *v.:* destroy completely.

emulate (em′yoo·lāt′) *v.:* follow the example of; imitate.

Connecting to the Literature

In Homer's *Odyssey,* Odysseus is a larger-than-life hero who does larger-than-life deeds. In the following nonfiction pieces, two highly successful film artists discuss the "little heroes" in our lives.

Where I Find My Heroes

from *McCall's Magazine*, November 1992

Oliver Stone

Oliver Stone became a movie director after serving in the Vietnam War. His films have explored historical subjects, such as the Vietnam War and President Kennedy's assassination.

It's not true that there are no heroes anymore—but it is true that my own concept of heroism has changed radically over time. When I was young and I read the Random House biographies, my heroes were always people like George Washington and General Custer[1] and Abraham Lincoln and Teddy Roosevelt. Men, generally, and doers. Women—with the exception of Clara Barton, Florence Nightingale, and Joan of Arc[2]—got short shrift.[3] Most history was oriented toward male heroes.

But as I've gotten older, and since I've been to war, I've been forced to reexamine the nature of life and of heroism. What is true? Where are the myths?

The simple acts of heroism are often overlooked—that's very clear to me not only in war but in peace. I'm not debunking[4] all of history: Crossing the Delaware[5] *was* a magnificent action. But I am saying that I think the meaning of heroism has a lot to do with evolving into a higher human being. I came into contact with it when I worked with Ron Kovic, the paraplegic[6] Vietnam vet, on *Born on the Fourth of July*. I was impressed by his life change, from a patriotic and strong-willed athlete to someone who had to deal with the total surrender of his body, who grew into a nonviolent and peaceful advocate of change in the Martin Luther King, Jr., and Gandhi[7]

---

1. **General Custer:** General George Armstrong Custer (1839–1876) was killed in a fierce battle against the Sioux and Cheyenne.
2. **Clara Barton** (1821–1912), **Florence Nightingale** (1820–1910), **and Joan of Arc** (1412–1431): Barton, a Civil War nurse, founded the Red Cross. Nightingale, an English nurse, is regarded as the founder of modern nursing. Joan of Arc led French troops to victory against the English during the Hundred Years' War.
3. **short shrift** *n.:* colloquial expression meaning "little time or attention."
4. **debunking** (dē·buŋk′iŋ) *v.:* discrediting something by exposing it as false or exaggerated.
5. **Crossing the Delaware:** On Christmas night in 1776, George Washington led soldiers from Valley Forge, Pennsylvania, across the Delaware River, surprising and defeating Hessian troops.
6. **paraplegic** (par′ə·plē′jik) *adj.:* having paraplegia, a condition in which a person loses sensation and movement in the lower half of the body.
7. **Gandhi:** Mohandas Gandhi (1869–1948) led India to independence from British rule using nonviolent resistance.

Vocabulary
advocate (ad′və·kit) *n.:* supporter.

tradition. So heroism *is* tied to an evolution of consciousness. . . .[8]

Since the war, I've had children, and I'm wrestling now with the everyday problems of trying to share my knowledge with them without overwhelming them. It's difficult to be a father, to be a mother, and I think that to be a kind and loving parent is an act of heroism. So there you go—heroes are everyday, common people. Most of what they do goes unheralded, unappreciated. And that, ironically, *is* heroism: not to be recognized.

Who is heroic? Scientists who spend years of their lives trying to find cures for diseases. The teenager who says no to crack. The inner-city kid who works at McDonald's instead of selling drugs. The kid who stands alone instead of joining a gang, which would give him an instant identity. The celebrity who remains modest and treats others with respect, or who uses his position to help society. The student who <u>defers</u> the immediate pleasure of making money and finishes college or high school. People who take risks despite fears. People in wheelchairs who don't give up. . . .

We have a lot of corruption in our society. But we mustn't assume that everything is always basely motivated. We should allow for the heroic impulse—which is to be greater than oneself, to try to find another version of oneself, to grow. That's where virtue comes from. And we must allow our young generation to strive for virtue, instead of ridiculing it.

---

8. **evolution of consciousness:** growth in awareness of one's self and one's role.

Vocabulary
defers (dē·furz′) *v.*: delays; puts off.

Saul Mendoza of the United States and Francesca Porcellato of Italy talk after the presentation of awards for winning competitions in the men's and women's Wheelchair Division of the New York City Marathon, November 4, 2001.

Berlin served as Germany's capital for most of the twentieth century. In 1933, the National Socialist German Workers Party, known as the Nazis, came to power, and Adolf Hitler became head of Germany. The Nazis began a series of discriminatory measures against Jews, which denied them rights given to other Germans. The Nazis eventually implemented what they called their Final Solution—confining Jews and other people considered undesirable in concentration camps, in which they were killed by gassing and other means or worked to death. By the end of World War II, over six million European Jews had perished in the Holocaust.

Kirk Douglas (1916–   ) is a Hollywood star known for his fiery performances in such roles as the artist Vincent van Gogh and Spartacus, a slave who led a rebellion against the Roman Empire. Like his father, Michael Douglas is an award-winning actor.

Heroes with Solid Feet

from *The New York Times*, April 23, 2001

Kirk Douglas

Beverly Hills, California

Recently, I journeyed to Berlin to accept the Golden Bear, a lifetime achievement award, from the Berlin Film Festival. Those awards make me smile—lifetime achievement? Is this the end? Not long ago my son Michael received a lifetime achievement award. If you last long enough, you may get dozens.

I accepted the Golden Bear because I was curious to see Berlin again. During my earlier visits there, the city had been divided by a wall.[1]

In a press conference at the film festival, one journalist asked loudly, "As a Jew, how does it affect you to be in Berlin?" A montage of pictures we have all seen raced through my mind. Shattering glass windows, Hitler salutes, Jews being herded into freight cars, piles of emaciated Jews, ovens, dark smoke coming out of chimneys.

"The last century has been a disaster," I said. "My generation did not do a good job—so many wars, so much killing and of course, here in Germany, the Holocaust, perhaps the worst crime of all, the attempt to annihilate a people as a final solution."

---

1. **divided by a wall:** reference to the wall built by the Communists in 1961 that separated Communist East Berlin and democratic West Berlin. The Berlin Wall was opened in 1989, when Germany was reunited under a democratic government.

Vocabulary

emaciated (ē·mā′shē·āt′id) *adj.*: extremely thin; wasted away.

annihilate (ə·nī′ə·lāt′) *v.*: destroy completely.

They were all listening.

"But I don't think children should be punished for the sins of their fathers. We should do all we can to give our children that chance."

The questioner persisted. "So why did you come back to Berlin?" I ignored him. But the question bothered me. I didn't know a proper reason for a Jew to be in Berlin.

The audience at the awards ceremony gave me a standing ovation when I gave my speech in German, a language I learned when I made two movies in Germany. The papers were filled with my smiling face. The television reports were very complimentary. That night my wife and I had a wonderful Wiener schnitzel[2]

2. **Wiener schnitzel** (vē′nər shnit′səl): German dish consisting of breaded veal cutlet.

with some friends and a Jewish friend of theirs, Inge Borck, who lived in Berlin throughout the war. She was such a happy person, smiling and laughing. But when I was told that her parents and grandparents had all been killed in the concentration camps, I blurted out, "So why do you stay in Berlin?"

Smiling, she gave me this answer: "I owe that to the little heroes."

"I don't understand," I said. With a sigh, she came over and sat closer.

"When the Gestapo[3] came to get them, my parents sent me to a small hotel to save my life. The owner was the first little hero. She kept me safe for a couple of nights.

3. **Gestapo** (gə·stä′pō): Nazi secret police.

The plaques in the Garden of the Righteous, in Israel, honor non-Jews who risked their lives to help Jews during the Holocaust.

During World War II, the Danish people helped more than seven thousand Jews escape the Nazis by smuggling them to Sweden. This boat was used in the rescue operation.

When it became dangerous, I met my second little hero. Or should I say heroine? She was our former housekeeper. She hid me for a while and endangered her own life. Then I lived in a cloister.[4] My little heroes were the nuns who took care of me when I was very sick. They never asked questions. When the situation became dangerous, my next little hero was a policeman who didn't agree with the Nazis. All through the war, I was lucky to find little heroes who helped me till the Russians came in."[5]

"So, why do you stay here?" I asked again. She looked at my perplexed face and said, "I thought about it, but I feel I owe it to the little heroes who helped me. Not everyone here was wicked."

Her story had a great impact on me. Of course, we are always looking for a big hero to emulate, and very often we see them topple from clay feet.[6] How much better to reach for the little heroes in life—and to try to be one. It's not always as hard as it was for the people in wartime Berlin. You aren't obligated to save a life—you only need to try to help other people.

And if everyone tried—well, just think of the lifetime achievements.

---

4. **cloister** (klois′tər) *n.*: place where a religious group, such as a group of nuns or monks, lives apart from the rest of society.
5. **Russians came in:** In the spring of 1945, Germany was defeated by British, United States, and Russian troops, ending World War II.

6. **topple from clay feet:** *Clay feet* is a figurative expression that refers to heroes who are discredited when their weaknesses are revealed. A statue in which the feet are made of clay, which can crumble easily, will not stand for long.

Vocabulary
emulate (em′yŏŏ·lāt′) *v.*: follow the example of; imitate.

Reading Check

1. What kinds of heroes does Oliver Stone say he had when he was young?

2. What is the **main idea** of "Where I Find My Heroes"?

3. What was Kirk Douglas's response when asked why he returned to Berlin?

4. Who is Inge Borck, and who were the "little heroes" she told Douglas about?

Test Practice

1. Oliver Stone's **intent, or purpose,** in writing "Where I Find My Heroes" is to —
   - **A** show how heroic he is
   - **B** praise Ron Kovic's heroism
   - **C** convince us of his vision of heroism
   - **D** publicize his movies

2. Which word *best* describes the **tone** of Oliver Stone's essay?
   - **F** uplifting
   - **G** concerned
   - **H** humorous
   - **J** angry

3. Kirk Douglas uses an **anecdote** when he —
   - **A** describes what happened at the Berlin Film Festival
   - **B** tells why he accepted the Golden Bear award
   - **C** explains that he learned German while making movies in Germany
   - **D** says everyone should try to be a "little hero"

4. Kirk Douglas uses **loaded words** in which of the following items?
   - **F** "If you last long enough, you may get dozens."
   - **G** "Jews being herded into freight cars, piles of emaciated Jews, ovens, dark smoke coming out of chimneys."
   - **H** "I didn't know a proper reason for a Jew to be in Berlin."
   - **J** " 'So, why do you stay here?' I asked again."

5. Douglas's **purpose, or intent,** in writing his op-ed article is to —
   - **A** persuade people never to forget the Holocaust
   - **B** prove that he was right to go to Berlin
   - **C** point out the importance of small acts of heroism
   - **D** explain how traditional heroes have clay feet

Constructed Response

SKILLS FOCUS

Reading Skills
Evaluate an author's argument, including intent and tone.

Select either Oliver Stone's essay or Kirk Douglas's op-ed article, and write an **evaluation** of the author's argument. First, explain the writer's **purpose, or intent,** and the main **opinion, or claim,** the writer is defending. Then, describe the means of support the author uses (facts, examples, loaded words, anecdotes, and so forth). Next, describe the **tone** of the piece. Finally, comment on how successful the author was in convincing you with his argument. Was your heart touched? Your mind? Both?

Word Knowledge: Using Context

PRACTICE 1

Use context clues in each sentence to help you fill in each blank with the appropriate word from the Word Bank.

1. Years of poor nutrition made the refugees weak and _____.
2. I always try to _____ people whom I admire, but I don't always succeed.
3. Sandra always _____ having fun after school until she has finished her homework.
4. There are laws to protect endangered species so that humans do not _____ certain animals.
5. Malcolm became an enthusiastic _____ of exercise after he started running and going to the gym regularly.

Word Bank

advocate
defers
emaciated
annihilate
emulate

Understanding Idioms

An **idiom** is an expression peculiar to a particular language that means something different from the literal meaning of its words. Kirk Douglas uses the idiom *clay feet,* which refers to a hero who is found to have hidden faults. The expression comes from the idea that a statue with clay feet will topple, since clay can easily crack and crumble.

Other common idioms include *a fish out of water* ("out of one's element"), *cry wolf* ("give a false alarm," based on a fable by Aesop), and *long in the tooth* ("somewhat old," based on judging a horse's age by the length of its teeth).

PRACTICE 2

Explain the meaning of each underlined idiom in the following sentences. Then, explain where you think each expression may have come from.

1. "Hold your horses," the teacher said. "The class hasn't been dismissed yet."
2. Sally is a couch potato who does nothing but watch television.
3. "Step on it!" called her mother. "You're going to be late for school!"
4. Natasha sent her letter to the editor by both e-mail and snail mail.
5. Pavel was star-struck after meeting the best surfer on the beach.

SKILLS FOCUS

Vocabulary Skills
Use words in context.
Understand idioms.

Before You Read

The Fenris Wolf

Make the Connection

Quickwrite ✏️

How do you feel when you hear someone talk about wolves or serpents? Note whether you associate each creature with good or with evil. Then, write down why you think you have formed these associations.

Literary Focus

Myths

Every society has its **myths,** stories that are connected to the traditions and religion of the culture that produced them. Myths tell people where they came from, where they are going, and how they should live. Myths predate science: They often provide imaginative explanations for the origins of things. They answer questions like *Why is there evil in the world?* or *Why do we die?* or *Why do the seasons change?*

Many archetypes (är′kə·tīps′) come from myths. **Archetypes** are very old patterns or images that recur over and over again in literature. Archetypes can be characters (such as the sacrificial hero), plots (such as the heroic quest), animals (such as lambs, wolves, and serpents), or settings (such as the place of perfect happiness).

In this myth you will find the archetype of the "big bad wolf." You will also find the archetype of the sacrificial hero—a hero who sacrifices himself or herself for the greater good.

Reading Skills 📖

Identifying Cause and Effect

Myths are narratives, which are built on a series of causes and effects. One event happens in a narrative, which causes another event to happen, which causes another event to happen, and so on. To keep track of causes and their effects, make a chart like the one below:

Background

Norse Mythology

"The Fenris Wolf" is a story from Norse mythology, the system of myths that developed thousands of years ago among the peoples of Scandinavia and Germany. The oldest surviving written versions of these tales came from Iceland in the thirteenth century. One collection, *The Elder Edda,* consists of poems compiled by an unknown person. The other collection, *The Younger Edda,* was written down by Snorri Sturluson, a wealthy and cultured man who was politically active in both Iceland and Norway. The tale of Fenris, or Fenrir as he is sometimes called, is found in Snorri Sturluson's collection.

There are variations in the Norse myths, as there are in the myths of most cultures. According to one version of the Norse creation story, life began in the boundary between fire and ice. Eventually, the first gods were born from a family of giants. These gods include those listed on the opposite page. Odin, Ve, and Vili created the earth and the first man and woman. They also created **Asgard** (äs′gärd′), where the gods live, and **Midgard** (mid′gärd′), where humans live.

One of the most remarkable and tragic aspects of Norse mythology is its bleak prophecy about how the world will end. In this prophecy, giants and monsters led by the evil god Loki will do battle with the other gods and goddesses. All the gods and goddesses, giants, and monsters will slay each other, and the entire earth will be consumed by fire. This final struggle is called **Ragnarok** (rag′nə · räk′).

However, Norse mythology does contain a faint glimmer of hope. The myths contain a prophecy that a new world will be created, free of misery and evil, following the destruction.

Norse Gods

Odin (ō′din): also known as **Woden** (wōd′′n), god of wisdom and victory; leader of the family of gods.

Ve (vā) and **Vili** (vil′ē): Odin's brothers.

Frigga (frig′ə) or **Frigg** (frig): Odin's wife, goddess of marriage and motherhood.

Thor (thôr): Odin's oldest son, god of thunder and lightning.

Balder (bôl′dər): Odin and Frigga's son, god of goodness and harmony; the most beautiful of the gods.

Tyr (tir) or **Tiu** (tē′oō): god of war; the bravest of the gods.

Loki (lō′kē): god of fire, mischief, and evil.

Frey (frā), or **Freyr** (frār): god of sun, rain, and harvests.

Freya (frā′ə): Frey's sister, goddess of love and fertility.

Bragi (brä′gē): god of poetry, eloquence, and music.

A CLOSER LOOK
Norse Mythology

The world of Norse mythology is a strange world. Asgard, the home of the gods, is unlike any other heaven men have dreamed of. No radiancy of joy is in it, no assurance of bliss. It is a grave and solemn place, over which hangs the threat of an inevitable doom. The gods know that a day will come when they will be destroyed . . . Asgard will fall in ruins. The cause the forces of good are fighting to defend against the forces of evil is hopeless. Nevertheless, the gods will fight for it to the end.

Necessarily the same is true of humanity. If the gods are finally helpless before evil, men and women must be more so. The heroes and heroines of the early stories face disaster. They know that they cannot save themselves, not by any courage or endurance or great deed. Even so, they do not yield. They die resisting. A brave death entitles them—at least the heroes—to a seat in Valhalla, one of the halls in Asgard, but there too they must look forward to final defeat and destruction. In the last battle between good and evil they will fight on the side of the gods and die with them.

This is the conception of life which underlies the Norse religion, as somber a conception as the mind of man has ever given birth to. The only sustaining support possible for the human spirit, the one pure unsullied good men can hope to attain, is heroism; and heroism depends on lost causes. The hero can prove what he is only by dying. The power of good is shown, not by triumphantly conquering evil, but by continuing to resist evil while facing certain defeat.

—Edith Hamilton, from *Mythology*

THE FENRIS WOLF

A NORSE MYTH

RETOLD BY OLIVIA COOLIDGE

The Norse god Tyr and the Fenris Wolf. Manuscript.

Though Loki, the fire god, was handsome and ready-witted, his nature was really evil. He was, indeed, the cause of most of the misfortunes which befell the gods. He was constantly in trouble, yet often forgiven because the gods valued his cleverness. It was he who found ways out of difficulty for them, so that for a long time they felt that they could not do without him.

In the early days Loki, though a god, had wedded a monstrous giantess, and the union of these two evil beings produced a fearful brood. The first was the great world serpent, whom Odin cast into the sea, and who became so large that he completely encircled the earth, his tail touching his mouth. The second was Hel, the grisly goddess of the underworld, who reigned in the horrible land of the dead. The third was the most dreadful of all, a huge monster called the Fenris Wolf.

When the gods first saw the Fenris Wolf, he was so young that they thought they could tame him. They took him to Asgard, therefore, and brave Tyr undertook to feed and train him. Presently, however, the black monster grew so enormous that his open jaws would stretch from heaven to earth, showing teeth as large as the trunks of oak trees and as sharply pointed as knives. The howls of the beast were so dreadful as he tore his vast meals of raw meat that the gods, save for Tyr, dared not go near him, lest he devour them.

At last all were agreed that the Fenris Wolf must be fettered[1] if they were to save their very lives, for the monster grew more ferocious towards them every day. They forged a huge chain, but since none was strong enough to bind him, they challenged him to a trial of strength. "Let us tie you with this to see if you can snap the links," said they.

The Fenris Wolf took a look at the chain and showed all his huge white teeth in a dreadful grin. "Bind me if you wish," he growled, and he actually shut his eyes as he lay down at ease to let them put it on.

The gods stepped back, and the wolf gave a little shake. There was a loud cracking sound, and the heavy links lay scattered around him in pieces. The wolf howled in triumph until the sun and moon in heaven trembled at the noise.

Thor, the smith,[2] called other gods to his aid, and they labored day and night at the second chain. This was half as strong again as the first, and so heavy that no one of the gods could drag it across the ground. "This is by far the largest chain that was ever made," said they. "Even the Fenris Wolf will not be able to snap fetters such as these."

Once more they brought the chain to the wolf, and he let them put it on, though this time it was clear that he somewhat doubted his strength. When they had chained him, he shook himself violently, but the fetters held. His great, red eyes burned with fury, the black hair bristled on his back, and he gnashed his teeth until the foam flew. He strained heavily against the iron until the vast links flattened and lengthened, but did not break. Finally with a great bound and a howl he dashed himself against the ground, and suddenly the chain sprang apart so violently that broken pieces were hurled about the heads of the watching gods.

Now the gods realized in despair that all their strength and skill would not avail to bind the wolf. Therefore Odin sent a messenger to the dwarf people under the earth, bidding them forge him a chain. The messenger returned with

> The wolf howled in triumph until the sun and moon in heaven trembled at the noise.

---

1. **fettered** (fet′ərd) *v.*: chained.

2. **smith** *n.*: blacksmith, someone who works at a forge, making and repairing metal objects, such as horseshoes.

a little rope, smooth and soft as a silken string, which was hammered on dwarfish anvils[3] out of strange materials which have never been seen or heard. The sound of a cat's footfall, the breath of a fish, the flowing beard of a woman, and the roots of a mountain made the metal from which it was forged.

The gods took the tiny rope to the Fenris Wolf. "See what an easy task we have for you this time," they said.

"Why should I bother myself with a silken string?" asked the wolf sullenly. "I have broken your mightiest chain. What use is this foolish thing?"

"The rope is stronger than it looks," answered they. "We are not able to break it, but it will be a small matter to you."

"If this rope is strong by enchantment," said the wolf in slow suspicion, "how can I tell that you will loosen me if I cannot snap it after all? On one condition you may bind me: You must give me a hostage from among yourselves."

"How can we do this?" they asked.

---

3. **anvils** (an'vəlz) *n.:* iron or steel blocks on which hot metal objects are hammered into shape.

The Fenris Wolf stretched himself and yawned until the sun hid behind clouds at the sight of his great, red throat. "I will let you bind me with this rope," he said, "if one of you gods will hold his hand between my teeth while I do it."

The gods looked at one another in silence. The wolf grinned from ear to ear. Without a word Tyr walked forward and laid his bare hand inside the open mouth.

The gods bound the great wolf, and he stretched himself and heaved as before. This time, however, he did not break his bonds. He gnashed his jaws together, and Tyr cried out in pain as he lost his hand. Nevertheless, the great black wolf lay howling and writhing and help-lessly biting the ground. There he lay in the bonds of the silken rope as long as the reign of Odin endured. The Fates declared, however, that in the last days, when the demons of ice and fire should come marching against the gods to the battlefield, the great sea would give up the serpent, and the Fenris Wolf would break his bonds. The wolf would swallow Odin, and the gods would go down in defeat. Sun and moon would be devoured, and the whole earth would perish utterly. ■

Meet the Writer

Olivia Coolidge

A Reteller of Tales

Olivia Coolidge (1908–   ) is best known for her retellings of the myths from ancient Greece, specifically aimed at young adults. Her interest in ancient legends has been evident from the beginning of her ca-reer. One of her earliest works, *Legends of the North,* is a collection of the Norse myths that contains "The Fenris Wolf" and other strange tales of the Northern gods, includ-ing the Norse creation myth and stories of the great Norse heroes. Coolidge has writ-ten about people from the distant past—ancient Egypt and Rome, for example—and from more recent historical periods as well. Her biographies of such figures as Abraham Lincoln, Tom Paine, and Gandhi, written for young adults, have been highly praised.

Reading Check

1. In a chart like the one below, outline the story as a series of **causes** and their **effects**. The first event and the final event are listed for you. Use as many boxes as you need to chart the causes and effects that lead from the first event to the final one.

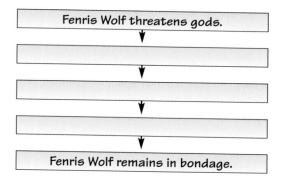

Fenris Wolf threatens gods.
↓
↓
↓
↓
Fenris Wolf remains in bondage.

Thinking Critically

2. Traditional folk and mythic literature often includes events that happen in threes. What event takes place three times in this myth? What is the result of the third event?

3. **Compare** and **contrast** the Fenris Wolf and his father, Loki. Remember to consider their relationship with the gods.

4. In Norse mythology, heroes face terrible enemies with great courage—even though they know they will be defeated in the end. What action in this myth shows that kind of heroic behavior?

5. In Norse mythology the dwarfs who live under Midgard have great cunning and skill. What is their rope made of? What do all these ingredients have in common? Why can't the Fenris Wolf break their rope?

6. This story is dramatically visual. What **similes** does the storyteller use to help you imagine the wolf's teeth?

What vivid **images** help you picture the Fenris Wolf?

7. The third binding of the Fenris Wolf is successful, yet the myth ends tragically. How does the story's ending reflect the bleak outlook of Norse mythology?

WRITING

Evildoers

In literature, wolves and serpents are often demonized—that is, they are associated with sneaky behavior, evil, and destruction. In a brief **essay,** explain why you think wolves and snakes are presented in a negative way. In your first paragraph, describe how wolves and serpents are usually presented, and give examples from stories you know. In your second paragraph, discuss why wolves and serpents might have gotten such bad reputations. You can **research** the wolf and the serpent on the Internet or in an encyclopedia. (Check your Quickwrite notes.)

Monsters and Endings

The Norse myth "The Fenris Wolf" and the Greek epic the *Odyssey* come from different traditions and different parts of the world. They have many similarities—for example, monsters with amazing powers are important in both works. The two works also have many differences. The Greek epic ends happily, while the Norse myth, true to Norse tradition, ends tragically, with a reference to the destruction of the earth. In a few paragraphs, **compare** and **contrast** both the role of monsters in the two works and the stories' endings. Be sure to include details to support your points.

Words from Norse Myths

The English language that we speak today has been enriched over the years by contributions from many languages, among them German, Latin, Greek, French, and Spanish. Old English, the ancestor of our modern English, was the language spoken by Anglo-Saxon tribes who migrated to England from areas in what are now Germany, Denmark, and other northern European countries. Because they originated in northern Europe, the Anglo-Saxon people shared much of the culture from which Norse mythology sprang. In modern English we still use many terms that derive from that ancient culture.

PRACTICE 1

1. Four of our weekdays are named for gods from Norse mythology. Look at the following list of Norse gods. Which days of the week are named for these gods? Use a dictionary to check your answers.

   a. Odin, or Woden   **c.** Tyr, or Tiu
   b. Frigga (or Frigg)   **d.** Thor

2. What is the origin of the names of the other days of the week? Look up *Monday, Saturday,* and *Sunday* in a dictionary. Then, write one or two sentences explaining the **origin,** or **derivation,** of each name. (For help researching word origins, see page 54.)

PRACTICE 2

Refer to the story and to a dictionary for help answering the following questions:

1. What Norse name is our word *hell* related to?

2. What Norse god gave us our word *thunder?*

Thor with his magic hammer.

SKILLS FOCUS

Vocabulary Skills
Understand words from Norse myths.

FICTION

Wealth at a Price

In the tiny village of La Plata, a fisherman, Kino, is doing his best to support his wife, Juana, and their baby son, Coyotito—but times are tough, and money is scarce. Kino's discovery of a valuable pearl seems to be the answer to all his prayers. The only trouble is that everyone else in his village thinks so too, and Kino must make a perilous escape from would-be thieves in order to protect his family and his fortune. John Steinbeck's novella **The Pearl** is a heart-rending moral tale of greed and its consequences.

FICTION

Tales from Greece and Rome

The author Edith Hamilton was one of our leading experts on classical myths, and her love of the subject can be found on every page of her collection **Mythology.** Most of the best-known Roman, Greek, and Norse myths are here—from the labors of Hercules to Jason's quest to the triumph of Perseus. Odysseus's long travels are also included, as are tales of Odin, Thor, and Loki. Hamilton's brisk retellings make each story an adventure with glorious heroes and monstrous villains.

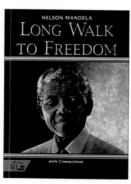

NONFICTION

A True-Life Epic

Long Walk to Freedom by Nelson Mandela is an inspiring chronicle of a man who fought to put an end to apartheid, the official policy of racial segregation and discrimination against blacks in South Africa. Mandela, whose humanitarian activism resulted in a twenty-seven-year imprisonment, wrote much of this autobiography while behind bars. His story is an epic journey that begins with Mandela's country childhood and ends with his winning the presidency in South Africa's first multiracial election.

This title is available in the HRW Library.

NONFICTION

Another Odyssey at Sea

Kon-Tiki is a real-life adventure story with a suspenseful plot that rivals anything in fiction or in film. Thor Heyerdahl journeyed 4,300 nautical miles across the Pacific Ocean—supported by nothing more than a handmade balsa-wood raft. Read this now-classic tale of Heyerdahl's voyage, and relive the dangers that threatened the Kon-Tiki crew: encounters with strange "monsters," leaks in the raft, and life-or-death struggles with a treacherous sea.

Persuading with Cause and Effect

Writing Assignment
Write an essay in which you examine the causes and effects of a situation and persuade the reader to take action to change it.

In the *Odyssey,* when Calypso tries to persuade Odysseus to remain with her, she explains the effects Odysseus will suffer if he leaves her island. If you were to use the same persuasive technique, you probably would want to be more successful than Calypso was with Odysseus. However, what *can* you do if you find yourself in a situation that you think needs to be changed? You might first want to ask yourself: "What caused this situation to happen? What effects will this situation have?" Then, ask: "What actions would fix this situation?"

Prewriting

Choose a Situation

Wanted: Change Agents Change agents are people who make things happen, often by persuading others to take action to change situations. By writing a **persuasive cause-and-effect essay,** you can become a change agent. To find a possible topic, create an *If-Then* log by looking at the world around you and asking yourself, *"If 'X' occurred, then* what would happen?" Next, consider the effects of the situation and the actions that might result in change. You might also brainstorm with other students about local situations or problems.

Make a list of promising topics for your persuasive paper. Then, review your list and choose the topic that you find most interesting and that might inspire the strongest response in your readers.

Consider Purpose, Audience, and Tone

Part of the Solution The **purpose** of your essay is both expository and persuasive; that is, you will *explain* the cause and effects of a situation to readers in order to *convince* them to take action. However, simply explaining the cause and effects of a situation may not motivate your readers. They also need to know a specific action they can take to correct or change the situation, and be persuaded to take that action.

In order to write persuasively about the action, you need to understand what your **audience**—your readers—will need and want to know. Ask yourself: "How much do my readers already know about the situation?" and "What are my readers' concerns or biases about the

Writing Skills
Write a persuasive cause-and-effect essay. Consider purpose, audience, and tone.

situation?" Knowing generally who your readers are and what reactions to expect from them can help you address any objections—or **counterclaims**—they may make. Addressing those objections in your essay will make your arguments more persuasive.

Your choice of words, details, and sentence structure express the **tone** of your writing—your attitude toward your subject and your audience. For most audiences, use a slightly formal tone so they will take your ideas seriously.

Analyze the Cause and Effects

What Happened and So What? The situation you've chosen is most likely part of a larger cause-effect relationship; that is, the situation has been caused by some previous action or decision. Ask yourself: "What is the initial *cause* of the situation I've chosen?" Analyze that cause so that you can explain to your readers why the situation or problem exists in the first place.

Next, turn your attention to the *effects* of the situation. When you write persuasively using cause and effect, you want your readers to agree that the situation you're describing needs to be changed. Therefore, think about the two or three most significant effects resulting from your situation. Those effects are probably negative ones; that's why there is a need for change.

Gather and Evaluate Evidence

Here's Why To be persuasive, provide precise and relevant **evidence** that supports your explanation of the cause and effects, and structure that evidence in a logical fashion. Evidence provides the proof your reader needs to accept your opinion. The following guide shows the kinds of supporting evidence you can use in your essay.

KINDS OF SUPPORTING EVIDENCE

Expert opinions are statements made by an authority on a subject.

Quotations present a person's word-for-word statement on a topic.

Facts are statements that can be proven true; **statistics** are facts in number form.

Anecdotes are brief stories that illustrate general ideas.

Commonly held beliefs are ideas that most people share.

A **case study** is an individual example used as the basis for generalizations.

An **analogy** is an explanation of something that readers do not know in terms of something familiar to them.

SKILLS FOCUS

Writing Skills
Structure ideas and arguments in a logical fashion. Use supporting evidence.

Look at the following notes one student made. Notice how the evidence supports the effect the student lists.

Effect: Heavy backpacks will cause health problems in students.

Evidence: A local chiropractor reports an increase in the number of students complaining of back and shoulder pain due to back-packs. (expert opinion)

A Matter of Appeal When you propose changes that you want your readers to adopt, you'll write persuasively, shaping your explanations and evidence with **rhetorical devices,** such as logical, emotional, or ethical appeals. To be convincing, use one or a combination of all three kinds of appeals within your essay. For example, look at the way one student experimented with the three different appeals to shape an explanation of a negative effect.

Effect: Health problems for students

Logical Appeal	Statistic showing the weight of a student's backpack and the resulting muscle strain
Emotional Appeal	Description of a student's chronic back pain from a heavy backpack
Ethical Appeal	Statement about the school's responsibility to maintain the physical well-being of the student in areas besides sports

Write Your Opinion Statement

DO THIS

Sound Off To voice your opinion, write an **opinion statement** to share your perspective on the changes needed for a situation. An opinion statement lets your readers know how you feel about the situation, and hints at the effects you will discuss.

Decide on a Call to Action

Do What I Say! After explaining the cause and effects of your situation, urge your readers to take action to improve the situation. To be convincing, address your readers' counterclaims, and clearly state the actions you think are necessary for changing the situation. You may want to give the readers a choice between two courses of action. For example, the student writing about heavy backpacks proposed that the school administration either reinstall school lockers or issue an extra set of textbooks for each classroom.

SKILLS FOCUS

Writing Skills
Establish your opinion statement.

PRACTICE & APPLY 1

Use the information on these pages to plan a persuasive cause-and-effect essay.

Writing

Persuading with Cause and Effect

A Writer's Framework

Introduction

- Begin with a bold statement or anecdote.

- Provide background information for the situation if necessary.

- Include a clear opinion statement. Indicate how you feel about the situation and hint at the effects you will discuss.

Body

- Explain the cause and the effects of the situation.

- Use persuasive appeals—logical, emotional, and ethical.

- Use evidence as support—facts, statistics, anecdotes, expert opinions, logical reasoning, or commonly accepted beliefs.

Conclusion

- Propose a specific call to action.

- Address any counterclaims a reader may have to your call to action.

- Restate your essay's opinion statement.

- End with a strong statement.

A Writer's Model

The highlighted words below indicate cause and effect.

A Weighty Case

Crowds of students once streamed toward Smith High School just before the first bell, headed for their lockers to deposit their bulging backpacks. However, now they are out of luck. Now there is no rest for the weary and heavy-laden at Smith High School, where lockers have been removed by school administrators because of their concerns about crowded hallways and tardiness. As a result, Smith High School students carry their heavy backpacks all day—an unfortunate situation that will cause other serious problems for students and should be changed.

According to a school announcement, the decision to remove the lockers was prompted by congested hallways. During every passing period between classes, clumps of students filled the halls so that other students could not get to class on time. Tardiness had become a real issue for the administration and teachers. The school administration's answer was to remove the lockers from the high school.

Without lockers, students have been forced to carry heavy backpacks all day. This situation creates not only an inconvenience, but also a health risk. A recent study shows that carrying an overloaded backpack can result in serious muscle strain in a student's

INTRODUCTION
Anecdote

Background information

Opinion statement

BODY
Description of cause

Effect 1: Logical appeal

Evidence: Case study

(continued)

(continued)

Evidence: Expert
opinion

Evidence: Quotation

Evidence: Statistics

Ethical appeal

Effect 2: Emotional
appeal

Evidence: Example

Emotional appeal
CONCLUSION
Call to action

Counterclaim
addressed

Another call
to action

Commonly held
belief

Restatement of
opinion
Final statement

back and shoulders. Alexa Nuñez, a local chiropractor, reports an increase in the number of high school students who suffer from back and neck pain caused by carrying heavy backpacks. She says, "Students are carrying heavy backpacks slung over one shoulder and increasing their risk of injury." Nuñez also says that the American Chiropractic Association recommends that a backpack should weigh no more than 10 percent of the student's body weight, or no more than 15 pounds. A backpack full of textbooks and supplies, however, weighs 25 or 30 pounds. Asking students to carry this weight all day means ignoring basic health guidelines.

Besides the harm caused by carrying these backpacks, there is an additional danger once students get to class. Because a stuffed backpack cannot fit under a desk, it ends up jamming the aisle. As a result, students and teachers cannot move freely around the classroom, and they may trip and fall. In case of a fire or even a fire drill, what if a student stumbles on a backpack, falls, and smashes her head? In the rush to escape, what if no one notices her? Is this a risk that Smith High administrators are willing to take?

Because of the hardships imposed on students by the school administration's decision, I ask for one of the following actions. First, I urge the school administration to reconsider its decision and restore the lockers for student use at least before school, during lunch, and after school. If students used their lockers at these times, they would not fill the halls during the passing periods, risk being tardy, or jam the aisles. The students would have to carry only half of their day's required books and perhaps cut the weight of their backpacks in half. Second, if the school cannot reinstall the lockers for some reason, I request that the school remedy the situation with a widely discussed and widely used method: Issue two sets of textbooks—one for the classroom and one for home. Everyone is concerned about student health, but the school should not expose students to real health risks in order to prevent possible, but highly unlikely, risks. Removing the lockers was a mistake because of the problems it has created for the students. To correct its mistake, Smith High School should reinstall the lockers or issue another set of textbooks for each student.

INTERNET

More Writer's
Models
Keyword: LE7 9-10

PRACTICE & APPLY 2 Write the first draft of your essay, using the framework and Writer's Model as guides. Remember to explain the cause and effects of the situation you have chosen and to use persuasive appeals.

Revising

Evaluate and Revise Your Draft

Checking It Twice If you are urging an audience to accept both your evaluation of a situation and your call to action, you'll want to present your explanation and persuasion in the best manner possible. Since errors detract from your presentation, try to read through your paper at least twice. If you have time, set your paper aside so that you can look at it with fresh eyes. Then, use the guidelines below to evaluate and revise your draft for content and organization. Use the guidelines on page 840 to revise for style, making sure you have used plenty of **cause-effect clue words.**

First Reading: Content and Organization Use the chart below to evaluate the content and organization of your essay. Answer the evaluation questions. Then, use the tips to pinpoint the revisions you need to make. As you revise, keep in mind your audience and your purpose for writing.

PEER REVIEW

Ask a classmate to read your essay and check to see if you have clearly explained the situation's cause and effects, used supporting evidence, and persuaded the reader to take action.

Rubric: Persuading with Cause and Effect

Evaluation Questions	▶ Tips	▶ Revision Techniques
❶ Does the essay include an opinion about the situation and hint at its effects?	**Highlight** the opinion statement. **Underline** the opinion. **Double underline** the hint at the effects of the situation.	**Add** an opinion statement that clearly states an opinion about the situation and hints at the effects.
❷ Does the essay explain the cause and effects of the situation?	**Circle** the situation. **Bracket** the cause. **Double bracket** the effects.	**Add** an explanation of the situation's cause. **Elaborate** by explaining the situation's effects.
❸ Does the essay include a variety of supporting evidence?	**Put a check** by each piece of evidence. **Label** each kind of evidence.	**Add** evidence—facts, statistics, anecdotes, expert opinions, and so on.
❹ Does the essay use logical, emotional, or ethical appeals?	**Put a box around** and **label** the sentences that show logical, emotional, or ethical appeals.	**Add** sentences that use one or a combination of logical, emotional, or ethical appeals.
❺ Does the conclusion address the reader's counterclaims and include a specific call to action and a last strong statement?	**Put a star by** the counterclaims. **Draw parentheses around** the call to action. In the margin, **draw an arrow** pointing to the final strong statement.	**Add** sentences that address counterclaims. **Reword** sentences to include a specific call to action and a final, strong statement.

> **Second Reading: Style** To keep your readers interested and really drive home the ideas in your essay, work on revising and improving your **style**—the way you express your thoughts. Use cause-effect clue words to link your ideas for the reader and to connect your sentences more clearly. Follow the guidelines below to revise for style.

Style Guidelines

Evaluation Question	▶ Tip	▶ Revision Technique
● Does the essay use cause-effect clue words to help explain the situation and its negative effects?	▶ **Highlight** any words that show either cause or effect.	▶ **Reword** sentences so that you use words that show cause and effects.

ANALYZING THE REVISION PROCESS

Study these revisions, and answer the questions that follow.

> Now there is no rest for the weary and heavy-laden at Smith
>
> High School, where lockers have been removed by school ad-
>
> *because of their concerns*
> reword   ministrators. ~~The school administrators are concerned~~ about
>
> *As a result,*
> reword   crowded hallways and tardiness. Smith High School students
>
> add   carry their heavy backpacks all day —*an unfortunate situation that will cause other serious problems for students and should be changed.*

Responding to the Revision Process

1. What is the effect of adding the words "because of their concerns" in the passage above?

2. How do the words "As a result," added to the last sentence, relate to the previous sentence?

3. How did the addition to the end of the last sentence clarify the opinion statement?

SKILLS FOCUS

Writing Skills
Revise for content and style.

PRACTICE & APPLY 3 Use the guidelines on pages 839 and 840 to revise the content, organization, and style of your essay. Make sure that you have clearly explained your situation's cause and effects, and have used cause-effect clue words.

Publishing

Proofread and Publish Your Essay

Getting It Right Remember that you never get a second chance to make a first impression. Make sure, therefore, that your essay is as error-free as possible so that you will create the right first impression on your readers and accomplish your goals. Before you make a final copy, check your essay thoroughly for grammar, usage, and mechanical errors. Correct any errors that you find.

Change Your World Try one of the following suggestions to share the ideas you presented in your essay.

- Submit your essay to people who can make the changes you propose. For instance, an essay about a school-related topic might be submitted to your school newspaper or to your school administration, while an essay about a neighborhood issue could be submitted to the neighborhood newsletter.

- Adapt your essay into an oral presentation that can be delivered to people who might be affected by the situation you are discussing, such as the school environment club or the city council.

- Videotape a reading of your presentation and show it to a public-speaking class for their review. Use their suggestions to make adjustments in your next presentation. For information on **adapting your essay for a persuasive speech,** see page 842.

- Exchange your paper with a pen pal from another country. Correspond with each other about the similarities and differences in persuading with cause and effect in the two cultures.

Reflect on Your Essay

A Job Well Done To reflect upon the decisions you made and the skills you gained while writing your essay, answer the following questions.

- Did you have trouble finding a situation with negative effects to discuss? Explain your answer.

- What was your best supporting piece of evidence? Why do you think that this was the case?

- Did writing this essay help you see how you could really take action and change a situation that has negative effects? Explain your reasoning.

PRACTICE & APPLY 4 Proofread, publish, and reflect on your essay, using the instructions on this page. Remember to have one of your peers review your essay and provide feedback so that you may have a final check on your work.

TIP A dangling modifier—a modifying word, phrase, or clause that does not clearly and sensibly modify—can muddle your explanation and confuse your readers. Carefully proofread your essay to correct dangling modifiers and to ensure that you follow the **conventions** of standard American English. For more on **dangling modifiers,** see Placement of Modifiers, 5f, in the Language Handbook.

SKILLS FOCUS

Writing Skills
Proofread, especially to correct dangling modifiers.

Giving a Persuasive Speech

A persuasive speech, like an essay that uses cause and effect to persuade, may change the audience members' beliefs, unite them behind a common cause, or inspire them to take action to solve a problem. A speech and an essay share the basic techniques of persuasion. In this workshop you will learn how to take advantage of those techniques and some additional strategies.

Adapt Your Essay

Tailor-Made To adapt your cause-effect essay for a speech, first think about your **audience.** Because a listening audience can't rehear a word, phrase, or sentence, be sure that your vocabulary is simple and easily understood. For a formal speech, however, maintain the same formal **tone** as you used in your essay.

Beginnings The art of verbal persuasion begins with the first words that you speak to your audience. Adapt the **introduction** of your essay so that you can make a dramatic impact from the very beginning. For example, use an intriguing literary quotation, an interesting anecdote, or a reference to an authority on the subject of your speech. Sometimes repeating your opinion statement to your audience reinforces the importance of your ideas.

Endings Conclude your speech by summarizing the effects of your situation. Restate your opinion in a memorable fashion. Then, make a lasting impression by saying your final sentence slowly enough that the audience can feel its impact. A great last line usually is rewarded by the audience's applause.

In the Middle, Make Your Case You will spend the majority of your time explaining why your audience should agree with your opinion statement. How will you formulate your arguments for your listeners? Keep the following suggestions in mind as you review the body paragraphs of your essay.

Listening and Speaking Skills
Deliver a persuasive speech.

INTERNET

Speeches
Keyword: LE7 9-10

- Remember that you have a limited amount of time to present your material. You may need to evaluate your description of the situation's cause, the explanation of its effects, and the supporting evidence you have used. Present only the information that will be most compelling to your audience, but make sure your evidence is both valid and credible. Each piece of evidence, as well as the **logical reasoning** that you use, should be relevant to your explanations of your situation and its effects.

- Choose the most effective **rhetorical devices**—emotional, logical, and ethical appeals—from your essay. Your appeals should suit your listening audience. For example, an audience of your classmates may respond to an effective emotional appeal. However, if you are addressing a school board, logical and ethical appeals would be more effective rhetorical devices for your persuasive speech.

One Jump Ahead Public speakers—from presidents to principals—know that one of the most effective strategies for convincing others is to anticipate and address the **concerns** and **counterclaims** of audience members who might disagree with them. If the audience for your speech is different from the audience for your essay, consider what different concerns or counterclaims the different audience might have and make adjustments in your speech.

TIP Counterclaims are also called **counterarguments.**

Additional Evidence If you find that you need additional evidence to be convincing, consider interviewing an authority on your subject. Before the interview, arrange a time and prepare a set of logical, appropriate questions. During the interview, record the responses, either by taking careful notes, or by asking permission to audiotape or videotape your interviewee. Listen carefully and politely; conduct the interview in a mature, respectful, and responsible manner. Answer any questions that may be asked of you by showing you have knowledge of the subject. After the interview, express your appreciation. Review your notes, and evaluate the effectiveness of the interview process. What, if anything, would you change and why?

Appealing Order To organize your speech, stick to the same basic organizational structure that you used for your essay. Use cause-effect clue words to help show the order of ideas and to make clear the relationship between the situation and its cause and effects.

Present Your Speech

Special Delivery To present a **formal speech**—a memorized speech—make a careful outline. You will memorize and practice the speech before you deliver it. To help you with your formal speech, create concise notes on the content of your speech and on the verbal and nonverbal techniques you intend to use at particular points. **Verbal techniques** include the tone, pitch, and volume of your voice. **Nonverbal techniques** include gestures, pauses, and eye contact. Use your notes to rehearse your speech before a mirror, an audience, a video camera, or an audio recorder. (For more on **verbal and nonverbal techniques,** see page 87.)

SKILLS FOCUS

PRACTICE & APPLY 5 Use the instruction in this workshop to adapt your persuasive cause-and-effect essay for a persuasive speech. Then, rehearse and deliver your speech.

Listening and Speaking Skills
Practice your presentation.

Evaluating an Argument: Intent and Tone

DIRECTIONS: Read the following article. Then, read and respond to the questions that follow.

Jackie Robinson

Henry Aaron

I was fourteen years old when I first saw Jackie Robinson. It was the spring of 1948, the year after Jackie changed my life by breaking baseball's color line. His team, the Brooklyn Dodgers, made a stop in my hometown of Mobile, Alabama, while barnstorming its way north to start the season, and while he was there, Jackie spoke to a big crowd of black folks over on Davis Avenue. I think he talked about segregation, but I didn't hear a word that came out of his mouth. Jackie Robinson was such a hero to me that I couldn't do anything but gawk at him.

They say certain people are bigger than life, but Jackie Robinson is the only man I've known who truly was. In 1947 life in America—at least my America, and Jackie's—was segregation. It was two worlds that were afraid of each other. There were separate schools for blacks and whites, separate restaurants, separate hotels, separate drinking fountains, and separate baseball leagues. Life was unkind to black people who tried to bring those worlds together. It could be hateful. But Jackie Robinson, God bless him, was bigger than all of that.

Jackie Robinson had to be bigger than life. He had to be bigger than the Brooklyn teammates who got up a petition to keep him off the ball club, bigger than the pitchers who threw at him or the base runners who dug their spikes into his shin, bigger than the bench jockeys who hollered for him to carry their bags and shine their shoes, bigger than the so-called fans who wrote him death threats.

When Branch Rickey first met with Jackie about joining the Dodgers, he told him that for three years he would have to turn the other cheek and silently suffer all the vile things that would come his way. Believe me, it wasn't Jackie's nature to do that. He was a fighter, the proudest and most competitive person I've ever seen. This was a man who, as a lieutenant in the army, risked a court-martial[1] by refusing to sit in the back of a military bus. But when Rickey read to him from *The Life of Christ,* Jackie understood the wisdom and the necessity of forbearance.[2]

---

1. **court-martial** (kôrt′mär′shəl) *n.*: military trial.
2. **forbearance** (fôr · ber′əns) *n.*: patience and self-control.

To this day, I don't know how he withstood the things he did without lashing back. I've been through a lot in my time, and I consider myself to be a patient man, but I know I couldn't have done what Jackie did. I don't think anybody else could have done it. Somehow, though, Jackie had the strength to suppress his instincts, to sacrifice his pride for his people's. It was an incredible act of selflessness that brought the races closer together than ever before and shaped the dreams of an entire generation.

Before Jackie Robinson broke the color line, I wasn't permitted even to think about being a professional baseball player. I once mentioned something to my father about it, and he said, "Ain't no colored ballplayers." There were the Negro Leagues, of course, where the Dodgers discovered Jackie, but my mother, like most, would rather her son be a schoolteacher than a Negro Leaguer. All that changed when Jackie started stealing bases in a Brooklyn uniform.

Jackie's character was much more important than his batting average, but it certainly helped that he was a great ballplayer, a .311 career hitter whose trademark was rattling pitchers and fielders with his daring base running. He wasn't the best Negro League talent at the time he was chosen, and baseball wasn't really his best sport—he had been a football and track star at UCLA—but he played the game with a ferocious creativity that gave the country a good idea of what it had been missing all those years. With Jackie in the infield, the Dodgers won six National League pennants.

I believe every black person in America had a piece of those pennants. There's never been another ballplayer who touched people as Jackie did. The only comparable athlete, in my experience, was Joe Louis.[3] The difference was that Louis competed against white men; Jackie competed with them as well. He was taking us over segregation's threshold[4] into a new land whose scenery made every black person stop and stare in reverence.[5] We were all with Jackie. We slid into every base that he swiped, ducked at every fastball that hurtled toward his head. The circulation of the Pittsburgh *Courier,* the leading black newspaper,

---

3. **Joe Louis:** Nicknamed "the Brown Bomber," Joe Louis (1914–1981) was world heavyweight champion from 1937 to 1949.
4. **threshold** (thresh′ōld′) *n.:* doorsill; here, a boundary marking the end of one thing and the start of something new.
5. **reverence** (rev′ə · rəns) *n.:* tremendous respect.

increased by 100,000 when it began reporting on him regularly. All over the country, black preachers would call together their congregations just to pray for Jackie and urge them to demonstrate the same forbearance that he did.

Later in his career, when the "Great Experiment"[6] had proved to be successful, Jackie allowed his instincts to take over in issues of race. He began striking back and speaking out. And when Jackie Robinson spoke, every black player got the message. He made it clear to us that we weren't playing just for ourselves or for our teams; we were playing for our people. I don't think it's a coincidence that the black players of the late '50s and '60s—me, Roy Campanella, Monte Irvin, Willie Mays, Ernie Banks, Frank Robinson, Bob Gibson, and others—dominated the National League. If we played as if we were on a mission, it was because Jackie Robinson had sent us out on one.

Even after he retired in 1956 and was inducted into the Hall of Fame in 1962, Jackie continued to chop along the path that was still a long way from being cleared. He campaigned for baseball to hire a black third-base coach, then a black manager. In 1969 he refused an invitation to play in an old-timers' game at Yankee Stadium to protest the lack of progress along those lines.

A great star from my generation, Frank Robinson (who was related to Jackie only in spirit), finally became the first black manager, in 1975. Jackie was gone by then. His last public appearance was at the 1972 World Series; he showed up with white hair, carrying a cane and going blind from diabetes. He died nine days later.

Most of the black players from Jackie's day were at the funeral, but I was appalled by how few of the younger players showed up to pay him tribute. At the time, I was 41 home runs short of Babe Ruth's[7] career record, and I felt that it was up to me to keep Jackie's dream alive. I was inspired to dedicate my home-run record to the same great cause to which he dedicated his life. I'm still inspired by Jackie Robinson. Hardly a day goes by that I don't think of him.

—from *American Legends: From the Time 100*

---

6. **"Great Experiment":** term used to describe the breaking of the color barrier in major-league baseball.
7. **Babe Ruth's:** George Herman Ruth (1895–1948), nicknamed "the Babe," was one of the most successful and popular baseball players in history. In 1974, Ruth's home-run record was finally beaten by Henry ("Hank") Aaron.

1. Henry Aaron's **intent,** or **purpose,** in writing this article is to —

   A   praise Jackie Robinson

   B   describe segregation in baseball

   C   explain the importance of being patient

   D   explain why he became a ballplayer

2. Which of the following words *best* describes the **tone** of this article?

   F   critical

   G   mournful

   H   admiring

   J   regretful

3. Which of the following statements uses **loaded words**?

   A   "I was fourteen years old when I first saw Jackie Robinson."

   B   "I didn't hear a word that came out of his mouth."

   C   "For three years he would have to turn the other cheek and silently suffer all the vile things that would come his way."

   D   "Jackie's character was much more important than his batting average. . . ."

4. All of the following statements are **facts** *except* —

   F   "He campaigned for baseball to hire a black third-base coach. . . ."

   G   "With Jackie in the infield, the Dodgers won six National League pennants."

   H   "I believe every black person in America had a piece of those pennants."

   J   "He retired in 1956 and was inducted into the Hall of Fame in 1962. . . ."

5. Aaron uses the **anecdote** about Robinson risking a court-martial to show that Robinson —

   A   did not respect laws

   B   was a proud person who fought for respect

   C   could not control his temper

   D   did not like being a soldier

6. Which of the following statements is the *most* accurate **evaluation** of Aaron's argument?

   F   It relies almost entirely on emotional appeals.

   G   Facts, statistics, and other objective evidence make up the argument's main support.

   H   It uses a mix of facts and emotional appeals to convince the reader.

   J   Aaron includes little support in his argument.

Constructed Response

7. According to Aaron, why did Jackie Robinson have to be "bigger than life"? Explain your answer using details from the text.

Collection 10: Skills Review

Vocabulary Skills

Test Practice

Synonyms

DIRECTIONS: Choose the *best* synonym for the underlined word in each sentence.

1. Odysseus overcame great <u>adversity</u> on his long, hard journey homeward.
   - **A** doubt
   - **B** hardship
   - **C** fear
   - **D** disappointment

2. The beautiful song of the sirens was haunting and filled with <u>ardor</u>.
   - **F** passion
   - **G** promise
   - **H** sorrow
   - **J** terror

3. Because Odysseus appeared as a poor old man, the suitors were <u>disdainful</u> of him.
   - **A** suspicious
   - **B** respectful
   - **C** ignorant
   - **D** scornful

4. The monster Scylla yapped <u>abominably</u>, frightening Odysseus's crew.
   - **F** cheerfully
   - **G** loudly
   - **H** disgustingly
   - **J** constantly

5. A brilliant general and a clever states-man, Odysseus was <u>formidable</u> in war and peace.
   - **A** helpful
   - **B** impressive

   - **C** untrustworthy
   - **D** beloved

6. The Cyclops was a fearsome <u>adversary</u>, but Odysseus tricked the one-eyed monster and escaped from his cave.
   - **F** burden
   - **G** giant
   - **H** opponent
   - **J** fighter

7. Odysseus only <u>glowered</u> at the suitors when they pleaded for their lives.
   - **A** stared
   - **C** laughed
   - **B** glanced
   - **D** screamed

8. Penelope was <u>aloof</u> to Odysseus until he proved his true identity by telling the secret of their bed.
   - **F** affectionate
   - **G** threatening
   - **H** distant
   - **J** disloyal

9. When Odysseus's men killed Helios's cattle, the god insisted that he should receive <u>restitution</u>.
   - **A** aid
   - **B** repayment
   - **C** sympathy
   - **D** forgiveness

SKILLS FOCUS

Vocabulary Skills
Identify synonyms.

Collection 10: Skills Review
Writing Skills

DIRECTIONS: Read the following paragraph from a draft of a student's cause-and-effect essay. Then, answer the questions below it.

(1) School administrators changed the dress code policy for students at Wabash High School in order to focus students' attention on academics instead of appearance. (2) The policy has proved most ineffective in reducing students' attention to appearance. (3) The students show how fashion-conscious they still are by buying a special kind of expensive blue shirt to add to the basic uniform. (4) Many students report in fact that wearing the school uniforms increases student body unity. (5) Some students also still discriminate against others who cannot create the elaborate hairstyles of the "in-crowd."

1. Which of the following sentences shows a cause-effect clue word or phrase?

A 1   **C** 3
B 2   **D** 4

2. Which sentence could be added to support the argument that students are still fashion-conscious despite wearing school uniforms?

F Parents love uniforms because their teens spend less on clothing.

G Students comb area stores for "cool" accessories—watches, earrings, and blazer lapel pins.

H The school uniform is a smart combination of school colors for the required blazer, skirt or trousers, and shoes.

J School uniforms have no effect on the fashion industry.

3. Which sentence could the writer add to address a reader's counterclaim that wearing school uniforms *has* refocused students' attention on academics?

A Grade point averages have not changed since students began wearing school uniforms.

B Administrators have lowered the academic standards since requiring school uniforms.

C Students care more about their social lives than their academics.

D Parents care more about student athletics than academics.

4. Which sentence should be deleted to improve the organization of the passage?

F 2   **H** 4
G 3   **J** 5

5. To present this passage formally as a speech, the writer could

A read from note cards for the presentation

B enliven the presentation with props or visuals

C make sudden loud noises to gain the audience's attention

D sustain a low and flat speaking voice to soothe the audience

SKILLS FOCUS

Writing Skills
Write a cause-and-effect essay.

Collection 11

Can This Be Love?

Literary Focus:

Analyzing Drama

Informational Reading Focus:

Synthesizing Sources:
Making Connections

INTERNET

Collection
Resources

Keyword: LE7 9-11

Russian Ballet I (1912) by August Macke.
Oil on paper (103 cm × 81 cm).

Kunsthalle, Bremen, Germany.

Elements of Literature

Drama *by* Diane Tasca
FORMS AND STAGECRAFT

Plays: Stories Acted Out

A **play** is a story acted out, live and on-stage. It presents characters performed by flesh-and-blood people in a physical setting, interacting before our eyes.

Like stories, plays consist of characters carrying out a series of actions, driven by a conflict of some kind. However, stories and plays differ markedly in their format. A story, as you know, is a prose narrative. A narrator in a short story describes the characters, action, and settings; the characters' words are usually marked by quotation marks.

In contrast, a play consists entirely of the characters' words and actions. The playwright may describe the setting and the characters' actions, but the audience never hears these stage directions. The audience sees and hears only the actors' interpretations of them.

> A play is
> a story acted out,
> live and onstage.

Dramatic Structure

You can expect the plot of a play to follow a rising-and-falling structure, much like that of a story. The plot is based on a **conflict,** whether a battle fought for a crown, as in Shakespeare's *Macbeth,* or one fought for a family heirloom, as in August Wilson's *The Piano Lesson.* Various conflicts—both internal and external—create tension for the characters. As the conflicts grow more complicated, the tension increases. Finally the tension reaches a **climax,** such as an argument, a chase, or a passionate love scene. Then the conflict is resolved, the action winds down, and the play ends.

The March Toward Tragedy

The oldest plays we know of were performed in ancient Greece as part of religious festivals. They included tragedies and comedies. The tragedies dealt with heroic characters and subjects that could not have been larger: fate, life, and death.

A **tragedy** is the presentation of serious and important actions that end unhappily. Some tragedies, like *Romeo and Juliet,* portray the suffering of innocent characters, but in most tragedies the central character is a noble figure, known as the **tragic hero,** who has a personal failing that leads to his or her downfall. This **tragic flaw** might be excessive pride, ambition, rebelliousness, or passion—imperfections that lead the otherwise noble hero to make choices that doom him or her to a tragic end.

The Dance of Comedy

A **comedy** is simply a play that ends happily. Many people would define a comedy as a funny play, and in fact most comedies are meant to make us laugh. However, comedies can have other, more important purposes as well, including making us think about issues and question things we take for granted.

Whereas the principal characters in classical tragedies were noble, the central characters in a comedy could be from any class—they could be princes, ordinary townspeople, servants. Like tragic heroes, characters in comedies almost always have flaws. Instead of marching to their doom, however, these flawed characters usually discover the error of their ways, and order is restored.

Like tragedy, comedy is rooted in **conflict,** but the conflict in comedies is usually romantic: Someone wants to marry someone else but faces an obstacle—for example, an opposing parent or a rival suitor. In comedy the obstacle is always overcome, but not before **complications** —often ridiculous but sometimes serious —heighten the suspense. The complications can involve misunderstandings, mistaken identities, disguises, and other transformations.

Modern Drama

Many of today's dramas do not have clear-cut distinctions between comedy and tragedy. Some plays have relatively happy endings, and others have relatively sad endings, but many plays mix the serious with the humorous. Unlike most of the classic tragedies of ancient Greece or Shakespeare's England, serious modern plays are not concerned with kings and queens. Instead, they tend to focus on the personal and domestic conflicts of ordinary people. The characters in contemporary plays, both serious and comedic, are usually ones their audiences will identify with rather than look up to. Thus a modern play like *The Diary of Anne Frank* exposes us to the horror of the Holocaust by showing its effect on the daily lives of a small group of characters who are much like the viewers watching the play.

From the Page to the Stage

Dramas are meant to be performed. While we can enjoy reading the written text of a play and can learn a great deal from it, we need to remember that it was written to be performed. It is the job of the people bringing the play to the stage—the actors, directors, and designers—to translate the playwright's intentions.

A **stage** can be grand or intimate in size. It can be positioned at one end of the theater in front of the audience, or it can be placed in the middle of the theater, surrounded by the audience. A stage is like a small world unto itself, with its own coordinates: not north, south, east, and west, but *upstage* (away from the audience), *downstage* (toward the audience), *stage right* and *stage left* (the actors' right and left when facing the audience).

Scene Design: Dressing the Stage

Every play takes place somewhere and at some time, and a **set** transforms a bare stage into that place and time. A set might be realistic and detailed, looking just like a handsome living room, a bustling office, or an autumn forest. It might be abstract or minimal, meeting the needs of the action with just a few movable boxes and screens. A set can change from scene to scene; sometimes the change is accomplished with elaborate motorized lifts and turntables, sometimes with just a change in the lighting.

Until the last few centuries most plays (including those of Shakespeare) were performed outdoors in natural light. Today most plays are performed indoors and so require artificial **lighting.** Lights can wash the entire stage with golden sunlight or cast blue twilight shadows, depending on their brightness, placement, and filter colors. They can create a warm, relaxed mood or a chilling, ominous tone.

Actors dress in **costumes** appropriate for their characters as well as for the time and place of the play. Costumes also suggest the social positions and professions of the characters. Like sets, costumes can be elaborate or minimal. In one production of a play, for example, a king might wear embroidered, fur-trimmed robes and a jeweled crown, but in another production the same king might wear black pants, a T-shirt, and a yellow cardboard crown.

When an actor waves a sword or talks on a cell phone, he or she is using a prop. **Props** (short for *properties*) are the portable items that actors carry or handle onstage (for example, books, letters, goblets, scepters, purses, umbrellas, suitcases).

All the elements of the scene design—sets, lights, costumes, and props—work together to support the action and create the appropriate mood. Above all, they help sustain the audience's belief in the reality of a play.

Characters Onstage

The conversation between characters in a play is called **dialogue.** A long speech by one character to one or more other characters onstage is a **monologue.** A speech by a character who is alone onstage, speaking to himself or herself or to the audience, is a **soliloquy.** Playwrights often use monologues and soliloquies to develop ideas or express complex emotions.

Sometimes a character speaks to the audience or to another character in an **aside,** dialogue that is not supposed to be heard by the other characters onstage.

Texts of plays include **stage directions,** which describe how the characters move around the stage and how they speak their lines. (When a play is published, stage directions usually appear in italics.) Actors, directors, and designers usually regard stage directions as suggestions rather than rigid specifications. Since every actor onstage is always doing something, even if he or she is not speaking, a playwright cannot specify every action every character performs. It is up to the actors to figure out how to fill out their characters' lives physically and emotionally onstage.

The actor decides (with the director's help) how to interpret the lines of a play—what the words mean, why the character says them, how the character feels while saying them. If you were to see two productions of the same play, the words would be the same, but the actors' actions and interpretations would certainly differ.

Drama is one of the oldest forms of literature, but it continues to speak to people today. Plays explore the human heart and psyche in a direct way. Following the memorable description Shakespeare's Hamlet gave four centuries ago, plays "hold, as 'twere, the mirror up to nature."

Practice

Choose a play or movie you remember seeing, and discuss its dramatic elements. Start by describing the **set** (or sets). Then, describe the actors' **costumes.** Next, evaluate the characters' **dialogue**—was it convincing? clever? silly? Finally, write a few **stage directions,** based on what you imagine them to have been.

Can This Be Love?

Make the Connection

Quickwrite ✎

How would you define that powerful emotion called love? Think of your own experiences or of love as depicted in TV shows and movies. What is love based on—personality, shared interests, or appearance, for example? What makes love ring true? Jot down your thoughts.

Exploring the Theme: Can This Be Love?

"Can this be love?" The selections in this collection all address that question. In the comedy *Visitor from Forest Hills,* a bride-to-be locks herself in a bathroom on her wedding day. Two teenagers fall in love at first sight and meet a tragic fate in Shakespeare's famous play *The Tragedy of Romeo and Juliet.* You'll also read articles about love that overcomes familial, ethnic, and religious prejudices. The selection that follows, a scene from *Cyrano de Bergerac,* centers on hidden identities and hidden love.

Literary Focus

Dialogue and Stage Directions in Drama

A **play** is a story acted out onstage. Playwrights use **dialogue,** or conversation between characters, to tell the audience about their characters and to move the plot forward. They often provide **stage directions** to indicate how characters should move onstage and how they should speak their lines. As you read the following scene, pay attention to what the characters say and how they say it. Note, as well, what the stage directions tell you about the characters' actions and reactions.

Background

This comic romance begins in France in 1640, when the French are fighting the Spanish. Christian is a strikingly handsome soldier, but he lacks the gift of eloquent, poetic language needed to win Roxane's love. Cyrano, who has a huge nose, is too ashamed of his appearance to reveal his love for Roxane. He has the heart and soul of a poet, however, and he offers to write love letters to Roxane for Christian. The scheme works so well that Roxane marries Christian in secret. In the scene from Act IV that follows, Roxane has placed herself in great danger by traveling to Christian and Cyrano's military camp to see her beloved Christian.

Literary Skills
Understand dialogue and stage directions in drama.

from

Cyrano de Bergerac

Edmond Rostand
translated by **Brian Hooker**

Characters

Christian • Cyrano • Roxane

Scene: *A military camp outside of Arras, France.*

Christian.

What is it?[1]

Cyrano.

If Roxane . . .

Christian.
Well?

Cyrano.

Speaks about your letters . . .

Christian.

Yes—I know!

Cyrano.
Do not make the mistake of showing . . .

Christian.

What?

Cyrano.
Showing surprise.

Christian.

Surprise—why?

---

1. The line spacing in this scene reflects the fact that the play was originally written in French verse.

Cyrano.

It is quite simple—I had forgotten it
Until just now. You have . . .

Christian.

Cyrano.

Have written oftener than you think.

Christian.

Cyrano.

I took upon me to interpret you;
And wrote—sometimes . . . without . . .

Christian.

Cyrano.
Perfectly simple!

Christian.

I must tell you! . . .

Speak quickly!—

You

Oh—have I!

My knowing. Well?

Oh yes, perfectly!
For a month, we have been blockaded[2] here!—
How did you send all these letters?

---

2. **blockaded** (blä·kād′id) *v*.: cut off by enemy troops and prevented from passing in or out.

DRAMA

❶ What do you notice about the way Cyrano and Christian speak to each other in the **dialogue** so far?

DRAMA

❷ Why do you think the **stage direction** indicates that Christian should speak "violently" here?

Cyrano.
                                          Before

Daylight, I managed—
Christian.
                                  I see. That was also

Perfectly simple! ❶

                    —So I wrote to her,
          How many times a week? Twice? Three times?
          Four?
Cyrano.
Oftener.
Christian.
                    Every day?
Cyrano.
                                  Yes—every day . . .

Every single day . . .
Christian.
          (*Violently*)
                              And that wrought³ you up

Into such a flame that you faced death— ❷
Cyrano.
          (*Sees* ROXANE *returning.*)
                                                  Hush—

Not before her!
          (*He goes quickly into the tent.* ROXANE *comes up to* CHRISTIAN.)
Roxane.
                    Now—Christian!
Christian.
          (*Takes her hands.*)
                                        Tell me now

Why you came here—over these ruined roads—
Why you made your way among mosstroopers⁴
And ruffians⁵—you—to join me here?
Roxane.
                                        Because—

Your letters . . .
Christian.
                    Meaning?

---

3. **wrought** (rôt) *v.:* alternate past-tense form of *work.*
4. **mosstroopers** (môs′trōōp′ərs) *n.:* raiders.
5. **ruffians** (ruf′ē•ənz) *n.:* tough, violent, lawless people.

Roxane.

It was your own fault
If I ran into danger! I went mad—
Mad with you! Think what you have written me,
How many times, each one more wonderful
Than the last!

Christian.

All this for a few absurd
Love-letters—

Roxane.

Hush—absurd! How can you know?
I thought I loved you, ever since one night
When a voice that I never would have known
Under my window breathed your soul to me . . .[6]
But—all this time, your letters—every one
Was like hearing your voice there in the dark,
All around me, like your arms around me . . .

(More lightly)

At last,
I came. Anyone would! Do you suppose
The prim Penelope had stayed at home
Embroidering,—if Ulysses wrote like you?
She would have fallen like another Helen—
Tucked up those linen petticoats of hers
And followed him to Troy![7] ❸

Christian.

But you—

Roxane.

I read them
Over and over. I grew faint reading them.
I belonged to you. Every page of them
Was like a petal fallen from your soul—
Like the light and the fire of a great love,
Sweet and strong and true—

**Introducing the
Collection Theme**

THEME

❸ How do Christian's
and Roxane's attitudes
toward the love
letters differ?

---

6. **ever since . . . soul to me:** Christian addressed Roxane one night as she stood on a balcony. She was frustrated by his inability to express his love eloquently until Cyrano, who was hiding in the bushes, stepped in. Under cover of darkness, Cyrano spoke so poetically that Roxane was deeply moved.

7. **Do you suppose . . . to Troy:** While she waits for her husband—the great Greek hero Ulysses, or Odysseus—to return home from the Trojan War, Penelope weaves and unweaves a shroud for her father-in-law as a trick to put off her suitors. Helen, the wife of King Menelaus of Sparta, runs off to Troy with Paris, a Trojan prince, thus sparking the Trojan War.

THEME

❹ In your own words, explain why Roxane asks Christian to forgive her.

Christian.

Sweet . . . and strong . . . and true . . .
You felt that, Roxane?—

Roxane.

You know how I feel! . . .

Christian.
So—you came . . .

Roxane.

Oh, my Christian, oh my king,—
Lift me up if I fall upon my knees—
It is the heart of me that kneels to you,
And will remain forever at your feet—
You cannot lift that!—

I came here to say
"Forgive me"—(It is time to be forgiven
Now, when we may die presently)—forgive me
For being light and vain and loving you
Only because you were beautiful. ❹

Christian.

(Astonished)

Roxane! . . .

Roxane.
Afterwards I knew better. Afterwards
(I had to learn to use my wings) I loved you
For yourself too—knowing you more, and loving
More of you. And now—

Christian.

Now? . . .

Roxane.

It is yourself
I love now: your own self.

Christian.

(Taken aback)

Roxane!

Roxane.

(Gravely)

Be happy!—
You must have suffered; for you must have seen
How frivolous[8] I was; and to be loved
For the mere costume, the poor casual body
You went about in—to a soul like yours,
That must have been torture! Therefore with words

---

8. **frivolous** (friv′ə•ləs) *adj.:* silly; not serious or sensible.

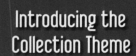

You revealed your heart. Now that image of you
Which filled my eyes first—I see better now,
And I see it no more! ❺
Christian.

        Oh!—

Roxane.

             You still doubt

Your victory?
Christian.

    (Miserably)

        Roxane!—

Roxane.

        I understand:
You cannot perfectly believe in me—

THEME

❺ Explain what
Roxane means by
the statement "I
see better now."

A love like this—
Christian.

I want no love like this!

I want love only for—
Roxane.

Only for what

Every woman sees in you? I can do
Better than that!
Christian.

No—it was best before!

Roxane.
You do not altogether know me . . . Dear,
There is more of me than there was—with this,
I can love more of you—more of what makes
You your own self—Truly! . . . If you were less
Lovable—
Christian.

No!

Roxane.

—Less charming—ugly even—

I should love you still.
Christian.

You mean that?

Roxane.

I do

Mean that!
Christian.

Ugly? . . .

Roxane.

Yes. Even then!

Christian.
(*Agonized*)

Oh . . . God! . . . ❻

Roxane.
Now are you happy?
Christian.
(*Choking*)

Yes . . .

Roxane.

What is it?

Christian.
(*Pushes her away gently.*)

Only . . .

THEME

❻ Why is Christian
so upset to learn
that Roxane would
love him even if he
were ugly?

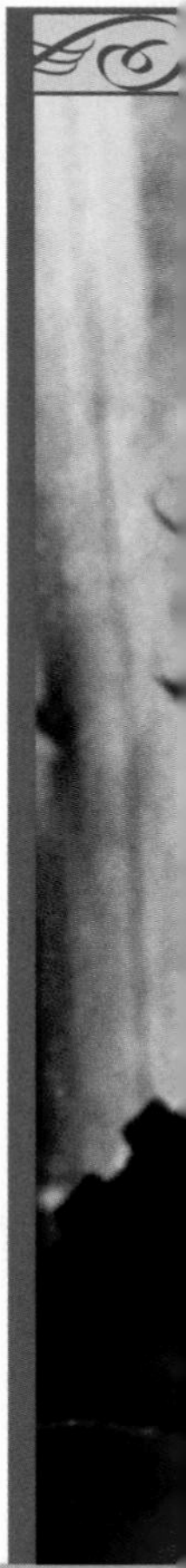

Nothing . . . one moment . . .
Roxane.

But—
Christian.

(Gesture toward the Cadets)

I am keeping you
From those poor fellows—Go and smile at them;
They are going to die!
Roxane.

(Softly)

Dear Christian!
Christian.

Go—

(She goes up among the Gascons[9] who gather round her respectfully.)
Cyrano!

---

9. **Gascons** (gas′kənz): people from Gascony, in southwestern France.

Introducing the Collection Theme

Cyrano.
(Comes out of the tent, armed for the battle.)
What is wrong? You look—

Christian.
She does not
Love me any more.

Cyrano.
(Smiles)
You think not?

Christian.
She loves
You.

Cyrano.
No!—

Christian.
(Bitterly)
She loves only my soul. ❼

Cyrano.
No!

Christian.
Yes—
That means you. And you love her.

Cyrano.
I?

Christian.
I see—
I know!

Cyrano.
That is true . . .

Christian.
More than—

Cyrano.
(Quietly)
More than that.

Christian.
Tell her so!

Cyrano.
No.

Christian.
Why not?

Cyrano.
Why—look at me!

DRAMA

❼ Explain why the **stage direction** "Bitterly" is crucial for understanding this line.

Christian.
She would love me if I were ugly.
Cyrano.

      (Startled)

                She—

Said that? ❽
Christian.

      Yes. Now then!
Cyrano.

      (Half to himself)

                It was good of her

To tell you that . . .
      (Change of tone)

                Nonsense! Do you believe

Any such madness—

                It was good of her

To tell you. . . .
      Do not take her at her word!
Go on—you never will be ugly—Go!
She would never forgive me.

Introducing the Collection Theme

DRAMA

❽ Consider what Cyrano says and how he says it. What is his reaction to hearing that Roxane would love Christian even if he were ugly? Why does he react in this way?

Christian.

That is what

We shall see.

Cyrano.

No, no—

Christian.

Let her choose between us!—

Tell her everything!

Cyrano.

No—you torture me—

Christian.
Shall I ruin your happiness, because
I have a cursed pretty face? That seems
Too unfair!

Cyrano.

And am I to ruin yours
Because I happen to be born with power
To say what you—perhaps—feel?

Christian.

Tell her!

Cyrano.

Man—

Do not try me too far!

Christian.

I am tired of being

My own rival! **9**

Cyrano.

Christian!—

Christian.

Our secret marriage—

No witnesses—fraudulent[10]—that can be
Annulled[11]—

Cyrano.

Do not try me—

Christian.

I want her love
For the poor fool I am—or not at all!
Oh, I am going through with this! I'll know,
One way or the other. Now I shall walk down
To the end of the post. Go tell her. Let her choose
One of us. **10**

---

10. **fraudulent** (frô′jə•lənt) *adj.*: deceitful; deliberately unlawful.
11. **annulled** (ə•nuld′) *v.*: declared invalid.

THEME

9 In what way has
Christian been his
"own rival"?

THEME

10 What does Christian
mean when he says he
wants Roxane to love
him "for the poor
fool" that he is?

Cyrano.
It will be you.

Christian.
God—I hope so!

Just as Cyrano is ready to tell Roxane the truth about the letters, Christian is killed. Cyrano feels he can't tell Roxane that he is the author of the letters. The grief-stricken Roxane does not learn the truth until fifteen years later, when Cyrano is dying.

Meet the Writer
Edmond Rostand

Early Success

Edmond Rostand (1868–1918) was born into a wealthy family in Marseille, France. Rostand's father hoped his son would pursue a career in law, but Rostand was drawn to the theater instead. In his youth he liked nothing better than to create costumes and stage sets for his puppet theater.

Rostand attended college in Paris, where he spent most of his time writing plays and poetry rather than concentrating on his studies. In 1890, he published his first book of poetry and married the poet Rosemonde Gérard. After his marriage he concentrated on writing plays and often wrote special parts for the famous actors of the time.

Rostand based his most famous play, *Cyrano de Bergerac,* on the life of a real

The Granger Collection, New York.

French writer and soldier. Performed in 1897, when Rostand was only twenty-nine years old, the play was greeted with great acclaim. During the first performance every seat in the theater was taken. After each act the audience got to its feet, cheering and applauding, sometimes for up to ten minutes. Rostand's later plays never quite matched this early success.

After You Read

Response and Analysis

Reading Check

1. What choice does Christian want to give Roxane at the end of the scene? Why?

Thinking Critically

2. **Dramatic irony** occurs when the audience knows something that a character does not know. Explain the dramatic irony in this scene.

3. What do you learn about the relationship between Cyrano and Christian from the **dialogue** in this scene? To answer, think about what the characters say and the way they speak to each other. (Remember to consider the **stage directions.**)

4. Think about how the collection theme "Can This Be Love?" relates to this selection. First, tell why Roxane initially falls in love with Christian. Then, explain how her love for him changes and why. What truth about love is revealed in this scene?

Exploring the Theme
Can This Be Love?

The selections in the rest of this collection all explore the nature of love. As you read each one, think about the lovers' relationship and the obstacles they face. Then, ask yourself the question "Can this be love?"

Extending and Evaluating

5. Do you think our society values people's appearance more than their character? Why or why not? To answer, consider the way relationships are depicted on TV, in movies, and in other forms of media. (Be sure to check your Quickwrite notes.)

6. Cyrano's letters bring about a dramatic change in Roxane's feelings. Do you believe words have the power to change the way we think, act, and feel, or do you believe actions speak louder than words? Support your response with examples.

SKILLS FOCUS

Literary Focus
Analyze dialogue and stage directions in drama.

Visitor from Forest Hills

Make the Connection

Quickwrite ✏️

Imagine an elegant album filled with typical wedding photographs: the bride and groom gazing at each other lovingly, the happy couple slicing the wedding cake, the dressed-up parents beaming proudly. Now, imagine the photos of a wedding at which everything has gone comically wrong: The bride's dog has eaten the wedding cake; sprinklers have gone off, soaking all the guests; the groom's father recognizes the bride's uncle as the third-grade bully. List a few of your own ideas for photos of the world's worst wedding.

Literary Focus

Comedy: Happy Endings

A **comedy** is a play that ends happily—with some laughter along the way. However, the best comedies are not aimed solely at the audience's funny bone. Like any good work of literature, a good comedy shows us something true about life—something that may not be funny at all. For example, in George Bernard Shaw's great comedy *Pygmalion* (the basis for the musical *My Fair Lady*), a highly educated professor successfully teaches a poor flower seller how to speak and behave like a lady. The play has many funny moments, but ultimately the professor discovers something serious: the human cost and responsibility of turning someone's life upside down.

Farce. Comedies can take various forms. One popular and very old type of comedy is **farce,** in which a playwright concentrates largely on ridiculous situations, comical physical actions (pies thrown in faces, wild chase scenes), and screwball dialogue. The characters in a farce are usually broad, one-dimensional **types,** who are representative of a group of people. In a way, type characters make literature possible—we recognize ourselves and others in stories. Stereotypes, however, are another matter. A **stereotype** represents a fixed, usually prejudicial idea about a group of people that is offensive and hurtful.

Both farce and comedy thrive on the contrast between characters with opposite natures. Opposites, of course, usually promise **conflict,** and conflict is the basis of drama. You are familiar with the humor that comes from a conflict of opposites in movies and television shows. In *The Odd Couple,* for example, two men share an apartment: One is a compulsively neat housekeeper; the other is very sloppy. This teaming of opposites is good for endless laughs. Other examples are the cowboy and the lady, the taxi driver and the princess, and the tough guy and the soft-hearted woman.

The battle of the sexes. Neil Simon's comedy *Visitor from Forest Hills* uses one set of opposites that has served comedy for many years: a man and a woman—usually husband and wife—who wage the so-called battle of the sexes. In such comedies the man is usually portrayed as a quick-tempered (though loving) husband and father, the domineering head of the household, and the woman is usually portrayed as a slightly muddled, or confused, wife and mother. Of course, it usually

(*continued*)

Literary Skills
Understand characteristics of comedy and farce.

INTERNET

Vocabulary Practice

Keyword: LE7 9-11

develops in these plays that although the wife *seems* flighty and disorganized, she is really more sensible than the husband.

When you read *Romeo and Juliet* (page 901), you will recognize the sixteenth-century squabbling of Lord and Lady Capulet, Juliet's parents, as not much different from the squabbling of Roy and Norma in *Visitor from Forest Hills*. It is all part of the battle of the sexes—and that battle, serious or hilarious, will probably go on forever.

Neil Simon, one of the most successful writers of comedy today, has said that he writes about potentially sad situations from a comic point of view. Think about his comment as you read *Visitor from Forest Hills*. What not-so-funny truth does it lead us to, laughing along the way?

Vocabulary Development

volatile (väl′ə·təl) *adj.:* explosive; likely to change rapidly.

incredulously (in·krej′oo·ləs·lē) *adv.:* unbelievingly; skeptically.

torrent (tôr′ənt) *n.:* flood; downpour.

vehemence (vē′ə·məns) *n.:* strong feeling or passion.

despondently (di·spän′dənt·lē) *adv.:* hopelessly.

interminable (in·tʉr′mi·nə·bəl) *adj.:* with no end in sight.

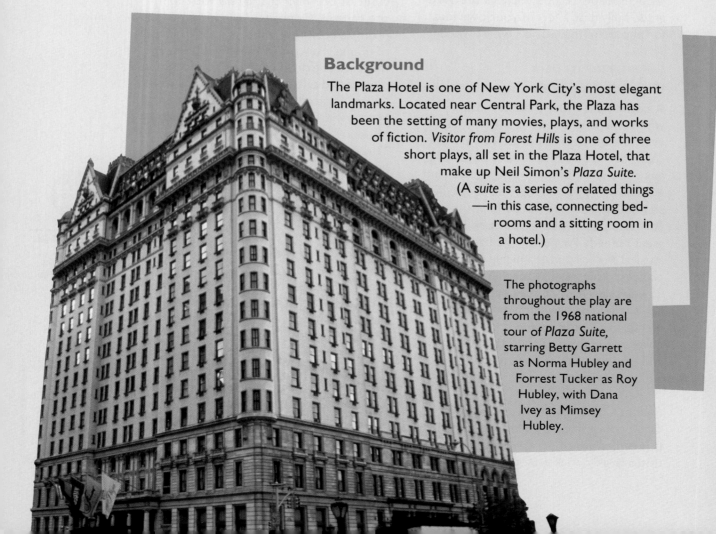

Background

The Plaza Hotel is one of New York City's most elegant landmarks. Located near Central Park, the Plaza has been the setting of many movies, plays, and works of fiction. *Visitor from Forest Hills* is one of three short plays, all set in the Plaza Hotel, that make up Neil Simon's *Plaza Suite*. (A *suite* is a series of related things —in this case, connecting bed-rooms and a sitting room in a hotel.)

The photographs throughout the play are from the 1968 national tour of *Plaza Suite*, starring Betty Garrett as Norma Hubley and Forrest Tucker as Roy Hubley, with Dana Ivey as Mimsey Hubley.

Visitor from Forest Hills

from Plaza Suite

Neil Simon

> ❝ **Mimsey! Are you coming out or do we have the wedding in the bathroom?** ❞

CAST OF CHARACTERS

Roy Hubley

Mimsey Hubley

and Borden Eisler

Norma Hubley

Suite 719 at the Plaza. It is three o'clock on a warm Saturday afternoon in spring.

The living room is bedecked with vases and baskets of flowers. In the bedroom one opened valise containing a young woman's street clothes rests on the floor. A very large box, which had held a wedding dress, rests on the luggage rack, and a man's suit lies on the bed. A fur wrap and gloves are thrown over the back of the sofa. Telegrams of congratulations and newspapers are strewn about.

The suite today is being used more or less as a dressing room, since a wedding is about to occur downstairs in one of the reception rooms.

As the lights come up, NORMA HUBLEY is at the phone in the bedroom, impatiently tapping the receiver. She is dressed in a formal cocktail dress and a large hat, looking her very best, as any woman would want to on her daughter's wedding day. But she is extremely nervous and harassed, and with good cause—as we'll soon find out.

Norma (*on the phone*). Hello? . . . Hello, operator? . . . Can I have the Blue Room, please . . . The Blue Room . . . Is there a Pink Room? I want the Hubley-Eisler wedding . . . The Green Room, that's it. Thank you . . . Could you please hurry, operator, it's an emergency . . . (*She looks over at the bathroom nervously. She paces back and forth.*) Hello? . . . Who's this? . . . Mr. Eisler . . . It's Norma Hubley . . . No, everything's fine . . . Yes, we're coming right down . . . (*She is smiling and trying to act as pleasant and as calm as possible.*) Yes, you're right, it certainly *is* the big day . . . Mr. Eisler, is my husband there? . . . Would you please? . . . Oh! Well, I'd like to wish you the very best of luck too . . . Borden's a wonderful boy . . . Well, they're *both* wonderful kids . . . No, no. She's as calm as a cucumber . . . That's the younger generation, I guess . . . Yes, everything seems to be going along beautifully . . . Absolutely beautifully . . . Oh, thank you. (*Her husband has obviously just come on the other end because the expression on her face changes violently and she screams a rasping whisper filled with doom. Sitting on the bed*) Roy? You'd better get up here right away, we're in big trouble . . . Don't ask questions, just get up here . . . I hope you're not drunk because I can't handle this alone . . . Don't say anything. Just smile

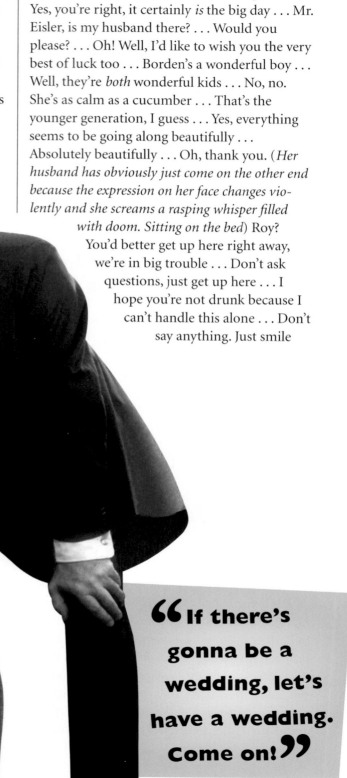

"If there's gonna be a wedding, let's have a wedding. Come on!"

872

and walk leisurely out the door . . . and then get the hell up here as fast as you can. (*She hangs up, putting the phone back on the night table. She crosses to the bathroom and then puts her head up against the door. Aloud through the bathroom door*) All right, Mimsey, your father's on his way up. Now, I want you to come out of that bathroom and get married. (*There is no answer.*) Do you hear me? . . . I've had enough of this nonsense . . . Unlock that door! (*That's about the end of her authority. She wilts and almost pleads.*) Mimsey, darling, please come downstairs and get married, you know your father's temper . . . I know what you're going through now, sweetheart, you're just nervous . . . Everyone goes through that on their wedding day . . . It's going to be all right, darling. You love Borden and he loves you. You're both going to have a wonderful future. So please come out of the bathroom! (*She listens; there is no answer.*) Mimsey, if you don't care about your life, think about mine. Your father'll kill me. (*The front doorbell rings.* NORMA *looks off nervously and moves to the other side of the bed.*) Oh, God, he's here! . . . Mimsey! Mimsey, please, spare me this . . . If you want, I'll have it annulled[1] next week, but please come out and get married! (*There is no answer from the bathroom but the front doorbell rings impatiently.*) All right, I'm letting your father in. And heaven help the three of us!

[*She crosses through the bedroom into the living room. She crosses to the door and opens it as* ROY HUBLEY *bursts into the room.* ROY *is dressed in striped trousers, black tailcoat, the works. He looks elegant but he's not too happy in this attire. He is a* <u>volatile</u>, *explosive man equipped to handle the rigors of the competitive business world, but a nervous, frightened man when it comes to the business of marrying off his only daughter.*]

Roy. Why are you standing here? There are sixty-eight people down there drinking my liquor. If there's gonna be a wedding, let's have a wedding. Come on! (*He starts back out the door but sees that* NORMA *is not going anywhere. She sits on the sofa. He comes back in.*) . . . Didn't you hear what I said? There's another couple waiting to use the Green Room. Come on, let's go! (*He makes a start out again.*)

Norma (*very calm*). Roy, could you sit down a minute? I want to talk to you about something.

Roy (*she must be mad*). You want to talk *now*? You had twenty-one years to talk while she was growing up. I'll talk to you when they're in Bermuda. Can we please have a wedding?

Norma. We can't have a wedding until you and I have a talk.

Roy. Are you crazy? While you and I are talking here, there are four musicians playing downstairs for seventy dollars an hour. I'll talk to you later when we're dancing. Come on, get Mimsey and let's go. (*He starts out again.*)

Norma. That's what I want to talk to you about.

Roy (*comes back*). Mimsey?

Norma. Sit down. You're not going to like this.

Roy. Is she sick?

Norma. She's not sick . . . exactly.

Roy. What do you mean, she's not sick exactly? Either she's sick or she's not sick. Is she sick?

Norma. She's not sick.

Roy. Then let's have a wedding! (*He crosses into the bedroom.*) Mimsey, there's two hundred dollars worth of cocktail frankfurters getting cold downstairs . . . (*He looks around the empty room.*) Mimsey? (*He crosses back to the living room to the side of the sofa. He looks at* NORMA.) . . . Where's Mimsey?

Norma. Promise you're not going to blame me.

Roy. Blame you for what? What did you do?

Norma. I didn't do anything. But I don't want to get blamed for it.

---

1. **annulled** (ə·nuld′) *v.*: ended legally.

Vocabulary
volatile (väl′ə·təl) *adj.*: explosive; likely to change rapidly.

Roy. What's going on here? Are you going to tell me where Mimsey is?

Norma. Are you going to take an oath you're not going to blame me?

Roy. *I take it! I take it!* NOW WHERE THE HELL IS SHE?

Norma. . . . She's locked herself in the bathroom. She's not coming out and she's not getting married.

[ROY *looks at* NORMA *incredulously. Then, because it must be an insane joke, he smiles at her. There is even the faint glint of a chuckle.*]

Roy (*softly*). . . . No kidding, where is she?

Norma (*turns away*). He doesn't believe me. I'll kill myself.

[ROY *turns and storms into the bedroom. He crosses to the bathroom and knocks on the door. Then he tries it. It's locked. He tries again. He bangs on the door with his fist.*]

Roy. Mimsey? . . . Mimsey? . . . MIMSEY? (*There is no reply. Girding himself, he crosses back through the bedroom into the living room to the sofa. He glares at* NORMA.) . . . All right, what did you say to her?

Norma (*jumping up and moving away*). I knew it! I knew you'd blame me. You took an oath. God'll punish you.

Roy. I'm not blaming you. I just want to know what *stupid* thing you said to her that made her do this.

Norma. I didn't say a word. I was putting on my lipstick, she was in the bathroom, I heard the door go click, it was locked, my whole life was over, what do you want from me?

Roy. And you didn't say a word?

Norma. Nothing.

Roy (*ominously moving toward her as* NORMA *backs away*). I see. In other words, you're trying to tell me that a normal, healthy, intelligent twenty-one-year-old college graduate, who has driven me crazy the last eighteen months with wedding lists, floral arrangements, and choices of assorted hors d'oeuvres,[2] has suddenly decided to spend this, the most important day of her life, locked in the Plaza Hotel john?

Norma (*making her stand at the mantel*). Yes! Yes! Yes! Yes! Yes!

Roy (*vicious*). YOU MUSTA SAID SOMETHING!

[*He storms into the bedroom.* NORMA *goes after him.*]

Norma. Roy . . . Roy . . . What are you going to do?

Roy (*stopping below the bed*). First I'm getting the college graduate out of the bathroom! Then we're gonna have a wedding and then you and I are gonna have a big talk! (*He crosses to the bathroom door and pounds on it.*) Mimsey! This is your father. I want you and your four-hundred-dollar wedding dress out of there in five seconds!

Norma (*standing at the side of the bed*). Don't threaten her. She'll never come out if you threaten her.

Roy (*to* NORMA). I got sixty-eight guests, nine waiters, four musicians, and a boy with a wedding license waiting downstairs. This is no time

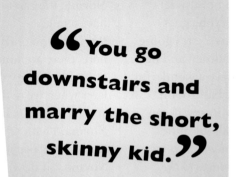

> " You go downstairs and marry the short, skinny kid. "

2. **hors d'oeuvres** (ôr'dʉrvz') *n.*: appetizers.

Vocabulary
incredulously (in·krej'oo·ləs·lē) *adv.*: unbelievingly; skeptically.

to be diplomatic. (*Bangs on the door*) Mimsey!
. . . Are you coming out or do we have the wedding in the bathroom?

Norma. Will you lower your voice! Everyone will hear us.

Roy (*to* NORMA). How long you think we can keep this a secret? As soon as that boy says "I do" and there's no one standing next to him, they're going to suspect something. (*He bangs on the door.*) You can't stay in there forever, Mimsey. We only have the room until six o'clock . . . *You hear me?*

[*There is still no reply from the bathroom.*]

Norma. Roy, will you please try to control yourself.

Roy (*with great display of patience, moves to the foot of the bed and sits*). All right, I'll stay here and control myself. You go downstairs and marry the short, skinny kid. (*Exploding*) *What's the matter with you?* Don't you realize what's happening?

Norma (*moving to him*). Yes. I realize what's happening. Our daughter is nervous, frightened, and scared to death.

Roy. Of what? OF WHAT? She's been screaming for two years if he doesn't ask her to marry him, she'll throw herself off the Guggenheim Museum . . . What is she scared of?

Norma. I don't know. Maybe she's had second thoughts about the whole thing.

Roy (*getting up and moving to the bathroom door*). Second thoughts? This is no time to be having *second thoughts.* It's costing me eight thousand dollars for the *first thoughts.* (*He bangs on the door.*) Mimsey, open this door.

Norma. Is that all you care about? What it's costing you? Aren't you concerned about your daughter's happiness?

Roy (*moving back to her below the bed*). Yes! Yes, I'm concerned about my daughter's happiness. I'm also concerned about that boy waiting downstairs. A decent, respectable, intelligent

young man . . . who I hope one day is going to teach that daughter of mine to grow up.

Norma. You haven't the faintest idea of what's going through her mind right now.

Roy. Do you?

Norma. It could be anything. I don't know, maybe she thinks she's not good enough for him.

Roy (*looks at her incredulously*). . . .Why? What is he? Some kind of Greek god? He's a plain kid, nothing . . . That's ridiculous. (*Moves back to the door and bangs on it*) Mimsey! Mimsey, open this door. (*He turns to* NORMA.) Maybe she's not in there.

Norma. She's in there. (*Clutches her chest and sits on the side of the bed*) Oh, God, I think I'm having a heart attack.

Roy (*listening at the door*). I don't hear a peep out of her. Is there a window in there? Maybe she tried something crazy.

Norma (*turning to him*). That's right. Tell a woman who's having a heart attack that her daughter jumped out the window.

Roy. Take a look through the keyhole. I want to make sure she's in there.

Norma. She's in there, I tell you. Look at this, my hand keeps bouncing off my chest. (*It does.*)

Roy. Are you gonna look in there and see if she's all right or am I gonna call the house detective?

Norma (*getting up and moving below the bed*). Why don't *you* look?

Roy. Maybe she's taking a bath.

Norma. Two minutes before her own wedding?

Roy (*crossing to her*). What wedding? She just called it off.

Norma. Wouldn't I have heard the water running?

Roy (*making a swipe at her hat*). With that hat you couldn't hear Niagara Falls! . . . Are you going to look to see what your daughter's doing in the bathroom or do I ask a stranger?

Norma (*crossing to the door*). I'll look! I'll look! I'll look! (*Reluctantly she gets down on one knee and* *looks through the keyhole with one eye.*) Oh, my God!

Roy. What's the matter?

Norma (*to him*). I ripped my stockings. (*Getting up and examining her stocking*)

Roy. Is she in there?

Norma. She's in there! She's in there! (*Hobbling to the far side of the bed and sitting down on the edge*) Where am I going to get another pair of stockings now? How am I going to go to the wedding with torn stockings?

Roy (*crossing to the bathroom*). If *she* doesn't show up, who's going to look at *you*? (*He kneels at the door and looks through the keyhole.*) There she is. Sitting there and crying.

Norma. I *told* you she was in there . . . The only one in my family to have a daughter married in the Plaza and I have torn stockings.

Roy (*he is on his knees, his eye to the keyhole*). Mimsey, I can see you . . . Do you hear me? . . . Don't turn away from me when I'm talking to you.

Norma. Maybe I could run across to Bergdorf's.[3] They have nice stockings. (*Crosses to her purse on the bureau in the bedroom and looks through it*)

Roy (*still through the keyhole*). Do you want me to break down the door, Mimsey, is that what you want? Because that's what I'm doing if you're not out of there in five seconds . . . Stop crying on your dress. Use the towel!

Norma (*crossing to* ROY *at the door*). I don't have any money. Give me four dollars, I'll be back in ten minutes.

Roy (*gets up and moves below the bed*). In ten minutes she'll be a married woman, because I've had enough of this nonsense. (*Yells in*) All right, Mimsey, stand in the shower because I'm breaking down the door.

Norma (*getting in front of the door*). Roy, don't get crazy.

Roy (*preparing himself for a run at the door*). Get out of my way.

---

3. **Bergdorf's:** Bergdorf Goodman, an expensive store near the Plaza Hotel.

Norma. Roy, she'll come out. Just talk nicely to her.

Roy (*waving her away*). We already had nice talking. Now we're gonna have door breaking. (*Through the door*) All right, Mimsey, I'm coming in!

Norma. No, Roy, don't! Don't!

[*She gets out of the way as* ROY *hurls his body, led by his shoulder, with full force against the door. It doesn't budge. He stays against the door silently a second; he doesn't react. Then he says, calmly and softly:*]

Roy. Get a doctor.

Norma (*standing below the door*). I knew it. I knew it.

Roy (*drawing back from the door*). Don't tell me I knew it, just get a doctor. (*Through the door*) I'm not coming in, Mimsey, because my arm is broken.

Norma. Let me see it. Can you move your fingers? (*Moves to him and examines his fingers*)

Roy (*through the door*). Are you happy now? Your mother has torn stockings and your father has a broken arm. How much longer is this gonna go on?

Norma (*moving* ROY's *fingers*). It's not broken, you can move your fingers. Give me four dollars with your other hand, I have to get stockings.

[*She starts to go into his pockets. He slaps her hands away.*]

Roy. Are you crazy moving a broken arm?

Norma. Two dollars, I'll get a cheap pair.

Roy (*as though she were a lunatic*). I'm not carrying any cash today. Rented, everything is rented.

Norma. I can't rent stockings. Don't you even have a charge plate? (*Starts to go through his pockets again*)

Roy (*slaps her hands away. Then pointing dramatically*). Wait in the Green Room! You're no use to me here, go wait in the Green Room!

Norma. With torn stockings?

Roy. Stand behind the rented potted plant. (*Takes her by the arm and leads her below the bed. Confidentially*) They're going to call from downstairs any second asking where the bride is. And *I'm* the one who's going to have to speak to them. *Me! Me! Me!* (*The phone rings. Pushing her toward the phone*) That's them. *You* speak to them!

Norma. What happened to *me me me*?

[*The phone rings again.*]

Roy (*moving to the bathroom door*). Answer it. Answer it.

[*The phone rings again.*]

Norma (*moving to the phone*). What am I going to say to them?

Roy. I don't know. Maybe something'll come to you as you're talking.

Norma (*picks the phone up*). Hello? . . . Oh, Mr. Eisler . . . Yes, it certainly is the big moment. (*She forces a merry laugh.*)

Roy. Stall 'em. Stall 'em. Just keep stalling him. Whatever you do, stall 'em! (*Turns to the door*)

Norma (*on the phone*). Yes, we'll be down in two minutes. (*Hangs up*)

> **" No, Roy, don't! Don't! "**

Roy (*turns back to her*). Are you crazy? What did you say that for? I told you to stall him.

Norma. I stalled him. You got two minutes. What do you want from me?

Roy (*shakes his arm at her*). You always panic. The minute there's a little crisis, you always go to pieces and panic.

Norma (*shaking her arm back at him*). Don't wave your broken arm at me. Why don't you use it to get your daughter out of the bathroom?

Roy (*very angry, kneeling to her on the bed*). I could say something to you now.

Norma (*confronting him, kneels in turn on the bed*). Then why don't you say it?

Roy. Because it would lead to a fight. And I don't want to spoil this day for you. (*He gets up and crosses back to the bathroom door.*) Mimsey, this is your father speaking . . . I think you know I'm not a violent man. I can be stern and strict, but I have never once been violent. Except when I'm angry. And I am really angry now, Mimsey. You can ask your mother.

[*Moves away so* NORMA *can get to the door.*]

Norma (*crossing to the bathroom door*). Mimsey, this is your mother speaking. It's true, darling, your father is very angry.

Roy (*moving back to the door*). This is your father again, Mimsey. If you have a problem you want to discuss, unlock the door and we'll discuss it. I'm not going to ask you this again, Mimsey. I've reached the end of my patience. I'm gonna count to three . . . and by God, I'm warning you, young lady, by the time I've reached three. . . *this door better be open!* (*Moving away to below the bed*) All right—One! . . . Two! . . . THREE! (*There is no reply or movement from behind the door.* ROY *helplessly sinks down on the foot of the bed.*) . . . Where did we fail her?

Norma (*crosses to the far side of the bed, consoling him as she goes, and sits on the edge*). We didn't fail her.

Roy. They're playing "Here Comes the Bride"

downstairs and she's barricaded in a toilet—we must have failed her.

Norma (*sighs*). All right, if it makes you any happier, we failed her.

Roy. You work and you dream and you hope and you save your whole life for this day, and in one click of a door, suddenly everything crumbles. Why? What's the answer?

Norma. It's not your fault, Roy. Stop blaming yourself.

Roy. I'm not blaming myself. I know *I've* done my best.

Norma (*turns and looks at him*). What does that mean?

Roy. It means we're not perfect. We make mistakes, we're only human. I've done my best and we failed her.

Norma. Meaning *I* didn't do my best?

Roy (*turning to her*). I didn't say that. I don't know what your best is. Only *you* know what your best is. Did you do your best?

Norma. Yes, I did my best.

Roy. And I did my best.

Norma. Then we *both* did our best.

Roy. So it's not our fault.

Norma. That's what I said before.

[*They turn away from each other. Then:*]

Roy (*softly*). Unless one of us didn't do our best.

Norma (*jumping up and moving away*). I don't want to discuss it any more.

Roy. All right, then what are we going to do?

Norma. I'm having a heart attack, *you* come up with something.

Roy. How? All right, I'll go down and tell them. (*Gets up and moves to the bedroom door*)

Norma (*moving to the door in front of him*). Tell them? Tell them what?

[*As they move into the living room, she stops him above the sofa.*]

Roy. I don't know. Those people down there deserve some kind of an explanation. They got all

dressed up, didn't they?

Norma. What are you going to say? You're going to tell them that my daughter is not going to marry their son and that she's locked herself in the bathroom?

Roy. What do you want me to do, start off with two good jokes? They're going to find out *some* time, aren't they?

Norma (*with great determination*). I'll tell you what you're going to do. If she's not out of there in five minutes, we're going to go out the back door and move to Seattle, Washington! . . . You don't think I'll be able to show my face in this city again, do you? (ROY *ponders this for a moment, then reassures her with a pat on the arm. Slowly he turns and moves into the bedroom. Suddenly, he loses control and lets his anger get the best of him. He grabs up the chair from*

"ROY!"

the dresser, and brandishing it above his head, he dashes for the bedroom door, not even detouring around the bed but rather crossing right over it. NORMA *screams and chases after him.*) ROY!

[*At the bathroom door,* ROY *manages to stop himself in time from smashing the chair against the door, trembling with frustration and anger. Finally, exhausted, he puts the chair down below the door and straddles it, sitting leaning on the back.* NORMA *sinks into the bedroom armchair.*]

Roy. . . . Would you believe it, last night I cried. Oh yes. I turned my head into the pillow and lay there in the dark, crying, because today I was losing my little girl. Some stranger was coming and taking my little Mimsey away from me . . . so I turned my back to you—and cried . . . Wait'll you hear what goes on *tonight*!

Norma (*lost in her own misery*). I should have invited your cousin Lillie. (*Gestures to the heavens*) She wished this on me, I know it. (*Suddenly* ROY *begins to chuckle.* NORMA *looks at him. He chuckles louder, although there is clearly no joy in his laughter.*) Do you find something funny about this?

Roy. Yes, I find something funny about this. I find it funny that I hired a photographer for three hundred dollars. I find it hysterical that the wedding pictures are going to be you and me in front of a locked bathroom! (*Gets up and puts the chair aside*) All right, I'm through sitting around waiting for that door to open. (*He crosses to the bedroom window and tries to open it.*)

Norma (*following after him*). What are you doing?

Roy. What do you think I'm doing?

[*Finding it impossible to open it, he crosses to the living room and opens a window there. The curtains begin to blow in the breeze.*]

Norma (*crosses after him*). If you're jumping, I'm going with you. You're not leaving *me* here alone.

Roy (*looking out the window*). I'm gonna crawl out along that ledge and get in through the bathroom window. (*He starts to climb out the window.*)

Norma. Are you crazy? It's seven stories up. You'll kill yourself. (*She grabs hold of him.*)

Roy. It's four steps, that's all. It's no problem, I'm telling you. Now will you let go of me.

Norma (*struggling to keep him from getting out the window*). Roy, no! Don't do this. We'll leave her in the bathroom. Let the hotel worry about her. Don't go out on the ledge. (*In desperation, she grabs hold of one of the tails of his coat.*)

Roy (*half out the window, trying to get out as she holds on to his coat*). You're gonna rip my coat. Let go or you're gonna rip my coat. (*As he tries to pull away from her, his coat rips completely up the back, right up to the collar. He stops and slowly comes back into the room.* NORMA *has frozen in misery by the bedroom door after letting go of the coat.* ROY *draws himself up with great dignity and control. He slowly turns and moves into the bedroom, stopping by the bed. With great patience, he calls toward the bathroom.*) Hey, you in there . . . Are you happy now? Your mother's got torn stockings and your father's got a rented ripped coat. Some wedding it's gonna be. (*Exploding, he crosses back to the open window in the living room.*) Get out of my way!

Norma (*puts hand to her head*). I'm getting dizzy. I think I'm going to pass out.

"You can pass out after the wedding . . ."

Roy (*getting her out of the way*). . . . You can pass out *after* the wedding . . . (*He goes out the window and onto the ledge.*) Call room service. I want a double Scotch the minute I get back.

[*And he disappears from view as he moves across the ledge.* NORMA *runs into the bedroom and catches a glimpse of him as he passes the bedroom window, but then he disappears once more.*]

Norma (*bemoaning her fate*). . . . He'll kill himself. He'll fall and kill himself, that's the way my luck's been going all day. (*She staggers away from the window and leans on the bureau.*) I'm not going to look. I'll just wait until I hear a scream. (*The telephone rings and* NORMA *screams in fright.*) Aggghhh! . . . I thought it was him . . . (*She crosses to the phone by the bed. The telephone rings again.*) Oh, God, what am I going to say? (*She picks it up.*) Hello? . . . Oh, Mr. Eisler. Yes, we're coming . . . My husband's getting Mimsey now . . . We'll be right down. Have some more hors d'oeuvres . . . Oh, thank you. It certainly *is* the happiest day of my life. (*She hangs up.*) No, I'm going to tell him I've got a husband dangling over Fifty-ninth Street. (*As she crosses back to the opened window, a sudden <u>torrent</u> of rain begins to fall. As she gets to the window and sees it*) I knew it! I knew it! It had to happen . . . (*She gets closer to the window and tries to look out.*) Are you all right, Roy? . . . Roy? (*There's no answer.*) He's not all right, he fell. (*She staggers into the bedroom.*) He fell, he fell, he fell, he fell . . . He's dead, I know it. (*She collapses onto the armchair.*) He's laying there in a puddle in front of Trader Vic's[4] . . . I'm passing out. This time I'm really passing out. (*And she passes out on the chair, legs and arms spread-eagled. The doorbell rings; she jumps right up.*) I'm coming! I'm coming! Help me, whoever you are, help me! (*She rushes through the bedroom into the living room and to the front door.*) Oh, please, somebody, help me, please!

---

4. **Trader Vic's:** restaurant formerly in the Plaza Hotel.

[*She opens the front door and* ROY *stands there dripping wet, fuming, exhausted, and with clothes disheveled[5] and his hair mussed.*]

Roy (*staggering into the room and weakly leaning on the mantelpiece. It takes a moment for him to catch his breath.* NORMA, *concerned, follows him.*). She locked the window too. I had to climb in through a strange bedroom. There may be a lawsuit.

[*He weakly charges back into the bedroom, followed by* NORMA, *who grabs his coattails in an effort to stop him. The rain outside stops.*]

Norma (*stopping him below the bed*). Don't yell at her. Don't get her more upset.

Roy (*turning back to her*). Don't get her *upset*? I'm hanging seven stories from a gargoyle in a pouring rain and you want me to worry about *her*? . . . You know what she's doing in there? She's playing with her false eyelashes. (*Moves to the bathroom door*) I'm out there fighting for my life with pigeons and she's playing with eyelashes . . . (*Crossing back to* NORMA) . . . I already made up my mind. The minute I get my hands on her, I'm gonna kill her. (*Moves back to the door*) Once I show them the wedding bills, no jury on earth would convict me . . . And if by some miracle she survives, let there be no talk of weddings . . . She can go into a convent. (*Slowly moving back to* NORMA *below the bed*) . . . Let her become a librarian with thick glasses and a pencil in her hair, I'm not paying for any more canceled weddings . . . (*Working himself up into a frenzy, he rushes to the table by the armchair and grabs up some newspapers.*) Now get her out of there or I start to burn these newspapers and smoke her out.

[NORMA *stops him, soothes him, and manages to*

---

5. **disheveled** (di·shev'əld) *adj.:* disordered; messy.

Vocabulary
torrent (tôr'ənt) *n.:* flood; downpour.

get him calmed down. She gently seats him on the foot of the bed.]

Norma (*really frightened*). I'll get her out! I'll get her out! (*She crosses to the door and knocks.*) Mimsey! Mimsey, please! (*She knocks harder and harder.*) Mimsey, you want to destroy a family? You want a scandal? You want a story in the *Daily News?* . . . Is that what you want? Is it? . . . Open this door! *Open it!* (*She bangs very hard, then stops and turns to* ROY.) . . . Promise you won't get hysterical.

Roy. What did you do? (*Turns wearily to her*)

Norma. I broke my diamond ring.

Roy (*letting the papers fall from his hand*). Your good diamond ring?

Norma. How many do I have?

Roy (*yells through the door*). Hey, you with the false eyelashes! (*Getting up and moving to the door*) . . . You want to see a broken diamond ring? You want to see eighteen hundred dollars' worth of crushed baguettes?[6] . . . (*He grabs* NORMA's *hand and holds it to the keyhole.*) Here! Here! *This* is a worthless family heirloom (*Kicks the door*)—and *this* is a diamond bathroom door! (*Controlling himself. To* NORMA) Do you know what I'm going to do now? Do you have any idea? (NORMA *puts her hand to her mouth, afraid to hear.* ROY *moves away from the door to the far side of the bed.*) I'm going to wash my hands of the entire Eisler-Hubley wedding. You can take all the Eislers and all the hors d'oeuvres and go to Central Park and have an eight-thousand-dollar picnic . . . (*Stops and turns back to* NORMA) I'm going down to the Oak Room with my broken arm, with my drenched rented ripped suit—and I'm gonna get blind! . . . I don't mean drunk, I mean totally blind . . . (*Erupting with great <u>vehemence</u>*) because I don't want to see you or *your* crazy daughter again, if I live to be a thousand.

---

6. **baguettes** (ba·gets′) *n.:* here, diamonds in the shape of long, narrow rectangles.

[*He turns and rushes from the bedroom, through the living room to the front door. As he tries to open it,* NORMA *catches up to him, grabs his tailcoat, and pulls him back into the room.*]

Norma. That's right. Run out on me. Run out on your daughter. Run out on everybody just when they need you.

Roy. You don't need me. You need a rhinoceros with a blowtorch—because no one else can get into that bathroom.

Norma (*with rising emotion*). I'll tell you who can get into that bathroom. Someone with love and understanding. Someone who cares about that poor kid who's going through some terrible decision now and needs help. Help that only *you* can give her and that *I* can give her. *That's* who can get into that bathroom now.

[ROY *looks at her solemnly . . . Then he crosses past her, hesitates and looks back at her, and then goes into the bedroom and to the bathroom door.* NORMA *follows him back in. He turns and looks at* NORMA *again. Then he knocks gently on the door and speaks softly and with some tenderness.*]

Roy. Mimsey! . . . This is Daddy . . . Is something wrong, dear? . . . (*He looks back at* NORMA, *who nods encouragement, happy about his new turn in character. Then he turns back to the door.*) . . . I want to help you, darling. Mother and I both do. But how can we help you if you won't talk to us? Mimsey, can you hear me? (*There is no answer. He looks back at* NORMA.)

Norma (*at the far side of the bed*). Maybe she's too choked up to talk.

Roy (*through the door*). Mimsey, if you can hear me, knock twice for yes, once for no.(*There are two knocks on the door. They look at each other encouragingly.*) Good. Good . . . Now, Mimsey, we

---

Vocabulary

vehemence (vē′ə·məns) *n.:* strong feeling or passion.

want to ask you a very, very important question. Do you want to marry Borden or don't you?

[*They wait anxiously for the answer. We hear one knock, a pause, then another knock.*]

Norma (*happily*). She said yes.

Roy (*despondently*). She said no. (*Moves away from the door to the foot of the bed*)

Norma. It was two knocks. Two knocks is yes. She wants to marry him.

Roy. It wasn't a double knock "yes." It was two single "no" knocks. She doesn't want to marry him.

Norma. Don't tell me she doesn't want to marry him. I heard her distinctly knock "yes." She went (*Knocks twice on the foot of the bed*) "Yes, I want to marry him."

Roy. It wasn't (*Knocks twice on the foot of the bed*) . . . It was (*Knocks once on the foot of the bed*) . . . and then another (*Knocks once more on the foot of the bed*) . . . That's "no," twice, she's not marrying him. (*Sinks down on the side of the bed*)

Vocabulary
despondently (di·spän′dənt·lē) *adv.*: hopelessly.

“Don't tell me she doesn't want to marry him.”

Norma (*crossing to the door*) Ask her again. (*Into the door*) Mimsey, what did you say? Yes or no? (*They listen. We hear two distinct loud knocks.* NORMA *turns to* ROY.) . . . All right? There it is in plain English . . . You never *could* talk to your own daughter. (*Moves away from the door*)
Roy (*getting up wearily and moving to the door*). Mimsey, this is not a good way to have a conversation. You're gonna hurt your knuckles . . . Won't you come out and talk to us? . . . Mimsey?
Norma (*leads* ROY *gently to the foot of the bed*). Don't you understand, it's probably something she can't discuss with her father. There are times a daughter wants to be alone with her mother. (*Sits* ROY *down on the foot of the bed and crosses back to the door*) Mimsey, do you want me to come in there and talk to you, just the two of us, sweetheart? Tell me, darling, is that what you want? (*There is no reply. A strip of toilet paper appears from under the bathroom door.* ROY *notices it, pushes* NORMA *aside, bends down, picks it up, and reads it.*) What? What does it say? (ROY *solemnly hands it to her.* NORMA *reads it aloud.*) "I would rather talk to Daddy."

[NORMA *is crushed. He looks at her sympathetically. We hear the bathroom door unlock.* ROY *doesn't quite know what to say to* NORMA. *He gives her a quick hug.*]

Roy. I—I'll try not to be too long.

[*He opens the door and goes in, closing it behind him quietly.* NORMA, *still with the strip of paper in her hand, walks slowly and sadly to the foot of the bed and sits. She looks glumly down at the paper.*]

Norma (*aloud*). . . . "I would rather talk to

> **"It's so bad you can't even tell me . . ."**

Daddy". . . Did she have to write it on this kind of paper? (*She wads up the paper.*) . . . Well—maybe I didn't do my best . . . I thought we had such a good relationship . . . Friends. Everyone thought we were friends, not mother and daughter . . . I tried to do everything right . . . I tried to teach her that there could be more than just love between a mother and a daughter . . . There can be trust and respect and friendship and understanding . . . (*Getting angry, she turns and yells toward the closed door.*) Just because *I* don't speak to my mother doesn't mean *we* can't be different!

[*She wipes her eyes with the paper. The bathroom door opens. A solemn* ROY *steps out, and the door closes and locks behind him. He deliberately buttons his coat and crosses to the bedroom phone wordlessly.* NORMA *has not taken her eyes off him. The pause seems* <u>interminable</u>.]

Roy (*into the phone*). The Green Room, please . . . Mr. Borden Eisler. Thank you. (*He waits.*)
Norma (*getting up from the bed*). . . . I'm gonna have to guess, is that it? . . . It's so bad you can't even tell me . . . Words can't form in your mouth, it's so horrible, right? . . . Come on, I'm a strong person, Roy. Tell me quickly, I'll get over it . . .
Roy (*into the phone*) Borden? Mr. Hubley . . . Can you come up to 719? . . . Yes, now . . . (*He hangs up and gestures for* NORMA *to follow him. He crosses into the living room and down to the ottoman,*[7] *where he sits.* NORMA *follows and stands*

---

7. **ottoman** (ät'ə·mən) *n.*: cushioned footstool.

Vocabulary
interminable (in·tʉr'mi·nə·bəl) *adj.*: with no end in sight.

waiting behind him. Finally) She wanted to talk to me because she couldn't bear to say it to both of us at the same time . . . The reason she's locked herself in the bathroom . . . is she's afraid.

Norma. Afraid? What is she afraid of? That Borden doesn't love her?

Roy. Not that Borden doesn't love her.

Norma. That she doesn't love Borden?

Roy. Not that she doesn't love Borden.

Norma. Then what is she afraid of?

Roy. . . . She's afraid of what they're going to become.

Norma. I don't understand.

Roy. Think about it.

Norma *(crossing above the sofa)*. What's there to think about? What are they going to become? They love each other, they'll get married, they'll have children, they'll grow older, they'll become like us. *(Comes the dawn. Stops by the side of the sofa and turns back to* ROY)—I never thought about that.

Roy. Makes you stop and think, doesn't it?

Norma. I don't think we're so bad, do you? . . . All right, so we yell and scream a little. So we fight and curse and aggravate each other. So you blame me for being a lousy mother and I accuse you of being a rotten husband. It doesn't mean we're not happy . . . does it? . . . *(Her voice rising)* Well? . . . Does it? . . .

Roy *(looks at her)*. . . . She wants something better. *(The doorbell rings. He crosses to open the door.* NORMA *follows.)* Hello, Borden.

Borden *(stepping into the room)*. Hi.

Norma. Hello, darling.

Roy *(gravely)*. Borden, you're an intelligent young man. I'm not going to beat around the bush. We have a serious problem on our hands.

Borden. How so?

Roy. Mimsey—is worried. Worried about your future together. About the whole institution of marriage. We've tried to allay her fears, but obviously we haven't been a very good example. It seems you're the only one who can communicate with her. She's locked herself in the bathroom and is not coming out . . . It's up to you now.

[*Without a word,* BORDEN *crosses below the sofa and up to the bedroom, through the bedroom below the bed and right up to the bathroom door. He knocks.*]

Borden. Mimsey? . . . This is Borden . . . Cool it! *(Then he turns and crosses back to the living room. Crossing above the sofa, he passes the Hubleys, and without looking at them, says)* See you downstairs!

[*He exits without showing any more emotion. The Hubleys stare after him as he closes the door. But then the bathroom door opens and* NORMA *and* ROY *slowly turn to it as* MIMSEY, *a beautiful bride, in a formal wedding gown, with veil, comes out.*]

Mimsey. I'm ready now!

[NORMA *turns and moves into the bedroom toward her.* ROY *follows slowly, shaking his head in amazement.*]

Roy. *Now* you're ready? *Now* you come out?

Norma *(admiring* MIMSEY). Roy, please . . .

Roy *(getting angry, leans toward her over the bed)*. I break every bone in my body and you come out for "Cool it"?

Norma *(pushing* MIMSEY *toward* ROY). You're beautiful, darling. Walk with your father, I want to look at both of you.

Roy *(fuming. As she takes his arm, to* NORMA) That's how he communicates? That's the brilliant understanding between two people? "Cool it"?

Norma *(gathering up* MIMSEY'*s train as they move toward the living room)*. Roy, don't start in.

Roy. What kind of a person is that to let your daughter marry?

[*They stop above the sofa.* MIMSEY *takes her bridal bouquet from the table behind the sofa while* NORMA *puts on her wrap and takes her gloves from the back of the sofa.*]

Norma. Roy, don't aggravate me. I'm warning you, don't spoil this day for me.

Roy. Kids today don't care. Not like they did in my day.

Norma. Walk. Will you walk? In five minutes he'll marry one of the flower girls. Will you walk—

[MIMSEY *takes* ROY *by the arm and they move to the door as* NORMA *follows.*]

Roy [*turning back to* NORMA] Crazy. I must be out of my mind, a boy like that. (*Opens the door*) She was better off in the bathroom. You hear me? Better off in the bathroom . . . (*They are out the door . . .*)■

CURTAIN

"She was better off in the bathroom."

Meet the Writer

Neil Simon

Laughing on the Outside

Over the years, Neil Simon (1927–   ) has had a string of successful plays running on Broadway. His plays are also performed in community and university theaters, on film, and on television. Simon has been making people laugh for more than fifty years.

Born and raised in New York City, Simon began writing comedy for television in the early 1950s. He moved on to the theater with his first play, *Come Blow Your Horn,* in 1961. Since then he has written hits for Broadway and the movies, such as *The Odd Couple, Chapter Two,* and *The Goodbye Girl.* Two of his comedies, *Barefoot in the Park* and *Plaza Suite,* had record-breaking runs on Broadway. Some of his more recent plays, *Brighton Beach Memoirs, Biloxi Blues,* and *Broadway Bound,* are based on his own boyhood and on his stint in the army.

Simon says that he is always looking at life as a play—he is always on the alert for new characters and new stories. In his half century as a professional writer, he has discovered almost everything there is to know about why people laugh. He says that audiences often laugh as a relief from the tension in a play. Simon tells about the time when *Plaza Suite* was about to open on Broadway:

66 The first act was too long—it wasn't that it was too long, we were getting too many laughs in a scene that we thought was basically serious. So Mike [Nichols, the director] and I started to cut out all of the laugh lines, and they started to laugh at other lines that they had never laughed at. They just wanted to laugh! 99

For Independent Reading

For more laughs, read *Barefoot in the Park,* a comic play about the difficult first weeks of a new marriage (for a short excerpt, see page 1052). You'll also enjoy *The Odd Couple,* a hilarious comedy about two men who are separated from their wives and are sharing an apartment, and *Broadway Bound,* Simon's humorous portrait of himself as a young writer dealing with his difficult family.

Reading Check

1. The **exposition** of a play presents the characters and their basic situation and **conflicts.** In *Visitor from Forest Hills,* the exposition is given in Norma's opening speech. How does Norma describe the way Mimsey feels? What is the *real* problem?

2. What different approaches does Norma first use to try to coax Mimsey out of the bathroom?

3. Many **farces,** or comedies, have a jack-in-the-box character, a character who establishes one attitude and then re-peats it each time he or she "pops up" in the play. We laugh at the character because he or she is so predictable. Roy Hubley is the jack-in-the-box in this play. What is he always concerned about? Find at least three lines that re-peat Roy's chief concern.

4. What do the Hubleys finally realize that Mimsey is afraid of?

5. Borden's appearance onstage signals the **climax** of the play. How does he resolve the Hubleys' problem?

Thinking Critically

6. What **farcical** (farcelike) actions do Norma and Roy Hubley engage in to get Mimsey to come out of the bath-room? **Contrast** how they look when the play begins with how they look when the play is over and they start downstairs.

7. Why do you think Borden's simple "Cool it!" works, whereas Norma and Roy's hysterics do not?

8. **Tension** is often created when a play's action runs against the clock. Why is time a crucial element in this play?

9. On the surface this play is about a frightened bride and her parents' comic efforts to get her to her wed-ding ceremony. Who, though, re-ceives most of the playwright's attention? Who or what would you say is the *real* subject of *Visitor from Forest Hills?*

10. Neil Simon's plays are usually **satiric**—that is, they make us laugh because they expose the foolishness of certain characters. What flaws in Roy and Norma is Simon making us laugh at?

Extending and Evaluating

11. Do you think most parents would behave like Roy and Norma if their daughter locked herself in a bathroom on her wedding day? Describe how some other parents might respond to the Hubleys' unusual problem.

WRITING

Extending the Play

Write a **farcical scene** showing Mimsey, Borden, Roy, and Norma twenty-five years after *Visitor from Forest Hills.* Begin the action at the wedding of Mimsey and Borden's daughter or son. Choose any part of the wedding ceremony or reception to dramatize, including the hour just before the wedding. (You might develop one of the photo ideas that you listed in your Quickwrite.) Invent a **conflict** so that your scene will have movement (a beginning, a middle, and an end). For example, do the bride and groom suddenly question whether they are truly in love? Express the conflict through the characters' **dialogue.** Be sure to include **stage directions** and **scene designs.**

SKILLS FOCUS

Literary Skills
Analyze characteristics of comedy and farce.

Writing Skills
Write a farcical scene.

Semantic Map

Making a semantic map is a good strategy for learning and using new words. A **semantic map** is a chart that can include a word's definition, questions and answers about when to use the word, the word's synonyms and antonyms (if there are any), and a sentence using the word. A sample map for the word *volatile* is shown here:

Word Bank

volatile
incredulously
torrent
vehemence
despondently
interminable

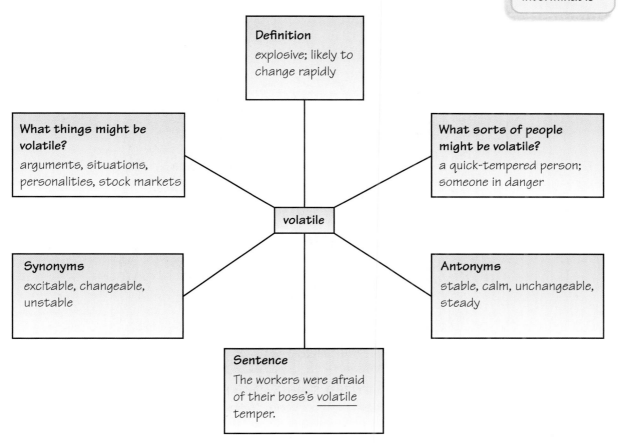

Definition
explosive; likely to change rapidly

What things might be volatile?
arguments, situations, personalities, stock markets

What sorts of people might be volatile?
a quick-tempered person; someone in danger

volatile

Synonyms
excitable, changeable, unstable

Antonyms
stable, calm, unchangeable, steady

Sentence
The workers were afraid of their boss's volatile temper.

PRACTICE

Work with a small group to make a **semantic map** for each of the other Word Bank words. Use a thesaurus or a dictionary for help identifying **synonyms** and **antonyms**.

SKILLS FOCUS

Vocabulary Skills
Create semantic maps.

WILLIAM SHAKESPEARE'S LIFE: A GENIUS FROM STRATFORD

by Robert Anderson

William Shakespeare (1783). Sketch by Ozias Humphrey.
By permission of the Folger Shakespeare Library, Washington, D.C.

He is the most famous writer in the world, but he left us no journals or letters—he left us only his poems and his plays. What we know about William Shakespeare's personal life comes mostly from church and legal documents—a baptismal registration, a marriage license, and records of real estate transactions. We also have a few remarks that others wrote about him during his lifetime.

We know that William was born the third of eight children around April 23, 1564, in Stratford, a market town about one hundred miles northwest of London. His father, John, was a shopkeeper and a man of some importance in Stratford, serving at various times as justice of the peace and high bailiff (mayor).

William attended grammar school, where he studied Latin grammar, Latin literature, and rhetoric (the uses of language). As far as we know, he had no further formal education.

At the age of eighteen, he married Anne Hathaway, who was eight years older than he was. Sometime after the birth of their second and third children (twins), Shakespeare moved to London, apparently leaving his family in Stratford.

We know that several years later, by 1592, Shakespeare had already become an actor and a playwright. By 1594, he was a charter member of the theatrical company called the Lord Chamberlain's Men, which was later to become the King's Men. (As the names of these acting companies indicate, theatrical groups depended on the support of a wealthy patron—the King's Men were supported by King James himself.) Shakespeare worked with this company for the rest of his writing life. Year after year he provided it with plays, almost on demand. Shakespeare was the ultimate professional writer. He had a theater that needed plays, actors who needed parts, and a family that needed to be fed.

Romeo and Juliet was probably among the early plays that Shakespeare wrote, between 1594 and 1596. By 1612, when he returned to Stratford to live the life of a prosperous retired gentleman, Shakespeare had written thirty-seven plays, including such masterpieces as *Julius Caesar, Hamlet, Othello, King Lear,* and *Macbeth.*

Shakespeare's plays are still produced all over the world. During a Broadway season in the 1980s, one critic estimated that if Shakespeare were alive, he would be receiving $25,000 a week in royalties for a production of *Othello* alone. The play was attracting larger audiences than any other nonmusical production in town.

Shakespeare died on April 23, 1616, at the age of fifty-two. He is buried under the old stone floor in the chancel of Holy Trinity Church in Stratford. Carved over his grave is the following verse (the spelling has been modernized):

Good friend, for Jesus' sake forbear
To dig the dust enclosèd here!
Blessed be the man that spares these stones
And cursed be he that moves my bones.

These are hardly the best of Shakespeare's lines (if indeed they are his at all), but like his other lines, they seem to have worked. His bones have lain undisturbed to this day.

Shakespeare and His Theater: A Perfect Match

by Robert Anderson

Sometimes playwrights influence the shape and form of a theater, but more often existing theaters seem to influence the shape and form of plays. It is important that we understand Shakespeare's theater because it influenced how he wrote his plays. Shakespeare took the theater of his time, and he used it brilliantly.

"The Wooden O"

In 1576, outside the city walls of London, an actor-manager named James Burbage built the first permanent theater in England. He called it the Theatre. Up to that time, touring acting companies had played wherever they could rent space. Usually this would be in the courtyards of inns. There the actors would erect a temporary platform stage at one end of the yard and play to an audience that stood around the stage or sat in the tiers of balconies that surrounded the courtyard. (Normally these balconies were used as passageways to the various rooms of the inn.) It was natural, then, that the first theater built by Burbage should derive its shape and form from the inns.

In 1599, Burbage's theater was torn down and its timbers were used by Shakespeare and his company to build the Globe Theatre. This was the theater for which Shakespeare wrote most of his plays.

In his play *Henry V*, Shakespeare called his theater a "wooden O." It was a large, round (or polygonal) building, three stories high, with a large platform stage that projected from one end into a yard open

The Globe Theatre (18th century), based on C. J. Visscher's engraved panoramic view of London (published 1616).
British Museum, London. The Granger Collection, New York.

to the sky. In the back wall of this stage was a curtained-off inner stage. Flanking the inner stage were two doors for entrances and exits. Above this inner stage was a small balcony or upper stage, which

SKILLS FOCUS

Pages 892–894 cover
Literary Skills
Understand the function of scene design in drama.

could be used to suggest Juliet's balcony or the high walls of a castle or the bridge of a ship. Trapdoors were placed in the floor of the main stage for the entrances and exits of ghosts and for descents into hell.

The plays were performed in the afternoon. Since the stage was open to the sky, there was no need for stage lighting. There were very few sets (scenery, furniture, and so on). The stage was "set" by the language. A whole forest scene was created in one play when a character announced, "Well, this is the Forest of Arden." But costumes were often elaborate, and the stage might have been hung with colorful banners and trappings. (The groundlings, those eight hundred or more people who stood shoulder to shoulder around the stage for the price of a penny, loved a good show. Most people still do.)

We can see that this stage, with its few sets and many acting areas—forestage, inner stage, and upper stage—made for a theater of great fluidity. That is, scene could follow scene with almost cinematic ease.

In one interesting aspect the theater in Shakespeare's day was very different from the theater we know today. Plays were originally performed by the all-male medieval trade guilds, so all women's parts were played by boys. It would be many years before women appeared on-stage in the professional English theater. In Shakespeare's day, Juliet would have been played by a trained boy actor.

"The Wooden O," the Globe Theatre. Drawing by David Gentleman.

The Modern Stage:
Back to Shakespeare's Theater

It has been said that all you need for a theater is "two planks and a passion." Since Shakespeare's time "the planks" (the stage) have undergone various changes. First, the part of the stage that projected into the yard grew narrower, and the small curtained inner stage grew larger, until there developed what is called the **proscenium stage.** Here there is no outer stage; there is only the inner stage, and a large curtain separates it from the audience. The effect is like looking inside a window or inside a picture frame. This is the stage most of us know today. It has been standard for well over a hundred years.

A cutaway of the Globe, showing the three stage levels and the dressing and prop rooms. Drawing by David Gentleman.

But recently we have seen a reversal of this design. Now more and more theaters (especially university and regional theaters) are building "thrust" stages, or arena stages. In this kind of theater, the audience once again sits on three or even four sides of the stage.

The Movies and the Theater: Words Versus Action

Like Shakespeare's stage, this kind of thrust stage, with its minimal scenery, allows playwrights (if they want) to move their stories rapidly from place to place. They can establish each new scene with a line like "Well, this is the Forest of Arden." As a result, playwrights have been tempted to write plays that imitate the style of movies. But this imitation rarely works. Theater and movies are different media. A theater audience does not necessarily want to be whisked from place to place. People who go to plays often prefer to spend a long, long time watching the subtle development of conflicts among a small group of people, all in one setting. For example, all of the action in Lorraine Hansberry's play *A Raisin in the Sun* takes place inside one small apartment on Chicago's South Side.

Movies are basically a *visual* medium and so must chiefly engage and delight the eye rather than the ear. (One movie director once referred to a dialogue in a movie as "foreground *noise*"!) The theater is much more a medium of *words*. When we go to see a play, it is the movement of the words rather than the movement of the scenery that delights us.

This difference between the appeal of a movie and the appeal of a play may account for the failure of some successful plays when they are translated to the screen. The movie producer will say, "Open up the story." In "opening up the story," the producer sometimes loses the concentration, the intensity, that was the prime virtue of the play.

HOW TO READ SHAKESPEARE

The Poetry

Whatever Shakespeare learned of rhetoric, or language, in grammar school, he parades with relish in *Romeo and Juliet*. He is obviously having a fine time here with puns and wordplay and all the other variations he can ring on the English language.

Romeo and Juliet is written in both prose and poetry. Prose is for the most part spoken by the common people and, occasionally, by Mercutio when he is joking. Most of the other characters speak in poetry.

Blank verse. The poetry is largely written in unrhymed iambic pentameter. In **iambic meter** each unstressed syllable is followed by a stressed syllable, as in the word *prefér*. In **iambic pentameter** there are five of these iambic units in each line. Unrhymed iambic pentameter is called **blank verse.** The word *blank* just means that there is no rhyme at the ends of lines.

Read aloud this perfect example of iambic pentameter, spoken by Romeo. The syllables marked with a stress (ˊ) should be stressed.

> But soft! What light through yonder window breaks?

Couplets. When Shakespeare uses rhymes, he generally uses **couplets,** two consecutive lines of poetry that rhyme. The couplets often punctuate a character's exit or signal the end of a scene. Read aloud Juliet's exit line from the balcony:

> Good night, good night! Parting is such sweet sorrow
> That I shall say good night till it be morrow.

Reading the lines. We have all heard people ruin a good poem by mechanically pausing at the end of each line, whether or not the meaning of the line called for a pause. (Maxwell Anderson, who wrote verse plays, had his plays typed as though they were prose, so that actors would not be tempted to pause at the end of each line. Consider using this technique when you stage a scene.)

Lines of poetry are either end-stopped or run-on. An **end-stopped line** has some punctuation at its end. A **run-on line** has no punctuation at its end. In a run-on line the meaning is always completed in the line or lines that follow.

Try reading aloud this passage from Act II, Scene 2, where Juliet speaks in end-stopped lines—lines ending with punctuation that requires her to pause:

> O, Romeo, Romeo! Wherefore art thou Romeo?
> Deny thy father and refuse thy name;
> Or, if thou wilt not, be but sworn my love,
> And I'll no longer be a Capulet.

Romeo's speech in the same scene has many run-on lines. Read these lines aloud; where does Romeo pause?

> The brightness of her cheek would shame those stars
> As daylight doth a lamp; her eyes in heaven
> Would through the airy region stream so bright
> That birds would sing and think it were not night.

The glory of *Romeo and Juliet* is its poetry and its theatricality. The play is fast moving, and the poetry suits the story of young people dealing with a matter very important to them—passionate, once-in-a-lifetime love.

The Words

Shakespeare wrote this play about four hundred years ago. It's not surprising, then, that many words are by now **archaic,** which means that they (or their particular meanings) have disappeared from common use. The sidenotes in the play will help you with these archaic words and with other words and expressions that might be unfamiliar to you. Here are some of the archaic words that are repeatedly used in the play:

'a: he.

a': on.

an' or **and:** if.

anon: soon; right away; coming.

but: if; except; only.

Good-den or **go-den** or **God-den:** Good evening (said in the late afternoon).

hap or **happy:** luck; lucky.

humor: mood; moisture.

Jack: common fellow; ordinary guy.

maid: unmarried girl.

mark: listen to.

Marry: mild oath, shortened from "by the Virgin Mary."

nice: trivial; foolish.

owes: owns.

shrift: confession or forgiveness for sins that have been confessed to a priest. After confession a person was said to be **shriven.**

soft: quiet; hush; slow up.

stay: wait.

still: always.

withal: with that; with.

wot: know.

The Tragedy of Romeo and Juliet

Make the Connection

Quickwrite ✏️

"Kids these days! They think that love conquers all, that nothing matters except how they feel about each other. They have no sense of responsibility to their families, no respect for tradition, no regard for those who are older and wiser. They don't know the problems they're going to have that all the love in the world won't solve for them."

What do you think of this complaint? Have you heard older people say these things about kids today? How would one of the kids respond to this speaker? Write a quick response from a kid's point of view.

Literary Focus

Tragedy

A **tragedy** is a narrative about serious and important actions that end unhappily. Usually a tragedy ends with the deaths of the **main characters.** In some tragedies the disaster hits totally innocent characters; in others the main characters are in some ways responsible for their downfall. Shakespeare's tragic plays usually follow this five-part pattern:

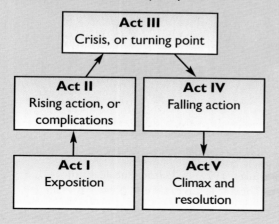

Act III
Crisis, or turning point

Act II
Rising action, or complications

Act IV
Falling action

Act I
Exposition

Act V
Climax and resolution

1. The **exposition** establishes the setting, introduces some of the main characters, explains background, and introduces the characters' main conflict.

2. The **rising action** consists of a series of complications. These occur as the main characters take action to resolve their problems.

3. The **crisis,** or **turning point,** is the moment when a choice made by the main characters determines the direction of the action: upward to a happy ending, which would be a **comedy,** or downward to **tragedy.** This turning point is the dramatic and tense moment when the forces of conflict come together. Look for the turning point in Act III.

4. The **falling action** presents events that result from the action taken at the turning point. These events usually lock the characters deeper and deeper into disaster; with each event we see the characters falling straight into tragedy.

5. The final and greatest **climax** occurs at the end of the play—usually, in tragedy, with the deaths of the main characters. In the **resolution** (or **denouement**) all the loose parts of the plot are tied up. The play is over.

The **Staging the Play** sidenotes throughout the play will help you visualize the play being performed—including the way the stage would be set, the way the actors would move and interact onstage, and the way they would say their lines.

(continued)

INTERNET

More About William Shakespeare

Keyword: LE7 9-11

Background

Most of Shakespeare's plays are based on stories that were already well-known to his audiences. (Shakespeare usually wrote about historical subjects.) *Romeo and Juliet* is based on a long narrative poem by Arthur Brooke, which was published in 1562 as *The Tragicall Historye of Romeus and Juliet.* Brooke's popular poem itself was based on older Italian stories.

Romeo and Juliet, a very young man and a nearly fourteen-year-old girl, fall in love at first sight. They are caught up in an idealized, almost unreal, passionate love. They are in love with love. In his prologue, Brooke preaches a moral, which people of his time expected. He says that Romeo and Juliet had to die because they broke the laws and married unwisely, against their parents' wishes. Shakespeare does away with this moralizing. He presents the couple as "star-crossed lovers," doomed to disaster by fate.

To understand what *star-crossed* means, you have to realize that most people of Shakespeare's time believed in astrology. They believed that the course of their lives was partly determined by the hour, day, month, and year of their birth—hence "the stars" under which they were born. Shakespeare himself may not have shared this belief. In a later play, *Julius Caesar,* he has a character question this age-old idea about astrology and the influence of the stars:

> The fault, dear Brutus, is not in our
>   stars,
> But in ourselves that we are underlings.

Although Shakespeare says in his prologue that Romeo and Juliet are star-crossed, he does not make them mere victims of fate. Romeo and Juliet make decisions that lead to their disaster. More important, other characters have a hand in the play's tragic ending. How important do *you* think fate is in affecting what happens to us? To what degree do you think we control our own destinies?

Romeo and Juliet (1977) by Milton Hebald, at the Delacorte Theater in Central Park, New York City.

❊ CHARACTERS ❊

THE MONTAGUES

Lord Montague

Lady Montague

Romeo, son of Montague

Benvolio, nephew of Montague and friend of Romeo

Balthasar, servant of Romeo

Abram, servant of Montague

THE CAPULETS

Lord Capulet

Lady Capulet

Juliet, daughter of Capulet

Tybalt, nephew of Lady Capulet

Nurse to Juliet

Peter, servant to the Nurse

Sampson
Gregory } servants of Capulet

An Old Man of the Capulet family

THE OTHERS

Prince Escalus, ruler of Verona

Mercutio, a relative of the Prince and friend of Romeo

Friar Laurence, a Franciscan priest

Friar John, another Franciscan priest

Count Paris, a young nobleman, a relative of the Prince

An Apothecary (a druggist)

Page to Paris

Chief Watchman

Three Musicians

An Officer

Citizens of Verona, Relatives of both families, **Maskers,**
Guards, Watchmen, and **Attendants**

Scene: Verona and Mantua, cities in northern Italy

"A pair of
star-crossed
lovers"
✧

THE TRAGEDY OF ROMEO AND JULIET

William Shakespeare

THE PROLOGUE

Enter CHORUS.

Chorus.
Two households, both alike in dignity,°
   In fair Verona, where we lay our scene,
From ancient grudge break to new mutiny,
   Where civil blood makes civil hands unclean.°
5   From forth the fatal loins of these two foes
   A pair of star-crossed lovers take their life;
Whose misadventured piteous overthrows
   Do with their death bury their parents' strife.
The fearful passage of their death-marked love,
10   And the continuance of their parents' rage,
Which, but° their children's end, naught could remove,
   Is now the two hours' traffic° of our stage;
The which if you with patient ears attend,
What here shall miss, our toil shall strive to mend.

                                [*Exit.*]

The photographs throughout the play are from the New York Shakespeare Festival's 1988 production of *Romeo and Juliet*, starring Cynthia Nixon as Juliet, Peter MacNicol as Romeo, and Anne Meara as the Nurse. All photographs taken by Martha Swope / TimePix.

1. dignity: status.

4. Where . . . unclean: That is, where civilians' passions ("civil blood") make their hands unclean (because they have been used for killing).

11. but: except for.

12. traffic: business.

? Staging the Play
14. *This prologue is spoken by a single actor called the Chorus. The Chorus welcomes the audience and gives them a taste of the story. What will the "two hours' traffic" of this stage be about? What will happen to the two lovers?*

✧ ACT I ✧

Scene 1. *Verona. A public place.*

Enter SAMPSON *and* GREGORY, *of the house of Capulet, with swords and bucklers (shields).*

Sampson. Gregory, on my word, we'll not carry coals.°
Gregory. No, for then we should be colliers.°
Sampson. I mean, and° we be in choler,° we'll draw.°
Gregory. Ay, while you live, draw your neck out of collar.°
5   **Sampson.** I strike quickly, being moved.
Gregory. But thou art not quickly moved to strike.
Sampson. A dog of the house of Montague moves me.
Gregory. To move is to stir, and to be valiant is to stand. Therefore, if thou art moved, thou run'st away.
10   **Sampson.** A dog of that house shall move me to stand. I will take the wall° of any man or maid of Montague's.
Gregory. That shows thee a weak slave; for the weakest goes to the wall.°
Sampson. 'Tis true; and therefore women, being the
15   weaker vessels, are ever thrust to the wall. Therefore I will push Montague's men from the wall and thrust his maids to the wall.
Gregory. The quarrel is between our masters and us their men.
20   **Sampson.** 'Tis all one. I will show myself a tyrant. When I have fought with the men, I will be civil with the maids—I will cut off their heads.
Gregory. The heads of the maids?
Sampson. Ay, the heads of the maids or their maidenheads.
25   Take it in what sense thou wilt.
Gregory. They must take it in sense that feel it.
Sampson. Me they shall feel while I am able to stand; and 'tis known I am a pretty piece of flesh.
Gregory. 'Tis well thou art not fish; if thou hadst, thou
30   hadst been Poor John.° Draw thy tool!° Here comes two of the house of Montagues.

[Enter two other servingmen, ABRAM *and* BALTHASAR.]

Sampson. My naked weapon is out. Quarrel! I will back thee.

? Staging the Play
Stage direction: Two servants enter, bragging and teasing each other. What actions do you imagine they are engaged in as they cross the city square?

1. carry coals: do dirty work (put up with insults). People often made jokes about men who carted coal.
2. colliers: coal dealers (men with dirty jobs). Notice how the servants start making jokes based on words that sound similar (*colliers, choler,* and *collar*).
3. and: if. **choler:** anger. **draw:** pull out swords.
4. collar: hangman's noose.
11. take the wall: take the best place on the path (which is closest to the wall).
13. goes to the wall: is defeated.

30. Poor John: kind of salted fish, a poor person's food. **tool:** sword.

? Staging the Play
Stage direction: Sampson's and Gregory's swaggering stops when they spy their enemies. How do their next speeches show that they are really cowards? What's Sampson doing when he says, "Quarrel! I will back thee"?

Gregory. How? Turn thy back and run?

Sampson. Fear me not.°

35 **Gregory.** No, marry. I fear thee!

Sampson. Let us take the law of our sides;° let them begin.

Gregory. I will frown as I pass by, and let them take it as they list.

Sampson. Nay, as they dare. I will bite my thumb° at them,
40 which is disgrace to them if they bear it.

Abram. Do you bite your thumb at us, sir?

Sampson. I do bite my thumb, sir.

Abram. Do you bite your thumb at us, sir?

Sampson (*aside to* GREGORY). Is the law of our side if I say
45 ay?

Gregory (*aside to* SAMPSON). No.

Sampson. No, sir, I do not bite my thumb at you, sir; but I
bite my thumb, sir.

Gregory. Do you quarrel, sir?

50 **Abram.** Quarrel, sir? No, sir.

Sampson. But if you do, sir, I am for you. I serve as good a
man as you.

Abram. No better.

Sampson. Well, sir.

[*Enter* BENVOLIO.]

55 **Gregory.** Say "better." Here comes one of my master's
kinsmen.

Sampson. Yes, better, sir.

Abram. You lie.

Sampson. Draw, if you be men. Gregory, remember thy
60 swashing° blow.

[*They fight.*]

Benvolio.
  Part, fools!
  Put up your swords. You know not what you do.

[*Enter* TYBALT.]

Tybalt.
  What, art thou drawn among these heartless hinds?°
  Turn thee, Benvolio; look upon thy death.

Benvolio.
65 I do but keep the peace. Put up thy sword,
  Or manage it to part these men with me.

---

34. Fear me not: Do not distrust me.

36. Let . . . sides: Let us stay on the right side of the law.

39. bite my thumb: insulting gesture.

? Staging the Play
41. *It takes the Montague servants some time to speak. How might their actions show that these four servants are very wary of one another?*

? Staging the Play
44. *An* **aside** *is dialogue spoken by a character to the audience or to another character that others onstage are not supposed to hear. Sampson and Gregory speak to each other in asides. Who is not supposed to overhear them?*

? 55. *How does Gregory's behavior change when he spots Tybalt in the distance?*

60. swashing: slashing with great force.

? Staging the Play
62. *What action is Benvolio involved in here?*

63. heartless hinds: cowardly hicks.

? Staging the Play
64. *In some productions, Tybalt's second line is spoken after a dramatic silence. Why should this line demand our attention?*

Tybalt.

> What, drawn, and talk of peace? I hate the word
> As I hate hell, all Montagues, and thee.
> Have at thee, coward!

[*They fight.*]

[*Enter an* OFFICER, *and three or four* CITIZENS *with clubs,*
bills, and partisans, or spears.]

70 **Officer.** Clubs, bills, and partisans! Strike! Beat them down!
> Down with the Capulets! Down with the Montagues!

[*Enter old* CAPULET, *in his gown, and his wife,* LADY
CAPULET.]

Capulet.

> What noise is this? Give me my long sword, ho!

Lady Capulet.

> A crutch, a crutch! Why call you for a sword?

Capulet.

> My sword, I say! Old Montague is come
75 > And flourishes his blade in spite of° me.

[*Enter old* MONTAGUE *and his wife,* LADY MONTAGUE.]

Montague.

> Thou villain Capulet!—Hold me not; let me go.

Lady Montague.

> Thou shalt not stir one foot to seek a foe.

[*Enter* PRINCE ESCALUS, *with his* TRAIN.]

Prince.

> Rebellious subjects, enemies to peace,
> Profaners of this neighbor-stainèd steel—
80 > Will they not hear? What, ho! You men, you beasts,
> That quench the fire of your pernicious rage
> With purple fountains issuing from your veins!
> On pain of torture, from those bloody hands
> Throw your mistempered° weapons to the ground
85 > And hear the sentence of your movèd prince.
> Three civil brawls, bred of an airy° word
> By thee, old Capulet, and Montague,
> Have thrice disturbed the quiet of our streets
> And made Verona's ancient citizens
90 > Cast by their grave beseeming° ornaments
> To wield old partisans, in hands as old,

67. *This is a key speech. What is Tybalt's mood? How is he shown to be opposite in nature to Benvolio?*

73. *In the midst of the tension over Tybalt, we have a comic touch. Why is Lady Capulet talking about a crutch?*
75. in spite of: in defiance of.

76. *Who is holding Montague back?*

Staging the Play
Stage direction: If you were directing this play, how would you stage the entrance of the prince? His dignified procession must contrast with the bloody rioting. How do you know from his speech that the prince is at first ignored by the brawlers?

84. mistempered: used with bad temper.

Staging the Play
85. *There is a dramatic pause before the next line is spoken. What are the brawlers doing now?*
86. airy: light or harmless.
90. grave beseeming: dignified, as they should be.

"Throw your mistempered weapons to the ground . . ."
✪

Cankered° with peace, to part your cankered° hate.
If ever you disturb our streets again,
Your lives shall pay the forfeit of the peace.
95   For this time all the rest depart away.
You, Capulet, shall go along with me;
And, Montague, come you this afternoon,
To know our farther pleasure in this case,
To old Freetown, our common judgment place.
100   Once more, on pain of death, all men depart.

[*Exeunt all but* MONTAGUE, LADY MONTAGUE, *and* BENVOLIO.]

Montague.
Who set this ancient quarrel new abroach?°
Speak, nephew, were you by when it began?
Benvolio.
Here were the servants of your adversary
And yours, close fighting ere I did approach.
105   I drew to part them. In the instant came
The fiery Tybalt, with his sword prepared,
Which, as he breathed defiance to my ears,
He swung about his head and cut the winds,
Who, nothing hurt withal, hissed him in scorn.
110   While we were interchanging thrusts and blows,
Came more and more, and fought on part and part,°
Till the prince came, who parted either part.
Lady Montague.
O, where is Romeo? Saw you him today?
Right glad I am he was not at this fray.

92. cankered: The first *cankered* means "rusted" (from lack of use in peaceful times); the second means "diseased," like a canker, a running sore.

? 100. *What has been happening in Verona? What is the prince's warning?*

101. new abroach: newly opened.

111. on part and part: some on one side, some on the other.

? Staging the Play
114. *For the first time, Romeo is mentioned—by his mother, whose parental concern is accented by a rhyme. Lady Montague does not say anything else in this scene. What do you imagine she is doing while her husband and Benvolio discuss her son?*

Benvolio.

115   Madam, an hour before the worshiped sun
       Peered forth the golden window of the East,
       A troubled mind drave me to walk abroad;
       Where, underneath the grove of sycamore
       That westward rooteth from this city side,
120   So early walking did I see your son.
       Towards him I made, but he was ware° of me
       And stole into the covert of the wood.
       I, measuring his affections by my own,
       Which then most sought where most might not be found,°
125   Being one too many by my weary self,
       Pursued my humor° not pursuing his,
       And gladly shunned who gladly fled from me.

Montague.

       Many a morning hath he there been seen,
       With tears augmenting the fresh morning's dew,
130   Adding to clouds more clouds with his deep sighs;
       But all so soon as the all-cheering sun
       Should in the farthest East begin to draw
       The shady curtains from Aurora's° bed,
       Away from light steals home my heavy° son
135   And private in his chamber pens himself,
       Shuts up his windows, locks fair daylight out,
       And makes himself an artificial night.
       Black and portentous must this humor prove
       Unless good counsel may the cause remove.

Benvolio.

140   My noble uncle, do you know the cause?

Montague.

       I neither know it nor can learn of him.

Benvolio.

       Have you importuned° him by any means?

Montague.

       Both by myself and many other friends;
       But he, his own affections' counselor,
145   Is to himself—I will not say how true—
       But to himself so secret and so close,
       So far from sounding° and discovery,
       As is the bud bit with an envious° worm
       Ere he can spread his sweet leaves to the air
150   Or dedicate his beauty to the sun.
       Could we but learn from whence his sorrows grow,
       We would as willingly give cure as know.

121. ware: aware.

124. He sought a place where no one could be found. (He wanted to be alone.)
126. humor: mood.

133. In Roman mythology, Aurora (ô·rôr′ə) is goddess of the dawn.
134. heavy: heavy-hearted.

139. *Romeo has been described by his father and his friend. What do we know of him so far?*

142. importuned: questioned.

147. So far from sounding: so far from being sounded out for his mood (as a river is sounded for its depth).
148. envious: evil.

[*Enter* ROMEO.]

Benvolio.
See, where he comes. So please you step aside;
I'll know his grievance, or be much denied.

Montague.
I would thou wert so happy° by the stay
To hear true shrift.° Come, madam, let's away.

[*Exeunt* MONTAGUE *and* LADY MONTAGUE.]

Benvolio.
Good morrow, cousin.

Romeo. Is the day so young?

Benvolio.
But new struck nine.

Romeo. Ay me! Sad hours seem long.
Was that my father that went hence so fast?

Benvolio.
It was. What sadness lengthens Romeo's hours?

Romeo.
Not having that which having makes them short.

Benvolio. In love?

Romeo. Out—

Benvolio. Of love?

Romeo.
Out of her favor where I am in love.

Benvolio.
Alas that love, so gentle in his view,°
Should be so tyrannous and rough in proof!°

> "Here's much to do with hate,
> but more with love."

Romeo.
Alas that love, whose view is muffled still,°
Should without eyes see pathways to his will!
Where shall we dine? O me! What fray was here?
Yet tell me not, for I have heard it all.
Here's much to do with hate, but more with love.°
Why then, O brawling love, O loving hate,
O anything, of nothing first created!

Staging the Play
Stage direction: *Romeo at first doesn't see his parents or Benvolio. How do you think he would be acting as he enters?*

155. happy: lucky.
156. shrift: confession.

Staging the Play
157. *Benvolio is trying to be casual. What attitude should Romeo convey in his answer to Benvolio's cheery greeting?*

165. *Romeo blurts out the truth. What is the cause of his strange behavior?*

166. view: appearance.
167. in proof: in reality.

168. muffled still: always blindfolded. Romeo is talking about Cupid (the god of love in Roman mythology), who was often depicted as blindfolded.

170. *Romeo wants to change the subject. Then he notices the signs of the street fighting. What does he say about the rivalry between the two families?*

172. more with love: They enjoyed fighting.

175 O heavy lightness, serious vanity,
Misshapen chaos of well-seeming forms,
Feather of lead, bright smoke, cold fire, sick health,
Still-waking sleep, that is not what it is!
This love feel I, that feel no love in this.
Dost thou not laugh?

180 **Benvolio.** No, coz,° I rather weep.

Romeo.
Good heart, at what?

Benvolio. At thy good heart's oppression.

Romeo.
Why, such is love's transgression.
Griefs of mine own lie heavy in my breast,
Which thou wilt propagate,° to have it prest°
185 With more of thine. This love that thou hast shown
Doth add more grief to too much of mine own.
Love is a smoke made with the fume of sighs;
Being purged, a fire sparkling in lovers' eyes;
Being vexed, a sea nourished with loving tears.
190 What is it else? A madness most discreet,°
A choking gall, and a preserving sweet.
Farewell, my coz.

Benvolio. Soft!° I will go along.
And if you leave me so, you do me wrong.

Romeo.
Tut! I have lost myself; I am not here;
195 This is not Romeo, he's some other where.

Benvolio.
Tell me in sadness,° who is that you love?

Romeo.
What, shall I groan and tell thee?

Benvolio. Groan? Why, no;
But sadly tell me who.

Romeo.
Bid a sick man in sadness make his will.
200 Ah, word ill urged to one that is so ill!
In sadness, cousin, I do love a woman.

Benvolio.
I aimed so near when I supposed you loved.

Romeo.
A right good markman. And she's fair I love.

Benvolio.
A right fair mark, fair coz, is soonest hit.

175–178. *All of these are* **contradictions,** *things that are really the opposite of the way they are described. How does Romeo bitterly relate these to the love he feels?*

180. coz: cousin (or other relative).

184. propagate: increase. **prest:** pressed; burdened.

190. discreet: discriminating.

191. *Romeo refuses to reveal more about his troubles and suggests to Benvolio that he is driven mad by love. What things does he compare love to, before he tries to get away from Benvolio?*
192. Soft: Wait.

196. sadness: seriousness.

Romeo.

205   Well, in that hit you miss. She'll not be hit
       With Cupid's arrow. She hath Dian's wit,°
       And, in strong proof° of chastity well armed,
       From Love's weak childish bow she lives uncharmed.
       She will not stay° the siege of loving terms,
210   Nor bide th' encounter of assailing eyes,
       Nor ope her lap to saint-seducing gold.°
       O, she is rich in beauty; only poor
       That, when she dies, with beauty dies her store.°

Benvolio.

       Then she hath sworn that she will still° live chaste?

Romeo.

215   She hath, and in that sparing makes huge waste;
       For beauty, starved with her severity,
       Cuts beauty off from all posterity.
       She is too fair, too wise, wisely too fair,
       To merit bliss° by making me despair.
220   She hath forsworn to love, and in that vow
       Do I live dead that live to tell it now.

Benvolio.

       Be ruled by me; forget to think of her.

Romeo.

       O, teach me how I should forget to think!

Benvolio.

       By giving liberty unto thine eyes.
       Examine other beauties.

225   **Romeo.**   'Tis the way
       To call hers, exquisite, in question° more.
       These happy masks° that kiss fair ladies' brows,
       Being black, put us in mind they hide the fair.
       He that is strucken blind cannot forget
230   The precious treasure of his eyesight lost.
       Show me a mistress that is passing fair:
       What doth her beauty serve but as a note
       Where I may read who passed that passing fair?
       Farewell. Thou canst not teach me to forget.

Benvolio.

235   I'll pay that doctrine, or else die in debt.°

                                        [*Exeunt.*]

206. Dian's wit: the cunning of Diana, the Roman goddess of chastity, the moon, and hunting, who was not interested in men.
207. proof: armor.
209. stay: submit to.
211. Nor ope . . . gold: In Greek mythology, the god Zeus visited Danae in the form of a shower of gold, and Danae bore Zeus a son.
213. when she dies . . . her store: Her store of beauty dies with her, since she'll have no children.
214. still: always.

219. bliss: heaven.

221. *What vow has the young woman made?*

226. call . . . in question: bring her beauty to mind.
227. masks: Women often wore masks to protect their faces from the sun.

233. *Why won't looking at other women help Romeo?*

235. or else die in debt: or die trying.

Staging the Play
235. *Benvolio can exit here as if running after Romeo. The pair will reenter later, Romeo still being pursued. How would the audience feel about Benvolio?*

Scene 2. *A street.*

Enter CAPULET, COUNT PARIS, *and the clown, his* SERVANT.

Capulet.
But Montague is bound° as well as I,
In penalty alike; and 'tis not hard, I think,
For men so old as we to keep the peace.

Paris.
Of honorable reckoning° are you both,
5   And pity 'tis you lived at odds so long.
But now, my lord, what say you to my suit?

Capulet.
But saying o'er what I have said before:
My child is yet a stranger in the world,
She hath not seen the change of fourteen years;
10   Let two more summers wither in their pride
Ere we may think her ripe to be a bride.

Paris.
Younger than she are happy mothers made.

> "Earth hath swallowed all my hopes
> but she;
> She is the hopeful lady of my earth."

Capulet.
And too soon marred are those so early made.
Earth hath swallowed all my hopes but she;
15   She is the hopeful lady of my earth.
But woo her, gentle Paris, get her heart;
My will to her consent is but a part.
And she agreed, within her scope of choice°
Lies my consent and fair according° voice.
20   This night I hold an old accustomed° feast,
Whereto I have invited many a guest,
Such as I love; and you among the store,
One more, most welcome, makes my number more.
At my poor house look to behold this night
25   Earth-treading stars° that make dark heaven light.
Such comfort as do lusty young men feel

1. is bound: is pledged to keep the peace.

4. reckoning: reputation.

? **12.** *Paris is very much at ease with old Capulet and more composed than the lovesick Romeo we just saw. What does Paris want?*

? **15.** *Why doesn't Capulet want his daughter to marry right away? How is Capulet now different from the man who drew his sword in Scene 1?*

18. within her scope of choice: among all she can choose from.
19. according: agreeing.
20. accustomed: traditional.

25. Earth-treading stars: that is, young girls.

When well-appareled April on the heel
Of limping winter treads, even such delight
Among fresh fennel° buds shall you this night
30 Inherit° at my house. Hear all, all see,
And like her most whose merit most shall be;
Which, on more view of many, mine, being one,
May stand in number,° though in reck'ning none.°
Come, go with me.

[*To* SERVANT, *giving him a paper.*]

                  Go, sirrah, trudge about
35 Through fair Verona; find those persons out
Whose names are written there, and to them say
My house and welcome on their pleasure stay.°

[*Exit with* PARIS.]

Servant. Find them out whose names are written here? It is
written that the shoemaker should meddle with his yard
40 and the tailor with his last, the fisher with his pencil and
the painter with his nets;° but I am sent to find those
persons whose names are here writ, and can never find°
what names the writing person hath here writ. I must to
the learned. In good time!°

[*Enter* BENVOLIO *and* ROMEO.]

Benvolio.
45   Tut, man, one fire burns out another's burning;
        One pain is less'ned by another's anguish;
    Turn giddy, and be holp by backward turning;°
        One desperate grief cures with another's languish.
    Take thou some new infection to thy eye,
50   And the rank poison of the old will die.
Romeo.
    Your plantain leaf is excellent for that.
Benvolio.
    For what, I pray thee?
Romeo.   For your broken° shin.
Benvolio.
    Why, Romeo, art thou mad?
Romeo.
    Not mad, but bound more than a madman is;
55   Shut up in prison, kept without my food,

---

29. fennel: an herb. Capulet
compares the young girls to fennel
flowers.
30. Inherit: have.

33. stand in number: be one of
the crowd (of girls). **though in
reck'ning none:** though none will
be worth more than Juliet is.

? Staging the Play
34. *Capulet can be played
many ways by actors. Some play
him here as a loving, considerate
father. Other actors interpret him
as a man who chiefly wants a
socially advantageous marriage for
his daughter. How would you play
this scene?*

37. stay: wait.

? Staging the Play
38. *Like the other servants
this one plays for comedy. He can't
read or write. How should he
show his bewilderment?*

39–41. shoemaker . . . nets: The
servant is quoting mixed-up
proverbs. He's trying to say that
people should attend to what they
do best.
42. find: understand.
44. In good time: Just in time.

? Staging the Play
44. *The servant looks up
from the note to see the young
gentlemen enter. He now tries to
get them to read the note, while
Benvolio chases Romeo across the
stage. How do Romeo's comments
in the following conversation
show that he is trying to change
the subject?*

**47. be holp by backward
turning:** be helped by turning in
the opposite direction.
52. broken: scratched.

Whipped and tormented and—God-den,° good fellow.

Servant. God gi' go-den. I pray, sir, can you read?

Romeo.

Ay, mine own fortune in my misery.

Servant. Perhaps you have learned it without book. But, I
60   pray, can you read anything you see?

Romeo.

Ay, if I know the letters and the language.

Servant. Ye say honestly. Rest you merry.

Romeo. Stay, fellow; I can read.

[*He reads the letter.*]

"Signior Martino and his wife and daughters;
65   County Anselm and his beauteous sisters;
The lady widow of Vitruvio;
Signior Placentio and his lovely nieces;
Mercutio and his brother Valentine;
Mine uncle Capulet, his wife and daughters;
70   My fair niece Rosaline; Livia;
Signior Valentio and his cousin Tybalt;
Lucio and the lively Helena."
A fair assembly. Whither should they come?

Servant. Up.

75   **Romeo.** Whither? To supper?

Servant. To our house.

Romeo. Whose house?

Servant. My master's.

Romeo.

Indeed I should have asked you that before.

80   **Servant.** Now I'll tell you without asking. My master is the
great rich Capulet; and if you be not of the house of
Montagues, I pray come and crush a cup of wine. Rest
you merry.

[*Exit.*]

Benvolio.

At this same ancient° feast of Capulet's
85   Sups the fair Rosaline whom thou so loves;
With all the admirèd beauties of Verona.
Go thither, and with unattainted° eye
Compare her face with some that I shall show,
And I will make thee think thy swan a crow.

Romeo.

90   When the devout religion of mine eye

---

56. God-den: good evening.

? Staging the Play
56. *Romeo turns to get away
and runs into the servant, who
has been listening to them in
stupefied silence. How should the
two gentlemen treat the servant in
this little encounter?*

? Staging the Play
70. *Rosaline, Capulet's niece,
is the young woman Romeo is in
love with. Some actors read this line
to betray to the audience Romeo's
secret. How would you have Romeo
read this line? How would he ask
his question in line 73?*

84. ancient: old; established by
an old custom.

87. unattainted: untainted;
unspoiled (by prejudice).

? 89. *What does Benvolio say
to lure Romeo to the party?*

Maintains such falsehood, then turn tears to fires;
And these, who, often drowned, could never die,
Transparent heretics,° be burnt for liars!
One fairer than my love? The all-seeing sun
95   Ne'er saw her match since first the world begun.
    Benvolio.
    Tut! you saw her fair, none else being by,
    Herself poised° with herself in either eye;
    But in that crystal scales° let there be weighed
    Your lady's love against some other maid
100   That I will show you shining at this feast,
    And she shall scant° show well that now seems best.
    Romeo.
    I'll go along, no such sight to be shown,
    But to rejoice in splendor of mine own.

                    [*Exeunt.*]

93. Transparent heretics: His eyes would be easily "seen through"—they would betray the truth.

97. poised: balanced (for comparison).
98. crystal scales: Romeo's eyes.

101. scant: scarcely.

Staging the Play
103. *If we know from the letter that Rosaline is to be at the party and that she is the one Romeo loves, we know why Romeo decides to go to Capulet's. Actors usually say these lines to indicate that the decision to go is crucial and fateful. What mood is Romeo in?*

> "One fairer than my love? The all-seeing sun Ne'er saw her match since first the world begun."
>
> ✧

913

40   And then my husband (God be with his soul!
        'A was a merry man) took up the child.
        "Yea," quoth he, "dost thou fall upon thy face?
        Thou wilt fall backward when thou hast more wit;°
        Wilt thou not, Jule?" and, by my holidam,°
        The pretty wretch left° crying and said, "Ay."
45   To see now how a jest shall come about!
        I warrant, and I should live a thousand years,
        I never should forget it. "Wilt thou not, Jule?" quoth he,
        And, pretty fool, it stinted° and said, "Ay."
    Lady Capulet.
        Enough of this. I pray thee hold thy peace.
    Nurse.
50   Yes, madam. Yet I cannot choose but laugh
        To think it should leave crying and say, "Ay."
        And yet, I warrant, it had upon its brow
        A bump as big as a young cock'rel's stone;
        A perilous knock; and it cried bitterly.
55   "Yea," quoth my husband, "fall'st upon thy face?
        Thou wilt fall backward when thou comest to age,
        Wilt thou not, Jule?" It stinted and said, "Ay."
    Juliet.
        And stint thou too, I pray thee, nurse, say I.
    Nurse.
        Peace, I have done. God mark thee to his grace!
60   Thou wast the prettiest babe that e'er I nursed.

42. wit: understanding.

43. by my holidam: by my holy relic (object associated with a saint).
44. left: stopped.

48. stinted: stopped.

Staging the Play
48. *Shakespeare often includes **comic scenes** and speeches in his tragedies. The nurse laughs heartily at her husband's joke. How would Lady Capulet react?*

Staging the Play
58. *How would Juliet react to her nurse's chatter? Do you think she finds the story funny?*

> "Thou wast the prettiest babe that e'er I nursed."
>
> ✧

Scene 3. A room in Capulet's house.

Enter Capulet's wife, LADY CAPULET, *and* NURSE.

Lady Capulet.
  Nurse, where's my daughter? Call her forth to me.
Nurse.
  Now, by my maidenhead at twelve year old,
  I bade her come. What,° lamb! What, ladybird!
  God forbid, where's this girl? What, Juliet!

[*Enter* JULIET.]

Juliet.
  How now? Who calls?
Nurse.   Your mother.
                                    Madam, I am here.
5 **Juliet.**
  What is your will?
Lady Capulet.
  This is the matter.—Nurse, give leave awhile;
  We must talk in secret. Nurse, come back again.
  I have rememb'red me; thou's° hear our counsel.
10 Thou knowest my daughter's of a pretty age.
Nurse.
  Faith, I can tell her age unto an hour.
Lady Capulet.
  She's not fourteen.
Nurse.   I'll lay fourteen of my teeth—
  And yet, to my teen° be it spoken, I have but four—
  She's not fourteen. How long is it now
  To Lammastide?°
15 **Lady Capulet.**   A fortnight and odd days.
Nurse.

3. What: impatient call, like "Hey!" or "Where are you?"

9. thou's: thou shalt.

? Staging the Play
10. *The nurse and Lady Capulet are opposites in nature. Lady Capulet sends the nurse off and then calls her back. Some actresses use this impulsive move to indicate Lady Capulet's reluctance to speak to her daughter about marriage. In contrast, how does the nurse react in this scene?*

13. teen: sorrow.
15. Lammastide: Christian church feast, held in England on

  And I might live to see thee married once,
  I have my wish.
Lady Capulet.
  Marry, that "marry" is the very theme
  I came to talk of. Tell me, daughter Juliet,
65 How stands your disposition to be married?
Juliet.
  It is an honor that I dream not of.
Nurse.
  An honor? Were not I thine only nurse,
  I would say thou hadst sucked wisdom from thy teat.
Lady Capulet.
  Well, think of marriage now. Younger than you,
70 Here in Verona, ladies of esteem,
  Are made already mothers. By my count,
  I was your mother much upon these years
  That you are now a maid. Thus then in brief:
  The valiant Paris seeks you for his love.
Nurse.
75 A man, young lady! Lady, such a man
  As all the world.—Why, he's a man of wax.°
Lady Capulet.
  Verona's summer hath not such a flower.
Nurse.
  Nay, he's a flower, in faith—a very flower.
Lady Capulet.
  What say you? Can you love the gentleman?
80 This night you shall behold him at our feast.
  Read o'er the volume of young Paris' face,
  And find delight writ there with beauty's pen;
  Examine every married lineament,°
  And see how one another lends content;°
85 And what obscured in this fair volume lies
  Find written in the margent of his eyes.
  This precious book of love, this unbound lover,
  To beautify him only lacks a cover.
  The fish lives in the sea, and 'tis much pride
90 For fair without the fair within to hide.°
  That book in many's eyes doth share the glory,
  That in gold clasps locks in the golden story;
  So shall you share all that he doth possess,
  By having him, making yourself no less.

? Staging the Play
62. *Line 62 suggests another dramatic pause. Often a director will have Juliet rush to the nurse and kiss her. Her fondness for and gaiety with the nurse must contrast with her reserve toward her mother. How should Juliet react when she speaks in line 66?*

76. man of wax: man like a wax statue, with a perfect figure.

? Staging the Play
79. *Notice that Juliet isn't answering. How do you suppose she is feeling during the conversation between the nurse and her mother about this man they want her to marry?*

83. married lineament: harmonious feature.
84. how one another lends content: how one feature makes another look good.
90. For fair without the fair within to hide: for those who are handsome outwardly also to be handsome inwardly.

? 94. *Lady Capulet has made an elegant appeal to Juliet, to persuade her to consider marrying Paris. Which **images** in this speech compare Paris to a fine book?*

"The valiant Paris
seeks you for his love."

917

Nurse.

95   No less? Nay, bigger! Women grow by men.

Lady Capulet.

Speak briefly, can you like of Paris' love?

Juliet.

I'll look to like, if looking liking move;
But no more deep will I endart mine eye
Than your consent gives strength to make it fly.

[*Enter* SERVINGMAN.]

100   **Servingman.** Madam, the guests are come, supper served
up, you called, my young lady asked for, the nurse cursed
in the pantry, and everything in extremity. I must hence
to wait. I beseech you follow straight.

[*Exit.*]

Lady Capulet.

We follow thee. Juliet, the county stays.°

Nurse.

105   Go, girl, seek happy nights to happy days.

[*Exeunt.*]

Scene 4. *A street.*

Enter ROMEO, MERCUTIO, BENVOLIO, *with five or six other*
MASKERS; TORCHBEARERS.

Romeo.

What, shall this speech be spoke for our excuse?°
Or shall we on without apology?

Benvolio.

The date is out of such prolixity.°
We'll have no Cupid hoodwinked° with a scarf,
5   Bearing a Tartar's painted bow of lath,
Scaring the ladies like a crowkeeper;°
Nor no without-book prologue,° faintly spoke
After the prompter, for our entrance;
But, let them measure° us by what they will,
10   We'll measure them a measure° and be gone.

Romeo.

Give me a torch. I am not for this ambling.
Being but heavy, I will bear the light.

---

96. A **character foil** *is a character who sets off another character by contrast so that each will stand out vividly. How does the nurse serve as a foil to Lady Capulet?*

99. *Juliet says she'll look at Paris to see if she likes him (if liking is brought about by looking). How does she show that she is a dutiful daughter?*

Staging the Play
100. *Another comical servant enters, speaking breathlessly, but our attention still must be on Juliet. In some productions we now hear the sounds of music coming from offstage, and Juliet exits excitedly, with little dancing motions. Do we really know much about Juliet yet?*

104. the county stays: the count waits.

105. *We meet Juliet for the first time in this scene. What is your first impression of her?*

Staging the Play
Stage direction: It's night. The stage is lit with torches and filled with masked young men. The mood is one of excitement—but we are watching Romeo. What does he say in the next speeches to indicate that he is still heavy-hearted?

1. shall . . . excuse?: Shall we introduce ourselves with the usual speeches? (Uninvited maskers were usually announced by a messenger.)

3. The date . . . prolixity: Such long-winded speeches are out of fashion now.

4. hoodwinked: blindfolded.

6. crowkeeper: scarecrow.

7. without-book prologue: memorized speech.

9. measure: examine; appraise.

10. measure them a measure: dance a dance.

Mercutio.

    Nay, gentle Romeo, we must have you dance.

Romeo.

    Not I, believe me. You have dancing shoes
15   With nimble soles; I have a soul of lead
    So stakes me to the ground I cannot move.

Mercutio.

    You are a lover. Borrow Cupid's wings
    And soar with them above a common bound.

Romeo.

    I am too sore enpiercèd with his shaft
20   To soar with his light feathers; and so bound
    I cannot bound a pitch° above dull woe.
    Under love's heavy burden do I sink.

Mercutio.

    And, to sink in it, should you burden love—
    Too great oppression for a tender thing.

Romeo.

25   Is love a tender thing? It is too rough,
    Too rude, too boist'rous, and it pricks like thorn.

Mercutio.

    If love be rough with you, be rough with love;
    Prick love for pricking, and you beat love down.
    Give me a case to put my visage in.
30   A visor° for a visor! What care I
    What curious eye doth quote deformities?°
    Here are the beetle brows shall blush° for me.

Benvolio.

    Come, knock and enter; and no sooner in
    But every man betake him to his legs.°

Romeo.

35   A torch for me! Let wantons light of heart
    Tickle the senseless rushes° with their heels;
    For I am proverbed with a grandsire phrase,°
    I'll be a candleholder and look on;
    The game was ne'er so fair, and I am done.°

Mercutio.

40   Tut! Dun's the mouse, the constable's own word!

Staging the Play

13. *Mercutio is a key character. Here he comes out of the crowd and speaks to Romeo. They engage in a verbal duel about love. In the following dialogue, how do Mercutio and Romeo differ in their attitudes toward love?*

21. bound a pitch: fly as high as a falcon.

23. *In what ways does Mercutio show that he is a good friend to Romeo? Would you want to be Mercutio's friend?*

Staging the Play

29. *Mercutio pauses and asks for a mask. What activity would he be engaged in here?*

30. visor: mask.
31. quote deformities: see imperfections (in the way he looks).
32. Here . . . blush: The mask's heavy eyebrows will blush for him.
34. betake . . . legs: begin dancing.
36. rushes: The dance floor is covered with rushes, plants with small, green flowers.
37. grandsire phrase: old man's saying.
39. The game . . . I am done: The game (dancing) was never very good, and I'm exhausted.

39. *Despite Mercutio's teasing and Benvolio's urging, what is Romeo determined to do at the dance?*

"O, then
I see
Queen Mab
hath been
with you."
✧

If thou art Dun,° we'll draw thee from the mire
Of this sir-reverence love,° wherein thou stickest
Upon to the ears. Come, we burn daylight, ho!

Romeo.
    Nay, that's not so.

Mercutio.   I mean, sir, in delay
45   We waste our lights° in vain, like lights by day.
Take our good meaning, for our judgment sits
Five times in that° ere once in our five wits.

Romeo.
    And we mean well in going to this masque,
But 'tis no wit° to go.

Mercutio.   Why, may one ask?

Romeo.
    I dreamt a dream tonight.

50 **Mercutio.**   And so did I.

Romeo.
    Well, what was yours?

Mercutio.   That dreamers often lie.

Romeo.
    In bed asleep, while they do dream things true.

Mercutio.
    O, then I see Queen Mab hath been with you.
She is the fairies' midwife, and she comes
55   In shape no bigger than an agate stone
On the forefinger of an alderman,
Drawn with a team of little atomies°
Over men's noses as they lie asleep;
Her wagon spokes made of long spinners'° legs,
60   The cover, of the wings of grasshoppers;
Her traces,° of the smallest spider web;
Her collars, of the moonshine's wat'ry beams;
Her whip, of cricket's bone; the lash, of film;°
Her wagoner, a small gray-coated gnat,
65   Not half so big as a round little worm
Pricked from the lazy finger of a maid;°
Her chariot is an empty hazelnut,
Made by the joiner squirrel or old grub,
Time out o' mind the fairies' coachmakers.
70   And in this state she gallops night by night
Through lovers' brains, and then they dream of love;
On courtiers' knees, that dream on curtsies straight;
O'er lawyers' fingers, who straight dream on fees;
O'er ladies' lips, who straight on kisses dream,

41. Dun: pun on Romeo's "done"; Dun was the common name used for a horse in an old game called "Dun is in the mire."

42. sir-reverence love: "Save your reverence" is an apologetic expression. Mercutio means "We'll save you from—pardon me for saying so—love."

45. lights: torches.

47. in that: in our good meaning.

49. no wit: not a good idea.

? Staging the Play
50. *Romeo's mood seems to have changed abruptly, and he has a sense of approaching doom. How would he speak this line about a dream? Would Mercutio's reply be kind or sharp?*

? 53. *Mercutio, as a ringleader and a born entertainer, serves as a **character foil** for the more serious and emotional Romeo. Mercutio grabs everyone's attention with this famous **monologue**—a long speech directed at other characters onstage. What point is Mercutio making about dreams and their significance? What does he claim Queen Mab has to do with Romeo? (Try reading this speech aloud. You might also want to draw a picture of Queen Mab.)*

57. atomies: tiny creatures.

59. spinners': spiders'.

61. traces: reins and harnesses for a wagon.

63. film: filament, or thread.

66. lazy finger of a maid: Lazy maids were said to have worms breeding in their fingers.

75	Which oft the angry Mab with blisters plagues,
	Because their breaths with sweetmeats tainted are.
	Sometime she gallops o'er a courtier's nose,
	And then dreams he of smelling out a suit;°
	And sometime comes she with a tithe pig's° tail
80	Tickling a parson's nose as 'a lies asleep,
	Then dreams he of another benefice.°
	Sometime she driveth o'er a soldier's neck,
	And then dreams he of cutting foreign throats,
	Of breaches, ambuscadoes, Spanish blades,
85	Of healths° five fathom deep; and then anon
	Drums in his ear, at which he starts and wakes,
	And being thus frighted, swears a prayer or two
	And sleeps again. This is that very Mab
	That plaits the manes of horses in the night
90	And bakes the elflocks° in foul sluttish hairs,
	Which once untangled much misfortune bodes.
	This is the hag,° when maids lie on their backs,
	That presses them and learns them first to bear,
	Making them women of good carriage.°
	This is she—
95	**Romeo.** Peace, peace, Mercutio, peace!
	Thou talk'st of nothing.
	Mercutio. True, I talk of dreams;
	Which are the children of an idle brain,
	Begot of nothing but vain fantasy;
	Which is as thin of substance as the air,
100	And more inconstant than the wind, who woos
	Even now the frozen bosom of the North
	And, being angered, puffs away from thence,
	Turning his side to the dewdropping South.
	Benvolio.
	This wind you talk of blows us from ourselves.
105	Supper is done, and we shall come too late.
	Romeo.
	I fear, too early; for my mind misgives
	Some consequence yet hanging in the stars
	Shall bitterly begin his fearful date
	With this night's revels and expire the term
110	Of a despisèd life, closed in my breast,
	By some vile forfeit of untimely death.

78. suit: person who might want to buy his influence at court.

79. tithe pig's: A tithe is a tenth of one's income, given to the church. Farmers often gave the parson one pig as a tithe.

81. benefice: church office that enabled a minister to make a living.`

85. healths: toasts to his health.

90. elflocks: locks of hair that were tangled by mischievous elves.

92. hag: nightmare. Nightmares were thought to be spirits who molested women at night.

94. women of good carriage: women who can bear children well.

[?] 94. *Mercutio's tone changes here. How are these last details getting into subjects that are more shocking and cynical? Romeo doesn't like this turn of events and cuts Mercutio off.*

[?] 103. *Mercutio could be comparing Romeo to the frozen north. If he is, what warning does he give his friend about remaining cold too long?*

[?] 106. *Romeo here expresses his feeling that something terrible will happen. Does he give any reasons for his fear? Which words in this speech suggest that he is going to the party because he is in the hands of fate?*

But he that hath the steerage of my course
Direct my sail! On, lusty gentlemen!
Benvolio. Strike, drum.

[*They march about the stage and retire to one side.*]

Scene 5. *A hall in Capulet's house.*

SERVINGMEN *come forth with napkins.*

First Servingman. Where's Potpan, that he helps not to take away? He shift a trencher!° He scrape a trencher!

Second Servingman. When good manners shall lie all in one or two men's hands, and they unwashed too, 'tis a
5 foul thing.

First Servingman. Away with the join-stools,° remove the court cupboard, look to the plate. Good thou, save me a piece of marchpane,° and as thou loves me, let the porter let in Susan Grindstone and Nell, Anthony, and Potpan!

10 **Second Servingman.** Ay, boy, ready.

First Servingman. You are looked for and called for, asked for and sought for, in the great chamber.

Third Servingman. We cannot be here and there too. Cheerly, boys! Be brisk awhile, and the longer liver
15 take all.

[*Exeunt.*]

[*Enter* CAPULET, LADY CAPULET, JULIET, TYBALT, NURSE, *and all the* GUESTS *and* GENTLEWOMEN, *meeting the* MASKERS.]

Capulet.
Welcome, gentlemen! Ladies that have their toes
Unplagued with corns will walk a bout° with you.
Ah, my mistresses, which of you all
Will now deny to dance? She that makes dainty,°
20 She I'll swear hath corns. Am I come near ye now?
Welcome, gentlemen! I have seen the day
That I have worn a visor and could tell
A whispering tale in a fair lady's ear,
Such as would please. 'Tis gone, 'tis gone, 'tis gone.
25 You are welcome, gentlemen! Come, musicians, play.

? Staging the Play
Stage direction: As you read these servants' speeches, note that one speaks in short emphatic phrases and bosses everyone else around. Which one is this? What mood do you think is suggested in this short scene?

2. trencher: wooden plate.

6. join-stools: wooden stools made by a carpenter (a joiner).

8. marchpane: marzipan.

17. bout: dance.

19. makes dainty: pretends to be shy.

[*Music plays, and they dance.*]

A hall,° a hall! Give room! And foot it, girls.
More light, you knaves, and turn the tables up,
And quench the fire; the room is grown too hot.
Ah, sirrah, this unlooked-for sport° comes well.

30 Nay, sit; nay, sit, good cousin Capulet;
For you and I are past our dancing days.
How long is't now since last yourself and I
Were in a mask?

Second Capulet. By'r Lady, thirty years.

Capulet.
What, man? 'Tis not so much, 'tis not so much;

35 'Tis since the nuptial of Lucentio,
Come Pentecost as quickly as it will,
Some five-and-twenty years, and then we masked.

Second Capulet.
'Tis more, 'tis more. His son is elder, sir;
His son is thirty.

Capulet. Will you tell me that?

40 His son was but a ward° two years ago.

Romeo (*to a* SERVINGMAN).
What lady's that which doth enrich the hand
Of yonder knight?

Servingman. I know not, sir.

Romeo.
O, she doth teach the torches to burn bright!

45 It seems she hangs upon the cheek of night
As a rich jewel in an Ethiop's ear—
Beauty too rich for use, for earth too dear!
So shows a snowy dove trooping with crows
As yonder lady o'er her fellows shows.

50 The measure° done, I'll watch her place of stand
And, touching hers, make blessèd my rude° hand.
Did my heart love till now? Forswear it, sight!
For I ne'er saw true beauty till this night.

Tybalt.
This, by his voice, should be a Montague.

55 Fetch me my rapier, boy. What! Dares the slave
Come hither, covered with an antic face,°
To fleer° and scorn at our solemnity?
Now, by the stock and honor of my kin,
To strike him dead I hold it not a sin.

Capulet.
60 Why, how now, kinsman? Wherefore storm you so?

Staging the Play
Stage direction: The dance, slow and stately, takes place at center stage. Old Capulet and his relative reminisce at one side, but our attention is focused on Romeo (in a mask) and Juliet, who is dancing with someone else. How does the following conversation contrast the two old men with Romeo and Juliet?

26. A hall: clear the floor (for dancing).
29. unlooked-for sport: He hadn't expected to find some of the dancers masked.

40. ward: minor.

Staging the Play
41. *In some productions, Romeo puts his torch down here, to draw our attention to his urgent question. Where would Juliet be onstage at this point?*

50. measure: dance.
51. rude: rough or simple.

53. *What has happened to Romeo?*

54. *Why would we feel a sense of fear when we see Tybalt stepping onto center stage again?*
56. antic face: hideous mask.
57. fleer: jeer.

"that which doth enrich the hand Of yonder knight?"

✦

Tybalt.
    Uncle, this is a Montague, our foe,
    A villain, that is hither come in spite
    To scorn at our solemnity this night.

Capulet.
    Young Romeo is it?

Tybalt.   'Tis he, that villain Romeo.

Capulet.

65   Content thee, gentle coz, let him alone.
    'A bears him like a portly° gentleman,
    And, to say truth, Verona brags of him
    To be a virtuous and well-governed youth.
    I would not for the wealth of all this town
70   Here in my house do him disparagement.
    Therefore be patient; take no note of him.
    It is my will, the which if thou respect,
    Show a fair presence and put off these frowns,

66. portly: well-mannered.

An ill-beseeming semblance for a feast.

Tybalt.

75   It fits when such a villain is a guest.
       I'll not endure him.

Capulet.   He shall be endured.
       What, goodman boy!° I say he shall. Go to!°
       Am I the master here, or you? Go to!
       You'll not endure him, God shall mend my soul!
80   You'll make a mutiny among my guests!
       You will set cock-a-hoop.° You'll be the man!

Tybalt.

       Why, uncle, 'tis a shame.

Capulet.   Go to, go to!
       You are a saucy boy. Is't so, indeed?
       This trick may chance to scathe° you. I know what.
85   You must contrary me! Marry, 'tis time—
       Well said, my hearts!—You are a princox°—go!
       Be quiet, or—More light, more light!—For shame!
       I'll make you quiet. What!—Cheerly, my hearts!

Tybalt.

       Patience perforce° with willful choler° meeting
90   Makes my flesh tremble in their different greeting.
       I will withdraw; but this intrusion shall,
       Now seeming sweet, convert to bitt'rest gall.

                                        [*Exit.*]

74. *What is Capulet's sensible reply to Tybalt's hostility? What feelings is Capulet revealing in his next speeches? Have Capulet's feelings about the Montagues changed since Scene 1?*

77. goodman boy: a scornful phrase. *Goodman* is below the rank of gentleman; *boy* is insulting. **Go to:** similar to "Go on" or "Cut it out."
81. set cock-a-hoop: start trouble.

84. scathe: hurt.

86. princox: rude youngster.

89. patience perforce: enforced patience. **choler:** anger.

92. *Paraphrase lines 54–92, putting the exchange between Capulet and Tybalt in modern-day language.*

"For saints have hands that pilgrims' hands do touch, And palm to palm is holy palmers' kiss."

✦

Romeo.

    If I profane with my unworthiest hand

      This holy shrine, the gentle sin is this:°

95   My lips, two blushing pilgrims, ready stand

      To smooth that rough touch with a tender kiss.

Juliet.

    Good pilgrim, you do wrong your hand too much,

      Which mannerly devotion shows in this;

    For saints have hands that pilgrims' hands do touch,

100   And palm to palm is holy palmers'° kiss.

Romeo.

    Have not saints lips, and holy palmers too?

Juliet.

    Ay, pilgrim, lips that they must use in prayer.

Romeo.

    O, then, dear saint, let lips do what hands do!

    They pray; grant thou, lest faith turn to despair.

Juliet.

105   Saints do not move,° though grant for prayers' sake.

Romeo.

    Then move not while my prayer's effect I take.

    Thus from my lips, by thine my sin is purged.

    [*Kisses her.*]

Juliet.

    Then have my lips the sin that they have took.

Romeo.

    Sin from my lips? O trespass sweetly urged!

    Give me my sin again. [*Kisses her.*]

110 **Juliet.**   You kiss by th' book.°

Nurse.

    Madam, your mother craves a word with you.

Romeo.

    What is her mother?

Nurse.   Marry, bachelor,

    Her mother is the lady of the house,

    And a good lady, and a wise and virtuous.

115   I nursed her daughter that you talked withal.°

    I tell you, he that can lay hold of her

    Shall have the chinks.°

Romeo.   Is she a Capulet?

    O dear account! My life is my foe's debt.°

Benvolio.

    Away, be gone; the sport is at the best.

? Staging the Play

93. *In contrast to the raging Tybalt, Romeo is now at center stage with Juliet. Romeo takes Juliet's hand, and in their next fourteen lines (lines 93–106), the two young speakers' words form a* **sonnet.** *Romeo pretends to be a pilgrim going to a saint's shrine. What religious images do the two young lovers use to talk of their feelings for each other?*

94. the gentle sin is this: this is the sin of a gentleman.

100. palmers': pilgrims going to a holy place. They often carried palm leaves to show they had been to the Holy Land.

? 100. *Romeo and Juliet bring the palms of their hands together here. What in their words suggests that this is what they are doing?*

105. do not move: do not make the first move.

? Staging the Play

107. *In the midst of the swirling dancers, Romeo and Juliet kiss. All of the audience's attention must be on this kiss. What do you fear as you watch, remembering that Tybalt is nearby?*

110. You kiss by th' book: You take my words literally (to get more kisses).

? Staging the Play

111. *As the nurse interrupts, the dance ends. Juliet runs off, and Romeo is left alone with the nurse. What do we know about the Capulets' plans for Juliet that Romeo does not know?*

115. withal: with.

117. chinks: money.

118. My life is my foe's debt: My foe now owns my life.

Romeo.

120   Ay, so I fear; the more is my unrest.

Capulet.

Nay, gentlemen, prepare not to be gone;
We have a trifling foolish banquet towards.°
Is it e'en so? Why then, I thank you all.
I thank you, honest gentlemen. Good night.
125   More torches here! Come on then; let's to bed.
Ah, sirrah, by my fay,° it waxes late;
I'll to my rest.

[*Exeunt all but* JULIET *and* NURSE.]

Juliet.

Come hither, nurse. What is yond gentleman?

Nurse.

The son and heir of old Tiberio.

Juliet.

130   What's he that now is going out of door?

Nurse.

Marry, that, I think, be young Petruchio.

Juliet.

What's he that follows there, that would not dance?

Nurse.

I know not.

Juliet.

Go ask his name.—If he be marrièd,
135   My grave is like to be my wedding bed.

Nurse.

His name is Romeo, and a Montague,
The only son of your great enemy.

Juliet.

My only love, sprung from my only hate!
Too early seen unknown, and known too late!
140   Prodigious° birth of love it is to me
That I must love a loathèd enemy.

Nurse.

What's this? What's this?

Juliet.   A rhyme I learnt even now
Of one I danced withal.

[*One calls within,* "Juliet."]

Nurse.   Anon, anon!°
Come, let's away; the strangers all are gone.

[*Exeunt.*]

120. *Romeo stands alone here, horrified. What activity goes on around him?*

122. towards: in preparation.

126. fay: faith.

Staging the Play
128. *Juliet has moved to the side of the stage. What feelings must she convey in this question? (She is not pointing to Romeo.)*

132. *Juliet has asked her nurse the names of several men at the dance. Why do you think she asks about Romeo last?*

140. Prodigious (prō·dij′əs): huge and monstrous.

Staging the Play
143. *What tone of voice would Juliet use here? What has she just realized?*

143. anon: at once.

"Thus from my lips, by thine my sin is purged." ✧

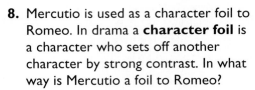

After You Read   Response and Analysis

Act I

Reading Check

1. What does the prologue say ends the rage between two families of Verona?

2. Who is Tybalt? What does he do that is dangerous?

3. What warning does Prince Escalus give the street brawlers in Scene 1?

4. In Scene 4, how does Mercutio try to snap Romeo out of his depression?

5. Where do Romeo and Juliet first meet?

Thinking Critically

6. Scene 1 shows how information can be conveyed through **dialogue,** or conversation between characters. Look at these three interactions: Gregory and Sampson; Benvolio and Tybalt; Benvolio and Montague. In a chart like the following one, list each pair of characters on the left. In the next column, write the line numbers of some of their dialogue. In the third column, explain what we learn from the dialogue.

Characters	Lines of Dialogue	What We Learn
Gregory and Sampson		
Benvolio and Tybalt		
Benvolio and Montague		

7. Before Romeo and Juliet meet in Scene 4, Shakespeare must set up obstacles to their love so that when they do meet, we will groan at the problems they are going to face. What problem, or **complication,** is presented in Scenes 2 and 3?

8. Mercutio is used as a character foil to Romeo. In drama a **character foil** is a character who sets off another character by strong contrast. In what way is Mercutio a foil to Romeo?

9. The title of this play tells us that it is a **tragedy**—a play in which the main characters come to an unhappy end. How do Romeo's and Juliet's reactions in Scene 5, when they learn each other's identity, **foreshadow,** or give clues to, their tragic end?

10. Shakespeare usually inserts **comic elements** into his tragedies. His servants and workers, for example, often tell funny stories, make puns, and kid around. List three examples of scenes from Act I that show comic elements.

Extending and Evaluating

11. Although the action of this play takes place in Italy in the fourteenth century, we can recognize similarities between the culture of that time and that of our own. Which **conflicts** in Act I could you imagine taking place today? What details would have to change, if any?

LISTENING AND SPEAKING
Speak the Speech

Choose a speech from this act, and prepare it for performance. Your first step is to write out or type the speech. Then, read it aloud several times so that you feel the rhythm created by the **blank verse.** However, watch for **end-stopped lines** and **run-on lines,** and don't let your reading become sing-song. If you have a partner you'd like to perform with, pick a **dialogue**—perhaps the love "duet" by Romeo and Juliet in Scene 5, lines 93–110.

SKILLS FOCUS

Literary Skills
Analyze characteristics of tragedy, including complication.

Listening and Speaking Skills
Present a speech from the play.

INTERNET

Projects and Activities

Keyword: LE7 9-11

After You Read | Vocabulary Development

Shakespeare's Words—Then and Now

As you saw in the list on page 896, many words in Shakespeare's plays have different meanings today. *Humor,* for example, comes from a Latin word for "moisture; fluid." In Shakespeare's time, people believed there were four fluids, or humors, in the body, which regulated a person's temperament, or disposition. *Humorous* eventually came to refer to a person who can see comedy in situations.

PRACTICE

Choose five words from the list on page 896, and use a good dictionary to research their **derivations,** or origins. (Which words are very old English words, rooted in Anglo-Saxon, or Old English?) Make a diagram like the one below, showing their origins, what each word meant in Shakespeare's day, and what it means today.

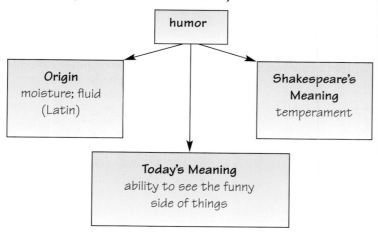

humor

Origin
moisture; fluid
(Latin)

Shakespeare's
Meaning
temperament

Today's Meaning
ability to see the funny
side of things

anon wot
withal shrift hap
maid
soft Jack

SKILLS FOCUS

Vocabulary Skills
Understand word origins.

✳ ACT II ✳

Enter CHORUS.

Chorus.
    Now old desire doth in his deathbed lie,
        And young affection gapes to be his heir;
    That fair° for which love groaned for and would die,
        With tender Juliet matched, is now not fair.
5   Now Romeo is beloved and loves again,
        Alike° bewitchèd by the charm of looks;
    But to his foe supposed he must complain,°
        And she steal love's sweet bait from fearful hooks.
    Being held a foe, he may not have access
10   To breathe such vows as lovers use to swear,°
    And she as much in love, her means much less
        To meet her new belovèd anywhere;
    But passion lends them power, time means, to meet,
    Temp'ring extremities° with extreme sweet.° [*Exit.*]

Scene 1. *Near Capulet's orchard.*

Enter ROMEO *alone.*

Romeo.
    Can I go forward when my heart is here?
    Turn back, dull earth, and find thy center° out.

[*Enter* BENVOLIO *with* MERCUTIO. ROMEO *retires.*]

Benvolio.
    Romeo! My cousin Romeo! Romeo!
Mercutio.   He is wise
    And, on my life, hath stol'n him home to bed.
Benvolio.
5   He ran this way and leapt this orchard wall.
    Call, good Mercutio.
Mercutio.   Nay, I'll conjure too.
    Romeo! Humors! Madman! Passion! Lover!
    Appear thou in the likeness of a sigh;
    Speak but one rhyme, and I am satisfied!
10   Cry but "Ay me!" pronounce but "love" and "dove";
    Speak to my gossip° Venus one fair word,

3. That fair: Rosaline.

6. Alike: both (both Romeo and Juliet).
7. complain: ask Juliet's father, his foe, for her hand in marriage.

10. use to swear: are used to promising.

14. extremities: difficulties. **extreme sweet:** very sweet delights.

? 14. *According to the Chorus, what has happened to Romeo's old love? What is his new problem? What line suggests that these young people fell in love at first sight?*

2. center: Juliet. The "dull earth" is Romeo, and Juliet is his soul.

? Staging the Play
Stage direction: *Although the stage direction says that Romeo "retires," a few lines later Benvolio says that Romeo ran and leapt over the wall. Since leaping a wall is difficult, most actors simply move behind it. How might the stage be designed so that we see Romeo hiding in Capulet's orchard and Benvolio and Mercutio on the other side of the wall?*

11. gossip: good friend. In Roman mythology, Venus is the goddess of love.

One nickname for her purblind° son and heir,
Young Abraham Cupid,° he that shot so true
When King Cophetua loved the beggar maid!°

15 He heareth not, he stirreth not, he moveth not;
The ape is dead,° and I must conjure him.
I conjure thee by Rosaline's bright eyes,
By her high forehead and her scarlet lip,
By her fine foot, straight leg, and quivering thigh,

20 And the demesnes° that there adjacent lie,
That in thy likeness thou appear to us!

Benvolio.
And if he hear thee, thou wilt anger him.

Mercutio.
This cannot anger him. 'Twould anger him
To raise a spirit in his mistress' circle°

25 Of some strange nature, letting it there stand
Till she had laid it and conjured it down.
That were some spite;° my invocation
Is fair and honest: in his mistress' name,
I conjure only but to raise up him.

Benvolio.
30 Come, he hath hid himself among these trees
To be consorted° with the humorous° night.
Blind is his love and best befits the dark.

> ## "If love be blind, love cannot hit the mark."

Mercutio.
If love be blind, love cannot hit the mark.
And wish his mistress were that kind of fruit

35 As maids call medlars when they laugh alone.
O, Romeo, that she were, O that she were
An open et cetera, thou a pop'rin pear!
Romeo, good night. I'll to my truckle bed;
This field bed is too cold for me to sleep.
Come, shall we go?

40 **Benvolio.**   Go then, for 'tis in vain
To seek him here that means not to be found.

[*Exit with others.*]

---

12. purblind (pur′blīnd′): blind.

13. Young Abraham Cupid: To Mercutio, Romeo seems the very figure of love—old like Abraham in the Bible and young like Cupid, the god of love in Roman mythology.

14. When . . . maid: from a popular ballad.

16. The ape is dead: Romeo is "playing" dead.

20. demesnes (di·mānz′): domains; regions.

? Staging the Play
22. *What is Benvolio's tone here? Why would Romeo be angry at Mercutio's remarks?*

24. circle: magical place.

27. spite: cause to be angry.

31. consorted: familiar.
humorous: damp.

Scene 2. *Capulet's orchard.*

Romeo (*coming forward*).
    He jests at scars that never felt a wound.

[*Enter* JULIET *at a window.*]

    But soft! What light through yonder window breaks?
    It is the East, and Juliet is the sun!
    Arise, fair sun, and kill the envious moon,
5   Who is already sick and pale with grief
    That thou her maid° art far more fair than she.
    Be not her maid, since she is envious.
    Her vestal livery° is but sick and green,°
    And none but fools do wear it. Cast it off.
10   It is my lady! O, it is my love!
    O, that she knew she were!
    She speaks, yet she says nothing. What of that?
    Her eye discourses;° I will answer it.
    I am too bold; 'tis not to me she speaks.
15   Two of the fairest stars in all the heaven,
    Having some business, do entreat her eyes
    To twinkle in their spheres till they return.
    What if her eyes were there, they in her head?
    The brightness of her cheek would shame those stars
20   As daylight doth a lamp; her eyes in heaven
    Would through the airy region stream so bright
    That birds would sing and think it were not night.
    See how she leans her cheek upon her hand!
    O, that I were a glove upon that hand,
    That I might touch that cheek!

Juliet.   Ay me!
25 **Romeo.**   She speaks.
    O, speak again, bright angel, for thou art
    As glorious to this night, being o'er my head,
    As is a wingèd messenger of heaven
    Unto the white-upturnèd wond'ring eyes
30   Of mortals that fall back to gaze on him
    When he bestrides the lazy puffing clouds
    And sails upon the bosom of the air.

Juliet.
    O Romeo, Romeo! Wherefore° art thou Romeo?
    Deny thy father and refuse thy name;
35   Or, if thou wilt not, be but sworn my love,
    And I'll no longer be a Capulet.

1. *Romeo has heard all the joking. Whom is he referring to here, and what kind of "wound" is he talking about?*

Staging the Play
2. *Romeo's* **soliloquy** *begins the balcony scene—one of the most famous and most beautiful in all dramatic literature—in which the two lovers woo and win each other. (In the Elizabethan theater [see page 892], a balcony was already built into the stage, so the* **scene design** *was not a problem. In modern theaters, however, it is often difficult to have a balcony high enough and yet still visible to people sitting in the back of the theater.) What is Juliet doing while Romeo is speaking aloud to himself?*

6. thou her maid: Juliet, whom Romeo sees as the servant of the virgin goddess of the moon, Diana in Roman mythology.
8. vestal livery: maidenly clothing. **sick and green:** Unmarried girls supposedly had "greensickness," or anemia.
13. discourses: speaks.

25. *Romeo and Juliet rarely talk of each other in straightforward prose. What are some of the* **figures of speech** *and* **images** *that Romeo uses to express his love here?*

33. Wherefore: why. In other words, "Why is your name Romeo?" (It is the name of her enemy.)

"But soft! What light through yonder window breaks? It is the East, and Juliet is the sun!"

✧

935

"O Romeo, Romeo! Wherefore art thou Romeo?"
✫

Romeo (*aside*).

Shall I hear more, or shall I speak at this?

Juliet.

'Tis but thy name that is my enemy.

Thou art thyself, though not° a Montague.

40   What's Montague? It is nor hand, nor foot,

Nor arm, nor face. O, be some other name

Belonging to a man.

What's in a name? That which we call a rose

By any other word would smell as sweet.

45   So Romeo would, were he not Romeo called,

Retain that dear perfection which he owes°

Without that title. Romeo, doff thy name;

And for thy name, which is no part of thee,

Take all myself.

Romeo.   I take thee at thy word.

50   Call me but love, and I'll be new baptized;

Henceforth I never will be Romeo.

Staging the Play
*Stage direction. Here Romeo is speaking an **aside**—a remark made to the audience or to another character that others onstage are not meant to hear.*

37. Juliet does not know that Romeo is standing beneath her balcony. What has Romeo now learned about her feelings for him?

39. though not: even if you were not.

Staging the Play
42. Short lines like this one usually indicate an interruption or pause. Here Juliet pauses to think about a question. What does she say in answer to this question about the true significance of a name?

46. owes: owns.

Staging the Play
*49. All of Romeo's and Juliet's speeches in this scene so far have been soliloquies. A **soliloquy** is a speech in which a character, who is usually alone onstage, expresses private thoughts or feelings that the audience hears. (A soliloquy is different from a **monologue**, which is directed to other characters onstage.) Here the lovers speak their thoughts out loud, but not to each other. Which of the lines that follow tell us that Romeo is now speaking to Juliet?*

Juliet.

What man art thou, that, thus bescreened in night,
So stumblest on my counsel?°

Romeo.   By a name
I know not how to tell thee who I am.

55 My name, dear saint, is hateful to myself
Because it is an enemy to thee.
Had I it written, I would tear the word.

Juliet.

My ears have yet not drunk a hundred words
Of thy tongue's uttering, yet I know the sound.

60 Art thou not Romeo, and a Montague?

Romeo.

Neither, fair maid, if either thee dislike.

Juliet.

How camest thou hither, tell me, and wherefore?
The orchard walls are high and hard to climb,
And the place death, considering who thou art,

65 If any of my kinsmen find thee here.

Romeo.

With love's light wings did I o'erperch° these walls;
For stony limits cannot hold love out,
And what love can do, that dares love attempt.
Therefore thy kinsmen are no stop to me.

Juliet.

70 If they do see thee, they will murder thee.

Romeo.

Alack, there lies more peril in thine eye
Than twenty of their swords! Look thou but sweet,
And I am proof° against their enmity.

Juliet.

I would not for the world they saw thee here.

Romeo.

75 I have night's cloak to hide me from their eyes;
And but° thou love me, let them find me here.
My life were better ended by their hate
Than death proroguèd,° wanting of thy love.

Juliet.

By whose direction found'st thou out this place?

Romeo.

80 By Love, that first did prompt me to inquire.
He lent me counsel, and I lent him eyes.
I am no pilot; yet, wert thou as far

53. **counsel:** private thoughts.

66. **o'erperch:** fly over.

73. **proof:** armored.

? Staging the Play
74. *Juliet is practical. She fears Romeo will be murdered. What is Romeo's tone—is he also fearful and cautious, or is he reckless and elated?*

76. **but:** if only.
78. **proroguèd:** postponed.

? 78. *The two lovers will repeatedly remind us that they prefer death to separation. What does this speech tell us of Romeo's intentions? Do you think he is seriously thinking of death here, or is he being impulsive and exaggerating—behaving as many people do when they've fallen head over heels in love?*

As that vast shore washed with the farthest sea,
I should adventure for such merchandise.

Juliet.
85   Thou knowest the mask of night is on my face;
Else would a maiden blush bepaint my cheek
For that which thou hast heard me speak tonight.
Fain would I dwell on form—fain, fain deny
What I have spoke; but farewell compliment.°
90   Dost thou love me? I know thou wilt say "Ay";
And I will take thy word. Yet, if thou swear'st,
Thou mayst prove false. At lovers' perjuries,
They say Jove laughs. O gentle Romeo,
If thou dost love, pronounce it faithfully.
95   Or if thou think'st I am too quickly won,
I'll frown and be perverse and say thee nay,
So thou wilt woo; but else, not for the world.
In truth, fair Montague, I am too fond,°
And therefore thou mayst think my havior° light;
100   But trust me, gentleman, I'll prove more true
Than those that have more cunning to be strange.°
I should have been more strange, I must confess,
But that thou overheard'st, ere I was ware,
My truelove passion. Therefore pardon me,
105   And not impute this yielding to light love,
Which the dark night hath so discoverèd.°

Staging the Play
85. *Juliet's thoughts race now, and she probably speaks rapidly here. Read this* **monologue** *aloud. Where does Juliet shift from embarrassment to frankness, to pleading, to anxiety, to doubt? Why is she worried that Romeo will think poorly of her?*

89. compliment: good manners.

98. fond: affectionate, tender.
99. havior: behavior.

101. strange: aloof or cold.

106. discoverèd: revealed.

> **"O gentle Romeo,**
> **If thou dost love, pronounce**
> **it faithfully."**

Romeo.
Lady, by yonder blessèd moon I vow,
That tips with silver all these fruit-tree tops—
Juliet.
O, swear not by the moon, the inconstant moon,
110   That monthly changes in her circle orb,
Lest that thy love prove likewise variable.
Romeo.
What shall I swear by?
Juliet.   Do not swear at all;
Or if thou wilt, swear by thy gracious self,

Staging the Play
109. *Why is Juliet afraid of having Romeo swear by the moon? If you were speaking these lines, would you make them comic, or would you make Juliet sound genuinely frightened?*

Which is the god of my idolatry,
And I'll believe thee.

115 **Romeo.**   If my heart's dear love—
Juliet.
Well, do not swear. Although I joy in thee,
I have no joy of this contract tonight.
It is too rash, too unadvised, too sudden;
Too like the lightning, which doth cease to be
120 Ere one can say it lightens. Sweet, good night!
This bud of love, by summer's ripening breath,
May prove a beauteous flower when next we meet.
Good night, good night! As sweet repose and rest
Come to thy heart as that within my breast!
Romeo.
125 O, wilt thou leave me so unsatisfied?
Juliet.
What satisfaction canst thou have tonight?
Romeo.
The exchange of thy love's faithful vow for mine.
Juliet.
I gave thee mine before thou didst request it;
And yet I would it were to give again.
Romeo.
130 Wouldst thou withdraw it? For what purpose, love?
Juliet.
But to be frank° and give it thee again.
And yet I wish but for the thing I have.
My bounty° is as boundless as the sea,
My love as deep; the more I give to thee,
135 The more I have, for both are infinite.
I hear some noise within. Dear love, adieu!

[NURSE *calls within.*]

Anon, good nurse! Sweet Montague, be true.
Stay but a little, I will come again.   [*Exit.*]
Romeo.
O blessèd, blessèd night! I am afeard,
140 Being in night, all this is but a dream,
Too flattering-sweet to be substantial.

[*Enter* JULIET *again.*]

Juliet.
Three words, dear Romeo, and good night indeed.

120. *Romeo is quick with vows and promises. Why has Juliet become fearful and cautious?*

131. frank: generous.

133. bounty: capacity for giving.

If that thy bent° of love be honorable,
Thy purpose marriage, send me word tomorrow,
145 By one that I'll procure to come to thee,
Where and what time thou wilt perform the rite;
And all my fortunes at thy foot I'll lay
And follow thee my lord throughout the world.

Nurse (*within*). Madam!

Juliet.
150 I come anon.—But if thou meanest not well,
I do beseech thee—

Nurse (*within*). Madam!

Juliet.   By and by I come.—
To cease thy strife° and leave me to my grief.
Tomorrow will I send.

Romeo.   So thrive my soul—

Juliet.
155 A thousand times good night!   [*Exit.*]

Romeo.
A thousand times the worse, to want thy light!
Love goes toward love as schoolboys from their books;
But love from love, toward school with heavy looks.

[*Enter* JULIET *again.*]

Juliet.
Hist! Romeo, hist! O for a falc'ner's voice
160 To lure this tassel gentle° back again!
Bondage is hoarse° and may not speak aloud,
Else would I tear the cave where Echo° lies
And make her airy tongue more hoarse than mine
With repetition of "My Romeo!"

Romeo.
165 It is my soul that calls upon my name.
How silver-sweet sound lovers' tongues by night,
Like softest music to attending ears!

Juliet.
Romeo!

Romeo.
              My sweet?

Juliet.   What o'clock tomorrow
Shall I send to thee?

Romeo.   By the hour of nine.

Juliet.
170 I will not fail. 'Tis twenty years till then.

143. **bent:** intention.

148. *What is Juliet making clear to Romeo here? Where does she show that she still fears he may be false with her?*

153. **strife:** efforts to win her.

Staging the Play
154. *With this fervent vow, Romeo swears by his immortal soul. What lines that follow indicate that Romeo turns around and heads away from Juliet's balcony?*

160. **tassel gentle:** male falcon.
161. **Bondage is hoarse:** Juliet is in "bondage" to her parents and must whisper.
162. **Echo:** In Greek mythology, a girl who could only repeat others' final words.

I have forgot why I did call thee back.

Romeo.

Let me stand here till thou remember it.

Juliet.

I shall forget, to have thee still stand there,
Remem'bring how I love thy company.

Romeo.

175   And I'll still stay, to have thee still forget,
Forgetting any other home but this.

Juliet.

'Tis almost morning. I would have thee gone—
And yet no farther than a wanton's° bird,
That lets it hop a little from his hand,
180   Like a poor prisoner in his twisted gyves,°
And with a silken thread plucks it back again,
So loving-jealous of his liberty.

Romeo.

I would I were thy bird.

Juliet.   Sweet, so would I.
Yet I should kill thee with much cherishing.
185   Good night, good night! Parting is such sweet sorrow
That I shall say good night till it be morrow.   [*Exit.*]

Romeo.

Sleep dwell upon thine eyes, peace in thy breast!
Would I were sleep and peace, so sweet to rest!
Hence will I to my ghostly friar's° close cell,
190   His help to crave and my dear hap° to tell.   [*Exit.*]

? 174. *When Juliet first
discovers that Romeo is in
the garden, she urges him to leave
for his own safety. Why does she
now want him to stay?*

178. **wanton's:** careless child's.

180. **gyves** (jīvz): chains, like the
threads that hold the bird captive.

? 184. *What terrible event
does this line foreshadow?*
? 185. *Why is parting "sweet"
to Juliet? (Is she enjoying this
prolonged farewell?)*

189. **ghostly friar's:** spiritual
father's.
190. **hap:** luck.

Scene 3. *Friar Laurence's cell.*

Enter FRIAR LAURENCE *alone, with a basket.*

Friar.

The gray-eyed morn smiles on the frowning night,
Check'ring the eastern clouds with streaks of light;
And fleckèd darkness like a drunkard reels
From forth day's path and Titan's burning wheels.°
5   Now, ere the sun advance his burning eye
The day to cheer and night's dank dew to dry,
I must upfill this osier cage° of ours
With baleful° weeds and precious-juicèd flowers.
The earth that's Nature's mother is her tomb.

? **Staging the Play**
1. *In the absence of lighting,
Shakespeare had his characters
"set the stage" in their speeches.
What "scene" does the friar set in
this* **soliloquy**? *How are his*
images *of night different from
Romeo's images in his "O blessèd,
blessèd night" speech in the last
scene?*

4. **Titan's burning wheels:**
wheels of the sun god's chariot.
7. **osier** (ō′ʒhər) **cage:** cage
woven of willow branches.
8. **baleful:** evil or poisonous.

"Within the infant rind of this weak flower
Poison hath residence and medicine power . . ."

10 What is her burying grave, that is her womb;
And from her womb children of divers kind
We sucking on her natural bosom find,
Many for many virtues excellent,
None but for some, and yet all different.
15 O, mickle° is the powerful grace that lies
In plants, herbs, stones, and their true qualities;
For naught so vile that on the earth doth live
But to the earth some special good doth give;
Nor aught so good but, strained° from that fair use,
20 Revolts from true birth,° stumbling on abuse.
Virtue itself turns vice, being misapplied,

15. **mickle:** great.

19. **strained:** turned aside.
20. **true birth:** true purpose.

And vice sometime by action dignified.

[*Enter* ROMEO.]

Within the infant rind° of this weak flower
Poison hath residence and medicine° power;
25 For this, being smelt, with that part cheers each part;°
Being tasted, stays all senses with the heart.
Two such opposèd kings encamp them still°
In man as well as herbs—grace and rude will;
And where the worser is predominant,
30 Full soon the canker° death eats up that plant.

Romeo.
Good morrow, father.

Friar.   Benedicite!°
What early tongue so sweet saluteth me?
Young son, it argues a distemperèd head°
So soon to bid good morrow to thy bed.
35 Care keeps his watch in every old man's eye,
And where care lodges, sleep will never lie;
But where unbruisèd° youth with unstuffed° brain
Doth couch his limbs, there golden sleep doth reign.
Therefore thy earliness doth me assure
40 Thou art uproused with some distemp'rature;
Or if not so, then here I hit it right—
Our Romeo hath not been in bed tonight.

Romeo.
That last is true. The sweeter rest was mine.

Friar.
God pardon sin! Wast thou with Rosaline?

Romeo.
45 With Rosaline, my ghostly father? No.
I have forgot that name and that name's woe.

Friar.
That's my good son! But where hast thou been then?

Romeo.
I'll tell thee ere thou ask it me again.
I have been feasting with mine enemy,
50 Where on a sudden one hath wounded me
That's by me wounded. Both our remedies
Within thy help and holy physic° lies.
I bear no hatred, blessèd man, for, lo,
My intercession° likewise steads° my foe.

Friar.
55 Be plain, good son, and homely° in thy drift.

? **22.** *How, according to the friar, can good turn to evil and evil turn to good?*

? **Staging the Play**
23. *Romeo enters quietly, unseen by the friar. As the friar explains that his flower contains the power to heal as well as kill, why might the audience fear for Romeo and Juliet?*

23. rind: outer covering.
24. medicine: medicinal.
25. For . . . part: When the flower is smelled, each part of the body is stimulated.
27. still: always.
30. canker: cankerworm, a larva that feeds on leaves.
31. Benedicite (be · ne · dis'i · tā): Latin for "bless you."
33. distemperèd head: troubled mind.

37. unbruisèd: innocent.
unstuffed: untroubled.

? **Staging the Play**
44. *Does the friar approve? If you were playing the friar, how would you speak to Romeo?*

52. holy physic: the friar's healing power (physic) to make Romeo and Juliet husband and wife.
54. intercession: request.
steads: helps.
55. homely: simple and straight-forward.

Riddling confession finds but riddling shrift.°

Romeo.

Then plainly know my heart's dear love is set
On the fair daughter of rich Capulet;
As mine on hers, so hers is set on mine,
60 And all combined,° save what thou must combine
By holy marriage. When and where and how
We met, we wooed, and made exchange of vow,
I'll tell thee as we pass; but this I pray,
That thou consent to marry us today.

Friar.

65 Holy Saint Francis! What a change is here!
Is Rosaline, that thou didst love so dear,
So soon forsaken? Young men's love then lies
Not truly in their hearts, but in their eyes.
Jesu Maria! What a deal of brine
70 Hath washed thy sallow cheeks for Rosaline!
How much salt water thrown away in waste
To season° love, that of it doth not taste!
The sun not yet thy signs from heaven clears,
Thy old groans ring yet in mine ancient ears.
75 Lo, here upon thy cheek the stain doth sit
Of an old tear that is not washed off yet.
If e'er thou wast thyself, and these woes thine,
Thou and these woes were all for Rosaline.
And art thou changed? Pronounce this sentence then:
80 Women may fall when there's no strength in men.

Romeo.

Thou chid'st me oft for loving Rosaline.

Friar.

For doting, not for loving, pupil mine.

Romeo.

And bad'st me bury love.

Friar. Not in a grave
To lay one in, another out to have.

Romeo.

85 I pray thee chide me not. Her I love now
Doth grace° for grace and love for love allow.
The other did not so.

Friar. O she knew well
Thy love did read by rote, that could not spell.°
But come, young waverer, come go with me.
90 In one respect I'll thy assistant be;
For this alliance may so happy prove

---

56. shrift: forgiveness (in the religious rite of confession).

56. *As we have seen, the play is mostly written in **blank verse,** but Shakespeare varies his verse forms from time to time. The prologues are written in **sonnet form**. The endings of scenes are marked by **rhymed couplets**. What is the **rhyme scheme** of this dialogue?*

60. combined: agreed.

Staging the Play
65. *In the early part of the play, Shakespeare keeps Romeo's intense love in perspective by letting us see how others regard him. We have heard Mercutio's sarcastic "The ape is dead." How does Friar Laurence continue with this scolding and ridicule? What actions do you imagine Romeo is engaged in as he listens to the priest?*

72. season: preserve; keep fresh. (In Shakespeare's day, food was seasoned with salt to keep it from spoiling.)

86. grace: favor.

88. Romeo recited words of love without understanding them.

To turn your households' rancor to pure love.

Romeo.

O, let us hence! I stand on° sudden haste.

Friar.

Wisely and slow. They stumble that run fast.   [*Exeunt.*]

Scene 4. *A street.*

Enter BENVOLIO *and* MERCUTIO.

Mercutio.

Where the devil should this Romeo be?
Came he not home tonight?

Benvolio.

Not to his father's. I spoke with his man.

Mercutio.

Why, that same pale hardhearted wench, that Rosaline,
5   Torments him so that he will sure run mad.

Benvolio.

Tybalt, the kinsman to old Capulet,
Hath sent a letter to his father's house.

Mercutio. A challenge, on my life.

Benvolio. Romeo will answer it.

10   **Mercutio.** Any man that can write may answer a letter.

Benvolio. Nay, he will answer the letter's master, how he
dares, being dared.

Mercutio. Alas, poor Romeo, he is already dead: stabbed
with a white wench's black eye; run through the ear with
15   a love song; the very pin° of his heart cleft with the blind
bow-boy's butt-shaft; and is he a man to encounter
Tybalt?

> "Alas, poor Romeo, he is already dead . . .
> run through the ear with a love song . . ."

Benvolio. Why, what is Tybalt?

Mercutio. More than Prince of Cats.° O, he's the coura-
20   geous captain of compliments. He fights as you sing
pricksong°—keeps time, distance, and proportion; he

92. *In Shakespeare's time it was not at all unusual to form alliances and settle disputes by arranging marriages. How does this explain Friar Laurence's decision to help the young couple?*

93. I stand on: I am firm about.

Staging the Play
94. *Romeo has gotten what he wants, and he dashes offstage. Nonetheless, why do the friar's last words leave us with a sense that danger lies ahead?*

7. *Now that the play's love story seems to be heading toward a marriage, Shakespeare turns again to the feuding families. Why is Tybalt looking for Romeo?*

15. pin: center (of a target).

19. Prince of Cats: Tybalt is the name of a cat in a fable who is known for his slyness.
21. sing pricksong: sing with attention to every note on a printed sheet of music.

rests his minim rests,° one, two and the third in your bosom! The very butcher of a silk button, a duelist, a duelist! A gentleman of the very first house,° of the first and second cause.° Ah, the immortal passado!° The punto reverso!° The hay!°

Benvolio. The what?

Mercutio. The pox of° such antic, lisping, affecting fantasticoes°—these new tuners of accent! "By Jesu, a very good blade! A very tall° man! A very good whore!" Why, is not this a lamentable thing, grand sir, that we should be thus afflicted with these strange flies, these fashionmongers, these pardon-me's, who stand so much on the new form° that they cannot sit at ease on the old bench? O, their bones,° their bones!

[*Enter* ROMEO.]

Benvolio. Here comes Romeo! Here comes Romeo!

Mercutio. Without his roe,° like a dried herring. O flesh, flesh, how art thou fishified! Now is he for the numbers° that Petrarch flowed in. Laura, to his lady, was a kitchen wench (marry, she had a better love to berhyme her), Dido° a dowdy, Cleopatra a gypsy, Helen and Hero hildings° and harlots, Thisbe a gray eye° or so, but not to the purpose. Signior Romeo, bonjour! There's a French salutation to your French slop.° You gave us the counterfeit° fairly last night.

Romeo. Good morrow to you both. What counterfeit did I give you?

Mercutio. The slip, sir, the slip. Can you not conceive?°

Romeo. Pardon, good Mercutio. My business was great, and in such a case as mine a man may strain courtesy.

Mercutio. That's as much as to say, such a case° as yours constrains a man to bow in the hams.

Romeo. Meaning, to curtsy.

Mercutio. Thou hast most kindly hit it.

Romeo. A most courteous exposition.

Mercutio. Nay, I am the very pink of courtesy.

Romeo. Pink for flower.

Mercutio. Right.

22. minim rests: shortest pauses in a bar of music.
24. first house: first rank.
25. first and second cause: dueling terms ("first," offense is taken; "second," a challenge is given). **passado:** lunge.
26. punto reverso: backhand stroke. **hay:** home thrust.

? Staging the Play
26. *Mercutio mocks Tybalt's dueling style. What do you picture Mercutio doing as he talks of duels? Is he also concerned for Romeo? How do his actions change in the next speech as he mocks people who want to wear the latest fashions?*

28. pox of: plague on (curse on).
29. fantasticoes: dandies; men who copy French fashions.
30. tall: brave.
34. new form: new fashions.
35. bones: pun on their use of the French *bon* ("good").
37. roe: pun on *roe*, female deer. *Roe* also means "fish eggs," so Mercutio is also suggesting that love has made Romeo gutless.
38. numbers: verses. Petrarch was an Italian poet who wrote verses to a woman named Laura.
41. Dido: queen of Carthage in the *Aeneid*, who loved Aeneas. (The women who follow also were famous lovers in history, legend, and literature: Cleopatra was the queen of Egypt, loved by Antony; Helen of Troy was loved by Paris; Hero was loved by Leander; Thisbe was loved by Pyramus.)
42. hildings: good-for-nothings. **gray eye:** gleam in the eye.
44. slop: loose trousers then popular in France.
45. counterfeit: slip.
48. conceive: understand.
51. case: set of clothes.

? 52. *Romeo is being lured by Mercutio to match wits. How can you tell that Romeo soon gets into the spirit of the game and for the moment forgets his romantic problems? In the following verbal duel the two friends use puns.*

Romeo. Why, then is my pump° well-flowered.°

60 **Mercutio.** Sure wit, follow me this jest now till thou hast worn out thy pump, that, when the single sole of it is worn, the jest may remain, after the wearing, solely singular.

Romeo. O single-soled jest, solely singular for the singleness!°

65 **Mercutio.** Come between us, good Benvolio! My wits faint.

Romeo. Swits° and spurs, swits and spurs; or I'll cry a match.

Mercutio. Nay, if our wits run the wild-goose chase, I am done; for thou hast more of the wild goose in one of thy

70 wits than, I am sure, I have in my whole five. Was I with you there for the goose?°

Romeo. Thou wast never with me for anything when thou wast not there for the goose.°

Mercutio. I will bite thee by the ear for that jest.

75 **Romeo.** Nay, good goose, bite not!

Mercutio. Thy wit is a very bitter sweeting;° it is a most sharp sauce.

Romeo. And is it not, then, well served in to a sweet goose?°

Mercutio. O, here's a wit of cheveril,° that stretches from an

80 inch narrow to an ell broad!°

Romeo. I stretch it out for that word "broad," which, added to the goose, proves thee far and wide a broad° goose.

Mercutio. Why, is not this better now than groaning for love? Now art thou sociable, now art thou Romeo; now

85 art thou what thou art, by art as well as by nature. For this driveling love is like a great natural° that runs lolling up and down to hide his bauble° in a hole.

Benvolio. Stop there, stop there!

Mercutio. Thou desirest me to stop in my tale against the

90 hair.°

Benvolio. Thou wouldst else have made thy tale large.°

Mercutio. O, thou art deceived! I would have made it short; for I was come to the whole depth of my tale, and meant indeed to occupy the argument no longer.

95 **Romeo.** Here's goodly gear!°

[*Enter* NURSE *and her man* PETER.]

A sail, a sail!

---

59. **pump:** shoe. **well-flowered:** pun on *well floored.* Men's shoes were "pinked," or cut with decorations.

64. **singleness:** pun on "silliness."

? Staging the Play
65. *What exaggerated action might Mercutio perform here?*

66. **Swits:** switches (a pun on wits).

71. **Was . . . goose?:** Was I right in calling you a goose?

73. **goose:** here, woman.

76. **bitter sweeting:** kind of apple.

78. **sweet goose:** sour sauce was considered best for sweet meat.

79. **cheveril:** kid leather (another reference to fashion).

80. **ell broad:** forty-five inches across.

82. **broad:** indecent.

86. **natural:** idiot.

87. **bauble:** cheap jewel.

? 87. *What does the loyal Mercutio think he has accomplished for Romeo by this game of wits?*

90. **against the hair:** against my inclination.

91. **large:** indecent.

95. **gear:** matter for teasing.

? 96. *After establishing the bad news that Tybalt is looking for Romeo, this scene turns into a playful duel of wits between Romeo and Mercutio. Wordplay of this sort was very popular with Elizabethan audiences but can be difficult for modern audiences to follow due to the many changes in word usage in four hundred years. The scene moves into a third phase as the nurse and her servant "sail" onstage. What does Romeo's comment suggest about the nurse's size?*

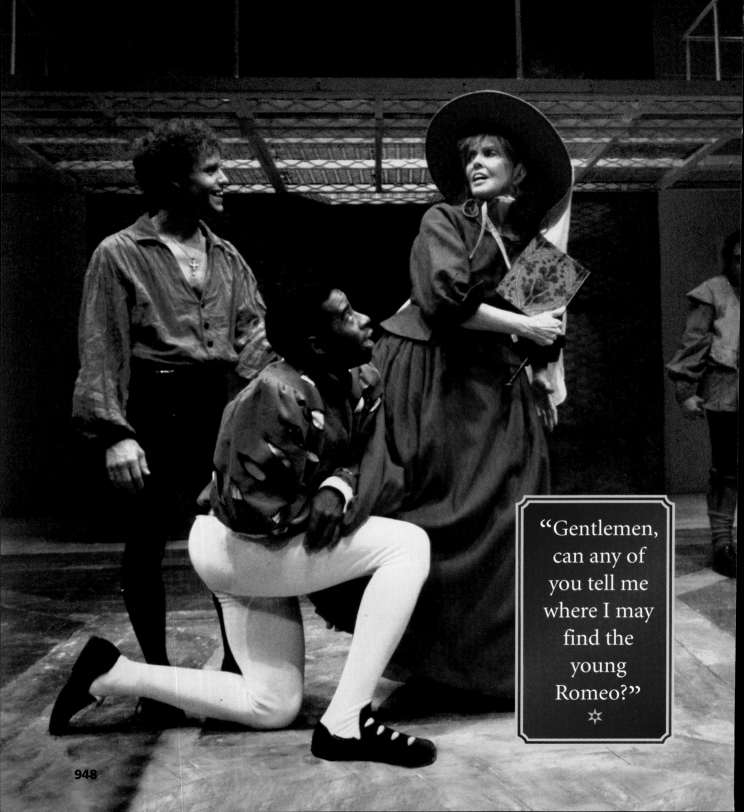

"Gentlemen, can any of you tell me where I may find the young Romeo?"
✦

948

Mercutio. Two, two! A shirt and a smock.°

Nurse. Peter!

Peter. Anon.

100 **Nurse.** My fan, Peter.

Mercutio. Good Peter, to hide her face; for her fan's the fairer face.

Nurse. God ye good morrow, gentlemen.

Mercutio. God ye good-den,° fair gentlewoman.

105 **Nurse.** Is it good-den?

Mercutio. 'Tis no less, I tell ye; for the bawdy hand of the dial is now upon the prick of noon.

Nurse. Out upon you! What a man are you!

Romeo. One, gentlewoman, that God hath made, himself
110 to mar.

Nurse. By my troth, it is well said. "For himself to mar," quoth 'a? Gentlemen, can any of you tell me where I may find the young Romeo?

Romeo. I can tell you; but young Romeo will be older when
115 you have found him than he was when you sought him. I am the youngest of that name, for fault of a worse.°

Nurse. You say well.

Mercutio. Yea, is the worst well? Very well took, i' faith! Wisely, wisely.

120 **Nurse.** If you be he, sir, I desire some confidence with you.

Benvolio. She will endite° him to some supper.

Mercutio. A bawd, a bawd, a bawd! So ho!

Romeo. What hast thou found?

Mercutio. No hare,° sir; unless a hare, sir, in a Lenten pie,°
125 that is something stale and hoar° ere it be spent.

[*He walks by them and sings.*]

> An old hare hoar,
> And an old hare hoar,
> Is very good meat in Lent;
> But a hare that is hoar
130 > Is too much for a score
> When it hoars ere it be spent.

Romeo, will you come to your father's? We'll to dinner thither.

Romeo. I will follow you.

135 **Mercutio.** Farewell, ancient lady. Farewell (*singing*) "Lady, lady, lady."   [*Exeunt* MERCUTIO, BENVOLIO.]

Nurse. I pray you, sir, what saucy merchant was this that

97. A shirt and a smock: a man (shirt) and a woman (smock).

104. God ye good-den: God grant you a good evening.

116. for fault of a worse: for want of a better.

121. endite (en·dīt′): invite. Benvolio mocks the nurse, for she said "confidence" but meant "conference."

Staging the Play
122. *Mercutio, who knows nothing of Romeo's plan to marry Juliet, thinks the nurse has come to arrange a secret date between Romeo and her mistress. He mocks and insults the nurse by suggesting that she is a bawd, or "procurer," for Juliet. Mercutio dominates the stage when he's on it. What do you imagine he's doing here?*

124. hare: slang for "morally loose woman." **Lenten pie:** rabbit pie, eaten sparingly during Lent, so that it is around for a long time and gets stale.

125. hoar (hôr): gray with mold (the old nurse has gray hair).

Staging the Play
131. *Mercutio teases the nurse about being a flirt by singing the chorus of an old song about a "chaste" lady. The nurse is outraged and struggles to keep her fine airs. How does Romeo try to calm her?*

was so full of his ropery?°

Romeo. A gentleman, nurse, that loves to hear himself talk
and will speak more in a minute than he will stand to in
a month.

Nurse. And 'a speak anything against me, I'll take him
down, and 'a were lustier than he is, and twenty such
Jacks; and if I cannot, I'll find those that shall. Scurvy
knave! I am none of his flirt-gills;° I am none of his
skainsmates.° And thou must stand by too, and suffer
every knave to use me at his pleasure!

Peter. I saw no man use you at his pleasure. If I had, my
weapon should quickly have been out, I warrant you. I
dare draw as soon as another man, if I see occasion in a
good quarrel, and the law on my side.

Nurse. Now, afore God, I am so vexed that every part about
me quivers. Scurvy knave! Pray you, sir, a word; and, as I
told you, my young lady bid me inquire you out. What
she bid me say, I will keep to myself; but first let me tell
ye, if ye should lead her in a fool's paradise, as they say, it
were a very gross kind of behavior, as they say; for the
gentlewoman is young; and therefore, if you should deal
double with her, truly it were an ill thing to be offered to
any gentlewoman, and very weak dealing.

Romeo. Nurse, commend me to thy lady and mistress. I
protest unto thee—

Nurse. Good heart, and i' faith I will tell her as much. Lord,
Lord, she will be a joyful woman.

Romeo. What wilt thou tell her, nurse? Thou dost not
mark° me.

Nurse. I will tell her, sir, that you do protest, which, as I take
it, is a gentlemanlike offer.

Romeo.
Bid her devise
Some means to come to shrift this afternoon;
And there she shall at Friar Laurence' cell
Be shrived° and married. Here is for thy pains.

Nurse. No, truly, sir; not a penny.

Romeo. Go to! I say you shall.

Nurse. This afternoon, sir? Well, she shall be there.

Romeo.
And stay, good nurse, behind the abbey wall.
Within this hour my man shall be with thee
And bring thee cords made like a tackled stair,°
Which to the high topgallant° of my joy

138. **ropery:** roguery; vulgar
ways.

145. **flirt-gills:** flirty girls.
146. **skainsmates:** loose women.

147. *Whom is the nurse
talking to here?*

Staging the Play
152. *In which part of this
speech does the nurse refer to
Mercutio? When does the nurse
turn to Romeo? How might her
manner change?*

160. *What warning does the
nurse give Romeo, and why
do you think she does this?*

166. **mark:** listen to.

172. **shrived** (shrīvd): forgiven of
her sins.

178. **tackled stair:** rope ladder.
179. **topgallant:** highest platform
on a sailing ship's mast.

180   Must be my convoy° in the secret night.
      Farewell. Be trusty, and I'll quit° thy pains.
      Farewell. Commend me to thy mistress.

Nurse.
      Now God in heaven bless thee! Hark you, sir.

Romeo.
      What say'st thou, my dear nurse?

Nurse.
185   Is your man secret? Did you ne'er hear say,
      Two may keep counsel, putting one away?

Romeo.
      Warrant thee my man's as true as steel.

Nurse. Well, sir, my mistress is the sweetest lady. Lord,
      Lord! When 'twas a little prating thing—O, there is a
190   nobleman in town, one Paris, that would fain lay knife
      aboard;° but she, good soul, had as lieve see a toad, a very
      toad, as see him. I anger her sometimes, and tell her that
      Paris is the properer man; but I'll warrant you, when I
      say so, she looks as pale as any clout° in the versal° world.
195   Doth not rosemary and Romeo begin both with a letter?

Romeo. Aye, nurse; what of that? Both with an R.

Nurse. Ah, mocker! That's the dog's name.° R is for the—
      no; I know it begins with some other letter; and she hath
      the prettiest sententious° of it, of you and rosemary, that
200   it would do you good to hear it.

Romeo. Commend me to thy lady.

Nurse. Ay, a thousand times. [*Exit* ROMEO.] Peter!

Peter. Anon.

Nurse. Before, and apace.   [*Exit after* PETER.]

Scene 5. *Capulet's orchard.*

Enter JULIET.

Juliet.
      The clock struck nine when I did send the nurse;
      In half an hour she promised to return.
      Perchance she cannot meet him. That's not so.
      O, she is lame! Love's heralds should be thoughts,
5   Which ten times faster glide than the sun's beams
      Driving back shadows over low'ring hills.
      Therefore do nimble-pinioned doves° draw Love,
      And therefore hath the wind-swift Cupid wings.
      Now is the sun upon the highmost hill

180. convoy: means of
conveyance.
181. quit: repay.

191. lay knife aboard: take a slice
(lay claim to Juliet).

194. clout: rag cloth. **versal:**
universal.

194. *The nurse becomes
confiding as she rattles on
and on. What trouble for Romeo
and Juliet does she talk about?
What is Juliet's feeling for Paris
now?*
197. In other words, a dog's growl
has an *r* sound (*r-r-r-r*).
199. sententious: The nurse
means "sentence."

Staging the Play
204. *Romeo abruptly rushes
offstage, leaving the nurse with
Peter. She bossily pushes Peter
ahead of her as she exits, to show
that she still has authority over
someone. How has this scene
advanced the love story? What
action has been set in motion?*

7. nimble-pinioned doves:
Nimble-winged doves were said to
pull the chariot of Venus, the
Roman goddess of love.

10   Of this day's journey, and from nine till twelve
      Is three long hours; yet she is not come.
      Had she affections and warm youthful blood,
      She would be as swift in motion as a ball;
      My words would bandy her° to my sweet love,
15   And his to me.
      But old folks, many feign as they were dead—
      Unwieldy, slow, heavy, and pale as lead.

      [Enter NURSE and PETER.]

      O God, she comes! O honey nurse, what news?
      Hast thou met with him? Send thy man away.
Nurse.
20   Peter, stay at the gate.   [Exit PETER.]
Juliet.
      Now, good sweet nurse—O Lord, why look'st thou sad?
      Though news be sad, yet tell them merrily;
      If good, thou sham'st the music of sweet news
      By playing it to me with so sour a face.
Nurse.
25   I am aweary, give me leave awhile.
      Fie, how my bones ache! What a jaunce° have I!
Juliet.
      I would thou hadst my bones, and I thy news.
      Nay, come, I pray thee speak. Good, good nurse, speak.
Nurse.
      Jesu, what haste! Can you not stay° awhile?
30   Do you not see that I am out of breath?
Juliet.
      How art thou out of breath when thou hast breath
      To say to me that thou art out of breath?
      The excuse that thou dost make in this delay
      Is longer than the tale thou dost excuse.
35   Is thy news good or bad? Answer to that.
      Say either, and I'll stay the circumstance.°
      Let me be satisfied, is't good or bad?
Nurse. Well, you have made a simple° choice; you know not
      how to choose a man. Romeo? No, not he. Though his
40   face be better than any man's, yet his leg excels all men's;
      and for a hand and a foot, and a body, though they be
      not to be talked on, yet they are past compare. He is not
      the flower of courtesy, but, I'll warrant him, as gentle as a
      lamb. Go thy ways, wench; serve God. What, have you
45   dined at home?

14. bandy her: send her back and forth, like a tennis ball.

? Staging the Play
17. *Juliet either has run onstage or is standing on the balcony. What is her mood in this* **soliloquy** *as she waits for the nurse to return?*

26. jaunce: tiring journey.

29. stay: wait.

? Staging the Play
30. *The actor playing the nurse can interpret her actions here in several ways. She could be genuinely weary; she could be teasing Juliet; or she could be fearful about the part she has agreed to play in the elopement. How do you think the nurse should play this scene?*

36. stay the circumstance: wait for the details.
38. simple: foolish.

? 38. *In* **comedy** *a character sometimes has one peculiarity that can always be counted on for a laugh. You push a button, and you get the same response. Such a character is sometimes called a jack-in-the-box. What is the nurse's almost inevitable way of responding when she is asked for information?*

Juliet.

No, no. But all this did I know before.

What says he of our marriage? What of that?

Nurse.

Lord, how my head aches! What a head have I!

It beats as it would fall in twenty pieces.

50   My back a'° t' other side—ah, my back, my back!

Beshrew° your heart for sending me about

To catch my death with jaunging up and down!

Juliet.

I' faith, I am sorry that thou art not well.

Sweet, sweet, sweet nurse, tell me, what says my love?

55   **Nurse.** Your love says, like an honest gentleman, and a
courteous, and a kind, and a handsome, and, I warrant, a
virtuous—where is your mother?

Juliet.

Where is my mother? Why, she is within.

Where should she be? How oddly thou repliest!

60   "Your love says, like an honest gentleman,

'Where is your mother?'"

Nurse.   O God's Lady dear!

Are you so hot?° Marry come up, I trow.°

Is this the poultice for my aching bones?

Henceforward do your messages yourself.

Juliet.

65   Here's such a coil!° Come, what says Romeo?

Nurse.

Have you got leave to go to shrift today?

50. **a':** on.

51. **Beshrew:** shame on.

? **52.** *What line in this speech indicates that Juliet has tried to humor the nurse by rubbing her back?*

? **Staging the Play**

61. *Juliet can play this scene in several ways. Do you imagine she is angry here? Is she bewildered? impatient? Is she mocking the old nurse?*

62. **hot:** angry. **Marry come up, I trow:** something like "By the Virgin Mary, come off it, I swear." **65.** **coil:** fuss.

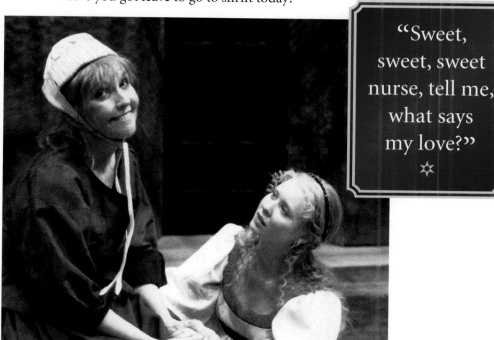

"Sweet, sweet, sweet nurse, tell me, what says my love?"

✦

Juliet.

I have.

Nurse.

Then hie° you hence to Friar Laurence' cell;
There stays a husband to make you a wife.
70   Now comes the wanton blood up in your cheeks.
They'll be in scarlet straight at any news.
Hie you to church; I must another way,
To fetch a ladder, by the which your love
Must climb a bird's nest soon when it is dark.
75   I am the drudge, and toil in your delight;
But you shall bear the burden soon at night.
Go; I'll to dinner; hie you to the cell.

Juliet.

Hie to high fortune! Honest nurse, farewell.   [*Exeunt.*]

Scene 6. *Friar Laurence's cell.*

Enter FRIAR LAURENCE *and* ROMEO.

Friar.

So smile the heavens upon this holy act
That afterhours with sorrow chide us not!

Romeo.

Amen, amen! But come what sorrow can,
It cannot countervail° the exchange of joy
5   That one short minute gives me in her sight.
Do thou but close our hands with holy words,
Then love-devouring death do what he dare—
It is enough I may but call her mine.

Friar.

These violent delights have violent ends
10   And in their triumph die, like fire and powder,°
Which, as they kiss, consume. The sweetest honey
Is loathsome in his own deliciousness
And in the taste confounds° the appetite.
Therefore love moderately: long love doth so;
15   Too swift arrives as tardy as too slow.

[*Enter* JULIET.]

Here comes the lady. O, so light a foot
Will ne'er wear out the everlasting flint.°
A lover may bestride the gossamers°
That idle in the wanton summer air,

68. hie (hī): hurry.

Staging the Play
69. *At last the nurse tells Juliet what she has been waiting to hear. What do you see Juliet doing as she hears the news?*

Staging the Play
78. *Even Juliet puns. What pun does she exit on? What is her mood?*

4. countervail: match or equal.

8. *We are continually prepared for the steps Romeo and Juliet might take if they are separated. What does Romeo say here to remind us again of how desperate their love is?*

10. powder: gunpowder.

13. confounds: destroys.

15. *What warning does the friar give about passionate love? What fear does he express for the future?*

17. flint: stone.

18. gossamers: finest spider threads.

20 And yet not fall; so light is vanity.°

Juliet.
Good even to my ghostly confessor.

Friar.
Romeo shall thank thee, daughter, for us both.

Juliet.
As much to him,° else is his thanks too much.

Romeo.
Ah, Juliet, if the measure of thy joy
25 Be heaped like mine, and that thy skill be more
To blazon° it, then sweeten with thy breath
This neighbor air, and let rich music's tongue
Unfold the imagined happiness that both
Receive in either by this dear encounter.

Juliet.
30 Conceit,° more rich in matter than in words,
Brags of his substance, not of ornament.°
They are but beggars that can count their worth;
But my true love is grown to such excess
I cannot sum up sum of half my wealth.

Friar.
35 Come, come with me, and we will make short work;
For, by your leaves, you shall not stay alone
Till holy church incorporate two in one.   [*Exeunt.*]

20. vanity: fleeting human love.

23. As much to him: the same to him.

26. blazon: describe.

29. *What is Romeo asking Juliet to do?*

30. Conceit: genuine understanding.
31. ornament: fancy language.

34. *What is Juliet's response to Romeo's request?*

Staging the Play
37. *What do you think the friar's tone is in this last speech? Is there a slightly humorous or teasing note here?*

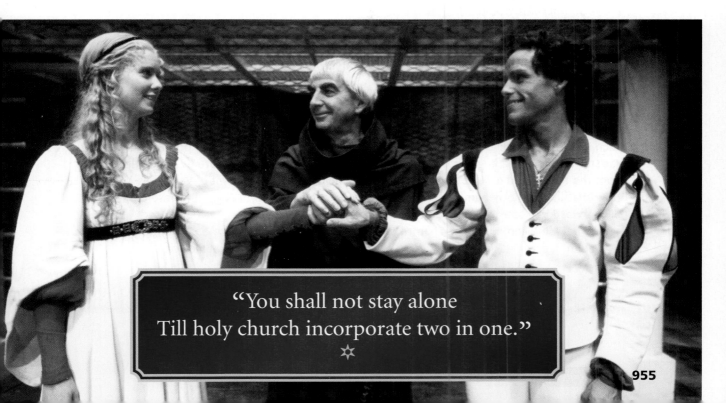

"You shall not stay alone
Till holy church incorporate two in one."

A CLOSER LOOK

No Female Actors and No R-Rated Love Scenes

On a visit to Venice in 1608, the English traveler Thomas Coryate recorded his astonishment: "For I saw women act, a thing I never saw before, though I have heard that it hath been sometimes used in London." Coryate was surprised because at the time in London, boy actors between the ages of about ten and eighteen regularly took the parts of women onstage.

The roots of this custom were bound up with the origins of medieval drama. Centuries earlier in English cathedrals, stories from the Bible were acted in brief plays. The performers—all male—came from the clergy, and they were assisted by choirboys. It wasn't until 1660 that women were permitted on the English stage—by the express order of King Charles II, whose fondness for the theater (and female actors) was to become a mark of his reign.

Boy actors were divided into two categories. There were members of all-boy companies, like the Children of St. Paul's Cathedral and the Children of the Chapel Royal. These young players enjoyed such popularity (and made so much money for their business managers) that star actors were in great demand. From the records of a 1602 legal case, we know that a schoolboy named Thomas Clifton was kidnapped and forced to join the Chapel Children. His father had to sue to get him back.

Other boy actors were apprentices to individual actors in the adult companies. These boys were preparing for a professional career. They took women's parts onstage for several years before and during adolescence. (It was one of these boy actors who took the part of Juliet.) When they were in their late teens, they switched to men's roles.

Some evidence suggests that Elizabethan actors trained their voices to be higher pitched, for both speaking and singing—so the difference between boys' voices and those of adults might have been less noticeable in Shakespeare's time. In any case, for a part such as Juliet—who is not yet fourteen when she makes her first appearance—the costume and makeup of a boy actor could have easily sustained the illusion. Unlike male and female actors in movies today, the young lovers in Shakespeare's play would have avoided physical contact. The words suggested the intensity of their feelings.

Casting boys as women on the Shakespearean stage had another unexpected twist. Plays with women in male disguise were highly popular at the time. Shakespeare wrote five such dramas, including *The Merchant of Venice, As You Like It,* and *Twelfth Night.* In these cases, boys played women who disguised themselves as young men. The mind boggles at the layers of illusion.

Act II

Reading Check

1. What plans do Romeo and Juliet make in Scene 2?

2. What fault does Friar Laurence find in Romeo in Scene 3?

3. We hear in Scene 4 that Tybalt is looking for Romeo. Why does he want Romeo?

4. How does Mercutio feel about Tybalt?

5. What part does the nurse play in Romeo and Juliet's schemes?

Thinking Critically

6. An **aside** is a short speech, usually delivered to the audience but sometimes to another character, that others onstage are not supposed to hear. Whom is Romeo talking to in his aside in Scene 2, line 37? Why is the aside effective?

7. This play in general and the balcony scene in particular are greatly admired for the beauty of the poetry. Pick one passage in Act II that especially appeals to you, and explain the poetic and literary devices involved. Is there **rhyme, rhythm,** or **alliteration**? What do the **figures of speech** mean? What senses do the **images** appeal to?

8. The nurse is one of Shakespeare's great **comic** characters. Do you think the nurse is a principled character, a person with a strong sense of right and wrong? Or does she seem to be easily corrupted, someone who will do whatever people want her to do? Find passages to support your answer.

9. Though Act II is a happy act, Shakespeare at times reminds us that this is a **tragedy** (a play that ends unhappily). Point out lines that **foreshadow,** or give clues to, possible trouble ahead.

10. The friar agrees to marry Romeo and Juliet because he wants them to be happy, but he also has another **motive.** What is that motive? What does it reveal about his **character**?

11. **Dramatic irony** occurs when the audience knows something that a character does not know. Since the prologue told us how the play will end, we sense this irony when we hear the friar's motive. What other moments of dramatic irony occur in this act?

Extending and Evaluating

12. Romeo's and Juliet's families hate each other, for reasons that we aren't told about. (The families themselves may even have forgotten.) Do you find the young lovers' situation believable? Can you think of any parallels today, and can you think of any real-life Romeos and Juliets?

Scene Design

Paint the Picture

Elizabethan playwrights created their **scene designs** mostly from words rather than the scenery, props, and lighting that might be used today. Pick a scene from Act II, and decide how you would design and stage it. If there is a wall or balcony in your scene, where would you place it? Where would the characters stand? Would you add furniture, trees, or other props? Would you include a backdrop showing a city street, a garden, a forest, or a castle? How would you light your scene? Make a drawing of your design, and add any description necessary to make your ideas clear to the viewer.

SKILLS FOCUS

Literary Skills
Analyze characteristics of tragedy, including dramatic irony. Describe scene design.

INTERNET

Projects and Activities

Keyword: LE7 9-11

Shakespeare's Language

Shakespeare's language is different from the English we use today. For one thing, many of Shakespeare's words and expressions are now **archaic.** They are out of use, or their meaning has changed. For another thing, Shakespeare often omits words. For example, in the Prologue the speaker says:

> "If you with patient ears attend,
> What here shall miss, our toil shall
>   strive to mend."

Shakespeare depends on your instinct and your ear to provide the missing words. He has also used the word *attend* in a way not commonly used today. Here's how we might say the same thing:

> If you listen patiently,
> Whatever you've missed from my
>   speech, we'll try to make clear by
>   our work onstage.

PRACTICE

The passages below are spoken by Juliet's nurse. Rewrite each one in the kind of English that you would use. Check the context, the side-notes, and a good dictionary for help.

1. "I pray you, sir, what saucy merchant was this that was so full of his ropery?" (pages 949–950, lines 137–138)

2. "Is your man secret? Did you ne'er hear say,
   Two may keep counsel, putting one away?" (page 951, lines 185–186)

3. "But she, good soul, had as lieve see a toad, a very toad, as see him." (page 951, lines 191–192)

4. "I am aweary, give me leave awhile.
   Fie, how my bones ache! What a jaunce have I!" (page 952, lines 25–26)

5. "Then hie you hence to Friar Laurence' cell;
   There stays a husband to make you a wife." (page 954, lines 68–69)

SKILLS FOCUS

Vocabulary Skills
Understand archaic language.

❈ ACT III ❈

Scene 1. *A public place.*

Enter MERCUTIO, BENVOLIO, *and* MEN.

Benvolio.
 I pray thee, good Mercutio, let's retire.
 The day is hot, the Capels° are abroad,
 And, if we meet, we shall not 'scape a brawl,
 For now, these hot days, is the mad blood stirring.

5 **Mercutio.** Thou art like one of these fellows that, when he
 enters the confines of a tavern, claps me his sword upon
 the table and says, "God send me no need of thee!" and
 by the operation of the second cup draws him on the
 drawer,° when indeed there is no need.

10 **Benvolio.** Am I like such a fellow?

 Mercutio. Come, come, thou art as hot a Jack in thy mood
 as any in Italy; and as soon moved to be moody, and as
 soon moody to be moved.

 Benvolio. And what to?

15 **Mercutio.** Nay, and there were two such, we should have
 none shortly, for one would kill the other. Thou! Why,
 thou wilt quarrel with a man that hath a hair more or a
 hair less in his beard than thou hast. Thou wilt quarrel
 with a man for cracking nuts, having no other reason but
20 because thou hast hazel eyes. What eye but such an eye
 would spy out such a quarrel? Thy head is as full of
 quarrels as an egg is full of meat; and yet thy head hath
 been beaten as addle° as an egg for quarreling. Thou hast
 quarreled with a man for coughing in the street, because
25 he hath wakened thy dog that hath lain asleep in the sun.
 Didst thou not fall out with a tailor for wearing his new
 doublet° before Easter? With another for tying his new
 shoes with old riband? And yet thou wilt tutor me from
 quarreling!

30 **Benvolio.** And I were so apt to quarrel as thou art, any man
 should buy the fee simple of° my life for an hour and a
 quarter.

 Mercutio. The fee simple? O simple!°

[Enter TYBALT *and others.]*

---

2. **Capels:** Capulets.

? 4. *Romeo's friends enter the stage. Again Shakespeare "sets the stage" by having the characters tell us what the weather is like. Why does this weather seem to breed trouble?*

9. **draws him on the drawer:** draws his sword on the waiter (who "draws" the drink).

? **Staging the Play**
16. *Mercutio mocks Benvolio, who is anything but a troublemaker. (Mercutio is the one who can't seem to resist a quarrel.) If you were playing Benvolio, what would you be doing as Mercutio goes on and on? If you were playing Mercutio, how would you behave as your comments became more and more exaggerated?*

23. **addle:** rotten.
27. **doublet:** jacket.

31. **buy the fee simple of:** buy insurance on.

33. **O simple:** O stupid.

Benvolio. By my head, here come the Capulets.

35 **Mercutio.** By my heel, I care not.

Tybalt.
Follow me close, for I will speak to them.
Gentlemen, good-den. A word with one of you.

Mercutio.
And but one word with one of us?
Couple it with something; make it a word and a blow.

40 **Tybalt.** You shall find me apt enough to that, sir, and you
will give me occasion.

Mercutio. Could you not take some occasion without giving?

Tybalt. Mercutio, thou consortest with Romeo.

Mercutio. Consort?° What, dost thou make us minstrels?

45 And thou make minstrels of us, look to hear nothing but
discords. Here's my fiddlestick;° here's that shall make
you dance. Zounds,° consort!

Benvolio.
We talk here in the public haunt of men.
Either withdraw unto some private place,

50 Or reason coldly of your grievances,
Or else depart. Here all eyes gaze on us.

Mercutio.
Men's eyes were made to look, and let them gaze.
I will not budge for no man's pleasure, I.

[*Enter* ROMEO.]

Tybalt.
Well, peace be with you, sir. Here comes my man.

Mercutio.
55 But I'll be hanged, sir, if he wear your livery.°
Marry, go before to field,° he'll be your follower!
Your worship in that sense may call him man.

Tybalt.
Romeo, the love I bear thee can afford
No better term than this: thou art a villain.°

Romeo.
60 Tybalt, the reason that I have to love thee
Doth much excuse the appertaining° rage
To such a greeting. Villain am I none.
Therefore farewell. I see thou knowest me not.

Tybalt.
Boy, this shall not excuse the injuries
65 That thou hast done me; therefore turn and draw.

---

44. Consort: Mercutio pretends to think that Tybalt means a *consort*, or group of musicians.
46. fiddlestick: bow for playing violinlike instruments (referring to his sword).
47. Zounds: slang for "by God's wounds."

? Staging the Play
Stage direction: Romeo is returning from his secret marriage—he has no thought about hatred and killing. What would he be doing as he enters? How would he react to the tense situation?

55. livery: servant's uniform. By *man*, Tybalt meant "target," but Mercutio uses the word to mean "servant."
56. field: dueling field.

59. villain: boor; clumsy, stupid fellow.

61. appertaining: appropriate.

? 58–65. *What insult does Tybalt use to try to make Romeo draw his sword?*

Romeo.

    I do protest I never injured thee,
    But love thee better than thou canst devise°
    Till thou shalt know the reason of my love;
    And so, good Capulet, which name I tender°
70   As dearly as mine own, be satisfied.

Mercutio.

    O calm, dishonorable, vile submission!
    Alla stoccata° carries it away.

    [*Draws.*]

    Tybalt, you ratcatcher, will you walk?°

Tybalt.

    What wouldst thou have with me?

75 **Mercutio.** Good King of Cats, nothing but one of your nine
    lives. That I mean to make bold withal,° and, as you shall
    use me hereafter, dry-beat° the rest of the eight. Will you
    pluck your sword out of his pilcher° by the ears? Make
    haste, lest mine be about your ears ere it be out.

80 **Tybalt.** I am for you.

    [*Draws.*]

Romeo.

    Gentle Mercutio, put thy rapier up.

Mercutio. Come, sir, your passado!

    [*They fight.*]

Romeo.

    Draw, Benvolio; beat down their weapons.
    Gentlemen, for shame! Forbear this outrage!
85   Tybalt, Mercutio, the prince expressly hath
    Forbid this bandying° in Verona streets.
    Hold, Tybalt! Good Mercutio!

    [TYBALT *under Romeo's arm thrusts* MERCUTIO *in, and flies.*]

Mercutio.   I am hurt.
    A plague a' both houses! I am sped.°
    Is he gone and hath nothing?

Benvolio.   What, art thou hurt?

Mercutio.

90   Ay, ay, a scratch, a scratch. Marry, 'tis enough.
    Where is my page? Go, villain, fetch a surgeon.

                            [*Exit* PAGE.]

---

67. devise: imagine.

69. tender: value.

? **70.** *Why does Romeo refuse to duel with Tybalt?*

? **Staging the Play**
71. *Mercutio doesn't know about Romeo's marriage to Juliet (a Capulet). Why is Mercutio so outraged? What feeling should Tybalt express (fear? annoyance?) as he asks Mercutio what he wants?*

72. Alla stoccata (ä′lä stə · kä′tä): Italian for "at the thrust"; a fencing term.

73. walk: make a move.

76. make bold withal: make free with (take away).

77. dry-beat: thrash.

78. pilcher: scabbard (sword holder).

? **Staging the Play**
Stage direction: The stage direction simply says "They fight," but how would you—as director—choreograph the action? The sword fight can range all over the stage, but where must the three characters be placed when Tybalt stabs Mercutio?

86. bandying: brawling.

88. sped: wounded.

Romeo.

    Courage, man. The hurt cannot be much.

Mercutio. No, 'tis not so deep as a well, nor so wide as a
church door; but 'tis enough, 'twill serve. Ask for me
95   tomorrow, and you shall find me a grave man. I am
peppered,° I warrant, for this world. A plague a' both
your houses! Zounds, a dog, a rat, a mouse, a cat, to
scratch a man to death! A braggart, a rogue, a villain, that
fights by the book of arithmetic!° Why the devil came
100   you between us? I was hurt under your arm.

Romeo.

    I thought all for the best.

Mercutio.

    Help me into some house, Benvolio,
    Or I shall faint. A plague a' both your houses!
    They have made worms' meat of me. I have it,
105   And soundly too. Your houses!

                   [*Exeunt* MERCUTIO *and* BENVOLIO.]

Romeo.

    This gentleman, the prince's near ally,°
    My very friend, hath got this mortal hurt
    In my behalf—my reputation stained
    With Tybalt's slander—Tybalt, that an hour
110   Hath been my cousin. O sweet Juliet,
    Thy beauty hath made me effeminate
    And in my temper soft'ned valor's steel!

[*Enter* BENVOLIO.]

Benvolio.

    O Romeo, Romeo, brave Mercutio is dead!
    That gallant spirit hath aspired° the clouds,
115   Which too untimely here did scorn the earth.

Romeo.

    This day's black fate on more days doth depend;°
    This but begins the woe others must end.

[*Enter* TYBALT.]

Benvolio.

    Here comes the furious Tybalt back again.

Romeo.

    Alive in triumph, and Mercutio slain?
120   Away to heaven respective lenity,
    And fire-eyed fury be my conduct now!

---

96. peppered: given a deadly wound (peppered food is ready to eat; Mercutio is "ready" to die).

99. fights by the book of arithmetic: fights according to formal rules of fencing.

Staging the Play
101. *How would Romeo say this pathetic line?*

Staging the Play
105. *What curse has Mercutio pronounced four times? Some actors playing Mercutio make him seem bitter about his approaching death and hostile to Romeo. Other Mercutios are gallant to the end and extend a hand to Romeo in friendship. How would you play this death speech?*

106. ally: relative. Mercutio is related to Verona's Prince Escalus.

114. aspired: climbed to.

116. depend: hang over.

Staging the Play
Stage direction: *Does it seem unlikely that Tybalt would return so soon? He must return, of course, so that Romeo can avenge Mercutio. An alternative would have been to have Romeo attack Tybalt as soon as he stabbed Mercutio, but then Shakespeare would have lost Mercutio's great dying speech. How would you stage Tybalt's return so that it seems believable?*

"O, I am fortune's fool!"
✪

Now, Tybalt, take the "villain" back again
That late thou gavest me; for Mercutio's soul
Is but a little way above our heads,
125   Staying for thine to keep him company.
Either thou or I, or both, must go with him.

Tybalt.
Thou, wretched boy, that didst consort him here,
Shalt with him hence.

Romeo.   This shall determine that.

[*They fight.* TYBALT *falls.*]

Benvolio.
Romeo, away, be gone!
130   The citizens are up, and Tybalt slain.
Stand not amazed. The prince will doom thee death
If thou art taken. Hence, be gone, away!

Romeo.
O, I am fortune's fool!

Benvolio.   Why dost thou stay?

[*Exit* ROMEO.]

[*Enter* CITIZENS.]

Citizen.
Which way ran he that killed Mercutio?
135   Tybalt, that murderer, which way ran he?

Benvolio.
There lies that Tybalt.

Citizen.   Up, sir, go with me.
I charge thee in the prince's name obey.

[*Enter* PRINCE, *old* MONTAGUE, CAPULET, *their* WIVES, *and all.*]

Prince.
Where are the vile beginners of this fray?

Benvolio.
O noble prince, I can discover° all
140   The unlucky manage° of this fatal brawl.
There lies the man, slain by young Romeo,
That slew thy kinsman, brave Mercutio.

Lady Capulet.
Tybalt, my cousin! O my brother's child!
O prince! O cousin! Husband! O, the blood is spilled
145   Of my dear kinsman! Prince, as thou art true,

132. *What details in Benvolio's speech tell us what Romeo is doing and how he is feeling after this second death?*

133. *What do you think Romeo means by calling himself "fortune's fool"? What does he realize will now happen to him and Juliet?*

Staging the Play
Stage direction: What do you imagine the stage looks like as the prince and the two families enter?

139. **discover:** reveal.
140. **manage:** course.

For blood of ours shed blood of Montague.
O cousin, cousin!

Prince.
Benvolio, who began this bloody fray?

Benvolio.
Tybalt, here slain, whom Romeo's hand did slay.
150 Romeo, that spoke him fair, bid him bethink
How nice° the quarrel was, and urged° withal
Your high displeasure. All this—utterèd
With gentle breath, calm look, knees humbly bowed—
Could not take truce with the unruly spleen°
155 Of Tybalt deaf to peace, but that he tilts°
With piercing steel at bold Mercutio's breast;
Who, all as hot, turns deadly point to point,
And, with a martial scorn, with one hand beats
Cold death aside and with the other sends
160 It back to Tybalt, whose dexterity
Retorts it. Romeo he cries aloud,
"Hold, friends! Friends, part!" and swifter than his
    tongue,
His agile arm beats down their fatal points,
And 'twixt them rushes; underneath whose arm
165 An envious° thrust from Tybalt hit the life
Of stout Mercutio, and then Tybalt fled;

151. **nice:** trivial. **urged:**
mentioned.

154. **spleen:** anger.
155. **tilts:** thrusts.

165. **envious:** full of enmity or
hatred.

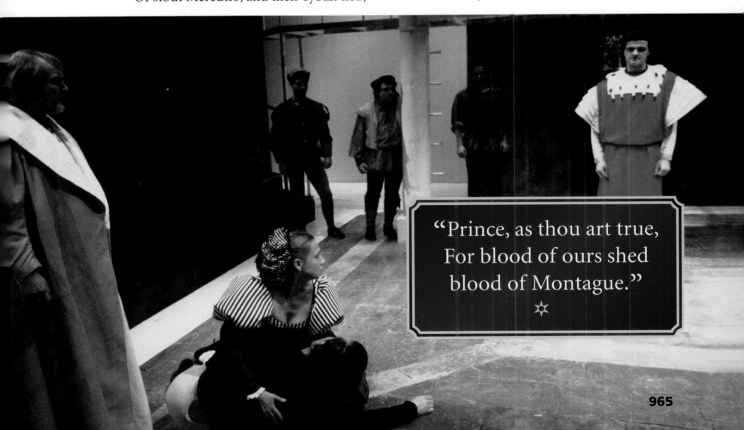

"Prince, as thou art true,
For blood of ours shed
blood of Montague."
✿

But by and by comes back to Romeo,
Who had but newly entertained° revenge,
And to't they go like lightning; for, ere I
170 Could draw to part them, was stout Tybalt slain;
And, as he fell, did Romeo turn and fly.
This is the truth, or let Benvolio die.

Lady Capulet.
He is a kinsman to the Montague;
Affection makes him false, he speaks not true.
175 Some twenty of them fought in this black strife,
And all those twenty could but kill one life.
I beg for justice, which thou, prince, must give.
Romeo slew Tybalt; Romeo must not live.

Prince.
Romeo slew him; he slew Mercutio.
180 Who now the price of his dear blood doth owe?

Montague.
Not Romeo, prince; he was Mercutio's friend;
His fault concludes but what the law should end,
The life of Tybalt.

Prince.   And for that offense
Immediately we do exile him hence.
185 I have an interest in your hate's proceeding,
My blood° for your rude brawls doth lie a-bleeding;
But I'll amerce° you with so strong a fine
That you shall all repent the loss of mine.
I will be deaf to pleading and excuses;
190 Nor tears nor prayers shall purchase out abuses.
Therefore use none. Let Romeo hence in haste,
Else, when he is found, that hour is his last.
Bear hence this body and attend our will.
Mercy but murders, pardoning those that kill.

[*Exit with others.*]

168. **entertained:** thought of.

172. *Is Benvolio's testimony about events fully accurate?*

176. *How does Lady Capulet think Tybalt was killed? Why does she think Benvolio is lying?*

186. **My blood:** that is, Mercutio, his blood relative.
187. **amerce:** punish.

194. *The prince has heard arguments from both families and has given judgment in the case. What is Romeo's punishment? Why won't the prince show Romeo greater mercy?*

Staging the Play
Stage direction: The families exit in separate processions, carrying their dead. How does this scene contrast with the fighting that has just taken place?

Scene 2. *Capulet's orchard.*

Enter JULIET *alone.*

Juliet.

    Gallop apace, you fiery-footed steeds,°
    Towards Phoebus' lodging! Such a wagoner
    As Phaethon° would whip you to the west
    And bring in cloudy night immediately.
5   Spread thy close curtain, love-performing night,
    That runaways' eyes may wink,° and Romeo
    Leap to these arms untalked of and unseen.
    Lovers can see to do their amorous rites,
    And by their own beauties; or, if love be blind,
10   It best agrees with night. Come, civil° night,
    Thou sober-suited matron all in black,
    And learn me how to lose a winning match,
    Played for a pair of stainless maidenhoods.
    Hood° my unmanned° blood, bating° in my cheeks,
15   With thy black mantle till strange° love grow bold,
    Think true love acted simple modesty.
    Come, night; come, Romeo; come, thou day in night;
    For thou wilt lie upon the wings of night
    Whiter than new snow upon a raven's back.
20   Come, gentle night; come, loving, black-browed night;
    Give me my Romeo; and, when he shall die,
    Take him and cut him out in little stars,
    And he will make the face of heaven so fine
    That all the world will be in love with night

> **"O, I have bought
> the mansion of a love,
> But not possessed it . . . "**

25   And pay no worship to the garish sun.
    O, I have bought the mansion of a love,
    But not possessed it; and though I am sold,
    Not yet enjoyed. So tedious is this day
    As is the night before some festival
30   To an impatient child that hath new robes
    And may not wear them. O, here comes my nurse,

? **1.** *In this famous **soliloquy**, Juliet yearns for the night, when she and Romeo will be together. What do we in the audience know that Juliet does not yet know?*

  1. steeds: horses. (In Greek mythology, horses pull the sun god Phoebus's chariot across the sky each day.)

  3. Phaethon (fā′ə·thän′): Phoebus's reckless son, who couldn't hold the horses' reins.

  6. That runaways' eyes may wink: so that the eyes of the sun god's horses may shut.

  10. civil: well-behaved.

  14. Hood: cover. **unmanned:** unmated. **bating:** fluttering.

  15. strange: unfamiliar.

? **24.** *Work with a small group to make a word map for the word* night. *Include all the associations, images, and synonyms that you can come up with. How do they compare with Juliet's view of night?*

? **Staging the Play**
26. *What is the "mansion of a love" that Juliet has bought?*

? **31.** *Where does Juliet, in lines of unconscious **foreshadowing,** make us think of Romeo's death?*

[*Enter* NURSE, *with a ladder of cords.*]

And she brings news; and every tongue that speaks
But Romeo's name speaks heavenly eloquence.
Now, nurse, what news? What hast thou there, the cords
That Romeo bid thee fetch?

35 **Nurse.**   Ay, ay, the cords.
Juliet.
    Ay me! What news? Why dost thou wring thy hands?
Nurse.
    Ah, weraday!° He's dead, he's dead, he's dead!
    We are undone, lady, we are undone!
    Alack the day! He's gone, he's killed, he's dead!
Juliet.
    Can heaven be so envious?
40 **Nurse.**   Romeo can,
    Though heaven cannot. O Romeo, Romeo!
    Who ever would have thought it? Romeo!
Juliet.
    What devil art thou that dost torment me thus?
    This torture should be roared in dismal hell.
45 Hath Romeo slain himself? Say thou but "Ay,"
    And that bare vowel "I" shall poison more
    Than the death-darting eye of cockatrice.°
    I am not I, if there be such an "Ay,"
    Or those eyes' shot that make thee answer "Ay."
50 If he be slain, say "Ay"; or if not, "No."
    Brief sounds determine of my weal or woe.
Nurse.
    I saw the wound, I saw it with mine eyes,
    (God save the mark!)° here on his manly breast.
    A piteous corse,° a bloody piteous corse;
55 Pale, pale as ashes, all bedaubed in blood,
    All in gore-blood. I swounded° at the sight.
Juliet.
    O, break, my heart! Poor bankrout,° break at once!
    To prison, eyes; ne'er look on liberty!
    Vile earth,° to earth resign; end motion here,
60 And thou and Romeo press one heavy bier!
Nurse.
    O Tybalt, Tybalt, the best friend I had!
    O courteous Tybalt! Honest gentleman!
    That ever I should live to see thee dead!

❓ Staging the Play
35. *How might the nurse speak this line?*

37. weraday: well-a-day (or alas).

❓ 39. *The nurse rattles on again—but this time, how does she seem to give the wrong news even as she delays it?*

47. cockatrice: legendary serpent that could kill by a glance.

53. God save the mark!: God forbid!
54. corse: corpse.

56. swounded: swooned (fainted).
57. bankrout: bankrupt.

59. Vile earth: Juliet refers to her own body.
❓ 60. *This is one of a series of odd scenes in which we cannot share a character's feelings because we know something that the character does not know. What does Juliet think has happened? How does she* **foreshadow** *her own death?*

Juliet.

What storm is this that blows so contrary?

65　Is Romeo slaught'red, and is Tybalt dead?

My dearest cousin, and my dearer lord?

Then, dreadful trumpet, sound the general doom!

For who is living, if those two are gone?

Nurse.

Tybalt is gone, and Romeo banishèd;

70　Romeo that killed him, he is banishèd.

Juliet.

O God! Did Romeo's hand shed Tybalt's blood?

Nurse.

It did, it did! Alas the day, it did!

Juliet.

O serpent heart, hid with a flow'ring face!

Did ever dragon keep so fair a cave?

75　Beautiful tyrant! Fiend angelical!

Dove-feathered raven! Wolvish-ravening lamb!

Despisèd substance of divinest show!

Just opposite to what thou justly seem'st—

A damnèd saint, an honorable villain!

80　O nature, what hadst thou to do in hell

When thou didst bower the spirit of a fiend

In mortal paradise of such sweet flesh?

Was ever book containing such vile matter

So fairly bound? O, that deceit should dwell

In such a gorgeous palace!

85　**Nurse.**　　　　　　　　　　　There's no trust,

No faith, no honesty in men; all perjured,

All forsworn, all naught, all dissemblers.°

Ah, where's my man? Give me some aqua vitae.°

These griefs, these woes, these sorrows make me old.

Shame come to Romeo!

90　**Juliet.**　　　　　　　　　Blistered be thy tongue

For such a wish! He was not born to shame.

Upon his brow shame is ashamed to sit;

For 'tis a throne where honor may be crowned

Sole monarch of the universal earth.

95　O, what a beast was I to chide at him!

Nurse.

Will you speak well of him that killed your cousin?

Juliet.

Shall I speak ill of him that is my husband?

Ah, poor my lord, what tongue shall smooth thy name

? Staging the Play
70. *Why do you think the nurse waits so long to give Juliet the correct news? Should we feel she is being self-centered here, or is she truly overwhelmed by the news she bears?*

? Staging the Play
73. *The news that Romeo has killed Tybalt is terrible for Juliet. Try writing stage directions that will help an actor express her horror.*

? 85. *A moment ago Juliet thought of Romeo as her "day in night." Now what does she think of him?*

87. dissemblers: liars.

88. aqua vitae (ak'wə vīt'ē): brandy (Latin for "water of life").

? 90. *What does the nurse think about these events? Where does she think the blame lies? Do you see her being selfish here, or is she wholly concerned for Juliet?*

? 97. *Why does Juliet turn against her nurse here?*

"'Tybalt is dead,
and Romeo—
banishèd.'"
✦

When I, thy three-hours wife, have mangled it?
100 But wherefore, villain, didst thou kill my cousin?
That villain cousin would have killed my husband.
Back, foolish tears, back to your native spring!
Your tributary drops° belong to woe,
Which you, mistaking, offer up to joy.
105 My husband lives, that Tybalt would have slain;
And Tybalt's dead, that would have slain my husband.
All this is comfort; wherefore weep I then?
Some word there was, worser than Tybalt's death,
That murd'red me. I would forget it fain;°
110 But O, it presses to my memory
Like damnèd guilty deeds to sinners' minds!
"Tybalt is dead, and Romeo—banishèd."
That "banishèd," that one word "banishèd,"
Hath slain ten thousand Tybalts. Tybalt's death
115 Was woe enough, if it had ended there;
Or, if sour woe delights in fellowship
And needly will be ranked with° other griefs,
Why followed not, when she said "Tybalt's dead,"
Thy father, or thy mother, nay, or both,
120 Which modern° lamentation might have moved?°
But with a rearward° following Tybalt's death,
"Romeo is banishèd"—to speak that word
Is father, mother, Tybalt, Romeo, Juliet,
All slain, all dead. "Romeo is banishèd"—
125 There is no end, no limit, measure, bound,
In that word's death; no words can that woe sound.
Where is my father and my mother, nurse?

Nurse.
Weeping and wailing over Tybalt's corse.
Will you go to them? I will bring you thither.

Juliet.
130 Wash they his wounds with tears? Mine shall be spent,
When theirs are dry, for Romeo's banishment.
Take up those cords. Poor ropes, you are beguiled,
Both you and I, for Romeo is exiled.
He made you for a highway to my bed;
135 But I, a maid, die maiden-widowèd.
Come, cords; come, nurse. I'll to my wedding bed;
And death, not Romeo, take my maidenhead!

Nurse.
Hie to your chamber. I'll find Romeo

---

103. tributary drops: tears poured out in tribute.

109. fain: willingly.

117. ranked with: accompanied by.

120. modern: ordinary. **moved:** provoked.
121. rearward: soldiers at the rear of a troop; here, an additional source of injury and pain after the bad news about Tybalt.

? **124.** *Juliet comprehends what has happened. Why does she fix on the word* banished?

? **Staging the Play**
127. *Juliet pauses before she speaks her last line here. How would she change her tone as she asks the nurse about her father and mother?*

? **137.** *Juliet addresses the rope ladder in this speech. What has she decided to do with the ropes?*

140   To comfort you. I wot° well where he is.
        Hark ye, your Romeo will be here at night.
        I'll to him; he is hid at Laurence' cell.

Juliet.
        O, find him! Give this ring to my true knight
        And bid him come to take his last farewell.

                                    [*Exit with* NURSE.]

Scene 3. *Friar Laurence's cell.*

Enter FRIAR LAURENCE.

Friar.
        Romeo, come forth; come forth, thou fearful man.
        Affliction is enamored of thy parts,
        And thou art wedded to calamity.

        [*Enter* ROMEO.]

Romeo.
        Father, what news? What is the prince's doom?
5   What sorrow craves acquaintance at my hand
        That I yet know not?
Friar.   Too familiar
        Is my dear son with such sour company.
        I bring thee tidings of the prince's doom.
Romeo.
        What less than doomsday° is the prince's doom?
Friar.
10   A gentler judgment vanished° from his lips—
        Not body's death, but body's banishment.
Romeo.
        Ha, banishment? Be merciful, say "death";
        For exile hath more terror in his look,
        Much more than death. Do not say "banishment."
Friar.
15   Here from Verona art thou banishèd.
        Be patient, for the world is broad and wide.
Romeo.
        There is no world without Verona walls,
        But purgatory, torture, hell itself.
        Hence banishèd is banished from the world,
20   And world's exile is death. Then "banishèd"
        Is death mistermed. Calling death "banishèd,"

139. wot: know.

? **3.** *When we last saw Romeo, he was speaking of himself as "fortune's fool" (Act III, Scene 1, line 133). Now, in the first lines of this scene, how does the friar remind us again that Romeo seems fated for ill fortune?*

9. doomsday: my death.

10. vanished: escaped.

Thou cut'st my head off with a golden ax
And smilest upon the stroke that murders me.
Friar.
O deadly sin! O rude unthankfulness!
25   Thy fault our law calls death; but the kind prince,
Taking thy part, hath rushed aside the law,
And turned that black word "death" to "banishment."
This is dear mercy, and thou see'st it not.
Romeo.
'Tis torture, and not mercy. Heaven is here,
30   Where Juliet lives; and every cat and dog
And little mouse, every unworthy thing,
Live here in heaven and may look on her;
But Romeo may not. More validity,°
More honorable state, more courtship lives
35   In carrion flies than Romeo. They may seize
On the white wonder of dear Juliet's hand
And steal immortal blessing from her lips,
Who, even in pure and vestal modesty,
Still blush, as thinking their own kisses sin;
40   But Romeo may not, he is banishèd.
Flies may do this but I from this must fly;
They are freemen, but I am banishèd.
And sayest thou yet that exile is not death?
Hadst thou no poison mixed, no sharp-ground knife,
45   No sudden mean of death, though ne'er so mean,
But "banishèd" to kill me—"banishèd"?
O friar, the damnèd use that word in hell;
Howling attends it! How hast thou the heart,
Being a divine, a ghostly confessor,
50   A sin-absolver, and my friend professed,
To mangle me with that word "banishèd"?

"'Tis torture, and not mercy."

Friar.
Thou fond° mad man, hear me a little speak.
Romeo.
O, thou wilt speak again of banishment.
Friar.
I'll give thee armor to keep off that word;
55   Adversity's sweet milk, philosophy,
To comfort thee, though thou art banishèd.

23. *Romeo and Friar Laurence have just had a* **dialogue**—*the talk between or among characters in a play—about the words* banished *and* banishment. *What do these words mean to Romeo? What do they mean to Friar Laurence?*

28. *Why is the friar angry at Romeo?*

33. validity: value.

52. fond: foolish.

Romeo.

Yet "banishèd"? Hang up philosophy!
Unless philosophy can make a Juliet,
Displant a town, reverse a prince's doom,
60   It helps not, it prevails not. Talk no more.

Friar.

O, then I see that madmen have no ears.

Romeo.

How should they, when that wise men have no eyes?

Friar.

Let me dispute with thee of thy estate.°

Romeo.

Thou canst not speak of that thou dost not feel.
65   Wert thou as young as I, Juliet thy love,
An hour but married, Tybalt murderèd,
Doting like me, and like me banishèd,
Then mightst thou speak, then mightst thou tear thy hair,
And fall upon the ground, as I do now,
70   Taking the measure of an unmade grave.

[*The* NURSE *knocks.*]

Friar.

Arise, one knocks. Good Romeo, hide thyself.

Romeo.

Not I; unless the breath of heartsick groans
Mistlike infold me from the search of eyes.

[*Knock.*]

Friar.

Hark, how they knock! Who's there? Romeo, arise;
75   Thou wilt be taken.—Stay awhile!—Stand up;

[*Knock.*]

Run to my study.—By and by!—God's will,
What simpleness is this.—I come, I come!

[*Knock.*]

Who knocks so hard? Whence come you? What's your
    will?

[*Enter* NURSE.]

Nurse.

Let me come in, and you shall know my errand.

? **60.** *It may seem that Romeo goes on too much. It is important, however, that we get the picture of this "fond mad man" in order to understand the action of the play. None of the other characters can understand Romeo's love. They are more levelheaded (perhaps less lucky in love?). How is Romeo's response to banishment like Juliet's?*

? **62.** *Whom is Romeo talking about?*

63. estate: situation.

? **Staging the Play**
70. *How do you think the friar responds to these harsh words?*

? **Staging the Play**
78. *There is a great deal of action in this scene while the knocks are heard at the door. What action is the friar engaged in, and what is Romeo doing?*

I come from Lady Juliet.

80 **Friar.**   Welcome then.

Nurse.

O holy friar, O, tell me, holy friar,
Where is my lady's lord, where's Romeo?

Friar.

There on the ground, with his own tears made drunk.

Nurse.

O, he is even in my mistress' case,°

85 Just in her case! O woeful sympathy!
Piteous predicament! Even so lies she,
Blubb'ring and weeping, weeping and blubb'ring.
Stand up, stand up! Stand, and you be a man.
For Juliet's sake, for her sake, rise and stand!

90 Why should you fall into so deep an O?°

Romeo (*rises*). Nurse—

Nurse.

Ah sir, ah sir! Death's the end of all.

Romeo.

Spakest thou of Juliet? How is it with her?
Doth not she think me an old murderer,

95 Now I have stained the childhood of our joy
With blood removed but little from her own?
Where is she? And how doth she? And what says
My concealed lady to our canceled love?

Nurse.

O, she says nothing, sir, but weeps and weeps;

100 And now falls on her bed, and then starts up,
And Tybalt calls; and then on Romeo cries,
And then down falls again.

Romeo.   As if that name,
Shot from the deadly level° of a gun,
Did murder her; as that name's cursèd hand

105 Murdered her kinsman. O, tell me, friar, tell me,
In what vile part of this anatomy
Doth my name lodge? Tell me, that I may sack°
The hateful mansion.

[*He offers to stab himself, and* NURSE *snatches the dagger away.*]

Friar.   Hold thy desperate hand.
Art thou a man? Thy form cries out thou art;

110 Thy tears are womanish, thy wild acts denote
The unreasonable fury of a beast.

84. case: condition.

90. O: fit of moaning ("oh, oh, oh").

[?] Staging the Play
90. *What action is the nurse engaged in as she speaks these lines?*

103. level: aim.

107. sack: plunder and destroy.

[?] Staging the Play
108. *Romeo is disarmed without a struggle. He probably stands broken as the friar, in this long speech, gradually reestablishes control over him. It is important to remember that to the people in this play, suicide was a mortal sin, which damned one to hell forever. Where does the friar angrily remind Romeo of this?*

Unseemly woman in a seeming man!
And ill-beseeming beast in seeming both!
Thou hast amazed me. By my holy order,
115 I thought thy disposition better tempered.
Hast thou slain Tybalt? Wilt thou slay thyself?
And slay thy lady that in thy life lives,
By doing damnèd hate upon thyself?
Why rail'st thou on thy birth, the heaven, and earth?
120 Since birth and heaven and earth,° all three do meet
In thee at once; which thou at once wouldst lose.
Fie, fie, thou sham'st thy shape, thy love, thy wit,
Which,° like a usurer, abound'st in all,
And usest none in that true use indeed
125 Which should bedeck° thy shape, thy love, thy wit.
Thy noble shape is but a form of wax,
Digressing from the valor of a man;
Thy dear love sworn but hollow perjury,
Killing that love which thou hast vowed to cherish;
130 Thy wit, that ornament to shape and love,
Misshapen in the conduct° of them both,
Like powder in a skill-less soldier's flask,
Is set afire by thine own ignorance,
And thou dismembered with thine own defense.°
135 What, rouse thee, man! Thy Juliet is alive,
For whose dear sake thou wast but lately dead.
There art thou happy.° Tybalt would kill thee,
But thou slewest Tybalt. There art thou happy.
The law, that threatened death, becomes thy friend
140 And turns it to exile. There art thou happy.
A pack of blessings light upon thy back;
Happiness courts thee in her best array;
But, like a misbehaved and sullen wench,
Thou pouts upon thy fortune and thy love.
145 Take heed, take heed, for such die miserable.
Go get thee to thy love, as was decreed,
Ascend her chamber, hence and comfort her.
But look thou stay not till the watch be set,
For then thou canst not pass to Mantua,
150 Where thou shalt live till we can find a time
To blaze° your marriage, reconcile your friends,
Beg pardon of the prince, and call thee back
With twenty hundred thousand times more joy
Than thou went'st forth in lamentation.

120. birth and heaven and earth: family origin, soul, and body.

123. Which: who (speaking of Romeo).

125. bedeck: do honor to.

131. conduct: management.

134. And . . . defense: Romeo's own mind (wit), which should protect him, is destroying him.

137. happy: lucky.

151. blaze: announce.

154. *What line in this speech suggests that Romeo has been standing listlessly? Find where the friar first shames Romeo, then appeals to his common sense, then offers him hope.*

155 Go before, nurse. Commend me to thy lady,
And bid her hasten all the house to bed,
Which heavy sorrow makes them apt unto.
Romeo is coming.

Nurse.

O Lord, I could have stayed here all the night
160 To hear good counsel. O, what learning is!
My lord, I'll tell my lady you will come.

Romeo.

Do so, and bid my sweet prepare to chide.

[NURSE *offers to go in and turns again.*]

Nurse.

Here, sir, a ring she bid me give you, sir.
Hie you, make haste, for it grows very late.   [*Exit.*]

Romeo.

165 How well my comfort is revived by this!

Friar.

Go hence; good night; and here stands all your state:°
Either be gone before the watch be set,
Or by the break of day disguised from hence.
Sojourn in Mantua. I'll find out your man,
170 And he shall signify from time to time
Every good hap to you that chances here.
Give me thy hand. 'Tis late. Farewell; good night.

Romeo.

But that a joy past joy calls out on me,
It were a grief so brief to part with thee.
175 Farewell.   [*Exeunt.*]

Scene 4. *A room in Capulet's house.*

Enter old CAPULET, *his wife,* LADY CAPULET, *and* PARIS.

Capulet.

Things have fallen out, sir, so unluckily
That we have had no time to move° our daughter.
Look you, she loved her kinsman Tybalt dearly,
And so did I. Well, we were born to die.
5 'Tis very late; she'll not come down tonight.
I promise you, but for your company,
I would have been abed an hour ago.

155. *The friar turns to the nurse. What are his instructions?*

Staging the Play
161. *The nurse's amazement at what she calls the friar's "learning" often brings a laugh from the audience and breaks the tension. Romeo thus far has said nothing. How do you imagine he shows that the friar's speech has brought him back to life?*

166. **state:** situation.

175. *In spite of Romeo's and Juliet's anguish, the problem at this point seems to have a simple solution. What plans have been made to resolve the young people's difficulties?*

2. **move:** persuade (to marry Paris).

7. *Dramatic irony* is felt *when the audience knows something that the characters onstage do* not *know. What intense dramatic irony does the audience feel as this scene unfolds? What do we know that the Capulets and Paris are ignorant of?*

Paris.

　　These times of woe afford no times to woo.
　　Madam, good night. Commend me to your daughter.

Lady Capulet.

10　　I will, and know her mind early tomorrow;
　　Tonight she's mewed up to her heaviness.°

Capulet.

　　Sir Paris, I will make a desperate tender°
　　Of my child's love. I think she will be ruled
　　In all respects by me; nay more, I doubt it not.
15　　Wife, go you to her ere you go to bed;
　　Acquaint her here of my son Paris' love
　　And bid her (mark you me?) on Wednesday next—
　　But soft! What day is this?

Paris.　　　　　　　　　　　　Monday, my lord.

Capulet.

　　Monday! Ha, ha! Well, Wednesday is too soon.
20　　A' Thursday let it be—a' Thursday, tell her,
　　She shall be married to this noble earl.
　　Will you be ready? Do you like this haste?
　　We'll keep no great ado—a friend or two;
　　For hark you, Tybalt being slain so late,
25　　It may be thought we held him carelessly,
　　Being our kinsman, if we revel much.
　　Therefore we'll have some half a dozen friends,
　　And there an end. But what say you to Thursday?

Paris.

　　My lord, I would that Thursday were tomorrow.

Capulet.

30　　Well, get you gone. A' Thursday be it then.
　　Go you to Juliet ere you go to bed;
　　Prepare her, wife, against this wedding day.
　　Farewell, my lord.—Light to my chamber, ho!
　　Afore me,° it is so very late
35　　That we may call it early by and by.
　　Good night.　　　　　　　　　　　　[*Exeunt.*]

> **"She shall be married to this noble earl."**

11. mewed up to her heaviness: shut away because of her great grief.
12. desperate tender: bold offer.

Staging the Play
19. *In some productions, Capulet is played as a foolish old man. Why might he want to get Juliet married as soon as possible? What do you think his mood is here?*

Staging the Play
32. *Capulet speaks this line to his wife. In some productions, Lady Capulet expresses uneasiness about her husband's plans here. Why would she be uneasy?*

34. Afore me: indeed.

36. *Just as we might feel the situation can be rescued, Shakespeare raises the stakes with this short scene. How does this development increase our tension in the scene that follows, the wedding-night scene?*

Scene 5. *Capulet's orchard.*

Enter ROMEO *and* JULIET *aloft.*

Juliet.

Wilt thou be gone? It is not yet near day.
It was the nightingale, and not the lark,
That pierced the fearful hollow of thine ear.
Nightly she sings on yond pomegranate tree.
5   Believe me, love, it was the nightingale.

Romeo.

It was the lark, the herald of the morn;
No nightingale. Look, love, what envious streaks
Do lace the severing clouds in yonder east.
Night's candles are burnt out, and jocund day
10   Stands tiptoe on the misty mountaintops.
I must be gone and live, or stay and die.

Juliet.

Yond light is not daylight; I know it, I.
It is some meteor that the sun exhales°
To be to thee this night a torchbearer
15   And light thee on thy way to Mantua.
Therefore stay yet; thou need'st not to be gone.

Romeo.

Let me be taken, let me be put to death.
I am content, so thou wilt have it so.
I'll say yon gray is not the morning's eye,
20   'Tis but the pale reflex° of Cynthia's brow;°
Nor that is not the lark whose notes do beat
The vaulty heaven so high above our heads.
I have more care to stay than will to go.
Come, death, and welcome! Juliet wills it so.
25   How is't, my soul? Let's talk; it is not day.

Juliet.

It is, it is! Hie hence, be gone, away!
It is the lark that sings so out of tune,
Straining harsh discords and unpleasing sharps.
Some say the lark makes sweet division;°
30   This doth not so, for she divideth us.
Some say the lark and loathèd toad change eyes;°
O, now I would they had changed voices too,

Staging the Play
Stage direction: *Given the design of Elizabethan theaters, this scene was probably played on the upper stage in Shakespeare's time. Modern directors often place the scene in Juliet's bedroom (with varying degrees of frankness). How would you design the scene for a movie or modern stage production?*

1. *Juliet's first words here alert us to the time: It must be near morning, when Romeo must go to Mantua. We hear the song of a lark, which sings at daybreak. The nightingale, on the other hand, sings at night. Why does Juliet insist she hears the nightingale?*

13. **exhales:** gives off. (It was believed that the sun drew up vapors and ignited them as meteors.)

20. **reflex:** reflection. **Cynthia's brow:** In Greek mythology, Cynthia is the goddess of the moon.

26. *What has Romeo said that makes Juliet suddenly practical and aware of danger?*
29. **division:** literally, a rapid run of notes, but Juliet is punning on the word's other meaning ("separation").
31. A fable to explain why the lark, which sings so beautifully, has ugly eyes and why the toad, which croaks so harshly, has beautiful ones.

"Farewell,
farewell!
One kiss,
and I'll
descend."

Since arm from arm that voice doth us affray,°
Hunting thee hence with hunt's-up° to the day.

35   O, now be gone! More light and light it grows.

Romeo.

More light and light—more dark and dark our woes.

[*Enter* NURSE.]

Nurse. Madam!

Juliet. Nurse?

Nurse.

Your lady mother is coming to your chamber.

40   The day is broke; be wary, look about.   [*Exit.*]

Juliet.

Then, window, let day in, and let life out.

Romeo.

Farewell, farewell! One kiss, and I'll descend.

[*He goes down.*]

Juliet.

Art thou gone so, love-lord, ay husband-friend?
I must hear from thee every day in the hour,

45   For in a minute there are many days.
O, for this count I shall be much in years
Ere I again behold my Romeo!

Romeo.

Farewell!
I will omit no opportunity

50   That may convey my greetings, love, to thee.

Juliet.

O, think'st thou we shall ever meet again?

Romeo.

I doubt it not; and all these woes shall serve
For sweet discourses in our times to come.

Juliet.

O God, I have an ill-divining soul!

55   Methinks I see thee, now thou art so low,
As one dead in the bottom of a tomb.
Either my eyesight fails, or thou look'st pale.

Romeo.

And trust me, love, in my eye so do you.
Dry° sorrow drinks our blood. Adieu, adieu!   [*Exit.*]

Juliet.

60   O Fortune, Fortune! All men call thee fickle.

33. affray: frighten.
34. hunt's-up: morning song for hunters.

? Staging the Play
41. *What is Juliet doing as she speaks these lines?*

? Staging the Play
43. *Where is Romeo now, as Juliet asks him to communicate with her?*

? Staging the Play
51. *Remember what the Chorus has told you in the Prologue about what will happen to Romeo and Juliet. How do you feel when you hear Juliet speak this line?*

? 57. *Friar Laurence might have sent Juliet with Romeo into exile in Mantua. We must remember, however, that Juliet is not quite fourteen. At this point in the story, Friar Laurence thinks the situation can be happily resolved. As the lovers part now, where does Juliet foresee Romeo's doom?*

59. Dry: thirsty (sorrow was thought to drain color from the cheeks).

If thou art fickle, what dost thou with him
That is renowned for faith? Be fickle, Fortune,
For then I hope thou wilt not keep him long
But send him back.

[*Enter Juliet's mother,* LADY CAPULET.]

Lady Capulet.
65   Ho, daughter! Are you up?
Juliet.
      Who is't that calls? It is my lady mother.
      Is she not down so late,° or up so early?
      What unaccustomed cause procures her hither?
Lady Capulet.
      Why, how now, Juliet?
Juliet.   Madam, I am not well.
Lady Capulet.
70   Evermore weeping for your cousin's death?
      What, wilt thou wash him from his grave with tears?
      And if thou couldst, thou couldst not make him live.
      Therefore have done. Some grief shows much of love;
      But much of grief shows still some want of wit.
Juliet.
75   Yet let me weep for such a feeling loss.°
Lady Capulet.
      So shall you feel the loss, but not the friend
      Which you weep for.
Juliet.   Feeling so the loss,
      I cannot choose but ever weep the friend.
Lady Capulet.
      Well, girl, thou weep'st not so much for his death
80   As that the villain lives which slaughtered him.
Juliet.
      What villain, madam?
Lady Capulet.   That same villain Romeo.
Juliet (*aside*).
      Villain and he be many miles asunder—
      God pardon him! I do, with all my heart;
      And yet no man like he doth grieve my heart.
Lady Capulet.
85   That is because the traitor murderer lives.
Juliet.
      Ay, madam, from the reach of these my hands.
      Would none but I might venge my cousin's death!

67. down so late: so late getting to bed.

Staging the Play
74. *Actors playing Lady Capulet have interpreted her character in different ways. Some portray her as loving toward Juliet. Others find in her speeches a signal to play her as distant and strong-willed, to contrast with Juliet's helplessness. What do you think Lady Capulet's tone is here, and how would you play the part?*

75. feeling loss: loss so deeply felt.

78. *All Juliet's lines in this scene have double meanings. Whom is she really grieving for?*

Staging the Play
82. *Juliet's first line here is an* **aside** *that her mother does not hear. In her next lines, how does Juliet convince her mother that she hates Romeo?*

Lady Capulet.
    We will have vengeance for it, fear thou not.
    Then weep no more. I'll send to one in Mantua,
90   Where that same banished runagate° doth live,
    Shall give him such an unaccustomed dram°
    That he shall soon keep Tybalt company;
    And then I hope thou wilt be satisfied.
Juliet.
    Indeed I never shall be satisfied
95   With Romeo till I behold him—dead—
    Is my poor heart so for a kinsman vexed.
    Madam, if you could find out but a man
    To bear a poison, I would temper° it—
    That Romeo should, upon receipt thereof,
100   Soon sleep in quiet. O, how my heart abhors
    To hear him named and cannot come to him,
    To wreak° the love I bore my cousin
    Upon his body that hath slaughtered him!
Lady Capulet.
    Find thou the means, and I'll find such a man.
105   But now I'll tell thee joyful tidings, girl.
Juliet.
    And joy comes well in such a needy time.
    What are they, I beseech your ladyship?
Lady Capulet.
    Well, well, thou hast a careful° father, child;
    One who, to put thee from thy heaviness,
110   Hath sorted out° a sudden day of joy
    That thou expects not nor I looked not for.
Juliet.
    Madam, in happy time!° What day is that?
Lady Capulet.
    Marry, my child, early next Thursday morn
    The gallant, young, and noble gentleman,
115   The County Paris, at Saint Peter's Church,
    Shall happily make thee there a joyful bride.
Juliet.
    Now by Saint Peter's Church, and Peter too,
    He shall not make me there a joyful bride!
    I wonder at this haste, that I must wed
120   Ere he that should be husband comes to woo.
    I pray you tell my lord and father, madam,
    I will not marry yet; and when I do, I swear

90. runagate (run′ə·gāt′): fugitive.

91. unaccustomed dram: unexpected drink (of poison).

? Staging the Play
93. *This is a hard and fearful threat. How does Juliet reply, and with what hidden emotions does she speak her next words? How does she continue to speak with double meanings?*

? Staging the Play
95. *How should lines 95–96 be said to indicate that Juliet intends* dead *to refer to her* heart?

98. temper: mix (she really means "weaken").

102. wreak: avenge (she really means "express").

? 105. *Has Juliet convinced her mother that she wants Romeo dead?*

? Staging the Play
107. *We know what the "tidings" are, but Juliet doesn't. How would she speak these lines?*

108. careful: full of caring (for Juliet).

110. sorted out: selected.

112. in happy time: at a lucky time.

? Staging the Play
120. *Juliet becomes sarcastic as she repeats her mother's words. Despite this shocking news, how does Juliet manage to make a reasonable protest to her mother?*

It shall be Romeo, whom you know I hate,
Rather than Paris. These are news indeed!

Lady Capulet.

125   Here comes your father. Tell him so yourself,
And see how he will take it at your hands.

[*Enter* CAPULET *and* NURSE.]

Capulet.

When the sun sets the earth doth drizzle dew,
But for the sunset of my brother's son
It rains downright.
130   How now? A conduit,° girl? What, still in tears?
Evermore showering? In one little body
Thou counterfeits a bark,° a sea, a wind:
For still thy eyes, which I may call the sea,
Do ebb and flow with tears; the bark thy body is,
135   Sailing in this salt flood; the winds, thy sighs,
Who, raging with thy tears and they with them,
Without a sudden calm will overset
Thy tempest-tossèd body. How now, wife?
Have you delivered to her our decree?

Lady Capulet.

140   Ay, sir; but she will none, she gives you thanks.
I would the fool were married to her grave!

Capulet.

Soft! Take me with you,° take me with you, wife.
How? Will she none? Doth she not give us thanks?
Is she not proud? Doth she not count her blest,
145   Unworthy as she is, that we have wrought°
So worthy a gentleman to be her bride?

Juliet.

Not proud you have, but thankful that you have.
Proud can I never be of what I hate,
But thankful even for hate that is meant love.

Capulet.

150   How, how, how, how, chopped-logic?° What is this?
"Proud"—and "I thank you"—and "I thank you not"—
And yet "not proud"? Mistress minion° you,
Thank me no thankings, nor proud me no prouds,
But fettle° your fine joints 'gainst Thursday next
155   To go with Paris to Saint Peter's Church,
Or I will drag thee on a hurdle thither.

130. conduit (kän′doo·it): water pipe (Juliet is weeping).

132. counterfeits a bark: imitates a boat.

Staging the Play
139. *Lord Capulet, self-satisfied and certain of his plan, tries to humor and tease the weeping Juliet. Again, what irony do we feel in this scene?*

142. Soft! Take me with you: Wait! Let me understand you.

145. wrought: arranged.

149. *How does Juliet show that she knows her father loves her even though she hates what he has done for her?*
150. chopped-logic: hair-splitting.
152. minion (min′yən): badly behaved girl.
154. fettle: make ready.

Out, you greensickness carrion! Out, you baggage!
You tallow-face!

Lady Capulet.   Fie, fie! What, are you mad?

Juliet.

Good father, I beseech you on my knees,
160   Hear me with patience but to speak a word.

Capulet.

Hang thee, young baggage! Disobedient wretch!
I tell thee what—get thee to church a' Thursday
Or never after look me in the face.
Speak not, reply not, do not answer me!
165   My fingers itch. Wife, we scarce thought us blest
That God had lent us but this only child;
But now I see this one is one too much,
And that we have a curse in having her.
Out on her, hilding!°

Nurse.   God in heaven bless her!
170   You are to blame, my lord, to rate° her so.

Capulet.

And why, my Lady Wisdom? Hold your tongue,
Good Prudence. Smatter with your gossips,° go!

? **Staging the Play**
158. *What insulting names does Capulet call Juliet? What would Capulet's actions be, as he speaks these vicious words to his only daughter? Whom is Juliet's mother talking to in her next line?*

? **Staging the Play**
160. *In the midst of this tragedy, we have a recognizable domestic scene, a family argument, which might have been played out in any century. What is Juliet doing as she talks to her father here? What does she do during her father's next speech?*

169. hilding: low, contemptible person.
170. rate: berate; scold.

172. Smatter with your gossips: chatter with your gossipy friends.

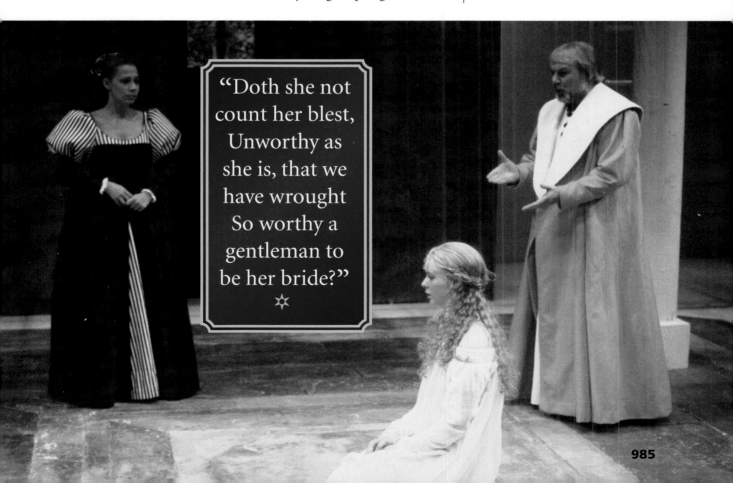

"Doth she not count her blest, Unworthy as she is, that we have wrought So worthy a gentleman to be her bride?"

Nurse.

    I speak no treason.

Capulet.   O, God-i-god-en!°

Nurse.

    May not one speak?

Capulet.   Peace, you mumbling fool!

175   Utter your gravity o'er a gossip's bowl,

    For here we need it not.

Lady Capulet.   You are too hot.

Capulet.

    God's bread!° It makes me mad.

    Day, night; hour, tide, time; work, play;

    Alone, in company; still my care hath been

180   To have her matched; and having now provided

    A gentleman of noble parentage,

    Of fair demesnes, youthful, and nobly trained,

    Stuffed, as they say, with honorable parts,

    Proportioned as one's thought would wish a man—

185   And then to have a wretched puling° fool,

    A whining mammet,° in her fortune's tender,°

    To answer "I'll not wed, I cannot love;

    I am too young, I pray you pardon me"!

    But, and you will not wed, I'll pardon you!°

190   Graze where you will, you shall not house with me.

    Look to't, think on't; I do not use to jest.

    Thursday is near; lay hand on heart, advise.°

    And you be mine, I'll give you to my friend;

    And you be not, hang, beg, starve, die in the streets,

195   For, by my soul, I'll ne'er acknowledge thee,

    Nor what is mine shall never do thee good.

    Trust to't. Bethink you. I'll not be forsworn.°   [*Exit.*]

Juliet.

    Is there no pity sitting in the clouds

    That sees into the bottom of my grief?

200   O sweet my mother, cast me not away!

    Delay this marriage for a month, a week;

    Or if you do not, make the bridal bed

    In that dim monument where Tybalt lies.

Lady Capulet.

    Talk not to me, for I'll not speak a word.

205   Do as thou wilt, for I have done with thee.   [*Exit.*]

Juliet.

    O God!—O nurse, how shall this be prevented?

173. God-i-god-en: Get on with you ("God give you good evening").

177. God's bread: oath on the sacrament of Communion (in the traditional Christian church service).

185. puling (pyool′iŋ): whining.
186. mammet: puppet. **in her fortune's tender:** with all her good fortunes.

188. *What does Lord Capulet think are Juliet's reasons for not wanting to marry Paris?*

189. I'll pardon you: I'll give you permission to go.
192. advise: consider.

197. forsworn: guilty of breaking my vow.

Staging the Play
197. *In most productions there is a moment of stunned silence onstage after Capulet leaves. What exactly will Lord Capulet do if Juliet refuses to marry Paris? In the next speech, how does Juliet appeal to her mother for help?*

My husband is on earth, my faith in heaven.°
How shall that faith return again to earth
Unless that husband send it me from heaven
210   By leaving earth? Comfort me, counsel me.
Alack, alack, that heaven should practice stratagems
Upon so soft a subject as myself!
What say'st thou? Hast thou not a word of joy?
Some comfort, nurse.

Nurse.   Faith, here it is.
215   Romeo is banished; and all the world to nothing°
That he dares ne'er come back to challenge you;
Or if he do, it needs must be by stealth.
Then, since the case so stands as now it doth,
I think it best you married with the county.
220   O, he's a lovely gentleman!
Romeo's a dishclout° to him. An eagle, madam,
Hath not so green, so quick, so fair an eye
As Paris hath. Beshrew° my very heart,
I think you are happy in this second match,
225   For it excels your first; or if it did not,
Your first is dead—or 'twere as good he were
As living here and you no use of him.

Juliet.
Speak'st thou from thy heart?

Nurse.
And from my soul too; else beshrew them both.
230   **Juliet.** Amen!
Nurse. What?
Juliet.
Well, thou hast comforted me marvelous much.
Go in; and tell my lady I am gone,
Having displeased my father, to Laurence' cell,
235   To make confession and to be absolved.
Nurse.
Marry, I will; and this is wisely done.   [*Exit.*]
Juliet.
Ancient damnation!° O most wicked fiend!
Is it more sin to wish me thus forsworn,
Or to dispraise my lord with that same tongue
240   Which she hath praised him with above compare
So many thousand times? Go, counselor!
Thou and my bosom henceforth shall be twain.°
I'll to the friar to know his remedy.
If all else fail, myself have power to die.   [*Exit.*]

207. my faith in heaven: my wedding vow is recorded in heaven.

? 210. *Romeo and Juliet constantly remind us that they have taken their marriage vows seriously. According to Juliet here, how can these vows be broken?*

215. all the world to nothing: it is a safe bet.

221. dishclout: dishcloth; limp and weak.

223. Beshrew: curse.

? 227. *What is the nurse's "comfort" and advice for Juliet? Which line in this speech suggests that Juliet has reacted with shock and that the nurse must pause? Did you expect such advice from the nurse?*

? Staging the Play
235. *In most productions the nurse embraces Juliet to comfort her. Now Juliet has made a decision. What do you see Juliet doing as she speaks?*

237. Ancient damnation: Damned old woman.

242. twain: two (thus, separate).
? 244. *What has Juliet decided about the nurse? We may wonder why Juliet doesn't just tell her parents why she cannot marry Paris. Why do you think she does not take this easy way out?*

Act III

Reading Check

1. What causes the fatal sword fight between Mercutio and Tybalt in Scene I? How is Mercutio killed?

2. Why does Romeo kill Tybalt?

3. Now the young lovers are in serious trouble. What does Juliet threaten in Scene 2, after hearing of Romeo's banishment?

4. What is the friar's plan to help them in Scene 3?

5. A new **complication** has arisen by the end of Scene 4. What plans have Juliet's parents made for her?

SKILLS FOCUS

Literary Skills
Analyze characteristics of tragedy, including complication, turning point, and suspense.

Writing Skills
Write a prologue.

Listening and Speaking Skills
Present scenes from the play.

INTERNET

Projects and Activities

Keyword: LE7 9-11

Thinking Critically

6. Romeo's killing of Tybalt is the **turning point** of the play—the point when something happens that turns the action toward either a happy ending (a **comedy**) or an unhappy ending (a **tragedy**). What actions does the killing set in motion, with what possible **tragic** consequences?

7. We already know (from the Prologue, page 901) that the play ends in the deaths of Romeo and Juliet. Their willingness to die comes as no surprise to us, because we have been warned. Point out the instances in this act where each of them mentions this willingness to die if they are separated.

8. How does the nurse offend Juliet in this act and cease to be her ally? How does this development add to the tragedy of the events that follow?

9. Romeo and Juliet are **dynamic characters,** characters who change during the course of the play. Describe how the lovers have changed in this act. What hard lessons have they learned about love?

10. By the end of Act III, we have reached the highest point of suspense. In drama, **suspense** causes us to wonder anxiously, "What will happen next?" Write down the questions you have at the end of Act III.

Extending and Evaluating

11. Does the last scene in this act remind you of encounters between parents and their teenage children that you've seen in movies or on TV shows or that you've read about in novels? Do Juliet and her parents remind you of real-life parents and teenagers today? Explain. Check your Quickwrite notes (page 897) before you answer.

WRITING

Write a Prologue

Did you notice that there is no prologue to Act III? Yet in this act we have some of the strongest action of the play. Write a **prologue** that **summarizes** the main events of the act. (If you want a challenge, try writing it in the form of a sonnet.)

LISTENING AND SPEAKING

Freeze! Speak!

Work in a group to create living pictures of the key action in each scene of Act III. For each scene, choose one character and one of that character's most significant lines. Then, arrange yourself in an appropriate opening position, and freeze. Taking turns with the other members of your group, come to life, say the line, change position, and freeze again. With your group, prepare a short opening and closing statement for the presentation.

Word Origins: What's in a Name?

In Act II, Scene 2, Juliet, upset to discover that the handsome young man she has just met is named Montague, speaks these famous lines about the insignificance of a name:

> "What's in a name? That which we call a rose
> By any other word would smell as sweet."

Names, however, *are* significant in Shakespeare's plays. They are often used to suggest something about a person's character or temperament.

PRACTICE

Use a dictionary and the sidenotes for help as you answer the following questions about the names of four characters in *Romeo and Juliet:*

1. Mercutio is named for the chemical element *mercury*, which itself is named for the Roman god Mercury, the messenger of the gods. Which characteristics of both the element and the god match Mercutio's character? What do we mean when we say that someone's temperament is *mercurial?*

2. Benvolio's name comes from the same Latin words as the adjective *benevolent.* What are these Latin words, and what do they mean? How does Benvolio's name match his character?

3. Tybalt is named for a cat that is known for its slyness in the fable "Reynard the Fox." How is Tybalt like the cat he is named for?

4. Paris has the same name as the Trojan prince in Homer's epic the *Iliad,* who persuades Helen to leave her husband and marry him. Although Count Paris never marries Juliet, what does he do in the play that is similar to what the Greek prince does in the epic?

5. If you were renaming these four characters for an updated version of the tragedy, what names would you give them?

SKILLS FOCUS

Vocabulary Skills
Understand word origins.

⁕ Act IV ⁕

Scene 1. *Friar Laurence's cell.*

Enter FRIAR LAURENCE *and* COUNT PARIS.

Friar.
> On Thursday, sir? The time is very short.

Paris.
> My father Capulet will have it so,
> And I am nothing slow to slack his haste.

Friar.
> You say you do not know the lady's mind.

5   Uneven° is the course; I like it not.

Paris.
> Immoderately she weeps for Tybalt's death,
> And therefore have I little talked of love;
> For Venus smiles not in a house of tears.
> Now, sir, her father counts it dangerous

10   That she do give her sorrow so much sway,
> And in his wisdom hastes our marriage
> To stop the inundation of her tears,
> Which, too much minded° by herself alone,
> May be put from her by society.

15   Now do you know the reason of this haste.

Friar (*aside*).
> I would I knew not why it should be slowed,—
> Look, sir, here comes the lady toward my cell.

[*Enter* JULIET.]

Paris.
> Happily met, my lady and my wife!

Juliet.
> That may be, sir, when I may be a wife.

Paris.
20   That "may be" must be, love, on Thursday next.

Juliet.
> What must be shall be.

Friar.   That's a certain text.

Paris.
> Come you to make confession to this father?

5. Uneven: irregular or unusual.

13. minded: thought about.

? **15.** *According to Paris, why is Capulet pushing his daughter to marry so quickly?*

Juliet.

    To answer that, I should confess to you.

Paris.

    Do not deny to him that you love me.

Juliet.

25   I will confess to you that I love him.

Paris.

    So will ye, I am sure, that you love me.

Juliet.

    If I do so, it will be of more price,

    Being spoke behind your back, than to your face.

Paris.

    Poor soul, thy face is much abused with tears.

Juliet.

30   The tears have got small victory by that,

    For it was bad enough before their spite.°

Paris.

    Thou wrong'st it more than tears with that report.

Juliet.

    That is no slander, sir, which is a truth;

    And what I spake, I spake it to my face.

Paris.

35   Thy face is mine, and thou hast slandered it.

Juliet.

    It may be so, for it is not mine own.

    Are you at leisure, holy father, now,

    Or shall I come to you at evening mass?

Friar.

    My leisure serves me, pensive daughter, now.

40   My lord, we must entreat the time alone.

Paris.

    God shield° I should disturb devotion!

    Juliet, on Thursday early will I rouse ye.

    Till then, adieu, and keep this holy kiss.   [*Exit.*]

Juliet.

    O, shut the door, and when thou hast done so,

45   Come weep with me—past hope, past care, past help!

Friar.

    O Juliet, I already know thy grief;

    It strains me past the compass of my wits.

    I hear thou must, and nothing may prorogue° it,

    On Thursday next be married to this county.

? 26. *In this scene, Juliet's action is to keep up appearances and ward off Paris, who presses his attentions on her. She does this by wittily playing with words. We are fascinated by two things here: what is being done and how it is being done. What double meanings does Juliet intend in the **dialogue** with Paris that follows?*

31. spite: injury or damage (to her face).

? Staging the Play

38. *Juliet must show here that the tension of keeping up this pretense is unbearable. Where do you think she pauses and changes her tone?*

41. God shield: God forbid.

? 45. *Paris has gone, and Juliet has endured his "holy kiss." What does she now ask Friar Laurence to do?*

48. prorogue (prō·rōg'): postpone.

Juliet.

50   Tell me not, friar, that thou hearest of this,
      Unless thou tell me how I may prevent it.
      If in thy wisdom thou canst give no help,
      Do thou but call my resolution wise
      And with this knife I'll help it presently.
55   God joined my heart and Romeo's, thou our hands;
      And ere this hand, by thee to Romeo's sealed,
      Shall be the label° to another deed,°
      Or my true heart with treacherous revolt
      Turn to another, this shall slay them both.
60   Therefore, out of thy long-experienced time,
      Give me some present counsel; or, behold,
      'Twixt my extremes and me this bloody knife
      Shall play the umpire, arbitrating that
      Which the commission° of thy years and art
65   Could to no issue of true honor bring.
      Be not so long to speak. I long to die
      If what thou speak'st speak not of remedy.

Friar.

      Hold, daughter. I do spy a kind of hope,
      Which craves as desperate an execution
70   As that is desperate which we would prevent.
      If, rather than to marry County Paris,
      Thou hast the strength of will to slay thyself,
      Then is it likely thou wilt undertake
      A thing like death to chide away this shame,
75   That cop'st° with death himself to scape from it;
      And, if thou darest, I'll give thee remedy.

Juliet.

      O, bid me leap, rather than marry Paris,
      From off the battlements of any tower,
      Or walk in thievish ways, or bid me lurk
80   Where serpents are; chain me with roaring bears,
      Or hide me nightly in a charnel house,°
      O'ercovered quite with dead men's rattling bones,
      With reeky° shanks and yellow chapless° skulls;
      Or bid me go into a new-made grave
85   And hide me with a dead man in his shroud—
      Things that, to hear them told, have made me tremble—
      And I will do it without fear or doubt,
      To live an unstained wife to my sweet love.

54. *What is Juliet holding in her hand? What is she threatening to do?*

57. label: seal. **deed:** contract (of marriage).

Staging the Play
62. *The friar has to put up with a good deal of brandishing of knives and daggers from Romeo and Juliet. Now that the nurse is no longer Juliet's ally, the friar has to be the confidant of both Juliet and Romeo. He must listen with patience to their threats of suicide if they cannot be together. What line in Juliet's speech indicates that she has paused and that the friar for a time is silent?*

64. commission: authority.

75. cop'st: negotiates.

Staging the Play
77. *What would Juliet's mood be as she delivers this speech? What is she willing to do rather than marry Paris?*

81. charnel house: house where bones from old graves are kept.

83. reeky: damp, stinking. **chapless:** jawless.

Friar.

Hold, then. Go home, be merry, give consent

90 To marry Paris. Wednesday is tomorrow.

Tomorrow night look that thou lie alone;

Let not the nurse lie with thee in thy chamber.

Take thou this vial, being then in bed,

And this distilling° liquor drink thou off;

95 When presently through all thy veins shall run

A cold and drowsy humor;° for no pulse

Shall keep his native° progress, but surcease;°

No warmth, no breath, shall testify thou livest;

The roses in thy lips and cheeks shall fade

100 To wanny° ashes, thy eyes' windows fall

Like death when he shuts up the day of life;

Each part, deprived of supple government,°

Shall, stiff and stark and cold, appear like death;

And in this borrowed likeness of shrunk death

105 Thou shalt continue two-and-forty hours,

And then awake as from a pleasant sleep.

Now, when the bridegroom in the morning comes

To rouse thee from thy bed, there art thou dead.

? **89.** *Juliet must pay strict attention to the friar's plan, as must the audience. On what day does the friar tell Juliet to take the potion?*

94. distilling: penetrating.

96. humor: fluid.

97. native: natural. **surcease:** stop.

100. wanny: pale.

102. government: control.

? **106.** *This may be the most implausible part of the play, but we have been prepared for it. Where have we seen the friar taking care of his herbs and heard him talk of magical potions before? What will happen to Juliet when she takes the drug?*

"Take thou this vial ..."

✦

993

Then, as the manner of our country is,
110   In thy best robes uncovered on the bier
Thou shalt be borne to that same ancient vault
Where all the kindred of the Capulets lie.
In the meantime, against° thou shalt awake,
Shall Romeo by my letters know our drift;°
115   And hither shall he come; and he and I
Will watch thy waking, and that very night
Shall Romeo bear thee hence to Mantua.
And this shall free thee from this present shame,
If no inconstant toy° nor womanish fear
120   Abate thy valor in the acting it.
Juliet.
Give me, give me! O, tell not me of fear!
Friar.
Hold! Get you gone, be strong and prosperous
In this resolve. I'll send a friar with speed
To Mantua, with my letters to thy lord.
Juliet.
125   Love give me strength, and strength shall help afford.
Farewell, dear father.   [*Exit with* FRIAR.]

113. **against:** before.
114. **drift:** intentions.

? **117.** *How is Romeo to be told of this plan? When is he to watch Juliet wake and take her to Mantua?*

119. toy: whim.

? **122.** *What does the friar give Juliet as she exits? What exactly is his plan?*

? **Staging the Play**
126. *In some productions the friar holds Juliet back for just a moment and silently blesses her. Why would this make us more anxious about the outcome of his plan?*

Scene 2. *A hall in Capulet's house.*

Enter father CAPULET, LADY CAPULET, NURSE, *and*
    SERVINGMEN, *two or three.*

Capulet.
So many guests invite as here are writ.
                    [*Exit a* SERVINGMAN.]
Sirrah, go hire me twenty cunning° cooks.
Servingman. You shall have none ill, sir; for I'll try if they
can lick their fingers.
Capulet.
5   How canst thou try them so?
Servingman. Marry, sir, 'tis an ill cook that cannot lick his
own fingers. Therefore he that cannot lick his fingers
goes not with me.
Capulet. Go, be gone.   [*Exit* SERVINGMAN.]
10   We shall be much unfurnished° for this time.
What, is my daughter gone to Friar Laurence?
Nurse. Ay, forsooth.

? **Staging the Play**
1. *Capulet is sending his servant off to invite guests to Juliet's wedding. How does this comic and busy domestic scene contrast with the previous one?*

2. cunning: skillful.

10. unfurnished: unsupplied (without food).

Capulet.

    Well, he may chance to do some good on her.
    A peevish self-willed harlotry it is.

[*Enter* JULIET.]

Nurse.

15   See where she comes from shrift with merry look.

Capulet.

    How now, my headstrong? Where have you been
      gadding?

Juliet.

    Where I have learnt me to repent the sin
    Of disobedient opposition
    To you and your behests, and am enjoined
20   By holy Laurence to fall prostrate here
    To beg your pardon. Pardon, I beseech you!
    Henceforward I am ever ruled by you.

Capulet.

    Send for the county. Go tell him of this.
    I'll have this knot knit up tomorrow morning.

Juliet.

25   I met the youthful lord at Laurence' cell
    And gave him what becomèd° love I might,
    Not stepping o'er the bounds of modesty.

Capulet.

    Why, I am glad on't. This is well. Stand up.
    This is as't should be. Let me see the county.
30   Ay, marry, go, I say, and fetch him hither.
    Now, afore God, this reverend holy friar,
    All our whole city is much bound to him.

Juliet.

    Nurse, will you go with me into my closet,°
    To help me sort such needful ornaments
35   As you think fit to furnish me tomorrow?

Lady Capulet.

    No, not till Thursday. There is time enough.

Capulet.

    Go, nurse, go with her. We'll to church tomorrow.

                   [*Exeunt* JULIET *and* NURSE.]

Lady Capulet.

    We shall be short in our provision.
    'Tis now near night.

Capulet.   Tush, I will stir about,
40   And all things shall be well, I warrant thee, wife.

---

14. Harlotry *means a "good-for-nothing," a prostitute. Whom is Capulet referring to as "it"?*

15. *Do you think Juliet really has a "merry look," or is the nurse trying to cover up?*

24. *Why do you think Capulet pushes the marriage up to Wednesday?*

26. becomèd: proper or becoming.

28. *According to this speech, what has Juliet been doing since she first addressed her father?*

33. closet: private room.

37. *The wedding has been changed to take place on Wednesday. Lady Capulet tries to change her husband's mind, perhaps in consideration of Juliet, but she is not successful. How will this affect the timing of the friar's plans?*

"I have a faint cold fear thrills through my veins"
✧

Go thou to Juliet, help to deck up her.
I'll not to bed tonight; let me alone.
I'll play the housewife for this once. What, ho!
They are all forth; well, I will walk myself
45　To County Paris, to prepare up him
Against tomorrow. My heart is wondrous light,
Since this same wayward girl is so reclaimed.

　　　　　　　　　　　　　[*Exit with* LADY CAPULET.]

Scene 3. *Juliet's chamber.*

Enter JULIET *and* NURSE.

Juliet.
　　Ay, those attires are best; but, gentle nurse,
　　I pray thee leave me to myself tonight;
　　For I have need of many orisons°
　　To move the heavens to smile upon my state,
5　Which, well thou knowest, is cross and full of sin.

[*Enter* LADY CAPULET.]

Lady Capulet.
　　What, are you busy, ho? Need you my help?

Juliet.
　　No, madam; we have culled such necessaries
　　As are behoveful° for our state° tomorrow.
　　So please you, let me now be left alone,
10　And let the nurse this night sit up with you;
　　For I am sure you have your hands full all
　　In this so sudden business.

Lady Capulet.　　　　　　　Good night.
　　Get thee to bed, and rest; for thou hast need.

　　　　　　　[*Exeunt* LADY CAPULET *and* NURSE.]

Juliet.
　　Farewell! God knows when we shall meet again.
15　I have a faint cold fear thrills through my veins
　　That almost freezes up the heat of life.
　　I'll call them back again to comfort me.
　　Nurse!—What should she do here?
　　My dismal scene I needs must act alone.
20　Come, vial.
　　What if this mixture do not work at all?
　　Shall I be married then tomorrow morning?
　　No, no! This shall forbid it. Lie thou there.

[*Lays down a dagger.*]

47. *Lord Capulet realizes all the servants are gone. What action is he involved in during this speech? What is his new mood?*

3. **orisons** (ôr′i · zənz): prayers.

Staging the Play
6. *In some productions, Lady Capulet is played here as loving and gentle with Juliet, perhaps suggesting that she is uneasy about her daughter's change of heart. What emotions should her next speech show?*

8. **behoveful:** suitable. **state:** ceremonies.

Staging the Play
14. *Here is a fine example of the Shakespearean* **soliloquy,** *where a character who is poised on the edge of action thinks over its pros and cons. What are the fears and doubts that Juliet must consider before taking the potion?*
Juliet is not standing still as she speaks these lines. What do you think she is doing?

What if it be a poison which the friar
25   Subtly hath ministered to have me dead,
      Lest in this marriage he should be dishonored
      Because he married me before to Romeo?
      I fear it is; and yet methinks it should not,
      For he hath still been tried° a holy man.
30   How if, when I am laid into the tomb,
      I wake before the time that Romeo
      Come to redeem me? There's a fearful point!
      Shall I not then be stifled in the vault,
      To whose foul mouth no healthsome air breathes in,
35   And there die strangled ere my Romeo comes?
      Or, if I live, is it not very like
      The horrible conceit of death and night,
      Together with the terror of the place—
      As in a vault, an ancient receptacle
40   Where for this many hundred years the bones

"Romeo, Romeo, Romeo, I drink to thee."

      Of all my buried ancestors are packed;
      Where bloody Tybalt, yet but green in earth,°
      Lies fest'ring in his shroud; where, as they say,
      At some hours in the night spirits resort—
45   Alack, alack, is it not like that I,
      So early waking—what with loathsome smells,
      And shrieks like mandrakes° torn out of the earth,
      That living mortals, hearing them, run mad—
      I, if I wake, shall I not be distraught,
50   Environèd with all these hideous fears,
      And madly play with my forefathers' joints,
      And pluck the mangled Tybalt from his shroud,
      And, in this rage, with some great kinsman's bone
      As with a club dash out my desp'rate brains?
55   O, look! Methinks I see my cousin's ghost
      Seeking out Romeo, that did spit his body
      Upon a rapier's point. Stay, Tybalt, stay!
      Romeo, Romeo, Romeo, I drink to thee.

      [*She falls upon her bed within the curtains.*]

29. still been tried: always been proved.

29. *Audiences always wonder why the friar has not simply told the families of Romeo and Juliet's secret wedding rather than involve them in such a dangerous plan. How does Juliet explain the friar's actions?*

42. green in earth: newly buried.

47. mandrakes: plants resembling the human body, which were said to grow beneath the gallows and to scream when torn up.

54. *Draw the mental picture you have of the tomb from Juliet's description of it.*

Scene 4. A hall in Capulet's house.

Enter LADY CAPULET *and* NURSE.

Lady Capulet.
   Hold, take these keys and fetch more spices, nurse.
Nurse.
   They call for dates and quinces in the pastry.

[*Enter old* CAPULET.]

Capulet.
   Come, stir, stir, stir! The second cock hath crowed,
   The curfew bell hath rung, 'tis three o'clock.
5   Look to the baked meats, good Angelica;
   Spare not for cost.
Nurse.   Go, you cotquean,° go,
   Get you to bed! Faith, you'll be sick tomorrow
   For this night's watching.
Capulet.
   No, not a whit. What, I have watched ere now
10   All night for lesser cause, and ne'er been sick.
Lady Capulet.
   Ay, you have been a mouse hunt° in your time;
   But I will watch you from such watching now.
                    [*Exeunt* LADY CAPULET *and* NURSE.]
Capulet.
   A jealous hood,° a jealous hood!

[*Enter three or four* FELLOWS *with spits and logs and baskets.*]

                              Now, fellow,
   What is there?
First Fellow.
15   Things for the cook, sir; but I know not what.
Capulet.
   Make haste, make haste.   [*Exit* FIRST FELLOW.]
                    Sirrah, fetch drier logs.
   Call Peter; he will show thee where they are.
Second Fellow.
   I have a head, sir, that will find out logs°
   And never trouble Peter for the matter.
Capulet.
20   Mass,° and well said; a merry whoreson, ha!

? **1.** *How does this peaceful domestic scene contrast with what has just happened? What is everyone preparing for?*

? **5.** *Angelica is the nurse's name. How does Lord Capulet treat her now, as opposed to how he treated her in Act III, Scene 5? What humor does the nurse add to this scene?*

   6. cotquean (kät′kwēn′): old woman (a man who acts like an old woman).

11. mouse hunt: woman chaser or night prowler.
? **12.** *What is Lady Capulet's tone here?*

13. hood: female.

18. I . . . logs: in other words, "I have a wooden head."

20. Mass: mild oath, "by the Mass."

Thou shalt be loggerhead.°

[*Exit* SECOND FELLOW, *with the others.*]
Good faith, 'tis day.
The county will be here with music straight,
For so he said he would. (*Play music offstage.*)
I hear him near.
Nurse! Wife! What, ho! What, nurse, I say!

[*Enter* NURSE.]

25   Go waken Juliet; go and trim her up.
I'll go and chat with Paris. Hie, make haste,
Make haste! The bridegroom he is come already:
Make haste, I say.   [*Exit.*]

Scene 5. *Juliet's chamber.*

Nurse.
Mistress! What, mistress! Juliet! Fast,° I warrant her, she.
Why, lamb! Why, lady! Fie, you slugabed.
Why, love, I say! Madam; sweetheart! Why, bride!
What, not a word? You take your pennyworths° now;
5   Sleep for a week; for the next night, I warrant,
The County Paris hath set up his rest°
That you shall rest but little. God forgive me!
Marry, and amen. How sound is she asleep!
I needs must wake her. Madam, madam, madam!
10   Ay, let the county take you in your bed;
He'll fright you up, i' faith. Will it not be?

[*Draws aside the curtains.*]

What, dressed, and in your clothes, and down again?
I must needs wake you. Lady! Lady! Lady!
Alas, alas! Help, help! My lady's dead!
15   O weraday that ever I was born!
Some aqua vitae, ho! My lord! My lady!

[*Enter* LADY CAPULET.]

Lady Capulet.
What noise is here?
Nurse.   O lamentable day!
Lady Capulet.
What is the matter?

---

21. **loggerhead:** blockhead.

? **Staging the Play**
21. *Capulet fusses around and has his nose in everything. What actions do you imagine the old man is involved in, in this scene?*

? 23. *The music is bridal music, for the wedding. What* **irony** *would the audience sense on hearing this music and knowing what has happened to Juliet?*

1. **Fast:** fast asleep.

? **Staging the Play**
1. *As the nurse speaks to Juliet and to herself, she is busy arranging clothes, opening windows, and doing things around the room. In what line here does she touch Juliet and discover she is cold?*

4. **pennyworths:** small naps.
6. **set up his rest:** become firmly resolved.

Nurse.   Look, look! O heavy day!

Lady Capulet.

O me, O me! My child, my only life!
20   Revive, look up, or I will die with thee!
Help, help! Call help.

[*Enter* CAPULET.]

Capulet.

For shame, bring Juliet forth; her lord is come.
Nurse.

She's dead, deceased; she's dead, alack the day!
Lady Capulet.

Alack the day, she's dead, she's dead, she's dead!
Capulet.

25   Ha! Let me see her. Out alas! She's cold,
Her blood is settled, and her joints are stiff;
Life and these lips have long been separated.
Death lies on her like an untimely frost
Upon the sweetest flower of all the field.
Nurse.

O lamentable day!
30   **Lady Capulet.**   O woeful time!
Capulet.

Death, that hath ta'en her hence to make me wail,
Ties up my tongue and will not let me speak.

[*Enter* FRIAR LAURENCE *and* PARIS, *with* MUSICIANS.]

Friar.

Come, is the bride ready to go to church?
Capulet.

Ready to go, but never to return.
35   O son, the night before thy wedding day
Hath Death lain with thy wife. There she lies,
Flower as she was, deflowerèd by him.
Death is my son-in-law, Death is my heir;
My daughter he hath wedded. I will die
40   And leave him all. Life, living, all is Death's.
Paris.

Have I thought, love, to see this morning's face,
And doth it give me such a sight as this?
Lady Capulet.

Accursed, unhappy, wretched, hateful day!
Most miserable hour that e'er time saw

? **Staging the Play**
29. *What actions are taking place onstage as the three actors now find Juliet "dead"?*

45   In lasting labor of his pilgrimage!
      But one, poor one, one poor and loving child,
      But one thing to rejoice and solace in,
      And cruel Death hath catched it from my sight.
Nurse.
      O woe! O woeful, woeful, woeful day!
50   Most lamentable day, most woeful day
      That ever ever I did yet behold!
      O day, O day, O day! O hateful day!
      Never was seen so black a day as this.
      O woeful day! O woeful day!
Paris.
55   Beguiled, divorcèd, wrongèd, spited, slain!
      Most detestable Death, by thee beguiled,
      By cruel, cruel thee quite overthrown.
      O love! O life!—not life, but love in death!
Capulet.
      Despised, distressèd, hated, martyred, killed!
60   Uncomfortable time, why cam'st thou now
      To murder, murder our solemnity?
      O child, O child! My soul, and not my child!
      Dead art thou—alack, my child is dead,
      And with my child my joys are burièd!
Friar.
65   Peace, ho, for shame! Confusion's cure lives not
      In these confusions. Heaven and yourself
      Had part in this fair maid—now heaven hath all,
      And all the better is it for the maid.
      Your part in her you could not keep from death,
70   But heaven keeps his part in eternal life.
      The most you sought was her promotion,
      For 'twas your heaven she should be advanced;
      And weep ye now, seeing she is advanced
      Above the clouds, as high as heaven itself?
75   O, in this love, you love your child so ill
      That you run mad, seeing that she is well.°
      She's not well married that lives married long,
      But she's best married that dies married young.
      Dry up your tears and stick your rosemary°
80   On this fair corse, and, as the custom is,
      And in her best array bear her to church;
      For though fond nature° bids us all lament,

48. *Here again, as with Juliet's bemoaning Romeo's supposed death in an earlier scene, we have Lord and Lady Capulet and the nurse expressing anguish when we, the audience, know that Juliet is not dead. We listen to them, but we are not moved in the way they are. What words of the Capulets here suggest a loving concern for Juliet that seemed to be missing from earlier scenes? Which character enters and plays dumb about the whole situation?*

58. *In your opinion, what might the nurse, Paris, and the Capulets think caused Juliet's death?*

64. *These expressions of grief are by now sounding mechanical and repetitive. Shakespeare might have written them this way to prevent grief at a false death from gaining our sympathy. How could these lines of the parents, of the nurse, and of Paris also suggest that the speakers' feelings might not be very deep?*

65. *The friar, of course, knows that Juliet is drugged, not dead. His words here suggest that there has been great confusion onstage. What consolation does he offer, and what sharp rebuke does he give the adults?*

76. well: that is, she is in heaven.

79. rosemary: herb that stands for remembrance.

82. fond nature: foolish human nature.

"Alack, my child is dead, And with my child my joys are burièd!"
✦

Yet nature's tears are reason's merriment.

Capulet.

All things that we ordainèd festival

85   Turn from their office to black funeral—

Our instruments to melancholy bells,

Our wedding cheer to a sad burial feast;

Our solemn hymns to sullen dirges change;

Our bridal flowers serve for a buried corse;

90   And all things change them to the contrary.

Friar.

Sir, go you in; and, madam, go with him;

And go, Sir Paris. Everyone prepare

To follow this fair corse unto her grave.

The heavens do lower° upon you for some ill;

95   Move them no more by crossing their high will.

[*Exeunt, casting rosemary on her and shutting the curtains. The* NURSE *and* MUSICIANS *remain.*]

First Musician.

Faith, we may put up our pipes and be gone.

Nurse.

Honest good fellows, ah, put up, put up!

For well you know this is a pitiful case.   [*Exit.*]

First Musician.

Ay, by my troth, the case may be amended.

[*Enter* PETER.]

100   **Peter.** Musicians, O, musicians, "Heart's ease," "Heart's ease"!

O, and you will have me live, play "Heart's ease."

First Musician. Why "Heart's ease"?

Peter. O, musicians, because my heart itself plays "My heart is full." O, play me some merry dump° to comfort me.

105   **First Musician.** Not a dump we! 'Tis no time to play now.

Peter. You will not then?

First Musician. No.

Peter. I will then give it you soundly.

First Musician. What will you give us?

110   **Peter.** No money, on my faith, but the gleek.° I will give you° the minstrel.

First Musician. Then will I give you the serving-creature.

Peter. Then will I lay the serving-creature's dagger on your pate. I will carry° no crotchets. I'll re you, I'll fa you. Do

115   you note me?

---

83. *Why does the friar say that reason tells us to be merry about death?*

90. *Does Capulet express any guilt? Is he still self-centered?*

94. **lower:** frown.

98. *These are the nurse's last lines in the play. True to her character, she jokes as she leaves, though she might do this to cover her grief. The musicians are talking about the cases for their instruments. What "case" is the nurse referring to?*

104. **dump:** sad tune.

110. **gleek:** jeer or insult.

111. **give you:** call you (to be called a minstrel was an insult to a musician).

114. **carry:** endure.

First Musician. And you re us and fa us, you note us.

Second Musician. Pray you put up your dagger, and put out your wit. Then have at you with my wit!

Peter. I will dry-beat° you with an iron wit, and put up my
120   iron dagger. Answer me like men.
        "When griping grief the heart doth wound,
        And doleful dumps the mind oppress,
        Then music with her silver sound"—
     Why "silver sound"? Why "music with her silver sound"?
125   What say you, Simon Catling?°

First Musician. Marry, sir, because silver hath a sweet sound.

Peter. Pretty! What say you, Hugh Rebeck?°

Second Musician. I say "silver sound" because musicians
     sound for silver.

130 **Peter.** Pretty too! What say you, James Soundpost?°

Third Musician. Faith, I know not what to say.

Peter. O, I cry you mercy,° you are the singer. I will say
     for you. It is "music with her silver sound" because
     musicians have no gold for sounding.°
135   "Then music with her silver sound
        With speedy help doth lend redress."   [*Exit.*]

First Musician. What a pestilent knave is this same!

Second Musician. Hang him, Jack! Come, we'll in here,
     tarry for the mourners, and stay dinner.
                               [*Exit with others.*]

119. dry-beat: beat soundly.

125. Catling: lute string.

127. Rebeck: fiddle.

130. Soundpost: peg on violinlike instrument.

132. cry you mercy: beg your pardon.

134. no gold for sounding: no money to jingle in their pockets.

Staging the Play
139. *Peter, who was always bossed about by the nurse, here has grabbed at the chance to boss the musicians, who are a step below him socially. What actions do you imagine during this exchange of insults? (Note that they all want to stay for dinner.) How does this scene provide relief for us and remind us that ordinary life goes on amid tragedy?*

A CLOSER LOOK

Shakespeare in the Video Store

Film and television have brought Shakespeare's plays to millions of viewers and confirmed the playwright's position as a world treasure. *Hamlet* has been by far the most popular of his plays, with more than sixty film versions of all or part of the tragedy (as of 2002). The earliest *Hamlet* movie was made in Paris in 1900. This black-and-white silent film had an interesting reversal of the custom of Shakespeare's time, in which boys took women's roles onstage: The role of Hamlet was played by the great Sarah Bernhardt (1844–1923).

For almost a century, film productions of Shakespeare have showcased some of our most distinguished actors: Laurence Olivier, Vanessa Redgrave, Richard Burton, John Gielgud, Katharine Hepburn, Mel Gibson, Glenn Close, Denzel Washington. Between 1978 and 1985, all of Shakespeare's plays were filmed for television. Now Shakespeare is accessible as never before: A performance of one of his plays is as close as your local library or video store.

Critics have pointed out drawbacks in the performance of these plays on screen. For example, they argue that film controls our perceptions of the plays and deprives us of the tension we feel when seeing the plays live, in a theater. Film and television productions of Shakespearean comedy are at another disadvantage, since the actors can't respond to the feedback of a live audience. Such feedback is unpredictable, but actors say it's critical in comedy.

Katharine Hepburn portrays William Shakespeare's Juliet in a 1933 film.

Laurence Olivier plays the Danish prince in a 1948 film version of Shakespeare's *Hamlet.*

Act IV

Reading Check

1. In Scene 1, what does Juliet threaten to do if the friar cannot help her?

2. What is the friar's plan for getting Romeo and Juliet together?

3. In Scene 2, another **complication** comes up. What change does Capulet make in the wedding plans?

4. What is the situation in the Capulet house at the end of Act IV?

Thinking Critically

5. Why is Juliet so willing to trust the friar? Do you think she is wise to follow his advice?

6. One of the pleasures of watching a play is knowing something that a character onstage does not know. Oddly enough, this experience of **dramatic irony** adds **suspense.** We wait anxiously to find out what will happen when the characters discover what we already know. Where do you sense dramatic irony in Scenes 2, 3, and 4?

7. What terrible trials does Juliet face in this act of the **tragedy**? How does she respond to these challenges?

Extending and Evaluating

8. Juliet's parents have plans for their daughter that make it seem impossible for the young couple to stay together. Does Shakespeare present the Capulets as villains? Does he help us see them as complex human beings? Explain your evaluation of these **characters,** using details from the play.

WRITING

Juliet's Thoughts

Write down Juliet's thoughts as you imagine them during this difficult time. (You could write as "I.") Write about her feelings toward her parents, Romeo, her nurse, Paris, and Friar Laurence. Let Juliet describe her feelings about the drug she is about to take and about her horror at being buried alive.

SKILLS FOCUS

Literary Skills
Analyze characteristics of tragedy, including complication, turning point, and suspense.

Writing Skills
Write the thoughts of a character.

INTERNET

Projects and Activities

Keyword: LE7 9-11

Paraphrasing and Context Clues

Paraphrasing means restating a text in your own words. A restatement, or paraphrase, simplifies a text, but it doesn't necessarily make it shorter. In fact, a paraphrase might be longer than the original passage, and of course it's never as interesting. Paraphrasing is a good way to check on your understanding of the original text. Here is a speech from Act IV of *Romeo and Juliet* and a paraphrase of the speech:

> **Paris.**
> My father Capulet will have it so,
> And I am nothing slow to slack his haste.
> —Scene I, lines 2–3

Paraphrase: My father-in-law Capulet wants it like that, and I have no desire to slow him down.

A Checklist for Paraphrasing

- Be sure you understand the main idea of the text.
- Look up unfamiliar words in a good dictionary.
- Replace difficult words with simple ones.
- If a word has multiple meanings, be sure to use **context clues** to determine the meaning appropriate to the passage. (Remember: The meaning intended by Shakespeare may now be archaic.)
- Restate figures of speech in your own words, clarifying what's being compared to what.
- Try to reproduce the tone or mood of the text. If the text is satiric, your paraphrase should also be satiric.
- Be sure your paraphrase has accounted for all details in the original.

PRACTICE

The following speeches are from Act IV. Paraphrase each one. Be sure to compare your paraphrases with those of your classmates. It's almost certain that no two paraphrases will be alike.

1. **Paris** (*speaking about Juliet*).
   Immoderately she weeps for Tybalt's death,
   And therefore have I little talked of love;
   For Venus smiles not in a house of tears.
   —Scene I, lines 6–8

2. **Juliet** (*to the Friar*).
   Be not so long to speak. I long to die
   If what thou speak'st speak not of remedy.
   —Scene I, lines 66–67

3. **Friar Laurence** (*to Juliet*).
   The roses in thy lips and cheeks shall fade
   To wanny ashes, thy eyes' windows fall
   Like death when he shuts up the day of life . . . .
   —Scene I, lines 99–101

4. **Juliet** (*holding the poison*).
   O, look! Methinks I see my cousin's ghost
   Seeking out Romeo, that did spit his body
   Upon a rapier's point. Stay, Tybalt, stay!
   —Scene 3, lines 55–57

SKILLS FOCUS

Reading Skills
Paraphrase speeches.

✦ ACT V ✦

Scene 1. *Mantua. A street.*

Enter ROMEO.

Romeo.
　　If I may trust the flattering truth of sleep,
　　My dreams presage° some joyful news at hand.
　　My bosom's lord° sits lightly in his throne,
　　And all this day an unaccustomed spirit
5　　Lifts me above the ground with cheerful thoughts.
　　I dreamt my lady came and found me dead
　　(Strange dream that gives a dead man leave to think!)
　　And breathed such life with kisses in my lips
　　That I revived and was an emperor.
10　　Ah me! How sweet is love itself possessed,
　　When but love's shadows° are so rich in joy!

[Enter Romeo's man BALTHASAR, *booted from riding.*]

　　News from Verona! How now, Balthasar?
　　Dost thou not bring me letters from the friar?
　　How doth my lady? Is my father well?
15　　How fares my Juliet? That I ask again,
　　For nothing can be ill if she be well.
Balthasar.
　　Then she is well, and nothing can be ill.
　　Her body sleeps in Capel's monument,
　　And her immortal part with angels lives.
20　　I saw her laid low in her kindred's vault
　　And presently took post° to tell it you.
　　O, pardon me for bringing these ill news,
　　Since you did leave it for my office,° sir.
Romeo.
　　Is it e'en so? Then I defy you, stars!
25　　Thou knowest my lodging. Get me ink and paper
　　And hire post horses. I will hence tonight.
Balthasar.
　　I do beseech you, sir, have patience.
　　Your looks are pale and wild and do import
　　Some misadventure.

2. **presage:** foretell.
3. **bosom's lord:** heart.

11. **shadows:** dreams.

> **❓ Staging the Play**
> **16.** *Some actors playing Romeo reveal in this line that they suspect bad news. What, meanwhile, would Balthasar be doing?*

21. **post:** post horse (horse kept at an inn and rented by travelers).
23. **office:** duty.

> **❓ Staging the Play**
> **23.** *Balthasar must show that he dreads giving his master the tragic news. What do we know that Balthasar does not know?*

> **❓ Staging the Play**
> **26.** *In some productions, actors move away here or hide their faces in their hands. Romeo could address the stars or fate defiantly or tonelessly, to suggest defeat. What would you say is Romeo's tone here?*

> **❓ 28.** *What does Balthasar suggest Romeo looks like, even though Romeo pretends to be calm?*

Romeo.   Tush, thou art deceived.

30   Leave me and do the thing I bid thee do.

Hast thou no letters to me from the friar?

Balthasar.

No, my good lord.

Romeo.   No matter. Get thee gone.

And hire those horses. I'll be with thee straight.

                                        [*Exit* BALTHASAR.]

Well, Juliet, I will lie with thee tonight.

35   Let's see for means. O mischief, thou art swift

To enter in the thoughts of desperate men!

I do remember an apothecary,

And hereabouts 'a dwells, which late I noted

In tattered weeds,° with overwhelming° brows,

40   Culling of simples.° Meager were his looks,

Sharp misery had worn him to the bones;

And in his needy shop a tortoise hung,

An alligator stuffed, and other skins

Of ill-shaped fishes; and about his shelves

45   A beggarly account° of empty boxes,

Green earthen pots, bladders, and musty seeds,

Remnants of packthread, and old cakes of roses

Were thinly scatterèd, to make up a show.

Noting this penury,° to myself I said,

50   "And if a man did need a poison now

Whose sale is present death in Mantua,

Here lives a caitiff° wretch would sell it him."

O, this same thought did but forerun my need,

And this same needy man must sell it me.

55   As I remember, this should be the house.

Being holiday, the beggar's shop is shut.

What, ho! Apothecary!

? **31.** *What letter is Romeo waiting for?*

? **Staging the Play**
34. *This line is spoken in a still, quiet moment. After a pause, what does Romeo immediately set out to do? Does he hesitate at all to consider his course of action, or does he plunge into it?*

39. weeds: clothes. **overwhelming:** overhanging.
40. simples: herbs.

45. account: number.

49. penury (pen′yoo · rē): poverty.

52. caitiff (kāt′if): miserable.

? **Staging the Play**
57. *What actions do you imagine Romeo is engaged in as he speaks these lines about the apothecary?*

> **"O mischief, thou art swift**
> **To enter in the thoughts**
> **of desperate men!"**

[*Enter* APOTHECARY.]

Apothecary.   Who calls so loud?

Romeo.

Come hither, man. I see that thou art poor.

Hold, there is forty ducats. Let me have
60   A dram of poison, such soon-speeding gear°
As will disperse itself through all the veins
That the life-weary taker may fall dead,
And that the trunk° may be discharged of breath
As violently as hasty powder fired
65   Doth hurry from the fatal cannon's womb.

Apothecary.
Such mortal drugs I have; but Mantua's law
Is death to any he that utters° them.

Romeo.
Art thou so bare and full of wretchedness
And fear'st to die? Famine is in thy cheeks,
70   Need and oppression starveth in thy eyes,
Contempt and beggary hangs upon thy back:
The world is not thy friend, nor the world's law;
The world affords no law to make thee rich;
Then be not poor, but break it and take this.

Apothecary.
75   My poverty but not my will consents.

Romeo.
I pay thy poverty and not thy will.

Apothecary.
Put this in any liquid thing you will
And drink it off, and if you had the strength
Of twenty men, it would dispatch you straight.

Romeo.
80   There is thy gold—worse poison to men's souls,
Doing more murder in this loathsome world,
Than these poor compounds that thou mayst not sell.
I sell thee poison; thou has sold me none.
Farewell. Buy food and get thyself in flesh.
85   Come, cordial and not poison, go with me
To Juliet's grave; for there must I use thee.   [*Exeunt.*]

Scene 2. *Friar Laurence's cell.*

Enter FRIAR JOHN.

John.
Holy Franciscan friar, brother, ho!

[*Enter* FRIAR LAURENCE.]

---

60. gear: stuff.

63. trunk: body.

67. utters: sells.

74. *What argument does Romeo use to persuade the apothecary to break the law?*

Staging the Play
79. *What actions do you think have taken place before the apothecary gives Romeo instructions for taking the poison?*

83. *What "poison" has Romeo "sold" the apothecary?*

85. *Why does Romeo call the poison a* cordial, *which is a kind of medicine that restores the heartbeat?*

Laurence.

This same should be the voice of Friar John.
Welcome from Mantua. What says Romeo?
Or, if his mind be writ, give me his letter.

John.

5   Going to find a barefoot brother out,
One of our order, to associate° me
Here in this city visiting the sick,
And finding him, the searchers° of the town,
Suspecting that we both were in a house
10   Where the infectious pestilence did reign,
Sealed up the doors, and would not let us forth,
So that my speed to Mantua there was stayed.

Laurence.

Who bare my letter, then, to Romeo?

John.

I could not send it—here it is again—
15   Nor get a messenger to bring it thee,
So fearful were they of infection.

Laurence.

Unhappy fortune! By my brotherhood,
The letter was not nice,° but full of charge,°
Of dear import; and the neglecting it
20   May do much danger. Friar John, go hence,
Get me an iron crow and bring it straight
Unto my cell.

John.   Brother, I'll go and bring it thee.   [*Exit.*]

Laurence.

Now must I to the monument alone.
Within this three hours will fair Juliet wake.
25   She will beshrew me much that Romeo
Hath had no notice of these accidents;°
But I will write again to Mantua,
And keep her at my cell till Romeo come—
Poor living corse, closed in a dead man's tomb!   [*Exit.*]

Scene 3. *A churchyard; in it, a monument belonging to the Capulets.*

Enter PARIS *and his* PAGE *with flowers and scented water.*

Paris.

Give me thy torch, boy. Hence, and stand aloof.
Yet put it out, for I would not be seen.

3. *In the previous scene we learned that Romeo had received no letters from the friar. How would the friar's question immediately put questions in the minds of the audience?*

6. associate: accompany.

8. searchers: health officers.

16. *Another accident! Why was the friar's letter never delivered to Romeo?*

18. nice: trivial. **charge:** importance.

26. accidents: happenings.

29. *If we can accept the "accidents" of fate, we have here something like a chase scene. We know, but the friar does not, that Romeo also is on his way to the tomb. Why is it essential that the friar get there first?*

Under yond yew trees lay thee all along,°
Holding the ear close to the hollow ground.
5   So shall no foot upon the churchyard tread
(Being loose, unfirm, with digging up of graves)
But thou shalt hear it. Whistle then to me,
As signal that thou hear'st something approach.
Give me those flowers. Do as I bid thee, go.

Page (*aside*).
10   I am almost afraid to stand alone
Here in the churchyard; yet I will adventure.°

[*Retires.*]

Paris.
Sweet flower, with flowers thy bridal bed I strew
(O woe! thy canopy is dust and stones)
Which with sweet water nightly I will dew;
15   Or, wanting that, with tears distilled by moans.
The obsequies° that I for thee will keep
Nightly shall be to strew thy grave and weep.

[BOY *whistles.*]

The boy gives warning something doth approach.
What cursèd foot wanders this way tonight
20   To cross° my obsequies and true love's rite?
What, with a torch? Muffle° me, night, awhile.

[*Retires.*]

[*Enter* ROMEO *and* BALTHASAR *with a torch, a mattock, and a*
crowbar of iron.]

Romeo.
Give me that mattock and the wrenching iron.
Hold, take this letter. Early in the morning
See thou deliver it to my lord and father.
25   Give me the light. Upon thy life I charge thee,
Whate'er thou hearest or see'st, stand all aloof
And do not interrupt me in my course.
Why I descend into this bed of death
Is partly to behold my lady's face,
30   But chiefly to take thence from her dead finger
A precious ring—a ring that I must use
In dear employment.° Therefore hence, be gone.
But if thou, jealous,° dost return to pry
In what I farther shall intend to do,
35   By heaven, I will tear thee joint by joint

? 9. *Paris is a surprise. He adds an interesting complication, as well as some action, to this scene. Why is Paris here?*

? Staging the Play
Stage direction: Paris and his page are alone onstage. Whom does the page speak his **aside** *to? Whom does he not want to hear it?*

11. adventure: risk it.

? Staging the Play
13. *In Shakespeare's theater we would see a tomb at the rear of the stage. Juliet's body, in its burial gown, would be placed in this tomb, on top of a raised structure. Tybalt's body would lie nearby. What atmosphere must be suggested in this scene? How would lighting be used on a modern stage to create such an atmosphere?*

16. obsequies (äb′si·kwēz′): observances or rituals.
20. cross: interrupt.
21. Muffle: hide.

? Staging the Play
22. *Paris enters with flowers and perfumed water, but Romeo enters with iron tools—a mattock, which is something like a hoe, and a crowbar. Like Paris, Romeo and his servant enter at the upper level. What strange excuse does Romeo give his servant for wanting to descend into the tomb alone?*

32. dear employment: important business.
33. jealous: curious.

And strew this hungry churchyard with thy limbs.
The time and my intents are savage-wild,
More fierce and more inexorable far
Than empty tigers or the roaring sea.

Balthasar.

40   I will be gone, sir, and not trouble ye.

Romeo.

So shalt thou show me friendship. Take thou that.
Live, and be prosperous; and farewell, good fellow.

Balthasar (*aside*).

For all this same, I'll hide me hereabout.
His looks I fear, and his intents I doubt.   [*Retires.*]

Romeo.

45   Thou detestable maw,° thou womb of death,
Gorged with the dearest morsel of the earth,
Thus I enforce thy rotten jaws to open,
And in despite° I'll cram thee with more food.

[ROMEO *opens the tomb.*]

Paris.

This is that banished haughty Montague
50   That murd'red my love's cousin—with which grief
It is supposed the fair creature died—
And here is come to do some villainous shame
To the dead bodies. I will apprehend him.
Stop thy unhallowèd toil, vile Montague!
55   Can vengeance be pursued further than death?
Condemnèd villain, I do apprehend thee.
Obey, and go with me; for thou must die.

Romeo.

I must indeed; and therefore came I hither.
Good gentle youth, tempt not a desp'rate man.
60   Fly hence and leave me. Think upon these gone;
Let them affright thee. I beseech thee, youth,
Put not another sin upon my head
By urging me to fury. O, be gone!
By heaven, I love thee better than myself,
65   For I come hither armed against myself.
Stay not, be gone. Live, and hereafter say
A madman's mercy bid thee run away.

Paris.

I do defy thy conjurations°
And apprehend thee for a felon here.

Romeo.

70   Wilt thou provoke me? Then have at thee, boy!

[*They fight.*]

Page.

O Lord, they fight! I will go call the watch.

[*Exit.* PARIS *falls.*]

Paris.

O, I am slain! If thou be merciful,
Open the tomb, lay me with Juliet.   [*Dies.*]

Romeo.

In faith, I will. Let me peruse this face.
75   Mercutio's kinsman, noble County Paris!
What said my man when my betossèd soul
Did not attend° him as we rode? I think
He told me Paris should have married Juliet.
Said he not so, or did I dream it so?
80   Or am I mad, hearing him talk of Juliet,
To think it was so? O, give me thy hand,
One writ with me in sour misfortune's book!
I'll bury thee in a triumphant grave.
A grave? O, no, a lanthorn,° slaught'red youth,
85   For here lies Juliet, and her beauty makes
This vault a feasting presence full of light.
Death, lie thou there, by a dead man interred.

[*Lays him in the tomb.*]

How oft when men are at the point of death
Have they been merry! Which their keepers° call
90   A lightning before death. O, how may I
Call this a lightning? O my love, my wife!
Death, that hath sucked the honey of thy breath,
Hath had no power yet upon thy beauty.
Thou art not conquered. Beauty's ensign° yet
95   Is crimson in thy lips and in thy cheeks,
And death's pale flag is not advancèd there.
Tybalt, liest thou there in the bloody sheet?
O, what more favor can I do to thee
Than with that hand that cut thy youth in twain
100   To sunder his that was thine enemy?
Forgive me, cousin! Ah, dear Juliet,
Why art thou yet so fair? Shall I believe
That unsubstantial Death is amorous,
And that the lean abhorrèd monster keeps

70. *What has Paris done to provoke Romeo?*

Staging the Play
74. *Whatever we thought of Paris before, we understand now that he loved Juliet. What does Romeo do here?*

77. attend: pay attention to.

82. *Remember that Romeo has spoken of himself as "fortune's fool." Why does he see Paris as another victim?*

84. lanthorn: lantern; here, a room with glass walls.

Staging the Play
85. *Romeo, dragging Paris's body across the stage, now sees Juliet. What words indicate that he sees the tomb transformed? Who is the "dead man" in line 87?*

89. keepers: jailers.

94. ensign (en′sīn′): flag (signal).

Staging the Play
97. *Romeo turns to see Tybalt's body. Is he angry at his enemy, or does he ask forgiveness?*

102. *Where in this speech does Romeo see life in Juliet, reminding us that she is not dead?*

105　Thee here in dark to be his paramour?
　　　For fear of that I still will stay with thee
　　　And never from this pallet of dim night
　　　Depart again. Here, here will I remain
　　　With worms that are thy chambermaids. O, here
110　Will I set up my everlasting rest
　　　And shake the yoke of inauspicious stars
　　　From this world-wearied flesh. Eyes, look your last!
　　　Arms, take your last embrace! And, lips, O you
　　　The doors of breath, seal with a righteous kiss
115　A dateless° bargain to engrossing° death!
　　　Come, bitter conduct;° come, unsavory guide!
　　　Thou desperate pilot,° now at once run on
　　　The dashing rocks thy seasick weary bark!
　　　Here's to my love! (*Drinks.*) O true apothecary!
120　Thy drugs are quick. Thus with a kiss I die.

[*Falls.*]

[*Enter* FRIAR LAURENCE, *with lanthorn, crowbar, and spade.*]

Friar.
　　　Saint Francis be my speed! How oft tonight
　　　Have my old feet stumbled at graves! Who's there?
Balthasar.
　　　Here's one, a friend, and one that knows you well.
Friar.
　　　Bliss be upon you! Tell me, good my friend,
125　What torch is yond that vainly lends his light
　　　To grubs and eyeless skulls? As I discern,
　　　It burneth in the Capels' monument.
Balthasar.
　　　It doth so, holy sir; and there's my master,
　　　One that you love.
Friar.　　　　　　　Who is it?
Balthasar.　　　　　　　　　Romeo.
Friar.
　　　How long hath he been there?
130　**Balthasar.**　　　　　　　　　　Full half an hour.
Friar.
　　　Go with me to the vault.
Balthasar.　　　　　　　　I dare not, sir.
　　　My master knows not but I am gone hence,
　　　And fearfully did menace me with death
　　　If I did stay to look on his intents.

? **Staging the Play**
108. *Romeo lies down beside Juliet. What other actions do you see him performing here?*

115. dateless: timeless.
engrossing: all-encompassing.
116. conduct: guide (the poison).
117. desperate pilot: Romeo himself.

? **Staging the Play**
120. *Actors playing Romeo interpret this last speech in different ways: Some play him as if he is in a dream; others as if he is mad; others as if he is in full control of himself; others as if he is desperate and out of his mind with grief, desire, and fear. What clues would direct the way you'd interpret Romeo's feelings as he gives his final soliloquy?*

? **Staging the Play**
130. *What feelings must the friar reveal when he hears that Romeo has gotten to the tomb before he has heard of the plan to drug Juliet?*

Friar.
135   Stay then; I'll go alone. Fear comes upon me.
       O, much I fear some ill unthrifty° thing.
Balthasar.
       As I did sleep under this yew tree here,
       I dreamt my master and another fought,
       And that my master slew him.
Friar.   Romeo!
140   Alack, alack, what blood is this which stains
       The stony entrance of this sepulcher?
       What mean these masterless and gory swords
       To lie discolored by this place of peace?

[*Enters the tomb.*]

       Romeo! O, pale! Who else? What, Paris too?
145   And steeped in blood? Ah, what an unkind° hour
       Is guilty of this lamentable chance!
       The lady stirs.

[JULIET *rises.*]

"O comfortable friar! Where is my lord?"

Juliet.
       O comfortable° friar! Where is my lord?
       I do remember well where I should be,
150   And there I am. Where is my Romeo?
Friar.
       I hear some noise. Lady, come from that nest
       Of death, contagion, and unnatural sleep.
       A greater power than we can contradict
       Hath thwarted our intents. Come, come away.
155   Thy husband in thy bosom there lies dead;
       And Paris too. Come, I'll dispose of thee
       Among a sisterhood of holy nuns.
       Stay not to question, for the watch is coming.
       Come, go, good Juliet. I dare no longer stay.
Juliet.
160   Go, get thee hence, for I will not away.

                                          [*Exit* FRIAR.]

       What's here? A cup, closed in my truelove's hand?

---

136. unthrifty: unlucky.

141. *Where is the friar as he discovers the bloodstains?*

145. unkind: unnatural.

Staging the Play
147. *This short line suggests that the friar rushes to Juliet and waits for her to speak. What must he be feeling?*

148. comfortable: comforting.

152. *For the friar this is a terrible moment. What is his reaction to the noise he hears?*

Staging the Play
159. *What plan does the friar propose to Juliet? What is Juliet doing or refusing to do as the friar repeatedly tries to move her?*

Staging the Play
160. *It is hard to believe that after all his concern for these two young lovers, the friar would become a coward at this moment and leave Juliet to harm herself. How must the friar act here to convince us that he is frantic and not very sensible?*

Poison, I see, hath been his timeless° end.
O churl!° Drunk all, and left no friendly drop
To help me after? I will kiss thy lips.
165   Haply some poison yet doth hang on them
To make me die with a restorative.

[*Kisses him.*]

Thy lips are warm!
Chief Watchman (*within*). Lead, boy. Which way?
Juliet.
Yea, noise? Then I'll be brief. O happy° dagger!

[*Snatches Romeo's dagger.*]

170   This is thy sheath; there rust, and let me die.

[*She stabs herself and falls.*]

[*Enter Paris's* BOY *and* WATCH.]

Boy.
This is the place. There, where the torch doth burn.
Chief Watchman.
The ground is bloody. Search about the churchyard.
Go, some of you; whoe'er you find attach.
                              [*Exeunt some of the* WATCH.]
Pitiful sight! Here lies the county slain;
175   And Juliet bleeding, warm, and newly dead,
Who here hath lain this two days burièd.
Go, tell the prince; run to the Capulets;
Raise up the Montagues; some others search.
                              [*Exeunt others of the* WATCH.]
We see the ground whereon these woes do lie,
180   But the true ground° of all these piteous woes
We cannot without circumstance° descry.

[*Enter some of the* WATCH, *with Romeo's man* BALTHASAR.]

Second Watchman.
Here's Romeo's man. We found him in the churchyard.
Chief Watchman.
Hold him in safety till the prince come hither.

[*Enter* FRIAR LAURENCE *and another* WATCHMAN.]

Third Watchman.
Here is a friar that trembles, sighs, and weeps.

162. timeless: untimely.
163. churl: rude fellow (spoken teasingly).

169. happy: lucky (to be here when she needs it).

Staging the Play
Stage direction: Do you see Juliet in her last moments as half-crazed? calm and purposeful? something else? Do you think this scene can be played only one way? Can it be played several ways? How would you play the scene?

180. ground: cause.
181. circumstance: details.

184. *How do the watchman's words help us picture the state the friar is in?*

"Drunk all,
and left no
friendly drop
To help me
after?"
✧

185   We took this mattock and this spade from him
       As he was coming from this churchyard's side.
Chief Watchman.
       A great suspicion! Stay the friar too.

[*Enter the* PRINCE *and* ATTENDANTS.]

Prince.
       What misadventure is so early up,
       That calls our person from our morning rest?

[*Enter* CAPULET *and his wife,* LADY CAPULET, *with others.*]

Capulet.
190   What should it be, that is so shrieked abroad?
Lady Capulet.
       O, the people in the street cry "Romeo,"
       Some "Juliet," and some "Paris"; and all run
       With open outcry toward our monument.
Prince.
       What fear is this which startles in your ears?
Chief Watchman.
195   Sovereign, here lies the County Paris slain;
       And Romeo dead; and Juliet, dead before,
       Warm and new killed.
Prince.
       Search, seek, and know how this foul murder comes.
Chief Watchman.
       Here is a friar, and slaughtered Romeo's man,
200   With instruments upon them fit to open
       These dead men's tombs.
Capulet.
       O heavens! O wife, look how our daughter bleeds!
       This dagger hath mista'en, for, lo, his house°
       Is empty on the back of Montague,
205   And it missheathèd in my daughter's bosom!
Lady Capulet.
       O me, this sight of death is as a bell
       That warns° my old age to a sepulcher.

[*Enter* MONTAGUE *and others.*]

Prince.
       Come, Montague; for thou art early up
       To see thy son and heir more early down.

? Staging the Play
193. *As the tomb begins to fill with people, noises and cries are heard offstage. What does Lady Capulet suggest is being "shrieked abroad" in Verona?*

203. house: sheath.

207. warns: summons.

Montague.

210   Alas, my liege, my wife is dead tonight!
       Grief of my son's exile hath stopped her breath.
       What further woe conspires against mine age?

Prince.

       Look, and thou shalt see.

Montague.

       O thou untaught! What manners is in this,
215   To press before thy father to a grave?

Prince.

       Seal up the mouth of outrage for a while,
       Till we can clear these ambiguities
       And know their spring, their head, their true descent;
       And then will I be general of your woes°
220   And lead you even to death. Meantime forbear,
       And let mischance be slave to patience.
       Bring forth the parties of suspicion.

Friar.

       I am the greatest, able to do least,
       Yet most suspected, as the time and place
225   Doth make against me, of this direful murder;
       And here I stand, both to impeach and purge°
       Myself condemnèd and myself excused.

Prince.

       Then say at once what thou dost know in this.

Friar.

       I will be brief, for my short date of breath°
230   Is not so long as is a tedious tale.
       Romeo, there dead, was husband to that Juliet;
       And she, there dead, that Romeo's faithful wife.
       I married them; and their stolen marriage day
       Was Tybalt's doomsday, whose untimely death
235   Banished the new-made bridegroom from this city;
       For whom, and not for Tybalt, Juliet pined.
       You, to remove that siege of grief from her,
       Betrothed and would have married her perforce
       To County Paris. Then comes she to me
240   And with wild looks bid me devise some mean
       To rid her from this second marriage,
       Or in my cell there would she kill herself.
       Then gave I her (so tutored by my art)
       A sleeping potion; which so took effect
245   As I intended, for it wrought on her
       The form of death. Meantime I writ to Romeo

215. *Whom is Montague talking to here?*

219. general of your woes: leader of your mourning.

226. impeach and purge: charge and punish.

229. date of breath: term of life.

Staging the Play
230. *All of what the friar says here is known by the audience. In some productions this long* **monologue** *is cut entirely, but it is important for us to imagine the effect the speech has on the Montagues, the Capulets, and the prince. This is the moment when they discover what we've known all along. Where do you think the friar must pause as the families cry out and weep?*

237. *Whom does the friar mean by "you"?*

That he should hither come as° this dire night
To help to take her from her borrowed grave,
Being the time the potion's force should cease.
250 But he which bore my letter, Friar John,
Was stayed by accident, and yesternight
Returned my letter back. Then all alone
At the prefixèd hour of her waking
Came I to take her from her kindred's vault,
255 Meaning to keep her closely at my cell
Till I conveniently could send to Romeo.
But when I came, some minute ere the time
Of her awakening, here untimely lay
The noble Paris and true Romeo dead.
260 She wakes; and I entreated her come forth
And bear this work of heaven with patience;
But then a noise did scare me from the tomb,
And she, too desperate, would not go with me,
But, as it seems, did violence on herself.
265 All this I know, and to the marriage
Her nurse is privy;° and if aught in this
Miscarried by my fault, let my old life
Be sacrificed some hour before his time
Unto the rigor of severest law.

Prince.
270 We still° have known thee for a holy man.
Where's Romeo's man? What can he say to this?

Balthasar.
I brought my master news of Juliet's death;
And then in post he came from Mantua
To this same place, to this same monument.
275 This letter he early bid me give his father,
And threat'ned me with death, going in the vault,
If I departed not and left him there.

Prince.
Give me the letter. I will look on it.
Where is the county's page that raised the watch?
280 Sirrah, what made your master in this place?

Boy.
He came with flowers to strew his lady's grave;
And bid me stand aloof, and so I did.
Anon comes one with light to ope the tomb;
And by and by my master drew on him;
285 And then I ran away to call the watch.

247. as: on.

261. *This line expresses the friar's view of life. How would the play have been different if both Romeo and Juliet had been able from the start to bear their trials "with patience"? How does this also apply to the adults in the play?*

266. to the marriage . . . privy: Juliet's nurse knows about the marriage.

269. *Does the friar accept responsibility for his part in the tragedy? What does he say?*

270. still: always.

"See what a scourge is laid
upon your hate,
That heaven finds means to kill
your joys with love . . ."

Prince.
　　This letter doth make good the friar's words,
　　Their course of love, the tidings of her death;
　　And here he writes that he did buy a poison
　　Of a poor pothecary and therewithal
290　　Came to this vault to die and lie with Juliet.
　　Where be these enemies? Capulet, Montague,
　　See what a scourge is laid upon your hate,
　　That heaven finds means to kill your joys with love,
　　And I, for winking at° your discords too,
295　　Have lost a brace° of kinsmen. All are punished.

Capulet.
　　O brother Montague, give me thy hand.
　　This is my daughter's jointure,° for no more
　　Can I demand.

Montague.　　　　But I can give thee more;
　　For I will raise her statue in pure gold,
300　　That whiles Verona by that name is known,
　　There shall no figure at such rate° be set
　　As that of true and faithful Juliet.

Capulet.
　　As rich shall Romeo's by his lady's lie—
　　Poor sacrifices of our enmity!

Prince.
305　　A glooming peace this morning with it brings.
　　　　The sun for sorrow will not show his head.
　　Go hence, to have more talk of these sad things;
　　　　Some shall be pardoned, and some punishèd;
　　For never was a story of more woe
310　　Than this of Juliet and her Romeo. [*Exeunt omnes.*]

"For never was a story of more woe
Than this of Juliet and her Romeo."

Your Laughter
Pablo Neruda

Take bread away from me, if you wish,
take air away, but
do not take from me your laughter.

Do not take away the rose,
5   the lanceflower that you pluck,
the water that suddenly
bursts forth in your joy,
the sudden wave
of silver born in you.

10   My struggle is harsh and I come back
with eyes tired
at times from having seen
the unchanging earth,
but when your laughter enters
15   it rises to the sky seeking me
and it opens for me all
the doors of life.

My love, in the darkest
hour your laughter
20   opens, and if suddenly
you see my blood staining
the stones of the street,
laugh, because your laughter
will be for my hands
25   like a fresh sword.

Next to the sea in the autumn,
your laughter must raise
its foamy cascade,
and in the spring, love,
30   I want your laughter like
the flower I was waiting for,
the blue flower, the rose
of my echoing country.

Laugh at the night,
35   at the day, at the moon,
laugh at the twisted
streets of the island,
laugh at this clumsy
boy who loves you,
40   but when I open
my eyes and close them,
when my steps go,
when my steps return,
deny me bread, air,
45   light, spring,
but never your laughter
for I would die.

How Do I Love Thee?
Elizabeth Barrett Browning

How do I love thee? Let me count the ways.
I love thee to the depth and breadth and height
My soul can reach, when feeling out of sight
For the ends of Being and ideal Grace.
5   I love thee to the level of everyday's
Most quiet need, by sun and candle light.
I love thee freely, as men strive for Right;
I love thee purely, as they turn from Praise.
I love thee with the passion put to use
10   In my old griefs, and with my childhood's
   faith.
I love thee with a love I seemed to lose
With my lost saints°—I love thee with the
   breath,
Smiles, tears, of all my life!—and, if God
   choose,
I shall but love thee better after death.

---

12. lost saints: childhood faith.

Act V

Reading Check

1. What news does Romeo's servant bring him in Scene 1?
2. Why does Romeo buy the poison?
3. Why doesn't Romeo receive the friar's letter explaining the latest plans?
4. What does Romeo find when he enters the tomb?
5. What finally happens to Romeo and then to Juliet?

Thinking Critically

Literary Skills
Analyze characteristics of tragedy, including dramatic irony and climax. Analyze soliloquy, monologue, and dialogue.

Writing Skills
Compare a play with a film. Prepare a plan for a modern version of a play. Write an essay analyzing the structure of the play. Write a character analysis.

Listening and Speaking Skills
Prepare an oral report about character types.

INTERNET
Projects and Activities
Keyword: LE7 9-11

6. What do you think caused the **tragedy** of Romeo and Juliet? Was it fate or human errors? Draw a web showing all the people or forces that might have been responsible.

Romeo's & Juliet's deaths

7. This act includes examples of **soliloquy** (a long speech in which a character alone onstage expresses thoughts aloud), **monologue** (a long speech that a character delivers to other characters onstage), and **dialogue** (a conversation between two or more characters). Find an example of each, and comment on what it adds to the play.

8. In which scene of this act do you think the **dramatic irony** peaked? Explain why you picked that scene.

9. The **climax** of a play is its most intense moment, when we know how the conflict will end. In a **tragedy** it is a moment when we are overcome by sadness, fear, or regret. The climax of Shakespeare's tragedies comes in the final act. When in this act do you think the climax occurs? What were your feelings at that moment?

10. In Scene 3, look back at the prince's speech about love killing the families' joys. It seems **ironic** that love could kill, so how in this play did love kill joy? In what way is the whole play about the way heaven scourges, or punishes, people for hating? Support your response with details from the text.

11. State the **theme** of the play (its main idea about life) as you see it. Then, compare your statement of theme with your classmates'. How do they vary?

Extending and Evaluating

12. Throughout the eighteenth and nineteenth centuries, *Romeo and Juliet* was often rewritten with a different ending, in which the young lovers live long and happily together. Explain whether you like the ending of the play as it was written or would prefer a happy ending. What changes, if any, would you make in the outcome?

Comparing Texts
Words of Love
The words that Romeo and Juliet speak to each other are words of love. "Your Laughter" and "How Do I Love Thee?" (see the **Connection** on page 1025) are about love too. In a brief essay, **compare** and **contrast** these two expressions of love. How does love transform each speaker? How does each speaker say that love conquers death and time? Which poem speaks most powerfully to you? Why?

Choose from among the following assignments to respond to the play.

WRITING

1. Review It

Look for a film version of *Romeo and Juliet* in your library or a video store. Then, write a short **essay** in which you **compare** one scene of the play with that scene in the film. Which did you find more effective? Why?

▷ **Use "Comparing a Play and a Film," pages 1040–1047, for help with this assignment.**

2. The Play Today

As a group, prepare a plan for an updated *Romeo and Juliet* that takes place in the United States. The chart below shows how Arthur Laurents and Stephen Sondheim changed the play to make it into a musical, *West Side Story* (1957). When you finish your rough plan, you might map your scenes. You might even write your own new *Romeo and Juliet.*

Romeo and Juliet	*West Side Story*
Verona, 1300s	New York, 1950s
Feuding families: Montagues versus Capulets	Gang war: Jets versus Sharks
Lovers: Romeo (Montague); Juliet (Capulet)	Lovers: Tony (Jet); Maria (sister of Shark)
Authority: prince	Authority: New York police officer
Friend/confidant: Benvolio (Romeo's); nurse (Juliet's)	Friend/confidant: Riff (Tony's); Anita (Maria's)
Leaders: Mercutio (Montagues); Tybalt (Capulets)	Leaders: Riff (Jets); Bernardo (Sharks)

3. Tracing the Action

The graphic on page 897 shows the pattern of a typical Shakespearean tragedy. In an **essay, analyze the structure** of *Romeo and Juliet* according to that pattern. Does the play match the structure? You might provide a graphic with your essay summarizing what happens in each act. You might even add illustrations showing the major action in each act.

4. Portrait of Juliet

Write a **character analysis** of Juliet, using the following comment by a critic as the basis of your thesis statement. Be sure to use details from the play to support what the critic says about Juliet and how the world treated her.

> Shakespeare's real miracle . . . was Juliet, transformed from an adolescent arrogantly eager to outdo her elders to an appealing child-woman, barely fourteen, who learns to mix courage with her innocence, yet falls victim to a world that only briefly and unintentionally, but fatally, treats her as a plaything.
>
> —J. A. Bryant, Jr.

LISTENING AND SPEAKING

5. Characters Endure

Prepare an **oral report** for the class in which you tell how the character types presented in *Romeo and Juliet* are found in movies, novels, and TV sitcoms and dramas today. Focus on these types: beautiful girl; handsome boyfriend; socially conscious mother; grumpy father; boyfriend approved by the girl's parents; older confidant; loyal best friend; hotheaded bully; dopey guys who follow the gang leader.

Figures of Speech

Shakespeare's characters use images and figures of speech so rich and so varied that the play, which has lived now for over four hundred years, will probably live as long as English continues to be spoken. As you're focusing on Shakespeare's language, you might try to imitate some of his figures of speech.

Similes. The simplest form of figurative language is the **simile,** a clearly stated comparison between two different things. A simile uses a word such as *like* or *as* or *than* in stating its comparison. For example, Romeo, dejected over Rosaline, says of love, "It pricks like thorn." Romeo's simile suggests that love can cause pain, just as a thorn can.

Metaphors. **Metaphors** omit words such as *like, as,* and *than* and directly equate two different things. When the nurse says of Paris "he's a flower, . . . a very flower," she immediately identifies Paris's good looks with a beautiful blossom. Metaphors may also be **implied.** The prince uses implied metaphors when he angrily accuses the citizens:

> "You men, you beasts,
> That quench the fire of
>   your pernicious rage
> With purple fountains
>   issuing from your veins!"

The prince compares the anger of the citizens to a fire, and he compares the blood issuing from the wounds to purple water spewing from fountains.

Personification. **Personification** is a special kind of metaphor, in which something that is not a person is spoken of as if it were human. When Benvolio says that the sun "peered forth the golden window of the East," he is personifying the sun by saying that it peered, as if it had two eyes.

Puns. Shakespeare's audiences loved **puns,** which are plays on the **multiple meanings** of words. (Many jokes today are based on puns. Question: "What has four wheels and flies?" Answer: "A garbage truck." This pun is based on two meanings of the word *flies.*) Many of the puns in *Romeo and Juliet* go over our heads today because jokes go out of fashion very quickly and because some of Shakespeare's wordplay involves words we don't use anymore or involves words whose meanings have changed.

Mercutio is the best punster in the play, though Romeo does pretty well in Act II, when he matches wits with his friend. When Mercutio spies Romeo coming down the street, he says Romeo comes "without his roe." *Roe* can refer to a female deer, so if Romeo is without his roe, he's without his girl. *Roe* also refers to fish eggs, so "without his roe" can mean that Romeo's been gutted (we'd say he's gutless), as a fish is when its eggs have been removed.

If you need help figuring out the examples of figurative language on the next page, go back to the play, and see if the **context** helps you.

SKILLS FOCUS

Vocabulary Skills
Understand figures of speech.

Similes. For each of the following quotations, identify the similes, and tell what two things are brought together. In what way are the two things alike?

1. **Romeo.**

   O, she doth teach the torches to burn
       bright!
   It seems she hangs upon the cheek of
       night
   As a rich jewel in an Ethiop's ear—
   Beauty too rich for use, for earth too
       dear!
           —Act I, Scene 5, lines 44–47

2. **Romeo.**

   Love goes toward love as schoolboys
       from their books;
   But love from love, toward school
       with heavy looks.
           —Act II, Scene 2, lines 157–158

3. **Lord Capulet.**

   Death lies on her like an untimely
       frost
   Upon the sweetest flower of all the
       field.
           —Act IV, Scene 5, lines 28–29

Metaphors. Here are some passages containing metaphors. Pick out each metaphor, and identify the two things that it compares.

1. **Romeo** (to Juliet).

   If I profane with my unworthiest hand
       This holy shrine, the gentle sin is
       this:
   My lips, two blushing pilgrims, ready
       stand
       To smooth that rough touch with
       a tender kiss.
           —Act I, Scene 5, lines 93–96

2. **Romeo** (under Juliet's balcony).

   But soft! What light through yonder
       window breaks?
   It is the East, and Juliet is the sun!
           —Act II, Scene 2, lines 2–3

3. **Juliet** (to Romeo).

   This bud of love, by summer's ripening
       breath,
   May prove a beauteous flower when
       next we meet.
           —Act II, Scene 2, lines 121–122

Personification. Here are some quotations from *Romeo and Juliet* that contain personifications. In each, what nonhuman thing is spoken of as if it were a person? (Hint: A passage can contain more than one personification.)

1. **Capulet.**

   When well-appareled April on the heel
   Of limping winter treads. . . .
           —Act I, Scene 2, lines 27–28

2. **Chorus.**

   Now old desire doth in his deathbed lie,
       And young affection gapes to be
       his heir. . . .
           —Act II, Chorus, lines 1–2

3. **Juliet.**

   Come, civil night,
   Thou sober-suited matron all in black,
   And learn me how to lose a winning
       match. . . .
           —Act III, Scene 2, lines 10–12

Puns. Here are two puns from the play. If you can explain the plays on meaning, you'll have caught the jokes.

1. **Mercutio** (after he is stabbed).

   Ask for me tomorrow, and you shall
   find me a grave man.
           —Act III, Scene 1, lines 94–95

2. **Romeo.**

   You have dancing shoes
   With nimble soles; I have a soul of lead
   So stakes me to the ground I cannot
       move.
           —Act I, Scene 4, lines 14–16

The History of the English Language

The English language has seen many changes since Shakespeare wrote *Romeo and Juliet* more than four hundred years ago. As you learned when reading the play, some of the words Shakespeare uses have different meanings today. For example, *still* now means "yet" instead of "always," and *owe* now means "be in debt" instead of "own; have." Other words found in Shakespeare's plays are considered **archaic:** They are no longer used. Examples are *thence* ("from there"), *sooth* ("truth"), and *wherefore* ("why").

In spite of those and other changes, Shakespeare's English, like ours, is considered Modern English, which began in the late 1400s. If you could travel back to a time before that date, you probably wouldn't be able to understand what anyone was saying. From their armchairs, however, linguists—people who study language—have traced the roots of English far back in time. The paragraphs that follow provide a brief overview of the history of the English language.

Proto-Indo-European

Before 3000 B.C., people living near the Caspian Sea (between the Middle East and Asia) spoke a language we call Proto-Indo-European. (*Proto*– means "first or earliest form," and *Indo*– refers to India.) Over the years, groups of these farmers, herders, and fighters traveled to distant places. In their new lands the Proto-Indo-European they spoke gradually developed into the languages we now call Farsi (or Persian), Hindi, Armenian, Sanskrit, Greek, Russian, Polish, Irish, Italian, French, Spanish, German, Dutch, Swedish, Norwegian—and English. From India to Scandinavia, all these languages have descended from the same Proto-Indo-European roots.

Old English

Much later (from 27 B.C. to A.D. 476), Roman armies conquered most of Europe, North Africa, and the Middle East. Their language, Latin, then influenced the languages of all those lands, including that of the Britons, a Celtic people living in the British Isles. In the fifth century A.D., England was invaded by Anglo-Saxons, who added their Old Germanic tongue to the Celtic of the native Britons. The next invaders to arrive were the Northmen, or Vikings, from Scandinavia, who added Norse to the mix. The language that resulted from all these influences we now call Old English. Like Proto-Indo-European, it was a spoken, or oral, language. Three words from Old English we still use today (among many others) are *horse, night,* and *wife.*

SKILLS FOCUS

Vocabulary Skills
Understand the history of the English language.

Middle English

The last invasion of England was in 1066, by William the Conqueror, from Normandy, in France. For about three hundred years after his conquest, French was spoken by the upper classes and used in the courts and government, while the Catholic clergy spoke and wrote in Latin. The common people—most of the population—continued to speak English, but they were soon borrowing many words from French, thus transforming the language into what is now called Middle English. This is the language of Geoffrey Chaucer's great work, *The Canterbury Tales*. Middle English has many similarities to Modern English, but it is different enough that most people today read Chaucer's poem in a Modern English translation. Three Middle English words (among many others) that were borrowed from French and are used today are *government, justice,* and *literature*.

Modern English

Modern English is generally considered to date from around the time Henry VII was crowned king of England, in 1485. He brought peace to the land and promoted all things English, including the language. Ten years earlier, in 1475, William Caxton had printed the first book in English, which helped to unify and spread the language. After Columbus landed in the New World in 1492, English sailors traveled throughout the Americas and Europe, further spreading the English language and, at the same time, enriching the language with new words. All these influences have given Modern English a vast and international vocabulary. From Spain we get *banana, hammock,* and *tobacco*; from Central America, *chocolate, potato,* and *tomato*; and from the Netherlands, *cruise, knapsack,* and *landscape*—to name a few examples.

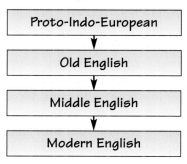

With the spread of science and technology, and especially with the widespread use of the Internet, English is now used worldwide. Still the language continues to pick up new words, such as *software, modem, e-mail*. How much do you think our language is changing? In another four hundred years, do you think people will still be able to read and understand the books we write today?

PRACTICE

Make a list of five words you use every day, and then look up their derivations in a good dictionary. Most dictionaries use abbreviations such as *IE* for "Indo-European," *OE* for "Old English," *ME* for "Middle English," *L* for "Latin," *Fr* for "French," and *Sp* for "Spanish." After you have located the original language for each of your words, share your findings with your classmates. Make a list on the chalkboard of the original languages. Then, from all the words chosen by the class, count the number of words that derive from each language. Do you find many sources for your derivations, or only a few?

Dear Juliet ◆ Romeo and Juliet in Bosnia

Synthesizing Sources: Making Connections

Shakespeare's plays were hits in his own day, four hundred years ago, and they have remained popular ever since because they speak to all kinds of people all over the world. We connect so readily with his plays because they have timeless, universal meaning. That is, they ask the big questions that people everywhere have always wrestled with: Where in the universe do human beings fit in? What do we live for? Why do we love?

Connect and compare. Whenever you read—whether it's a play by Shakespeare, a short story, or a newspaper or Internet article—you look for connections between what you're reading and the world you know. You think about how the subject—a heartache, a family crisis, a societal wrong—**connects** with your own experience. You ask yourself whether the work rings true.

You should also connect and compare your reading with other works you have read. For example, remembering a character in a novel who faces difficulties being with the one she loves, you might **compare** her responses with Juliet's. Each work you read on a subject thus adds to your overall understanding of the topic.

Put it all together. One way to increase your understanding is to **synthesize**—or bring together into a whole—what you have learned from different sources on a topic. To do this, first **paraphrase** the ideas in each source—that is, restate them in your own words. Then, **connect** each source with the others—tell how they are similar and how they are different. Finally, explain what all the works have added to your understanding of life.

Vocabulary Development

carnage (kär′nij) *n.:* slaughter; bloodshed.

reminiscing (rem′ə·nis′iŋ) *v.:* thinking, talking, or writing about one's memories.

relentless (ri·lent′lis) *adj.:* not stopping; persistent; harsh.

mundane (mun′dān′) *adj.:* everyday; commonplace.

compulsory (kəm·pul′sə·rē) *adj.:* required by rule or law.

vulnerable (vul′nər·ə·bəl) *adj.:* affected by a specific influence.

primal (prī′məl) *adj.:* original; primitive.

esteem (ə·stēm′) *n.:* respect.

eradicating (ē·rad′i·kāt′iŋ) *v.* used as *n.:* wiping out; destroying.

dilemma (di·lem′ə) *n.:* difficult choice; serious problem.

Connecting to the Literature

Sometimes a well-known literary work like *Romeo and Juliet* takes on a reality of its own. The following nonfiction articles connect true-life stories with Shakespeare's play. "Dear Juliet" tells of lovelorn individuals who address their letters to Romeo or Juliet, Verona, Italy. "Romeo and Juliet in Bosnia" relates the story of a Bosnian couple who shared the tragic fate of Shakespeare's young lovers.

SKILLS FOCUS

Reading Skills
Synthesize information from several sources on a single topic.

INTERNET
Interactive Reading Model
Keyword: LE7 9-11

DEAR JULIET

from *The Wall Street Journal*, November 10, 1992

Lisa Bannon

> *A*ny man that can write may
> answer a letter.
> —William Shakespeare
> from *Romeo and Juliet*, Act II, Scene 4

VERONA, ITALY—Fate bequeathed[1] a strange legacy[2] to this small city in northern Italy.

As the setting for Shakespeare's sixteenth-century tragedy *Romeo and Juliet,* Verona inherited the curiosity of literary scholars, a celebrated theatrical tradition, and several hundred thousand tourists a year.

In the bargain, the city also became the star-crossed lovers' capital of the world.

"We don't know how it started exactly," explains Giulio Tamassia, the bespectacled city spokesman for matters relating to Romeo and Juliet. "But one day in the thirties, these letters started arriving unprompted—addressed to Juliet. At a certain point somebody decided Juliet should write back."

Juliet's Address

What began sixty years ago as an occasional correspondence has grown into an industry. This year more than one thousand letters from the lovelorn will arrive in Verona, addressed to Shakespeare's tragic heroine. Many of them land on Mr. Tamassia's desk, with no more address than: Juliet, Italy.

"They tend to be sentimental," says Mr. Tamassia, rifling through stacks of musty airmail in the cramped studio that serves as Juliet's headquarters. Inside big pink folders are thousands of sorrowful letters, break-your-heart tales of love and loss. They come from all over—a teenage girl in Guatemala,[3] a businessman in Boston, a high school teacher in London. Some but not many are written by students in Shakespearean language. About two percent of letters received are addressed to Romeo, but Juliet replies.

"Writing the letter itself is really the first step toward solving the problem," says Mr. Tamassia, a fifty-nine-year-old retired businessman who wants it known at the outset that he himself is not Juliet. He is more her correspondence secretary.

"People express feelings in the letters that they would never admit to the person they love. Juliet's story inspires them," he says.

---

1. **bequeathed** (bē·kwē*th*d′) *v.:* handed down or passed on, as in a will.
2. **legacy** (leg′ə·sē) *n.:* gift handed down to someone, as in a will.
3. **Guatemala** (gwät′ə·mä′lə): nation in Central America.

A Saudi Version

After much rummaging, he pulls out one of his favorites—describing a modern equivalent of the Montague-Capulet family rivalry.

Hala, an eighteen-year-old Saudi Arabian,[4] wrote in March that she had fallen in love with the only son of her family's mortal enemy.[5] Years ago, in Pakistan,[6] her great-grandfather was responsible for the execution of a man who was using his property for smuggling heroin. From that time on, war was declared between the two families.

Now Hala was in love with a descendant[7] of the executed man. "I am torn between the love for my family, which has made me what I am today, and my love for Omer, the man of my dreams," she wrote.

"Please reply quickly . . . my love, my life and future all depend on your answer."

---

4. **Saudi Arabian:** native of Saudi Arabia, a nation in the Middle East.
5. **mortal enemy:** extremely hostile enemy.
6. **Pakistan:** Asian nation west of India. The feud described in the letter began in Pakistan, which is a great distance from Saudi Arabia, where the writer of the letter lives.

---

7. **descendant** (dē·sen′dənt) *n.:* offspring of an ancestor, such as a child, grandchild, or great-grandchild.

This house and balcony in Verona, Italy, are popularly claimed to have been Juliet's.

Romeo and Juliet in Bosnia

from *The New York Times,* May 8, 1994

Bob Herbert

Bosnia and Herzegovina (hert′sə·gō·vē′nə) is a small nation on the Balkan peninsula in eastern Europe. It recently became independent, but its problems are centuries old, since the population has long been divided among three hostile groups: Muslims, Serbs, and Croatians. The divisions are both ethnic and religious, since the Serbs and Croatians are Christians (the Serbs, members of the Eastern Orthodox Church; the Croats, members of the Roman Catholic Church). The area has been plagued by violence, in which warring ethnic groups have battled one another. Sarajevo (sar′ə·yā′vō) is the capital of Bosnia and Herzegovina.

If you watch *Frontline* Tuesday night on PBS, you will see the story of two ordinary young people, Bosko Brkic, an Eastern Orthodox Serb, and Admira Ismic, a Muslim, who met at a New Year's Eve party in the mid-1980s, fell in love, tried to pursue the most conventional of dreams, and died together on a hellish bridge in Sarajevo.

The documentary, called "Romeo and Juliet in Sarajevo," achieves its power by focusing our attention on the thoroughly human individuals caught up in a horror that, from afar, can seem abstract and almost unimaginable. It's one thing to hear about the carnage caused by incessant[1] sniper fire and the steady rain of mortar shells on a city; it's something quite different to actually witness a parent desperately groping for meaning while reminiscing about a lost daughter.

For viewers overwhelmed and desensitized by the relentless reports of mass killings and mass rapes, the shock of "Romeo and Juliet in Sarajevo" is that what we see is so real and utterly familiar. We become riveted by the mundane. Bosko and Admira could be a young couple from anywhere, from Queens, or Tokyo, or Barcelona.

We learn that they graduated from high school in June of 1986 and that both were crazy about movies and music. Admira had a cat named Yellow that she loved, and Bosko liked to play practical jokes.

Admira's father, Zijo, speaking amid clouds of cigarette smoke, says, "Well, I knew from the first day about that relationship and I didn't have anything against it. I thought it was good because her guy was so likable, and after a time I started to love him and didn't regard him any differently than Admira."

Admira's grandmother, Sadika Ismic, was

---

1. **incessant** (in·ses′ənt) *adj.:* never stopping; continual.

Vocabulary

carnage (kär′nij) *n.:* slaughter; bloodshed.

reminiscing (rem′ə·nis′iŋ) *v.:* thinking, talking, or writing about one's memories.

relentless (ri·lent′lis) *adj.:* not stopping; persistent; harsh.

mundane (mun′dān′) *adj.:* everyday; commonplace.

not so sanguine.[2] "Yes, I did have something against it," she says. "I thought, 'He is Serb, she is a Muslim, and how will it work?'"

For Admira and Bosko, of course, love was the answer to everything. While Bosko was away on compulsory military service soon after high school, Admira wrote: "My dear love, Sarajevo at night is the most beautiful thing in the world. I guess I could live somewhere else but only if I must or if I am forced. Just a little beat of time is left until we are together. After that, absolutely nothing can separate us."

Sarajevo at the time was a cosmopolitan[3] city coming off the triumph of the 1984 Winter Olympics. With a population of Serbs, Croats, Muslims, Jews, and others, the city had become a symbol of ethnic and religious tolerance, a place where people were making a serious attempt to live together in peace.

But civilization is an exceedingly fragile enterprise, and it's especially vulnerable to the primal madness of ethnic and religious hatreds. Simple tolerance is nothing in the face of the relentless, pathetic, and near-universal need to bolster the esteem of the individual and the group by eradicating the rights, and even the existence, of others.

When the madness descended on Sarajevo, Bosko Brkic faced a cruel dilemma. He could not kill Serbs. And he could not go up into the hills and fire back down on his girlfriend's people. Says his mother, Rada: "He was simply a kid who was not for the war."

Bosko and Admira decided to flee Sarajevo. To escape, they had to cross a bridge over the Miljacka River in a no man's land[4] between the Serb and Muslim lines. Snipers from both sides overlooked the bridge.

It has not been determined who shot the lovers. They were about two thirds of the way across the bridge when the gunfire erupted. Both sides blame the other. Witnesses said Bosko died instantly. Admira crawled to him. She died a few minutes later. The area in which they were shot was so dangerous that the bodies remained on the bridge, entwined, for six days before being removed.

Only the times and places change. Bosnia today, Rwanda and Burundi[5] tomorrow. Jews versus Arabs, Chinese versus Japanese, blacks versus whites. There are various ostensible reasons for the endless conflicts—ideological[6] differences, border disputes, oil—but dig just a little and you will uncover the ruinous ethnic or religious origins of the clash.

The world stands helpless and sometimes depressed before the madness. Millions upon millions dead, millions more to die. It is not just the curse of our times. It seems to be the curse of all time.

---

4. **no man's land** *n.*: battle zone claimed by both sides in a war but controlled by neither, often where much of the fighting takes place.
5. **Rwanda and Burundi:** African nations that have been the scene of ethnic warfare between the Watusi, or Tutsi, and the Hutu peoples.
6. **ideological** (i′dē·ə·lä′ji·kəl) *adj.*: based on political, social, or economic beliefs.

Vocabulary
compulsory (kəm·pul′sə·rē) *adj.*: required by rule or law.

vulnerable (vul′nər·ə·bəl) *adj.*: affected by a specific influence.

primal (prī′məl) *adj.*: original; primitive.

esteem (ə·stēm′) *n.*: respect.

eradicating (ē·rad′i·kāt′iŋ) *v.* used as *n.*: wiping out; destroying.

dilemma (di·lem′ə) *n.*: difficult choice; serious problem.

---

2. **sanguine** (saŋ′gwin) *adj.*: optimistic; hopeful; cheerful.
3. **cosmopolitan** (käz′mə·päl′ə·tən) *adj.*: worldly; sophisticated.

Reading Check

1. As explained in "Dear Juliet," who is Giulio Tamassia, and what does he do?

2. What problem did Hala, the Saudi Arabian girl, write to Juliet about?

3. What difference exists between Admira and Bosko, the couple described in "Romeo and Juliet in Bosnia"?

4. What happened to Admira and Bosko?

Test Practice

1. Which of the following statements *best* expresses the **main idea** of "Dear Juliet"?

   A Many people all over the world fall in love with someone their parents hate.

   B Many people with problems relating to love look to Romeo and Juliet for answers.

   C It is important to answer letters promptly to help people with their problems.

   D Giulio Tamassia helps everyone who writes to him as best he can.

2. In *both* "Romeo and Juliet in Bosnia" and Shakespeare's *Romeo and Juliet* —

   F characters named Romeo and Juliet die

   G innocent lovers die because of a larger conflict

   H the destructiveness and pointlessness of war are described

   J young people are rejected by their families because of a feud

3. What is Bob Herbert's *main* **purpose** in writing "Romeo and Juliet in Bosnia"?

   A To point out parallels between the story of Admira and Bosko and the story of Shakespeare's lovers

   B To show that love can triumph over death

   C To highlight the universal madness of conflicts like the one in Bosnia

   D To show that love is universal

4. Which element in "Dear Juliet" offers the strongest parallel to both *Romeo and Juliet* and "Romeo and Juliet in Bosnia"?

   F The plight Hala describes in her letter

   G Tamassia's sympathy for the letter writers

   H The need of people to write to Juliet

   J The fact that the letters come from all over the world

5. Which statement **synthesizes** themes from *Romeo and Juliet,* "Dear Juliet," and "Romeo and Juliet in Bosnia"?

   A Conflict often destroys love.

   B People in love look to others for help.

   C Loyalty makes love strong.

   D People in love often face difficulties.

Constructed Response

Connect one of these informational pieces to another work you have read or seen—a story about love, for example, or a news report about innocent victims. In a short essay, first **paraphrase** the ideas in each work. Then, discuss their similarities and differences. Finally, **synthesize** what you have learned about life from the two works.

SKILLS FOCUS

Reading Skills
Synthesize information from several sources on a single topic.

Denotations and Connotations

Connotations are the emotions and associations that are suggested by a word and that go beyond the word's literal meaning found in a dictionary—its **denotation.** Often connotations show shades of meaning or intensity.

> **Word Bank**
>
> carnage
> reminiscing
> relentless
> mundane
> compulsory
> vulnerable
> primal
> esteem
> eradicating
> dilemma

PRACTICE

Use the plus sign (+) or the minus sign (–) to show how each of the following pairs of words compare in intensity. Use the plus sign if the word on the right seems stronger than the numbered Word Bank word on the left. Use the minus sign if the word on the right seems weaker. Use a dictionary for help. Then, discuss your answers with a classmate. You probably won't agree on all of your decisions.

1. carnage   (   ) killing

2. reminiscing   (   ) remembering

3. relentless   (   ) continuing

4. mundane   (   ) common

5. compulsory   (   ) necessary

6. vulnerable   (   ) sensitive

7. primal   (   ) first

8. esteem   (   ) regard

9. eradicating   (   ) erasing

10. dilemma   (   ) choice

"INEPT".....HERE IT IS..."UNFIT, AWKWARD, CLUMSY, OR BUNGLING"

2-18 © 1992 United Feature Syndicate, Inc.

PEANUTS reprinted by permission of United Feature Syndicate, Inc.

SKILLS FOCUS

Vocabulary Skills
Understand word denotations and connotations.

PLAY

From Balcony to Barrio

Tony and Maria are in love, but they come from different social worlds—Tony is Italian American, and Maria is Puerto Rican. Add to their problems the fact that Tony is the former ringleader of the Jets—a tough street-fighting gang—and Maria's brother, Bernardo, is the leader of the equally fearsome Sharks. If the story line sounds familiar, it should: The musical *West Side Story* takes its cue from *Romeo and Juliet.* This updated spin on Shakespeare's tale of star-crossed lovers is set in New York City in the 1950s.

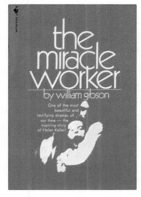

PLAY

Against the Odds

Six-year-old Helen Keller was considered a hopeless case. Blind, hearing impaired, and unable to speak, Helen was an angry prisoner of her own body. A teacher, Annie Sullivan, was asked to help—if help was possible. Slowly but surely the patient instructor taught Helen to "see" with her hands, to learn sign language, and to open herself to a world beyond darkness and silence. William Gibson's play **The Miracle Worker** stands as a classic story of two amazing young women—one a student, the other a teacher.

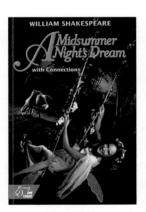

PLAY

Deep in the Forest

A wedding, an argument, a series of bungling play rehearsals, and misfortunes in love—these four plot elements are woven together in William Shakespeare's comedy **A Midsummer Night's Dream.** This play, which some critics consider Shakespeare's funniest and most imaginative, features characters ranging from fairies and fools to a king and a queen—all of whose paths intersect in surprising ways.

This title is available in the HRW Library.

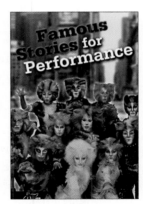

PLAYS

The Play's the Thing

Famous Stories for Performance includes stage plays and teleplays as well as some famous tales adapted for performance with a new dramatic spin. Here you'll find comedy (*Pyramus and Thisby* by William Shakespeare), a tragic true story (*Brian's Song* by William Blinn), and a legend to make the hair on the back of your neck stand up (*The Legend of Sleepy Hollow* by Washington Irving).

This title is available in the HRW Library.

Comparing a Play and a Film

Writing Assignment
Write an essay in which you compare a scene from a film with the play from which it was adapted and evaluate the film techniques the director uses.

Now that you've read William Shakespeare's *Romeo and Juliet*, you might feel compelled to go out and rent a video version of it. Since you already know the story's tragic ending, you'd think that you wouldn't be too upset when it's shown. Still, you might find yourself feeling choked up and sad in a way that you weren't when you read the original. Somehow, the filmmakers have affected you in a way the words written on the page didn't. How did they do that?

Prewriting

Choose a Film

Cameras . . . Rolling! Begin by choosing a film that has been adapted from a play. There are many films to choose from. For example, several of Shakespeare's plays have been adapted into films, including *Much Ado About Nothing, Romeo and Juliet,* and *A Midsummer Night's Dream.* You might prefer, instead, a more modern play, such as *The Odd Couple* or *The Glass Menagerie.* You may even find that there is more than one film version of a play that you've enjoyed.

Look for film adaptations of plays in video stores and libraries. If you have trouble finding or choosing a film adaptation, look for movie reviews in newspapers and magazines and on the Internet. Consider asking friends, teachers, or family members to recommend a film adaptation they've enjoyed.

Focus on One Scene

The Scene's the Thing You won't be able to analyze an entire film in a 1,500-word essay, so you'll focus your analysis on one important scene. Find that scene by watching a video of the film. As you watch, take notes on your responses to each scene. Is there a scene that draws a strong emotional reaction from you? Is there a scene that makes you think about your own life or the larger world? After you've watched the film, review your notes. The scene to which you had the strongest reactions will be the best one for you to focus on in your analysis.

Compare the Film with the Play

Altered Tales Now, read the same scene in the play and take notes on any differences between the written text of the play and the scene in the film. Filmmakers creating movies based on plays often use

SKILLS FOCUS

Writing Skills
Write an essay comparing a scene from a play with its film adaptation.

narrative techniques to make changes to the written play. For example, they may choose to cut dialogue, combine several characters into one, and change the setting of a scene. To analyze the film's narrative techniques, ask yourself the questions in the chart below.

IDENTIFYING NARRATIVE TECHNIQUES IN A FILM

Plot, Characters, and Setting: Did the filmmaker make changes to the characters, plot, or settings? For example, have characters, plot events, or settings been added or eliminated? If so, how do these changes affect the story?

Dialogue: Did the filmmaker cut or add lines of dialogue? Do cuts make the story simpler? Do additions help make ideas from the play clearer?

Theme: Did the filmmaker keep the original theme, or message, of the story? How does a change in theme change the viewer's reaction to the story?

Every Picture Tells a Story In addition to narrative techniques, filmmakers also have various **film techniques,** such as lighting, camera angles and shots, sound, and special effects, with which to tell their stories. These techniques enable the filmmaker to create reactions in viewers that are very different from what readers experience. For example, when you watch a film, you often see close-up shots that show characters' emotions. However, when you read a play, you rely only on word clues to understand the characters' feelings. To analyze the film techniques used in the scene you've chosen, ask yourself the following questions.

IDENTIFYING FILM TECHNIQUES

Camera Shots and Angles: What types of camera shots are used—close-ups, long shots? From what angles does the camera shoot the characters and actions? What effects do the shots and angles create?

Lighting: How is lighting used in the scene? Does the lighting affect the mood of the scene?

Sound: What music or sound effects are present in the scene? How do they affect your reactions to the scene?

Special Effects: What special effects are included that you would not expect to see in a stage production of the play? Are the special effects distracting? Are they helpful to your understanding of the story?

On the next page are some of the notes one viewer took of the examples of narrative and film techniques he found while comparing a scene from Shakespeare's *Romeo and Juliet* to Franco Zeffirelli's 1968 film version of the play. He will use this information as **evidence** in his paper to support his thesis statement.

Plot
- The duel between Paris and Romeo at the tomb is cut out altogether.

Dialogue
- Only Prince Escalus speaks at the end. Friar Laurence's explanation of the events is cut.

Lighting
- Romeo first sees Juliet in blue-tinted darkness. White light shines on her alone.
- At the end, they are shown in golden light, as if to show the purity of their love.

Sound
- Ominous music plays as Romeo enters the tomb, but fades to crickets chirping.

Write Your Thesis Statement

What Say You? A filmmaker combines narrative and film techniques to create intellectual and emotional responses, known as **aesthetic effects,** in the film's viewers. The **thesis,** or main idea, of your essay identifies the effects created by the techniques.

To write a **thesis statement,** ask yourself, "What response was the filmmaker trying to create?" and "How did the techniques affect me as a viewer?" You'll find the answers to these questions in your notes. The example below shows one student's working thesis statement.

> Franco Zeffirelli uses narrative and film techniques to reduce the final scene to an emotional essence—the two young lovers and their tragic fate.

Organize Your Essay

Getting Your Act Together Your essay really has two parts: the first part compares the narrative techniques of the film with the original play, and the second part analyzes and evaluates the film techniques. To help your readers see how your ideas fit together, organize your essay in these two ways:

- **Point-by-point order:** Discuss the narrative techniques by comparing each narrative technique from the play to the corresponding one from the film.

- **Order of importance:** Discuss the film techniques by evaluating the most important film technique first and the least important one last, or vice versa.

| DO THIS →

SKILLS FOCUS

Writing Skills
Establish a thesis statement.
Organize the essay.

PRACTICE & APPLY 1 Compare a film adaptation of a play with the original by analyzing the filmmaker's use of narrative and film techniques. Then, write your thesis statement and organize your ideas.

Writing

Comparing a Play and a Film

A Writer's Framework

Introduction

- Engage your readers immediately with an interesting opening, such as a question, a quote from the play, or a relevant anecdote.
- Identify the original play and the film and their creators.
- Clearly state your thesis.

Body

- Compare the narrative techniques, and organize them in point-by-point order.
- Analyze and evaluate the film techniques, and organize them in order of importance.
- Include specific references to the play and film to support your discussion.

Conclusion

- Remind readers of your thesis by restating it.
- Include a concluding thought or question to leave readers with something to think about.

A Writer's Model

A Rose by Any Other Name

Can Franco Zeffirelli's *Romeo and Juliet* smell quite as sweet as Shakespeare's original play? The 1968 film adaptation remains largely faithful to the original. The unfolding of the tragic love theme in both the play and the film is dramatic and moving. However, Zeffirelli uses narrative and film techniques to reduce the final scene to its emotional essence—the two young lovers and their tragic fate.

The final scene when Romeo and Juliet die serves as a good example of the choices Zeffirelli makes to get to the play's emotional essence. He changes the scene by cutting out plot events and dialogue, and by moving the final setting to a different location. Zeffirelli cuts out the scene at the tomb where Paris arrives, fights with Romeo, and is killed. By cutting the duel, the audience can focus on the tragic events that are about to unfold. Also, at the very end of the play, the entire cast comes onstage, and the Friar explains the tragedy. Zeffirelli moves this gathering to another place and time—the steps of the church on the following morning. The Friar's speech of explanation is cut out entirely, and the Prince bitterly tells the Capulets and Montagues that "all are punished" (V.3.295). The Prince's speech leaves the viewers to consider how the story would have ended if the Capulets and Montagues were not enemies.

INTRODUCTION
Introduction of film, play, and creators

Thesis statement

Comparison of narrative techniques

Plot

Setting

Dialogue

(continued)

(continued)

Discussion of
film techniques

Camera shots

Zeffirelli also uses a variety of film techniques to create an emotional response beyond that created by the language of the play. Different camera shots allow the viewer to understand the emotions portrayed in the last scene when Romeo and Juliet die. For example, a long shot from the side provides an overview of the scene. Viewers see Juliet's still form and Romeo's anguished face as he speaks to her. Then, the camera moves to a close-up of Romeo's face as he sobs and drinks the poison. Viewers can experience Romeo's sadness and desperation as they watch him in this shot. Next, viewers see the extreme close-up on Juliet's left hand—the same one Romeo kissed as he died—as the hand stirs with life. Viewers feel hope and anguish at the same time, because even though Juliet is alive, she will soon find that her true love is not. The camera moves back to show Juliet's discovery of Romeo dead by her side. She then stabs herself and rests her head on Romeo's chest. The final close-up shot of the two lovers' faces illustrates the irony of the situation. In life the two could not be together, but in death they can.

Sound and lighting

Music and lighting also play a role in bringing out the emotional aspects of the scene. As Romeo enters this scene, he's shown on horseback approaching the tomb at night as ominous, sad music plays. The quiet of the nighttime graveyard is emphasized when the music fades and only the sound of chirping crickets remains. When Romeo enters the tomb, he sees Juliet in the blue-tinted darkness. A soft white light shines on her alone, giving a false sense of peace. As Romeo kisses her, the music swells in the full orchestral version of their love theme. Music is also played softly as Juliet's hand feels the edge of the stone bier and then her dress, but trumpets interrupt the soft music when Juliet sees Romeo dead. The rest of the scene is shot in a beautiful golden light focused on the two lovers alone, illustrating the purity of their love.

CONCLUSION

Restatement of
thesis

Concluding thought

By concentrating on the deaths of Juliet and Romeo, Zeffirelli creates an emotionally wrenching and powerful scene that expresses the heart of Shakespeare's famous tragedy. Zeffirelli's treatment of this ancient tale of love allows the viewer to experience fully the tragedy of these "star-crossed lovers" (Prologue, line 6).

go.
hrw
.com

INTERNET

More Writer's
Models

Keyword: LE7 9-11

PRACTICE & APPLY 2 Use the framework and Writer's Model to write the first draft of your essay. Be sure to include parenthetical citations whenever you quote lines from the play. For more on **giving credit to sources,** see page 716.

Revising

Revise Your Essay

The Big Picture The revision process is as important as any other phase of the writing process. Some even say it's the *most* important stage. When you revise, you shape both your ideas and how you express them so that they can best achieve their desired effects: strong content, clear organization, and effective style.

PEER REVIEW

As you revise, exchange papers with a classmate. He or she can help ensure that your ideas are organized in two ways: point-by-point and order of importance.

▷ **First Reading: Content and Organization** Evaluate the content and organization of your essay using the guidelines below as a **think sheet.** First, answer the questions in the left-hand column. If you need help answering them, refer to the tips in the middle column. Then, make the changes suggested by using the revision techniques in the right-hand column.

Rubric: Comparing a Play and a Film

Evaluation Questions	▶ Tips	▶ Revision Techniques
❶ Is the opening engaging? Are the original play, its film version, and their creators introduced in the first paragraph?	▶ **Underline** the engaging opening. **Bracket** the introduction of the subjects.	▶ **Add** a relevant anecdote, an interesting quotation, or an intriguing question. **Add** a sentence introducing the play, film, and their creators.
❷ Does the introduction include a clear thesis statement that identifies the response the filmmaker was trying to create?	▶ **Highlight** the thesis statement. **Circle** the part that identifies the filmmaker's intended response.	▶ **Add** a thesis statement, or **reword** the thesis statement to identify the response the filmmaker intended.
❸ Does evidence support the discussion of each narrative and film technique?	▶ **Put a star** by each example from the play or film.	▶ **Add** evidence, or **elaborate** on existing evidence.
❹ Is the essay well organized so that the reader can easily follow ideas?	▶ **Label** the specific narrative techniques. **Number** the film techniques.	▶ **Rearrange** the narrative techniques so that they are in point-by-point order. **Reorder** the film techniques so that they are arranged in order of importance.
❺ Does the conclusion restate the thesis? Does it contain an interesting concluding thought or question?	▶ **Highlight** the sentence that restates the thesis. **Circle** the concluding thought or question.	▶ **Add** a sentence restating the thesis. If necessary, **add** a concluding thought or summary.

→ **Second Reading: Style** Once you've revised the content and organization of your essay, you can concentrate on its style, or how you've expressed your ideas. One way to improve the style is to use active instead of passive voice. When a writer uses the **active voice,** the subject of the verb performs the action. When a writer uses the **passive voice,** the subject of the verb receives the action. The passive voice takes the attention away from the subject. Look at the following examples.

Passive Voice The tomb **is broken** into by Romeo.
Active Voice Romeo **breaks** into the tomb.

Notice how simple and direct the second sentence is. Follow the guidelines below to make sure your essay uses the active voice.

Style Guidelines

Evaluation Question	▶ **Tip**	▶ **Revision Technique**
● Does the essay contain verbs in the active voice?	▶ **Double underline** all *be* verbs (e.g., *be, am, is, are, was, were, been*). Do not underline *be* verbs that express a state of being or that are in quotations.	▶ **Reword** half of the *be* verb sentences so that the subject of the sentence performs the verb.

ANALYZING THE REVISION PROCESS
Study these revisions, and answer the questions that follow.

The Friar's speech of explanation is cut out entirely, and

reword
Prince bitterly tells the
the ᴧCapulets and Montagues ~~are bitterly told by the Prince~~ that

elaborate
"all are punished."ᴧ*The Prince's speech leaves the viewers to consider how the story would have ended if the Capulets and Montagues were not enemies.*

Responding to the Revision Process
1. Why do you think the writer revised the first sentence?
2. How does adding the last sentence improve the passage?

SKILLS FOCUS

Writing Skills
Revise for content and style.

PRACTICE & APPLY ③ Revise the content, organization, and style of your essay, using the guidelines in this section. Exchange essays with a peer to get another person's ideas on how you might revise. Reviewing a peer's essay may even give you ideas on how to revise your own.

Publishing

Proofread and Publish Your Essay

A Last Look After you've revised your essay, be sure to proofread it. Check for and correct any errors in grammar, usage, and mechanics. Have someone else—a classmate, parent, or friend—proofread your essay, too. Two sets of eyes are always better than one since the other person may catch errors that you missed.

Finally, It's Showtime! Now that you have written, revised, and proofread your essay, it's time for others to read it. Here are some suggestions for publication.

- Watch the film with your family and let them read your essay. Be prepared to discuss your essay and listen to their ideas, thoughts, feelings, and opinions, too.

- With a group of classmates, form a panel discussion about the techniques filmmakers use in their movies. Use your essays as a springboard into the discussion.

- Post your essay to an online movie database or video store. Many invite people to send in comments—both positive and negative—of the videos they discuss or sell.

Reflect on Your Essay

That's a Wrap! After a sporting event, coaches and athletes often review videotapes of the game, match, or race to evaluate individual or team performance. This gives them the opportunity to see what they did well and where they may need improvement before their next outing. You, too, should look back on what you have done. Think about what you've learned in the process of writing this essay. Ask yourself the following questions to improve future writing assignments. The questions will also give you insight on how well you understand media presentations.

- What revisions do you think strengthened your essay the most? Why?

- What additional narrative and film techniques would you have used if you were doing a film adaptation of the same play? Explain each of your answers.

- How did writing this essay help you better understand the choices made by filmmakers?

PRACTICE & APPLY 4 Proofread your essay one last time. Publish your essay by using one of the ideas on this page, or think of your own publishing idea. Finally, write down answers to the reflection questions above.

> **TIP** Careful proofreading will help you make sure that your essay follows the **conventions** of standard American English. For example, you may have listed several different narrative or film techniques in one sentence. Check to make sure that you have used commas correctly between items in a series. For more on **serial commas,** see Commas, 12f, in the Language Handbook.

SKILLS FOCUS

Writing Skills
Proofread, especially for correct use of serial commas.

Analyzing and Evaluating Speeches

Speaking Assignment
Analyze and evaluate a historically significant speech to uncover its impact on an audience.

In *Romeo and Juliet,* Prince Escalus issues a speech to convince the Capulets and Montagues, who "have thrice disturbed the quiet of our streets," to stop their feuding. In history, as in literature, speakers often use the power of persuasion to convince others to take action. In this workshop you'll have the opportunity to look at a **historically significant speech** and determine what made it so persuasive.

Select a Speech

Actions Speak Louder You can find many historically important speeches as written texts, audio recordings, and videotapes at the library, in your history textbook, and on the Internet. Consider what historical events interest you, and do a little research to find what great speeches were given at that point in time. Instead, you may wish to start with an issue that interests you, such as civil rights, space exploration, or freedom of religion, and see what great speeches have been given on either side of those issues. Try to find a speech that you can listen to and watch instead of just read. Great speakers often rely on not only their words, but also their voices, gestures, and body postures to communicate their messages.

Analyze Content

Getting into the Arguments Begin your analysis by viewing the speech you've selected. Pay close attention to the content, the **important points** the speaker wants to make. As you identify these important points, you will probably notice that the speech contains persuasive elements. Keep in mind, though, that a speaker cannot persuade an audience just by stating an opinion. He or she must provide **arguments** that convince listeners to change their minds or take action. Here are some common types of arguments you will find.

Listening and Speaking Skills
Analyze a historically significant speech.

INTERNET
Speeches
Keyword: LE7 9-11

- **Causation** shows how a cause-effect relationship supports the speaker's opinion.

- **Analogies** make literal comparisons between things that are generally unlike.

- **Appeals to authority** refer to a trustworthy or knowledgeable authority or expert.

- **Emotional appeals** use language to stir feelings of happiness, sadness, or anger in listeners.

- **Logical appeals** speak to the listeners' minds through facts, statistics, anecdotes (brief stories), and examples.

Rhetorical Devices   To make their arguments effective and memorable, speakers must master rhetoric, the art of speaking or writing well. Over thousands of years, people who speak effectively have developed **rhetorical devices**—certain ways of using language to make their messages attention-getting, persuasive, and memorable. The following chart lists and defines some rhetorical devices you might find when listening to a speech.

TIP Some speakers use elaborate language to cover up a lack of substance or to mislead listeners. Because of this misuse, some people have negative feelings about the word *rhetoric*.

RHETORICAL DEVICES

Allusion: an indirect reference to literature or an actual person, event, or place

Metaphor: an imaginative comparison between unlike things

Repetition: repeating the same important words or phrases

Diction: word choice that creates specific reactions from the audience

Parallelism: using the same **syntax,** or sentence structure, to point out a similarity in ideas

Analyze Organization

Follow Me   Speakers organize their messages according to two different approaches. With the **deductive** approach, they state their thesis first, then deliver their reasons and support. Speakers using this approach start with general ideas, then move to more specific ones. With the **inductive** approach, speakers present reasons and support first, building to a thesis statement. Speakers using the inductive approach usually move their audience from thinking about specific ideas to more general ones. Whichever approach speakers choose, they must make sure that the organization of their ideas is **clear** and **coherent.**

Analyze Delivery

How Are We Feeling Today?   In addition to **language,** a speaker's **delivery,** or use of voice and body, often sets the tone and mood of the speech. **Tone** is the speaker's attitude toward the subject and audience. **Mood** is the overall impression the speech makes on the audience. A speaker must choose a tone that is appropriate for the audience and purpose. For instance, a speaker who uses an angry tone when speaking to people who disagree with his opinion might antagonize his listeners, creating a hostile mood. A thoughtful, respectful tone, on the other hand, creates a more positive mood.

SKILLS FOCUS

Listening and Speaking Skills
Analyze rhetorical devices, organization, delivery, tone, and mood.

Quick guide!

Speakers often use verbal and nonverbal delivery techniques, like those shown in the following chart, to convey tone and mood, and to get their points across to an audience.

DELIVERY TECHNIQUES

Verbal	Nonverbal
Emphasis is the stress a speaker puts on certain words and phrases. Speakers emphasize key ideas or points in their speeches by saying those words with a little more volume.	**Gestures** are body movements that emphasize emotions or ideas. Good speakers use natural gestures, such as nodding their heads, shrugging their shoulders, or pointing at the audience.
Pauses are small silences in speaking. A good speaker uses pauses to let his or her ideas soak in. Pauses also tell you that what the speaker has just said or is about to say is important.	**Facial expressions** clue listeners in to the speaker's feelings. For example, a smile can suggest warmth and sincerity, while a frown might show that the speaker is angry and wants you to know why.
Enunciation is the clarity with which speakers pronounce their words. Good speakers always want their ideas to be clearly understood. Poor enunciation makes listeners strain, giving them the impression that the speaker does not care about them or the topic.	**Posture** is how the speaker stands. A speaker standing straight and alert suggests confidence in his or her topic, while a slouching speaker suggests that he or she is disinterested and does not truly care about the topic.

A Speaker's Model The following is an excerpt from John F. Kennedy's 1962 "We choose to go to the moon . . . " speech, which helped convince Americans to support the U.S. space exploration program. The annotations in the model's margin identify arguments and rhetorical devices used in the speech. If you're able to listen to or view this speech, pay close attention to Kennedy's use of verbal and nonverbal techniques.

Causation
Emotional appeal

Metaphor and repetition

If . . . history . . . teaches us anything, it is that man, in this quest for knowledge and progress, is determined and cannot be deterred. The exploration of space will go ahead, whether we join in it or not, and it is one of the great adventures of all time, and no nation which expects to be the leader of other nations can expect to stay behind in this race for space.

Those who came before us made certain that this country rode the first waves of the industrial revolution, the first waves of modern invention, and the first waves of nuclear power, and this generation does not intend to founder in the backwash of the coming age of space. We mean to be part of it—we mean to lead it. For the eyes of the world now look into space, to the moon and to the planets beyond, and we have vowed that we shall not see it governed by a hostile flag of conquest, but by a banner of freedom and peace. We have vowed that we shall not see space filled with weapons of mass destruction, but with instruments of knowledge and understanding.

    Yet the vows of this Nation can only be fulfilled if we in this Nation are first, and, therefore, we intend to be first. In short, our leadership in science and industry, our hopes for peace and security, our obligations to ourselves as well as others, all require us to make this effort, to solve these mysteries, to solve them for the good of all men, and to become the world's leading space-faring nation.

Emotional appeal
Parallelism

Repetition

Causation
Repetition

Evaluate a Speech

Put It All Together The most important test of a good persuasive speech is your own reaction. A speech should make you think more deeply about a subject and might change your mind or prompt you to take action. Use the following questions to evaluate the effectiveness and quality of a persuasive speech, stating your own **judgments** about it.

EVALUATING PERSUASIVE SPEECHES

Content and Organization	Delivery
What **arguments** and **rhetorical devices** did the speaker use? Was there a variety of arguments and devices?	How did the speaker make good use of **emphasis, enunciation,** and **pauses**? Were his or her **diction** and **syntax** clear?
What **evidence** (facts, statistics, or expert testimony) did the speaker provide to support his or her ideas?	Did the speaker use **facial expressions, gestures,** and **posture** to express tone and mood? If so, describe them.
Were the speaker's main points **clear** and **coherent**—connected to each other and to the main idea? Describe the organizational pattern.	Did the speaker's **overall delivery** capture your attention and help you understand the speech? Explain.

PRACTICE & APPLY 5 Use the information in this workshop to select and analyze a historically significant speech. Then, write a one-paragraph evaluation of the speech's quality and effectiveness. Depending on your access to audio-visual resources, choose one of two options:

- View a recorded speech (on tape or disc, or on the Internet), analyzing the content, organization, and delivery.

- Read the text of a written speech, concentrating on its content and organization. Pay close attention to how the language affects the mood and tone of the speech.

SKILLS FOCUS

Listening and Speaking Skills
Evaluate a historically significant speech.

Test Practice

Analyzing Drama

DIRECTIONS: Read this excerpt from a comedy. Then, read and respond to the questions that follow.

from Barefoot in the Park

Neil Simon

Here's the climactic scene, Act II, Scene 2, of Neil Simon's comedy Barefoot in the Park. *As the scene opens, a young couple—Corie and Paul—have just returned from a late evening with Corie's widowed mother and their colorful next-door neighbor. This neighbor is a gourmet, and he has taken Paul, Corie, and her mother to an unusual restaurant on Staten Island, in New York City. Now he is politely accompanying Corie's mother home to New Jersey. Corie has had a perfectly wonderful evening; Paul has not had a good time at all.*

Corie. What are you so angry about, Paul?

Paul (*crossing to the closet*). I just told you. I felt terrible for your mother. (*He gets the wallet out of his jacket pocket.*)

Corie (*following after him to the front of the couch*). Why? Where is she at this very minute? Alone with probably the most attractive man she's ever met. Don't tell me *that* doesn't beat . . . hair curlers and *The Late Late Show.*

Paul (*crossing onto bedroom landing*). Oh, I can just hear it now. What sparkling conversation. He's probably telling her about a chicken cacciatore he once cooked for the High Lama of Tibet, and she's sitting there shoving pink pills in her mouth.

Corie (*taking her coat from the couch and putting it on the armchair at right*). You can never tell what people talk about when they're alone.

Paul. I don't understand how you can be so unconcerned about this. (*He goes into the bedroom.*)

Corie (*moving to the stairs*). Unconcerned . . . I'm plenty concerned. Do you think I'm going to get one wink of sleep until that phone rings tomorrow? I'm scared to death for my mother. But I'm grateful there's finally the opportunity for something to be scared about . . . (*She moves right, then turns back.*) What I'm really concerned about is you!

Paul (*bursts out of the bedroom, nearly slamming through the door*). Me? Me?

Corie. I'm beginning to wonder if you're capable of *having* a good time.

Paul. Why? Because I like to wear my gloves in the winter?

Corie. No. Because there isn't the least bit of adventure in you. Do you know what you are? You're a Watcher. There are Watchers in this world and there are Do-ers. And the Watchers sit around watching the Do-ers do. Well, tonight you watched and I did.

Paul (*moves down the stairs to* CORIE). Yeah . . . Well, it was harder to watch what you did than it was for you to *do* what I was watching. (*He goes back up the stairs to the landing.*)

SKILLS FOCUS

Pages 1052–1055 cover **Literary Skills** Understand elements of drama.

Corie. You won't let your hair down for a minute? You couldn't even relax for one night. Boy, Paul, sometimes you act like a . . . a . . . (*She gets her shoes from under the couch.*)

Paul (*stopping on the landing*). What . . . ? A stuffed shirt?

Corie (*drops the shoes on the couch*). I didn't say that.

Paul. That's what you're implying.

Corie (*moves to the right armchair and begins to take off her jewelry*). That's what you're anticipating. I didn't say you're a stuffed shirt. But you are extremely proper and dignified.

Paul. I'm proper and dignified? (*He moves to* CORIE.) When . . . ? When was I proper and dignified? . . .

Corie. Always. You're always dressed right, you always look right, you always say the right things. You're very close to being perfect.

Paul (*hurt to the quick*). That's . . . that's a *rotten* thing to say.

Corie (*moves to* PAUL). I have never seen you without a jacket. I always feel like such a slob compared to you. Before we were married, I was sure you slept with a tie.

Paul. No, no. Just for very *formal* sleeps.

Corie. You can't even walk into a candy store and ask the lady for a Tootsie Roll. (*Playing the scene out, she moves down to right side of the couch.*) You've got to walk up to the counter and point at it and say, "I'll have that thing in the brown-and-white wrapper."

Paul (*moving to the bedroom door*). That's ridiculous.

Corie. And you're not. That's just the trouble. (*She crosses to the foot of the stairs.*) Like Thursday night. You wouldn't

walk barefoot with me in Washington Square Park. Why not?

Paul (*moving to the head of the stairs*). Very simple answer. It was seventeen degrees.

Corie (*moves back to the chair and continues taking down her hair*). Exactly. That's very sensible and logical. Except it isn't any fun.

Paul (*moves down the stairs to the couch*). You know, maybe I *am* too proper and dignified for you. Maybe you would have been happier with someone a little more colorful and flamboyant . . . like the Greek! (*He starts back to the bedroom.*)

Corie. Well, he'd be a lot more laughs than a stuffed shirt.

Paul (*turns back on the landing*). Oh, oh . . . I thought you said I wasn't.

Corie. Well, you are now.

Paul (*reflectively*). I'm not going to listen to this . . . I'm not going to listen . . . (*He starts for the bedroom.*) I've got a case in court in the morning.

Corie (*moves left*). Where are you going?

Paul. To sleep.

Corie. *Now?* How can you sleep now?

Paul (*steps up on the bed and turns back, leaning on the door jamb*). I'm going to close my eyes and count knichis.° Good night!

Corie. You can't go to sleep now. We're having a fight.

Paul. *You* have the fight. When you're through, turn off the lights. (*He turns back into the bedroom.*)

Corie. Ooh, that gets me insane. You can even control your emotions.

Paul (*storms out to the head of the stairs*).

° **knichis** (nē′chēz) *n. pl.:* unusual appetizer they had eaten with dinner.

Look, I'm just as upset as you are. . . . (*He controls himself.*). But when I get hungry, I eat. And when I get tired, I sleep. You eat and sleep, too. Don't deny it, I've seen you . . .

Corie (*moves right with a grand gesture*). Not in the middle of a crisis.

Paul. What crisis? We're just yelling a little.

Corie. You don't consider this a crisis? Our whole marriage hangs in the balance.

Paul (*sits on the steps*). It does? When did that happen?

Corie. Just now. It's suddenly very clear that you and I have absolutely *nothing* in common.

Paul. Why? Because I won't walk barefoot in the park in winter? . . .

Corie (*seething*). Don't oversimplify this. I'm angry. Can't you see that?

Paul (*brings his hands to his eyes, peers at her through imaginary binoculars, and then looks at his watch*). Corie, it's two-fifteen. If I can fall asleep in about half an hour, I can get about five hours' sleep. I'll call you from court tomorrow, and we can fight over the phone. (*He gets up and moves to the bedroom.*)

Corie. You will *not* go to sleep. You will stay here and fight to save our marriage.

Paul (*in the doorway*). If our marriage hinges on breathing fish balls and pooflapoo pie, it's not worth saving. . . . I am now going to crawl into our tiny little single bed. If you care to join me, we will be sleeping from left to right tonight. (*He goes into the bedroom and slams the door.*)

Corie. You won't discuss it . . . You're *afraid* to discuss it . . . I married a coward!! . . . (*She takes a shoe from the couch and throws it at the bedroom door.*)

Paul (*opens the door*). Corie, would you bring in a pail? The closet's dripping.

Corie. Ohh, I hate you! I really, really hate you!

Paul (*storms to the head of the stairs*). Corie, there is one thing I learned in court. Be careful when you're tired and angry. You might say something you will soon regret. I-am-now-tired-and-angry.

Corie. And a coward.

Paul (*comes down the stairs to her at right of the couch*). And I will now say something I will soon regret . . . OK, Corie, maybe you're right. Maybe we have nothing in common. Maybe we rushed into this marriage a little too fast. Maybe Love isn't enough. Maybe two people should have to take more than a blood test. Maybe they should be checked for common sense, understanding, and emotional maturity.

Corie (*that hurt*). All right . . . Why don't you get it passed in the Supreme Court? Only those couples bearing a letter from their psychiatrists proving they're well adjusted will be permitted to be married.

Paul. You're impossible.

Corie. You're unbearable.

Paul. You belong in a nursery school.

Corie. It's a lot more fun than the Home for the Fuddy Duddies.

Paul (*reaches out his hand to her*). All right, Corie, let's not get . . .

Corie. Don't you touch me . . . Don't you touch me . . .

1. Corie is mad at Paul because he —
   A   insulted her mother
   B   didn't like the restaurant
   C   has a court case in the morning
   D   doesn't know how to have fun

2. Paul describes Corie's **character** as —
   F   impossible
   G   charming
   H   mature
   J   serious

3. Because *Barefoot in the Park* is a **comedy,** you can predict that by the end of the play —
   A   Paul and Corie will resolve their differences
   B   Paul and Corie will get divorced
   C   there will be a funny scene with the neighbor
   D   Corie's mother will move in with them

4. If the play were a **tragedy** instead of a comedy, it might end with —
   F   Corie's mother getting married
   G   the death of Paul and Corie
   H   Paul and Corie moving to another apartment
   J   Paul's winning his case in court

5. This excerpt from the play consists of —
   A   monologues
   B   narration
   C   dialogue
   D   asides

6. Which of the following stage directions tells you something about the **scene design**?
   F   *hurt to the quick*
   G   *crossing onto bedroom landing*
   H   *He controls himself.*
   J   *reaches out his hand to her*

7. If this scene were followed by a **soliloquy,** it might be delivered by —
   A   Paul telling Corie how he really feels about her
   B   Paul and Corie apologizing to each other for getting so angry
   C   Corie alone talking about how much she loves Paul
   D   Corie's mother telling Paul and Corie what a good time she had

Constructed Response

8. Although the playwright presents a comical argument in this excerpt, what serious topic does he also want the audience to think about? Use evidence from the play excerpt to support your opinion.

Collection 11: Skills Review

Vocabulary Skills

Multiple-Meaning Words

DIRECTIONS: Choose the answer in which the underlined word is used in the same way it is used in the passage from *Visitor from Forest Hills*.

1. *"In the bedroom one opened valise containing a young woman's street clothes rests on the floor."*
   A The kindergartner rests after lunch every day.
   B Our success rests on the efforts of everyone on the team.
   C The singer caught his breath during rests in the music.
   D The book rests on the table, opened to her favorite story.

2. *"ROY turns and storms into the bedroom."*
   F Heavy storms are predicted for tonight.
   G The attacking army storms the enemy's camp.
   H Angry at her friend, she storms out of the house.
   J The mayor was faced with storms of criticism.

3. *"He dashes for the bedroom door, not even detouring around the bed. . . ."*
   A The death of the hero dashes the reader's hope for a happy ending.
   B Every morning, Anika dashes out of the house to catch the bus.
   C The ocean current dashes the boats onto the sandbar.
   D Use dashes in a sentence to indicate breaks in thought.

4. *"NORMA is crushed. He looks at her sympathetically."*
   F When Jamal heard the sad news, he was crushed.
   G Passengers on the crowded bus were crushed in the aisle.
   H The rebellion against the dictator was crushed by the troops.
   J We add syrup to crushed ice to make a refreshing summer treat.

5. *"NORMA has frozen in misery by the bedroom door after letting go of the coat."*
   A Frightened by the noise, the children were frozen in their tracks.
   B The countess's frozen manners cast a chill on the party.
   C I lost my right glove, and now my hand is frozen.
   D The children skated happily on the frozen pond.

6. *"The front doorbell rings."*
   F Sarena and Soo Lin exchange friendship rings.
   G The clock in the town hall rings every hour.
   H The clowns perform in all three rings of the circus.
   J You can tell a tree's age by looking at its rings.

SKILLS FOCUS

Vocabulary Skills
Understand multiple-meaning words.

Collection 11: Skills Review

Writing Skills

DIRECTIONS: Read the following paragraph from a draft of a student's essay comparing a film scene with the play on which it is based. Then, read and answer the questions below it.

(1) While much of the dialogue in the film *The Miracle Worker* is directly from the pages of William Gibson's play, some differences do exist. (2) In the play, Annie tells James Keller that losing her brother, Jimmie, has taught her the importance of never giving up. (3) In the film, this scene is replaced with several in which Annie is haunted by Jimmie's voice in her dreams. (4) In these scenes, film techniques enhance the emotional appeal. (5) Tense and piercing music grows in the background as Annie responds in whispers to Jimmie's desperate cries. (6) The different camera shots also draw an emotional reaction.

1. Which sentence could be added before sentence 2 to provide a clear thesis statement?

   A   The film is much better than the play's text because it shows what Annie looks like.

   B   The film uses narrative and film techniques to create sympathy for Annie Sullivan.

   C   The film follows the play so closely that you can read the words from the play as the actors are saying them.

   D   In the film, conversation is not as important as the action, so many dialogue scenes have been cut.

2. What could be added to sentence 2 to make the sentence clearer?

   F   an identification of the act and scene

   G   a list of characters in the scene

   H   an explanation of Jimmie's death

   J   the year the film was made

3. Which sentence could be added to elaborate on sentence 4?

   A   The scenes include various camera shots and angles.

   B   The sound techniques in the film are no more effective than in the script.

   C   The scenes foreshadow that Annie will not be a good teacher.

   D   The dark lighting in these scenes produces sympathy for Annie.

4. What sentence below could be added to support the point in sentence 6?

   F   Annie's complex character makes viewers feel sympathy for her.

   G   The audience can't see Jimmie, yet they know that he's crying.

   H   The camera zooms in to reveal the tormented features of Annie's face.

   J   The light doesn't darken or change when Annie hears Jimmie's voice.

SKILLS FOCUS

Writing Skills
Write an essay comparing a scene from a play with its film adaptation.

Collection 12

Creating Computer Games

Informational Reading Focus:
Consumer and Workplace Documents

by Flo Ota De Lange *and*
Sheri Henderson

Introduction

The World of Computer Game Development

The only way of discovering the limits of the possible is to venture a little way past them into the impossible.

—Sir Arthur C. Clarke's Second Law

Developing Computer Games

In this collection you'll take a journey into the world of computer game development. Along the way you'll imagine that you're a computer-game-savvy high school student who wants to break into the field. Here's a little background on the subject.

If you have been using computers and playing computer games your entire life, it's easy to think that they've always been around; but in fact they had a beginning. The first video computer game was created in 1962 by Steve Russell, and it was played on a $120,000 computer about the size of a car.

Computer games and computer technology have come a long way in a short time. Not so long ago computers were too huge for anyone to imagine that they could ever be portable. Today computers can be carried in one hand, and computer games are mass marketed and played by people all around the world.

Using Informational Materials

What brought about such far-reaching changes so quickly? Vision, talent, focus, hard work, and communication. Communication? Yes. The transformation of that first video computer game into a growth industry involved a lot of communication using various **informational materials: consumer documents, public documents, workplace documents, technical documents, business letters,** and more.

It may seem that computer games, with all their excitement, flashy colors, and action, have nothing in common with black-and-white informational materials printed on a page. But if you dig a little deeper, all sorts of connections can be uncovered. (Here's an interesting connection we discovered: Steve Russell based that first computer game on the science fiction writings of E. E. "Doc" Smith. Doc Smith not only wrote great science fiction stories, but he also held a doctorate in chemical engineering. He was the researcher who figured out how to get powdered sugar to stick to doughnuts!)

As you move through this collection, you'll learn about, and become skilled in using, consumer documents, workplace documents, bibliographies, business letters, and other communication tools. Keep in mind that these informational materials enable people to move beyond the possible into the impossible. Right now someone somewhere is dreaming about cracking open the future of computer games. Could that person be you?

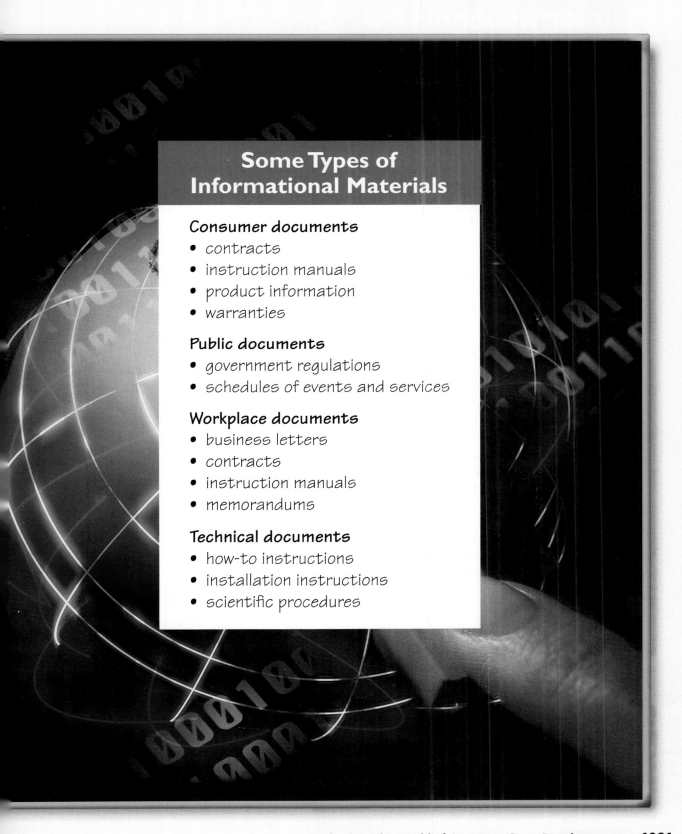

Some Types of Informational Materials

Consumer documents
- contracts
- instruction manuals
- product information
- warranties

Public documents
- government regulations
- schedules of events and services

Workplace documents
- business letters
- contracts
- instruction manuals
- memorandums

Technical documents
- how-to instructions
- installation instructions
- scientific procedures

Reading Consumer Documents

Consumer Documents: From the Manufacturer to You

Picture before you an unopened box. In it is the latest and greatest computer game console. Its graphics capabilities will have you thinking real instead of virtual. And the sound chip! Just wait until your friends hear this!

Like most people, you rivet your attention on getting that game console unpacked and loaded. In your hurry to get it out of its box, you let a sheaf of official-looking papers slide to the floor. There they lie, hidden in a scramble of packing litter—the **consumer documents: the warranty,** the **product information,** and the **instruction manual.** They are down on the floor in danger of being thrown out when the parental command rescues them: "Puh*leez* clean this mess up."

These consumer documents can make a big difference in how much you enjoy your new game. Before you put them away in a safe place, it's important to read them carefully. To be sure you understand what you are reading, let's take a brief look at the elements and features of consumer documents.

Elements of Consumer Documents

All computer game consoles include certain **elements,** such as a control device, sound and video capability, and a way to load and run the programs. However, you chose the game console in the box in front of you because it offers specific **features** you want, such as a programmable wireless joystick, surround-sound, 3-D video resolution, and DVD. These elements and features combine to make the game fun to play.

The consumer documents that came with the game are also important to your satisfaction. Here are some types of consumer documents and the **elements,** or types of information, that each document provides:

- **product information**—descriptions of what the game console will do
- **contract**—information on the legal uses of the game's software
- **warranty**—details on what happens if the game console does not work as promised and what you must do to receive service
- **instruction manual**—instructions on how to use the game console
- **technical directions**—directions for installation and use

Pages 1062–1064 cover
Reading Skills
Understand elements of consumer documents.

INCLUDES:
- Console
- Instruction Manual
- Warranty
- Technical Directions

Features of Consumer Documents

All electronic equipment comes with these same types of consumer documents, but the documents' features may vary from product to product. For instance, all warranties specify what the manufacturer will do if the product fails, but one company might offer only repair while another will give you a choice of getting your money back. When two products seem nearly identical, the features mentioned in the consumer materials can tip your decision: Does the contract offer technical support that is available 24/7? Is the instruction manual reader friendly?

As you read the following consumer documents, marginal notes will help you identify key elements and features.

WYSIWYGAME ARTS

Limited Warranty
WYSIWYGame Arts makes the following limited warranties. These limited warranties extend to the original consumer purchaser or any person receiving this product as a gift from the original consumer purchaser and to no other purchaser or transferee.

Element: warranty eligibility.
Feature: extends to original buyer or person who receives product as gift.

Limited Ninety [90] Day Warranty
WYSIWYGame Arts warrants this product and its parts against defect in materials and workmanship for a period of ninety [90] days after the date of original retail purchase. During this period, WYSIWYGame Arts will replace any defective product or part without charge to you. For replacement you must deliver the entire product to the place of purchase.

Element: short-term warranty.
Features: 90 days; defects in materials and workmanship; replacement without charge; must return to seller.

Limited One [1] Year Warranty of Parts
WYSIWYGame Arts further warrants the parts of this product against defects in materials or workmanship for a period of one year after the date of original retail purchase. During this period, WYSIWYGame Arts will replace a defective part without charge to you, except that if a defective part is replaced after ninety [90] days from the date of the original retail purchase, you pay labor charges involved in the replacement. You must also deliver the entire product to an authorized WYSIWYGame Arts service station. You pay all transportation and insurance charges for the product to and from the service station.

Element: parts warranty.
Features: What specific features do you find?

Owner's Manual and Warranty Registration
Read the owner's manual thoroughly before operating this product. WYSIWYGame Arts does not warrant any defect caused by improper installation or operation. Complete and mail the attached registration card within fourteen [14] days; the warranty is effective only if your name, address, and date of purchase are on file as the new owner of a WYSIWYGame Arts product.

Element: disclaimer.
Features: Under what conditions will the company NOT guarantee the product?

Element: specifications.
Features: What kind of information do the specifications provide? Why might you need to know this information?

CPU	800 MHz
Video Card	250 MHz GPU
Resolution	1920 × 1080 maximum
Memory	128 MB
Storage	Memory Card • Hard Drive
Sound Card	64 Channels
DVD	Yes
Media	12X DVD-ROM 6.2 GB Capacity
Hard Drive	8 GB
Modem	Yes
Ethernet Port	Yes
Controllers	4

WYSI WYGAME ARTS

Element: safety information.
Features: What are the most important things you should do to protect the product?

Safety Information

Please follow these important safeguards regarding the use and installation of your game console:

1. When installing your game console, be certain that the unit receives proper ventilation. Vents in the console covering are provided for this purpose. Never block or cover these vents with any objects such as fabric, books, magazines, etc.

2. Do not install your game console in a bookcase or entertainment rack where it cannot receive proper ventilation.

3. Do not place the game console in direct sunlight or near a heat source, such as a radiator or hot-air duct.

4. Do not set the game console on a soft surface, such as a bed, sofa, or rug, since doing so may result in damage to the appliance.

5. Unplug this appliance from the wall outlet, and contact a qualified service person under the following conditions:

   a. The power-supply cord or plug is damaged.

   b. Liquid has been spilled on, or objects have fallen into, the game console.

   c. The game console has been exposed to rain or water.

   d. The game console does not operate normally after you follow the operating instructions.

   e. The game console has been dropped, or the cabinet has been damaged.

   f. The game console exhibits a distinct change in performance.

Do not attempt to service this product yourself. Opening or removing the outside covers may expose you to dangerous voltage or other hazards. All service must be done by qualified service personnel.

Reading Check

1. What **features** are offered by the limited ninety-day warranty?

2. What are the differences between the **features** of the ninety-day warranty and the one-year warranty?

3. Where do you look to find out how many sound channels your WYSIWYGame has? What do you find out?

4. If you accidentally dump a can of soda on your game console, what should you do? Where do you find this advice?

Test Practice

1. If you want to tell a friend how powerful your game console is, you would look —
   A   in the warranty under "Warranty Registration"
   B   in the instruction manual under "Safety Information"
   C   in the product information
   D   in the warranty under "Limited One [1] Year Warranty of Parts"

2. Items 1–3 under "Safety Information" are intended to protect the unit from —
   F   chilling
   G   overheating
   H   static electricity
   J   humidity

3. "Safety Information" and "Limited Warranty" are *similar* in that both address —
   A   problems with the product
   B   how to operate the product
   C   how to buy the product
   D   how to set up the product

4. According to the manufacturer's warranty, if you have *not* sent in your owner's registration card and your game console breaks six months after you bought it —
   F   WYSIWYGame Arts will pay only for a defective part
   G   WYSIWYGame Arts will pay all costs for the repair
   H   you will have to pay all costs to an authorized service station; the company will not pay for anything
   J   you will have to pay only for transportation and insurance

5. Consumer documents exist to protect —
   A   the user
   B   the manufacturer
   C   both of the above
   D   neither of the above

Application

Find the consumer documents that came with a piece of equipment you or someone you know owns. (The equipment might be a cell phone, a pager, a camera, any kitchen appliance, or any piece of electronic equipment.) Read the consumer documents carefully to identify all of the elements and features and to **compare and contrast** them with the WSIWYGame Arts documents.

SKILLS FOCUS

Reading Skills
Analyze elements of consumer documents.

Following Technical Directions

Finding Information on the Internet

Before you start to invent the best computer game ever, you might want to learn something about the history of computer game design and development. A good place to start your research, naturally, is on the Internet. There are a lot of computer games out there, so you'll want to make your research as easy as possible.

Your first step is to choose a **search engine**[1] you like and feel comfortable with. When you have found one, it is a good idea to customize your **browser**[2] so that your favorite search engine is your home page. How do you do that? It's easy. You just follow the directions.

---

1. **search engine:** tool that enables you to search World Wide Web pages for a specific topic.
2. **browser:** software program that enables you to access the World Wide Web. Note that a browser is not the same as a search engine.

Reading Technical Directions

Directions for using computers (as well as other scientific, mechanical, and electronic products and activities) are called **technical directions.** You follow technical directions when you read informational materials that tell you how to

- do an experiment in a chemistry lab
- fix a flat on your bicycle for the first time
- program the remote control to access your favorite radio stations
- operate your new microwave oven
- install virus-protection software on your computer

Technical directions may seem complicated and difficult when you first look at them, but if you pay attention and follow each step carefully, they will help you do the things you want to do.

FAQs° About Search Engines

Q: What does a search engine do?
A: A search engine helps you locate information that is available on the World Wide Web.

Q: How does a search engine do this?
A: There are many different search engines, and they all vary somewhat, but each one matches the words of your search request with the keywords in a Web site. It eliminates what doesn't match your request and tells you what does match.

Q: What is an example of a search request?
A: Say you wanted to know about computer games. You would choose a specific search engine, and in the search box you would type, for example, the keyword *computer games.* The search

engine might deliver the first 10 most relevant entries of a possible 2.4 million results.

Q: That's way too many results. How do I narrow my search?
A: You narrow your search by requesting what you specifically want to know about computer games. For example, if you want to know about the most popular computer games, you might phrase your search request in this way: *computer games+most popular.* The search engine might then give you the first 10 most relevant entries of a possible 751,000 results.

Q: That's still too many. How can I narrow my search further?

° **FAQs:** Frequently Asked Questions.

A: If you want to narrow your search further, on some search engines you can use quotation marks to search for phrases instead of individual words: *"computer games"*+*"most popular."* A search phrased in this way might return the first 10 most relevant entries of a possible 21,600 results.

Q: There are so many search engines. How do I decide which one to use?
A: The best way is to experiment with some of the most popular search engines. You might ask your computer-savvy friends which ones they use and then put their recommendations on your Favorites or Bookmarks list. Once you've decided which search engine works best for you, you can make that Web site your home page by customizing your browser.

Q: How do I customize my browser?
A: Customizing your browser involves following technical directions, which are a sequence of steps. First, decide on a search engine, and go to its Web site. Then, find the directions for customizing the browser you are using, and follow them.

Q: Will the directions work with every browser in use today?
A: No, they will work only with the version of the browser they were written for.

Customizing Your Browser

The sample below shows instructions that are typical of those you might find for customizing a browser. They use a made-up search engine called QuickFind. Reading QuickFind's instructions will make you familiar with the process of following **technical directions,** so that when you choose your own favorite search engine—and there are many out there to pick from—you'll have no trouble following the instructions. You will be ready to make your favorite search engine's Web site your home page.

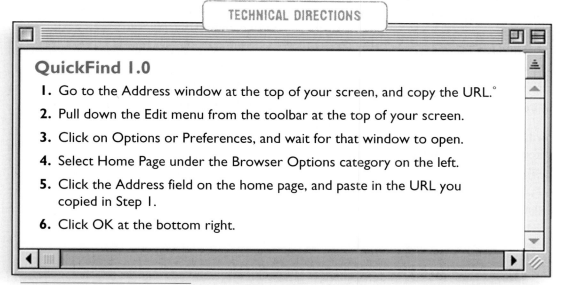

TECHNICAL DIRECTIONS

QuickFind 1.0

1. Go to the Address window at the top of your screen, and copy the URL.°
2. Pull down the Edit menu from the toolbar at the top of your screen.
3. Click on Options or Preferences, and wait for that window to open.
4. Select Home Page under the Browser Options category on the left.
5. Click the Address field on the home page, and paste in the URL you copied in Step 1.
6. Click OK at the bottom right.

° **URL:** uniform resource locator, a site's Internet address.

Whichever search engine you choose, there is one last step to follow: Check your work. Quit your browser, and then open it again. The browser should automatically open to the search engine you've selected. If it doesn't, repeat the process, making sure to follow each step carefully.

Reading Check

1. What does a search engine do?

2. How might you choose a search engine?

3. When using QuickFind, what is your first step in customizing your browser?

4. What is the very last step you should take when customizing any browser?

Test Practice

1. According to "FAQs About Search Engines," which of the following key-words would you use to search for the most popular computer games?

  A   mostpopularcomputergames

  B   most+popular+computer+games

  C   computer games+most popular

  D   What are the most popular computer games?

2. According to "FAQs About Search Engines," on some search engines you can narrow a search by enclosing key phrases in —

  F   question marks

  G   quotation marks

  H   slashes

  J   parentheses

3. According to the QuickFind 1.0 technical directions for customizing a browser, the first thing you do is —

  A   click on the URL

  B   paste the URL

  C   click on Options

  D   go to the Address window

4. According to the QuickFind 1.0 directions for customizing a browser, which of the following steps comes last?

  F   Copy the URL in the Address window.

  G   Pull down the Edit menu.

  H   Click on Address.

  J   Click on OK.

5. The *best* way to access your favorite search engine *quickly* is to —

  A   look for it on the Internet

  B   make it your home page

  C   ask your computer-savvy friends

  D   follow technical directions

Application

SKILLS FOCUS

Reading Skills
Analyze technical directions.

Find a set of **technical directions** for completing a totally unfamiliar process—something you've never done before. You might try one of the examples listed in the second column on page 1066. For a real challenge (and a glimpse of adult life), try completing a 1040EZ income tax form or learning a new trick in your word-processing program, such as creating and using macros. Whatever you set out to do, carefully follow the directions in an **instruction manual.** Report to the class on what you tried to do, how well you did, and how helpful the directions were.

Citing Internet Sources

You're the Expert

One way to learn more about the computer game industry is to experience the business from the inside. Perhaps your school offers an internship program in which students work at local businesses during the summer.

Since you already own its game console and play its games, your summer internship with WYSIWYGame Arts seems like a wonderful opportunity—the perfect match. You arrive on your first day eager to learn at the side of real experts in the field. Then you are given your first assignment—to write a report.

It turns out that WYSIWYGame Arts considers *you* the real expert in the field of being a teenage consumer. The company wants to know what you like about its products, what you use, and what you want to see improved. Writing about what you like and use will be easy, but writing about what you want improved will be more complicated.

All the gamers you know, including you, want better game graphics. However, if getting better graphics were easy, it would have been done already. So what is really involved? What are the limitations on graphics? What advances have to be made in hardware before software evolves? So many unanswered questions, so little time to do research, but what better place to start researching a fast-moving field like computer games than the Internet?

Documenting Internet Sources

A research report must include an orderly list of **Works Cited** that enables others to find and read the sources you used in your report. Since online information is easily updated (in some cases, daily), citing **Internet sources** requires more information than you may be accustomed to providing in citations of print materials.

You are not, of course, responsible for changes made in a site between the time you make your notation and the time your reader goes there to find the work. You are responsible for giving your reader as much information as you have. In particular, it is crucial that you reproduce the URL (uniform resource locator) —the site's Internet address—exactly so that a reader may access the site.

To see some examples of **citations** for **consumer, public,** and **workplace documents** you might find on the Internet, look at the chart on page 1070. (Some of the sites are made up; some are real.) The examples follow the Modern Language Association (MLA) style. If you have any questions about how to document your sources, look for the MLA style book in the library. In preparing a list of sources, the style you follow is less important than choosing one style and sticking to it. Always ask what style your teacher wants you to use.

Pages 1069–1071 cover
Reading Skills
Understand how to cite Internet sources in a *Works Cited* list.

General Format for an Online Source

Author's Last Name, Author's First Name (if known).
"Title of Work." Title of Web Site or Database.
Date of electronic publication. Name of
Sponsoring Institution. Date information was
accessed <URL>.

Note: If an electronic address, or URL, must be
broken at the end of a line, break the address
immediately after one of the slash marks. Do not
add a hyphen or any other mark of punctuation
to indicate the division of an address.

Sample Works Cited Citations for Consumer, Public, and Workplace Documents

Product Information from a Commercial Site

"About the New WYSIWYGame Arts Console." WYSIWYGame Arts Console Page. 7 June 2001.
    WYSIWYGame Arts 27 July 2001 <http://www.wysiwygame.com/console/index.asp>.

Article from an Online Nonprofit Magazine Dedicated to Protecting Consumers

Sleuthing, I. B. "And the Winner Is—Testing Today's Game Consoles." Digital 25 June 2001. 7 Aug.
    2001 <http://www.digital.org/main/article/gamcon/1.html>.

Article from a Reference Database (Encyclopedia)

"Programming Language." Electronic Library Presents: Encyclopedia.com. The Columbia Electronic
    Encyclopedia, Sixth Ed. 2000. Columbia UP. 15 July 2001 <http://www.encyclopedia.com/
    articlesnew/10538biblio.html>.

Part of an Online Book Found on a Public-Library Site (Also Available in Print)

Case, Loyd. "Chapter 4—Graphics." Building the Ultimate Game PC. Indianapolis: Macmillan, 2000.
    netLibrary. 3 Aug. 2001 <http://emedia.netlibrary.com/nlreader/
    dll?bookid=38549&filename=Page_v.html>.

Copyright Forms from the Library of Congress (Government Office)

United States. Library of Congress. US Copyright Office. Form VA—For a Work of the Visual Arts.
    Washington: GPO, 1999. 2 Aug. 2001 <http://www.loc.gov/copyright/forms/formva.pdf>.

Information from a Company's FAQ Page

"Resource Code Game Software Developers May Use When Programming for Our Products."
    ShellGame, Inc. 7 June 2001 <http://www.shellgame.com/corp/faqs/faqslist.html>.

Posting to a Discussion List (Message Board)

GameDawg. "Why More Polygons Mean Awesome Graphics." Online postage. 23 June 2001. Way
    Kool Net. 16 Aug. 2001 <http://www.waykoolnet.com/mboards/
    boards.cgi?board=prgm&read=9218>.

Quotation from an E-mail Communication

Nguyen, W. "Re: WYSIWYGame Arts Graphics." E-mail to the author. 21 Aug. 2001.

Using Note Cards

Ready to try a few Internet citations on your own? When you are researching on the Internet, it is a good idea to record your sources on three-by-five-inch cards like the ones below. (Most of these are made-up sources.)

Source type: Consumer information

What it is: Online magazine article

Author(s): Art C. Graphic

Title: "Writing Game Software Without Writing Code"

Other information: from JoyClick magazine, printed 7/17/01. I found it on 8/5/01.

URL: www.joyclickmag.com/main/articles/artg/1.html

Source type: Workplace document

What it is: Company software instruction manual

Author(s): V. Phat

Title: "User's Manual for Compiler Version 2.2"

Other information: There is no print version (they change it too often). You have to print from the WYSIWYGame Arts company intranet. It had last been updated 6/27/01 when I accessed this info on 7/3/01.

URL: www.wysiwygame.com/manuals/compiler2.2.html

Source type: Public document

What it is: Government information service

Author(s): Federal Consumer Information Service, a division of the U. S. General Services Administration

Title: "Recalls"

Other information: Note to myself: This is where I found out about the computer-chip recall from that company WYSIWYGame Arts was considering switching to for its chips. Boy, was the boss surprised when I showed him that! I found the recall on 8/3/01 using my usual search engine. There was no notation of when the site had last been updated.

URL: http://www.pueblo.gsa.gov/recallsdesc.html

Formatting Your Works Cited List

The last step in writing a report is to compile all the sources you have cited in a *Works Cited* list. Follow these formatting steps:

- At the top of the page, center the title *Works Cited*.
- Alphabetize your sources by the author's last name. If no author is listed, alphabetize a source by the first two words in the title, ignoring *A, An,* and *The.*

- If two or more sources are by the same author, use the author's full name in the first entry only. For the other entries, type three dashes in place of the name, followed by a period and the rest of the citation.

- Double-space the list, and begin each entry at the left margin. If an entry runs longer than one line, indent the following lines five spaces.

Reading Check

1. What is the purpose of a *Works Cited* list?

2. List some special problems involved in citing works from Internet sources.

3. In what order should you list your sources in a *Works Cited* list?

4. In a *Works Cited* list, if you have two sources by the same author, how do you list the second source?

Test Practice

1. On a *Works Cited* list an author's name appears —
   A after the title of the work cited
   B last, at the end of the citation
   C first, with the first name first
   D first, with the last name first

2. The most crucial information to reproduce accurately in an Internet citation is the —
   F URL
   G date you accessed the site
   H title of the site
   J author of the site

3. In an Internet citation the URL appears —
   A at the very beginning
   B directly after the author's name
   C directly after the title
   D at the very end

4. According to MLA style, what is the correct way to cite the following URL in a *Works Cited* list?
   F hrw.com
   G www.hrw.com
   H http://www.hrw.com
   J <http://www.hrw.com>.

5. The Web site you wish to use as a source does not list an author. How would you alphabetize the entry in your *Works Cited* list?
   A Use Anonymous as the author's name.
   B Alphabetize by the first two words in the title, ignoring *A, An,* or *The.*
   C Type two dashes and a period, and then alphabetize by the title.
   D Alphabetize by the month you accessed the Web site.

Application

SKILLS FOCUS

Reading Skills
Analyze how to cite Internet sources in a *Works Cited* list.

Now you're ready to search the **Internet** for three more *credible* sources on computer game graphics to use in your report. Remember to gather as much information as you can for your citations, and record that information on a note card for each source.

Then, prepare a *Works Cited* list using your three sources and the three sources shown on the three-by-five-inch note cards on page 1071. Follow the MLA style used in the examples on page 1070.

Analyzing Functional Workplace Documents

Workplace Documents for Computer Games

Say you have finished designing your first computer game. What now? Do you want to limit distribution to family and friends, or do you want to make your game more widely available, perhaps as downloadable shareware on the Internet? If it's the latter, then it's time to talk about control structures in cyberspace.

If you put a work you have authored on the World Wide Web, you want to control what happens to it there. In order to do that, you must first establish your ownership of the work by copyrighting it (using that well-known copyright symbol, "©") with the U.S. Copyright Office for a fee.

A **copyright** is an exclusive right granted to you as the author of a work. It gives you the sole right—the *proprietary rights*—to reproduce and distribute that work.

As the owner of the copyright, you may then license others to use the work. You do that by means of a **legal agreement,** or **license,** between you and the user of that software. (This agreement is sometimes called a **shareware license agreement,** or **end user software license.**) The license grants the user of copyrighted software certain rights, but it does not grant any proprietary (or ownership) rights. Those remain with you.

An end user software license, or shareware license agreement, is a kind of **contract.** It is a **functional workplace document** that helps people get things done. In this case, the goal is to inform people how they may, and may not, use your software.

On the next page you'll find an example of a shareware agreement.

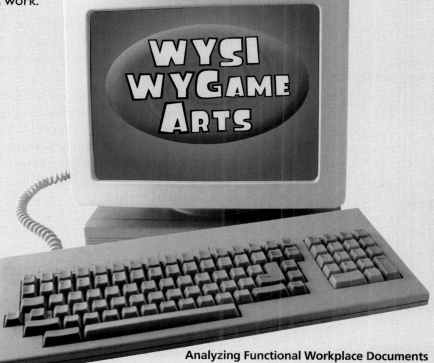

SKILLS
FOCUS

Pages 1073–1077 cover
Reading Skills
Analyze the structure and format of functional workplace documents.

WYSI WYGame Arts

Shareware Agreement

This is a legal agreement between you, the end user, and WYSIWYGame Arts, the proprietor. By using this WYSIWYGame Arts software [hereafter called the SOFTWARE], you indicate your acceptance of these terms.

1. **GRANT OF LICENSE**—WYSIWYGame Arts grants you the right to use the SOFTWARE on a single computer. The SOFTWARE is considered in use on a computer when it is loaded into RAM or installed in permanent memory.

2. **PROPRIETARY RIGHTS**—The SOFTWARE is owned exclusively by WYSIWYGame Arts. This license does not transfer any ownership rights of the SOFTWARE to you.

3. **RESTRICTIONS**—You may not translate, reverse program, decompile, disassemble, or otherwise reverse engineer the SOFTWARE.

4. **NO WARRANTY**—This SOFTWARE is licensed to you "as is" and without any warranty of any kind, expressed or implied, including but not limited to warranties of merchantability and fitness for a particular purpose.

5. **LIMITATION OF LIABILITY**—In no event shall WYSIWYGame Arts' liability related to any of the SOFTWARE exceed the license fees, if any, actually paid by you for the SOFTWARE. WYSIWYGame Arts shall not be liable for any damages whatsoever arising out of, or related to, the use of or inability to use the SOFTWARE, including but not limited to direct, indirect, special, incidental, or consequential damages.

Features of the Shareware Agreement

The shareware agreement at the left makes effective use of **structure** and **format** to achieve its purpose. Some of its features are

- a centered **title** (**header**) that clearly states the purpose of the document
- a new **section** for each major topic
- **spacing** between each major section
- **numerical identification** of each major section
- **section headers** in boldface capital letters

The agreement also follows a **logical sequence.** It first states that using the software indicates the user's agreement to the terms, and then it lists those terms. They progress as follows:

1. what the license allows
2. who owns the software
3. restrictions on use of the software
4. warranty (none)
5. liability of the owner (none)

Analyzing Workplace Documents

Let's take a closer look at the structure, format, and sequence of effective functional workplace documents.

Structure

Functional workplace documents are usually divided into sections, each with its own header. Each **section** is often one short paragraph in length, sometimes just one sentence. The **headers** might be titles, subtitles, or numbers. Separating each main idea into its own section makes it easy for the reader to locate information. It also highlights each major point so that the reader will be sure to consider them all.

Format

The **format,** or design, of a document is important to its effectiveness. It focuses the reader's attention on key words, sections, and ideas. Some of the elements involved in designing or creating the format of a functional workplace document are

- **formatting elements**—bold or italic type, margin widths, indentations, and line spacing
- **graphic elements**—drawings, photos, and other artwork
- **design elements**—placement of text and graphic elements on the page, use of white space, and choice of colors

Sequence

The **sequence,** or order, in which ideas are presented can make a big difference to the reader's understanding. Most history books present information in a **chronological sequence;** that is, in the order in which events happened in time. Imagine how difficult it would be if the books had an **alphabetical sequence** by the last names of the participants, as in a bibliography?

A functional workplace document should present its information in a logical sequence. Two examples are

- **Step-by-step sequence**. This type of sequence describes a process and tells what to do first, second, third, and so on. An example is the instructions in "Customizing Your Browser," page 1067.
- **Point-by-point sequence**. This type of sequence is based on the relationship of the points to each other. Sometimes the order of the points is not particularly important, as long as each point is stated clearly. An example is the "WYSI-WYGame Arts Shareware Agreement" on page 1074.

Analyzing a Web Site

The "WYSIWYGame Arts Shareware Agreement" on page 1074 effectively uses a simple structure and format to draw the reader's attention to its features. Now, let's assess the more complicated format of the Web site on which that agreement—and your software—are posted. How has the Webmaster at WYSIWYGame Arts used the structure and format of the Web site to draw the viewer's attention to your game?

WEB SITE

Location: http://www.wysiwygamearts.com/games/tsmgo/description

Game Description

You, Candy Rapper, are trying to get to the stadium to sing at the big benefit concert to aid the farmworkers. En route, though, you are stopped by different characters—Opal Opera and Coyote Cowboy, for example—who demand that you play them *their* songs before they let you pass. With a quick check of the playlist, you dial up a song on your boombox. If you play the right song, you gain points and move on toward the stadium. If not, you lose points and have to stay until you find the right song. Can you make it to the stadium in time? If you do, you perform to a standing ovation accompanied by a fireworks display.

Would you recommend this game?

YES **NO** **Post My Opinion**

Game Facts

Version:	1.0
Ages:	10–16
Date added:	April 6, 2002
File size:	5.5MB
Approximate download time:	13 min. at 56 kbps
Downloads:	8
Opinions (5):	80% yes; 20% no
License:	Shareware

DOWNLOAD NOW

Reading Check

1. What does the shareware agreement allow you to do?

2. List three structural or formatting features of the shareware agreement.

3. What is the main purpose of the Web site?

4. What **graphics** does the Web site use?

Test Practice

1. The **section headers** on the shareware agreement are —
   - **A** boldface and colorful
   - **B** boldface and numbered
   - **C** boldface and bulleted
   - **D** italicized and capitalized

2. On the Web site the name of the computer game is displayed —
   - **F** in a long paragraph
   - **G** next to the company logo
   - **H** under a "Download Now" button
   - **J** next to "Read User Opinions"

3. A repeated **graphic** icon on the Web site draws the reader's attention to —
   - **A** where to download
   - **B** the search button
   - **C** the company logo
   - **D** the game's name

4. The Web site uses *all* of the following elements of **structure** and **format** *except* —
   - **F** bold and colored print
   - **G** graphics and bullets
   - **H** chronological sequence
   - **J** placement of text and graphics on the page

5. The Web site uses the structural element of a bulleted list to —
   - **A** describe the game
   - **B** repeat the company name
   - **C** list game facts
   - **D** identify internal links

6. The main purpose of "Game Description" on the Web site is to help you decide if you want to —
   - **F** find out about the author
   - **G** download the game
   - **H** suggest improvements for the game
   - **J** submit an original game of your own

SKILLS FOCUS

Reading Skills
Analyze the structure and format of functional workplace documents.

Application

Choose three structural, formatting, or graphic features of the Web site (pages 1076–1077), and describe how each contributes to WYSIWYGame Arts' purpose in creating this site.

Evaluating the Logic of Functional Documents

Using Functional Documents

Functional documents with clear and logical instructions help people get things done. By contrast, documents that are illogically sequenced or missing steps are impossible to use. Such documents offer to get you somewhere, but when you attempt to follow their directions, you end up in Wonderland, thinking, "Off with their heads!"

When you are downloading a software game, putting together your kid sister's new swing set, or following the prompts on an ATM or voice-mail system, you are using functional documents. It may seem odd to think of on-screen or voice prompts as documents, but it makes sense if you remember this: Someone wrote the words and decided on the sequence of the procedures that you see on the ATM screen or hear when you reach a voice-mail system. When instructions are well written, these documents are easy to follow. When they are not well written, they can cause serious misunderstandings.

When a functional document is poorly written, chances are that either a crucial piece of the information you need has been left out or the information is not presented in a logical, step-by-step sequence. Either way you end up scratching your head and thinking, "Huh?"

Missing a Step

Let's say, for example, that you are installing memory chips in a laptop computer that has been designed to let you do this. The first step tells you, in big block letters, to unplug the computer and remove the battery. You follow each of the next twenty steps flawlessly. The illustrations actually match what you see, and you are confident that you have done everything correctly. The last step tells you to turn the computer on. You take a deep breath, press the On switch, and . . . Nothing. No lights, no whirring, no little *chucka-chucka-chucka* sounds. Finally, you think, "Duh. Plug it in."

We've all been there. The instructions omitted that vital step. As obvious as the step may have seemed to the person who wrote the document, it is still necessary to tell you when it's safe to plug the computer back in, especially after you've been instructed to unplug it. Such a failure in logic creates confusion, and creating confusion is not what a functional document should do.

SKILLS FOCUS

Pages 1079–1082 cover **Reading Skills** Evaluate the logic of functional documents.

Steps Out of Order

Logical sequencing requires not only that **all the steps be there** but also that they appear **in the correct order.** If a step is out of order, a great deal of confusion and frustration can result. For example, take a look at the following functional document:

Installing Your Wireless Internet Access

1. Your new wireless system will use your existing cable-modem service to access the Internet. Test to see whether the cable connection is working by going to your home page in the usual way. If the connection is working, go on to steps 2–7.

2. Shut down your computer.

3. Unplug the cable modem from your computer.

4. Turn the wireless system on.

5. Restart the computer.

6. Check to see that the wireless system has taken you back to your home page.

7. Plug the cable modem you unplugged from your computer into the wireless system.

What's Wrong with This Document?

Hold on here. Put your hand over the paragraphs under this one, and pretend you really are installing wireless Internet access. What confuses you? Critique the sequencing flaw in the document on page 1080, "Installing Your Wireless Internet Access." Talk over the sequencing with a partner, and then go on reading below.

What did you decide? Step 7 is clearly out of order. You are now faced with a quandary: You know step 7 should occur sometime after step 3, but should it come between steps 3 and 4, steps 4 and 5, or steps 5 and 6? You have no way of knowing. You are faced with a series of bad choices:

- **Plan A.** Try each of the above choices (the possible places to put step 7) to see if one of them works—but will doing so damage the equipment?

- **Plan B.** Call tech support—but how long until someone answers?

- **Plan C.** Return the product—but will the company take it back?

Let's say you took the risk and used plan A to solve the problem. It worked perfectly once you tried step 7 between steps 3 and 4. Of course, you later found it necessary to go to plan B after all. It is frequently true that a poorly written document will have more than one unclear section. Fortunately, tech support for the product was available twenty-four hours a day and immediately offered a simple solution. (Remember the importance of checking the warranty and the availability of technical support before you buy a product? It paid off here.)

Editing for Logic and Clarity

Let's get back to your newly designed software game. You want the downloading instructions on the WYSIWYGame Arts Web site to be easy and clear for your reader to follow. Below are the instructions provided by the technical-support crew at WYSIWYGame Arts. Critique the logic and clarity of their instructions. Make notations where you think a reader might misunderstand the instructions, and suggest how those misunderstandings might be avoided.

Back   **Forward**   **Reload**   **Home**   **Search**

TECHNICAL DIRECTIONS

Location: http://www.wysiwygamearts.com/games/tsmgo/download

The Show Must Go On

Five Easy Steps to Downloading Software

1. Click on Download Now.
2. Decompress your download.
3. Install the game software on the hard drive of your PC.
4. Clean up your desktop directory.
5. Download decompression software.

STEP 1—Click on Download Now

a. The download window will appear.

b. Click on OK for the download to begin.

c. Your browser will automatically download the file to the folder you have specified.

STEP 2—Decompress Your Download on a PC

Note: This game has been compressed for faster file downloading. PC files will download in .ZIP format.

a. Double-click on the game icon with the .ZIP extension. Your decompression software will automatically load.

b. Click on Extract.

c. Select the destination folder, and click on Extract again. The file will appear in that folder.

STEP 3—Install the Game Software on the Hard Drive of Your PC

a. Click on Install on the button bar, or click on Next as prompted.

b. Follow the prompts.

STEP 4—Clean Up Your Desktop Directory

Delete the compressed file ending in .ZIP, and empty the trash or recycle bin. Once the game software has been installed, you will no longer need this file.

STEP 5—Download Decompression Software

ZIP Click here for .ZIP, .arc, .arj, .gz, and .z files.

Files that end in .exe or .sea do not need compression software.

Reading Check

1. Why is a **logical sequence** important in **functional documents**?

2. List two errors often found in the sequencing of poorly written documents.

3. In "Five Easy Steps to Downloading Software," what two main steps do you have to do before you can install the game software on your hard drive?

4. To decompress files on a PC, what format will you download in?

Test Practice

1. In "Five Easy Steps to Downloading Software" (page 1082), which step is out of sequence?
   A "Click on Download Now"
   B "Decompress Your Download on a PC"
   C "Install the Game Software on the Hard Drive of Your PC"
   D "Download Decompression Software"

2. Where *should* the step that is out of sequence be placed?
   F After step 1
   G After step 2
   H After step 3
   J After step 4

3. The most logical order for giving instructions in any functional document (including "Five Easy Steps to Downloading Software") is —
   A alphabetical order
   B order of importance
   C step-by-step order
   D spatial order

4. Step 2, "Decompress Your Download on a PC," will probably leave an inexperienced computer user *most* uncertain about which question?
   F I'm supposed to double-click on *what*?
   G *What* do I have to do to make the decompression software load?
   H *How* do I select a destination folder (and what is it)?
   J Why exactly did I think I wanted this computer game anyway?

5. According to step 4, to clean up your desktop, what should you do once the game software is installed?
   A Download the .ZIP file.
   B Delete the compressed .ZIP file.
   C Decompress the .ZIP file.
   D Create a new folder.

Application

Write a brief critique of the functional document "Five Easy Steps to Downloading Software" (page 1082). Are the procedures presented in a logical sequence? Is the information clear and easily understood? What possible misunderstandings could occur? How could such misunderstandings be prevented? Write your suggestions for changes.

SKILLS FOCUS

Reading Skills
Analyze the logic of functional documents.

Writing Business Letters

Marketing Your Computer Game

So here you are, further down the road of computer game design and development. You've acquired some meaningful hands-on experience, and you're wondering how you can parlay that experience into the next step—whatever that step may be. A new step may seem intimidating, but remember Sir Arthur C. Clarke's second law: "The only way of discovering the limits of the possible is to venture a little way past them into the impossible." Now is the time to get out into the world and make connections.

To market your computer game, you will need to write **business letters**— probably lots of them.

Elements of a Business Letter

When you write a **thank-you letter** to Aunt Cele for your birthday gift (a hand-knit red plaid scarf), you can call the scarf "cool" and use an informal, chatty style. In contrast, the **style** and **tone** of a business letter are **formal.** Focus on these elements whenever you write a business letter:

- **Clarity.** Provide all the information the recipient of the letter needs to know, and say it clearly and briefly.
- **Courtesy.** Even if you're writing a **complaint letter,** be polite. You're asking the recipient to *do* something, and you'll be more successful if you remain courteous.
- **Style.** The **style** of a business letter is **formal.** That means it contains no slang, no contractions, no sentence fragments.

- **Tone.** The recipient of the letter is probably someone you don't know. Be respectful and formal.
- **Vocabulary.** Use appropriate vocabulary, the language you would use in a formal speaking situation. You may need to define terms the recipient of the letter might not know.

Format of a Business Letter

If you want to make a good impression, you can't write letters in just any form. It is important to follow the proper **format** and conventional **style** for a business letter, as shown on pages 1085–1087.

A business letter has these six parts:

- heading
- inside address
- salutation
- body
- closing
- signature

The example on page 1087 uses the **block-style format,** in which all six parts of the letter (heading, inside address, salutation, body, closing, and signature) align at the left margin.

In the **modified-block-style format,** the heading, closing, and signature are indented, as is every paragraph. See the letter on page 1086 for an example of the modified block style.

Pages 1084–1087 cover
Writing Skills
Write a business letter.

Your Street Address
Your City, State, and ZIP code
Date on which letter is written

— Heading.

Recipient's Title [Ms., Dr., etc.] and First and Last Name
Recipient's Business Title
Company Name
Street Address
City, State, and ZIP code

— Inside address.

Dear [Title and Last Name of Recipient]: — Salutation, followed by a colon.

In this paragraph, tell the recipient why you are writing. Make the statement or request in clear and purposeful language.

Body: paragraph 1.

In this paragraph, include information relevant to your goal, such as facts about your background or questions you have.

Body: paragraph 2.

Here you thank the recipient in advance for whatever actions he or she may take in regard to your request in the first paragraph.

Body: paragraph 3.

Sincerely,

Your Name

Closing, followed by a comma.

Your Name

Four blank lines for signature—full name without title—followed by your typed name.

Two Sample Business Letters

Now that you have a sample of the business-letter format, let's look at two actual letters.

8 Chimney Rock Way
Suburbanite, CA 98990
April 6, 2002

Mr. S. K. Miyamoto
Conference Project Manager
WYSIWYGame Arts
41311 On Donner Highway
Cybercity, CA 99880

Dear Mr. Miyamoto:

    I am writing to request the chance to attend your upcoming "Making Games Fun Again" conference in May. I see from information provided on the WYSIWYGame Arts Web site that attendance can be arranged through your office.

    I am making this request on account of a lifelong interest in computer games. I am a high school student who has taught myself C++ programming. I have designed several successful computer games, which I am making available as downloadable shareware on my Web site. My Web site has attracted the attention of other gamers.

    Thank you in advance for your time and attention. I hope to have the opportunity to meet you in person.

Sincerely yours,

Judy Realdata

Judy Realdata

Analyzing the Model Letter

Judy Realdata's letter (on page 1086) should have a positive effect on Mr. Miyamoto. The **vocabulary** is appropriate—Judy is writing to a business executive. The writer's formal **tone** shows respect and reflects the fact that the writer and the recipient do not know each other.

The letter's **central idea** (in this case, a **request**) is clearly stated in the first paragraph. The **style**—a conventional format, with a standard font and spaces between paragraphs—makes the letter easy to read. Now, let's see what response the letter received.

WYSIWYGame Arts
41311 On Donner Highway
Cybercity, CA 99880

BUSINESS LETTER

April 18, 2002

Ms. Judy Realdata
8 Chimney Rock Way
Suburbanite, CA 98990

Dear Ms. Realdata:

Thank you for your letter of April 6. In regard to your request, WYSIWYGame Arts would like to invite you not only to attend our "Making Games Fun Again" conference in May but also to be the conference's West Coast high school representative.

Please reply in writing by April 30. Once we have your acceptance, we will provide additional information about the conference.

We look forward to hearing from you.

Sincerely,

S. K. Miyamoto

S. K. Miyamoto
Conference Project Manager

PRACTICE

Judy Realdata's carefully prepared letter got an even better response than she'd hoped. Your assignment is to write Judy's reply. Be sure to follow the proper **form** for a business letter and use a **tone** and **style** appropriate to your audience. This assignment gives you practice in writing a business letter, so that you can make business connections that will help you design the best computer game ever.

Writing the Minutes of a Meeting

Taking Notes at a Meeting

The big day arrives. You are the West Coast high school representative for the WYSIWYGame Arts "Making Games Fun Again" conference. On the first morning you are scheduled to attend a meeting of all the high school representatives from around the country. You are all set to sit back and enjoy yourself. But what's this? You are asked to take **minutes of the meeting,** which is quite a responsibility. Not only that, but you are also asked to go to the business office at the conference center and run off copies of your minutes. Your minutes of the meeting will be distributed to everyone at the conference and sent to a list of interested students from countries all over the world.

Writing a Clear and Logical Summary

Taking notes of what is said in the meeting doesn't seem to be a problem because you take notes in your classes every day. But minutes are different from classroom notes. Both involve listening carefully and noting important information.

When it comes to writing the minutes, however, you'll be writing a **formal report** (no slang or informal language) in complete sentences. In your minutes you'll **summarize** in a sentence or two each speaker's main ideas. You'll report your information **clearly, briefly,** and **accurately,** covering the complete meeting in **chronological order.** You'll also include certain **formal conventions,** such as the names of those who attended and who were unable to attend, the person who chaired (ran) the meeting, and the time that the meeting began and ended.

Formatting Minutes

How do you transform your notes into a presentable form? Lucky for you, your packet of materials for the conference includes a copy of the minutes of last year's meeting. On the following pages you'll see an example of the standard **format** for presenting the minutes of a meeting.

SKILLS FOCUS

Pages 1088–1091 cover
Writing Skills
Write the minutes of a meeting.

WYSIWYGame Arts
WYSIWYGame Arts Conference 2001
Creating New Graphics!

Meeting of High School Representatives, May 9, 2001

Present:
Laura Lee, Mark Hadley, Pedro Valdez, Samantha Soltano, Abdul Akbar, Jimmy Johnson, Lin Huang, Kim Soo Long, Jerry Gralnik, Renee Letendre, Brian Parke.

Regrets:
Katie Dee.

Call to order:
The meeting was called to order at 9:05 a.m. by Laura Lee, WYSIWYGame Arts Student Coordinator, as chair.

Approval of minutes:
The minutes of the 2001 Meeting of High School Representatives were approved by Mark Hadley, Lin Huang, and Renee Letendre, the only representatives present who had attended that meeting.

Business conducted:

The agenda was approved as submitted by Laura Lee.

The representatives introduced themselves, told where they came from, and said a few words about their experience with computer game design.

The main topic of discussion was high school consumers' complaints about the 3-D Pinball game. Apparently the game appears choppy when played. The ball and flippers do not move smoothly, and the picture in the background is often distorted and fragmented. The game works despite those flaws, and some consumers are not bothered by these problems.

A game console was provided, and ten minutes was allotted for those few representatives who had never played 3-D Pinball to see what the game looks like. The consensus of the representatives was that the complaints were justified and had to be addressed.

Laura Lee opened the floor to suggestions for correcting the graphics problems. Kim Soo Long suggested that a new gaming project be started to replace 3-D Pinball completely. Brian Parke said that the company should inspect the hardware—the game console. He believes that the problem lies in the actual game console rather than in the 3-D Pinball software. Jimmy Johnson argued that since other games work well and do not have problems similar to those of 3-D Pinball, the problems must be in the actual game. Pedro Valdez suggested that the group create new graphics for 3-D Pinball and then do thorough tests to ensure that the problems do not reoccur.

Votes taken:
A vote was taken to decide the course of action. The high school representatives voted 9–3 in favor of deleting the current graphics and creating new ones that would be compatible with the game console. It was voted unanimously that another meeting was needed to decide on the new graphics. This meeting is scheduled for May 10, 2001, at 9:00 a.m.

Adjournment:
The current meeting was adjourned at 10:45 a.m.

Minutes prepared by Lin Huang, high school representative

Elements of a Meeting's Minutes

You now know what minutes of a meeting look like. They include the following **elements:**

- the name of the organization and committee, workshop, and so on, that is meeting
- the date of the meeting and the time at which the meeting began
- a list of those present
- a list of those who sent regrets (did not attend)
- a detailed and accurate report of the business of the meeting
- a report of any votes taken and their outcome
- the time of adjournment
- the name of the person writing the minutes

PRACTICE

Choose one of the following activities:

1. Make up minutes for the WYSI-WYGame Arts 2002 "Making Games Fun Again" conference.

2. Take minutes at a meeting of an organization to which you belong.

3. Take minutes at a local council, school-board, or other meeting to which the public is invited.

Whichever activity you choose, be sure to report information clearly, briefly, and accurately. Summarize the important topics that were covered at the meeting, including speakers' main ideas and the outcome of any votes. Write in complete sentences, and follow the standard format for presenting minutes.

Consumer and Workplace Documents

Test Practice

DIRECTIONS: Read and respond to the following questions about consumer and workplace documents.

1. Which **consumer document** is *most* likely to help you if you have trouble figuring out how to operate a device?

   A A contract

   B An instruction manual

   C A warranty

   D Product information

2. The **purpose** of a **limited warranty** is to provide —

   F some protection if a product is defective

   G a lifetime provision for repair of a product

   H directions for operating a product

   J a lifetime money-back guarantee of a product

3. For most product **warranties** to be effective, the manufacturer usually requires that the purchaser —

   A mail a registration card to the manufacturer in order to register purchase of the product

   B pay full price, not a reduced price, for the product

   C wait at least thirty days before requesting repairs

   D sign a legal contract with the manufacturer

4. In which of these **consumer documents** are you *most* likely to find out how many phone numbers you can enter in a cell phone's memory?

   F A warranty

   G Product information

   H Safety information

   J A contract

5. What does a **search engine** enable you to do?

   A Design a Web page

   B Send an e-mail message

   C Join an online chat room

   D Locate information that is available on the Web

6. According to MLA style, what is the correct way to cite a URL?

   F Within parentheses

   G Within slash marks

   H Within angled brackets

   J Within dashes

7. In preparing a *Works Cited* list, you should —

   A use cursive handwriting

   B always follow MLA style

   C not be concerned about using a consistent style

   D follow the style that your teacher requests

SKILLS FOCUS

Pages 1092–1093 cover **Reading Skills** Analyze elements of consumer and workplace documents.

Collection 12: Skills Review

8. In preparing a *Works Cited* list, you should —

   F divide a URL only after a period

   G divide a URL only after a slash

   H divide a URL anywhere in the address as long as you use a hyphen

   J not divide a URL at all

9. The **purpose** of a **functional workplace document** is to —

   A eliminate some jobs

   B increase paperwork

   C help people get things done

   D lessen people's dependence on computers

10. A **shareware agreement** is a type of —

   F software program

   G contract

   H warranty

   J Web browser

11. What type of **sequence** do *most* **functional documents** follow?

   A Alphabetical

   B Logical

   C Spatial

   D Chronological

12. Which element is *not* part of the **format,** or **design,** of a document?

   F Boldface type

   G Drawings

   H Color

   J Point-by-point sequence

13. A set of **technical directions** is badly flawed if it —

   A omits a step

   B puts a step in the wrong order

   C does either of the above

   D does none of the above

14. Which item is *not* necessary to include in the **minutes of a meeting**?

   F The names of those present

   G The time at which the meeting adjourns

   H A record of votes taken

   J The kind of refreshments served at the meeting

Constructed Response

15. Think about a product you've purchased or used recently, and write a **business letter** to the manufacturer explaining what you think of it. Be sure to include all six parts of the business-letter format. If you don't know the mailing address of the manufacturer, just make it up.

Resource Center

The Parisian Novels (The Yellow Books), Vincent van Gogh, 1888.

Reading Matters

Why Reading Matters

> *I read good enough. I mean, most of the time I don't know the answers to the questions that are at the end of the chapter like in my science book or even at the end of stories we read in English, but that's okay, because those questions are hard. Right? Anyway, how are those questions going to help me in real life, you know, when I'm out of school and working?*
>
> —Collin, grade 10

Collin takes driver's ed, plays basketball, works at a bagel shop on weekends, and struggles in school. He'd like to make better grades, but because he doesn't read well, he has problems doing his homework and studying for tests. But when you ask (as I did) how he reads, he says, "Good enough." It's good enough for him because he doesn't see the connection between being able to read well and doing well in school and in the job he'll someday have as an adult.

He asks how answering the questions in his social studies, science, and literature books is going to help him in "real life." Well, being able to answer questions in school helps in two ways. First, answering questions is a quick way to show yourself and your teachers what you understand about content. Second, since most of the questions you answer either force you to recall specific information or push you to figure out more complex problems, answering questions can help you become a better thinker. Being a better thinker is helpful in any job.

It all starts with reading. If you can't read the stories and essays in your textbooks or the questions or the tests, then all sorts of negative things begin to happen. That's because no matter where you live, no matter what you do, you are surrounded by print—from textbooks, e-mail messages, and Web pages to how-to instruction manuals and magazines. In a literate society, reading is critical.

The following section is designed to help you with reading. In it you'll find strategies that will help you better comprehend the texts you read. Take some time right now to flip through the pages of this section. You'll see that each lesson is brief—so you can learn a lot in a little bit of time. You can return to this section as often as you need to. Use the strategies suggested here with the selections in this book. Then, try them as you read other texts. The more you think about the topics covered in this section and practice what's suggested here, the better you'll be at reading.

That's important because, after all, *reading matters*.

—Kylene Beers

When the Text Is Tough

Remember the reading you did back in first, second, and third grades? Big print. Short texts. Easy words. Now in high school, however, the texts you read are often filled with small print, long chapters, and complicated plots or topics. Also, you now find yourself reading a variety of material—from your driver's-ed handbook to college applications, from job applications to income-tax forms, from e-mail to e-zines, from classics to comics, from textbooks to checkbooks.

Doing something every day that you find difficult and tedious isn't much fun—and that includes reading. So, this section of this book is designed for you, to show you what to do when the text gets tough. Let's begin by looking at some *reading* matters.

READING UP CLOSE: HOW TO USE THIS SECTION

- **This section is for you.** Turn to it whenever you need to remind yourself about what to do when the text gets tough. Don't wait for your teacher to assign this section for you to read. It's your handbook. Use it.

- **Read the sections that you need.** You don't have to read every word. Skim the headings, and find the information you need.

- **Use this information for help with reading for other classes,** not just for the reading you do in this book.

- **Don't be afraid to re-read the information you find in Reading Matters.** The best readers constantly re-read information.

- **If you need more help, then check the index.** The index will direct you to other pages in this book with information on reading skills and strategies.

Improving Your Comprehension

Have you seen the reruns of an old weekly television show called *Lost in Space*? Perhaps you saw the more recent movie version of it? If so, you probably remember the robot that constantly tried to warn the young boy, Will Robinson, when danger was near by waving his robot arms and announcing loudly, "Danger approaching, Will Robinson!" Then Will would look up from whatever he was doing, notice whatever evil was moments away, and take action. But until the robot warned him, Will would ignore all warning signs that danger was at hand.

Wouldn't it be nice if something would warn us as we were about to enter a dangerous area when we were reading—a part of the text that we might not understand? Perhaps our own little robots could pop up in books, saying, "Danger, reader! Misunderstandings approaching!" Then we'd know to slow down, pay attention, and carefully study the text we were reading.

Actually those signs do appear, but not as arm-waving robots in the margins of books. Instead, the signs appear in our minds as we are reading. However, unless we are paying attention, we often read on past them, not noticing the warnings they offer. What we need to do is learn to recognize the danger signs so that like Will Robinson, we will know when to look up and take action.

READING UP CLOSE

Looking for the Danger Signs

Study each of the signs to the right, and decide what type of danger each could signify when you read. You might want to copy these signs onto stick-on notes to put on your texts as you read.

Danger Sign 1

You can't remember what you read.

This happens to all readers occasionally. You read something, and your attention wanders for a moment, but your eyes don't quit moving from word to word. In a few minutes you realize you are several pages beyond the last point where you can remember thinking about what you were reading. Then you know you need to back up and start over.

Forgetting what you've read is a danger sign only if it happens to you frequently. If you constantly complete a reading assignment but don't remember anything that you've been reading, then you probably are in the habit of letting your mind focus on something else while your eyes are focusing on the words. That's a habit you need to break.

READING UP CLOSE

▶ **Measure Your Attention Quotient**

Take the following survey to see what your attention quotient is. The lower the score, the less attention you pay to what you are reading.

When I read, I . . .

1. let my mind wander
  a. most of the time
  b. sometimes
  c. almost never

2. forget what I'm reading
  a. most of the time
  b. sometimes
  c. almost never

3. get confused and stay confused
  a. most of the time
  b. sometimes
  c. almost never

4. discover I've turned lots of pages and don't have a clue as to what I've read
  a. most of the time
  b. sometimes
  c. almost never

5. rarely finish whatever I'm supposed to be reading
  a. most of the time
  b. sometimes
  c. almost never

Tips for Staying Focused

1. Don't read from the beginning of the assignment to the end without pausing. Set up **checkpoints** for yourself, either every few pages or every five minutes. At those checkpoints, stop reading and ask yourself some basic questions—"What's happening now? What do I not understand?"

2. As you read, keep paper and pen close by. **Take notes** as you read, in particular jotting down questions you have about what confuses you, interests you, or perhaps even surprises you.

Danger Sign 2
You don't "see" what you are reading.

The ability to **visualize**—or see in your mind—what you are reading is important for comprehension. To understand how visualizing makes a difference, try this quick test. When you get home, turn on a television to a program you enjoy. Then, turn your back to the television set. How long will you keep "watching" the program that way? Probably not long. Why not? Because it would be boring if you couldn't see what was happening. The same is true of reading: If you can't see in your mind what is happening on the page, then you probably will tune out quickly. You can improve your ability to visualize text by practicing the following strategies:

1. **Read a few sentences; then, pause, and describe what is happening on the page.** Forcing yourself to describe the scene will take some time at first, but it will help in the long run.

2. **On a sheet of paper or a stick-on note, make a graphic representation of what is happening as you are reading.** For instance, if two characters are talking, draw two stick figures with arrows pointing between them to show yourself that they are talking.

3. **Discuss a scene or a part of a chapter with a buddy.** Talk about what you "saw" as you were reading.

4. **Read aloud.** If you are having trouble visualizing the text, it might be because you aren't really "hearing" it. Try reading a portion of your text aloud, using good expression and phrasing. As you hear the words, you may find it easier to see the scenes.

READING UP CLOSE

▶ **Visualizing What You Read**

Read the following excerpt from "Blues Ain't No Mockin Bird" by Toni Cade Bambara, and discuss what you "see":

"The puddle had frozen over, and me and Cathy went stompin in it. The twins from next door, Tyrone and Terry, were swingin so high out of sight we forgot we were waitin our turn on the tire. Cathy jumped up and came down hard on her heels and started tap-dancin. And the frozen patch splinterin every which way underneath kinda spooky. 'Looks like a plastic spider web,' she said. 'A sort of weird spider, I guess, with many mental problems.' But really it looked like the crystal paperweight Granny kept in the parlor."

Reading Matters

Danger Sign 3

You constantly answer "I don't know" to questions at the end of reading selections.

If you consistently don't know the answers to questions about what you've been reading, then you probably would benefit from the following strategies:

Think-Aloud. Comprehension problems don't appear only after you *finish* reading. Confusion occurs *as* you read. Therefore, don't wait until you complete your reading assignment to try to understand the text; instead, work on comprehending while reading by becoming an active reader.

Active readers **predict, connect, clarify, question,** and **visualize** as they read. If you don't do those things, then you need to pause while you read to

- make predictions

- make connections

- clarify in your own thoughts what you are reading

- question what you don't understand

- visualize the text and observe key details

Use the Think-Aloud strategy to practice your active-reading skills. Read a selection of text aloud to a partner. As you read, pause to make comments and ask questions. Your partner's job is to tally your comments and classify each according to the list above.

READING UP CLOSE

▶ **One Student's Think-Aloud**

Here's Jamail's Think-Aloud for "Cranes" (p. 272):

<u>Page 272, sixth paragraph</u>: In this part, Sŏngsam suddenly sees a childhood friend he used to know. I also saw a friend of mine the other day, and the last time I had seen him was in first grade. (**Connection**)

<u>Page 272, eleventh paragraph</u>: Sŏngsam says, "I'll take the fellow with me." I bet he plans to find out why Tŏkchae joined the Farmers Communist League. (**Prediction**)

<u>Page 274, thirteenth paragraph</u>: Why does Tŏkchae say his father is ill? (**Question**)

<u>Page 275, fourth paragraph</u>: Oh, now I see. Tŏkchae explains that he didn't escape because he didn't want to leave his sick father. (**Clarification**)

Retelling. While the Think-Aloud strategy keeps you focused as you read, the Retelling strategy helps you after reading. Read the tips for retelling on the next page, and then practice retelling small portions of your reading assignments. You might ask a friend to listen to you retell what you have read, or you might record yourself as you retell a selection.

Retelling Prompts for Fiction

1. State what text you are retelling.
2. Give characters' names, and explain who they are.
3. Sequence the events using words like *first, second, third, then, later, next,* and *last.*
4. Identify the conflict in the story.
5. Explain the resolution of the conflict.
6. Tell what you enjoyed or did not enjoy about the text.

Retelling Prompts for Informational Texts

State what text you are retelling, and identify the **structure** of the text.

- If the structure is a **sequence** (the water cycle), use words like *first, second, third, then, later, afterwards, following that, before,* and *last.*

- If the structure is **comparison and contrast** (the differences between World War I and World War II), use words or phrases such as *by comparison, by contrast, on the other hand, yet, but, however, nevertheless, conversely, then again,* or *in opposition.*

- If showing **cause-and-effect relationships,** use words like *reason, motive, basis,* and *grounds* to discuss **causes,** and use words like *outcome, consequence, result,* and *product* to discuss **effects.**

READING UP CLOSE

▶ **Evaluate Your Retelling**

Listen to your retelling, and ask yourself:

1. Does my retelling make sense?
2. Does it have enough information?
3. Is the information in the correct order?
4. Could a drawing or a diagram help my retelling?
5. If someone listening to my retelling hadn't read the text, what would that person visualize?
6. To improve my next retelling, should I focus on characters, sequence of events, amount of detail, or general conclusions?

Re-reading and Rewording. The best way to improve your comprehension is simply to **re-read.** The first time you read something, you get the basic idea of the text. The next time you read it, you revise your understanding. Try thinking of your first reading as a draft—just like the first draft of an essay. As you revise your essay, you are improving your writing. As you revise your reading, you are improving your comprehension.

Sometimes, as you re-read, you find some specific sentences or even passages that you just don't understand. When that's the case, you need to spend some time closely studying those sentences. One effective way to tackle tough text is to **reword** it:

1. On a sheet of paper, write the sentences that are confusing you.
2. Leave a few blank lines between each line you write.
3. Then, choose the difficult words, and replace them in the space above.
4. While you wouldn't want to reword every line of a text, this is a powerful way to help you understand key sentences.

READING UP CLOSE

▶ **One Student's Rewording**

After ninth-grader Callie read the article "Romeo and Juliet in Bosnia" (p. 1035), she copied a few sentences she didn't understand. After re-reading them, she reworded them, using a thesaurus.

1. "But ~~civilization~~ is ~~an exceedingly fragile enterprise,~~ and it's

   society   *a very weak thing,*

   ~~especially vulnerable to~~ the ~~primal madness~~ of ~~ethnic~~ and

   really in danger of   *primitive craziness*   *racial*

   religious hatreds."

2. "When the madness ~~descended~~ on Sarajevo, Bosko Brkic faced a

   came down

   ~~cruel dilemma.~~"

   bad problem.

Summarizing Narrative Text.   Understanding a long piece of text is easier if you can summarize chunks of it. If you are reading a **narrative,** or a story, then use a strategy called **Somebody Wanted But So (SWBS)** to help you write a summary of what you are reading. SWBS is a powerful way to think about the characters in a story and note what each did, what conflict each faced, and what the resolution was. As you write an SWBS statement for different characters in the same story, you are forcing yourself to rethink the story from different **points of view.** By analyzing point of view in this way, you get a better understanding of the impact of the author's choice of narrator.

Here are the steps for writing SWBS statements:

1. Write the words *Somebody, Wanted, But,* and *So* across four columns.
2. In the "Somebody" column, write a character's name.

3. Then, in the "Wanted" column, write what that character wanted to do.

4. Next, in the "But" column, explain what happened that kept the character from doing what he or she wanted.

5. Finally, in the "So" column, explain the eventual outcome.

6. If you're making an SWBS chart for a long story or novel, you'll need to write several statements at different points in the story.

READING UP CLOSE

▶ **One Student's SWBS Chart**

Here is Ben's SWBS chart for "The Scarlet Ibis" (p. 415):

Somebody	Wanted	But	So
Brother	wanted Doodle to be like other kids,	but Doodle's physical problems kept that from happening,	so Brother pushed Doodle too hard and then had to live with guilt when Doodle died.
Doodle	wanted to please Brother,	but he couldn't do all Brother demanded of him,	so he died.

Summarizing Expository Text.

If summarizing the information in **expository,** or informational, texts is difficult, try a strategy called GIST.

Steps for GIST

1. Divide the text you want to summarize into three or four sections.

2. Read the first section.

3. Draw twenty blank lines on a sheet of paper.

4. Write a summary of the first section of text using exactly twenty words—one word for each blank.

5. Read the next section of text. In your next set of twenty blanks, write a new summary statement that combines your first summary with whatever you want to add from this second section of text. It's important to note that even though you've now got two chunks of text to cover, you still have only twenty blanks to fill, not forty.

READING UP CLOSE

▶ **One Student's GIST**

After reading "How Did They Disappear?" (p. 588), Erin wrote the following GIST statements:

GIST 1 (for the first and second paragraphs)
Some scientists believe the earth's rock layers reveal that dinosaurs became extinct after a comet or asteroid struck the earth.

GIST 2 (adding the third paragraph)
Some scientists believe iridium in rock layers indicates a comet or asteroid struck the earth, resulting in the dinosaurs' extinction.

GIST 3 (completing the page)
Some scientists believe a comet or asteroid struck Mexico, and the resulting greenhouse effect caused the extinction of the dinosaurs.

6. Repeat this one or two more times, depending on how much more text you have. When you are finished, you'll have a twenty-word statement that gives you the gist, or overall idea, of what the entire text is about.

Key Words. Sometimes you don't want to write a summary of what you've been reading. Sometimes you just want to jot down some key words to remind yourself about a specific topic. To keep your key words organized, don't forget your ABCs. Fill a page with boxes, as in the example below. You can use your computer to make this page or just grab a pencil and notebook paper. Once your boxes are drawn, all you have to do is decide what information to include.

For instance, Meredith uses her Key Word chart while reading "Thank You, M'am" on page 109. She puts Roger's name in blue at the top of the page and Mrs. Luella Bates Washington Jones's name in red. As Meredith reads the story and thinks of words to describe each character, she puts those key character-description words in the correct box in the correct color. So, she writes "preachy" in red (because she thinks that word describes Mrs. Jones) in the O–P box. She writes "ashamed" in blue (because this word is for Roger) in the A–B box. When completed, the chart could be a starting point for writing a paper that compares and contrasts Roger and Mrs. Jones.

READING UP CLOSE

▶ **Using a Key Word Chart**

Here is Meredith's Key Word chart for "Thank You, M'am." Read the story, and find more key words to describe the two main characters.

Roger   Mrs. Luella Bates Washington Jones

A–B	C–D	E–F	G–H	I–J	K–L
ashamed					

M–N	O–P	Q–R	S–T	U–V–W	X–Y–Z
	preachy				

Improving Your Reading Rate

If your reading concerns are more about getting through the words than figuring out the meaning, then this part of Reading Matters is for you.

If you think you are a slow reader, then reading can seem overwhelming. But you can change your reading rate—the pace at which you read. All you have to do is practice. The point isn't to read so fast that you just rush over words— the I'mgoingtoreadsofastthatallthewordsruntogether approach. Instead, the goal is to find a pace that keeps you moving comfortably through the pages. Why is it important to establish a good reading rate? Let's do a little math to see why your silent reading rate counts.

As you figure out the problem, you see that it takes 100 minutes to read 10 pages at the slowest pace and only 20 minutes at the fastest pace. See the chart at the right for all the times.

Reading Rate and Homework

Now, assume that with literature homework, science homework, and social studies homework, in one night you have 40 pages to read. If you are reading at 40 WPM, you are spending over *6 hours* just reading the information; but at 100 WPM, you would spend only about 2 hours and 45 minutes. And at 200 WPM, you'd finish in 1 hour and 20 minutes.

MATH PROBLEM!

If you read 40 words per minute (WPM) and there are 400 words on a page, then how long will it take you to read 1 page? 5 pages? 10 pages? How long will it take if you read 80 WPM? 100 WPM? 200 WPM?

	1 page @400 words/page	5 pages @400 words/page	10 pages @400 words/page
40 WPM	10 minutes	50 minutes	100 minutes
80 WPM	5 minutes	25 minutes	50 minutes
100 WPM	4 minutes	20 minutes	40 minutes
200 WPM	2 minutes	10 minutes	20 minutes

READING UP CLOSE

▶ **Tips on Varying Your Reading Rate**

- Increasing your rate doesn't matter if your comprehension goes down.

- Don't rush to read fast if that means understanding less.

- Remember that your rate will vary as your purpose for reading varies. You'll read more slowly when you are studying for a test than when you are skimming a text.

Figuring Out Your Reading Rate

To determine your silent-reading rate, you'll need three things: a watch or clock with a second hand, a book, and someone who will watch the time for you. Then, follow these steps:

1. Have your friend time you as you begin reading to yourself.

2. Read at your normal rate. Don't speed just because you're being timed.

3. Stop when your friend tells you one minute is up.

4. Count the number of words you read in that minute. Write down that number.

5. Repeat this process several more times, using different passages.

6. Then, add the number of words together, and divide by the number of times you timed yourself. That's your average rate.

> **Example**
>
> 1st minute   180 words
> 2nd minute   215 words
> 3rd minute   190 words
>
> 585 words ÷ 3 = 195 WPM

Reading Rate Reminders

You can improve your reading rate by using the following strategies:

1. **Make sure you aren't reading just one word at a time with a pause between each word.** Practice phrasing words in your mind as you read. For instance, look at the sample sentence, and pause only where you see the slash marks. One slash (/) means pause a bit. Two slashes (//) mean pause a bit longer.

> Jack and Jill/ went up the hill/ to fetch a pail of water.// Jack fell down/ and broke his crown/ and Jill came tumbling after.//

Now, read it again, pausing after each word:

> Jack/ and/ Jill/ went/ up/ the/ hill/ to/ fetch/ a/ pail/ of/ water.// Jack/ fell/ down/ and/ broke/ his/ crown/ and/ Jill/ came/ tumbling/ after.//

Hear the difference? Word-at-a-time reading is much slower than phrase reading. If you are reading one word at a time, you'll want to practice reading by phrases. You can hear good phrasing by listening to a book on tape.

2. **Make sure you aren't sounding out each word.** At this point in school, you need to be able to recognize whole words and save the sounding-out strategy for words you haven't seen before. In other words, you ought to be able to read *material* as "material" and not

"ma-ter-i-al," but you might need to move more slowly through *metacognition* so that you read that word as "met-a-cog-ni-tion."

3. **Make sure when you are reading silently that you really are reading silently.** Don't move your lips or read aloud very softly when reading. These habits slow you down. Remember, if you need to slow down (for instance, when the information you are reading is confusing you), then reading aloud to yourself is a smart thing to do. But generally, silent reading means reading silently!

4. **Don't use your finger to point to words as you read.** If you find that you always use your finger to point to words as you read (instead of just occasionally, when you are really concentrating), then you are probably reading one word at a time. Instead, use a bookmark to help yourself stay on the right line, and practice your phrase reading.

5. **As you practice your fluency, remember that the single best way to improve your reading rate is simply to read more!** You won't get better at what you never do. Also, always remember that your rate will vary as your purpose for reading varies. So, time yourself, determine your reading rate, start reading more, and remember these *dos* and *don'ts*. Soon you'll find that reading too slowly isn't a problem anymore.

READING UP CLOSE

▶ Recalculating Your Reading Rate

After putting into practice some of the advice on improving your reading rate provided above, recalculate your average rate. Once again, use the instructions in Figuring Out Your Reading Rate (page 1106). This time, however, read one passage from the following material:

1. Page 39:   "Can Animals Think?"
2. Page 127:   "Helen on Eighty-sixth Street"
3. Page 530:   "The Sounds of Poetry"

After you've counted the number of words you read in each passage in one minute, divide by three. The result will be your average rate.

Remember: It's important to slow down your rate when you are confused about what you are reading.

Writer's Handbook

The Writing Process

Good writing doesn't just appear, ready-made, out of nowhere. The writer of an enjoyable piece uses a process to create it. The writing process has four stages, each with several steps. The chart below lists what happens during each stage.

STAGES OF THE WRITING PROCESS	
Prewriting	• Choose your topic.
	• Identify your purpose and audience.
	• Generate ideas, and gather information about the topic.
	• Begin to organize the information.
	• Draft a sentence that expresses your main point and your perspective on the topic.
Writing a Draft	• Grab your readers' attention in the introduction.
	• Provide background information.
	• State and support your main points, and elaborate on them.
	• Follow a plan of organization.
	• Wrap up with a conclusion.
Revising	• Evaluate your draft.
	• Revise the draft's content, organization, and style.
Publishing	• Proofread, or edit, your final draft.
	• Publish, or share your finished writing with readers.
	• Reflect on your writing experience.

You can always return to an earlier stage in the process to improve your writing. For example, if in revising you find that you need more information, you can return to prewriting to gather ideas and then draft a new paragraph.

As you progress through the stages of the writing process, make sure you do the following:

● **Keep your ideas focused.** Your writing should be **coherent,** with ideas clearly connected to one another. To keep your writing on track, pin down the specific purpose you want the piece to achieve and establish a coherent thesis. Every idea in a piece must support your thesis or the controlling impression you want to create. Eliminate anything that doesn't fit your distinct perspective or that might detract from a tightly reasoned argument. Your focus should be clear and consistent throughout a piece of writing.

● **Use a consistent tone.** To unify the ideas in a piece of writing, keep your tone consistent. Avoid jumping from a serious, formal tone to a casual or sarcastic tone midway through a piece. Choose your tone by thinking about your specific audience. What tone would they appreciate? Does that tone fit your topic?

● **Plan to publish.** Develop each piece as though it might be published, or shared with an audience. When you proofread, use the following questions to guide you. The numbers in parentheses indicate the sections in the Language Handbook that contain instruction on these topics.

GUIDELINES FOR PROOFREADING

1. Is every sentence complete, not a fragment or run-on? (9a, b)

2. Are punctuation marks used correctly? (12a–r, 13a–j, 14a–o)

3. Are the first letters of sentences and proper nouns and adjectives capitalized? (11a, d)

4. Does each verb agree in number with its subject? (2a) Are verb forms and tenses used correctly? (3a–e)

5. Are subject and object forms of personal pronouns used correctly? (4a–c) Does every pronoun agree with a clear antecedent in number and gender? (4i)

To mark proofreading corrections, use the symbols below.

PROOFREADING SYMBOLS

Symbol	Example	Meaning of Symbol
≡	Fifty-first street	Capitalize a lowercase letter.
/	Jerry's Aunt	Lowercase a capital letter.
∧	the capital of Ohio	Insert a missing word, letter, or punctuation mark.
⌐	beside the river lake	Replace a word.
ℰ	Where's the the key?	Delete a word, letter, or punctuation mark.
∪	thier	Change the order of letters.
¶	¶ "Hi," he smiled.	Begin a new paragraph.

Paragraphs

A **paragraph** is made up of sentences grouped together for a reason—usually to present and support a single idea. Each paragraph in a composition is like a member of a team, working with other paragraphs to develop ideas. Think of a paragraph as a link in a chain connecting ideas.

Paragraphs are used to divide an essay into blocks of separate thoughts or to divide a story into a series of events. Paragraphs signal readers that a new thought or a new speaker is coming. They also allow readers to pause to digest what they've read so far.

Parts of a Body Paragraph

Although some paragraphs—especially in narrative writing—do not have a central focus, most paragraphs do emphasize one **main idea.** Paragraphs like this, often called **body paragraphs,** usually have three major parts: a **topic sentence,** which states the paragraph's main idea; additional **supporting sentences** that elaborate on and support the topic sentence; and (often, but not always) a concluding **clincher** sentence.

The Main Idea and Topic Sentence   Together, the sentences in a paragraph make its main idea clear. Many paragraphs express the main idea in a single sentence, called a **topic sentence.**

Although a topic sentence can be placed at any point in the paragraph, it often appears as the first or second sentence. A topic sentence at the beginning of a paragraph helps a reader know what to expect in the rest of the paragraph. The diagram below shows the typical three-part structure of a body paragraph that begins with a topic sentence.

TIP   Although many paragraphs you read will not have topic sentences, it's a good idea to use them in your own writing to keep you focused on your main idea and to organize your support.

Typical Body Paragraph Structure

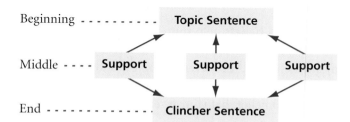

A topic sentence placed at the end of a paragraph can be an effective way to create surprise or summarize ideas. As you read the following paragraph, notice how the writer sews all the details together with a topic sentence at the very end.

> In the summer, hosts of big red-and-yellow grasshoppers, with heads shaped like horses, will descend and eat holes in all the softer leaves. Walking sticks fly like boomerangs. Shining brown leaf-shaped palmetto bugs scurry like cockroaches. Spiders like tiny crabs hang in stout webs. The birds snap at small moths and butterflies of every kind. A blue racer, the snake that moves across the cleared land like whiplash, will with one flick destroy the smooth, careful cup of the ant lion in the hot sand. The whole world of the pines and of the rocks hums and glistens and stings with life.
>
> Marjory Stoneman Douglas, *The Everglades: River of Grass*

TIP Supporting sentences don't just provide evidence, but also elaborate on it. Every piece of support must clearly relate to the main idea; you may need to use supporting sentences to explain this connection or simply to explain a piece of evidence to make it more clear.

Supporting Sentences To make your main idea clear and interesting, **elaborate** on it, or develop it in detail. Use supporting sentences to give the types of specific evidence below for the main idea.

Sensory Details **Sensory details** are collected through the senses of sight, hearing, smell, touch, or taste.

Facts and Statistics A **fact** is a statement that can be proved true. A **statistic** is a fact based on numbers, such as "During the Civil War, the South lost about 260,000 soldiers, and the North lost about 360,000." Choose facts and statistics from reliable, unbiased sources.

Examples **Examples** are specific instances or illustrations of a general idea. A cow is an example of an animal.

Other Types of Supporting Evidence Some types of supporting evidence are useful only in certain kinds of writing.

- **Scenarios** are general descriptions of potential events or common situations. They can support ideas in persuasive writing and in cause-and-effect or problem-solution essays.

- **Commonly held beliefs** help support appeals in persuasive pieces. For example, to encourage voter registration, you could note the commonly held belief that everyone's vote should count. You could also grab attention at the beginning of a research report by stating a commonly held belief that your research disproves.

- **Hypotheses** are unproven theories that serve as the basis for investigation. They can support ideas in cause-and-effect papers or in research reports by providing background information or by presenting possible results of events or situations.

- **Definitions** provide support in expository and persuasive pieces by clarifying for readers exactly what a particular term means.

The Clincher Sentence Some paragraphs, especially long ones, end with a **clincher**—a sentence that emphasizes the paragraph's main idea. A clincher pulls together details and signals the end of the paragraph, often using a transition such as *therefore* or *as a result*.

The Makings of a Good Paragraph

A good paragraph has **unity** and **coherence.** Use the following guidelines to give your own writing these two important qualities.

Unity When a paragraph has **unity,** all its sentences work together as a unit to express or support one main idea. Sentences can work as a unit by supporting a main idea that is either stated or implied, or by expressing a related series of actions. Sentences that interrupt the consistent focus of a paragraph destroy its unity.

Coherence A paragraph lacking **coherence** fails to make clear how the ideas it presents fit together. Create coherence by using a clear **order,** or structure, of ideas and by making strong **connections** between ideas.

Order of Ideas How you structure ideas in a paragraph can help your readers follow those ideas. Here are four ways to organize a paragraph:

- Use **chronological order,** relating events in the order they happened, to explain a process, tell a story, or explain a cause-and-effect sequence.

- Use **spatial order,** describing things according to where they are located in relation to one another or to a viewer (for example, moving from nearest to farthest or from left to right), for descriptive writing.

- Use **order of importance,** showing the importance of details in relation to one another, to build up to or down from your most important point. Place that point prominently—first or last.

- Use **logical order,** grouping related ideas together, to **compare and contrast subjects** (explaining how they are alike and different) or to **define a subject.** The paragraph below defines *mummies*.

> A mummy is the preserved body of a human being or an animal, by any means, either deliberate or accidental. Mummies survive from many ancient cultures, some preserved in a wet state, others dry. The bog bodies of northern Europe, such as the 2,000-year-old Lindow Man, found in Cheshire, England, in 1984, belonged to people who had either fallen, or been thrown, into wet, marshy places. The exclusion of oxygen and acidity in the peat of the bog effectively preserved their bodies. Most mummies, though, were preserved by being dried, or desiccated. Many civilizations, including the Egyptian, Chinese, and some South American cultures, tried to achieve this artificially.
> Christine El Mahdy, *Mummies, Myth and Magic in Ancient Egypt*

Definition

Specific example

Details

Details
Details

TIP Direct references and transitional words and phrases can make connections *between* paragraphs as well as *within* paragraphs.

Connections Between Ideas Along with putting ideas in an order that makes sense, you create coherence in a paragraph by showing how ideas are connected. You can show connections by using **direct references** and by using **transitional words and phrases.**

- **Direct References** **Direct references** link ideas by referring to a noun or pronoun used earlier in a paragraph. You can make direct references by using a noun or pronoun that refers to a noun used earlier, by repeating a word used earlier, or by using a word or phrase with the same meaning as one used earlier.

- **Transitional Words and Phrases** A **transitional expression**—whether a word, a phrase, or a sentence—shows *how* ideas are connected, often by using a conjunction or preposition. The chart below shows transitions that fit certain types of writing.

TRANSITIONAL WORDS AND PHRASES			
Comparing Ideas	also and	another moreover	similarly too
Contrasting Ideas	although however	in spite of instead	on the other hand yet
Showing Cause and Effect	as a result because consequently	for since so	so that thus therefore
Showing Chronological Order	after at last before	eventually finally first	meanwhile next then
Showing Spatial Order	above across around behind	beyond down here inside	into next to over under
Showing Importance	first last	mainly more important	then to begin with

PRACTICE & APPLY Draft a paragraph on a topic of your choice. First, identify your main idea. As you write, give your paragraph a clear topic sentence, several types of support for your main idea, and a clincher sentence; unity and coherence, with all ideas creating a controlling impression; and an easy-to-follow structure with clear connections between ideas.

The Writer's Language

Revising to Improve Style

When you revise a draft, be sure to look at your **style**—the way you express your ideas. Consider your **audience** and **purpose,** and examine your draft for **precise language, action verbs, sensory details, appropriate modifiers,** and the **active voice.**

Who and Why   As you re-read your draft, answer these questions:

- **What is my purpose?** Ask yourself *why* you are writing this piece and what you hope it will achieve. Make sure your **tone**—your attitude toward your topic—fits this purpose.

- **Who is my audience? Does my essay speak directly to them?** Consider whether your **level of formality** is appropriate. Avoid making your writing too formal or too informal for your audience.

The Finer Points   When revising, consider your **word choice**— particularly precise language, action verbs, sensory details, and appropriate modifiers. Also, use the **active voice** as much as possible. Read this example:

> I was hungry. I went home after school. Thoughts of eating were starting to come into my mind. I opened the refrigerator door and looked inside. There was nothing good to eat. The loud refrigerator door closed. Then I saw exactly what I wanted to eat—food that had been made for my mother for her birthday. I ate it all and then had to replace it.

Because it lacks stylistic elements such as precise language and sensory detail, this paragraph fails to create a complete picture.

Precise Language   To paint a clear picture of a subject, use **precise verbs, nouns,** and **adjectives.** For example, the phrase "nothing good to eat" doesn't show what is in the refrigerator. Are there moldy green leftovers? a wilted head of lettuce? Create a vivid picture for readers.

Action Verbs   Avoid overusing dull verbs, such as *be, go, have,* and *do.* To improve the dull sentence "I went home after school," try substituting the more vivid *ran, galloped, dragged,* or *hurried* for the verb *went.* **Action verbs** such as these *show* what happened. When revising, replace dull verbs, especially *be*-verbs, with more-vivid action verbs.

Sensory Details   Words and phrases that appeal to the senses— sight, hearing, taste, touch, and smell—are called **sensory details.** For example, noting the sound of the narrator's growling stomach would help readers experience his hunger.

Appropriate Modifiers **Appropriate modifiers** clearly relate to the correct word. For example, in the paragraph on page 1115, the use of "loud" as an adjective implies that the refrigerator door is loud all by itself. Instead, the adverb "loudly" should modify the verb *closed*. Also, consider whether you really *need* a modifier; a more precise noun or verb is often a better solution, as in the revised sentence, "I slammed the refrigerator door."

Active Voice Use the **active** rather than the **passive voice** whenever possible in your writing. The phrase "food that had been made for my mother" is in the passive voice. The action just "happens" to the subject. To show *who* performed the action, the phrase should be turned around: "food I had made for my mother." To find passive constructions in your writing, first look for *be*-verbs. Then, decide whether the action of the sentence is being done *by* the subject or *to* the subject. If the subject is receiving the action, revise.

Read the following revision of the passage on page 1115. Notice how precise language, action verbs, sensory details, appropriate modifiers, and the active voice make the writing more vivid and entertaining.

A Writer's Model

Action verbs

Precise language and sensory detail

Action verb

Precise language and active voice

My stomach growled, and I galloped home from school—all I could think about was food. I opened the refrigerator door and peeked inside. A wilted head of lettuce stared back at me, along with a mysterious something, squishy and greenish brown in a plastic bag. "Yuck," I thought, hungrier than ever. I slammed the refrigerator door. Suddenly, my mouth watered as I saw just what I wanted to eat on the kitchen counter. The muffins I had made for my mother for a birthday breakfast were irresistible. By the time I thought about what I was doing, I had wolfed down all of them. Now I had to figure out how to replace the birthday treat before my mother got home!

PRACTICE & APPLY Revise the following paragraph to improve its style. Make up details as needed.

A collection of Native American items is on display at a museum in town. They have arrowheads, blankets, and cooking pots. Some of the arrowheads are small, and some are larger. The blankets are colorful, and the cooking pots are interesting. One of the pots can be touched. A lecture is given. The exhibit is unique.

Designing Your Writing

No matter how well-written a document's content might be, if it is sloppy, confusing, or hard to read, it won't make a strong impact on the audience. Some readers may give up trying to read a badly designed document. Others may assume that a writer who is careless about design is also careless about facts. Use the suggestions in this section to get your ideas across clearly.

Page Design

Easy on the Eyes If you want your documents to make a good impression, make sure they are visually appealing and easy to read. You can improve the readability and impact of your papers by using some of the design elements below, whether you create those documents by hand or using a word-processing program.

DESIGN ELEMENTS

Element	Definition	Purpose
Bullets	A *bullet* (•) is an icon used to make information stand out.	Bullets are most often used for lists.
Captions	A *caption* is text printed beneath an illustration.	Captions explain photos, maps, and graphs.
Columns and blocks of text	*Columns* arrange text in two or more separate sections printed side by side. A *block* is a section of text shorter than a page—for example, one story would fill a rectangular block on the front page of the newspaper. Columns and blocks of text are separated from each other by white space.	Columns and blocks make text easier to read.
Headings and subheadings	A *heading* gives readers a general idea of what a section of text, such as a chapter, will be about. A *subheading* is used to indicate subsections of the text.	Headings and subheadings give readers clues about the content and organization of the document.
Leading	*Leading* (rhymes with *heading*) is the amount of white space *between* lines of text. This text is single-spaced.	For school papers, use double-spaced text, which gives your teacher space to comment on your ideas.
Margins	*Margins* are the white space at the top, bottom, and both sides of a page.	Page margins of about one inch create a visual break for readers and make text easier to read.

A Capital Idea Your choice of type can impact a document's readability and attractiveness. You can vary the **case** of type (from the usual mostly **lowercase,** or small type) to add interest to a document and make it easier to navigate.

- **Uppercase,** or all capital, letters attract readers' attention and may be used in headings or titles. Remember that words in uppercase letters can be difficult to read. Use uppercase letters for emphasis, not for large bodies of text.

- **Small caps** are uppercase letters that are reduced in size. Usually they appear in abbreviations of time, such as 9:00 A.M. and A.D. 1500.

Font-astic! A **font** is one complete set of characters (such as letters, numbers, and punctuation marks) of a given size and design. Here are the types of fonts.

Quick guide

TYPES OF FONTS		
Category	**Explanation**	**How They Are Used**
decorative, or **script,** fonts	elaborately designed characters that convey a distinct mood or feeling	Decorative fonts are difficult to read and should be used sparingly for an artistic effect.
serif fonts	characters with small strokes (serifs) attached at each end	Because the strokes on serif characters guide the reader's eyes from letter to letter, serif type is often used for large bodies of text.
sans serif fonts	characters formed of neat straight lines, with no serifs at the ends of letters	Sans serif fonts are easy to read and are used for headings, subheadings, callouts, and captions.

Graphics and Visuals

The Big Picture Some information is difficult to communicate in words but easy to communicate visually. Fortunately, advanced publishing software has made creating many kinds of visuals easy. A graphic program may allow you to enter your information and choose the most appropriate type of visual. You can also create nearly any type of graphic by hand.

Choosing the right visual to show a piece of information will help you avoid confusing your readers. Include a **caption** or **title** that explicitly tells readers what they are to see in the visual and why it is there. Use **color** sparingly to emphasize ideas, not as decoration. The following pages explain some useful types of visuals.

- **Charts** show relationships among ideas or data. Two types of charts you are likely to use are flowcharts and pie charts. A **flowchart** uses geometric shapes linked by arrows to show the sequence of events in a process.

EXAMPLE

Writing the First Draft of a Research Paper

Brainstorm possible topics

↓

Choose one topic

↓

Research the topic and take notes

↓

Organize ideas

↓

Write a first draft

A **pie chart** shows the parts of a whole. This type of chart is a circle that is divided into wedges. Each wedge represents a certain percentage of the total. A legend tells what idea or characteristic of the whole is represented by each wedge color.

EXAMPLE

Career Goals of Seniors at Felicity High School

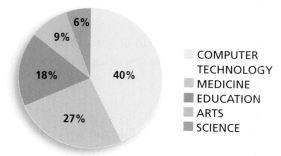

6%
9%
18%
27%
40%

- COMPUTER TECHNOLOGY
- MEDICINE
- EDUCATION
- ARTS
- SCIENCE

- **Graphs** use numbers to present facts and figures. There are two types of graphs, both used to show how one thing changes in relation to another. A **bar graph** can be used to compare quantities at a glance, to show trends or changes over time, or to indicate the parts of a whole. Bar graphs, such as the example at the top of the next page, are formed along a vertical and horizontal axis.

EXAMPLE

Number of Students Voting in School Elections by Class

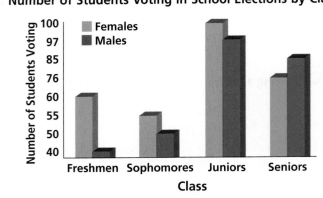

A **line graph** can be used to show changes or trends over time, to compare trends, or to show how two or more variables interact.

EXAMPLE

Number of Students Voting in School Elections

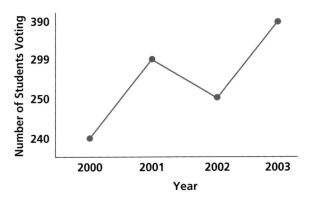

● **Maps** represent part of the earth or space. Maps of the earth may show geographical features, roads, cities, and other important locations.

Other types of visuals you might use to present information include **illustrations** showing your subject, **diagrams** clarifying a process you explain, and **time lines** pinpointing historical events you discuss.

PRACTICE & APPLY Choose the visual you think would most effectively communicate the information below. Then, use the guidelines in this section to create the visual.

Diameters of selected solar system planets in kilometers

Mercury 4,878   Jupiter 142,800
Earth 12,756   Neptune 49,528

Test Smarts

by **Flo Ota De Lange** *and* **Sheri Henderson**

Strategies for Taking Multiple-Choice Tests

Whatever you choose to do in the future, a high school diploma can open doors for you. It is a basic requirement for many, many jobs as well as for getting into college. But to get that diploma, you'll have to pass a lot of tests—pop quizzes in class, midterm exams, finals, your state's standardized tests required for graduation, and the SAT or ACT if you are thinking about college.

Taking tests doesn't have to be the scary nightmare many students make it out to be. With some preparation you'll do just fine. The first thing you have to do, of course, is study. Read all your assignments at least once, and make sure you have mastered the skills being taught.

Even when you know all the material, however, you might not do well on a test if you get nervous or are not familiar with the kinds of questions being asked. This section will give you some strategies that will help you approach your tests with confidence and let your abilities shine through.

Stay Calm

It's test time. You have studied the material, and you know your stuff, but you're still nervous. That's OK. A little nervousness will help you focus, but so will a calm body. Take a few deep breaths—five slow counts in, five slow counts out. Now you're ready to begin the test.

Track Your Time

First, estimate how much time you have for each question. Then, set checkpoints for yourself—how many questions should be completed at a quarter of the time, half of the time, and so on. That way you can **pace yourself** throughout the test. If you're behind, you can speed up. If you're ahead, you can—and should—slow down.

Master the Directions

Read the directions carefully to be sure you know exactly what to do and how to do it. If you are supposed to fill in an oval, fill it in cleanly and carefully. Be careful also to match the number of the question to the number on the answer sheet. Do just what the directions say to do.

Study the Questions

Read each question once, twice, three times—until you are certain you know what the question is asking. Watch out for words like *not* and *except;* they tell you to look for choices that are false, different, or opposite in some way.

Anticipate Answers

Once you are sure you understand the question, **anticipate the answer.** Then, read the choices. If the answer you gave is there, it is probably correct. To be sure, though, check out each choice. If you don't know the answer, eliminate any choices you think are wrong. Then, make an educated—not a wild—guess about the choices that remain. Be careful to **avoid distracters,** answers that are true but don't fit the question.

Don't Give Up

If you are having a hard time with a test, take a deep breath and **keep on going.** On most tests the questions do not get more difficult as you go, and an easier question is probably coming up soon. The last question on a test is worth just as many points as the first, so give it your all—all the way to the end.

Types of Test Questions

You will feel a lot more confident taking a test if you are familiar with the kinds of questions given. The following pages describe and give examples of the different types of multiple-choice questions you'll find on many of your tests. Tips on how to approach the questions are also included.

Reading-Comprehension Questions

Reading-comprehension questions seek to determine not only whether you have gotten the facts straight but also how well you can think critically about what you have read. You have to make accurate **inferences** and **predictions** as well as determine the author's attitude, purpose, and meaning.

The readings and the questions may be long and complicated or short and easy. Pay attention to the purpose of the question, and you will have a good chance of selecting the correct answer.

Following the informational reading below, you will find examples of some of the most common types of reading-comprehension questions.

DIRECTIONS: Read the following selection. Then, choose the best answer for each question that follows.

Dr. Jonas Salk began researching poliomyelitis after World War II, when epidemics of the disease were intensifying. Poliomyelitis, or polio, attacks the nervous system, causing pain and stiffness and often paralysis or even death. Salk worked on developing a vaccine to prevent this incurable disease.

First he studied how polio affects the body. He reasoned that polio is a virus that enters the body through the mouth or nose, eventually reaching the intestines. From there the virus spreads to the central nervous system by means of either blood or nerves. Once the virus enters a nerve cell, it changes how the cell functions. Instead of expelling the virus, the cell reproduces it. The virus then enters the surrounding nerve cells. When enough nerve cells are altered or killed, the nervous system is affected, and paralysis results.

Once Salk knew how the virus spreads through the body, he looked for a substance that would kill it. After lengthy experimentation he discovered that a formaldehyde solution would destroy the virus. He then developed a vaccine using the dead virus. In 1954, the National Foundation for Infantile Paralysis, the current March of Dimes Birth Defects Foundation, gave him the money that enabled him to test the vaccine. After giving the vaccine to nearly two million schoolchildren and testing the results, he proved that the vaccine was both safe and effective.

FACTUAL-RECALL QUESTIONS ask you to do a **close reading** to find **details** or **facts** straight from the selection. Search carefully. The words may not be identical, but the answer will be there.

1. Jonas Salk's purpose in researching polio was to —

   A determine how viruses cause disease

   B study how the human nervous system works

   C cure people who had been paralyzed by polio

   D develop a vaccine to prevent polio

Answer: **D is the correct answer.** The purpose of Salk's research is directly stated at the end of the first paragraph: to develop a vaccine that would prevent people from getting polio. Choices **A** and **B** are both far too broad; Salk wasn't interested in how viruses in general cause disease or in how the human nervous system works. Choice **C** may be tempting, but if you read the article carefully, you know that Salk wasn't searching for a way to cure paralyzed polio victims.

2. All of the following are effects of the polio virus's entering a nerve cell *except* —

   A the cell reproduces the virus

   B the virus leaves the cell and enters the surrounding nerve cells

   C the cell expels the virus

   D the virus changes how the cell functions

Answer: **C is the correct answer.** Notice the word *except* in the question. It makes choices **A, B,** and **D** wrong because they are all clearly described in the second paragraph as effects of the polio virus on a nerve cell.

INFERENCE QUESTIONS ask you to connect **clues.** You read between the lines to make an **educated guess.** An inference question sometimes requires you to apply what you already know.

3. Salk's vaccine had to be tested in two million schoolchildren before —

   A he could develop a formula for the vaccine

   B he could get any money to test the vaccine

   C he could determine how the polio virus spreads

   D it could be approved for general use

Answer: **D is the correct answer** even though it is not directly stated in the text. After Salk's polio vaccine was proved safe and effective on two million schoolchildren, you can infer that the next step (note the word *before*) would be its approval for general use in the population. Choice **A** is incorrect because the vaccine couldn't have been tested if Salk hadn't already developed a formula for the vaccine. **B** is incorrect because the article states directly that the National Foundation for Infantile Paralysis funded the testing of his virus. **C** is incorrect because Salk had to know how the polio virus spreads before he could develop a vaccine.

MAIN-IDEA QUESTIONS ask you to state the selection's **main idea** or **draw a conclusion.**

Sometimes a main-idea question asks you to choose the **best title** for a selection.

4. The main idea of this article is —

   A how Dr. Jonas Salk developed the polio vaccine

   B how a new vaccine is developed

   C how polio affects someone who has the virus

   D how the polio virus spreads

Answer: **A is the correct answer. B** is too broad; the article specifically focuses on Dr. Salk and the polio vaccine. **C** and **D** are incorrect because even though these topics are mentioned in the article, they are not the main focus of the article.

5. Which of the following would make the *best* title for the selection?

   A Dr. Jonas Salk Stalks the Polio Virus

   B How Polio Affects the Nervous System

   C How Viruses Reproduce

   D Testing a New Vaccine

Answer: **A is the correct answer,** the only choice that covers the whole article. **B** covers only part of the article. **C** and **D** are too broad and do not mention polio; also answer **C** is not discussed in the article.

EVALUATION QUESTIONS ask you to use your own knowledge and life experience to give an **opinion** about the selection. Sometimes an evaluation question asks about the writer's purpose or style of writing.

6. The information in this article is probably —

   A unreliable because the writer is not identified

   B unreliable because much of it is opinions, not facts

   C reliable because it gives facts that can be verified in other sources

   D reliable because the writer is an expert on infectious diseases

Answer: **The correct answer is C.** The article's dates and other facts can be verified in other sources. **A** is incorrect because although it's true the writer isn't identified, that doesn't mean the article is unreliable. Encyclopedia articles, for example, often do not identify the writer. **B** is incorrect because the article contains only facts, no opinions. **D** is incorrect because the writer isn't identified.

Vocabulary Questions

Vocabulary questions test your understanding of word meanings, both in and out of context. Some are simple and some are tricky. Read the question carefully.

DIRECTIONS: Read the following auto-biographical excerpt. Then, choose the best answer for each question that follows.

The Chicken

As I was walking down Stanton Street early one Sunday morning, I saw a chicken a few yards ahead of me. I was walking faster than the chicken, so I gradually caught up. By the time we approached Eighteenth Avenue, I was close behind. The chicken turned south on Eighteenth. At the fourth house along, it turned in the walk, hopped up the front steps, and rapped sharply on the metal storm door with its beak. After a moment, the door opened and the chicken went in.

> —Linda Elegant
> Portland, Oregon
> from *I Thought My Father Was God and Other True Tales from the National Story Project*

DEFINITION OR SYNONYM QUESTIONS are the simplest type of vocabulary question. They ask for a definition or synonym of a word. There are no clues to help you. You are expected to know the word's meaning.

7. <u>Gradually</u> means —
   A quickly
   B hurriedly
   C quietly
   D little by little

Answer: **D is the correct answer.**

CONTEXT-CLUE QUESTIONS ask you to define an unfamiliar word. You will find clues to the word's meaning in the **context,** the sentence in which the word appears or the sentences immediately before or after it.

8. What does <u>pullet</u> mean in the following sentence? "This fine specimen was a mature hen, well beyond the <u>pullet</u> stage."
   A old hen
   B young hen
   C rooster
   D roasted chicken

Answer: **B is the correct answer. C** and **D** are incorrect because you know from the context that a pullet is a young hen. **A** is incorrect because the contrasting context clue, *mature,* tells you that a pullet must be young.

MULTIPLE-MEANINGS QUESTIONS ask you to recognize which meaning of a familiar word is being used in a sentence. Then you choose the sentence that uses the word in the same way it is used in the original sentence.

9. "The chicken <u>turned</u> south on Eighteenth."
   A Kerry often <u>turned</u> a pretty phrase when she spoke.
   B Jim <u>turned</u> his jacket inside out.
   C The traffic <u>turned</u> right onto the bridge.
   D The top <u>turned</u> around quickly

Answer: **C is the correct answer.** The chicken isn't speaking, reversing something, or spinning, so you look for an answer using *turned* with the meaning "changed direction," which fits the context.

SENTENCE-COMPLETION OR FILL-IN-THE-BLANK QUESTIONS ask you to choose the appropriate word for the context of the sentence. When these questions have two blanks in an item, the trick is to find the answer that fits both blanks correctly. As a short-cut, first determine which choices contain a word that fits the first blank. Then, consider only those choices when filling in the second blank.

> **10.** "The Chicken" is _____, but it also raises more _____ than it answers.
>
> **A** amusing, anger
>
> **B** sickening, thoughts
>
> **C** funny, questions
>
> **D** autobiographical, pullets

Answer: First, look for choices that will not work in the first blank; you can eliminate those choices immediately. Choice **B** will clearly not work in the first blank: "The Chicken" can be considered amusing, funny, or autobiographical, but it is not sickening. Then, review the remaining choices: **A, C,** and **D.** The only word that works in the second blank is *questions;* the selection does raise more questions than it answers. Therefore, **the correct answer is C.**

ANALOGY QUESTIONS ask you to recognize the relationship between a pair of words and to identify a second pair of words that has the same relationship. An analogy question is written in this form: A : B :: C : D, which can be read as "A is to B as C is to D."

The tricky part of these questions is figuring out the relationship. There are many types of relationships, including the following ones:

- **degree** *(pink : red :: beige : brown)*
- **size** *(hummingbird : ostrich :: house cat : tiger)*
- **part to whole** *(leg : lion :: fin : fish)*
- **cause and effect** *(cold : shiver :: hot : sweat)*
- **synonyms** *(happy : cheery :: sad : glum)*
- **antonyms** *(happy : sad :: nice : mean)*

Once you figure out the relationship between the first pair of words, try expressing it as a sentence—for example, *A leg is a part of a lion.*

Then, pick from the choices the pair of words that has the same relationship—for example, *A fin is a part of a fish.* (For more about analogies, see pages 279 and 672.)

> **11.** Pullet : hen ::
>
> **A** scaffold : building
>
> **B** tree : seed
>
> **C** girl : boy
>
> **D** tadpole : frog

Answer: Try turning the first pair of words into a sentence, as in *A pullet is a young hen.* Now, try each answer out within the same sentence: *A scaffold is a young building. A tree is a young seed. A girl is a young—* Well, you get the idea. **D is the only workable answer.**

Multiple-Choice Writing Questions

Multiple-choice writing questions are designed to test your knowledge of standard written English. To answer them, you will need to know the rules of punctuation, such as when and how to use commas, quotation marks, end marks, italics, and so on. You will also need to know some basic rules of grammar: active versus passive voice, subject-verb agreement, correct verb tense, correct sentence structure, correct diction, parallel construction in sentences and paragraphs, to name a few. Here are some sample questions:

IDENTIFYING-SENTENCE-ERRORS QUESTIONS ask you to look at underlined sections of a sentence and choose the section that includes an error. You are not expected to correct the error.

> **12.** Tara and her sister <u>are planning</u> a twenty-fifth
>   A
>
> anniversary party for their <u>parents, and</u> they
>   B
>
> have invited their <u>parents'</u> closest friends and
>   C
>
> relatives as well as <u>him and I.</u> <u>No error.</u>
>   D   E

Answer: **The correct answer is D** because D contains an error. Instead of the subject pronoun *I*, the sentence should have the object pronoun *me* because *him and me* are direct objects in this sentence.

IMPROVING-SENTENCES QUESTIONS

may ask you to choose the correct version of an underlined section of a sentence:

13. A Magazine Article written in 1949 forecast "Computers of the future may weigh no more than 1.5 tons."

   A In 1949, a magazine article forecast "Computers

   B A magazine article written in 1949 fore-cast, "Computers

   C A magazine article in 1949 forecast, computers

   D A Magazine Article written in 1949 fore-casts "Computers

Answer: **B is the correct answer** because *magazine article* should not be capitalized and because a comma and quotation mark should precede the direct quotation.

14. Irving Fisher professor of economics at Yale University says in 1929, "Stocks have reached what looks like a permanently high plateau."

   A Irving Fisher, professor of economics at Yale University, said in 1929, "Stocks

   B Irving Fisher, professor of economics at Yale University says in 1929, "Stocks

   C Irving Fisher, professor of economics at Yale University, says in 1929, "Stocks

   D Irving Fisher professor of economics at Yale University said in 1929, "Stocks

Answer: **A is the correct answer** because it corrects the two errors in this sentence: It uses commas to set off the appositive *professor of economics at Yale University,* and it changes the verb to the past tense, *said.*

IMPROVING-THE-PARAGRAPH QUESTIONS

are preceded by a paragraph. You may be asked to pick a choice that combines or rewrites portions of sentences. You may be asked to decide which sentences could be added to or removed from the paragraph. You may be asked which sentence could be used to strengthen the argument of the writer. You may be asked to pick a thesis statement for the paragraph. As an example, refer to our paragraph-length selection, "The Chicken," on page 1124. Then, look at the questions below:

15. Which of the sentences would *not* fit well into "The Chicken"?

   A It isn't every day that you meet a chicken out for a morning walk.

   B It is still more unusual to see a chicken knock on a door and go in when the door opens.

   C I thought about knocking on the door myself to ask about the chicken but was afraid the chicken might answer.

   D The numbered streets in my neighbor-hood go up to Twenty-fifth Street.

Answer: You caught the word *not* in the question, didn't you? **D is the answer;** it is the only sentence that would *not* fit into the paragraph. **A, B,** and **C** would fit because they have the appropriate tone and humor.

16. Which of the following items could be added to "The Chicken" to support the main idea?

   A A chicken can make a good pet.

   B The world is full of unusual and unex-pected pleasures.

   C Why did the chicken cross the road?

   D Is this a knock-knock joke?

Answer: Do we even have to say, "**The correct answer is B**"?

Strategies for Taking Writing Tests

Writing a Response to Literature

On tests, you will often be asked to write an essay responding to a literary selection. Your response should demonstrate your understanding of the selection as a whole, including its main ideas and the author's purpose. Follow the steps below to write such a response for a test. The sample responses provided are based on the prompt to the right. ("Thank You M'am" begins on page 109.)

THINKING IT THROUGH · Writing a Response to Literature

STEP 1 **Read the prompt carefully, and then read the selection for general understanding.** Get to know the selection's plot, characters, setting, and theme, and consider all parts of the prompt.

I need to take a close look at one of the two characters in this story and draw a conclusion about that person based on details from the story.

STEP 2 **Choose a topic, and take notes from the piece on your main points.**

I'll write about Mrs. Jones. My main points will have to do with her actions, her words, and her situation. Her actions show some anger but mostly kindness. Her words have an indignant tone but also are basically kind. Her situation is that she is not financially well off, but she still gives Roger food, money, and advice.

STEP 3 **Generate a thesis for your essay.** To develop a thesis, draw a conclusion based on your main points.

Even though she is angry with Roger for trying to take from her, and she doesn't have much anyway, Mrs. Jones is kinder to him than most people in the same situation would be. My thesis will be: Despite Roger's actions and her own circumstances, Mrs. Jones shows a kindness that will change his life.

STEP 4 **Support your thesis and main points.** Find details that prove your thesis, and look for relevant subtle or complex ideas in the selection. To elaborate on your evidence, use your own knowledge and experience.

I need to discuss how Mrs. Jones shows trust in Roger despite his attempt to steal her purse and how she hints that her past was not perfect, either. I think she understands that he can be better than his actions if he is shown some kindness.

STEP 5 **Draft your essay.** Arrange your ideas to show clearly how they relate to each other and to your thesis. Use an objective, serious tone, with precise language and a variety of sentence types. Revise your essay to make sure it shows a thorough understanding of the selection. Then, proofread and correct any errors.

Writing a Response to Expository Text

When you read and respond to **expository,** or informative, text, you use a different set of skills than for literary texts. If you are asked to write a response to an expository selection on a test, use the steps below. The sample responses provided are based on the prompt to the right. ("Far-out Housekeeping on the ISS" begins on page 56.)

Prompt

In "Far-out Housekeeping on the ISS," what specific purpose is the writer trying to achieve? How do the article's content and organization help achieve this purpose? In an essay, examine the writer's purpose using details from the article.

THINKING IT THROUGH

Writing a Response to Expository Text

STEP 1 **Read the selection for understanding, and take notes of important points.** Note the main idea and organization of the piece. Use the selection's headings, boldface terms, and graphics to add to your understanding.

The article explains what people on the International Space Station eat, how they contact their families, what happens to waste, and what the astronauts do for fun.

STEP 2 **Read the prompt, and identify your task and your answer.**

I need to identify the purpose of the article and how the organization and details support that purpose. I think the purpose is to give people who are curious about the space station a look at the everyday activities there and to make the astronauts seem more like regular people and less like movie heroes.

STEP 3 **Skim the selection looking for support.** Note relevant and interesting evidence that backs up the answer you identified in Step 2.

The article discusses eating, taking out the trash, and having fun. This makes the astronauts seem more like me. Using the astronauts' own words from interviews also makes them seem like regular people.

STEP 4 **Elaborate on your ideas, and draft a thesis statement.** Make connections to your own knowledge, and consider the meaning of each piece of evidence. Draft a sentence that clearly states your overall impression, or thesis.

I think when you find out you have something in common with someone, it makes it easier to relate to them—that's what this article does, by helping readers imagine themselves doing normal things, but in space. My thesis will be: This article was written to help curious readers imagine themselves as astronauts by showing what everyday life in space is like.

STEP 5 **Draft your essay.** Choose an arrangement that fits the selection and the prompt. Make that pattern clear to readers by using transitional words and phrases such as *for one thing, also,* and *finally* for logical order or *first, furthermore,* and *most important* for order of importance. Proofread your draft to make sure you use language conventions correctly.

Writing a Biographical Narrative

In a **biographical narrative,** you must present an event from another person's life in such a way that readers can share in the experience. Here are the steps to follow if you are asked to write a biographical narrative for a test. The sample responses below are based on the prompt to the right.

Prompt

Think of a person you know well, and write an essay describing an incident in that person's life that demonstrates an important part of his or her personality or character.

THINKING IT THROUGH · Writing a Biographical Narrative

STEP 1 Carefully read the prompt, and choose a subject. Make sure you address all parts of the prompt.

The prompt asks me to tell about something that someone I know experienced. I need to pick an experience that shows my subject's personality or character. I'll write about my best friend, Maia, because I've known her since we were little.

STEP 2 Choose an incident to relate, and identify its parts. Outline in sequence the smaller events that make up your chosen experience.

I'll write about the time when Maia and I were eight and she fell off her bike.
1. It was her first time riding without her dad helping.
2. I encouraged her to go down a hill on our street.
3. She looked nervous but tried it anyway.
4. She lost control and landed in the bushes.
5. Even though she got scratched, she got back on her bike and rode back home with me. She didn't even seem that upset.

STEP 3 Identify important details about the character, events, and setting. Details should be relevant and specific to bring the incident to life.

I'll describe the steep hill with the sharp curve at the bottom, Maia's wide eyes and wrinkled forehead before we rode, the path her bike took before landing at the bottom, and her resolve when she got back up.

STEP 4 Draw a conclusion based on the events. Decide why the incident is significant, and plan a thesis statement to guide you as you plan and draft.

This event is important because it shows how Maia tries things even if she's nervous and how she keeps trying if she doesn't get it right the first time. My thesis will be: Maia showed her bravery and resolve even when she was only an eight-year-old riding a bike.

STEP 5 Use your notes to write a draft of your biographical narrative. Include an introduction to give readers a context for the narrative. Keep your tone consistent, focus on the subject rather than on yourself, and build toward the event's climax. Then, correct any errors in grammar, usage, and mechanics.

Writing an Expository Composition

An **expository composition** provides information about a topic unfamiliar to readers. When you write an expository composition for a test, you must explain ideas clearly and support those ideas with relevant evidence. Follow the steps below. A sample prompt is to the right.

Prompt

Think about a favorite place to visit. Write an essay in which you explain why this place is so important or enjoyable to you.

THINKING IT THROUGH · Writing an Expository Composition

STEP 1 Carefully read the prompt, and choose a topic. Make sure you address all parts of the prompt and choose a topic you know well.

I need to pick out the things that make a place special to me. I'll write about Hastings, the town in the mountains where my grandparents live.

STEP 2 Divide the topic into parts. Outline the main categories of information you will provide about your topic.

I like Hastings because: 1. I get to see lots of relatives when we have family reunions there. 2. It's a beautiful area. 3. I like how remote it is, especially compared with where I live.

STEP 3 Brainstorm details about each part of the topic. Details should answer questions readers will have about the topic and correct any misunderstandings or biases they might have. Try to answer the *5W-How?* questions *(Who? What? Where? When? Why? How?)* with your details.

1. I can go into detail about my favorite relatives and reunion activities.
2. I can explain what makes it beautiful, describing some of the mountain scenery.
3. I can point out how few TV and radio signals you can get, how you can walk for hours without hearing a human sound, and how there's only one tiny grocery store.

STEP 4 Synthesize your ideas to plan a thesis. Draft a thesis statement that explains the point the information about your topic makes.

All of my details show how different Hastings is from where I live. My thesis will be: In Hastings I can see distant relatives, experience the beauty of the mountains, and enjoy being totally alone if I feel like it—all things I could never do at home.

STEP 5 Use your notes to write a draft of your expository composition. Write an attention-getting introduction. Rather than stringing together a lot of obvious facts about your topic, dig deeper and connect these more interesting ideas to your thesis. End with a conclusion that echoes your thesis. Revise to make sure all of your support is relevant. Then, proofread to make sure you have correctly used English-language conventions.

Writing a Persuasive Composition

Writing tests often ask you to write a **persuasive essay** on a given issue. You must decide your opinion or position on the issue, organize your response, write, and proofread—all in a limited amount of time. Use the following strategy to develop a convincing, well-supported essay under pressure. The sample responses provided are based on the prompt to the right.

Prompt

The city council is considering an ordinance banning cycling on all sidewalks. Consider the effects such an ordinance would have, and decide whether you support or oppose the measure. Then, write an essay in which you express and support your opinion on the issue.

THINKING IT THROUGH • **Writing a Persuasive Composition**

STEP 1 Read the prompt carefully, and identify your task. Answer all parts of the prompt.

I need to think about the effects of banning cycling on sidewalks and be able to support my opinion on the issue.

STEP 2 State your opinion on the topic.

Based on my experience, I think this ordinance would be a bad idea.

STEP 3 Plan reasons using the THEMES strategy. Choose reasons that will address positive or negative effects in some of the following categories: **T**ime, **H**ealth, **E**ducation, **M**oney, **E**nvironment, and **S**afety.

Safety: Banning cycling on sidewalks will force people to ride bikes on often-dangerous city streets.

Health: An effect of banning cycling on sidewalks is that people may choose not to ride bikes at all; less exercise may cause health problems.

Environment: The ban may cause people to drive rather than ride a bike for short errands, adding to air pollution.

STEP 4 Develop evidence to support each of your reasons. To elaborate on your evidence, use your own knowledge and experience.

I can discuss the positive effects of bicycling on our community and include personal anecdotes about trying to avoid potholes, parked cars, and reckless drivers while riding my own bike. I can also make an ethical appeal to protect young children who ride bikes to school from harm.

STEP 5 Draft your essay. Begin with an attention getter, and state your opinion up front. Arrange reasons in order of importance, and explain how each piece of evidence relates to its reason. End with a call to action, if your position requires readers to act rather than simply to agree with you. Then, find and correct any errors in grammar, usage, and mechanics.

Handbook of Literary Terms

For more information about a topic, turn to the page(s) in this book that are indicated on a separate line at the end of the entry. For example, to learn more about *alliteration,* turn to page 532.

On another line are cross-references to entries in this handbook that provide closely related information. For instance, at the end of *Alliteration* is a cross-reference to *Assonance.*

ALLEGORY **A narrative in which characters and settings stand for abstract ideas or moral qualities.** In addition to the literal meaning of the story, an allegory contains a symbolic, or **allegorical,** meaning. Characters and places in allegories often have names that indicate the abstract ideas they stand for: Justice, Deceit, Vanity. George Orwell's novel *Animal Farm* is a well-known modern allegory.

See pages 403, 436.

ALLITERATION **Repetition of the same or very similar consonant sounds usually at the beginnings of words that are close together in a poem.** In this example the sound "fl" is repeated in line 1, and the "s" sound is repeated in line 2:

> Open here I flung the shutter, when with many a
>   flirt and flutter,
> In there stepped a stately Raven of the saintly days
>   of yore.
>
> —Edgar Allan Poe, from "The Raven"

See pages 532, 551.
See also *Assonance, Onomatopoeia, Rhyme.*

ALLUSION **Reference to a statement, a person, a place, or an event from literature, history, religion, mythology, politics, sports, science, or pop culture.** In calling one of his stories "The Gift of the Magi" (page 349), O. Henry uses an allusion to the wise men from the East called the Magi, who presented the infant Jesus with the first Christmas gifts.

"I think I'll wait for the next elevator."

Drawing by Chas. Addams; © 1988 The New Yorker Magazine, Inc.

AMBIGUITY **An element of uncertainty in a text, in which something can be interpreted in a number of different ways.** Ambiguity adds a layer of complexity to a story, for it presents us with a variety of possible interpretations, all of which are valid. Edgar Allan Poe's "The Cask of Amontillado" (page 211) is ambiguous because we don't know if we should trust the narrator's claims. **Subtleties,** or fine distinctions in meaning, in a text help create ambiguity. The significance of these subtleties is open to question.

See pages 334–335, 359.

ANALOGY **Comparison made between two things to show how they are alike in some respects.** During the Revolutionary War the writer Thomas Paine drew an analogy between a thief breaking into a house and the king of England interfering in the affairs of the American Colonies (*The Crisis,* No. 1). Similes are a kind of analogy. However, an analogy usually clarifies something, while a simile shows imaginatively how two different things are alike in some unusual way.

See page 370.

ANECDOTE Very, very brief story, usually told to make a point. Historians and other writers of nonfiction often use anecdotes to clarify their texts or to provide human interest.

ASIDE Words that are spoken by a character in a play to the audience or to another character but that are not supposed to be overheard by the others onstage. Stage directions usually tell when a speech is an aside. For example, in Shakespeare's *Romeo and Juliet* (page 901), there are two asides in the opening scene. Sampson speaks to Gregory in an aside, and Gregory responds to him in another aside as they pick a fight with the servants of the house of Montague. Sampson and Gregory hear each other's asides, and so do we in the audience, but Montague's servants do not.

See page 854.

ASSONANCE Repetition of similar vowel sounds that are followed by different consonant sounds, especially in words that are close together in a poem. The words *base* and *fade* and the words *young* and *love* contain examples of assonance. The lines that follow are especially musical because of assonance:

> Seeing the snowman standing all alone
> In dusk and cold is more than he can bear.
> The small boy weeps to hear the wind prepare
> A night of gnashings and enormous moan.
>
> —Richard Wilbur, from "Boy at the Window"

See page 532.
See also *Alliteration, Onomatopoeia, Rhyme.*

AUTHOR The writer of a literary work.

AUTOBIOGRAPHY An account of the writer's own life. An example of a book-length autobiography is *When I Was Puerto Rican* by Esmeralda Santiago (see page 625). Judith Ortiz Cofer's "Volar" (page 669) is an example of an autobiographical essay.

See also *Biography.*

BALLAD Song that tells a story. Folk ballads are composed by unknown singers and are passed on for generations before they are written down. **Literary ballads,** on the other hand, are poems composed by known individuals and are written in imitation of the old folk ballads. "Ballad of Birmingham" by Dudley Randall (page 540) is a modern literary ballad. Ballads usually tell sensational stories of tragedy or adventure. They use simple language and a great deal of repetition and usually have regular rhythm and rhyme schemes, which make them easy to memorize.

See page 539.

BIOGRAPHY An account of a person's life, written or told by another person. A classic American biography is Carl Sandburg's multivolume life of Abraham Lincoln. Today biographies are written about movie stars, TV personalities, politicians, sports figures, self-made millionaires, even underworld figures. Biographies are among the most popular forms of contemporary literature. On page 222 is an excerpt from Kenneth Silverman's biography of Edgar Allan Poe.

See also *Autobiography.*

BLANK VERSE Poetry written in unrhymed iambic pentameter. *Blank* means the poetry is not rhymed. *Iambic pentameter* means that each line contains five iambs, or metrical feet that consist of an unstressed syllable followed by a stressed syllable ($\smile$ $'$). Blank verse is the most important poetic form in English epic and dramatic poetry. It is the major verse form used in Shakespeare's plays.

See page 895.
See also *Iambic Pentameter, Meter.*

CHARACTER Person in a story, poem, or play. Sometimes, as in George Orwell's novel *Animal Farm,* the characters are animals. In myths the characters are divinities or heroes who have superhuman powers, such as Poseidon and Athena and Odysseus in the *Odyssey* (page 750). Most often a character is an ordinary human being, like Mme. Loisel in Guy de Maupassant's "The Necklace" (page 198).

The process of revealing the personality of a character in a story is called **characterization.** A writer can reveal a character by

1. letting us hear the character speak
2. describing how the character looks and dresses
3. letting us listen to the character's inner thoughts and feelings
4. revealing what other characters in the story think or say about the character

5. showing us what the character does—how he or she acts

6. telling us directly what the character's personality is like: cruel, kind, sneaky, brave, and so on

The first five ways of revealing a character are known as **indirect characterization.** When a writer uses indirect characterization, we have to use our own judgment to decide what a character is like, based on the evidence the writer gives us. But when a writer uses the sixth method, known as **direct characterization,** we don't have to decide for ourselves; we are told directly what the character is like.

Characters can be classified as static or dynamic. A **static character** is one who does not change much in the course of a story. By contrast, a **dynamic character** changes as a result of the story's events.

Characters can also be classified as flat or round. A **flat character** has only one or two traits, and these can be described in a few words. Such a character has no depth, like a piece of cardboard. A **round character,** like a real person, has many different character traits, which sometimes contradict one another.

Static and flat characters often function as **subordinate characters** in a story. This means that they may play important roles in a story but they are not the main actors in the plot.

The fears or conflicts or needs that drive a character are called **motivation.** A character can be motivated by many factors, such as vengeance, fear, greed, love, even boredom.

See pages 96–97, 138–139.

CLIMAX Moment of great emotional intensity or suspense in a plot. The major climax in a story or play usually marks the moment when the conflict is decided one way or another.

See pages 2, 897.

COMEDY In general, a story that ends happily. The hero or heroine of a comedy is usually an ordinary character who overcomes a series of obstacles that block what he or she wants. Many comedies have a boy-meets-girl plot, in which young lovers must face obstacles to their marrying. At the end of such comedies, the lovers marry, and everyone celebrates, as in Shakespeare's play *A Midsummer Night's Dream.* In structure and characterization, a comedy is the opposite of a **tragedy.**

See pages 852–853, 869.
See also *Comic Relief, Drama, Tragedy.*

COMIC RELIEF Comic scene or event that breaks up a serious play or narrative. Comic relief allows writers to lighten the tone of a work and show the humorous side of a dramatic theme. In Shakespeare's tragedy *Romeo and Juliet* (page 901), the nurse and Mercutio provide comic relief.

CONFLICT Struggle or clash between opposing characters or opposing forces. In an **external conflict,** a character struggles against an outside force. This outside force might be another character, or society as a whole, or something in nature. "The Most Dangerous Game" by Richard Connell (page 17) is about the external conflict between the evil General Zaroff and the hunter Rainsford. By contrast, an **internal conflict** takes place entirely within a character's own mind. An internal conflict is a struggle between opposing needs or desires or emotions within a single person. In James Hurst's "The Scarlet Ibis" (page 415), the young narrator struggles with an internal conflict—between love for his brother and hatred of his brother's disabilities. Many works, especially longer ones, contain both internal and external conflicts, and an external conflict often leads to internal problems.

See pages 2, 138, 247, 852.

CONNOTATION All the meanings, associations, or emotions that have come to be attached to some words, in addition to their literal dictionary definitions, or denotations. For example, *skinny* and *slender* have the same literal definition, or **denotation**—"thin." But their connotations are completely different. If you call someone skinny, you are saying something unflattering. If you call someone slender, you are paying him or her a compliment. The British philosopher Bertrand Russell once gave a classic example of the different connotations of words: "I am firm. You are obstinate. He is a pigheaded fool." Connotations, or the suggestive power of certain words, play an important role in creating **mood** or **tone.**

See pages 310, 512, 622.
See also *Diction, Mood, Tone.*

COUPLET Two consecutive lines of poetry that rhyme. Alexander Pope wrote this sarcastic couplet for a dog's collar (Kew is a place in England):

> I am his Highness' dog at Kew;
> Pray tell me, Sir, whose dog are you?
>
> —Alexander Pope

Couplets work nicely for humor and satire because the punch line comes so quickly. However, they are most often used to express a completed thought. In Shakespeare's plays an important speech or scene often ends with a couplet.

See pages 498, 895.

DESCRIPTION **Type of writing intended to create a mood or emotion or to re-create a person, a place, a thing, an event, or an experience.** Description is one of the four major techniques used in writing. (The others are **narration, exposition,** and **persuasion.**) Description works by creating images that appeal to the senses of sight, smell, taste, hearing, or touch. Writers use description in all forms of fiction, nonfiction, and poetry.

See also *Imagery*.

DIALECT **Way of speaking that is characteristic of a particular region or a particular group of people.** Dialects may have a distinct vocabulary, pronunciation system, and grammar. In a sense, we all speak dialects; but one dialect usually becomes dominant in a country or culture and becomes accepted as the standard way of speaking. In the United States, for example, the formal language is known as standard English. (This is what you usually hear spoken by TV newscasters on the national channels.)

See page 607.

DIALOGUE **The conversation between characters in a story or play.** Dialogue is an important factor in characterization and in moving the plot forward. Dialogue forms the structure of most plays. The following dialogue is taken from Edgar Allan Poe's "The Cask of Amontillado" (page 211):

> "You do not comprehend?" he said.
> "Not I," I replied.
> "Then you are not of the brotherhood."
> "How?"
> "You are not of the Masons."

> "Yes, yes," I said, "yes, yes."
> "You? Impossible! A Mason?"
> "A Mason," I replied.
> "A sign," he said.
> "It is this," I answered, producing a trowel from beneath the folds of my roquelaure.
> "You jest," he exclaimed, recoiling a few paces.
> "But let us proceed to the amontillado."

DICTION **A writer's or speaker's choice of words.** Diction is an essential element of a writer's **style.** Some writers use simple, down-to-earth, or even slang words (*house, home, digs*); others use ornate, official-sounding, or even flowery language (*domicile, residence, abode*). The **connotations** of words are an important aspect of diction.

See pages 512, 572, 607, 623.
See also *Connotation, Tone*.

DRAMA **Story that is written to be acted for an audience.** The action of a drama is usually driven by a character who wants something and takes steps to get it. The elements of a dramatic plot are **exposition, complications, climax,** and **resolution.** The term *drama* is also used to describe a serious play that is neither a **comedy** nor a **tragedy.**

See pages 852–854, 897.
See also *Comedy, Tragedy*.

DRAMATIC MONOLOGUE **A poem in which a speaker addresses one or more silent listeners, often reflecting on a specific problem or situation.** Though the person addressed in a dramatic monologue does not speak, we often can discover something about the listener or listeners—as well as the speaker—by paying close attention to the speaker's words. The speaker in Edgar Lee Masters's dramatic monologue "Lucinda Matlock" is an outspoken old woman who addresses the younger generation from the graveyard in Spoon River:

> What is this I hear of sorrow and weariness,
> Anger, discontent, and drooping hopes?
> Degenerate sons and daughters,
> Life is too strong for you—
> It takes life to love Life.

See page 96.

EPIC **Long story told in elevated language (usually poetry), which relates the great deeds of a larger-than-life hero who embodies the values of a particular society.** Most epics include elements of myth, legend, folk tale, and history. Their tone is serious and their language is grand. Most epic heroes undertake quests to achieve something of tremendous value to themselves or their people. Often parts of the hero's quest are set in both heaven and hell. Homer's *Iliad* and *Odyssey* (page 750) are the best-known epics in Western civilization. The great epic of ancient Rome is Virgil's *Aeneid,* which, like the *Iliad* and *Odyssey,* is based on events that happened during and immediately after the Trojan War. The great epic of India is the *Mahabharata.* The great epic of Mali in Africa is *Sundiata.* Spain's epic is *El Cid.*

See pages 740–746.

EPITHET **Adjective or descriptive phrase that is regularly used to characterize a person, place, or thing.** We speak of "Honest Abe," for example, and "America the Beautiful."

Homer created so many epithets in his *Iliad* and *Odyssey* that his name is permanently associated with a type of epithet. The **Homeric epithet** in most English translations consists of a compound adjective that is regularly used to modify a particular noun. Three famous examples from the *Odyssey* are "*wine-dark* sea," "*rosy-fingered* dawn," "the *gray-eyed* goddess Athena."

See page 815.

ESSAY **Short piece of nonfiction that examines a single subject from a limited point of view.** Most essays can be categorized as either **personal** or **formal.**

A **personal essay** (sometimes called an **informal essay**) generally reveals a great deal about the writer's personality and tastes. Its tone is often conversational, sometimes even humorous.

A **formal essay** is usually serious, objective, and impersonal in tone. Its purpose is to inform its readers about some topic of interest or to persuade them to accept the writer's views. The statements in a formal essay are supported by facts and logic.

EXPOSITION **Type of writing that explains, gives information, defines, or clarifies an idea.** Exposition is one of the four major techniques used in writing. (The others are **narration, description,** and **persuasion.**) We find exposition in news articles, in histories, in biographies (and even in cookbook recipes). In fact, each entry in this Handbook of Literary Terms is an example of exposition.

Exposition is also the term for that beginning part of a plot that gives information about the characters and their problems or conflicts.

See pages 2, 897.
See also *Plot.*

FABLE **Very brief story in prose or verse that teaches a moral, or a practical lesson about how to get along in life.** The characters in most fables are animals that behave and speak like human beings. Some of the most popular fables are those attributed to Aesop, who scholars believe was a slave in ancient Greece.

See also *Folk Tale, Tall Tale.*

FIGURE OF SPEECH **Word or phrase that describes one thing in terms of another and is not meant to be understood on a literal level.** Most figures of speech, or **figurative language,** involve some sort of imaginative comparison between seemingly unlike things.

Some 250 different types of figures of speech have been identified. The most common are the **simile** ("I wandered lonely as a cloud"), the **metaphor** ("Fame is a bee"), and **personification** ("The wind stood up and gave a shout").

See pages 504–505.
See also *Metaphor, Personification, Simile.*

FLASHBACK **Scene in a movie, play, short story, novel, or narrative poem that interrupts the present action of the plot to flash backward and tell what happened at an earlier time.** That is, a flashback breaks the normal time sequence of events in a narrative, usually to give the readers or viewers some background information that helps them make sense of a story. Much of the *Odyssey* (page 750) is told in the form of a flashback, as Odysseus describes his previous adventures to the Phaeacian court of King Alcinous. Hwang Sunwŏn successfully incorporates flashbacks into his short story "Cranes" (page 272). As Sŏngsam recalls scenes from his childhood, we are transported to the past so that we can fully understand Sŏngsam's present conflict. Flashbacks are extremely common storytelling devices in movies. In fact, the word *flashback* comes from film criticism, and it has spread to the rest of literature.

See pages 3, 44.

FLASH-FORWARD A scene in a movie, play, short story, novel, or narrative poem that interrupts the present action of the plot to shift into the future. Writers may use a flash-forward to create **dramatic irony.** By means of the flash-forward, we know the future, but the story characters do not.

See page 3.

FOIL Character who is used as a contrast to another character. A writer uses a foil to accentuate and clarify the distinct qualities of two characters. The word *foil* is also used for a thin sheet of shiny metal that is placed beneath a gem to intensify its brilliance. A character who is a foil, like the metal behind the gem, sets off or intensifies the qualities of another character. In Shakespeare's *Romeo and Juliet* (page 901), the cynical, sophisticated Mercutio is a foil to the romantic, naive Romeo.

See page 930.

FOLK TALE Story that has no known author and was originally passed on from one generation to another by word of mouth. Unlike myths, which are about gods and heroes, folk tales are usually about ordinary people. Folk tales tend to travel, and you'll often find the same motifs—elements such as characters, images, and story lines—in the tales of different cultures. For example, there are said to be nine hundred versions of the folk tale about Cinderella.

See also *Fable, Tall Tale*.

FORESHADOWING The use of clues to hint at events that will occur later in a plot. Foreshadowing is used to build suspense and, sometimes, anxiety in the reader or viewer. In a drama the gun found in a bureau drawer in Act 1 is likely to foreshadow violence later in the play. In "The Cask of Amontillado" (page 211), Poe uses foreshadowing skillfully. For example, when Montresor produces a trowel from beneath his cloak, Poe is foreshadowing the means Montresor will use to murder his enemy. When later he begins to build a wall around Fortunato, we remember that trowel.

See pages 3, 16.

FREE VERSE Poetry that does not have a regular meter or rhyme scheme. Poets writing in free verse try to capture the natural rhythms of ordinary speech. To create its music, free verse may use **internal rhyme, alliteration, onomatopoeia, refrain,** and **parallel structure.** For an example of a poem written in free verse, read "Daily" (page 486).

See pages 531–532, 544.
See also *Meter, Rhythm*.

GENRE (zhän′rə) **The category that a work of literature is classified under. Five major genres in literature are nonfiction, fiction, poetry, drama, and myth.** Collections 7, 10, and 11 of this book are organized by genre: by poetry, by epic and myth, and by drama.

See page 294.

HAIKU Japanese verse form consisting of three lines and, usually, seventeen syllables (five in the first line, seven in the second, and five in the third). The writer of a haiku uses association and suggestion to describe a particular moment of discovery or enlightenment. A haiku often presents an image of daily life that relates to a particular season.

See page 494.

HYPERBOLE (hī·pur′bə·lē) **Figure of speech that uses exaggeration to express strong emotion or to create a comic effect.** Writers often use hyperbole, also called **overstatement,** to intensify a description or to emphasize the essential nature of something. If you say that a limousine is as long as an ocean liner, you are using hyperbole.

IAMBIC PENTAMETER Line of poetry that contains five iambs. An **iamb** is a metrical foot, or unit of measure, consisting of an unstressed syllable followed by a stressed syllable (˘ ′). *Pentameter* comes from the Greek *penta* (five) and *meter* (measure). Here is one iamb: arise. Here is a line measuring five iambs:

> But soft! What light through yonder window breaks?
>
> —William Shakespeare, from *Romeo and Juliet*

Iambic pentameter is by far the most common verse line in English poetry.

See pages 498, 895.
See also *Blank Verse, Meter*.

IDIOM Expression peculiar to a particular language that means something different from the literal meaning of each word. "It's raining cats and dogs" and "We heard it through the grapevine" are idioms of American English. One of the difficulties of translating a work from another language is translating the idioms.

See page 825.

IMAGERY Language that appeals to the senses. Most images are visual—that is, they create pictures in the reader's mind by appealing to the sense of sight. Images can also appeal to the senses of hearing, touch, taste, or smell or even to several senses at once. Imagery is an element in all types of writing, but it is especially important in poetry. The following lines contain images that make us see, hear, and even smell what the speaker experiences as he travels to meet someone he loves.

> Then a mile of warm sea-scented beach;
> Three fields to cross till a farm appears;
> A tap at the pane, the quick sharp scratch
> And blue spurt of a lighted match . . .
>
> —Robert Browning, from "Meeting at Night"

See pages 474–475.
See also *Description*.

INVERSION Reversal of the normal word order of a sentence. The elements of a standard English sentence are subject, verb, and complement, and in most sentences that is the order in which they appear. *(Ray rowed the boat.)* Writers use inversion for emphasis and variety. They may also use it for more technical reasons—to create end rhymes or to accommodate a given meter. In a statement about Ulysses S. Grant and Robert E. Lee, the historian Bruce Catton wrote, "Daring and resourcefulness they had too. . . ." Catton inverts the order of the parts of the sentence so that the important words (*daring* and *resourcefulness*) come first.

IRONY Contrast between expectation and reality—between what is said and what is really meant, between what is expected to happen and what really does happen, or between what appears to be true and what is really true.

In **verbal irony,** a writer or speaker says one thing but really means something completely different.

If you call a clumsy basketball player the new Michael Jordan, you are using verbal irony. The murderer in Edgar Allan Poe's "The Cask of Amontillado" (page 211) is using verbal irony when he says to his unsuspecting victim, "Your health is precious."

Situational irony occurs when there is a contrast between what would seem appropriate and what really happens or when there is a contradiction between what we expect to happen and what really does take place.

Dramatic irony occurs when the audience or the reader knows something important that a character in a play or story does not know. In Shakespeare's *Romeo and Juliet* (page 901), we know, but Romeo *does not,* that when he finds Juliet in the tomb, she is drugged, not dead. Thus we feel a terrible sense of dramatic irony as we watch Romeo kill himself upon discovering her body.

See pages 334–335, 348.
See also *Satire, Tone*.

LYRIC POETRY Poetry that does not tell a story but is aimed only at expressing a speaker's emotions or thoughts. Most lyrics are short, and they usually imply, rather than directly state, a single strong emotion. The term *lyric* comes from the Greek. In ancient Greece, lyric poems were recited to the accompaniment of a stringed instrument called a lyre. Today poets still try to make their lyrics "sing," but they rely only on the musical effects they create with words (such as **rhyme, rhythm,** and **onomatopoeia**).

See page 500.
See also *Sonnet*.

METAPHOR Figure of speech that makes a comparison between two unlike things, in which one thing becomes another thing without the use of the word *like, as, than, or resembles.* The poet Robert Burns's famous comparison "O my love is like a red, red rose" is a simile. If he had written, "O my love *is* a red, red rose" or "O my love bursts into bloom," he would have been using a metaphor.

Notice that the comparison in the second metaphor above is implied, or suggested, rather than directly stated, as it is in the first metaphor. An **implied metaphor** does not tell us directly that one thing *is* something else. Instead, it uses words that suggest the nature of the comparison. The phrase "bursts into bloom" implies that the feeling of love is like a budding flower.

An **extended metaphor** is a metaphor that is extended, or developed, over several lines of writing or even throughout an entire poem.

A **dead metaphor** is a metaphor that has been used so often that we no longer realize it is a figure of speech—we simply skip over the metaphorical connection it makes. Examples of dead metaphors are *the roof of the mouth, the eye of the storm, the heart of the matter,* and *the arm of the chair.*

A **mixed metaphor** is the inconsistent mixture of two or more metaphors. Mixed metaphors are a common problem in bad writing, and they are often unintentionally funny. You are using a mixed metaphor if you say, "Put it on the back burner and let it germinate" or "Let's set sail and get this show on the road."

See pages 504–505, 511.
See also *Figure of Speech, Personification, Simile.*

METER **Generally regular pattern of stressed and unstressed syllables in poetry.** When we want to indicate the metrical pattern of a poem, we mark the stressed syllables with the symbol (**′**) and the unstressed syllables with the symbol (**˘**). Indicating the metrical pattern of a poem in this way is called **scanning** the poem, or **scansion** (skan′shən). Notice the pattern of stressed and unstressed syllables in the first four lines of this poem:

> Slowly, silently, now the moon
> Walks the night in her silver shoon;
> This way, and that, she peers, and sees
> Silver fruit upon silver trees. . . .
>
> —Walter de la Mare, from "Silver"

See pages 530–531.
See also *Blank Verse, Iambic Pentameter, Rhythm.*

MOOD **A story's atmosphere or the feeling it evokes.** Mood is often created by a story's setting. A story set in a wild forest at night, with wolves howling in the distance, will probably convey a mood of terror, tension, or uneasiness. A story set in a cozy cottage or garden full of sunlight and the chirps of birds will probably create a mood of peace.

See pages 60, 573, 580.
See also *Setting.*

MYTH **Traditional story that is rooted in a particular culture, is basically religious, and usually serves to explain a belief, a ritual, or a mysterious natural phenomenon.** Most myths grew out of religious rituals, and almost all of them involve the influence of gods on human affairs. Every culture has its own mythology. For many centuries the myths of ancient Greece and Rome were very influential in the Western world.

"The Fenris Wolf" (page 828) is a story from Norse mythology, the system of myths developed thousands of years ago by the people of Scandinavia. The myths were part of an oral tradition; the oldest surviving written versions of these ancient tales came from Iceland in the thirteenth century. There are variations in the Norse myths, as there are in the myths of most cultures.

See pages 744, 826–827.

NARRATION **Type of writing or speaking that tells about a series of related events.** Narration is one of the four major techniques used in writing. (The others are **description, exposition,** and **persuasion.**) Narration can be any length, from a brief paragraph to an entire book. It is most often found in short stories, novels, epics, and ballads. But narration is also used in any piece of nonfiction that relates a series of events that tell what happened—such as a biography, an essay, or a news story—and even in a scientific analysis or a report of a business meeting.

See also *Point of View.*

NARRATOR **The voice telling a story.** The choice of a narrator is very important in storytelling. For example, Edgar Allan Poe chose the murderer himself to tell the story "The Cask of Amontillado" (page 211). This choice of a narrator not only increases our sense of horror but also raises many questions, which make us uneasy. For one thing we wonder whether this narrator is telling the truth. We also wonder whom the narrator is talking to as he relates the details of his crime.

See pages 170–171.
See also *Point of View.*

NONFICTION **Prose writing that deals with real people, things, events, and places.** The most popular forms of nonfiction are **biography** and **autobiography.** Other examples include essays, newspaper stories, magazine articles, historical writing, scientific reports, and even personal diaries and letters.

NOVEL Fictional prose narrative usually consisting of more than fifty thousand words. In general, the novel uses the same basic literary elements as the short story (**plot, character, setting, theme,** and **point of view**) but develops them more fully. Many novels have several subplots, for instance. Modern writers often do away with one or more of the novel's traditional elements. Some novels today are basically character studies, with only the barest, stripped-down story lines.

ONOMATOPOEIA (än′ō·mat′ō·pē′ə) **Use of a word whose sound imitates or suggests its meaning.** Onomatopoeia is so natural to us that we begin using it instinctively as children. *Crackle, pop, fizz, click, zoom,* and *chirp* are examples of onomatopoeia. Onomatopoeia is an important element in the music of poetry.

> And in the hush of waters was the sound
> Of pebbles, rolling round;
> Forever rolling, with a hollow sound:
>
> And bubbling seaweeds, as the waters go,
> Swish to and fro
> Their long cold tentacles of slimy gray. . . .
>
> —James Stephens, from "The Shell"

See pages 532, 551.
See also *Alliteration, Assonance, Rhyme.*

PARADOX Statement or situation that seems to be a contradiction but reveals a truth. Paradoxes in literature are designed to make readers stop and think. They often express aspects of life that are mysterious, surprising, or difficult to describe. When O. Henry, in "The Gift of the Magi" (page 349), refers to the impoverished Della and Jim as "one of the richest couples on earth," he is stating a paradox.

PARALLELISM Repetition of words, phrases, or sentences that have the same grammatical structure or that state a similar idea. Parallelism, or **parallel structure,** helps make lines rhythmic and memorable and heightens their emotional effect:

> It was the best of times, it was the worst of times, it was the age of wisdom, it was the age of foolishness, it was the epoch of belief, it was the epoch of incredulity, it was the season of Light, it was the season of Darkness, it was the spring of hope, it was the winter of despair, we had everything before us, we had nothing before us, we were all going direct to Heaven, we were all going direct the other way. . . .
>
> —Charles Dickens, from *A Tale of Two Cities*

See page 435.

PERSONA Mask or voice assumed by a writer. Authors often take on other identities in their works. In a short story a writer may assume a persona by using a first-person narrator. When a poet is not the speaker of a poem, the poet is creating a persona.

See pages 210, 548.
See also *Point of View, Speaker.*

PERSONIFICATION Kind of metaphor in which a nonhuman thing or quality is talked about as if it were human. Here are a few lines in which poetry itself is personified—that is, it is described as behaving and feeling the way people do:

> This poetry gets bored of being alone,
> it wants to go outdoors to chew on the winds,
> to fill its commas with the keels of rowboats. . . .
>
> —Hugo Margenat, from "Living Poetry"

See pages 505, 526.
See also *Figure of Speech, Metaphor.*

PLOT Series of related events that make up a story or drama. Plot is what happens in a story, novel, or play. An outline showing the "bare bones" of a plot would include the story's **basic situation,** or **exposition;** the **conflict,** or problem; the **main events** (including **complications**); the final **climax,** or moment of great emotional intensity or suspense, when we learn what the outcome of the conflict is going to be; and the **resolution,** or **denouement.**

See pages 2–3, 897.

Handbook of Literary Terms

POETRY Type of rhythmic, compressed language that uses figures of speech and imagery to appeal to the reader's emotions and imagination. The major forms of poetry are the **lyric poem** and **narrative poem.** Two types of narrative poetry are the **epic** and the **ballad.** One popular type of lyric poetry is the **sonnet.** Beyond this, poetry is difficult to define, though many readers feel it is easy to recognize. The poet Wallace Stevens, for example, once described poetry as "a search for the inexplicable."

See also *Ballad, Epic, Lyric Poetry, Sonnet.*

POINT OF VIEW Vantage point from which a writer tells a story. In broad terms there are three possible points of view: omniscient, first person, and third person limited.

In the **omniscient** (or "all-knowing") **point of view,** the person telling the story knows everything there is to know about the characters and their problems. This all-knowing narrator can tell us about the past, the present, and the future of all the characters. He or she can even tell us what the characters are thinking. The narrator can also tell us what is happening in other places. In the omniscient point of view, the narrator is not in the story at all. In fact, the omniscient narrator is like a god telling the story.

In the **first-person point of view,** one of the characters is telling the story, using the pronoun *I.* We get to know this narrator very well, but we can know only what this character knows, and we can observe only what this character observes. All of our information about the events in the story must come from this one character. When a story is told from the first-person point of view, readers often must ask if the narrator is unreliable. An **unreliable narrator** does not always know what is happening in the story, or he or she might be lying or telling us only part of the story.

In the **third-person-limited point of view,** the narrator, who plays no part in the story, zooms in on the thoughts and feelings of just one character. With this point of view, we observe the action through the eyes and with the feelings of this one character.

See pages 170–171, 188, 197, 210.
See also *Narrator, Persona.*

PROTAGONIST Main character in fiction or drama. The protagonist is the character we focus our attention on, the person who sets the plot in motion.

The character or force that blocks the protagonist is the **antagonist.** Most protagonists are rounded, dynamic characters who change in some important way by the end of the story, novel, or play. The antagonist is often but not always the villain in the story. Similarly, the protagonist is often but not always the hero.

See page 138.

PUN Play on the multiple meanings of a word or on two words that sound alike but have different meanings. Most often puns are used for their humorous effects; they are used in jokes all the time. ("What has four wheels and flies?" Answer: "A garbage truck.") Shakespeare was one of the great punsters of all time. The servants in *Romeo and Juliet* (page 901) make crude puns as they clown around at the start of the play. Later, Romeo and his friend Mercutio trade wits in a series of more sophisticated puns. Since word meanings change so quickly, some of Shakespeare's puns are barely understandable to us today, just as puns popular today may be puzzling to people a hundred years from now.

See page 1028.

"Does the doctor make mouse calls?"

Drawing by Bernard Schoenbaum; © 1991 The New Yorker Magazine, Inc.

REFRAIN Repeated word, phrase, line, or group of lines. Though refrains are usually associated with songs and poems, they are also used in speeches and other forms of literature. Refrains are most often used to build rhythm, but they may also provide commentary or build suspense.

See page 539.

Handbook of Literary Terms

RHYME **Repetition of accented vowel sounds, and all sounds following them, in words that are close together in a poem.** *Choice* and *voice* are rhymes, as are *tingle* and *jingle*.

End rhymes occur at the ends of lines. In this poem the words *defense/tense, know/go,* and *Spain/Maine* are end rhymes:

Old Mary

My last defense
Is the present tense.
It little hurts me now to know
I shall not go
Cathedral-hunting in Spain
Nor cherrying in Michigan or Maine.

—Gwendolyn Brooks

Internal rhymes occur in the middle of a line. This line has an internal rhyme (*dreary* rhymes with *weary*):

Once upon a midnight dreary, while I pondered, weak and weary

Edgar Allan Poe, from "The Raven"

When two words have some sound in common but do not rhyme exactly, they are called **approximate rhymes** (or **half rhymes, off rhymes,** or **slant rhymes**). In Brooks's poem on this page, the words *now* and *know* are approximate rhymes.

The pattern of end rhymes in a poem is called a **rhyme scheme.** The rhyme scheme of a stanza or a poem is indicated by the use of a different letter of the alphabet for each new rhyme. For example, the rhyme scheme of Brooks's poem is *aabbcc.*

See pages 530, 537.

RHYTHM **Musical quality in language produced by repetition.** Rhythm occurs naturally in all forms of spoken and written language. The most obvious kind of rhythm is produced by **meter,** the regular repetition of stressed and unstressed syllables found in some poetry. But writers can also create rhythm by using rhymes, by repeating words and phrases, and even by repeating whole lines or sentences. This stanza by Walt Whitman is written in free verse and so does not follow a metri-cal pattern. Yet the lines are rhythmical because of Whitman's repeated use of certain sentence structures, words, and sounds.

Give me the splendid silent sun with all his
    beams full-dazzling,
Give me juicy autumnal fruit ripe and red
    from the orchard,
Give me a field where the unmowed grass grows,
Give me an arbor, give me the trellised grape,
Give me fresh corn and wheat, give me
    serene-moving animals teaching content,
Give me nights perfectly quiet as on high
    plateaus west of the Mississippi, and I
    looking up at the stars. . . .

—Walt Whitman, from "Give Me the
    Splendid Silent Sun"

See pages 530–531.
See also *Free Verse, Meter.*

SATIRE **Type of writing that ridicules something—a person, a group of people, humanity at large, an attitude or failing, a social institution—in order to reveal a weakness.** Most satires are an attempt to convince us of a point of view or to persuade us to follow a course of action. They do this by pointing out how the opposite point of view or action is ridiculous or laughable. Satire often involves **exaggeration**—the act of overstating something to make it look worse than it is.

See also *Irony, Tone.*

SCENE DESIGN **Sets, lights, costumes, and props, which bring a play to life onstage. Sets** are the furnishings and scenery that suggest the time and place of the action. **Props** (short for *properties*) are all the objects that the actors use onstage, such as books, telephones, suitcases.

See pages 853–854.

SETTING **The time and place of a story or play.** Most often the setting of a narrative is established early in the story. For example, in the fourth paragraph of "The Cask of Amontillado" (page 211), Edgar Allan Poe tells his readers, "It was about dusk, one evening during the supreme madness of the carnival season. . . ." Setting often contributes to a story's emotional effect. In "The Cask of Amontillado" the descriptions of the gloomy Montresor palace, with its damp catacombs full of bones, help create the story's mood of horror. Setting can also contribute to the conflict in a story, as the harsh environment does in Eugenia W. Collier's "Marigolds" (page 141). Setting can also be used to reveal character, as it does in Truman Capote's "A Christmas Memory" (page 63).

See pages 60–61.

See also *Mood*.

SHORT STORY **Short, concentrated, fictional prose narrative.** Some say Edgar Allan Poe was the first short-story writer. He was also one of the first to attempt to define the short story. He said "unity of effect" is crucial, meaning that a short story ought to concentrate on a single purpose. Short stories are usually built on a plot that consists of these "bare bones": the **basic situation** or **exposition, complications, climax,** and **resolution.** Years ago, most short stories were notable for their strong plots. Today's short-story writers tend to be more interested in character.

SIMILE **Figure of speech that makes a comparison between two unlike things, using a word such as *like, as, resembles, or than*.** Shakespeare, in one of his famous sonnets, uses a simile with an ironic twist, comparing two things that are *not* alike:

> My mistress' eyes are nothing like the sun

We would expect a love poem to compare the light in a lover's eyes to the bright sun. But instead, Shakespeare puts a twist into a common comparison—in order to make a point about the extravagant similes found in most love poems of his day.

See pages 504, 745–746.

See also *Figure of Speech, Metaphor*.

SOLILOQUY **Long speech in which a character who is onstage alone expresses his or her thoughts aloud.** The soliloquy is a very old dramatic convention, in which the audience is supposedly overhearing the private thoughts of a character. Perhaps the most famous soliloquy is the "To be or not to be" speech in Shakespeare's play *Hamlet*. There are also several soliloquies in *Romeo and Juliet*, including Friar Laurence's soliloquy at the opening of Act II, Scene 3

(pages 941–943); Juliet's at the end of Act IV, Scene 3 (pages 997–998); and Romeo's in Act V, Scene 3 (pages 1015–1016).

SONNET **Fourteen-line lyric poem that is usually written in iambic pentameter and that has one of several rhyme schemes.** The oldest kind of sonnet is called the **Italian sonnet,** or **Petrarchan sonnet,** after the fourteenth-century Italian poet Petrarch. The first eight lines, or **octet** or **octave,** of the Italian sonnet pose a question or problem about love or some other subject. The concluding six lines, or the **sestet,** are a response to the octet. The octet has the rhyme scheme *abba abba;* the sestet has the rhyme scheme *cde cde.*

Another important sonnet form, widely used by Shakespeare, is called the **Shakespearean sonnet.** It has three four-line units, or **quatrains,** followed by a concluding two-line unit, or **couplet.** The most common rhyme scheme for the Shakespearean sonnet is *abab cdcd efef gg.*

See page 498.

See also *Lyric Poetry*.

SPEAKER **Voice that is talking to us in a poem.** Sometimes the speaker is identical with the poet, but often the speaker and the poet are not the same. The poet may be speaking as a child, a woman, a man, a whole people, an animal, or even an object. For example, the speaker of Maya Angelou's poem "Woman Work" (page 485) is a hard-working woman with several children, who cuts cane and cotton and lives in a hut—not Maya Angelou at all.

See page 548.

See also *Persona*.

STANZA **Group of consecutive lines in a poem that form a single unit.** A stanza in a poem is something like a paragraph in prose: It often expresses a unit of thought. A stanza may consist of any number of lines. The word *stanza* is Italian for "stopping place" or "place to rest." Emily Dickinson's poem " 'Hope' is the thing with feathers" (page 511) consists of three four-line stanzas, or **quatrains,** each one expressing a unit of thought.

STYLE **The particular way in which a writer uses language.** Style is created mainly through **diction** (word choice), use of **figurative language,** and sentence patterns. Style can be described as plain, ornate, formal, ironic, conversational, and so on.

See pages 572–573.

SUSPENSE **Uncertainty or anxiety the reader feels about what is going to happen next in a story.** In "The Most Dangerous Game" (page 17) our curiosity is aroused at once when we hear about Ship-Trap Island and sailors' fear of it. When Rainsford lands on that very island and is hunted by the sinister General Zaroff, suspense keeps us on the edge of our seats. We wonder: Will Rainsford be another victim who is hunted down and killed by the evil and weird Zaroff?

See also *Foreshadowing, Plot.*

SYMBOL **Person, place, thing, or event that stands for itself and for something beyond itself as well.** For example, a scale has a real existence as an instrument for measuring weights, but it also is used as a public symbol of justice. Other familiar public symbols are the cross that symbolizes Christianity, the six-pointed star that symbolizes Judaism, the star and crescent that symbolizes Islam, and the bald eagle that symbolizes the United States. These are public symbols that most people know, but in literature, writers sometimes create new, private symbols that can be understood only from their context. One of the great symbols in literature is Herman Melville's great white whale, used as a symbol of the mystery of evil in the novel *Moby-Dick.*

See pages 402–403, 430.

TALL TALE **Exaggerated, far-fetched story that is obviously untrue but is told as though it should be believed.** Most tall tales are humorous. Tall tales are especially popular in the United States. As tall tales are passed on, they often get taller and taller—more and more exaggerated. The tales told about Paul Bunyan, the superheroic logger of the Northern forests, are tall tales.

See also *Fable, Folk Tale.*

THEME **Central idea of a work of literature.** A theme is not the same as a subject. The subject of a work can usually be expressed in a word or two: love, childhood, death. The theme is the idea the writer wishes to reveal *about* that subject. The theme is something that can be expressed in at least one complete sentence. For example, one theme of Shakespeare's *Romeo and Juliet* (page 901) might be stated in this way: "Love is more powerful than hatred." Theme is not usually stated directly in a work of literature. Most often, the reader has to think about all the elements of the work and use them to make an inference, or educated guess, about what its theme is. Some themes are so commonly found in the literature of all cultures and all ages that they are called **universal themes.** Here are some universal themes found in stories throughout the ages and expressed in the *Odyssey* (page 750): "Heroes must undergo trials and endure losses before they can claim their rightful kindom." "Arrogance and pride can bring destruction." "Love will endure and triumph over evil."

See pages 246–247, 260.

TONE **Attitude a writer takes toward a subject, a character, or the audience.** Tone is conveyed through the writer's choice of words and details. For example, Gary Soto's "The Grandfather" (page 431) is affectionate and nostalgic in tone. James Thurber's "The Princess and the Tin Box" (page 394) is humorous and lightly mocking in tone.

See pages 171, 573.
See also *Connotation, Diction, Irony, Satire.*

TRAGEDY **Play that depicts serious and important events in which the main character comes to an unhappy end.** In a tragedy the main character is usually dignified and courageous. His or her downfall may be caused by a character flaw, or it may result from forces beyond human control. The tragic hero usually wins some self-knowledge and wisdom, even though he or she suffers defeat, perhaps even death.

See pages 852, 897.
See also *Comedy, Drama.*

VOICE **The writer's or speaker's distinctive use of language in a text.** Voice is created by a writer's **tone** and choice of words. Some writers have such a distinctive voice that you can identify their works on the basis of voice alone. The detached, objective tone and simple language in "Old Man at the Bridge" (page 162), for example, make it instantly recognizable as one of Ernest Hemingway's short stories.

See pages 171, 548.

Handbook of Reading and Informational Terms

For more information about a topic, turn to the page(s) in this book indicated on a separate line at the end of most entries. To learn more about *Inference,* for example, turn to page 108.

The words in **boldface** are other key terms, with definitions provided in context. On another line there are cross-references to entries in this Handbook that provide closely related information. For instance, *Logic* contains a cross-reference to *Logical Order.*

ARGUMENT **A series of statements in a text designed to convince us of something.** What the writer or speaker wants to prove is called the **claim** (or the **opinion**). An argument might appeal to both our reason and our emotions. An argument in a scientific or historical journal, for instance, would probably present only **logical appeals,** which include sound reasons and factual evidence. An argument in a political text would probably also include **emotional appeals,** which are directed more to our "hearts" than to our minds. Some arguments use **loaded words** (words loaded with emotional connotations) and **anecdotes** (brief, personal stories) that also appeal to our feelings. It is important to be able to recognize emotional appeals used in arguments—and to be aware of how they can trick an audience.

Arguments can be found in editorials, magazine articles, political speeches, professional journals, and primary source material.

See pages 370–371, 598–599, 818.

CAUSE AND EFFECT **A text structure that shows how or why one thing leads to another.** The **cause** is the reason that an action takes place. The **effect** is the result or consequence of the cause. A cause can have more than one effect, and an effect may have several causes. Writers may explain causes only or effects only.

A text may be organized in a cause-effect chain. One cause leads to an effect, which causes another effect, and so on. Notice the cause-effect chain in the following paragraph from "An Arctic Floe of Climate Questions" (page 603):

> But some alarm bells did ring, because there is growing concern that we humans are fouling things up through our burning of gas, oil, and coal, which releases so-called greenhouse gases such as carbon dioxide into the air. These gases, which trap heat, may be causing the world's temperature to steadily creep higher and higher. And an absence of ice at the North Pole seemed like one more ominous sign of impending trouble.

Effect:
Alarm bells rang.

↓

Cause:
Concern was growing about the burning of gas, oil, and coal.

↓

Effect:
They release heat-trapping gases.

↓

Cause/Effect:
World's temperatures climb higher.

↓

Effect:
Ice absent at the North Pole.

Writers use the cause-effect pattern in both narrative and informational texts. In most short stories, events in the plot are connected in a cause-effect chain. Some words and phrases that signal the cause-effect pattern are *because, depended on, inspired, produced, resulting in, led to,* and *outcome.* Never assume, either in your reading or in real life, that one event causes another just because it happened before it.

See pages 436, 580.
See also *Text Structures.*

CHRONOLOGICAL ORDER The arrangement of details in time order, that is, in the order in which they occurred. Chronological order is used in a narrative, which describes a series of events, and in texts that explain the steps in a process.

See pages 44, 1075.
See also *Text Structures.*

CLAIM The idea or opinion that a writer tries to prove or defend in an argument. The claim is stated as a **generalization,** a broad statement or conclusion that covers many situations (or follows from the evidence). The following statements are examples of claims stated as generalizations:

> Edgar Allan Poe died as a result of rabies poisoning. ("Poe's Death is Rewritten as Case of Rabies, Not Telltale Alcohol," page 225)
>
> Everyday acts of heroism are often overlooked. ("Where I Find My Heroes," page 819)

The author of the argument then supports the claim with either logical appeals (reasons backed by factual evidence), emotional appeals, or both.

See page 370.
See also *Argument, Generalization.*

COHERENT Logically integrated, consistent, and understandable. A text is **coherent** (kō·hir′ənt) when its ideas are arranged in an order that makes sense to the reader. To aid in coherence, writers help readers follow a text by using **transitions,** words and phrases that show how ideas are connected.

Common Transitional Words and Phrases	
Comparing Ideas also, and, too, moreover, similarly, another	**Contrasting Ideas** although, still, yet, but, on the other hand, instead
Showing Cause-Effect for, since, as a result, therefore, so that, because	**Showing Importance** first, last, to begin with, mainly, more important
Showing Location above, across, over, there, inside, behind, next to, through, near	**Showing Time** before, at last, now, when, eventually, at once, finally

COMPARISON/CONTRAST A method of organizing information by showing similarities and differences among various groups of details.

See pages 281, 446, 1032.
See also *Text Structures.*

CONSUMER DOCUMENTS Informative texts, such as a warranties, contracts, instruction manuals. Here are some points to keep in mind when you read consumer documents:

1. Try to read the consumer document before you buy the product. Then, you can ask the clerk to explain anything you don't understand.

2. Read all of the pages in whatever language comes most easily to you. (Many documents are printed in two or three languages.) You will often find important information where you least expect it, such as at the end of the document.

3. Read the fine print. *Fine,* here, means "tiny and barely readable." Some fine-print statements in documents are required by law. They are

designed to protect you, the consumer, so the company may not be interested in emphasizing these points.

4. Don't expect the document to be interesting or easy to read. If you don't understand a statement and you can't ask someone at the store that sold you the product, call or write to the company that made it. You should complain to the company if you find its consumer document confusing.

5. Before you sign anything, read everything on the page, and be sure you understand what you're agreeing to. Ask to take the document home, and have your parent or guardian read it. If you are not of legal age, an adult may be responsible for whatever you've signed. Make a copy of any document that you've signed—and keep the copy in a place where you can find it.

See pages 1062–1064.

CONTEXT CLUES **The words and sentences surrounding a word.** Context clues can sometimes help you guess at the meaning of an unfamiliar word. You will find examples below of three types of context clues. In the examples, the unfamiliar word appears in **boldface**. The context clue is underlined.

Definition: Look for words that define the unfamiliar word, often by giving a synonym or a definition for it.

> Mathilde brought no **dowry** to her marriage—no <u>property or money to give her marriage a good start</u>.

Example: Look for examples that reveal the meaning of the unfamiliar word.

> She wanted **tapestries** on her walls, like those <u>beautiful embroidered hangings that decorated her friend's home</u>.

Contrast: Find words that contrast the unfamiliar word with a word or phrase you already know.

> M. Loisel was **distracted,** but Mathilde was <u>fully involved</u> in the party.

See pages 196, 368.

CREDIBILITY **The believability of a writer's argument.** To evaluate credibility, you first need to determine the author's claim, or opinion. Then you need to look at the **reasons** (statements that explain *why* the author holds the opinion) and the **evidence** (information that supports each reason). To be credible, evidence must be **relevant,** that is, directly related to the argument; **comprehensive,** that is, sufficient to be convincing; and **accurate,** that is, from a source that can be trusted as factually correct or otherwise reliable.

The writer's **intent** should also be considered. If you're reading an opinion essay, for instance, be sure to note any credentials or background information about the writer. Does the writer work for an institution that represents a particular point of view? Has the writer published a book on the same topic? Do emotional appeals and fallacious reasoning reveal a bias even though the writer pretends to be fair to both sides of the argument?

Notice the **tone** of the text. An argument that is based on logical appeals will usually have a serious, sincere tone. An angry or self-righteous tone might make you question the credibility of the argument.

See pages 370–371, 598–599, 675.
See also *Argument.*

DICTIONARY You use a dictionary to find the precise meaning and usage of words. The elements of a typical entry are explained below.

1. **Entry word.** The entry word shows how the word is spelled and divided into syllables. It may also show capitalization and other spellings.

2. Pronunciation. Phonetic symbols (such as the *schwa,* ə) and **diacritical marks** (such as the *dieresis,* ä) show how to pronounce the entry word. A key to these symbols and marks usually appears at the bottom of every other page of a dictionary. In this book a pronunciation guide appears at the bottom of every other page of the Glossary (pages 1206–1211).

3. Part-of-speech label. This label tells how the entry word is used. When a word can be used as more than one part of speech, definitions are grouped by part of speech. The sample entry shows three definitions of *indulge* as a transitive verb *(vt.)* and one as an intransitive verb *(vi.).*

4. Other forms. Sometimes the spellings of plural forms of nouns, principal parts of verbs, and comparative and superlative forms of adjectives and adverbs are shown.

5. Word origin. A word's origin, or **etymology** (et′ə·mäl′ə·jē), shows where the word comes from. *Indulge* comes from the Latin *indulgere,* which probably comes from the prefix *in–,* meaning "not," added to the Greek *dolichos,* "long" and the Gothic *tulgus,* "firm."

6. Examples. Phrases or sentences show how the entry word is used.

7. Definitions. If a word has more than one meaning, the meanings are numbered or lettered.

8. Special-usage labels. These labels identify special meanings or special uses of the word. Here, *Archaic* indicates an outdated meaning.

9. Related word forms. Other forms of the entry word are listed. Usually these are created by the addition of suffixes.

10. Synonyms and antonyms. Synonyms (words similar in meaning) and **antonyms** (words opposite in meaning) may appear at the end of the entry.

A dictionary is available as a book, a CD-ROM, or part of a word-processing program or Web site.

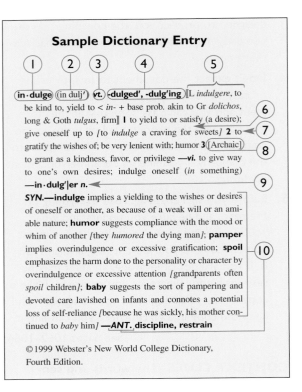

Sample Dictionary Entry

in·dulge (in dulj′) **vt. -dulged′, -dulg′ing** [L *indulgere,* to be kind to, yield to < *in-* + base prob. akin to Gr *dolichos,* long & Goth *tulgus,* firm] **1** to yield to or satisfy (a desire); give oneself up to *[to indulge a craving for sweets]* **2** to gratify the wishes of; be very lenient with; humor **3** [Archaic] to grant as a kindness, favor, or privilege —**vi.** to give way to one's own desires; indulge oneself (*in* something) —**in·dulg′|er** *n.*
SYN.—**indulge** implies a yielding to the wishes or desires of oneself or another, as because of a weak will or an amiable nature; **humor** suggests compliance with the mood or whim of another *[they humored the dying man];* **pamper** implies overindulgence or excessive gratification; **spoil** emphasizes the harm done to the personality or character by overindulgence or excessive attention *[grandparents often spoil children];* **baby** suggests the sort of pampering and devoted care lavished on infants and connotes a potential loss of self-reliance *[because he was sickly, his mother continued to baby him]* —**ANT.** discipline, restrain

© 1999 Webster's New World College Dictionary, Fourth Edition.

See also *Text Structures.*

EVIDENCE Specific information or proof that backs up the reasons in an argument. Factual evidence includes statements that can be proved by direct observation or by checking reliable reference sources. **Statistics** (facts in the form of numbers) and **expert testimony,** statements from people who are recognized as experts or authorities on an issue, may all be considered factual evidence.

In fields where discoveries are constantly being made, such as in astronomy and genetics, facts need to be checked in a recently published source. Remember that a Web site on the Internet may be current, but it may not be reliable. Anybody can post a statement on the Internet. If you suspect that a statement presented as a fact is not true, try to find the same fact in another source.

See pages 221, 370, 598–599.

FALLACIOUS (fə·lā′shəs) **REASONING** **Faulty reasoning, or mistakes in logical thinking.** (The word *fallacious* comes from a Latin word meaning "deceptive" or "tricky." The word *false* comes from the same root word, as does the word *fallacy.*) Fallacious reasoning leads to false or incorrect conclusions. Here are some types of fallacious reasoning:

1. **Begging the question,** also called **circular reasoning,** assumes the truth of a statement before it has been proved. You appear to be giving a reason to support your opinion, but all you're doing is restating your opinion in different words.

> All students in the ninth grade need to get a laptop computer because it's essential for every ninth grader to have one.

2. **Name calling** uses labels to attack a person who holds an opposing view instead of giving reasons or evidence to atttack the opposing view itself. This fallacy includes criticizing the person's character, situation, or background.

> Why should I listen to someone who doesn't even know who won the World Series?

3. **Stereotyping** gives all members of a group the same (usually undesirable) characteristics. It assumes that everyone (or everything) in that group is alike. (The word *stereotype* comes from the word for a metal plate that was used to print the same image over and over.) Stereotypes are often based on misconceptions about racial, social, religious, gender, or ethnic groups.

> Small towns are boring. Cats are self-centered.

4. **Hasty generalization** is a broad, general statement or conclusion that is made without sufficient evidence to back it up. A hasty generalization is often made on the basis of one or two experiences or observations.

> **Insufficient evidence:** I read about a healthy eighty-eight-year-old woman who smokes a pack of cigarettes every day. My grandfather smokes, too, and he's in great shape physically.
>
> **Hasty generalization:** Smoking does not affect your health.

If any exceptions to the conclusion can be found, the generalization is not true.

5. **Either/or fallacy** assumes that there are only two possible choices or solutions (usually extremes), even though there may be many.

> Either I get a cell phone, or you're never going to know where I am after school.

6. **False cause and effect** occurs when one event is said to be the cause of another event just because the two events happened in sequence. You cannot assume that an event caused whatever happened afterward.

> Her grades improved when she got a job after school.

See page 598.

GENERALIZATION **A broad statement that applies to or covers many individuals, experiences, situations, observations, or texts.** A **valid generalization** is a type of conclusion that is drawn after considering as many of the facts as possible. Here are some specific facts from "Community Service & You" (page 120) and a generalization based on them. Notice that each fact is one piece of evidence. The generalization then states what the evidence adds up to, drawing a conclusion that applies to all members of the group.

> **Specific facts:** Thousands of young people volunteer to tutor children. Others help in massive projects to clean up beaches and rivers. Still others work at soup kitchens, shelters, and playgrounds—all without earning a cent.
>
> **Generalization:** Many young people get involved in voluntary community service.

A generalization jumps from your own specific experiences and observations to a larger, general understanding.

See pages 370, 598.

GRAPHS Graphic depiction of information.
Line graphs generally show changes in quantity over time. **Bar graphs** usually compare quantities within categories. **Pie graphs,** or **circle graphs,** show proportions by dividing a circle into different-sized sections, like slices of a pie.

How to Read a Graph

1. **Read the title.** The title will tell you the subject and purpose of the graph.

2. **Read the headings and labels.** These will help you determine the type of information presented.

3. **Analyze the details.** Read numbers carefully. Note increases or decreases. Look for the direction or order of events and trends and for relationships.

See pages 1119–1120.

INFERENCE A guess based on observation and prior experience. When you make inferences about a literary work, you use evidence from the text as well as from other texts you have read and from your own prior experience. One way to analyze a character, for instance, is to consider what the person says and how he or she interacts

with other characters. In the story "Thank You, M'am" (page 109), after the woman is almost mugged, she says to the boy who tried to steal her pocketbook:

> "You ought to be my son. I would teach you right from wrong. Least I can do right now is to wash your face. Are you hungry?"

From these statements, you can infer that the woman is strong and not easily intimidated. You can infer that she is also kind, that she understands why the boy tried to steal from her. Values are important to her, and she is determined to do what she can to help him.

When you're writing about a story or an informational text, you must be sure your inferences are supported by details in the text. **Supported inferences** are based directly on evidence in a text that you can point to and on reasonable prior knowledge. Some interpretation of the evidence is possible, but you cannot ignore or contradict facts that a writer gives you.

See pages 108, 140, 686.

INFORMATIVE TEXTS Texts that communicate information and data. When you're reading informative texts, you need to read slowly, looking for main ideas and important details. Slow and careful reading is especially important when you're trying to get meaning from consumer, workplace, and public documents. These documents are often not written by professional writers, so they may be difficult to read.

See also *Consumer Documents, Public Documents, Workplace Documents.*

LOGIC Correct reasoning. A logical text presents reasons supported by evidence (facts and examples). A text is illogical when it does not provide reasons backed by evidence. Notice how each sentence in this text, from "A Country Divided" (page 282), gives evidence that supports the sentence that precedes it.

Through the long years of British rule, the Irish fought for their freedom. They fought with what weapons they had, in rebellions great and small—rebellions that the vast British army always put down. The Irish fought with words as well as weapons. They organized and signed petitions, held massive nonviolent protests, and after Catholics regained the vote in 1829, they lobbied in the English Parliament for their freedom.

See pages 370, 598–599, 818.
See also *Logical Order.*

LOGICAL ORDER **A method of organizing information by putting details into related groupings.** Writers use logical order most often when they want to classify information, that is, to examine a subject and its relationship to other subjects. When you classify, you can divide a subject into its parts (considering global warming in different parts of the world, as in "An Arctic Floe of Climate Questions," page 603). You can define a new term or idea (defining a *polynya* in the same article). Or you can use the comparison-contrast pattern to show similarities and differences among various groups (comparing beneficial and harmful results of global warming, as in "Rising Tides," page 600).

See page 1075.
See also *Text Structures.*

MAIN IDEA **The writer's most important point, opinion, or message.** The main idea may be stated directly, or it may be only suggested or implied. If the idea is not stated directly, it's up to you to look at the details and decide on the idea that they all seem to support. Try to restate the writer's main idea in your own words.

In an argument, the main idea (the generalization that the writer is trying to prove) is called the **claim,** or **opinion.**

Main idea of an essay: Every person who tries to help others is a hero (for "Heroes with Solid Feet," page 821).

Claim of an argument: The jury system is the best means we have for maintaining justice in a democracy (for "A Defense of the Jury System," page 372).

See page 430.

MAPS **A drawing showing all or part of the earth's surface or of bodies in the sky. Physical maps** illustrate the natural landscape of an area, using shading, lines, and color to show landforms and elevation. **Political maps** show political units, such as states and nations. They usually also show borders and capitals and other major cities. **Special-purpose maps** present specific information, such as the routes of the explorers. The special-purpose map on page 750 shows the route of Odysseus's journey. Use these guidelines to help you read the map on the next page.

How to Read a Map

1. **Determine the focus of the map.** The map's title and labels tell you its focus—its subject and the geographical area it covers.

2. **Study the legend.** The **legend,** or **key,** explains the symbols, lines, colors, and shadings used in the map.

3. **Check directions and distances.** Maps often include a **compass rose,** a diagram that shows north, south, east, and west. If there isn't one, assume that north is at the top, west to the left, and so on. Many maps also include a scale that relates distances on the map to actual distances.

4. **Look at the larger context.** The **absolute location** of any place on earth is given by its **latitude** (the number of degrees north or south of the equator) and its **longitude** (the number of degrees east or west of the **prime meridian,** or 0 degrees longitude). Some maps also include **locator maps,** which show the area depicted in relation to a larger area.

Handbook of Reading and Informational Terms

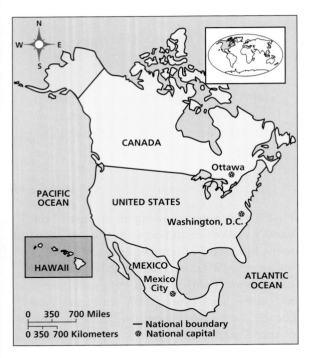

OPINION A statement of a person's belief, idea, or attitude. A **fact** is something that can be verified or proved by direct observation or by checking a reliable reference source. An **opinion** cannot be proved to be either true or false—even when it is supported by facts. The following statement is an unsupported opinion:

> William Shakespeare is the greatest writer that the world has ever known.

A **valid opinion** is an opinion that is supported by verifiable facts. In the following example, the verifiable facts are underlined:

> I think that William Shakespeare was a great writer because <u>most of his plays and poems are still read and enjoyed today, four hundred years after they were written.</u>

When you read a persuasive text, remember that statements of opinion can't be proved, but they can and should be supported by facts and logical reasoning.

See pages 311, 675.

ORDER OF IMPORTANCE A means of organizing information by ranking details in the order of their importance.

Writers of persuasive texts have to decide whether to give the strongest reason first or to present the weakest reason first and end with the strongest point. Informational texts such as news articles always begin with the most important details because they want to grab the readers' attention immediately. The structure of a news article looks like an upside-down triangle, with the least important details at the bottom.

See pages 458, 465.
See also *Text Structures.*

OUTLINING A way of organizing information to show relationships among key details in a text. You can use outlining as a writer and as a reader. Outlining puts main ideas and details in a form that you can review quickly. An **informal outline,** sometimes called a working outline, should have at least three main ideas. You put supporting details under each main idea, like this:

> **Informal Outline**
> I. First main idea
>   A. First detail supporting first main idea
>   B. Second detail supporting first main idea
>   C. Third detail supporting first main idea
> II. Second main idea
>   [etc.]

A **formal outline** is especially useful if you're writing a research paper. You might start with a working outline and then revise it into a formal one. Your teacher may ask you to submit a formal outline with your completed research paper.

Formal outlines use Roman numerals (I, II, III), capital letters (A, B, C) and Arabic numerals (1, 2, 3) to show order, relationship, and relative importance of ideas. The headings in a formal outline should have the same grammatical structure, and you must be consistent in your use of either phrases or sentences. (You can't move back and forth between them.) There should always be at least two divisions under each heading or none at all.

Here is the beginning of a formal outline of "Far-out Housekeeping on the ISS" (page 56):

Formal Outline

I. Setting up housekeeping routines
  A. Discussion with two astronauts about the excitement and routine of living in space
  B. Quotation from Lieutenant Commander Burbank
    1. Space as a hostile environment
    2. Dependence on the Station and on people on the ground
II. Everyday life in space
  A. Different kinds of food
  B. Communicating with home
  C. Recycling and trash

See pages 713–715.

PARAPHRASING Restating each sentence of a text in your own words. Paraphrasing is usually done only for difficult texts. Paraphrasing a text helps you to be certain you understand it. When you paraphrase, you follow the author's sequence of ideas. You carefully reword each line (if it's a poem) or sentence (if it's prose) without changing the author's ideas or leaving anything out. You restate each figure of speech to be sure you understand the basis of the comparison. If sentences are missing words or if the words are wrenched out of the usual order, you rephrase the sentence.

A paraphrase is longer than a **summary,** which is a brief statement of the main ideas in a text. Here are a paraphrase and a summary of a paragraph from "Address to Congress, November 27, 1963" (page 680).

Paraphrase: No speech could honor President Kennedy's memory more than

passing the civil rights bill as soon as possible. He fought to pass this bill and we have talked long enough about it—for more than a hundred years. Now it's time for the next chapter—making equal rights the law.
Summary: Passing the civil rights bill would be the best way to honor President Kennedy's memory.

See pages 446, 1008.

PRIMARY SOURCE An original, firsthand account. Primary sources may include an autobiography; an eyewitness testimony; a letter, speech, or literary work; a historical document; or information gathered from firsthand surveys or interviews. For example, Albert Einstein's "Letter to President Roosevelt," (page 448), is a primary source. It's important to use primary sources wherever they are available on a topic, but you need to research widely to make sure that a primary source is not biased.

Be sure to keep track of your primary sources by numbering each source and recording the necessary publishing information. If you quote directly from the primary source, be sure to use quotation marks and to give credit to your source.

See page 674.
See also *Secondary Source.*

PUBLIC DOCUMENTS Informative texts put out by the government or public agencies. Public documents include political platforms, public policy statements, speeches, and debates. These documents inform the public about government policy, laws, municipal codes, records, schedules, and the like.

See pages 680, 1061.

RESEARCH QUESTIONS Questions that are focused on a specific subject, which the researcher searches to answer. Such questions are essential tools for focusing your research.

One way to generate research questions is to use a KWL chart as a research guide. (See page 38 for an example.) This kind of chart is an easy way to organize questions and answers, especially if you know how to set up columns and rows on your computer. In the K column, you note what you already know about the subject. In the W column, you note what you'd like to find out. As you do your research, complete the L column by answering the questions you've asked in the W column.

Research questions can also be generated by brainstorming or by using the *5W-How* questions: *Who? What? When? Where? Why?* and *How?* As you seek primary and secondary source information at libraries and museums, in various electronic media (Internet, films, tapes), and from personal interviews, you will come up with more research questions. Always remember to keep your questions focused on the specific subject you have chosen.

See page 38.

ROOTS, PREFIXES, SUFFIXES

English words are often made up of two or more word parts. These words parts include

- **roots, which carry a word's core meaning**
- **prefixes, added onto the beginning of a word or in front of a word root to form a new word**
- **suffixes, added onto the end of a word or after a word root to form a new word**

Most word roots come from Greek and Latin. Prefixes and suffixes come from Greek, Latin, and Anglo-Saxon.

Greek Roots	Meaning	Examples
–dem–	people	de**dem**ocracy, epi**dem**ic
–hydr–	water	de**hydr**ate, **hydr**ogen
–psyche–	mind, soul	**psych**ic, **psych**ology
–syn–, –sym–	together	**syn**thesize, **sym**phony

Latin Roots	Meaning	Examples
–cog–	think, know	in**cog**nito, re**cog**nize
–dic–, –dict–	say, speak	**dict**ion, inter**dict**
–juven–	young	**juven**ile, re**juven**ate
–mar–	war	**mar**tial, **mar**tinet
–somn–	sleep	**somn**olent, **somn**ambulate

Greek Prefixes	Meaning	Examples
a–	lacking, without	**a**moral, **a**typical
neo–	new	**neo**classic, **neo**natal

Latin Prefixes	Meaning	Examples
e–, ef–, ex–	away, from, out	**ef**face, **ex**punge
retro–	back	**retro**active, **retro**spective

Anglo-Saxon/Old English Prefixes	Meaning	Examples
be–	around	**be**friend, **be**grime
over–	above	**over**bite, **over**see
mis–	badly, not	**mis**hap, **mis**copy

Greek Suffixes	Meaning	Examples
–logue –ism	speech act, manner	dia**logue**, epi**logue** critic**ism**, ostrac**ism**
Latin Suffixes	**Meaning**	**Examples**
–esce –tude	become, grow quality of being	coal**esce**, effer**vesce** apti**tude**, multi**tude**
Anglo-Saxon/Old English Suffixes	**Meaning**	**Examples**
–less –ful –en	lacking, without full of, marked by become	aim**less**, rest**less** rest**ful**, wonder**ful** strength**en**, light**en**

SECONDARY SOURCE **A secondhand account written by a writer who did not participate directly in the events he or she interprets, relates, or analyzes.** Secondary sources may include encyclopedias, magazine articles, textbooks, biographies, and technical journals. The news feature "Dear Juliet" (page 1033) is an example of a secondary source. A research paper may include both primary and secondary sources.

See page 674.

SPATIAL (spā′shəl) **ORDER** **A means of organizing information by showing where things are located.** (The word *spatial* is related to the word *space*. Spatial order shows where things are located in space.) Spatial order is often used in descriptive writing. Here is an example from "The Most Dangerous Game" (page 17). Phrases showing spatial order are underlined.

> The baying of the hounds drew <u>nearer, then still nearer, nearer, ever nearer.</u> <u>On a ridge</u> Rainsford climbed a tree. <u>Down a watercourse, not a quarter of a mile away,</u> he could see the bush moving.

See pages 458, 465.
See also *Text Structures*.

SYNTHESIZING **Putting all the different sources of information together in a process that gives you a better understanding of the whole subject.** In order to synthesize information, you first gather information about a topic from several sources. Then you find each writer's main ideas. Paraphrasing ideas, restating them in your own words, can help you understand difficult texts. Next you examine the ideas in each source, and you compare and contrast the ideas you've found. To synthesize what you have learned, you draw conclusions about the information you have gathered.

See page 281, 446.
See also *Generalization*.

TEXT STRUCTURES **Any organizational patterns that writers use to make their meaning clear.** In imaginative literature, text structures range from the plot structures in stories and dramas to the sonnet structure in poetry.

In nonfiction and informational texts, the writer's intent or purpose in creating the text determines how the text will be organized. Don't expect writers of informational texts and nonfiction to use the same structure throughout an entire text. Most writers switch from one type of structure to another and may even combine structures. The four basic ways of arranging ideas or details in nonfiction and informational texts are:

1. **Chronological order, time order** or **sequence**—putting events or steps in the order in which they occur. For an example of chronological order, see "A Warm, Clear Day in Dallas" (page 676). Most narrative and historical texts are written in chronological order. Chronological order is also found in writing that explains a process such as technical directions and recipes. This type of chronological order is called **step-by-step order.**

2. **Spatial order**—the order that shows where things are located. This pattern is used in descriptive writing. It is especially useful in helping readers visualize setting. See the first paragraph of "Teaching Chess, and Life" (page 119).

3. **Order of importance**—ranking details from most important to least important or from least important to most important. Writers of persuasive texts in particular have to decide which order makes the strongest impact: putting the strongest reason first and the weaker ones later or saving the strongest reason for last. For an example of a text that uses order of importance, see "Peace Isn't Impossible" (page 290). News articles always begin with the most important details because they want to grab the readers' attention immediately.

4. **Logical order**—classifying details into related groups. One type of logical order is the **comparison and contrast** text structure, which shows similarities and differences among various groups. See a comparison of judges and juries in "A Defense of the Jury System" (page 372).

Other methods used to organize texts include:

- **cause and effect**—showing how events happen as a result of other events. See "Romeo and Juliet in Bosnia" (page 1035).

- **problem-solution**—explaining how a problem may be solved. See "Far-out Housekeeping on the ISS" (page 56).

- **question-answer**—asking questions, then giving the answers. See "Can Animals Think?" (page 39).

Recognizing these structures will help you understand the ideas in a text. The following guidelines can help you recognize text structures:

1. Search the text for the main idea. Look for clue words (**transitions**) that signal a specific pattern of organization. Also note colors, special type, headers, numbered lists, and icons that may be used to highlight terms or indicate text structure.

2. Analyze the text for other important ideas. Think about how the ideas connect, and look for an obvious pattern.

3. Remember that a writer might use one organizational pattern throughout a text or combine two or more patterns.

4. Draw a graphic organizer that maps how the text is structured. Some common graphic organizers are a **causal chain** (for the cause-effect text structure), a **flowchart** (showing chronological sequence), and a **Venn diagram** (showing similarities and differences).

See pages 44, 1075.
See also *Chronological Order, Logical Order, Order of Importance, Spatial Order.*

WORKPLACE DOCUMENTS Job-related texts, such as job applications, memos, instructional manuals, and employee handbooks. When you read workplace documents, keep these points in mind (in addition to the points about reading consumer documents, cited on pages 1148–1149):

1. Take all the time you need to read and understand the document. Don't let anyone rush you or tell you that a document is unimportant or just a formality.

2. Read technical directions carefully, even if they're just posted on the side of a device you're supposed to operate. Read all of the directions before you start. Ask questions if you're not sure how to proceed. Don't try anything out before you know what will happen next.

3. The employee handbook contains the "rules of the game" at that particular business. It tells you about holidays, work hours, break times, and vacations as well as other important company policies. Read the employee handbook from cover to cover.

See also *Consumer Documents.*

Language Handbook

1 THE PARTS OF SPEECH

PART OF SPEECH	DEFINITION	EXAMPLES
NOUN	Names person, place, thing, or idea	captain, swimmers, Maria Tallchief, team, Stratford-on-Avon, stories, "The Scarlet Ibis," justice, honesty
PRONOUN	Takes place of one or more nouns or pronouns	
Personal	Refers to one(s) speaking (first person), spoken to (second person), spoken about (third person)	I, me, my, mine, we, us, our, ours you, your, yours he, him, his, she, her, hers, it, its, they, them, their, theirs
Reflexive	Refers to subject and directs action of verb back to subject	myself, ourselves, yourself, yourselves, himself, herself, itself, themselves
Intensive	Refers to and emphasizes noun or another pronoun	(See Reflexive.)
Demonstrative	Refers to specific one(s) of group	this, that, these, those
Interrogative	Introduces question	what, which, who, whom, whose
Relative	Introduces subordinate clause and refers to noun or pronoun outside clause	that, which, who, whom, whose
Indefinite	Refers to one(s) not specifically named	all, any, anyone, both, each, either, everybody, many, none, nothing
ADJECTIVE	Modifies noun or pronoun by telling *what kind, which one, how many,* or *how much*	**an old, flea-bitten** dog, **a Sioux** custom, **that** one, **the twelve red** roses, **more** water
VERB	Shows action or state of being	
Action	Expresses physical or mental activity	paint, jump, write, know, imagine
Linking	Connects subject with word identifying or describing it	appear, be, seem, become, feel, look, smell, sound, taste
Helping (Auxiliary)	Combines with another verb to form a verb phrase	be, have, may, can, shall, will, would
ADVERB	Modifies verb, adjective, or adverb by telling *how, when, where,* or *to what extent*	drives **carefully, quite** dangerous, **shortly afterward,** arrived **there late**
PREPOSITION	Relates noun or pronoun to another word	across, between, into, near, of, on, with, aside from, instead of, next to
CONJUNCTION	Joins words or word groups	
Coordinating	Joins words or word groups used in same way	and, but, for, nor, or, so, yet

(continued)

PART OF SPEECH		DEFINITION	EXAMPLES
	Correlative	A pair of conjunctions that join parallel words or word groups	both . . . and, either . . . or, neither . . . nor, not only . . . but (also)
	Subordinating	Begins subordinate clause and connects it to independent clause	as though, because, if, since, so that, than, when, where, while
INTERJECTION		Expresses emotion	hey, oops, ouch, wow

Determining Parts of Speech

The way a word is used in a sentence determines the word's part of speech.

EXAMPLES
The fine feathers of young birds are called **down.**
   [noun]
She wore a **down** vest. [adjective]
Did the tackle **down** the ball in the end zone?
   [verb]
Her poster fell **down.** [adverb]
My cousin lives **down** the street from my school.
   [preposition]

Let's get a drink of **water.** [noun]
Did you **water** the plants? [verb]
Most **water** sports offer good exercise. [adjective]

He promised us **that** he would meet us after the game. [conjunction]
That CD didn't cost much. [adjective]
I never said **that.** [pronoun]

Avoiding Overused Adverbs

The adverbs *really, too, so,* and *very* are often overused. To keep your writing lively, replace those inexact, overused words with more specific adverbs such as *completely, definitely, entirely, especially, extremely, generally, largely, mainly, mostly, particularly, rather,* and *unusually.*

Try It Out

For each of the following sentences, replace the italicized adverb with a more specific adverb.

1. Elie Wiesel's speech was *very* direct.
2. It *really* focused on personal responsibility.
3. People accept injustice *too* easily.
4. One person's actions can be *very* important.
5. The worst part was to be *so* forgotten.

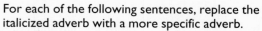

2 AGREEMENT

AGREEMENT OF SUBJECT AND VERB

2a. **A verb should always agree with its subject in number. Singular subjects take singular verbs. Plural subjects take plural verbs.**

SINGULAR   **She searches** for Mme. Forestier's necklace.

  PLURAL   **They search** for Mme. Forestier's necklace.

SINGULAR   Miss Lottie's flower **garden was destroyed.**

  PLURAL   Miss Lottie's **marigolds were destroyed.**

COMPUTER NOTE

Some word-processing programs can identify problems in subject-verb agreement. If you have access to such a program, you can use it to help you search for errors when you are proofreading your writing. If you are not sure whether a problem identified by the word processor is truly an error, look it up in this section of the Language Handbook.

 For information about identifying subjects and verbs, see 8b–g.

2b. The number of the subject is not changed by a phrase following the subject.

SINGULAR   The **sign** near the glass doors **explains** the theme of the exhibit.
PLURAL   Several **paintings** by Emilio Sánchez **were hanging** in the gallery.

SINGULAR   **Romeo,** together with Benvolio and Mercutio, **goes** to Lord Capulet's party.
PLURAL   The **combs** made of pure tortoise shell **were** expensive.

☞ For information about kinds of phrases, see 6a–g.

The number of the subject is not changed by a negative construction following the subject.

EXAMPLE
A **human being,** not a tiger nor any other animal, **becomes** the prey hunted by General Zaroff in "The Most Dangerous Game."

2c. The following indefinite pronouns are singular: *anybody, anyone, anything, each, either, everybody, everyone, everything, neither, nobody, no one, nothing, one, somebody, someone, something.*

EXAMPLES
Each of the poems about farm workers **was written** by Gary Soto.
Has anyone else in your study group **read** all of *The Miracle Worker*?

2d. The following indefinite pronouns are plural: *both, few, many, several.*

EXAMPLES
Both of the poems about the San Joaquin Valley **were written** by Gary Soto.
Have many in your study group **read** *The Miracle Worker*?

2e. The indefinite pronouns *all, any, most, none,* and *some* are singular when they refer to singular words and are plural when they refer to plural words.

SINGULAR   **Some** of the show **is** funny.
PLURAL   **Some** of the skits and other acts **are** funny.

SINGULAR   **All** of the house **looks** clean.
PLURAL   **All** of the houses **look** clean.

2f. A *compound subject,* which is two or more subjects that have the same verb, may be singular, plural, or either.

(1) Subjects joined by *and* usually take a plural verb.

EXAMPLE
Both **Leslie Marmon Silko** and **Mari Evans are** poets.

A compound subject that names only one person or thing takes a singular verb.

EXAMPLES
My **pen pal and best friend is** my cousin.
Macaroni and cheese makes a good side dish.

(2) Singular subjects joined by *or* or *nor* take a singular verb.

EXAMPLES
Either the **principal** or the **coach has** to approve it.
Neither **Della** nor **Jim was** disappointed.

(3) When a singular subject and a plural subject are joined by *or* or *nor,* the verb agrees with the subject nearer the verb.

EXAMPLES
Neither the losers nor the **winner was** happy with the outcome of the match.
Neither the winner nor the **losers were** happy with the outcome of the match.

 NOTE   If such a construction sounds awkward, revise the sentence to give each part of the subject its own verb.

EXAMPLE
The **losers were** not happy with the outcome of the match, and neither **was** the **winner.**

 For more information about subjects, see 8b, c, e, and g.

2g. *Don't* and *doesn't* must agree with their subjects.

With the subjects *I* and *you* and with plural subjects, use *don't (do not).*

EXAMPLES
I **don't** know.
You **don't** seem happy.
Some people **don't** care.

With other subjects, use *doesn't (does not).*

EXAMPLES
He **doesn't** drive.
Donna **doesn't** work.
It **doesn't** have one.

2h. A collective noun takes a singular verb when the noun refers to the group as a unit and takes a plural verb when the noun refers to the individual parts or members of the group.

A *collective noun* is singular in form but names a group of persons or things.

SINGULAR	The class **has** elected its officers. [class = a unit]
PLURAL	The class **have** completed their projects on *Romeo and Juliet*. [class = individual students]

Common Collective Nouns

army	club	group	public
assembly	committee	herd	squad
audience	couple	jury	staff
band	crew	majority	swarm
cast	crowd	number	team
chorus	family	pack	troop
class	flock	pair	wildlife

2i. A verb agrees with its subject, not with its predicate nominative.

SINGULAR	The main **attraction is** the marching bands.
PLURAL	The marching **bands are** the main attraction.

2j. A verb agrees with its subject even when the verb precedes the subject, as in sentences beginning with *here* or *there* and in questions.

SINGULAR	Here **is** [*or* here's] my **drawing** of the Cyclops.
PLURAL	Here **are** my **drawings** of the Cyclops.
SINGULAR	When in the program **does** the **skater perform** her triple axel?
PLURAL	When in the program **do** the **fans start** clapping to the music?

NOTE Contractions such as *here's, there's,* and *where's* should be used only with subjects that are singular in meaning.

2k. An expression of an amount (a length of time, a statistic, or a fraction, for example) is singular when the amount is thought of as a unit or when it refers to a singular word and is plural when the amount is thought of as many parts or when it refers to a plural word.

SINGULAR	**Twenty dollars is** the amount Della receives for her hair. [Twenty dollars is the single amount Della receives.]
PLURAL	**Twenty dollars were stuck** together. [Twenty individual dollars were stuck together.]
SINGULAR	**Three fourths** of the barrel **is** full. [*Three fourths* refers to *barrel,* a singular word.]
PLURAL	**Three fourths** of the barrels **have been** loaded. [*Three fourths* refers to *barrels,* a plural word.]

2l. The title of a creative work (such as a book, song, film, or painting) or the name of an organization, a country, or a city (even if it is plural in form) takes a singular verb.

EXAMPLES
"Marigolds" is a story by Eugenia W. Collier.
Friends of the Earth was founded in 1969.
The Netherlands has thousands of canals.

2m. A few nouns, although plural in form, take singular verbs.

EXAMPLE
The **news** of the nominee for the Supreme Court **was** a surprise to many observers.

Some nouns that end in –s take a plural verb even though they refer to a single item.

EXAMPLES
The **scissors need** to be sharpened.
Were these **pants** on sale?
The **pliers are** next to the wrench.

AGREEMENT OF PRONOUN AND ANTECEDENT

A pronoun usually refers to a noun or another pronoun. The word that a pronoun refers to is called its *antecedent.*

2n. A pronoun agrees with its antecedent in number and gender. Singular pronouns refer to singular antecedents. A few personal pronouns indicate gender: feminine, masculine, or neuter. Plural pronouns refer to plural antecedents. No plural pronouns indicate gender.

MASCULINE	he	him	his	himself
FEMININE	she	her	hers	herself
NEUTER	it	it	its	itself

EXAMPLES

Juliet stabs **herself.** [singular, feminine]

General Zaroff thinks that Rainsford has escaped **him.** [singular, masculine]

After eating the Lotus plant, the **men** did not want to return to **their** homeland. [plural]

2o. A singular pronoun is used to refer to *anybody, anyone, anything, each, either, everybody, everyone, everything, neither, nobody, no one, nothing, one, somebody, someone,* or *something.* The gender of any of these pronouns can sometimes be determined by a word in a phrase following the pronoun.

EXAMPLES

Each of the **boys** held some pebbles in **his** hand.

Everyone on the **girls'** tennis team won **her** match.

When the antecedent could be either masculine or feminine, use both the masculine and the feminine pronoun forms connected by *or.*

EXAMPLE

Everybody should choose **his or her** friends carefully.

Avoiding the *His or Her* Construction

When an antecedent could be either masculine or feminine, you can avoid the *his or her* construction by using plural nouns and pronouns. You can also change the possessive *his or her* to an article (*a, an, the*) or eliminate it altogether.

ORIGINAL

A person should choose his or her friends carefully.

REVISED

People should choose **their** friends carefully.
A person should choose **a** friend carefully.
People should choose friends carefully.

Try It Out

Revise each of the following sentences to eliminate the *his or her* construction.

1. Each person had to hide his or her talents.
2. Could anyone take off his or her handicap bag?
3. Everybody had to be equal to his or her neighbor.
4. Did Harrison or the dancer realize his or her fate?
5. Neither he nor she wore his or her handicaps.

2p. A singular pronoun is used to refer to two or more singular antecedents joined by *or* or *nor.*

EXAMPLES

Paula or Janet will present **her** interpretation of Denise Levertov's "The Secret."

Neither **Richard nor Bob** has read **his** report on Ray Bradbury.

If a sentence sounds awkward when the antecedents are of different genders, revise it.

| AWKWARD | Either Ben or Maya will read his or her report on O. Henry. |
| REVISED | Either **Ben** will read **his** report on O. Henry, or **Maya** will read **hers.** |

2q. A plural pronoun is used to refer to two or more antecedents joined by *and.*

EXAMPLES

Romeo and Juliet marry despite the feud between **their** families.

Doodle and his **brother** spent much time with each other; **they** became very close.

2r. The number of a relative pronoun (such as *who, whom, whose, which,* or *that*) depends on the number of its antecedent.

EXAMPLES

Aretha is one **friend who** always **keeps her** word. [*Who* refers to the singular noun *friend.* Therefore, the singular forms *keeps* and *her* are used to agree with *who.*]

Many who volunteer find **their** experiences rewarding. [*Who* refers to the plural pronoun *many.* Therefore, the plural forms *volunteer* and *their* are used to agree with *who.*]

 For more about relative pronouns in adjective clauses, see 7d.

3 USING VERBS

THE PRINCIPAL PARTS OF VERBS

3a. The four principal parts of a verb are the *base form,* the *present participle,* the *past,* and the *past participle.* These principal parts are used to form all the different verb tenses.

3b. A *regular verb* forms its past and past participle by adding *–d* or *–ed* to the base form.

3c. An *irregular verb* forms its past and past participle in some other way than by adding *–d* or *–ed* to the base form.

COMMON REGULAR VERBS

BASE FORM	PRESENT PARTICIPLE	PAST	PAST PARTICIPLE
ask	(is) asking	asked	(have) asked
attack	(is) attacking	attacked	(have) attacked
raise	(is) raising	raised	(have) raised
plan	(is) planning	planned	(have) planned
try	(is) trying	tried	(have) tried

COMMON IRREGULAR VERBS

BASE FORM	PRESENT PARTICIPLE	PAST	PAST PARTICIPLE
be	(is) being	was, were	(have) been
begin	(is) beginning	began	(have) begun
bring	(is) bringing	brought	(have) brought
burst	(is) bursting	burst	(have) burst
drink	(is) drinking	drank	(have) drunk
drive	(is) driving	drove	(have) driven
eat	(is) eating	ate	(have) eaten
fall	(is) falling	fell	(have) fallen
find	(is) finding	found	(have) found
freeze	(is) freezing	froze	(have) frozen
go	(is) going	went	(have) gone
keep	(is) keeping	kept	(have) kept
lay	(is) laying	laid	(have) laid
lead	(is) leading	led	(have) led
lie	(is) lying	lay	(have) lain
ride	(is) riding	rode	(have) ridden
rise	(is) rising	rose	(have) risen
set	(is) setting	set	(have) set
shake	(is) shaking	shook	(have) shaken
sing	(is) singing	sang	(have) sung
sit	(is) sitting	sat	(have) sat
steal	(is) stealing	stole	(have) stolen
swim	(is) swimming	swam	(have) swum
tear	(is) tearing	tore	(have) torn

NOTE The examples in the chart at the left include *is* and *have* in parentheses to show that helping verbs (forms of *be* and *have*) are used with the present participle and past participle forms.

TIPS FOR SPELLING Drop the final silent e in the base form of a verb when adding *–ing* and *–ed* to form the present participle and past participle.

PRESENT PARTICIPLES
share + –ing = shar**ing**
dive + –ing = div**ing**

PAST PARTICIPLES
raise + –ed = rais**ed**
receive + –ed = receiv**ed**

EXCEPTIONS
dye + –ing = dye**ing**
singe + –ing = singe**ing**

 For more about correct spelling when adding suffixes to words, see 15e–j.

NOTE If you are not sure about the principal parts of a verb, look in a dictionary. Entries for irregular verbs give the principal parts. If no principal parts are listed, the verb is a regular verb.

TENSE

3d. **The *tense* of a verb indicates the time of the action or the state of being expressed by the verb. Verbs in English have six tenses: *present, past, future, present perfect, past perfect,* and *future perfect.* The tenses are formed from the verb's principal parts.**

(1) The ***present tense*** is used mainly to express an action or a state of being that is occurring now.

EXAMPLES
The car **turns** into the driveway.
They **like** my idea for a science project.

The present tense is also used

- to show a customary or habitual action or state of being
- to express a general truth—something that is always true
- to make historical events seem current (such use is called the **historical present**)
- to discuss a literary work (such use is called the **literary present**)
- to express future time

EXAMPLES
Every November she **bakes** fruitcakes for her friends. [customary action]
The sun **sets** in the west. [general truth]
In 1905, Albert Einstein **proposes** his theory of relativity. [historical present]
Maya Angelou's *I Know Why the Caged Bird Sings* **tells** the story of her childhood. [literary present]
Finals **begin** next week. [future time]

(2) The ***past tense*** is used to express an action or a state of being that occurred in the past but that is not occurring now.

EXAMPLES
Jim **gave** Della a set of combs.
The children **annoyed** Miss Lottie.

A past action or state of being can also be shown with the verb *used* followed by an infinitive.

EXAMPLE
We **used to live** in Chicago.

(3) The ***future tense*** (formed with *will* or *shall* and the verb's base form) is used to express an action or a state of being that will occur.

EXAMPLES
I **shall play** the part of Romeo.
They **will arrive** soon.

A future action or state of being can also be shown in other ways.

EXAMPLES
They **are going to win.**
We **leave** for the theater **in an hour.**

(4) The ***present perfect tense*** (formed with *have* or *has* and the verb's past participle) is used to express an action or a state of being that occurred at some indefinite time in the past.

EXAMPLES
Doodle **has learned** how to walk.
We **have read** the *Odyssey.*

The present perfect tense is also used to express an action or a state of being that began in the past and continues into the present.

EXAMPLE
We **have lived** in the same house for nine years.

(5) The ***past perfect tense*** (formed with *had* and the verb's past participle) is used to express an action or a state of being that was completed in the past before some other past action or event.

EXAMPLES
Lizabeth regretted what she **had done.** [The doing occurred before the regretting.]
When you called, I **had** already **eaten** supper. [The eating occurred before the calling.]

(6) The ***future perfect tense*** (formed with *will have* or *shall have* and the verb's past participle) is used to express an action or a state of being that will be completed in the future before some other future occurrence.

EXAMPLES
By the time Mom returns, I **will have done** my chores. [The doing will be completed before the returning.]
He **will have finished** his Hebrew lessons before his bar mitzvah. [The finishing will be completed before the bar mitzvah.]

Each of the six verb tenses has an additional form called the ***progressive form.*** The progressive form expresses a continuing action or state of being. It consists of the appropriate tense of *be* plus the verb's present participle. For the perfect tenses, the progressive form also includes one or more helping verbs.

Present Progressive	am, are, is giving
Past Progressive	was, were giving
Future Progressive	will (shall) be giving
Present Perfect Progressive	has, have been giving
Past Perfect Progressive	had been giving
Future Perfect Progressive	will (shall) have been giving

3e. Do not change needlessly from one tense to another.

INCONSISTENT	Jim sold his watch and buys Della a set of combs. [change from past to present tense]
CONSISTENT	Jim **sold** his watch and **bought** Della a set of combs. [past tense]

Using Appropriate Verb Tenses

Using different verb tenses is often necessary to show the order of events that occur at different times.

NONSTANDARD	I regretted that I chose such a broad topic.
STANDARD	I **regretted** that I **had chosen** such a broad topic. [Since the action of choosing was completed before the action of regretting, the verb should be *had chosen*, not *chose*.]

Try It Out

For each of the following sentences, change the verb tenses to show the order of events that occur at different times. If a sentence is correct, write *C*.

1. Before he went away, they spent much time together.
2. When they gathered enough nuts, they go shopping.
3. By the time the moon rises tonight, they will finish.
4. She told ghost stories and was superstitious.
5. He was grateful for all they shared during the past year.

ACTIVE AND PASSIVE VOICE

3f. A verb in the *active voice* expresses an action done by its subject. A verb in the *passive voice* expresses an action received by its subject.

A verb in the passive voice is always a verb phrase that includes a form of *be* and the main verb's past participle.

ACTIVE VOICE	Rainsford **surprised** General Zaroff. [The subject, *Rainsford,* performs the action.]
PASSIVE VOICE	General Zaroff **was surprised** by Rainsford. [The subject, *General Zaroff,* receives the action.]
ACTIVE VOICE	William Gibson **wrote** *The Miracle Worker.*
PASSIVE VOICE	*The Miracle Worker* **was written** by William Gibson.

3g. Use the passive voice sparingly.

The passive voice is not any less correct than the active voice, but it is less direct, less forceful, and less concise. As a result, a sentence written in the passive voice can often be wordy and can sound awkward or weak.

AWKWARD PASSIVE	Mme. Forestier's necklace was borrowed by Mme. Loisel.
ACTIVE	Mme. Loisel **borrowed** Mme. Forestier's necklace.

The passive voice is useful, however, in certain situations:

1. when you do not know the performer of the action

EXAMPLE
The Globe Theater **was built** in 1599.

2. when you do not want to reveal the performer of the action

EXAMPLE
Unfounded accusations **were made** against the candidate.

3. when you want to emphasize the receiver of the action

EXAMPLE
Abraham Lincoln **was elected** president of the United States in 1860.

COMPUTER NOTE Some software programs can identify and highlight passive-voice verbs. If you use such a program, keep in mind that it can't tell why you used the passive voice. If you did so for one of the reasons listed under 3g above, you may want to leave the verb in the passive voice.

4 USING PRONOUNS

CASE

Case is the form that a noun or pronoun takes to indicate its use in a sentence. In English, there are three cases: *nominative, objective,* and *possessive.* Most personal pronouns have a different form for each case.

NOTE The form of a noun is the same for both the nominative and the objective case. For the possessive case, however, a noun changes its form, usually by adding an apostrophe and an *s* to singular nouns and only an apostrophe to plural nouns.

NOMINATIVE	The **sniper** fired his rifle.
OBJECTIVE	Someone shot the **sniper.**
POSSESSIVE	Who was the **sniper's** enemy?

The Nominative Case

4a. A subject of a verb is in the nominative case.

EXAMPLES
She was glad that **they** were elected. [*She* is the subject of *was; they* is the subject of *were elected.*]
Is **Della** or **he** disappointed? [*Della* and *he* are the compound subject of *is.*]

4b. A predicate nominative is in the nominative case.

A *predicate nominative* follows a linking verb and explains or identifies the subject of the verb.

EXAMPLES
The woman who borrows the necklace is **she.** [*She* follows *is* and identifies the subject *woman.*]
The main characters are **he** and his **brother** Doodle. [*He* and *brother* follow *are* and identify the subject *characters.*]

NOTE Expressions such as *It's me, That's him,* and *Could it be her?* are informal usage. Avoid such expressions in formal speaking and writing.

The Objective Case

4c. A direct object of a verb is in the objective case.

A *direct object* follows an action verb and tells *whom* or *what.*

EXAMPLES
Lizabeth destroyed **them.** [*Them* tells *what* Lizabeth destroyed.]
Friar Laurence helps **her** and **him.** [*Her* and *him* tell *whom* Friar Laurence helps.]

PERSONAL PRONOUNS

SINGULAR

	NOMINATIVE	OBJECTIVE	POSSESSIVE
FIRST PERSON	I	me	my, mine
SECOND PERSON	you	you	your, yours
THIRD PERSON	he, she, it	him, her, it	his, her, hers, its

PLURAL

	NOMINATIVE	OBJECTIVE	POSSESSIVE
FIRST PERSON	we	us	our, ours
SECOND PERSON	you	you	your, yours
THIRD PERSON	they	them	their, theirs

NOTE Notice in the chart at the left that *you* and *it* are the only personal pronouns that have the same form in both the nominative case and the objective case.

☞ For more information on possessive personal pronouns, see 14c.

Language Handbook

4d. An indirect object of a verb is in the objective case.

An *indirect object* comes before a direct object and tells *to whom* or *to what* or *for whom* or *for what.*

EXAMPLES
Buddy gave **her** a kite. [*Her* tells *to whom* Buddy gave a kite.]
Molly made **him** and **me** a tape. [*Him* and *me* tell *for whom* Molly made a tape.]

4e. An object of a preposition is in the objective case.

An *object of a preposition* comes at the end of a phrase that begins with a preposition.

EXAMPLES
Mme. Loisel borrows a necklace from **her.**
This gift is for **him** and **her.**

SPECIAL PRONOUN PROBLEMS

4f. The pronoun *who* (*whoever*) is in the nominative case. The pronoun *whom* (*whomever*) is in the objective case.

NOMINATIVE **Who** wrote *Black Boy*? [*Who* is the subject of *wrote.*]

OBJECTIVE From **whom** did Mme. Loisel borrow the necklace? [*Whom* is the object of the preposition *from.*]

When choosing between *who* and *whom* in a subordinate clause, be sure to base your choice on how the pronoun functions in the subordinate clause.

EXAMPLES
The sniper learned **who** his enemy had been. [*Who* is the predicate nominative identifying the subject *enemy.*]
The sniper learned the identity of the man **whom** he had shot. [*Whom* is the direct object of *had shot.*]

NOTE In spoken English, the use of *whom* is becoming less common. In fact, when speaking, you may correctly begin any question with *who.* In written English, however, you should distinguish between *who* and *whom.*

INFORMAL **Who** did you see at the mall?
FORMAL **Whom** did you see at the mall?

INFORMAL **Who** did you go skating with?
FORMAL With **whom** did you go skating?

TIPS FOR WRITERS

Using *Whom* in Formal Situations
Frequently, *whom* is left out of subordinate clauses.

EXAMPLE
The person [**whom**] I have always admired most is Dr. Margaret Mead. [*Whom* is understood to be the direct object of *admired.*]

Leaving out *whom* in such cases tends to make writing sound more informal. In formal situations, it is generally better to include *whom.*

Try It Out
For each of the following sentences, insert *whom* where appropriate. Make any other changes needed for the sentence to sound correct in a formal situation.

1. The girl they admired was reading.
2. Do you know boys like the ones he speaks of?
3. They talked about the woman each of them would marry.
4. The field of carpentry appealed to the boy that kind of work was easy for.
5. The other boy Gary Soto wrote of said that he would go to school.

4g. An appositive is in the same case as the noun or pronoun to which it refers.

An *appositive* is a noun or pronoun placed next to another noun or pronoun to identify or explain it.

EXAMPLES
In the story, the main characters, **Doodle and he,** are brothers. [The appositive, *Doodle and he,* is in the nominative case because it identifies the subject, *characters.*]
Miss Lottie did not say a word to either of the children, **Lizabeth or him.** [The appositive, *Lizabeth or him,* is in the objective case because it identifies an object of a preposition, *children.*]

Sometimes the pronouns *we* and *us* are used with noun appositives.

EXAMPLES
We cast members have a dress rehearsal tonight. [The pronoun *we* is in the nominative case because it is the subject of *have.*]
The principal praised **us** members of the Ecology Club. [The pronoun *us* is in the objective case because it is the direct object of *praised.*]

4h. A pronoun following *than* or *as* in an incomplete construction is in the same case as it would be if the construction were completed.

Notice how the meaning of each of the following sentences is determined by the pronoun form in the incomplete construction.

EXAMPLES
I wrote you more often than **he** [wrote you].
I wrote you more often than [I wrote] **him.**

Did you help Ada as much as **I** [helped Ada]?
Did you help Ada as much as [you helped] **me**?

Clear Pronoun Reference

4i. A pronoun should refer clearly to its antecedent.

An *antecedent* is the word a pronoun stands for.

(1) Avoid an *ambiguous reference,* which occurs when a pronoun can refer to any one of two or more antecedents.

AMBIGUOUS	Miss Lottie saw Lizabeth when she was in the garden. [*She* can refer to either Miss Lottie or Lizabeth.]
CLEAR	When **Miss Lottie** was in the garden, **she** saw Lizabeth.
CLEAR	When **Lizabeth** was in the garden, Miss Lottie saw **her.**

(2) Avoid a *general reference,* which occurs when a pronoun refers to a general idea rather than to a specific antecedent.

GENERAL	Rainsford had escaped. This annoyed General Zaroff. [*This* has no specific antecedent.]
CLEAR	That Rainsford had escaped annoyed General Zaroff.

(3) Avoid a *weak reference,* which occurs when a pronoun refers to an implied antecedent.

WEAK	Ralph enjoys writing poetry, but he never shows them to anyone else. [*Them* most likely refers to the unstated plural noun *poems,* but the writer has used the singular noun *poetry* instead.]
CLEAR	Ralph enjoys writing poetry, but he never shows his poems to anyone else.

(4) Avoid using an *indefinite reference,* which occurs when a pronoun (such as *you, it,* or *they*) refers to no particular person or thing.

INDEFINITE	In the owner's manual, they explain how to program the VCR. [*They* has no antecedent.]
CLEAR	The owner's manual explains how to program the VCR.

 NOTE The indefinite use of *it* is acceptable in familiar expressions such as *It is snowing, It seems as though . . . ,* and *It's late.*

---

5 USING MODIFIERS

WHAT IS A MODIFIER?

A *modifier* is a word or group of words that limits the meaning of another word or group of words. The two kinds of modifiers are *adjectives* and *adverbs.* An *adjective* limits the meaning of a noun or a pronoun. An *adverb* limits the meaning of a verb, an adjective, or another adverb.

Adjective or Adverb?

Although many adverbs end in *–ly,* many others do not. Furthermore, not all words with the *–ly* ending are adverbs. Some adjectives also end in *–ly.* Therefore, you can't tell whether a word is an adjective or adverb simply by looking for the *–ly* ending.

ADVERBS NOT ENDING IN –LY	arrive **soon**	sit **here**
	not angry	run **loose**
	walk **home**	**very** hot
ADJECTIVES ENDING IN –LY	**daily** diet	**holy** place
	curly hair	**silly** joke

In addition, some words can be used as either adjectives or adverbs.

ADJECTIVES	ADVERBS
He is an **only** child.	She has **only** one sister.
I have an **early** class.	I get up **early.**
Tina has a **fast** bicycle.	The baby is **fast** asleep.
We caught the **last** bus.	We left **last.**

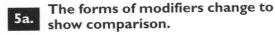

Language Handbook

COMPARISON OF MODIFIERS

5a. The forms of modifiers change to show comparison.

The three degrees of comparison are *positive, comparative,* and *superlative.*

Regular Comparison

(1) Most one-syllable modifiers form the comparative and superlative degrees by adding *–er* and *–est.*

POSITIVE	COMPARATIVE	SUPERLATIVE
deep	deeper	deepest
gentle	gentler	gentlest
careful	more careful	most careful
slowly	more slowly	most slowly
significantly	more significantly	most significantly
fresh	less fresh	least fresh
common	less common	least common

Irregular Comparison

(5) Some modifiers form the comparative and superlative degrees in other ways.

POSITIVE	COMPARATIVE	SUPERLATIVE
bad	worse	worst
good/well	better	best
little	less	least
many/much	more	most

Use of Comparative and Superlative Forms

5b. Use the comparative degree when comparing two things. Use the superlative degree when comparing more than two.

COMPARATIVE Rainsford was **more resourceful** than Zaroff had expected him to be.

SUPERLATIVE "The Most Dangerous Game" is one of the **most suspenseful** stories I have ever read.

(2) Some two-syllable modifiers form the comparative and superlative degrees by adding *–er* and *–est.* Other two-syllable modifiers form the comparative and superlative degrees by using *more* and *most.*

(3) Modifiers of more than two syllables form the comparative and superlative degrees by using *more* and *most.*

(4) All modifiers, no matter how many syllables they have, show decreasing degrees of comparison by using *less* and *least.*

Drop the final silent e before adding *–er* or *–est.*

EXAMPLES
strange + –er = strang**er**
noble + –est = nobl**est**

☞ For more information about correct spelling when adding suffixes to words, see 15e–j.

NOTE Do not add *–er, –est, more,* or *most* to irregular comparative and superlative forms. Use *worse,* not *worser* or *more worse,* and *best,* not *bestest.*

☞ For information about using *good* and *well,* see Part 16: Glossary of Usage; for information about using *bad* and *badly,* see Part 16: Glossary of Usage.

5c. Include the word *other* or *else* when comparing one thing with others in the same group.

ILLOGICAL Ruth is more agile than any member of her gymnastics team. [Ruth is a member of her team. Logically, she cannot be more agile than herself.]

LOGICAL Ruth is more agile than any **other** member of her gymnastics team.

ILLOGICAL Carlos ran faster than everyone. [*Everyone* includes Carlos. Logically, he cannot run faster than himself.]

LOGICAL Carlos ran faster than everyone **else.**

5d. Avoid a *double comparison*—the use of both *–er* and *more* (or *less*) or both *–est* and *most* (or *least*) to modify the same word.

EXAMPLES

William Sydney Porter, **better** [*not* more better] known as O. Henry, wrote "The Gift of the Magi."

This is the **cheapest** [*not* most cheapest] bicycle in the store.

5e. Avoid comparing items that cannot logically be compared.

ILLOGICAL	The average temperature in Dallas is higher than Spokane. [illogical comparison between a temperature and a city]
LOGICAL	The average temperature in Dallas is higher than **the average temperature in** Spokane.
ILLOGICAL	A coral snake's venom is more dangerous than a rattlesnake. [illogical comparison between a snake's venom and a snake]
LOGICAL	A coral snake's venom is more dangerous than a **rattlesnake's** [*or* **rattlesnake's venom**].

State both parts of an incomplete comparison if there is any chance of misunderstanding.

UNCLEAR	I visited her more than Elise.
CLEAR	I visited her more than **I visited** Elise.
CLEAR	I visited her more than Elise **visited her.**

PLACEMENT OF MODIFIERS

5f. Avoid using a *dangling modifier*—a modifying word or word group that does not sensibly modify any word or word group in the same sentence.

DANGLING	Working together, our goal can be attained within a few months.
CLEAR	Working together, we can attain our goal within a few months.
CLEAR	We can attain our goal within a few months by working together.

You may correct a dangling modifier

- by adding a word or words that the dangling modifier can sensibly modify
- by adding a word or words to the dangling modifier
- by rewording the sentence

DANGLING	Peering over the parapet, an armored car was seen. [Who or what was peering over the parapet?]
CLEAR	Peering over the parapet, the **sniper** saw an armored car.
DANGLING	To understand Denise Levertov's poetry, some knowledge of figurative language is necessary. [Who needs to know figurative language?]
CLEAR	To understand Denise Levertov's poetry, the **reader** needs some knowledge of figurative language.
DANGLING	While burying the scarlet ibis, a hymn is sung. [Who or what is burying the scarlet ibis?]
CLEAR	While burying the scarlet ibis, **Doodle** sings a hymn.

 NOTE A sentence may appear to have a dangling modifier when *you* is the understood subject. In such cases, the modifier is not dangling; it modifies the understood subject.

EXAMPLE

To find the correct spelling, [**you**] look up the word in a dictionary.

For more information about understood subjects, see 8g.

5g. Avoid using a *misplaced modifier*—a modifying word or word group that sounds awkward or unclear because it seems to modify the wrong word or word group.

To correct a misplaced modifier, place the modifier as near as possible to the word or word group you intend it to modify.

MISPLACED	Doodle reveals to his family that he has learned to walk on his sixth birthday. [Does Doodle reveal or does he learn on his sixth birthday?]
CLEAR	**On his sixth birthday,** Doodle reveals to his family that he has learned to walk.
MISPLACED	Born eight weeks ago, we adopted one of the puppies. [Were we or the puppies born eight weeks ago?]
CLEAR	We adopted one of the puppies **born eight weeks ago.**

For more information on phrase and clause modifiers, see 6a–g and 7a–f.

6 PHRASES

6a. **A *phrase* is a group of related words that is used as a single part of speech and that does not contain both a verb and its subject.**

EXAMPLES

has been sitting [verb phrase; no subject]
about you and me [prepositional phrase; no subject or verb]

If a group of words has both a subject and a verb, it is called a clause. For more information about clauses, see 7a–f.

PREPOSITIONAL PHRASES

6b. **A *prepositional phrase* begins with a preposition and ends with a noun or pronoun that is called the *object of the preposition*. A prepositional phrase may also contain modifiers of the object of the preposition.**

EXAMPLES

The sniper ran **across the street.** [The noun *street* is the object of the preposition *across*.]
In front of him was Fortunato. [The pronoun *him* is the object of the compound preposition *in front of*.]
Kyoko called **to Nancy and me.** [Both *Nancy* and *me* are objects of the preposition *to*.]

(1) A prepositional phrase that modifies a noun or pronoun is called an ***adjective phrase.***

An adjective phrase tells *what kind* or *which one*.

EXAMPLES

Lizabeth destroyed Miss Lottie's garden **of marigolds.** [*Of marigolds* modifies the noun *garden,* telling *what kind*.]
All **of them** watched Doodle bury the scarlet ibis. [*Of them* modifies the pronoun *all,* telling *which ones*.]

An adjective phrase usually follows the word it modifies. That word may be the object of another preposition.

EXAMPLE

"Poison" is the title **of a story by Roald Dahl.** [*Of a story* modifies the noun *title. By Roald Dahl* modifies the noun *story,* the object of the preposition *of*.]

More than one adjective phrase may modify the same noun or pronoun.

EXAMPLE

The bottle **of vitamins on the shelf** is almost empty. [*Of vitamins* and *on the shelf* modify the noun *bottle*.]

(2) A prepositional phrase that modifies a verb, an adjective, or an adverb is called an ***adverb phrase.***

An adverb phrase tells *when, where, how, why,* or *to what extent*.

EXAMPLES

By his sixth birthday Doodle could walk. [*By his sixth birthday* modifies *could walk,* telling *when*.]
Had a snake crawled **under the sheet**? [*Under the sheet* modifies *had crawled,* telling *where*.]
She answered **with a smile.** [*With a smile* modifies *answered,* telling *how*.]
Everyone remained quiet **because of the snake.** [*Because of the snake* modifies *quiet,* telling *why*.]
Is the water warm enough **for swimming**? [*For swimming* modifies *enough,* telling *to what extent*.]

An adverb phrase may come either before or after the word or word group it modifies.

EXAMPLES

For Christmas, Buddy gave her a kite.
Buddy gave her a kite **for Christmas.**

More than one adverb phrase may modify the same word or group of words.

EXAMPLE

In November she and Buddy bake fruitcakes **for their friends.** [*In November* tells *when* they bake the fruitcakes, and *for their friends* tells *why* they bake them.]

 For more information about placement of modifying phrases, see 5f, g.

VERBALS AND VERBAL PHRASES

A ***verbal*** is a form of a verb used as a noun, an adjective, or an adverb. A ***verbal phrase*** consists of a verbal and its modifiers and complements. The three kinds of verbals are *participles, gerunds,* and *infinitives*.

Participles and Participial Phrases

6c. A *participle* is a verb form that can be used as an adjective. A *participial phrase* consists of a participle and all the words related to the participle.

(1) *Present participles* end in *–ing.*

EXAMPLES
Doodle collapsed in the **pouring** rain. [The present participle *pouring* modifies the noun *rain.*]
Lying quietly in his bed, Harry told Timber about the snake. [The participial phrase *lying quietly in his bed* modifies the noun *Harry.* Both the adverb *quietly* and the adverb phrase *in his bed* modify the present participle *lying.*]

(2) Most *past participles* end in *–d* or *–ed.* Others are irregularly formed.

EXAMPLES
Lizabeth sat in the **ruined** garden and cried. [The past participle *ruined* modifies the noun *garden.*]
The speaker, **known for her strong support of recycling,** was loudly applauded. [The participial phrase *known for her strong support of recycling* modifies the noun *speaker.* The adverb phrase *for her strong support* modifies the past participle *known.* The adjective phrase *of recycling* modifies *support.*]

Do not confuse a participle used as an adjective with a participle used as part of a verb phrase.

| ADJECTIVE | Fortunato, **struggling** to free himself, begged Montresor to unchain him. |
| VERB PHRASE | Fortunato, who **was struggling** to free himself, begged Montresor to unchain him. |

For more information about participles, see 3a–c. For more about the placement of participial phrases, see 5f, g.

Gerunds and Gerund Phrases

6d. A *gerund* is a verb form ending in *–ing* that is used as a noun. A *gerund phrase* consists of a gerund and all the words related to the gerund.

EXAMPLES
Violently destroying the marigolds was Lizabeth's last act of childhood. [The gerund phrase is the subject of *was.* The adverb *violently* modifies the gerund *destroying,* and *marigolds* is the direct object of *destroying.*]

They enjoy **making fruitcakes together.** [The gerund phrase is the direct object of *enjoy. Fruitcakes* is the direct object of the gerund *making,* and the adverb *together* modifies *making.*]
His job is **giving the customers their menus.** [The gerund phrase is the predicate nominative explaining the subject *job. Customers* is the indirect object and *menus* is the direct object of the gerund *giving.*]
Rainsford escaped from Zaroff by **leaping into the sea.** [The gerund phrase is the object of the preposition *by.* The adverb phrase *into the sea* modifies the gerund *leaping.*]

Do not confuse a gerund with a present participle used as an adjective or as part of a verb phrase.

EXAMPLE
Following the basketball coach's advice, she was **planning** to go on with her **training.** [*Following* is a present participle modifying *she. Planning* is part of the verb phrase *was planning. Training* is a gerund used as the object of the preposition *with.*]

 NOTE When preceding a gerund, a noun or pronoun should be in the possessive form.

EXAMPLES
Pedro's constant practicing improved **his** playing.

Infinitives and Infinitive Phrases

6e. An *infinitive* is a verb form, usually preceded by *to,* that can be used as a noun, an adjective, or an adverb. An *infinitive phrase* consists of an infinitive and all the words related to the infinitive.

| NOUN | **To proofread your writing carefully** is important. [The infinitive phrase is the subject of *is. Writing* is the direct object of the infinitive, *to proofread,* and the adverb *carefully* modifies *to proofread.*] |

Why did she finally decide **to buy that video?** [The infinitive phrase is the direct object of *decide. Video* is the direct object of the infinitive *to buy.*]
Zaroff's plan was **to hunt Rainsford.** [The infinitive phrase is the predicate nominative identifying the subject *plan. Rainsford* is the direct object of the infinitive *to hunt.*]

ADJECTIVE Friar Laurence's plan **to help Romeo and Juliet** failed. [The infinitive phrase modifies the noun *plan*. *Romeo* and *Juliet* are the direct objects of the infinitive *to help*.]

ADVERB Fortunato was eager **to taste the amontillado.** [The infinitive phrase modifies the adjective *eager*. *Amontillado* is the direct object of the infinitive *to taste*.]

Sometimes the *to* of the infinitive is omitted.

EXAMPLE

You should go [to] get a warmer jacket.

 NOTE Do not confuse an infinitive with a prepositional phrase that begins with *to*.

EXAMPLE

Doodle and he went **to the creek** [prepositional phrase] **to swim.** [infinitive]

6f. An infinitive may have a subject, in which case it forms an *infinitive clause*.

EXAMPLE

Juliet trusted Friar Laurence and asked **him to help her.** [The infinitive clause is the direct object of *asked*. *Him* is the subject of the infinitive *to help*. *Her* is the direct object of *to help*.]

Notice in the example that a pronoun functioning as the subject of an infinitive clause takes the objective form.

 **Using Verbals and Verbal Phrases**

You can use verbals and verbal phrases to clarify relationships between ideas and to make your writing more interesting and concise.

ORIGINAL Coyotes barked near the river. Momaday heard them at dusk.

REVISED Momaday heard coyotes **barking near the river at dusk.** [present participial phrase]

Try It Out ✐

Combine each of the following pairs of sentences by using the predicate of one sentence to form a verbal or verbal phrase that can be placed in the other sentence. Revise your sentence as needed to make it clear and concise.

1. N. Scott Momaday often rode his horse. For him, this activity was "an exercise of the mind."

2. He rode his horse, Pecos, over the hills of New Mexico. Along the way, he imagined that he was traveling with Billy the Kid.

3. Sometimes he and Billy saved a wagon train in trouble. Such a rescue was one of Momaday's favorite adventures.

4. Pecos could outrun the other horses in Jemez. Momaday was proud of his horse's ability.

5. Scents of pine and cedar smoke filled the air. A fresh, cold wind carried them from the canyon.

APPOSITIVES AND APPOSITIVE PHRASES

6g. An *appositive* is a noun or a pronoun placed beside another noun or pronoun to identify it or explain it. An *appositive phrase* consists of an appositive and its modifiers.

EXAMPLES

Kurt Vonnegut wrote the story **"Harrison Bergeron."** [The appositive *"Harrison Bergeron"* identifies the noun *story*.]

In the movie, Anne Bancroft played the role of Annie Sullivan, **Helen's teacher.** [The appositive phrase *Helen's teacher* explains the noun *Annie Sullivan*.]

Odysseus blinded Cyclops, **the one-eyed giant.** [The appositive phrase *the one-eyed giant* explains the noun *Cyclops*.]

An appositive phrase usually follows the noun or pronoun it refers to. For emphasis, however, it may come at the beginning of a sentence.

EXAMPLE

A noble leader of his people, Chief Joseph spoke with quiet dignity.

Appositives and appositive phrases are usually set off by commas. However, if the appositive is closely related to the preceding noun or pronoun, it should not be set off by commas.

EXAMPLES

My brother **Richard** goes to college. [The writer has more than one brother, and the appositive identifies which brother goes to college. Because this information is essential to the meaning of the sentence, it is not set off by commas.]

My brother, **Richard,** goes to college. [The writer has only one brother; therefore, the appositive is not necessary to identify him. Because the information is nonessential, it is set off by commas.]

7 CLAUSES

7a. A *clause* is a group of words that contains a verb and its subject and that is used as part of a sentence.

KINDS OF CLAUSES

7b. An *independent* (or *main*) *clause* expresses a complete thought and can stand by itself as a sentence.

EXAMPLES
Della gives Jim a watch chain, and **Jim gives Della a set of combs.**

When I wrote my report on William Shakespeare, **I quoted from *Romeo and Juliet, Hamlet,* and *Macbeth.***

7c. A *subordinate* (or *dependent*) *clause* does not express a complete thought and cannot stand alone.

SUBORDINATE CLAUSES
whom you know
because I told him the truth
what the show is about

SENTENCES
Will the player **whom you know** autograph our baseball gloves?

Because I told him the truth, Dad wasn't too angry about the broken window.

Stephanie wants to know **what the show is about.**

7d. An *adjective clause* is a subordinate clause that modifies a noun or pronoun.

An adjective clause, which always follows the word it modifies, usually begins with a *relative pronoun,* such as *who, whom, whose, which,* or *that.* Besides introducing an adjective clause, a relative pronoun has its own function within the clause.

EXAMPLES
In "The Gift of the Magi," Della and Jim, **who are deeply in love,** make sacrifices to buy gifts for each other. [The adjective clause modifies *Della* and *Jim. Who* is the subject of *are.*]

Not all the stories **that Edgar Allan Poe wrote** deal with horror or terror. [The adjective clause modifies *stories. That* is the direct object of *wrote.*]

I read about Sequoyah, **whose invention of a written language aided other Cherokees.** [The adjective clause modifies *Sequoyah. Whose* modifies *invention.*]

A relative pronoun is sometimes left out of an adjective clause.

EXAMPLES
Was *The Miracle Worker* the first play [that] **William Gibson wrote**?

The mechanic [whom] **you recommended** fixed my stepfather's motorcycle.

Occasionally, an adjective clause begins with the *relative adverb* where or when.

EXAMPLES
We visited the town **where Shakespeare was born.**

Summer is the season **when I feel happiest.**

Revising for Sentence Variety

Although short sentences can be effective, it's a good idea to alternate between shorter sentences and longer ones. To change choppy sentences into smoother writing, revise them into adjective clauses that express the same ideas.

CHOPPY   Mary Cassatt was an American painter. I enjoy her works. She was an Impressionist.

SMOOTH   I enjoy the works of Mary Cassatt, who was an American Impressionist painter.

Try It Out ✎

Use adjective clauses to combine each of the following pairs of short, choppy sentences.

1. Many people do not have homes. They wander the cities.
2. Ann appears in this article. She is one of these homeless people.
3. At one time, Ann had lived in a house. It had yellow siding.
4. Now she has only a coat. The coat is dirty and creased.
5. People like Ann need help, not labels. Their lives are hard.

7e. An *adverb clause* is a subordinate clause that modifies a verb, an adjective, or an adverb.

An adverb clause, which may come before or after the word it modifies, tells *how, when, where, why, to what extent (how much),* or *under what condition.* An adverb clause begins with a **subordinating conjunction,** such as *although, because, if, so that,* or *when.*

EXAMPLES

Because we students did so well in the discussion of *Romeo and Juliet,* our teacher did not assign any homework. [The adverb clause modifies *did assign,* telling *why.*]

I wrote a poem about war **after I read "The Sniper."** [The adverb clause modifies *wrote,* telling *when.*]

If Harry moves, he may disturb the sleeping snake. [The adverb clause modifies *may disturb,* telling *under what condition.*]

His pitching arm is stronger today **than it ever was.** [The adverb clause modifies *stronger,* telling *to what extent.*]

Doodle's brother was able to run faster **than Doodle could.** [The adverb clause modifies *faster,* telling *how much.*]

7f. A *noun clause* is a subordinate clause used as a subject, a predicate nom-inative, a direct object, an indirect object, or an object of a preposition.

The words commonly used to begin noun clauses include *that, what, whether, who,* and *why.*

SUBJECT	**What Odysseus did** was clever.
PREDICATE NOMINATIVE	The captains are **who pick the players for their teams.**
DIRECT OBJECT	The sniper discovered **that his brother was the enemy.**
INDIRECT OBJECT	The clerk should tell **whoever calls** the sale prices.
OBJECT OF PREPOSITION	He knew the price of **whatever they requested.**

The word that introduces a noun clause may or may not have a function within the noun clause.

EXAMPLES

Lizabeth regretted **what she had done.** [*What* is the direct object of *had done.*]

Mme. Loisel learned **that the necklace was fake.** [*That* has no function in the clause.]

Sometimes the word that introduces a noun clause is not stated, but its meaning is understood.

EXAMPLE

His mother said [that] **he could go to the concert.**

8 SENTENCE STRUCTURE

SENTENCE OR SENTENCE FRAGMENT?

8a. A *sentence* is a group of words that contains a subject and a verb and that expresses a complete thought.

A sentence should begin with a capital letter and end with a period, a question mark, or an exclamation point. A group of words that either does not contain a subject and verb or does not express a complete thought is called a *sentence fragment.*

FRAGMENT	Romeo banished from Verona?
SENTENCE	Why was Romeo banished from Verona?
FRAGMENT	What a clever plan!
SENTENCE	What a clever plan he had!

FRAGMENT	When the Montagues and the Capulets learned of the deaths of Romeo and Juliet.
SENTENCE	When the Montagues and the Capulets learned of the deaths of Romeo and Juliet, they ended their feud.

COMPUTER NOTE

Many style-checking software programs can identify sentence fragments. If you have access to such a program, use it to help you evaluate your writing. Then, revise each fragment to make sure that all your sentences express complete thoughts.

SUBJECT AND PREDICATE

8b. A sentence consists of two parts: the subject and the predicate. The *subject* tells *whom* or *what* the sentence is about. The *predicate* tells something about the subject.

In the following examples, all the words labeled *subject* make up the **complete subject,** and all the words labeled *predicate* make up the **complete predicate.**

SUBJECT   PREDICATE
Tybalt | was Juliet's cousin.

          SUBJECT   PREDICATE
Two of Prince Escalus's kinsmen | died.

     SUBJECT   PREDICATE
The setting of the play | is fourteenth-century Italy.

PREDICATE   SUBJECT   PREDICATE
Why did | Juliet | take the sleeping potion?

The Simple Subject

8c. The *simple subject* is the main word or group of words that tells *whom* or *what* the sentence is about.

EXAMPLES
An **excerpt** from Richard Wright's *Black Boy* appears in this book. [The complete subject is *an excerpt from Richard Wright's* Black Boy.]
The talented **Georgia O'Keeffe** is known for her paintings of huge flowers. [The complete subject is *the talented Georgia O'Keeffe.*]

The Simple Predicate

8d. The *simple predicate,* or *verb,* is the main word or group of words that tells something about the subject.

A simple predicate may be a single word or a **verb phrase** (a verb with one or more helping verbs).

EXAMPLES
Montresor **led** Fortunato to the catacombs. [The complete predicate is *led Fortunato to the catacombs.*]
Did Mme. Loisel **find** the necklace? [The complete predicate is *did find the necklace.*]

NOTE   In this book, the term *subject* refers to the simple subject, and the term *verb* refers to the simple predicate unless otherwise indicated.

The Compound Subject and the Compound Verb

8e. A *compound subject* consists of two or more subjects that are joined by a conjunction—usually *and* or *or*—and that have the same verb.

EXAMPLES
Does **Rainsford** or **Zaroff** win the game?
Romeo, Benvolio, and **Mercutio** attend the Capulets' party.

8f. A *compound verb* consists of two or more verbs that are joined by a conjunction—usually *and, but,* or *or*—and that have the same subject.

EXAMPLES
Della **sold** her hair and **bought** Jim a watch chain.
Timber **looked** for the snake but **did** not **find** it.

Finding the Subject of a Sentence

8g. To find the subject of a sentence, ask "Who?" or "What?" before the verb.

EXAMPLE
The price of those videos seems high. [What seems high? The price seems high. *Price* is the subject.]

(1) The subject of a sentence is never in a prepositional phrase.

EXAMPLES
Her **garden** of marigolds was ruined. [What was ruined? *Garden* was ruined. *Marigolds* is the object of the preposition *of.*]
On the rooftop crouched the **sniper.** [Who crouched? *Sniper* crouched. *Rooftop* is the object of the preposition *on.*]

(2) The subject of a sentence expressing a question usually follows the verb or a part of the verb phrase. Turning the question into a statement may help you find the subject.

QUESTION   Did **she** give Buddy a kite?
STATEMENT **She** did give Buddy a kite.

QUESTION   Is the *Odyssey* an epic?
STATEMENT The *Odyssey* is an epic.

(3) The word *there* or *here* is never the subject of a sentence.

EXAMPLES
There are your **keys.** [What are there? *Keys* are.]
Here is your **pencil.** [What is here? *Pencil* is.]

(4) The subject of a sentence expressing a command or request is always understood to be *you,* although *you* may not appear in the sentence.

EXAMPLE
[**You**] Listen carefully to his question. [Who is to listen? *You* is understood.]

The subject of a command or request is *you* even when the sentence contains a **noun of direct address,** a word naming the one or ones spoken to.

EXAMPLE
Ellen, [**you**] please read the part of Juliet.

COMPLEMENTS

8h. A *complement* is a word or group of words that completes the meaning of a verb.

Three kinds of complements are the *subject complement,* the *direct object,* and the *indirect object.*

The Subject Complement

8i. A *subject complement* is a word or word group that completes the meaning of a linking verb and that identifies or modifies the subject.

The two types of subject complements are the *predicate nominative* and the *predicate adjective.*

(I) A *predicate nominative* is a noun or pronoun that follows a linking verb and that renames or identifies the subject of the verb.

EXAMPLES
"The Most Dangerous Game" is an exciting **story.** [The noun *story* identifies the subject *"The Most Dangerous Game."*]
The only people in line were **they.** [The pronoun *they* renames the subject *people.*]
The main characters are **Helen Keller** and **Annie Sullivan.** [The nouns *Helen Keller* and *Annie Sullivan* identify the subject *characters.*]

(2) A *predicate adjective* is an adjective that follows a linking verb and that modifies the subject of the verb.

EXAMPLES
The necklace was **inexpensive.** [The adjective *inexpensive* modifies the subject *necklace.*]
Miss Lottie looked **sad.** [The adjective *sad* modifies the subject *Miss Lottie.*]
The corn tastes **sweet** and **buttery.** [The adjectives *sweet* and *buttery* modify the subject *corn.*]

The Direct Object and the Indirect Object

8j. A *direct object* is a noun or pronoun that receives the action of a verb or that shows the result of the action. It tells *whom* or *what* after a transitive verb.

EXAMPLES
The sniper killed his own **brother.** [killed whom? brother]
Although his watch was his most prized possession, Jim sold **it.** [sold what? it]
Shakespeare wrote not only great **plays** but also beautiful **sonnets.** [wrote what? plays and sonnets]

8k. An *indirect object* is a noun or pronoun that precedes the direct object and that usually tells *to whom* or *for whom* (or *to what* or *for what*) the action of the verb is done.

EXAMPLES
Sheila read the **children** a story by Truman Capote. [read to whom? children]
Frank gave the **Red Cross** a donation. [gave to what? Red Cross]
She made her **neighbors** and other **friends** fruitcakes for Christmas. [made for whom? neighbors and friends]

 NOTE A complement may precede the subject and the verb.

DIRECT OBJECT What a good **friend** Buddy has!
PREDICATE ADJECTIVE How **happy** Della and Jim are!

CLASSIFYING SENTENCES ACCORDING TO PURPOSE

8l. Sentences may be classified as *declarative, imperative, interrogative,* or *exclamatory.*

(I) A *declarative sentence* makes a statement. It is followed by a period.

EXAMPLES
One of my favorite stories is "Thank You, M'am."
Jonathan, the CD-ROM you ordered a while back has finally arrived.
It's raining.

(2) An *imperative sentence* makes a request or gives a command. It is usually followed by a period. A very strong command, however, is followed by an exclamation point.

EXAMPLES
Please open your books to page 3. [request]
Be careful of the undertow. [mild command]
Stop! [strong command]

NOTE In a command or a request, the understood subject is *you.*

(3) An *interrogative sentence* asks a question. It is followed by a question mark.

EXAMPLES
Did Friar Laurence's plan fail?
What did Romeo do when he found Juliet lying there so still and pale?

(4) An *exclamatory sentence* expresses strong feeling. It is followed by an exclamation point.

EXAMPLES
What a mess we're in now!
The battery is dead!

CLASSIFYING SENTENCES ACCORDING TO STRUCTURE

8m. **Sentences may be classified as *simple, compound, complex,* or *compound-complex.***

(1) A *simple sentence* has one independent clause and no subordinate clauses.

EXAMPLE
Frankenstein and *Dracula* were both written during the nineteenth century.

(2) A *compound sentence* has two or more independent clauses but no subordinate clauses.

EXAMPLES
Rita wanted to see an adventure film, **but** Carlos preferred a comedy. [two independent clauses joined by a comma and the coordinating conjunction *but*]
Harriet Tubman was a leader of the Underground Railroad; she rescued more than three hundred people. [two independent clauses joined by a semicolon]
Romeo killed Tybalt, Juliet's cousin; **as a result,** Romeo was banished from Verona. [two independent clauses joined by a semicolon and the transitional expression *as a result*]

(3) A *complex sentence* has one independent clause and at least one subordinate clause.

EXAMPLES
Juliet declared her love for Romeo before she spoke to him. [The independent clause is *Juliet declared her love for Romeo.* The subordinate clause is *before she spoke to him.*]
On Shakespeare's gravestone is an inscription that places a curse on anyone who moves his bones. [The independent clause is *on Shakespeare's gravestone is an inscription.* The subordinate clauses are *that places a curse on anyone* and *who moves his bones.*]

(4) A *compound-complex sentence* contains two or more independent clauses and at least one subordinate clause.

EXAMPLE
William Golding received the Nobel Prize in 1983; his best-known novel is *Lord of the Flies,* which he published in 1954. [The independent clauses are *William Golding received the Nobel Prize in 1983* and *his best-known novel is* Lord of the Flies. The subordinate clause is *which he published in 1954.*]

 For more on clauses, see 7a–f.

 **Varying Sentence Structure**

Paragraphs in which all the sentences have the same structure can make for monotonous reading. To help keep your readers interested, evaluate your writing to see whether you've used a variety of sentence structures. If you have not, use revising techniques—add, cut, replace, and reorder—to vary the structure of your sentences.

Try It Out

The following paragraph is composed of simple sentences. Revise the paragraph, using a variety of sentence structures.

[1] "The Most Dangerous Game" begins with a conversation about hunting. [2] Rainsford is the protagonist. [3] He and Whitney are on a yacht in the Caribbean. [4] They're near the eerie Ship-Trap Island. [5] Rainsford loves hunting. [6] According to Rainsford, sympathy for the hunted animal is foolish. [7] Later Rainsford falls overboard and swims to the island. [8] He meets General Zaroff at the general's chateau. [9] Zaroff hunts human beings for sport. [10] Soon Rainsford the hunter becomes the hunted.

9 WRITING COMPLETE SENTENCES

SENTENCE FRAGMENTS

9a. Avoid using a *sentence fragment*—a part of a sentence that has been punctuated as if it were a complete sentence.

Here are two ways to correct a sentence fragment:

1. Add words that will make the thought complete.

FRAGMENT	Shortly after his birth, was baptized in a small church in Stratford. [The verb *was baptized* has no subject. Who was baptized?]
SENTENCE	Shortly after his birth, **Shakespeare** was baptized in a small church in Stratford.
FRAGMENT	Odysseus a great hero of the Greeks. [The verb is missing. What about Odysseus?]
SENTENCE	Odysseus **became** a great hero of the Greeks.
FRAGMENT	For the balcony scene in *Romeo and Juliet*. [The subject and the verb are missing. What about the balcony scene?]
SENTENCE	**The actors are preparing** for the balcony scene in *Romeo and Juliet*.

2. Attach the fragment to a sentence that comes before or after it.

EXAMPLE	One of my favorite stories by Edgar Allan Poe is "X-ing a Paragrab." [sentence] A comic tale of a feud between two newspaper editors. [fragment]
REVISED	One of my favorite stories by Edgar Allan Poe is "X-ing a Paragrab," **a comic tale of a feud between two newspaper editors.** [appositive phrase]
EXAMPLE	When she takes off her coat. [fragment] Mme. Loisel discovers that she is no longer wearing the necklace. [sentence]
REVISED	**When she takes off her coat,** Mme. Loisel discovers that she is no longer wearing the necklace. [subordinate clause]

EXAMPLE	Odysseus figured out a way for his men and him. [sentence] To escape from the Cyclops. [fragment]
REVISED	Odysseus figured out a way for his men and him **to escape from the Cyclops.** [infinitive phrase]

 For more information about sentence fragments, see 8a.

RUN-ON SENTENCES

9b. Avoid using a *run-on sentence*—two or more complete sentences that run together as if they were one complete sentence.

There are two kinds of run-on sentences.

- A *fused sentence* has no punctuation between the complete sentences.
- A *comma splice* has only a comma between the complete sentences.

FUSED SENTENCE	Della sold her hair to buy Jim a chain for his watch Jim sold his watch to buy Della combs for her hair.
COMMA SPLICE	Della sold her hair to buy Jim a chain for his watch, Jim sold his watch to buy Della combs for her hair.

Here are five ways to correct a run-on sentence:

1. Make two sentences.

REVISED	Della sold her hair to buy Jim a chain for his watch. Jim sold his watch to buy Della combs for her hair.

2. Use a comma and a *coordinating conjunction*—*and, but, or, yet, for, so,* or *nor*.

REVISED	Della sold her hair to buy Jim a chain for his watch, **and** Jim sold his watch to buy Della combs for her hair.

3. Use a semicolon.

REVISED	Della sold her hair to buy Jim a chain for his watch; Jim sold his watch to buy Della combs for her hair.

4. Use a semicolon and a *conjunctive adverb,* such as *therefore, instead, meanwhile, still, also,* or *however.* Follow a conjunctive adverb with a comma.

REVISED   Della sold her hair to buy Jim a chain for his watch; **however,** Jim sold his watch to buy Della combs for her hair.

5. Change one of the complete thoughts into a subordinate clause.

REVISED   Della sold her hair to buy Jim a chain for his watch **while Jim sold his watch to buy Della combs for her hair**.

☞ For more information about combining sentences, see 10a–e.

COMPUTER NOTE   Style-checking software can help you evaluate your writing for the use of clear, complete sentences. Many such programs can identify and highlight sentence fragments. You can also use the "Search" command offered by computer programs to identify sentences in which you've used a comma and a coordinating conjunction—one search for each different conjunction and the comma in front of it. These searches can help you check to make sure that the ideas you've combined in a compound sentence are complete and are closely related and equally important.

TIPS FOR WRITERS

Identifying Run-on Sentences

One way to spot run-on sentences is to read your writing aloud. A natural, distinct pause in your speech often means that you need to separate sentences in some way. You can also check for run-ons by identifying subjects and verbs. Checking for clauses will help you find where one complete thought ends and another begins.

RUN-ON   The family thought that Doodle would die they built him a coffin.

REVISED   **Because** the family thought that Doodle would die, they built him a coffin.

REVISED   The family thought that Doodle would die, **so** they built him a coffin.

REVISED   The family thought that Doodle would die; **consequently,** they built him a coffin.

Try It Out ✎

Revise each of the following run-on sentences.

1. Doodle and his brother had an active fantasy world, they created stories and imaginary plans.
2. Doodle was afraid of being left behind, he cried when his brother started to leave.
3. Brother taught Doodle to walk Brother was ashamed of Doodle.
4. Doodle didn't think that he could walk after much help and practice, he did.
5. He could walk perhaps he could run.

10 WRITING EFFECTIVE SENTENCES

SENTENCE COMBINING

10a.   **Combine related sentences by taking a key word (or by using another form of the word) from one sentence and inserting it into another.**

ORIGINAL   Edgar Allan Poe led a short life. His life was tragic.

COMBINED   Edgar Allan Poe led a short, **tragic** life.

ORIGINAL   Edgar Allan Poe wrote strange stories. He wrote stories of suspense.

COMBINED   Edgar Allan Poe wrote strange, **suspenseful** stories.

TIPS FOR SPELLING   When you change the form of a key word, you often need to add an ending that makes the word an adjective or an adverb. Usually this ending is *–ed, –ing,* or *–ly.*

10b. Combine related sentences by taking (or creating) a phrase from one sentence and inserting it into another.

ORIGINAL *A Fire in My Hands* is a collection of poems. The poems were written by Gary Soto.

COMBINED *A Fire in My Hands* is a collection of poems **by Gary Soto.** [prepositional phrase]

ORIGINAL Romeo kills Tybalt. Tybalt is Juliet's cousin.

COMBINED Romeo kills Tybalt, **Juliet's cousin.** [appositive phrase]

10c. Combine related sentences by using a coordinating conjunction (*and, but, or, or nor*) to make a compound subject, a compound verb, or both.

ORIGINAL After lunch Doodle went to Horsehead Landing. His brother went, too.

COMBINED After lunch **Doodle and** his **brother** went to Horsehead Landing. [compound subject]

ORIGINAL Ernesto Galarza's family immigrated to the United States. They eventually settled in Sacramento, California.

COMBINED Ernesto Galarza's family **immigrated** to the United States **and** eventually **settled** in Sacramento, California. [compound verb]

 Using Compound Subjects and Compound Verbs

When you combine sentences by using compound subjects and compound verbs, make sure that your new subjects and verbs agree in number.

ORIGINAL Della has little money. Jim also doesn't have much.

COMBINED **Della and Jim have** little money. [The compound subject *Della and Jim* takes the plural verb *have*.]

Try It Out

Combine each of the following pairs of sentences into one sentence that has a compound subject or a compound verb.

1. Mrs. Johnson's husband moved to Oklahoma. He studied religion.
2. The cotton gin would not hire her. Neither would the lumber mill.
3. She didn't want to become a servant. She saw another possibility.
4. The cotton gin workers walked to her stand and bought lunch. The lumber workers also walked to her stand and bought lunch there.
5. In time, syrup was sold at the store. Canned goods were, too.

10d. Combine related sentences by creating a compound sentence.

You can form a compound sentence by linking two or more independent clauses with a comma and a coordinating conjunction, a semicolon, or a semicolon and a conjunctive adverb.

ORIGINAL Buddy makes his friend a kite. She makes him one, too.

COMBINED Buddy makes his friend a kite**, and** she makes him one, too. [comma and coordinating conjunction]

COMBINED Buddy makes his friend a kite**;** she makes him one, too. [semicolon]

COMBINED Buddy makes his friend a kite**; meanwhile,** she makes him one, too. [semicolon and conjunctive adverb]

10e. Combine related sentences by creating a complex sentence.

You can form a complex sentence by joining one independent clause with one or more subordinate clauses (adjective clause, adverb clause, or noun clause).

ORIGINAL Gwendolyn Brooks often writes about Chicago. She has won a Pulitzer Prize for her poetry.

COMBINED Gwendolyn Brooks, **who has won a Pulitzer Prize for her poetry,** often writes about Chicago. [adjective clause]

ORIGINAL Zaroff turned on the light. He saw Rainsford.

COMBINED **When Zaroff turned on the light,** he saw Rainsford. [adverb clause]

ORIGINAL The snake in "Poison" is just an illusion on Harry's part. Many readers think this.

COMBINED Many readers think **that the snake in "Poison" is just an illusion on Harry's part.** [noun clause]

For more information about compound and complex sentences, see 8m.

Varying Sentence Structures

 In your writing, try to use a mix of simple, compound, complex, and compound-complex sentences.

EXAMPLE

As the music and the thump of the drums grew louder, the people lined up along the street. [complex] Finally, with a blast of brass, the high school band rounded the corner. [simple] First came the drum major; setting the tempo with her baton, she proudly raised her feet as high as possible. [compound] Behind her, leading the parade of colorful floats, the musicians marched in their bright purple-and-red jackets. [simple sentence]

Try It Out

The following paragraph is composed of simple sentences. Revise the paragraph, using varied sentence structures.

[1] The boy had known hunger before. [2] This hunger was different. [3] It could not be satisfied by just a few bites. [4] It gnawed at his insides and made him weak. [5] His mother got a job. [6] She sent him to the store for groceries. [7] Some boys took his money. [8] She gave him more money and sent him again. [9] Again, the boys took his money. [10] His mother gave him a stick this time and told him to fight.

IMPROVING SENTENCE STYLE

10f. Use the same grammatical form (*parallel structure*) to express equal ideas.

NOT PARALLEL	Buddy and she liked baking fruit-cakes and to fly kites. [gerund phrase paired with infinitive phrase]
PARALLEL	Buddy and she liked **baking fruitcakes** and **flying kites.** [gerund phrase paired with gerund phrase]
PARALLEL	Buddy and she liked **to bake fruitcakes** and **to fly kites.** [infinitive phrase paired with infinitive phrase]

NOT PARALLEL	Harry received help from not only Timber but also from Ganderbai. [noun paired with prepositional phrase]
PARALLEL	Harry received help from not only **Timber** but also **Ganderbai.** [noun paired with noun]
PARALLEL	Harry received help not only **from Timber** but also **from Ganderbai.** [prepositional phrase paired with prepositional phrase]

10g. Avoid using stringy sentences—sentences that have too many independent clauses strung together with coordinating conjunctions like *and* or *but.*

You may revise a stringy sentence in one of two ways.

1. Break the sentence into two or more sentences.
2. Turn some of the independent clauses into subordinate clauses or into phrases.

STRINGY	The fire alarm rang, and everyone started to file out of school, but then our principal came down the hall, and he said that the bell was a mistake, and we went back to our classes.
REVISED	The fire alarm bell rang, and everyone started to file out of school. Then our principal came down the hall to say that the bell was a mistake. We went back to our classes.
REVISED	When the fire alarm bell rang, everyone started to file out of school. Then our principal came down the hall. He said that the bell was a mistake, and we went back to our classes.

 For more information about phrases, see 6a–g. For more about clauses, see 7a–f.

COMPUTER NOTE Whenever you revise your writing on a computer, you can use functions such as "Copy," "Cut," and "Move" to experiment with your sentences. Try a variety of sentence beginnings and structures. Then, decide which ones work best with the other sentences in a particular paragraph.

10h. Avoid using unnecessary words.

Here are three tips for avoiding wordiness.

1. Don't use more words than you need to use.
2. Don't use difficult words where simple ones will do.
3. Don't repeat yourself unless it's absolutely necessary.

WORDY	Fortunato is a wine connoisseur who has much knowledge of and great appreciation for fine wines.
REVISED	Fortunato is a connoisseur of fine wines.
WORDY	In the event that they were able to find the missing necklace belonging to Mme. Forestier by the last day of the month of February, the Loisels could return the other necklace.
REVISED	If they could find Mme. Forestier's necklace by the end of February, the Loisels could return the other necklace.

10i. Use a variety of sentence beginnings.

The basic structure of an English sentence is a subject followed by a verb. The following examples show how you can revise sentences to avoid beginning with the subject every time. Notice that a comma follows the introductory word, phrase, or clause in each revision.

SUBJECT FIRST	Della excitedly opened her present.
ADVERB FIRST	**Excitedly,** Della opened her present.
SUBJECT FIRST	You must study to make good grades.
INFINITIVE PHRASE FIRST	**To make good grades,** you must study.
SUBJECT FIRST	Romeo fell in love with Juliet as soon as he saw her.
ADVERB CLAUSE FIRST	**As soon as Romeo saw Juliet,** he fell in love with her.

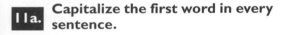

11 CAPITALIZATION

11a. Capitalize the first word in every sentence.

EXAMPLES
The two boys in "The Talk" discuss their plans.
Stop!

(1) Capitalize the first word of a direct quotation.

EXAMPLE
Maria asked me, "**H**ave you written your report on Gary Soto?"

(2) Traditionally, the first word of a line of poetry is capitalized.

EXAMPLES
Two roads diverged in a wood, and I—
I took the one less traveled by,
And that has made all the difference.
— Robert Frost, "The Road Not Taken"

NOTE Some writers do not follow these practices. When you are quoting, use capital letters exactly as they are used in the source of the quotation.

For more information about using capital letters in quotations, see pages 13d, e.

11b. Capitalize the first word both in the salutation and in the closing of a letter.

EXAMPLES
To Whom It May Concern:
Dear Ann,   Dear Sir:
Sincerely,   Yours truly,

11c. Capitalize the pronoun *I* and the interjection *O*.

EXAMPLES
Mom says that **I** can go this weekend.
Who says "Romeo can, / Though heaven cannot.
   O Romeo, Romeo"?

11d. Capitalize proper nouns and proper adjectives.

A **common noun** is a general name for a person, a place, a thing, or an idea. A **proper noun** names a particular person, place, thing, or idea. A **proper adjective** is formed from a proper noun.

Proper nouns and proper adjectives are always capitalized. Common nouns are not capitalized unless they begin a sentence, begin a direct quotation, or are part of a title.

COMMON NOUNS	PROPER NOUNS	PROPER ADJECTIVES
poet	Homer	Homeric simile
planet	Mars	Martian landscape

In proper nouns that have more than one word, do *not* capitalize articles (*a, an, the*), prepositions of fewer than five letters (such as *at, for,* and *with*), coordinating conjunctions (*and, but, for, nor, or, so, yet*), or the sign of the infinitive (*to*) unless they are the first word of the proper noun.

EXAMPLES
American Society for the Prevention of Cruelty to Animals
National Campers and Hikers Association
"Writing a Paragraph to Inform"

(1) Capitalize the names of persons and animals.

PERSONS	Sandra Cisneros	Langston Hughes
ANIMALS	Old Yeller	Brer Rabbit

(2) Capitalize geographical names.

For names with more than one word, capitalization may vary. Always check the spelling of such a name with the person whose name it is, or look in a reference source.

EXAMPLES
Kees van Dongen   Henry Van Dyke

Abbreviations such as *Ms., Mr., Dr.,* and *Gen.* should always be capitalized.

EXAMPLES
Mr. James Thurber   Dr. Mary McLeod Bethune

Capitalize the abbreviations *Jr.* and *Sr.* after a name, and set them off with commas.

EXAMPLE
In 1975, Gen. Daniel James, Jr., became the first African American four-star general in the U.S. Air Force.

TYPE OF NAME	EXAMPLES	
Towns and Cities	San Francisco	St. Charles
Counties, Townships, and Parishes	Hayes Township Union Parish	Kane County Manhattan
States and Territories	Florida Guam	North Carolina Northwest Territory
Countries	Canada	United States of America
Continents	Africa	North America
Islands	Long Island	Isle of Palms
Mountains	Rocky Mountains	Mount McKinley
Other Land Forms and Features	Cape Hatteras Kalahari Desert	Niagara Falls Mammoth Cave
Bodies of Water	Pacific Ocean Cross Creek	Gulf of Mexico Blue Springs
Parks	Yellowstone National Park Cleburne State Recreation Area	
Regions	the North New England	the Middle West the Great Plains
Roads, Streets, and Highways	Route 66 Gibbs Drive	Pennsylvania Turnpike Thirty-first Street

NOTE Words such as *north, west,* and *southeast* are not capitalized when they indicate direction.

EXAMPLES
north of town
traveling southeast

NOTE In a hyphenated number, the second word begins with a small letter.

EXAMPLE
Thirty-first Street

NOTE Words like *city, river, street,* and *park* are capitalized only when they are part of a name.

EXAMPLES
go to the park
go to Central Park

across the river
across the Pecos River

(3) Capitalize the names of organizations, teams, business firms, institutions, buildings and other structures, and government bodies.

TYPE OF NAME	EXAMPLES
Organizations	United Nations National Basketball Association
Teams	Tampa Bay Buccaneers Minnesota Twins
Business Firms	Quaker Oats Company Aluminum Company of America
Institutions	United States Naval Academy Bethune-Cookman College
Buildings and Other Structures	Apollo Theater Taj Mahal Golden Gate Bridge
Government Bodies	Federal Bureau of Investigation House of Representatives

NOTE Capitalize words such as *democratic* or *republican* only when they refer to a specific political party.

EXAMPLES
The new leaders promised **d**emocratic reforms.
The **D**emocratic candidates for mayor held a rally.

The word *party* in the name of a political party may be capitalized or not.

EXAMPLE
Federalist **P**arty *or* **p**arty

(4) Capitalize the names of historical events and periods, special events, holidays, and other calendar items.

TYPE OF NAME	EXAMPLES	
Historical Events and Periods	French Revolution Boston Tea Party	Middle Ages Mesozoic Era
Special Events	Interscholastic Debate Tournament Kansas State Fair	
Holidays and Calendar Items	Labor Day Saturday December Fourth of July National Book Week	

NOTE Do not capitalize the name of a season unless it is being personified or used in the name of a special event.

EXAMPLES
I'm on the committee for the **W**inter Carnival.
Soon **A**utumn will begin painting the leaves in bright colors.

(5) Capitalize the names of ships, trains, aircraft, spacecraft, monuments, awards, planets, and other particular places, things, or events.

TYPE OF NAME	EXAMPLES		
Ships and Trains	*Mayflower* *Silver Meteor*		
Aircraft and Spacecraft	*Spirit of St. Louis* Lockheed **C-5A G**alaxy *Pioneer 10* Hubble Space Telescope		
Monuments and Memorials	Washington Monument Statue of Liberty Vietnam Veterans Memorial		
Awards	Pulitzer Prize Congressional Medal of Honor Stanley Cup Key Club Achievement Award		
Planets, Stars, and Constellations	Mercury Dog Star Ursa Major Pluto Big Dipper Rigel		

NOTE The word *earth* is not capitalized unless it is used along with the names of other heavenly bodies that are capitalized. The words *sun* and *moon* are not capitalized.

EXAMPLES
The **m**oon is a satellite of the **e**arth.
Venus is closer to **E**arth than Mars is.

(6) Capitalize the names of nationalities, races, and peoples.

EXAMPLES
Greek   African Americans   Hispanic   Cherokee

(7) Capitalize the brand names of business products but not the common nouns that follow the names.

EXAMPLES
Chevrolet **v**an   Teflon **p**an

11e. Do *not* capitalize the names of school subjects, except for languages or course names followed by a number.

EXAMPLES
algebra   English   Typing I

11f. Capitalize titles.

(1) Capitalize the title of a person when it comes before the person's name.

EXAMPLES
President Clinton   Mr. Vonnegut

Usually, do not capitalize a title that is used alone or following a person's name, especially if the title is preceded by *a* or *the*.

EXAMPLE
Cleopatra reigned as the **q**ueen of Egypt between 51 and 30 B.C.

When a title is used alone in direct address, it is usually capitalized.

EXAMPLE
I think, Senator, that the issue is critical.

(2) Capitalize words showing family relationship when used with a person's name but *not* when preceded by a possessive.

EXAMPLES
Aunt Clara   my **m**other
Harold's **g**randmother

(3) Capitalize the first and last words and all important words in titles of books, periodicals, poems, stories, essays, speeches, plays, historical documents, movies, radio and television programs, works of art, musical compositions, and cartoons.

TYPE OF TITLE	EXAMPLES
Books	*The Pearl* *I Know Why the Caged Bird Sings*
Periodicals	*The Atlantic Monthly* *Field and Stream*
Poems	"The Road Not Taken" "The Girl Who Loved the Sky"
Stories	"The Cask of Amontillado" "The Most Dangerous Game"
Essays and Speeches	"The Death of a Tree" "Work and What It's Worth"
Plays	*The Miracle Worker* *The Phantom of the Opera*
Historical Documents	Declaration of Independence Emancipation Proclamation
Movies	*Dances with Wolves* *Stand and Deliver*
Radio and Television Programs	*All Things Considered* *Nova* *Star Trek: The Next Generation*
Works of Art	*American Gothic* *The Thinker*
Musical Compositions	"The Tennessee Waltz" "The Flight of the Bumblebee"
Cartoons	*Calvin and Hobbes* *The Neighborhood*

NOTE Unimportant words in a title are articles (*a, an, the*), prepositions of fewer than five letters (such as *for* and *from*), and co-ordinating conjunctions (*and, but, so, nor, or, yet, for*).

NOTE The words *a, an,* and *the* written before a title are capitalized only when they are part of the official title. The official title of a book is found on the title page. The official title of a newspaper or a periodical is found on the masthead, which is usually on the editorial page.

EXAMPLES
The Autobiography of
  Malcolm X
the *Austin American-Statesman*
A Tale of Two Cities

☞ For information about when to use italics for titles, see 13a. For information about when to use quotation marks for titles, see 13j.

(4) Capitalize the names of religions and their followers, holy days and celebrations, holy writings, and specific deities.

TYPE OF NAME	EXAMPLES	
Religions and Followers	Judaism Taoism	Quaker Muslim
Holy Days and Celebrations	Passover Ramadan	Good Friday Lent
Holy Writings	Bible Koran	Upanishads Genesis
Specific Deities	Allah	Brahma	Zeus

COMPUTER NOTE

Some software programs can identify errors in capitalization. However, even the most complete programs may not include all the terms you need. In addition, the program may be based on rules that vary from the ones you've been given to follow. If your software allows it, modify the capitalization of words already in the program, and add terms that you use frequently.

12 PUNCTUATION

END MARKS

Sentences

***End marks**—periods, question marks, and exclamation points—are used to indicate the purpose of a sentence.*

For a discussion of how sentences are classified according to purpose, see 8l. For information on using quotation marks with end marks, see 13f.

12a. **A statement (or declarative sentence) is followed by a period.**

EXAMPLE
Dorothy M. Johnson wrote "A Man Called Horse."

12b. **A question (or interrogative sentence) is followed by a question mark.**

EXAMPLE
Did Penelope recognize Odysseus?

 NOTE Be sure to distinguish between a declarative sentence that contains an indirect question and an interrogative sentence, which asks a direct question.

INDIRECT QUESTION	He asked me **what was worrying her.** [declarative]
DIRECT QUESTION	What is worrying her? [interrogative]

A direct question may have the same word order as a declarative sentence. Since it *is* a question, however, it is followed by a question mark.

EXAMPLES
A cat can see color?   The plane was late?

12c. **An exclamation is followed by an exclamation point.**

EXAMPLE
Wow! What a great play *The Miracle Worker* is!

12d. **A command or request (or imperative sentence) is followed by either a period or an exclamation point.**

A mild command or an imperative sentence that makes a request is followed by a period. An imperative sentence that shows strong feeling is followed by an exclamation point.

EXAMPLES
Please be quiet. [request]
Turn off your radio. [mild command]
Be quiet! [strong command]

Sometimes a command or request is stated in the form of a question. Because of its purpose, however, the sentence is really an imperative sentence and should be followed by a period or an exclamation point.

EXAMPLES
Could you please send me twenty-five copies.
Will you stop that!

Abbreviations

12e. An abbreviation is usually followed by a period.

TYPES OF ABBREVIATIONS	EXAMPLES
Personal Names	A. E. Housman Eugenia W. Collier
Organizations and Companies	Assn. Co. Inc. Ltd. Corp.
Titles Used with Names	Mr. Mrs. Jr. Dr.
Times of Day	A.M. P.M.
Years	B.C. (written after the date) A.D. (written before the date)
Addresses	Ave. St. Blvd. Pkwy.
States	Calif. Mass. Tex. N. Dak.

NOTE Two-letter state abbreviations without periods are used only when the ZIP Code is included. Each letter of the abbreviation is capitalized, and no comma separates the abbreviation from the ZIP Code.

EXAMPLE

Cincinnati, OH 45233

NOTE In most cases, an abbreviation is capitalized only if the words it stands for are capitalized. If you are unsure whether to capitalize an abbreviation or to use periods with it, look in a recent dictionary.

If a statement ends with an abbreviation, do not use an additional period as an end mark. However, do add a question mark or an exclamation point if the sentence should have one.

EXAMPLES

Mrs. Tavares will be arriving at 3 P.M.
Can you go to meet her at 3 P.M.**?**

Abbreviations for government agencies and international organizations and some other frequently used abbreviations are written without periods. Abbreviations for most units of measurement are commonly written without periods, especially in science books.

EXAMPLES

CD, VCR, FM, IRS, TV, UFO
cm, kg, lb, ml

NOTE Include a period with the abbreviation for *inch* (*in.*) so that it will not be confused with *in,* the word.

COMMAS

12f. Use commas to separate items in a series.

EXAMPLES

Odysseus slays Antinous, Eurymachus, and Penelope's other suitors.
We can meet before school, at lunch, or after school.

(1) If all items in a series are joined by *and* or *or,* do not use commas to separate them.

EXAMPLE

The names of the characters in "Poison" are Harry **and** Timber **and** Dr. Ganderbai.

Some words—such as *bread and butter, rod and reel,* and *law and order*—are used in pairs and may be considered one item in a series.

EXAMPLE

My favorite breakfast is milk, **biscuits and gravy,** and fruit.

(2) Independent clauses in a series are generally separated by semicolons. Short independent clauses, however, may be separated by commas.

EXAMPLE

The sky darkened, branches swayed, the cold deepened, and snow fell.

12g. Use commas to separate two or more adjectives preceding a noun.

EXAMPLE

Montresor leads Fortunato to the dark, cold vaults below the palazzo.

When the last adjective in a series is thought of as part of the noun, the comma before the adjective is omitted.

EXAMPLE

The Loisels bought an expensive **diamond necklace.**

12h. Use commas before *and, but, or, nor, for, so,* and *yet* when they join independent clauses.

EXAMPLE
General Zaroff was confident he would kill Rainsford, **but** the hunt did not go as he had planned.

You may omit the comma before *and, but, or,* or *nor* if the clauses are very short and there is no chance of misunderstanding.

12i. Use commas to set off nonessential clauses and nonessential participial phrases.

A *nonessential* (or *nonrestrictive*) clause or participial phrase adds information that is not needed to understand the main idea in the sentence.

NONESSENTIAL CLAUSE   Langston Hughes, **who was a key figure in the Harlem Renaissance,** often used the rhythms of jazz in his poetry.

Omitting the adjective clause in this example would not change the main idea of the sentence: *Langston Hughes often used the rhythms of jazz in his poetry.*

An *essential* (or *restrictive*) clause or phrase provides information that is needed to understand the sentence, and commas are *not* used.

ESSENTIAL PHRASE   Actors **missing more than two rehearsals** will be replaced.

Omitting the participial phrase above would affect the meaning of the sentence: The phrase tells *which actors.*

12j. Use commas after certain introductory elements.

(1) Use a comma after a word such as *next, yes,* or *no* as well as after an introductory interjection such as *why, well,* or *oops.*

EXAMPLES
Yes, I've read "Salvador Late or Early."
Ah, there's nothing like cold water on a hot day!

(2) Use a comma after an introductory participial phrase.

EXAMPLE
Having passed Penelope's last test, Odysseus reclaims his home and his kingdom.

(3) Use a comma after the last of two or more introductory prepositional phrases.

EXAMPLE
Of all of his novels, Charles Dickens liked *David Copperfield* best.

(4) Use a comma after an introductory adverb clause.

EXAMPLE
Until he meets Juliet, Romeo is madly in love with Rosaline.

12k. Use commas to set off elements that interrupt a sentence.

EXAMPLES
Dr. Ganderbai, **in fact,** worked very hard.
The storm, **the worst this winter,** raged for days.

(1) Appositives and appositive phrases are usually set off by commas.

EXAMPLE
My sister gave me a copy of *Gorilla, My Love,* **Toni Cade Bambara's first collection of stories.**

 NOTE   An appositive that tells which one(s) of two or more is a *restrictive appositive* and should not be set off by commas.

EXAMPLE
The television special is about Graham Greene the British writer, not Graham Greene the Canadian actor.

(2) Words used in direct address are set off by commas.

EXAMPLE
Linda, please read the part of Juliet.

(3) Parenthetical expressions are set off by commas.

Parenthetical expressions are side remarks that add minor information or that relate ideas to each other.

EXAMPLE
He was not angry and, **on the contrary,** was actually glad that you told him about the error.

A contrasting expression introduced by *not* or *yet* is parenthetical and is set off by commas.

EXAMPLE
It is the spirit of the giver, **not the cost of the gift,** that counts.

12l. Use commas in certain conventional situations.

(1) Use a comma to separate items in dates and in addresses (except between a two-letter state abbreviation and a ZIP Code).

EXAMPLES
My family moved to Oakland, California, on Wednesday, December 5, 1990.
On December 5, 1990, our address became 25 Peralta Road, Oakland, CA 94611.

(2) Use a comma after the salutation of a friendly letter and after the closing of any letter.

EXAMPLES
Dear Ms. Chen,   Yours truly,

(3) Use a comma to set off an abbreviation such as *Jr.,* *Sr.,* or *M.D.,* including after the abbreviation unless it ends the sentence.

EXAMPLE
Dr. Martin Luther King, Jr., delivered that speech.

SEMICOLONS

12m. Use a semicolon between independent clauses if they are not joined by *and, but, or, nor, for, so,* or *yet.*

EXAMPLE
I enjoyed reading *The Miracle Worker;* it tells what Helen Keller's youth was like.

12n. Use a semicolon between independent clauses joined by a conjunctive adverb—such as *however, therefore,* and *furthermore*—or a transitional expression—such as *for instance, in fact,* and *that is.*

EXAMPLES
Sherlock Holmes is a fictional character; **however,** many people are convinced that he actually did exist.
My parents are strict; **for example,** I can watch TV only on weekends.

Notice in the two examples above that a comma always follows a conjunctive adverb or a transitional expression that joins independent clauses.

12o. Use a semicolon (rather than a comma) before a coordinating conjunction to join independent clauses that contain commas.

EXAMPLE
Doodle's mother, father, and brother went back inside the house; **but** Doodle remained outside to bury the scarlet ibis.

12p. Use a semicolon between items in a series if the items contain commas.

EXAMPLE
I have postcards from Paris, France; Rome, Italy; Lisbon, Portugal; and London, England.

COLONS

12q. Use a colon to mean "note what follows."

(1) In some cases a colon is used before a list of items, especially after the expressions *the following* and *as follows.*

EXAMPLE
The reading list includes the following titles: "The Gift," "The Sniper," and "The Necklace."

Do not use a colon before a list that follows a verb or a preposition.

INCORRECT	The list of literary terms includes: *conflict, climax,* and *resolution.*
CORRECT	The list of literary terms includes *conflict, climax,* and *resolution.*
INCORRECT	In the past five years, my family has lived in: Texas, Oregon, Ohio, and Florida.
CORRECT	In the past five years, my family has lived in Texas, Oregon, Ohio, and Florida.

(2) Use a colon before a long, formal statement or a long quotation.

EXAMPLE
O. Henry had this to say about Della and Jim: "But in a last word to the wise of these days, let it be said that of all who give gifts, these two were the wisest."

12r. Use a colon in certain conventional situations.

(1) Use a colon between the hour and the minute.

EXAMPLES
9:30 P.M.   8:00 A.M.

(2) Use a colon after the salutation of a business letter.

EXAMPLES
Dear Ms. González: Dear Sir or Madam:
To Whom It May Concern:

(3) Use a colon between chapter and verse in referring to passages from the Bible.

EXAMPLES
Esther 3:5   Exodus 1:6–14

(4) Use a colon between a title and a subtitle.

EXAMPLE
"Shakespeare and His Theater: A Perfect Match"

13 PUNCTUATION

ITALICS

When writing or typing, indicate italics by underlining. If your composition were to be printed, the typesetter would set the underlined words in italics. For example, if you typed the sentence

> Alice Walker wrote <u>The Color Purple</u>.

it would be printed like this:

> Alice Walker wrote *The Color Purple*.

COMPUTER NOTE If you use a computer, you can probably set words in italics yourself. Most word-processing software and many printers are capable of producing italic type.

13a. Use underlining (italics) for titles of books, plays, films, periodicals, works of art, recordings, long musical works, television series, trains, ships, aircraft, and spacecraft.

TYPE OF TITLE	EXAMPLES	
Books	*Black Boy*	*Odyssey*
Plays	*The Miracle Worker* *Romeo and Juliet*	
Films	*The Lion King*	*Jurassic Park*
Periodicals	*Seventeen*	*USA Today*

NOTE The articles *a, an,* and *the* written before a title are italicized only when they are part of the official title. The official title of a book appears on the title page. The official title of a newspaper or periodical appears on the masthead, which is usually found on the editorial page.

EXAMPLE

We subscribe to ***The Wall Street Journal*** and **the** *Austin American-Statesman*.

TYPE OF TITLE	EXAMPLES
Works of Art	*Death of Cleopatra* *Mona Lisa*
Recordings	*Music Box* *Two Worlds, One Heart*
Long Musical Works	*The Magic Flute* *Rhapsody in Blue*
Television Series	*60 Minutes* *The Simpsons*
Trains and Ships	*Orient Express* *U.S.S. Nimitz*
Aircraft and Spacecraft	*Spirit of St. Louis* *Apollo 13*

 For examples of titles that should be placed in quotation marks rather than be italicized, see 13j.

13b. Use underlining (italics) for words, letters, and figures referred to as such and for foreign words not yet a part of English vocabulary.

EXAMPLES

The word *excellent* has two *l*'s.
The *3* on that license plate looks like an *8.*
The *corrido* is a fast-paced ballad.

QUOTATION MARKS

13c. Use quotation marks to enclose a *direct quotation*—a person's exact words.

EXAMPLES

She asked, "How much does the necklace cost?"
"The Loisels pay thirty-six thousand francs," answered Lamont.

Do not use quotation marks for indirect quotations.

DIRECT QUOTATION	Stephanie said, "I'm going to plant some marigolds." [the speaker's exact words]
INDIRECT QUOTATION	Stephanie said that she was going to plant some marigolds. [not the speaker's exact words]

An interrupting expression is not a part of a quotation and should never be inside quotation marks.

EXAMPLE

"Let's fly our kites," Jennifer suggested, "before the breeze dies down."

When two or more sentences by the same speaker are quoted together, use one set of quotation marks.

EXAMPLE

Brennan said, "I'm making a fruitcake. Do you like fruitcake?"

13d. A direct quotation begins with a capital letter.

EXAMPLES

Mrs. Perez asked, "**W**ho is Mercutio?"
Charles answered, "**O**ne of Romeo's friends."
[Although this quotation is not a sentence, it is Charles's complete remark.]

 NOTE If a direct quotation is obviously a fragment of the original quotation, it should begin with a lowercase letter.

EXAMPLE

To Romeo, Juliet is like "**a** wingèd messenger of heaven."

13e. When a quoted sentence is divided into two parts by an interrupting expression, the second part begins with a lowercase letter.

EXAMPLE

"I wish," she said, "**t**hat we went to the same school."

If the second part of a quotation is a new sentence, a period (not a comma) follows the interrupting expression, and the second part begins with a capital letter.

EXAMPLE

"I requested an interview," the reporter said**.** "She told me she was too busy."

13f. When used with quotation marks, other marks of punctuation are placed according to the following rules.

(1) A comma or a period is always placed inside the closing quotation marks.

EXAMPLES

"I haven't seen the film version of *Romeo and Juliet*," remarked Jeannette, "but I understand it's excellent."

(2) A semicolon or a colon is always placed outside the closing quotation marks.

EXAMPLES

My mom's favorite poem is Maya Angelou's "Woman Work"; in fact, I can recite it.
Find examples of the following figures of speech in "I Wandered Lonely as a Cloud": simile, personification, and alliteration.

(3) A question mark or an exclamation point is placed inside the closing quotation marks if the quotation is a question or an exclamation; otherwise, it is placed outside.

EXAMPLES

"Where does Romeo first meet Juliet?" asked Mr. Suarez.
"Help me, please!" she exclaimed.
Which of the characters says "Parting is such sweet sorrow"?
It is *not* an insult to be called a "bookworm"!

13g. When you write dialogue (a conversation), begin a new paragraph every time the speaker changes.

EXAMPLE

The gait of my friend was unsteady, and the bells upon his cap jingled as he strode.
"The pipe," said he.
"It is farther on," said I; "but observe the white web-work which gleams from these cavern walls."
——Edgar Allan Poe, "The Cask of Amontillado"

13h. When a quoted passage consists of more than one paragraph, put quotation marks at the beginning of each paragraph and at the end of only the last paragraph.

EXAMPLE

"At nine o'clock this morning," read the news story, "someone entered the Millford Bank by the back entrance, broke through two thick steel doors guarding the bank's vault, and escaped with sixteen bars of gold.
"No arrests have yet been made, but state and local police are confident the case will be solved within a few days.
"FBI agents are due to arrive on the scene later today."

13i. Use single quotation marks to enclose a quotation within a quotation.

EXAMPLE

"Do you agree with O. Henry that Della and Jim 'were the wisest'?" asked Greg.

13j. Use quotation marks to enclose titles of articles, short stories, essays, poems, songs, individual episodes of TV shows, and chapters and other parts of books and periodicals.

 For examples of titles that should be italicized rather than enclosed in quotation marks, see 13a.

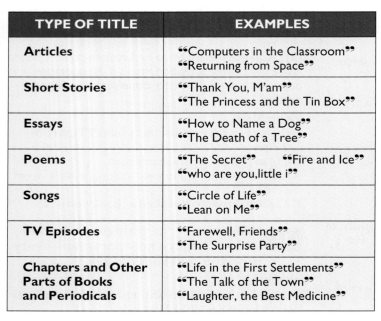

TYPE OF TITLE	EXAMPLES
Articles	"Computers in the Classroom" "Returning from Space"
Short Stories	"Thank You, M'am" "The Princess and the Tin Box"
Essays	"How to Name a Dog" "The Death of a Tree"
Poems	"The Secret" "Fire and Ice" "who are you,little i"
Songs	"Circle of Life" "Lean on Me"
TV Episodes	"Farewell, Friends" "The Surprise Party"
Chapters and Other Parts of Books and Periodicals	"Life in the First Settlements" "The Talk of the Town" "Laughter, the Best Medicine"

 NOTE Neither italics nor quotation marks are used for the titles of major religious texts or for the titles of legal or historical documents.

RELIGIOUS TEXTS
New Testament   Koran   Rig-Veda

LEGAL AND HISTORICAL DOCUMENTS
Declaration of Independence
Code of Hammurabi

EXCEPTION
Names of court cases are usually italicized.

EXAMPLE
Brown v. *Board of Education of Topeka*

Using Italics for Emphasis

Occasionally, writers will use italics (underlining) to emphasize a particular word or phrase. This technique can be especially effective in written dialogue. The italic type helps to show how the sentence is spoken by the character. Read the following sentences aloud. Notice that by italicizing different words, the writer can alter the meaning of the sentence.

EXAMPLES
"Are you *certain* that she said to be here at nine o'clock?" asked Suzanne. [Are you certain, not just guessing?]

"Are you certain that *she* said to be here at nine o'clock?" asked Suzanne. [Did she say so, or did someone else?]

"Are you certain that she said to be here at *nine* o'clock?" asked Suzanne. [Did she say nine o'clock, or was it eight?]

Although italicizing (underlining) words for emphasis is a handy technique, it should not be overused, because it can quickly lose its effectiveness.

Try It Out

Revise the following dialogue by adding commas, end marks, quotation marks, and paragraph breaks where necessary. In addition, underline words you think the speakers would emphasize.

[1] You know what really bothers me about a lot of stories? said Kyle. [2] What? inquired Erin. [3] I can never—well, not never, but often I can't—figure out if a story is fiction or if it really happened, he explained. [4] Yeah she nodded I know what you mean. That reminds me of the story A Man Called Horse. Did it really happen or not? [5] I don't know he answered When I saw the movie, I thought it did, but now I'm not so sure. [6] Erin added, It's the same with stories that don't give the narrator's name. [7] I always wonder whether the narrator is the writer or not. [8] Yes, and the more I like the story, the more I wonder! Kyle agreed. [9] Erin replied Hey let's check the book out again and see if we can find out if Horse was a real person or not. [10] As they read the notes and comments about the story, Kyle said with surprise Wow it says here that Dorothy Johnson also wrote the story The Man Who Shot Liberty Valance!

14 PUNCTUATION

APOSTROPHES

Possessive Case

The **possessive case** of a noun or pronoun shows ownership or relationship.

OWNERSHIP	Mme. Forestier's necklace
RELATIONSHIP	Buddy's friend

14a. To form the possessive case of a singular noun, add an apostrophe and an *s*.

EXAMPLES
Miss Lottie's marigolds   a bus's wheel

> **NOTE** For a proper name ending in *s*, add only an apostrophe if adding 's would make the name awkward to pronounce.

EXAMPLES
West Indies' island   Mrs. Saunders' class

14b. To form the possessive case of a plural noun ending in *s*, add only the apostrophe. To form the possessive case of a plural noun that does not end in *s*, add an apostrophe and an *s*.

EXAMPLES
birds' feathers   Capulets' party
children's shoes   deer's food

TIPS FOR SPELLING

Do not use an apostrophe to form the *plural* of a noun. Usually an apostrophe shows ownership or relationship.

PLURAL	Doodle and he are **brothers**.
POSSESSIVE	The **brothers'** relationship is special.

14c. Possessive personal pronouns—*my, mine, your, yours, his, her, hers, its, our, ours, their,* and *theirs*—do not require an apostrophe.

EXAMPLES
This is **our** plant.
This plant is **ours.**

14d. Indefinite pronouns—such as *everybody* and *neither*—in the possessive case require an apostrophe and an *s*.

EXAMPLES
nobody's wish   another's viewpoint

14e. In compound words, names of organizations and businesses, and word groups showing joint possession, only the last word is possessive in form.

EXAMPLES
brother-in-**law's** gift   City **Garage's** tow trucks
United **Fund's** drive   Della and **Jim's** home

14f. When two or more persons possess something individually, each of their names is possessive in form.

EXAMPLE
Poe's and **Dahl's** stories

Contractions

14g. Use an apostrophe to show where letters, words, or numerals have been omitted in a contraction.

EXAMPLES
let us . . . . **let's**   you are . . . . . . **you're**
1991 . . . . **'91**   of the clock . . . **o'clock**

Ordinarily, the word *not* is shortened to *–n't* and added to a verb with no change to the verb's spelling.

EXAMPLES
are not . . . . . . **aren't**   has not . . . . . **hasn't**
EXCEPTIONS
will not . . . . . . **won't**   cannot . . . . . . **can't**

Do not confuse contractions with possessive pronouns.

CONTRACTIONS	PRONOUNS
Who's [Who is] at bat?	**Whose** bat is that?
It's [It is] roaring.	Listen to **its** roar.
You're [You are] late.	**Your** friend is late.
There's [There is] a kite.	That kite is **theirs.**
They're [They are] here.	**Their** bus is here.

Plurals

14h. Use an apostrophe and an *s* to form the plurals of all lowercase letters, some capital letters, and some words that are referred to as words.

EXAMPLES
Grandma always tells me to mind my *p*'s and *q*'s.
Those *U*'s look like *V*'s. [Without an apostrophe, the plural of *U* would spell *Us*. An apostrophe and an *s* are used to form the plural of *V* to make the style consistent.]
His *hi*'s are always cheerful. [Without an apostrophe, the plural would spell the word *his*.]

Using Apostrophes
In your reading you may have noticed that some writers do not use apostrophes to form the plurals of numbers, capital letters, symbols, and words used as words.

EXAMPLE
Their music was popular in the **1970s.**

However, using an apostrophe is never wrong. Therefore, it is often best to use the apostrophe.

Try It Out
For each of the following sentences, add an apostrophe wherever it is needed.

1. As in your studies are great, but Bs are good, too.
2. If you use *its*, make sure that they clearly refer to specific words.
3. Try not to include *I*s in the opening paragraph of a business letter.
4. The *I0*s in this chart indicate the highest scores.
5. These *his*s should be *theirs*s.

HYPHENS

14i. Use a hyphen to divide a word at the end of a line.

EXAMPLE
"The Most Dangerous Game" is a very suspense-ful story.

When you divide a word at the end of a line, keep in mind the following rules.

(1) Do not divide one-syllable words.

(2) Divide a word only between syllables.

EXAMPLES
fi-an-cé   wor-thy

 NOTE If you need to divide a word and are not sure about its syllables, look it up in a current dictionary.

(3) Words with double consonants may usually be divided between those two consonants.

EXAMPLES
rib-bon   man-ners
EXCEPTION
Words that end in double consonants followed by a suffix are divided before the suffix.
fall-ing   will-ing

(4) Usually, a word with a prefix or a suffix may be divided between the prefix or suffix and the base word (or root).

EXAMPLES
pro-gressive   govern-ment

(5) Divide an already hyphenated word only at a hyphen.

EXAMPLES
man-of-war   daughter-in-law

(6) Do not divide a word so that one letter stands alone.

14j. Use a hyphen with compound numbers from *twenty-one* to *ninety-nine* and with fractions used as adjectives.

EXAMPLES
twenty-four chairs
one-half cup [*One-half* is an adjective.]
one half of the money [*Half* is a noun.]

14k. Use a hyphen with the suffix *–elect* and with all prefixes before a proper noun or proper adjective.

EXAMPLES
president-elect   pre-Revolutionary

14l. Hyphenate a compound adjective that precedes the noun it modifies.

EXAMPLES
a well-written book   a world-famous skier

Do not use a hyphen if one of the modifiers is an adverb that ends in *–ly*.

EXAMPLE
a **bitterly cold** day

NOTE Some compound adjectives are always hyphenated, whether they precede or follow the nouns they modify.

EXAMPLE

an up-to-date dictionary
a dictionary that is up-to-date

If you're not sure whether a compound adjective should be hyphenated, check a recent dictionary.

DASHES

14m. Use a dash to indicate an abrupt break in thought or speech or an unfinished statement or question.

EXAMPLE

Judy—Ms. Lane, I mean—will be your new coach.

14n. Use a dash to mean *namely, that is, in other words,* and similar expressions that introduce an explanation.

EXAMPLES

Dr. Ganderbai considered using an anesthetic— ether or chloroform. [namely]
William Sydney Porter—O. Henry—is my favorite writer. [that is]

NOTE When you type or input your writing on a word processor, you may indicate a dash by using two hyphens. (Do not leave a space before, between, or after the hyphens.) If you are using a computer, you may also find a dash available in your word processing software. When you write by hand, use an unbroken line about as long as two hyphens.

PARENTHESES

14o. Use parentheses to enclose material that is not considered of major importance in a sentence.

EXAMPLES

Richard Wright **(**1908–1960**)** wrote *Black Boy.*
Aunt Constance **(**Mother's aunt and my great-aunt**)** will meet us at the airport.

Capitalize and use end punctuation for parenthetical matter that stands alone as a sentence. Do not capitalize and use end punctuation for parenthetical matter contained within a sentence.

EXAMPLES

Complete the form. **(P**lease print or type**.)**
The protagonist **(**the author did not give him a name**)** is a sniper.

15 SPELLING

UNDERSTANDING WORD STRUCTURE

Many English words are made up of roots and affixes (prefixes and suffixes). The **root** of a word is the part that carries the word's core meaning. A **prefix** is one or more letters or syllables added to the beginning of a word or word part to create a new word. A **suffix** is one or more letters or syllables added to the end of a word or word part to create a new word. Learning how to spell commonly used word parts and how to combine them can help you spell thousands of words.

COMMONLY USED ROOTS		
ROOTS	**MEANINGS**	**EXAMPLES**
–aud–, –audit– –bene– –chron– –cycl– –dem–	hear well, good time circle, wheel people	audible, auditorium benefit, benevolent chronological, synchronize cyclone, bicycle democracy, epidemic

(continued)

Language Handbook

COMMONLY USED ROOTS (continued)

ROOTS	MEANINGS	EXAMPLES
–gen–	birth, kind, origin	generate, generic, generous
–graph–	write, writing	autograph, geography
–hydr–	water	hydrant, hydrate
–log–, –logue–	study, word	logic, mythology, dialogue
–micr–	small	microbe, microscope
–morph–	form	metamorphosis, polymorph
–phil–	like, love	philanthropic, philosophy
–phon–	sound	phonograph, euphony
–port–	carry, bear	export, important
–psych–	mind	psychology, psychosomatic
–verse–, –vert–	turn	reverse, convert
–vid–, –vis–	see	television, evident

COMMONLY USED PREFIXES

PREFIXES	MEANINGS	EXAMPLES
anti–	against, opposing	antipathy, antithesis
bi–	two	bimonthly, bisect
contra–	against	contradict, contrast
de–	away, off, down	defect, desert, decline
dis–	away, off, opposing	dismount, dissent
hemi–	half	hemisphere, hemicycle
hyper–	excessive, over	hyperactive, hypertension
inter–	between, among	intercede, international
mis–	badly, not, wrongly	misfire, misspell
over–	above, excessive	oversee, overdo
post–	after, following	postpone, postscript
re–	back, backward, again	revoke, reflect, reforest
tra–, trans–	across, beyond	traffic, transport
un–	not, reverse of	untrue, unfold

COMMONLY USED SUFFIXES

SUFFIXES	MEANINGS	EXAMPLES
–able	able, likely	capable, changeable
–cy	state, condition	accuracy, normalcy
–er	doer, native of	baker, westerner
–ful	full of, marked by	thankful, masterful
–ic	dealing with, caused by, person or thing showing	classic, choleric, heretic
–ion	action, result, state	union, fusion, dominion
–ish	suggesting, like	smallish, childish
–ist	doer, believer	monopolist, capitalist
–ly	like, characteristic of	friendly, cowardly
–ness	quality, state	softness, shortness
–or	doer, office, action	director, juror, error
–ous	marked by, given to	religious, furious
–tion	action, condition	selection, relation
–tude	quality, state	fortitude, multitude

SPELLING RULES

ie and ei

15a. **Write *ie* when the sound is long *e*, except after *c*.**

EXAMPLES
ach**ie**ve ch**ie**f n**ie**ce **cei**ling dec**ei**t rec**ei**ve
EXCEPTIONS
either l**ei**sure n**ei**ther s**ei**ze prot**ei**n

15b. **Write *ei* when the sound is not long *e*.**

EXAMPLES
for**ei**gn forf**ei**t h**ei**ght h**ei**r r**ei**gn w**ei**gh
EXCEPTIONS
ancient consc**ie**nce fr**ie**nd misch**ie**f v**ie**w

–cede, –ceed, and –sede

15c. **The only English word ending in *–sede* is *supersede*. The only words ending in *–ceed* are *exceed*, *proceed*, and *succeed*. Most other words with this sound end in *–cede*.**

EXAMPLES
ac**cede**   inter**cede**   re**cede**
con**cede**   pre**cede**   se**cede**

Adding Prefixes

15d. **When adding a prefix, do not change the spelling of the original word.**

EXAMPLES
im + mortal = **im**mortal   mis + step = **mis**step
re + elect = **re**elect   over + run = **over**run

Adding Suffixes

15e. **When adding the suffix *–ness* or *–ly*, do not change the spelling of the original word.**

EXAMPLES
fair + ness = fair**ness**   sure + ly = sure**ly**
EXCEPTIONS
For most words ending in *y*, change the *y* to *i* before adding *–ness* or *–ly*:
empty—empt**i**ness   easy—eas**i**ly

However, most one-syllable words ending in *y* follow rule 15e.

EXAMPLES
dry + ness = dry**ness**   sly + ly = sly**ly**

15f. **Drop the final silent *e* before a suffix beginning with a vowel.**

EXAMPLES
hope + ing = hop**ing**   strange + est = strang**est**
EXCEPTIONS
Keep the final silent *e*

- in words ending in *ce* or *ge* before a suffix that begins with *a* or *o*: knowledg**eable**, outrag**eous**
- in *dye* and in *singe*, before *–ing*: dy**eing**, sing**eing**
- in *mile* before *–age*: mil**eage**

15g. **Keep the final silent *e* before a suffix beginning with a consonant.**

EXAMPLES
nine + ty = nine**ty**   entire + ly = entire**ly**
EXCEPTIONS
nine + th = nin**th**   awe + ful = aw**ful**
judge + ment = judg**ment**
argue + ment = argu**ment**

15h. **For words ending in *y* preceded by a consonant, change the *y* to *i* before any suffix that does not begin with *i*.**

EXAMPLES
fifty + eth = fift**ieth**   mystery + ous = myster**ious**

15i. **For words ending in *y* preceded by a vowel, simply add the suffix.**

EXAMPLES
joy + ful = joy**ful**   boy + hood = boy**hood**
EXCEPTIONS
day + ly = da**i**ly   pay + ed = pa**id**
say + ed = sa**id**   lay + ed = la**id**

15j. **Double the final consonant before a suffix that begins with a vowel if the word *both* (1) has only one syllable or has the accent on the last syllable *and* (2) ends in a single consonant preceded by a single vowel.**

EXAMPLES
drop + ing = dro**pping**
occur + ence = occu**rrence**
strum + ed = stru**mmed**
thin + er = thi**nner**

NOTE   The final consonant in some words may or may not be doubled. Both spellings are equally correct.

EXAMPLES
travel + er = trave**ler** *or* trave**ller**
shovel + ed = shove**led** *or* shove**lled**

Forming Plurals of Nouns

15k. To form the plurals of most English nouns, add –s.

EXAMPLES

boats   houses   nickels   Lincolns

15l. To form the plurals of other nouns, follow these rules.

(1) For nouns ending in *s, x, z, ch,* or *sh,* add –es.

EXAMPLES

glasses   boxes   waltzes   beaches   Bushes

(2) For nouns ending in *y* preceded by a consonant, change the *y* to *i* and add –es.

EXAMPLES

armies   babies   skies   mysteries

EXCEPTION

For proper nouns, add –s: Hardys

(3) For nouns ending in *y* preceded by a vowel, add –s.

EXAMPLES

joys   keys   Momadays

(4) For some nouns ending in *f* or *fe,* add –s. For others, change the *f* or *fe* to *v* and add –es.

EXAMPLES

beliefs   roofs   safes   giraffes
calves   wives   leaves   shelves

EXCEPTION

For proper nouns, add –s: Radcliffs, Rolfes

(5) For nouns ending in *o* preceded by a vowel, add –s.

EXAMPLES

radios   patios   Marios   stereos

(6) For nouns ending in *o* preceded by a consonant, add –es.

EXAMPLES

echoes   heroes   vetoes   tomatoes

EXCEPTIONS

For some common nouns ending in *o* preceded by a consonant, especially musical terms, and for proper nouns, add only –s: tacos, pianos, Sotos

(7) The plurals of a few nouns are formed in irregular ways.

EXAMPLES

children   feet   men   teeth   mice

(8) For a few nouns, the singular and the plural forms are the same.

SINGULAR AND PLURAL

deer   Japanese   Navajo   sheep   trout   series

(9) For a compound noun written as one word, form the plural of only the last word of the compound.

EXAMPLES

iceboxes   blackberries   businesspeople

(10) For a compound noun that is hyphenated or written as separate words, form the plural of the noun that is modified.

EXAMPLES

sisters-in-law   runners-up   music boxes

(11) For some nouns borrowed from other languages, the plurals are formed as in the original languages.

EXAMPLES

crisis—crises   phenomenon—phenomena

A few nouns borrowed from other languages have two plural forms.

EXAMPLES

appendix—appendices *or* appendixes
formula—formulas *or* formulae

(12) For numerals, symbols, some capital letters, and words used as words, add an –s or both an apostrophe and an –s.

EXAMPLES

6—6s *or* 6's   R—Rs *or* R's
&—&s *or* &'s   and—ands *or* and's

To prevent confusion, always use an apostrophe and an –s to form the plurals of lowercase letters, certain capital letters, and some words used as words.

EXAMPLES

Your *i*'s look like *e*'s. [Without an apostrophe, the plural of *i* would look like *is.*]
Ramón got all **A**'s last semester. [Without an apostrophe, the plural of A would look like *As.*]
Her ***and so*'s** began to get tiresome. [Without the apostrophe, the plural of *so* would look like *sos.*]

COMPUTER NOTE

Spell-checking software can help you proofread your writing. Even the best spelling checkers aren't foolproof, however. Some accept British and archaic spellings, and most do not identify words that are spelled correctly but are used incorrectly (such as *affect* for *effect*). Always double-check your writing to make sure that your spelling is error free.

The Glossary of Usage is an alphabetical list of words, expressions, and special terms with definitions, explanations, and examples. Some examples have usage labels. *Standard* or *formal* usages are appropriate in serious writing and speaking, such as in compositions and in speeches. *Informal* words and expressions are standard English usages generally appropriate in conversation and in everyday writing such as in personal letters. *Nonstandard* usages do not follow the guidelines of standard English.

---

accept, except   *Accept* is a verb that means "receive." *Except* may be either a verb or a preposition. As a verb, *except* means "leave out." As a preposition, *except* means "excluding."

EXAMPLES
We **accept** your apology.
All children under age three will be **excepted** from the fee. [verb]
Everyone **except** Bob and me has seen the exhibit. [preposition]

advice, advise   *Advice* is a noun meaning "suggestion about what to do." *Advise* is a verb meaning "offer a suggestion; recommend."

EXAMPLES
He gave me some excellent **advice.**
She **advised** me to finish high school.

affect, effect   *Affect* is a verb meaning "influence." As a verb, *effect* means "accomplish." As a noun, *effect* means "result (of an action)."

EXAMPLES
What he said did not **affect** my decision.
The mayor has **effected** many changes during her administration. [verb]
What **effect** will the new factory have on the environment? [noun]

ain't   Avoid using this word in formal speaking and in all writing other than dialogue; it is nonstandard English.

all together, altogether   *All together* means "everyone or everything in the same place." *Altogether* is an adverb meaning "entirely."

EXAMPLES
When we were **all together,** we voted.
He was **altogether** wrong.

a lot   Do not write the expression *a lot* as one word.

EXAMPLE
In addition to short stories, Edgar Allan Poe also wrote **a lot** [*not* alot] of poetry.

among   See **between, among.**

and etc.   The abbreviation for the Latin phrase *et cetera,* meaning "and other things" is *etc.* Thus, do not use *and* with *etc.*

EXAMPLE
My younger sister collects stickers, bottle caps, string, **etc.** [*not* and etc.]

anyways, anywheres   Use these words (and others like them, such as *everywheres, somewheres,* and *nowheres*) without the final *s.*

EXAMPLES
I have to baby-sit tonight **anyway** [*not* anyways].
The Loisels could not find the necklace **anywhere** [*not* anywheres].

as   See **like, as.**

as if   See **like, as if.**

at   Do not use *at* after *where.*

NONSTANDARD   Where was Romeo at?
STANDARD   **Where** was Romeo?

bad, badly   *Bad* is an adjective. *Badly* is an adverb. In standard English, only *bad* should follow a linking verb, such as *feel, look, sound, taste,* or *smell,* or forms of the verb *be.*

EXAMPLE
The fruitcake doesn't taste **bad** [*not* badly].

being as, being that   Use *since* or *because* instead of these expressions.

EXAMPLE
Because [*not* being as] President Clinton admired Maya Angelou's writing, he invited her to write a poem for his inauguration.

beside, besides   *Beside* is a preposition that means "by the side of" or "next to." As a preposition, *besides* means "in addition to" or "other than." As an adverb, *besides* means "moreover."

EXAMPLES
His rifle lay **beside** him.
Who **besides** Timber tried to help? [preposition]
I don't want to go; **besides,** it's snowing. [adverb]

between, among Use *between* when you are referring to two things at a time, even though they may be part of a group consisting of more than two.

EXAMPLES

There was a feud **between** the Montagues and the Capulets.

The manager could not decide which of the four players to select, because there was not much difference **between** them. [Although there are more than two players, each one is being compared with the others separately.]

Use *among* when referring to a group rather than to separate individuals.

EXAMPLE

We were able to collect only ten dollars **among** the four of us.

bust, busted Avoid using these words as verbs. Use a form of either *burst* or *break,* depending on the meaning.

EXAMPLES

The balloon **burst** [*not* busted] loudly.

The firefighters **broke** [*not* busted] a window.

consul, council, counsel *Consul* is a noun meaning "representative of a foreign country." *Council* is a noun meaning "group called together to accomplish a job." As a noun, *counsel* means "advice." As a verb, it means "give advice."

EXAMPLES

The French **consul** outlined his government's plan.

The city **council** will debate the issue.

I'm grateful for your **counsel.** [noun]

Did the doctor **counsel** her to get more rest? [verb]

could of See **of.**

discover, invent *Discover* means "be the first to find, see, or learn about something that already exists." *Invent* means "be the first to do or make something."

EXAMPLES

Marguerite Perey **discovered** the element francium.

The zipper was **invented** in 1893.

double negative A double negative is the use of two negative words when one is enough. Avoid using double negatives.

Common Negative Words

barely	never	no one	not (–n't)
hardly	no	nowhere	nothing
neither	nobody	none	scarcely

NONSTANDARD	I had not read none of Emily Dickinson's poems.
STANDARD	I **had not read any** of Emily Dickinson's poems.
STANDARD	I **had read none** of Emily Dickinson's poems.
NONSTANDARD	Doodle couldn't hardly walk.
STANDARD	Doodle **could hardly** walk.

double subject See **he, she, it, they.**

effect See **affect, effect.**

etc. See **and etc.**

everywheres See **anyways, anywheres.**

except See **accept, except.**

fewer, less *Fewer* tells "how many"; it is used with plural nouns. *Less* tells "how much"; it is used with singular nouns.

EXAMPLES

There are **fewer** gypsy moths this year than there were last year.

Reading the *Odyssey* took **less** time than we had thought.

good, well *Good* is an adjective. *Well* may be used as an adjective or an adverb. Never use *good* to modify a verb; instead, use *well* as an adverb meaning "capably" or "satisfactorily."

EXAMPLE

Sandra Cisneros writes **well** [*not* good].

As an adjective, *well* means "healthy" or "satisfactory in appearance or condition."

EXAMPLES

Lying in his bed, Harry did not look **well.**

Friar Laurence thought that all would be **well** with the Montagues and the Capulets.

NOTE *Feel good* and *feel well* mean different things. *Feel good* means "feel happy or pleased." *Feel well* means "feel healthy."

EXAMPLES

The news made her feel **good.**

I didn't feel **well,** so I went home.

had ought, hadn't ought Unlike other verbs, *ought* is not used with *had.*

EXAMPLES

I think Doodle's brother **ought** [*not* had ought] to be more patient; he **ought not** [*not* hadn't ought] to push Doodle so hard.

hardly   See **double negative**.

he, she, it, they   Do not use an unnecessary pronoun after the subject of a verb. This error is called the *double subject*.

NONSTANDARD	Miss Lottie she likes to grow marigolds.
STANDARD	Miss Lottie likes to grow marigolds.

hisself, theirselves   Do not use these words for *himself* and *themselves*.

EXAMPLE
Romeo unburdens **himself** [*not* hisself] to Friar Laurence.

imply, infer   *Imply* means "suggest indirectly." *Infer* means "interpret" or "draw a conclusion (from a remark or an action)."

EXAMPLES
Doug **implied** that he will vote for me.
From Doug's remark, I **inferred** that he will vote for me.

inside of   See **of**.

invent   See **discover, invent**.

it   See **he, she, it, they**.

its, it's   *Its* is the possessive form of *it*. *It's* is the contraction of *it is* or *it has*.

EXAMPLES
The bird stopped **its** singing.
It's [it is] an easy problem.
It's [it has] been raining since noon.

kind of, sort of   In formal situations, avoid using these terms to mean *somewhat* or *rather*.

INFORMAL	Zaroff was kind of surprised to see that Rainsford was still alive.
FORMAL	Zaroff was **somewhat** [*or* **rather**] surprised to see that Rainsford was still alive.

kind of a, sort of a   Avoid using *a* after *kind of* and *sort of* in formal situations.

INFORMAL	What kind of a snake was it?
FORMAL	What **kind of** snake was it?

kind(s), sort(s), type(s)   Use *this* or *that* with the singular form of each of these nouns. Use *these* or *those* with the plural form.

EXAMPLES
I like **this kind** of jeans better than any of **those** other **kinds**.

lay   See **lie, lay**.

learn, teach   *Learn* means "acquire knowledge." *Teach* means "instruct" or "show how."

EXAMPLES
Doodle **learns** to walk.
His brother **teaches** him to walk.

leave, let   *Leave* means "go away" or "depart from." *Let* means "allow" or "permit." Avoid using *leave* for *let*.

EXAMPLE
Let [*not* leave] her speak if she insists.

less   See **fewer, less**.

let   See **leave, let**.

lie, lay   The verb *lie* means "rest" or "stay, recline, or remain in a certain position." *Lie* never takes an object. Its principal parts are *lie, lying, lay, lain*. The verb *lay* means "put (something) in a place." Its principal parts are *lay, laying, laid, laid*. *Lay* usually takes an object.

EXAMPLES
Is there a real snake **lying** on Harry's stomach? [no object]
He **laid** her gift on the table. [*Gift* is the object of *laid.*]

like, as   In formal English, use *like* to introduce a prepositional phrase, and use *as* to introduce a subordinate clause.

EXAMPLES
Does Juliet look **like** Rosaline? [The preposition *like* introduces the phrase *like Rosaline.*]
Juliet does **as** Friar Laurence suggests. [The subordinating conjunction *as* introduces the clause *as Friar Laurence suggests.*]

like, as if   In formal situations, *like* should not be used for the compound conjunction *as if* or *as though*.

EXAMPLE
Juliet looks **as though** [*not* like] she is alive.

might of, must of   See **of**.

moral, morale   As an adjective, *moral* means "good; virtuous." As a noun, it means "lesson of conduct." *Morale* is a noun meaning "spirit; mental condition."

EXAMPLES
In Pearl Buck's short story "The Old Demon," Mrs. Wang's **moral** values compel her to help the Japanese pilot. [adjective]
James Thurber's fables end with **morals** quite unlike the ones in traditional fairy tales. [noun]
The employees' **morale** is high.

nowheres   See **anyways, anywheres.**

of   *Of* is a preposition. Do not use *of* in place of *have* after verbs such as *could, should, would, ought (to), might,* and *must.* Also, do not use *had of* for *had.*

NONSTANDARD	You would of enjoyed our production of *The Miracle Worker.*
STANDARD	You **would have** [*or* would've] enjoyed our production of *The Miracle Worker.*
NONSTANDARD	If I had of known it was your birthday, I would of given you a card.
STANDARD	If I **had** known it was your birthday, I **would have** given you a card.

Also, do not use *of* after other prepositions such as *inside, off,* or *outside.*

EXAMPLES
The sniper's enemy fell **off** [*not* off of] the roof.
The sleeping Juliet is carried **inside** [*not* inside of] the Capulets' tomb.

off of   See **of.**

ought   See **had ought, hadn't ought.**

ought to of   See **of.**

peace, piece   *Peace* means "calmness; absence of war or strife." *Piece* means "part of something."

EXAMPLES
After the long war, **peace** was welcome.
Do you have a **piece** of paper I can borrow?

principal, principle   As a noun, *principal* means "the head of a school." As an adjective, it means "main or most important." *Principle* is a noun meaning "a rule of conduct" or "a general truth."

EXAMPLES
Ted had a long talk with the **principal.** [noun]
Winning is not our **principal** goal. [adjective]
My friends have high **principles.**
I don't know the **principles** of physics.

rise, raise   The verb *rise* means "go up" or "get up." *Rise* almost never takes an object. Its principal parts are *rise, rising, rose, risen.* The verb *raise* means "cause (something) to rise" or "lift up." *Raise* usually takes an object. Its principal parts are *raise, raising, raised, raised.*

EXAMPLES
Everyone **rose** when the judge entered the room. [no object]
The sniper **raised** his revolver and fired. [*Revolver* is the object of *raised.*]

scarcely   See **double negative.**

set   See **sit, set.**

she   See **he, she, it, they.**

should of   See **of.**

sit, set   The verb *sit* means "rest in an upright, seated position." *Sit* almost never takes an object. Its principal parts are *sit, sitting, sat, sat.* The verb *set* means "put (something) in a place." *Set* usually takes an object. Its principal parts are *set, setting, set, set.*

EXAMPLES
The campers were **sitting** around the fire. [no object]
Ganderbai **set** the bag on a chair. [*Bag* is the object of *set.*]

some, somewhat   In formal situations, do not use *some* to mean "to some extent" or "slightly." Instead, use *somewhat.*

INFORMAL	My spelling has now improved some.
FORMAL	My spelling has now improved **somewhat.**

somewheres   See **anyways, anywheres.**

sort(s)   See **kind(s), sort(s), type(s)** and **kind of a, sort of a.**

sort of   See **kind of, sort of.**

teach   See **learn, teach.**

than, then   *Than* is a conjunction used in comparisons. *Then* is an adverb meaning "at that time" or "next."

EXAMPLES
This box is heavier **than** that one.
Did the sniper know **then** who his enemy was?
First, I read *Romeo and Juliet;* **then,** I watched the film version.

that   See **who, which, that.**

their, there, they're   *Their* is a possessive form of *they.* As an adverb, *there* means "at that place." *There* is also used to begin a sentence. *They're* is the contraction of *they are.*

EXAMPLES
Their daughter, Juliet, was in love with a Montague.
Harry Pope lay **there** quietly.
There is a conflict between Odysseus and the Cyclops.
They're throwing pebbles at Miss Lottie's flowers.

theirs, there's *Theirs* is a possessive form of the pronoun *they. There's* is the contraction of *there is.*

EXAMPLES
Our team was ready to play, and so was **theirs.**
There's a sniper on the rooftop.

theirselves See **hisself, theirselves.**

them *Them* should not be used as an adjective. Use *those.*

EXAMPLE
Their unselfish love is symbolized by **those** [*not* them] gifts.

then See **than, then.**

there See **their, there, they're.**

there's See **theirs, there's.**

they See **he, she, it, they.**

they're See **their, there, they're.**

this, that, these, those See **kind(s), sort(s), type(s).**

try and Use *try to,* not *try and.*

EXAMPLE
Timber and Ganderbai **try to** [*not* try and] keep Harry calm.

type(s) See **kind(s), sort(s), type(s).**

unless See **without, unless.**

way, ways Use *way,* not *ways,* in referring to a distance.

EXAMPLE
Odysseus traveled quite a long **way** [*not* ways] to get back home.

well See **good, well.**

what Use *that,* not *what,* to introduce an adjective clause.

EXAMPLE
The poem **that** [*not* what] I wrote about was Naomi Shihab Nye's "Daily."

when, where Do not use *when* or *where* to begin a definition.

NONSTANDARD	A "bomb" in football is when a backfielder throws a long pass.
STANDARD	A "bomb" in football is a long pass thrown by a backfielder.

Also, do not use *where* for *that.*

EXAMPLE
I read in this book **that** [*not* where] Robert Frost won the Pulitzer Prize four times.

where . . . at See **at.**

who, which, that *Who* refers to persons only; *which* refers to things only; *that* may refer to either persons or things.

EXAMPLES
Isn't Walt Whitman the poet **who** [*or* that] wrote *Leaves of Grass*? [person]
They decided to replace Mme. Forestier's necklace, **which** they did not know was fake. [thing]
The necklace **that** the Loisels bought cost thirty-six thousand francs. [thing]

who's, whose *Who's* is the contraction of *who is* or *who has. Whose* is the possessive form of *who.*

EXAMPLES
Who's [who is] the narrator of "A Christmas Memory"?
Who's [who has] been helping Helen?
Whose autobiography is titled *Black Boy*?

without, unless Do not use the preposition *without* in place of the conjunction *unless.*

EXAMPLE
I will not be able to sing **unless** [*not* without] my cold gets better.

would of See **of.**

your, you're *Your* is a possessive form of *you. You're* is the contraction of *you are.*

EXAMPLES
What is **your** opinion of General Zaroff?
You're [you are] my best friend.

Glossary

The glossary that follows is an alphabetical list of words found in the selections in this book. Use this glossary just as you would use a dictionary—to find out the meanings of unfamiliar words. (Some technical, foreign, and more obscure words in this book are not listed here but instead are defined for you in the footnotes that accompany many of the selections.)

Many words in the English language have more than one meaning. This glossary gives the meanings that apply to the words as they are used in the selections in this book. Words closely related in form and meaning are usually listed together in one entry (for instance, *compassion* and *compassionate*), and the definition is given for the first form.

The following abbreviations are used:

adj.	adjective
adv.	adverb
n.	noun
v.	verb

Each word's pronunciation is given in parentheses. A guide to the pronunciation symbols appears at the bottom of this page. For more information about the words in this glossary or for information about words not listed here, consult a dictionary.

A

abhor (ab·hôr′) *v.*: hate.

abolish (ə·bäl′ish) *v.*: put an end to. *Abolition* is the noun form of this word.

abominable (ə·bäm′ə·nə·bəl) *adj.*: extremely unpleasant or disgusting. —**abominably** *adv.*

absorb (ab·sôrb′) *v.*: take in.

acclaim (ə·klām′) *v.*: receive strong approval; applaud.

acquiesce (ak′wē·es′) *v.* (used with *in*): accept; comply with.

admonish (ad·män′ish) *v.*: scold mildly.

admonition (ad′mə·nish′ən) *n.*: scolding; warning.

adorn (ə·dôrn′) *v.*: add beauty to; decorate.

adulation (a′joo·lā′shən) *n.*: intense or excessive admiration or praise.

adversary (ad′vər·ser′ē) *n.*: enemy; opponent.

adversity (ad·vur′sə·tē) *n.*: hardship; great misfortune.

advocate (ad′və·kāt′) *v.*: support; argue in favor of.

advocate (ad′və·kit) *n.*: supporter.

affluent (af′loo·ənt) *adj.*: wealthy.

aghast (ə·gast′) *adj.*: terrified; horrified.

agile (aj′əl) *adj.*: moving with ease.

allegiance (ə·lē′jəns) *n.*: loyalty.

aloof (ə·loof′) *adj.*: at a distance; unfriendly.

annihilate (ə·nī′ə·lāt′) *v.*: destroy completely; wipe out.

ardor (är′dər) *n.*: passion; enthusiasm.

arid (ar′id) *adj.*: lacking enough water for many types of plants to grow; dry.

ascetic (ə·set′ik) *adj.*: severe; also, self-disciplined.

ascribe (ə·skrīb′) *v.*: assign or attribute something to a cause.

aspire (ə·spīr′) *v.*: seek to gain; desire. —**aspiring** *v.* used as *n.*

astronomer (ə·strän′ə·mər) *n.*: scientist who studies the stars and planets.

austere (ô·stir′) *adj.*: very plain; severe.

avail (ə·vāl′) *v.*: be of use; help.

avert (ə·vurt′) *v.*: turn away. —**averted** *v.* used as *adj.*

awry (ə·rī′) *adv.*: in the wrong manner.

B

balmy (bäm′ē) *adj.*: mild; pleasant.

beckon (bek′ən) *v.*: gesture or signal to request someone to approach or follow.

beguile (bē·gīl′) *v.*: charm; deceive.

beleaguer (bē·lē′gər) *v.*: surround and attack. —**beleaguered** *v.* used as *adj.*

belligerent (bə·lij′ər·ənt) *adj.*: angry and aggressive or ready to start a fight.

bigotry (big′ə·trē) *n.*: strong prejudice against a particular group of people.

blight (blīt) *v.*: destroy or prevent growth. —**blighted** *v.* used as *adj.*

bureaucratic (byoor′ə·krat′ik) *adj.*: relating to rigid government routine.

C

candor (kan'dər) *n.*: honesty; frankness.

carnage (kär'nij) *n.*: widespread killing; slaughter; bloodshed.

cascade (kas·kād') *n.*: waterfall.

catastrophic (kat'ə·sträf'ik) *adj.*: disastrous.

chronic (krän'ik) *adj.*: frequently occurring.

clarity (klar'ə·tē) *n.*: clearness.

clench (klench) *v.*: tightly close. —**clenched** *v.* used as *adj.*

coerce (kō·ʉrs') *v.*: force.

compulsory (kəm·pul'sə·rē) *adj.*: required by rule or law.

conceivable (kən·sēv'ə·bəl) *adj.*: capable of being imagined or understood.

condolence (kən·dō'ləns) *n.*: expression of sympathy.

condone (kən·dōn') *v.*: overlook or excuse an offense.

connoisseurship (kän'ə·sur'ship) *n.*: expert knowledge.

conscientious (kän'shē·en'shəs) *adj.*: careful and thoughtful. —**conscientiously** *adv.*

conspicuous (kən·spik'yoo·əs) *adj.*: obvious; noticeable; notable.

conspiracy (kən·spir'ə·sē) *n.*: secret, often unlawful plan carried out by a group.

constitute (kän'stə·toot') *v.*: make up; form.

contrition (kən·trish'ən) *n.*: deep feelings of guilt and repentance.

controversial (kän'trə·vur'shəl) *adj.*: stirring up disagreement between groups holding opposing views.

conviction (kən·vik'shən) *n.*: strong belief.

covet (kuv'it) *v.*: long for. —**coveted** *v.* used as *adj.*

D

decrepit (dē·krep'it) *adj.*: falling apart.

default (dē·fôlt') *n.*: failure to do something.

defer (dē·fur') *v.*: delay; put off.

defiant (dē·fī'ənt) *adj.*: openly and boldly resisting or opposing.

deficient (dē·fish'ənt) *adj.*: lacking.

deliberation (di·lib'ər·ā'shən) *n.*: careful thought, especially in making a decision.

delirious (di·lir'ē·əs) *adj.*: temporarily confused and seeing imaginary things, often because of injury or fever.

delirium (di·lir'ē·əm) *n.*: extreme mental disturbance, often accompanied by hallucinations (seeing things that are not there).

demise (dē·mīz') *n.*: death; end.

denounce (dē·nouns') *v.*: accuse publicly; condemn. —**denouncing** *v.* used as *adj.*

depreciate (dē·prē'shē·āt') *v.*: make something seem less important; lower the value of.

depression (dē·presh'ən) *n.*: major economic downturn. *Depression* also means "sadness."

designate (dez'ig·nāt') *v.*: point out; indicate.

desolate (des'ə·lāt') *v.*: produce a feeling of loneliness and sadness. —**desolating** *v.* used as *adj.*

despondent (di·spän'dənt) *adj.*: hopeless. —**despondently** *adv.*

devious (dē'vē·əs) *adj.*: sneaky; deceptive.

dilapidated (də·lap'ə·dāt'id) *adj.*: in poor condition; shabby and neglected; falling apart.

dilemma (di·lem'ə) *n.*: difficult choice; serious problem.

dire (dīr) *adj.*: terrible.

disarming (dis·ärm'in) *adj.*: removing or lessening suspicions or fears.

disconsolate (dis·kän'sə·lit) *adj.*: causing sadness or depression; also, very unhappy.

discreet (di·skrēt') *adj.*: showing good judgment in what one says or does; especially being silent or careful.

disdainful (dis·dān'fəl) *adj.*: scornful; regarding someone as beneath you.

disposition (dis'pə·zish'ən) *n.*: usual frame of mind; temperament.

distracted (di·strakt'id) *adj.*: unable to concentrate on something.

distraught (di·strôt') *adj.*: deeply troubled, as with worry or grief.

divergent (dī·vur'jənt) *adj.*: separate; going in different directions.

diverting (də·vurt'in) *adj.*: entertaining.

doggedness (dôg'id·nis) *n.*: stubbornness; persistence.

---

at, āte, cär; ten, ēve; is, īce; gō, hôrn, look, tool; oil, out; up, fur; ə *for unstressed vowels, as* a *in* ago, u *in* focus; ' *as in* Latin (lat''n); chin; she; thin; *the*; zh *as in* azure (azh'ər); ŋ *as in* ring (riŋ)

E

eclipse (i·klips´) v.: conceal from view; overshadow.

elation (ē·lā´shən) n.: great joy.

elect (ē·lekt´) v.: choose.

emaciated (ē·mā´shē·āt´id) adj.: extremely thin; wasted away.

embody (em·bäd´ē) v.: convey the impression of; represent.

emulate (em´yoo·lāt´) v.: follow the example of; imitate.

endeavor (en·dev´ər) n.: **1.** serious attempt, effort, or undertaking. v.: **2.** try.

enduring (en·door´iŋ) adj.: strong and lasting.

enthrall (en·thrôl´) v.: fascinate.

enunciate (ē·nun´sē·āt´) v.: pronounce; articulate.

equitable (ek´wit·ə·bəl) adj.: fair; just.

eradicate (ē·rad´i·kāt´) v.: wipe out; destroy; eliminate completely; get rid of. —**eradicating** v. used as n.

esteem (ə·stēm´) n.: respect.

exasperation (eg·zas´pər·ā´shən) n.: great annoyance.

exhilarate (eg·zil´ə·rāt´) v.: gladden; excite.

exorbitant (eg·zôr´bi·tənt) adj.: much too high in price or amount.

expendable (ek·spen´də·bəl) adj.: worth sacrificing to gain an objective.

expire (ek·spīr´) v.: die.

exuberant (eg·zoo´bər·ənt) adj.: elaborate; extreme; also, high-spirited.

F

fanatic (fə·nat´ik) n.: person whose extreme devotion to a cause is excessive or unreasonable.

fervent (fur´vənt) adj.: passionate.

formidable (fôr´mə·də·bəl) adj.: awe-inspiring by reason of excellence; strikingly impressive; causing fear or dread.

futile (fyoot´'l) adj.: useless; vain.

G

genial (jēn´yəl) adj.: cheerful and friendly.

giddy (gid´ē) adj.: dizzy.

glower (glou´ər) v.: glare; stare angrily.

gurgle (gur´gəl) v.: make a bubbling sound while flowing.

H

hoist (hoist) v.: lift or pull up.

hover (huv´ər) v.: stay suspended over something.

hyperactive (hī´pər·ak´tiv) adj.: abnormally active; very lively.

I

idle (īd´'l) adj.: without aim or purpose. —**idly** adv.

ignorance (ig´nə·rəns) n.: lack of knowledge.

imminent (im´ə·nənt) adj.: near; about to happen.

immolation (im´ə·lā´shən) n.: destruction.

immortal (i·môrt´'l) adj.: lasting or living forever.

impartial (im·pär´shəl) adj.: fair; unbiased.

impend (im·pend´) v.: be about to happen. —**impending** v. used as adj.

implication (im´pli·kā´shən) n.: possible connection or consequence.

impose (im·pōz´) v. (used with upon): take advantage of.

imposing (im·pō´ziŋ) adj.: large and impressive looking.

impoverish (im·päv´ər·ish) v.: make poor. —**impoverished** v. used as adj.

imprudent (im·prood´'nt) adj.: unwise.

impulse (im´puls´) n.: sudden desire to do something.

impunity (im·pyoo´ni·tē) n.: freedom from punishment or harm.

inaugurate (in·ô´gyə·rāt´) v.: formally begin.

incantation (in´kan·tā´shən) n.: chant of words or phrases that is meant to produce a magical result.

incessant (in·ses´ənt) adj.: constant; continuous. —**incessantly** adv.

incite (in·sīt´) v.: stir up. —**inciting** v. used as n.

inconsolable (in´kən·sōl´ə·bəl) adj.: unable to be comforted; brokenhearted.

incredulous (in·krej´oo·ləs) adj.: unbelieving; skeptical. —**incredulously** adv.

indiscriminate (in´di·skrim´i·nit) adj.: careless.

inevitable (in·ev´i·tə·bəl) adj.: unavoidable; certain to happen.

infallibility (in·fal´ə·bil´i·tē) n.: inability to make a mistake.

infatuated (in·fach´oo·āt´id) adj.: carried away by shallow or foolish love.

insensible (in·sen´sə·bəl) adj.: not fully conscious or aware.

instigate (in′stə·gāt′) v.: give rise to. *Instigate* is generally used to mean "urge on to some action, usually negative, or set something in motion."

intangible (in·tan′jə·bəl) adj.: cannot be touched or held.

interminable (in·tur′min·nə·bəl) adj.: with no end in sight.

intimidate (in·tim′ə·dāt′) v.: frighten. —**intimidating** v. used as adj.

intolerance (in·täl′ər·əns) n.: prejudice; hostility to other groups.

invariable (in·ver′ē·ə·bəl) adj.: always; without changing. —**invariably** adv.

invincible (in·vin′sə·bəl) adj.: unconquerable.

iridescent (ir′i·des′ənt) adj.: rainbowlike; displaying a shifting range of colors.

irrational (i·rash′ə·nəl) adj.: not based on reason or logic.

L

labyrinthine (lab′ə·rin′thin) adj.: like a maze; complicated.

languor (laŋ′gər) n.: weakness; weariness.

lavish (lav′ish) v.: give generously.

legislation (lej′is·lā′shən) n.: law or body of laws.

linger (liŋ′gər) v.: continue to stay; be reluctant to leave.

litany (lit′′n·ē) n.: repetitive prayer or recitation.

literal (lit′ər·əl) adj.: actual. —**literally** adv.

luminous (lōō′mə·nəs) adj.: shining; glowing.

lurk (lurk) v.: lie in wait, ready to attack.

M

mainstay (mān′stā′) n.: principal support.

malicious (mə·lish′əs) adj.: showing a desire to harm another; spiteful.

malign (mə·līn′) v.: falsely accuse of bad conduct; slander. —**maligned** v. used as adj.

mar (mär) v.: damage; spoil.

marauder (mə·rôd′ər) n.: person who roams in search of loot, or goods to steal.

meager (mē′gər) adj.: thin; small; inadequate.

menace (men′əs) v.: threaten. —**menacing** v. used as adj.

mentorship (men′tər·ship) n.: advice or lessons from a mentor, or wise teacher.

misanthropic (mis′ən·thräp′ik) adj.: disliking other human beings.

monotony (mə·nät′′n·ē) n.: lack of variety.

mundane (mun′dān′) adj.: everyday; commonplace.

N

negotiation (ni·gō′shē·ā′shən) n.: discussion aimed at reaching an agreement.

nimble (nim′bəl) adj.: quickly moving.

noncommittal (nän′kə·mit′′l) adj.: not admitting or committing to any particular purpose or point of view.

O

obscure (əb·skyoor′) v.: conceal; cover up.

obsession (əb·sesh′ən) n.: persistent idea or desire that consumes a person's attention.

obstinate (äb′stə·nət) adj.: stubborn.

obstruction (əb·struk′shən) n.: obstacle; barrier.

odyssey (äd′i·sē) n.: extended journey marked by wandering, adventure, and changes of fortune.

omen (ō′mən) n.: thing or event believed to be a sign of a future occurrence.

ominous (äm′ə·nəs) adj.: threatening.

optimist (äp′tə·mist) n.: person who is always hopeful.

P

pandemonium (pan′də·mō′nē·əm) n.: great confusion; chaos.

paradox (par′ə·däks′) n.: something that has or seems to have contradictory qualities.

paraphernalia (par′ə·fər·nāl′yə) n.: equipment; gear.

pauper (pô′pər) n.: very poor person.

perennial (pə·ren′ē·əl) adj.: year-round; continual.

phenomenon (fə·näm′ə·nən) n.: extraordinary thing or occurrence.

at, āte, cär; ten, ēve; is, īce; gō, hôrn, look, tōol; oil, out; up, fur; ə *for unstressed vowels, as* a *in* ago, u *in* focus; ′ *as in* Latin (lat′′n); chin; she; thin; *the*; zh *as in* azure (azh′ər); ŋ *as in* ring (riŋ)

pious (pī′əs) *adj.*: showing religious devotion.

placid (plas′id) *adj.*: calm; quiet. —**placidly** *adv.*

pliant (plī′ənt) *adj.*: flexible.

poignant (poin′yənt) *adj.*: sharply painful; moving. —**poignantly** *adv.*

polytheism (päl′i·thē·iz′əm) *n.*: belief in more than one god.

portent (pôr′tent) *n.*: thing that warns of events about to occur.

precarious (pri·ker′ē·əs) *adj.*: unsteady; insecure. —**precariously** *adv.*

precipitous (prē·sip′ə·təs) *adj.*: very steep.

preclude (prē·klo͞od′) *v.*: make impossible in advance; prevent.

primal (prī′məl) *adj.*: original; primitive.

primeval (prī·mē′vəl) *adj.*: primitive; of the earliest times.

privation (prī·vā′shən) *n.*: hardship; lack of the things needed for a happy, healthy life.

procure (prō·kyoor′) *v.*: get; obtain.

profusion (prō·fyo͞o′zhən) *n.*: large supply; abundance.

prolong (prō·lôn′) *v.*: extend. —**prolonged** *v.* used as *adj.*

prosaic (prō·zā′ik) *adj.*: ordinary.

protracted (prō·trakt′id) *adj.*: extended.

protrude (prō·tro͞od′) *v.*: stick out. —**protruding** *v.* used as *adj.*

putrid (pyo͞o′trid) *adj.*: offensive to the senses; disgusting.

R

radical (rad′i·kəl) *adj.*: extreme; thorough.

rampart (ram′pärt′) *n.*: broad embankment surrounding a castle, fort, or city for defense against attack.

rancor (raŋ′kər) *n.*: bitter hatred; ill will.

ransack (ran′sak′) *v.*: search thoroughly.

ravage (rav′ij) *v.*: destroy violently; ruin.

recede (ri·sēd′) *v.*: become more distant; move back; become less. —**receding** *v.* used as *adj.*

recoil (ri·koil′) *v.*: move backward, as in fear. —**recoiling** *v.* used as *adj.*

reconciliation (rek′ən·sil′ē·ā′shən) *n.*: friendly end to a quarrel.

refuge (ref′yo͞oj) *n.*: shelter; protection from danger or difficulty.

reiterate (rē·it′ə·rāt′) *v.*: repeat.

relentless (ri·lent′lis) *adj.*: not stopping; persistent; harsh.

reminisce (rem′ə·nis′) *v.*: think, talk, or write about one's memories. —**reminiscing** *v.*

remit (ri·mit′) *v.*: return payment.

remorse (ri·môrs′) *n.*: deep guilt.

renunciation (ri·nun′sē·ā′shən) *n.*: formal act of giving up something.

reprove (ri·pro͞ov′) *v.*: disapprove of.

resilient (ri·zil′yənt) *adj.*: able to return to its original shape quickly after being stretched or compressed; elastic.

resolve (ri·zälv′) *n.*: strength of purpose; determination.

restitution (res′tə·to͞o′shən) *n.*: compensation; repayment.

retort (ri·tôrt′) *v.*: reply sharply.

retribution (re′trə·byo͞o′shən) *n.*: punishment.

reunification (rē·yo͞o′nə·fi′kā′shən) *n.*: joining together of things that had been divided.

revelry (rev′əl·rē) *n.*: merrymaking; festivity.

revoke (ri·vōk′) *v.*: cancel; withdraw.

ruse (ro͞oz) *n.*: trick.

S

sacrilegious (sak′rə·lij′əs) *adj.*: disrespectful toward religion.

scourge (skʉrj) *n.*: cause of serious trouble or great suffering.

scrutiny (skro͞ot′'n·ē) *n.*: close inspection.

serene (sə·rēn′) *adj.*: peaceful; calm.

silhouette (sil′ə·wet′) *n.*: outline. —**silhouetted** *v.* used as *adj.*

singe (sinj) *v.*: slightly burn. —**singed** *v.* used as *adj.*

solace (säl′is) *n.*: comfort; easing of grief.

spectral (spek′trəl) *adj.*: ghostly; unreal.

spurn (spʉrn) *v.*: reject someone or something for being unworthy; scorn.

stellar (stel′ər) *adj.*: of or like a star.

stifle (stī′fəl) *v.*: smother. —**stifled** *v.* used as *adj.*

stupor (sto͞o′pər) *n.*: dull, half-conscious state.

subliminal (sub·lim′ə·nəl) *adj.*: below the level of awareness.

succession (sək·sesh′ən) *n.*: series.

succor (suk′ər) *n.*: help given to someone in distress; relief.

suffuse (sə·fyo͞oz′) *v.*: spread over or through.

sulk (sulk) *v.*: show resentment and ill-humor.

sullen (sul′ən) *adj.*: resentful; gloomy. —**sullenly** *adv.*

superficial (so͞o′pər·fish′əl) *adj.*: not deep or thorough; shallow.

supplication (sup′lə·kā′shən) *n.*: humble plea or request.
surmount (sər·mount′) *v.*: overcome.
sustain (sə·stān′) *v.*: support; nourish.

T

terrestrial (tə·res′trē·əl) *adj.*: earthly; of this world.
tolerance (täl′ər·əns) *n.*: respect for others who differ from you; freedom from prejudice.
torrent (tôr′ənt) *n.*: flood; downpour.
transmit (trans·mit′) *v.*: pass on.
tremulous (trem′yoo·ləs) *adj.*: trembling; shaking.
truculent (truk′yoo·lənt) *adj.*: fierce.
tumult (too′mult) *n.*: commotion; uproar; confusion.

U

unconscious (un·kän′shəs) *adj.*: not awake and alert.
undaunted (un·dôn′tid) *adj.*: not discouraged by a difficulty or setback.
undulate (un′jə·lāt′) *v.*: move in waves.
  —**undulating** *v.* used as *adj.*
unrelenting (un·ri·len′tiŋ) *adj.*: not letting up or weakening.
unruffled (un·ruf′əld) *adj.*: calm; not disturbed.

V

vanquish (vaŋ′kwish) *v.*: defeat.
vehemence (vē′ə·məns) *n.*: strong feeling or passion.
vexation (vek·sā′shən) *n.*: disturbance; distress.
vigilant (vij′ə·lənt) *adj.*: watchful.
virtuous (vur′choo·əs) *adj.*: good and moral; honorable.
vitalize (vīt′′l·īz) *v.*: give life to; energize.
volatile (väl′ə·təl) *adj.*: explosive; likely to change rapidly.
vulnerable (vul′nər·ə·bəl) *adj.*: affected by a specific influence.

at, āte, cär; ten, ēve; is, īce; gō, hôrn, look, tool; oil, out; up, fur; ə *for unstressed vowels, as* a *in* ago, u *in* focus; ′ *as in* Latin (lat′′n); chin; she; thin; *the*; zh *as in* azure (azh′ər); ŋ *as in* ring (riŋ)

Spanish Glossary

A

abhor/aborrecer *v.* despreciar; odiar algo en particular.

abolish/abolir *v.* suprimir; eliminar.

abominable/abominable *adj.* espantoso; detestable; horrible.

absorb/absorber *v.* amortiguar; *s.* absorbencia.

acclaim/ovación *v.* aclamar (a un ministro, por ejemplo); ovacionar; aplaudir.

acquiesce/consentir *v.* asentir en; conformarse con; aceptar; acatar.

admonish/amonestar *v.* reprender; advertir; aconsejar.

admonition/amonestación *s.* advertencia; consejo severo; reprensión.

adorn/adornar *v.* embellecer; decorar.

adulation/adulación *s.* alabanza; elogio; aplauso; admiración intensa o excesiva.

adversary/adversario *s.* enemigo; contrincante; antagonista.

adversity/adversidad *s.* infortunio; desgracia; desventura; revés.

advocate/defender *v.* abogar por; recomendar; preconizar.

advocate/defensor *s.* abogado de una causa; *adj.* partidario.

affluent/próspero, a *adj.* acaudalado; rico; opulento.

aghast/espantado, da *adj.* horrorizado; pasmado.

agile/ágil *adj.* ligero; alerta; veloz; que se desplaza con agilidad o ágilmente.

allegiance/lealtad *s.* devoción; sumisión.

aloof/reservado, da *adj.* guardado; cauto; desconfiado.

annihilate/aniquilar *v.* destruir; exterminar.

ardor/ardor *s.* emoción intensa; pasión; entusiasmo.

arid/árido, da *adj.* seco; estéril; improductivo.

ascetic/ascético *adj.* austero; sobrio; disciplinado.

ascribe/atribuir *v.* imputar; hacer cargo.

aspire/aspirar *v.* ambicionar; desear.

　　—**aspiring/ambicioso** *adj.* en potencia.

astronomer/astrónomo *s.* científico que estudia las estrellas y los planetas.

austere/austero *adj.* severo; muy sencillo; puritano.

avail/servir *v.* sacar partido de; valerse de; utilizar.

avert/evitar *v.* alejar; apartar.

awry/descarriado *adj./v.* torcido; salir mal, errado.

B

balmy/agradable *adj.* suave; balsámico; fragrante.

beckon/hacer señas *v.* atraer; llamar la atención; indicar que alguien se acerque.

beguile/seducir *v.* engañar.

beleaguer/sitiar *v.* asediar; cercar.

belligerent/agresivo *adj.* beligerante; combativo.

bigotry/intolerancia *s.* fanatismo; intransigencia; prejuicio intenso hacia un grupo particular de personas.

blight/arruinar *v.* destruir; destrozar; marchitar.

bureaucratic/burocrático *adj.* administrativo; moroso.

C

candor/sinceridad *s.* franqueza; imparcialidad; candidez; ingenuidad.

carnage/matanza *s.* carnicería; hecatombe; destrucción.

cascade/cascada *s.* salto de agua; chorro; torrente.

catastrophic/catastrófico *adj.* calamitoso; trágico, funesto.

chronic/crónico *adj.* empedernido; inexorable, frecuente, asiduo.

clarity/claridad *s.* sinceridad; sencillez; llaneza.

clench/apretar *v.* presionar; remachar un clavo.

coerce/coercer *v.* forzar; obligar.

compulsory/obligatorio *adj.* requerido por una regla o por la ley; forzoso.

conceivable/concebible *adj.* imaginable; que puede ser concebido o comprendido.

condolence/condolencia *s.* acompañar en el sentimiento; dar el pésame por.

condone/condonar v. perdonar; permitir que continúe (una ofensa, por ejemplo).

connoisseurship/pericia s. conocimiento experto, conocedor.

conscientious/concienzudo adj. esmerado; escrupuloso. —**conscientiously/escrupulosamente** adv. en forma esmerada y cuidadosa.

conspicuous/visible adj. obvio; llamativo; notable; patente; que llama la atención.

conspiracy/conspiración s. plan secreto y que suele ser ilegal llevado a cabo por un grupo.

constitute/constituir v. realizar; formar; nombrar a un puesto.

contrition/contrición s. sentimientos de culpabilidad; arrepentimiento.

controversial/polémico adj. que lleva a desacuerdos entre grupos con opiniones contrarias; controvertible.

conviction/convicción s. certidumbre; también condena; sentencia.

covet/codiciar v. ansiar; anhelar; desear con fuerte anhelo. —**coveted/codiciado** v. usado como; adj. codiciable; algo deseado.

D

decrepit/decrépito adj. vetusto; ruinoso.

default/negligencia s. omisión; falta; ausencia.

defer/diferir v. aplazar; delegar; también someter.

defiant/provocativo adj. provocador; desafiante; tono de voz retador.

deficient/deficiente adj. atrasado; que carece de.

deliberation/deliberación s. discusión; lentitud; pensar bien antes de tomar una decisión.

delirious/delirante adj. inmoderado; extravagante; que siente confusión o alucina debido a un accidente o una fiebre elevada.

delirium/delirio s. disturbio mental intenso que suele conllevar alucinaciones.

demise/fallecimiento s. cesión de bienes; transmisión de soberanía.

denounce/denunciar v. realizar una acusación pública; condenar.

depreciate/depreciar v. disminuir el valor de; menospreciar.

depression/depresión s. crisis económica; abatimiento.

designate/designar v. nombrar alguien para un puesto; señalar; denominar.

desolating/desolador adj. triste; que produce congoja o desamparo.

despondent/desanimado adj. sin esperanza; abatido.

devious/sinuoso adj. torcido; artificioso; disimulado.

dilapidated/derruido adj. desvencijado; muy estropeado; en malas condiciones.

dilemma/dilema s. decisión difícil; problema grave; conflicto.

dire/terrible adj. espantoso; horrible; medida extrema o necesidad urgente.

disarming/seductor adj. que desarma.

disconsolate/desconsolado adj. que causa tristeza o depresión; afligido; dolorido.

discreet/discreto adj. que demuestra circunspección; prudente en sus decisiones y acciones; silencioso o precavido.

disdainful/desdeñoso adj. despectivo; indiferente; altivo.

disposition/disposición s. carácter; temperamento; propensión, también disposición o determinación testamentaria.

distracted/distraído adj. que no se puede concentrar.

distraught/turbado adj. azorado; desconcertado; que sufre una gran preocupación.

divergent/divergente adj. separado; que sigue direcciones separadas.

diverting/divertido adj. que entretiene o divierte.

doggedness/tenacidad s. persistencia; obstinación.

E

eclipse/eclipsar v. deslucir; oscurecer; privar.

elation/júbilo s. gran alegría; regocijo; deleite.

elect/elegir v. optar; votar.

emaciated/demacrado adj. extremadamente delgado; consumido.

embody/encarnar v. personificar; representar; figurar.

emulate/emular v. seguir el ejemplo de; imitar; copiar.

endeavor/esfuerzo s. intento serio; empeño; tentativa.

enduring/duradero adj. perdurable; resistente; paciente.

enthrall/cautivar v. fascinar; hechizar; encantar.

enunciate/enunciar v. formular un principio; articular sonidos; pronunciar; proclamar.

equitable/justo adj. equitativo; imparcial; ecuánime.

eradicate/erradicar v. desarraigar plantas; extirpar una mala costumbre; eliminar; arrancar.

esteem/estima *s.* aprecio; consideración.

exasperation/exasperación *s.* irritación; agitación; inquietud.

exhilarate/alegrar *v.* animar; levantar el ánimo; regocijar.

exorbitant/exorbitante *adj.* desorbitado; desmesurado; excesivo.

expendable/prescindible *adj.* innecesario; gastable; que se puede sacrificar por una causa.

expire/expirar *v.* morir; fallecer; caducar; espirar aire.

exuberant/exuberante *adj.* pródigo; excesivo; intenso; abundante.

F

fanatic/fanático *adj./s.* entusiasta; extremista; persona cuya pasión por una causa puede ser excesiva o irrazonable.

fervent/ardiente *adj.* ferviente; vehemente; apasionado.

formidable/formidable *adj.* tremendo; terrible; impresionante; que inspira la admiración de otros; que causa pavor.

futile/vano *adj.* inútil; frívolo; pueril.

G

genial/simpático *adj.* afable; cordial.

giddy/mareado *adj.* vertiginoso; atolondrado; frívolo.

glower/mirar con ira *v.* fijar una mirada furiosa.

gurgle/borbotear *v.* gorjear.

H

hoist/izar *v.* levantar algo pesado; subir una mercancía a un barco.

hover/flotar en el aire *v.* un helicóptero que se cierna; una mariposa que revolotea; rondar alrededor de alguien; esbozar una sonrisa.

hyperactive/hiperactivo *adj.* excesivamente activo; inquieto; revuelto.

I

idle/ocioso *adj.* perezoso, sin objetivo ni meta; desocupado; temor infundado; conversación frívola; capital improductivo; máquina parada.

ignorance/ignorancia *s.* falta de conocimientos; desconocimiento; no saber.

imminent/inminente *adj.* perentorio; urgente; imperioso; cercano

immolation/inmolación *s.* sacrificio; expiación; destrucción.

immortal/inmortal *adj.* que vive para siempre; eterno; indestructible.

impartial/imparcial *adj.* justo; sin prejuicios; razonable.

impend/cernerse *v.* a punto de ocurrir; pender; amenazar.

implication/implicación *s.* conexión o consecuencia posible; complicidad; repercusión.

impose/imponer *v.* instituir condiciones; engañar; aprovecharse de; abusar de.

imposing/imponente *adj.* de apariencia grande e impresionante; grandioso; inmenso.

impoverish/empobrecer *v.* agotar; arruinar; extenuar.

imprudent/imprudente *adj.* irreflexivo; precipitado.

impulse/impulso *s.* deseo repentino; estímulo.

impunity/impunidad *s.* exención; perdón.

inaugurate/inaugurar *v.* introducir; dar posesión de un cargo; descubrir una estatua; abrir.

incantation/conjuro *s.* evocación; sortilegio; hechizo; conjunto de palabras o frases que deben producir un resultado mágico.

incessant/incesante *adj.* constante; continuo; perpetuo.

incite/incitar *v.* fomentar; estimular; provocar; atizar.

inconsolable/inconsolable *v.* desconsolado; apenado; desesperado.

incredulous/incrédulo *adj.* descreído; desconfiado; receloso.

indiscriminate/indistinto *adj.* sin criterio; confuso; indeterminado.

inevitable/inevitable *adj.* necesario; irremediable; fijo.

infallibility/infalibilidad *s.* acierto; perspicacia; agudeza.

infatuated/encaprichado *adj.* persistir por una idea; estar locamente enamorado de una persona.

insensible/insensible *adj.* inconsciente; inerte.

instigate/instigar *v.* llevar o incitar a una acción negativa; fomentar una insurrección.

intangible/intangible *adj.* que no se puede tocar; impalpable; inmaterial; tenue.

interminable/interminable *adj.* sin fin; imperecedero; eterno; perpetuo.

intimidate/intimidar *v.* acobardar; amedrentar; atemorizar; asustar.

intolerance/intolerancia *s.* prejuicio; hostilidad hacia otros grupos; intransigencia; sectarismo.

invariable/invariable *adj.* inmutable; inalterable; sin cambio. **–invariably/invariablemente** *adv.* eternamente; perpetuamente.

invincible/invencible *adj.* que no se puede conquistar; invulnerable; inmune.

iridescent/iridiscente *adj.* irisado; refulgente; parecido a un arco iris.

irrational/irracional *adj.* insensato; absurdo; que no se basa en la razón o la lógica.

L

labyrinthine/laberíntico *adj.* complicado; enredado; embrollado.

languor/languidez *s.* cansancio; fatiga; apatía.

lavish/prodigar *v.* regalar; dar generosamente; agraciar.

legislation/legislación *adj.* ley o conjunto de leyes; código.

linger/quedarse *v.* rezagarse; retrasarse; no querer marcharse.

litany/letanía *s.* discurso; oración o recitación repetitiva.

literal/literal *adj.* actual; en el sentido exacto de la palabra; prosaico. **–literally/literalmente** *adv.* al pie de la letra.

luminous/luminoso *adj.* radiante; resplandeciente; brillante.

lurk/esconderse *v.* estar al acecho; aguardar; rondar.

M

mainstay/fundamento *s.* razón; principio; cimiento.

malicious/malicioso *adj.* pícaro; pérfido; deseoso de hacer el mal.

malign/calumniar *v.* difamar; hablar mal de otro.

mar/estropear *v.* echar a perder; desfigurar; deformar.

marauder/merodeador *s.* delincuente; malandrín; maleante; persona furtiva.

meager/escaso *adj.* insuficiente; parco; pobre; mediocre; flaco.

menace/amenazar *v.* intimidar; inquietar; atemorizar. **–menacing/amenazador** *adj.* inquietante; retador.

mentorship/tutoría *s.* tutela; lecciones o consejos impartidos por un mentor, o persona sagaz.

misanthropic/misantrópico *adj.* sentir antipatía por los seres humanos.

monotony/monotonía *s.* invariabilidad; fastidio; repetición.

mundane/mundano *adj.* frívolo; común; vano.

N

negotiation/negociación *s.* gestión; transacción; contrato; discusión con el fin de llegar a un acuerdo.

nimble/ágil *adj.* vivo; ligero.

noncommittal/evasivo *adj.* ambiguo; precavido; que no compromete a nada.

O

obscure/oscurecer *v.* ocultar; disimular; esconder.

obsession/obsesión *s.* idea o deseo persistente que consume la atención; manía; capricho.

obstinate/obstinado *adj.* terco.

obstruction/obstrucción *s.* dificultad; obstáculo; barrera.

odyssey/odisea *s.* largo viaje en el que abundan las aventuras, los reveses y las peripecias; éxodo.

omen/presagio *s.* augurio; predicción; evento o cosa capaz de predecir un futuro acontecimiento.

ominous/siniestro *adj.* inquietante; adverso.

optimist/optimista *adj.* alegre; confiado; que mantiene vivas las esperanzas.

P

pandemonium/caos *s.* gran confusión; anarquía; jaleo.

paradox/paradoja *s.* concepto que parece disponer de características contradictorias; incongruencia; contrasentido.

paraphernalia/equipo *s.* avíos; trastos; equipaje.

pauper/pobre *s.* persona indigente, mendiga.

perennial/eterno *adj.* continuo; perenne.

phenomenon/fenómeno *s.* entidad o evento extraordinario; prodigio.

pious/piadoso *adj.* devoto; religioso; practicante; creyente.

placid/plácido adj. apacible; tranquilo; sosegado.

pliant/flexible adj. elástico; maleable; tolerante.

poignant/conmovedor adj. patético; triste; melancólico; dolor agudo; mordaz.

polytheism/politeísmo s. fe en más de un solo Dios; paganismo.

portent/presagio s. augurio; predicción; profecía; presentimiento.

precarious/precario adj. inestable; inseguro.

precipitous/empinado adj. inclinado; precipitado; pronunciado.

preclude/impedir v. imposibilitar; evitar; excluir; frenar; descartar.

primal/primitivo adj. original; primordial; fundamental.

primeval/prístino adj. inicial; intacto.

privation/privación s. estrechez; miseria; carencia de lo necesario para una vida feliz.

procure/proporcionar v. obtener; conseguir; lograr.

profusion/profusión s. abundancia; prodigalidad; exuberancia; plétora.

prolong/prolongar v. extender; amplificar.

prosaic/prosaico adj. pedestre; ordinario.

protracted/prolongado adj. extendido; amplificado.

protrude/sobresalir v. resaltar; despuntar; predominar.

putrid/podrido adj. que ofende los sentidos; putrefacto; depravado; repugnante.

R

radical/radical adj. fundamental; extremado; soberano.

rampart/muralla s. muralla de un castillo; defensa; cerca.

rancor/rencor s. odio; resentimiento; aversión.

ransack/saquear v. registrar; despojar; rastrear.

ravage/destrozar v. asolar; desfigurar; causar estragos; arrasar.

recede/retroceder v. retirarse; volverse atrás.

recoil/rechazar v. echarse atrás; retroceder; sentir repugnancia por; tener horror.

reconciliation/reconciliación s. conciliación; acuerdo amistoso.

refuge/refugio s. protección; amparo.

reiterate/reiterar v. repetir; insistir; confirmar.

relentless/implacable adj. sin cese; persistente; tenaz.

reminisce/recordar v. pensar en el pasado; evocar.

remit/remitir v. realizar un pago; enviar; expedir; facturar.

remorse/remordimiento s. culpabilidad profunda; contrición; arrepentimiento.

renunciation/renuncia s. dimisión; sacrificio.

reprove/censurar v. condenar; criticar; reprender.

resilient/resistente adj. elástico; que puede volver rápidamente a su forma original.

resolve/resolución s. decisión; propósito; valor.

restitution/restitución s. indemnización; compensación; pago.

retort/réplica s. argumento; objeción.

retribution/castigo s. sanción; pena; venganza.

reunification/reunificación s. unificar lo que se hallaba dividido; reunir; concentrar.

revelry/regocijo s. jolgorio; celebración; fiesta.

revoke/revocar v. cancelar; anular; disolver.

ruse/ardid s. astucia; treta.

S

sacrilegious/sacrílego adj. que no respeta la religión; impío; profano.

scourge/plaga s. castigo divino; gran sufrimiento; calamidad.

scrutiny/escrutinio s. inspección o examinación detallada; investigación.

serene/sereno adj. suave; sosegado; tranquilo.

silhouette/silueta s. contorno; perfil; trazo.

singe/chamuscar v. tostar; quemar ligeramente.

solace/consuelo s. alivio; desahogo.

spectral/espectral adj. fantasmagórico; ilusorio.

spurn/despreciar v. rechazar; menospreciar; desfavorecer; desdeñar.

stellar/estelar adj. que trata de las estrellas; papel principal.

stifle/sofocar v. ahogar; oprimir.

stupor/estupor s. insensibilidad; letargo.

subliminal/subconsciente adj. inconsciente; mecánico; instintivo.

succession/sucesión s. serie; continuación; proceso; descendencia.

succor/socorro s. ayuda; sosiego; auxilio; refuerzo.

suffuse/cubrir v. bañar una sala de luz; inundar; difundirse.

sulk/enfurruñarse v. poner mala cara; resentir.

sullen/hosco adj. ceñudo; resentido; huraño; arisco.

superficial/superficial adj. frívolo; que solamente toca la superficie; somero.

supplication/súplica *s.* ruego; demanda humilde; solicitud.

surmount/superar *v.* prevalecer; adelantar; sobrepasar.

sustain/mantener *v.* sostener; conservar; alimentar; nutrir.

T

terrestrial/terrestre *adj.* terrenal; material; físico.

tolerance/tolerancia *s.* respeto por la opinión de los demás; falta de prejuicios; paciencia.

torrent/torrente *s.* arroyo; cascada; llover a cántaros; tumulto.

transmit/transmitir *v.* ceder; traspasar; entregar.

tremulous/trémulo *adj.* tembloroso; estremecido; palpitante.

truculent/feroz *adj.* salvaje; cruel; agresivo.

tumult/tumulto *s.* conmoción; disturbio; alboroto; confusión.

U

unconscious/inconsciente *adj.* sin conocimiento; desvanecido.

undaunted/intrépido *adj.* impávido; que no se deja desalentar o no se descorazona ante dificultades; valeroso; enérgico.

undulate/ondular *v.* hacer ondear; rizar; encrespar.

unrelenting/implacable *adj.* riguroso; que no cede.

unruffled/sereno *adj.* tranquilo; imperturbable; firme; liso.

V

vanquish/vencer *v.* conquistar; dominar sus sentimientos; rendir; imponerse.

vehemence/vehemencia *s.* violencia; fuerte sentimiento o pasión; elocuencia; convicción.

vexation/fastidio *s.* molestia; disturbio; disgusto.

vigilant/vigilante *adj.* alerta; precavido; cuidadoso.

virtuous/virtuoso *adj.* bueno y moral; honorable; honrado.

vitalize/vitalizar *v.* vivificar; animar; rejuvenecer; robustecer.

volatile/volátil *adj.* voluble; inconstante; inestable; explosivo.

vulnerable/vulnerable *adj.* fácil de impresionar; afectado por una influencia particular; sensible; frágil.

Acknowledgments

Da Capo Press, a member of Perseus Books, L.L.C.: "Prologue: How to Eat a Guava" from *When I Was Puerto Rican* by Esmeralda Santiago. Copyright © 1993 by Esmeralda Santiago.

Gary N. Da Silva: *Visitor from Forest Hills* from *Plaza Suite* by Neil Simon. Copyright © 1969 and renewed © 1997 by Neil Simon. CAUTION: Professionals and amateurs are hereby warned that PLAZA SUITE is fully protected under the Berne Convention and the Universal Copyright Convention and is subject to royalty. All rights, including without limitation professional, amateur, motion picture, television, radio, recitation, lecturing, public reading and foreign translation rights, computer media rights and the right of reproduction, and electronic storage or retrieval, in whole or in part and in any form, are strictly reserved and none of these rights can be exercised or used without written permission from the copyright owner. Inquiries for stock and amateur performances should be addressed to Samuel French, Inc., 45 West 25th Street, New York, NY 10010. All other inquiries should be addressed to Gary N. Da Silva, 111 N. Sepulveda Blvd., Suite 250, Manhattan Beach, CA 90266-6850.

Dell Publishing, a division of Random House, Inc.: "Harrison Bergeron" from *Welcome to the Monkey House* by Kurt Vonnegut, Jr. Copyright © 1961 by Kurt Vonnegut, Jr.

Doubleday, a division of Random House, Inc.: Quote by Bill Moyers from *The Power of Myth* by Joseph Campbell and Bill Moyers. Copyright © 1988 by Apostrophe S Productions, Inc., and Bill Moyers and Alfred Van der Marck Editions, Inc. for itself and the estate of Joseph Campbell. "The Road Block" ("Get out of my road") by Miura Chora from *An Introduction to Haiku* by Harold G. Henderson. Copyright © 1958 by Harold G. Henderson.

Dunham Literary as agents for Wendi Kaufman: Adapted from "Helen on 86th Street" by Wendi Kaufman from *The New Yorker*, November 24, 1997. Copyright © 1997 by Wendi Kaufman. Author's comment on "Helen on 86th Street" by Wendi Kaufman. Copyright © 2000 by Wendi Kaufman.

Dutton, a division of Penguin Group (USA) Inc. and electronic format by permission of **International Creative Management, Inc.:** "Can Animals Think?" edited and adapted from *The Parrot's Lament* by Eugene Linden. Copyright © 1999 by Eugene Linden. Originally published in *Time*, 1999.

Anita Endrezze: "The Girl Who Loved the Sky" from *At the Helm of Twilight* by Anita Endrezze. Copyright © 1988 by Anita Endrezze. Published by Broken Moon Press, 1992.

Mari Evans: "If There Be Sorrow" from *I Am a Black Woman* by Mari Evans. Copyright © 1970 by Mari Evans. Published by William Morrow & Co.

The Feminist Press at The City University of New York, www.feministpress.org: "To Da-Duh, In Memoriam" from *Reena and Other Stories* by Paule Marshall. Copyright © 1983 by Paule Marshall.

Benedict R. C. Fitzgerald: From "Book 1: A Goddess Intervenes," from "Book 5: Sweet Nymph and Open Sea," from "Book 9: New Coasts and Poseidon's Son," from "Book 10: The Grace of the Witch," from "Book 11: A Gathering of Shades," from "Book 12: Sea Perils and Defeat," from "Book 16: Father and Son," from "Book 17: The Beggar at the Manor," from "Book 21: The Test of the Bow," from "Book 22: Death in the Great Hall," and from "Book 23: The Trunk of the Olive Tree" from *The Odyssey* by Homer, translated by Robert Fitzgerald. Copyright © 1961, 1963 by Robert Fitzgerald; copyright renewed © 1989 by Benedict R. C. Fitzgerald, on behalf of the Fitzgerald children.

Florida Classics Library: From *The Everglades: River of Grass* by Marjory Stoneman Douglas. Copyright 1947 by Marjory Stoneman Douglas.

Frances Goldin Literary Agency: "American Hero" from *Ceremonies: Prose and Poetry* by Essex Hemphill. Copyright © 1992 by Essex Hemphill.

GRM Associates, Inc., representing the Ann Elmo Agency: From *Children and the Death of a President: Multi-Disciplinary Studies,* edited by Martha Wolfenstein and Gilbert Kliman. Copyright © 1965 by Gilbert Kliman and Martha Wolfenstein.

Harcourt, Inc.: Definition #15, #25 and #36 from "Tentative (First Model) Definitions of Poetry" from *Good Morning, America* by Carl Sandburg. Copyright 1928 and renewed © 1956 by Carl Sandburg. "Boy at the Window" and excerpt from *Things of This World* by Richard Wilbur. Copyright 1952 and renewed © 1980 by Richard Wilbur.

Harcourt, Inc. and electronic format by permission of **The Wendy Weil Agency, Inc.:** "Women" from *Revolutionary Petunias & Other Poems* by Alice Walker. Copyright © 1970 and renewed © 1998 by Alice Walker.

Harcourt, Inc. and electronic format by permission of **The Wylie Agency, Inc.:** "The Happy Man's Shirt" from *Italian Folktales, Selected and Retold by Italo Calvino,* translated by George Martin. Copyright © 1956 by Giulio Einaudi editore, s.p.a.; English translation copyright © 1980 by Harcourt, Inc.

HarperCollins Publishers, Inc.: "The World Is Not a Pleasant Place to Be" from *My House* by Nikki Giovanni. Copyright © 1972 by Nikki Giovanni. "The Cyclops in the Ocean" from *Those Who Ride the Night Winds* by Nikki Giovanni. Copyright © 1983 by Nikki Giovanni. "Initiation" from *Johnny Panic and the Bible of Dreams* by Sylvia Plath. Copyright © 1952, 1953, 1954, 1955, 1956, 1957, 1960, 1961, 1962, 1963 by Sylvia Plath. Copyright © 1977, 1979 by Ted Hughes. From *Edgar A. Poe: Mournful and Never-Ending Remembrance* by Kenneth Silverman. Copyright © 1991 by Kenneth Silverman.

Joy Harris Literary Agency: "The Sea Call" from *The Odyssey: A Modern Sequel* by Nikos Kazantzakis, translated by Kimon Friar. Copyright © 1958 by Helen Kazantzakis and Kimon Friar; copyright renewed © 1986 by Simon & Schuster.

The Albert Einstein Archives, the Hebrew University of Jerusalem, Israel: From *Einstein on Peace,* edited by Otto Nathan and Heinz Norden. Copyright © 1960 by Otto Nathan.

David Higham Associates Limited and Estate of Roald Dahl: From "Survival" from *Going Solo* by Roald Dahl. Copyright © 1986 by Roald Dahl. "Beware of the Dog" (slightly abridged) from *Over to You: Ten Stories of Flyers and Flying* by Roald Dahl. Copyright © 1945 by Roald Dahl. Published by Penguin Inc. "Poison" from *Someone Like You* by Roald Dahl. Copyright 1950 by Roald Dahl. Published by Alfred A. Knopf, a division of Random House, Inc.

Hill and Wang, a division of Farrar, Straus and Giroux, LLC: "Thank You, M'am" from *Short Stories* by Langston Hughes. Copyright © 1996 by Ramona Bass and Arnold Rampersad. All rights reserved.

Henry Holt and Company, LLC: "The Chicken" by Linda Elegant from *I Thought My Father Was God: And Other True Tales From NPR's National Story Project,* edited and introduced by Paul Auster. Copyright © 2001 by Henry Holt and Company, LLC. "Dust of Snow," "Fire and Ice," and "Once by the Pacific" from *The Poetry of Robert Frost,* edited by Edward Connery Lathem. Copyright 1951, © 1956 by Robert Frost; copyright 1923, 1928, © 1969 by Henry Holt and Company.

Henry Holt and Company, LLC: From pages 158–165 from *Cyrano de Bergerac* by Edmond Rostand, translated by Brian Hooker. Copyright 1923 by Henry Holt and Company, LLC.

Houghton Mifflin Company: "The Fenris Wolf" from *Legends of the North* by Olivia E. Coolidge. Copyright © 1951 and renewed © 1979 by Olivia E. Coolidge. All rights reserved. Adapted and reprinted from *One Belfast Boy* by Patricia McMahon. Copyright © 1999 by Patricia McMahon. All rights reserved.

James R. Hurst: "The Scarlet Ibis" by James R. Hurst from *The Atlantic Monthly,* July 1960. Copyright © 1960 by The Atlantic Monthly.

Sharon Ingram: From the diary of Sharon Ingram from *Children of "The Troubles": Our Lives in the Crossfire of Northern Ireland* by Laurel Holliday. Copyright © 1997 by Sharon Ingram. Published by Pocket Books, a division of Simon & Schuster, New York, 1997.

Stephen King: Adapted from "Eyeglasses for the Mind," an interview with Stephen King, by George Christian from *Houston Chronicle*, September 30, 1979. Copyright © 1979 by Houston Chronicle.

Alfred A. Knopf, a division of Random House, Inc.: From *Jurassic Park* by Michael Crichton. Copyright © 1990 by Michael Crichton.

Alfred A. Knopf, a division of Random House, Inc. and electronic format by permission of **Harold Ober Associates Incorporated:** "Mother to Son" from *The Collected Poems of Langston Hughes.* Copyright © 1994 by The Estate of Langston Hughes.

Juliet S. Kono: "Internment" from *Hilo Rains* by Juliet S. Kono. Copyright © 1988 by Juliet S. Kono.

Jean Fong Kwok: "Disguises" by Jean Fong Kwok from *Story*, 1997. Copyright © 1997 by Jean Fong Kwok.

Li-Young Lee: Untitled essay by Li-Young Lee from *Chinese American Poetry: An Anthology*, edited by L. Ling-chi Wang and Henry Yiheng Zhao. Copyright © 1991 by Li-Young Lee.

Peter H. Lee: "Cranes" by Hwang Sun-won from *Flowers of Fire: Twentieth Century Korean Stories*, edited by Peter H. Lee. Copyright © 1974 by Peter H. Lee.

Little, Brown and Company, Inc. and electronic format by permission of **Alice R. Abbott:** From "Mythology of the Norsemen" from *Mythology* by Edith Hamilton. Copyright © 1942 by Edith Hamilton; copyright renewed © 1969 by Dorian Fielding Reid and Doris Fielding Reid.

Liveright Publishing Corporation: "in Just-" from *Complete Poems: 1904-1962* by E. E. Cummings, edited by George J. Firmage. Copyright 1923, 1951, © 1991 by the Trustees for the E. E. Cummings Trust; copyright © 1976 by George James Firmage. From "A Poet's Advice to Students" from *A Miscellany Revised* by E. E. Cummings, edited by George J. Firmage. Copyright © 1955, 1965 by the Trustees for the E. E. Cummings Trust; copyright © 1958, 1965 by George J. Firmage. "Those Winter Sundays" from *Collected Poems of Robert Hayden*, edited by Frederick Glaysher. Copyright © 1966 by Robert Hayden.

The Literary Trustees of Walter de la Mare and the Society of Authors as their representative: From "Silver" from *The Complete Poems of Walter de la Mare*. Published in the United States in 1970.

Margaret McCrory: "Internment" by Margaret McCrory from *Children of "The Troubles": Our Lives in the Crossfire of Northern Ireland* by Laurel Holliday. Copyright © 1997 by Margaret McCrory. Published by Pocket Books, a division of Simon & Schuster, New York, 1997.

George J. Mitchell c/o Verner, Liipferd, et al.: From "Peace Isn't Impossible" by George J. Mitchell from *Newsweek*, June 30, 1997, page 23. Copyright © 1997 by George J. Mitchell.

New Directions Publishing Corp.: "Your Laughter" from *The Captain's Verses* by Pablo Neruda. Copyright © 1972 by Pablo Neruda and Donald D. Walsh.

The New York Times Company: From "In America; Romeo and Juliet in Bosnia" by Bob Herbert from *The New York Times*, May 8, 1994. Copyright © 1994 by The New York Times Company. From "Sunday View; Perfectly Tuned Actors Hit a High Note" by Margo Jefferson from "Arts & Leisure" from *The New York Times*, April 23, 1995. Copyright © 1995 by The New York Times Company. "Rising Tides" by Bob Herbert from *The New York Times*, February 22, 2001. Copyright © 2001 by The New York Times Company.

The New York Times Syndication Sales: "Heroes with Solid Feet" by Kirk Douglas from *The New York Times*, April 23, 2001. Copyright © 2001 by The New York Times. "An American Story" by Anthony Lewis from *The New York Times*, November 26, 1993. Copyright © 1993 by The New York Times.

Naomi Shihab Nye: "Daily" from *Hugging the Jukebox* by Naomi Shihab Nye. Copyright © 1982 by Naomi Shihab Nye.

Harold Ober Associates Incorporated: "The Old Demon" by Pearl S. Buck from *Cosmopolitan*, February 1939. Copyright 1939 and renewed © 1966 by Pearl S. Buck.

The Orange County Register: From "Ex-Refugee Is Nominated for Justice Post" by Dena Bunis and Anh Do from *The Orange County Register*, Thursday, May 10, 2001. Copyright © 2001 by The Orange County Register.

Pantheon Books, a division of Random House, Inc.: "The Trapper Trapped" from *African Folktales* by Roger D. Abrahams. Copyright © 1983 by Roger D. Abrahams.

Paramount Pictures: From *Barefoot in the Park* by Neil Simon. Copyright © 1964, 2002 by Paramount Pictures. All rights reserved.

Pearson Education, Inc.: From *Three Genres: The Writing of Poetry, Fiction and Drama*, Seventh Edition, by Stephen Minot. Copyright © 2002 by Prentice Hall, Inc.

People Weekly: From "Feeding Frenzy" by Peter Ames Carlin and Don Sider from *People*, June 2, 1997. Copyright © 1997 by Time, Inc. All rights reserved.

The Peters Fraser & Dunlop Group Limited (www.pfd.co.uk) on behalf of the Estate of Liam O'Flaherty: "The Sniper" from *Spring Sowing* by Liam O'Flaherty. Copyright © 1924 by the Estate of Liam O'Flaherty.

Burton R. Pollin: "If Only Poe Had Succeeded When He Said Nevermore to Drink" by Burton R. Pollin from *The New York Times*, Editorial Desk, September 23, 1996. Copyright © 1996 by Burton R. Pollin.

Aaron M. Priest Literary Agency, Inc.: "Full Circle" by Sue Grafton from *A Woman's Eye*, edited by Sara Paretsky.

Princeton University Press: "Ithaka" from *Collected Poems* by C. P. Cavafy, translated by Edmund Keeley and Philip Sherrard. Copyright © 1992 by Princeton University Press.

Random House, Inc.: "Woman Work" from *And Still I Rise* by Maya Angelou. Copyright © 1978 by Maya Angelou. From *On the Pulse of Morning* by Maya Angelou. Copyright © 1993 by Maya Angelou. From "Blues Ain't No Mockin Bird" from *Gorilla, My Love* by Toni Cade Bambara. Copyright © 1971 by Toni Cade Bambara.

Random House, Inc. and electronic format by permission of **The Truman Capote Literary Trust, Alan U. Schwartz, Trustee:** *A Christmas Memory* by Truman Capote. Copyright © 1956 by Truman Capote.

Pierre Salinger: From Foreword by Pierre Salinger from *Where Were You When President Kennedy Was Shot? Memories and Tributes to a Slain President as Told to Dear Abby*. Foreword copyright © 1993 by Pierre Salinger.

Scholastic, Inc.: From Afterword from *Heroes & Monsters of Greek Mythology* by Bernard Evslin et al. Copyright © 1967 by Scholastic, Inc. All rights reserved.

Meredith Anne Schwartz: "Penelope to Ulysses" by Meredith Schwartz from *Dead Center Literary Magazine*, 1992. Copyright © 1992 by Meredith Anne Schwartz. Published by Highland Park High School, Highland Park, New Jersey.

Science@NASA: From "Far-out Housekeeping on the ISS" by Ron Koczor from *Science@NASA* Web site, at http://science.nasa.gov/headlines/y2000/ast29nov_1.htm. Copyright © 2000 by NASA.

Scovil, Chichak, & Galen: "Dog Star" from *The Nine Billion Names of God: The Best Short Stories of Arthur C. Clarke*. Copyright © 1962 by Galaxy Publishing Corporation.

Scribner, an imprint of Simon & Schuster Adult Publishing Group: "Old Man at the Bridge" from *The Short Stories of Ernest Hemingway*. Copyright 1938 by Ernest Hemingway; copyright renewed © 1966 by Mary Hemingway.

Scribner, an imprint of Simon & Schuster Adult Publishing Group and electronic format by permission of **June Coffin:** "Forgive My Guilt" from *Selected Poems of Robert P. Tristram Coffin*. Copyright 1939 by The Macmillan Company; copyright renewed © 1967 by Margaret Coffin Halvosa.

Scripps Howard Foundation: "Wounded and Trapped" by Ernie Pyle from Scripps Howard wire copy, August 22, 1944. Copyright © 1944 by Scripps Howard Foundation.

Simon & Schuster, Inc.: Excerpt (retitled "The History Behind the Ballad") from *Parting the Waters: America in the King Years, 1956–63* by Taylor Branch. Copyright © 1988 by Taylor Branch.

The Estate of William Stafford: "The Osage Orange Tree" by William Stafford. Copyright 1959 by William Stafford. Originally published in *The Oregon Centennial Anthology*, 1959.

Gloria Steinem: Quote by Alice Walker from "Do You Know This Woman? She Knows You: A Profile of Alice Walker" by Gloria Steinem from *Ms. Magazine*, June 1982. Copyright © 1982 by Ms. Foundation for Education and Communication, Inc.

Oliver Stone: "Where I Find My Heroes" by Oliver Stone from *McCall's Magazine*, November 1992. Copyright © 1992 by Oliver Stone.

Rosemary A. Thurber and The Barbara Hogenson Agency: "The Princess and the Tin Box" from *The Beast in Me and Other Animals* by James Thurber. Copyright © 1948 by James Thurber; copyright renewed © 1976 by Helen Thurber and Rosemary A. Thurber. All rights reserved.

Time Inc.: "Jackie Robinson" by Henry Aaron from *American Legends: From the Time 100*. Copyright © 2001 by Time Inc.

Tribune Media Services International, Inc.: "An Arctic Floe of Climate Questions" by Robert Cooke from *Newsday*, April 18, 2001. Copyright © 2001 by Newsday, Inc.

Charles E. Tuttle Co., Inc., Boston, MA and Tokyo, Japan: "The old pond" by Matsuo Bashō, "A morning glory" by Chiyo, and "A dragonfly!" by Kobayashi Issa from *Zen Art for Meditation* by Stewart W. Holmes and Chimoyo Horioka. Copyright in Japan © 1973 by Charles E. Tuttle Co., Inc. All rights reserved.

The University of Georgia Press: Slight adaptation of "American History" from *The Latin Deli: Prose and Poetry* by Judith Ortiz Cofer. Copyright © 1993 by Judith Ortiz Cofer.

The University of North Carolina Press: From "Ain't I a Woman?" by Sojourner Truth, adapted by Erlene Stetson, from *Sojourner Truth: God's Faithful Pilgrim* by Arthur Huff Fauset. Copyright © 1938 by The University of North Carolina Press.

University of Pittsburgh Press: "Starfish" from *Emplumada* by Lorna Dee Cervantes. Copyright © 1981 by Lorna Dee Cervantes.

University Press of New England: "The Grandfather" from *A Summer Life* by Gary Soto. Copyright © 1990 by University Press of New England.

Suzanne Vega: Lyrics from "Calypso" from *Solitude Standing* by Suzanne Vega. Copyright © 1978 by Suzanne Vega.

Viking Penguin, a division of Penguin Putnam Inc.: "I May, I Might, I Must" from *The Complete Poems of Marianne Moore*. Copyright © 1959 by Marianne Moore; copyright renewed © 1987 by Lawrence E. Brinn and Louise Crane, Executors of the Estate of Marianne Moore.

The Wall Street Journal: From "Juliet of Verona Gets a Lot of Letters from the Lovelorn" by Lisa Bannon from *The Wall Street Journal*, November 10, 1992. Copyright © 1992 by Dow Jones & Company, Inc. All rights reserved worldwide.

Weekly Reader Corporation: From "Community Service & You" by T. J. Saftner from *Career World*, September 1998. Copyright © 1998 by Weekly Reader Corporation. All rights reserved.

Wesleyan University Press: "The Base Stealer" from *The Orb Weaver* by Robert Francis. Copyright © 1960 by Robert Francis. "A Blessing" from *Collected Poems* by James Wright. Copyright © 1963, 1971 by James Wright.

Wiley Publishing, Inc.: Entry for "indulge" and pronunciation key from *Webster's New World™ College Dictionary, Fourth Edition*. Copyright © 1999, 2000 by Wiley Publishing, Inc. All rights reserved.

World Book, Inc.: From "John Fitzgerald Kennedy" by Eric Sevareid from *The World Book Encyclopedia*, vol. 11, pp. 266–268. Copyright © 2001 by World Book, Inc., www.worldbook.com.

Sources Cited

Quote by Brenda Platt from "Is recycling a waste?" by Mark Fearer from *Colorado's Holistic Journal* Web site, accessed January 31, 2002 at http://www.nexuspub.com/july97/recycle.htm.

Quote by Bridie Murphy from *Children of "The Troubles": Our Lives in the Crossfire of Northern Ireland* by Laurel Holliday. Published by Pocket Books, New York, 1997.

Quote by Truman Capote from "The Private World of Truman Capote" (Part 1), an interview by Anne Taylor Fleming, from *The New York Times Magazine*, July 9, 1978. Published by The New York Times Company, New York, NY, 1978.

From "What is a mummy?" from *Mummies, Myth and Magic in Ancient Egypt* by Christine El Mahdy. Published by Thames & Hudson Ltd., London, 1989.

Program Staff Credits: Kristen Azzara, Julie Beckman-Key, Tom Browne, Matt Bucher, Susan Cakars, Kimberly Cammerata, Melissa Ciano, Gail Coupland, Grant Davidson, Nina Degollado, Scott Deneroff, Christine Devall, Liz Dickson, Lydia Doty, Amy Fleming, Emily Force, Betty Gabriel, Jeff Galvez, Mikki Gibson, Guy Guidici, Leora Harris, Sally Hartin-Young, Anne Heausler, Sean Henry, Eric Higgerson, Julie Hill, Julie Hoover, Julia Hu, Liz Huckestein, Rodney Jester, Stephanie Jones, Dolores Keller, Marcia Kelley, Juliana Koenig, Karen Kolar, Jane Kominek, Cathy Kuhles, Elizabeth LaManna, Jamie Lane, Carolyn Logan, Belinda Lopez, Mary Malone, Kris Marshall, Carol Marunas, Pat McCambridge, Mark McDonald, Dick Metzger, Betty Mintz, Mary Monaco, Laura Mongello, Victoria Moreland, Cynthia Muñoz, Michael Neibergall, Steve Oelenberger, Karen Peterfreund, Marie Price, Jeff Raun, Amber Rigney, Mike Rinella, Kathryn Rogers, Beth Sample, Susan Sato, Annette Saunders, Peter Sawchuk, Kathleen Scheiner, Gloria Shahan, Mary Shaw, Dakota Smith, Emily R. Stern, Jeff Streber, Ralph Tachuk, Jennifer Tench, Carol Trammel, Lisa Vecchione, Katie Vignery, Ken Whiteside, Tamesa Williams, Evan Wilson, Sari Wilson, Richard Wright, Michael Zakhar, Sara Zettner

Picture Credits

Page A6: Courtesy Louis K. Meisel Gallery; **A7:** Demetrio Carrasco/Stone/Getty Images; **4:** Terra Foundation for American Art, Chicago/Art Resource, NY; **6–7:** Courtesy Galerie Thaddaeus Ropac, Paris; **11:** Photograph by Ellen Labenski, courtesy Pace Wildenstein, New York; **14:** © Bettmann/CORBIS; **17:** © John Lund/Stone; **23:** © Julio Larraz; **25:** National Gallery, London/ SuperStock; **27:** © Erich Lessing/Art Resource, NY; **33:** © John Lund/Stone; **35:** Brandt & Brandt Literary Agents, Inc.; **39:** © David Hosking/Photo Researchers, Inc.; **41:** © David E. Myers/Stone; **51:** AP Photo/Fiona Hanson; **52:** © Peter Beck/CORBIS/Stock Market; **56:** (top) STS-101 Crew/NASA; (bottom) NASA; **57:** STS-106 Crew/NASA; **65:** © Getty Images; **67:** Photo by: Kirk Eck; **73:** © Nancy Crampton; **77:** (top left) Cover from *The Hobbit.* Copyright © 1966 by J.R.R. Tolkien. Reprinted by permission of Houghton Mifflin Company, HarperCollins in Canada. All rights reserved; (top right) Cover art courtesy Paul Goble; (bottom left) Cover from *Apollo 13* by Jim Lovell and Jeffrey Kluger, reprinted by permission of Houghton Mifflin Company (Boston: Houghton Mifflin, 2000). All rights reserved; (bottom right) From *Woodsong* by Gary Paulsen, cover by Neil Waldman. Copyright © 1991 by Neil Waldman for cover illustration. Used by permission of Penguin Putnam, Inc.; **99:** © Royalty-Free/CORBIS; **102–103:** © Darren Winter/CORBIS; **105:** CNAC/MNAM/Dist. Réunion des Musées Nationaux/Art Resource, NY; **106:** © Gregory Pace/CORBIS/SYGMA; **113:** © Henri Cartier-Bresson/ Magnum Photos, Inc.; **119:** Mitsu Yasukawa/New York Daily News; **121:** © James A. Sugar/CORBIS; **123:** © Patty DiRienzo/Silver Image; **135:** Courtesy of Wendi Kaufman, care of Russell and Volkening; **149:** Charles S. Colier; **150:** Corel; **153:** (top left) *A Tree Grows in Brooklyn* by Betty Smith. HarperCollins Publishers; (top right) From *American Dragons: Twenty Five Asian American Voices* by Lawrence Yep. Jacket art by Kam Mak. Used by permission of HarperCollins Publishers; (bottom left) Jacket illustration from *Inside the Walls of Troy* © Joel Peter Johnson. Used by permission of Nancy Bruck; (bottom right) *Black Boy* by Richard Wright. Cover painting © David Diaz. HarperCollins Publishers; **168:** Photograph © Geoffrey Clements/CORBIS; **171:** © cartoonbank.com; **172:** Photo: Adam Rzepka. CNAC/MNAM/Dist. Réunion des Musées Nationaux/Art Resource, NY; **174:** Art Museum of Estonia, Tallinn, Estonia/ Bridgeman Art Library; **186:** © Jeanne Freibert/CORBIS SYGMA; **202:** © Getty Images; **207:** Brown Brothers; **211:** © RB Studio/ CORBIS/Stock Market; (background) © Francisco Hidalgo/Getty Images; **213:** © Mimmo Jodice/CORBIS; **214:** © RB Studio/CORBIS/ Stock Market; **216:** © Scala/Art Resource, NY; **217:** © RB Studio/ The Stock Market; **218:** © Bettmann/COR-BIS; **226:** R. Krubner/H. Armstrong Roberts; **231:** (top left) Cover from *To Kill a Mockingbird* by Harper Lee. Used by permission of Warner Books, Inc.; (top right) Cover from *The Circuit* by Francisco Jimenez, courtesy University of New Mexico Press; (bottom left) *Frankenstein: Or the Modern Prometheus* by Mary Shelley. Cover © HRW, illustration by Cliff Nielsen; (bottom right) From *Chinese Cinderella* by Adeline Yan Mah. Used by permission of Dell Publishing, a division of Random House, Inc.; **251:** Demetrio Carrasco/ Stone/Getty Images; **252–253:** David Zimmerman/Masterfile; **254:** LLC.FogStock/Index Stock Imagery; **256:** Victoria and Albert Museum, London/Art Resource, NY; **258:** Photo by Shauna Angel Blue; **262:** © Underwood & Underwood/CORBIS; **265:** © Walshe/Getty Images;

266: © E. O. Hoppé/Mansell/TimePix; **270:** Roine Magnusson/Image Bank; **283:** © Bettmann/CORBIS; **287:** Corel; **288, 297:** © Getty Images; **298:** Corel; **301:** © Getty Images; **302:** © Theo Westenberger Photography; **303:** © Morton Beebe/CORBIS; **305:** © Tom Bean/CORBIS; **306–308:** (background) Corel; **312:** Richard Tompkins/Gamma Press USA, Inc.; **314:** New York Times; **315:** AP Photo/Ron Edmonds; **319:** (top left) Cover from *Year of Impossible Goodbyes* by Sook Myul Choi (Boston: Houghton Mifflin, 1991). Reprinted by permission of Houghton Mifflin Company. All rights reserved; (top right) *Things Fall Apart* by Chinua Achebe. Cover © HRW, art by Earl Keleny; (bottom left) University of Washington Press; (bottom right) *A Stillness in Appomattox* by Bruce Caton. Cover © HRW, photo by Andrew Yates, design by Will Hornaday; **335:** © cartoonbank.com; **339:** Digital Zoo/Getty Images; **341:** Ryan McVay/Getty Images; **344:** © Martin Harvey/CORBIS; **346:** © Nancy Crampton; **347:** © Vanni/Art Resource, NY; **355:** © Bettmann/ CORBIS; **356:** Corel; **366:** © Getty Images; **371:** © Getty Images; **373:** Reuters/TimePix; **376–377:** Peter Lindstrom; **378:** © Tom Hollyman/Photo Researchers, Inc.; **379:** © Rob Atkins/Getty Images; **381:** (top left) *Holes* by Louis Sachar. Cover © HRW, art by Sally Vitsky/Artco LLC; (top right) *Fair Is Fair: World Folktales of Justice*; (bottom left) From the book *My World and Welcome To It*: copyright © 1940 by James Thurber. Copyright © renewed 1968 by Helen Thurber and Rosemary A. Thurber. Reprinted by permission arrangement with Rosemary A. Thurber and The Barbara Hogenson Agency. All rights reserved; (bottom right) *Barefoot Heart: Stories of a Migrant Child* by Elva Traviño Hart: © 1999. Cover design by John Wincek: Aerocraft Charter Art Service. Used by permission of Bilingual Press/Editorial Bilingüe: Arizona State University: Tempe, Ariz.; **400:** David Heald © The Solomon R. Guggenheim Foundation: New York; **404:** © Grant Heilman/Grant Heilman Photography. All rights reserved; **409:** The Bridgeman Art Library; **412:** Associated Press photo; **415:** © Margarette Mead/ Getty Images; **416:** Corel; **420, 423:** © Getty Images; **425:** Corel; **427:** © Giraudon/Art Resource, NY; **431:** © Eric and David Hosking/CORBIS; **432:** © Craig Lovell/CORBIS; **433:** Courtesy of Gary Soto; **437:** ©Walter Bibkow/FPG; **438–439:** © Getty Images; Walter Bibkow/FPG; **441:** © Pete Turner/Image Bank; **442:** © Keren Su/Image Bank; **443, 447:** © Getty Images; **450:** © Getty Images; **452:** © Getty Images; **455:** (top left) *The Little Prince* by Antoine de Saint-Exupéry. Cover illustration © 1943 by Harcourt: renewed 1971 by Consuelo de Saint-Exupéry. Used by permission of Harcourt, Inc.; (top right) *The Chosen* by Chaim Potok. Cover © HRW, illustration by Phillip Dvorak/Chip Caton Represents; (bottom left) *Death Be Not Proud*; (bottom right) From *Living Up the Street* (jacket cover) by Gary Soto: text © 1985 by Gary Soto. Cover art © 1985 by Carmen Lomas Garza. Used by permission of Random House Children's Books, a division of Random House, Inc.; **477:** © age fotostock/superStock; **478:** (background) © ThinkStock/Super-Stock. (inset) Reprinted with permission from the publisher Arte Público Press, University of Houston, © 2000; **480–481:** Yva Momatiuk/ John Eastcott/Miden Pictures; **482:** Wesleyan University Press; **483:** E. R. Degginger/Photo Researchers, Inc.; **484–485:** © Getty Images; **487:** (top) © Nancy Crampton; (bottom) Photo by Michael Nye; **489:** © Bettmann/CORBIS; **490:** (composite) © Craig Hammell/ CORBIS/Stock Market; Mark A. Johnson/The Stock Market; © Getty Images; **491:** © AP Photos; **495:** Photograph © 1982 The Metropolitan Museum of Art; **497:** © Seattle Art Museum/CORBIS; **498:** © Getty Images; **499:** © Douglas Peebles/CORBIS; **501:** © Tim Page/CORBIS; **506:** © Alex Buckingham/Getty Images; **508–509:** Tim Turner/FoodPix; **509:** Copyright © 2001 Eric Chang;

Illustrations

Maps

Index of Skills

The boldface page numbers indicate an extensive treatment of the topic.

LITERARY SKILLS

Actions, **97**
Allegory, **403, 436,** 444, 466–469, **1133**
Alliteration, **532,** 547, **551,** 554, 568, 957, **1133,** 1138
Allusion, **126,** 136, 529, **1133**
Alter ego, 744
Ambiguity, **334–335, 336,** 339, 345, 347, 359, 367, **1133**
Analysis questions (Interpretations), 36, 53, 75, 116, 136, 151, 195, 208, 219, 267, 278, 303, 309, 316, 357, 367, 380, 428, 434, 444, 483, 488, 492, 497, 503, 507, 510, 515, 519, 522, 525, 529, 536, 538, 543, 547, 550, 554, 596, 621, 628, 671, 703, 787, 813, 831, 888, 930, 957, 988, 1007, 1026
Anapest, **531**
Antagonist, 138, 1142
Apostrophe, 488
Approximate rhyme, **530,** 532, 538, **1143**
Archetype, **826**
Aside, **854,** 903, 936, 957, 982, 1013, **1134**
Assonance, **1134**
Atmosphere, **60.** *See also* Mood.
Audience, 852, 853, 854, 869, 892, 893, 894, 957
Autobiography, **1134,** 1140
Ballad, **539,** 543, **1134**
Basic situation, **2,** 1141
Biographical approach, **644–645, 646,** 659
Biography, **1134,** 1140
Blank verse, **895,** 944, **1134**
Catalog poem, **484,** 488
Character, 53, **60,** 75, **96–97, 98**–107, 136, 162–165, 195, **247,** 248, 251, 255, 267, **270,** 278, 303, 357, 367, 396, 413, 444, 469, 671, 703, 736, 739, **1134–1135**
   actions of, **97,** 98
   appearance and, **96–97,** 98
   comic, 957
   dialogue and, **96, 108,** 116, 165, 930
   in drama, **852–854, 897,** 957, 1007, 1055
   dramatic monologue and, **96,** 114, 116, **1136**
   dynamic/static, **139,** 988, 1135
   flat/round, **139,** 1135
   foil, 921, 930, **1138**

interactions, **138–139**
main, 703, **897**
motivations of. *See* Motivation.
other characters' response to, **97**
private thoughts and, **97**
soliloquy and. *See* Soliloquy.
speech and, **96**
subordinate, **138,** 151, 749, 1135
traits, 116, **126,** 136, 165, 219, **789,** 813
types, 869
Character foil, 921, 930, **1138**
Characterization, 53, 164, 208, 316, 367, 434, 579, **1134–1135**
   direct/indirect, **97,** 1135
Chronological order, **3, 44,** 53
Climax, **2, 4, 852,** 888, **897,** 1026, **1135,** 1141
Comedy, **852–853, 869,** 897, 952, 988, 1055, **1135,** 1136
Comic relief, **1135**
   elements, 930
   scenes, 915
Compare and contrast, 628, 831
   characters, 36
   poems, 515, 519
   theme across genres, **294,** 328–329
   universal themes, **260**
Complication, **2, 4, 853,** 930, 988, 1007, 1141
Conflict, **2, 4, 138, 140,** 143, 148, **247,** 248, 250, 254, 256, 257, 259, **261,** 444, 621, 671, **686,** 703, 736–739, 787, **852, 853, 869,** 888, 930, **1135,** 1141
   external, **2, 4,** 15, **138,** 139, **140,** 151, 164, 248, 259, 267, 736, **749,** 787, **1135**
   internal, **2, 4,** 15, 53, **138,** 139, **140,** 151, 164, 248, 259, 267, 278, **1135**
Connotation, **310, 435, 512,** 515, 607, **622, 1038, 1135,** 1136
Contradiction, 357, **376,** 380, 908
Contrast, 357, 497, 888
Costumes, **854**
Couplet, 498, **895, 1135–1136,** 1144
Crisis, **897**
Dactyl, **531**
Denotation, **310, 435, 512, 622, 1038,** 1135
Denouement, **2, 897,** 1141
Details, **62,** 65, 66, 68, 69, 71, 75, **414,** 417, 422, 424, 426, 428
Dialect, **607,** 621, **1136**
Dialogue, **96, 108,** 116, 165, **854, 855,** 868, 930, 973, 991, 1026, **1136**
Diction, 171, 210, **512,** 515, 523, **572, 607,** 621, **623,** 628, 639, **1136**

Direct characterization, **97**
Direct metaphor, **505, 516**
Drama, **852–854, 855**–868, 1052–1055, **1136**
   aside, **854,** 903, 936, 957, 982, 1013
   comedy, **852–853, 869,** 897, 952, 988, 1055
   dialogue, **854, 855,** 868, 930, 973, 991, 1026, 1136
   modern, **853**
   monologue, 520, 522, **854,** 921, 936, 938, 1021, 1026
   scene design, **853–854, 892–894,** 934, 957, 1055, 1143
   soliloquy, **96, 854,** 934, 936, 941, 952, 967, 997, 1016, 1026, 1055, **1144**
   stage, 853
   stage direction, **854, 855,** 868, 897, 902, 904, 918, 923, 924, 932, 936, 960, 961, 962, 964, 966, 979, 1018
   See also Tragedy.
Dramatic irony, **334,** 543, 813, 868, 957, 977, 1007, 1026, **1139**
Dramatic monologue, **96,** 114, 116, **1136**
Dynamic character, **139,** 988
End rhyme, **530,** 537, 543, **1143**
End-stopped line, in poetry, **508,** 510, **896**
English sonnet, 498, 503
Epic, 736, **740–746, 1137**
Epic simile, **745–746,** 788
Epithet, **815, 1137**
Evaluation questions, 36, 53, 75, 116, 136, 151, 195, 208, 219, 267, 278, 303, 309, 316, 357, 367, 380, 428, 434, 444, 483, 547, 596, 787, 813, 888, 930, 957, 988, 1007, 1026
Exact rhyme, **530,** 532
Exposition, **2,** 888, **897, 1137,** 1141
Extended metaphor, **511,** 515, **520,** 522
External conflict, **2, 4, 138,** 139, **140,** 151, 164, 248, 259, 267, 736, **749,** 787, **1135**
Fable, **1137**
Falling action, **897**
Farce, **869,** 888
Figures of speech, 71, **152, 429,** 479, **504–505, 508,** 510, **516,** 572, 580, 582, 596, **607,** 621, **788,** 934, 957, **1028–1029, 1137**
   personification, 444, **505, 526,** 529, 536, **1028,** 1029, **1141**
   pun, **1028,** 1029, **1137,** 1142

Scanning, of poetry, **531, 533,** 536, 1140
Scene design, **853–854, 892–894,** 934, 957, 1055, 1143
Sensory details, **62,** 75
Sentence structure, 547, **551,** 554, 572, 574, 607
Sestet, 498, 1144
Set. *See* Scene design.
Setting, **60–61, 62,** 75, 116, 151, 219, 278, 303, 309, 413, 483, 492, **580,** 596, 671, **1143–1144**
Shakespearean sonnet, 498, 1144
Short story, **1144**
Simile, **152, 305,** 309, **429, 504,** 505, **506,** 507, **508,** 515, 516, 522, 536, 538, 554, 568, 639, 831, **1028,** 1029, 1137, **1144**
Situational irony, **334, 348,** 357, 813, **1139**
Soliloquy, **96, 854,** 934, 936, 941, 952, 967, 997, 1016, 1026, 1055, **1144**
Sonnet, **498,** 503, 927, 944, **1144**
Speaker, 536, 547, **548,** 550, 567, **1144**
Spondee, **531**
Stage. *See* Scene design.
Stage direction, **854, 855,** 868, 897, 902, 904, 918, 923, 924, 932, 936, 960, 961, 962, 964, 966, 979, 1018
Staging the Play, 897, 901, 902, 903, 904, 905, 907, 909, 911, 912, 913, 914, 915, 916, 918, 919, 921, 923, 924, 927, 928, 932, 933, 934, 936, 937, 938, 940, 941, 943, 944, 945, 946, 947, 949, 950, 951, 952, 953, 954, 955, 959, 960, 961, 962, 964, 966, 967, 968, 969, 971, 974, 975, 977, 978, 979, 981, 982, 983, 984, 985, 986, 987, 991, 992, 994, 997, 1000, 1001, 1005, 1009, 1010, 1011, 1013, 1014, 1015, 1016, 1017, 1018, 1020, 1021, 1024
Stanza, **1144**
Static character, **139**
Stereotype, 869
Story map. *See* Graphic organizers.
Style, **572–573, 574**–579, **580,** 582, 587, 596, **607,** 621, **623,** 638–639, 1136, **1144–1145**
Subject, of literary work, 246
Subordinate character, **138,** 151, 749
Subtlety, 367, 1133
Surprise ending, **188,** 267, 348, 357
Suspense, 703, 988, 1007, **1145**
Symbol, 278, 380, **402–403, 404**–413, **414,** 428, **430,** 434, 466–469, 515, 813, **1145**
Tall tale, **1145**
Theme, 53, 136, **246–247, 248–259, 261,** 267, **270,** 278, **295,** 303, **305,** 309, 316, 397, 428, 444, 469, 573, 596, 621, 628, 639, **660,** 671, 1026, **1145**
    comparing, **260, 294**
    across genres, **246, 294,** 328–329
    universal, **246, 260,** 1145

Third-person-limited point of view, **170–171, 197,** 208, 1142
Time and sequence
    chronological order, **3, 44,** 53
    flashback, **3, 44,** 53, 278, **1137**
    flash-forward, **3,** 1138
    foreshadowing, **3, 16,** 36, 53, 787, 930, 957, 967, 968, **1138**
Title, 16, 36, 53, 187, **247,** 248, 253, 258, 259, **295,** 303, 347, 357, 483, 596, 659, 671, 703
Tone, **60, 171,** 195, 208, 210, 219, 241, 309, 367, 380, 397, 434, 469, 483, 488, **523,** 525, 547, **548,** 550, 568, **573, 623,** 628, 639, 1135, **1145**
Tragedy, **852–853, 897,** 930, 957, 988, 1007, 1026, 1055, 1135, 1136, **1145**
Tragic flaw, **852**
Tragic hero, **852**
Trochee, **531**
Turning point, **897,** 988
Unreliable narrator, **170,** 210, 219
Venn diagram. *See* Graphic organizers.
Verbal irony, **334,** 335, 367, 380, **1139**
Voice, **171, 172,** 173, 187, **210,** 219, 240–241, **548,** 550, **1145**

INFORMATIONAL READING SKILLS

Accuracy, 675
Alphabetical sequence, 1075
Analogy, 370, **1133**
Analyzing, 42, 59, 88–91, **118,** 121, 122, 124, 229–230, 292–293, 374, 449, 453–454, 605–606, 679, 680, 681, 683, 684–685, 728–731, 824, 844–847, 1037, 1065, 1068, 1072, 1083
    functional workplace documents, **1073–1078**
    sources, **674–675**
    Web site, **1076**
    workplace documents, **1075**
Anecdote, 370, 371, 598, **818, 824,** 847, 1134, 1147
Argument, **370–371, 598–599, 818,** 844–847, 1147
    claim, **370,** 373, 374, **598,** 600, 603, 604, 605, 606, 824, 1147, **1148,** 1153
    credibility, **370–371,** 374, **598–599,** 606, **1149**
    evidence, **370,** 373, 374, **598–599,** 600, 604, 606, 1149, **1150**
    fallacies, logical, **598,** 1151
    generalization, **370,** 372, 598, 602, 1148
    intent, author's, **371, 599,** 602, 605, 606, **818,** 824, 847, 1149
    logical appeals, **370, 598,** 818, 1147
    opposing, **598–599,** 603
    tone, author's, 371, 374, **599,** 605, **818,** 824, 847, 1149

    See also Emotional appeals.
Attacking the person, 598
Audience, 121, **281,** 446, **674,** 675, 684
Autobiography, 1134, 1140
Begging the question, **1151**
Bias, 675
Bibliography, 118
Biography, **1134,** 1140
Browser, 1066, **1067**
Business letter, 1060, **1084–1087**
Call to action, 599, 602
Cause and effect, 599, **1147,** 1158
    false, 598, **1151**
Chronological sequence, 1075, 1148, **1158**
Circular reasoning, 598, **1151**
Citing Internet sources, **1069–1071**
Claim, **370,** 373, 374, **598,** 600, 603, 604, 605, 606, 824, 1147, **1148,** 1153
Compare and contrast, 221, 229, 230, **281, 446,** 599, **1032,** 1065, 1148, 1158
Computer games, developing, **1060**
Conclusions, drawing, 230, 281, 293
Connecting to the Literature, 38, 55, 118, 221, 281, 371, 446, 599, 675, 818, 1032
Connections, making, 221, 281, 293, 446, 454, **1032**
Consumer documents, 1060, 1061, **1062–1064,** 1092, **1148–1149**
    citing, **1069–1071**
Contract, 1062, 1073
Copyright, 1073
Credibility, **370–371,** 374, **598–599,** 606, **675,** 1149
Design elements, 1075
Either/or fallacy, **1151**
Elaborating, **118,** 120, 124, **675,** 685
Emotional appeals, **370,** 371, 598, 600, 606, **818,** 1147
    anecdote, 370, 371, 598, **818,** 824, 847, 1134, 1147
    loaded words, 370, 371, 374, 598, 600, **818,** 824, 847, 1147
Essay, **1137**
Evaluating, 120, 124, 676, 678, 684, 731
    argument, **370–371,** 372, 373, 374, **598–599,** 600, 602, 603, 604, 606, **818,** 824, 844–847
    functional documents, **1079–1083**
    sources, **118,** 675
Evidence, 221, 229, **370,** 373, 374, **598–599,** 600, 604, 606, 1149, **1150**
Extending information, 685
Facts, 118, 122, 281, 370, 598, **675,** 678, 685, 847, 1154
Fallacies, logical, **598, 1151**
False cause and effect, 598, **1151**
5W-How? questions, 38
Format, of documents, **1075,** 1078
Functional documents, 1073, **1075, 1079–1082,** 1083

Generalization, **370**, 372, 602, 1148, **1151–1152**
  hasty, 598, **1151**
Graphic elements, 1075, 1078
Graphic organizers
  evaluating-arguments chart, 371, 599, 606
  KWL chart, 38
  main idea chart, 221
Graphs, **1152**
Hasty generalization, 598, **1151**
Header, 1075, 1078
Icon, as Web link, 55, 58
Informative texts, **1152**
Instruction manual, 1062, 1068
Intent, author's, **371, 599**, 602, 605, 606, **818**, 824, 847, 1149. See also Purpose.
Internal Web link, 55
Internet, 55, 59, **1066–1067**
  citing, Internet sources, **1069–1072**
Interviewing, 124
KWL chart. See Graphic organizers.
License, 1073
Loaded words, 370, 371, 374, 598, 600, **818**, 824, 847, 1147
Logic, **1152–1153**
Logical appeals, **370, 598**, 818, 1147
Logical order, **1075, 1153**, 1158
Main idea, 118, 124, 221, 229, 292, 453, 674, 824, 1037, **1153**
Maps, reading, **1153–1154**
Name-calling, as logical fallacy, **1151**
Nonfiction sources, 55, 1140
Online sources. See Internet.
Opinion, 118, 122, 281, **370**, 374, 598, 603, 604, 606, **675**, 678, 685, 824, **1154**
Order of importance, **1154, 1158**
Paraphrasing, 221, 230, 281, 293, **446**, 447, 451, 452, 453, 598, 602, 604, 1032, 1037, **1155**
Periodicals, 55
Point-by-point sequence, 1075
Primary source, **118**, 124, 281, **674**, 683, 685, 728–731, **1155**
Problem-solution (text structures), 1158
Product information, 1062
Public documents, 1060, 1061, **1155**
  citing, **1069–1071**
Purpose, author's, 121, **281**, 292, 446, 449, **674, 675**, 679, 684, 731, **818**, 824, 847, 1037
Question-answer (text structures), 1158
Reading Comprehension (Reading Check), 42, 59, 124, 229, 292, 374, 453, 605, 684, 824, 1037, 1065, 1068, 1072, 1078, 1083
Reading Comprehension (Test Practice), 42, 59, 88–91, 124, 229–230, 292–293, 374, 453–454, 605–606, 684–685, 728–731, 824, 1037, 1065, 1068, 1072, 1078, 1083

Reasons, **370**, 598
Reference books, 55
Research
  citing sources, **1069–1072**
  questions, generating, **38**, 42, 88–91, **1155–1156**
  sources, **55**, 59, **118**, 124, **674–675**, 679, 683, 685, 728–731
  tools, **1066**
Search engine, 55, **1066–1067**
Secondary source, **118**, 124, 281, **674**, 679, 728–731, **1157**
Sequence, of ideas, **1075**, 1080, 1083. See also Text structures.
Sources
  analyzing, **118**, 121, 122, 449, **674–675**, 679, 680, 681, 683, 728–731
  citing, **1069–1072**
  elaborating from, **118**, 120, 124, **675**, 685
  evaluating, **118**, 120, 124, **675**, 676, 678, 684
  print resources, **55**
  See also Internet, Primary source, Secondary source, Synthesizing.
Spatial order, **1157, 1158**
Statistics, 374, 598
Step-by-step sequence, 1075
Stereotyping, **1151**
Structure, of document, **1075**, 1078
Style, writer's, 675
Summarizing, 293, **1155**
Synthesizing
  sources, **221**, 230, **281**, 293, **1032**, 1037, **1157**
  works by one author, **446**, 454
Technical directions, 1062, **1066**, 1067, 1068
Technical documents, 1060, 1061
Text structures, **1157–1158**
Tone, **371**, 374, **599**, 605, **675**, 680, 681, 731, **818**, 824, 847, 1149
Verifying, 684, 731
Warranty, 1062
Web
  link, **55**, 56, 58, 59
  search engine, 55, **1066–1067**
  site, 55, 1076, 1078
Workplace documents, 1060, 1061, 1073, **1075, 1158**
  citing, **1069–1071**
Works Cited list, 118, **1069–1072**
World Wide Web. See Web.

VOCABULARY SKILLS

Analogy, **152, 279, 672, 1125**
Antonym, 152, 368, 685
Archaic words, **896, 958**, 1030
Borrowed words, **317**
Connotation, 43, **310, 435, 622**, 685, **1038**
Context, **375**, 522
  clues, 166, **196, 368**, 470, 640, 825, **1124**

Denotation, **310, 435, 622, 1038**
Derivations (word origins), **54**, 125, 220, **230**, 268, 317, 445, 597, **816–817, 832**, 931, 989, **1030–1031, 1156–1157**
Diction, 358, 622
Dictionary, 43, **54**, 125, 293, 317, 445, 454, 493, 597, 704, 816, 817, 832, 889, 958, 989, 1008, 1031, 1038, **1149–1150**
Epic simile, **788**
Epithet, 815, **1137**
Etymology, **54**, 220, 597. See also Derivations.
Figures of speech, **152, 429, 788, 1028–1029**
  metaphor, **152, 1028**, 1029
  personification, **1028**, 1029
  pun, **1028**, 1029
  simile, **152, 429, 1028**, 1029
Graphic organizers
  jargon chart, 704
  multiple-meanings chart, 522
  semantic map, 125, 137, 454, 493, 622, 704, 788, 889
  synonym chart, 43, 117, 209, 304
  word-derivation map, 220, 317, 445, 597, 931
  word-family chart, 293
Greek roots, 230, 597. See also Derivations.
History of English language, **1030–1031**
Homeric simile, **788**
Idiom, **825, 1139**
Jargon, **704**
Latin roots, 230, 597, 989, 1030. See also Derivations.
Metaphor, **152, 1028**, 1029
Middle English, 1031
Modern English, 1030, 1031
Multiple-choice tests, **1124–1125**
  analogy questions, **1125**
  context-clue questions, **1124**
  definition or synonym questions, **1124**
  multiple-meaning questions, **1124**
  sentence-completion or fill-in-the-blank questions, **1125**
Multiple-meaning words, 92, 330, **522**, 1056, **1124**
Myths, words derived from, 54, **816–817, 832**
Norse words, **832**, 1030
Old English, 1030
Prefix, **37**, 220, **597, 1156–1157**
Proto-Indo-European language, 1030
Restatement, 196, 368
Roots, **230, 1156**. See also Derivations.
Root words, 220, 445, **597**. See also Derivations.
Semantic map. See Graphic organizers.
Simile, **152, 429, 1028**, 1029
Suffix, **1156–1157**
Synonym, **43, 117**, 152, **209**, 242, **304**, 368, 398, 454, 493, 685, 732, **815**, 848, 1124

Technical vocabulary, **704**
Test practice, 92, 166, 242, 330, 398, 470, 640, 732, 848, 1056
Thesaurus, 43, **304**, 454, 493, 889
Vocabulary Development, 37, 43, 54, 76, 92, 117, 125, 137, 152, 166, 196, 209, 220, 230, 242, 268, 279, 293, 304, 310, 317, 330, 358, 368, 375, 398, 429, 435, 445, 454, 470, 493, 522, 597, 606, 622, 640, 672, 685, 704, 732, 788, 815, 816–817, 825, 832, 848, 889, 931, 958, 989, 1028–1029, 1030–1031, 1038, 1056
Vocabulary resource file, **76**
Word bank, 493
Word families, **293**
Word origins. See Derivations.

READING SKILLS

Allusions, 126, 136
Cause and effect, **436**, 444, **580**, 585, 589, 596, 826, 831, **1147**, 1158
Chronological order, 44, 53, 1148, **1158**
Clarifying the text, 1100
Comparing and contrasting themes, 260, 294
Conclusions, drawing, **210**, 212, 213, 215, 217
Connecting literature and news, 295, 303
Connections, making, 1100
Context clues, 188, **1008**, **1149**
Details
  inference from, 107, **414**, 417, 422, 424, 426, 428
  reading for, **62**, 65, 66, 68, 69, 71, 75
Fact and opinion, distinguishing between, **311**, 316, 1122, 1123
GIST, **1103–1104**
Graphic organizers
  cause-and-effect chart, 444, 596, 826, 831
  fact-and-opinion chart, 311
  key word chart, 1104
  summary chart, 787
  theme chart, 260, 294
Independent reading (Read On). See **Independent Reading.**
Inference, 107, **108**, 116, 430, **686**, 688, 691, 694, 695, 697, 698, 699, 703, **1152**
  from details, 107, **414**, 417, 419, 422, 424, 426, 428
  logical order, **1158**
  about motivation, **140**, 270, **359**, 362, 363, 364, 366, 367
  in multiple-choice tests, 1122, **1123**
Main idea, **430**, 434, **1123**, **1153**
Monitor your comprehension, **749**, 751, 753, 754, 757, 758, 763, 768, 770, 774, 777, 780, 782, 783, 785, 786, 787, 792, 794, 795, 800, 801, 802, 803, 805, 806, 808, 809

Monitoring reading, **188**, 195
Multiple-choice tests, **1121–1123**
  evaluation questions, **1123–1124**
  factual-recall questions, **1122–1123**
  inference questions, **1123**
  main-idea questions, **1123**
  strategies, for taking, **1121–1122**
Notes, taking, 1098
Opinion. See Fact and opinion, distinguishing between.
Oral presentation, 751
Order of importance, **1158**
Organizing events, 44
Paraphrasing, 808, **1008**, **1155**
Predictions, making, **16**, 18, 21, 22, 26, 29, 30, 34, 36, **261**, 267, **348**, 357, 802, 1100
Problem-solution (text structures), 1158
Question-answer (text structures), 1158
Questioning the text, 1100
Reading a poem, **508**, 510
Reading checkpoints, **1098**
Reading rate, **1105–1107**
  determining, **1106**
  strategies for improving, **1106–1107**
  varying, **1105**
Re-reading, 188, **1101–1102**
Retelling, **1100–1101**
Rewording, **1102**
Setting a purpose for reading (Before You Read),16, 44, 62, 108, 126, 140, 188, 197, 210, 261, 270, 295, 305, 311, 348, 359, 376, 414, 430, 436, 480, 484, 489, 494, 498, 500, 506, 508, 511, 512, 516, 520, 523, 526, 533, 537, 539, 544, 548, 551, 580, 607, 623, 660, 686, 749, 789, 826–827, 869–870, 897–898
Setting a purpose for reading (Reading Informational Materials), 38, 55, 118, 221, 281, 370–371, 446, 598–599, 674–675, 818, 1032, 1062–1063, 1066, 1069, 1073, 1079
Somebody wants . . . , but . . . , so . . . formula, **197**, 208, **1102–1103**
Spatial order, **1158**
Summarizing
  expository text, **1103–1104**, 1155
  narrative text, 188, **197**, 208, 309, **660**, 671, 787, **1102–1103**
Text structures, **1101**, **1157–1158**
Think-Aloud strategy, **1100**
Visualizing, **607**, 611, 615, 618, 619, 621, 768, 777, 801, **1099**, 1100

WRITING SKILLS

Accuracy, 711, 1088
Action, 79
Action verb, 1115
Active voice, 1046, **1115–1116**
Act-summary graphic, 1027
Adjectives, cutting deadwood, 462

Aesthetic effect, 1042
"After" narrative, 267
Allegory, 444
Alliteration, 547, 554
Ambiguity, 558, 632
Ambiguous sequel, 367
Analogy, 384, 835
Analysis log, 232, 233, 557
Analysis of a poem, **556–563**
  choosing and analyzing a poem for, 556–557
  evaluating and revising, 561–562
  gathering supporting evidence for, 558
  organizing your analysis for, 558
  peer review of, 561
  prewriting, 556–558
  proofreading, 563
  publishing, 563
  reflecting on writing, 563
  writer's framework, 559
  writer's model, 559–560
  writing first draft of, 559–560
  writing your thesis for, 557
Analysis of a short story, **630–637**
  analyzing literary elements for, 630–631
  choosing a story for, 630
  evaluating and revising, 635–636
  organizing your analysis for, 632
  peer review of, 635
  prewriting, 630–632
  proofreading, 637
  publishing, 637
  reflecting on writing, 637
  supporting your thesis statement for, 632
  writer's framework, 633
  writer's model, 633–634
  writing a thesis statement for, 631
  writing first draft of, 633–634
Analysis of nonfiction, **232–239**
  analyzing character, events, and setting for, 232–233
  choosing a biography for, 232
  evaluating and revising, 237–238
  organizing your analysis for, 234
  peer review of, 237
  prewriting, 232–234
  proofreading, 239
  publishing, 239
  reflecting on writing, 239
  writer's framework, 235
  writer's model, 235–236
  writing and supporting a thesis statement for, 234
  writing first draft of, 235–236
Analyzing
  biography, 232
  the cause and effects for persuasion with cause and effect, 835
  character, events, and setting for analysis of nonfiction, 232–233
  literary elements for analysis of a short story, 630–631
  structure of play, 1027

Genres, comparing and contrasting, 628, 1027
  chart, 628
Gestures, 79
Graph, 1119
Graphic organizers
  act-summary graphic, 1027
  analysis log, 232, 233, 557
  bar graph, 1119–1120
  block-method chart, 280
  body paragraph structure, 1111
  character chart, 97
  controlling-impression diagram, 458
  credibility chart, 606
  details chart, 79, 457
  Editor in Charge: Content and Organization. See Editor in Charge: Content and Organization.
  Editor in Charge: Style Guidelines. See Editor in Charge: Style Guidelines.
  elaboration chart, 558
  flowchart, 1119
  genre-comparison chart, 628
  journal-entry chart, 536
  kinds of supporting evidence chart, 835
  line graph, 1120
  media questions chart, 321
  movie-proposal chart, 814
  news-story chart, 321–322
  opinion statement charts, 382, 383
  pie chart, 1119
  play-change chart, 1027
  point-by-point-method chart, 318
  Quick guide! See Quick guide!
  style chart, 621
  summarizing-acts graphic, 1027
  think sheet, 83, 159, 160
  worlds chart, 548
Graphics and visuals, 1118–1120
Group work, 358, 463
Haiku, 497
Heading, 714, 1117
Historical setting, 645
  chart, 645
Hyperlink, 463
Hypothesis, 712, 1112
Identifying purpose and audience for a research paper, 707–708
Illustration, 1120
Imagery, 492, 529, 628
Images, 380, 475, 488, 507, 510, 547
Imagined thoughts, 1007
Implied metaphor, 519
Inference, 233
Informal outline, 714
Informal style, 573
Integrating quotations for a research paper, 717
Interior monologue, 79, 156
Internal conflict, 155
Internet, 232, 563, 831, 1040
Interview, 515, 709

recording source information for, 711
Introduction
  of analysis of nonfiction, 235
  of analysis of a poem, 559
  of analysis of a short story, 633
  of autobiographical narrative, 81
  of comparison-contrast essay, 280, 318
  of comparison of media coverage, 323
  of comparison of a play and a film, 1043
  of description of a place, 459
  of persuasion with cause and effect, 837
  of persuasive essay, 385
  of research paper, 718
Ironic ending, 208
Irony, 543
Journal entry, 309
  chart, 536
Key literary elements, 557
Key point, 631, 632
Kinds of supporting evidence chart, 835
Leading, 1117
Letter, 116, 221, 309, 357, 380
  to editor, 374
Library, 708
Lighting, 1041, 1042
Line graph, 1120
Literary club, 637
Literary elements, 556
Logic, 325
Logical appeal, 383, 836
Logical order, 713
Logical organization, 384
Logical reasoning, 836
Lowercase, 1118
Magazine article, recording source information for, 710
Main character, 155
Main idea, 631
Map, 1120
Margin, 1117
Media questions chart, 321
Meeting
  minutes of a. See Minutes of a meeting.
  taking notes at a, **1088**
Metaphor, 515, 519, 522, 538, 557, 631
Microfilm and microfiche, 708
Middle of short story, 157
Minutes of a meeting, **1088**
  elements of, **1091**
  format for, **1088–1089**
  writing, **1088–1091**
Models. See Writer's Models.
Modern Language Association (MLA) format, 710
Modified-block-style format, 1084, 1086
Mood, 492, 631
Motivation page, 278
Movie-proposal chart, 814
Multiple-choice tests

identifying-sentence-errors questions, 1125–1126
  improving-sentence questions, 1126
  improving-the-paragraph questions, 1126
Multiple meanings, 434
Narration
  autobiographical narrative, 78–85
  short story, 154–161
Narrative details, 155
Narrative techniques, 1041
Narrator, 155
New beginning, 219
New ending, 195
News article, 515
Newspaper article, recording source information for, 710
News-story chart, 321–322
Note cards, 712, 713
Notes, taking, 348
  at a meeting, **1088**
Nuance, 558, 632
Objectivity, 321
Online book stores, 637
Online catalog, 708
Online database, 708
Online sources, recording source information for, 711
Opening statement, 988
Opinion, expert, 384
Opinion statement, 382, 836
  charts, 382, 383
Order of importance, 234, 458, 558, 632, 713, 1042, 1113
Organizing
  information and developing an outline for a research paper, 713–715
  your analysis
    of nonfiction, 234
    of a poem, 558
    of a short story, 632
  your details
    for autobiographical narrative, 79–80
    for description of a place, 458
  your essay
    for comparison of media coverage, 322
    for comparison of a play and a film, 1042
Outlining, 714, 1154–1155
Pace, 79, 155
Page design, 161, 389, 1117
Paragraph(s)
  analyzing free verse, 547
  analyzing style, 621
  about characters, 357
  clincher sentence, 1113
  coherence, 1113
  comparing and contrasting genres, 628
  comparing reports, 303
  in contrasting styles, 573
  describing experience, 267
  describing leaving, 303

INDEPENDENT READING

Index of Art

Index of Authors and Titles